STEPHEN CRANE

A CRITICAL BIBLIOGRAPHY

STEPHEN CRANE

A CRITICAL BIBLIOGRAPHY

by R. W. Stallman

THE IOWA STATE UNIVERSITY PRESS/AMES

1972

ROBERT WOOSTER STALLMAN is Professor, Department of English, University of Connecticut. Author of *The Houses That James Built* (1961) and of *Stephen Crane: A Biography* (1968), he has edited *Stephen Crane: An Omnibus* (1952), *Stephen Crane: Sullivan County Tales and Sketches* (1968), *The Stephen Crane Reader* (1972), and *The Art of Stephen Crane* (in preparation, 1973). His critical essays on Crane, Conrad, Henry James, and Kafka have been reprinted in many anthologies. An honorary member of Phi Beta Kappa (1969), he received the University of Connecticut's third annual award for Faculty Excellence in Teaching and Research (1968).

© 1972 R. W. Stallman

Composed and printed by The Iowa State University Press

First edition, 1972

Library of Congress Cataloging in Publication Data

Stallman, Robert Wooster, 1911–
  Stephen Crane.

  1. Crane, Stephen, 1871–1900–Bibliography.
Z8198.2.S76   818'.4'09   79–103837
ISBN 0–8138–0357–8

FOR

ROBERTA SMITH

REFERENCE LIBRARIAN, UNIVERSITY OF CONNECTICUT

CONTENTS

PREFACE

1

"POOR CRANE was at one time 'puffed,' but he was never properly appreciated. We were great friends from the first, after his arrival in England," Joseph Conrad wrote Peter F. Somerville in 1912. "Believe me my dear Sir no paper, no review, would look at anything that I or anybody else could write about Crane. They would laugh at the suggestion. Crane? Who's Crane? Who cares for Crane? . . . Mere literary excellence won't save a man's memory. In fifty years' time some curious literary critic (of the professional scribbler kind) will perhaps rediscover him as a curiosity and write a short paper in order to earn five guineas. Sad but true. I hardly meet anyone now who knows or remembers anything of him. For the younger oncoming writers he does not exist, simply." (*Letters,* 1960, pp. 321–22.)

However, in much shorter time than Conrad prophesied, Crane was rediscovered in the 1920s, notably by Vincent Starrett's "Stephen Crane: An Estimate" (1920) and his edition of *Men, Women and Boats* (1921); but more importantly by Thomas Beer's *Stephen Crane* (1923). The decade of the 1920s introduced Crane with memoirs by Ford Madox Ford (1921), Ralph D. Paine (1922), Joseph Conrad, (1925, 1926, 1928), Willis Fletcher Johnson (1926), Robert H. Davis (1926), and Charles Michelson (1927). The Davis and Michelson memoirs appeared as Introductions to Wilson Follett's twelve-volume edition, *The Work of Stephen Crane* (1925–1927). Other useful Introductions are by Amy Lowell, Willa Cather, Joseph Hergesheimer, and Sherwood Anderson.

ix

It was a rich decade of memoirs and impressionistic appraisals of Crane, notable especially for Beer's biography, Van Wyck Brooks's "A Reviewer's Notebook," in *Freeman* (1922), and Edmund Wilson's "A Vortex in the Nineties: Stephen Crane," in *New Republic* (1924). When Wilson compiled *The Shock of Recognition* (1943) he could find nothing better for an appraisal of Crane than H. G. Wells's "Stephen Crane From an English Standpoint," in *North American Review* (1900). However, he might have included also Van Wyck Brooks's short study, a most perceptive critical note.

However, no Crane revival occurred in the 1920s; nor in the 1930s, a decade which introduced Crane with critical essays by Matthew Josephson (1930), Henry Hazlitt (1931), Harlan Hatcher (1934), Harry Hartwick (1935), and Vernon Loggins (1937). The decade took off from Wilson Follett's cleverly titled survey "The Second Twenty-Eight Years: A Note on Stephen Crane" (1929) and ended with the pioneer scholarship of Lyndon U. Pratt, who initiated our present-day probing for the facts about Crane's life and works (1939–1970). I refer to Pratt's "The Formal Education of Stephen Crane" and "An Addition to the Canon of Stephen Crane," both articles published in 1939.

The single most important contribution in the 1940s to the slowly rising recognition of Crane was the Vincent Starrett and Ames W. Williams *Stephen Crane: A Bibliography* (1948). It superseded Vincent Starrett's *Stephen Crane: A Bibliography* (1923) and B. J. R. Stolper's *Stephen Crane: A List of His Writings* (1930). At this writing (1970) there have been five Stephen Crane bibliographies, five biographies (not including Thomas L. Raymond's monograph, 1923), and five book-length studies, the latest being Jean Cazemajou's *Stephen Crane (1871–1900) Écrivain Journaliste* (Paris, 1969).

The 1940s began with Carl Van Doren's *Stephen Crane: Twenty Stories* (1940), with an outstanding Introduction. Other critical appraisals worth mentioning were by Mark Van Doren (1942) and H. L. Mencken (1949). Russell Nye considered "Stephen Crane as Social Critic" (1940). Doctoral dissertations began with Jean V. Whitehead's "The Art of Stephen Crane," Cornell (1944); John C. Bushman's "The Fiction of Stephen Crane and Its Critics," Illinois (1944); and Victor Elconin's "Studies in the Fiction of Stephen Crane," Ohio State (1947). Lewis Leary bibliographed Crane in his *Articles on American Literature Appearing in Current Periodicals, 1920–1945* (1947). Elconin, in bringing to light unknown-to-exist Crane periodical publications in the *New York Tribune*, in "Stephen Crane at Asbury Park," began in 1948 that quest for additions to the Crane canon, for published and unpublished writings, for manuscripts and letters, which subsequent scholars have unearthed again and again during the past two decades. In Lars Ahnebrink's *The Beginnings of Naturalism in American Fiction* (Uppsala, 1950) was the beginning of interest in Crane by foreign scholars.

In the 1950s *The Red Badge of Courage,* translated, appeared in France, Russia, and Thailand. My Introduction to the Modern Library edition of *The Red Badge of Courage* (1951) was translated into the Greek and published in Athens in 1956. In Germany, according to one of my Hamburg correspondents, interest in Crane began shortly after the publication of *Stephen Crane: An Omnibus* (1952), and in 1954 *The Red Badge of Courage* appeared in Mannheim, translated into the German by Hans Umstätter, and in 1955 *Stephen Crane: Das blaue Hotel* appeared in Munich, translated by Hermann Stresau. Another Hamburg (1970) correspondent, F. H. Bastein, has provided my Crane bibliography with a dozen or more writings and editions by German scholars. These are additional to the entries supplied by Ursula Christmann in 1966. Also unsolicited were Professor Yoshie Itabashi's list of writings on Crane by Japanese scholars and critics and George Monteiro's list of South American writers on Crane. For entries of Italian writers on Crane I am indebted to Professor Sergio Perosa, and of French writers and translators of Crane I am indebted to Professor Jean Cazemajou. Crane is made known in Switzerland by H. W. Hausermann's *Moderne amerikanische Literatur* (Bern and Munich, 1965).

This bibliography records something of the international scope of Crane's present-day reputation, the record of publications on him by foreign scholars and critics (albeit not complete), in France, Germany, Russia, Sweden, Italy, Japan, Holland, Brazil, and Argentina. Appearing here for the first time are a considerable number of foreign writings (not listed in other American bibliographies), notably by writers on Crane in South America, Japan, and Germany.

2

The Crane revival began in the early 1950s with the publication of John Berryman's *Stephen Crane* (1950), William Gibson's *Selected Prose and Poetry,* the first Crane paperback textbook (1950), and Stallman's Introduction to the Modern Library edition of *The Red Badge of Courage* (1951), his "Stephen Crane: A Revaluation," in John Aldridge's *Critiques and Essays on Modern Fiction* (1952), and especially with *Stephen Crane: An Omnibus* (1952; London, 1954).

In 1953 appeared John E. Hart's *"The Red Badge of Courage* as

Myth and Symbol" and Maxwell Geismar's reading of *The Red Badge* in *Rebels and Ancestors,* which interpretation seems similar to my own. In *The Poetry of Stephen Crane* (1957) and in his not-so-well-known Introduction to *The Red Badge of Courage and Other Stories* (1957), Daniel G. Hoffman buttressed and extended my 1951 "Notes Toward an Analysis of *The Red Badge of Courage.*" The battle over interpretations of *The Red Badge* has continued into the 1970s. The first shots were fired by Winifred Lynskey, who contested the note by R. B. Sewall in *The Explicator* (1945) in her note of 1949 on *The Red Badge* in that same journal. Considerable opposition exists to my reading of biblical echoes and religious symbolism in *The Red Badge;* notably by Philip Rahv, who denies the presence of irony and symbol in Crane's fiction (1956), and by S. B. Greenfield (1958). However, the fact is that biblical echoes and religious symbolism toolmark not only *The Red Badge,* but also *Maggie* and many other Crane works—even "A Mystery of Heroism," as James W. Gargano proves, I think, in *Modern Language Notes* (1959). Or again as George Monteiro proves in "Whilomville as Judah: Crane's 'A Little Pilgrimage,' " *Renascence* (1967). As for biblical echoes in *The Red Badge,* early advocates of that reading include James B. Colvert, James Trammell Cox, and Eric Solomon, whose studies—all three—appeared in the Stephen Crane Special Number of *Modern Fiction Studies* (Autumn, 1959).

The Crane revival of the 1950s was buttressed by the publication of *Stephen Crane's Love Letters to Nellie Crouse* (1954); by *Stephen Crane (1871–1900): An Exhibition of His Writings Held in the Columbia University Libraries September 17–November 30, 1956,* edited by Jean H. Baum, with a Foreword by Lewis Leary; by Corwin Knapp Linson's memoirs, *My Stephen Crane* (1958); and by that first collection of critical studies in *Modern Fiction Studies,* a collection richly rewarding for its multiplicity of insights about Crane's art. The 1940s ended with Melvin Schoberlin's edition of *The Sullivan County Sketches* (1949); the 1950s ended with *MFS's* tribute to Crane, in which he was also bibliographed by Maurice Beebe and Thomas A. Gullason. The first annotated bibliography appeared in Edwin H. Cady's excellent and interesting monograph *Stephen Crane* (1962). The 1960s began with Lillian Gilkes' *Cora Crane: A Biography of Mrs. Stephen Crane* (1960) and *Stephen Crane: Letters,* edited by Stallman and Gilkes (1960).

However, I am tracing here mainly the critical concern about Crane's works 1920–1960. (My Preface is supplemented by Jean Cazemajou's Introduction, which carries the survey beyond the 1960s.) Early and noteworthy critical studies were John W.

Shroeder's "Stephen Crane Embattled" (1950) and Walter Sutton's "Pity and Fear in 'The Blue Hotel' " (1952). Also noteworthy were Charles C. Walcutt's *American Literary Naturalism: A Divided Stream* (1956); James Trammel Cox's "Stephen Crane as Symbolic Naturalist: An Analysis of 'The Blue Hotel' " (1957); James B. Colvert's "Style and Meaning in 'The Open Boat' " (1958); and Bernard Weisberger's study of *The Red Badge of Courage* in *Twelve Original Essays on Great American Novels,* edited by Charles Shapiro (1958).

The impetus for the Crane revival was the upsurge of Criticism. Other revivals included critical concern with the works of Joseph Conrad, Franz Kafka, William Faulkner, Herman Melville, Twain, and Poe, preceded somewhat by the Henry James revival. In the 1940s, while doing my doctorate and writing my dissertation on John Dryden, I read for the first time Crane's *The Red Badge of Courage,* and a decade later I applied Kenneth Burke's categories of form (in *Counter-Statement,* 1931) to Crane's fiction and poetry, as noted in "Stephen Crane: A Revaluation," in John Aldridge's *Critiques* (1952), p. 259.

3

Crane, said a friend, was always acting as though to make himself good copy for a biography. "I go through the world unexplained, I suppose," Crane wrote Nellie Crouse. His implied wish to be explained suggests that he thought of himself as a complicated person needing to be explained, which in fact he was. He had reason to think that he would be biographed because Willis Clarke interviewed the dying Crane at Brede Manor for just that purpose, and Cora Taylor (Crane's commonlaw wife) may very well have assured him that she would write his biography. However, she decided some months after his death that she just couldn't do it, and Willis Clarke came to the same conclusion.

While it most likely occurred to the dying Crane that he would be biographed, it could not possibly have occurred to him that he would also be bibliographed. I think cool-cat Crane, as it were, would have scoffed at a bibliographer as being "uptight" and "flaky"!

Recorded here in this first comprehensive and annotated Stephen Crane bibliography is the history of Crane's importance in American literature. His impact on twentieth century critics and scholars—meteoric since the early 1950s—is rendered undeniable by this journal of interest in his incredible achievement as novelist, short story writer, journalist, war correspondent, and poet. In each of these fields he remains today an indisputable master craftsman. As

Hemingway put it: "The good writers are Henry James, Stephen Crane, and Mark Twain. That's not the order they're good in. There is no order for good writers." (In *Green Hills of Africa*.)

This book is organized into six parts. Parts A, B, and C comprise a descriptive bibliography of Crane's books, contribution to books, *miscellanea* and *curiosa,* and published letters. Parts A and B are facsimile sections of the Williams and Starrett *Stephen Crane: A Bibliography* (1948). Their descriptive bibliography of Crane's works, to which on occasion footnotes of correction or additional information have been appended, remain authoritative, valid, and worth preserving, although modern descriptive techniques differ from those of Ames W. Williams and Vincent Starrett. I have not tampered with their descriptive bibliography of Crane's books and contributions to books because first, I am not a professional bibliographer, and also, because it remains as useful today as it was in 1948. My book incorporates the relevant portions of their book by the kind permissions of Mr. Starrett and Mr. Williams in 1955. At that time I had intended to publish a Crane bibliography bringing their compilation of writings on Crane up-to-date, with Clifton Waller Barrett then offering to underwrite its publication costs. However, I lagged for more than a decade until finally the writing of *Stephen Crane: A Biography* trapped me into assembling my bibliographical notes into the present volume and also into annotating my collection of photocopy and xerox of everything written by or on Crane (not counting foreign writings on Crane).

I rejoice in a backward glance that I postponed writing the bibliography and the biography of Crane back in 1955 because since then an incredible amount of writings on Crane has seen print—more than 1,000 articles in the last two decades, far more than any biographer could possibly utilize. As for writings by Crane, several dozens of manuscripts have been brought to light and published since 1955, as well as numerous letters *by* Crane, additional to the first collection in *Omnibus* (1952); and again letters *on* Crane, also innumerable. My Crane biography (1968), even after the second edition, contains more errors than I'd care to admit, and so will this Crane bibliography. However, as Ryder said of a certain sky he had been ten years painting, "My sky begins to look interesting," so too does this Crane bibliography. Novelists get even with their enemies by putting them in their novels.

This Crane bibliography transcends the *W-S Bibliography* in scope and in depth of its listings of writings by Crane and also in its

listings of writings on Crane, of course. It has been impossible to
indicate where new material has been added to the *W-S Bibliography*, but their 1948 cutoff date provides the reader one clue. This
Crane bibliography supplements as companion volume *Stephen
Crane: A Biography*, wherein it was promised as forthcoming in
1968.*

Part D presents contemporary reviews and some parodies of
Crane's works (1893–1904), annotated. The *W-S Bibliography* is
unannotated in "Contemporary Reviews," pp. 77–82, which lists but
a fraction of the present collection. Here for the first time are almost
all of the known-to-exist contemporary reviews. They comprise
within *Stephen Crane: A Critical Bibliography* a book in themselves.

The reviewed works in Part D, as in Part F (writings about
Stephen Crane), are annotated so as to provide multiple critical
viewpoints and a history of the critical reception of Crane's works
at the start, his reputation then. The critical insights of many of
these reviewers (as on *The Red Badge*, for instance) anticipated by
sixty years what many present-day critics offer as new insights.

The format in Part D, as again in Part F, differs from that in the
W-S Bibliography where, for example, the 1893 Hamlin Garland
review of *Maggie* is cited thus: *Arena*, Vol. 8, pp. xi–xii, June
1893. By Hamlin Garland. Our format runs thus: *Lotus*, 2, no. 6
(October, 1896), 208–211. By Jonathan Penn. "A Little Study of
Stephen Crane."

Although Crane publicly bluffed it that he never read reviews of
his works, he nevertheless subscribed to a clipping bureau. In
November, 1895, he received forty-one reviews of *The Red Badge of
Courage* and wrote Willis B. Hawkins: "And, oh, say, most of 'em
were not only favorable but passionately enthusiastic." *The Red
Badge* was among the best sellers in January, 1896, and in the same
Bookman we learn that Crane's war book, "owing no doubt to the
generous appreciation of the book in England, is attracting considerable attention now, although when this work first appeared very
little call indeed was experienced for it." Here is supporting evidence that *The Red Badge of Courage* was acclaimed more in
America after it had been critically received very favorably in
England. A running argument raged on this side of the Atlantic
about this question: Did England or America first discover Crane's

---

* See *Crane*, pp. 633–634. "To footnote every quoted passage in a text which jux-
taposes on the same page quotations from disparate sources would encumber this biography with an elephantine appendix of data irrelevant to the text. For the same
reason, it is impossible to provide a complete checklist of writings on Crane. . . . and
so the Crane scholar is asked to consult my forthcoming *Stephen Crane: A Critical
Bibliography* (Iowa State University Press)."

war book? Some critical warfare occurred in these contemporary reviews, and critical warfare—acrimonious skirmishes, sometimes vicious—occurs again in present-day writings by scholars and critics on Crane (Part F).

Part E presents the writings of Stephen Crane arranged alphabetically by individual titles, as given in the *W-S Bibliography,* pp. 83-133. However, the present volume adds numerous variant newspaper reprints with variant titles; all in all, more than a hundred new titles occur here, scattered throughout this section. Some few of these are my findings, but the majority of new titles are the kind gift of Fredson Bowers, while a considerable number—mainly in the *Nebraska State Journal*—were contributed by Bernice Slote.

Here for the first time (in Part E) is a collation of Crane manuscripts and typescripts—prose and poetry—listed with their location in various Crane collections: Barrett Crane Collection (coded BCC), Columbia University Crane Collection (coded CUCC), etc. *See* Code, p. xxxxi.

Here for the first time (in Part E) individual poems are bibliographed—by title or by first line—with location of manuscript or typescript, if any such exist, and the publication of the given title in *The Black Riders* or in *War Is Kind* with citation of reprints in *The Work of Stephen Crane,* vol. 6 (1926); *The Collected Poems of Stephen Crane,* 1930; *The Poetry of Stephen Crane,* 1957; and *The Poems of Stephen Crane,* 1966.

For titles of prose works, likewise, first publication and subsequent reprintings are cited. The list of books and journals in which Crane's writings obtained first publication or obtained reprinting (1920–1970), not including here first editions of Crane's works (from 1893 *Maggie* to 1904 *The O'Ruddy),* are given in the List of Shortened Titles.

For example: "Joys of Seaside Life" is listed for first publication in the *New York Tribune,* July 17, 1892, part 2, p. 18. Next in *UW* (1963) and in *NYCS* (1966). The latter, to decode them, are *Uncollected Writings* and *The New York City Sketches of Stephen Crane.*

In Part E appear some titles made known here for the first time by the fact that they are not included in the Crane collection catalogues, BCC and/or CUCC catalogues. The listings in *Stephen Crane (1871–1900): An Exhibition of His Writings* (1956) are incomplete. The card catalogue of CUCC, which improves upon *Exhibition,* has been here collated with the BCC catalogue. As the CUCC catalogue quotes no part of the title's text, and as the text of a given Crane manuscript bears either no title or a title differing from that listed title in *Exhibition* or in the CUCC card catalogue, some confusion might (in some few instances) result. For instance, "Indian Fights in the 12th Cavalry," listed in *Exhibition,* p. 55, is listed in the CUCC card catalogue as "Twelfth Cavalry and the Indian Wars," AMs., 17 pp. Where possible confusion of identity of a title exists, the variant titles are cross-referenced. For example, "Apaché Crossing" is cross-identified to "Graveyard in Apaché Crossing," and under the latter entry its holograph manuscript is listed and then its first publication in *Prairie Schooner* (1969).

The Barrett Crane Collection catalogue is also incomplete. It lists Crane's Pocket Notebook, but not its contents, for instance. Also, it omits mention of the fact that on verso of page "3" of the final holograph manuscript of *The Red Badge of Courage* appears an untitled fragment of a story about Gustave and Marie, first made known in *Stephen Crane: An Omnibus* (1952). Almost every scrap of Crane manuscripts has by now (1970) seen print, but not "Gustave and Marie"—the title given it in *Omnibus.*

A selection of some of Crane's best manuscripts began to appear in *Bulletin of the New York Public Library* in 1956 and 1957: "Stephen Crane: Some New Stories." They were drawn from Crane's Pocket Notebook, from typescripts by Edith Crane, and from manuscripts in the BCC. The Notebook and the Edith Crane typescripts, which were then owned by Bacon Collamore, are now in BCC, together with the manuscripts of the Edith Crane typescripts. *The Notebook of Stephen Crane,* edited by Donald J. Greiner and Ellen B. Greiner, was published in 1969.

When Crane became the Diamond as Big as the Ritz in the 1960s, nothing then could possibly damage his reputation no matter what scrap he had written; and so more Crane manuscripts appeared in *Bulletin* and in *Studies in Short Fiction* (1963 and 1964). "Drama in Cuba" appeared in *Bulletin* in 1963, and "Three Mexican Sketches" in 1967. Another prize was "Dan Emmonds" in *SinSF* (1963). However, "The Camel," I having lagged too long, was published in *CSS&S* (1963).

Part F, writings about Crane, begins with notices about him in 1888 and ends with books and articles, scholarly and critical, in 1970. Listings extend into 1972, but the terminal year of comprehensive listings is 1969. These writings about Crane are arranged by year and with authors then listed alphabetically under the given year. Arranged thus, they total more than 2,100 and chart year by year the rising reputation of Crane, notably since the early 1950s.

Translations of Crane's works are entered here in Part F under the name of the translator. They are not listed in Part E, writings of Crane. Not included are textbooks excepting those with introductions which ask for and reward some critical annotation. Not included are anthologies of Crane's works unless they include introductions of possible merit. Not included are dissertations (except for the early ones of the 1940s), and abstracts of dissertations, although once or twice I have made an exception. Neither are yearly bibliographies included except for a few important exceptions.

A bibliography is at its most interesting when it reads like a journal. My annotations provide a critique of Crane scholarship and criticism. Critic X is cross-referenced with critic Y; I annotate their contradictory standpoints and comment. I trace antecedents of their standpoints and critical echoes. Critics subsequent to X and Y echo their standpoints, sometimes without acknowledging X and Y, who in turn were ignorant of Crane's contemporary reviewers who had said the same thing. My annotations occasionally amount to no more than "Nothing new here." The author may think otherwise, but he is mistaken; writings on Crane presenting something new in Crane scholarship or saying something new in Crane criticism are usually annotated. What gets annotated is what interests me, and in that sense this is a kind of "autobibliography." However, my annotations quote from other Crane critics on X and Y. They include quotations from reviews of Eric Solomon's *Stephen Crane: From Parody to Realism* (1966), for instance. And so my annotated critiques are not solely personal judgments.

Some of the known reviews of books on Crane are cited in Part F, writings on Crane; but reviews are scarce on Olov Fryckstedt's *Stephen Crane: Uncollected Writings* (1963), Edwin Cady's *Stephen Crane* (1963), and Thomas A. Gullason's edition of *The Complete Short Stories and Sketches of Stephen Crane* (1963), which was reviewed almost not at all.

The richest and best of recent short critical studies of Crane are unquestionably Sergio Perosa's "Naturalism and Impressionism in Stephen Crane's Fiction" (1964) and James B. Colvert's "Stephen Crane's Magic Mountain" (1967)—both essays made known for the first time in *Stephen Crane: A Collection of Critical Essays,* edited by Maurice Bassan (1967).

Another brilliant critical study is Daniel Knapp's "Son of Thunder," in *Nineteenth Century Fiction,* 24 (1969).

R. W. STALLMAN

23 December 1970

ACKNOWLEDGEMENTS

TO: Fredson Bowers for checking the galleys of BOOKS AND CONTRIBUTIONS TO BOOKS and THE WRITINGS OF STEPHEN CRANE, to which latter section he contributed variant periodical titles numbering about a hundred new entries, an incomparable find by which this Crane bibliography is enlarged and enriched. I thank him also for his constant aid in the minute particulars.

I am greatly indebted also

TO: Bernice Slote (University of Nebraska) for her contribution of variant periodical titles and for new entries of Omaha newspapers.

TO: Jean Cazemajou (University of Bordeaux) for listing French writers on Crane and for French translations of Crane's works.

TO: Sergio Perosa (University of Venice) for listing Italian writers on Crane.

TO: George Monteiro (Brown University) for his contribution of South American writers on Crane, translations of Crane into Spanish and Portuguese, and several periodical items.

TO: Olga Vasilievskaya (Moscow) for the entries on Crane by Russian writers and translators.

TO: Mrs. Yoshie Itabashi (Tokyo) for contributing a list of Japanese writers and translators.

TO: F. H. Bastein (Hamburg) for submitting a list of German writers on Crane and translators of his works.

TO: Ursula Christmann (Hamburg) for submitting a list of German writers on Crane.

TO: Austin Fox (Buffalo) for his generous offer of the new entries here on Crane and Elbert Hubbard.

TO: Kenneth Lohf (Librarian for Rare Books and Manuscripts, Butler Library, Columbia University) for his kind aid on Crane bibliographical queries.

TO: Herald Merklen (Research Librarian, New York Public Library) for his many kindnesses in tracing Crane publications in periodicals.

TO: University of Connecticut graduate assistants: John Conway, whose library researches contributed considerably to the making of this book; Mrs. Bobby Rawlings and Ellen Silverman, for their kind aid in preparing the manuscript in its midway drafts. My debt is also to Robert Onopa (University of Hawaii, University of Liberia), who prepared the first draft of the manuscript half a decade ago while a graduate student in English 379 at the University of Connecticut.

TO: Miss Gillian Kyles and Mrs. B. Yalden-Thomson, secretaries to Fredson Bowers.

TO: Mrs. Richard L. Stevens (Sparrowbush, N.Y.) for her gift of the new Crane photograph, and to Victor Cassella, an undergraduate student in my 212 who researched the manufacturer's dates for the rifles of the hunters in that photograph.

TO: Mrs. Rowena James (Editor, Iowa State University Press) for her extraordinary generosity in giving this manuscript so much of her time, labor, and scholarly care.

TO: my wife Virginia.

TO: Dr. Hugh Clark and the University of Connecticut Research Foundation for grants in aid of research on the Crane Bibliography.

TO: Miss Roberta Smith (Reference Librarian, University of Connecticut), who co-authored *Stephen Crane: A Critical Bibliography* by producing hundreds of answers to hundreds of bibliographical queries since the beginning of this project in 1954–1955.

The *MLA International Bibliography of Books and Articles on the Modern Languages and Literatures,* and *American Literature; a Journal of Literary History, Criticism, and Bibliography,* have been invaluable resources.

INTRODUCTION

CRANE CRITICISM TODAY (1948–1970)
by Jean Cazemajou

A REVIVAL OF INTEREST in Crane, after the two decades of silence following his death, began in 1923 when Thomas Beer published his highly impressionistic biography, prefaced by Joseph Conrad. However, both Beer and Conrad contributed more to the literature of devotion than to a correct assessment of Crane's achievement, and the same criticism could be levelled at most of the introductions to the twelve volumes of *The Work of Stephen Crane*, edited by Wilson Follett and published between 1925 and 1927.

Thus, as noted in the Preface to this work, the twenties did not throw much light on Crane's complex personality. Scholars preferred to regard it as mysterious and elusive, and left to future critics the task of assessing his work more soberly. During the thirties and forties, scholars were merely content to see this writer through their own specific bias, mostly social and economic. Serious Crane criticism began in the 1950s and was launched by an invaluable book, *Stephen Crane: A Bibliography* (1948), prepared by Ames W. Williams and Vincent Starrett.

The essence of Crane's personality emerged from a variety of stereotypes when, in the 1950s, a new approach was started, attempting to explore the symbols of his prose and verse in the light of Freudian, Jungian, and, occasionally, Christian patterns. In his biography, *Stephen Crane* (1950), John Berryman, while trying to decode the cipher of Crane's mind, emphasized a deep-seated wish for "moral rescue" and a castration complex. If such hypotheses

xxi

were sometimes overexploited in this book for the sake of logic, they
have nevertheless proved to be useful pointers to a new generation
of critics. Most of the American doctoral dissertations on Crane
written in the 1950s and 1960s have regarded Berryman's interpretation as a guide or, at least, a landmark. Daniel G. Hoffman, in his
Columbia University doctoral thesis published in 1957, *The Poetry
of Stephen Crane,* pursued the same enquiry, focusing his attention
mainly on Crane's religious heritage, which contributed so much
to the inner landscape of his poetry.

R. W. Stallman had, by then, strongly established his Christian
exegesis, formulated in his introduction to the Modern Library
edition of *The Red Badge of Courage* (1951) and expanded in his
essay: "Stephen Crane: A Revaluation" (in *Critiques and Essays
in Modern Fiction,* edited by John Aldridge, 1952). By the end
of 1952, Professor Stallman had completed *Stephen Crane: An
Omnibus,* which brought together the essential writings of Crane,
critical introductions, and large extracts of the manuscript of *The
Red Badge of Courage.* This *Omnibus,* more than any single book,
except Berryman's, contributed to the Crane revival. In 1960, with
the help of Lillian Gilkes, Stallman provided future biographers
with a very useful edition of Crane's *Letters.* The same year, Lillian
Gilkes published a biography of Cora Crane, the woman who shared
the last three years of the writer's life. Miss Gilkes' painstaking research helped to clear up many mysterious episodes in Crane's life
and systematically explored his relationship with the English literary
scene.

The sixties have come to a close and Crane is now recognized as a
classic, thanks to the efforts made by scholars the world over in order
to interpret his contribution to American literature. R. W. Stallman's gigantic biography, published in 1968, will remain an important landmark. Its virtues are numerous: Stallman has thoroughly
depicted Crane's background and minutely traced the genesis of most
of his works. His study is extremely well documented on almost
any dramatic episode of Crane's life, the Dora Clark affair, the
Commodore disaster, the experience of war reporting in Greece and
Cuba, for instance. Indeed Stallman's monumental work deserves
to be ranked with Mark Schorer's biography of Sinclair Lewis, which
seems to have been its model.

Joseph Katz, editor of the *Stephen Crane Newsletter,* has been one
of the most active researchers and editors in the Crane vineyard.
His major contributions are *The Poems of Stephen Crane* (1966)—
the best edition of Crane's poetry now in print—and *The Portable
Stephen Crane* (1969), which contains, besides an excellent intro-

duction and a chronology, the most famous novels—*Maggie, George's Mother, The Red Badge of Courage*—, nineteen short stories and a selection of letters, poems, and newspaper articles.

Among the forthcoming selections, Professor Stallman's *The Stephen Crane Reader*—a recast version of his *Stephen Crane: Stories and Tales*, Vintage Books, 1955—, due to appear in 1972, is well worth mentioning for it will contain a very comprehensive selection of Crane's writings.

During the sixties critics in the United States as well as in the rest of the world have introduced Crane's work to an increasingly larger audience. In the United States one of the most important directions followed by Crane scholars had to do with his stylistic identity: was he an impressionist, a realist, a naturalist, a decadent, a symbolist, an existentialist, a social reformer, or something else? Then-unexplored facets of specific works (*Maggie, George's Mother, The Red Badge of Courage, The O'Ruddy*, for the novels, "The Open Boat," "The Blue Hotel," "The Bride Comes to Yellow Sky," and "The Monster," for the short stories, and some of the more representative poems) came under the scrutiny of enthusiastic scholars. Among the general books of the sixties devoted to *fin-de-siècle* writers, four studies contain long essays on Crane: they are the work of Warner Berthoff, Robert Schneider, Larzer Ziff, and Jay Martin. All of them serve to document the quality of Crane's achievement and contain interesting insights: Jay Martin, for instance, was one of the first among the general critics to try and rehabilitate the journalist.

Meanwhile, Japan, Germany, France, Sweden, Norway, Great Britain, the Soviet Union, and Italy began to show signs of a Crane revival in their turn. Japanese critics followed closely in the wake of the Americans. English reticence was shaken occasionally by writings of V. S. Pritchett; and Neville Denny, Professor at University College in Nairobi (Kenya), wrote a long essay on the role of imagination and experience in Crane's work. German criticism, apart from a few doctoral dissertations completed on both sides of the Berlin wall, was focused on Crane's relationship with Conrad, on the short-story writer, the novelist, and the poet.[1] For Sweden

---

[1] Hans Petersen's doctoral dissertation, *"Der künstlerische Werdegang Stephen Cranes,"* Ernst-Moritz-Arndt Universität, Greifswald, 1929, is available on microfilm. Two doctoral dissertations were under way in 1964 in Western Germany: Dietmar Haack was working on *"Die Erzählkunst Stephen Cranes: Theoretische Prinzipien und dichterisches Werk"* (at the Freie Universität, Berlin). Someone else (not named) at the University of Giessen was writing on *"Die Satzsprache in den Kurzgeschichten Stephen Cranes."*
Among the most interesting articles were: F. Schoenberner, *"Die romantische Begründung des amerikanischen Realismus,"* Prisma 23-24 (1948), 49-50; Gerard Wilk,

and Norway the two leading scholars appear to have been Olov W. Fryckstedt—a spiritual heir of Lars Åhnebrink—and Orm Overland: they both staked out their claims very clearly, Fryckstedt devoting most of his attention to Crane's journalism with Overland trying to define his "impressionism." In France, the interest raised by Crane in the sixties was partly linked with the preparation of two *"thèses d'Etat,"* one on Hamlin Garland and one on Crane himself. The Crane-Garland relationship—also studied by Donald Pizer in the United States—, the Freudian pulsions in the oneiric substructure of *The Red Badge,* the genesis of the New York City Sketches, the parodies of Crane's work, the posthumous completion of *The O'Ruddy* by Robert Barr, Crane's first taste of boarding school at Pennington Seminary, and his links with the world of the small American town were successively analyzed.[2]

Although Crane was occasionally mentioned in the Soviet Union by prominent critics of American literature such as A. A. Elistratova and R. M. Samarin, the most important critic was Olga Vasilievskaya who, in a study published in 1967, tried to outline the development of his work and emphasized his gradual conquest of a personal form of realism.

Professor Sergio Perosa of Venice, Italy, devoted a long essay—later included in a book—to Stephen Crane's method and, instead of trying to trace the influences that shaped his talent, Perosa declared: "He was mistaken for a disciple, a follower. In fact he was a precursor who instinctively applied the principles [of literary renewal] at the very moment they were being formulated in England."

Perhaps of greatest interest among the insights of the sixties was the contention that the essence of Crane's personality lay in a love for experimentation and a basic commitment to the journalistic experience.[3] These two features were somewhat lost in two biographies of the early sixties—Ruth Franchere's *Stephen Crane* (1961), a rather sketchy book meant for young readers, and Louis Zara's *Dark Rider* (1961), a fictionalized jazzed up biography—but began

---

"Stephen Crane: Dil nis eines amerikanischen Dichters," Der Monat, 5, no. 59 (1953), 518–527; E. Gerlach, *"Stephen Crane: Hemingways grosser Lehrmeister,"* Welt-Stimmen, 24 (1955), 410–422; Peter Baasner, "Stephen Crane and Joseph Conrad," *Kleine Beiträge zur amerikanischen Literatur Geschichte* (1961), pp. 34–39; Rudolf Kerscher, *"Whilomville Stories: Stephen Cranes vergessene Kindheitserzäklungen,"* Die neueren Sprachen, 15 (1966), 77–86.

[2] A very interesting doctoral dissertation published in France in the 1960s gives a good survey of Crane's times: Marianne Debouzy, *La genèse de l'esprit de révolte dans le roman américain 1875–1915,* Paris, Minard, 1968.

[3] John Berryman, "Stephen Crane, *The Red Badge of Courage"* in *The American Novel,* ed. Wallace Stegner. New York, 1965, p. 88: "He is inventing [in *The Red Badge*], he is experimenting."

to come into clearer focus in the very perceptive study that Edwin H. Cady published the following year.

With each new addition to the canon our assessment of Crane's impact has been based on more substantial evidence: gradually it became apparent that his most characteristic medium was neither poetry, which he often used as a period mask, nor the novel form in which he seemed to flounder like a fallen albatross. His best medium was the short story and, occasionally, the feature article. The necessity for a modern critic to be able to see the whole of Crane's work at a glance made research into his journalistic publications all the more imperative, and, in this field, Olov W. Fryckstedt's *Stephen Crane: Uncollected Writings* (1963) came out most opportunely to fill an obvious gap. The legendary figure of a self-centered reporter and an "irresponsible" war correspondent was shattered by the publication of this book. Crane the journalist turned out to be not a paragon of the Fourth Estate but a newspaperman full of passion, eager to learn, and taking his missions quite seriously. Two other books, *The War Dispatches of Stephen Crane* and *The New York City Sketches and Related Pieces,* both edited by R. W. Stallman and E. R. Hagemann, supplemented Fryckstedt's pioneering work and helped re-create the background of the journalistic experience.

In the year 1966 the critics went *"Maggie*-mad." The 1893 edition, an extremely rare book which had sold for $3700 in the hungry thirties and which could only be found in the vaults of a few American University libraries, was suddenly released from its prisons: three new editions of *Maggie,* vintage 1893, saw the light of day thanks to Joseph Katz, Maurice Bassan, and Donald Pizer. Another scholar, Thomas A. Gullason, had, by that time, brought securely between the covers of two handy volumes the work of the short-story writer and that of the novelist but, useful as these new publications were, they did not always provide the best possible text.

One thing still seemed to keep the critics in abeyance—Crane's literary achievement seen as a whole. No complete study of his prose writings had been attempted until Eric Solomon published his *Stephen Crane: From Parody to Realism* in 1966. This book, full of sharp insights, suffered from the too systematic approach outlined in its title. In 1967 the Soviet critic Olga Vasilievskaya tackled the problem of Crane's literary development in her turn. According to her, his progress as a writer led from the "naturalism" of *Maggie* to the "realism" of the Spanish-American war stories, and her demonstration was, on the whole, convincing. The same year, Maurice Bassan edited a "Twentieth Century Views" volume devoted to

Stephen Crane, which contained well-known interpretations and a new essay by James B. Colvert, "Stephen Crane's Magic Mountain." The latter singled out the metaphor of the solitary pilgrim facing the "silent mountain"—a recurrent image in Crane's verse—as central to an understanding of his message. This collection of essays forms, with the *Modern Fiction Studies* "Stephen Crane number," the best sampling of major critical views on this writer. In 1968, *The Fiction of Stephen Crane* by Donald B. Gibson—a 1962 doctoral dissertation at Brown University—applied again Freudian patterns but often failed to convince.

In 1968, *The Sullivan County Sketches,* Crane's early journalism in New York State, came out in a new edition, much enlarged because of Professor Stallman's recent "finds" consisting of seven new items, for the most part unsigned chronicles from the *New York Tribune.* "The Blue Hotel," superlative among short stories, entered the case-book niche the same year thanks to Joseph Katz. As for the undersigned writer he published three contributions, two in French—a book-length study, *Stephen Crane, Écrivain Journaliste,* and a long essay on *The Red Badge* included in a textbook analyzing *Maggie* and *The Red Badge*—and one in English, a pamphlet in the Minnesota series on American writers.

At the close of the sixties an ambitious project, made possible by a grant from the National Endowment for the Humanities, was under way at the University of Virginia: the preparation of a definitive edition of *The Works of Stephen Crane* under the supervision of Professor Fredson Bowers. Volume I: *Bowery Tales,* and Volume VII: *Tales of Whilomville* came out in 1969, the former prefaced by James B. Colvert and the latter by J. C. Levenson. Both books, elegantly printed, had carefully established the Crane text according to the techniques of modern textual scholarship. *Bowery Tales* included *Maggie* and *George's Mother,* while *Tales of Whilomville* brought together "The Monster," "His New Mittens," and the thirteen "Whilomville Stories" published in *Harper's Magazine* between August, 1899, and August, 1900, and, later the same year, in book form by the same publisher.

In volume I, James B. Colvert comes to the following conclusion concerning the genesis of *Maggie:* "The external evidence for a Syracuse version of the novel seems weak and inconclusive." He rejects the hypothesis of a European influence on Crane in his Bowery novels. Professor Colvert instead traces some of Crane's stylistic devices to the work of Mark Twain and Edgar Allan Poe and his literary creed to a corpus of ideas combining Rudyard Kipling's and Hamlin Garland's respective brands of impressionism.

For *Maggie* Professor Bowers has used the privately printed 1893 edition as copy-text, which appears as a wise choice since the 1896 edition was not entirely prepared under Crane's supervision. Professor Bowers has carried out very thorough editorial work with a view to incorporating what he presumes to have been Crane's literary aims in the writing and rewriting of this book. Most of the emendations and alterations introduced by the present editor are sound and reasonable, but we wonder whether deleting the paragraph immediately preceding Maggie's death in chapter XVII—the "fat man" paragraph—actually reflects Crane's "desire for simplicity" or rather a mawkish impulse of the 1896 editor.[4] In our opinion, the "fat man" whose body shakes "like that of a dead jelly fish" does not have "a distracting effect" in the overall picture but, on the contrary, brings the prostitute's despair to its climax.[5] She has now reached the end of her walk, and the repulsion she feels at the sight of that drunken tramp fully justifies her suicide. This final paragraph is relevant both dramatically and stylistically. Leaving it out causes the picture to lose some of its dynamic quality, and the next paragraph, which concludes the chapter, then dangles like a broken limb.

In the preface to volume VII, Professor J. C. Levenson provides us with a chronology of composition for the tales included in the volume—a painstaking task which involved collating much circumstantial evidence. Future literary historians will certainly appreciate finding there a clearer picture of the genesis of Crane's Whilomville tales than anywhere else in print, but these stories needed a reassessment and are excellent material for a linguistic and sociological analysis, as Alfred Kazin pointed out. Levenson's preface, rich as it is, somewhat neglects these two approaches.

As they stand, the first two volumes of *The Works of Stephen Crane* now in print are a credit to their editors, publishers, and printers and augur well for the ones to come.

Much progress has been accomplished from the impressionism of the 1920s to the more scientific criticism of the 1960s, and Crane has not suffered too much from his new condition as classic writer, which has caused his frequent translation into foreign languages and his entrance into the realm of high-school text books. *The Red Badge of Courage,* especially, has been offered to countless schoolboys and students in very attractive editions, among which the "Norton Critical Edition" best exemplifies what scholarship and good pedagogy can do when they join hands.

---

[4] The phrase "desire for simplicity" was used by Professor Levenson in a note on *Maggie:* it corroborates Professor Fredson Bowers' viewpoint.

[5] This phrase is part of Professor Bowers' Preface.

Although critics of all faiths and creeds—including marxism and existentialism—have tried to interpret the work of Crane, the chances are that the literary warfare between two rival schools will remain the most memorable episode of the last two decades. Disciples of the Chicago school of criticism have emphasized such elements as plot and character and insisted on the "organic" quality of Crane's stories which, according to them, are quite meaningful at the literary level. On the contrary, the supporters of symbolic criticism have continually looked for the underlying significance of Crane's irony and, contending that his language is "the language of symbol and paradox," have argued that it should never be taken at its face value. In the foreground of that battlefield appear the followers of R. W. Stallman and his opponents.[6]

Does the spate of articles published in the 1950s and 1960s—more than 1,000 articles according to Professor Stallman—indicate the high watermark of Crane scholarship? If we judge by numbers alone, yes. But most of these articles have a tendency to overlap and often deal with minor aspects of Crane as a writer and as a man. They are, for the most part, focused on recondite facets of his achievement and seldom offer reassessments of his better tales or poems. Very few of them attempt to synthesize the whole prospect on a given issue. Among the exceptions some deserve mention: George W. Johnson's "Stephen Crane: Metaphor of Decorum," a June, 1963, *PMLA* essay, and Max Westbrook's "Stephen Crane's Social Ethic," both of which stress the positive side of Crane's social philosophy. On *The Red Badge of Courage*, which was the topic of a large section of Crane criticism in the sixties, Daniel Weiss's psychoanalytic reading had the merit of being the work of a serious and highly qualified practitioner. About the genesis of this novel a close analysis of the manuscript, conducted by William L. Howarth, started, in 1965, the spadework for the textual criticism of what will be one day volume II of *The Works of Stephen Crane*.

As we view this twenty-year span of criticism in perspective, we are bound to conclude that Crane's literary expression was *both* organic and symbolic, which should encourage critics to form a united front. And indeed many tasks remain to be carried out before the scholars can rest satisfied. Crane, like Mark Twain but to a lesser extent, was fascinated by language and, in his short creative

[6] This quotation is from *Stephen Crane: An Omnibus*, ed. R. W. Stallman. New York, 1952, p. xlv. As for the "organic" interpretation, it is best expressed in the following articles: Philip Rahv, "Fiction and the Criticism of Fiction," *Kenyon Review*, 18 (Spring, 1956), 276–299; Norman Friedman, "Criticism and the Novel: Hardy, Hemingway, Crane, Woolf, Conrad," *Antioch Review*, 18 (Fall, 1958), 343–370; Stanley B. Greenfield, "The Unmistakable Stephen Crane," *PMLA*, 73 (December, 1958), 562–572.

period, helped to record the military academy and university student slang, the journalistic jargon, and the Bowery dialect of his times, as well as the rhetoric and powerful imagery of small-town Methodism, which was his personal heritage. It is the merging of those various layers of speech, with their major and minor fringes of connotations, that constitutes the specific quality of Crane's literary expression. So the first trail opening out in front of the scholar is a linguistic one, and such research might eventually be greatly assisted by the publication of a *Stephen Crane Concordance,* when the University of Virginia edition of *The Works of Stephen Crane* is completed.

Another task of equal importance will require a closer study of his psychological workshop and should analyze the inner mechanisms of his various modes of expression. It is no longer enough to say, as Thomas Beer did, that "the mistress of this boy's life was fear," because fear is a most common human emotion anyway. The interesting thing about Crane's "fear" is that it generated in him an acute awareness of religious drives, such as guilt, remorse, and voluntary retribution. This second phase of exploration, made possible by the previous one, would be an attempt at discovering what Tzvetan Todorov, in a recent essay, called: "a theory of the structure and operations of literary expression."[7] This theory probably functioned at an unconscious level in the case of Crane but, unless this "figure in the carpet" is made visible, the reality of his message will remain a blur.

A purely descriptive conception of literature leaves the modern mind unsatisfied because, as Todorov pointed out (p. 100), " . . . in a certain sense, any literary work is in itself its best description." So, in order to avoid the deficiencies and drawbacks of a mere inventory, the probing of language ought to be vertical rather than horizontal. We are inclined to go along with Roland Barthes' contention when he wrote: "Nothing is more vital to a society than the classification of its languages."[8]

Crane's work will not offer us such a wide variety of layers of American speech as Mark Twain, Sinclair Lewis, or H. L. Mencken explored in their lifetime, but this dialectical approach should throw light on two prospects: the American religious mind in a period of transition and one of the first attempts at creating a new language—an early blueprint of mass-media American English.

It is true that Crane's name figures prominently in the story of

[7] Tzvetan Todorov, "Poétique," in *Qu'est-ce que le structuralisme?* Oswald Ducrot, et al. Paris, Le Seuil, 1968, p. 102.
[8] Roland Barthes, *Critique et vérité.* Paris, Le Seuil, 1966, p. 45.

American journalism, but his place there has not always been correctly assigned. This is due in part to a confusion between hierarchy and classification. We are only beginning to become aware of the various levels of communication in human speech, and, investing a formal and artificial mode of expression with a privileged status has often led literary historians, in the past, to neglect other media currently in use. In the case of Crane, his impact on the American language was certainly felt in a variety of fields, and his specific contribution to American journalese should not be ignored.

But Crane the iconoclast also spoke of *new* spiritual values in the words and metaphors of an *old* faith. At a time when his country was undergoing profound social and economic changes, it would be interesting to see how these changes were registered in a language that was still, to a large extent, shaped by the Bible and by the hymns of the Methodist Episcopal Church. The study of literature and that of sociology will then overlap, since Crane's religious heritage and his special link with large audiences may also serve to explore the American folk mind, which has depended so much upon the evolution of religion and mass-media culture in America.

The last word on Crane has not been written yet, but it is comforting to realize that a more coherent image of his achievement is gradually taking shape. Even if it is too ambitious to hope that literary criticism may be turned into a science, we are bound to observe that all the "charisms" and "mysteries" mentioned in the past did not explain anything at all. Modern literary criticism, if it wishes to survive, must aim at something more meaningful.*

University of Bordeaux

* This introduction is recast from Cazemajou, "Deux Decennies de Rede Couverte (1948–1968)," *Langues Moderne,* 63 (January-February, 1969), 54–60.

INTRODUCTION

by *Vincent Starrett*

STILL SADLY IMPERATIVE, in spite of Thomas Beer's biography, now more than twenty years old, is a careful chronology and factual study of the life of Stephen Crane. Broadly his exits and entrances are accounted for, but to the fascinated student and admirer of this remarkable figure in American letters—perhaps the most startling figure after Poe—the numerous lacunae in published reports are tantalizing and exasperating.

Writing of the Beer opus, in the *Colophon,* a number of years ago, I used the following words: "Mr. Beer's admirable study, in my opinion a masterpiece, is far from being a documented biography. His impressionism keeps coming between one and what one wants most to know. The book is a study of the times, in strong light, and across that light moves an inconspicuous figure called Stephen Crane." Thomas Beer, who was then living, agreed. "Henry Mc-Bride's comment on my book, I think, is final," he wrote me in a friendly letter. "He said, 'I spent ten years planning a study of Crane and ended by deciding there was no such animal, although I knew him for eleven years.'"

Nevertheless, some day somebody will try again to write the "Life" of Stephen Crane, and the materials are available. In part they are to be found in the writings of the man himself—in his fiction as well as in his journalism—and in part in the now numerous

From *Stephen Crane: A Bibliography* (1948).

reminiscences of those who knew him. After his death, in 1900, many reminiscent articles were printed in the newspapers and magazines; these were largely explored by Thomas Beer. After Beer's biography was published more articles appeared, inspired by the book; some of these are of considerable importance and all are interesting. Those that are important correct the biography in significant particulars.

There is still a large body of unpublished material, some of it in process of being lost, some of it in the hands of collectors. For example, three interesting women who knew Crane in his early days, and were influential in his life, are nowhere mentioned by Beer in his biography. These are Lily Brandon, Nancy Crouse, and Amy Leslie—the latter well known in her later years as drama critic of the *Chicago Daily News*. Some of Lily Brandon's letters from Stephen Crane were destroyed soon after arrival, as ascertained by Mr. Williams in a personal interview; but others survived and he was able to obtain copies of them. Seven youthful and revealing (and very charming) letters to Miss Crouse are extant; copies of these are in various hands. It is not known at present what became of Crane's letters to Miss Leslie—who was a dancer of lively temper on the New York stage when Stephen knew her—but whispers of the relationship are to be found in old files of the Manhattan newspapers. Several efforts were made to relieve Miss Leslie of her letters, shortly before her death, and all were wrathfully repulsed.*

Much work has yet to be done on the woman who married Crane, the extraordinary Cora Taylor. Thomas Beer shirked her story conspicuously, possibly because he could not lay hands on the provable facts. These have now been made available, in part, in Messrs. Cabell's and Hanna's work on the St. Johns River, in the *Rivers of America* series; they are handled in appalling taste, but reveal a chapter of life worthy the attention of a Maupassant. More sympathetically viewed, Thomas Beer's "fair, affable woman, older than himself, who had fallen in love with him at Jacksonville and had come after him to Greece"—obviously she is the original of Nora, in *Active Service*—is seen to be a memorable and courageous figure in one of the great true stories of literature. She is entitled to fairer consideration than ever she has received in the curious mythology that has grown up around the name and fame of her husband. Karl Edwin Harriman, who knew and liked her, might have given us a valuable remedial study—albeit a bit on the romantic side—and indeed it was in his mind to do so; he died, however, with only one chapter of his memories of Crane completed.

* It is possible that ultimately she destroyed them.

It is proper, I believe, to say that Crane was born out of season; but the line means little—all geniuses are born out of season. Poe, our classic example, lived and wrote and died in our *Martin Chuzzlewit* period. Crane came to writing stature when the American reading public, generally speaking, was devouring the pious sentimentalities of "Ian Maclaren" and the sanctimonious claptrap of Hall Caine; a time when Howells, our most realistic novelist, was capable of having one New York clubman call another "You goose!" The America of his day was ill-prepared to appreciate the then painful realism he put into such tales as *Maggie, George's Mother,* and a little later *The Red Badge of Courage.* Because Crane was an anti-sentimentalist and a truthteller, his country failed to rejoice that it had produced one of the most vivid geniuses of modern fiction.

He died young, but before he died he succeeded in scandalizing the conventional people of two nations. Little or nothing was then known of his history. Legends, many of them sordid, all of them fantastic, grew up around his sudden celebrity. His picturesque exterior, as James Huneker remarked, offered a field for the imagination of some of his contemporaries and they "turned a little Flaubert into a big Verlaine." Crane himself did little to suppress the legends; they probably amused him. He was aware of them, however, and occasionally made a wry comment. "When people see a banker taking a glass of beer in a café," he once wrote to a friend, "they say, 'There is Smith.' When they behold a writer taking a glass of beer, they say, 'Send for the police!' No great law of nature can be proved from this, but it pretty often hits me that people are ingenious [ingenuous?] blockheads."

The mythology encountered by every researcher who probes at all deeply into the mystery of Stephen Crane's personality—it is described at some length by Beer in an appendix to the biography—has given him a subterranean reputation for profligacy that is more plausible than true. The legendary Stephen Crane is, indeed, a wonderfully wayward and attractive figure in the line of Villon, Byron, Poe, Verlaine, and other men of genius whom we almost prefer to think of as unregenerate sinners; but the real Stephen Crane is even more attractive. When the full story is told, there will be enough of the wayward genius in it to satisfy the most fastidious *precieuse,* but it will also be a profoundly moving human adventure.

Not all the bizarre tales told of him are untrue; rather, they are not *wholly* untrue. "I followed my son through a street of broken windows, and found him dead of old age at five-and-twenty," was not written about Stephen Cane, but might be accepted as a parody of his way of life. Actually, he died of tuberculosis exacerbated, at least, by exposure while acting as a war correspondent in Cuba. But he lived violently, it is clear; it was the way he preferred to live. He was a preacher's son, a newspaperman, a bohemian of bohemians, who claimed for himself complete freedom of thought and action; and he outraged conventions, which he despised, with cool deliberation and malice. He knew peculiar people, he had a clinical curiosity about low life, he frequented barrooms, swore picturesquely, and played poker. He loaned money to prostitutes and consorted with outcasts. He fought with policemen and got into scrapes that landed him in the headlines. He was frequently broke. His respect for Christianity, as he saw it practised, and for the Ten Commandments, was perhaps negligible. He liked horses, dogs, children, boats, baseball, revolver shooting, wine and women within reason (he was peculiarly romantic about prostitutes), and had sometimes an excellent conceit of himself. He married the Madame of a Jacksonville bawdy-house, who made him a faithful and devoted wife before returning to her old trade when his premature death left her in straits. He hated humbugs of all kinds, and said so with more honesty than tact. He was arrogant and humble, modest and immodest, sophisticated and immature. He wrote as he pleased, thought as he pleased, and for the most part lived as he pleased. He didn't give a damn. Such is our hero.

I will add only that those who knew him best found him wholesome, courageous, honorable, generous, modest, kindly, and singularly charming. "There was in Crane a strain of chivalry which made him safe to trust with one's life," said Joseph Conrad, who knew and loved him. In the words of Thomas L. Raymond, "he wore his own red badge of courage."

Crane was not a bookish man; he was not "literary." His reading was miscellaneous, desultory, and unguided. In general, he disliked the writers of his time whom it was the fashion to like—including Stevenson. Zola and Flaubert had their points, but on the whole he found them dull. He criticized Mark Twain sharply, and confined his admiration to *Life on the Mississippi*. When asked if he admired Mallarmé, he confessed that he didn't know much about "Irish authors." He never got around to Balzac or Stendhal. He appears to have liked Kipling, and later Conrad, while Tolstoy was the writer he admired "most of all," although he would have liked to rewrite *War and Peace*—"He [Tolstoy] could have done the whole business in one third of the time and made it just as wonderful. It goes on and on like Texas."

But the fact is, he seldom read books; he didn't have time.

It is not my intention here to debate his own place in literature;

but he has an important place and it is permanent and interesting. His *Maggie* was perhaps the first hint of naturalism in American fiction; but his reputation does not depend on his early studies of slum life along the Bowery. It depends, in part, on *The Red Badge of Courage,* a study in the psychology of fear, one of the great allegories of war; and more and more it is coming to depend on his short stories, which—I think—is as it should be. He was at his best in the short story; at least three of his several dozen specimens are admitted masterpieces—"The Open Boat," "The Monster," "The Blue Hotel." In these, as in the *Red Badge,* it is his highstrung impressionism that makes all the difference between a merely good story and a great one, the extraordinary style that made him, in the words of Carl Van Doren, a "kind of poet among storytellers." It was, of course, the self-conscious violence of his word-painting, amounting to genius, that led to misapprehension of his work in the beginning, and gave the parodists and the conventional critics a Roman holiday at his expense; but it is this startling personal idiom, this grim flippancy, this "inspired audacity of epithet," as Conrad called it, that will make him to the end of our literature one of the most interesting of "little masters." Plus, of course, the ruthless honesty with which he reported life.

I like as well as any I have seen the words of Will Irwin, who said, with admirable finality, that Stephen Crane "spoke in a voice and with a manner which no one had ever used before him. He was like one of those musical phenomena whom humanity spawns occasionally—a child possessing the technique of maturity. His vision was childlike in its unspoiled clarity, his writing was essentially mature. He died early, leaving behind his instrument; and no one after him has ever been able to play it."

Of himself Stephen Crane once wrote in a letter to an editor: "The one thing that deeply pleases me is the fact that men of sense invariably believe me to be sincere. I know that my work does not amount to a string of dried beans—I always calmly admit it—but I also know that I do the best that is in me without regard to praise or blame. When I was the mark for every humorist in the country, I went ahead; and now when I am the mark for only fifty per cent of the humorists of the country, I go ahead; for I understand that a man is born into the world with his own pair of eyes, and he is not at all responsible for his vision—he is merely responsible for his quality of personal honesty. To keep close to this personal honesty is my supreme ambition."

Twice since his death Crane has been "discovered" and there has been a new flurry of interest in his work. Recently critics have been surprised to recognize in him a brilliant contemporary; but the creative writers of our time made the discovery first. His influence may be felt in the work of Sherwood Anderson, Sinclair Lewis, Willa Cather, Ernest Hemingway, even Theodore Dreiser. Crane himself remains unique, but he is also a shining forerunner—the first modern American storyteller.

Some day, as I was saying, there will be a new biography of Stephen Crane; there will have to be. In my opinion, and that of Mr. Williams, most of the material for it is now listed between these covers. We have, we hope, provided an index of sources. All that is needed is the biographer. Our work, a labor of love, has been done with this new biographer in mind. We envy him his subject and wish him godspeed. Having no talent for reticence, we record our own belief that in Stephen Crane he will be dealing with a genius beside whom, without derogation, most of the writing men of our time have been merely so many industrious craftsmen.

CHRONOLOGY

1871   Born on November 1 in the parsonage of the Central Methodist Church in Newark, New Jersey, he was the fourteenth child of the Reverend Dr. Jonathan Townley Crane and Mary Helen Peck. No baptismal record exists at the Central (or First) Methodist Church probably because he was baptised in the parsonage; hence his middle name, which he once initialed T. (for Truesdell?) remains unknown.

1878   Dr. Crane moves his family from Paterson, New Jersey, from the Cross Street Church to the Drew Methodist Church in Port Jervis, New York. That town is the "Whilomville" of Crane's *Whilomville Stories* (1900).

1880   Dr. Crane dies in February, and Mrs. Crane settles in Asbury Park, where son Townley has opened a newspaper agency. Mrs. Crane reports Methodist "holy show" meetings for the *Tribune,* and Stephen when in his late teens reports shore news in Townley's column "On the New Jersey Coast" and renders pen-portraits of Asbury Park, notably in "The Pace of Youth" (1895) and in "Stephen Crane at Asbury Park" (1896).

1885   Stephen writes his first story, "Uncle Jake and the Bell Handle," and and attends the Pennington Seminary from September, 1885, to December, 1887. He next attends Claverack College, the Hudson River Institute, from January, 1888, to June, 1890. Here General John B. Van Petten, his history teacher, recounts his battle memories of Antietam.

1890   He enters Lafayette College as a mining-engineering student and joins Delta Upsilon fraternity. He survives Lafayette one semester, flunking out.

1891   Enters Syracuse University and excels in baseball as shortstop. Decides to become a writer instead of a professional baseball player. His D. U.

fraternity brothers testify that Crane began writing *Maggie* in the cupola of the fraternity house this spring. He publishes "Great Bugs," a journalistic hoax, in the *New York Tribune*, reports Hamlin Garland's summer lecture on W. D. Howells ("Howells Discussed at Avon-By-The-Sea"), and, falling in love with Miss Helen Trent, he composes his first poems, which antedate other "lines" in *The Black Riders* (1895). His mother dies on December 7.

1892   The *Tribune* publishes his first New York City sketches and more than a dozen Sullivan County tales and sketches. In July he boasts he can write a better war novel than Zola's *La Débâcle,* then reviewed in the *Tribune.* This occasion marks the beginning of *The Red Badge of Courage,* at which he perhaps made a beginning draft in late 1892. In December he recasts *Maggie,* published in March, 1893, and by June, 1893, he begins *George's Mother* on verso of the manuscript of "The Holler Tree," a Sullivan County tale. All these works, so diversified in style, Crane wrote in the short span of 1892–1894, earning thus William Dean Howells' sobriquet, "Here is a writer who has sprung into life fully armed." At Asbury Park he falls in love with Mrs. Lily Brandon Munroe. She figures in "The Captain," a New York City tale (1892) and also in Crane's "Intrigue Poems," published in *War Is Kind* (1899). The United Mechanics labor union took offense at the *Tribune*'s August 21 report of their parade in Asbury Park, and Stephen—as well as his brother Townley—was fired. That disaster ended Townley's career as journalist, but not Stephen Crane's.

1893   Publishes *Maggie* in March at his own expense under the pseudonym "Johnston Smith." Howells in April reads him some Emily Dickinson, and *that* turns on his "poetic spout."

1894   In January-February he shows Hamlin Garland the manuscript of his poems, and in April the manuscript of *The Red Badge of Courage. The Red Badge* in abridged form (18,000 words) appears in the *Philadelphia Press,* December 3–8, and perhaps in other papers. The *New York Press* publishes his New York City sketches, 1894–1896.

1895   Crane proposes to Mrs. Munroe and is rejected; he journeys into the West and Mexico to write sketches for the Bacheller-Johnson Syndicate. In Lincoln, Nebraska, Willa Cather meets him and is reminded of Edgar Allan Poe. *The Black Riders* is published in May. *The Red Badge of Courage: An Episode of the American Civil War,* published by Appleton on October 1, receives extraordinary acclaim. English reviewers add to the applause, and his war novel becomes a best seller (fourteen printings by 1897).

1896   Appleton publishes in hard cover the 1893 paperback *Maggie* (a variant text) and *The Little Regiment and Other Episodes of the American Civil War.* Edward Arnold publishes *George's Mother* in June. *The Third Violet* appears serially in *Inter Ocean* (and in book form in 1897). En route to Cuba to report the Cuban insurrection, Crane meets Cora Taylor at her Hotel de Dream in Jacksonville, Florida;

she falls in love with him and follows him to Greece the next year as the *New York Journal*'s "first" woman war correspondent.

1897   Shipwrecked off Florida coast on January 2, after which he writes "The Open Boat" out of his *Commodore* disaster. Reports the Greco-Turkish War (April–May) for the *Journal* and the *Westminster Gazette,* and settles in England at Oxted, Surrey, with Cora; they never marry. Travels to Ireland in September, meets Joseph Conrad in October, and forms friendships with Ford Madox Ford, Harold Frederic, H. G. Wells, and Henry James. He writes "The Monster," "The Bride Comes to Yellow Sky," and "The Blue Hotel."

1898   In April, *The Open Boat and Other Tales of Adventure* is published, and Crane goes to Cuba as war correspondent for Pulitzer's *New York World,* where he is fired midway through the war, and then for Hearst's *New York Journal.* During the Puerto-Rican campaign his colleagues vote Crane the best of the war correspondents in the Cuban War. In addition to dozens of war dispatches, his stories appear in periodicals: "The Bride Comes to Yellow Sky" (February), "Death and the Child" (March), "The Monster" (August), and "The Blue Hotel" (November).

1899   After hiding out in Havana at the end of the war and lingering since November 21, 1898, in New York, where he arrived from Havana on the *Vigilancia,* Crane returns at last to Cora and England on January 11 on the *Manitou.* He and Cora live extravagantly in Brede Manor in Sussex, and Crane writes at a feverish pace to pay the resulting debts. In October the Cranes visit Ireland, and in December they give a holiday party at Brede Manor for H. G. Wells and other literary friends; Crane coughs up blood. His publications this year include *War Is Kind* (May), *Active Service,* a novel based on Crane's Greco-Turkish War experiences (October), *The Monster and Other Stories* (December), and "War Memories" of the Cuban War, which appeared in Lady Randolph Churchill's *Anglo Saxon Review* (December). He begins his Irish romance *The O'Ruddy,* completed by Robert Barr (1903).

1900   Crane reports on the Boer War. In March he collapses with tubercular hemorrhages, and two months later Conrad, H. G. Wells, and Robert Barr see him for the last time at Dover before his final voyage—to Calais and (by private railway coach hired by Cora) to the Black Forest. At Badenweiler, Germany, the exhausted Crane dies on June 5 of tuberculosis *and* of a recurrent attack of the malaria he had caught in Cuba. The *New York Tribune*'s unsigned reporter—Wallace Stevens—said in the *Tribune* obituary that Stephen Crane was buried in Evergreen Cemetery at Elizabeth, New Jersey. Crane is buried at Hillside, New Jersey.

LIST OF
SHORTENED TITLES

BC	Berg Collection, New York Public Library
BCC	Barrett Crane Collection (University of Virginia Library)
BCCC	Bacon Collamore Crane Collection
Beer's *SC*	*Stephen Crane,* Thomas Beer (1923)
BT	*Bowery Tales,* I, ed. Fredson Bowers (1969).
Berryman's *Crane*	*Stephen Crane,* John Berryman (1950)
Bulletin	*Bulletin of the New York Public Library*
Cora Crane	*Cora Crane: A Biography of Mrs. Stephen Crane,* Lillian Gilkes (1960)
Crane	*Stephen Crane: A Biography,* R. W. Stallman (1968)
CSS&S	*The Complete Short Stories and Sketches of Stephen Crane,* ed. Thomas A. Gullason (1963)
CUCC	Columbia University Crane Collection (Butler Library)
Exhibition	*Stephen Crane: 1871–1900: An Exhibition of His Writings. . . .,* ed. Joan H. Baum (1956)
Houses	*The Houses That James Built and Other Literary Studies,* R. W. Stallman (1961)
Letters	*Stephen Crane: Letters,* ed. R. W. Stallman and Lillian Gilkes (1960)
MSC	*My Stephen Crane,* Corwin K. Linson, ed. Edwin H. Cady (1958)
Notebook	*The Notebook of Stephen Crane,* ed. Donald J. and Ellen B. Greiner (1969)
NYCS	*New York City Sketches of Stephen Crane and Related Pieces,* ed. R. W. Stallman and E. R. Hagemann (1966)
Omnibus	*Stephen Crane: An Omnibus,* ed. R. W. Stallman (1952)
O'Ruddy	*The O'Ruddy,* IV, ed. Fredson Bowers (1971).
Poems	*The Collected Poems of Stephen Crane,* ed. Wilson Follett (1930)

Poetry	*The Poetry of Stephen Crane,* Daniel G. Hoffman (1957)
RW	*Reports of War,* IX, ed. Fredson Bowers (1971).
SCC	Stephen Crane Collection, Syracuse University Library
SCraneN	*The Stephen Crane Newsletter*
SCS	*The Sullivan County Sketches of Stephen Crane,* ed. Melvin Schoberlin (1949)
SCTS	*Stephen Crane: Sullivan County Tales and Sketches,* ed. R. W. Stallman (1968)
SHR	*Southern Humanities Review*
SinSF	*Studies in Short Fiction*
TA	*Tales of Adventure,* V, ed. Fredson Bowers (1970)
TLS	*London Times Literary Supplement*
TW	*Tales of War,* VI, ed. Fredson Bowers (1970)
TWH	*Tales of Whilomville,* VII, ed. Fredson Bowers (1969)
UW	*Stephen Crane: Uncollected Writings,* ed. Olov Fryckstedt (1963)
War Dispatches	*The War Dispatches of Stephen Crane,* ed. R. W. Stallman and E. R. Hagemann (1964)
Work	*The Work of Stephen Crane,* ed. Wilson Follett (1925–1927)
W-S Bibliography	*Stephen Crane: A Bibliography,* Ames W. Williams and Vincent Starrett (1948)

A

BOOKS AND CONTRIBUTIONS TO BOOKS
(Facsimile)

Books and Contributions to Books

1

MAGGIE

1893

MAGGIE / A / GIRL OF THE STREETS / (A STORY OF NEW YORK) / BY / JOHNSTON SMITH / COPYRIGHTED

Signatures: [1-10]⁸, [11]². Size of leaf: 7 13/16 x 5 3/8 inches. Wove paper; edges untrimmed; no endpapers.

Pagination: [1], title-page, as above; [2], blank; [3], 4-163, text; [164], blank.

Binding: Yellow paper wrappers. Front cover: (at right) Price, 50 cents / (three rules in red) / MAGGIE / A Girl of the Streets (A STORY OF NEW YORK) / By / JOHNSTON SMITH / Copyrighted / (three rules in red) /. Spine and back wrapper: blank. Lettered in black.

Publication: Probably in March or April, 1893. The first edition.

Publication Price: Fifty cents.

Note: On January 19, 1893, the Library of Congress received the following brief letter in the handwriting of Stephen Crane, bearing the letterhead of the Pendennis Club, 1064 Eastern Boulevard [New York City]:

> Librarian of Congress:
> Enclosed find a printed copy of the title page of a book written by me, and one dollar, for which please send a copy of the record of the copyright which is applied for, to
> Stephen Crane
> 1064 Eastern Boulevard
> N. Y.

13

The title-page, typewritten on an accompanying sheet of paper, bears the legend:

A GIRL OF THE STREETS,
A STORY OF NEW YORK.
-BY-
STEPHEN CRANE.

Stephen Crane

Considering the date of the application, the fact that "Maggie" is not included in the title, and that the pseudonym "Johnston Smith" is absent, a question arises as to when the book actually emerged in print.

According to Thomas Beer, Crane showed the manuscript to his friend Wallis McHarg sometime in January 1892; Beer quotes the author as saying, "I wrote it in two days before Christmas" (*i.e.*, Christmas 1891). McHarg, like other readers of the manuscript, criticized Crane for his failure to endow the characters with the dubious distinction of proper names. Beer further relates that Crane wrote McHarg a short note dated February, without mention of the year, stating that his brother William had named the book. It was now "Maggie: A Girl of the Street."

The fact that Crane copyrighted the story on January 19, 1893, without the title "Maggie" would indicate that Beer was incorrect in assuming the date of Crane's note to McHarg to be February 1892. In all likelihood, the note was written one year later. William Crane, therefore, did not christen the heroine until late in February 1893, after the application for the copyright had been made. It follows that the book was actually published sometime between late February and May 1893, since a printed copy was reviewed by Hamlin Garland in the June 1893 issue of *The Arena*. Unfortunately for the record, Crane failed to make the requisite copyright deposit of two copies of the book in the Library of Congress. To add to the confusion surrounding this book, Edward Marshall erroneously implied that *Maggie* was published by the Arena Company of Boston, Massachusetts, in an article on William Dean Howells entitled, "Greatest Living American Writer," which appeared in *The New York Press*, April 15, 1894. Despite numerous investigations, the identity of the publisher remains a mystery, but it is known that the volume was produced by a firm of religious and medical printers in New York City. Crane's initial contact with the Arena Company was established through Hamlin Garland about a year after *Maggie* appeared in print.

Stephen Crane

2
THE BLACK RIDERS
1895

THE BLACK RIDERS AND / OTHER LINES BY STE- / PHEN CRANE / BOSTON COPELAND AND DAY MDCCCXCV

Signatures: [1]⁴, [2]², [3-7]⁸, [8]⁴. Leaves [1₁] and [8₄] used as endpapers. Size of leaf: 6 x 4 3/16 inches. Wove paper; all edges untrimmed.

Pagination: [i-vi], blank; [vii], title-page, as above; [viii], copyright notice: ENTERED ACCORDING TO THE ACT OF CONGRESS / IN THE YEAR MDCCCXCV BY COPELAND AND DAY / IN THE OFFICE OF THE LIBRARIAN OF CONGRESS / AT WASHINGTON /; [ix], dedication: TO HAMLIN GARLAND; [x], blank; 1-76, text; [77], colophon: PRINTED BY JOHN WILSON AND SON CAMBRIDGE; [78-86], blank.

Binding: Cream laid paper over boards. Front cover: THE BLACK RIDERS / AND OTHER / LINES / BY / STEPHEN / CRANE / (a conventionalized orchid design rises in the lower left corner and curves upward to the right, almost touching the R of "OTHER") /. The initial letters of all six lines are aligned. Spine: THE / BLACK / RIDERS / STEPHEN / CRANE / COPELAND / AND / DAY / 1895 /. Back cover: (identical with the front, except that the lettering and orchid design are reversed, the title appearing in descending order to the right and the last letter of each line being aligned). Lettered and decorated in black. The binder's name, DUDLEY & HODGE, is stamped at the bottom of the front inside cover.

Publication: Announced in *The Publishers' Weekly* of May 11, 1895. Copyright applied for on January 14, 1895. Copyright deposit made on May 11, 1895. The first edition.

Stephen Crane *Publication Price*: One dollar.

Note: This small volume, Crane's first published book excepting the ill-fated *Maggie*, was produced by the youthful firm of Copeland and Day who, at the turn of the century, were among the first of American publishers to issue works of literary merit in an attractive format. Considering the experimental proclivities of the publishers, it is not surprising that many variant bindings of this title occur. For some time bibliophiles have been seriously concerned about the precedence of the various binding states. Recently a number of letters between Crane, Frederic C. Gordon, the decorator, and the publishers have been discovered. One letter, quoted below, describes Gordon's original cover design.

> Messrs. Copeland & Day
>   Gentlemen—
>   In another package I mail you a design for cover of Mr. Crane's poems. It is drawn twice the dimensions of the book. The same design, with title and author's name omitted is intended for the back of the book.
>   The orchid, with its strange habits, extraordinary forms and curious properties, seemed to me the most appropriate floral motive, an idea in which Mr. Crane concurred before he left New York. I have just mailed him a tracing of the design.
>   Will you kindly let me know whether it suits your requirements.
>   Very truly yours,
>   F. C. Gordon

Evidently the design met with the requirements of the publishers, at least temporarily, since the compilers possess a copy decorated exactly as described. This copy (2a) is bound in gray laid paper with faint red and blue threadings as are found in banknotes, over boards. On the front cover, the first line of the title, "The Black Riders," is indented one space to the right of the succeeding five lines. Lettering and decorations are in black. This binding state is undoubtedly confined to a very few copies. The impressions thereon appear sharp and fresh in comparison with those of the other state.

Stephen Crane

An edition said to be limited to fifty copies (2b) was issued, printed in green ink on Japan vellum and bound in white vellum over boards. A white paper label on the spine is printed in black: (double rule) / THE / BLACK / RIDERS /-/ CRANE /-/ 1895 / (double rule) /. The signatures are sewed with green silk. Of this edition two variant bindings have been noted: one bound in white vellum and decorated as in the state collated above, but in gilt instead of black; the other bound in full green levant by Cobden-Sanderson, stamped "The Doves Bindery, 18 C-S 96." inside the back cover.

The collations and contents of the foregoing editions are identical. It is noted, however, by careful comparison that certain typefaces appear worn in the green ink edition, which indicates that it was printed subsequently to the ordinary trade edition. This hypothesis is substantiated by the fact that the first announcement by Copeland and Day of an edition limited to fifty copies printed in green ink appears in *The Bookman*, Vol. 3, p. ix, April 1896, one year later than the publication of the trade edition. The success of *The Red Badge of Courage* apparently prompted the issuance of this handsome edition, which retailed at the price of three dollars a copy.

A third edition (2c), so stated on the verso of the title-page, was issued in 1896 by Copeland and Day and William Heinemann jointly.

No stated "second" edition of this title is known, and it is therefore logical to assume that the publishers considered the limited edition (2b) to be, in fact, the second edition.

Two poems in this collection were separately reprinted, as follows: "I saw a man pursuing the horizon," *The Philistine*, Vol. 1, p. 27, June 1895; "I stood upon a high place," *The Bookman*, Vol. 3, p. 196, May, 1896; *The Philistine*, Vol. 8 [back wrapper], February 1898.

3

THE RED BADGE OF COURAGE

1895

Stephen
Crane The Red Badge / Of Courage / (helmet design) / An Episode
of the American Civil War / (five fleurons) / By / (four
fleurons) / Stephen Crane / (three fleurons) / (publisher's
device) / (two fleurons) / (three fleurons) / New York /
D. Appleton and Company / 1895

Signatures: [1]⁸, 2-15⁸. Size of leaf: 7 1/4 x 4 7/8 inches. Laid
paper with horizontal wire marks; top edge stained yellow,
other edges rough-trimmed; light brown coated endpapers. The
title-page, inserted between leaves [1₁] and [1₂], is printed on
lighter weight paper than the text, and is identical in grade with
the inserted flyleaves.

Pagination: [i-ii], blank; [iii], title-page, as above, in Old English type, lettered in black and decorated in red with the exception of the publisher's device which is in black; [iv], copyright
notice: COPYRIGHT, 1894, / BY STEPHEN CRANE. / COPYRIGHT,
1895, / BY D. APPLETON AND COMPANY. /; 1-233, text; [234],
blank; [235-238], publisher's announcements: D. APPLETON &
CO.'S PUBLICATIONS. (See *Note*.)

Binding: Tan buckram. Front cover: (ornament) / THE RED
BADGE / OF COURAGE / BY / STEPHEN CRANE / (ornament) /.
Spine: (ornament) / THE RED / BADGE OF / COURAGE / (ornament) / CRANE / (ornament) / APPLETONS /. Back cover: blank.
Ornaments and all initial letters except B of "BY" in red; other
letters in black. Initial T on front cover is set in a square gilt
panel studded with black lozenges.

Publication: Announced in *The Publishers' Weekly* of October 5, 1895. Copyright applied for on September 27, 1895. Copyright deposit made on September 28, 1895. The first edition.

Publication Price: One dollar.

18

Note: At least two states of this edition exist. In the first state, page [235] advertises three works by Gilbert Parker, and the last page of advertisements [238] ends with *The Land of the Sun*, by Christian Reid. Copies of this state are printed on laid paper with *horizontal* wire marks. In the second state (3a), page [235] advertises *The Red Badge of Courage*, there is no mention of Gilbert Parker, and page [238] contains advertisements of the works of A. Conan Doyle. Copies of this state are printed on wove paper or on laid paper with *vertical* wire marks.

There has been much creasing of brows over this key book in any Crane collection, and for the most part deduction and discussion have focussed on the word *congratulated* on page 225. According to Merle Johnson, three states exist, indicated as follows: in the first, the half-word *lated*, in the last line of page 225, is perfect; in the second, the type at this point is mutilated; in the third, the type has been patched and the final letter *d* is out of perpendicular. (Copies of the volume with gilt tops, a considerable number of which exist to trouble the problem, were of the second state in all instances examined by him, Mr. Johnson indicated.) Actually, there is considerable evidence of broken type elsewhere in the volume, as David A. Randall has pointed out; but in any case a better test would seem to be made available by the testimony of the advertisements, which the present investigators believe to be the controlling factor in the situation. Pre-publication copies of this volume may exist (copies of the 1896 *Maggie*, *The Little Regiment* and *The Third Violet* in this state have come to light, as hereinafter noted), examination of which would be an interesting adventure; but it is difficult to see how they might change the present set-up. The Library of Congress copyright copy, deposited September 28, 1895, printed on laid paper with horizontal wire marks, shows the first state of the advertisements, and has the perfect type on page 225. All copies of the first state examined by Mr. Randall and by the immediate researchers conform to these apparent requirements. It is agreed that intermediate states may exist (as between the first and second states described), showing paper variants; but these would not change

Stephen Crane

the status of the first state as set forth. In all copies of the first edition the title page is tipped in. Finally, it may be noted that the word *bank* on page 4, line 11, should be *bunk*. This misprint persists in all Appleton editions until 1900.   [SEE NOTE]

4

THE RED BADGE OF COURAGE

1896

The Red Badge / of Courage / An Episode of / The American Civil War / By / Stephen Crane / London / William Heinemann / 1896

Signatures: [a]², A-I⁸, K-M⁸, N¹, [O]⁴. Size of leaf: 7 1/2 x 4 3/4 inches. Laid paper; top edge untrimmed; other edges rough-trimmed; white wove endpapers; inserted front flyleaf decorated in black, green, tan, and yellow.

Pagination: [i], half-title: The Red Badge / of Courage /; [ii], The Pioneer Series. (Old English type) (list of 11 titles); [iii], title-page, as above; [iv], copyright notice: *All rights reserved*; [1], 2-194, text; 194, colophon: *Printed by* BALLANTYNE, HANSON & CO. / *Edinburgh and London* /; [195-202], publisher's announcements: The Pioneer Series (Old English type).

Binding: Olive green cloth. Front cover: decorative panel in upper right corner containing: *The / Red Badge / of / Courage* / (line) / *Stephen Crane* /. Spine: *The / Red Badge / of / Courage* / (line) / *Stephen / Crane* / HEINEMANN. /. Back cover: *The Pioneer Series* (within a decorative panel). Lettered and decorated in white.

Publication: Announced in *The Publishers' Circular* of November 30, 1895. The first English edition.

Publication Price: Two shillings six pence.

Note: This volume was also issued in paper wrappers (4a), the front wrapper of which is lettered and decorated as follows:

20

Note to Section 3: "On the analogy of *Maggie*, *The Little Regiment*, and *The Third Violet* Williams and Starrett speculate that pre-publication copies of *The Red Badge of Courage* may exist. It is a pleasure to announce that they are indeed in existence both at the British Museum and Bodleian libraries, where Heinemann used them as deposits for copyright."—Fredson Bowers, "*The Red Badge of Courage* and Other Crane 'Advance Copies,'" *Studies in Bibliography*, 22 (1969), 275.

THE PIONEER SERIES. / (line) / The Red Badge / of Courage. / (panel containing the figures of four Japanese, two with banners and two with trumpets) / London: WILLIAM HEINEMANN. /. The title is lettered in black; other lettering in green. The figures in the panel are colored in black, green, tan, and yellow. The cloth-bound book is, in fact, the cheaper binding state recased with the above described front wrapper retained as a flyleaf.

Stephen Crane

Although the title-page is dated 1896, the book was actually published during the week of November 30, 1895. The British Museum copy was deposited on November 25, 1895.

[SEE NOTE]

5

A SOUVENIR AND A MEDLEY
1896

A SOUVENIR / AND / A MEDLEY: / SEVEN POEMS AND / A SKETCH / BY / STEPHEN CRANE. / WITH DIVERS / AND / SUNDRY / COMMUNICATIONS / FROM / CERTAIN EMINENT / WITS. / DONE INTO PRINT / AT / THE ROYCROFT PRINTING SHOP, / WHICH IS IN EAST AURORA, N. Y. / EIGHTEEN HUNDRED AND NINETY-SIX.

Signatures: [1-6]⁴. Stapled. Size of leaf: 7 1/2 x 5 inches. Laid paper; all edges untrimmed.

Pagination: [1], title-page, as above; [2], (eight lines by Crane from *The Black Riders*) / Copyright 1896 / by / The Roycroft Printing Shop. /; [3], CONTENTS (see *infra*); [4], blank; 5, FOREWORD; [6], blank; 7-46, text; 47, (advertisement of books published by Way & Williams); 48, (advertisement of *The Philistine*).

Binding: Gray paper wrappers. Front cover: The Roycroft Quarterly (all in black) / A SOUVENIR AND A MEDLEY: / SEVEN POEMS AND A SKETCH BY / STEPHEN CRANE (all the foregoing in red) / (decorative design in black, symbolizing "The Black Riders," signed "Collin") / May '96. PRICE 25 CENTS. NO. 1 (all in red) /. The title and design are bordered on all sides by a

21

Note to Section 4: Binding: (l. 4) HEINEMANN should be *HEINEMANN*.

single black rule. The spine is blank and the back cover bears an advertisement of The Roycroft Printing Shop.

Stephen Crane

Contents: I. Foreword. II. Glints of Wit and Wisdom: Being replies from sundry Great Men who missed a good Thing. III. Some Historical documents by W. Irving Way, Philip Hale and Livy S. Richard. IV. As to the Man. [by] E. H. V. Seven Poems by Stephen Crane. 1.—The Chatter of a Death Demon. 2.—A Lantern Song. 3.—A Slant of Sun on Dull Brown Walls. 4.—I have heard the Sunset Song of the Birches. 5.—What Says the Sea? 6.—To the Maiden the Sea was Blue Meadow. 7.—Fast Rode the Knight. VI. A Great Mistake. [by] Stephen Crane. VII. A Prologue. [by] Stephen Crane.

Publication: May 1896. The first edition.

Publication Price: Twenty-five cents.

Note: All of the poems in this volume with the exception of "Fast rode the knight" appeared in earlier issues of *The Philistine*. "Fast rode the knight" appears here for the first time in print, likewise the prose sketch, "A Prologue."

Although the title-page reads "Seven Poems," the book, in fact, contains eight, including "I saw a man pursuing the horizon" which appears on p. [2].

Two leaflets entitled, *The Members of the Society* . . . and *'The Time Has Come,'* . . . are collected as companion pieces. The latter leaflet contains the first appearance of the poem, "I have heard the sunset song of the birches." See: PHILISTINES' DINNER IN HONOR OF STEPHEN CRANE in "Writings Biographical and Bibliographical About Stephen Crane," for a complete description of these items.

6

GEORGE'S MOTHER
1896

GEORGE'S MOTHER / BY / STEPHEN CRANE / AUTHOR OF "THE RED BADGE OF COURAGE," / "THE BLACK RIDERS," ETC. / EDWARD ARNOLD

22

/ NEW YORK (vertical line) LONDON / 70 FIFTH AVENUE (vertical line continued) 37 BEDFORD STREET / 1896

Signatures: [1]⁸, 2-11⁸, [12]⁶. Size of leaf: 6 13/16 x 4 1/4 inches. Laid paper; all edges trimmed; white wove endpapers.

Stephen Crane

Pagination: [1], half-title: GEORGE'S MOTHER; [2], blank; [3], title-page, as above; [4], copyright notice: COPYRIGHT, 1896 / BY EDWARD ARNOLD / TROW DIRECTORY / PRINTING AND BOOKBINDING COMPANY / NEW YORK /; [5-6], blank; [7], 8-177, text; [178], blank; [179-186], publisher's announcements: Other Works of FICTION / RECENTLY PUBLISHED BY / EDWARD ARNOLD. /; [187], blank; [188], blank.

Binding: Tan cloth. Front cover: *George's* (ornament) / (ornament) *Mother* / *Stephen* / *Crane* (the whole enclosed within a heavy rule) /. Spine: (rule) / George's / Mother / (ornament) / Stephen / Crane / Arnold / (rule) /. Back cover: blank. Lettered and decorated in black.

Publication: Announced in *The Publishers' Weekly* of June 6, 1896. Copyright applied for on May 15, 1896. Copyright deposit made on May 29, 1896. The first edition.

Publication Price: Seventy-five cents.

Note: This edition was probably issued simultaneously with the English, despite the fact that the latter was announced a week later in *The Publishers' Circular*.

Investigation suggests that prior to publication Crane tentatively called this work "A Woman Without Weapons."

7

GEORGE'S MOTHER

1896

GEORGE'S MOTHER / BY / STEPHEN CRANE / AUTHOR OF / 'THE RED BADGE OF COURAGE,' 'THE BLACK RIDERS,' ETC. / EDWARD ARNOLD / LONDON NEW YORK / 37 BEDFORD STREET 70 FIFTH AVENUE / 1896

23

Signatures: [1]⁸, 2-12⁸. Size of leaf: 6 13/16 x 4 7/16 inches. Wove paper; all edges trimmed; white coated endpapers.

Stephen Crane

Pagination: [1], half-title: GEORGE'S MOTHER; [2], blank; [3], title-page, as above; [4], copyright notice: COPYRIGHT, 1896 / BY EDWARD ARNOLD /; [5-6], blank; [7], 8-185, text; [186], blank; [187-192], publisher's announcements: *Selections from /* MR. EDWARD ARNOLD'S LIST. /.

Binding: Black cloth. Front cover: George's Mother / by / Stephen Crane (the whole enclosed within a heavy rule) /. Spine: (rule) / George's / Mother / (rule) / Stephen / Crane / Arnold / (rule) /. Back cover: blank. Lettered and decorated in white.

Publication: Announced in *The Publishers' Circular* of June 13, 1896. British Museum deposit made June 30, 1896. The first English edition.

Publication Price: Two shillings.

Note: Page 34 is incorrectly numbered 4.

8

MAGGIE

1896

Maggie / A Girl of the Streets / (ornament) / By / Stephen Crane / Author of The Red Badge of Courage / (publisher's design) / New York / D. Appleton and Company / 1896

Signatures: 1 unsigned leaf, [1]⁸, 2-11⁸, 1 unsigned leaf. Size of leaf: 7 3/16 x 4 3/4 inches. Wove paper; top edge trimmed and stained yellow; other edges untrimmed; white wove endpapers and flyleaves.

Pagination: [i], half-title: MAGGIE / A GIRL OF THE STREETS /; [ii], publisher's advertisement: The Red Badge of Courage.

(Old English type) (with press notices); [iii], title-page, as above, in Old English type; [iv], copyright notice: COPYRIGHT, 1896, / BY D. APPLETON AND COMPANY. / Copyright, 1893, by Stephen Crane. /; v-vi, PUBLISHER'S NOTE.; 1-158, text; [159-170], publisher's announcements: D. APPLETON & CO.'S PUBLICATIONS. *Stephen Crane*

Binding: Tan buckram. Front cover: (ornament) / MAGGIE (followed by a fleuron, both in cover color except initial M, which is in gilt; the whole set within a black scroll bordered above and below in gilt) / BY / STEPHEN CRANE / (ornament) /. Spine: (ornament) / MAGGIE / (ornament) / CRANE / (ornament) / APPLETONS /. Back cover: blank. Ornaments and all initial letters in red except M of "MAGGIE" on front cover and B of "BY"; other letters in black, except as noted.

Publication: Announced in *The Publishers' Weekly* of June 13, 1896. Copyright applied for on May 28, 1896. Copyright deposit made on June 3, 1896. The second edition.

Publication Price: Seventy-five cents.

Note: In the first state the book, including endpapers and flyleaves, is constructed of wove paper, with fore and bottom edges rough-trimmed. The second state (8a), which contains an eleven-line title-page in Roman type, is constructed of deckle-edge laid paper bearing a watermark similar to the publisher's design on the title-page.

A plausible theory has been advanced by John T. Winterich for Appleton's substitution of the Roman type title-page for the earlier one in Old English type. In his opinion the first state did not sufficiently emphasize the fact that the book was written by the author of *The Red Badge of Courage*. Hence, in order to capitalize upon the success of that book, the Roman type title-page replaced the Old English.

An apparently unique copy (8b) has been noted, bound in buff wrappers, lacking advertisements, and with a tipped-in London title-page. The front wrapper reproduces the title-page described above, including the publisher's design, but omits the

25

imprint which is supplied in rubber stamp as follows: Wm.
Heinemann, / Publisher, / 21, Bedford Street, / London, /W.C.
/. The spine is blank. All edges are trimmed. The tipped-in title-

Stephen page reads: MAGGIE / A GIRL OF THE STREETS / BY / STEPHEN CRANE
Crane / AUTHOR OF / THE RED / BADGE OF / COURAGE / LONDON / WIL-
LIAM HEINEMANN / 1896 /. The make-up and typeface of the
page is that of the Appleton second state without the Appleton
device or imprint. The verso of the half-title is blank, unlike
either of the Appleton states—which carry an advertisement of
The Red Badge of Courage—but there exists upon it a faint impression of the removed title-page which was that of the Appleton first state.   [SEE NOTE]

9

MAGGIE

1896

Maggie / A Child of the Streets / By / Stephen Crane / Author
of / "The Red Badge of Courage" / London / William Heinemann / 1896

Signatures: [a]⁴, A-I⁸, K⁴. Size of leaf: 6 7/16 x 4 5/16 inches.
Laid paper; top edge gilt; other edges untrimmed; white wove
endpapers.

Pagination: [i], half-title: Maggie; [ii], (titles of other books
by Crane: "The Red Badge of Courage," with brief press notices, "The Black Riders," and "The Little Regiment"); [iii],
title-page, as above; [iv], copyright notice: *All rights reserved*;
v-vii, An Appreciation (signed) W. D. HOWELLS; [viii], blank;
1-147, [148], text; [1], 2-4, publisher's announcements: A Selection (Old English type) / FROM / MR. WILLIAM HEINE-
MANN'S LIST./.

Binding: Dark blue buckram over flexible boards. Front cover:
(ornament) / MAGGIE (followed by a fleuron, both in cover
color; the whole set within a gilt scroll bordered in cover color)
/ STEPHEN CRANE /. Spine: (rule in blind) / MAGGIE / (star orna-

26

Note to Section 8: On the "apparently unique copy (8 b)" of *Maggie*, the 1896 New
York edition, a mint copy is preserved in the Barrett Collection in the University of
Virginia Library and a rebound copy in the British Museum. Williams and Starrett are
mistaken in assigning the date June 8, 1896 to their no. 9, the 1896 London edition of
Maggie, "which was not deposited in the Museum. . . ."—Fredson Bowers, *Studies in
Bibliography*, 22 (1969), 273, 274.

ment) /̣ STEPHEN / CRANE / HEINEMANN / (rule in blind) /. Back cover: blank. Ornaments and all letters in gilt, except as noted. Front and back covers bordered in blind.

Publication: Announced in *The Publishers' Circular* of September 19, 1896. British Museum deposit made June 8, 1896. The first English edition.

Publication Price: Two shillings.

Stephen Crane

10
THE LITTLE REGIMENT
1896

The Little Regiment / And Other Episodes of the American / Civil War / By / Stephen Crane / Author of the Red Badge of Courage, and Maggie / (publisher's design) / New York / D. Appleton and Company / 1896

Signatures: 1 unsigned leaf; [1]⁸, 2-13⁸; 1 unsigned leaf. Size of leaf: 7 3/16 x 4 7/8 inches. Laid deckle-edge paper; top edge stained yellow; white laid endpapers and flyleaves.

Pagination: [i], half-title: THE LITTLE REGIMENT / AND OTHER EPISODES OF THE AMERICAN / CIVIL WAR /; [ii]. Other Books by Stephen Crane. (Old English type) (*The Red Badge of Courage* and *Maggie*, each with press notices); [iii], title-page, as above, in Old English type; [iv], copyright notice: COPYRIGHT, 1896, / BY D. APPLETON AND COMPANY: / Copyright, 1895, 1896, by Stephen Crane. /; v, table of contents: (see *infra*); [vi], blank; 1-196, text; [197-202], publisher's announcements: D. APPLETON & CO.'S PUBLICATIONS. (See *Note*.)

Binding: Tan buckram. Front cover. (ornament) / THE LITTLE / REGIMENT / BY / STEPHEN CRANE / (ornament)/. Spine: (ornament) / THE / LITTLE / REGIMENT / (ornament) / CRANE / (ornament) / APPLETONS /. Back cover: blank. Ornaments and all initial letters except B of "BY" in red; other letters in black.

27

Initial letter T is set in a square gilt panel studded with black lozenges.

Stephen Crane

Contents: The Little Regiment; Three Miraculous Soldiers; A Mystery of Heroism; An Indiana Campaign; A Gray Sleeve; The Veteran.

Publication: Announced in *The Publishers' Weekly* of December 5, 1896. Copyright applied for on October 7, 1896. Copyright deposit made on October 30, 1896. The first edition.

Publication Price: One dollar.

Note: In the first state the endpapers and flyleaves are laid paper. Page [197] bears the caption, GILBERT PARKER'S BEST BOOKS. The last page of advertisements [202] concludes with THE LILAC SUNBONNET BY S. R. CROCKETT.

In the second state (10a) the endpapers and flyleaves are wove paper. Page [197] advertises THE BEGINNERS OF A NATION by Edward Eggleston. The last page of advertisements [202] announces THE STORY OF THE WEST SERIES, edited by Ripley Hitchcock.

A probable advance copy (10b) has been noted, bound in buff, unlettered wrappers, with all edges uncut. The publisher's announcements on the verso of the half-title and at the end of the book are absent.

11

THE BLACK RIDERS

1896

THE BLACK RIDERS AND / OTHER LINES BY STE- / PHEN CRANE (three leaf ornaments) / (ornament) / LONDON: WILLIAM HEINE- MANN / MDCCCXCVI

Signatures: 3 unsigned leaves, [1-4]⁸, 2 unsigned leaves, [5]⁴. Size of leaf: 6 x 4 3/16 inches. Wove paper; top edge gilt; other edges untrimmed; white wove endpapers.

Pagination: [i], half-title: THE BLACK RIDERS / AND OTHER LINES / ; [ii], *By the same Author* / THE RED BADGE OF COURAGE / (line) / MAGGIE / A Child of the Streets / (line) / THE LITTLE REGI- *Stephen* MENT / (line) [*Shortly* / *This Edition is limited* / *to Five Hun-* *Crane* *dred copies* /; [iii], title-page, as above; [iv], PRINTED BY JOHN WILSON AND SON CAMBRIDGE U.S.A. / *All rights reserved* /; [v], dedication: TO HAMLIN GARLAND; [vi], blank; 1-76, text.

Binding: Black morocco. Front cover: THE BLACK RIDERS / AND OTHER / LINES / BY / STEPHEN / CRANE / (a conventionalized orchid design in blind rises in the lower left corner and curves upward to the right, almost touching the R of "OTHER")/. The initial letters of all six lines are aligned. Spine: THE / BLACK / RIDERS / STEPHEN / CRANE / HEINEMANN /. Back cover: (orchid design in blind as on front cover, but reversed). Lettered in gilt.

Publication: Announced in *The Publishers' Circular* of November 14, 1896. British Museum deposit made on November 13, 1896. The first English edition.

Publication Price: Three shillings.

12

THE LITTLE REGIMENT

1897

The Little Regiment / And Other Episodes of the / American. Civil War / By / Stephen Crane / Author of / "The Red Badge of Courage," "Maggie" / Etc. / London / William Heinemann / 1897

Signatures: [a]⁴, A-I⁸, K⁴, [L]⁸. Size of leaf: 7 1/2 x 4 3/4 inches. Laid paper; top edge untrimmed; other edges rough-trimmed; white wove endpapers; inserted front flyleaf decorated in black, green, yellow, and tan.

Pagination: [i], *By the same Author* (advertisement of *The Red Badge of Courage* with press notices); [ii], *By the same*

Author (advertisement of *Maggie* with press notices); [1], half-
title: The Little Regiment; [2], The Pioneer Series. (Old English type) (list of 17 titles); [3], title-page, as above; [4],
Stephen copyright notice: *All rights reserved*; 5, Contents (see *infra*);
Crane [6], blank; [1], half-title (repeated): The Little Regiment; [2],
blank; 3-150, text; 150, colophon: *Printed by* BALLANTYNE, HAN-
SON & CO. / *Edinburgh and London* /; [151-152], blank; [153-
168], publisher's announcements: The Pioneer Series (Old English type).

Binding: Olive green cloth. Front cover: decorative panel in
upper right corner containing: *The / Little / Regiment* / (line)
/ *Stephen Crane.* /. Spine: *The / Little / Regiment* / (decoration) / *Stephen Crane.* / HEINEMANN. /. Back cover: decorative
panel containing: *The Pioneer Series.* Lettered and decorated in
white.

Contents: The Little Regiment; Three Miraculous Soldiers; A
Mystery of Heroism; An Indiana Campaign; A Grey Sleeve;
The Veteran.

Publication: Announced in *The Publishers' Circular* of February 13, 1897. British Museum deposit made October 30, 1896.
The first English edition.

Publication Price: Three shillings, cloth; two shillings six pence,
wrappers.

Note: This volume was also issued in paper wrappers (12a), the
front wrapper of which is lettered and decorated as follows:
THE PIONEER SERIES. / (line) / The Little Regiment / (panel
containing the figures of four Japanese, two with banners and
two with trumpets) / London: WILLIAM HEINEMANN. /. The
title is lettered in black; other lettering in green. The figures in
the panel are colored in black, green, tan, and yellow. The cloth
bound book is, in fact, the cheaper binding state recased, with
the above described front wrapper retained as a flyleaf.

30   [SEE NOTE]

Note to Section 12: Williams and Starrett err on the British Museum deposit date. The
Museum does not own the regular Heinemann edition. Cited from Fredson Bowers,
Studies in Bibliography, 22 (1969), 274.

13
THE THIRD VIOLET
1897

Stephen Crane

The Third Violet / By / Stephen Crane / Author of The Red Badge of Courage, / The Little Regiment, and Maggie / (publisher's design) / New York / D. Appleton and Company / 1897

Signatures: 1 unsigned leaf; [1]⁸, 2-13⁸; 1 unsigned leaf. Size of leaf: 7 3/16 x 4 7/8 inches. Wove paper; top edge stained yellow; other edges rough-trimmed; white wove endpapers and flyleaves.

Pagination: [i], half-title: THE THIRD VIOLET; [ii], Other Books by Stephen Crane. (Old English type) (titles of three books by Crane, each with brief press comments); [iii], title-page, as above, in Old English type; [iv], copyright notice: COPYRIGHT, 1897, / BY D. APPLETON AND COMPANY. / Copyright, 1896, by Stephen Crane. /; 1-203, text; [204], blank.

Binding: Tan buckram. Front cover: (ornament) / THE THIRD / VIOLET / BY / STEPHEN CRANE / (ornament) /. Spine: (ornament) / THE / THIRD / VIOLET / (ornament) / CRANE / (ornament) / APPLETONS /. Back cover: blank. Ornaments and all initial letters except B of "BY" in red; other letters in black. First initial letter T is set in a square gilt panel studded with black lozenges.

Publication: Announced in *The Publishers' Weekly* of May 15, 1897. Copyright applied for April 15, 1897. Copyright deposit made on April 30, 1897. The first edition.

Publication Price: One dollar.

Note: A probable advance copy (13a) has been noted bound in buff wrappers and lacking the publisher's announcements on the verso of the half-title, but otherwise identical with the

above. The front wrapper reproduces the title-page exactly.
The spine is blank, and all edges are trimmed.

The English edition was published simultaneously by Wil-
Stephen liam Heinemann.

Crane   [SEE NOTE]

14

THE THIRD VIOLET

1897

THE THIRD VIOLET / BY / STEPHEN CRANE / AUTHOR OF / 'THE RED
BADGE OF COURAGE,' ETC. / LONDON / WILLIAM HEINEMANN /
1897 / [*All rights reserved*]

Signatures: 2 unsigned leaves, 1-13⁸, 14⁶, A⁸, A2⁸. Signature A2
between leaves A₄ and A₅. Size of leaf: 7 7/16 x 5 inches. Laid
paper; bottom edge trimmed; other edges untrimmed; white
wove endpapers.

Pagination: [i], half-title: THE THIRD VIOLET; [ii], *By the same
Author.* / (titles of four books by Crane, three with brief press
comments) / LONDON: WM. HEINEMANN. /; [iii], title-page, as
above; [iv], blank; [1], 2-220, text; 220, colophon: BILLINGS AND
SONS, PRINTERS, GUILDFORD; [1-32], publisher's announcements:
(list beginning with *Illumination* by Harold Frederic and concluding with *The Island Of Doctor Moreau* by H. G. Wells).

Binding: Tan buckram. Front cover: THE / THIRD / VIOLET /
(flower ornament in gilt) / STEPHEN CRANE /. Spine: THE /
THIRD / VIOLET / STEPHEN / CRANE / HEINEMANN /. Back cover:
(publisher's monogram in blind).

Publication: Announced in *The Publishers' Circular* of May 15,
1897. British Museum deposit made April 30, 1897. The first
English edition.

Publication Price: Six shillings.

Note: A variant binding state has been noted (14a) in which
the front and back covers are slotted to accommodate a purple

32

Note to Section 13: "The Appleton edition of *The Third Violet* in 1897 seems to have
been prepared in a special edition but was not used, since both the British Museum
copy (not date-stamped) of the American edition . . . is a regular trade copy and the
Heinemann 1897 copy (also without date-stamp) is preserved there. The Bodleian Library, also, does not have a special copy. However, Columbia University Library pre-
serves . . . a special copy in plain buff wrappers lacking the preliminary unsigned
leaf. . . ."—Fredson Bowers, *Studies in Bibliography*, 22 (1969), 275.

ribbon, a half inch in width, which passes horizontally across the middle of both covers and beneath the spine. The ends of the ribbon are pasted beneath the endpapers. In all other respects the volume is identical with that collated. No priority has *Stephen* been determined, although the British Museum copy bears evi- *Crane* dence of having had the ribbon band. It is possible that the bindings described above as tan buckram were originally a blue or violet buckram. A number of copies of the book suggest this possibility, particularly where a book has been protected from the light for many years. Also, since the cover and spine are stamped in gold, which is hardly discernible against the present tan background, it is logical to conclude that the publisher used a binding with a greater contrast. The American edition of this title was published simultaneously by D. Appleton and Company.

15

THE OPEN BOAT

1898

The Open Boat / And Other Tales of Adventure / By / Stephen Crane / Author of "Red Badge of Courage," / "The Third Violet," etc. / (leaf ornament) / New York / Doubleday & McClure Co. / 1898

Signatures: [1-21]⁸, [22]². Size of leaf: 6 7/16 x 3 15/16 inches. White laid paper with horizontal wire marks; all edges trimmed; white laid endpapers with vertical wire marks.

Pagination: [i], half-title: The Open Boat / And Other Tales of Adventure /; [ii], blank; [iii], title-page, as above; [iv], copyright notice: Copyright, 1898, by / DOUBLEDAY & MCCLURE CO. /; [v], dedication: TO / THE LATE WILLIAM HIGGINS / AND TO CAPTAIN EDWARD MURPHY AND / STEWARD C. B. MONTGOMERY / OF THE SUNK STEAMER / COMMODORE / [vi], blank; [vii], Contents: (see *infra*); [viii], blank; [1], divisional title: The Open Boat / A Tale Intended to be after the Fact: / Being the Ex-

33

perience of Four Men / From the Sunk Steamer / "Commodore" /; [2], blank; 3-336, text.

Stephen
Crane

Binding: Green cloth, lettered and decorated in silver and dark green. Front cover: THE OPEN / BOAT / Stephen / Crane /. A narrow dark green border surrounds the cover, which depicts the ocean in silver and dark green; the outline of a small boat appears on the horizon. Spine: (line) / THE / OPEN / BOAT / DOUBLEDAY / AND /MCCLURE CO. / (line) /. Ocean design as on front cover, in silver and dark green. Back cover: blank.

Contents: The Open Boat; A Man and Some Others; One Dash —Horses; Flanagan; The Bride Comes to Yellow Sky; The Wise Men; Death and the Child; The Five White Mice.

Publication: Announced in *The Publishers' Weekly* of April 30, 1898. Copyright applied for and deposit made on April 18, 1898. The first edition.

Publication Price: One dollar.

Note: The fourth edition of *Merle Johnson's American First Editions* states that there are three issues of this volume, about 1,500 copies in all, and that no priority has been established. No information is given which enables the collector to differentiate between the alleged three issues.

H. Bacon Collamore has compared a number of copies of this book, and, in a note in the *Colophon*, Vol. 3, No. 3, Summer 1938, reveals that the publisher's name—DOUBLEDAY / AND / MCCLURE CO. / at the base of the spine exists in two states: (1) measuring 11/32 of an inch from top to bottom of the three lines, and bearing two dots under the first C of "MCCLURE"; (2) measuring 15/32 of an inch, with two small horizontal lines under the first C of "MCCLURE." Mr. Collamore suggests that a number of binders may have worked on the book simultaneously, using different types of the publisher's name in stamping the spine, and that the resulting variance does not necessarily indicate separate issues. This edition was issued simultaneously with the English, despite the fact that the latter was announced a week earlier in *The Publishers' Circular*.

34

16

THE OPEN BOAT

1898

The Open Boat / and Other Stories / By / Stephen Crane / Author of / "The Red Badge of Courage," "The Little Regiment," / "The Third Violet," etc. / London / William Heinemann / 1898

Signatures: [A]⁴, B-I⁸, K-U⁸, [X]¹⁶. Size of leaf: 7 7/16 x 5 inches. Laid paper; all edges untrimmed; white wove endpapers.

Pagination: [i], half-title: The Open Boat / and Other Stories /; [ii], New Novels for 1898 (Old English type) (list of Heinemann novels beginning with *Dreamers of the Ghetto*, by I. Zangwill and ending with *Ezekiel's Sin*, by J. A. Pearce); [iii], title-page, as above; [iv], copyright notice: *All rights reserved*; [v], dedication: To the Memory of / THE LATE WILLIAM HIGGINS / and to / CAPTAIN EDWARD MURPHY and STEWARD C. B. MONTGOMERY / Of the sunk Steamer 'Commodore.' /; [vi], blank; [vii], CONTENTS (see *infra*); [viii], blank; [1], divisional title: Part I / Minor Conflicts /; [2], blank; [3], 4-207, text; [208], blank; [209], divisional title: Part II / Midnight Sketches /; [210], blank; 211-301, text; [302], colophon: RICHARD CLAY & SONS, LIMITED, / LONDON & BUNGAY. /; [303-304], STEPHEN CRANE'S WORKS (advertisements of five titles by Crane, some with press notices); [1-2], 3-32, publisher's announcements, dated March 1898.

Binding: Green cloth. Front cover: THE OPEN BOAT (lettered in blue) /. Spine: THE / OPEN / BOAT / STEPHEN / CRANE / HEINEMANN (lettered in gilt) /. Back cover: (publisher's design in blind).

Contents: *Part I Minor Conflicts*: The Open Boat; A Man and Some Others; The Bride comes to Yellow Sky; The Wise Men; The Five White Mice; Flanagan and His Short Filibustering Adventure; Horses; Death and the Child; *Part II Midnight*

35

Stephen Crane

Sketches: An Experiment in Misery; The Men in the Storm; The Duel that was not Fought; An Ominous Baby; A Great Mistake; An Eloquence of Grief; The Auction; The Pace of Youth; A Detail.

Publication: Announced in *The Publishers' Circular* of April 23, 1898. The British Museum copy was deposited on April 18, 1898. The first English edition.

Publication Price: Six shillings.

Note: All nine stories included in "Midnight Sketches" were omitted from the American edition. A new binding of the original edition (16a) in tan linen, designed by William Nicholson, was issued in June 1900, described as follows: Front cover: The Open Boat (lettered in black) / *By Stephen Crane* (lettered in red) / (pictorial design, in black and red, representing an open lifeboat) /. Spine: The / Open / Boat (all the foregoing lettered in black) / *By Stephen* / *Crane* (the foregoing lettered in red) / (publisher's windmill design in black and red) / *Heinemann* (red) /. Back cover: (lifeboat design as on front cover). [SEE NOTE]

17

PICTURES OF WAR
1898

Pictures of War / By / Stephen Crane / Author of / "The Open Boat," "The Third Violet," etc. / London / William Heinemann / 1898

Signatures: [a]⁴, b⁸, A-I⁸, K-U⁸, X⁸, Y⁴, A⁸, A2⁸. Signature A2 between leaves A_4 and A_5. Size of leaf: 7 7/16 x 5 inches. Wove paper; bottom edge trimmed; other edges untrimmed; white wove endpapers.

Pagination: [i-ii], Stephen Crane's Works (advertisements of *The Third Violet, Maggie, The Black Riders* and *The Open*

36

Note to Section 16: "Both the British Museum and the London Library copies (the latter rebound) of the Heinemann *Open Boat* of 1898 lack the bound-in publisher's advertisements mentioned in Williams and Starrett."—Fredson Bowers, *Studies in Bibliography*, 22 (1969), 276.

Boat, all with press notices except *The Black Riders*); [iii], half-title: Pictures of War; [iv], New Novels for 1898 (Old English type) (list of new Heinemann novels beginning with *Dreamers of the Ghetto* by I. Zangwill and ending with *The Nigger of the "Narcissus"* by Joseph Conrad); [v], title-page, as above; [vi], copyright notice: NEW EDITION / *The Red Badge of Courage, 1st Impression, 1895 / 2nd, 3rd, 4th, 5th, and 6th Impressions, 1896 / The Little Regiment, and other Stories, 1st / Impression, 1897 / This Edition enjoys Copyright in all countries / signatory to the Berne Treaty, and is / not to be imported into the United States / of America. /*; [vii], Contents (see *infra*); [viii], blank; ix-xxiv, An Appreciation (signed) GEORGE WYNDHAM; [1], 2-344, text; 344, colophon: Printed by BALLANTYNE, HANSON & CO. / Edinburgh & London /; [1-32], (list of Heinemann books beginning with *The Nigger of the 'Narcissus'* by Joseph Conrad and concluding with *The Scourge-Stick* by Mrs. Campbell-Praed).

Binding: Tan linen. Front cover: Pictures of War (lettered in black) / *By Stephen Crane* (lettered in orange) / (sword decoration in orange) /. Spine: Pictures / of War (lettered in black) / *By Stephen / Crane* (lettered in orange) / (publisher's windmill design in orange and black) / *Heinemann* (lettered in black) /. Back cover: (sword decoration in orange). Cover design by William Nicholson.

Contents: The Red Badge Of Courage; The Little Regiment; Three Miraculous Soldiers; A Mystery Of Heroism; An Indiana Campaign; A Grey Sleeve; The Veteran.

Publication: Announced in *The Publishers' Circular* of July 16, 1898. The first edition of this title.

Publication Price: Six shillings.

Note: This volume does not contain any new material except the appreciation by George Wyndham. It is possible that the title of this collection was suggested by Crane.

37

Stephen Crane

18
SPANISH-AMERICAN WAR SONGS
1898

Stephen
Crane SPANISH-AMERICAN / WAR SONGS / A COMPLETE COLLECTION OF
NEWSPAPER VERSE DUR- / ING THE RECENT WAR WITH SPAIN /
(line) / Compiled and Edited / BY SIDNEY A. WITHERBEE. /
(line) / SIDNEY A. WITHERBEE, PUBLISHER, / DETROIT, MICH. /
1898

Signatures: [1]¹⁰, [2-61]⁸, [62]⁴. Size of leaf: 9 3/4 x 6 inches.
Laid paper; all edges untrimmed; white laid endpapers.

Pagination: [1], title-page, as above; [2], copyright notice:
(line) / Copyright 1898, / BY SIDNEY A. WITHERBEE, / Detroit,
Mich. / (line) / *Press of John F. Eby & Company* / *65-67-69*
Congress St. West—Detroit /; [i], ii-iii, PRESIDENT MCKINLEY'S
TRIBUTE TO THE / SOLDIERS IN THE TRENCHES AND / THE MEN BE-
HIND THE GUNS. /; [iv], blank; [3], Dedication. / (line) / (line)
/ To the heroes who went to the front, and to / those who
could not go, and to their wives and / mothers and sweethearts,
I dedicate this book. / (Old English type); [4], blank; [5], 6,
PREFACE, (signed) SIDNEY A. WITHERBEE.; [7], 8-984, text.

Binding: Royal blue cloth. Front cover: SPANISH- / AMERICAN /
WAR SONGS. / (decorative line) / TWO VIEWS OF WAR. / (line) /
HENRY ROBINSON PALMER. / (line) / Stirring drums in a sunny
street, / A bonnie flag in the azure sky, / A lurid melody,
tramping feet, / And hope in many an eye. / (three dots) /
Death in a still and shadowed room, / A pallid, boyish face at
rest, / A sunbeam quivering in the gloom, / And woe in a
woman's breast. (all of the above within a decorative panel) /.
Spine: Spanish- / American / War Songs. (all within a decorative panel) /. Back cover: blank. Lettered and decorated in gilt.

Publication: Announced in *The Publishers' Weekly* of December 10, 1898. Copyright applied for on October 3, 1898. The
first edition.

38

Publication Price: Two dollars and fifty cents.

Note: This large anthology of newspaper verse contains on pp. 182-183 the first book appearance of "The Blue Battalions."

Stephen Crane

19

THE LANTHORN BOOK

1898

The Lanthorn Book / BEING A SMALL / COLLECTION OF / TALES AND VERSES / READ AT / The Sign o' the Lanthorn / 126 WILLIAM STREET / NEW YORK

Signatures: [1]⁴, [2-8]⁸, [9]⁴. First and final signatures used as endpapers; leaves [1_1], [1_2], and [9_3], [9_4], are pasted to the front and back covers, respectively. Size of leaf: 11 x 8 inches. White wove deckle-edge paper.

Pagination: [i], half-title: The / Lanthorn / Book / EDITION LIMITED / TO ONE HUNDRED / AND TWENTY-FIVE / COPIES (four dots) /; [ii-iii], blank; [iv], This Book is / No. /; [v], title-page, as above, the first, fourth, and sixth lines in red, others in black; [vi-viii], blank; [ix], (2 dots) CONTENTS (2 dots) (all in red) (see *infra*); [x-xi], blank; [xii], copyright notice: Copyright, 1898, / by the / SIGN O' THE LANTHORN / and Published at / 126 William St., New York /; [xiii], preface; [xiv-xvi], blank; [1-96], text. Titles and initial letters of the stories and verses are rubricated.

Binding: Shelf-edge bound in sheep; green cloth sides. Front cover: four-inch square tan paper label designed by Carroll J. Post, Jr., decorated and bordered in black, lettered in brown: (lanthorn and bracket) / The / Lanthorn / Book. /. Spine and back cover: blank.

Contents: The Wise Men [by] Stephen Crane; The Answer of the Sea [by] John Langdon Heaton; The Night of a Thousand Years [by] Irving Bacheller, illustrated by G. Y. Kauffman; Larry and the Squg [by] Willis Brooks Hawkins, illustrated by

39

the author; The Wheel [by] Post Wheeler, illustrated by F. H. King; It Came to Pass [by] Charles B. Lewis (M Quad); Veiled Gods [by] Charles Kelsey Gaines.

Stephen
Crane   *Publication*: Other than the year, the date of publication of this volume has not been determined. There is no record in the Library of Congress that this volume was copyrighted despite the fact that it bears such notice. Since Crane was in the United States for an extended period only during November and December of 1898, it seems likely that this book must have appeared during that time.

Note: The edition was limited to one hundred and twenty-five copies and all contributions were to be signed by the contributors, but it is alleged that Crane signed less than a dozen copies.

20

WAR IS KIND

1899

WAR (bird decoration) is / KIND *by* / STEPHEN / CRANE / (harp decoration) / DRAWINGS / *by* WILL / BRADLEY / NEW YORK / FREDERICK A / STOKES *Company* / MDCCCXCIX

Signatures: [1]⁴, [2]², [3-13]⁴. Leaves [1₁] and [13₄] used as endpapers. Size of leaf: 8 3/8 x 5 1/8 inches. Gray deckle-edge cartridge paper.

Pagination: [1-4], blank; [5], title-page, as above, in six horizontal panels of rules, one blank; bordered on the right by a vertical seventh panel containing two candles and bird decoration; [6], copyright notice: Copyright, 1899, by / Frederick A. Stokes Company / *Arranged and Printed by Will Bradley at the / University Press, Cambridge and New York* /; [7], (spear decoration); [8], (full page illustration); 9-96, text; [97-98], blank.

Binding: Gray cartridge paper boards. Front cover: Symbolic design in panels, including trees, a woman with a sword, a harp, and an urn. The lower right panel is lettered: WAR IS / KIND *by* / STEPHEN / CRANE /. Spine: gray paper label, 1 5/8 x 3/4 inches, lettered: WAR / IS / KIND (all in a panel) / STEPHEN / CRANE (in a separate panel) /. Both of the foregoing panels are enclosed in a larger panel of rules. Back cover: blank. *Stephen Crane*

Publication: Announced in *The Publishers' Weekly* of May 20, 1899. Copyright applied for on March 20, 1899. Copyright deposit made on April 17, 1899. The first edition.

Publication Price: Two dollars and fifty cents.

Note: Six copies of the original edition (20a) were prepared with Heinemann title-pages for copyright purposes. The book was not published in England.

Later editions of this title are in a smaller format. A "New Edition" is dated 1902.

Prior appearances of poems in this volume follow:
Do not weep, maiden, for war is kind.
   Literary Digest, Vol. 12, p. [520], February 29, 1896.
What says the sea, little shell?
   Philistine, Vol. 2, pp. [94-95], February 1896.
   Roycroft Quarterly, p. 31, May 1896.
To the maiden
   Philistine, Vol. 2, p. [152], April 1896.
   Roycroft Quarterly, p. 32, May 1896.
I explain the silvered passing of a ship at night,
   Bookman, Vol. 4, p.149, October, 1896.
I have heard the sunset song of the birches,
   'The Time Has Come,' . . . [East Aurora, New York: The Roycroft Printing Shop, 1895.]
   Philistine, Vol. 2, p. [62], January 1896.
   Roycroft Quarterly, p. 30, May 1896.
Fast rode the knight
   Roycroft Quarterly, p. 33, May 1896.
   Philistine, Vol. 3, p. [20], June 1896.
You tell me this is God?
   Philistine, Vol. 6, [back wrapper], April 1898.

On the desert
Philistine, Vol. 6, pp. 166-167, May 1898.
A slant of sun on dull brown walls,
Stephen   *Philistine*, Vol. 2, p. [216], December 1895.
Crane   *Roycroft Quarterly*, p. 29, May 1896.
In the night
Chap-book, Vol. 4, p. 372, March 1896.
Literary Digest, Vol. 12, p. 671, April 4, 1896.
The chatter of a death-demon from a tree-top.
Philistine, Vol. 1, p. [93], August 1895.
Roycroft Quarterly, p. 27, May 1896.
The impact of a dollar upon the heart
Philistine, Vol. 6, [back wrapper], February 1898.
Each small gleam was a voice,
Philistine, Vol. 1, p. [124], September 1895.
Roycroft Quarterly, p. 28, May 1896.

21

ACTIVE SERVICE

1899

ACTIVE / SERVICE / A Novel (Old English type) / BY / STEPHEN
CRANE / AUTHOR OF "THE RED BADGE OF COURAGE," / "GEORGE'S
MOTHER," ETC., ETC. / (decorative leaf) / NEW YORK / FRED-
ERICK A. STOKES COMPANY / PUBLISHERS

Signatures: [1-22]⁸. Size of leaf: 7 3/8 x 4 7/8 inches. Laid
paper; all edges trimmed; white wove endpapers.

Pagination: [i], half-title: ACTIVE SERVICE; [ii], blank; [iii], title-
page, as above; [iv], copyright notice: *Copyright, 1899, / By
Stephen Crane / Copyright, 1899, / By Frederick A. Stokes
Company /*; [v], dedication: TO E. A.; [vi], blank; [1], 2-345,
text; [346], blank.

Binding: Light green cloth. Front cover: ACTIVE / SERVICE (leaf
design in upper right the width of the above two lines) / STE-
PHEN (star) CRANE / (large formalized tree design signed T B H

at bottom /. Spine: ACTIVE / SERVICE / (leaf design) / STEPHEN / CRANE / (formalized tree design) / STOKES /. Back cover: blank. Lettered in dark green; decorated in pale green.

Publication: Announced in *The Publishers' Weekly* of October 14, 1899. Copyright applied for on September 11, 1899. Copyright deposit made on October 7, 1899. The first edition.

Stephen Crane

Publication Price: One dollar and twenty-five cents.

Note: The second edition of this book, so stated on the title-page, was issued in gray cloth, lettered in pink, decorated in light green.

22

ACTIVE SERVICE

1899

Active Service / By / Stephen Crane / Author of / "Pictures of War," "The Third Violet," etc. / London / William Heinemann / 1899

Signatures: [A]², B-I⁸, K-U⁸, X⁶, A⁸, A2⁸. Size of leaf: 7 7/16 x 5 inches. Wove paper; top edge rough-trimmed; white wove endpapers.

Pagination: [i], half-title: Active Service; [ii], New 6 s. Novels. (a list of new Heinemann novels beginning with THE SLAVE by Robert Hichens and ending with THE MARKET PLACE by Harold Frederic); [iii], title-page, as above; [iv], copyright notice: *This Edition enjoys Copyright in all / Countries signatory to the Berne / Treaty, and is not to be imported / into the United States of America. / All rights, including translation, reserved. /*; [1], 2-315, text; [316], colophon: RICHARD CLAY & SONS, LIMITED, / LONDON & BUNGAY. /; [1-32], (a list of Heinemann books beginning with THE OPEN QUESTION by Elizabeth Robins and concluding with SOLDIERS OF FORTUNE by Richard Harding Davis).

Binding: Tan linen. Front cover: Active Service (lettered in black) / By Stephen Crane (lettered in orange) / (sword deco-

43

ration in orange) /. Spine: Active / Service (lettered in black) / *By Stephen* / *Crane* (lettered in orange) / (publisher's windmill design in orange and black) / Heinemann (lettered in
Stephen black). Back cover: (sword decoration in orange).

Crane *Publication*: Announced in *The Publishers' Circular* of November 11, 1899. British Museum deposit made on November 2, 1899. The first English edition.

Publication Price: Six shillings.

23

THE MONSTER

1899

THE MONSTER / AND / OTHER STORIES / (line) / BY / STEPHEN CRANE / ILLUSTRATED / (line) / (publisher's design) / (line) / NEW YORK AND LONDON / HARPER & BROTHERS PUBLISHERS / 1899

Signatures: [a]⁴, [A]⁸, B-I⁸, K-M⁸. Size of leaf: 7 1/2 x 5 1/8 inches. Calendered paper; top edge stained red; other edges untrimmed; white laid endpapers.

Pagination: 2 blank preliminary pages: [i], title-page, as above, enclosed by rules; [ii], copyright notice: Copyright, 1899, by HARPER & BROTHERS. / (line) / *All rights reserved.* /; [iii], CONTENTS (see *infra*); [iv], blank; v-[vi], ILLUSTRATIONS (see *infra*); [1], half-title: THE MONSTER; [2], blank; 3-188, [189], text; [190], blank; [191], publisher's advertisements: BY LILLIAN BELL; [192], BY RICHARD HARDING DAVIS.

Binding: Red cloth. Front cover: THE MONSTER / AND OTHER STORIES / (design of three medallions linked by a chain) / STEPHEN / (dot) CRANE (dot) /. Spine: / THE / MONSTER / AND / OTHER / STORIES / STEPHEN / CRANE / HARPERS /. Back cover: blank. All lettering in gilt; decorated in black.

Contents: The Monster; The Blue Hotel; His New Mittens.

Illustrations: Frontispiece facing p. [i]; illustrations facing pp.

44

10, 14, 16, 18, 20, 30, 36, 58, 68, 74, 100; on pp. 165, 166, 167, 168, 169, 175, 177, 179, 180, 181, 185, 186, 188.

Publication: Announced in *The Publishers' Weekly* of December 9, 1899. Copyright applied for on November 2, 1899. Copyright deposit made on December 2, 1899. The first edition.

Stephen Crane

Publication Price: One dollar and twenty-five cents.

24

BEST THINGS FROM AMERICAN LITERATURE
1899

BEST THINGS / FROM / AMERICAN / (five flower ornaments) LITERATURE / (line) *Edited by* IRVING BACHELLER / (line) / With numerous unique and original Illustrations, / including facsimile Reproductions of Authors' MSS. / NEW YORK / THE CHRISTIAN HERALD / LOUIS KLOPSCH, Proprietor / 1899

Signatures: [1-26]⁸. Size of leaf: 8 9/16 x 6 1/2 inches. White calendered paper; all edges trimmed; white laid endpapers.

Pagination: [1], half-title: BEST THINGS / FROM AMERICAN LITERATURE /; [2], blank; frontispiece, portrait of Irving Bacheller; [3], title-page, as above, in a panel of rules; [4], copyright notice: COPYRIGHT 1899 BY LOUIS KLOPSCH; [5], PREFACE; [6], blank; [7], 8-9, INDEX TO SELECTIONS; [10], 11-12, INDEX TO AUTHORS; [13], 14-15, INDEX TO ILLUSTRATIONS; 16, portrait of Richard Harding Davis; 17-416, text.

Binding: Light green cloth. Front cover: BEST / THINGS / FROM / AMERICAN / LITERATURE (within a scroll) / (lamp within a laurel wreath) / PROFUSELY ILLUSTRATED /. Figure of a muse holding a torch occupies left half of cover. The figure, first four lines of title, scroll, and lamp are tan, outlined in brown. "Literature," "Profusely Illustrated," and wreath are in brown. The entire cover is bordered by three rules, alternately brown, tan, and brown. Spine: (three alternate rules of brown and tan) / BEST / THINGS / FROM / AMERICAN / LITERATURE / (five alter-

45

Stephen Crane

nate rules of brown and tan) / COMPILED / BY / ADDISON / IRVING / BACHELLER (the five above lines superimposed upon a torch, which is tan with brown flame) / (five alternate rules in brown and tan) / THE / CHRISTIAN HERALD / NEW YORK. / (three alternate rules in brown and tan) /. Title lettered in gilt; other lettering in brown. Back cover: blank.

Publication: Copyright applied for and deposit made on December 4, 1899. Distributed as a premium to subscribers of *The Christian Herald.*

Note: This large anthology of selections by sixty-four American authors contains the first book appearance of "A Tale of Mere Chance" and the first American book appearance of "A Detail."

25

BOWERY TALES

1900

Bowery Tales / George's Mother / Maggie / By / Stephen Crane / Author of / "The Red Badge of Courage," etc. / London / William Heinemann / 1900

Signatures: [A]², B-I⁸, K-P⁸, Q⁶, A⁸, A2⁸. Signature A2 between leaves A₄ and A₅. Size of leaf: 7 9/16 x 5 inches. Laid paper, untrimmed; white wove endpapers.

Pagination: [i], half-title: Bowery Tales; [ii], BY THE SAME AUTHOR (list of 5 titles); [iii], title-page, as above; [iv], copyright notice: GEORGE'S MOTHER / *First Impression* (EDWARD ARNOLD), 1896 / MAGGIE / *First Impression, 1896 / This Edition enjoys Copyright in / all Countries signatory to the / Berne Treaty, and is not to be / imported into the United States / of America. /*; [1], divisional title: GEORGE'S MOTHER; [2], blank; 3-109, text; [110], blank; [111], divisional title: MAGGIE; [112], blank; 113-114, An Appreciation (signed) W. D. HOWELLS; 115-236, text; 236, colophon: *Richard Clay & Sons, Limited,*

London & Bungay.; [1-32], publisher's announcements (list beginning with THE OPEN QUESTION by Elizabeth Robins and concluding with THEY THAT WALK IN DARKNESS by I. Zangwill).

Stephen Crane

Binding: Tan buckram. Front cover: Bowery Tales (lettered in black) / *By Stephen Crane* (lettered in orange) /. Spine: Bowery / Tales (lettered in black) / *By Stephen / Crane* (lettered in orange) / (publisher's windmill design in orange and black) / *Heinemann* (lettered in black) /. Back cover: blank.

Publication: Announced in *The Publishers' Circular* of June 30, 1900. The first edition of this title.

Publication Price: Six shillings.

Note: This volume does not contain any new material. Crane may have suggested the title.

A binding variant (25a) is noted in the Times Book Club edition, which is *blue* cloth lettered in black. In this edition the circular Times imprint (The Times 1785) replaces the publisher's name and design at the foot of the spine. There are no advertisements in this edition. Simultaneous publication is probable, but the regular edition is commonly preferred.

26

WHILOMVILLE STORIES

1900

Whilomville Stories / *by* / *Stephen Crane* / *Illustrated by* / *Peter Newell* / (publisher's design) / *New York and London* / *Harper & Brothers* / *Publishers* / *1900*

Signatures: [a]⁴, A-I⁸, K-M⁸, N⁴. Size of leaf: 7 1/2 x 4 7/8 inches. Laid paper; all edges trimmed; white laid endpapers.

Pagination: [i], title-page, as above; [ii], copyright notice: Copyright, 1900, by STEPHEN CRANE / (line) / *All rights reserved* /; [iii], CONTENTS (see *infra*); [iv], blank; v-vi, ILLUSTRA-

TIONS (see *infra*); [vii], half-title: WHILOMVILLE STORIES; [viii], blank; 1-198, [199], text; [200], blank.

Stephen Crane

Binding: Light green cloth. Front cover: WHILOMVILLE / STORIES / *by* / STEPHEN CRANE / (decorations: five formalized trees) /. Spine: WHILOM- / VILLE / STORIES / (line) / CRANE / (decoration: single tree) / HARPERS /. Back cover: blank. Lettered in gold and decorated in dark green and coral.

Contents: The Angel Child; Lynx-Hunting; The Lover and the Telltale; "Showin' Off"; Making an Orator; Shame; The Carriage-Lamps; The Knife; The Stove; The Trial, Execution, and Burial of Homer Phelps; The Fight; The City Urchin and the Chaste Villagers; A Little Pilgrimage.

Illustrations: Frontispiece: portrait, facing p. [i]. Illustrations facing pp. 10, 12, 14, 16, 18, 22, 24, 26, 36, 50, 60, 70, 84, 92, 94, 96, 102, 104, 112, 118, 124, 136, 138, 146, 150, 154, 158, 164, 174, 184, 186, 188, 196.

Publication: Announced in *The Publishers' Weekly* of August 25, 1900. Copyright applied for on August 15, 1900. Copyright deposit made on August 16, 1900. The first edition.

Publication Price: One dollar and fifty cents.

Note: A perplexing situation arises in connection with the two copyright copies of this book, both of which were received at the Library of Congress on the same day. One volume bears the copyright notice in the name of STEPHEN CRANE and the second (26a), in the name of WILLIAM HOWE CRANE. In all other respects the two books are identical. The copyright application was actually made by the latter on the day preceding the deposit, as executor of the estate of Stephen Crane. One tenable explanation of this variance is that the book was being printed at the time of the author's death and that the plate of page [ii] was amended before the first issue was completely run off. Since the Library of Congress copy bearing the Stephen Crane notice is apparently unique, it would seem logical to assume that the printed sheets bearing such notice were withdrawn by

48

Harpers prior to publication and corrected ones bearing the William Howe Crane notice substituted. At least one set of sheets containing the original notice escaped detection and remains extant to confound bibliographers. Undoubtedly this *Stephen* book is the veritable first issue despite its apparent rarity. Tech- *Crane* nically, however, it may be classified as a pre-publication issue and that fact may offer some small measure of consolation to the collectors destined to be without a copy. A third (26b) and much later state of this title has no date on the title-page and the illustrations are reduced to fifteen in number.

Later editions of this book lack the date on title-page, and are bound in dark green undecorated cloth lettered in gold.

27

WHILOMVILLE STORIES

1900

Whilomville / Stories / *by* / *Stephen Crane* / *Illustrated by* / *Peter Newell* / (publisher's design) / *London and New York* / *Harper & Brothers* / *Publishers* / *1900* [All the above within a decorative border.]

Signatures: [a]⁴, A-I⁸, K-M⁸, N⁴. Size of leaf: 7 3/4 x 5 1/8 inches. Laid paper; top edge trimmed; other edges untrimmed; white wove endpapers.

Pagination: [i], title-page, as above; [ii], Copyright notice: Copyright, 1900, by WILLIAM HOWE CRANE. / (line) / *All rights reserved.* /; [iii], CONTENTS (see *infra*); [iv], blank; v-vi, ILLUSTRATIONS (see *infra*); [vii], half-title: WHILOMVILLE STORIES; [viii], blank; 1-198, [199], text; [200], blank.

Binding: Dark blue cloth. Front cover: WHILOMVILLE / STORIES / STEPHEN CRANE / (decorations: four formalized inverted tulips) /. Spine: WHILOM- / VILLE / STORIES / (a line) / CRANE / HARPERS /. Back cover: blank.

Contents: The Angel Child; Lynx-Hunting; The Lover and the

49

Telltale; "Showin' Off"; Making an Orator; Shame; The Carriage-Lamps; The Knife; The Stove; The Trial, Execution, and
Burial of Homer Phelps; The Fight; The City Urchin and the

Stephen Chaste Villagers; A Little Pilgrimage.

Crane *Illustrations*: Frontispiece: portrait, facing p. [i]. Illustrations
facing pp. 10, 12, 14, 16, 18, 22, 24, 26, 36, 50, 60, 70, 84, 92, 94,
96, 102, 104, 112, 118, 124, 136, 138, 146, 150, 154, 158, 164, 174,
184, 186, 188, 196.

Publication: Announced in *The Publishers' Circular* of November 17, 1900. The British Museum deposit was made on February 19, 1901. The first English edition.

Publication Price: Five shillings.

28

WOUNDS IN THE RAIN

1900

WOUNDS IN / THE RAIN / (line) / *War Stories* / (line) / BY /
STEPHEN CRANE / *Author of* / "The Red Badge of Courage,"
"Active Service," / "War is Kind," etc. / (line) / (leaf orna-
ment) / (line) / New York (Old English type) / Frederick A.
Stokes Company / *Publishers*

Signatures: 2 unsigned leaves, [1]⁸, 2-22⁸. Signature 17 misnumbered 18. Size of leaf: 7 5/16 x 4 15/16 inches. Laid paper;
all edges trimmed; top edge gilt; white wove endpapers.

Pagination: [i], half-title: (2 red lines) / WOUNDS *in the* RAIN /
(2 red lines) /; [ii], blank; [iii], title-page, as above, with the
title, author, and publisher in red; remainder in black; all within
a panel of black rules; [iv], copyright notice: Copyright, 1899,
by / S. S. MCCLURE COMPANY. / Copyright, 1899, by / THE
CURTIS PUBLISHING COMPANY. / Copyright, 1899, by / FRANK
LESLIE PUBLISHING HOUSE (Incorporated). / Copyright, 1900, by
/ FREDERICK A. STOKES COMPANY. / (line) / *All Rights Reserved.*
/; [v], dedication: TO / Moreton Frewen (Old English type) /

50

THIS SMALL TOKEN OF THINGS / WELL REMEMBERED BY / HIS FRIEND / STEPHEN CRANE. / BREDE PLACE, SUSSEX, *April, 1900.* /; [vi], blank; [vii], CONTENTS: (see *infra*); [viii], blank; [1], 2-347, text; [348], blank.

Binding: Dark green cloth. Front cover: WOUNDS *in* / THE RAIN / *By* STEPHEN CRANE / (leaf ornament) /. Entire cover bordered in a chain design. Spine: Wounds / *in the* / Rain / CRANE / (leaf ornament) / *Stokes* /. Back cover: blank. Lettered and decorated in gilt.

Contents: The Price of the Harness; The Lone Charge of William B. Perkins; The Clan of No-Name; God Rest Ye, Merry Gentlemen; The Revenge of the Adolphus; The Sergeant's Private Madhouse; Virtue in War; Marines Signalling under Fire at Guantanamo; This Majestic Lie; War Memories; The Second Generation.

Publication: Announced in *The Publishers' Weekly* of October 13, 1900. Copyright applied for on September 1, 1900. Copyright deposit made on September 4, 1900. The first edition.

Publication Price: One dollar and fifty cents.

Note: Although the English edition was announced several weeks earlier than the American, it is probable that both editions were published simultaneously, since the English edition was printed from the American plates.

Stephen Crane

29

WOUNDS IN THE RAIN

1900

WOUNDS IN THE RAIN / A COLLECTION OF STORIES RELATING TO / THE SPANISH-AMERICAN WAR OF 1898 / BY / STEPHEN CRANE / METHUEN & CO. / 36 ESSEX STREET W. C. / LONDON / 1900

Signatures: [i]⁴, 1-21⁸, 22⁶, [A]⁸, A2⁸, A3⁴. Signature A2 between leaves [A]₄ and [A]₅; signature A3 between leaves A2₄ and A2₅. Size of leaf: 7 1/2 x 4 7/8 inches. Laid paper; top edge trimmed; white wove endpapers.

Pagination: [i], half-title: WOUNDS IN THE RAIN; [ii], BY THE SAME AUTHOR (list of ten books); [iii], title-page, as above; [iv], blank; [v], dedication: TO / Moreton Frewen (Old English type) / THIS SMALL TOKEN OF THINGS / WELL REMEMBERED BY / HIS FRIEND / STEPHEN CRANE. / BREDE PLACE, SUSSEX, *April,* 1900. /; [vi], blank; [vii], CONTENTS: (see *infra*); [viii], blank; [1], 2-347, text; 347, colophon: *Printed from American Plates* / Edinburgh: T. & A. CONSTABLE, Printers to Her Majesty. /; [348], blank; [1], 2-47, (catalog and announcements of Methuen and Company, dated August 1900); [48], blank.

Binding: Red cloth. Front cover: WOUNDS / IN THE / RAIN / BY / STEPHEN / CRANE (all enclosed in a panel of rules) /. Spine: WOUNDS / IN THE / RAIN / STEPHEN / CRANE (all enclosed in a panel of rules) / METHUEN (within a separate panel of rules) /. Back cover: blank. Lettered and ruled in gilt.

Contents: The Price of the Harness; The Lone Charge of William B. Perkins; The Clan of No-Name; God Rest Ye, Merry Gentlemen; The Revenge of the Adolphus; The Sergeant's Private Madhouse; Virtue in War; Marines Signalling under Fire at Guantanamo; This Majestic Lie; War Memories; The Second Generation.

Publication: Announced in *The Publishers' Circular* of September 22, 1900. British Museum deposit made September 1, 1900. The first English edition.

Publication Price: Six shillings.

30

GREAT BATTLES OF THE WORLD

1901

GREAT BATTLES / OF THE WORLD / (line) / BY STEPHEN CRANE / AUTHOR OF "THE RED BADGE OF COURAGE," ETC. / ILLUSTRATED BY

/ JOHN SLOAN / (line) / (ornament) / (line) / PHILADELPHIA /
J. B. LIPPINCOTT / COMPANY MDCCCCI

Signatures: [1], 2-17⁸, 18⁴. Size of leaf: 7 11/16 x 5 inches. Laid
paper; top edge gilt; other edges trimmed; white laid endpapers. *Stephen Crane*

Pagination: [i], half-title: GREAT BATTLES / OF THE WORLD /;
[ii], blank; [1], title-page, as above, enclosed by rules; the first
three lines of type and ornament in red; other lines in black;
[2], copyright notice: COPYRIGHT, 1900 / BY / J. B. LIPPINCOTT
COMPANY / *Electrotyped and Printed by* / *J. B. Lippincott Com-*
pany, Philadelphia, U.S.A. /; 3-4, NOTE (signed) HARRISON S.
MORRIS; 5, CONTENTS (see *infra*); [6], blank; (pages 7-8 not present, due to the misnumbering of prior pages); 9, ILLUSTRATIONS
(see *infra*); [10], blank; 11-278, text; [279-280], blank.

Binding: Red cloth (also light blue). Front cover: Great Battles
/ of the World / (line) / (crossed swords design in a vertical
panel) / (line) / Stephen Crane ·/. All of the above within a
panel. The sword blades and the ribbon binding them are in
silver; all other lettering and decorations in gilt. Spine: (line) /
Great / Battles / of the / World / (line) / Crane / Lippincott
/ (line) /. Back cover: blank.

Contents: The Battle of Bunker Hill; Vittoria; The Siege of
Plevna; The Storming of Burkersdorf Heights; A Swede's Campaign in Germany: I. Leipzig, II. Lutzen; The Storming of Badajos; The Brief Campaign against New Orleans; The Battle of
Solferino.

Illustrations: frontispiece facing p. [1]; illustrations facing pp.
58, 70, 108, 162, 220, 230, 272.

Publication: Announced in *The Publishers' Weekly* of December 8, 1900. Copyright applied for and deposit made on October
24, 1900. The first edition.

Publication Price: One dollar and fifty cents.

Note: The second edition of this work is so indicated on the

53

half-title; still later issues may be recognized by the word "for-lorn" correctly spelled in the fifth line of page 212—in the first and second editions the word is spelled "folorn."

31

THE MONSTER

1901

THE MONSTER / AND / OTHER STORIES / (line) / BY / STEPHEN CRANE / ILLUSTRATED / (line) / (publisher's design) / (line) / LONDON AND NEW YORK / HARPER & BROTHERS PUBLISHERS / 1901

Signatures: [a]⁴, [A]⁸, B-I⁸, K-P⁸, Q⁶. Size of leaf: 7 3/16 x 4 7/8 inches. Calendered paper; all edges trimmed; white wove endpapers.

Pagination: [i], half-title: THE MONSTER / AND / OTHER STORIES /; [ii], blank; [iii], title-page, as above, enclosed by rules; [iv], copyright notice: Copyright, 1899, by HARPER & BROTHERS. / (line) / *All rights reserved.* /; v, CONTENTS (see *infra*); [vi], blank; vii-viii, ILLUSTRATIONS (see *infra*); [i], divisional title: THE MONSTER; [2], blank; 3-252, text; 252, colophon: LONDON: PRINTED BY WILLIAM CLOWES AND SONS, LIMITED, / STAMFORD STREET AND CHARING CROSS. /.

Binding: Red cloth. Front cover: THE MONSTER / AND OTHER STORIES / design of three medallions linked by a chain) / STEPHEN / (dot) CRANE (dot) /. Spine: THE / MONSTER / AND OTHER / (dot) STORIES (dot) / STEPHEN / (dot) CRANE (dot) / HARPERS /. Back cover: blank. All lettering in gilt; decorated in black.

Contents: The Monster; The Blue Hotel; His New Mittens; Twelve O'clock; Moonlight on the Snow; Manacled; An Illusion in Red and White.

Illustrations: frontispiece facing p. [iii]; illustrations facing pp. 10, 14, 16, 18, 20, 30, 36, 58, 68, 74, 100; on pp. 165, 166, 167, 168, 169, 175, 177, 179, 180, 181, 185, 186, 188.

54

Publication: Announced in *The Publishers' Circular* of February 23, 1901. British Museum deposit made February 25, 1901. The first English edition.

Publication Price: Five shillings.

Note: This volume contains the first book appearance of the following stories: "Twelve O'clock"; "Moonlight on the Snow"; "Manacled"; "An Illusion in Red and White." These stories were not included in the New York edition of 1899.

32
GREAT BATTLES OF THE WORLD
1901

GREAT BATTLES / of the World. By / Stephen Crane, Author / of "The Red Badge of / Courage," etc. Illus- / trated by John Sloan / London: Chapman & Hall Limited, / Henrietta Street, Covent Garden, W. C. / 1901

Signatures: [A]⁶, B-I⁸, K-S⁸, [T]². Size of leaf: 7 1/2 x 5 inches. Wove paper; top edge trimmed; other edges untrimmed; white laid endpapers.

Pagination: [i-ii], blank; [iii], half-title: GREAT BATTLES / OF THE WORLD /; [iv], blank; [v], title-page, as above, the first and seventh lines of type printed in red; others in black; [vi], blank; [vii-viii], NOTE (signed) HARRISON S. MORRIS; [ix], CONTENTS (see *infra*); [x], blank; [xi], ILLUSTRATIONS (see *infra*); [xii], blank; 1-271, [272], text; [272], colophon: *Printed by* R. & R. CLARK, LIMITED, *Edinburgh*; 1-4, publisher's announcements, beginning with FACT AND FABLE by Effie Johnson and terminating with THE SALTONSTALL GAZETTE.

Binding: Brick red cloth. Front cover: GREAT BATTLES / of the World. By / Stephen Crane, Illus- / trated by John Sloan /. Spine: GREAT / BATTLES / OF THE / WORLD / STEPHEN / CRANE / CHAPMAN / AND HALL /. Back cover: blank. Lettered in gilt.

Contents: Vittoria; The Siege of Plevna; The Storming of Burkersdorf Heights; A Swede's Campaign in Germany: I. Leipzig, II. Lutzen; The Storming of Badajoz; The Brief Cam-
Stephen paign against New Orleans; The Battle of Solferino; The Battle
Crane of Bunker Hill.

Illustrations: frontispiece facing p. [v]; illustrations facing pp. 33, 50, 85, 177, 196, 214, 253.

Publication: Announced in *The Publishers' Circular* of June 15, 1901. British Museum deposit made July 31, 1901. The first English edition.

Publication Price: Six shillings.

Note: First edition sheets were later bound (32a) in red pictorial cloth, decorated in blue and black, and lettered in gilt as in the above described binding. A Victoria Cross in gilt appears on the spine between "CRANE" and "CHAPMAN." All edges are gilt.

33

LAST WORDS

1902

LAST WORDS / BY / STEPHEN CRANE / AUTHOR OF / "RED BADGE OF COURAGE," "ACTIVE SERVICE," "PICTURES OF WAR," / "THE THIRD VIOLET," "THE OPEN BOAT," / "WOUNDS IN THE RAIN," ETC. / London (Old English type) / DIGBY, LONG & CO. / 18 Bouverie Street, Fleet Street, E. C. / 1902

Signatures: [A]⁴, B-I⁸, K-U⁸, X-[Y]⁸. Size of leaf: 7 3/4 x 5 inches. Laid paper; top edge untrimmed; other edges rough-trimmed; white laid endpapers.

Pagination: [i], blank; [ii], blank; [iii], half-title: LAST WORDS; [iv], blank; [v], title-page, as above; [vi], blank; [vii]-viii, table of contents (see *infra*); 1-320, text; [1], 2-14, [15-16], publisher's announcements, dated March 1902.

Binding: Red cloth over beveled boards. Front cover: Last *Stephen*
Words / STEPHEN CRANE / Author of / "The Red Badge of *Crane*
Courage," etc. / (design in blind at foot of cover) /. Spine: LAST
/ WORDS / (rule) / STEPHEN CRANE / DIGBY, LONG & CO. /. Back
cover: (publisher's design in blind). Lettered and ruled in gilt.

Contents: The Reluctant Voyagers; The Kicking Twelfth; The
Upturned Face; The Shrapnel of Their Friends; "And If He
Wills, We Must Die"; The Surrender of Forty Fort; "Ol' Bennet" and the Indians; The Battle of Forty Fort; London Impressions; Great Grief's Holiday Dinner; The Silver Pageant;
A Street Scene; Minetta Lane; Roof Gardens; In the Broadway
Cars; The Assassins in Modern Battles; An Old Man Goes Wooing; Ballydehob; The Royal Irish Constabulary; A Fishing Village; Four Men in a Cave; The Mesmeric Mountain; The
Squire's Madness; A Desertion; How the Donkey Lifted the
Hills; A Man by the Name of Mud; A Poker Game; The Snake;
A Self-Made Man; A Tale of Mere Chance; At Clancy's Wake;
An Episode of War; The Voice of the Mountain; Why Did the
Young Clerk Swear?; The Victory of the Moon.

Publication: Announced in *The Publishers' Circular* of March
29, 1902. British Museum deposit made May 16, 1902. The first
edition.

Publication Price: Six shillings.

Note: The first edition sheets were later bound in cheaper
grades of cloth—brown (33a), blue-gray (33b), and red (33c);
lettered in black and lacking the publisher's design in blind on
the back cover. No copy of the Philadelphia edition, alleged to
have been published by Henry T. Coates and Company, has
been discovered. The records of the company reveal no entry
pertaining to such a title and it is probable that the edition is
apocryphal.

57

34
THE O'RUDDY
1903

THE O'RUDDY / A ROMANCE / BY / STEPHEN CRANE / *Author of
"The Red Badge of Courage," "Active / Service," "Wounds in
the Rain,"* etc. / AND / ROBERT BARR / *Author of "Tekla," "In
the Midst of Alarms," / "Over the Border," "The Victors,"* etc.
/ With frontispiece by / C. D. WILLIAMS / (ornament) / NEW
YORK / FREDERICK A. STOKES COMPANY / PUBLISHERS

Signatures: [1-22]⁸. Size of leaf: 7 7/16 x 5 inches. Wove paper;
all edges trimmed; white wove endpapers.

Pagination: [i], half-title: THE O'RUDDY; [ii], blank; inserted
frontispiece in color facing page [iii]; [iii], title-page, as above,
the whole surrounded by a narrow black rule, in turn enclosed
in a heavier black rule; [iv], copyright notice and printer's imprint: *Copyright, 1903,* / BY FREDERICK A. STOKES COMPANY /
All rights reserved / Published in October, 1903 / (line) / UNI-
VERSITY PRESS · JOHN WILSON / AND SON · CAMBRIDGE, U. S. A.;
1-356, text.

Binding: Light tan cloth. Front cover: The / O'Ruddy / (costumed figure occupying left half of cover to within an inch of
top and bottom) / By / Stephen Crane / and (four dots) /
Robert Barr /. "The O'Ruddy" lettered in green and outlined
in black; costumed figure outlined in black, coat of green; other
lettering in black. Spine: The / O'Ruddy / (shamrock) / *Stephen / Crane / & / Robert / Barr* / STOKES /. "The O'Ruddy,"
shamrock design, and "Stokes" in black; other lettering in green.
Back cover: blank.

Publication: Announced in *The Publishers' Weekly* of December 5, 1903. Copyright applied for on October 27, 1903. Copyright deposit made on November 2, 1903. The first edition.

Publication Price: One dollar and fifty cents.

Note: Later editions of this title are so specified.   [SEE NOTE]

58.

Note to Section 34: "The Williams and Starrett collation for the Stokes edition is
faulty, since instead of being [1-22]⁸ as described, it is in fact 1-22⁸ 23⁴ with the third
leaf of the gatherings carrying the signature."—Fredson Bowers, *Studies in Bibliography,*
22 (1969), 276.
    For other data about the Stokes New York first edition in both the British Museum
and the Bodleian Library, see the same work.

35

THE O'RUDDY

1904

Stephen Crane

THE O'RUDDY / A ROMANCE / BY / STEPHEN CRANE / AND / ROBERT BARR / METHUEN & CO. / 36 ESSEX STREET W. C. / LONDON / 1904

Signatures: 2 unsigned leaves, 1-22⁸, 23², [A]⁸, A2⁸, A3⁴. Signature A2 between leaves [A]₄ and [A]₅; signature A3 between leaves A2₄ and A2₅. Size of leaf: 7 1/2 x 5 inches. Wove paper; top edge trimmed; fore edge rough-trimmed; bottom edge untrimmed; white wove endpapers.

Pagination: [i], half-title: THE O'RUDDY; [ii], BY STEPHEN CRANE / THE RED BADGE OF COURAGE / WOUNDS IN THE RAIN / BY ROBERT BARR / TEKLA / IN THE MIDST OF ALARMS / OVER THE BORDER / THE VICTORS /; [iii], title-page, as above; [iv], blank; 1-356, text; 356, colophon: *Printed by* MORRISON & GIBB LIMITED, *Edinburgh*; [1, 2], 3-40, (catalog of books published by Methuen and Company, dated March 1904).

Binding: Red cloth. Front cover: THE O'RUDDY / BY / STEPHEN / CRANE / AND / ROBERT / BARR (all enclosed in a panel of rules) /. Spine: THE / O'RUDDY / STEPHEN / CRANE / AND / ROBERT / BARR (all enclosed in a panel of rules) / METHUEN (within a separate panel of rules) /. Back cover: blank. Lettered and ruled in gilt.

Publication: Announced in *The Publishers' Circular* of July 16, 1904. British Museum deposit made July 7, 1904. The first English edition.

Publication Price: Six shillings.

36

MEN, WOMEN AND BOATS

1921

MEN, WOMEN AND BOATS / (line) / BY STEPHEN CRANE / (line) / EDITED WITH AN INTRODUCTION BY / VINCENT STARRETT / (line) /

59

(publisher's design) / (line) / BONI AND LIVERIGHT / (line) /
PUBLISHERS (two triangles of three dots each) NEW YORK

Stephen *Signatures*: [1-8]⁸. Size of leaf: 6 1/2 x 4 1/4 inches. Wove
Crane paper; all edges trimmed; top edge stained brown or blue, de-
pending on color of binding; decorated endpapers with initials
"M L", signed "Horace Brodzky—19."

Pagination: [i], half-title: THE MODERN LIBRARY / OF THE WORLD'S
BEST BOOKS / MEN, WOMEN AND BOATS /; [ii], (notice of advertisements at end of book); [iii], title-page, as above, in a panel
of double rules; [iv], copyright notice: MEN, WOMEN AND BOATS
/ (line) / COPYRIGHT, 1921, BY / BONI & LIVERIGHT, INC. / PRINTED
IN THE UNITED STATES OF AMERICA /; [1], NOTE (signed) V. S.;
[2], blank; [3], half-title: MEN, WOMEN AND BOATS; [4], blank;
[5], CONTENTS (see *infra*); [6], blank; [7], STEPHEN CRANE: AN
ESTIMATE; [8], blank; 9-20, text (introduction); [21], divisional title: THE OPEN BOAT; [22], blank; 23-245, text; [246-252],
publisher's announcements: Modern Library of the World's
Best Books.

Binding: Brown or blue flexible imitation leather. Front cover:
Publisher's design in a panel of rules, 1 x 3/4 inches, containing:
MODERN / (line) / LIBRARY / (line) / B L (within a circle) /.
The entire cover is rimmed by a rule in blind. Spine: (two
lines) / MEN / WOMEN / AND / BOATS / (three dots) / STEPHEN
/ CRANE / MODERN / LIBRARY / (line) /. Back cover: blank. Let-
tered and decorated in gilt.

Contents: Stephen Crane: An Estimate [by Vincent Starrett];
The Open Boat; The Reluctant Voyagers; The End of the
Battle; The Upturned Face; An Episode of War; An Experi-
ment in Misery; The Duel That Was Not Fought; A Desertion;
A Dark Brown Dog; The Pace of Youth; Sullivan County
Sketches:—A Tent in Agony, Four Men in a Cave, The Mes-
meric Mountain; The Snake; London Impressions; The Scotch
Express.

Publication: Announced in *The Publishers' Weekly* of September 24, 1921. The first edition.

Publication Price: Ninety-five cents.

Note: The first edition of this volume may be identified by the omission of a word on page 69, line 19. In later editions, the word "immediately" was inserted after the word "almost."

The following stories appear in this volume for the first time in a book: A Dark Brown Dog; A Tent in Agony; The Scotch Express. The story, "The End of the Battle," appeared in *Last Words* entitled, "And if He Wills, We Must Die." The former title, however, was used in the original periodical publication.

Stephen Crane

37

ET CETERA

1924

ET CETERA / A Collector's / Scrap-Book / (mounted knight and esquire design) / CHICAGO / PASCAL COVICI, *Publisher* / 1924

Signatures: [1-17]^8. Size of leaf: 9 1/4 x 6 1/4 inches. Simulated parchment paper; top edge stained red with gilt superimposed; other edges untrimmed; mottled gray endpapers.

Pagination: [i], (mounted knight and esquire design); [ii-iv], blank; [v], half-title: ET CETERA; [vi], blank; [vii], title-page, as above, within a decorative panel; first line of title and knight and esquire design in red; [viii], copyright notice: Copyright 1924 / PASCAL COVICI · Publisher / Chicago / This Edition is Limited to / Six Hundred and Twenty-five Copies / Of Which This is / (publisher's device) /; [ix], Edited by / CHARLES VINCENT STARRETT /; [x], blank; [xi-xii], *Contents*; [xiii-xv], *Foreword* (signed) VINCENT STARRETT; [xvi], blank; [xvii], half-title (repeated): ET CETERA; [xviii], blank; 1-244, text; [245], 246-251, Gossip (signed) V. S.; [252], blank; 253, *Acknowledgement*; [254], blank.

61

Binding: Half beige cloth with gray board sides. Front cover: blank. Spine: gray paper label, 1 5/8 x 1 1/4 inches, lettered and decorated in black: (ornament) / Et Cetera / *A Collector's* *Stephen* / *Scrap-book* / (ornament) / (knight and esquire design at *Crane* foot of spine, stamped in gilt). Back cover: blank.

Publication: Copyright applied for and deposit made on May 31, 1924. The first edition.

Publication Price: Seven dollars and firty cents.

Note: This volume of miscellaneous selections contains the first book appearance of "At the Pit Door" and "The Great Boer Trek."

38

THE WORK OF STEPHEN CRANE

1925 - 1926 - 1927

THE WORK OF / STEPHEN CRANE / *Edited by Wilson Follett* / ·I· / THE RED BADGE / OF COURAGE / *and* / THE VETERAN / *Introduction by* / JOSEPH HERGESHEIMER / *New York* / ALFRED · A · KNOPF

Signatures: 2 unsigned leaves, [1]¹⁰, [2-13]⁸. Size of leaf: 7 1/2 x 5 1/4 inches. Laid paper watermarked "S. C."; all edges untrimmed; mauve endpapers.

Pagination: 2 preliminary blank leaves, [i], half-title: STEPHEN CRANE / (ornament) / *The Red Badge of Courage* / *The Veteran* /; [ii], blank; [iii], title-page, as above, within a mauve ornamental border; [iv], (imprint of Plimpton Press and copyright notices); [v], CONTENTS OF VOLUME I / (ornament) / *Introduction* / PAGE IX / THE RED BADGE OF COURAGE / PAGE 21 / THE VETERAN / PAGE 203 / (ornament) /; [vi], blank; [vii], half-title: (ornament) / *Introduction* / (ornament) /; [viii], blank; ix-xvii, *Introduction* (signed) JOSEPH HERGESHEIMER; [xix], half-title: THE RED BADGE / OF COURAGE / (ornament) /; [xx], blank; 21-209, text; [210], colophon.

62

Binding: Buff cloth sides; black cloth spine. Front cover: (octagonal black cloth label, 2 1/4 x 1 1/2 inches, with the initials "S. C." within an ornamental gilt panel). Spine: (ornament) / THE RED / BADGE / OF / COURAGE / (ornament) / THE / WORK / *Stephen* OF / *Stephen* / *Crane* / (ornament) / I /. Back cover: blank. *Crane* Lettered and decorated in gilt.

Publication: Copyrights applied for and deposits made on the following dates: Vol. I, November 23, 1925; Vol. II, December 14, 1925; Vols. III, IV, V, March 31, 1926; Vols. VI, VII, VIII, August 16, 1926; Vols. IX, X, October 26, 1926; Vol. XI, December 9, 1926; Vol. XII, February 7, 1927. The first edition.

Publication Price: Seven dollars and fifty cents a volume.

Note: This edition, designed by Elmer Adler and limited to 750 numbered copies, was published over a period of three years, and comprises 12 uniform volumes. The contents of the respective volumes are as follows:

II
TALES OF TWO WARS
Introduction by Robert H. Davis
The Little Regiment; Three Miraculous Soldiers; A Mystery of Heroism; An Indiana Campaign; A Grey Sleeve; The Clan of No Name; Virtue in War; His Majestic Lie; The Second Generation.

III
THE MONSTER and THE THIRD VIOLET
Introduction by Wilson Follett

IV
ACTIVE SERVICE
Introduction by Carl Van Doren

V
WHILOMVILLE STORIES
Introduction by William Lyon Phelps
The Angel Child; Lynx Hunting; The Lover and the Telltale; Showin' Off; Making an Orator; Shame; The Carriage Lamps; The Knife; The Stove; The Trial, Execution and Burial of Homer Phelps; The Fight; The City Urchin and the Chaste Villagers; A Little Pilgrimage; His New Mittens.

63

Stephen
Crane

VI
THE BLACK RIDERS and Other Lines
Introduction by Amy Lowell
The Black Riders; War Is Kind; Intrigue.

VII - VIII
THE O'RUDDY
Introduction by Thomas Beer

IX
WOUNDS IN THE RAIN
Introduction by Willa Cather
The Price of the Harness; The Lone Charge of William B. Perkins; God
Rest Ye, Merry Gentlemen; The Revenge of the Adolphus; The Ser-
geant's Private Madhouse; Marines Signalling Under Fire at Guantanamo;
An Episode of War; The Kicking Twelfth; Ol' Bennet and the Indians;
War Memories.

X
MAJOR CONFLICTS
Introduction by H. L. Mencken
George's Mother; The Blue Hotel; Maggie.

XI
MIDNIGHT SKETCHES and Other Impressions
Introduction by Sherwood Anderson
Midnight Sketches: An Experiment in Misery; The Men in the Storm;
The Duel That Was Not Fought; The Pace of Youth; The Auction; A
Detail; An Eloquence of Grief; A Desertion; An Ominous Baby; A Great
Mistake; A Dark Brown Dog. *The Reporter Errant*: London Impressions;
The Scotch Express; Irish Notes (Ballydehob; The Royal Irish Constabu-
lary; An Old Man Goes Wooing; A Fishing Village); A Street Scene in
New York. *Minor Conflicts*: The Reluctant Voyagers; Sullivan County
Sketches (A Tent in Agony; Four Men in a Cave; The Mesmeric Moun-
tain); The Snake; A Self-Made Man; A Poker Game; The Silver Pageant;
Three Fables (How the Donkey Lifted the Hills; The Victory of the
Moon; The Voice of the Mountain); The Squire's Madness; A Tale of
Mere Chance; A Prologue.

XII
THE OPEN BOAT and Other Tales
Introduction by Charles Michelson
The Open Boat; A Man and — Some Others; The Bride Comes to Yel-
low Sky; Twelve O'clock; Moonlight on the Snow; The Wise Men; The
Five White Mice; Flanagan and His Short Filibustering Adventure;
Horses—One Dash; An Illusion in Red and White; Manacled; Death and
the Child.

64

39

THE COLLECTED POEMS OF STEPHEN CRANE

1930

Stephen

THE / COLLECTED POEMS / OF / STEPHEN CRANE / EDITED BY *Crane*
WILSON FOLLETT / S. / C. / (publisher's design) / *Nineteen hundred and thirty* / NEW YORK · ALFRED · A · KNOPF · LONDON

Signatures: [1-9]⁸. Size of leaf: 7 1/2 x 5 1/8 inches. Laid paper; top edge stained blue; other edges rough-trimmed; white wove endpapers.

Pagination: [i-ii], blank; [iii], half-title: *The* / COLLECTED POEMS / *of* / STEPHEN CRANE / (ornament) /; [iv], BOOKS /BY MODERN POETS / (ornament in blue) / (there follows a list of titles beginning with COLLECTED POEMS by A. E. Coppard and concluding with INDIAN EARTH by Witter Bynner) /; [v], title-page, as above, with the pen facsimile initials "S." and "C." enclosed by a decorative panel consisting of double rows of blue brackets; the publisher's design is enclosed by blue brackets; periods in the last line also in blue; [vi], copyright notice: *Copyright 1922 / by William H. Crane / Copyright 1895, 1899, 1926, 1929, 1930 / by Alfred A. Knopf, Inc. / Manufactured in the United States of America* /; [vii], contents: (see *infra*); [viii], blank; [1], divisional title: (ornament) / THE BLACK RIDERS / AND OTHER LINES / (ornament) /; [2], blank; 3-73, text; [74], blank; [75], divisional title: (ornament) / WAR IS KIND / AND OTHER LINES / (ornament) /; [76], blank; 77-125, text; [126], blank; [127], divisional title: *Three Poems* (followed by note); [128], blank; 129-132, text; [133], colophon; [134-136], blank.

Binding: Blue cloth. Front cover decorated with panel (2 3/16 x 1 1/2 inches) containing pen facsimile initials "S." and "C." Spine: (ornament) / THE / COL- / LECTED / POEMS / OF / *Stephen* / *Crane* / (ornament) / ALFRED A. / KNOPF /. Back cover: (publisher's design in blind). Lettered and decorated in silver.

Contents: The Black Riders And Other Lines; War Is Kind And Other Lines; Three Poems.

65

Publication: Announced in *The Publishers' Weekly* of March 27, 1930. Copyright applied for and deposit made on March 31, 1930. The first edition.

Publication Price: Two dollars and fifty cents.

Note: The first state of this volume may be identified by the running head "The Black Riders" at the top of the left-hand page throughout the book.

The poem "There was one I met upon the road" appears in the original editions of both *The Black Riders And Other Lines* and *War Is Kind*. In this volume, the poem is omitted from the "War Is Kind" section. Included in the "War Is Kind" section is "The Blue Battalions" which first appeared in *The Philistine*, Vol. 7, pp. 9-10, June 1898, and later, in *Spanish-American War Songs*, Detroit: Sidney A. Witherbee, Publisher, 1898. "Three Poems" are here published for the first time in book form, having made their initial appearance in *The Bookman*, Vol. 69, pp. 120-122, April 1929.

40

A BATTLE IN GREECE

1936

A BATTLE / IN / GREECE / BY STEPHEN CRANE / (ornament—three dots) / Decorated by / VALENTI ANGELO / for the Peter Pauper Press / Mount Vernon / 1936

Signatures: [1-6]⁴. Leaves [1₁] and [6₄] used as endpapers. Size of leaf: 9 5/8 x 6 1/4 inches. Wove paper; top edge stained red; other edges untrimmed.

Pagination: [i-iv], blank; [v], half-title: A BATTLE IN GREECE; [vi], blank; [1], title-page, as above, lettered in red, within a decorative panel depicting a battle scene in blue and gray; [2], blank; [3], 4-30, text; [31], blank; [32], colophon: Four hundred and twenty-five copies of this / book have been set in Electra type and printed / on Archer paper at the Walpole

Printing Office / in Mount Vernon, New York. (star ornament)
The text is / reprinted from a copy of the newspaper, now / in
the possession of Mr. Harry Stone, in which / the story made its
original appearance. /; [33-38], blank.

Binding: Vertically streaked mauve paper over boards. Front
cover: white paper label, 2 1/4 x 1 3/8 inches, lettered and bordered in black: A BATTLE / IN / GREECE / (battle scene silhou-
ette in red) /. Spine: white paper label, 2 1/4 x 5/16 inches,
lettered in red and bordered in black at each end: A BATTLE IN
GREECE. Back cover: blank.

Publication: Announced in *The Publishers' Weekly* of December 19, 1936. The first edition.

Publication Price: Four dollars.

Note: This battle sketch is reprinted from the *New York Journal* of June 13, 1897. The story originally appeared in the *Westminster Gazette* in three parts, on June 3, 4, and 11, 1897, as "A
Fragment of Velestino" in a series of articles by Crane entitled
"With Greek and Turk."

41

THE BLOOD OF THE MARTYR

1940

THE BLOOD / OF THE / MARTYR / BY / Stephen Crane / (decorative line) / Peter Pauper Press

Signatures: [1-5]⁴. Leaves [1₁] and [5₄] used as endpapers. Size
of leaf: 6 3/8 x 4 6/8 inches. Gray laid paper; fore edge deckled;
other edges trimmed.

Pagination: [i-viii], blank; [ix], title-page, as above, lettered in
red, enclosed by a blue decorative panel of oriental motif; [x],
blank; [1-20], text; [21], colophon: Two hundred copies of
this book, / decorated by Valenti Angelo, / have been set in
Electra / types and printed on / Winterbourne paper. / No

67

copies are / for sale / (dot) / Peter Pauper Press / Mount Vernon / New York /; [22-28], blank.

Binding: Slate blue wall paper decorated in white and silver over boards. Front cover: red paper label, 1 7/8 x 1 1/8 inches, lettered and decorated in gilt: THE / BLOOD / OF THE / MARTYR / (two dots) / STEPHEN / CRANE (all of the above within a panel of two gilt rules, a gilt star ornament in each corner] /. Spine and back cover blank.

Published: December 1940, for private distribution. The first edition.

Note: This brief satirical play was reprinted from the *Sunday Magazine* (New York *Press*) Vol. 1, pp. 9-11, April 3, 1898, the periodical in which it made its original appearance.

42
THE PUBLIC PAPERS OF A BIBLIOMANIAC
1942

THE / PUBLIC PAPERS / OF A / BIBLIOMANIAC / Together with Some Private Leaves / from a Collector's Scrapbook / BY CHARLES HONCE / PRELUDE BY ELLERY QUEEN (in oblong box) / MOUNT VERNON / THE GOLDEN EAGLE PRESS / 1942

Signatures: [1-12]⁸. Size of leaf: 9 1/2 x 6 1/4 inches. White laid paper; top edge gilt, other edges untrimmed. White laid endpapers.

Pagination: [i-ii], blank; [iii], half-title: THE / PUBLIC PAPERS / OF A / BIBLIOMANIAC /; [iv-v], blank; [vi], frontispiece (caricature of Stephen Crane by Fornaro, printed in magenta; [vii], title-page as above (first six words printed in magenta); [viii], *Copyright, 1942, by* CHARLES HONCE / *Printed in* THE UNITED STATES OF AMERICA /; [ix], FOR / FREDERIC DANNAY / WHO WRITES LONG DETECTIVE / STORIES AND COLLECTS SHORT / ONES AND WHO NOW IS TRAVEL- / ING THE PERILOUS TRAILS OF / BIBLI-

OGRAPHY /; [x], blank; [xi], ELLERY QUEEN / HAS THE FLOOR /; [xii], blank; [xiii-xvii], misnumbered xi-xv, SOME CURIOUS CHANGES / IN BOOK TITLES* /; [xviii], blank; [xix-xx], misnumbered xvii-xviii, THE ROLL CALL; [1], THE / PUBLIC PAPERS / OF A / BIBLIOMANIAC /; [2], blank; 3-170, text; [171-172], blank. *Stephen Crane*

Binding: Tan buckram. Front cover: blank. Spine: THE PUBLIC PAPERS / OF A BIBLIOMANIAC / CHARLES HONCE (The foregoing in gold letters running upward and enclosed by gold line at top and bottom of title.) Back cover: blank.

Publication: Intended to be a book for Christmas 1942, it actually did not appear until March 1943, carrying the season's greetings of Emmanuella and Charles Honce, and explaining the delay on an inserted sheet. One hundred copies printed by S. A. Jacobs in Emmanuella type.

Note: A miscellany of literary material, containing (pp. 115-125) a section entitled "Legends of Stephen Crane," concerning his burial place, the Asbury Park parade story, and similar memorabilia; also the first book appearance of the parade story, "On the New Jersey Coast," by Stephen Crane, reprinted from the *New York Tribune* of August 21, 1892. The book's frontispiece is a drawing by Carlo de Fornaro, printed in color, of "Stephen Crane à la Beardsley."

69

B

MISCELLANEA AND CURIOSA
(Facsimile)

Miscellanea and Curiosa

43

PIKE COUNTY PUZZLE

1894

PIKE COUNTY PUZZLE / (line) / "HSTR WTH XZOASCVAR"—*Senger* / (line) / VOL. I CAMP INTERLAKEN, PENN., AUGUST 28, 1894 NO. I / (line)

Note: A four-page parody newspaper, measuring 14 1/2 x 11 11/16 inches, the mast head of which reads as above. There are four columns to each page, composed of humorous and fictitious news events, editorials, advertisements and personals. It is possible that the entire paper was written by Crane, who is listed as "Office Boy" in the box at the upper left-hand corner of page two. Only one edition of the paper is known to have been published.

44

THE TIME HAS COME

1895

See: PHILISTINES' DINNER IN HONOR OF STEPHEN CRANE in "Writings Biographical and Bibliographical About Stephen Crane" for a detailed description of this item.

45

A LOST POEM

1932

A LOST POEM / BY (seven ornaments) / STEPHEN CRANE / (decoration)

Leaflet consisting of a single sheet of laid paper measuring 12 1/2

71

x 9 7/8 inches, watermarked "Wayside Text U. S. A." and folded twice.

Stephen Crane

Pagination: [i], title-page, as above; [ii-iii], blank; [iv], Of this first printing / One hundred copies have been issued / for the friends of / HARVEY TAYLOR / HARVARD PRESS / New York /; [v], text; [vi-viii], blank.

Note: This poem was later reprinted in *The Golden Book*, Vol. 19, p. 189, February 1934.

46

LEGENDS

1942

LEGENDS / BY / STEPHEN CRANE / (sombrero ornament) / YSLETA / EDWIN B. HILL / 1942

Signatures: [1]⁴. Size of leaf: 6 1/2 x 4 7/8 inches. Deckle edge laid paper watermarked "Cranes."

Pagination: [i-ii], blank; [iii], title-page, as above, [iv-v], text; [vi], colophon: These lines, intended for publication in *The Black ·/ Riders*, first appeared in *The Bookman*, May, 1896 / (line) / Privately printed, April, 1942, at Ysleta, Texas, in an edition / of only forty-five copies, for the friends of Vincent Starrett / and Ames W. Williams; and no copy is for sale. /; [vii-viii], blank.

Binding: Buff deckle edge wrappers. Front wrapper: LEGENDS / (orchid design) / BY / STEPHEN / CRANE /. All of the foregoing is within a panel of rules measuring 3 1/4 x 2 1/4 inches. Back wrapper, blank. Lettered and decorated in black.

47

A SONG CYCLE

1901

As sung by the / Famous Baritone / DAVID BISPHAM. / A SONG

CYCLE / FROM / STEPHEN CRANE'S BLACK RIDERS / SET TO / MUSIC / BY /WILLIAM / SCHUYLER. / Consecration / Good Bye / Long-ing / Darkness / The March of / the Mountains / PUBLISHERS / Thiebes-Stierlin Music Co. / THE PIANO & MUSIC HOUSE OF ST. LOUIS. / Copyright 1900 by Thiebes-Stierlin Music Co.

Stephen Crane

Size of leaf: 13 3/4 x 10 inches. White calendered paper wrappers; printed in black and red.

Pagination: [1], front wrapper, as above, all enclosed by a border of four rules except the copyright notice which is at the bottom of the page; title, within a decorative scroll, supported by a cluster of orchids; 2-7, text; [8], back wrapper: SELECT MUSIC FOR THE PIANOFORTE. / (publisher's advertisements, beginning with *"The Enchanted Well"* and concluding with *"Creole Shawl Dance"*).

48
PLACES AMONG THE STARS
1933

PLACES AMONG THE STARS / SONG FOR HIGH OR MEDIUM VOICE BY / ROLAND FARLEY / POEM BY STEPHEN CRANE / NEW MUSIC PRESS / INC. / 435 PARK AVENUE NEW YORK CITY

Size of leaf: 12 1/4 x 9 3/8 inches. White calendered paper wrappers decorated with yellow vertical stripes and printed in black.

Pagination: [1], front wrapper, as above, all enclosed within a scroll; [2], blank; 3-5, text; [6], back wrapper: Other Compositions / (publisher's advertisements, beginning with *"A Lark Went Singing"* and concluding with *"Wind Flowers"*).

Note: The poem is from *The Black Riders and Other Lines.*

49

LINES

Stephen   1947
  Crane LINES / *By* (seven dashes) / STEPHEN CRANE

Leaflet consisting of a single sheet of laid paper measuring
12 1/2 x 9 7/8 inches, watermarked "Utopian" and folded twice.

Pagination: [i], title-page, as above, with three short horizontal
lines before and after LINES; [ii-iii], blank; [iv], **Of** this original
draft of / "I explain the silvered / passing" one hundred / copies
have been / printed for the / friends of MELVIN H. SCHOBERLIN /
on the first day of / the new year. /THE MOGOLLON PRESS / *Baltimore* / *1947* /; [v], text; [vi-viii], blank.

74

C

PUBLISHED LETTERS

STEPHEN CRANE: LETTERS
1960

STEPHEN CRANE: / LETTERS edited by / R. W. STALLMAN AND
LILLIAN GILKES / With an Introduction by R. W. Stallman / (ornament)
/ New York University Press / 1960 *Frontispiece:* Portrait of Stephen Crane
painted by Corwin Knapp Linson in 1894; reproduced from the original in the
possession of Clifton Waller Barrett. *Dedication page: To* / WILSON FOL-
LETT / *and* / AMES W. WILLIAMS / *and* / VINCENT STARRETT
Introduction by R. W. Stallman (vii–xv, 3–5).

> *Letters* had its beginning in the collection of Crane letters published in
> *Omnibus* (1952), pp. 581–696. This first collection of Crane letters pre-
> sented 120 in all, fifty-seven of which appeared in *Omnibus* for the first
> time.
> Fifty-six new Stephen Crane letters and inscriptions are here published
> for the first time, together with fifty Cora Crane letters, letters of Joseph
> Conrad, Edward Garnett, H. G. Wells, Paul Revere Reynolds, and Crane's
> letters to Lily Brandon Munroe and to Nellie Crouse. All in all, 184 new
> letters and autographs are here published for the first time. *Letters* in-
> corporates the letters in *Stephen Crane's Love Letters to Nellie Crouse
> With Six Other Letters,* ed. Edwin H. Cady and Lester G. Wells (1954).
> *Letters* charts the main events in Crane's career and thus provides the
> first documented chronology. While the chronology gets redefined, new
> chapters are added to the biography; notably by Crane's love letters to
> Nellie Crouse and Lily Brandon Munroe, but also by the letters of Hamlin
> Garland, W. D. Howells, Joseph Conrad, Harold Frederic, H. G. Wells,
> and other literary figures, friends of Crane, and recipients of his letters or
> Cora's. In sum, by the interrelationship of all these letters a pattern not
> known to any one of these contributors emerges, and thus also some new
> lights are thrown upon Stephen Crane. In Beer's *SC* (1923) Lily Brandon
> Munroe and Nellie Crouse are not mentioned at all, and Cora Taylor ap-
> pears only peripherally in two scant references. For the sake of the Crane
> family Beer felt obliged not to divulge the truth about Cora Taylor, and
> he also deferred to the Crane family by silencing some of the truth about
> Stephen Crane lest it offend. The Edith Crane-Beer correspondence, in the
> files of R. W. S., discloses that situation.
> *Letters* incorporates the Crane letters first published in Beer's *SC*. How-
> ever, some snippits of Crane letters deriving from Beer's *SC,* as well as
> portions of letters from Henry James, Bernard Shaw, and others, appear
> in the footnotes and editorial notes to *Letters* and are not listed in the
> list of Letters comprising the CATALOGUE, pp. 349–366.
> Source locations for letters are identified by the various libraries, various
> retainers or collectors of the originals, and various books where they first
> saw print, as in Beer's *SC,* Berryman's *Crane,* or *Omnibus.* It reprints the

letters in *W-S Bibliography*, p. 75, which lists letters published 1895–1937. The Crane to Brandon and Crouse letters then were known to exist but were not yet published.

Letters: Suggested Corrections:*

P. 3: "She [Mary Helen Peck Crane] had had a university education. . . ." However, Mrs. Crane was long dead before C.C.N.Y. admitted the first woman student. (Helen Crane claimed that her grandmother had attended City College, New York.)

P. 112: Letter, no. 140, to Ripley Hitchcock. Crane is here mistaken in that the horse he asks Hitchcock money for was a gelding, not a mare. Elbert Hubbard II trained and cared for the little brown horse Peanuts until Crane sent for him; Peanuts was then shipped to Hartwood in Spring of 1896. *See* Peanuts note 38.

P. 134: Letter, no. 179 and note 81. Charley, Crane's poker table friend referred to also in letter no. 157, p. 123, was Charley Hooke, a writer.

P. 180, note 34: Mrs. Munroe, "having divorced her husband sometime before 1898." However, according to Louis Zara, author of *Dark Rider: A Novel Based on the Life of Stephen Crane* (1961), Lily Brandon Munroe did not divorce her husband until after Crane's death in 1900. (Letter by Zara to R. W. S., April 3, 1960, to which I am indebted for these entries.)

P. 198: Telegram, no. 259 and note 78. Misdated. "Dec. 28 1898" should read 1896. This error is compounded in note 67 (last line), p. 194.

P. 241, note 186. "Edmund's daughter" (Agnes) should read William's daughter Agnes. This error is repeated p. 249, note 205.

Letters: Some Additions *(see also* Addenda):

My Stephen Crane, by Corwin Knapp Linson, ed. Edwin H. Cady (1958), pp. 41, 82, 87, 90, 94. A few of these are in *Letters* (1960) and in *Crane* (1968).

Bulletin, 64 (June, 1960), 339. In "Stephen Crane's Last Novel," by Daniel G. Hoffman. From a press clipping for June 10, 1900, in an unidentified periodical, commented upon in *Newark Call,* June 17, 1923, which reprints the Crane letter. This *Call* clipping is in the Crane Collection, Newark Public Library.

> Dear Sir: I am about to attempt a novel upon Revolutionary times in the Province of New Jersey, and I would be very glad if you could tell me the titles of some of the books on the manners and customs of the times in the Province. I am particularly interested in Elizabethtown, and would be much obliged and gratified if you could give me the title of a good history of that city./Faithfully yours, *Stephen Crane*

* For other corrections to *Letters, see* Fox (1969), Gullason (1969), Katz (1969), and Monteiro (1969). New Crane letters are in the ADDENDA.

Times Literary Supplement, September 22, 1961 (Letters to the Editor). "A Stephen Crane Letter," by William White. The original is in the Charles Feinberg collection, Detroit, Michigan. Crane to William, March 2nd—'99.

"This letter shows, to quote Professor Stallman again, 'how feverishly he [Crane] worked his bankrupt body against the clock.'"

The Poems of Stephen Crane, ed. Joseph Katz (1966). Crane letter to Dr. A. L. Mitchell appearing on verso of a photograph of Crane, dated January 29, 1896. In Lilly Library, Indiana University.

Mr. Frewen of England, by Anita Leslie (London, 1966). Quotes from three Crane letters, new to *Letters.* Quoted in *Crane* (1968).

The Stephen Crane Newsletter, 1, no. 1 (Fall, 1966), and subsequent issues present some new Crane letters and correct *Letters.* However, some of these seemingly new Crane letters had appeared first in *Letters* and are duplicates except in punctuation and/or in spelling. *See SCraneN,* Part F.

Nineteenth-Century Fiction, 23 (September, 1968), 220–225. "Stephen Crane, Samuel Carlton, and a Recovered Letter," by Joseph Katz.

American Literature, 41 (March, 1969), 104–106. "The Letters of Stephen Crane: Additions and Corrections," by Thomas A. Gullason. Crane to Ted (Edmund B. Crane), July 22 [1897], of which the last two sentences appear in *Letters.*

Dukedom Large Enough, by David A. Randall (1969), pp. 227–228. Reproduces Crane to Paul Reynolds letter, January 27, 1899. Not in *Paul Revere Reynolds,* by Frederick Lewis Allen (1944).

Berg Collection, New York Public Library. Crane to Daniel G. Thompson, March 21 [1896].

Library of Congress. Crane to Mrs. Moreton Frewen, 1 ALS. Crane to Mr. Moreton Frewen, 4 ALS. Quoted in Gilkes' *Cora Crane.* Formerly owned by Mr. Roger Frewen of Brede Place, Sussex, England.

Seven Gables Bookshop, Inc. New Crane letter—undated (? 1897)—here published for the first time. In signing it "Your uncle / Stephen" Crane was lightly joking because Crane was uncle to no one named Frank. He wrote someone named Frank at the *New York Journal* to find out whether the *Journal* owed him money for a certain article he had written about "the Portsmouth fluke." He had probably submitted to the *Journal* an article about the new dry docks installed at Portsmouth in 1896, or about the ships in those dry docks, 1897, and now he is back from the Greco-Turkish War and wonders whether the *Journal,* for whom he had reported from the battlefields of Greece, owes him some money. Just back from Greece, he is hard up; just back from Paris, he signs his query to the *Journal*'s bookkeeping office "Au Revoir."

This enigmatic Crane letter reads thus:

Telegrams.   *Ravensbrook,*
Crane, Oxted   *Oxted,*
                                         Surrey.

My dear Frank: Please ask / the *Journal* if they owe me / anything for the Portsmouth / fluke. Explain your advance / and ask them, please, if there / is any more up their sleeves / Au Revoir, / Your uncle / Stephen.

This new Crane letter, submitted to R. W. S. by John S. Van E. Kohn of the Seven Gables Bookshop, Inc., New York City (July 8, 1971), is here published by permission of the Seven Gables Bookshop, Inc.

D

CONTEMPORARY REVIEWS AND PARODIES

M A G G I E
1893

Arena, 8 (June, 1893), xi–xii. By Hamlin Garland. "An Ambitious French Novel and a Modest American Study."

It is a singular thing that French writers like Bourget "should confine themselves so largely to morbid sexuality and to the criminal classes. They make unpardonably dull books, because there is so little real life in them. Most of them are pathological, as Nordan called it, diseased not healthy. Compopalis is very didactic in the study of morbid passions. . . . It is not salacious; it is only a study of the abnormal pursued in the evident belief that there is more human nature in crime and vice than in the commonplace, wholesome action of men and women. This is a mistake, from my point of view."

Maggie: A Story of New York, by Stephen Crane (published by the author) "is of more interest to me, both because it is the work of a young man, and also because it is a work of astonishingly good style. It deals with poverty and vice and crime also, but it does so, not out of curiosity, not out of salaciousness, but because of a distinct art impulse, the desire to utter in truthful phrase a certain rebellious cry. It is the voice of the slums. It is not written by a *dilettante;* it is written by one who has lived the life.* The young author, Stephen Crane, is a native of the city, and has grown up in the very scenes he describes. His book is the most truthful and unhackneyed study of the slums I have yet read, fragment though it is. It is pictorial, graphic, terrible in its directness. It has no conventional phrases. It gives the dialect of the slums as I have never before seen it written—crisp, direct, terse. . . ."

However, "The story fails of rounded completeness. It is only a fragment. It is typical only of the worst elements of the city alley. The author should delineate the families living on the next street, who live lives of heroic purity and hopeless hardship." Mr. Crane has "met and grappled with the actualities of the street in almost unequalled grace and strength. With such a *technique* already at command, with life mainly *before him,* Stephen Crane is to be henceforth reckoned with." Garland compares briefly Richard Harding Davis's "Van Bibber"—to see "the extremes of New York as stated by two young men. Mr. Crane need not fear comparisons so far as *technique* goes, and Mr. Davis will need to step forward right briskly or he may be overtaken by a man who impresses the reader with a sense of almost unlimited resource."

Bookman, 1 (May, 1895), 229–230. Unsigned [by Harry Thurston Peck]. "Stephen Crane." Portrait.

On the 1893 *Maggie* and *The Black Riders.* (Annotated, *The Black Riders.*)

---

* However, Garland withdrew his admiration for Crane once Crane became involved in scandalous adventures among opium-eaters and street-walkers in 1896. Both Garland and Howells were squeamish about the realism of one who really "lived the life."

Bookman, 2 (November, 1895), 217–220. By N. H. B. [Nancy Banks]. "The Novels of Two Journalists."

Reviews *The Red Badge of Courage, Maggie,* and Edward E. Townsend's *A Daughter of the Tenements. Maggie* "is among the saddest books in our language." Crane and Townsend are both journalists, but Crane does not write like a journalist when he undertakes literature. The root of literature lies in Mr. Crane's works, "but the root seems to be terribly buried, and much in need of being assisted into sunlight and a natural, normal growth."

Critic, 28 (February 22, 1896), 135.

Journal (New York) March 8, 1896, p. 26. By Alfred Henry Lewis.

Press (New York), April 15, 1894.*

Times (New York), November 4, 1894. By Holland [E. J. Edwards]. "Realism and a New Realist. / How Howells' Praise Came to a Young Author in a Dark Hour. . . ." Also in *Philadelphia Press,* probably November 4, 1894.

A clipping in the Crane scrapbook in CUCC bears in Crane's script: "The Philadelphia Press," undated. (Traced from that source to the *New York Times.)* Crane also wrote on this clipping's margin: "This is a fake—not only a fake but a wretched, inartistic fake written by a very stupid man. But it was a great benefit." E. J. Edwards, "a very stupid man," had befriended Crane by sharing his room with him.

Holland reports that in the interesting interview in the *Press* last Sunday (Crane's "Howells Fears Realists Must Wait," *Philadelphia Press,* October 28, 1894) there appeared praise by Howells of "the work of an author whom he called Stephen Crane." Howells praised him for his realism (in *Maggie*), "approaching, as he told a friend, even that of Tolstoi." Crane's realism "is certainly cold, awful, brutal realism, and it reveals a power which when the author has learned of experience and has disciplined his artistic sense may give us something that may be compared to Tolstoi with respect to art as well as realism. But it is possible to tell a story of realism quite as suggestive and not so shocking as that one told in Mr. Crane's book, and it is a realism in which he had an unconscious part."

Pen-portrait of Crane in a publisher's office, no doubt the *New York Press*'s office of Edward Marshall. Approached by a friend (Curtis Brown), Crane is told that Howells has read his book and says it's great. Holland reports also the reading of Crane's poems at the Uncut Leaves Society in April, 1894, by John Barry, a reading which "created something of excitement and interest." (Holland does not identify the book of realism as *Maggie,* nor the friendly editors, Marshall and Brown, both of the *New York Press,* as was E. J. Edwards.)

Union (Port Jervis), March 13, 1893.

The first known review of a Crane work. *See* Thomas A. Gullason in *English Language Notes,* June, 1968.

World (New York), February 23, 1896, p. 18. By Jeannette L. Gilder. Portrait.

---

* In the same issue of the *Press,* in part 2, p. 2, appears Edward Marshall's "Greatest Living Writer" (Howells).

THE BLACK RIDERS
1895

Academy, 51 (January 16, 1897), 76. "Stephen Crane."
 The Black Riders "strikes with a fearless novelty and eccentricity."

Argonaut (San Francisco), July 13, 1896.
 An obscure reporter a few months ago, "his extraordinary 'Lines' drew attention to his originality and his *Red Badge of Courage* set him among the new lights to be counted with."

Athenaeum, 24, no. 3626 (April 24, 1897), 540.
 "*The Black Riders, and Other Lines,* by Mr. Stephen Crane, hardly deserves the pretty printing and get-up which Mr. Heinemann has given it. These lines have no rhyme or rhythm, but are occasionally forcible by sheer abruptness. Mr. Crane is too young in experience to write apologues and fables of destiny and man. The futility of human wisdom and the doctrine that every man is a law unto himself are themes so well worn as to need a master hand to illuminate them afresh, to which Mr. Crane, with all his promise, cannot pretend."

Atlantic Monthly, 77 (February, 1896), 271–272.
 "The strange little lines of which *The Black Riders* is made up are not even rhymed, and have but a faint rhythmic quality. Surpassing the college exercise in verse, to which the shrewd instructor made objection that every line began with a capital letter, these small skeletons of poetry are printed entirely in capitals, and in the modern fashion which hangs a few lines by the shoulders to the top of the page, as if more had meant to come below, but had changed its mind. The virtue of these lines, however, is that they often have enough freshness of conception to set the reader thinking, and so perhaps the blank spaces are filled. The spirit of the lines is generally rebellious and modern in the extreme, occasionally blasphemous to a degree which even cleverness will not reconcile to a liberal taste. One feels that a long journey has been taken since the *Last Poems* of Mr. Lowell were read. But it is too much to think that the writer always takes himself seriously. Many of the lines are intentionally amusing, and the satiric note sometimes serves to mollify the profanity. The parable form into which many of the fragments are cast gives them half their effectiveness. The audacity of their conception, suggesting a mind not without kinship to Emily Dickinson's, supplies the rest."

Book Buyer, 12 (June, 1895), 298.

Bookman, 1 (May, 1895), 229–230. Unsigned [by Harry Thurston Peck]. "Stephen Crane: Author of *The Black Riders, and Other Lines.*" Portrait by David Ericson.
 The copy of *Maggie* in the 1893 edition which came unto the possession of the writer [Harry Thurston Peck] "was addressed to the Rev. Thomas Dixon a few months ago, before the author went West on a journalistic trip to Nebraska, and has these words written across the cover: 'It is inevitable that this book will greatly shock you, but continue, pray, with great courage to the end, for it tries to show that environment is a tremendous thing in this world, and often shapes lives regardlessly. If one could prove that theory, one would make room in Heaven for all sorts of souls (notably an occasional

street girl) who are not confidently expected to be there by many excellent people.' "

The realism of *Maggie*—"a story that might have taken a greater hold on the public than even *Chimmie Fadden,* had the publishers been less timid— is of that daring and terrible directness which in its iconoclasm is the very characteristic of rugged undisciplined strength in a youth of genius. We hear the echo of this mood in number XLV of his 'Lines': 'Tradition, thou art for suckling children. . . .' Mr. Crane started to write for the press when only sixteen, and he has been at newspaper work ever since." Sketches the history of Crane's publications of *Maggie* and *The Red Badge,* announcing as forth- coming *A Woman without Weapons (George's Mother).* Mr. Crane is now in Mexico.

His *Black Riders* is "certain to make a sensation." All the stanzas "were written in a sudden fit of inspiration, in less than three days, and were polished and finished and sent off within a fortnight. The cover design of *The Black Riders* was drawn by Mr. F. C. Gordon, whose work on the beauti- ful holiday edition of Tennyson's *Becket,* published last Christmas, met with signal approbation. . . . What Hamlin Garland said of the author a few years ago may be now repeated with a more certain assurance of fulfilment: 'With such a technique already in command, with life mainly before him, Stephen Crane is to be henceforth reckoned with.' The accompanying portrait of Mr. Crane is taken from a sketch in black and white by Mr. David Ericson, through whose courtesy we are able to reproduce it here."

Bookman, 1 (May, 1895), 254. By Harry Thurston Peck.*

"Mr. Stephen Crane is the Aubrey Beardsley of poetry. . . .

" . . . But just as Mr. Beardsley with all his absurdities is none the less a master of black and white, so Mr. Crane is a true poet whose verse, long after the eccentricity of its form has worn off, fascinates us and forbids us to lay the volume down until the last line has been read. Even in the most fantastic of his conceits there are readily to be found a thought and a meaning. In fact, if Walt Whitman had been caught young and subjected to aesthetic influences, it is likely that he would have mellowed his barbaric yawp to some such note as that which sounds in the poems that are now before us. . . . [Quotes some samples from the volume.]

"On the whole, Mr. Crane's work has traces of *Entartung,* but he is by no means a decadent, but rather a bold—sometimes too bold—original, and power- ful writer of eccentric verse, skeptical, pessimistic, often cynical; and one who stimulates thought because he himself thinks. It is no exaggeration to say that the small volume that bears his name is the most notable contribution to liter- ature to which the present year has given birth."

* John Berryman in *Stephen Crane* (1950), pp. 113, 118, quotes only this review as favorable to *The Black Riders;* it was the only one known to him. He cites *Munsey's, Life,* and *Literary Digest,* and on this slight evidence he claims that "The ferocity of the attacks on *The Black Riders* has been, if anything, under- stated," that the book "was 'vituperated' into six printings within a year," and that Crane's poems accumulated "upwards of a hundred parodies, and certain good-natured epithets. Not only were they 'absurd,' 'besotted,' 'idiotic,' 'lunatic,' but they were 'hamfat,' 'garbage,' 'rot,' and also 'opium-laded,' 'bassoon-poetry,' 'gas-house ballads.' " Berryman never saw any reviews using such epithets. His unacknowledged source for them is Elbert Hubbard, who claimed to have kept a scrapbook of *Black Riders* reviews. No such scrapbook exists among Elbert Hub- bard's papers (according to Elbert Hubbard II in a letter to R. W. S.); no such scrapbook ever did exist, nor the vituperative reviews fabricated by E. H.

Bookman, 13 (April, 1901), 148. By John D. Barry. "A Note on Stephen Crane."

Commercial Advertiser (New York), August 7, 1896. "The Art of Stephen Crane."

Commercial Tribune (Cincinnati), October 18, 1896.

"I observe that Stephen Crane, the Boy Phenomenon, who writes tales of war and terrible conflicts, has struck bottom in his cistern of blood, and is resting for a while. He has a lurid and fervid imagination, and a rattling, clattering way of telling stories which must have made his schoolmates shiver in days gone by. As for his poetry, I am forcibly reminded of an old fellow in the South who once told me he knew what poetry was—yes, indeed. 'It's words, with capital letters in the beginning of every line.' And in Mr. Crane's case, I would add, with small capital letters throughout the rest of his text—and that's about all."

Current Literature, 18 (July, 1895), 9. "Stephen Crane, Author of *The Black Riders*."
   See annotation, *Maggie* (1896).

Daily Chronicle (London), April 26, 1897, p. 3. "Stephen Crane as Fabulist."

Daily Eagle (Brooklyn), June 7, 1896, p. 19. "Stephen Crane's Recent Work."
   "Attention is called also to some evidences of Mr. Crane's work in another direction. He has been published in a new and prettily printed quarterly issued from the Roycroft Press in East Aurora, in this state, though the book [*A Souvenir and a Medley*] is in larger part given over to a narrative of the dinner eaten in that village by Mr. Crane and the Society of Philistines, with letters received from Mr. Bok, Mr. Howells and other remarkable men on that occasion. There is truly nothing remarkable in the eight or ten specimens of the young man's art contained in the book except their audacity. To be great in our time poetry must be difficult to understand. Most of the verses in the magazines have to be studied very hard in order to find out what the poet was thinking about, and sometimes it is not worth while. Mr. Crane usually speaks clearly in spite of his affectations, and his purpose is to put an incident or situation before the reader, rather than to inspire, to moralize, or even to suggest. Some of his things are merely crazy, like his *Black Riders*, which sets forth that the writer saw a man chasing the horizon, and when accosted with the remark, 'You can never—' merely sang out, 'You lie,' and sped on. If that means that the chaser was pursuing ideals, it is not put in a very happy way, because one thinks of that sort of a chase as a progress, but this is only going 'round and round.' But no matter what it means to the poet. So long as it does not reach the heart of the people it might as well have been unwritten. We have no puzzle poetry among the Iliads and the Paradises. Not all of the spasmodic utterances of Mr. Crane are of this kind, however. He occasionally has an idea that is expressed as clearly as it is tersely. His economy of words is as great as Emerson's—if there is a little difference in their freight—and he occasionally draws for us an impressionistic picture that entertains the fancy for a moment."

Echo (Chicago), 2, no. 5 (January 1, 1896), 5. Pen drawing by Homer Davenport.
   "It is, of course, quite impossible to question Mr. Stephen Crane's originality. Whatever else his lines may not be, they are at least on a key of their own." However, their manner is not so new. "Ever since the *Black Riders* came out, the parodists of the daily press have hailed this sort of writing as an absolutely new variety,—something instantly fit for burlesque. When, as a

matter of fact, this method was in vogue with our humorous versifiers as long as three or four years ago. Tom Hall, for instance, wrote on this plan in *Life* ere ever Mr. Crane was heard of. . . . So the manner is merely an echo. And as for the matter—I am pagan enough to prefer Mr. Hall's."

Godey's Magazine, 135 (September, 1896), 317–319. By "Chelifer" [Rupert Hughes]. "The Rise of Stephen Crane."

"All in all, Mr. Crane's vigor is so great and his individuality so distinct that he takes a hardly disputed place at the very head of the American story-writers of the younger school."

Harper's Magazine, 131 (September, 1915), 634. By W. D. Howells.

Mr. Stephen Crane "has done the most striking thing of the year in his little book of 'lines,' called *The Black Riders*, but I believe it will be the opinion of most who read it that the effect would have been three times as great from a third of the quantity. . . . I cannot see how the thought in the following lines, which seems to me fresh, and fine and true, would have been any less so if it had been cast in the mould which need not have been broken to secure them the stamp of novelty: 'In the desert / I saw a creature, naked, bestial, . . .' But after all, how a man gives you his thought is not so important as what thought he gives you, and we can well be patient with Mr. Crane's form as long as he can endure it himself. There is passion in the little poem below which I suppose could not be more intense if it were duly rhymed and measured: 'Should the wide world roll away. . . .' There is thinking, I am sure, in all these strange poems. . . .

"Often there is a teasing dream-quality in them: a promise of significance that fades from them when you examine them in the waking light." Recasts the lines "I was in the darkness" in the form of prose, "to prove that it owes nothing of its poetry to the typographic mask of metre."

Herald (Boston), April 3, 1895.

Herald (Rochester), January 23, 1896.

Quotes the *Philistine*: "The polychrome Bible has been such a success in shedding light on dark places that I understand Stephen Crane has seriously contemplated a polychrome edition of his verse. The fatal objection was Mr. Crane's dislike of the color scheme. He is said to have announced his decision in similar terms to those used by Dean Richmond once when it was proposed to experiment in the painting of some New York Central freight cars. 'You can paint them cars any damn color you like,' said Mr. Richmond, 'so long as you paint 'em red.' "

Literary Digest, 12 (February 29, 1896), 520.

"Is there room for a second Walt Whitman? But perhaps that question can not be answered until it has been decided what proportion of the poetic firmament Whitman is really to fill. Meantime the star of Mr. Stephen Crane is in the ascendant. The following, which is taken from *The Bookman*, is a specimen of Mr. Crane's workmanship." Here quoted is the poem which became the title poem for *War Is Kind* (1899): "Do not weep, maiden, for war is kind."*

Literary World (Boston), January 11, 1896. By John D. Barry.

On *The Black Riders* and *The Red Badge of Courage*.

* Crane wrote "War Is Kind" in 1895. The *W-S Bibliography*, p. 41, cites its original publication in *Literary Digest* for February 29, 1896. However, it first appeared in *Bookman*, February, 1896.

Literature, 4 (April 1, 1899), 349. "Authors and Publishers."

Lotus, 1 (February 1, 1896), 135. "Comment."

"However, if the ineligibility of Bliss Carman should be pressed and the committee on the Monroe doctrine should instruct for a native product, I humbly suggest Mr. Gillett Burgess of San Francisco, a child of nature sometime known as 'Mother Goose' Burgess. Here is found all that STEPHEN CRANE lacks in originality, united with the flow of a Whitman, the deep sentiment of a Bik, the lyric style of a Dole."

Lotus, 1, no. 6 (April 15, 1896), 274. "Comment."

"I might, for instance, in a moment of incaution, confess to a secret delight in *Munsey* pictures, or to a fondness for the general quality of culture omitted in the *Ladies' Home Journal.* I might admit of an admiration for the vigorous character and picturesque phrases of Stephen Crane's poetry."

Lotus, 1, no. 12 (May 15, 1896), 341. "Comment."

"Were it not for the confidence which I place in the abiding sincerity of the two young men who edit *The Bookman,* I should have fallen into grievous error, as did several of my friends, concerning the beautiful illustrations of Stephen Crane's poetry in the May number. They are not burlesques. A few may call them freakish, but the magnificent absence of detail and technique will appeal to every one of true artistic taste. By special arrangements with *The Bookman* I am able to reproduce two drawings."

Lotus, 2, no. 6 (October, 1896), 208–211. By Jonathan Penn. "A Little Study of Stephen Crane."

"The Stephen Crane 'boom' is being insidiously undermined by the effronts of Stephen Crane, and it can now be considered in the lurid red light, as Crane would say, of bitter and inexorable fact. . . .

"Here is a young man who owes his amazing success in literature to his keen power of introspection and intuition. . . .

"He recognized the power of the ludicrous and irrelevant in immediately arresting attention. The recipe for the successful mixing of the new mysticism is a furious scepticism of all the old orthodoxies, with an unlimited credulity for all the bogies of the nursery. This puts one upon a familiar footing with the Almighty, and Mr. Crane's first success was achieved in this foggy region, where the soul of man encounters God in the palpable diminution of a Shape, and spits scorn upon the mechanical horrors of the universe. *The Black Riders, and Other Lines* deals almost exclusively with great moral questions. It is lunacy revealing the irony of sanity, and its goblin atmosphere admirably suits the literary epicure who has enough catholicity to thoroughly enjoy the surprises of folly. It is a book of horrors for the tea-table; and for all who love the meaningless and mysterious rhapsodies of an intellectual booze it is an inspired book. It is filled with the ludicrous sobriety of a sincere lunatic or a 'wanton cynic,' and so deserves its decided success as a genuine curiosity of literature, with those who have a greater craving for what is curious than for what is really literature. On the other hand, criticism declares: Here is originality of design and expression without significance or merit; audacity of conception without real and sincere thought—in a word, a mere farce of literary chicane. 'A new Boozy Prophet,' I thought—but he has turned out better. . . .

"I spent one wild night of hilarity with *The Black Riders, and Other Lines,* and the profound sagacity of this literary delirium at once convinced me that the author was a genius in his unerring perception of his own gift of illogic and confusion, and of the public's susceptibility to any startling bait of lunacy. A writer without any sense of humor is relieved of all fatal hesitancy, and he is sure of a public, for the sense of humor is very rare. This is one of Mr. Crane's strong qualities. He writes completely incomprehensible jangles of words with the rapt sobriety of Saint John. With such a talent he cannot fail of achieving preeminence and the sympathy of a large audience."

Mercure de France, 25 (January, 1898), 330. By Henry-D. Davray, "The Black Riders and Other Lines."

Munsey's Magazine, 13 (July, 1895), 430.
   "Stephen Crane is one of these newly heralded geniuses. . . , one of the fads among a certain class."

Nation, 61 (October 24, 1895), 296. By T. W. Higginson.
   "It is an attraction which makes young people learn it by heart, carry it into the woods with them, sleep with it under their pillows, and perhaps suggest that it should be buried with them in their early graves. Undoubtedly it offers new sensations: the brevity of its stanzas; its rhymelessness and covert rhythm, as of a condensed Whitman or an amplified Emily Dickinson; a certain modest aggressiveness, stopping short of actual conceit. The power lies largely in the fact that this apparent affectation is not really such, and that there is behind it a vigorous earnestness and a fresh pair of eyes. Even the capitalization of every word seems to imply that the author sought thus to emphasize his 'lines'—just as Wordsworth printed 'The White Doe of Rylstone,' in quarto—to express his sense of their value. A mere experiment will show how much each page loses by being reduced to what printers call 'lower-case' type; and yet this result itself seems unsatisfactory because anything which is really good, one might say, could bear to be printed in letters as small as in those microscopic newspapers sent out of Paris under pigeons' wings during the siege. The total effect of the book is that of poetry torn up by the roots—a process always interesting to the botanist, yet bad for the blossoms. As formless, in the ordinary sense, as the productions of Walt Whitman, these 'lines' are in other respects the antipodes of his; while Whitman dilutes mercilessly, Crane condenses almost as formidably. He fulfils Joubert's wish, to condense a page into a sentence and a sentence into a word. He grasps his thought as nakedly and simply as Emily Dickinson; gives you a glance at it, or, perhaps, two glances from different points of view, and leaves it there. If it be a paradox, as it commonly is, so much the better for him. . . .
   "Better, perhaps, than any of these polemics are those 'lines' which paint with a terseness like Emily Dickinson's, some aspect of nature. Since Browning's fine description, in 'England in Italy [sic],' of the 'infinite movement' of a chain of mountains before the traveller, the same thing has not been more vividly put than here (p. 38):

> On the horizon the peaks assembled,
> And, as I looked,
> The march of the mountains began.
> As they marched, they sang,
> 'Aye, we come! we come!'

That is all; but it is fine, it tells its own story. If it be asked whether it is also poetry, one can only remember Thoreau's dictum, that no matter how we define poetry, the true poet will presently set the whole definition aside. If it be further asked whether such a book gives promise, the reply must be that experience points the other way. So marked a new departure rarely leads to further growth. Neither Whitman nor Miss Dickinson ever stepped beyond the circle they first drew."

Philistine, 1 (June, 1895), 27. By Elbert Hubbard.

Press (New York), January 17, 1897, p. 24.

Spectator, 77 (September 12, 1896), p. 346. "Publications of the Week," "Crane, Stephen, *The Black Riders."*

Sunny South (Atlanta), July 18, 1896. By Minnie Kidd.
"The poems are throbbing with strange, weird force. They take hold of one with mesmeric power."

Times (London), January 7, 1897, p. 10. "Publications To-Day."

Times (London), February 4, 1897, p. 7. "Books of the Week."

Times Democrat (New Orleans), October 11, 1896.
"*The Bookman,* apart from its unaccountable partiality for the disjointed effusions of Stephen Crane, very often prints good verse."

Tribune (New York), June 9, 1895, p. 24.
Nothing more amazing and ludicrous than the New Poet, of which the latest example is Mr. Stephen Crane, whose *Black Riders and Other Lines* "is said to have been written 'in a sudden fit of inspiration.' Sudden or not, the visitation to which we owe Mr. Crane's 'lines' does not seem to have come from Parnassus. On the contrary, this young gentleman, over whom some noise is getting itself made, stays on a level of dull prose, disdaining to use—if he could—the means whereby even the minor poet can sometimes give his work a lilt." The sooner that Mr. Crane and his compeers abandon the hypothesis that irregularity of form is a virtue "the better for them all. The only poets of consequence in this century who rebelled against form, Browning and Whitman, failed to win perfection and are still insecure as to their niches in the temple of pure poetic fame."
The *Tribune* quotes Crane's "Many red devils ran from my heart" and remarks: "Does Mr. Crane really believe that he is writing of things from his heart? If so, why have not his 'lines' some poetic vitality, some obvious reason for being? In their futility and affectation they strike the impartial reader as so much trash." (However, the *Tribune,* having fired Crane in late 1892, remained not at all "the impartial reader" of his many books and in an obituary for June 29, 1900, his achievement was belittled by the *Tribune's* reporter, who was undoubtedly Wallace Stevens.) *See Crane,* p. 520.

Weekly Sun (London), March 8, 1896, p. 2. "Mr. Stephen Crane, Author of *The Red Badge of Courage."*

Whitehall Review (London), May 8, 1897, p. 26. "Literary Gossip."

World (New York), February 23, 1896, p. 18. By Jeanette L. Gilder. Portrait.

THE RED BADGE OF COURAGE
1895

NOTE: Additional reviews (all favorable) appeared in the following American news-papers for October, 1895: *New York Herald, Brooklyn Daily Eagle, Cleveland World, St. Paul Pioneer Press, Boston Daily Advertiser, Kansas City Journal, Boston Courier, Sioux City Times, Minneapolis Journal, New Haven Leader,* and *Hartford Times.*

In *Crane,* reviews of *The Red Badge* are quoted and commented on in chap. 10, pp. 180–188.

Academy, 49 (February 15, 1896), 135.* By John Barrow Allen.

The author of *The Red Badge of Courage,* "in quaint, bantering style, describes some military operations, and presents us with a running analysis of a young soldier's varying emotions during the course of the campaign. It must be confessed that the narrative soon becomes tiresome. A serio-comic effect seems to be intended throughout, and Mr. Crane is no doubt highly gifted with that grotesqueness of fancy which is peculiarly a Transatlantic production; but the humour is scarcely of a sort to be appreciated by readers on this side, and not a few of them will lay the book down before getting half way through."

However, the *Academy* in its reviews of *The Little Regiment* and even *The Third Violet* "used *The Red Badge of Courage* as a touchstone of Crane's genius, while the *Academy* went on through the years practically to adopt Crane. It was in its pages that Edward Garnett's appreciation first appeared; its editor, C. Lewis Hind, became one of Crane's friends and saw to it that each Crane publication was warmly praised by the journal's review-ers." In Eric Solomon's *Stephen Crane in England* (1964), p. 17.

Academy, 51 (January 16, 1897), 76.

Athenaeum, no. 3552 (November 23, 1895), 717.

Lists *The Red Badge* among books received, while scorching Thomas Hardy's *Jude the Obscure* as a "titanically bad book."

Athenaeum, 24 (January 16, 1897), 76.

Reviews also *Maggie: A Child of the Streets.*

Atlantic Monthly, 77 (February, 1896), 271–272.

Atlantic Monthly, 77 (March, 1896), 422. "Comment on New Books."

"The process of becoming a hero is so naturally unfolded that the reader no more than the hero himself is aware of the transfer from indecision and cowardice to bravery. This picture, so vivid as to produce almost the effect of a personal experience, is not made by any finished excellence of literary workmanship, but by the sheer power of an imaginative description. The style is as rough as it is direct. The sentences never flow; they are shot forth in sharp volleys. But the original power of the book is great enough to set a new fashion in literature."

Beacon (Boston), October 12, 1895.

"To read the book is like looking upon a painting of Verestchagin."

Black and White, 10 (December 21, 1895), p. 805. "Concerning Recent Fiction."

* Not p. 315 as given in *W-S Bibliography,* p. 78.

Book Buyer, 13 (April, 1896), 140–141. Photograph.*

Reproduces in holograph: "I have never been in a battle, of course, and I believe that I got my sense of the rage of conflict on the football field. Stephen Crane."

"In a conversation, recently, Mr. Crane said that he began the tale as a pot-boiler, intending to make a short story for a newspaper; that he selected a battle as his subject as affording plenty of 'color' and range for the imagination, although he had, of course, never been in a battle in his life.

"He was born in this State, and received his education at Lafayette College and Syracuse University, leaving both places before finishing the prescribed course of study. While at Lafayette he played baseball, but later developed a special fondness for football, and about the time he was at work upon *The Red Badge,* was also engaged in coaching, and playing quarter-back upon, a football team in Lakeview, a suburb of Paterson, N.J. And, speaking of the whirling excitement of this game, he said: 'I do believe I got my sense of the rage of conflict on the football field.' "

Bookman, 1 (May, 1895), 229–230. By Harry Thurston Peck. "Stephen Crane. / Author of *The Black Riders and Other Lines."* Portrait.

Reviews mainly *The Red Badge of Courage.*

Bookman, 2 (August–September, 1895), 12–13.

Announcement on *The Red Badge of Courage.*

Bookman, 2 (November, 1895), 217–220. By N. H. B. [Nancy Banks].

Reviews *Red Badge* and Edward W. Townsend's *A Daughter of The Tenements.* Each a newspaper man, and each in his first novel deals with the slums, "finding the light of his art in the shadows of the under-world which his profession forced him to penetrate. *Maggie: A Girl of the Streets,* Mr. Crane's first expression of the deep feeling of life thus imbibed is among the saddest books in our language." (Here is one of the very few reviews of the 1893 *Maggie.*)

The Red Badge is a powerful, but morbid book, distorted in emotion and "much in need of being assisted into sunlight and a natural, normal growth. . . .

"As if further to confuse his intense work, Mr. Crane has given it a double meaning—always a dangerous and usually a fatal method in literature. The young soldier, starting out to face his first trial by fire, may be either an individual or man universal; the battle may be either the Battle of the Wilderness or the Battle of Life."

Bookman, 2 and 3 (1896). Best Seller List.

First notice of *The Red Badge of Courage* as a best seller is noted in *Bookman,* January, 1896. A best seller in New York and Buffalo. "Letters" in this same *Bookman* mentions *RBC* in New York Letters and in London Letters. Chicago Letters says that *The Red Badge of Courage,* "owing no doubt to the generous appreciation of the book in England, is attracting considerable attention now, although when this work first appeared very little call indeed was experienced for it."

---

* The photograph by Mr. King appeared first in the *Critic,* March 7, 1896, and then in *Inter Ocean* and *Philadelphia Press,* March 15. Crane here wears a high-winged collar and cravat; he has no moustache.

By February, 1896, the *Bookman*'s Best Seller List included *The Red Badge* as a best seller in New York, Albany, Chicago, Louisville, Rochester. Again, it was mentioned in the New York and London Letters.

It was on the *Bookman*'s Best Seller List for March, 1896, in New York City, Albany, Boston, Chicago, Cincinnati, Cleveland, Hartford, Kansas City, Los Angeles, New Haven, Philadelphia, Pittsburgh, Salt Lake City, San Francisco, St. Louis, Washington D.C.; and again it was mentioned in the *Bookman*'s New York and London Letters.

In April, 1896, the *Bookman* listed it as a best seller in New York City, Boston, Cincinnati, Cleveland, Denver, Kansas City, Los Angeles, Louisville, Philadelphia, Pittsburgh, Portland, Rochester, San Francisco, St. Louis, Washington, D.C.; and again it was mentioned in the *Bookman*'s Letters from London, New York City, and Chicago.

In May, 1896, it was listed as a best seller in Albany, Boston, Buffalo, Denver, Indianapolis, Los Angeles, Portland, Salt Lake City, St. Paul, Washington, D.C.; and again *The Red Badge* was mentioned in the New York City and Chicago Letters.

The *Bookman*, June, 1896, listed it as a best seller in Atlanta, Detroit, Los Angeles, Philadelphia; and again *The Red Badge* was mentioned in the New York City and Chicago Letters. *Maggie* was listed as a best seller in uptown New York City.*

Bookman, 2 (February, 1896), 468–470. Photograph of Crane.

"It is gratifying to record the immense success which Mr. Crane's new novel, *The Red Badge of Courage,* is having in England. . . . Why is it, we might ask again, that in America critics are less sure and readers slower to discover a good book in spite of the genius in it?" He has not received in his own country the recognition which his recent novel should evoke. The narrative of *The Red Badge* "is stamped with truth. The youth's mind as well as the field of active service in which he is a recruit is a battleground." (This echoes the London *Bookman* for January, 1896.)

On Crane's speech at the banquet honoring him at the Society of the Philistines affair, "a very hilarious affair at which he made a speech, a regular *Black Rider* poem that scintillated with flashes of wit, to the merriment of all. 'Since he had recovered from College,' he had thrown off the sophomoric yoke, and was doing what he could to give to the world the best that he had. 'I write what is in me,' said he, 'and it will be enough to follow with obedience the promptings of that inspiration, if it be worthy of so dignified a name.' In introducing the guest of honour, Mr. Elbert Hubbard spoke of the 'strong voice now heard in America, the voice of Stephen Crane.' The Philistines had had a hard time from the beginning, when driven out of their country by a tribe of invaders who had been slaves in Egypt, and had 'the pull with the publishers!' Mr. Harry P. Taber, the editor of the 'periodical of protest,' presided gracefully as toastmaster."

Quotes some of the tributes to Crane from the banquet's menu folder, including Hayden Carruth's parody: "I saw a man reading an invitation." Re-

---

* Recast from a letter of William Werner to R. W. S. (undated. 1952–1953?). On the newspaper version of the 1894 *Red Badge of Courage*, see W. L. Werner, "Stephen Crane and *The Red Badge of Courage*," *New York Times Book Review*, September 30, 1945. No mention of Werner's article is made by Joseph Katz in his edition of the 1894 *RBC* (1967), nor does Katz include Werner in Katz's *Checklist of Stephen Crane* (1969).

ports on Crane's reception in England, the critics vying with one another in singing the praises of *The Red Badge of Courage*, "until we understand that Mr. Crane bids fair to be the author of the hour in London."

Bookman, 3 (March, 1896), 16.

Bookman, 3 (March, 1896), 90. "The Book Mart."

Bookman, 3 (April, 1896), 111–112.

Bookman, 3 (April, 1896), 178.

Bookman, 11 (July, 1900), 406.

"In some respects *The Red Badge* is inferior to *Maggie*. There is real power in the latter book. Here and there a phase of proletarian life is caught with photographic fidelity. On the other hand, it is too strained—too intense—it is all out of proportion. Truck-drivers are torn with Promethean woes and stirred with Homeric passions. They bellow—they exchange epithets—and the universe resounds. The sordid squabbles of besotted tenement-house family become Titanic struggles, and mud-puddles are magnified to measureless oceans."

Quotes Robert Barr on Crane as the one most likely to produce the Great American Novel.

Bookman, 35 (May, 1904), 235–236. *"Redeeming The Red Badge of Courage."*

Bookman (London), 9 (January, 1896), 131.

"The youth's mind is a battle-ground too. . . . What military courage means exactly for the average man you will learn here. The narrative is stamped with truth. Just so did the youth feel, you believe; just so did he act."

Book News (Philadelphia), 14 (November, 1895), 72. By Talcott Williams.

Book News (Philadelphia), September, 1896. By E. St. Elmo Lewis. Pen-portrait of Crane.

Book News (Philadelphia), January, 1897.

"The Red Badge of Courage has had many opinions. I add one more by the last of the great commanders of the war, a man of thought and half a century's experience in the field. 'What do I think of it,' said he, bristling. 'I think it is a boy's book about a man's work.' "

Call (Philadelphia), January 26, 1897.

Quotes an unidentified New York paper ridiculing the English claim that *The Red Badge* was first appreciated by English reviewers.* "Americans are not in the habit of shouting reproachfully at England that she is imitating them. Thomas De Quincey and Herbert Spencer were appreciated in this country before England recognized them; Robert Louis Stevenson had a host of enthusiastic admirers here before England discovered him. . . . But we do not think it worth while to keep up an incessant chatter over our acumen, and we have hardly smiled at England's change from scorn of our 'Trilby' enthusiasm [shared by Crane] to hysterics which far outdid our example. And how about Carlyle. I have an impression that Emerson 'boomed' him in this country long before his own people awakened to his greatness. And did not Mrs. Browning find many of her earliest admirers among us? Yet the English reviewer clings to his *Red Badge* myth: 'After English praise, the author's countrymen reconsidered their verdict.' "

* *See Critic* for January 23, 1897, below.

Chap-Book (Chicago), November, 1895.

Commercial Advertiser (New York), August 7, 1896. "The Art of Stephen Crane."

Criterion, 22 (January 6, 1900), 24. By "Chelifer" [Rupert Hughes]. "The Genius of Stephen Crane."

Reviews *The Monster, Active Service;* and *Red Badge of Courage* and *Maggie* reappraised. Calls *War Is Kind* "that crazy nightmare."

"Yet, withal, Mr. Crane seems to me to be the most definite and individual of all our book-writers; and I credit him with having written some of the best pages America has contributed to literature, in *Maggie, The Red Badge,* certain of the *Black Riders* lines, 'The Open Boat,' and in the two books just published from his hand." *(Active Service* and *The Monster.)*

Critic, n.s., 25, no. 719 (November 30, 1895), 363.

"A strong book, then, is *The Red Badge of Courage,* and it is a true book; true to life, whether it be taken as a literal transcript of a soldier's experience in his first battle, or (as some have fancied) a great parable of the inner battle which every man must fight. . . . In assembling the good qualities of the book, we must name also the quick eye for color which is shown on every page, and not for the mere externals of color alone, but for the inner significance of its relation to the events and emotions under hand. Metaphors and similes, too, abound in rich profusion, not strung on for effect, but living and actual as Homer's."

Critic, n.s., 25 (December 28, 1895). By Arthur Waugh. "London Letter."

Waugh remarks on *The Red Badge*'s "great and deserved success during the last fortnight." His London Letter is dated December 13.

Critics, n.s., 25 (January, 1896), 135. By Arthur Waugh. "London Letter."

Critic, n.s., 25 (February 22, 1896), 135.

Critic, n.s., 25,* no. 733 (March 7, 1896), 163. "The Author of *The Red Badge.*" Portrait. Quoted in *Inter Ocean* for March 15.

Reports Crane's first visit with Ripley Hitchcock at Appleton, bearing with him some short stories and a letter of introduction from a well-known author. *The Red Badge of Courage* was written "when Mr. Crane was between twenty-one and twenty-two years of age [begun thus in November, 1892], and is a remarkable performance when one considers that he had had no personal experience of war. When asked where he got his minute knowledge of battle scenes and sensations, he replied that he drew upon his imagination. He had talked to old soldiers, but they had never told him just the things he wanted to know about. They would describe the position of the troops, and tell how this regiment marched up here while another one marched down there; but as for their sensations in the fight they seemed to have forgotten them. And yet old soldiers who have read Mr. Crane's story say that he has painted a most realistic picture."

Crane's publication history, the *Bookman* drawing on Crane's letter to the *Critic* (February 15, 1896), which is available in *Letters,* p. 117.

"According to an article by Mr. J. N. Hilliard, recently printed in the Rochester *Union and Advertiser* [for February 8], Mr. Crane comes of a family of clergymen and soldiers." (This important note about Crane's heritage was also made in 1896 articles by Gaines and by Peaslee.)

---

* Also marked o.s., 28 (January–June, 1896).

Mr. Crane's home is in the hills of Sullivan County, where he spends most of his time on horseback. "He has, we hear, just signed an agreement with Mr. McClure to write for *McClure's Magazine* on a salary. This is a comfortable arrangement, but it is not always the best thing for an author, particularly a young one."

The portrait reproduced here "is from a photograph taken by Mr. F. H. King of this city. It is regarded by Mr. Crane as a good likeness, and it has not hitherto been published." (It is reprinted in *Inter Ocean* for March 15, 1896.) "Mr. Crane is small and slight, with a dark and rather sallow complexion and light hair, which the camera, it seems, is not always truthful in picturing."

Critic, n.s., 25, no. 745 (May 30, 1896), 392.

Summarizes the case made by Appleton & Co. *versus* General McClurg's letter to the *Dial* concerning *The Red Badge of Courage.* See *Dial,* April 16 and May 1, 1896.

Critic, n.s., 26, no. 753 (July 25, 1896), 62.

Quotes *Illustrated London News:* "General Sir Evelyn Wood—than whom a braver man never lived—has expressed the opinion that Mr. Crane's work is quite the finest thing in that line that has ever been done, and that the intuitions of the boy who has never seen war are worth far more than the experiences of any writer known to him, even though he may have been in the thick of the fiercest battle." The *Critic* adds that those who, like General McClurg, fail to see the merit of *The Red Badge* take it to be intended as a description of the sensations and experiences of the typical youth. "It is not that. It is a study of the effect of his first battle upon a youth of a certain *temperament.* Given the temperament, and the sensations are natural enough."

Critic, n.s., 27 (January 23, 1897), 60.

Scoffs at London newspapers carrying obituaries of Crane in spite of reports that he had reached land safely after leaving the ill-fated *Commodore.* "It is interesting to observe that *The Daily News* in its demi-obituary notice solemnly reasserts the exploded fable that *The Red Badge* was 'first praised in England.' The true facts in the case have been pointed out again and again, but evidently without reaching at least some English editors. *The Red Badge* was published in this country two months before its actual publication in England, and had nearly passed through its second edition before English readers saw the book, to say nothing of the fact that it had been 'discovered' and reviewed from Maine to California before a single English reviewer had received the book." Lists many English authors who were first discovered here, such as Robert Louis Stevenson. "And did not Mrs. Browning find many of her earliest admirers among us? Yet the English reviewer clings to his 'Red Badge' myth:—'After English praise, the author's countrymen reconsidered their verdict.' "

Current Literature, 19 (March, 1896), 190–191: "*The Red Badge of Courage:* Crane's Success." From the *Saturday Review.* Photograph from the *Bookman.*

Current Literature, July, 1895, quoted a portion of *The Red Badge* from advance sheets, under the title "In the Heat of Battle." Under the same title in *Current Literature,* August, 1896, *The Little Regiment* is quoted—portions of it—from *McClure's Magazine.*

Daily Chronicle (London), November 30, 1895, p. 4.

Daily Eagle (Brooklyn), June 7, 1896, p. 19.

Daily Telegraph (London), November 29, 1895, p. 7. By W. L. Courtney. "Books of the Day."

Daily Telegraph (London), December 8, 1897, p. 7. By W. L. Courtney. *The Nigger of the "Narcissus."*

"Everyone will remember what a singular effect Mr. Stephen Crane produced some little time ago by his *Red Badge of Courage.* Mr. Joseph Conrad has chosen Mr. Stephen Crane for his example, and has determined to do for the sea and the sailor what his predecessor had done for war and warriors. The style, though a good deal better than Mr. Crane's, has the same jerky and spasmodic quality; while a spirit of faithful and minute description—even to the verge of the wearisome—is common to both."

Dial, 20 (February 1, 1896), 80. By William M. Payne.* "Recent Fiction."

"*The Red Badge of Courage* is a book that has been getting a good deal of belated praise within the past few weeks, but we cannot admit that much of it is deserved. There is almost no story to Mr. Crane's production, but merely an account, in roughshod descriptive style, of the thoughts and feelings of a young soldier during his first days of active fighting. The author constructs for his central character a psychological history that is plausible, but hardly convincing. We do not know, nor does the writer, that it is what actually does go on in the mind of a man who is passing through his baptism of fire. It may be retorted that we do not know any the more that Count Tolstoi is giving us the real thing in his war-stories, or Stendhal in the *Chartreuse de Parme,* but the descriptions in these books at least seem inevitable while we are reading them, and Mr. Crane's descriptions do not."

Dial, 20 (April 16, 1896), 227–228. By A. C. McClurg. "The Red Badge of Hysteria."†

The Red Badge of Courage "is a vicious satire upon American soldiers and American armies. The hero of the book (if such he can be called—'the youth' the author styles him) is an ignorant and stupid country lad, who, without a spark of patriotic feeling, or even of soldierly ambition, has enlisted in the army from no definite motive that the reader can discover, unless it be because other boys are doing so; and the whole book, in which there is absolutely no story, is occupied with giving what are supposed to be his emotions and his actions in the first two days of battle. His poor weak intellect, if indeed he has any, seems to be at once and entirely overthrown by the din and movement of the field, and he acts throughout like a madman. Under the influence of mere excitement, for he does not even appear to be frightened, he first rushes madly to the rear in a crazy panic, and afterward plunges forward to the rescue of the colors under exactly the same influences. In neither case has reason or any intelligent motive any influence on his action. He is throughout an idiot or a maniac, and betrays no trace of the reasoning being. No thrill of patriotic devotion to cause or country ever moves his breast, and not even an emotion of manly courage. Even a wound which he finally gets comes from a comrade who strikes him on the head with his musket to get rid of him; and this is the only 'Red Badge of Courage' (!) which we discover in

* The *W-S Bibliography* errs in listing this entry as by General A. C. McClurg whose article in fact appeared in *Dial,* April 16.

† The above data correct *W-S,* p. 78. McClurg enlisted as a private in the Union Army in 1863 and became a brigadier general.

the book. A number of other characters come in to fill out the two hundred and thirty-three pages of the book, such as 'the loud soldier,' 'the tall soldier,' etc., but not one of them betrays any more sense, self-possession, or courage than does 'the youth.' On the field all is chaos and confusion. 'The young lieutenant,' 'the mounted officer,' even 'the general,' are all utterly demented beings, raving and talking alike in an unintelligible and hitherto unheard of jargon, rushing about in a very delirium of madness. No intelligent orders are given; no intelligent movements are made. There is no evidence of drill, none of discipline. There is a constant, senseless, and profane babbling going on, such as one could hear nowhere but in a mad-house. Nowhere are seen the quiet, manly, self-respecting, and patriotic men, influenced by the highest sense of duty, who in reality fought our battles.

"It can be said most confidently that no soldier who fought in our recent War ever saw any approach to the battle scenes in this book—but what wonder? We are told that it is the work of a young man of twenty-three or twenty-four years of age, and so of course must be a mere work of diseased imagination. And yet it constantly strains after so-called realism. The result is a mere riot of words.

"Although its burlesques and caricatures are quite enough to dismiss it from attention, it is worth while to give some samples of its diction to show that there is in it an entire lack of any literary quality. Notice the violent straining after effect in the mere unusual association of words, in the forced and distorted use of adjectives. Notice, too, the absurd similes, and even the bad grammar. Startling sentences are so frequent they might be quoted indefinitely; but here are a few. . . .

"It is extraordinary that even a prejudiced animus could have led English writers to lavish extravagant praise on such a book; it is still more extraordinary that an attempt should be made to foist it upon the long-suffering American public, and to push it into popularity here. Respect for our own people should have prevented its issue in this country.

"There may have been a moderate number of men in our service who felt and acted in battle like those in this book; but of such deserters were made. They did not stay when they could get away: why should they? The army was no healthy place for them, and they had no reason to stay; there was no moral motive. After they had deserted, however, they remained 'loud soldiers,' energetic, and blatant—and they are possibly now enjoying good pensions. It must have been some of these fellows who got the ear of Mr. Crane and told him how they felt and acted."

Dial, 20 (May 1, 1896), 263–264. By J. L. Onderdonk. "A Red Badge of Bad English."

"The animus of the articles in British magazines during our Civil War, as quoted by 'A. C. McC.' in your issue of April 16, sufficiently explains the English enthusiasm for that literary absurdity called *The Red Badge of Courage*. The trend of the whole work—to prove the absence of such a thing as a gentleman in the union army—may be justly expected to arouse the resentment of the class of whom 'A. C. McC.' is such a striking and honorable example. If this work is realism, it is realism run mad, rioting in all that is revolting to man's best instincts, and utterly false to nature and to life."

The examples of "hysterical composition" given by General McClurg are here supplemented with further examples of Crane's vulgarisms, split infinitives and other grammatical wrenchings of the language. "Amid so much that is strained and affected there is not one agreeable character, hardly one praiseworthy sentiment, and certainly not a new or original thought."

Dial, 20 (May 1, 1896), 263. By D. Appleton & Company (Ripley Hitchcock). *"The Red Badge of Courage*—A Correction."

Corrects McClurg in *Dial* for April 16, who said that the American papers had said very little about the merits or demerits of *The Red Badge of Courage,* that the book was reprinted in America, and that "respect for our own people should have prevented its issue in this country." Contends that our country was in fact the first to recognize Mr. Crane's genius and that "our people have read his book so eagerly that it continues to be the most popular work of fiction in the market, and it has been the one most talked of and written about since October last." Contends that American journals gave it "an almost universal chorus of eulogy," listing titles of twenty American papers.

Dial, 20 (May 16, 1896), 297–298. By Sydney Brooks. "Mr. Stephen Crane and His Critics."

Your correspondent "A. C. McC" for April 16 "came out on the warpath, arrested Mr. Crane as a literary spy, court-martialled him, and shot the poor fellow off-hand." To him, the English praised the book because its American hero was a coward; "Mr. Crane's one unforgivable crime lies in portraying a Northerner who fled from the field. Scarcely less wrong-headed is your correspondent's criticism of the book as a piece of literature. He had missed the whole point of the tale. Part of Mr. Crane's plan, I take it, was to give an idea of the impressions made on a raw recruit by the movements of a regiment in battle. Who can doubt that to a man who but yesterday was working at the plough the whole thing appears one intolerable confusion?"

Most of the literary expressions crucified by "A. C. McC" strike Mr. Brooks as "admirable and picturesque." (Brooks was one of the first English reviewers of *The Red Badge.)*

Dial, 21 (July 1, 1896), 6. "The Fiction of the Season."

Discussion, 20 (May 1–16, 1896), 263, 297–298.

Edinburgh Review, 187 (April, 1898), 411–414. By Stephen Gwynne. "Novels of American Life."

Crane's great flaw is his straining after effects. Gwynne denies "the reality of Crane's red haze and lurid dream of war; after all, Baden-Powell had said that man was more alert in combat. Therefore the psychological portrait of Henry Fleming was valueless." Quoted from Eric Solomon, *Stephen Crane in England: A Portrait of the Artist* (1964). Solomon concludes, p. 20, that no American criticism was more negative than Gwynne's sustained attack on not only *The Red Badge,* but also on *The Third Violet,* and *Maggie.* However, the general tone of English reviews of *The Red Badge* was "warm."

Examiner (San Francisco), July 26, 1896. By Ambrose Bierce.

Fortnightly Review, 67, n.s., 61 (January, 1897), 63–66. By H. D. Traill. "The New Realism." Reprinted in his *The New Fiction,* London, 1898.

Free Press (Detroit), October 7, 1895.

"Stephen Crane describes in a style that reminds one of Victor Hugo in its terse brief sentences, its aptness of comparison and its strength of scene painting, what men feel and see in war."

Globe (London), January 15, 1896, p. 4.

Globe (St. Paul), October 20, 1895.

Godey's Magazine, 133 (September, 1896), 317–319. By "Chelifer" [Rupert Hughes].* "The Rise of Stephen Crane."
  The Red Badge "bristles more with false grammar than with bayonets." Reviews also *Black Riders, Maggie,* and *George's Mother.*

Graphic, 53 (April 11, 1896), 444.

Guardian (Manchester), January 29, 1896, p. 178.
  Calls *The Red Badge* "a new departure . . . throughout we feel that the analysis is true to life and that this is what a battle really means to a private soldier. . . . Another blow has been given to the glamour and false charm of war."

Guardian (Manchester), March 26, 1898.
  Compares Walt Whitman's *Specimen Days* with *The Red Badge of Courage.* (The two works are discussed by V. S. Pritchett in his *Living Novel,* 1949, "Two Writers and Modern War.")

Harper's Magazine, 92 (May, 1896), 961–962. By Charles Dudley Warner. "Color in Literature."†
  Discusses *The Red Badge of Courage* without naming the title or the author. "I liked the book very much. I was carried along by its intensity and felt at the end as if I had experienced a most exciting and melodramatic dream, which I could not shake off when waking. I do not know how much of this effect was due to the scheme of color. It is almost a poem—quite, except in form. It is real, in a way. But what worried me was the thought of the verdict of the Realists. Would they not call it lurid realism?"

Harper's Weekly, 39 (October 26, 1895), 1013. By W. D. Howells.
  Introduces the new author, whom he mentioned some time ago "as so good but so impossible of general acceptance because of our conventional limitations in respect of swearing, and some other traits of the common parlance. He has now attempted to give a close-at-hand impression of battle as seen by a young volunteer in the Civil War, and I cannot say that to my inexperience of battle he has given such a vivid sense of it as one gets from some other authors." He objects to the dialect as unconvincing. "There are divinations of motive and experience which cannot fail to strike the critical reader from time to time; and decidedly on the psychological side the book is worthwhile as an earnest of the greater things that we may hope from a new talent working upon a high level, not quite clearly as yet, but strenuously."
  The Red Badge gives a sense of deaf and blind turmoil, "but we might get that from fewer pages than Mr. Crane employs to impart it. The more valuable effect of the book is subjective: the conception of character in the tawdry-minded youth whom the slight story gathers itself about, and in his common-ness (which we cannot shrink from without vulgarity) is potently illustrated throughout in their speech and action and motive; and the cloud of bewilder-

---

* Rupert Hughes was a member of Delta Upsilon at Cornell University.
  † Crane's novel did not appeal to Warner, co-author (with Mark Twain) of *The Gilded Age,* because he disapproved of sensationalism. Elsewhere in this "Editor's Study" he pronounced great literature to be "always calm, and produces its effect by less apparent effort." Compare Howells' review of *The Red Badge* in *Harper's Weekly,* 39 (October 26, 1895), 1013. Warner's article was first brought to light by Thomas F. O'Donnell, *American Literature,* 35 (November, 1953): "Charles Dudley Warner on *The Red Badge of Courage.*"

ment in which they all have their being after the fighting begins, the frenzy, the insensate resentment, are graphically and probably suggested. The dialect employed does not so much convince me; I have not heard people speak with those contractions, though perhaps they do it; and in commending the book I should dwell rather upon the skill shown in evolving from the youth's crude expectations and ambitions a quiet honesty and self-possession manlier and nobler than any heroism he had imagined."

Harper's Weekly, 40, no. 2054 (May 2, 1896), 451. By W. M. P. [William M. Payne]. "This Busy World—Chicago."

"Mr. Stephen Crane's Novel, *The Red Badge of Courage*, has been the occasion of a most extraordinary aberration of critical judgment on the part of writers who should have known better, both in England and the United States. When the English reviewers discovered the book they simply went daft over it, praising it in highly extravagant terms. . . . At last, a genuine veteran of the war, General A. C. McClurg of Chicago, has found breath to protest against the monstrous extravagance and to publish in *The Dial* a communication aptly named '*The Red Badge of Hysteria.*' . . ."

Home Journal (Boston), October 19, 1895.

Inter Ocean (Chicago), March 15, 1896, p. 24. "Stephen Crane: Author of *The Red Badge* and 'Three Miraculous Soldiers.'" Photograph.

Reprinted from the *Critic,* March 7, 1896, which recasts information on Crane's publication history from his letter to the *Critic,* February 15, 1896. The photograph is the same as used in Gaines's article in *Philadelphia Press,* March 15, 1896, and in *Chicago Record,* January 16, 1897, a review of *The Little Regiment.*

Journal (New York), May 22, 1896. By Percival Pollard. "In the Matter of a Badge."

On Crane and Verestchagin.

Journal (New York), August 23, 1896.

Literary Digest, 13 (March 14, 1896).

"It is scarcely to the credit of America that this book . . . was first pronounced a work of genius in England, where its success is great and growing. The story has now caught the attention of the American public, and it is said that during the first week in February the publishers were unable to supply the demand."

Literary Digest, 15 (June 19, 1897), 218.

On *The Red Badge* and *The Third Violet.*

Literary Digest, 20 (February 10, 1900), 182.

Literary World (Boston), January 11, 1896. By John D. Barry.

Reviews also *The Black Riders.*

"It is a satisfaction to note that the unique and promising work which Mr. Stephen Crane has done during the past three years has at last won distinguished recognition. I wish that this recognition came from Mr. Crane's own countrymen. . . . I cannot think of the case of another American writer who was accepted as a man of consequence in England before winning marked recognition in his own country, and I doubt if Mr. Crane's recent experience has a precedent."

Lotus, 2, no. 6 (October, 1896), 208–211. By Jonathan Penn. "A Little Study of Stephen Crane."

"This book [*The Red Badge*] shows Crane in his highest mood of insight and imagination. It is doubtful if he will ever reach the same high plane again, for he shows a decided weakness in his tendency to persist in mannerisms that become familiar upon a second acquaintance, and so lose their effectiveness. The extraordinary success of *The Red Badge of Courage* in England, where every American writer since Hawthorne has been dismissed with contempt, has awakened a general belief that Crane is to be America's young hopeful in letters. But, unfortunately, Crane, like many other young hopefuls, does not apparently realize the truth of Lowell's saying, that a naive thing repeated is naive no longer. The fondness Mr. Crane shows for chromatic effects—a sort of 'poster' commentary—cannot be such a consistent passion with all his readers."

Mail and Express (New York), October 26, 1895.

Methodist Times (London), 12 (April 23, 1896), 274.

Nation, 63 (July 2, 1896), 15. By A. C. Sedgwick.

"The book is undeniably clever; its vice is over-emphasis. Mr. Crane has not learnt the secret that carnage is itself eloquent, and does not need epithets to make it so. What is a 'crimson roar'? Do soldiers hear crimson roars, or do they hear simply roars? If this way of getting expression out of language is allowable, why not extend it to the other senses, and have not only crimson sounds, but purple smells, prehensile views, adhesive music? Color in language is just now a fashionable affectation; Mr. Crane's originality does not lie in falling into it. *George's Mother* is the story of a degenerate drunkard who breaks his mother's heart; *Maggie* is a story of the Bowery, in the 'dialect' of *Chimmie Fadden*.

"Taking all three stories together, we should classify Mr. Crane as a rather promising writer of the animalistic school. His types are mainly human beings of the order which makes us regret the power of literature to portray them. Not merely are they low, but there is little that is interesting in them. We resent the sense that we must at certain points resemble them. Even the old mother is not made pathetic in a human way; her son disgusts us so that we have small power of sympathy with her left. Maggie it is impossible to weep over. We can feel only that it is a pity that the gutter is so dirty, and turn in another direction. In short, Mr. Crane's art is to us very depressing."

National Observer, 15 (January 11, 1896), 272.

New Review (London), 14 (January, 1896), 30–40. By George Wyndham. "A Remarkable Book." Reprinted as "An Appreciation," the Introduction to *Pictures of War* (London, 1898).

Mr. Crane "is a great artist, with something new to say, and consequently, with a new way of saying it. His theme, indeed, is an old one, but old themes re-handled anew in the light of novel experience are the stuff out of which masterpieces are made, and in *The Red Badge of Courage* Mr. Crane has surely contrived a masterpiece." As an artist he "achieves by his singleness of purpose a truer and completer picture of war than either Tolstoi, bent also upon proving the insignificance of heroes, or Zola, bent also upon prophesying the regeneration of France. That is much; but it is more than his work of art, when completed, chimes with the universal experience of mankind; that his heroes find in their extreme danger, if not confidence in their leaders and conviction in their cause, at least the conviction that most men do what they can or, at most, what they must. We have few good accounts of battles—many of shipwrecks. . . . It is but a further step to recognize all life for a battle and this earth for a vessel lost in space. We may then infer that virtues easy in moments of distress may be useful also in everyday experience. . . .

"Mr. Crane, for his distinction, has hit on a new device. . . . In order to show the features of modern war he takes a subject—a youth with a peculiar temperament, capable of exaltation and yet morbidly sensitive. Then he traces the successive impressions made on such a temperament, from minute to minute, during two days of heavy fighting. He stages the drama of war, so to speak, within the mind of one man, and then admits you as to a theatre. You may, if you please, object that this youth is unlike most other young men who serve in the ranks, and that the same events would have impressed the average man differently; but you are convinced that this man's soul is truly drawn, and that the impressions made in it are faithfully rendered. The youth's temperament is merely the medium which the artist has chosen: that it is exceptionally plastic makes for the deeper incision of his work. It follows from Mr. Crane's method that he creates by his art even such a first-hand report of war as we seek in vain among the journals and letters of soldiers. But the book is not written in the form of an autobiography; the author narrates. . . . Had he put his descriptions of scenery and his atmospheric effects, or his reports of overheard conversations into the mouth of his youth, their very excellence would have belied all likelihood. Yet in all his descriptions and all his reports he confines himself only to such things as that youth heard and saw, and, of these, only to such as influenced his emotions. By this compromise he combines the strength and truth of a monodrama with the directness and colour of the best narrative prose. . . .

"Mr. Crane has composed his palette with these colours, and has painted a picture that challenges comparison with the most vivid scenes of Tolstoi's *La Guerre et la Paix* or of Zola's *La Débâcle*. This is unstinted praise, but I feel bound to give it after reading the book twice and comparing it with Zola's Sedan and Tolstoi's account of Rostow's squadron for the first time under fire. Indeed, I think that Mr. Crane's picture of war is more complete than Tolstoi's, more true than Zola's." Wyndham quotes a passage from *The Red Badge*, and remarks that this passage challenges comparison with Zola's scene in *La Débâcle*, in which the lieutenant expires among the morsels of a bullet-eaten flag. "Mr. Crane has probably read *La Débâcle*, and wittingly threw down his glove. One can only say that he is justified of his courage."

News (Providence, R.I.), October 9, 1895.

North American Review, 175 (December, 1902), 770–771. By W. D. Howells. "Frank Norris."
On Crane and Norris.

Outlook, 52 (December 21, 1895), p. 1090.
"The story is not pleasant by any means, but the author seems to lay bare the very nerves of his character; practically, the book is a minute study of one man's mind in the environment of war in all its horrible details."

Overland Monthly, n.s., 28 (August, 1896), 235.

Pall Mall Gazette, 61 (November 26, 1895), p. 4. By H. B. Marriott-Watson. "The Heart of a Soldier."
Crane's insight and his power of realization "amount to genius."

Philistine, 3 (July, 1896), 33–38. By Thomas Wentworth Higginson. "Book and Heart. A Bit of War Photography."
On Tolstoi and Crane's *Red Badge of Courage.*

Plain Dealer (Cleveland), October 27, 1895.
"It is perfectly apparent that the experiences described were those of the author."

Post (Chicago), October 26, 1895. "A Strong Tale of War."
"The style is as keen and bright as a swordblade and a Kipling has done nothing better in this line."

Press (New York), October 13, 1895, part 5, p. 4. Unsigned [by Edward Marshall].
"Stephen Crane is not the blithering idiot he was set down to be when his crazy little volume of 'lines'—*The Red* [*sic*] *Riders*—was recently put forth upon the world, thereby giving a great many newspaper writers an opportunity to be funny, and incidentally to make memorable the name of Crane. Now he comes, clothed and in his right mind, with a story as remarkable for its insight and its originality as his verse was remarkable for what it did not mean. . . . No one before except Tolstoi, so far as we know, has described so vividly the curious petty details of personal conduct and feeling when the fight is thickest. . . . At times the description is so vivid as to be almost suffocating. The reader is right down in the midst of it where patriotism is dissolved into its elements and where only a dozen men can be seen, firing blindly and grotesquely into the smoke. This is war from a new point of view, and it seems more real than when seen with an eye only for large movements and general effects.
"One should be forever slow in charging an author with genius, but it must be confessed that *The Red Badge of Courage* is open to the suspicion of having greater power and originality than can be girdled by the name of talent."

Public Opinion, 20 (April 23, 1896), 536.
Quotes from *Bachelor of Arts* (New York).

Public Opinion, 20 (May 21, 1896), 661. "Concerning 'Color' in Literature."
Condenses an article in the *Springfield Republican.*

Republic (St. Louis), August 25, 1896. By Ambrose Bierce. Reprinted from *New York Press.* See Bierce on Crane also in *San Francisco Examiner,* July 26, 1896.

St. James's Gazette (London), December 7, 1895, p. 5. "Mars Revealed."

Saturday Evening Post, 72 (November 18, 1899), 413. By Kenneth Herford. "Young Blood—Stephen Crane."

Saturday Review (London), 81 (January 4, 1896), 3.
"We hope to treat this work [*The Red Badge*] at length next week; but we wish to draw our readers' attention to it at once, as containing, in our opinion, the most realistic description ever published of modern war."

Saturday Review (London), 81 (January 11, 1896), 44–45. "In the School of Battle: The Making of a Soldier."
Tolstoi, in *War and Peace* and in his sketches of Sebastopol, renders the effect of battle on the ordinary man; "but he takes no one man through the long series of experiences and impressions which Mr. Crane describes in its effects on young Henry Fleming. . . . With less imagination, but with an accumulated mass of studied knowledge altogether too laboured, M. Zola in

La Débâcle has done some excellent literary work, but work not so convincing as Kipling's (in *The Drums of Fore and Aft*), and work certainly far inferior to Mr. Stephen Crane's, whose picture of the effect of actual fighting on a raw regiment is simply unapproached in intimate knowledge and sustained imaginative strength. This we say without forgetting Mérimée's celebrated account of the taking of the redoubt. . . .

"Whether Mr. Crane has had personal experience of the scenes he depicts we cannot say from external evidence; but the extremely vivid touches of detail convince us that he has. Certainly, if his book were altogether a work of the imagination, unbased on personal experience, his realism would be nothing short of a miracle." Here follows an excellent synopsis of the action of the novel.

Excerpt from the above is quoted in *Public Opinion*, 20 (January, 1896), 131.

Sketch (London), December 18, 1895, p. 4, supplement. "How A Hero Was Made."

Speaker (London), 13 (January 11, 1896), 50.

Speaker (London), 17 (January 15, 1898), 83–84.
On Crane's *The Red Badge* and Conrad's *The Nigger of the "Narcissus."*

Spectator, 76 (June 27, 1896), 924. "*The Red Badge of Courage*."

"*The Red Badge of Courage: An Episode of the American War* is a remarkable book, and has been received by English reviewers with an unanimity of praise which we are in no wise desirous that its author—a young man, as it is understood—should have been deprived of. But we believe that Mr. Stephen Crane, the author in question, has received his good marks not exactly on right grounds. His episode has been praised as a novel; we are inclined to praise it chiefly as an interesting and painful essay in pathology. The substance and "thesis" of the book, as the serious theatrical reviewers might say, consists in a presentation of the effects of physical danger, in the thousand forms which danger wears in modern warfare, upon the human nervous system. Nor is this all; the nervous system on which Mr. Crane chooses to illustrate his prelection is not a normal organism but an abnormal one,—morbid, hypersensitive, and over-conscious. . . .

"As an achievement in imagination, in the art of placing one's self in the situation of another—of an exceptional other in exceptional surroundings—Mr. Crane's document can hardly be praised too much. It convinces; one feels that not otherwise than as he describes did such a man fall wounded and another lie in the grasp of corruption. But when we are asked to say that a specialised record of morbid introspection and an exact description of physical horrors is good art we demur; there *is* art in *The Red Badge of Courage*—an infelicitous title by the way—but the general effect which it leaves behind it is not artistic."

Sunday Times (Glasgow, Scotland), March 28, 1898.
Crane as another Verestchagin.

Times (Boston), October 27, 1895.

Times (London), November 27, 1895, p. 12. "Publications To-Day."

Times (London), January 23, 1896, p. 12. "*The Red Badge of Courage*. Second edition."

Times (London), February 18, 1896, p. 13.

Times (Minneapolis), October 13, 1895.

Times (New York), October 19, 1895, p. 3. "A Green Private under Fire."

"A recent autobiographical account of actual experiences in our civil war bears testimony that every soldier is frightened at the moment of entering battle, and his fright increases rather than diminishes as he grows old in service and more familiar with the dangers he has to encounter. It is true, also, that once in battle all men are much alike. They fight like beasts. Cowards and skulkers are the exception, and cowardice is often the result of some sudden physical disability.

"The young private soldier who is the central personage in this remarkable work was a farm boy in one of the Middle States, probably Ohio, though certain peculiarities of the dialect in which Mr. Crane chooses to clothe the speech of all his persons, belong also to Western Pennsylvania and the Hoosier country. Except for those few expressions, such as 'Watch out' for 'Look out,' the talk is a very fair phonetic equivalent for the common speech in parts of this State and Connecticut. The boy does not enlist at the beginning of the war, but his duty to go to the front weighs upon him day and night. He is the only son of his mother, and she a widow and a typical American woman of the old New-England stock, who ever conceals her emotions, and seems to possess no imaginative faculty whatever. She is peeling potatoes when her boy, in his new blue clothes, says 'Good-bye,' and the exhortation she then delivers is perfectly practical and devoid of all sentiment. There is a black-eyed girl, nameless in the story, who looks after the youth as he trudges down the road, but when he looks back pretends to be gazing at the sky.

"In other words, the early environment of Mr. Crane's hero is absolutely typical, differing in no particular from that of tens of thousands of young men who went to the front in the interval between the Sumter episode and the fall of Richmond. But as to his temperament and the quality of his mind, we cannot speak so positively. He is certainly of a more emotional type than any one of his comrades. His aspirations, perhaps, are no higher than theirs, his mental capacity no larger, his will, certainly, no stronger. But there is a touch of poetry in his nature which most men lack.

"Probably Mr. Crane has put some of his own mental traits into the composition of his otherwise commonplace hero. Therefore, it is not possible to accept this graphic study of his mind under the stress of new and frightful experiences as an exact picture of the mental states of every green soldier under his first fire. All its complexities are surely not typical.

"Yet it is as a picture which seems to be extraordinarily true, free from any suspicion of identity, defying every accepted tradition of martial glory, that the book commends itself to the reader. The majesty, the pomp and circumstance of glorious war, Mr. Crane rejects altogether. War, as he depicts it, is a mean, nasty, horrible thing; its seeming glories are the results of accident or that blind courage when driven to bay and fighting for life that the meanest animal would show as strongly as man. For it must be remembered that the point of view is consistently that of the humblest soldier in the ranks, who never knows where he is going or what is expected of him until the order comes, who never comprehends the whole scheme, but only his small share of it, who is frequently put forward as an intentional sacrifice, but yet is a sentient human being, who is bound to have his own opinions founded on the scanty knowledge he possesses, his own hopes and fears and doubts and prejudices.

"Private Henry Fleming goes to the war a hot-headed young patriot with his mind brimful of crude ideas of glory, and a settled conviction that his capacity for heroism is quite out of the common. Weary months of drill in camp reduce him seemingly to the proper machinelike condition. He learns many things, among them that the glories of war have been greatly exaggerated in books, that the enemy is not composed chiefly of bragging cowards, that victory is rare and dear, and that the lot of a private soldier is very hard. On the eve of his first battle he has about abandoned all hope of ever getting a chance to distinguish himself. Yet when the hour comes it brings depression instead of exhilaration. He communes with himself, and fears that he is a coward.

"The battle Mr. Crane describes is one of those long and bloody conflicts of our civil war that we now freely admit were badly mismanaged through the lack of good generalship, which had no particular result except the destruction of human life, and were claimed as prodigious victories by both sides. The green regiment is part of a brigade which is the centre at first, and for a long while it has nothing to do. Then it has to stand on the edge of a piece of woods and receive the enemy's fire, and return it. This is a short and sharp proceeding, and while it lasts Private Henry Fleming acquits himself creditably. When the enemy's fire stops, he feels himself a hero and feels also that he has done the greatest day's work of his life. The nervous tension has been awful, the revulsion of feeling is correspondingly great. When the enemy's fire is resumed, a few minutes later, he is entirely unprepared. Panic seizes him, he drops his musket and runs for his life.

"All that day he is a skulker in the rear of a great battle. His emotions, his mental vagaries, his experiences with the dead and dying, and the terrible nervous ordeal he undergoes are depicted by Mr. Crane with a degree of vividness and original power almost unique in our fiction. The night of the first day finds him back in the camp of his own regiment, lauded by his surviving comrades as a wounded hero. His scalp was cut by a blow of a musket by a retreating soldier, whose flight he tried to stop, for no reason, and he has tied his handkerchief over the wound. He is physically exhausted, and his conscience troubles him sorely.

"In the next day's conflict he remains with his regiment. His nervous excitement has increased, but he is no longer so greatly shocked by the spectacle of the dead and dying. He has lost all control of his tongue, and he jabbers oaths incessantly. When his regiment is called upon to repel an advance of the enemy, he excels all his comrades in the ferocious rapidity of his fire. He is again extolled as a hero, but scarcely comprehends the praise. His regiment, esteemed by the division officers, apparently with good reason, as nearly worthless is selected to make a charge which is intended merely to check a contemplated attack of the enemy on the left until reinforcements can be forwarded to that point. It is not expected that any member of the regiment will return alive, and some rude remarks of a staff officer to this effect reach the ears of the men and transform them into demons, but very impotent and purposeless demons. The order is only half carried out. A file of soldiers in gray, behind a rail fence, keeps the blue fellows at bay. They stand like lost sheep, and scarcely return the fire which is destroying them. Yet, on their retreat they combat bravely enough with a small Confederate body which tries to cut them off. Returning to their own lines, they are received with derision, while their Colonel is roundly abused by his superior. The charge has been a failure, yet it has transformed Private Henry Fleming. He has saved the colors, and he has sounded his own depths. He feels that he will never run away again.

" 'At last his eyes seem to open to some new ways. He found that he could look back upon the brass and bombast of his earlier gospels and see them truly. He was gleeful when he discovered that he now despised them. With this conviction came a store of assurance. He felt a quiet manhood, non-assertive, but of sturdy and strong blood. He knew that he would no more quail before his guides wherever they should point. He had been in touch with the great death, and found that, after all, it was but the great death. He was a man.'

"The book is written in terse and vigorous sentences, but not without some unpleasant affectations of style which the author would do well to correct. His natural talent is so strong that it is a pity its expression should be marred by petty tricks. When he begins a sentence with 'too,' for instance, he makes a sensitive reader squirm. But he is certainly a young man of remarkable promise."

Times (New York), January 26, 1896, p. 22. By Harold Frederic. "Stephen Crane's Triumph."

"When one searches for comparisons, they can only be found by culling out selected portions from the trunks of masterpieces and considering these detached fragments one by one, with reference to the *Red Badge*, which is itself a fragment, and yet is complete. Thus one lifts the best battle pictures from Tolstoi's great *War and Peace*, from Balzac's *Chousans*, from Hugo's *Les Misérables*, and the forest fight in *'93* from Prosper Mérimée's assault of the redoubt, from Zola's *La Débâcle* and *Attack on the Mill* (it is strange enough that equivalents in the literature of our own language do not suggest themselves) and studies them side by side with this tremendously effective battle painting by the unknown youngster. Positively they are cold and ineffectual beside it. The praise may sound exaggerated, but really it is inadequate. These renowned battle descriptions of the big men are made to seem all wrong. *The Red Badge* impels the feeling that the actual truth about a battle has never been guessed before."

Times (New York), April 3, 1896.

"D. Appleton & Co., who brought out *The Red Badge of Courage*, have watched with amusement, if not amazement, the claims of the English 'discoverers' of Mr. Crane. The true and exact history of the publication of *The Red Badge of Courage* is that it was read and accepted by D. Appleton & Co. in December, 1894, almost a year before the book was printed. It was the intention then to publish the volume immediately, but Mr. Crane was absent from the city [he was in Mexico] and could not be reached conveniently when the proofs were ready, and the work was, as a consequence, delayed. The electrotype plates were all made in the Spring of 1895, but as it was deemed inadvisable to put the book on the market at that time of the year the publication was deferred until Autumn. The book was brought out on the 1st of October in this country. Although the work was copyrighted abroad at the same time, it did not appear and was not reviewed in Europe until nearly two months afterward."

Times Supplement (New York), July 14, 1900, p. 467. "Mr. Crane's Master Work."

On Crane in 1894, his connection with Ripley Hitchcock, whose edition of *The Red Badge* (1900) prompted this article.

Town Topics (New York), June 25, 1896.

Transcript (Boston), October 26, 1895.

The Red Badge is a book "with a mighty theme. It is designated on the title page as merely 'an episode of the civil war,' but it is something more than this. It is a tremendous grasping of the glory and carnage of all war. . . . [It] forces upon the reader the conviction of what fighting really means."

Tribune (New York), October 29, 1896, p. 8. "Stephen Crane."*

Notes on the English reception of *The Red Badge.* London went mad over Crane, "the Genius of 1896." "Once a year at least, sometimes twice, London must have its 'genius.' For a while it had Mr. Wilde. He lasted longer than London wanted him to. . . . When Mr. Crane turned up with his *Red Badge of Courage* (it is curious, this passion of the English for colors), there was a void that ached for him. He filled it, this 'genius of 1896.' It will be interesting to see who takes his place."

Tribune (Scranton), January, 1896.

Union (Port Jervis, N.Y.), November (n.d.), 1895. "An Extraordinary Work: Stephen Crane's Talent Recognized by the Reviews and Newspapers of the United States."

An omnibus of reviews in quotation.

Reprinted for the first time in *Letters,* pp. 296–297.

Union and Advertiser (Rochester), February 8, 1896, p. 2. By John Northern Hilliard. "The Hideousness of War: Stephen Crane and *The Red Badge.*" Quoted in *Inter Ocean,* March 15, 1896, p. 24. Photograph.

"A unique figure in contemporary literature is Stephen Crane. The success of his book, *The Red Badge of Courage,* has placed him in a position to be envied by all writers to whom individuality means much. He is a Verestchagin in print, this young man who has revealed the utter hideousness of warfare as no writer has yet done, not even the microscopic Zola in his realistic and sanguinary descriptions of carnage. After reading Mr. Crane's book no one can ever be inspired with the glory of war. His story is plain, unvarnished and hideously grim, utterly despoiling the traditional heroism and romance. Mr. Hamlin Garland, stern realist as he is, presented a story of the war in his *Main Traveled Roads,* entitled 'The Return of a Private,' a story capable of filling the reader with intense disgust at the thing men call war. Mr. Garland wrote from the point of view of a private, and, it is needless to say, Mr. Crane takes the same mound of observation. Heretofore the story of the war has been written by those who saw in its awful carnage an unlimited field in which romanticism could flourish. They have seen only its picturesque features and have upheld the Homeric idea of conflict. Men are to-day essentially the same in primal instincts as in the earlier days of the world. One of these natural instincts is the passion for killing, which sophists assert is the inheritance of Cain. On the subject of who was responsible for Cain's herditary defect the same gentry are discreetly silent. However much we may deplore

---

* The *Tribune,* who fired Crane in September, 1892, consistently belittled in *Tribune* reviews all Crane books and in June, 1900, belittled his achievement in the *Tribune* obituary (unsigned) by Wallace Stevens. Crane wrote Hawkins on November 19, 1895, that about six in the batch of *Red Badge* reviews "are roasts. One is a copy of the *Tribune*'s grind." In *Letters,* p. 76.

the idea of war in this day of civilization the fact is still evident that all the
world holds dear today is due to the slaughter of men. Had it not been for
this same warfare I very much doubt that Mr. Stephen Crane would have conceived his crimson masterpiece, *The Red Badge of Courage*. . . .

"He possesses an intellect that is keen and strong; he has power and imagination, and, above all else, he is original. He is Stephen Crane first, last and
all the time. He calmly disdains all masters living as dead. He does not worship tradition; he defies it. He has 'recovered from college,' as he aptly
termed it in a speech at the Philistine banquet given at Buffalo last December.
He presents original ideas in an original manner, and in a way that must attract the attention of the world.

"Mr. Crane's first book, I believe, was called *Maggie, a Girl of the Streets*,
written over the nom de plume of 'Johnston Smith.' Hamlin Garland reviewed it enthusiastically in the *Arena* and made the prophecy that Stephen
Crane would live to be reckoned with. Mr. Howells was also deeply impressed
with the story, written as it was by a young fellow twenty-one years of age.
The next volume bearing the signature of Stephen Crane was issued last year
by Copeland & Day of Boston, and under the unique title of *The Black Riders*.
This was a book of verse, or rather it was styled verse; for, as a matter of fact,
there is not a rhyme in it and it is as sterile of meter as boarding house milk
is of cream. . . .

"The critics of this country seem slow in recognizing *The Red Badge*,
but this is true of all works of sterling worth. They will come to it in time.
The English critics hail it as an American achievement of which to be proud,
and their laudatory notices would be enough to turn the head of almost anyone except—Stephen Crane. He has despoiled war of traditional heroism and
romance. His soldiers fight in ungainly attitudes, crouched and twisted into
all kinds of shapes, snarling, cursing, babbling like driveling idiots, perspiring,
dirty, and thoroughly animal. Under Crane's treatment this war hero becomes
a disgusting spectacle, stripped of all the noble traits of manhood. They are
not men, they are little else than animals, fired with the lust of slaughter. The
story has no particular plot, no inner mechanism. The book is a study of war,
or possibly a panorama. There is no hero, only a type. . . .

"Stephen Crane is a young man of 24 years and his promises are great. He
is a native of New York State, and lives on a large estate at Hartwood, where
he spends his time writing books and riding horseback. Mr. Crane told me
recently that he was at times bitterly ashamed of his name, and when in
peculiar moments he sees it in print it strikes him as being the homeliest name
in created things. He has every reason to be proud of it, however. The first
Stephen Crane to appear in America arrived in Massachusetts from England in
1635. His son, Stephen Crane, settled in Connecticut, and the Stephen Crane
of the third American generation settled in New Jersey on lands that now
hold the cities of Newark and Elizabeth. At the time of the trouble of England he was president of both Colonial Assemblies that met in New York.
He was sent by the State of New Jersey to the Continental Congress, and
served in that body until a week beore the Declaration was signed, when the
Tories made such trouble in New Jersey that he was obliged to return and
serve as speaker in the colony's assembly. He died in the old homestead at
Elizabeth when the British troops were marching past to what turned out to
be the defeat at Trenton. His eldest son commanded the Sixth New Jersey infantry during the Revolution, and ultimately died the ranking major-general in

the regular army from an old wound received in the expedition to Quebec. The second son was commodore in the navy at a time when the rank of admiral was unknown. The youngest son, while proceeding to his father's bedside, was captured by some Hessians, and, upon his refusing to tell the road by which they intended to surprise a certain American outpost, they beat him with their muskets, and then having stabbed him with their bayonets, they left him dead in the road. In those old times the Crane family did their duty. Upon the author's mother's side everyone was a Methodist clergyman of the old 'ambling-nag, saddle-bag, exhorting kind.' Her father was a clergyman of that church, an author of numerous theological works and an editor of various church periodicals. He was a graduate of Princeton, and the novelist pays him the tribute of being a man with a 'great, fine, simple mind.' Stephen Crane, the subject of this sketch, went to Lafayette College, but did not graduate. He preferred baseball to mining-engineering. He also attended Syracuse University, where he attempted literature, but baseball again interfered. He is a member of the Delta Upsilon fraternity. His work in fiction was for the New York *Tribune,* when he was only eighteen years old. One of the stories of the series found its way into the *Cosmopolitan.* He began writing at sixteen. At twenty he wrote his first novel, *Maggie,* which gained him the friendship of Hamlin Garland and William Dean Howells. He was in his twenty-first year when he began his *Red Badge of Courage,* and completed it in his twenty-second year. In a letter which I received from Mr. Crane but a few days ago he said that he had just completed a new novel which he calls *The Third Violet,* a story of life among the younger and poorer artists of New York. At present Mr. Crane is living on an estate of 3,500 acres belonging to his brother in Hartwood, Sullivan county, this state. His father died when he was seven years old and his mother when he was nineteen.

"For a man so young to have accomplished so much is indeed a miracle. In his case it is not genius alone, but talent allied with perseverance, originality and a capacity for hard work. His achievements have been notable ones; his future seems very brilliant. Stephen Crane is to be a potent factor in American literature."

University Herald (Syracuse), January, 1895.*

World (New York), February 23, 1896, p. 18. By Jeannette L. Gilder. "Stephen Crane's Study of War." Portrait.

Recounts the history of *Maggie,* briefly reports on the contents of *The Red Badge,* and concludes that Zola in *The Débâcle,* rather than Mr. Crane, is the Verestchagin of literature. Announces Crane's forthcoming "With the Regiment" in *McClure's Magazine (The Little Regiment).* "Mr. Crane says that this is his last war story and he should know. . . . If he turns his back upon the Muse and gives himself time to write prose he will make a mark that it will be hard to erase."

World (New York), March 6, 1896, p. 6.

World (New York), March 29, 1896, p. 22.

"Mr. Stephen Crane says that he is very much flattered by the kind reception of his *Red Badge of Courage,* but he is getting just a little weary of being told by every other man that he meets that he is the one who discovered him."

* For this item I am indebted to Lester G. Wells of Syracuse University Library. (Letter of August 19, 1953, to R. W. S.)

World (New York), July 26, 1896, p. 18. By William Dean Howells. "New York Low Life in Fiction."

Claims that *The Red Badge of Courage* "owed its excellence to the training the author had given himself in setting forth the life he knew in these earlier books of later publication [*Maggie* and *George's Mother*]. He learned to imagine vividly from seeing clearly."* Contends that "As pieces of art they are altogether superior to it, and as representations of life their greater fidelity cannot be questioned."

MAGGIE
1896

Academy, 49 (December 26, 1896), 600.

Reports a comparison between *Maggie* and Arthur Morrison's *A Child of the Jago* made by the *Saturday Review,* whose critic "is doubtful if Mr. Crane could equal Mr. Morrison's fight between Perrott and Leary, although he thinks that the concluding chapter of *Maggie* is perhaps beyond the author of *A Child of the Jago*—or is it 'Jay' go?"

Academy, no. 1289, n.s., 51 (January 16, 1897), 76. "Stephen Crane."

"It is sincerely to be hoped that there is no truth in the report of Mr. Stephen Crane's death in Cuba. He is—we are loth to write in the past tense—emphatically a young man with a future, and the new literature could ill afford to lose him.

"About six years ago there appeared in New York a small book in paper covers, entitled *Maggie: A Child of the Streets,* by Johnston Smith. This very modest *brochure,* which was sold at fifty cents, bore no publisher's imprint, and it may well be supposed that only a few copies were issued. The reason for this is not far to seek. *Maggie* is not a pleasant book, and in those days the public was not ripe for the reception of instantaneous literary photographs of slum life. No firm cared or dared to associate its name with such a publication. But we have changed all that. One man stood out alone from the mass of unsympathetic reviewers. Mr. Hamlin Garland, perhaps the most genuine of American critics, read *Maggie* with intense interest, and loudly proclaimed the advent of an author 'to be reckoned with.' But the public refused to be interested, and *Maggie* was forgotten by all but a chosen few, who still treasure the little book in paper covers.

"Stephen Crane—for 'Johnston Smith' and Stephen Crane are, of course, one and the same—is now about twenty-six years old. At the age of sixteen he was writing for several New York papers. He has been writing ever since, and journalism still claims him as one of her most devoted children. At the time of the publication of *Maggie* he had been working for some time for the Bachelor Syndicate, and it was for them that he wrote his next book, *The Red Badge of Courage.* This proved very successful as a serial, but the publication

---

* However, *George's Mother* was not begun until the spring or early summer of 1893 (on verso of "The Holler Tree," a Sullivan County tale), and it was put aside until he completed *The Red Badge,* begun perhaps in the winter of 1892–1893.

in book form was for some reason delayed. Mr. Crane next attracted attention by a small volume of 'lines'—he does not call them poems—entitled *The Black Riders,* which has recently been published in this country. Like so many American authors, he owes his success to British enthusiasm. It was not until *The Red Badge of Courage* was brought out in this country, in the autumn of 1895, that America 'found' its author. Mr. Crane would be the first to acknowledge his indebtedness to the English critics and the English public, who, with one accord, forced his name into well-deserved prominence.

"Such, then, in brief, is the history of his short career. Apart from the mass of journalistic work, his literary baggage consists of three slender volumes. *Maggie* is one of the most downright earnestly-written books ever published. The gruesome tragedy of environment, with all its sordidness of detail, is hammered in with brief, pitiless sentences. Mr. Crane's command of language is remarkable; he does not spare his readers one jot or tittle of the horror of New York slum life. *The Black Riders* strikes a note of fearless novelty and eccentricity. The 'lines' were hurriedly dashed off in a moment of inspiration. They are essentially pessimistic, often cynical. Of *The Red Badge of Courage* little need be said. That such a photograph of the American War should be produced by a young man of twenty-four is little short of marvellous. Every page reads like the confessions of a veteran, every line reeks of battle smoke, and in every sentence we hear the booming of countless cannon and the ping of the merciless bullets.

"Mr. Crane has at least four new volumes in the hands of the publishers. *The Little Regiment,* a war story, will appear almost immediately; followed by *A Woman without Weapons. The Third Violet,* and another novel of slum life may be expected very shortly."

Argonaut (San Francisco), July 15, 1896. "Stephen Crane's Daughter of the Tenements."

"*Maggie: A Girl of the Streets,* by Stephen Crane, is not a new book in every sense of the term, inasmuch as it was written and put in type but not published three years ago, but it is the book of the week and will undoubtedly be widely read. Its author was an obscure reporter up to a few months ago, but his extraordinary little compositions, called 'Lines,' drew attention to his originality, and his *Red Badge of Courage* set him among the new lights to be counted with.

"*Maggie* is like Mr. Crane's other recently published story, *George's Mother,* in being a series of pictures among the degraded poor of a great city.

"It is told in a score of scenes, each portrayed with a graphic power that one can not help wishing had been better used. The characters are all strongly drawn and possessed of distinct individuality, and the reader will not soon forget them. But they are not the kind of beautiful pictures to hang on memory's wall."

Argonaut (San Francisco), August 31, 1896. "Stephen Crane's *Maggie.*"

"Some weeks ago we made brief notice of Stephen Crane's story of *Maggie,* but its popularity has grown to such an extent that we have decided to put before our readers a few of the more striking scenes—or, rather, a few of those scenes in which the daughter of the tenements who gives her name to the story is chiefly concerned. Though her brother, Jimmie, appears more frequently than she in the pages of the book, and his life and mental processes are shown in greater detail, we agree with the author's implied judgment, in naming the book after her, that the young woman of the slums is a more important social problem than her belligerent brother; in these extracts, therefore, we shall follow her fortunes. . . ."

Athenaeum, no. 3600 (October 24, 1896), 562. "Our Library Table."

Banner (Nashville), August 15, 1896.

"A noticeable thing about the book is the resemblance of its methods to those of Victor Hugo, a resemblance merely suggestive at first, but which becomes more pronounced on a second reading." Some of Crane's sentences might have been taken verbatim from some volume of Hugo.

Our fascination with *Maggie,* however, "is a miserable and depressing one, and the average reader will regret his inability to lay the book aside until its dreary story is finished. . . . And it is in this that the story is a failure, in spite of its strength. It is too hopeless, too full of misery, degradation and dirt. The reader flounders in a mire of pessimism, never once receiving from the author the offer of a helping hand or a word of encouragement, and the memory of the book is a nightmare, and the thought of it inexpressibly hopeless and depressing. And yet it is not an unmoral book. . . . And, indeed, as a philanthropic work, the story is a strong sermon, urging the need of greater charity of sentiment, as well as of gold for the poverty-hardened people of the slums.

"But as a literary production, and as such it invites our attention, it is a magnificent piece of realism, which loses its artistic value because its shadows are too deep and its lights too faint and evasive, missing, indeed, the highest aim of literature, which is to give some small degree of pleasure, at least, to the world, and to prove itself not a clog, but an inspiration in the uplifting of humanity."

Beacon (Boston), June 27, 1896.

"As a study of New York tenement-house life the book certainly leaves nothing to be desired in the way of aggressive and pitiless realism. The father of Maggie is a sullen sot, her mother is a brawling drunkard, her brother is a typical Bowery tough, and her 'best friend' for a time is Pete, the barkeeper. With these and other characters, all of them firmly yet roughly outlined, Mr. Crane unfolds a picture that in its sordidness and pathos amounts to a positive revelation. No reasonable person could think of reading the story of Maggie for entertainment, but those who are not afraid to face the realities of existence, and who are willing to look upon humanity at its worst, will find the book a source of edification, if not of pleasure. Mr. Crane seems to be the first of American novelists to go in the slums of a great city with the intent of telling the truth, instead of seeking for humorous or romantic 'material.' He has drawn a picture that takes hold upon the mind and that in its strenuous fidelity is filled with a potent meaning."

Beacon (Boston) July 27, 1896.

Book Buyer, n.s., 13 (July, 1896), 357–358.

"Mr. Stephen Crane's *Maggie: A Girl of the Streets,* upholds the reputation he won by the *Red Badge,* if one may say so of a book written before what is called his 'masterpiece.' The book which made Mr. Crane famous was not a sustained narrative, but a sequence of extraordinary tableaux. The same lack of any structural quality is apparent in *Maggie,* but there is the same vehemence, the same selection of forcible and picturesque words, the same blinding glare of primary colors flashing out into a panorama of illumination.

Maggie suffers in some degree from the fact that nothing but scenes of slaughter and death can properly be painted with such broad strokes of brilliant color. Also, while it was amazing that Mr. Crane could have imagined the scenes of battle and made them seem so inevitably faithful, there is nothing amazing in a writer's knowledge of the details of slum life of New York. Yet the book is sufficiently remarkable to justify an expression of hearty admiration. *Maggie* is written as pitilessly as *L'Assommoir,* and deserves praise, in a degree, for the same literary qualities.

"Another story by Mr. Crane is published simultaneously with *Maggie. George's Mother* is a sketch of a respectable young workingman's slipping down into drunkenness, and the consequent breaking of his Puritan mother's heart. If one may pursue the color figure (which Mr. Crane's language always suggests), the subject seems more suitable for drawing in shades of grey, while Mr. Crane's brushes are full of red and yellow paint. The words used seem too tumultuous for what he describes. The successive stages of a debauch are piled high with such terrors of description as seemed fitting in the battle scenes of the *Red Badge,* but they overload the idea of George's getting drunk. The descriptions of the mother's fury of housekeeping are brilliant, but the edge is too keen; as has been said by them of old time, Thou shalt not slice turnips with a razor. Still, the book is strong, melodramatic, and sure to attract attention; and except that the key is too high, there is nothing commonplace about it."

Bookman (London), 10 (October, 1896), 19–20.

"Mr. Stephen Crane impresses us with the conviction that he tells the truth as he knows it. *The Red Badge of Courage* showed his refusal to sentimentalise. Sentimentality is so far away from the story of *Maggie* that one expects every moment to come on some exaggeration of sordidness, some morbid revelling in the ugly and the brutal; yet nothing of the kind happens. His mind is as unusually restrained as it is watchful. Romance is not wanting. . . . 'Maggie perceived that he was the ideal man. Her dim thoughts were often searching for far-away lands where the little hills sing together in the morning.' There is running through the miserable story the fair light of a trustful, grateful nature, a 'blossom in a mud-puddle,' gentle even when cruelty and treachery have done their worst. And as such, Maggie is as real as the redoubtable savage Jimmie, or the terrible mother, nearly as real as the magnificent Pete. There Mr. Crane surpasses nearly all his models of the sternly realistic school,* who fail so often in their finer, their more beautiful portraits. New York life—nearly at its lowest, surely—is the material of the book, and the material is used by a daring and a relentless hand. But Mr. Crane has reticence and sympathy, and these, as much as his astonishing cleverness, have given him the high rank he holds already in America and England."

Book News, 14 (July, 1896), 524. By Talcott Williams.

Bulletin (Pittsburgh), August 8, 1896.

"This unpleasant story will make Stephen Crane's admirers wish they had stopped at his *Red Badge of Courage.* Its heavy vulgarity leads nowhere and effects nothing."

"A Child of the Streets," unidentified English review of the Heinemann 1896 edition.†

* *See Fortnightly Review* (January, 1897), for opposing view.
† Crane subscribed to The Author's Clipping Bureau (Boston), whose clippings, bearing identification of source and date, he pasted into a scrapbook. CUCC. Clippings of English reviews bear no Author's Clipping Bureau identification tags.

"*Maggie* is surely a fine tribute to the art in a book that the reviewer should be compelled to praise it against his will [sic]. . . . The story is told with a masterly simplicity which shows up the squalor and horror of the scenes with a lurid clearness that is sometimes revolting and always pitiful and apalling. Mr. Crane's realism is merciless and unsparing; in these chapters are set before us in cold blood hideous phases of misery, brutality, drunkenness, vice; while oaths and blaphemies form the habitual speech of the men and women who live and move in this atmosphere of vileness. Yet every scene is alive and has the unmistakable stamp of truth upon it. The reader does not feel that he is reading about these horrors; he feels as if the outer walls of some tenement houses in the slums had been taken away and he could see—and see with comprehension—the doings of the teeming inmates. Over the whole grimly powerful tragedy is the redeeming grace of the author's implied compassion; but he never mars the effect of the story by speaking this compassion or by pointing a moral. He has drawn a vivid picture of life at its lowest and worst; he has shown us the characters as they would be, with no false glamour of an impossible romance about them; and the moral may confidently be left to look after itself, since it stares from every page. Maggie herself is a wonderfully well-drawn character, and the book, repellent though it is, is in its way a triumph."

Chronicle (San Francisco), August 9, 1896. "Stephen Crane's *Maggie.*"

"In *Maggie* Stephen Crane has made a far stronger study of tenement-house life than in *George's Mother.* . . . This sketch of the tenements is brutal in its frankness. There is no attempt, as in Ned Townsend's latest story, to idealize the characters. The coarseness, the sordidness of life in these overcrowded buildings of New York is something which affects one like the reek of the Mulberry Bend gutters on a hot August night. The genius of the writer is revealed in the simplicity of his means of producing powerful effects. He shows the savagery of the instincts of the tenement child; the hatred of the police officer as the embodiment of the law that is detested; the evil influence of the saloon which casts its light into the darkest alleys and converts frowsy homes into hells of cruelty and misery. The dialect of the tenements is imitated to perfection, but it becomes very monotonous except to a student of this barbaric slang. . . .

". . . The story is a powerful sermon on the need of missionary work among the heathen in the tenements of our big cities, and it cannot fail to open the eyes of many who have only taken a sentimental interest in a class that seems to be no nearer to them than the natives of the Congo."

Commercial Advertiser (New York), (July 1?), 1896.

"It is as realistic as anything that Émile Zola has ever written. Though some of its chapters are enough to give one the 'creeps,' none can deny that the characters which he draws with such a master hand are absolutely true to life. The dialect is also natural, and nothing is lacking to give Devil's Row and Rum Alley, slums of the darker New York, such prominence as they never had before. It may, in fact, be said that Mr. Crane has discovered those localities and revealed them to the astonished gaze of the world for the first time. The reader, in going over the pages of *A Girl of the Streets,* is reminded of nothing so much as the slimy things that crawl and blink when a long undisturbed stone is moved and the light is thrown upon them. . . . Analytical powers are the chief feature of the novel. It is free from maudlin sentiment.

No missionary ever ventures near Rum Alley. Its denizens are left to their own resources, and they simmer in them."

Courier (Boston), June 28, 1896.

"The story of Darkest America has been told in the most realistic way by Stephen Crane. In all the work that he has ventured upon, he has rendered the seamy side of modern existence, the real life of the slums, with a force and actuality of description that has not been equalled by any depiction of low life. Every sentence bristles with the steely sinews of the Nemesis that lays its heavy burdens upon the dwarfish development of these poor, puny lives. Every phrase is a noteworthy one, a revelation of a people waiting for a savior. This story of *Maggie, a Girl of the Streets,* is a story of one of that much-to-be-pitied class of human beings of whom the more favored of the earth catch but a passing glimpse, as the tale of some downfall is rehearsed in the police court, and revamped, usually in sarcastic vein, in the great dailies; a story of an unfortunate with a spark of soul dormant and unkindled for all time. The author paints this girl as black as her circumstances cause her to be; and in fact, the coloring of the whole story is deeply defined and real. We meet with people in books that we would shun upon the streets, and it is well if we do not draw our literary skirts aside from them, for it is absolutely necessary to us that we know something of 'how the other half lives,' even if we must learn the same from books. There are no sweet characters in Mr. Crane's stories, and they are thus incomplete. And he realizes this, for he lifts his pen suddenly as if in anticipation of the pure reality, the missionary angel of real life, that his abrupt endings would suggest.

"It was left for Stephen Crane to write such works as these; works that, though unconsciously to himself, are in collaboration with the most earnest reforms and the education of the lower classes. For these are not ideal people that he pictures to us; he reveals them to us as they are, in all their poverty, disgrace and moral turpitude, rooting them out of their dens, exhibiting their vices, and telling a plain, unvarnished tale of those who suffer, and—are dumb, leaving no stone for the knight of reform to stumble over in the dark. This is his purpose, no doubt, to clear the way, to map out the route, honestly and fearlessly. He would have us view, as he does, the nakedness of the problem, the gaping, sanguineous wound, the personification of despair, the stubborn truth,—and thus bids us suggest the remedy. He has little to offer beside this monochrome, these gray days, these starvelings, that live bitterly and, die hopelessly, but he spells their fortunes with an artist's inspiration and cleverness. *The Red Badge of Courage* has lent us a craving that will not be satisfied, for more from this author, and this story will have fully as many readers as did his masterpiece. The publishers inform us that *Maggie* has never been published before, even in serial form."

Critic, n.s., 25 (February 22, 1896), 135.

"*Maggie* was not an immoral story, as many persons imagined from its title; it was coarse in the way that *Chimmie Fadden* is coarse, but there was more objection to bad language from the mouth of a girl-tough than from a boy. The book, however, will be republished—or published, we should say perhaps, for the first publication was little more than a printing—by the Messrs. Appleton, who will also publish a new story by Mr. Crane, called *The Third Violet,* which is a story of life among the younger and poorer artists of New York. Mr. Crane has also just finished another story, 'With the Regiment,' which will be published serially in *McClure's*. He writes to us that this will be his last battle story."

Critic, n.s., 25 (June 13, 1896), 421. "Two Books by Stephen Crane."
Reviews also *George's Mother*.

"The problem which we have always with us, which presses more and more for an answer, and which we are only beginning to study, is that upon which Mr. Crane aims to throw some light in these two books. He offers no solution; he does not even state the problem. He simply turns on the light, and we perceive at once what the actual conditions of life are to the other nine-tenths, in New York. What rules in New York, rules in every large city of the world supposed to be civilized—but with a difference. There is what may be called a special atmosphere here; and it is Mr. Crane's chief merit as a novelist of low life that he has known how to reproduce it with fidelity. It is naturally denser in low places, such as those which he has chosen to illumine, but it is the same atmosphere, only more rarefied, higher up. Broaden the traits a very little, and the supremely contemptuous truck-driver, whose glory is in a phenomenal 'jam,' and whose habit, on ordinary occasions, it is to fix 'his eye on a high and distant object, commanding his horses to start, and then going into a trance of observation,' indifferent as to what may happen to mere foot-passengers—this haughty and self-contained being may represent the modern Juggernaut, Trade, quite as well as any other 'driver' or 'pusher' behind desk or counter. Not one of them but rejoices in like manner in the glory of the fray; not one but observes with the same air of abstract content the crushing progress of the machine. . . .

"It is greatly to Mr. Crane's credit that he indulges in no rhetoric and is never denunciatory. It is such an easy trick of art, and such a convenience to good people who want a definite object of attack, to throw all the blame for our social disorder upon some particular class—the monopolists, the rum-sellers, the politicians, the clergy,—that it is little wonder that such is the course usually pursued by writers who take their themes from the slums. But their books are bad art, and only add to the muddle they profess to depict. Mr. Crane is not yet a skilled artist: he indulges too frequently in needless repetition, and is not always as careful as he should be about the construction of his sentences. But he knows that the essential thing in his line of work is to focus the vital facts in a given field of observation, without distortion; and this he succeeds in doing."

Current Literature, 18 (July, 1895), 9. "Stephen Crane, Author of *The Black Riders*."

Quotes Crane's inscription to the Rev. Thomas Dixon, written on a copy of *Maggie* a few months before Crane went West on a journalistic trip to Nebraska. "The realism of his *Maggie*—a story that might have taken a greater hold on the public than even *Chimmie Fadden* had the publishers been less timid—is of that daring and terrible directness which in its iconoclasm is the very characteristic of rugged undisciplined strength in a youth of genius." Mentions the serialization of *The Red Badge* by the Bacheller Syndicate and announces its forthcoming publication by Messrs. Appleton & Co., "who think very highly of his work. Among other manuscripts which are now in the publisher's hands is one entitled *A Woman without Weapons*. It is a story of New York life, like *Maggie,* but its scenes are laid on the borderland of the slums, and not down in the Devil's Row and Rum Alley."

Daily Tatler, 1 (November 11, 1896), 5.

"Now why is Stephen Crane credited in England with *Maggie: A Child of the Streets* when over here it is *Maggie: A Girl of the Streets?* Is it that the former title strikes the British publisher as a bit more innocuous, in like case with his preferring *Illumination* to Mr. Frederic's more profane title [*The Damnation of Theron Ware*].

"The *Literary World* remarks that 'there is nothing pleasing or pretty about Mr. Crane's work: but it has its place undoubtedly, and if it keeps the complacent among Christians to a period of thoughtful introspection it will amply justify its existence.' This is a trifle ambiguous, but the inference seems to be that, in the reviewer's experience, the complacent among Christians need the lesson conveyed by Maggie's wicked life and consequent untimely death."

Dial, 20 (February 1, 1896), 79–80. By William Morton Payne.

Dispatch (St. Paul), October 3, 1896.

Identical with the *New York Press* review for October 17, 1896.

Edinburgh Review, 187 (April, 1897), 411–414. By Stephen Gwynne. "Novels of American Life."

Fortnightly Review, 67, n.s., 61 (January, 1897), 63–66. By H. D. Traill. "The New Realism." Reprinted in his *The New Fiction,* London, 1898.

Traill denies realism to *Maggie* and *George's Mother.*

Globe (Boston), November 5, 1896.

"The fame of Stephen Crane has spread abroad in the wild way in which it has here, and a London critic writes in this wise of the young and glowing colorist: 'Mr. Crane always shouts in his writings, in fact he positively blares, with never a pause. To read his latest book, *Maggie,* is to put one's ears into the bell of a cornet blown by giant lungs. It leaves one limp, exhausted, maltreated. The book is like a lump of red, raw beef. It is food for tigers, not for women and men. Mr. Crane may be as clever as Mr. Howells makes him out to be, but he is abusing his talents. Even supposing he does split our ear drums with his loud bass what shall it profit him or us?' "

Godey's Magazine, 131 (October, 1895), 431–432. By "Chelifer" [Rupert Hughes]. "The Justification of Slum Stories."

"The highest office of the writer of fiction is the education of human sympathy. To widen, deepen, refine, mellow, generalize, particularize, stimulate, in one word, to educate the brotherly and sisterly feelings of mankind, is the sacred and Christly priesthood of the story-teller. The unpardonable literary sin of omission is the failure to entertain; the most heinous positive offence is the mismanagement of the reader's sympathy. Herein is the real responsibility of a writer of fiction, for there is no sillier heresy than the loud-mouthed anarchy that art has nothing to do with morals. If a novelist defends thievery, he is a criminal, if he stirs up sympathy for a certain thief, that is quite a different matter; if he glorifies licentiousness, he is Sir Pandarus; if he becomes the apologist of a sore-tried backslider, he is following the hallowed footsteps of Him who said, 'Neither do I condemn thee.' The artist need not shackle himself with a Blue-book moral code. I can't see why every novel should be written with one eye on 'the young person,' whose chief innocence is ignorance. But the artist must have some code of morals, and must feel responsible to it. Literary ethics is a principle necessary to valuable fiction.

"One of the greatest fallacies among critics of high degree is the denial to tales of low life of all right to existence. They whine, 'We have sorrow enough and to spare. Why show us the dark side of those things that we could never put an end to if we tried? Art is only meant to amuse.' They are not consistent enough to stick to Joe Miller and the *Pickwick Papers,* but they languish back to old romances or grasp at latter-day pseudo-historical novels and claim to be exactly satisfied. Then if fair maidens wail their souls out, or if heroic knights gasp in deep dungeons, or if fate goes hard with anyone in doublet and hose, they shed a melodious tear and purr as they weep. Yet other enemies of low life stick to society stories and revel in the pitiful existence of high-born dames mismated. No woe is too dire, so long as the characters are correct in attire, but the moment the scene changes and slouchy laborers are the Sirs Launcelot, and Queen Guinevere is a factory girl, all is vulgar, plebeian, too heart-rending to be read. Even the comic side of low life is not bright enough, and humanity is no longer humanity, but a race divided into two species, society and simianity. Of course no one can object to stories of high life, but the whole loaf is better than half the bread. Literature is the greatest of all democratizing forces. . . .

"No better proof of the comedy possible in works on low life could be asked for than the writings of Mr. Edward W. Townsend, whose *Chimmie Fadden* has become a household familiar, and whose vivid language has infected the nation. Of course 'Chimmie' figures principally in a scenery of high life, but the character-drawing is perfect and there are not a few visits to that seventh paradise, the 'Bow'ry.' Any writer who realizes the picturesqueness and charm of such a character deserves all he can realize on it.

"But probably the strongest piece of slum writing we have is *Maggie,* by Mr. Stephen Crane, which was published some years ago with a pen-name for the writer and no name at all for the publishers. But merit will out, and the unclaimed foundling attracted no little attention, though by no means as much as it deserves. The keenness of the wit, the minuteness of the observation, and the bitterness of the cynicism resemble Morrison's work. The foredoomed fall of a well-meaning girl reared in an environment of drunkenness and grime is told with great humanity and fearless art, and there is a fine use of contrast in the conclusion of the work, where the brutal mother in drunken sentimentality is persuaded with difficulty to 'forgive' the dead girl whom she compelled to a harsh fate by the barren cruelty of home-life.

"The subjects chosen by all these writers compel an occasional plainness of speech which may give a shock to spasmic prudishness, but there is nothing to harm a healthy mind, and they all should have the effect of creating a better understanding and a wiser, more active sympathy for the unfortunates who must fill the cellar of the tenement we call life. To do this is far better even than to be artistic."

Godey's Magazine, 133 (September, 1896), 317–319. By "Chelifer" [Rupert Hughes]. "The Rise of Stephen Crane."

Harper's Weekly, 39 (June 8, 1895), 532–533. By W. D. Howells. In "Life and Letters."

Harper's Weekly, 39 (October 26, 1895).

Home Journal (New York), July 8, 1896.

"One of our most noted contemporary literary critics, preeminent for his good taste, fairness, and discrimination, has sharply castigated this book. But whatever may be the general trend of the notices it has received, it is inconceivable that any reader, even with moral tone not above the average, could go over these pages without a shock to his sensibilities, and the pressure of the old question, 'Cui bono?' No good at all, must be the answer that springs to the lips of every right-thinking man or woman that turns over the leaves of Mr. Crane's *Maggie*. His previous and successful literary venture, *The Red Badge of Courage*, merits the warm commendation it has received. This later story, it appears, has lain 'in type and copyright' three years. Were the writer and the publishers demurring with themselves whether pages on pages reeking with profanity, blasphemy, the low, brutal dialect of the slums, and the babble and drivel of half-drunken men and women, could find acceptance among the better and purer classes of the reading world? The 'publisher's note' calls this book 'a real and strenuous tale of New York life.' But why give to American readers such a revolting phase of 'New York life,' merely as a story, without the justification of a single suggestion for uplifting so vile and debased a class from its vileness and debasement?"

Ideas (Boston), July 4, 1896.
"And the pity of it all is so manifest in Mr. Crane's realistic story—which is the work of a master hand indeed. The writer must have absorbed the meaning of the life here described deeply into his consciousness, it must have lingered there, to enable him to so accurately depict characters and scenes of which the average intelligent reading public catches but incidental outward glimpses without sympathetically understanding their causes and interludes. . . .

"The story is so very real that its effect is almost harrowing—at any rate Stephen Crane shows himself an adept in getting at the heart-fibres of what he depicts, enrolling himself among those who believe in revealing truth herself, not in scurrying around the edges simply. His pictures are vivid indeed and glow with that life alone derivable from an understanding of their individual entities as scenes in life's kaleidoscope. The words used are graphic, many a phrase quite irresistible in its fitness.

"Necessarily quite different from *The Red Badge of Courage* and probably not to be as popularly appreciated, *Maggie* is a subject worthy of Mr. Crane's pen, and most worthily treated. There are bits of luridness that have a saddening effect, but the sadness of an audience often produces more lucrative thought than does its merriment. And Stephen Crane's individuality and power in writing are so vitally fertile that his books will always awaken heart-whole interest."

Illustrated American, 20 (July 11, 1896), 94. By Edward Bright. "A Melodrama of the Streets."*

Journal (Boston), June 2, 1896.
"The *New York Times* says: 'We are informed from the best source that the story [*Maggie*] has never been actually published before, even in serial form.' The *Times* has been misinformed. Mr. Crane's grim tale of slum life was published a few years ago, in book form, with paper covers. The author used a pseudonym. We read the story as told in the first edition and we

---

* For this and several other notices about Crane and his works in *Illustrated American*, I am indebted to George Monteiro's article about Crane's appearances in that journal, in *Serif*, 6, no. 4 (December, 1969), 49–54.

remember reviews of it. If we are not mistaken Messrs. Howells and Hamlin Garland indulged themselves in noisy praise."

Journal (New York), March 8, 1896, p. 26. By Alfred Henry Lewis.

Life (Brooklyn), August 22, 1896. "Mr. Crane Again."

"The chief fault of Mr. Stephen Crane's style grows out of his attempt to give a lurid color, a striking emphasis, to every trait and every action of his characters, and to every incident that he describes. The result of this method is to make it seem as if he were, as he really is, 'writing at the top of his voice' all the time. His lavish use of epithets gives an air of exaggeration, almost of grotesquerie, to all of his pictures—makes them seem uncouth and formless. But it is a method that has the merit of making things vivid and of arresting the attention. And it would be silly to deny that this young writer has both imagination and force.

"These are rare and valuable qualities. I have been more impressed by their presence in his story of the tenement-house girl, *Maggie* (Appleton), than I was by his war pictures in *The Red Badge of Courage*. Some of his figures, too, are amazingly effective. 'Over on the island,' he says in painting the outlook from the tenement-house window, 'a worm of yellow convicts came from the shadow of a gray ominous building and crawled slowly along the river's bank.' The most encouraging thing, however, in the book is the evidence which it affords that this young author has acquired the art of character painting, and is a student, and a careful student, who is not without a sense of humor, of human nature. The people who surround this girl of the tenements are of the lowest sort, but they all, father, brother, lover, neighbor and mother, are drawn to the life. By all odds the best thing in the book is the conception of Maggie's mother, a drunken wretch who spends half her time on the island, bewailing the disgrace which the wayward daughter brings upon the family. And equally admirable is the touch by which the old woman, when the news of Maggie's death is brought, goes out and gets the worsted boots which the baby girl used to wear and mourns over them. It is the Irish nature that is revealed in the language, and the act which gives the scene its value."

Literary Digest, 13 (August 8, 1896), 459–460.

"Though issued after the *Red Badge of Courage, Maggie: A Girl of the Streets,* was printed and copyrighted (but not published) three years ago. The publishers describe it as a 'real and strenuous tale of New York life.' Strenuous it is, but it is more "impressionistic' than 'real,' and, true to the impressionistic practise, alike in point and in letters, the essential figure is the least delineated. Maggie is far less important to the canvas than her brother Jimmie, or her sottish mother, or the coarse and tawdry Bowery bartender who is the villain of the piece, and her destroyer.

"The book is strong in fights. It begins with a fight, continues with fights, and culminates in a really considerable 'scrap' between Pete, the Bowery hero—who 'showed that he was a lion of lordly characteristics by the air with which he spat'—and Jimmie, and a 'pal.' This notable encounter takes place in Peter's saloon, whither (to avenge his sister's betrayal) Jimmie has come to taunt the betrayer into combat. . . .

"The reader is left to infer that poor Maggie, after a half-hearted attempt to live on the streets, drowns herself. Whereupon the mother has a fit of maudlin grief, while Pete 'has a good time.' Mr. Crane's 'color' eccentrics are not so prominent as in his late work. Jimmie, it is true, 'lived some red years,' and we are told of 'squat, ignorant stables,' and 'yellow silk women' who play in a Bowery orchestra. But such verbal displays are rare."

Littell's Living Age, 212 (February 20, 1897), 564–572.
      Reprint's Traill's review in *Fortnightly Review* (January, 1897).

Mail and Express (New York), November 6, 1896.
      "It is a miserable and inevitable tragedy, told in relentless stages, but not brutally. It is a terrible satire, but the writer has stopped short of cynicism— not far enough, however, to make *Maggie* palatable to the lovers of only pleasant things." Quoted from an unidentified London journal, which also observes that "Mr. Heinemann has given to Mr. Stephen Crane's *Maggie* something of the appearance of an old-fashioned Sunday school prize book. This is surely dangerous."

Munsey's Magazine, 15 (August, 1896), 630.

Munsey's Magazine, 16 (December, 1896), 373–374.

Nation, 63 (July 2, 1896), 15.
      "We can feel only that it is a pity that the gutter is so dirty, and turn in another direction."

News (Indianapolis), August 14, 1896.
      "He has gone to the lowest depths of degradation for material, and he does not spare the reader in telling of his observations. . . .
      "This is by no means a cheerful tale. There is something inexorable in the movement of the incidents of the girl's life. It is all very pitiful, and it is told with power. There is no half-way in Mr. Crane's realism. It is, as we said in the beginning, debatable, whether the *Red Badge of Courage* is a fair presentation of the life of a green soldier; but this other story offers a picture of slum life in New York, which, we suspect, is not far from true. The great question is not of veracity, but is as to the right of an author to use an undeniable power in presenting a tale of unrelieved misery, despair and sin. It is to be hoped that Mr. Crane will turn his talents to the writing of some less wretched tale. He might at least blend his colors a trifle."

North American Review, 175 (December, 1902), 770–771. By W. D. Howells. "Frank Norris."
      On Crane and Norris.

Pall Mall Gazette, 63 (October 22, 1896), 4.

Pioneer Press (St. Paul), June 28, 1896, p. 11. Portrait.
      "Stephen Crane's *Maggie* is as relentless and wretched a story of its kind as could well be imagined." In *The Red Badge of Courage* "there is a considerable stirring of the better part of human nature. Patriotism, generosity, compassion, courage, play some part in its composition. In *Maggie* there is almost nothing but bitterness. Maggie's own natural inclinations to decency are strong enough merely to emphasize her sorrows more keenly. . . . Painful as the story is, however, and detestable as are its details, it demonstrates the author's power in several directions. He compels his readers to see and hear with him; he places himself on the inside of his puppets and lays bare their mental processes in a singularly skillful fashion."

Pioneer Press (St. Paul), August 30, 1896, p. 20.

Press (New York), July 12, 1896, p. 26.
(Annotated, *George's Mother.*)

Press (New York), October 17, 1896. Unsigned [by Edward Marshall?].

"*Maggie* is a story of New York life. It was written prior to the *Red Badge of Courage,* a book which, within a year, has made Mr. Crane the most talked of writer on the American continent. *Maggie* is, without doubt, a story of 'strenuous New York life,' in the depicting of which Mr. Crane has brought to his aid the strong dramatic painting which has made his *Red Badge of Courage* such a powerful story. There can hardly be anything more graphic than the picture furnished of the miserable hovel in which Maggie lived and the fights in which her father and mother indulged.

"There are some who may think that Mr. Crane is too lurid; that there is slightly too much 'red' about his work. There is probably a too decided martial spirit, but this may be attributed to the realistic picture which Mr. Crane portrays. And Mr. Crane is nothing if he is not realistic. There is realism in every chapter of *Maggie*—it is the realism of every day life. Mr. Crane wields a trenchant pen, and there has not been published a sterner picture of life in the slums of New York than is here presented."

Recorder (New York). Undated.*

"About a year ago a novel called *Maggie* was published here in New York. The name of the author was given as 'Johnston Smith.' The book attracted the attention of Hamlin Garland, who wrote an enthusiastic review of it in the *Arena.* It is learned that the name on the title page was the pseudonym of Stephen Crane, a young newspaper writer of this city. Mr. Crane is only 21 years of age [twenty-two in the spring-and-summer of 1894], and his work gives fine promise. Its notable characteristic is its fidelity to life and its unconventionality of treatment. Mr. Crane recently completed a second novel, which will be brought out in a few months [*The Red Badge of Courage*]."

Republican (Denver), July 26, 1896.

"In less artistic hands the story would be commonplace enough. It is only the sadly familiar one of 'One more unfortunate, / Weary of breath, / Sadly importunate, / Gone to her death.' But this writer casts no lurid flame of sensationalism over the scenes. From the first, Maggie was forced to bear heavy burdens which should have been carried by the older and stronger members of her family. Then, too, heredity and environment, the two bugbears of to-day, are strong factors to contend with and when, as in this case, their chief elements are drunkenness and even worse vices, the end is not hard to foresee. Mr. Crane tells his pitiful story with a restraint of language, yet vivid realism which makes its portraiture very powerful."

Saturday Evening Gazette (Boston), June 20, 1896.

"*The Red Badge of Courage* was not Stephen Crane's first notable literary effort. *Maggie,* which antedates that remarkable book by several years, bears the touches of a master-hand, and would enhance the reputation of any writer of these times. It is one of those commonplace but intensely pitiful tragedies which are being enacted in our great cities continually—the simple story of a

---

* Above this clipping in his scrapbook Crane wrote: "The Recorder, New York." CUCC.

girl who went down to ruin because all the overwhelming forces of heredity and environment were against her, a story of those overcrowded tenements which are a disgrace to our civilization. . . .

"In the hands of an artist like Mr. Crane the simple story becomes an awful arraignment of our humanity. Such books are needed to impress upon the fortunate portion of mankind the truth that their fair cities bear ulcerous spots which threaten hideous mischief."

Saturday Review (London), 82 (November 28, 1896), 557.

Saturday Review (London), 82 (December 19, 1896), 655. By H. G. Wells.

Sketch (London), October 14, 1896, p. 516.

Times (Boston), July 12, 1896.

"*The Red Badge of Courage* was not the first of Mr. Stephen Crane's efforts as an author, but it has sounded with such force in the literary world that anything from his pen is now eagerly sought. Before this famous book, however, an entirely different story had been written by Mr. Crane, *Maggie,* which has just been published by the Appletons. Like all his other works it bears the touch of a master's hand in the emphatic vigor of its descriptions and characters, and evidences his closeness of observation in their fidelity to life. . . .

"The pitiful tragedy of the plot is being enacted over and over again all about us. It tells of a girl whose dormant soul was never kindled, who was ruined by the overwhelming forces of heredity and environment. Maggie is far better than her associates in the story, all of whom drink and swear and fight, and after she had fallen, so ignorant was she that she never dreamed she was bad. After her sin had been discovered by her besotted parents, and her brother, who was sinning against other girls as she had been sinned against, she was cast adrift by them all, friendless and helpless. Despite the sadness of her death one does not wish that she might have liveed longer.

"There is not a gleam of sunshine in the whole book, but in Mr. Crane's hands this simple, ordinary story is so horribly real that it makes an indelible appeal to the fortunate portion of mankind, to right the wrongs which are making such hideous mischief all about us."

Times (London), September 17, 1896. "Publications To-Day."

Times (New York), May 31, 1896, p. 31. Reprinted in *A Century of Books: 1851–1951. New York Times Supplement,* 1951.

Mr. Crane took out a copyright on this story in 1893, and a new copyright ˊ was taken out this year, "which indicates revisions. But we are informed from the best source that the story has never been actually published before, even in serial form. . . . Whether or not Mr. Crane in 1893 found difficulty in securing a publisher, it will now seem hardly credible to readers that he went long in pursuit of one.

"The story is a sad one. Not one gleam of light or of humor falls across its sombre pages. . . . Mr. Crane cannot have seen all that he describes, and yet the reader feels that he must have seen it all. This, perhaps, is the highest praise one can give the book. . . . It is a powerful portrayal, and, if somber and repellent, none the less freighted with appeal to those who are able to assist in righting wrongs."

Times (Richmond), July 26, 1896.

"Many readers will find it impossible to become interested in it, because, as they will tell you, 'it deals with such low people.' These will belong to the class who consign Mr. Dickens to the back shelves, or tolerate him coldly, as a person who devoted great talents to a low use. Mr. Crane can afford to dispense with their admiration. As a matter of fact, in the ghastly story of this girl of the streets, he has revealed the tragedy in the degradation of the lowest ten thousand with the pen of a master. We hear that Mr. Crane boasts of his lack of what we understand as culture, but with all admiration for unusual genius, we think his inattention to his grammar is to be regretted. It is a fault that was very apparent in *The Red Badge of Courage,* and it is not less so in this latest volume. Nevertheless, it is about the only fault the book possesses, in our judgment."

Town Topics (New York), June 25, 1896.
　　"I recall no tale that approaches *Maggie* in the illustration of drunkenness, promiscuous pugilism, joyless and repellent dialogue, and noise. Of course, I like it. Mr. Howells has educated me in realism, and I hope I know a good thing in that line when I see it. . . .
　　"An admirer of Mr. Crane's said to me recently, 'He gives a picture; he makes you see things.' I should say so! I cover my eyes from the high color. My own flesh seems to be black and blue. Methinks I see the jawless soldier of *The Red Badge of Courage* beckoning for beer at the 'family entrance,' and hear the death demon chattering on top of the hot-water urn. Poor Maggie, broken-hearted, crockery-scarred, is dead in the ooze. What eyes the whisky bottle has; how the cash register and the stationary corkscrew stare and glower! Evil and sorrow! Sorrow and evil! Oh, my! Oh, my!"

Tribune (New York), May 31, 1896, p. 26.

Truth, 15 (October 10, 1896) 12. Unsigned [by James L. Ford].
　　"This week it is my whim to analyze 'The Red Boom of Crane.' It is flickering out in the sad gray dawns of the slums, where his keen faculty for the dissection of crimson psychology has got diluted and lost in the enumeration of the endless swilling of golden swill." *Maggie* is a decline from *The Red Badge of Courage.*

Wave (San Francisco), July 4, 1896, p. 13. Unsigned [by Frank Norris]. "Stephen Crane's Stories of Life in the Slums."
　　"*George's Mother* seems to me better than *Maggie.* For a short novel it is less pretentious, has fewer characters and more unity, conveying one distinct impression." Good as *Maggie* is, "and told in Mr. Crane's catching style, the impression left with the reader is one of hurry; the downfall of Maggie, the motif of the tale, strikes one as handled in a manner almost too flippant for the seriousness of the subject."
　　Crane has written *Maggie* somewhat on the plan of the episode of Nana in Zola's *L'Assommoir.* In ordinary hands the tale would be " 'twice told.' But Mr. Crane is, of course, out of the ordinary. I think that the charm of his style lies chiefly in his habit and aptitude for making phrases—short, terse epigrams struck off in the heat of composition, sparks merely, that cast a momentary gleam of light upon whole phases of life. There are hundreds of them throughout this tale of *Maggie.* Indeed, it is the way Mr. Crane tells his story. The picture he makes is not a single carefully composed painting, serious, finished, scrupulously studied, but rather scores and scores of tiny flashlight photographs, instantaneous, caught, as it were, on the run. Of a

necessity, then, the movement of his tale must be rapid, brief, very hurried, hardly more than a glimpse. . . .

"The reader is apt to feel that the author is writing, as it were, from the outside. There is a certain lack of sympathy apparent. Mr. Crane does not seem to *know* his people. You are tempted to wonder if he has ever studied them as closely as he might have done. He does not seem to have gotten *into* their life and to have written from what he saw around him. . . .

"His people are types, not characters; his scenes and incidents are not particularized. It is as if Mr. Crane has merely used the 'machinery' and 'business' of slum life to develop certain traits or to portray certain emotions and passions that might happen anywhere. With him it is the broader, vaguer, human interest that is the main thing, not the smaller details of a particular phase of life."

Westminster Gazette (London), July 31, 1896.

Womankind (Springfield, Ohio), August, 1896. By Marco Morrow. "Stories of the Slums."

"Two new stories of the slums will be widely read: *Maggie: A Girl of the Streets,* because its author, Stephen Crane, has made a reputation, and *Yekl,* because its author, Abraham Cahan, is new and treats of a people almost new to literature, in a vigorous manner.

"*Maggie,* which, as is generally known, is the first novel of Mr. Crane, written when he was twenty-one, is a depressing picture of the squalor—physical, mental and spiritual—of an increasing class of Americans. It is not the story of 'A Girl of the Streets'—rather a record of her evolution, how she unwittingly and unwillingly became the thing she despised.

"Mr. Crane is a realist, but unlike so many imitators of Zola, he does not revel in dirt and filth and nastiness as if he enjoyed it; he simply puts it in his picture because he cannot draw true and leave it out; he simply calls things by their real names, and we remember what he says, while if he had called the dungheap the conventional strawpile, he and his book would make small impression.

"There is much delicacy shown in many places in the book, where the would-be-Zolas would have gorged themselves and their readers on filth.

"*Maggie* does not take hold of one as did *The Red Badge of Courage;* but in one respect it is superior to that much lauded story. When he wrote *Maggie,* Mr. Crane had not yet acquired the poster art; he had not learned the bad habit of laying gaudy chromo colors over everything he touches, else he would have called his story 'The Blue Blazed Path of the Scarlet Woman.'

"One of the most delightful features of *Maggie* is the many passages, mere touches, that teem with the richest suggestions. In a line or two—without saying anything about them, himself, at all, Mr. Crane shows the utter futility of the ordinary 'mission' methods for reaching such people as Maggie and her brother; again in a line he reveals the contemptible Pharisaical spirit of certain of the clergy; and in the brutal laugh and jest that greet the successive appearances of the old drunken mother in the police court, he hints at the wickedness and folly of our present methods of dealing with such pitiable creatures.

"Mr. Crane is an artist; his characters and the setting are true, and while *Maggie* may add nothing to the reputation he has already made, it is a book to read and remember."

World (New York), February 23, 1896, p. 18. By Jeannette L. Gilder. Portrait by Mortimer.
  Reviews also *The Red Badge of Courage.*

World (New York), July 26, 1896, p. 18. By William Dean Howells. "New York Low Life in Fiction."
  (Annotated, Howells [1896].)

Yale Courant, 33, no. 3 (November, 1896), 81. By S. R. K. [Sidney R. Kennedy].

GEORGE'S MOTHER
1896

Academy, 50 (July 25, 1896), 64. By Frank Rinder.
  "*George's Mother*, despite certain marked defects, is a strong study of life among the poor of an American city. . . . George is less satisfactorily portrayed. It is hard to think of him as one who dreamed 'of the indefinite woman and the fragrance of roses that came from her hair, . . . of the chariot of pink clouds coming for him.' In several places the author permits his ready pen to run away with him, notably in the scene where the temporarily penitent George accompanies his mother to a prayer-meeting. In the circumstances, surely it is too much to say that, because the old lady insisted on marching slowly up the aisle to a foremost place, 'he felt he could have assassinated her,' and 'his hands were to him like monstrous swollen hides.' "

Academy, 51 (January 16, 1897), 76.
  H. G. Wells votes for *Maggie* and *George's Mother* for the best books of the year.

Academy, 55 (December 17, 1898), 483–484. By Edward Garnett. "Stephen Crane: An Appreciation."

Athenaeum, 24 (June 27, 1896), 842.
  "When *The Red Badge of Courage* appeared those who were struck by it were divided in opinion as to whether the author would ever accomplish the production of another successful book, and opinion will probably continue to be divided on this point, even after the publication of *George's Mother*, which is now issued by Mr. Edward Arnold. Mr. Stephen Crane has produced in it a striking scene of the relations, in a rough world, between a boy and his mother. It is painful, it is strong; but it will not have for the public the interest they found in *The Red Badge of Courage.*"

Book Buyer, n.s., 13 (July, 1896), 357–358.
  Reviews also *Maggie: A Girl of the Streets.*

Bookman, 3 (July, 1896), 446–447. By Harry Thurston Peck.
  "When an English author by chance attains a sudden and definite success, he is always extremely solicitous that his earlier and imperfect books should not be dragged out and thrust upon the public in a violent effort to take advantage of his 'boom.' He rather suppresses them altogether. . . . We commend this precedent to Mr. Crane, and beg to suggest that an author who

within a single year has forced critics to compare his work with that of the greatest living realists, ought not, as a mere matter of self-respect, to take over his literary ash-barrel and ask us to accept his old bones and junk as virgin gold."

Book News, 14 (July, 1896), 524.

Critic, n.s., 25 (February 22, 1896), 24–25.

Critic, n.s., 25 (June 13, 1896), 421. "Two Books by Stephen Crane."
Reviews also *Maggie: A Girl of the Streets.*
"*George's Mother,* dwelling in the same tenement, is another of the crushed ones. She is a country-bred, mildly fanatical little woman, and her life is one long and spirited warfare against the devils of dirt and sin. Religious enthusiasm flourishes in her, it might be said on air. She attends on Thursday evenings a small conventicle, austere in its appointments, the refuge of a few souls from imminent perdition. Her great grief is that her only surviving son will not accompany her there. For George, imaginative like his mother, has found another refuge, where also a chosen few, out of place in a harsh world, 'fitted for a tree-shaded land, where everything was peace,' are used to congregate. Here the decorations are of a more cheerful character. A rite frequently repeated consists in the bringing of fresh glasses and the taking away of others that have been emptied. It is a paradise of wit and fancy, affection and sentiment, where whiskey prophesies smooth things by the mouths of its worshippers. But, as a consequence of too frequent attendance at his shrine, George loses his job. It is an article of faith with his coreligionists, as with those of other persuasions, not to lend money. He is mourned over a little; then dropped.

"And now the manly and martial qualities of the youths whose glorious deeds half fill the former book engage his attention. They, at least, squarely face the world as it is, undismayed, needing neither refuge nor consolation. They successfully tackle its most perplexing problems, have their way by force of fists and obtain what they want without paying for it. They are the lords of life, the cream and fine flower of our civilization, its most expressive product. Shaking off his dreams, George violently fights his way into full communion with these choice spirits. The little mother finds her mystic warfare becoming too much for her: she is overpowered by the demons and dies tormented by visions like those that scare the dying sinner in mediaeval picture-books."

Daily Eagle (Brooklyn), June 7, 1896, p. 19. "Stephen Crane's Recent Work."
"It is one of the misfortunes of literature incident to the weakness of human nature that when an author has made a pronounced success, there is at once a demand for everything he has written, without much regard for its intrinsic merit." We are told that *George's Mother* "was written a year ago. That was before Mr. Crane had found fame as a story writer with the aid of his *Red Badge of Courage.* Since the publication of that book he has been hailed with a degree of praise and adulation that is not good for any young man. . . . Yet he has given us nothing since the appearance of *The Red Badge of Courage* which can be accepted as any fulfillment of the promise in that volume. He has printed some verses, so-called, and written certain 'lines' which are claimed by his admirers to be poetry. . . . We are told that he has certain books in preparation which will see the light next fall, one of which Mr. Howells is said to regard as greater than *The Red Badge of Courage.* It would have been better for Mr. Crane's reputation as a literary worker,

and as the possessor of some quality which is called genius, if he had had the courage to suppress *George's Mother* and had been content to rest upon fame acquired, until such time as the reading world could have formed its judgment as to the soundness of Mr. Howells' estimate. He has gained nothing that will last by the issue of the new book.

"It purports to be an episode of east side tenement life. It cannot be said to rise to the dignity of a story, for there is no plot. It is simply a succession of dull and uninteresting events. The book means nothing. The writer has simply described certain common enough incidents in the life of the tenement districts, which do not possess any striking significance. A good share of the book—which is not large—is taken up with the description of a booze in a saloon and a debauch in the home of the persons who figure on the canvas. Now, the idiosyncrasies of a 'drunk' participated in by a collection of 'tanks' in the back room of an east side gin mill may have some scientific interest for students of mental pathology, but it is pretty poor stuff to put into literature. Indeed, it is a misuse of terms to call it literature. . . . The world is not interested in descriptions of the successive stages through which a party of inebriates progress to complete drunkenness. If Mr. Crane is possessed of the pearls of genius he has no right to waste his God given gifts upon swine."

As a picture of the East Side, *George's Mother* does not compare with Townsend's or Julian Ralph's sketches for "strength of drawing or brilliancy of coloring." Reports Crane's contributions to a new quarterly printed in East Aurora, the *Roycroft Quarterly;* but there is nothing remarkable about these specimens of the young man's art "except their audacity."

Daily Tatler, 1 (November 12, 1896), 6-7. By John D. Barry. "A Literary Phoenix."

Barry reports that he couldn't read *The Red Badge of Courage* and that reviewers of *George's Mother* hacked it. A certain reviewer chose a certain quotation which was the only detachable bit that could misrepresent the story as vulgar and commonplace, which is the way he wanted to misrepresent it. "Out of the context it had no meaning; in its place it was the keystone of the whole structure. But the reviewer didn't speak of that; he had a point to make. The first chapter of *George's Mother* seemed to me just gratuitously low. When I had finished the last I knew what the first chapter meant, and I changed my mind. In other words, the construction of the story is absolutely logical.

"But Mr. Crane's book is its own justification; it teaches us what the lesson of the life it depicts would teach us if we were to know it at first hand, the dreadful pity of it. I do not see how any one could resent or blame the characters in *George's Mother;* given the conditions surrounding them, and they had to be what they were. In this lies the whole pathos of all human life. The mystery of the treatment which *George's Mother* has received bewilders me when I think of the intense humanity of the story. It is the most heartrending picture of mother-love that I have ever seen in literature, and mother-love is a theme that ought to touch even critics. Yet the book is not for one instant either mawkish or morbid! . . . The description of their going to meeting together is a unique example of impressionism in literature, as wonderful as a picture by Claude Monet. For the matter of that the whole book is the work of a master of literary impressionism.

"Whatever Mr. Crane may be in *The Red Badge of Courage,* he is not a realist in *George's Mother.* The little mother is real, but the son stands for a class, not an individual. Mr. Crane's conversation I don't believe in for a moment, nor do I believe that life is exactly as he depicts it, any more than I think the pictures of the impressionists are like the life they see. But the impressionists think they see what they describe, and that is enough. In *George's Mother* Mr. Crane has written a great book, and I shall be amazed if it does not have a revival."

Fortnightly Review, 67, n.s., 61 (January, 1897), 63–73. By H. D. Traill. "The New Realism."

Globe (Boston), July 5, 1896.

Godey's Magazine, 133 (September, 1896), 316–319. By "Chelifer" [Rupert Hughes]. "The Rise of Stephen Crane."

Illustrated American, July 18, 1896. By Herbert P. Williams. "Mr. Crane as Literary Artist."

Illustrated London News, 109 (October 3, 1896), 439.

Journal (Boston), August 15, 1896.

Literary Digest, 13 (July 4, 1896), 297–298. "Stephen Crane's New Story."
Provides a synopsis of the story with generous quotations. "The death of 'the little old woman,' with her poor dazed mind wandering back to George's boyhood, is one of the features of the tale. Mr. Crane's celebrity as a 'colorist' is well sustained in this work by such touches as the following: 'The broad avenue glistened with that deep-bluish tint which is so widely condemned when it is put into pictures. . . . Kelcy fell with a yellow crash.'"

Lotus, 2 (September, 1896), 893. By Neith Boyce.

Lotus, 2, no. 6 (October, 1896), 208–211. By Jonathan Penn. "A Little Study of Stephen Crane."
"We cannot accept the rather grotesque characters and descriptions of East Side life in *Maggie* and *George's Mother* as equally veritable and valuable pictures of the human consciousness as the convincing psychological pictures of the war. These are written in the unmistakable staccato style of the 'star' reporter on a newspaper of 'the largest circulation in the cosmos.' The stories as simple fiction are unsatisfactory, and as studies of real life they seem a little fatuous. They are both concerned mainly with a series of minutely described drinking feats, ending in certain little unpleasantnesses. The story of *George's Mother* consists entirely of the history of a protracted 'jag.' But it is to be doubted whether the guzzling bouts of the canaille can really occupy an unequivocal place in literature. Considering their insignificant claims, on esthetic grounds, to the consideration of intelligent people, it is becoming a matter of serious moment whether the inarticulate lower classes do not occupy altogether too much prominence in fiction. This is especially to be deplored since our sentimental epoch has relegated all literature but the novel to ignominy and oblivion.

"A careful and impartial, though not at all unappreciative, reading of all of Mr. Crane's published work leads the writer to the conclusion that here is another clever writer who will take his place among the other popular and prolific entertainers of current literature. But to claim for him, as has been done by English and American critics, an assured pre-eminence as a writer of genius, is an extravagance of the cordiality that lacks judgment. Of course this is all a matter of individual judgment, and this opinion is offered as quite tentative, with all proper diffidence—though the diffidence happens to come last, like a kiss in a lover-letter."

Monthly Illustrator, 13 (August, 1896), 27–30. By Clarence Loomis Peaslee. "Stephen Crane's College Days."

Munsey's Magazine, 15 (August, 1896), 630.

Nation, 63 (July 2, 1896), 15.

North American Review, 175 (December, 1902), 770–771. By W. D. Howells. "Frank Norris."
   On Crane and Norris.

Pall Mall Gazette, 62 (June 26, 1896), 10.

Pall Mall Gazette, 63 (August 5, 1896), 4.

Press (New York), May 3, 1896, p. 30.

Press (New York), July 12, 1896, p. 26. Unsigned [by Edward Marshall?].
   "No doubt there will be a tempest of criticism and applause about Stephen Crane's ears as soon as the public begins to talk about his latest two books, *George's Mother,* published by Edwin Arnold, and *Maggie,* published by D. Appleton & Co. Certainly there will be talk about these two books, as there must be about any two so indifferent to tradition, so boldly divergent from the beaten path. Both stories are wonderfully sharp photographs of squalid life, with no retouching, no apparent effort at pleasing arrangement, no softening shadows, not one jot or tittle of compromise with facts, as Stephen Crane sees them, for the sake of making them less unpleasant. Whether or not these stories are literature depends on one's definition of literary art. It is generally agreed that one part of the art is in the omission of all that is unnecessary—all that detracts from the main idea that is to be expressed. So far, Mr. Crane is a rare artist. But if one insists that what remains after the omission of detracting details should be, not an exact copy of nature, but a rearrangement for the purpose of gaining beauty or effectiveness, then this surprising young man falls short. Furthermore, a great deal depends on the choice of a subject, and the subjects of both of these new Crane stories are distinctly disagreeable. One doesn't care much what becomes of the characters. The George of the first volume is a young workman of the sort that one meets much more frequently in life than in books. He might have been a somewhat worthy citizen if his mother had known what to do with him. She was an irritably good woman, who wanted him to go to prayer meeting. He went once out of sheer exasperation, and thereafter went to the devil faster than ever. One certainly cannot read of George's drinkings and fightings and occasional glimmers of intelligence without getting valuable sociological information. No philanthropist interested in the welfare of commonplace young men like George should fail to read the story and get the benefit of Mr. Crane's wonderfully keen faculty for observation. It is the clearest and most intelligent study of a life that thousands of young men live that we remember to have seen. But it isn't good fiction, for the reader feels no particular personal interest in either George or his mother; and its author can retort, 'Who said it was fiction?' much as he responded when some critic asserted that his famous 'Lines' were not poetry.
   "One gets more into sympathy with *Maggie, A Girl of the Streets.* It is assured from the beginning that in the ordinary course of events she will go to

the bad. Mr. Crane makes one feel the morally downward pull of her surroundings with a power all the greater because he skillfully avoids all hint of sermonizing and almost all comment of any sort.

"Two or three years ago the author of *Maggie* offered the story to practically every publisher in town. None would accept it, and Mr. Crane finally published a limited edition of it at his own expense. It was understood that the story was wicked; but that charge is absurd. A more convincing picture of the utter horror, despair and squalor of vice could not well be made.

"In *Maggie,* as in Mr. Crane's other stories, the parts of speech break forth frequently into open revolt against common usage, but it must be admitted that there is often method in their madness. We take Mr. Crane to be generally an earnest, honest young man, whose adjectives slip out of the traces and run wild sometimes from inherent intensity, and not because of affectation."

Public Opinion, 21 (July 9, 1896), 57.

Publisher's Weekly, June 6, 1896.

Saturday Review (London), 82 (September 5, 1896), 262–263. Unsigned [by H. G. Wells]. "The New American Novelists."*

Crane is indebted to Tolstoi, whose distinction lies "in the extraordinary use in narrative of sustained descriptions of the mental states of his characters. Great lengths of story are told in a kind of monologue in the third person. Mr. Crane outdoes his master in this direction in the present book almost as much as in *The Red Badge of Courage.* . . ." In *George's Mother* "There are no purple passages, no decorations, no digressions. In the suppression of the author's personality both these writers [Crane and Sherwin Cody] are as rigorous as the earlier Mr. George Gissing, and there these disciples of Tolstoi join hands with our inheritors of Turgenev. There is no 'style,' no 'Charm'; from the standpoint of Mr. Le Gallienne such books as Mr. Crane's cannot be literature."

Spectator, 77 (July 4, 1896).

Times (London), June 6, 1896, p. 12.

Tribune (New York), July 1, 1896.

Wave (San Francisco), July 4, 1896. Unsigned [by Frank Norris].† "Stephen Crane's Stories of Life in the Slums. / *Maggie* and *George's Mother.*"
Prefers *George's Mother* to *Maggie.*

World (New York), May 31, 1896. By Jeannette L. Gilder. "Romance by Swinburne and Realism by Crane: The English Poet Turns an Arthurian Legend into Saccharine Verse, While the Young American Author Tells a Dark Tale of Modern Life." Portrait.‡

"It can hardly be called a novel, for it is barely a novelette. There is no plot, as plots go, and the characters are few and play no very important part in the tale. George and his mother are the principal characters. There is no action, unless the drunken row at 'Old Bleeker's' can be called action. Mr. Crane's idea, as I understand it, is simply to show the hopelessness of the lives of certain of the working classes, and that they do not make them any the

* For this H. G. Wells identification I am indebted to Eric Solomon in his *Stephen Crane in England* (1964), from which I have also drawn reviews (listed in his footnotes) on other Crane works.
† Identified by Franklin Walker (1932).
‡ The same as in the *Bookman* for February, 1896: Crane with tousled hair, head leaning on fist, and wearing a corduroy jacket.

less hopeless by drink and debauchery. The scenes, I should think, had been sketched from life and the conversation taken down in shorthand. In *Chimmie Fadden* we have the romance of the slums. In *George's Mother* we get their hard and stern reality. . . . There is not as much originality in this story as in *The Red Badge of Courage,* but those who admired that grim study of war will admire this no less grim study of the slums."

Claims that *George's Mother* was written before *The Red Badge of Courage* and that "it lay in a publisher's safe until the author called for it and took it elsewhere."*

World (New York), July 26, 1896, p. 18. By William Dean Howells. "New York Low Life in Fiction."

Reprinted as "An Appreciation," in *Maggie: A Child of the Streets.* London: William Heinemann, 1896. (Howells reviews here also *The Red Badge of Courage.)*

George's Mother "is scarcely a study at all, while *Maggie* is really and fully so. It is the study of a situation merely: a poor, inadequate woman, of a commonplace religiosity, whose son goes to the bad. The wonder of it is the courage which deals with persons so absolutely average, and the art that graves them with the beauty of the author's compassion for everything that errs and suffers." Crane's "simple country folk are contrasted with simple city folk of varying degrees of badness. Mr. Crane has the skill to show how evil is greatly the effect of ignorance and imperfect civilization."

THE LITTLE REGIMENT
1896

Academy, 51 (February 13, 1897), 209. "Notes and News."

Academy, 51 (February 20, 1897), 231–232.

"Mr. Crane has attempted the bold and dangerous task of writing two books on exactly the same subject, from exactly the same standpoint, and making use of exactly the same background. This has proved a stumbling-block to many more experienced authors, and it is high praise to say that *The Little Regiment,* in every way a companion volume to *The Red Badge of Courage,* is not one whit behind it in power or picturesqueness.

"Mr. Crane relies for his effects on daring and original colour similes. He is a word artist of infinite resource, and for everything he invents a special line. The sense of smell which plays such a prominent part in Zola's *Débâcle* is conspicuous by its absence. We certainly miss the *odeur de la guerre.*

---

* However, *George's Mother* was begun on verso of the manuscript of "The Holler Tree," a Sullivan County tale written in 1892–1893, on verso of which he also began "The Reluctant Voyagers," which was written in the late spring or early summer of 1893, shortly after *Maggie* was published and he had met then Corwin Knapp Linson. The evidence that Crane began *The Red Badge* in late 1892 includes his statement to Hilliard: "In the latter part of my twenty-first year I began *The Red Badge of Courage,* and completed it early in my twenty-second year [1893]. The following year I wrote the poems contained in the volume known as *The Black Riders.*" (In *Rochester Post Express,* April 18, 1900, p. 4.) What lay in a "publisher's safe until the author called for it and took it elsewhere," *contra* Miss Gilder, was the manuscript of *The Red Badge.*

"Mr. Crane's peculiar genius is admirably adapted to the exigencies of the short story. He writes at such fever heat, and puts so much of the rush and turmoil of battle into his short, quivering sentences, that a long-continued story like *The Red Badge of Courage* comes as a strain to the mind of the average reader, who closes the book with a genuine sigh of relief."

Academy, 51 (May 22, 1897), 541. "Mr. Stephen Crane's New Book."

Athenaeum, 24, no. 3617 (February 20, 1897), 245.

Crane here equals his *Red Badge* and excels his *Maggie*. "The extraordinary power of imagination which transports the reader into the very firing line of the Northern troops of 1863 is displayed by a writer born, if we mistake not, many years after the close of the scenes which he describes, and is, for this reason, more wonderful than that of Defoe. Mr. Crane's English, when he writes in his own person, is his own, and follows no known rule as to the use and even the meaning of words. It is in dialogue that he is at his strongest, for in this the words are used as the soldiers would have used them."

Beacon (Boston), September 12, 1896.

Book Buyer, n.s., 13 (January, 1897), 983–984.

"The power of Mr. Crane's art is undeniable. His method is frankly individualistic. He ignores literary conventions and escapes the commonplace. His impressions are rendered with a vividness and nervous energy that compel attention, as is evidenced by the recognition which his work has already received. Whether his war stories have the characteristics that will enable the normally minded lover of literature to turn to them again and again, for their permanent pleasure-giving quality, is quite another matter. They are seriously handicapped by morbid psychology and by mannerisms. Interesting as is the color-notation, for instance, it is frequently obtruded upon the reader at the very moment when his attention should be engrossed with the personages or the action of the story. A sympathetic spectator of the struggle would not notice—nor wish to notice—many of the nuances of atmospheric effect to which Mr. Crane invites his scrutiny, and it is sometimes difficult to resist the conclusion that the author himself did not at bottom care so much for the essentials as for the picturesque accidents of the tale. He takes great risks, likewise, as very impressionist must, in his phraseology. . . .

"Again, Mr. Crane's favorite motive, the mania of terror, precludes him from characterizing his personages. 'The tall soldier' or 'the other soldier' is indeed characterization enough, if abject fear or emotional insanity is a moment later to obliterate the human traits of these men. In 'The Veteran,' the finest story in the volume, we are informed that at the alarm of fire the old man's face 'ceased instantly to be a face; it became a mask, *a gray thing,* with horror written about the mouth and eyes.' "

Bookman (London), 11 (March, 1897), 179–180. "The Little Regiment."

"The best of Mr. Crane's work in the field where as yet he has best exerted himself, gives the impression of a perfectly independent discovery and adoption of Tolstoy's method—one of Tolstoy's methods, to be exact, that in which he appears as a highly organised sensitivist. Impressionist the Russian novelist has been called, but the nerves have even more to do with the effect produced than have the eyes—take the most striking scenes in *The Cossacks,* for example. Mr. Crane is too young in his art to be beyond criticism; but he has earned the right to be recognised no imitator, even when he is recalling to us a strange, rare power of an elder and a greater brother. He sees things in the same way, and even more habitually. . . . As a story-teller he has yet much to learn—those in this volume are not all successes—but in description of the kind that is worth anything at all in literature, which seizes on the essential, where the seeker of the picturesque nearly always fails, into which the simple truth-teller sometimes blunders, and where only rare artists know their way, he is already a master."

Book News (Philadelphia), January, 1897.

Daily Eagle (Brooklyn), June 7, 1896, p. 19.

Daily Eagle (Brooklyn), December 20, 1896. "Stephen Crane's War Sketches."
　"They are not tales, they do not describe connected events, there is no thought of plot running through them. They are simply episodes wherein the personal sensations and the conduct inspired by personal emotions and passions are described." Some of these tales are *The Red Badge* all over again, with the same power of analysis and the same portrayal of primary emotions; "one would like to know whether the soldier really felt that way in a battle. How truthful is the author's picture. . . . Is it true art to invent emotions and attribute them to men under certain conditions when there may be some doubts as to their fidelity to nature?"
　After "The Little Regiment" the most striking tale is "A Mystery of Heroism." "It shows a clearer insight into the mainsprings of human action than is found elsewhere in any of these sketches. One cannot help realizing that here, at least, the author is standing on firm ground."

Daily Florida Citizen (Jacksonville), December 20, 1896.

Daily Tatler, 1 (November 9, 1896), 5. "The Little Regiment." Unsigned [by George Parsons Lathrop].
　"Aside from and beneath his bizarre color-schemes, his profanity and bad English, and his magnificent collection of adjectives, there is a marvelous fount of originality, a great and daring imagination, and a power of forcible, graphic description. Added to these is a decided talent for exaggeration, which is perhaps the keynote of his popularity. But 'nothing is reprehensible if you're clever at it,' and clever at his exaggerations Mr. Crane certainly is. It goes without saying that these war stories cannot compare with *The Red Badge of Courage* in merit. Mr. Crane's bright sayings are decidedly of the note-book order, and no note-book, however fat, could stand such repeated drafts upon it."

Edinburgh Review, 187 (April, 1898), 411–412. By S. L. Gwynn.
　Reviews also *The Red Badge.*

Examiner (San Francisco), January 10, 1897.
　"A reader of Stephen Crane will find that that erratic writer has much in common with Hamlin Garland. Both men show much affectation in style and both are young, too, and they have good knowledge of the language. But as an offensive stylist Mr. Crane leads Mr. Garland. He is more violent, and at the same time his work is more permeable by the light by which we discern superficiality. For, in his case, the superficial is very poorly concealed. He is not easy reading. You are constantly annoyed by the blare of word-trumpets. . . . There is no denying the value of Stephen Crane's work, and that he has his place in letters is not to be gainsaid. . . . But Mr. Crane must flit more easily or he will never soar. For the present he insists upon a literary

style that flies up and flaps its callow wings in your face, sometimes emitting in that unpleasant proximity an adolescent crow."

Express (Los Angeles), March 27, 1897.

"How would it do for John L. Sullivan and Stephen Crane to collaborate? They certainly are striking writers, says the Riverside Enterprise."

Ideas (Boston), January 2, 1897.

Lady's Pictorial (London), October 2, 1896.

"I am amongst the very few who are not enthusiastic admirers of Mr. Crane. I acknowledge his cleverness and his gift of graphic description, but his themes are so uniformly gruesome that I have never been able to enjoy thoroughly one of his books. And now, having made such a palpable hit with the *Red Badge of Courage,* he gives us a series of five stories, which might have served as studies for the more important work. I prefer the studies to the finished picture, for there is less bloodshed and more real heroism. The men of 'The Little Regiment' take part in no big fights, but the adventures that befall them bring out now and then the best, instead of the worst, side of human nature. 'The Veteran' and 'The Three Miraculous Soldiers' are perhaps the best of the five stories in the volume. 'A Grey Sleeve' too, is pretty and pathetic."

Literary Review (Boston), March 15, 1897.

"We cannot call Mr. Crane a story teller; rather he is a sketcher, with decided impressionistic tendencies. Neither do his sketches hold for us what they tell; instead, it is by the manner in which they tell it. However, Mr. Crane's war episodes are like clippings out of the great book of war itself, realistic in the best sense, and in *The Little Regiment* he fully sustains the surprising power he first displayed in *The Red Badge of Courage.*"

News (Baltimore), January 16, 1897.

Pioneer Press (St. Paul), February 7, 1897.

Press (New York), November 29, 1896, p. 30.

"Stephen Crane has been doing spiritless hack work for newspapers of late, and those who held *The Red Badge of Courage* to be one of the most original and imaginative and intuitive of American novels probably agreed, if they read any of this unofficial writing of Mr. Crane's, in feeling that the young man had gone to the literary dogs, and that his early promise, renewed but not fulfilled by *George's Mother,* had gone to protest. It seems, however, that Mr. Crane has not gone to the . . . bow-wows by any means, for *The Little Regiment* . . . has all the power of the best of his previous work, and additional good qualities which will, we believe, lead those who admire this extraordinary author to vote it the finest thing he has done. . . . It is noticeable and significant that opinion about this author has been more positive, one way or the other, than about any other writer of the day. . . .

"Mr. Crane's adjectives are as striking as Walt Whitman's. Many of them are strokes of genius, and in this latest work fewer of them than formerly create a suspicion of affectation. Speaking of Walt Whitman, it seems to us that Mr. Crane resembles him rather remarkably in style, independence of tradition and general philosophy of life."

Public opinion, 21 (December 24, 1896), 840. "Briefer Notices."

Record (Chicago), January 16, 1897, p. 11. Photograph.*

* The same photograph—taken by F. H. King, the artist (as Crane called him)— as reproduced in the *Critic,* March 7, 1896; in *Inter Ocean* and in *Philadelphia Press,* March 15, 1896. Crane here wears a stiff collar and cravat; he has no moustache.

"Mr. Crane is not a scientist. His mind does not turn to the abstract. He is above all an impressionist, who now and then transcends in a happy combination of colors, but more by chance than real intention. There is a superficiality about the tales of *The Little Regiment* which is unfortunate."

Sketch (London), February 24, 1897, p. 310. "The Literary Lounger."

Speaker (London), 15 (March 20, 1897), 331.

Spectator, 78 (February 6, 1897), 223. "Heinemann"'s New Books," "*The Little Regiment and Other Episodes of the American Civil War* by Stephen Crane, the author of *The Red Badge of Courage*. 'Pioneer Series,' cloth 3s net; paper 2/6 net."

Spectator, 78 (February 27, 1897), 310.

"In one notable respect he shows a distinct advance on *The Red Badge of Courage*. Alongside of the horrors, the privations, and the discomfort of war he now sets before us the humours, the ironies, and the romance of campaigning. The motive of the story which gives its name to the collection is fraternal affection concealed under a covering of porcupine quills, but none the less deep and genuine. Dan and Billie are always quarrelling, but when the latter is missing Dan is paralysed with grief. But yet when Billie returns wounded but safe, they instantly relapse into their former attitude of mutual and critical antagonism. In 'Three Miraculous Soldiers' the central figure is a girl at a farmhouse, the scene of a painfully thrilling episode of concealment and detection. 'A Mystery of Heroism' is a shrewd commentary on that passage in Aristotle's Ethics which deals with the lower and irrational forms of courage. 'The Indiana Campaign' is a purely humorous sketch of a modern *miles gloriosus*, while 'A Grey Sleeve' is a charming little sketch of love born at first sight amid the reek of the battle-smoke. The descriptive style of this little book is not less impressive than its psychological insight. How fine, for example, is the opening sentence on p. 30: 'After the red round eye of the sun had stared long at the little plain and its burden, darkness, a sable mercy, came heavily upon it, and the wan hands of the dead were no longer seen in strange frozen gestures.'"

Times (London), February 8, 1897, p. 10. "Publications To-Day."

Times (London), March 10, 1897, p. 15. "Recent Novels."

Times (New York), May 1, 1896. By Harold Frederic.

World (Cleveland), January 23, 1897.

World (New York), September 13, 1896.

World (New York), October 25, 1896, p. 25. By Jeannette L. Gilder. "Stephen Crane's New Book of Stories."

"Mr. Stephen Crane is reported to have said that, when he finished *The Little Regiment and Other Episodes of the American Civil War*, he would write no more war stories. . . . I am compelled to say that if Mr. Crane has turned his back upon the war story he has snubbed his best friend." This volume is much superior to *Maggie* and *George's Mother,* although they share the same tricks of style as in *The Red Badge*. For "Mr. Crane is fond of awkward sentences, and he often labors painfully for excentricity of expression, but at the same time he shows in this book that he can tell a good story when he does not try too hard."

Yorkshire Post (Leeds, England), August 18, 1897.

"The humours, as well as the tragedy of the American Civil War are described with admirable skill. There is a quaint story of fraternal love, and a little sentiment of a more conventional order. There is individuality about every one of the stories, and not one can be called weak."

THE THIRD VIOLET
1897

Academy, 51 (May 22, 1897), 541. "Mr. Stephen Crane's New Book." (Quoted in *Book Buyer* and in *Literary Digest.*)

"A precipitate outpouring of lively pictures, a spontaneous dazzle of colour, a frequent success in the quest of the right word and phrase, were among the qualities which won for *The Red Badge of Courage* immediate recognition as the product of genius. . . . These qualities, with less of their excesses, are manifest in *The Third Violet;* and the sincere psychology, the scientific analysis, which in the earlier work lay at the root of the treatment of its subject-matter, are no less sure in the author's portrayal of more daily emotions—of the hackneyed, yet never to be outworn, themes of a man's love, a woman's modesty, and the snobbery which is very near to us all. Of the hundreds who strive after this inward vision, and this power of just expression, once in a decade of years, or in a score, one attains to them; and the result is literature."

Surveys in detail the various episodes of the novel and on the ambiguous ending concludes that "Even the gift of the third violet—so strongly is his prejudice against himself entrenched—he [artist Hawker] interprets into an insolent triumphing over the hopelessness of his passion. Very delicately the inarticulate crisis of mutual intelligence arrives, and 'later she told him that he was perfectly ridiculous.' . . .

"By this latest product of his genius our impression of Mr. Crane is confirmed: that for psychological insight, for dramatic intensity, and for potency of phrase he is already in the front rank of English and American writers of fiction: and that he possesses a certain separate quality which places him apart. It is a short story and slender; but taking it in conjunction with what he has previously given us, there remains, in our judgment, no room for doubt."

Athenaeum, 24, no. 3630 (May 22, 1897), 678. (Quoted in *Literary Digest* and *Book Buyer.*)

Complains that the book is spoiled for English readers because of its American slang. For instance, who would guess that by "bug" Crane means a flying insect? " 'Snickered,' we suppose, means sniggered. 'So long,' of course, we know to be a salutation at departure, but in England that fact is not generally known, though it is known in parts and among certain classes."

The Third Violet makes Crane more the rival of Henry James than of Kipling because Crane is intensely American. "We have never come across a book that brought certain sections of American society so perfectly as does *The Third Violet*. The picture is an extremely pleasant one, and its truth appeals to the English reader, so that the effect of the book is to draw him nearer to his American cousins."

Book Buyer, n.s., 14 (July, 1897), 560.

Book Buyer, n.s., 14 (July, 1897), 609–610. By Gerald Stanley Lee. "Of Mr. Stephen Crane."

"Mr. Crane reads his title clear. If he had called it 'The Second Violet,' it would have lacked character. 'The First Violet' would have been little better. . . . One violet lacks plot, relation, progress, culmination. It is out of the question. But there are numbers enough. Why did not Mr. Crane call it 'The Fourth Violet'? Because there is creative accuracy and inevitableness in *The Third Violet*. Three violets settle things. . . .

"The author of *The Red Badge of Courage* has been obliged to pay rather soon in life the penalty of succeeding too well. Like all more promising men, he is either very good indeed or very bad." However, Mr. Crane has earned the benefit of our doubt. "The quality that earns it for him is the challenging quality in all that he does. He makes men take sides."

Bookman, 5 (July, 1897), 436.

Bookman (London), 12 (June, 1897), 72.

"This is an idyll, and it is written for the most part in slang, and in the elliptical and vituperative language in vogue to-day amongst young persons on the best of terms with one another. Yet it is an idyll, and a very pretty one. . . . By the bye, there is Trilby in the tale—this time Florinda, with fine arms instead of feet; and there are a troop of Trilby—that is, Florinda admirers." In this slighter effort we feel the same directness as in *The Red Badge* and *Maggie*, "the same true reading of the workings of the mind, the same contempt for conventions and clap-trap sentiment."

Book News, 15 (July, 1897), 562. By Harrison S. Morris.

"Conceived in the style of Maeterlinck and brought forth in the way of Ibsen, the tales of Stephen Crane are teeming with modernity. They are undigested, ungrammatical, slangy, boyish, and yet they rise often into the loftier simplicity of literature. *The Third Violet* is a story as abrupt in form as the *Sentimental Journey*, but there the analogy disappears. Were it told in straightforward chapters, each blending with the next, it is doubtful if it would arrest a reader. Even the dash of Bohemia in the metropolis is tame beside the reality, and here we should have fancied Mr. Crane to be strong and picturesque. His vein is naturally an heroic one. He needs the tragic background of war or peril. In 'The Open Boat,' which has just appeared in *Scribner's Magazine*, he surpasses himself in his achievements as well as in defects. In *The Third Violet*, his theme is the flirtation on a hotel porch, terminating in the capture of an heiress. Imagine the panting sentences of *The Red Badge of Courage*, thus degraded, and you have the result."

Book News, 15 (July, 1897), 584. "Mr. Crane's New Book."

Quotes the London *Academy* (as do also *Book Buyer* and *Literary Digest*). "Briefly, the story is that of an impecunious landscape painter's love for a rich girl. He meets her at a mountain summer resort [in Sullivan County]. She gives him two violets during their stay out of town over which he moons upon his return to New York, until she presents him with the third violet and accepts him as her husband."*

Chap-Book, 7 (June 15, 1897), 104.

Critic, n.s., 27 (June 26, 1897), 438.

Mr. Crane has divested this novel of the excellences in his *Red Badge* "with

---

* However, the ambivalence of the ending makes it uncertain.

a thoroughness that seems almost intentional, and yet it is inconceivable that even for an experiment in inanity a writer should be willing to follow up a book like *The Red Badge* with such a vacuous trifle as *The Third Violet*. The author not only shows no grasp of character, but omits to present any characters to grasp." Presents a brief *résumé* of the contents of the book and remarks: "It will be perceived that the author has practically left the entire novel to the reader's imagination. . . . You can have *Hamlet* with Hamlet left out, perhaps, but you cannot omit the entire cast, the stage, and the manager, and claim that you are presenting a play. Maeterlinck says that he is not sure that a 'static theatre' is out of the question, and he has gone some distance toward proving its possibility. However this may be, Mr. Crane has not yet proved that a novel can exist when the author neglects all consideration of characters, action and environment, and we venture to believe that he will never do so. . . . Taking the book as a whole, the author has prepared for those who would gladly be his admirers as many kinds of disappointment as 200 pages can possibly contain."

"The only writers whom English critics seem to consider typically American are Mrs. Gertrude Atherton and Mr. Stephen Crane. No American who has any respect for his country's literature can read with patience the praise bestowed by certain English papers—*The Athenaeum* and *The Academy* among others—on Mr. Crane's latest story, *The Third Violet*." They only care "for things American when they are 'freakish.' No one can accuse me of Anglophobia, but I must admit that I lose patience when I see such a book as Mr. Crane's *Third Violet* singled out for unqualified praise in England."

Edinburgh Review, 187 (April, 1898), 413–414.
  Reviews also *The Red Badge of Courage* and *Maggie*.

Godey's Magazine, 135 (September, 1897), 331. By "Chelifer" [Rupert Hughes].
  "The Bookery."

Lady's Pictorial (London), October 23, 1897.
  "There is only one interesting creature in the book, namely 'Stanley,' the dog."

Literary Digest, 15 (June 19, 1897), 218.
  "The English reviewers claim to have been the first to discover Mr. Stephen Crane, and they are by no means ashamed as yet, of their discovery. . . . The *Athenaeum* and the *Academy*, of London, find in it [*The Third Violet*] ample reason to repeat their affirmations concerning the author's genius and to place him in the front rank of English and American writers." The *New York Home Journal*, on the contrary, concludes: "It is impossible to see the argument for writing books of this character. This young author, however, has unquestionably more than an average ability. The mystery remains that he should direct it into such channels. There is not a word to be said in favor of *The Third Violet*, whose reason, even for its name, does not appear till we reach the last page." (The *Literary Digest* contends that "the gift of the third violet leads to mutual understanding.")

Literary World (London), July 9, 1897.
  "*The Third Violet* is a pleasing and passable story."

Pall Mall Gazette, 50 (January 15, 1898), 425. By Arthur Quiller-Couch.

Public Opinion, 23 (September 2, 1897), 309. "American Fiction and Local Color."

Condensed from the *Times Democrat* (New Orleans). In *The Red Badge* and *The Third Violet* Crane is "wild and woolly and take liberties with the rules of grammar."

Queen, the Lady's Newspaper and Court Chronicle (London), 52, no. 2652 (October 23, 1897), p. 793.

The Third Violet is "a distinct blot on Mr. Crane's reputation; it is scarcely deserving of even strong censure. . . . There is scarcely any story in the book. This, of course, we may not expect from Mr. Crane, as his strong point is not plot. But we ask, what has he given us instead? Literally nothing. . . . Mr. Crane is out of his own province when he enters the arena of love. We hope that *The Third Violet*, which is a hopelessly scentless one, will be the last of its kind, and that instead of violets Mr. Crane will give us war—war—war."

Scotsman (Edinburgh), May 13, 1897.

Spectator, 78 (May 29, 1897), 771.

"Inverting the procedure of Virgil, who passed from bucolic strains to the *horrentia Martis arma*, Mr. Stephen Crane has in *The Third Violet* turned aside from the battlefield into the realm of the pastoral idyll. Mr. Crane is at no pains to subdue the strenuous accents of his explosive style to the gentler tones naturally associated with such unheroic themes as lawn-tennis and picnics, and the incongruity between matter and manner is, in consequence, rather glaring. When his 'summer folk' leave the train they 'burst forth with the enthusiasm of escaping convicts.' Elsewhere we read how 'a little brook, a brawling, ruffianly little brook, swaggered from side to side down the glade, swirling in white leaps over the great dark rocks, and shouting challenge to the hillsides.' This is carrying the 'pathetic fallacy' to extremes; and life-like as Mr. Crane's pictures are, they have something of the spasmodic jerkiness of the kinetoscope. But though his story lacks restfulness and reserve, it fascinates by its fresh and vivid charm. The comedies of courtship have seldom been more unconventionally portrayed than in the conversations—short and sharp, like a cross-fire of rifles—between Billie Hawker and his lady-love. Hawker is an artist, of humble parentage but remarkable talent, who falls hopelessly in love at first sight with a beautiful New York heiress, and is driven by sheer diffidence to assume a mask of indifference and even rudeness. But his efforts are as futile as those of the ostrich to avoid concealment, and the tortures he endures at the hands of his homely sisters, his artist friends, and, above all, of a good-hearted but irrepressibly humorous journalist named Hollanden, keep the reader in a constant simmer of amusement tinged with pity. Agreeable relief is lent to the rural scenes by some remarkably spirited and genial pictures of Bohemian life in what may be called the Quartier Latin of New York, and a note of genuine pathos is struck in the unrequited and unselfish devotion of Florinda O'Connor—a very pleasing variant on the Trilby type—to the unresponsive Hawker. Nor should we fail to mention the humblest, but not the least engaging, of the dramatis personae—'Stanley,' Hawker's dog, who is quite one of the most delightful animals we have encountered in recent fiction."

THE OPEN BOAT
1898

Academy, 53 (May 14, 1898), 522, supplement. Unsigned [by Edward Garnett?].
"Here is Mr. Crane again: this time with a volume made up out of odds and ends; excellent odds, laudable ends. He is the same Mr. Crane we know: when he is objective a cinematograph, astonishing in spite of the drawbacks incidental to a machine in the process of evolution; when he is in the subjective realm, where as often as not he delights to be, the analytical chemist of the subconscious and the occasional betrayer of the night side of heroism. In this capacity it is his function to tell us what a man thinks when he thinks he is thinking of nothing, or of something else. And this is a task of singular difficulty, because, in order successfully to perform it, the observer, having but one subject to experiment upon—himself—has first of all to set himself thinking vacuity and then to think how he thinks it; and this demands a clear head. . . .
"It may or may not be great art, but we jump to a recognition of it as an expression of truth. And no one has done the thing just that way before. Therefore one may say of him what can be said of but few of the men and women who write prose fiction: that he is not superfluous."

American (Philadelphia), August 6, 1898.

Athenaeum, no. 3680 (May 7, 1898), 597.

Book News, 16 (May, 1898), 547. By Talcott Williams.
"In many respects, to-day, the most original and interesting prose figure in American letters, Mr. Crane here as elsewhere plays the camera and seems to see nothing but the developing plate on which much appears, yet under the limitations of the photograph. This is well. It is not all. . . . The young literateur once waited in some city and wrote as things came. To-day, he is the most active-footed of men and creates emotions where they are to be found: the result is, he never thinks and his work is full only of impressions and facts, as witness Crane, Davis, Doyle, and even Kipling. It is in silence things grow."

Current Literature, 24 (July, 1898), 24.
Quotes *Literature*'s review of *The Open Boat*. "His book must not be regarded as a collection of short stories. They are incidents rather than stories, and are selected, not for their dramatic interest, which the author apparently wishes to exclude, but as a vehicle for the telling touches in which he paints the aspects of nature, or analyzes human emotions. When a writer works in this manner, generally, it must be admitted, with less success than Mr. Crane, his friends, as a rule, urge him to sustained efforts of which he is not capable, and lament that he does not write a 'regular novel.' For ourselves, we see no evidence in these sketches that Mr. Crane is equal to any such undertaking. The sketches are complete in themselves, and owe their effectiveness to that fact, and by no means to their intrinsic interest; nor do they seem to contain raw material that might be further developed. This is their peculiarity, that they all have the one same merit, without which, to say the truth, they would be somewhat poor reading. Some of them are so extremely slight that one is tempted to think that almost any other ordinary incident would have served Mr. Crane's purpose equally well. We can assure him that the value of his

work and the reader's pleasure would be much increased if he chose his subjects as carefully as the words in which he describes them. In *The Red Badge of Courage* he had an excellent subject, certain aspects of which are repeated in one of these sketches; the rest, however, appeal too exclusively to our appreciation of his power of vivid presentment, and that, in our opinion, is their chief defect."

Daily Chronicle (London), April 15, 1898, p. 3. "Writers and Readers."

Daily Telegraph (London), April 27, 1898. By W. L. Courtney.

Guardian (Manchester), May 27, 1898.
    In Cora Crane's red scrapbook. BCC.

Literature (London), 2 (May 7, 1898), 535–536.
    We do not dissent "from the praise that has been bestowed upon him, although his admirers have been a little extravagant in their laudation. As far as we can judge—and Mr. Crane has not as yet written a great deal—his position in literature is in some ways peculiar. He has in a very unusual degree the power of bringing a scene, no matter what, before our eyes by a few graphic phrases. His subjects are not always interesting; it is his way of presenting them that is everything. In this respect he resembles those painters who care little for the subject but more for the method of their art, and are called, for want of a better term, Impressionists. To this extent, with his carefully-chosen details, his insistence on the main theme, and his avoidance of irrelevance, Mr. Crane is an Impressionist, and not a mere descriptive writer." Quotes from *The Open Boat* as an example of where Crane's strength lies. *Literature*'s review is quoted in *Current Literature*, 24 (July, 1898), 24.

Outlook (London), 1 (May 7, 1898), 437. "Mr. Stephen Crane's New Book."*
    "Some years ago Mr. Crane wrote a little book called *The Red Badge of Courage*, which may stand as the finest delineation of modern warfare, comparable only to Tolstoi's *Peace and War* [sic] and *Sevastopol*. But the great Russian's point of view is that of a man disillusioned and entirely without hope in this world; stoically courageous if you will, but pessimistic always. He is a glass vessel of a sad even hue, which is continually replenished with the water of truth. But 'nothing is, but thinking makes it so.' And Mr. Crane, with a vision as keen, though of narrower range, an intuition as extraordinary, and a courage as complete as his Russian forerunner, accepts the universe with a sort of sardonic cheerfulness. The Russian divines upon the veiled countenance of destiny a profound and sinister intention, an implacable austerity; and, to point another modern, typical instance, M. Marcel Schwob beholds, with a nightmare vision, the monstrous disfeatures of a leper behind a mask of gold. But the hand of destiny has spread in the sight of Mr. Crane a feast of interests so manifold and surprising that, perhaps, he does not greatly concern himself with the eternal face behind the veil.

    "'What is truth?' said jesting Pilate. We need not pause for an answer; let us rather call to mind how that the observer and the observed are spun of the same stuff at the loom of fate. Man is neither a mirror nor a phonograph; and the objective point of view, upon which the French, with the fatuous dogmatism which is a characteristic of that amiable nation, have sometimes insisted, can have no real existence.

---

* The London *Outlook* superseded the *New Review*.

"So Mr. Crane, not untinctured with the Great American Spirit, sure of himself, sure of his method, takes a piece of life in his hand, saying, 'Come, listen to me, and this dusty clot of confusion shall become suddenly luminous, and shall thrill you with a certain emotion.'

"In *The Open Boat* Mr. Crane has given us the realism of shipwreck, as the late Charles Dickens, in the 'Wreck of the *Golden Mary,*' gave us the romance. The author is always more interested in the manner in which a given event comes to pass than in the event itself. He is ever intensely preoccupied with the psychology of circumstance. And it is this preoccupation which both secures to him the mastery of the *conte,* the short story proper, and denies him success in the relation of a story whose interest lies in its appropriate culmination. For the *conte* is an impression pure and simple, whose existence depends upon the selection and presentation of detail. Other stories, be they long or short—it is immaterial so they be complete—depend for their interest upon the solution of a problem. Hence it is that in 'The Wise Men' and the 'Five White Mice,' wherein we care nothing for the problem's solution, and wherein the presentment does not greatly interest; and in 'Flanagan,' where there ought to be a problem to solve, and is not, the artist has failed of his effect. And hence it is that in 'Horses,' where (for once) the problem is presented along with a wonderful piece of psychology, and in 'Death and the Child,' and in all of Part II, the 'Midnight Sketches,' he has achieved admirable success.

"In 'Death and the Child' Mr. Crane touches the epic. Beginning with the picture of a headlong flight ('it was a freshet that might sear the face of the tall, quiet mountain; it might draw a livid line across the lands, this downpour of fear with a thousand homes adrift in the current'), it goes on to the presentment of battle and the invasion of overmastering fear, and ends with the wonderful vision of cowardice confronted with the child—'the primitive courage, the sovereign child, the brother of the mountains, the sky and the sea.'

"The measure of Mr. Crane's achievement varies, of course, with his subject. His writing, save for a vulgarism here and there, is most subtle and vividly exact. After 'Death and the Child' perhaps the minute ingenuity of his method is most plainly observable in 'A Detail,' a tiny sketch, two pages long, which ends this volume of singular, unequal, and exceedingly clever work."

Publisher's Weekly, 53 (April 30, 1898), 732.

St. James Gazette (London), July 1, 1898, p. 5.

Saturday Review (London), 85 (June 11, 1898), 785. Unsigned.*

"The various stages in the development of Mr. Stephen Crane towards mastery of his art are of more than common interest, and not the least value of the present volume consists in the fact that it shows with unmistakable plainness how earnestly he is endeavouring to find his style, to arrive at the true formula of self-expression. No one who read *The Red Badge of Courage* for the first time could lay down the book without feeling that he had been listening to a new voice, and a voice that had something new to say. The story told was engrossing, compelling; it revealed a section of the psychology

---

* Not by H. G. Wells, *contra* Eric Solomon (1964).

of war which Mr. Kipling had not shown us; and it proclaimed itself the work of a man who, already master of his material, lacked only mastery of style. In the volume before us Mr. Crane is at his best and his worst—though even the worst is something to be grateful for. One story in the book—to wit, 'Death and the Child'—comes as near perfection as one could wish. The description of the bumptious Greek who is prompted to fight for his country by vanity alone, and sees his egotism and cowardice laid bare at the touch of an unfrightened child, is as subtle and convincing an invention as we can recall; and the story, handled with admirable simplicity and skill, is the most artistic thing Mr. Crane has yet accomplished. 'Flanagan' is only less valuable because the material is of cheaper fibre; the art with which it is woven is not a whit less praiseworthy. Immediately thereafter, in order of merit, we put 'The Bride comes to Yellow Sky'—a singularly vivid and picturesque sketch of Texan life. It will perhaps surprise Mr. Crane that we prefer all these to the story he has placed in the forefront of the book. 'The Open Boat' has some undeniably fine passages, and certainly reads like a transcript from actual experience; but we find in it several examples of Mr. Crane's least pleasant mannerisms. The trick of vain repetition is the most obvious; the most serious, that of such enigmatic abruptness as serves only to bewilder the reader. It is all very well to leave something to the imagination, and, within certain limits, to set the reader wondering what happened afterwards. Mr. Crane, however, goes farther than this, and carries to extremity the old device of the writers of sensational serials. We would not wish to convey that any of these faults are very serious or likely to remain uncorrected; they are merely impedimenta which Mr. Crane will assuredly drop in his further progress. We should like to persuade him, moreover, that some of his shorter sketches were hardly worth doing. There is nothing in the second half of this book which rises much above the level of clever descriptive journalism, and he may safely leave such matters to Mr. Richard Harding Davis and the other journalists of his class. From the author of 'Death and the Child' we are entitled to expect work which shall deal with more passionate issues, and the best in this book is so good that Mr. Crane is hardly likely to disappoint the highest expectations."

Spectator, 81 (July 23, 1898), 120–121.

"Mr. Stephen Crane grows, and this is no small thing to say of a writer who sprang full-armed on the public with his first book. When it transpired that *The Red Badge of Courage* was the work of a mere boy, that it was the result of intuition, not experience, one felt misgivings whether the experience when it came would not blur the visions which came unsought into the crystal mirror of Mr. Crane's imagination. His new volume, *The Open Boat.* based in regard to the story which gives its name to the collection on Mr. Crane's escape from the steamer *Commodore,* conclusively dispels this anxiety. Mr. Crane has never done anything finer than this truly wonderful picture of four men battling for their lives in a cockleshell off the coast of Florida. How finely it begins: 'None of them knew the colour of the sky. Their eyes glanced level, and were fastened upon the waves that swept toward them. These waves were of the hue of slate, save for the tops, which were of foaming white, and all of the men knew the colours of the sea.' Here at once we are confronted with a device—borrowed, perhaps, from Maeterlinck—which Mr. Crane employs with great effect in this and other sketches,—the device of iteration. In the dialogue it emphasises the dreary monotony of the long agony; in the descriptive passages it is like the *ritornello* of a song; but in both the effect is entirely artistic. Very touching again, is the way Mr. Crane illustrates the 'subtle brotherhood' established between the four comrades by the stress of a common peril, and the crowning of the poor 'oiler' when within an ace of rescue brings the recital to a harrowing conclusion. . . .

"In 'A Man, and Some Others' we have a wonderfully vivid account of a night attack by Mexican 'greasers' on the camp of a 'sheep-herder' and a chance comrade,—both Americans. . . . We have no space left to dwell in detail on the humour of the strange homecoming of the town-marshal of Yellow Sky and his newly wedded wife, on the thrilling night-escape on horseback of an American traveller from a den of Mexican cut-throats, or on the splendid portrait of the filibustering Captain Flanagan, whose expedition, for reasons which Mr. Crane so vividly sets forth, never became historic. We hope, however, that we have said enough to induce the curious reader to make acquaintance with the most striking and irresistible of all the younger American writers."

Times (London), April 20, 1898, p. 12. "Publications To-Day."

Times (London), August 12, 1898, p. 2.

Times (New York), May 1, 1898, p. 19. Unsigned [by Harold Frederic].

"The most important literary event of these last few days has been the issue of Stephen Crane's new book, of which the title story, 'The Open Boat,' would, even if he had written nothing else, have placed him where he now undoubtedly stands. The heart of a nation of sailors goes out to him who spelled at the oar with the oiler, while even the most microscopic critic can find no wasted stroke of the pen in his pages. The genius of this young son of America is being keenly felt here, and there is a quickening touch in this volume of stories which will put a new face on British appreciation, though the average indolent reviewer has been too staggered by their form to be able to see the true inwardness of his poems, for the British critic, with all his good qualities, is at heart a literary Tory and somewhat cramped by the iron rules of precedent. Just as it has been candidly said of the present Poet Laureate that he is too facile a maker of rhymes ever to be a poet, so it is true of Stephen Crane that he is too real a poet to be a rhymster. No living English prose writer of his years approaches his wonderful gift of original and penetrating observation, while no writer of English is to-day prouder of being an American. Possibly this steady, unswerving loyalty to his native land has helped to make him so many friends among Englishmen, who, even when men of letters, are sportsmen enough to like that man who stands up for his own regiment. Maybe Crane little knows himself what a powerful factor he has been of late in drawing England Westward."

Tribune (Chicago), April 30, 1898.

Tribune (New York), April 24, 1898, p. 17. "Fiction."

University Forum (Syracuse), 3 (May 4, 1898), 343–344.

WAR IS KIND
1899

Book Buyer, 18 (June, 1899), 368.

Book Buyer, 20 (July, 1900), 434.

Bookman, 9 (July, 1899), 466–467. By John Curtis Underwood.

"No one who reads this book can say justly that Mr. Crane is not a poet. He has enriched our literature with prose that rises almost to the level of epic song at times, but he will never be able to make prose of poetry, and his wisdom in following Walt Whitman's footsteps is not overwhelmingly apparent. He has neither the supreme sense of melody that harmonises Whitman's rugged lines nor the force and breadth of grasp that makes the 'Song of the Open Road' the biggest thing in American literature. Among the best things in the book are the epigrams. They are obviously prose, nothing more. Stripped of the gray paper, the black drawings, the printing of four solitary lines at the top of one page, they stand for the thought in them, but the illusive glamour of verse has fled. And the author seems naively conscious of this. . . .

"Technically, the book is in some respects an advance on *The Black Riders*, Mr. Crane's former metrical effort. . . . Evidently he takes himself seriously, in spite of what seems occasional freakishness. There is room for his individuality in fiction—so striking a personality will always find hearers—but in the strait domain of true poesy he can only win to greatness by a closer regard for the conventionalities of rhyme and reason that the centuries have taught us are the best. The less said of Mr. [Will] Bradley's drawings the better."

Leader (Pittsburgh), June 3, 1899. By Willa Cather.

"Either Mr. Crane is insulting the public or insulting himself, or he has developed a case of atavism and is chattering the primeval nonsense of the apes. His *Black Riders*, uneven as it was, was a casket of polished masterpieces when compared with *War Is Kind*. And it is not kind at all, Mr. Crane: when it provokes such verses as these, it is all that Sherman said it was."

Criterion, 21 (June 3, 1899), 26–27. By C[helifer]. "Mr. Crane's Crazyquilting."

"To be ironical is all right, but why drive the iron in so far? We all know that war was brutal, that it killed lovers, husbands and sons, but we never thought of telling the sweethearts, wives and mothers that war, therefore, was kind. The burglar held the old lady on the red-hot stove. Oh, he was a kind man! That is the apparent recipe." However, Crane is an artist. "He is frugal of words and has the magic of style and the wizardry of effects."

Critic, 35 (August, 1899), 681.

Literature, 4 (April 1, 1899), 349. "Authors and Publishers."

Munsey's Magazine, 21 (September, 1899), 946.

Nation, 69 (November 16, 1899), 378. By T. W. Higginson. "Recent Poetry."

Mr. Will Bradley's share in *War Is Kind* as the illustrator "is perhaps worse than Mr. Crane's, being purely imitative, but even Mr. Crane has written his own epitaph neatly on one page as follows (p. 56):

> A man said to the universe:
> "Sir, I exist!"
> "However," replied the universe,
> "The fact has not created in me
> "A sense of obligation."

Republican (Springfield), June 4, 1899, p. 12. "Stephen Crane and Will Bradley."
  Reprinted from the *New York Sun.*
Saturday Evening Post, 172 (July 22, 1899), 63. By Agnes Repplier. "A Novelty in Verse."
Times (New York), May 27, 1899, p. 339. By Ashley A. Smith.

ACTIVE SERVICE
1899

Academy, 58 (January 6, 1900), 13–14.
  "The hero of this novel is the editor of the Sunday edition of a New York paper, Rufus Coleman, a down-East Yankee of the most resourceful and clear-headed type. Coleman falls in love with Marjory Wainright, daughter of a college professor. The professor declines the young man as a son-in-law, and then, his daughter proving obstinate, takes her and his wife to Greece, with a party of young students. Rufus follows as correspondent of his paper, and there follows also a *divette* named Nora Black who has something more than a preference for the great young Sunday editor. The presence of all the characters in Greece can only be explained by the fact that Mr. Crane has spent some time in Greece as a war-correspondent, and must have a large quantity of descriptive stuff to 'work off.' Otherwise it has no significance. Mr. Crane makes of the Turko-Greek war a rather effective background to a romantic love-tale with a 'happy' conclusion. The book is full of those feats of description for which the author is famous—some of them really excellent, others nothing but trickeries in which a certain effect is obtained by applying to men the epithets of things and to things the epithets of men. But let us admit that Mr. Crane can handle the epithet and the simile with surprising, almost miraculous dexterity. The best chapter in the book is that in which is set forth the strenuous life of the sixteenth floor of the *New York Eclipse* building. It is a piece of sheer impudent vivacity, the end justifying the means. If it had not succeeded it would have been obviously crude; but it does succeed, and the sixteenth floor of the *Eclipse* building lives for you as in a biograph."
Athenaeum, 24, no. 3630 (May 22, 1897), 541.

Athenaeum, no. 3759 (November 11, 1899), 650. "New Books."
  Downright bad in style and grammar. The characters are admirably sketched and sustained. There is tenderness and brilliance and real insight into the minds and ways of women and of men; but the last chapter is an "addition to a book suggestively complete without it. . . . But the real blemish is the worse than mannerism of the style, which must detract from the triumphs to which the author's genius ought to lead."
Bookman, 17 (December, 1899), 89.
  "Mr. Crane shows his usual power of describing scenes he actually knows, whether in college class-rooms, in newspaper offices, or on Greek roads, in vivid, energetic language. You will read to the end to see whether Marjorie and love crown Coleman at last, or whether he is drowned in champagne and

despair by the strong hand of Miss Nora Black; and a book that you must read to the end is not to be sniffed at. But, nevertheless, this one is careless and formless. Mr. Crane has a talent which he should take more seriously."

Book News, 18 (December, 1899), 202. Unsigned [by Talcott Williams]. "With the New Books." Quoted from the *Mail and Express*.

"Mr. Crane has taken the new Sunday supplement newspaper man, had him fall in love with the daughter of a professor of Greek, put the professor, his family, and a chorus of students in the vortex of the Greek war and let the hero rescue them, with a comic opera singer thrown in to play Potiphar's wife to the Sunday supplement man's Joseph. This ought to be interesting to the end, but it is interesting only about to the middle, the illusion of reality being lost midway."

Criterion, 22 (January 6, 1900), 24. By "Chelifer" [Rupert Hughes]. "The Genius of Stephen Crane."

The hero in *Active Service* "is far from ideal; he stumbles into heroism more or less unintentionally; he takes good and ill fortune with a bad grace generally; he is in short a hero by accident, an average flawful character, peevish and irritable at worst and not very good at best. But because he is like the great average of humanity, he is the more worthy of consideration. Though the book drags a bit at first, it later enchains and hales along the interest unflaggingly, and this without sacrificing probabilities.

"The heroine is a fine study, an American girl, whose deep emotions are held in strict leash by a sturdy self-respect. Her frumpish and shallow mother and her petty and professorial father are well characterized, and an actress is brought in to mix things up. As a psychological study of motives the book is keen; as a piece of narrative construction, the latter half of it shows an ability Mr. Crane has given little evidence of before.

"But, chiefly, the book is worthy for its details. There is an abundance of that minute observation that distinguishes Mr. Crane's manner. There is, furthermore, a warmth of amorous life that is unusual in his prose; the love of the heroine for the man is beautifully painted, and when, after many misunderstandings, they reach the great understanding in a crisis of danger, there is a nobility of situation. All is petty again when a silly contretempts cuts the Gordian knot of love. There is a deep and faithful pathos in the scene where the heroine, so strong in public, is found, by her foolish old father, alone in the dark and crying over her broken heart. Then, when the man of text-books becomes for the nonce a man of action and re-unites the lovers, there is a new height of power, all is ecstatic, rose-colored and blissful.

"The last page of the book is simply a ravishment of beauty. A most notable feature of Mr. Crane's style is the hunt for the one fit word. Always with him it is the unexpected, the unusual, the vivid epithet."

Daily Chronicle (London), November 10, 1899, p. 4.

Dial, 27 (December 16, 1899), 492.

Graphic (London), 60 (December 16, 1899), 834.

Leader (Pittsburgh), November 11, 1899. By Willa Cather. "Books and Magazines."

Literature, 5 (November 25, 1899), 518.

Munsey's Magazine, 22 (January, 1900), 616.

Nation, 69 (November 30, 1899), 413.

144

Outlook, 4 (December 16, 1899), 656–657. "Mr. Stephen Crane in Action."

Active Service "is sketchy, arbitrary; it has not the subtle lines of pure art. Naturally, the novel is clever and brilliant; it is life, more or less, and is full of effective pages. But with all this it is not fine art. The fact is we have learnt to demand more from Mr. Crane than *Active Service* gives us. We demand that his own peculiar gift, his clairvoyance, in laying bare the psychology of men's blind emotions should flash on us dramas of real significance. *The Red Badge of Courage, George's Mother,* and *The Third Violet* were great discoveries in impressionism; they showed human nature such cunning, arbitrary, irrational stuff, such fiery mud, that Mr. Crane really invented a new mode of analysing men. And his short stories made every artist open his eyes. But *Active Service* is a step of repetition."

Public Opinion, 27 (November 23, 1899), 665.

Scotsman (Edinburgh), November 6, 1899, p. 3.

Spectator, 83 (November 11, 1899), 701.

"Mr. Crane's plot is ingenious and entertaining, and the characterisation full of those unexpected—occasionally unedifying—strokes in which he excels."

Times (London), November 2, 1899, p. 11. "Publications To-Day."

Vanity Fair, April 12, 1900, p. 264.

THE MONSTER
1899

Academy, 60 (March 2, 1901), 177.

"It has been suggested that, in his volume of short stories entitled *The Monster,* the late Mr. Stephen Crane was less original than usual, that he was indebted to *Uncle Tom's Cabin* for the idea of the title story, and that 'The Blue Hotel' resembles a story by a distinguished compatriot [Bret Harte] called 'Snow-Bound at Eagle's.' These suggestions hardly carry conviction, and we are not surprised to learn from Mrs. Crane that the stories which are thus criticized were founded on her late husband's personal experiences. Mrs. Crane writes: 'The Blue Hotel was one of Mr. Crane's own experiences when he went West for the Bachelor Syndicate of New York . . . Uncle Tom's Cabin did not suggest The Monster.' Mr. W. W. Howells says: 'The Monster is the greatest short story ever written by an American. Henry Johnson was a real man—that is, he was burned horribly about the face; but he was a hero only as he was a horror. Out of the crepe-bound face of a Negro whom Mr. Crane saw came the story of *The Monster.*' "

Academy, 60 (March 16, 1901), 334.

Athenaeum, no. 3829 (March 16, 1901), 334.

Book Buyer, 20 (April, 1900), 244.

Book News, 18 (February, 1900), 337–338. By Julian Hawthorne.

"I call this an outrage on art and humanity; and the splendid descriptive ability of the author, his vividness and veracity, only render it more flagrant. Something is fundamentally out of gear in a mind that can reconcile itself to such a performance. . . . Of constructive ability he shows not a vestige. His outfit for literary purposes consists of a microscopic eye, and a keen sense of the queer, the bizarre, the morbid. His minute analysis produces nothing. He is anything but an artist." (However, Howells called "The Monster"—according to Mrs. Stephen Crane—the "greatest short story ever written by an American." *See Academy,* March 2, 1901.)

Criterion, 22 (January 6, 1900), 24. By "Chelifer" [Rupert Hughes].

"That Stephen Crane is a genius I have been convinced ever since I read that little fatherless yellow-covered book 'Maggie, a Tale of the Streets, by Johnston Smith.' To this belief I have clung in spite of many jolts and jars. . . ." These jolts and jars include *Black Riders,* much of *George's Mother,* the general idea of *The Third Violet,* "and almost all of that crazy nightmare, *War is Kind.* Yet, withal, Mr. Crane seems to me to be the most definite and individual of all our book-writers; and I credit him with having written some of the best pages America has contributed to literature, in *Maggie, The Red Badge,* certain of the *Black Riders* lines, 'The Open Boat,' and in the two books just published by his hand [*Active Service* and *The Monster*]. . . .

" 'The Monster' is an incursion into the realms of the horrible without once losing sight of realism or plausibility. There is no strain on credulity, no mysticism of any sort. . . . The scene of the fire in the laboratory is a most gorgeous study in high colors, that ought to be quoted for its high beauty. The second story, 'The Blue Hotel,' is a wonderful thing in its way, full of stirring action and most subtly motivated. A big genius, this young fellow Crane!"

Critic, 36 (February, 1900), 182.

Daily News, February 20, 1901.

Independent, 52 (February 1, 1900), 324.

Literary Digest, 19 (December 23, 1899), 770.

Public Opinion, 27 (December 28, 1899), 826.

Morning Post (London), February 23, 1901, p. 6.

Spectator, 86 (February 16, 1901), 244.

WOUNDS IN THE RAIN
1900

Academy, 59 (October 6, 1900), 281.

"No one can escape, in reading this last of Mr. Crane's extraordinary work, from the reflection that it ridiculously resembles his first. Almost every impression was preconceived in *The Red Badge of Courage,* and for verisimilitude the author might have stayed for the one as for the other in his own armchair, and never have gone at all to the wars. This might lead to either of two conclusions: that the reporter was obsessed by the author's battles in the brain, or that the author had successfully divined truth which the reporter's observation could but verify." Crane here is concerned with the inner man; the objective operations are of secondary importance. What mainly interests him are "the sharpening of the senses or their temporary anaesthesia, the effects of fear, the strange sources from which in emergency courage may derive. . . . Mr. Crane preserved to the last his Japanese-like sensitiveness to the paradox of perspective." Claims "The Second Generation" to be the finest work in the volume. "On the whole, however, this posthumous volume is a brilliant last word from one who had discovered himself completely from the beginning."*

Athenaeum, no. 3805 (September 29, 1900), 410.

"The Price of the Harness" is as good as any part of *The Red Badge,* and the characters in "The Second Generation" are developed "in touches worthy of Ibsen." The *Athenaeum*'s reviewer thinks that the title of the volume—*Wounds in the Rain*—is "inapplicable." (However, the leitmotif of "wound" and of "rain" obviously link the stories comprising *Wounds in the Rain.)* *See* Thomas Gullason (1959).

Book Buyer, n.s., 21 (November, 1900), 300. By Carolyn Shipman.

"How would he have developed had he lived? This question is of perpetual interest when a man dies who appears to be riding on the crest of his highest wave. With Stevenson there could be only one answer: Towards greater perfection of art and ripeness of sane thought. With Stephen Crane the answer is not so sure. . . . Some of the early crudeness has disappeared in these vivid pictures of soldier life, and with it some of the Manet splashes of color in word-painting. The vigor and fearlessness are here, without the apparent aim at effect. The book is a distinct advance, but we shall never know whether or not it would have been its author's swansong before literary death. Those who knew the man say No."

Bookman, 12 (December, 1900), 320–321. Photograph.

Critic, n.s., 35 (January, 1901), 88.

The war stories, the record of Crane's personal experiences in Cuba, are "as vivid as the record of imaginary experiences in *The Red Badge of Courage.* They could not well be more so. Indeed, Mr. Crane's war stories, written after he had been through two campaigns, strongly confirm the story of a battle written before he had ever smelt gunpowder. . . . *Wounds in the Rain* is the work of a born story-teller."

Nation, 71 (November 29, 1900), 429–430.

"It is impossible rigidly to divide fact from fiction in Mr. Crane's *Wounds in the Rain,* but, roughly speaking, the events narrated are now historical,† while the actors are mostly the unknown who get into print only under fictitious names. The manner in which these sketches and memories are written is that of a clever and vivacious journalist, tempered by afterthought and softened by the desire to give literary effectiveness to descriptions of episodes in which the note of life is distressing or violent or brutal. The volume contains some of the best work that Mr. Crane has left behind him."

Outlook, 66 (October 27, 1900), 519.

Public Opinion, 29 (November 15, 1900), 634.

---

* On this point *see* Introduction, *SCTS,* p. 12

† The fictitious names are identified, as well as the specific terrain of skirmish or battle which Crane camouflaged in his *Wounds in the Rain,* in *Crane,* chaps. 21–22.

WHILOMVILLE STORIES
1900

Academy, 58 (June 9, 1900), 116, 123. By Edward Garnett. "Stephen Crane."

Academy, 59 (November 17, 1900), 468.

Academy, 59 (December 15, 1900), 603. Unsigned [by Edward Garnett].
"No man—as we have before now pointed out—manifested so little progress as Mr. Crane: almost he may be said, in a literary sense, to have been born an adult. Thus these attempts upon Tom Sawyer subjects may be either early essays of the time when Crane was looking about the globe for the matter proper to his genius, or they may have been the fruit of recreatory moments during his short, brilliant career as a war correspondent or psychological artist of the battlefield.* Extremely slight they are; in some the framework is almost too frail to bear the canvas on which he paints; but everywhere in the treatment of these children, no less than in the minute touches by which his ultra-sensitised mind reflected the humours, the gaieties, the bizarreries of the struggle against an armed landscape that is modern war, you find the marks of the wonderful beyondness that was his convincing effect."

Athenaeum, no. 3814 (December 1, 1900), 722.

Bookman, 12 (October, 1900), 165.

Book News, 19 (October, 1900), 87–88. "Whilomville Stories."
"The indefatigable genius of the healthy small boy to make trouble for himself and for those whose fortune, or misfortune if you like, it is to cross his path, is the keynote of the late Stephen Crane's collection of childhood sketches, put together under the title of *Whilomville Stories,* as clever a study of the psychology of boyhood, though in a vastly different vein, as has appeared since Kenneth Graham put forth his *Golden Age.* . . .
"Stephen Crane caught the spirit of boyhood and demonstrated again that which needed no demonstration, the correctness of his imaginative faculty. This, with his happy power of depiction, gives the stories a literary worth distinct from their value as a mere source of amusement.
"Jimmie Trescott, who is really the central figure in the book, is a thoroughly lovable little rascal. 'The Angel Child,' 'The Dalzel Boy,' and the other types which figure in the stories, are well drawn, and immediately recognizable as among the companions of our own childhood. Incidentally, the sketches of negro character, which are interpolated, although not pertinent to the general theme of the stories, are certainly well done. It is not every one who has a real love for children, such as was possessed by Stephen Crane. Nor does the world of grown-up men and some women particularly censure the man from whose heart this quality is lacking, the man who is popularly said to have forgotten that he was once a boy himself. Perhaps it is rather a hard test to apply to a person, this love of children, too severe a standard by which to measure men who are the product of a highly nervous civilization. But there are those who are blessed with that tenderness of heart which finds pleasure, and not annoyance, in the peculiar monstrosities ever present in the normal boyish mind.

* Crane began his Whilomville stories in 1898.

"While Jimmie Trescott is hardly likely to live, as a character, among other children of fiction who have survived oblivion in the past, he is nonetheless a character rather than a type."

Critic, 37 (October, 1900), 374.

"*Whilomville Stories* shine superior to much of the late Stephen Crane's work. They are by no means masterpieces, these acutely human little sketches, for simplicity is ever lacking. They show observation and sympathy, but are in many places baroque, overweighted. Throughout his career Mr. Crane was a consistent victim of the shoddy in word or phrase. That which stood most in his way was an absence of fine, discriminating, aesthetic perception. Hence his splendors are largely tinsel, his triumphs often tawdry. Though brilliant and colorful, Mr. Crane's pages do not burn with anything approaching Pater's 'gem-like flame'; they are mere flashes in the pan."

Independent, 52 (September 6, 1900), 2070–2071.

Literature (London), 8 (March 2, 1901), 165. "Whilomville Stories and Others."

Munsey's Magazine, 24 (December, 1900), 470.

Nation, 72 (February 28, 1901), 181–182.

"Mr. David Dwight Wells's literary reputation is damaged by *Parlous Times*, and Mr. Crane's might justly be annihilated by *Whilomville Stories*. It would be comforting to think that he meant to satirize one group of American children for the eternal good of all American children, but, on reflection, there is nothing to support such a kindly opinion. One of Mr. Crane's greatest defects was his capacity for admiring the wrong things, and at Whilomville there appear to have been no correcting influences or objects. No children in the world are good enough to read these tales without losing the bloom of their virtues."

Outlook, 66 (September 8, 1900), 133.

Public Opinion, 29 (September 13, 1900), 346. "Stephen Crane."

Republican (Springfield, Ohio), August 26, 1900, p. 15. "Stephen Crane's Boy Stories."

These stories "represent the fiction art of their author as worthily as almost anything he has written. . . . H. G. Wells refers his art to the spirit of the modern studio, and draws an interesting parallel between Crane's writing and a certain sort of painting that has greatly developed in recent years. The essential traits of his work are (1) extreme impressionism, (2) the striking word, (3) dialect caught with the minutest care, (4) short monotonous sentences which hammer in the picture to be impressed, (5) the phenomenally vigorous elimination of everything else."

Spectator, 85 (December 15, 1900), 891.

Times (London), November 13, 1900.

Times, (New York), September 8, 1900, p. 605. "Stories by Stephen Crane."

GREAT   BATTLES   OF   THE   WORLD
1900

Athenaeum, no. 3844 (June 29, 1901), 819.

Critic, n.s., 35 (January, 1901), 88.
    Reviews in comparison *Great Battles of the World* and *Wounds in the Rain.*
In *Great Battles* the author is giving "an historical account of battles which
have been repeatedly described by eye-witnesses and later historians, with
whose works the world is familiar. The author is constrained by the knowledge that his fancy must render a rigid account of itself, that he will be
detected in the slightest departure from the well-known facts in each case.
Hence no one should be surprised at finding his *Great Battles of the World*
very unlike Mr. Crane's other war books, and less significant than his fictitious
battle-pieces. The accounts of Bunker Hill, Vittoria, New Orleans, etc., are
well enough in their way, but there is nothing notable about them. Any experienced storyteller could have written them, whereas no one but Crane
could have written *The Red Badge.*"*

Daily Eagle (Brooklyn), November 10, 1900, p. 13.
    "We are so accustomed to regarding Stephen Crane as an almost matchless
describer of battle scenes that it seems novel to encounter him in a work that
is essentially historical in its character. And it will become apparent as the
reader peruses these sketches that when his imaginative genius is limited by
the necessity of confining himself to the facts of the history, that his spon-
taneity and the brilliancy of his descriptive style suffers. While these descriptive sketches are vigorously written and while their author did not fail when
opportunity offered to take advantage of picturesque situations, the reader
will find them different in several ways from *The Red Badge of Courage.* The
author is obliged to devote so much space to the historical setting of the battle
he is describing that he loses a little of that imaginative quality which enabled
him to give so forceful a description of an actual fight. While these sketches
are better than many other descriptions of the same fights, it can hardly be
said that they have added greatly to Mr. Crane's reputation as a writer of what
may be called battle pieces. A good many authors have described battles on
land and sea. It should be borne in mind that Mr. Crane's reputation in this
direction was achieved not in the description of any actual conflict in its
entirety from the standpoint of the historian, but from his imaginative picture
of the individual experiences and emotions of a single unit in the conflict. His
Red Badge of Courage is not an account of any one battle. It is a wonderfully
vivid and brilliant psychological study of how one private soldier and con-
structively any one, or a dozen or a hundred or a thousand of his comrades
feel under like conditions in the throes of a conflict under fire. Similarly his
volume of sketches of the Cuban campaign, recently published, in which he
gives chapters of personal experiences in the fighting before Santiago are
pictures from the individual point of view rather than accounts of the battle.
He tells in those sketches what he saw and felt. In the new book he takes up
the role of the historian. They are good historical sketches, but it is not a

---

* *Great Battles* was researched for Crane by Kate Lyon (Mrs. Harold Frederic),
and she also wrote most of the battle pieces.

great book. They are good bird's-eye views of the battles named, but they will not take rank in literature with *The Red Badge of Courage."*

Dial, 30 (February 16, 1901), 114. "Some of the Great Battles of the World."

Public Opinion, 29 (December 6, 1900), 722.

LAST WORDS
1902

NOTE: The title was originally "The Last Voyagers." A good many pieces in *Last Words* are early writings—not Last Words.

Athenaeum, no. 3883 (March 29, 1902), 399.

THE O'RUDDY
1903

Athenaeum, no. 4007 (August 13, 1904), 200.

Bookman, 18 (January, 1904), 565.

Book News, 22 (December, 1903), 428.

Critic, 37 (July, 1900), 15-16.

Daily Post (Birmingham), July 15, 1904, p. 4.

Dial, 36 (February 16, 1904), 121. By William Morton Payne.

Herald (New York), June 21, 1900, p. 10. By Robert Barr.

Independent, 56 (February 4, 1904), 273.

Literary World (Boston), 34 (October, 1903), 277.

Morning Leader (London), July 15, 1904, p. 3.

Morning Post (London), July 14, 1904, p. 8.

Nation, 77 (November 19, 1903), 414.
    A note announcing publication of *The O'Ruddy* by Stephen Crane and Robert Barr.

Outlook (London), 13 (July 16, 1904), 5.

Pall Mall Gazette, 79 (July 16, 1904), 5.

Public Opinion, 25 (December 24, 1903), 824.

Saturday Review, 98 (August 6, 1904), 177.

Scotsman, July 14, 1904, p. 2.

Times (New York), November 21, 1903, p. 836. "King of the Irelands."

Times Literary Supplement (London), July 8, 1904, p. 215.
    "The O'Ruddy is a ruffling Irishman of good family who comes over to England to fight duels and win a bride."

Times Literary Supplement (London), July 29, 1904, p. 237.

T. P.'s Weekly (London), September 2, 1904, p. 297.

Tribune (New York), 63 (November 22, 1903), 12.

CONTEMPORARY PARODIES

NOTE: For additional parodies *see The Time Has Come* (East Aurora, N.Y., 1895); *American Literature*, 30 (November, 1958), 393–344; *War Dispatches*, pp. 50–54; and *Crane*, appendix 8, pp. 552–554.

Bookman, 4 (December, 1896), 332. By W. S. Bean. "Lines after Stephen Crane."

Clack Book, 2 (December, 1896), 97. By Harvey Worthington Loomis. "A Philistine."

Critic, 27 (May 1, 1897). By Charles Battell Loomis. Also in J. B. Gilder's the *Month*, June, 1897.
     Reprinted in *War Dispatches*, pp. 50-51.

Journal (Indianapolis), September 9, 1896.

Life, 27 (April 23, 1896), 332. By Paul M. Paine. "The Blue Blotch of Cowardice."
     A parody of *The Red Badge of Courage* purporting to be "An Incident of the Pursuit of the Insurgents, with Profuse Apologies to Mr. Stephen Crane." Paine's parody begins: "Above, the sun hung like a custard pie in a burnt blanket."

Lotus, 1, no. 6 (February 15, 1896), 158-159. "Comment."
     "An exchange has neatly parodied two verses of Stephen Crane's latest, which appeared in the *Bookman*, entitled 'War is Kind'. This is the Crane version:

> 'Mother, whose heart hung humble as a button /
> On the bright splendid shroud of your son.'

Here the parody:

> 'Stephen, Whose verse Ham Garland, like a glutton, /
> Gulps with bright splendid mouth like a gun's.'

Apropos of the Crane mania, a Scotch friend sent me a bit of doggerel clipped from a provincial paper:

> 'If I had riches, name, and fame, /
> I would them all forego-ra /
> If I could be a Stephen Crane, /
> And hang in East Aurora.'

True to his honest nature, he would leave nothing unexplained, and adds by way of postscript, 'The sober truth is, Crane didna hang in East Aurora, but De'el tak' me if he sudna hae doon the trick.' "

Lotus, 1, no. 8 (March 15, 1896), 208. "Comment."
     "First Child: 'I am taking just the sweetest little magazine. My mama got it for me, and she read aloud to me Mr. Crane's poem which he calls "Verses," because my mama says no other name is big enough. She says one

line is just grand; I remember her words—"a grand conception"—that was it. She made me memorize it and hoped it would have a wholesome effect on me. This is the line; I said it to my doggie all the way to school this morning: "A noise of Men at work came the clear blue miles." ' Second Child: 'That's funny, but I don't think it's nearly so pretty as my purple cow book with red grass and lovely green roses. I look at the art designs in it every morning after I get through with my lesson in the Arabella and Araminta stories. And my mama says that juvenile literature is very elevating and she is going to make an artist of me.' Garlin Hamland: 'Bless you both, my children. In spite of finicky criticism, youth sends back its best arterial blood into the nation.' "

Musical Courier, 27 (August 3, 1898), 20. By James Huneker. "By Stephen Crane."

 Reprinted in *War Dispatches*, p. 54.

 The *Musical Courier* prefaces Huneker's parody with this note: "The *Buffalo Enquirer* prints the following war correspondence from the front. It neglects to state whether the dispatches were received by wire or by freight."

Philistine, 1 (July, 1895), 70. "An Earnest Cry & Prayer" ("Ye kin of unco' writing men"). Unsigned.

Philistine, 1 (July, 1895), 70. "The Spotted Sprinter" ("I saw a man making a fool of himself"). Unsigned.

Philistine, 1 (September, 1895), 136. By Nelson Ayres.

Philistine, 6 (April, 1898), 146–147. By E. M.

Philistine, 8 (February, 1899). "I Saw a Man Tugging at his Boot-Straps."

Philistine, 8 (March, 1899, back wrapper). Cartoon by W. W. Denslow. "I Saw a Man Tugging at his Boot Straps."

Public Opinion, 26 (June 1, 1899), 697. "First Find a Grisly Theme."

Town Topics (New York), July 23, 1896. "Mr. Crane and Mr. Popp / Oh, for God's sake can't you stop / Won't you ever shut up shop?"

Tribune (New York) May 18, 1897. "I Have Seen a Battle."

 Reprinted in *War Dispatches*, pp. 51–52.

Wave (San Francisco), December 24, 1897. Unsigned [by Frank Norris]. "The Green Stones of Unrest / By S——n C——e."

 Reprinted in *Frank Norris of the "Wave,"* ed. Oscar Lewis. San Francisco, 1931, pp 82–85.

 Reprinted in *War Dispatches*, pp. 52–53.

E

WRITINGS OF STEPHEN CRANE
ARRANGED ALPHABETICALLY
BY INDIVIDUAL TITLES

ACROSS THE COVERED PIT
　Typescript by Edith Crane, 4 pp., originally in the BCCC, which describes
　　the Crane holograph Ms. of 29 leaves of yellow paper 6⅜ × 10 in. Also notes
　　two identical typed copies marked "From S. Seth / Acting for A. T.
　　Vance / 1133 Broadway." That is evidence Crane was seeking a publisher.
　Holograph Ms. in BCC (acquired 1961) but not listed in BCC catalogue.
　Most of Crane's Sullivan County tales and sketches were published in the
　　New York Tribune for 1892, but not this one. *W-S Bibliography* (1948)
　　declares: "Unpublished. Concerns a clergyman who liked to explore caves."
　　This Sullivan County tale provides a companion-piece to Crane's "Four
　　Men in a Cave" (1892).
　First published in *Bulletin,* 61 (January, 1957), 39–41.
　In *CSS&S* (1963).
　In *NYCS* (1966).
　In *SCTS* (1968).

ACTIVE SERVICE
　TMs., 212 pp., complete except for 12 pp. CUCC.
　W-S Bibliography: "Copyrighted by S. S. McClure on July 21, 1899, for serial
　　publication. Appearance unknown." However, see below:
　Chicago Times-Herald, August 6–October 1, 1899. In 9 installments.
　Buffalo Courier, August 27–October 29, 1899, beginning serial publication.
　　With one chapter omitted.
　New York: Frederick A. Stokes Company, 1899.
　London: William Heinemann, 1899.
　London: International Association of Newspapers and Authors, 1901.
　New York: Melville Publishing Co., 1903.
　In *Work,* vol. 4 (1926).
　In *The Complete Novels of Stephen Crane.* Garden City: Doubleday & Co.,
　　1967.

ADVENTURES OF A NOVELIST
　See DORA CLARK.

AH, HAGGARD PURSE
　AMs., 1 p. CUCC.
　In *Poetry* (1957).
　In *Poems of Stephen Crane* (1966).

"ALL FEELING GOD" (BATTLE HYMN)
　See BATTLE HYMN.

NOTE: The abbreviations used throughout this section are: AMs., autograph manuscript; An., autograph note; AMsS., autograph manuscript signed; Ms., manuscript;
TMs., typed manuscript; TMsS., typed manuscript signed; Ts., typed manuscript, original; Tsc., typed manuscript, carbon.

ALONG THE SHARK RIVER*
New York Tribune, August 15, 1892, p. 4 [unsigned].
In *UW* (1963).

AMERICANS AND BEGGARS IN CUBA
AMs., 3 pp., unfinished news article written in pencil on back of stationery from the Grand Hotel "Pasaje," Havana, in September, 1898. CUCC.
In *War Dispatches* (1964), here reproduced from the holograph Ms. for the first time.

AN AMERICAN TRAMPS EXCURSION (story)
See BILLIE ATKINS WENT TO OMAHA.

ANCIENT CAPITAL OF MONTEZUMA. / STEPHEN CRANE DESCRIBES THE JOURNEY FROM SAN ANTONIO TO MEXICO
Press proof "for July 21. . . . Copyright, 1895, Bacheller, Johnson & Bacheller."† "Stephen Crane in Mexico." CUCC.
Cincinnati Commercial Tribune, July 21, 1895, p. 18. "Two Tourists in Mexico."
Dallas Morning News, July 21, 1895, p. 8. "From Stephen Crane."
Galveston Daily News, July 21, 1895, p. 10. "From Stephen Crane."
Nebraska State Journal, July 21, 1895, p. 13. "Stephen Crane in Mexico."
Philadelphia Press, July 21, 1895, p. 32.
Philadelphia Press, July 21, 1895, p. 32. "Stephen Crane in Mexico." (A variant title of *Philadelphia Press* edition the same day.)
Rochester Democrat and Chronicle, July 21, 1895, p. 16.
New Orleans Times-Democrat, July 23, 1895, p. 8. "Crane in Mexico."
In *UW* (1963).

"AND IF HE WILLS, WE MUST DIE"
TMsS., 8 pp. BCC. Typed manuscripts in BCC, although designated as TMsS., are signed by Cora Crane thus: "By Stephen Crane," in a script closely resembling Crane's own handwriting. Facsimile reproduction of the typescript's first page is in *The Works of Stephen Crane,* ed. Fredson Bowers, vol. VI, *Tales of War* (1970).
Illustrated London News, 117 (July 28, 1900), 121–122. Reprinted August 11, 1900, pp. 185–186.
Philadelphia Press, July 28, 1900. "End of the Battle."
Frank Leslie's Popular Monthly, 50 (October, 1900), 533–538.
In *Last Words.* London: Digby, Long & Co., 1902.
In *Men, Women and Boats.* New York: Boni and Liveright, 1921.
In *Work,* vol. 9 (1926).

---

* Discovered in *American Literature,* 20 (November, 1948), 275–279. "Stephen Crane at Asbury Park," by Victor A. Elconin. Not included in Elconin's discoveries is "Stephen Crane at Asbury Park," although that is the title of his Crane findings. *See* ASBURY PARK AS SEEN BY STEPHEN CRANE.
Elconin's discoveries include the above title and "Crowding Into Asbury Park," "Gay Bathing Suit and Novel Both Must Go," "Joys of Seaside Life," "Meetings Begun at Ocean Grove," "On the Board Walk," "On the New Jersey Coast: Summer Dwellers," "On the New Jersey Coast: Guests Continue to Arrive," "Seaside Assembly's Work at Avon," "Seaside Assembly." Unsigned, they are by Crane. Other *Tribune* reports listed by Elconin are not by Crane. *See NYCS,* p. xiii.
† The dateline is faked; Crane was back in the East by May 16, 1895. *See Crane* (1968).

In *Maggie, and Other Stories.* New York: Modern Library, 1933.

In *The Upturned Face and Other Stories.* Girard, Kans.: Haldeman-Julius (n.d.).

In *CSS&S* (1963).

In *TW* (1970).

ANECDOTE OF A TRAVELLER ON THE ROYAL PRUSSIAN RAILWAY.
See PRUSSIAN OFFICIAL'S STUPIDITY.

ANGEL CHILD
Holograph Ms. owned by Melvin H. Schoberlin.
Harper's Magazine, 99 (August, 1899), 358–364.
In *Whilomville Stories.* New York: Harper & Brothers, 1900.
In *Whilomville Stories.* London: Harper & Brothers, 1900.
In *Work,* vol. 5 (1926).
In *CSS&S* (1963).
In *TWH* (1969).

APACHÉ CROSSING
See GRAVEYARD IN APACHÉ CROSSING.

ARTILLERY DUEL WAS FIERCELY FOUGHT ON BOTH SIDES
New York World, July 3, 1898, p. 2.
In *UW* (1963).
In *War Dispatches* (1964).

ART IN KANSAS CITY
AMs., 2 pp., with Crane's inscription on verso of p. 2 ("Uncle Clarence / Art in Kansas City / Unfinished."). CUCC. Ts. copy by Edith Crane. BCC. *W-S Bibliography* notes it as "untraced; perhaps unpublished. Probably written in 1895. . . ."

SinSF, 1, no. 2 (Winter, 1964).

SCraneN, 2, no. 1 (Fall, 1967), with Joseph Katz issuing "Art in Kansas City" without acknowledgement of its prior publication.

ART STUDENTS' LEAGUE
An untitled but complete article filling 25 pages of the Crane Notebook in BCC. Portions of the holograph manuscript are quoted with commentary, for the first time, in *Bulletin,* 60 (September, 1956), 457–459. "Stephen Crane: Some New Stories (Part 1)" by R. W. Stallman.
Another sketch of the Art Students' League Building—two pages untitled—is in CUCC, as noted in the above, p. 458*n*.

In *NYCS* (1966).

In *Notebook* (1969).

ASBURY PARK AS SEEN BY STEPHEN CRANE
New York Journal, August 16, 1896, p. 33.
Kansas City Star, August 22, 1896. Press clipping in CUCC. "Stephen Crane at Asbury Park."
In *UW* (1963). Mislocated under the heading "New York and Florida," p. xiii.
In *NYCS* (1966). "Stephen Crane at Asbury Park."

ASS AND THE MOUNTAIN
See HOW THE DONKEY LIFTED THE HILLS.

ASSASSINS IN MODERN BATTLES
TMsS., 7 pp., with autograph corrections, signed by Cora Crane's hand. BCC.
New York Journal, April 24, 1898, p. 21. Titled also "The Little Stilettos of
the Modern Navy Which Stab in the Dark / By / Stephen Crane / Who
Wrote the / Greatest Battle Story / of the Age. The Assassins in Modern
Battles."
See DESTROYERS, ETC.
Denver Republican, May, 1, 1898, p. 30.
In *Last Words.* London: Digby, Long & Co., 1902.
In *War Dispatches* (1964). "The Little Stilettos of the Modern Navy Which
Stab in the Dark."

AT CLANCY'S WAKE
TMsS., 4 pp., with autograph corrections in Cora Crane's hand. BCC. Press
clipping, source unidentified. CUCC.*
Truth, 12 (July 3, 1893), 40.
In *Last Words.* London: Digby, Long & Co., 1902.
In *NYCS* (1966).

AT THE PIT DOOR
Philistine, 11 (September, 1900), 97–104.
In *Et Cetera: A Collector's Scrap-Book.* Chicago, Ill.: Pascal Covici, 1924.
In *CSS&S* (1963).
In *UW* (1963).

AUCTION
In *The Open Boat and Other Stories.* London: William Heinemann, 1898.
In *Work,* vol. 11 (1926).
In *CSS&S* (1963).
In *NYCS* (1966).

AYE, WORKMAN, MAKE ME A DREAM
TMs., 1 p., poem. CUCC.
In *Poems of Stephen Crane* (1966). Not in *Poetry* (1957).

BALLYDEHOB†
TMs., pp., with autograph corrections. BCC.
Westminster Gazette, October 22, 1897, pp. 1–2.
Westminster Budget, 10 (November 5, 1897), 15.
In *Last Words.* London: Digby, Long & Co., 1902.
In *Work,* vol. 11 (1926).

BATTLE HYMN ("ALL FEELING GOD")
TMs., 2 pp., poem. Also a copy in Cora Crane's hand. CUCC.
Cora Crane's note: "The ms. . . . has just been discovered in saddle-bags

---

* The CUCC catalogue does not list this press clipping. However, it is signed
by Crane "Truth, New York." So I traced it there. It is not included in *UW,*
nor in *CSS&S.* William R. Linneman's findings, "Stephen Crane's Contributions to
Truth," *American Literature,* 31 (May, 1959), 196–197, do not include "At Clancy's
Wake." He does not admit how he discovered three Crane contributions to *Truth;*
namely, by Crane's inscription on the unidentified press clipping "Truth, New
York." Linneman describes his three finds but did not reproduce them in *AL.*

† This is no. 2 of "Irish Notes." They include "Queenstown," "Ballydehob,"
"The Royal Irish Constabulary," "A Fishing Village," "An Old Man Goes Wooing,"
in *Westminster Gazette,* October 19, October 22, November 5, November 12, and
November 23, 1897.

used by Stephen Crane during the late war with Spain." It was discovered by Charles Michelson, who sent a copy of the "autograph battle hymn" to the *Pall Mall Magazine,* and then apologized to Cora for having done so. *See Crane,* p. 525. The manuscript has not survived, and the poem's possible publication remains in doubt.

In *Poetry* (1957), here for the first time.

In *Poems of Stephen Crane* (1966).

BATTLE IN GREECE
See A FRAGMENT OF VELESTINO.

BATTLE OF BUNKER HILL
AMs., 1 p., one sentence. CUCC. Not listed in CUCC catalogue.

Lippincott's Magazine, 65 (June, 1900), 924–932.

In *Great Battles of the World.* London: Chapman & Hall Limited, 1901.

In *Great Battles of the World.* Philadelphia: J. B. Lippincott Co., 1901.

In *Great Battles of the World.* London: Hodder & Stoughton, 1914.

SCraneN, 3, no. 2 (Winter, 1968), 5–6, 7. Reproduces the holograph Ms.

BATTLE OF FORTY FORT
AMsS., 3 pp., finished in Edith Richie's hand. BCC.

Cassell's Magazine, n.s., 23 (May, 1901), 591–594.

In *CSS&S* (1963).

BATTLE OF SOLFERINO
Lippincott's Magazine, 66 (October, 1900), pp. 613–627.

In *Great Battles of the World.* London: Chapman & Hall Limited, 1901.

In *Great Battles of the World.* Philadelphia: J. B. Lippincott Company, 1901.

In *Great Battles of the World.* London: Hodder & Stoughton, 1914.

BEAR AND PANTHER
New York Tribune, July 17, 1892, p. 18 [unsigned]. One of several newly discovered Sullivan County sketches and tales, this one datelined: Hartwood, N.Y., July 12.

In *SCTS* (1968).

Southern Humanities Review, 2, no. 1 (Winter, 1968), 32–33. Prior to Gullason in *SHR,* Stallman's edition of *SCTS*—with an Introduction dated "27 September, 1967"—was published in May, 1968.

BILLIE ATKINS WENT TO OMAHA
TMsS., 4 pp., corrections in ink. CUCC.

See EXCURSION TICKET.

New York Press, July 8, 1894, part 4, p. 2.

In *CSS&S* (1963).

In *UW* (1963).

In *NYCS* (1966).

BIRTHDAY WORD FROM NOVELIST STEPHEN CRANE
New York Journal, November 8, 1896, p. 14. Reproduces holograph Ms.: "It is a condition of most of us who are in journalism that we do not know how to define it because your newspaper seems to change and advance each day. / Stephen Crane."

First reprinted in *Crane* (1968).

BLACK DOG: A NIGHT OF SPECTRAL TERROR
TMs., 5 pp. "By Stephen Crane" in Cora Crane's hand. CUCC.

New York Tribune, July 24, 1892, part 2, p. 19.
In *SCS* (1949).
In *CSS&S* (1963).
In *SCTS* (1968).

BLACKGUARD OF A POLICE OFFICER
Holograph Ms., 1 p. folio. CUCC.
First published in *NYCS* (1966).

BLACK RIDERS AND OTHER LINES
Boston: Copeland and Day, 1895.
Boston & London: Copeland and Day & William Heinemann, 1896.
London: William Heinemann, 1896.
In *An American Anthology: 1787–1899. Selections Illustrating the Editor's Critical Review of American Poetry in the Nineteenth Century.* Boston and New York: Houghton Mifflin and Company, 1900. Reprints from *The Black Riders* the title poem, "Black riders came from the sea," and three other *Black Riders* poems: "Behold, the grave of a wicked man" (titled Why?), "Once I knew a fine song" (titled 'Scaped), and "A youth in apparel that glittered" (titled Content). And four poems from *War Is Kind* (1899).
Boston: Sherman, French & Co., 1912.
In *Work,* vol. 6 (1926).
In *Poems* (1930).
[N. p.] [n. d.] Edition of 400 copies reprinted by Small, Maynard & Co. for H. P. Davis.
In *Poetry* (1957).
In *Poems of Stephen Crane* (1966)
Consult the collation of this title for separate appearances of individual poems.
NOTE: *The Black Riders* was set to music by William Schuyler. *See Saturday Review of Literature,* 10 (December 16, 1933). "Unpublished Crane Material," by B. J. R. Stolper.

BLACK RIDERS CAME FROM THE SEA
Holograph Ms., 1 p., dated March 19, 1896, signed. A presentation copy written while Crane was in Washington, D.C. The only known holograph copy. Special Collections, University of California, Los Angeles.
In *A Roycroft Anthology.* East Aurora, N.Y.: The Roycrofters, 1917, p. 26.
Facsimile reproduction in "A Manuscript of 'Black Riders Came From the Sea,'" by Richard M. Weatherford, *SCraneN,* 4, no. 4 (Summer, 1970), 3–4.

BLOOD OF THE MARTYR
New York Press Sunday Magazine, 1 (April 3, 1898), 9–11.
In *Blood of the Martyr.* Mount Vernon, N.Y.: Peter Pauper Press, 1940.
In *UW* (1963).

BLUE BADGE OF COWARDICE
Boston Globe, May 12, 1897, p. 7. "Cursed the Prince."
Buffalo Evening News, May 12, 1897, pp. 1, 7. "Pitiable Scenes at Volo."
Chicago Tribune, May 12, 1897, pp. 1, 3. "Stephen Crane Describes Flight of Greeks from Volo."
Kansas City Star, May 12, 1897, p. 2. "Stephen Crane's Impressions. / The Young Author on Smolenski's Retreat / and Misery of Fugitives."
New York Journal, May 12, 1897, p. 3.
Philadelphia Press, May 12, 1897, p. 2. "Stephen Crane Sees Volo's Fear."

San Francisco Examiner, May 12, 1897, pp. 1–2. "Horrors / of War in / Defeat. / Stephen Crane Depicts / the Scenes at / Volo."
In *UW* (1963); reprints *New York Journal.*
In *War Dispatches* (1964); reprints *New York Journal.*

BLUE BATTALIONS ("WHEN A PEOPLE REACH THE TOP OF A HILL")
AMs., 1 p., poem. CUCC.
Philistine, 3 (June, 1898), 9–10.
In *Spanish American War Songs.* Detroit: Sidney A. Witherbee, 1898. Here published as a Cuban War lyric, although not one. Written in 1897 after the Greco-Turkish War.
In *War Is Kind* (1899).
In *Work,* vol. 6 (1926).
In *Poems* (1930).
In *Poetry* (1957).
In *Poems of Stephen Crane* (1966).

BLUE HOTEL
AMs., 1 p., marked "8" in Cora Crane's hand. This is a fragment from the end of the first section of "The Blue Hotel," appearing on verso of the first page of Cora Crane's manuscript, "Peter the Great." On verso of the second page of "Peter the Great" appears a portion of "Death and the Child," also in Cora Crane's hand. CUCC.
Facsimile reproduction of the manuscript in *The Works of Stephen Crane,* ed. Fredson Bowers, vol. V, *Tales of Adventure* (1970). Quoted in Introduction by J. C. Levenson, pp. xcix–c. Joseph Katz describes the manuscript in *SCraneN,* 3 (Fall, 1968), 1–2. Facsimile, p. 3.
Collier's Weekly, 22 (November 26, 1898), 14–16.
Collier's Weekly, 22 (December 3, 1898), 14–16.
In *The Monster and Other Stories.* New York: Harper & Brothers, 1899.
In *The Monster and Other Stories.* London: Harper & Brothers, 1901.
In *Work,* vol. 10 (1926).
Golden Book, 5 (May, 1927), 593–606.
In *Maggie, together with George's Mother and The Blue Hotel.* New York: Alfred A. Knopf, 1931.
Das Blaue Hotel. Berlin: F. A. Herbig (193–?).*
In *Twenty Stories.* New York: Alfred A. Knopf, 1940.
In *Twenty Stories.* Cleveland & New York: World Publishing Company, 1945.
In *Omnibus* (1952).
In *CSS&S* (1963).
In *Stephen Crane: The Blue Hotel.* Columbus, Ohio: Charles E. Merrill Publishing Company, 1969.
In *TA* (1970).

BOTTLES AND BOTTLES AND BOTTLES
TMs., 1 p., poem. CUCC.
In *Poetry* (1957), for the first time.
In *Poems of Stephen Crane* (1966).

---

* As given in *W-S,* p. 87. However, in this bibliography foreign editions of Crane's works are listed in Part F by name of translator.

BOWERY TALES
 London: William Heinemann, 1900. Reprints *George's Mother* and *Maggie*
 with "An Appreciation" by W. D. Howells, which first appeared in Heinemann's 1896 clothbound edition of *Maggie: A Child of the Streets.*
 Consult collation of this title.

BOY AND HIS DOG
 See SMALL BLACK AND WHITE AND TAN HOUND.

BRIDE COMES TO YELLOW SKY
 Chapman's Magazine, 9 (February, 1898), 115–126.
 McClure's Magazine, 10 (February, 1898), 377–384.
 In *The Open Boat and Other Stories.* London: William Heinemann, 1898.*
 In *The Open Boat and Other Tales of Adventure.* New York: Doubleday &
  McClure, 1898.
 In *The Open Boat and Other Tales of Adventure.* New York: Doubleday,
  Page & Co., 1905.
 Golden Book, 5 (April, 1927), 437–442.
 In *Work,* vol. 12 (1927).
 In *Twenty Stories.* New York: Alfred A. Knopf, 1940.
 In *Twenty Stories.* Cleveland & New York: World Publishing Company, 1945.
 In *The American West.* Cleveland & New York: World Publishing Company,
  1946.
 In *Omnibus* (1952).
 In *CSS&S* (1963).
 In *TA* (1970).

BRIEF CAMPAIGN AGAINST NEW ORLEANS
 Lippincott's Magazine, 65 (March, 1900), 405–411.
 In *Great Battles of the World.* London: Chapman & Hall Limited, 1901.
 In *Great Battles of the World.* Philadelphia: J. B. Lippincott Company, 1901.
 In *Great Battles of the World.* London: Hodder & Stoughton, 1914.

BROKEN-DOWN VAN
 See TRAVELS IN NEW YORK: THE BROKEN-DOWN VAN.

CAGED WITH A WILD MAN
 See FREIGHT CAR INCIDENT.

CAMEL
 TMs., 3 pp. BCC. TMs., 3 pp., copy. CUCC†
 Exhibition, p. 55, errs: "Typescript 2 pp." The CUCC catalogue rightly
 lists it as TMs., 3 pp. Cora Crane submitted "The Camel" for publication
 after Crane's death, but she did not succeed in placing it.
 In *CSS&S* (1963).
 See SinSF, 1, no. 2 (Winter, 1963–1964), 147–148.

---

 * Crane wrote Paul Reynolds that *Illustrated Bits* "plagiarized 'The Bride
Comes to Yellow Sky.'" *See Letters,* p. 188.
 † The typescript in BCC was originally in the BCCC. Mr. Collamore granted
me copies of his Crane materials in the early 1950s. However, "The Camel" and
many other writings by Crane, including typescripts by Edith Crane, did not seem
worth publishing at that time when strategically the all-important thing was to
make known the best of Crane and not to damage his reputation by unpublished
first drafts such as "The Camel," a humorous but trivial thing.

CANTHARIDES

Unpublished. A lost collection of erotic verses.

CAPTAIN

New York Tribune, August 7, 1892, part 2, p. 19 [unsigned].
In *CSS&S* (1963).
In *UW* (1963).

CAPTURED MAUSERS FOR VOLUNTEERS

New York World, July 17, 1898, p. 17. Appearing on same p. is Frank Norris,
"Comida: An Experience in Famine."
Philadelphia Press, July 17, 1898, p. 3. "Hard to Fight / an Unseen Foe /
Stephen Crane on Disadvan- / tages of Springfields Com- / pared with
Mauser Rifles." Contains two paragraphs not in *New York World*.
In *UW* (1963); reprints *New York World*.
In *War Dispatches* (1964); reprints *New York World*.

CARRIAGE-LAMPS

Harper's Magazine, 100 (February, 1900), 366–372.
In *Whilomville Stories*. New York: Harper & Brothers, 1900.
In *Whilomville Stories*. London: Harper & Brothers, 1900.
In *Mark Twain's Library of Humor: The Primrose Way*. New York and
London, 1906, pp. 149–165.
In *Work*, vol. 5 (1926).
In *Twenty Stories*. New York: Alfred A. Knopf, 1940.
In *Twenty Stories*. Cleveland & New York: World Publishing Company, 1945.
In *CSS&S* (1963).
In *TWH* (1969).

CAT'S MARCH

A lost tale written in Cuba and typed by Acton Davies. It is interesting to
know that the story was about the artist's model in *The Third Violet*. It
appears that she married "Pennoyer" and settled down with him in a
small town, where the respectable women gave her a bad time of it. Manuscript said to have been destroyed.
See Beer's *SC* (1923).

CHANT YOU LOUD OF PUNISHMENTS

AMs., 1 p., poem. TMs., 1 p. CUCC.
Bookman, 69 (April, 1929), 122.
In *Poems* (1930); reprinted from *Bookman*.
In *Poetry* (1957).
In *Poems of Stephen Crane* (1966).
See THREE POEMS.

CHARITY IN THE SLUMS

Unpublished Crane essay which Elbert Hubbard bought for his *Philistine*
but never published.
See Beer's *SC* (1923) pp, 110–111.

CHASED BY A BIG SPANISH MAN-O-WAR

New York World, July 3, 1898, Supplement, p. 4.
In *UW* (1963).
In *War Dispatches* (1964).

CHATTER OF A DEATH-DEMON FROM A TREE-TOP

TMs., 1 p., poem. CUCC.

Philistine, 1 (August, 1895), 93.
Roycroft Quarterly, 1 (May, 1896), 28.
In *War Is Kind* (1899). Omits the line: "Lift your grey face!"
Fra, 3, no. 2 (November, 1909), 56.
In *A Roycroft Anthology*. East Aurora, N.Y.: The Roycrofters, 1917, p. 102.
In *Work*, vol. 6 (1926).
In *Poems* (1930).
In *Poetry* (1957).
In *Poems of Stephen Crane* (1966).

CRANE'S CARDTABLE COVER
Holograph Ms., cardtable cover on which Crane doodled while keeping score
at a game of cards. BCC.
See STEPHEN CRANE, STEPHEN CRANE, CHAUNCEY DEPEW.

CHRISTMAS DINNER WON IN BATTLE
Page proof, 2 pp., corrections in Cora Crane's hand. CUCC. (The proof is
for Tillotson's Northern Newspaper Syndicate, England.)
Plumber's Trade Journal, 17 (January 1, 1895), 26–27.
In *CSS&S* (1963).
In *UW* (1963).
In *NYCS* (1966).

CITY OF MEXICO
Three AMsS., 4 pp. each; untitled. CUCC.
First published in *Bulletin*, 71 (November, 1967), 554–562. "Three Mexican
Sketches." Each sketch is datelined "City of Mexico." No. 1 begins: "The
main streets of this city. . . ." No. 2 begins: "The Viga canal. . . ." No. 3
begins: "Above all things, the stranger finds. . . ."*

CITY URCHIN AND THE CHASTE VILLAGERS
AMs., 5 pp., partly in the handwriting of Edith Richie. Crane's hand begins
when the dialogue begins. CUCC. Described in Textual Introduction by
Fredson Bowers, in *The Works of Stephen Crane*, ed. Fredson Bowers, vol.
VII, *Tales of Whilomville* (1969), pp. 124–126.†
Harper's Magazine, 101 (July, 1900), 216–221.
In *Whilomville Stories*. New York: Harper & Brothers, 1900.
In *Whilomville Stories*. London: Harper & Brothers, 1900.
In *Work*, vol. 5 (1926).
In *CSS&S* (1963).
In *TWH* (1969).

CLAN OF NO-NAME
Black and White, Christmas Number, 1899, pp. 13–16.

---

* *See* Bassan, *Stephen Crane's Maggie: Text and Context* (1966), p. 96, which
quotes for the first time one paragraph from one of these three City of Mexico
sketches.
See also Above All Things/By Stephen Crane. Privately printed pamphlet, edited
and published "for the friends of Mr. and Mrs. Joseph Katz, January, 1968." This
pamphlet reprint of City of Mexico, no. 3, makes no acknowledgement of its prior
publication in *Bulletin* (1967), nor of its source in CUCC, nor of the copyright
owner of all Crane manuscripts, Alfred A. Knopf, Inc.
† Bowers quotes this interesting letter of Edith Richie Jones (April 26, 1942), in
Berg Collection, New York Public Library. "Sometimes in a train or outdoors or
in a room he'd say: 'Anyone got a pencil & paper? I've just thought of something.'
Then Cora or I wd write it down & afterwards type it. He rarely altered any of
it but seemed to have it all straight in his mind when he began."

Chicago Times-Herald, March 19, 1899, Sunday Illustrated Section, part 5, pp. 1–2.
New York Herald, March 19, 1899, section 8, p. 2.
San Francisco Examiner, March 19, 1899, Sunday Magazine, p. 29.
In *Wounds in the Rain.* London: Methuen & Co., 1900.
In *Wounds in the Rain.* New York: Frederick A. Stokes Company, 1900.
In *Work,* vol. 2 (1925).
In *CSS&S* (1963).
In *Poems* (1966).
In *TW* (1970).

CONCERNING THE ENGLISH ACADEMY
Bookman, 7 (March, 1898), 22–24.
In *UW* (1963).

CONEY ISLAND'S FAILING DAYS
New York Press, October 14, 1894, part 5, p. 2.
In *CSS&S* (1963).
In *UW* (1963).
In *NYCS* (1966).

CONGRESS
See SESSION OF CONGRESS.

CORPORAL O'CONNOR'S STORY
AMs., 1 p., fragment on verso of a scrap of paper with the title. CUCC.
In *"The Red Badge of Courage" by Stephen Crane: A Facsimile Reproduction of the New York* Press *Appearance of December 9, 1894.* Gainesville, Fla.: Scholars' Facsimiles & Reprints, 1967.

However, this fragment about "Mr. Steele [McG‑‑‑‑‑‑ not legible] fresh from his studies" of "Descarte" provides no internal evidence that this barely legible scrap of paper was Crane's first attempt at *The Red Badge of Courage.* To claim it as such is pure speculation. *Contra* Joseph Katz, Introduction, p. 15.

CRANE AT VELESTINO
See STEPHEN CRANE AT VELESTINO.

CRANE TELLS THE STORY OF THE DISEMBARKMENT
Boston Globe, July 7, 1898, p. 2.
New York World, July 7, 1898, p. 8.
In *UW* (1963).
In *War Dispatches* (1964). *See* note p. 154.

CROWDING INTO ASBURY PARK
New York Tribune, July 3, 1892, p. 28 [unsigned].
In *UW* (1963).

CROWDS AT NEW YORK THEATRE
Lost Crane manuscript mentioned by Cora Crane in letter to Mr. G. H. Perris (August, 1900), in Yale University Library.

CRY OF THE HUCKLEBERRY PUDDING
Syracuse University Herald, 21 (December 23, 1892), 51–54.
Chap Book (Syracuse University literary magazine), 2 (May, 1930), 3–7.
In *SCS* (1949).
In *CSS&S* (1963).
In *SCTS* (1968).

DAN EMMONDS
TMs., 10 pp., incomplete tale. CUCC.
First published in *SinSF*, 1, no. 1 (Fall, 1963), 1–7.
In *CSS&S* (1963).
See Monteiro, "Dan Emmonds: A Case Reargued" (1969).

DARK BROWN DOG
Crane sent this tale to his London agent James B. Pinker in early 1900. It
was written, however, in his New York City days, 1892–1896. Compare
"Dark Brown Dog" with "A Great Mistake."
Cosmopolitan, 30 (March, 1901, 481–486.
In *Men, Women and Boats*. New York: Boni and Liveright, 1921.
In *Work*, vol. 11 (1926).
Golden Book, 12 (December, 1930), 55–57.
In *Maggie, and Other Stories*. New York: The Modern Library, 1933.
Reader's Digest, 30 (May, 1937), 129–132. Abridged.
In *The Fireside Book of Dog Stories*, ed. Jack Goodman. New York: Simon
& Schuster, 1943.
In *The Pace of Youth and Other Stories*. Girard, Kans.: Haldeman-Julius
(n.d.).
In *The Upturned Face and Other Stories*. Girard, Kans.: Haldeman-Julius
(n.d.)
In *CSS&S* (1963).
In *NYCS* (1966).

DEATH AND THE CHILD
AMs., 1 p., marked "3" in Cora Crane's hand. A fragment appearing on verso
of the second page of Cora Crane's review of "Peter the Great," a play
by Lawrence Irving. (On verso of the first page of her review appears a
fragment of a draft of "The Blue Hotel," discovered by Lillian Gilkes.)
CUCC.
   Facsimile reproduction of the manuscript in *The Works of Stephen Crane*,
ed. Fredson Bowers, vol. V, *Tales of Adventure* (1970). Quoted in Intro-
duction by J. C. Levenson, pp. lxxviii–lxxx. *See SCraneN*, 3 (Spring,
1969), 1–2.
Black and White (London), 15 (March 5, 1898), 332–334; 15 (March 12, 1898),
368–370. "The Death and the Child."
Harper's Weekly, 42, (March 19, 1898), 281–282; (March 26, 1898), 297–298.
In *The Open Boat and Other Stories*. London: William Heinemann, 1898.
In *The Open Boat and Other Tales of Adventure*. New York: Doubleday
& McClure, 1898.
In *The Open Boat and Other Tales of Adventure*. New York: Doubleday,
Page & Co., 1905.
In *Work*, vol. 12 (1927).
In *Twenty Stories*. New York: Alfred A. Knopf, 1940.
In *Twenty Stories*. Cleveland and New York: World Publishing Company,
1945.
In *CSS&S* (1963).
In *War Dispatches* (1964).
SCraneN, 3, no. 3 (Spring, 1969), 1, 2. Reproduces the cancelled holograph
Ms., 1 p., from CUCC.

DENIES MUTILATION OF BODIES. ONLY MUTILATED BY BULLETS.
Signed.*

Boston Globe, June 16, 1898, p. 5.
Philadelphia Press, June 17, 1898, p. 2.
In RW (1971). "Only Mutilated by Bullets."

DESERTION

TMsS., 5 pp., with autograph corrections. BCC. Not to be confused with "A Desertion," title of a manuscript in SCC.

Harper's Magazine, 101 (November, 1900), 938–939.
In Last Words. London: Digby, Long & Co., 1902.
In Men, Women and Boats. New York: Boni and Liveright, 1921.
In Work, vol. 11 (1926).
In Maggie, and Other Stories. New York: The Modern Library, 1933.
In The Upturned Face and Other Stories. Girard, Kans.: Haldeman-Julius (n.d.).
In CSS&S (1963).
In NYCS (1966).
In Notebook (1969). Four pages of an early draft appear in Crane's notebook in BCC.

A DESERTION

Holograph Ms., 2 pp. SCC.
First published in NYCS (1966).

DESTROYERS, ETC.

An., 6 pp., notes on warships. CUCC.
These notes on torpedo boats, which form the basis of ASSASSINS IN MODERN BATTLES are published in RW (1971), pp. 513–514.

DETAIL

AMs., an early draft, 7 pp., owned by Melvin H. Schoberlin.
Buffalo Evening News, August 30, 1896, p. 9.
Dallas Morning News, August 30, 1896, p. 16.
Nebraska State Journal, August 30, 1896, p. 10.
Chicago Daily News, August 31, 1896, p. 8.
Pocket Magazine, 2 (November, 1896), 145–148.
In The Open Boat and Other Stories. London: William Heinemann, 1898.
In Best Things from American Literature. New York: The Christian Herald, 1899.
Academy, 58 (June 9, 1900), 491. Quotes from "A Detail."
In Work, vol. 11 (1926).
In CSS&S (1963).
In NYCS (1966).

DEVIL'S ACRE

New York World, October 25, 1896, p. 23.
In UW (1963).
In NYCS (1966).

DIAMONDS AND DIAMONDS

TMs., 6 pp., with autograph corrections. BCC.
The typescript was done on sheets—watermarked "Indian Colonial"—measuring 12 13/16 × 7 7/8 in. The sheets are ruled vertically by lines

* This corrects War Dispatches, p. 160.

spaced 1 1/16 in. apart. It was typed by Cora Crane during Crane's last years in England. Cora typed it on their newly purchased typewriter—purchased on credit.

First published in *Bulletin*, 60 (October, 1956), 482–486.

In *CSS&S* (1963).*

In *NYCS* (1966).

DOGS OF WAR

New York Journal, May 30, 1897, p. 18.

San Francisco Examiner, June 13, 1897, p. 4.

In *UW* (1963); reprints *New York Journal*.

In *War Dispatches* (1964); reprints *New York Journal*.

DO NOT WEEP, MAIDEN, FOR WAR IS KIND

AMs., 1 p., poem, unsigned, dated 1895. On recto of third leaf of his *The Red Badge of Courage* presented to William Dean Howells and misdating it in 1896. BC. Inscribed: "To W. D. Howells this small and belated book as a token of the veneration and gratitude of Stephen Crane for many things he has learned of the common man and, above all, for a certain re-adjustment of his point of view victoriously concluded some time in 1892. August 17, 1895." TMs., 1 p., title poem of *War Is Kind*. CUCC. A reproduced holograph, 1 p. SCC.

See HOARSE BOOMING DRUMS.

Bookman, 2 (February, 1896), 476. Reprinted in *Literary Digest* and *Public Opinion*.

Chicago Times Herald, February 9, 1896, p. 4.

Public Opinion, 20 (February 27, 1896), 277.

Literary Digest, 12 (February 29, 1896), 520.

In *Bookman*, 9 (July, 1899), 400. Holograph Ms. in facsimile, titled "Lines."

In *War Is Kind* (1899).

In *Work*, vol. 6 (1926).

In *Poems* (1930).

In *Poetry* (1957).

In *Poems of Stephen Crane* (1966).

DORA CLARK ("ADVENTURES OF A NOVELIST")

TMs., 6 pp., with autograph corrections; leaf 5 is wanting and leaves 1 and 3 are mutilated; untitled. Crane does not name the girl, and he describes himself as a "reluctant laggard witness." BCC.

Crane's own account of the Dora Clark affair, which was published as "Adventures of a Novelist." *New York Journal*, September 20, 1896, pp. 17–18.

Bulletin, 60 (October, 1956), 478. Describes the typescript, but errs in calling the untitled TMs. "Dora Clark," since it is "Adventures of a Novelist."

In *UW* (1963).

In *NYCS* (1966).

DOWN IN A COAL MINE

See IN THE DEPTHS OF A COAL MINE.

DRAMA IN CUBA

TMs., 31 pp. (2 acts, 4 scenes), an incomplete Spanish-American War play. TMs., 12 pp., first act only. CUCC.

* No acknowledgement is made by Thomas A. Gullason here to its first publication in *Bulletin* (1956).

First published in *Bulletin*, 67 (October, 1963), 498–511.
In *War Dispatches* (1964).

THE DRESS OF OLD MEXICO
See HATS, SHIRTS AND SPURS IN MEXICO.

DUEL THAT WAS NOT FOUGHT
Holograph Ms. in Notebook of Stephen Crane. Incomplete draft, 8 pp. BCC.
New York Press, December 9, 1894, part 3, p. 2.
In *The Open Boat and Other Stories*. London: William Heinemann, 1898.
In *Men, Women and Boats*. New York: Boni and Liveright, 1921.
In *Work*, vol. 11 (1926).
In *Maggie, and Other Stories*. New York: The Modern Library, 1933.
In *The Upturned Face and Other Stories*. Girard, Kans.: Haldeman-Julius
(n.d.).
In *CSS&S* (1963).
In *NYCS* (1966).
In *Notebook* (1969).

EACH SMALL GLEAM WAS A VOICE
TMs., 1 p., poem. CUCC.
Philistine, 1 (September, 1895), 124.
Roycroft Quarterly, 1 (May, 1896), 28.
In *War Is Kind* (1899).
Fra, 3, no. 5 (August, 1909), 121.
In *Roycroft Anthology*. East Aurora, N.Y.: The Roycrofters, 1917, p. 86.
In *Work*, vol. 6 (1926).
In *Poems* (1930).
In *Poetry* (1957).
In *Poems of Stephen Crane* (1966).

EASTERN QUESTION
Holograph Ms., untitled, 6 pp. of which the first and most of the second are
in Cora Crane's hand, Crane taking over at the sentence: "And yet it puts
to flight the brains of Europe." CUCC. At top of first sheet the figure 2000
(representing wordage) is encircled, and underlined is the phrase "not
used."
First reproduced in *War Dispatches* (1964).

ELLA FLOCK
New York Tribune, August 21, 1892, pp. 29–30.
Crane's report of a piano concert by Miss Ella L. Flock appears in a paragraph expunged from the reprint of "On the New Jersey Coast" in *NYCS*
(1966), pp. 272–273. The lost paragraph is rediscovered by Fredson Bowers
(1970–71).

ELOQUENCE OF GRIEF
AMs., 2 pp., story of a girl arrested for stealing, fragment of Crane's draft of
"An Eloquence of Grief." (On verso is "Notes about Prostitutes.") BCC,
listed as "Story of a Girl Arrested for Stealing."
In *The Open Boat and Other Stories*. London: William Heinemann, 1898.
In *Work*, vol. 11 (1926).
In *CSS&S* (1963).

First published in *NYCS* (1966), "An Eloquence of Grief" and "Story of a Girl Arrested for Stealing," p. 261, untitled.

END OF THE BATTLE
See "AND IF HE WILLS, WE MUST DIE."

EPISODE OF WAR
TMs., 5 pp. with corrections in an unidentified hand. BCC. Titled "The Loss of an Arm" in Crane's holograph list of some of his writings; in CUCC. Since no entry in Crane's list is later than "The Man in the White Hat," in *Westminster Gazette* (1897), it follows that "An Episode of War" was written prior to the Cuban War (1898) and is in fact a Civil War story.*
Gentlewoman (London), Christmas, 1899, pp. 24–25.
In *Last Words.* London: Digby, Long & Co., 1902.
In *Men, Women and Boats.* New York: Boni and Liveright, 1921.
In *Work,* vol. 9 (1926).
In *Maggie, and Other Stories.* New York: The Modern Library, 1933.
In *Twenty Stories.* New York: Alfred A. Knopf, 1940.
In *Twenty Stories.* Cleveland & New York: World Publishing Company, 1945.
In *The Upturned Face and Other Stories.* Girard, Kans.: Haldeman-Julius (n.d.).
In *Omnibus* (1952).
In *CSS&S* (1963).
In *TW* (1970).

ETERNAL PATIENCE
See THE THIRD VIOLET.

EUROPEAN GOSSIP OF DRESS AND SPORT
New York Press, August 22, 1897.
See Cora Crane (1960), p. 117. Written jointly Crane and Cora.

EVENING ON THE ROOF
Galley proof, 1 p. BCC.
Cincinnati Commercial Tribune, August 9, 1896, p. 18. "The Roof Garden."
Denver Republican, August 9, 1896, p. 21. "Roof Gardens of New York."
Omaha Daily Bee, August 9, 1896, p. 13. "Queer Side of New York Life."
Pittsburgh Leader, August 9, 1896, p. 20. "The Roof Gardens."
Portland Oregonian, August 9, 1896, p. 16. "Roof Gardens of New York."
Washington Post, August 9, 1896, p. 20. Not titled "Roof Gardens" as given in *W-S Bibliography,* p. 118. Titled "Evening On the Roof."
In *Last Words.* London: Digby, Long & Co., 1902. "Roof Gardens and Gardeners of New York." Same title in galley proof, BCC.
In *NYCS* (1966). "Evening on the Roof."

EXCURSION TICKET
Page proof, 3 pp., with corrections in Crane's hand. CUCC. This is BILLIE ATKINS WENT TO OMAHA.

EXPERIMENT IN LUXURY
New York Press, April 29, 1894, part 3, p. 2.
In *CSS&S* (1963).

---

* I am here indebted to Prof. Fredson Bowers (letter to R. W. S., Summer, 1970). The above note corrects *Omnibus,* and *Crane,* and all anthologies and textbooks reprinting "An Episode of War," including *CSS&S* (1963) and *The Portable Stephen Crane* (1969). *See TW* (1970).

In *UW* (1963).

In *NYCS* (1966).

EXPERIMENT IN MISERY

New York Press, April 22, 1894, part 3, p. 2.

In *The Open Boat and Other Stories*. London: William Heinemann, 1898.

In *Men, Women and Boats*. New York: Boni and Liveright, 1921.

In *Work*, vol. 11 (1926).

In *Maggie, and Other Stories*. New York: The Modern Library, 1933.

In *Twenty Stories*. New York: Alfred A. Knopf, 1940.

In *Twenty Stories*. Cleveland & New York: World Publishing Company, 1945.

In *The Upturned Face and Other Stories*. Girard, Kans.: Haldeman-Julius, (n.d.).

In *Omnibus* (1952). Reprints for the first time the opening and closing passages appearing in the *New York Press* version, where this tale had a different beginning and ending. See *Omnibus*, pp. 31, 42.

In *CSS&S* (1963). The text is not that of the *New York Press*, although it claims to be so.

In *NYCS* (1966). Reprints the complete version of the *New York Press* text.

EXPLOSION OF SEVEN BABIES: A SULLIVAN COUNTY SKETCH

AMsS., 8 pp. BCC. (Title as given above.) TMs., 8 pp. CUCC. Photocopy of holograph Ms. BC.

Home Magazine, 16 (January, 1901), 75–80. "Sullivan County Episode: An Explosion of Seven Babies."

In *SCS* (1949).

In *CSS&S* (1963).

In *SCTS* (1968).

FAST RODE THE KNIGHT

Holograph, 1 p., poem [signed "Stephen Crane"]. SCC. TMs., 1 p. CUCC. *Roycroft Quarterly*, May, 1896, p. 33.

Philistine, 3 (June, 1896), 20.

In *War Is Kind* (1899).

In *Work*, vol. 6 (1926).

In *Poems* (1930).

In *Poetry* (1957).

In *Poems of Stephen Crane* (1966).

FEARS REALISTS MUST WAIT

See HOWELLS FEARS REALISTS MUST WAIT.

FIGHT

AMsS., 8 pp. CUCC.

Harper's Magazine, 101 (June, 1900), 56–63.

In *Whilomville Stories*. New York: Harper & Brothers, 1900.

In *Whilomville Stories*. London: Harper & Brothers, 1900.

Everybody's Magazine, 55 (October, 1926), 104–109.

In *Work*, vol. 5 (1926).

In *CSS&S* (1963).

In *TWH* (1969).

FILIBUSTERING

Denver Republican, May 2, 1897, p. 21. "The Filibustering Industry."

Pittsburgh Leader, May 2, 1897, p. 24.

St. Paul Pioneer Press, May 3, 1897, p. 3. "The Filibustering Industry."

Prairie Schooner, 43 (Fall, 1969), 287–292.

In *RW* (1971).

FIRE

See WHEN EVERY ONE IS PANIC STRICKEN.

FIRE TRIBE AND THE PALEFACE

AMs., 6 pp., dramatization of chapter 3 of the story of the same name. CUCC. Unpublished (1970).

FIRE TRIBE AND THE WHITE-FACE (a Spitzbergen story)

TMs., 16 pp., incomplete carbon copy (pp. 6–21). TMs., 27 pp., with photostats. TMs., 14 pp. AMsS., 15 pp., with pages 11–14 in Cora Crane's hand. CUCC. Unpublished (1970). Only this version is listed in *Exhibition*, p. 55.

FIRS

No information available.

FISHERMEN

TMs., 8 pp. BCC. Cora's typescript made from an early version of "the Octopush."

FISHING VILLAGE

TMs., 2 pp. BCC.

Westminster Gazette, November 12, 1897, pp. 1–2.

Westminster Budget, 10 (November 19, 1897), 13.

Philistine, 9 (August, 1899), 71–77.

In *Last Words*. London: Digby, Long & Co., 1902.

In *Work*, vol. 11 (1926).

In *CSS&S* (1963).

FIVE WHITE MICE

Holograph Ms., printer's copy, in Huntington Library.*

Facsimile reproduction of the first page of Crane's manuscript in *The Works of Stephen Crane*, ed. Fredson Bowers, vol. V, *Tales of Adventure* (1970), p. xiv.

New York World, April 10, 1898, Sunday Supplement, p. 32.

In *The Open Boat and Other Stories*. London: William Heinemann, 1898.

In *The Open Boat and Other Tales of Adventure*. New York: Doubleday & McClure, 1898.

In *The Windmill*, edited by L. Callender. London: William Heinemann, Ltd., 1923.

In *Work*, vol. 12 (1927).

In *Twenty Stories*. New York: Alfred A. Knopf, 1940.

In *Twenty Stories*. Cleveland & New York: World Publishing Company, 1945.

In *CSS&S* (1963).

FLANAGAN AND HIS SHORT FILIBUSTERING ADVENTURE

Illustrated London News, 111 (August 28, 1897), 279–282.

McClure's Magazine, 9 (October, 1897), 1045–1052.

---

* Crane gave the manuscript to Joseph Conrad. *See Letters*, pp. 176–177. It was acquired by John Quinn in 1912 and is now in the Henry E. Huntington Library.

In *The Open Boat and Other Stories*. London: William Heinemann, 1898.
In *The Open Boat and Other Tales of Adventure*. New York: Doubleday & McClure, 1898.
In *The Open Boat and Other Tales of Adventure*. New York: Doubleday, Page & Co., 1905.
In *Work*, vol. 12 (1927).
In *CSS&S* (1963).

FLOWERS IN ASPHALT

A novel begun in October, 1898, according to James Huneker, which was to have been "longer than anything he had done." The story was that of a boy prostitute. Manuscript untraced.

A FLURRY OF CONDENSED MILK

AMs., 3 pp., Sullivan County sketch, incomplete. CUCC. Unpublished (1970).

FOLLOWERS OF WAR

See GREEK WAR CORRESPONDENTS.

A FOREIGN POLICY, IN THREE GLIMPSES

Typescript, 6 pp., by Edith Crane from the holograph Ms. of 17 leaves of heavy, unlined yellow paper measuring 7×9 in. Holograph Ms. in BCC (acquired 1961). Not listed in BCC catalogue. *W-S Bibliography* lists it erroneously as " 'A Foreign Policy in Two Glimpses.' Unpublished. An essay written while Crane was a student at Syracuse University." The BCC's list of manuscripts (dated November 20, 1969) claims "A Foreign Policy in Three Glimpses" to be unpublished, whereas almost every one of the Crane titles so listed as unpublished has appeared in print, most of them a decade ago.

First published in *Bulletin*, 61 (January, 1957), 43–46.
In *CSS&S* (1963).*

FORTH WENT THE CANDID MAN

AMs., 1 p. TMs., 1 p., poem. CUCC.
In *Work*, vol. 6 (1926).
In *Poems* (1930).
In *Poetry* (1957).
In *Poems of Stephen Crane* (1966).

FOUR MEN IN A CAVE

AMs., 4 pp., first draft of a Sullivan County tale (incomplete). CUCC. TMsS., with unidentified autograph corrections, 7 pp. BCC. Subtitled: "Likewise Four Queens, and a Sullivan County Hermit," the early draft locates the game of poker in the woods, not in the cave.
New York Tribune, July 3, 1892, part 2, p. 14.
In *Last Words*. London: Digby, Long & Co., 1902.
In *Men, Women and Boats*. New York: Boni and Liveright, 1921.
In *Work*, vol. 11 (1926).
In *Maggie, and Other Stories*. New York: The Modern Library, 1933.
In *The Pace of Youth and Other Stories*. Girard, Kans.: Haldeman-Julius (n.d.).
In *SCS* (1949).
In *CSS&S* (1963).
Readers and Writers, 1 (April–May, 1967), 30–31.
In *SCTS* (1968).

* In which no mention is made of its prior publication in *Bulletin*.

FOUR OF OUR MEN
  See IN THE FIRST LAND FIGHT 4 OF OUR MEN ARE KILLED.

FRAGMENT OF VELESTINO (FROM "WITH GREEK AND TURK")
  Westminster Gazette (London), June 3, 4, 8, 1897, pp. 1–2 in each issue. Not datelined.
  New York Journal, June 13, 1897, pp. 24–25. "That was the Romance, / This is the / Reality, / The Battle To-day in Greece / —a Fact. / by / Stephen Crane."
  San Francisco Examiner, June 27, 1897, p. 21. "That was the Romance: 'The Red Badge of Courage.' / This is the Reality: A Battle of To-Day in Greece. / By Stephen Crane."
  New York Journal, October 15, 1899, p. 25. "France's Would-Be Hero."
  San Francisco Examiner, October 15, 1899, p. 15.
  In *Battle in Greece.* Mount Vernon, N. Y.: Peter Pauper Press, 1936.
  In *UW* (1963); reprints *New York Journal* under headline "A Battle in Greece."
  In *War Dispatches* (1964); reprints *Westminster Gazette* under headline "A Fragment of Velestino." Here the portions omitted from *New York Journal* are indicated in *War Dispatches'* text of *Westminster Gazette* by the device of brackets.

FREE SILVER DOWN IN MEXICO
  Cincinnati Commercial Tribune, June 30, 1895, p. 9. "Wages and Living in Free Silver Mexico."
  Dallas Morning News, June 30, 1895, p. 12. "Free Silver Mexico."
  Minneapolis Tribune, June 30, 1895, p. 4. "The Land of Free Silver."
  Nebraska State Journal, June 30, 1895, p. 13. "In Free Silver Mexico."
  Philadelphia Press, June 30, 1895, p. 31.
  Galveston Daily News, July 1, 1895, p. 4. "Free Silver Mexico."
  Semi-Weekly State Journal (Nebraska), July 5, 1895, p. 7. "In Free Silver Mexico."
  Chicago Daily News, July 23, 1895, p. 2. "In Free Silver Mexico."
  In *UW* (1963).

FREIGHT CAR INCIDENT
  TMsS., 5 p., titled "An Auction Sale of Real Estate in Texas, U.S.A." (story). CUCC.
  Corrected proof. CUCC.
  Brooklyn Daily Eagle, April 12, 1896, p. 19.
  Buffalo Sunday News, April 12, 1896, p. 9.
  Louisville Courier-Journal, April 12, 1896, section 3, p. 8.
  Nebraska State Journal, April 12, 1896, p. 11.
  St. Louis Globe-Democrat, April 12, 1896, p. 41.
  Rochester Democrat and Chronicle, April 12, 1896, p. 16.
  Philadelphia Press, April 19, 1896, 37. "Caged With a Wild Man."
  English Illustrated Magazine, 15 (June, 1896), 273–275. "A Texan Legend."
  In *CSS&S* (1963).
  In *UW* (1963). "Caged With a Wild Man."

FRESH BITS OF GOSSIP ON EUROPEAN AFFAIRS
  Cora's Ms. CUCC.
  New York Press, August 15, 1897, p. 23.

GALVESTON, TEXAS, IN 1895
Westminster Gazette, November 6, 1900, pp. 1–2.
Westminster Budget, November 16, 1900, p. 22. A shortened version.
In *UW* (1963).

GAY BATHING SUIT AND NOVEL BOTH MUST GO
New York Tribune, August 5, 1888 [unsigned].

GEORGE'S MOTHER
AMs., 2 pp., written on versos of the fifth and sixth leaves of the Sullivan County sketch, "The Holler Tree." Appearing also on versos of same manuscript is the first draft of "The Reluctant Voyagers," not noticed by Maurice Bassan in his discovery of the early draft of the opening of *George's Mother. See* his "An Early Draft of *George's Mother," American Literature,* 36 (January, 1965), 518–522. BCC.

Facsimile reproduction of the manuscripts of *George's Mother* in *The Works of Stephen Crane,* ed. Fredson Bowers, vol. I, *Bowery Tales* (1969). Quoted in diplomatic reprint in Textual Introduction by Fredson Bowers, pp. 111–112.

Prior to publication *George's Mother* was tentatively titled "A Woman Without Weapons." John Berryman (1950) confounded "Dan Emmonds" with *George's Mother. See Crane* (1968), chap. 12 and note 6, p. 585; also, on "The Holler Tree" and "The Reluctant Voyagers," *see* p. 210.

London: Edward Arnold, 1896.
New York: Edward Arnold, 1896.
In *Bowery Tales.* London: William Heinemann, 1900.
In *Work,* vol. 10 (1926).
In *Maggie together with George's Mother and The Blue Hotel.* New York: Alfred A. Knopf, 1931.
In *Omnibus* (1952).
In *The Complete Novels of Stephen Crane.* Garden City: Doubleday & Company, 1967.

GHOST
"Play supposedly written in collaboration with Joseph Conrad and others. Unpublished and manuscript probably lost." *W-S Bibliography,* p. 97.

AMs., 3 pp., by an unknown hand; TMs., 2 pp.* All in all, five pages, of which p. 3 is in Cora Crane's hand. CUCC. Typescript, 7 pp. BC. Holograph Ms., 1 p., in Cora Crane's Scrapbook. BCC. Formerly owned by Mr. Roger Frewen of Brede Place.
See Hoffman, "An Unwritten Life of Stephen Crane" (1953).

In *Letters,* pp. 246–247. "Manuscript Page of 'The Ghost,' " in Crane's hand, here published for the first time, by courtesy of Mr. Roger Frewen of Brede Place.† In *Crane,* p. 557.

Printed program of "The Ghost" is in CUCC. It is signed by Robert Barr, Edwin Pugh, H. G. Wells, Joseph Conrad, Henry James, E. E. Mason, H. B. Marriott-Watson, and Stephen Crane. An unsigned copy of the printed program is in BC.

* As given in CUCC catlogue. Facsimile of the first page of the printed program appeared in *Academy* (London), January 6, 1900.

† For writings *about* the play *see* " 'The Ghost' at Brede Place," in *Letters,* pp. 244–247. Also, pp. 258–259, note 6. *See also* John D. Gordan, "The Ghost at Brede Place" (1952); *Columbia University Columns,* February, 1953; *Exhibition* (1956), p. 48; R. W. Stallman, "Stephen Crane: Some New Stories (Part III)," *Bulletin* (1957); Gilkes' *Cora Crane* (1960); *Crane* (1968), pp. 556–57.

GHOSTLY SPHINX OF METEDECONK
New York Press, January 13, 1895, part 5, p. 1 [unsigned].*
Proceedings of the New Jersey Historical Society, 71 (October, 1953), 239–253.
In *UW* (1963).

GHOSTS ON THE JERSEY COAST
Press clipping in Crane's Scrapboook. CUCC.†
New York Press, November 11, 1894, part 4, p. 2.
Proceedings of the New Jersey Historical Society, 71 (October, 1953), 239–253.
In *UW* (1963).

GHOUL'S ACCOUNTANT
New York Tribune, July 17, 1892, part 2, p. 17.
In *SCS* (1949).
In *CSS&S* (1963).
In *SCTS* (1968).

GOD CAME TO A MAN
AMs., 3 pp., poem. On verso of p. 2 is an expense account in Crane's hand.
TMs., 2 pp. CUCC. TMs. and carbon typescripts of holograph from CUCC
in SCC.
In *Poetry* (1957).
In *Poems of Stephen Crane* (1966).

GOD REST YE, MERRY GENTLEMEN
New York Herald, March 19, 1899.
Cornhill Magazine, 79 (May, 1899), 577–592.
Saturday Evening Post, 171 (May 6, 1899), 705–707.
In *Wounds in the Rain.* London: Methuen & Co., 1900.
In *Work,* vol. 9 (1926).
In *CSS&S* (1963).
In *TW* (1970).

GRAND OPERA IN NEW ORLEANS
Dallas Morning News, March 24, 1895, p. 16. "A Century of Music."
Minneapolis Tribune, March 24, 1895, p. 17. "Unique: Music With a History
of More Than a Hundred Years."
Nebraska State Journal, March 24, 1895, p. 11. "Opera in New Orleans."
Philadelphia Press, March 24, 1895, part 3, p. 25.
Rochester Democrat Chronicle, March 24, 1895, p. 10.
Galveston Daily News, March 25, 1895, p. 4. "A Century of Music."
Public Opinion, 18 (July 4, 1895), 770. "Grand Opera for the People."
In *UW* (1963).
See *Papers of the Bibliographical Society of America,* 63 (First Quarter, 1969),
29–30; 65 (First Quarter, 1971), 70–72.

GRAND RAPIDS AND PONCE
New York Journal, August 17, 1897, p. 4.
Kansas City Star, August 21, 1898, p. 5. "The Wonders of Ponce."
SCraneN, 4 (Fall, 1969), 1–3. "The Wonders of Ponce."
In *RW* (1971).

* Some error exists in the above *New York Press* pagination, according to New
York Public Library.
† In *Exhibition* (1956), mistitled "Ghosts on the New Jersey Coast."

GRATITUDE OF A NATION

AMs., 5 pp., with the poem appended to this sketch, "A soldier young in years, young in ambitions." CUCC.

In *The Red Badge of Courage and Other Stories.* New York: Harper & Brothers, 1957. The poem is lacking.

In *Poems of Stephen Crane* (1966). The prose article with the preface poem.

GRAVEYARD IN APACHÉ CROSSING

AMs., 4 pp., incomplete. CUCC.

First published in *Prairie Schooner,* 43 (Summer, 1969), 184–186. "Stephen Crane's 'Apaché Crossing': The Text of an Unfinished Story." With a "Note on 'Apaché Crossing,'" p. 186, by R. W. Stallman.

GREAT BATTLES OF THE WORLD

Researched by Kate Lyon, Harold Frederic's common-law wife. She also wrote most of the sketches.

London: Chapman & Hall Limited, 1901.

Philadelphia: J. B. Lippincott Company, 1901.

London: Hodder & Stoughton, 1914.

Not included in *Work,* vols. 1–12 (1925–1927).

GREAT BOER TREK

Holograph Ms. In collection of Charles Feinberg, Detroit, Mich. TMsS., 15 pp., with autograph corrections. BCC.

Cosmopolitan, 29 (June, 1900), 153–158.

In *Et Cetera: A Collector's Scrap-Book.* Chicago: Pascal Covici, 1924.

In *UW* (1963).

In *War Dispatches* (1964).

GREAT BUGS IN ONANDAGA

New York Tribune, June 1, 1891, p. 1 [unsigned].

Syracuse Standard, June 1, 1891. "Huge Electric Light Bugs. / What a Wild-Eyed Patriot from the Sand Hills Thought He Saw." Quotes the first half of the sketch in quotation marks word for word (except for several small variations).

Courier, 3 (March, 1963), 1–3. "The Iron Monster, the Crackling Insects of Onondaga County, and Stephen Crane," by Lester G. Wells. However, no mention is here made that this journalistic hoax of Crane was discovered by Ames W. Williams. He omitted it from *Stephen Crane: A Bibliography* (1948) "because he had no proof of authorship."*

In *UW* (1963).

In *Great Bugs in Ononadaga / By Stephen Crane.* Syracuse: Syracuse University Library Associates, 1964. A pamphlet, ed. John S. Mayfield, combining related materials in *Courier* for March and September, 1963.

In *NYCS* (1966), Preface, pp. xiv–xvi. Misdated 18 June 1891, with no acknowledgement to *Courier* for March, 1963, because the discoverer—Ames W. Williams—was not here announced by Lester G. Wells. No acknowledgement to *Courier* for March, 1963, is made in *UW* (1963).

GREAT GRIEF'S HOLIDAY DINNER

TMsS., 10 pp., signed with S. C.'s name by Cora Crane. BCC.

New York Press, October 28, 1894, part 4, p. 6 [unsigned]. "Stories Told by

---

* See *Poetry* (1957), p. 147n.

an Artist." The scene is the Art Students' League Building. Corinson is re-
cast from the now familiar Corwin Knapp Linson. Great Grief is Stephen
Crane, lying on the bed in Linson's studio (as photographed in Linson's *My
Stephen Crane,* 1958), smoking his pipe and "waiting for fame." "In a
Park Row Restaurant" appeared in the same issue of the *New York Press.*
In *Last Words.* London: Digby, Long & Co., 1902.
In *CSS&S* (1963).
In *NYCS* (1966). *See* note, p. 76.

GREAT MISTAKE

Philistine, 2 (March, 1896), 106–109.
Roycroft Quarterly, 1 (May, 1896), 34–37.
In *The Open Boat and Other Stories.* London: William Heinemann, 1898.
Fra, 3 (September, 1909), 151.
In *Work,* vol. 11 (1926).
In *CSS&S* (1963).
In *NYCS* (1966).

THE GRECO-TURKISH PROBLEM

AMsS., 6 pp., untitled and unpublished news article begun by Cora Crane
and finished by Stephen. Marked "Not used." CUCC.

GREED RAMPANT

TMs., 6 pp., on back side of press dispatch paper (measuring $8 \times 10\frac{1}{2}$ in.),
signed in Crane's hand. From the TMs. by Edith Crane in BCC. Unpub-
lished. Holograph Ms. (acquired 1961) in BCC. Not listed in BCC Catalogue.
Bulletin, 61 (January, 1957), 37–38. Here first described and quoted from.
Probably one of Crane's first attempts at fashioning a play; possibly it was
written at Syracuse University (1891). A satiric drama spoofing at both
Jews and Gentiles, with the ironic twist that the Gentiles are quite as greedy
as the Jews—and more successful.

GREEKS WAITING AT THERMOPYLAE

Chicago Tribune, May 24, 1897, p. 2. "Greek Army Gathering Again at Pass
of Thermopylae."
New York Journal, May 24, 1897, p. 10. In Greater New York edition. In
out-of-town edition, p. 2. The text is identical.
Philadelphia Press, May 24, 1897, p. 2. "Stephen Crane at Thermopylae."
San Francisco Examiner, May 24, 1897, p. 1. "At Thermopylae They Wait."
In *UW* (1963); reprints *New York Journal.*
In *War Dispatches* (1964); reprints *New York Journal.*

GREEK WAR CORRESPONDENTS

Denver Republican, May 16, 1897, p. 17.
Pittsburgh Leader, May 16, 1897, p. 21. "The War Correspondents."
Portland Oregonian, May 16, 1897, p. 18. "Followers of War."
St. Paul Pioneer Press, May 16, 1897, p. 19. "Greek War Correspondence."
Prairie Schooner, 43 (Fall, 1969), 293–296. "Stephen Crane: Two Uncollected
Articles," by Bernice Slote. The other article is "Filibustering."

GREY AND BOILING STREET

TMs. (copy), 1 p., poem. CUCC.
In *Poetry* (1957).
In *Poems of Stephen Crane* (1966).

GREY SLEEVE

Omaha Evening Bee, October 10, 1895, p. 7; October 12, 1895, p. 24.

Kansas City Star, October 10, 11, 12, 1895, pp. 7, 9, 7.

Minneapolis Tribune, October 10, 11, 12, 1895, pp. 6, 6, 8.

New Orleans Times-Picayune, October 13, 1895, p. 18.

Omaha Weekly Bee, October 30, 1895, p. 1.

San Francisco Chronicle, January 19, 1896, p. 13.

English Illustrated Magazine, 14 (January, 1896), 437–477.

Chicago Times Herald, 62 (March 22, 1896), 38.

Pocket Magazine, 2 (May, 1896), 69–103.

Leslie's Weekly, 82 (May 28, 1896), 367–369.

DeMorest's Family Magazine, 32 (September, 1896), 627–632.

In *The Little Regiment.* New York: D. Appleton & Co., 1896.

In *The Little Regiment.* London: William Heinemann, 1897.

Philadelphia Press, October 12, 14, 15, 1898, p. 11 each issue.

In *Pictures of War.* London: William Heinemann, 1898.

In *The International Library of Masterpieces, Literature, Art and Rare Manuscripts.* New York: The International Bibliophile Society, 1899 and 1901.

In *Pictures of War.* London: William Heinemann, 1916.

Golden Book, 2 (July, 1925), 5–11.

In *Work,* vol. 2 (1925).

In *The International Library of Masterpieces, Literature, Art and Rare Manuscripts,* vol. 9. New York: The International Bibliophile Society, 1930.

In *Twenty Stories.* New York: Alfred A. Knopf, 1940.

In *Twenty Stories.* Cleveland and New York: World Publishing Company, 1945.

In *CSS&S* (1963).

In *TW* (1970).

GROCER BLOCKADE

New York Journal, September 23, 1898, p. 6.

New York Herald, June 24, 1900.

In *UW* (1963).

In *War Dispatches* (1964).

Crane recast the same ideas in "The Grocer Blockade" in "This Majestic Lie" (1900).

GUSTAVE AND MARIE

Holograph Ms., 1 p., numbered page "3" on verso of page 137 of the final manuscript of *The Red Badge of Courage,* Ms. LV. (Designated Ms. LV in *Omnibus,* 1952. Ms. SV is the earlier draft appearing on verso of LV.) This unfinished tale about Marie and Gustave in their Parisian boudoir is preserved in the bound volume of *The Red Badge of Courage* in BCC. Not listed in BCC Catalogue (1970).

In *Omnibus* (1952). Here first announced and described.

Bulletin, 60 (September, 1956), 456–457.

HALF A DAY IN SUDA BAY

See IMPRESSION OF THE "CONCERT."

HAROLD FREDERIC

Chicago Chap-Book, 8 (March 15, 1898), 358–359.

HARTWOOD PARK
Lost Crane manuscript mentioned by Cora Crane in letter to G. H. Perris (August, 1900), in Yale University Library.

HARVARD UNIVERSITY AGAINST THE CARLISLE INDIANS
New York Journal, November 1, 1896, p. 5 [signed].
In *UW* (1963). "Harvard University Against the Carlisle Indians, Described by Stephen Crane."

HATS, SHIRTS AND SPURS IN MEXICO
Buffalo Evening News, October 18, 1896, p. 9. "Swells and Spurs in Mexico."
Dallas Morning News, October 18, 1896, p. 10. "The Mexican Dude."
Detroit Free Press, October 18, 1896, p. 2. "Stephen Crane in Mexico." This is not the only text of Crane's several Mexican sketches titled "Stephen Crane in Mexico."
Galveston Daily News, October 18, 1896, p. 10. "Hats, Shirts and Spurs."
Louisville Courier-Journal, October 18, 1896, section 3, p. 2. "Hats, Shirts and Spurs: Mexican Requisites."
Nebraska State Journal, October 18, 1896, p. 9. "The Dress of Old Mexico."
Philadelphia Press, October 18, 1896, p. 34.
Rochester Democrat and Chronicle, October 18, 1896, p. 9.
St. Louis Globe-Democrat, October 18, 1896, p. 33. "Mexican Caballeros."
San Francisco Chronicle, October 18, 1896, p. 12. "Hats, Shirts and Spurs in Mexico."
Chicago Daily News, October 29, 1896, p. 5. "A Mexican Dude's Hat."
In *UW* (1963).

HAVANA'S HATE DYING, / SAYS STEPHEN CRANE
New York Journal, September 3, 1898, p. 5.
Kansas City Star, September 11, 1898, p. 5. "The Spirit in Havana."
In *UW* (1963); reprints *New York Journal.*
In *War Dispatches* (1964); reprints *New York Journal.*

HAVE YOU EVER MADE A JUST MAN?
TMs., 1 p., poem. CUCC.*
In *War Is Kind* (1899).
In *Work,* vol. 6 (1926).
In *Poems* (1930).
In *Poems of Stephen Crane* (1966).

HAYTI AND SAN DOMINGO FAVOR THE U.S.
New York World, May 24, 1898, p. 7.
In *UW* (1963).
In *War Dispatches* (1964).

HEARD ON THE STREET ELECTION NIGHT
A conversation piece of 6 pp. in the Crane Notebook. BCC.† Press clipping. CUCC [unpaged, unsigned].
New York Press, November ?, 1894 [unsigned].
Bulletin, 60 (September, 1956), 460–462. "Election Night: New York, 1894." The *New York Press* version is an expanded account from the Crane Notebook.
In *UW* (1963).

---

* Not in *Poetry* (1957).
† First noticed and commented on in Berryman's *Crane* (1950).

In *NYCS* (1966).
In *Notebook* (1969).
In *The Portable Stephen Crane*. New York: Viking Press, 1969.

HENRY M. STANLEY
Vidette (Claverack College), 1 (February, 1890), 8, 9.
Research Studies of the State College of Washington, 7 (March, 1939), 55–58.

HIS NEW MITTENS
Cornhill Magazine, n.s., 29 (November, 1898), 630–639.
McClure's Magazine, 12 (November, 1898), 54–61.
In *The Monster and Other Stories*. New York: Harper & Brothers, 1899.
In *The Monster and Other Stories*. London: Harper & Brothers, 1901.
In *Work*, vol. 5 (1926).
In *Omnibus* (1952).
In *CSS&S* (1963).
In *TWH* (1969).

HOARSE BOOMING DRUMS OF THE REGIMENT ("DO NOT WEEP, MAIDEN, FOR WAR IS KIND")
AMsS., 1 p., inscribed "Stephen Crane / Washington, D.C. / March 18, 1896." Laid in a copy of *The Red Badge of Courage*. BCC.
See DO NOT WEEP, MAIDEN, FOR WAR IS KIND.

HOLLER TREE
AMs., 9 pp., with 2 pp. of first draft of *George's Mother* on versos of pp. 5 and 6. BCC. Also appearing on versos of Ms. of "The Holler Tree" is a portion of "The Reluctant Voyagers."
Golden Book, 19 (February, 1934), 189–191.
In *SCS* (1949).
In *CSS&S* (1963).
In *SCTS* (1968).

HORSES—ONE DASH
See ONE DASH—HORSES. Title as given in American edition of *The Open Boat and Other Tales of Adventure* (1898), whereas the title is "Horses—One Dash" in the English edition, *The Open Boat and Other Stories* (1898).

HOW AMERICANS MAKE WAR. / SOME CRITICISMS AND A CONCLUSION
London Daily Chronicle, July 25, 1899, p. 9.
San Francisco Examiner, August 28, 1899, p. 6. Reprints Crane's letter-article from *London Daily Chronicle* as if it were a news story.

HOWELLS DISCUSSED AT AVON BY-THE-SEA
New York Tribune, August 18, 1891, p. 5, [unsigned].
Modern Language Notes, 30 (January, 1955), 37–39.
In *UW* (1963).
In *NYCS* (1966).

HOWELLS FEARS REALISTS MUST WAIT
Louisville Courier-Journal, October 28, 1894, p. 20. "Howells Talks Out."
New York Times, October 28, 1894, p. 20.
Philadelphia Inquirer, October 28, 1894, p. 9. "Realists Must Wait. Says W. Dean Howells."
Boston Globe, November 4, 1894, p. 32.
St. Paul Pioneer Press, November 6, 1894, p. 4. "The Realists Must Wait."

Americana, 37 (April, 1943), 257–295.

In *Omnibus* (1952).

In *UW* (1963).

In *NYCS* (1966).

SCraneN, 4, no. 4 (Summer, 1970), 7–9. Copy of proof sheet distributed by S. S. McClure to syndicated newspapers, reproduced in illegible print here: "Howells Fears Realists Must Wait." McClure's proof is in CUCC.

HOW PRINCETON MET HARVARD AT CAMBRIDGE AND WON, 12 TO 0

New York Journal, November 8, 1896, pp. 1–2. [signed].

In *UW* (1963).

HOW SAMPSON CLOSED HIS TRAP

New York World, May 27, 1898, p. 3.

Philadelphia Press, May 27, 1898, p. 2. "Sampson's Fleet on the Alert."

Chicago Tribune, May 28, 1898, p. 13. "In the Wake of Sampson Off the Cuban Coast."

HOW THE DONKEY LIFTED THE HILLS

TMs., 3 pp. BCC.

Nebraska State Journal, June 6, 1895, p. 4. "Mexican Tales / By Stephen Crane: How the Donkey Lifted the Hills."

Pocket Magazine, 4 (June, 1897), 144–151.

In *Last Words.* London: Digby, Long & Co., 1902.

In *Work,* vol. 11 (1926).

In *CSS&S* (1963).

In *SCTS* (1968).

HOW THEY COURT IN CUBA

New York Journal, October 25, 1898, p. 6.

San Francisco Examiner, November 13, 1898, p. 4.

In *UW* (1963); reprints *New York Journal.*

In *War Dispatches* (1964); reprints *New York Journal.*

HOW THEY LEAVE CUBA

New York Journal, October 6, 1898, p. 6.

In *UW* (1963).

In *War Dispatches* (1964).

HUNGER HAS MADE CUBANS FATALISTS

Boston Globe, July 12, 1898, p 3. "Journey to Hills. / Stephen Crane Describes Trip / With Scovel."

New York World, July 12, 1898, p. 4.

Philadelphia Press, July 12, 1898, p. 3. "How the Army Prepared to Capture Santiago."

In *UW* (1963); reprints *New York World.*

In *War Dispatches* (1964); reprints *New York World.*

HUNTING WILD HOGS

New York Tribune, February 28, 1892, p. 17 [unsigned].

In *SCTS* (1968).

SHR, 2, no. 1 (Winter, 1968), 12–17.

I EXPLAIN THE SILVERED PASSING OF A SHIP AT NIGHT

AMs., 1 p., poem. TMs., 1 p., and TMs., 1 p. CUCC.

Bookman, 4 (October, 1896), 149.
In *War Is Kind* (1899).
In *Work*, vol. 6 (1926).
In *Poems* (1930).
In New Year's card, privately printed for Melvin Schoberlin. Baltimore: Mogollon Press, 1947.
In *Poetry* (1957), pp. 121–123.
In *Poems of Stephen Crane* (1966).

IF YOU WOULD SEEK A FRIEND AMONG MEN

AMs., 1 p., poem. TMs., 1p.; in Cora Crane's hand: "Not used in war is kind." CUCC.
In *Poetry* (1957).
In *Poems of Stephen Crane* (1966).

I HAVE HEARD THE SUNSET SONG OF THE BIRCHES

TMs., 1 p. CUCC.
"*The Time Has Come, . . .*" East Aurora, N.Y.: The Roycroft Printing Shop, 1895.
Philistine, 2 (January, 1896), 62.
Roycroft Quarterly, 1 (May, 1896), 30.
Fra, 4, no. 4 (January, 1910), 120. "The Maniac's Complaint."
In *A Roycroft Anthology*, East Aurora, N.Y.: The Roycrofters, 1917, p. 73.
In *War Is Kind* (1899).
In *Work*, vol. 6 (1926).
In *Poems* (1930).
In *Poetry* (1957).
In *Poems of Stephen Crane* (1966).

ILLUSION IN RED AND WHITE

Galley proofs, 2 pp. BCC. For Tillotson's Northern Newspaper Syndicate, England.
New York World, May 20, 1900, supplement, p. 2.
St. Louis Post Dispatch, May 20, 1900, Sunday Magazine Section, p. 6.
Bolton (Lancaster, England) *Evening News*, December 28, 1901.
In *The Monster and Other Stories*. London: Harper & Brothers, 1901.
In *Work*, vol. 12 (1927).
In *Twenty Stories*. New York: Alfred A. Knopf, 1940.
In *Twenty Stories*. Cleveland & New York: World Publishing Company, 1945.
In *CSS&S* (1963).

I LOOKED HERE

AMs., 1 p., poem. SCC.
In *Black Riders* (1895).
In *Work*, vol. 6 (1926).
In *Poems* (1930).
In *Poetry* (1957).
In *Poems of Stephen Crane* (1966).

IMPACT OF A DOLLAR UPON THE HEART ("SOME THINGS")

TMsS., 1 p., poem, inscribed in Cora Crane's hand: "By Stephen Crane." CUCC.
Philistine, 6 (February, 1898), back cover. Also, p. 77, announcement (by Elbert Hubbard) that "Arrangements have been made with Stephen

Crane (there's only one) to supply 'Lines' for the back of every *Philistine* for a decade."
Philistine, 9 (October, 1899), 149–150. Reprints the poem.
In *War Is Kind* (1899).
In *Work,* vol. 6 (1926).
In *Poems* (1930).
In *Poetry* (1957).
In *Poems of Stephen Crane* (1966).

IMPRESSION OF THE "CONCERT" (FROM "WITH GREEK AND TURK")
Part I of a series titled "With Greek and Turk" in London *Westminster Gazette.* Part II consists of "A Fragment of Velestino," appearing in *Westminster Gazette* a month after Part I, for which the editor issued an apology. In much shortened form "A Fragment of Velestino" appeared in *New York Journal,* June 13, 1897. Parts III and IV are "A Fragment of Velestino" (Continued). Parts V and VI—titled "Some Interviews"—appeared in the *Westminster Gazette* on June 14 and 15, 1897, and Part VII—titled "The Man in the White Hat"—concluded the series on June 18, 1897. "Some Interviews" collates with what the *New York Journal* published on June 20 titled "My Talk With Soldiers Six." Throughout the series *Westminster Gazette* spelled Velestino as "Velestimo."
Westminster Gazette (London), May 3, 1897, pp. 1–2. "An Impression of the Concert."
Portland Oregonian, May 8, 1897, p. 6. "At the Seat of War."
Boston Globe, May 9, 1897, p. 33. "Stephen Crane at Crete."
Detroit Free Press, May 9, 1897, p. 17. "The Frowning Fleet of the Powers in Suda Bay."
Louisville Courier-Journal, May 9, 1897, p. 12. "Stephen Crane's Pen Picture of the Powers' Fleet Off Crete."*
New York Sun, May 9, 1897, p. 6. "Half a Day in Suda Bay."
Pittsburgh Leader, May 9, 1897, p. 19. "Europe's Mailed Arm."
St. Paul Pioneer Press, May 9, 1897, p. 20. "The Fleets Now Off Crete."
Omaha Daily Bee, May 10, 1897, p. 6. "Fleet of the Great Powers Preserving 'The Peace of Europe.'" Reprinted in *Omaha Weekly Bee,* May 12, 1897, p. 2.
In *UW* (1963). "Half a Day in Suda Bay."
In *War Dispatches* (1964). "Stephen Crane's Pen Picture of the Powers' Fleet Off Crete."†

INACTION DETERIORATES THE KEY WEST FLEET
Chicago Tribune, May 6, 1898, p. 2. "Men are Anxious to Fight."
New York World, May 6, 1898, p. 3.
Omaha Daily Bee, May 6, 1898, p. 6. "Men on War Ships are Uneasy."
Omaha Evening Bee, May 6, 1898, p. 7. "Men on War Ships are Uneasy."
Philadelphia Press, May 6, 1898, p. 2. "Chafe Over Idleness."
In *UW* (1963); reprints *New York World.*

IN A LARGE VAULTED HALL
Holograph Ms., 1 p. SCC. Unpublished.

---

* *W-S Bibliography* lists the *Louisville Courier-Journal, New York Sun,* and *Detroit Free Press,* without quoting the variant titles. It says "Title varies slightly." See *W-S Bibliography,* p. 101, under IMPRESSION OF THE "CONCERT."
† Datelined "On Board French Steamer *Guardiana* April 28." Misspelled "Guardiana" for *Guadiana.*

IN A PARK ROW RESTAURANT
Holograph Ms. in the Crane Notebook, 10 draft pp. BCC.
TMsS., 3 pp., signed by Cora Crane. It derives from the Notebook, and differs
from the *New York Press* version.
New York Press, October 28, 1894, part 5, p. 3.
In *CSS&S* (1963).
In *UW* (1963).
In *NYCS* (1966). *See* note, p. 83.
In *Notebook* (1969).

INDIANA CAMPAIGN
Buffalo Commercial, May 23, 1896, p. 4; May 25, 1896, p. 5.
Kansas City Star, May 23, 1896, p. 7; May 25, 1896, p. 7.
Minneapolis Tribune, May 23, 1896, p. 6; May 25, 1896, p. 4.
Nebraska State Journal, May 23, 1896, p. 5; May 25, 1896, p. 4.
New York Times, May 23, 1896, part 1, p. 9; May 25, 1896, part 2, p. 9.
San Francisco Chronicle, June 14, 1896, p. 12.
St. Louis Post-Dispatch, June 23, 1896, p. 9.
Pocket Magazine, 2 (September, 1896), 92–114.
English Illustrated Magazine, 16 (December, 1896), 320–326.
In *The Little Regiment.* New York: D. Appleton & Co., 1896.
In *The Little Regiment.* London: William Heinemann, 1897.
In *Pictures of War.* London: William Heinemann, 1898.
In *Work,* vol. 2 (1925).
In *CSS&S* (1963).
In *TW* (1970).

INDIAN FIGHTERS IN THE 12TH CAVALRY
See TWELFTH CAVALRY AND THE INDIAN WARS.

IN FRONT OF SANTIAGO
See STEPHEN CRANE'S VIVID STORY OF THE BATTLE OF SAN
JUAN.

IN HAVANA AS IT IS TODAY
New York Journal, November 12, 1898, p. 6.
In *UW* (1963).
In *War Dispatches* (1964).

IN HEAVEN, SOME LITTLE BLADES OF GRASS
AMs., 1 p., poem. SCC.
In *Black Riders* (1895).
In *Work,* vol. 6 (1926).
Golden Book, 9 (April, 1929), 43. "The Blades of Grass."
In *Poems* (1930).
In *Poetry* (1957).
In *Poems of Stephen Crane* (1966).

IN MINETTA LANE
See STEPHEN CRANE IN MINETTA LANE.

IN OLD MEXICO
See MEXICAN SIGHTS AND STREET SCENES.

INTERMINGLED
AMs., 1 p., incomplete, poem. CUCC.

In *Poetry* (1957).

In *Poems of Stephen Crane* (1966).

IN THE BROADWAY CARS

New York Sun, n.d., press clipping. CUCC.

New York Press, n.d., 2 pp. BCC. This is same clipping as in CUCC. Crane in error wrote "Press" instead of "Sun."

Denver Republican, July 26, 1896, p. 24.

New York Sun, July 26, 1896, p. 3.

Pittsburgh Leader, July 26, 1896, p. 22. "The Broadway Cable cars."

In *Last Words.* London: Digby, Long & Co., 1902.

In *Once Upon a City.* New York: Macmillan, 1958. Quotes from "In the Broadway Cars," p. 10.

In *NYCS* (1966).

IN THE COUNTRY OF RHYMERS AND WRITERS

AMs., 13 pp., unfinished tale. CUCC. Two of the holograph sheets provide a first draft version of a portion which Crane in parts rejected and in other parts recopied with slight variants here and there.

Reproduced for the first time in *SinSF,* 1, no. 2 (Winter, 1964), 149–152.

IN THE DEPTHS OF A COAL MINE

AMs., 19 pp., with pp. 12–14, 20–21 missing. With autograph corrections. Crane's first draft, according to C. K. Linson's annotation. BCC.

Press copy signed by Crane in Crane Scrapbook. CUCC.

Buffalo Morning Express, July 22, 1894, p. 17. "The Depths of a Coal Mine."

Detroit Free Press, July 22, 1894, p. 2. "Down in a Coal Mine."

Philadelphia Inquirer, July 22, 1894, p. 21. "The Depths of a Coal Mine."

St. Louis Republic, July 22, 1894. "Down in a Coal Mine."

St. Paul Pioneer Press, July 22, 1894, p. 13. "Depths of a Coal Mine."

McClure's Magazine, 3 (August, 1894), 195–209.

In *My Stephen Crane.* Syracuse: Syracuse University Press, 1958, pp. 69–70. Here is a portion expunged from the printed text.

In *UW* (1963).

In *NYCS* (1966). Reprints the text of "In the Depths of a Coal Mine" and quotes the passage from the manuscript not printed prior to *My Stephen Crane.*

IN THE FIRST LAND FIGHT 4 OF OUR MEN ARE KILLED

New York World, June 12, 1898, p. 1 [unsigned]. City edition.

New York World, June 13, 1898, p. 1 [unsigned]. "Four of Our Men Killed Including Surgeon John Blair Gibbs." (In Brooklyn and suburban editions of *World.*) Dictated to Ernest McCready by Crane at Guantánamo Bay on June 12 and filed for the *New York World* by McCready of the *New York Herald.* The *World*'s byline reads "Special Cable dispatch to the *World,*" whereas the usual *World* byline for Crane reads "Special from a Staff Correspondent." All other known Crane dispatches in the *New York World* bear his name. *See Crane,* p. 606.

In *A Treasury of Great Reporting.* New York: Simon and Schuster, 1949, 1962. "A World Correspondent Immortalizes an Incident on the Shores of Guantánamo Bay."

IN THE NIGHT

TMs., 1 p., poem. Page proof, 1 p., with autograph corrections in Cora Crane's hand. CUCC. Ms. inscribed "Stephen Crane / Hartwood / Sullivan Co.

/ N. Y. / Stephen Crane." Tipped into *Chap-Book,* 4, no. 8 (March, 1896). University of North Carolina Library.

Chap-Book, 4, no. 8 (March, 1896), 372.

Literary Digest, 12 (April 4, 1896), 671.

In *War Is Kind* (1899).

In *Work,* vol. 6 (1926).

In *Poems* (1930).

In *Poetry* (1957).

In *Poems of Stephen Crane* (1966).

See *Papers of the Bibliographical Society of America,* 58 (1964), 173–179.

IN THE TENDERLOIN: A DUEL BETWEEN AN ALARM CLOCK AND A SUICIDAL PURPOSE

Ms., 3 pp., draft fragment in Crane Notebook. BCC.

Town Topics, 36 (October 1, 1896), 14.

Tales From Town Topics, 33 (September, 1899), 119–123. First made known in *Papers of the Bibliographical Society of America,* 35 (Fourth Quarter, 1941), 297.

In *CSS&S* (1963).

In *UW* (1963).

In *NYCS* (1966).

IN THE "TENDERLOIN" BY STEPHEN CRANE. THE SECOND OF A SERIES OF SKETCHES OF NEW YORK LIFE BY THE FAMOUS NOVELIST

New York Journal, November 1, 1896, p. 25. The first in the *Journal's* series began with "The Tenderloin as It Really Is." Not in *CSS&S.*

In *UW* (1963).

In *NYCS* (1966).

INTRIGUE

TMs. (I, 12 pp.; II, 8 pp.; III, 1 p.; IV, 1 p.; V, 1 p.). CUCC.

In *War Is Kind* (1899).*

In *Work,* vol. 6 (1926).

In *Poems* (1930).

In *Poetry* (1957).

In *Poems of Stephen Crane* (1966).

In *Crane* (1968), chap. 25, pp. 422–442.

I SAW A MAN PURSUING THE HORIZON

In *Black Riders* (1895).

Philistine, 1 (June, 1895), 27. A reprint since *Black Riders* was published May 11, 1895.

Roycroft Quarterly, 1 (May, 1896), 2.

In *Work,* vol. 6 (1926).

Golden Book, 11 (April, 1930), 36.

In *Poems* (1930).

In *Poetry* (1957).

In *Poems of Stephen Crane* (1966).

I STOOD UPON A HIGH PLACE

In *Black Riders* (1895).

Bookman, 3 (April, 1896), 196. Reprinted from *The Black Riders.*

---

* That *War Is Kind* contains the Intrigue Poems is not mentioned in *W-S Bibliography.*

Philistine, 8 (March, 1899), back cover. With a cartoon in red and black of a
demon leering at the poet.
In *Work,* vol. 6 (1926).
In *Poems* (1930).
In *Poems of Stephen Crane* (1966). Not in *Poetry* (1957).

JACK
TMs., 5 pp., copied from Stephen Crane's AMs. by Edith Crane, unpublished.
Three unfinished drafts about a dog. BCC.
AMs., 9 pp. BCC.
Described in *Bulletin,* 61 (January, 1957), 38.
    A dog story in three drafts: first draft on 3 leaves of lined paper (8 × 12½
in.); second draft, lacking title, on 7 handwritten pages of thin, yellowish
paper (6⅜ × 10 in.); third draft, lacking title, on 9 pages.
    W-S Bibliography says that the scene of this dog story was laid in the
Mongaup Valley. "A version of this story was rejected by *St. Nicholas* in
1891 because of a plethora of dog stories at the time."

JAGS OF PULQUE DOWN IN MEXICO
Galveston Daily News, August 10, 1895, p. 9. "Pulque Jag Is Heavy."
Cincinnati Commercial Tribune, August 11, 1895, p. 17. "A Jag on Pulque."
Philadelphia Press, August 11, 1895, p. 26. "Jags of Pulque Down in Mexico."
Rochester Democrat and Chronicle, August 11, 1895, p. 10.
Salt Lake City Tribune, August 11, 1895, p. 15. "A Jag of Pulque Is Heavy."
Nebraska State Journal, August 12, 1895, p. 5. "A Jag of Pulque Is Heavy."
In *UW* (1963).

JOYS OF SEASIDE LIFE
New York Tribune, July 17, 1892, part 2, p. 18 [unsigned].
In *UW* (1963).
In *NYCS* (1966).

JUDGMENT OF THE SAGE
Bookman, 2 (January, 1896), 412.
In *CSS&S* (1963).
In *UW* (1963).
In *NYCS* (1966).

KICKING TWELFTH
TMsS., 11 pp., notation by Cora Crane. BCC. Manuscript in Edith Richie's
hand. In Berg Collection, New York Public Library. Facsimile reproduction
in *The Works of Stephen Crane,* ed. Fredson Bowers, vol. VI, *Tales of War*
(1970).
Pall Mall Magazine, 20 (February, 1900), 173.*
Ainslee's Magazine, 6 (August, 1900), 46–51.
Crystal Palace Magazine, 1, no. 1 (October, 1900), 2–3.
Leslie's Magazine, October, 1900. "Kim Up, the Kickers."
In *Last Words.* London: Digby, Long & Co., 1902.

    * Not *Pall Mall Gazette,* as given in *W-S Bibliography,* p. 103. Cora edited *Lost
Words* and gave the title *Spitzbergen Tales* to four war tales or stories: "The
Kicking Twelfth," "The Upturned Face," "The Shrapnel of Their Friends," and
" 'And If He Wills, We Must Die.' "

In *Work,* vol. 9 (1926).
In *CSS&S* (1963).
In *TW* (1970).

KID WHO STOLE A LEMON

No. 27 in Crane's holograph list of titles of his works, the journal publishing the given title, the location of the Ms., and the word count. Here the wordage is 1,000, and the journal is the *Philistine* (untraced). List in CUCC. *See* GREAT MISTAKE.

KILLING HIS BEAR

New York Tribune, July 31, 1892, part 2, p. 18.
Pamphlet issued as Christmas token. New York: Gabriel and Lee Engel, 1949.
In *SCS* (1949).
In *CSS&S* (1963).
In *SCTS* (1968).

KING'S FAVOR

Tsc., 1 p., fragment. SCC.
Syracuse University Herald, 19 (May, 1891), 128–131, [signed].
The Argot (literary journal at Syracuse University), 3 (March, 1935), 1, 8.
In *CSS&S* (1963).
In *UW* (1963).

KNIFE

AMs., 8 pp. CUCC.
Harper's Magazine, 100 (March, 1900), 591–598.
In *Whilomville Stories.* New York: Harper & Brothers, 1900.
In *Whilomville Stories.* London: Harper & Brothers, 1900.
In *Work,* vol. 5 (1926).
In *Omnibus* (1952).
In *CSS&S* (1963).
In *TWH* (1969).

A LAD AND A MAID AT A CURVE IN THE STREAM

AMs., 1 p., poem. TMs., 1 p. CUCC.
In *Poetry* (1957).
In *Poems of Stephen Crane* (1966).

LANDLADY'S DAUGHTER

AMs., 18 pp.; AMs., 5 pp. (first draft). Both drafts untitled and unfinished. CUCC, titled "New York Boarding House."
First reproduced in *NYCS* (1966); titled "The Landlady's Daughter."

LAST OF THE MOHICANS

New York Tribune, February 21, 1892, p. 12 [unsigned].
American Literature, 39 (November, 1967), 392–396.
In *SCTS* (1968).
SHR, 2, no. 1 (Winter, 1968), 11–12.

LAST PANTHER

New York Tribune, April 3, 1892, part 2, p. 17.
In *SCTS* (1968). Here for the first time reprinted from *New York Tribune.*
SHR, 2, no. 1 (Winter, 1968), 17–20.

LAST WORDS

London: Digby, Long & Co., 1902.
See Crane (1968), p. 527. *"Last Words,* with eight pieces published here for

the first time (1902) was at first titled *Reluctant Voyagers* until Cora protested to Perris against that title. A good many pieces were not Crane's last words; they were early writings."

LEGENDS (I. "A MAN BUILDED A BUGLE." II. "WHEN THE SUICIDE ARRIVED AT THE SKY." III. "A MAN SAID: 'THOU TREE!'" IV. "A WARRIOR STOOD UPON A PEAK AND DEFIED THE STARS." V. "THE WIND THAT WAVES THE BLOSSOMS SANG.")

> *Bookman*, 3 (April, 1896), 206. Illustrated by Miss Melanie Elisabeth Norton. Reprints, pp. 196, 197, "I Stood Upon a High Place" and "Should the Wide World Roll Away." Editorial note, p. 196.
> In *Legends by Stephen Crane*. Ysleta: Edwin B. Hill, 1942. Limited to 45 copies.
> In *Poems of Stephen Crane* (1966). The poems are listed by title, but not under "Legends."

"LINES"

> Ts., 3 pp. SCC.
> The title "Lines," is given to several poems in the *Philistine*, including "You Tell Me This Is God?" and "When a People Reach the Top of a Hill" and "On the Desert." And in *Bookman*, 4, no. 2 (October, 1896), 149: "Lines"— "I explain the silvered path of a ship at night."

LINES BY STEPHEN CRANE

> TMs., 1 p. (title page only). CUCC.

LISTS OF CRANE'S STORIES AND POEMS AND PLACES OF PUBLICATION

> Lists of Crane's stories and places of publication, A.d.s. (autograph document signed). Lists of sketches and stories; where published and serialized, with numbers of words, A.d., 8 pp. (4 pp. are in Cora Crane's hand). List of poems with places of publication, A.n., 2 pp. In CUCC.

LITERARY NOTES

> Trivia, 3 pp. in Crane Notebook. BCC.
> *Bulletin*, 60 (September, 1956), 462. Quotes a sample.
> In *Notebook* (1969).

LITTLE BIRDS OF THE NIGHT

> *See* LOST POEM.

LITTLE INK, MORE OR LESS!

> TMs., 1 p., poem. CUCC. Holograph, lacking first six lines, in SCC.
> In *War Is Kind* (1899).
> In *Work*, vol. 6 (1926).
> In *Poems* (1930).
> In *Poetry* (1957).
> In *Poems of Stephen Crane* (1966).
> *See* WHAT? YOU DEFINE ME GOD WITH THESE TRINKETS?

LITTLE PILGRIM

> AMsS., 3 pp., titled "A Little Pilgrimage." CUCC.
> *Harper's Magazine*, 101 (August, 1900), 401–404.
> In *Whilomville Stories*. New York: Harper & Brothers, 1900.
> In *Whilomville Stories*. London: Harper & Brothers, 1900.
> In *Work*, vol. 5 (1926).

In *CSS&S* (1963).

In *TWH* (1969).

LITTLE REGIMENT

AMs., 1 p. (p. 9 only). CUCC. Facsimile reproduction of the manuscript in *The Works of Stephen Crane*, ed. Fredson Bowers, vol. VI, *Tales of War* (1970).

Chapman's Magazine, 4 (June, 1896), 214–232.

McClure's Magazine, 7 (June, 1896), 12–22.

Current Literature, 20 (August, 1896), 145–146. Reprints a portion of "The Little Regiment," titled "In the Heat of Night."

New York: D. Appleton & Co., 1896.

London: William Heinemann, 1897.

In *Pictures of War*. London: William Heinemann, 1898.

In *Pictures of War*. London: William Heinemann, 1916.

In *Work*, vol. 2 (1925).

In *Twenty Stories*. New York: Alfred A. Knopf, 1940.

In *Twenty Stories*. Cleveland & New York: World Publishing Company, 1945.

In *CSS&S* (1963).

In *TW* (1970).

LITTLE STILETTOS OF THE MODERN NAVY WHICH STAB IN THE DARK

See ASSASSINS IN MODERN BATTLES.

LONDON IMPRESSIONS

TMsS., 15 pp., with autograph corrections. BCC.

Saturday Review, 84 (July 31, 1897), 105–106; (August 7, 1897), 132–133; (August 14, 1897), 158–159.

In *Last Words*. London: Digby, Long & Co., 1902.

In *Men, Women and Boats*. New York: Boni and Liveright, 1921.

In *Work*, vol. 11 (1926).

In *Maggie, and Other Stories*. New York: The Modern Library, 1933.

In *The Pace of Youth and Other Stories*. Girard, Kans.: Haldeman-Julius (n.d.).

LONDON SOCIETY WOMEN'S BRACERS

Ms. CUCC. *See Cora Crane* (1960), p. 117.

New York Press, August 22, 1897, p. 23.

LONE CHARGE OF WILLIAM B. PERKINS

Westminster Gazette, 13, no. 1819 (January 2, 1899), 1–2.

Westminster Budget, January 6, 1899, p. 20.

McClure's Magazine, 13 (July, 1899), 279–282.

In *Wounds in the Rain*. London: Methuen & Co., 1900.

In *Wounds in the Rain*. New York: Frederick A. Stokes Company, 1900.

In *Work*, vol. 9 (1926).

In *CSS&S* (1963).

In *TW* (1970).

LOSS OF AN ARM ("AN EPISODE OF WAR")

No. 5 in Crane's holograph list of titles of his works, the journal publishing the given title, the location of the Ms., and the word count. Here the word-age is 1,500 and the journal is *Youth's Companion* (untraced). List in CUCC.

Collate this title with EPISODE OF WAR.

LOST POEM ("LITTLE BIRDS OF THE NIGHT")
Holograph Ms., 2 pp., in the Crane Notebook. BCC.*
In *Lost Poem by Stephen Crane.* New York: The Harvard Press [1932].
   "Of this first printing one hundred copies have been issued for the friends
   of Harvey Taylor."
Golden Book, 19 (February, 1934), 189. Errs in claiming that "Lost Poem" is
   the first of unpublished Crane manuscripts to be reproduced.
In *Poetry* (1957); *see* Appendix.
In *Poems of Stephen Crane* (1966).
In *Notebook* (1969).

LOVELY JAG IN A CROWDED CAR
New York Press, January 6, 1895, part 5, p. 6.
In *CSS&S* (1963).
In *UW* (1963).
In *NYCS* (1966).

LOVER AND THE TELL-TALE
AMsS., 4 pp. BCC. Facsimile reproduction of the first page of the manuscript
   in *The Works of Stephen Crane,* ed. Fredson Bowers, vol. VII, *Tales of
   Whilomville* (1969), p. 133. Bowers, p. 121, describes the manuscript thus:
   "Four leaves of quarto paper 263 × 212 mm., titled 'The Lover and the
   Tell-Tale / By Stephen Crane.' To the left of the title is inscribed 'For
   Mrs Edward Pease / S. C.' Written in blue ink. The first leaf seems to show
   the sign of perforations at the top, as from a pad, and is shorter than the
   others (without these perforations), measuring 237× 212 mm. On the verso
   of each leaf are circled word counts in ink and the added cumulative totals
   up to 2030 of fol. 4."†
Harper's Magazine, 99 (October, 1899), 759–763.
In *Whilomville Stories.* New York: Harper & Brothers, 1900.
In *Whilomville Stories.* London: Harper & Brothers, 1900.
In *Work,* vol. 5 (1926).
In *Twenty Stories.* New York: Alfred A. Knopf, 1940.
In *Twenty Stories.* Cleveland & New York: World Publishing Company, 1945.
In *CSS&S* (1963).
In *TWH* (1969).

LYNX-HUNTING
AMs., 10 pp. CUCC.
Harper's Magazine, 99 (September, 1899), 552–557.
In *Whilomville Stories.* New York: Harper & Brothers, 1900.
In *Whilomville Stories.* London: Harper & Brothers, 1900.
In *Work,* vol. 5 (1926).
In *Twenty Stories.* New York: Alfred A. Knopf, 1940.

---

   * BCC lists the Crane Notebook, but omitted from the BCC catalogue is this
poem. *See Notebook.*
   † The manuscripts of "The Lover and the Tell-Tale" and "The Angel Child"
were obtained from Michael Pease in 1948 by Commander Melvin H. Schoberlin,
USN (Ret.), who owns the latter manuscript. He made a gift of the manuscript
of "The Lover and the Tell-Tale" to the Barrett Crane Collection.
   Letters about the origin of this Whilomville story—by Michael Pease, Cora
Crane, and Schoberlin—are in BCC. However, for letter of Michael Pease to
R. W. S., *see Crane* (1968).

In *Twenty Stories.* Cleveland & New York: World Publishing Company, 1945.
In *CSS&S* (1963).
In *TWH* (1969).

MAGGIE

[New York]: [printer unknown]. [1893]. Published at the author's expense.
Maggie, A Girl of the Streets. (A Story of New York), by Johnston Smith.
[New York, 1893.] Crane inscription on verso of title page, signed and
dated August 29, 1896: " 'And the wealth of the few shall be built upon
the patience of the poor.' Prophecy not made BC 1090." BCC. *See Exhibition,* p. 15. Crane inscription on the jacket-cover of the copy he sent
to Hamlin Garland (March ?, 1893): "It is inevitable that you will be
greatly shocked by this book but continue please with all possible courage
to the end. For it tries to show that environment is a tremendous thing in
the world and frequently shapes lives regardless. If one proves that theory
one makes room in Heaven for all sorts of souls (notably an occasional
street girl) who are confidently not expected to be there by many excellent people.

"It is probable that the reader of this small thing may consider the
Author to be a bad man, but, obviously, this is a matter of small consequence to

The Author"

In Lilly Library, Indiana University. In *Letters,* p. 14. The same is inscribed on a copy of the 1893 *Maggie* to Dr. Lucius L. Button (March ?
1893). In *Letters,* p. 14, differing from the above by its variant punctuation. Crane inscribed no doubt a number of copies with this same message,
sending one in early 1895 to the Reverend Thomas Dixon. The inscribed
Maggie to Button appears in John T. Winterich's *23 Books The Stories
Behind Them.* Berkeley, California: The Books Arts Club of the Univer-
sity of California, 1938; New York: J. B. Lippincott Company, 1939.
New York: D. Appleton & Co., 1896, *Maggie: A Girl of the Streets.*
Copyright applied for May 28, 1896; deposit made June 6, 1896.
London: William Heinemann, 1896. Titled *Maggie: A Child of the Streets.*
Advance copy of U.S. printing deposited June 8, 1896. English edition pub-
lished September 19, 1896.
In *Bowery Tales.* London: William Heinemann, 1900.
London: William Heinemann, [1915].
London: William Heinemann, [1918].
In *Work,* vol. 10 (1926).
Two Worlds Monthly, 1, no. 4 (November ?, 1926), 427–472.
New York: Newland Press, [1930].
New York: Alfred A. Knopf, 1931.
In *Maggie and Other Stories.* New York: The Modern Library, 1933.
In *Twenty Stories.* New York: Alfred A. Knopf, 1940.
In *Twenty Stories.* Cleveland & New York: World Publishing Company,
[1945].
In *Great American Short Novels.* New York: Dial Press, 1946.
In *Omnibus* (1952).
In *The Complete Novels of Stephen Crane.* Garden City, N.Y.: Doubleday &
Company, 1967.

In *Bowery Tales: Maggie and George's Mother,* vol. I. Charlottesville, Va.:
University Press of Virginia, 1969.
NOTE: *Maggie* in its 1893 text was first reprinted in *Stephen Crane's Maggie: Text and
Context,* ed. Maurice Bassan (1966). Facsimile reproductions of the first edition were
edited by Joseph Katz (1966) and by Donald Pizer (1968). The 1893 *Maggie* is reprinted
in *The Portable Stephen Crane,* ed. Joseph Katz (1969), and in *The Stephen Crane
Reader,* ed. R. W. Stallman (1972).

MAJESTIC LIE
See THIS MAJESTIC LIE.

MAKING AN ORATOR
AMs., 8 pp., first 3 pp. in Cora Crane's hand. CUCC. Facsimile reproduc-
tion of the fourth page, showing Stephen and Cora Crane's handwriting,
is in *The Works of Stephen Crane,* ed. Fredson Bowers, vol. VII, *Tales
of Whilomville* (1969), p. 148. Described in Textual Introduction by
Fredson Bowers, p. 122.
Manuscripts of *Whilomville Stories*—except for "Shame" and "The
Carriage-Lamps"—are preserved.
Harper's Magazine, 100 (December, 1899), 25–28.
In *Whilomville Stories.* New York: Harper & Brothers, 1900.
In *Whilomville Stories.* London: Harper & Brothers, 1900.
In *Work,* vol. 5 (1926).
In *CSS&S* (1963).

MANACLED
Argosy, 71 (August, 1900), 364–366.
Index of Pittsburg Life, November 3, 1900, p. 15.
Truth, 19 (November, 1900), 265–266.
In *The Monster and Other Stories.* London: Harper & Brothers, 1901.
In *Work,* vol. 12 (1927).
In *NYCS* (1966).

MAN ADRIFT ON A SLIM SPAR
AMsS., 1 p., poem. AMs. (copy), 1 p., signed "Stephen Crane" but in Cora
Crane's hand. CUCC.
See THREE POEMS.
Bookman, 69 (April, 1929), 120.
In *Poems* (1930).
In *Poetry* (1957).
In *Poems of Stephen Crane* (1966).

MAN AND SOME OTHERS
Century, 53 (February, 1897), 601–607.
In *The Open Boat and Other Stories.* London: William Heinemann, 1898.
In *The Open Boat and Other Tales of Adventure.* New York: Doubleday
& McClure, 1898.
In *The Open Boat and Other Tales of Adventure.* New York: Doubleday,
Page & Co., 1905.
In *Work,* vol. 12 (1927).
In *CSS&S* (1963).

MAN BY THE NAME OF MUD
TMs.S., 4 pp., with autograph corrections. BCC. Signature supplied by Cora.

In *Last Words*. London: Digby, Long & Co., 1902.
In *CSS&S* (1963).
In *NYCS* (1966).

MAN FROM DULUTH
Metropolitan Magazine, 13 (February, 1901), 175–181.
Crampton's Magazine, 17 (May, 1901), 353–360.
In *CSS&S* (1963).
In *UW* (1963).
In *NYCS* (1966).

MANIAC'S COMPLAINT
See I HAVE HEARD THE SUNSET SONG OF THE BIRCHES.

MAN IN THE WHITE HAT (FROM "WITH GREEK AND TURK")
Westminster Gazette, June 18, 1897, pp. 1–2. Part VII of series captioned "With Greek and Turk."
See IMPRESSION OF THE "CONCERT."
Denver Republican, July 11, 1897, p. 21. "White Hat in Greece."
New York Sun, July 11, 1897, section 2, p. 2. "Under the White Hat."
Philadelphia Inquirer, July 11, 1897, p. 28. "The White Hat in Greece."
Pittsburgh Leader, July 11, 1897, p. 21. "The White Hat in Greece."
Portland Oregonian, July 11, 1897, p. 19.
In *UW* (1963); reprints *Westminster Gazette*.
In *War Dispatches* (1964); reprints *Westminster Gazette*.

MARDI GRAS FESTIVAL
Nebraska State Journal, February 16, 1896, p. 11. "The Fete of Mardi Gras."
Philadelphia Press, February 16, 1896, p. 30.
New Orleans Times-Democrat, February 17, 1896, p. 9.
Rochester Democrat and Chronicle, February 17, 1896, p. 9.
Cincinnati Commercial Tribune, February 23, 1896. "The Fete of Mardi Gras."
In *UW* (1963).

MARINES SIGNALLING UNDER FIRE AT GUANTANAMO
McClure's Magazine, 12 (February, 1899), 332–336.
In *Wounds in the Rain*. London: Methuen and Co., 1900.
In *Wounds in the Rain*. New York: Frederick A. Stokes Company, 1900.
In *Work*, vol. 9 (1926).
In *War Dispatches* (1964).
In *TW* (1970).

MATINEE GIRLS
Holograph Ms., 3 pp., in the Crane Notebook. BCC.
Bulletin, 60 (September, 1956), 459–460.
In *NYCS* (1966).
In *Notebook* (1969).

MEETINGS BEGUN AT OCEAN GROVE
New York Tribune, July 2, 1892, p. 4 [unsigned].
In *UW* (1963).
A portion quoted in *NYCS* (1966), p. xiii.

MEMOIRS OF A PRIVATE
New York Journal, September 25, 1898, p. 26.

In *UW* (1963).

In *War Dispatches* (1964).

"MEMORANDUM OF TRIP FROM NEW YORK TO PARIS TO MARSEILLES"

An., 1 p. CUCC.

MEN IN THE STORM

Arena, 10 (October, 1894), 662–667. Contains a variant opening reprinted for the first time in *NYCS* (1966). This opening phrase reads: "At about three o'clock of the February afternoon. . . ."

Philistine, 4 (January, 1897), 37–48.

In *The Open Boat and Other Stories.* London: William Heinemann, 1898.

In *Work,* vol. 11 (1926).

In *Omnibus* (1952).

In *CSS&S* (1963).

In *NYCS* (1966), reproducing the text of *Arena* (1894).

MERRY-GO-ROUND

A projected novel about the adventures of the daughter of a travelling carousel's owner, her father, and her lover. "The Pace of Youth" provides one of the final chapters of this projected novel about Asbury Park.

MERRY THRONG AT HOT SPRINGS

Proof of *Nebraska State Journal* in CUCC.

Buffalo Sunday News, March 3, 1895, p. 8. "Seen at Hot Springs."

Cincinnati Commercial Tribune, March 3, 1895, p. 17. "Arkansas Hot Springs."

Dallas News, March 3, 1895, p. 16.

Galveston Daily News, March 3, 1895, p. 11. "Hot Springs Scenes."

Nebraska State Journal, March 3, 1895, p. 10. "Seen at Hot Springs."

Philadelphia Press, March 3, 1895, part 3, p. 29.

Rochester Democrat-Chronicle, March 3, 1895, p. 7.

In *UW* (1963); reprints *Philadelphia Press.*

MESMERIC MOUNTAIN

TMs., 5 pp., with autograph corrections perhaps in Cora Crane's hand. BCC.

In *Last Words.* London: Digby, Long & Co., 1902.

In *Men, Women and Boats.* New York: Boni and Liveright, 1921.

In *Work,* vol. 11 (1926).

In *Maggie, and Other Stories.* New York: Modern Library, 1933.

In *The Pace of Youth and Other Stories.* Girard, Kans.: Haldeman-Julius (n.d.).

In *SCS* (1949).

In *CSS&S* (1963).

In *SCTS* (1968).

MEXICAN SIGHTS AND STREET SCENES

Press clipping, undated, from *New York Sun.* CUCC. Not yet traced.

Savannah Morning News, May 16, 1895, p. 9. "Stephen Crane in Mexico."

Buffalo Sunday News, May 19, 1895, p. 11. "Crane in Mexico."

Dallas Morning News, May 19, 1895, p. 18. "Crane Sees Mexico."

Galveston Daily News, May 19, 1895, p. 13. "Crane Sees Mexico."

Louisville Courier-Journal, May 19, 1895, part 2, p. 7. "In Old Mexico."

Nebraska State Journal, May 19, 1895, p. 13. "Stephen Crane in Mexico."

Philadelphia Press, May 19, 1895, p. 33.

Rochester Democrat and Chronicle, May 19, 1895, p. 9.
Chicago Daily News, June 6, 1895, p. 10. "In the City of Mexico."
In *UW* (1963); reprints *Philadelphia Press.*

MINETTA LANE
See STEPHEN CRANE IN MINETTA LANE.

"MISCELLANEOUS FRAGMENTS"
AMs., 17 pp., with one page in Cora Crane's hand. CUCC. Includes a Ms.
fragment replying to London *Times,* November 21, 1899. Crane's reply
is in *TW,* p. 516.

MISS LOUISE GERARD—SOPRANO
Musical News, December, 1894, p. 3 [unsigned]. Press clipping in CUCC.
Musical Courier, 19, no. 20 (December 26, 1894), 30.
In *UW* (1963).
In *NYCS* (1966).

MONSTER
AMs., 1 p., last page only (p. 68). CUCC. Also, holograph note in Crane's
hand appearing at the reverse end of Cora Crane's manuscript book, a note
listing names, 2 pp.

> Dr. Edmund Trescott (M.D.) ("Ned") Lives corner of Niagra Avenue and On-
> tario St. New House. Loves good horses.
> Grace, his wife. Originally from Connecticut.
> Jimmie their son. Only child. Strict obedience to father.

On a new leaf appears the name of one of Dr. Trescott's friends in
"The Monster": Judge Denning Hagenthorpe.
Facsimile reproduction of the single surviving leaf of "The Monster" is re-
produced in *The Works of Stephen Crane,* ed. Fredson Bowers, vol. VII,
Tales of Whilomville (1969). Text quoted in Introduction by J. C. Leven-
son, p. xxxi.

Harper's Magazine, 97 (August, 1898), 343–376.
New York: Harper & Brothers, 1899.
London: Harper & Brothers, 1901.
In *Work,* vol. 3 (1926).
In *Twenty Stories.* New York: Alfred A. Knopf, 1940.
In *Twenty Stories.* Cleveland & New York: World Publishing Company, 1945.
In *CSS&S* (1963).

MOONLIGHT ON THE SNOW
Holograph Ms. on verso of letterhead of the Royal Pavilion Hotel, and
a holograph fragment, also in CUCC. Discovered by Fredson Bowers.
Facsimile reproduction of both fragment autographs starts in *The Works of
Stephen Crane,* ed., Fredson Bowers, vol. V, *Tales of Adventure* (1970).
Page proofs, 23 pp., with autograph corrections. BCC.
Frank Leslie's Popular Monthly, 49 (April, 1900), 606–618.
In *The Monster and Other Stories.* London: Harper & Brothers, 1901.
In *Work,* vol. 12 (1927).
In *CSS&S* (1963).
SCraneN, 3, no. 4 (Summer, 1969), 1–2. "An Early Draft of 'Moonlight on
the Snow.'"

MOURNFUL OLD BUILDING STOOD
AMs., 2 pp., incomplete, untitled. Two drafts are in CUCC. On the second
draft is a note in Crane's hand: "to be looked over."

"A Mournful Old Building," in which Crane regards a building as a metaphor of man's plight (as again in *Maggie*), is a variant sketch of "The Art Students' League Building" and these versions are echoed in *The Third Violet* (1896, 1897).
Quoted briefly in *Bulletin*, 60 (1956).
First published in *NYCS* (1966).

MR. BINKS' DAY OFF
New York Press, July 8, 1894, part 4, p. 2.
In *CSS&S* (1963).
In *UW* (1963).
In *NYCS* (1966).

MR. CRANE, OF HAVANA
New York Journal, November 9, 1898, p. 6.
In *UW* (1963).
In *War Dispatches* (1964).

MR. STEPHEN CRANE ON THE NEW AMERICA*
Outlook (London), 3 (February 4, 1899), pp. 12–13. Crane quoted by an anonymous interviewer.
In *UW* (1963).
In *War Dispatches* (1964).

MY CROSS
TMs., 1 p., poem. CUCC.
In *Poetry* (1957).
In *Poems of Stephen Crane* (1966).

MYSTERY OF HEROISM
Kansas City Star, August 1, 1895, p. 8; August 2, 1895, p. 10.
Minneapolis Tribune, August 1, 1895, p. 4; August 2, 1895, p. 4.
Omaha Daily Bee, August 1, 1895, p. 7; August 2, 1895, p. 7.
Omaha Evening Bee, August 1, 1895, p. 7; August 2, 1895, p. 7.
Philadelphia Press, August 1, 1895, p. 11; August 2, 1895, p. 9.
San Francisco Chronicle, August 14, 1895, p. 11; August 15, 1895, p. 11.
Chicago Times-Herald, October 27, 1895, p. 33.
Novels and Stories (1896), pp. 17, 19, 21, 23.
In *The Little Regiment.* New York: D. Appleton & Co., 1896.
In *The Little Regiment.* London: William Heinemann, 1897.
In *Pictures of War.* London: William Heinemann, 1898.
In *Pictures of War.* London: William Heinemann, 1916.
In *Work,* vol. 2 (1925).
In *Twenty Stories.* New York: Alfred A. Knopf, 1940.
Scholastic, 38 (February 17, 1941), 29–30, 34–35.
In *Twenty Stories.* Cleveland & New York: World Publishing Company, 1945.
In *Omnibus* (1952).
In *CSS&S* (1963).
In *TW* (1970).

MY TALK WITH "SOLDIERS SIX" ("SOME INTERVIEWS")
Westminster Gazette, June 14, 1897, p. 2; June 15, 1897, pp. 1–2. Parts V and VI of series captioned "With Greek and Turk."
See IMPRESSION OF THE "CONCERT."
New York Journal, June 20, 1897, p. 18.

* Listed in *W-S Bibliography* as "Stephen Crane on the New Americas."

San Francisco Examiner, July 4, 1897, p. 6.
In *UW* (1963); reprints *New York Journal.*
In *War Dispatches* (1964). "Some Interviews."

NAKED WOMAN AND A DEAD DWARF
TMs., 1 p. CUCC.*
Bookman, 69 (April, 1929), 122.
In *Poems* (1930); reprinted from *Bookman.*
In *Poetry* (1957).
In *Poems of Stephen Crane* (1966).
See THREE POEMS.

NARROW ESCAPE OF THE THREE FRIENDS
New York World, May 29, 1898, p. 23.
In *UW* (1963).
In *War Dispatches* (1964).

NEBRASKANS' BITTER FIGHT FOR LIFE
New Orleans Times-Democrat, February 23, 1895, p. 9. "Nebraskans' Fight."
Buffalo Evening News, February 24, 1895.
Cincinnati Commercial Tribune, February 24, 1895, pp. 17–18. "Nebraska's Fight for Life."
Dallas Morning News, February 24, 1895, p. 18.
Galveston Daily News, February 24, 1895, p. 10.
Nebraska State Journal, February 24, 1895, p. 14. "Waiting for the Spring."
New York Press, February 24, 1895, p. 2. "A State's Hard Fight."
Philadelphia Press, February 24, 1895, part 3, p. 25.
Salt Lake City Tribune, February 24, 1895, p. 14.
In *UW* (1963).
Prairie Schooner, 38 (Spring, 1964), 15–26. "Waiting for the Spring."

NEW INVASION OF BRITAIN
Chicago Record, May 8, 1897, p. 4. "Stephen Crane on Bounders."
Omaha Daily Bee, May 9, 1897, p. 20 [unsigned].
Omaha Weekly Bee, May 9, 1897, p. 20. [unsigned].
Pittsburgh Leader, May 9, 1897, p. 22.
In *UW* (1963).

NEW YORK BOARDING HOUSE
See LANDLADY'S DAUGHTER.

NEW YORK LIFE BY THE FAMOUS NOVELIST: STEPHEN CRANE
See IN THE TENDERLOIN.

NEW YORK'S BICYCLE SPEEDWAY
Press clipping signed, dated "For July 5," in the Crane Scrapbook. CUCC.
W-S Bibliography, p. 128, errs in claiming it appeared in *New York Sun,* July 5, 1895, part 3, p. 5. "Transformed Boulevard." This appeared in *New York Sun,* July 5, 1896, p. 5. The text is identical with the press clipping. Only the title differs, the *Sun* publishing the same day the same sketch under variant titles.
Boston Globe, July 5, 1896, p. 30. "Mighty Army of Wheels."
New York Sun, July 5, 1896 p. 5. "Transformed Boulevard."
Pittsburgh Leader, July 5, 1896, p. 22. "A Bicycle Speedway."

Poetry (1957), p. 286, cites an AMsS., 1 p. but no such manuscript exists.

In *UW* (1963). "New York's Bicycle Speedway."
In *NYCS* (1966). "New York's Bicycle Speedway." *See* note, p. 149.

NIGHT ATTACKS ON THE MARINES AND A BRAVE RESCUE
New York World, July 16, 1898, p. 2.
In *UW* (1963).
In *War Dispatches* (1964).

NIGHT AT THE MILLIONAIRE'S CLUB*
Press clipping, signed by Crane "Truth, New York." CUCC.
Truth (New York), 13 (April 21, 1894), 4.
In *UW* (1963).
In *NYCS* (1966).

NOTEBOOK OF STEPHEN CRANE
Holograph Ms. written on leaves measuring 8⅝ × 5⅛ in. BCC.
Bulletin, 60 (September, 1856), 455–462. Reproduces from Crane's Pocket
Notebook of 1892–1894 the untitled but complete article filling 25 pp.,
"The Art Students' League," portions of that sketch; "Matinee Girls," a
fragment of 3 pp.; "Election Night: New York 1894"; and one sample of
"Literary Notes."
In *NYCS* (1966). Reproduces the entire "Art Students' League Building" and
"A Mournful Old Building," here for the first time, the latter from Ms. in
CUCC. They are related pieces. Also reproduces "Election Night," from
Crane's Notebook; also, "Matinee Girls."
In *Notebook* (1969). "There are 76 unnumbered leaves, of which 17 are torn
out. It is bound at the top with flimsy cardboard covers, and on the in-
side back cover the name 'Stephen Crane' is printed upside down in light
pencil. Next to 'Stephen Crane' is a sticker with the name of 'Harry Ba-
con Collamore,' who owned the Notebook before Barrett."
Crane wrote consecutively on the rectos, except for one leaf, "and then
reversed the Notebook and began writing again on the versos."
The Notebook contains seven major sketches, Literary Notes, the poem
"Little Birds of the Night," and other fragments. The seven major
sketches, all published in *NYCS* (1966), are: "The Art Students' League
Building," "The Duel That Was Not Fought," "Matinee Girls," "The
Park Row Restaurant," "Heard on the Street Election Night," "A Deser-
tion," and "A Street Scene."

NOTES ABOUT PROSTITUTES
Holograph Ms., 2 pp. folio, written on legal cap paper with a portion of
"An Eloquence of Grief," namely "The Story of a Girl Arrested for
Stealing," on recto. On verso "Notes about Prostitutes," which is not
listed in the BCC catalogue (1970). BCC.
Crane wrote these drafts during the court trial of Dora Clark (1896).†
Bulletin, 60 (October, 1956), 477–478. Here first described and quoted from.
First published in *NYCS* (1966).

NOTES FOR SULLIVAN COUNTY SKETCHES
An., 3 pp. CUCC.

NOT MUCH OF A HERO
New York Tribune, May 1, 1892, part 2, p. 15.
SHR, 2, no. 1 (Winter, 1968).

* *See also* footnote to WHY DID THE YOUNG CLERK SWEAR?
† *See Crane,* chap. 12, The Dora Clark Affair.

OCTOPUSH
  New York Tribune, July 10, 1892, part 2, p. 17.
  In *SCS* (1949).
  In *CSS&S* (1963).
  In *SCTS* (1968).
  See THE FISHERMEN.

OGDEN GOELET'S NEW YACHT
  Ms. CUCC, a Crane newsletter. Not in CUCC catalogue.
  New York Press, August 22, 1897, p. 23. *See Cora Crane,* pp. 117, 376, 395.

OH, A RARE OLD WINE YE BREWED FOR ME
  AMs., 1 p., poem. AMs., 1 p., copy signed "Stephen Crane" in Cora Crane's
  hand. CUCC.
  In *Poetry* (1957).
  In *Poems of Stephen Crane* (1966).

"OL' BENNET" AND THE INDIANS
  AMs., 4 pp., in Edith Richie's hand. CUCC. Holograph Ms., 4 pp., SCC.
  Galley proofs, 3 pp., *Cassell's Magazine* (1900). BCC.
  Cassell's Magazine, n.s., 22 (December, 1900), 108–111.
  In *Last Words.* Digby, Long & Co., 1902.
  In *Work,* vol 9 (1926).
  In *Twenty Stories.* New York: Alfred A. Knopf, 1940.
  In *Twenty Stories.* Cleveland & New York: World Publishing Company,
  1945.
  In *CSS&S* (1963).

OLD MAN GOES WOOING
  Westminster Gazette, November 23, 1897, pp. 1–2.
  Westminster Budget, November 26, 1897.
  Philistine, 9 (July, 1899), 44–50. "An Old Man Goes A-Wooing." A bastard-
  ized text, as is the title.
  In *Last Words.* London: Digby, Long & Co., 1902.
  In *CSS&S* (1963). The text is not the one Gullason cites, p. 380; it is not the
  Philistine's text as claimed.

OMINOUS BABY
  Crane wrote a sequel to "An Ominous Baby" on pink-lined pad sheets, titled
  "An Ominous Baby—Tommie's Home Coming." In *MSC* (1958), pp. 40–41.
  This new passage from the sequel is quoted for the first time in *NYCS*
  (1966), pp. 59–60. Neither BCC nor CUCC catalogues list the above data.
  "An Ominous Baby" links with "A Great Mistake" (1896).
  Arena, 9 (May, 1894), 819–821.
  Philistine, 3 (October, 1896), 133–137.
  In *The Open Boat And Other Stories.* London: William Heinemann, 1898.
  In *Work,* vol. 11 (1926).
  In *CSS&S* (1963).
  In *NYCS* (1966).

ONCE A MAN, CLAMBERING TO THE HOUSETOPS
  AMs., 1 p., poem, on verso of Ms. of "Gratitude, the sense of obligation,"
  inscribed: "Stephen Crane / Hartwood Club / Port Jervis N.Y. / The
  name of this club / shall be the. . . ." CUCC.
  In *War Is Kind* (1899).
  In *Work,* vol. 6 (1926).

In *Poems* (1930).
In *Poetry* (1957).
In *Poems of Stephen Crane* (1966).

ONE CAME FROM THE SKIES
AMs., 1 p., poem; TMs., 1 p. CUCC.
Ts., 1 p. and Tsc. (2 pp. of holograph in CUCC). SCC. (Also found in "Lines.")
In *Poetry* (1957).
In *Poems of Stephen Crane* (1966).

ONE DASH—HORSES
Buffalo Commercial, January 3, 1896, p. 4; January 4, 1896, p. 4.
Kansas City Star, January 3, 1896, p. 7; January 4, 1896, p. 7.
Nebraska State Journal, January 3, 1896, p. 5; January 4, 1896, p. 5.
Philadelphia Press, January 4, 1896, p. 11; January 6, 1896, p. 10.
New Orleans Times-Picayune, January 5, 1896, p. 22. "One Dash With Horses."
New Review, 14 (February, 1896), 140–151.
Pocket Magazine, 3 (June, 1896), 70–101.
In *The Open Boat and Other Stories.* London: William Heinemann, 1898. "Horses—One Dash."
In *The Open Boat and Other Tales of Adventure.* New York: Doubleday & McClure, 1898.
In *The Open Boat and Other Tales of Adventure.* New York: Doubleday, Page & Co., 1905.
In *Work,* vol. 12 (1927).
In *Twenty Stories.* New York: Alfred A. Knopf, 1940.
In *Twenty Stories.* Cleveland & New York: World Publishing Company, 1945.
In *CSS&S* (1963).
In *TA* (1970).

ON THE BOARDWALK
New York Tribune, August 14, 1892, part 2, p. 17 [unsigned].
In *UW* (1963).

ON THE BROWN TRAIL
AMs., 1 p., poem. AMs., 1 p., copy by Cora Crane signed "Stephen Crane" in Cora Crane's hand. CUCC.
In *Poetry* (1957).
In *Poems of Stephen Crane* (1966).

ON THE DESERT
TMs., 1 p., poem, included with "You tell me this is God?" Also, *Philistine* proof sheet, corrected in Crane's hand? CUCC.
AMsS., 1 p., inscribed: "Stephen Crane. . . . Please send proof." BCC.
Philistine, 6 (May, 1898), 166–167.
In *War Is Kind* (1899).
In *Work,* vol. 6 (1926).
In *Poems* (1930).
In *Poetry* (1957).
In *Poems of Stephen Crane* (1966).

ON THE NEW JERSEY COAST / GUESTS CONTINUE TO ARRIVE IN LARGE NUMBERS / PARADES AND ENTERTAINMENTS. . . .

New York Tribune, August 21, 1892, p. 22 [unsigned]. Crane's sketch of the parade of the Junior Order of United American Mechanics at Asbury Park, for which sketch the *Tribune* fired him.

See ELLA FLOCK.

Newark Sunday Call, January 14, 1931.

Library (Public Library of Newark), 5, no. 1 (September, 1932), 3. "Presidential Parade."

In *The Public Papers of a Bibliomaniac*. Mount Vernon, N.Y.: The Golden Eagle Press, 1942.

American Literature, 20 (November, 1948), 284–286. "Stephen Crane at Asbury Park," by Victer A. Elconin.

In *SCS* (1949), Introduction, pp. 7–8.

In *Omnibus* (1952).

In *Nineteenth Century Fiction*, 8 (September, 1953), 99–117.

In *UW* (1963).

In *NYCS* (1966).

ON THE NEW JERSEY COAST / SUMMER DWELLERS AT ASBURY PARK AND THEIR DOINGS. . . .

New York Tribune, July 24, 1892, p. 22 [unsigned].

In *UW* (1963).

In *NYCS* (1966).

OPEN BOAT

AMs., 1 p., dedication and list of contents for the English edition of *The Open Boat and Other Stories*. CUCC.

Scribner's Magazine, 21 (June, 1897), 728–740.

London: William Heinemann, 1898.

New York: Doubleday & McClure, 1898.

New York: Doubleday, Page & Co., 1905.

In *Men, Women and Boats*. New York: Boni and Liveright, 1921.

In *Work*, vol. 12 (1927).

Golden Book, 11 (January, 1930), 83–92.

In *Maggie, and Other Stories*. New York: The Modern Library, 1933.

Scribner's Magazine, 101 (January, 1937), 45–53.

In *Twenty Stories*. New York: Alfred A. Knopf, 1940.

In *Twenty Stories*. Cleveland & New York: World Publishing Company, 1945.

In *Omnibus* (1952).

In *CSS&S* (1963).

OPIUM'S VARIED DREAMS

Buffalo Morning Express, May 17, 1896, section 2, p. 3. "The Opium Smokers of New York."

Denver Republican, May 17, 1896, p. 21. "White Smokers of Opium."

Detroit Free Press, May 17, 1896, p. 20. "Opium Smokers."

Kansas City Star, May 17, 1896, p. 16. "They Who Smoke Opium."

New York Sun, May 17, 1896, part 3, p. 3 [unsigned].

Philadelphia Inquirer, May 17, 1896, p. 28. "Slaves of the Opium Habit."

Portland Oregonian, May 17, 1896, p. 17. "Slaves of the Opium Habit."

In *UW* (1963); reprints *New York Sun*.

In *NYCS* (1966); reprints *New York Sun*.

O'RUDDY

Holograph Ms., 102 leaves, written on rectos only, all in Crane's hand except for parts of two or three leaves, written probably by Helen Crane at Brede Place.

"The MS is complete up to almost the end of Chapter XXV, ending with the text of the first edition page 226, line 7. It is evident that a leaf is missing that finished Chapter XXV. This is consistent with the evidence that Crane's share went up to Chapter XXVI, where [Robert] Barr started. . . .

"The manuscript has a number of stylistic differences from the first edition, and three long passages in the MS were not printed in the first edition, in each case I think because they were considered a bit sexy (by the standards of the day, which were remarkably purist). The *Idler* version has even deeper censorship of this theme." (From letter of Fredson Bowers to R. W. S., August 4, 1970.)

The holograph Ms. is owned by Mrs. Donald Klopfer of New York City.* The page proofs, in their early state, for the Robert Barr part of *The O'Ruddy,* starting with Chapter XXVI, together with a statement by Robert Barr that this was where his writing of *The O'Ruddy* began, are in the possession of Matthew J. Bruccoli.

AMs., 2 pp., in Cora Crane's hand. AMs., 8 pp., in Cora Crane's hand. AMs., 1 p., list of four chapter headings. TMs., 4 pp., Chapter XXIV, incomplete. TMs., 4 pp., Chapter XXIV, incomplete. TMs., 4 pp., Chapter XXIV incomplete. TMs., 4 pp., Chapter XXIV, incomplete. CUCC.

New York: Frederick A. Stokes Company, 1903.

Idler, 24 (January, 1904), 351–377; February, 1904, 469–488; March, 1904, 635–664; 25 (April, 1904), 65–90; May, 1904, 171–187; June, 1904, 307–326; July, 1904, 413–435.

London: Methuen & Co., 1904.

In *Work,* vols. 7 and 8 (1926).

In *The Complete Novels of Stephen Crane.* Garden City, N.Y.: Doubleday & Co., 1967.

In *O'Ruddy* (1971).

OUIDA'S MASTERPIECE
Book Buyer, n.s., 13 (January, 1897), 968–969.

In *UW* (1963).

OUR SAD NEED OF DIPLOMATS
New York Journal, November 17, 1898, p. 6.

In *UW* (1963).

In *War Dispatches* (1964).

PACE OF YOUTH
Dayton Daily Journal, January 17, 1895, p. 4; January 18, 1895, p. 4.

Kansas City Star, January 17, 1895, p. 8; January 18, 1895, p. 7.

Minneapolis Tribune, January 18, 1895, p. 4; January 19, 1895, p. 4.

Nebraska State Journal, January 18, 1895, p. 5; January 19, 1895, p. 5.

New York Press, January 18, 1895, p. 7; January 19, 1895, p. 7.

San Francisco Examiner, June 30, 1895, Fiction Supplement.

In *The Open Boat and Other Stories.* London: William Heinemann, 1898.

---

* *See* David A. Randall, *Dukedom Large Enough* (1969), p. 229. Identifies owner of Ms. and remarks: "It is completely in Crane's hand with a few pages by Cora till about a quarter through Chapter XXV."

In *Men, Women and Boats*. New York: Boni and Liveright, 1921.
In *Work*, vol. 11 (1926).
In *Maggie, and Other Stories*. New York: The Modern Library, 1933.
In *The Pace of Youth and Other Stories*. Girard, Kans.: Haldeman-Julius (n.d.).
In *CSS&S* (1963).
In *NYCS* (1966).
In *TA* (1970).

PANDO HURRYING TO SANTIAGO
New York World, July 1, 1898, p. 2.
In *UW* (1963).

PARK ROW RESTAURANT
See IN A PARK ROW RESTAURANT.

THE PATENT OF A LORD
TMs., 1 p., poem, copy. CUCC.*
In *Poetry* (1957).

PATRIOT SHRINE OF TEXAS
See STEPHEN CRANE IN TEXAS.

PICTURES OF WAR
London: William Heinemann, 1898.
London: William Heinemann, 1916.
See collation of this title.

PIKE COUNTY PUZZLE
A mock newspaper written and published through the *Gazette* newspaper printers of Port Jervis, New York, by Stephen Crane and Louis Senger. Dated August 28, 1894, 4 pp. Photostat of original in the Stallman Crane Collection, gift of Anna Wells of the Poughkeepsie Public Library.
Reprinted by *SCraneN*, Columbus, Ohio, 1967. Brochure.

PLANS FOR NEW JERSEY NOVEL
An., 2 p. CUCC.

PLANS FOR NEW NOVEL
An., 1 p., Revolutionary War novel and the Crane family's part therein. CUCC.

PLAY SET IN A FRENCH TAVERN
AMs., 18 pp., first act of an untitled play. Unpublished.
TMs., 14 pp. CUCC.

POKER GAME
TMs., 4 pp., with autograph corrections. BCC. Facsimile reproduction in *The Works of Stephen Crane,* ed. Fredson Bowers, vol. V, *Tales of Adventure* (1970).
In *Last Words*. London: Digby, Long & Co., 1902.
In *Work*, vol. 11 (1926).
In *CSS&S* (1963).
In *NYCS* (1966).
In *TA* (1970).

PORTO RICAN "STRADDLE"
New York Journal, August 18, 1898, p. 3.
Kansas City Star, August 28, 1898, p. 5. "It was Hard to Choose / But the

---

* One of several poems not included in *Poems of Stephen Crane* (1966).

Porto Rican Soldiers Finally Joined / the American Side. / Stephen Crane in the New York Journal."
In *UW* (1963); reprints *New York Journal.*
In *War Dispatches* (1964); reprints *New York Journal.*

PORTRAIT OF SMOLENSKI
Ms., 5 pp., untitled; written in Cora Crane's hand with corrections in her hand and a few in Crane's hand. Dictated by Crane to Cora. CUCC.
In *Cora Crane* (1960), pp. 100–101, portions quoted, but not accurately. Source not cited.
In *RW* (1971).

PREDECESSOR
Title of a Western play which Crane and Conrad proposed writing in collaboration.
See Crane, p. 339 and note 2, p. 602. John Berryman in *Stephen Crane* (1950) says that "Conrad and Crane wrote 'The Blood of the Martyr.' " However, the play of their intended collaboration was "The Predecessor."

PRICE OF THE HARNESS [THE WOOF OF THIN RED THREADS]
Blackwood's Edinburgh Magazine, 164 (December, 1898), 829–841. "The Price of the Harness." Crane here added: "He laid his face to his rifle as if it were his mistress."
Nolan, here seemingly a fictionalized person, is in fact named Nolan in Crane's list of seventeen volunteers in Company C, in Crane's *New York World* dispatch, "Night Attacks on the Marines and a Brave Rescue," July 16, 1898. Nolan figures again in "Regulars Get No Glory," *New York World,* July 20, 1898.
Cosmopolitan, 26 (December, 1898), 164–172. "The Woof of Thin Red Threads." This title derives from part 5, from a phrase therein.
In *Wounds in the Rain.* London: Methuen & Co., 1900.
In *Wounds in the Rain.* New York: Frederick A. Stokes Company, 1900.
In *Work,* vol. 9 (1926).
In *Twenty Stories.* New York: Alfred A. Knopf, 1940.
In *Twenty Stories.* Cleveland & New York: World Publishing Company, 1945.
In *CSS&S* (1963).
In *War Dispatches* (1964).
In *TA* (1970).

PRIVATE'S STORY
New York Journal, September 26, 1898, p. 6.
In *UW* (1963).
In *War Dispatches* (1964).

PROLOGUE
Roycroft Quarterly, 1 (May, 1896), 38.
Philistine, 3 (July, 1896), 39.
In *Work,* vol. 11 (1926).
In *NYCS* (1966).
In *Crane* (1968), Appendix, pp. 545–546. Identifies the source of this prose drama in the Reverend Thomas de Witt Talmage's *Night Side of New York Life* (1878).*

* *See The Portable Stephen Crane,* ed. Joseph Katz (1969), which reprints "A Prologue" as a poem, p. 550. However, Katz did not include it as a poem, which it isn't, in *The Poems of Stephen Crane* (1966).

PRUSSIAN OFFICIAL'S STUPIDITY
AMs., 2 pp. CUCC.
New York Press, August 15, 1897.

PURSUIT OF THE BUTTER & EGGS MAN
No. 26 in Crane's holograph list of titles of his works, the journal publishing the given title, the location of the Ms., and the word count. Here the word age is 500, and the journal is "The Press" (untraced). List in CUCC.

QUEENSTOWN
New York Journal, October 18, 1897, p. 6.
Westminster Gazette, October 19, 1897, pp. 1–2.
Kansas City Star, October 24, 1897, p. 5.
Westminster Budget, 10 (October 29, 1897), 7–8.
In *UW* (1963).*

RAFT STORY ("SIX YEARS AFLOAT")
Holograph Ms., 8 pp., folio, unsigned. Each page numbered in Crane's hand, with the first page signed "Raft Story." Each page measures approximately $8 \times 12\frac{1}{8}$ in. And each is lined—31 lines per sheet—but without ruled margin. BC.

Press proof dated "For Aug. 2"—in CUCC—is identical with the manuscript except for a few typographical errors, a few changes in punctuation, one in spelling *(increased* for *encreased),* and one transposed phrase *(is in fact* for *in fact is).* No further changes were made before Crane sent the sketch to the editor or printer.

The manuscript provides additional evidence of Crane's remarkable gift for spinning out a sketch or tale with no need to make revisions.

The proof-sheet is headlined "Six Years Afloat / The Captain of the *Tillie B.* Reports / That He Sighted . . . / . . . the Famous Lumber Raft Lost . . . in / . . . 1890. . . ." Signed.

New York Press, August 2, 1896, p. 18. "Six Years Afloat."
Pittsburgh Leader, August 2, 1896, p. 20. "Six Years Afloat."
Portland Oregonian, August 2, 1896, p. 18. "Six Years Afloat."
Bulletin, 60 (October, 1956), 478–482.
In *CSS&S* (1963), with no acknowledgement to *Bulletin.*
In *UW* (1963), with no acknowledgement to *Bulletin.*

RED BADGE OF COURAGE
AMsS., 176 pp. BCC. Photostat of AMs., 1 p. (page 1). BCC. AMs., 2 pp., pp. 99 and 101 of the final holograph Ms., CUCC. AMs., 1 p., p. 98 of the final holograph Ms. BC. AMs., 1 p., p. 98 of the final holograph Ms., in Houghton Library.† (For first publication of these five new holograph Ms. pages see below.) AMsS., 57 pp. of an earlier draft appearing upside down in the bound notebook. BCC.

Photocopy of the bound notebook manuscripts is in the possession of

---

* Not in *The Complete Short Stories and Sketches of Stephen Crane,* ed. Thomas A. Gullason (1963), which volume is not complete in that it omits many dozens of Crane sketches: Mexican, Asbury Park, New York City, several Irish Notes, battle sketches, etc.

† Crane used the back side of Houghton 98 to keep scorings for a card game.

Stallman Crane Collection (a gift of Mr. Clifton Waller Barrett, December, 1951). BC has a photocopy, as does also the University of Texas Library.

Philadephia Press, December 3–8, 1894, p. 11 each day. The shortened newspaper version.

Minneapolis Tribune, December 4–8, 10, 1894, pp. 4, 4, 4. Short version.

Nebraska State Journal, December 4–9, 1894, pp. 4, 5, 5, 5, 5, and 9, respectively. The shortened newspaper version.

New York Press, December 9, 1894, pp. 4, 5, 6. The shortened newspaper version.

San Francisco Examiner, July 14, 21, 28, 1895, pp. 23, 24. Short version.

Current Literature, 18 (August, 1895), 142. Reprints a portion of the novel from advance sheets.

New York: D. Appleton and Company, 1895.

London: William Heinemann, 1896.

New York: D. Appleton and Company, 1896.

In *Pictures of War.* London: William Heinemann, 1898.

New York: D. Appleton and Company, 1900. Introduction by Ripley Hitchcock.

Fra, 18, no. 1 (October, 1916), 27–28. "The Color-Bearer." A portion of the novel reprinted.

New York: D. Appleton and Company, 1916. Introduction by Ripley Hitchcock.

In *Pictures of War.* London: William Heinemann, 1916.

New York: D. Appleton and Company, 1917. Introduction by Ripley Hitchcock.

New York: D. Appleton and Company, 1917. Introduction by Arthur Guy Empey.

London: William Heinemann, 1925. Introduction by Joseph Conrad. Reprinted in *Last Essays.* New York and London, 1926. "His War Book."

New York: D. Appleton and Company, 1925–1931.

In *Work,* vol. 1 (1925). Introduction by Joseph Hergesheimer.

New York: D. Appleton and Company, 1926–1941. Students' Edition.

New York: Random House, [1930]. Limited to 980 copies; printed at the Grabhorn Press; decorated by Valenti Angelo.

New York: D. Appleton and Company, 1933–1940.

London: Jonathan Cape, [1937]. Introduction by Joseph Conrad.

London: William Collins Sons & Co., Ltd., 1939. Introduction by F. Brereton. Illustrated by H. Monroe.

In *Men at War,* ed. Ernest Hemingway. New York: Crown Publishers, [1942].

New York: The Modern Library, [1942]. Introduction by Max J. Herzberg.

New York: Pocket Books, Inc., 1942. Introduction by Max J. Herzberg.

New York: The Heritage Press, [1944]. Introduction by Carl Van Doren. Illustrated by John Steuart Curry.

New York: Limited Editions Club, 1944. Introduction by Carl Van Doren. Illustrated by John Steuart Curry.

New York: Armed Services Edition, [1945].

Cleveland and New York: World Publishing Company, 1951. Introduction by William Targ. Illustrated by Winslow Homer.

London: Folio Society, 1951. Introduction by John T. Winterich. Reproduces for the first time the final holograph Ms. in the text of the First American Edition (1895) by the device of brackets. However, it is a faulty text of the

Ms., with numerous errors and a few omisssions. The Ms. of the earlier and shorter version is not reproduced here.

New York: Modern Library, 1951. Introduction by R. W. Stallman.

In *Omnibus*. New York: Alfred A. Knopf, 1952. London: William Heinemann, 1954. Reproduces in the text of the First American Edition (1895); by the device of brackets, the final holograph Ms. and, in footnotes to the text, the earlier Ms. draft. Here both manuscripts are brought together for the first time.

In BCC they are preserved in a bound book with the front cover stamped in gold lettering: THE RED BADGE OF COURAGE / STEPHEN CRANE. These loose sheets were bound into book form by Willis Brooks Hawkins, to whom Crane sent them as a gift on January 27, 1896. (*See Letters*, p. 107.) What his friend received consisted in fact of two manuscripts.

The final manuscript consists of 176 sheets of blue-ruled paper having a one-inch red-lined margin. On verso of 57 leaves appears portions of an earlier draft.

The pages of this earlier and shorter draft are not numbered consecutively, and in the bound book they appear upside down. That is because Crane stacked the sheets in haphazard order and used the clean back sides, turned upside down, for writing his final manuscript. (For example, on verso of pages 70–75 appear pp. 47, 52, 46, 45, 42, 64.) On verso of p. 137 of the long and final version (Ms. LV) appears a page from an unpublished short story, a page which happened to to get stacked in with the sheets of *The Red Badge* manuscript.

While transcribing from the short and earlier version (Ms. SV) Crane added to Ms. LV new matter. But then, having finished this enlarged draft, he cut it down, canceling many passages in order to speed up the pace of the narrative. He crossed out the used pages of his earlier draft by downward wavy pencil-strokes so as to avoid possible confusion with his new and final version.

Although most of Ms. SV has the appearance of being a transcription because it contains very few instances of corrected phrases, the procedure of composition in several passages seems more characteristic of the mind inventing rather than of the mind merely copying. One striking instance occurs toward the end of Ms. SV (p. 76). The signs of original composition that I think are evidenced here are the false starts, the unfinished and uncorrected syntax and sense, and the noticeable uncertainties of intention. Similar examples occur at the beginning of Ms. SV—on pp. 10, 13, and 49.

Was there a draft earlier than Ms. SV? All the evidence—including Crane's own account—contradicts any supposition that Ms. SV might be the original first draft. *See Omnibus*, pp. 205–206. Again, there can be no question that Ms. LV was transcribed from Ms. SV.

In recasting Ms. SV into Ms. LV Crane tended toward the gradual elimination of of all unnecessary words, paragraphs, and in one instance an entire chapter—Chapter XII. One part of this expunged Chapter XII is found on three pages of the earlier draft (Ms. SV). After copying it from Ms. SV, Crane removed from Ms. LV six pages, and then he renumbered his chapter headings, Chapter XIII being renumbered XII and some subsequent chapters being renumbered accordingly. He failed to renumber Chapter XVII, which should be XVI, etc. Consequently, the final chapter in

Ms. LV, which is in fact Chapter XXIV, is designated in Ms. LV as Chapter XXV.

Before sending the loose sheets to Hawkins, Crane had removed fifteen pages of Ms. LV. The only portions of the printed 1895 text, the First American Edition, which are *not* found in the final handwritten manuscript are (1) the final image of Chapter XXIV, and (2) the last half of Chapter IV beginning with the paragraph: "The din in front swelled to a tremendous chorus." However, one part of this last half of Chapter IV remains in Ms. SV. It appears on p. 36 of Crane's paginated Ms. SV, which p. 36 appears on verso of p. 127 Ms. LV. Ms. SV contains only one complete chapter, Chapter VI, pp. 46–52 by Crane's pagination. Two other chapters are almost complete, lacking only one page each; they are Chapters VII and XI.

Of the fifteen leaves not bound in the *Red Badge of Courage* manuscript book in BCC, five pages have come to light since *Omnibus* (1952). *See* below.

In *The Red Badge of Courage and Selected Stories.* New York: New American Library, 1960. Reproduces in the text of the First American Edition (1895); by the device of brackets, the final holograph Ms. and, in footnotes to the text, pp. 209–220, the canceled passages in that manuscript (Ms. LV) and in the earlier draft (Ms. SV), the shorter version.

Brought together here for the first time are five new pages of Ms. LV. Brought to light since *Omnibus* (1952) were two of these five pages, designated as Houghton 98 and Berg 98.* The other three pages, designated as CUCC 99 and 101 and Houghton 102, are reproduced here for the first time.

In *Stephen Crane: The Red Badge of Courage and Other Stories.* London: Oxford University Press (World's Classics), 1960. Reprinted in paperback, 1969.

In *Stephen Crane's The Red Badge of Courage: Text and Criticism.* New York: Harcourt, Brace and Company, 1960.

In *Stephen Crane: The Red Badge of Courage: An Annotated Text: Background and Sources: Essays in Criticism.* New York: W. W. Norton & Company, 1962.

In *The Complete Novels of Stephen Crane.* Garden City, N.Y.: Doubleday & Company, 1967.

In *"The Red Badge of Courage" by Stephen Crane: A Facsimile Reproduction of the New York Press Appearance of December 9, 1894.* Gainesville, Fla.: Scholars' Facsimiles & Reprints, 1967.

The Red Badge of Courage and Selected Prose and Poetry. New York: Holt, Rinehart and Winston, Inc., 1968. First editions in shorter form, 1950, 1956.

In *The Stephen Crane Reader.* Glenview, Ill.: Scott, Foresman and Company, 1972. Reproduces the text of the First American Edition (1895) together with Ms. SV and Ms. LV and the five Ms. LV pages from the libraries of Houghton, Columbia University, and New York Public Library.

RED BADGE OF COURAGE WAS HIS WIG-WAG FLAG

New York World, July 1, 1898, p. 3.

In *UW* (1963).

In *War Dispatches* (1964).

REFORMER

Poem written for the *Arena* but lost before publication and never rewritten. Read by Hamlin Garland.

* Collated in *Papers of the Bibliographical Society of America,* 49 (1955), 273–277.

REGULARS GET NO GLORY
  Boston Globe, July 19, 1898, p. 6. "Private Nolan. / Stephen Crane Says a Word / For the Regular."
    On Nolan *see* "Night Attacks on the Marines," where Crane reports on a volunteer named Noland. *See also* "The Price of the Harness," "War Memories," and *Crane.*
  Philadelphia Press, July 19, 1898, p. 2. "Stephen Crane Sketches the Common Soldier."
  New York World, July 20, 1898, p. 6.
  In *UW* (1963); reprints *New York World.*
  In *War Dispatches* (1964); reprints *New York World.*

RELUCTANT VOYAGERS
  AMs., 2 pp., written on versos of Ms. of "The Holler Tree," on versos of which Ms. appears also first draft of *George's Mother.** BCC, which has also a proof headed Northern Newspaper Syndicate. As "The Reluctant Voyagers" was written in May–June, 1893 (*see MSC*), it follows that *George's Mother* and probably also "The Holler Tree" were written at that time.
  Broadside release, 2 pp., on a sheet 14 inches by 22 inches. BCC.
  Boston Sunday Journal, 10 (February 11, 18, 1900), 296–303, 367–371, respectively.
  Chicago Times-Herald, February 11, 1900, part 3, p. 4; February 18, 1900, part 3, p. 4.
  New York Press, February 11, 1900, Sunday Magazine, pp. 6–11; February 18, 1900, Sunday Magazine, pp. 3–6.
  Philadelphia Press, February 11 and 18, 1900, p. 2.
  In *Last Words.* London: Digby, Long & Co., 1902.
  In *Men, Women and Boats.* New York: Boni & Liveright, 1921.
  In *Work,* vol. 11 (1926).
  In *Maggie, and Other Stories.* New York: Modern Library, 1933.
  In *CSS&S* (1963).

REMINISCENCE OF INDIAN WAR
  New York Daily Tribune, June 26, 1892, part 2, p. 17 [unsigned].
  SHR, 2, no. 1 (Winter, 1968), 29–32.

REPORT FROM ATHENS
  See SPIRIT OF THE GREEK PEOPLE.

REVENGE OF THE ADOLPHUS
  Strand Magazine, 18 (September, 1899), 724–733.
  Collier's Weekly, 24 (October 28, 1899), 13–14, 19, 24–25.
  In *Wounds in the Rain.* London: Methuen & Co., 1900.
  In *Wounds in the Rain.* New York: Frederick A. Stokes Company, 1900.
  In *Work,* vol. 9 (1926).
  In *CSS&S* (1963).
  In *TW* (1970).

RIGHT OF ARREST
  AMs., 1 p. CUCC.

ROOF GARDENS
  See EVENING ON THE ROOF.

----

* *See* Maurice Bassan, "First Draft of *George's Mother,*" *American Literature* (January, 1965), which omits mention of the Ms. of "The Reluctant Voyagers."

ROOSEVELT'S ROUGH RIDERS' LOSS DUE TO A GALLANT BLUNDER
New York World, June 26, 1898, p. 2.
Philadelphia Press, June 26, 1898, p. 3. "Stephen Crane Calls it a Blunder."
In *UW* (1963); reprints *New York World.*
In *War Dispatches* (1964); reprints *New York World.*

A ROW OF THICK PILLARS
TMs., 1 p., poem. CUCC.
In *Poetry* (1957).
In *Poems of Stephen Crane* (1966).

ROYAL IRISH CONSTABULARY
TMs., 4 pp. BCC.
Westminster Gazette, November 5, 1897, pp. 1–2.
Westminster Budget, November 12, 1897.
In *Last Words.* London: Digby, Long & Co., 1902.
In *Work,* vol. 11 (1926).

RUMBLING, BUZZING, TURNING, WHIRLING WHEELS
See WHEELS.

RUMORS STARTLE ASBURY
New York World, July 8, 1892, p. 11.

SAILING DAY SCENES
Press clipping—undated, unsigned—on which Crane wrote "The Press, New York" [*New York Press?*]. CUCC. Located by Fredson Bowers in *New York Press,* June 10, 1894, Part IV, p. 2.
In *UW* (1963).
In *NYCS* (1966).

SAMPSON INSPECTS HARBOR AT MARIEL
Chicago Tribune, May 1, 1898, p. 2. "Crane Sees Cabanas Shelled."
New York World, May 1, 1898, p. 3.
Omaha Daily Bee, May 1, 1898, p. 1. "Guns Speak Again."
Philadelphia Press, May 1, 1898, p. 2. "Stephen Crane's Story of a Skirmish."
In *UW* (1963); reprints *New York World.*
In *War Dispatches* (1964); reprints *New York World.*

SAN ANTONIO*
Pittsburgh Leader, January 8, 1899, p. 23.
Omaha Daily Bee, January 11, 1899, p. 12.
Omaha Weekly Bee, January 11, 1899, p. 12.

SAYINGS OF THE TURRET JACKS IN OUR BLOCKADING FLEETS
New York World, May 15, 1898, p. 33.
In *UW* (1966).

SCOTCH EXPRESS
AMsS., 12 pp. CUCC.
McClure's Magazine, 12 (January, 1899), 273–283.
Cassell's Magazine, n.s., 18 (January, 1899), 163–171.
In *Men, Women and Boats.* New York: Boni & Liveright, 1921.

* Discovered by Bernice Slote and reprinted for the first time in *Prairie Schooner,* 43 (Summer, 1969), 176–183.

In *Work,* vol. 11 (1926).

In *Maggie, and Other Stories.* New York: The Modern Library, 1933.

SEASIDE ASSEMBLY'S WORK AT AVON

New York Tribune, August 29, 1892, p. 4 [unsigned]. Possibly by Stephen Crane.

SEASIDE HOTEL HOP

New York Tribune, September 11, 1892, p. 15 [unsigned].

In *UW* (1963).

SECOND GENERATION

Cornhill Magazine, 80, n.s., 7 (December, 1899), 734–753.

Saturday Evening Post, 172 (December 2, 1899), 449–452.

In *Wounds in the Rain.* London: Methuen & Co., 1900.

In *Wounds in the Rain.* New York: Frederick A. Stokes Company, 1900.

In *Work,* vol. 2 (1925).

In *CSS&S* (1963).

In *TW* (1970).

SELF-MADE MAN

TMsS., 8 pp., with autograph corrections (Stephen Crane's signature by Cora Crane). BCC.

Cornhill Magazine, 79 (March, 1899), 324–329.

In *Last Words.* London: Digby, Long & Co., 1902.

In *Work,* vol. 11 (1926).

In *CSS&S* (1963).

In *NYCS* (1966).

SERGEANT'S PRIVATE MADHOUSE

Saturday Evening Post, 167 (September 30, 1899), 214–215.

English Illustrated Magazine, 22 (December, 1899), 243–249.

In *Wounds in the Rain.* London: Methuen & Co., 1900.

In *Wounds in the Rain.* New York: Frederick A. Stokes Company, 1900.

In *Work,* vol. 9 (1926).

In *The Saturday Evening Post Treasury.* New York, 1954, pp. 51–54.

In *CSS&S* (1963).

In *TW* (1970).

SESSION OF CONGRESS

An unfinished news article, AMs., 3 pp., unfinished. CUCC. Quoted in *Crane* (1986), pp. 201–202. Not listed in CUCC catalogue (1970).

SHAME

Harper's Magazine, 100 (January, 1900), 321–325.

In *Whilomville Stories.* New York: Harper & Brothers, 1900.

In *Whilomville Stories.* London: Harper & Brothers, 1900.

In *Work,* vol. 5 (1926).

In *Twenty Stories.* New York: Alfred A. Knopf, 1940.

In *Twenty Stories.* Cleveland & New York: World Publishing Company, 1945.

In *CSS&S* (1963).

In *TWH* (1969).

SHE CAME, SHE CONQUERED AND SHE RODE AWAY

Untraced. Story of a mining camp, manuscript of which was seen by Frank Noxon.

SHOULD THE WIDE WORLD ROLL AWAY

AMs., 1 p., poem. Inscribed ". . . Stephen Crane 1894." SCC.

In *Black Riders* (1895).
Bookman, 3 (April, 1896), 197. Reprints the poem. Reprints also "I Stood Upon a High Place," p. 196, and "Legends," p. 206.
In *Work,* vol. 6 (1926).
In *Poems* (1930).
In *Poetry* (1957).
In *Poems of Stephen Crane* (1966).

SHOWIN' OFF
AMsS., 4 pp. CUCC.
Harper's Magazine, 99 (November, 1899), 855–860.
In *Whilomville Stories.* New York: Harper & Brothers, 1900.
In *Whilomville Stories.* London: Harper & Brothers, 1900.
In *Work,* vol. 5 (1926).
In *CSS&S* (1963).
In *TWH* (1969).

SHRAPNEL OF THEIR FRIENDS
AMs., 3 pp. (pages 7, 8, 9 only). By an unidentified hand. CUCC.
TMsS., 7 pp., with autograph corrections (Stephen Crane's signature and notation "Spitzbergen Tale" in an unknown handwriting, not Cora Crane's.) BCC. Facsimile reproduction in *The Works of Stephen Crane,* ed. Fredson Bowers, vol. VI, *Tales of War* (1970).
Ainslee's Magazine. 5 (May, 1900), 303–305.
Black and White, 17 (September, 1900), 490–491.
In *Last Words.* London: Digby, Long & Co., 1902.
In *Work,* vol. 9 (1926).
In *CSS&S* (1963).
In *TW* (1970).

SIEGE
Untraced. A Cromwellian tale written at Brede Place in August, 1899. The manuscript, which was seen by Karl Harriman, is said to have been destroyed.

SIEGE OF PLEVNA
Lippincott's Magazine, 65 (May, 1900), 759–765.
In *Great Battles of the World.* Philadelphia: J. B. Lippincott Company, 1901.
In *Great Battles of the World.* London: Chapman & Hall Limited, 1901.
In *Great Battles of the World.* London: Hodder & Stoughton, 1914.

SILVER PAGEANT
TMsS., 2 pp., with Stephen Crane's signature by Cora Crane. BCC.
In *Last Words.* London: Digby, Long & Co., 1902.
In *Work,* vol. 11 (1926).
In *CSS&S* (1963).
In *NYCS* (1966).

SIXTH AVENUE
AMs., 1 p.; the opening paragraph of a sketch intended for the *New York Press.* CUCC.
First published in *NYCS* (1966).
　　　Crane lived with Charles J. Pike on and off for eighteen months during 1895–1896 in Pike's third-floor studio on the corner of Sixth Avenue and

33rd Street (at 281 Sixth Avenue). Sixth Avenue figures in several of Crane's sketches in *NYCS*.

SIX YEARS AFLOAT
See RAFT STORY.

SKETCHES FROM LIFE: UNCLE JAKE AND THE BELL HANDLE
AMsS., 14 pp., written on lined tablet paper in Crane's "large, open, clearly readable hand," dated 1885. CUCC.
Bulletin, 64 (May, 1960), 273–278.
In *CSS&S* (1963). Not in *UW* (1963).

SKETCHES OF NEBRASKA LIFE
No. 25 in Crane's holograph list of titles of his works, the journal publishing the given title, the location of the Ms., and the word count. Here the wordage is 1,000, and Crane's note reads: "MS to be recovered from Bacheler" [misspelled for Bacheller].

SLANT OF SUN ON DULL BROWN WALLS
TMs., 1 p., poem. Included on this page is "The Wayfarer." CUCC.
Roycroft Quarterly, 1 (May, 1896), 29.
In *War Is Kind* (1899).
Fra, 5, no. 1 (April, 1910), 29.
In *Work,* vol. 6 (1926).
In *Poems* (1930).
In *Poems of Stephen Crane* (1966).

SMALL BLACK AND WHITE AND TAN HOUND
AMs., 2 pp; AMs. 1 p., untitled sketch, unfinished. CUCC. *Exhibition,* p. 55, is in error.
Fine Arts Magazine (University of Connecticut), 6 (1961). Facsimile reproduction of the holograph Ms. on front and back sides of the cover.

SMOLENSKI
See PORTRAIT OF SMOLENSKI.

SNAKE*
AMsS., 5 pp. BCC.
TMs., 3 pp. BCC.
Cincinnati Commercial Tribune, June 14, 1896, p. 20. "The Man and the Snake."
Dallas Morning News, June 14, 1896, p. 9.
Detroit Free Press, June 14, 1896, p. 17.
Galveston Daily News, June 14, 1896, p. 20.
St. Louis Globe-Democrat, June 14, 1896, p. 36.
Minneapolis Tribune, July 6, 1896, p. 4. "The Snake."
Pocket Magazine, 2 (August, 1896), 125–132.
In *Last Words.* London: Digby, Long & Co., 1902.
In *Men, Women and Boats.* New York: Boni and Liveright, 1921.
In *Work,* vol. 11 (1926).
In *Maggie, and Other Stories.* New York: Modern Library, 1933.
In *The Pace of Youth and Other Stories.* Girard, Kans.: Haldeman-Julius (n.d.).

* Written at Hartwood, according to Mr. David Balch of Hartwood, N.Y. (to R. W. S.). Included, though not for that reason, as a Sullivan County sketch in *SCTS* (1968).

In *CSS&S* (1963).
In *SCTS* (1968).

SOLDIER, YOUNG IN YEARS, YOUNG IN AMBITION
AMs., 1 p., poem, appended to the article "Gratitude of a Nation," 5 pp. CUCC.
In *Poetry* (1957).
Fine Arts Magazine (University of Connecticut), 9 (1964), 23. Note by R. W. Stallman. Reproduces the holograph Ms., in facsimile, and photograph of Crane.
In *Poems of Stephen Crane* (1966).

SOLDIER'S BURIAL THAT MADE A NATIVE HOLIDAY
New York Journal, August 15, 1898, p. 2.
San Francisco Examiner, August 15, 1898, p. 1. "A Grave Beneath the Palms."
Kansas City Star, August 22, 1898, p. 5. "Death Did Not Quiet Them."
In *UW* (1963); reprints *New York Journal.*
In *War Dispatches* (1964); reprints *New York Journal.*

SOME CURIOUS LESSONS FROM THE TRANSVAAL
New York Journal, January 7, 1900, p. 27.
San Francisco Examiner, January 7, 1900, p. 24. "Wherein the Transvaal is Now Affording Lessons to the World."
In *UW* (1963); reprints *New York Journal.*
In *War Dispatches* (1964); reprints *New York Journal.*

SOME HINTS FOR PLAY-MAKERS*
Truth, 12 (November 4, 1893), 4–5.
In *UW* (1963).
In *NYCS* (1966).

SOME INTERVIEWS (FROM "WITH GREEK AND TURK")
See MY TALK WITH SOLDIERS SIX.

SOME THINGS
See IMPACT OF A DOLLAR UPON THE HEART.

SPANIARDS TWO
New York Journal, November 11, 1898, p. 6.
In *UW* (1963).
In *War Dispatches* (1964).

SPANISH AMERICAN WAR PLAY
See DRAMA IN CUBA.

SPANISH DESERTERS AMONG THE REFUGEES AT EL CANEY
New York World, July 8, 1898, p. 4.
In *UW* (1963).
In *War Dispatches* (1964).

SPIRIT OF THE GREEK PEOPLE
AMs., 2 pp., untitled. CUCC.
An unfinished article datelined "Athens, Greece. April 17, 1897."
In *Exhibition* (1956), p. 55. "Report From Athens."
In *War Dispatches* (1964), here for the first time.

SQUIRE'S MADNESS
AMs., 9 pp.; begun by Crane and finished by Cora Crane; pp. 1–6 in

* *See also* footnote to WHY DID THE YOUNG CLERK SWEAR?

Crane's hand, unsigned; pp. 6–9 in Cora Crane's hand, signed. CUCC. TMs., 11 pp., with autograph corrections. BCC.

Crampton's Magazine, 16 (October, 1900), 93–99.
Cincinnati Commercial Tribune, June 2, 1901, p. 22.
Minneapolis Tribune, June 2, 1901, p. 3.
New Orleans Times-Democrat, June 2, 1901, p. 8.
Washington Post, June 2, 1901, p. 35.
Buffalo Morning Express, June 9, 1901, p. 2.
San Francisco Chronicle, June 9, 1901, p. 26.
In *Last Words.* London: Digby, Long & Co., 1902.
In *Work,* vol. 11 (1926).
In *CSS&S* (1963).

STATE'S HARD FIGHT
See NEBRASKANS' BITTER FIGHT FOR LIFE.

STEPHEN CRANE AND JULIAN RALPH TELL OF WAR'S HORRORS AND TURKEY'S BOLD PLAN

Buffalo Evening News, May 23, 1897, pp. 1, 8. "Dead and Dying. / Picture of a Hospital Beat and / the Closing Scenes of / the War. / By Stephen Crane."
Chicago Tribune, May 23, 1897, pp. 1–2. " 'Mid Dead and Dying / Stephen Crane Tells of Some / of the Horrors of War."
New York Journal, May 23, 1897, p. 37.
Philadelphia Press, May 23, 1897, p. 2. "Stephen Crane on Waning War / The Young Novelist Cables 'The Press' a Brilliant Story of / the Closing Days of Greece's Struggle / with Turkey."
San Francisco Examiner, May 23, 1897, p. 13. "Vanished Greek and Victorious Turk."
In *UW* (1963); reprints *New York Journal,* with title "Stephen Crane Tells of War's Horrors."
In *War Dispatches* (1964); reprints *New York Journal* with title "War's Horrors and Turkey's Bold Plan–I, by Julian Ralph. II, by Stephen Crane. The *Journal's* headline subsumes both articles under title "Stephen Crane and Julian Ralph Tell of War's Horrors and Turkey's Bold Plan." On same p. 37 appears John Bass, "How Novelist Crane Acts on the Battlefield." Reprinted for the first time in *War Dispatches,* pp. 42–43.

STEPHEN CRANE AT ASBURY PARK
See ASBURY PARK AS SEEN BY STEPHEN CRANE.

STEPHEN CRANE AT THE FRONT FOR THE WORLD

Boston Globe, July 7, 1898, p. 2. "Globe Extra / 5 O'Clock. / Crane in War. / Young Novelist Writes About Reality."
New York World, July 7, 1898, p. 8. On the same page appears "Crane Tells Story of the Disembarkment."
In *UW* (1963); reprints *New York World.*
In *War Dispatches* (1964); reprints *New York World.*

STEPHEN CRANE AT VELESTINO

Boston Globe, May 11, 1897, p. 7. "Velestino a Grecian Gettysburg."
Buffalo Evening News, May 11, 1897, pp. 1, 5. "Red Badge of Courage. / Graphic Description of the Battle of Velestino."
Chicago Tribune, May 11, 1897, p. 1. "Stephen Crane Describes a Big Battle."

Kansas City Star, May 11, 1897, p. 1. "Crane's Story of a Battle / the Author of 'The Red Badge of / Courage' Sees War."

New York Journal, May 11, 1897, pp. 1–2. The out-of-town edition, signed.

New York Journal, May 11, 1897, pp. 1–2 [unsigned]. "Crane at Velestino."*

Philadelphia Press, May 11, 1897, p. 2. "Stephen Crane in Battle."

San Francisco Examiner, May 11, 1897, pp. 1–2. "Crane at Velestino."

Beatrice Daily Express (Nebraska), May 12, 1897, p. 1.

Kearney Daily Hub, May 12, 1897, p. 1 [unsigned]. "Battle of Velestino."

Omaha Weekly Bee, May 12, 1897, p. 2. "Greek Troops Behave Well."

Omaha World Herald, May 12, 1897, p. 5. "Stephen Crane at Velestino."

Portland Oregonian, May 12, 1897, pp. 1–2. "The Battle of Velestino."

Salt Lake City Tribune, May 12, 1897, p. 2 [unsigned]. "How Greeks Fought / Graphic Story of the Battle / of Velestino. / Victory Turned to Defeat."

Omaha Weekly World-Herald, May 14, 1897, p. 10. "Stephen Crane at Velestino."

In *UW* (1963). "Stephen Crane at Velestino."

In *War Dispatches* (1964); reprints *New York Journal*'s edition titled "Crane at Velestino."

STEPHEN CRANE CALLS IT A BLUNDER
See ROOSEVELT'S ROUGH RIDERS' LOSS DUE TO A GALLANT BLUNDER.

STEPHEN CRANE FEARS NO BLANCO
New York Journal, August 31, 1898, p. 5.
In *UW* (1963).
In *War Dispatches* (1964).

STEPHEN CRANE IN HAVANA
New York Journal, October 9, 1898, p. 27.
In *UW* (1963).
In *War Dispatches* (1964).

STEPHEN CRANE IN MEXICO
See ANCIENT CAPITAL OF MONTEZUMA.
See also MEXICAN SIGHTS AND STREET SCENES.
"Stephen Crane in Mexico" is a variant title for both "Ancient Capital of Montezuma" and "Mexican Sights and Street Scenes," although these sketches are not one and the same. Likewise, a variant title for "Hats, Shirts and Spurs in Mexico" is "Stephen Crane in Mexico."

STEPHEN CRANE IN MINETTA LANE
TMsS., 10 pp., with autograph corrections. BCC. Press clipping in the Crane Scrapbook, from *Minneapolis Tribune.* CUCC.
Dallas Morning News, December 20, 1896, p. 11. "In Minetta Lane."
Galveston Daily News, December 20, 1896, p. 24. "In Minetta Lane."
Minneapolis Tribune, December 20, 1896, p. 21.
New York Herald, December 20, 1896, section 5, p. 5. "What Life was Like . . . in Minetta Lane."
Philadelphia Press, December 20, 1896, p. 34.
Nebraska State Journal, December 21, 1896, p. 3. "Murderous Minetta Lane."

* This city edition is difficult to obtain. Copy at Rutgers University Library and photocopy in the Stallman CC. The out-of-town edition is at the Library of Congress.

San Francisco Chronicle, January 10, 1897, p. 2. "Stephen Crane in Minetta Lane."

In *Last Words.* London: Digby, Long & Co., 1902. "Minetta Lane."

In *NYCS* (1966). "Stephen Crane in Minetta Lane." Not in *CSS&S* (1963).

STEPHEN CRANE IN TEXAS

Louisville Courier-Journal, January 8, 1899, section 3, p. 4. "Some Lively Impresions of the Lone Star State."

Omaha Daily Bee, January 8, 1899, p. 15. "Patriot Shrine of Texas."

Pittsburgh Leader, January 8, 1899, p. 23.

St. Louis Globe-Democrat, January 8, 1899, section 3, p. 6. "Stephen Crane in Texas."

Savannah Morning News, January 8, 1899, p. 10. "Stephen Crane Writes of Texas."

STEPHEN CRANE MAKES OBSERVATIONS IN CUBA'S CAPITAL

New York Journal, October 2, 1898, p. 26.

In *UW* (1963).

In *War Dispatches* (1966).

STEPHEN CRANE ON HAVANA: WHY CUBA IS BY NO MEANS A KLONDIKE

New York Journal, November 6, 1898, p. 26.

In *UW* (1963).

In *War Dispatches* (1964). *See* note, p. 222.

STEPHEN CRANE ON THE NEW AMERICA

See MR. STEPHEN CRANE ON THE NEW AMERICA.

STEPHEN CRANE SAYS: EDWIN MARKHAM IS HIS FIRST CHOICE FOR THE AMERICAN ACADEMY

New York Journal, March 31, 1900, p. 8.

In *UW* (1963).

STEPHEN CRANE SAYS GREEKS CANNOT BE CURBED

Chicago Tribune, April 30, 1897, p. 2. "Stephen Crane Arrives in Athens."

New York Journal, April 30, 1897, p. 1.

Philadelphia Press, April 30, 1897, p. 1. "Stephen Crane is at Athens."

San Francisco Examiner, April 30, 1897, p. 1. "Stephen Crane, 'Examiner- / Journal' Correspondent. / The Distinguished Author has been sent to the Scene of the Turko- / Grecian War by 'The Examiner-Journal,' and to-day his first dispatch / is Presented."

In *UW* (1963); reprints *New York Journal.*

In *War Dispatches* (1964); reprints *New York Journal.*

STEPHEN CRANE SAYS: THE BRITISH SOLDIERS ARE NOT FAMILIAR WITH THE "BUSINESS END" OF MODERN RIFLES

AMs., 3 pp. Untitled news article. CUCC.

New York Journal, February 14, 1900, p. 8.

San Francisco Examiner, February 14, 1900, p. 3. "Tommy Atkins Ignorant of Modern Rifle's Power."

In *UW* (1963).

STEPHEN CRANE SAYS: WATSON'S CRITICISMS OF ENGLAND'S WAR NOT UNPATRIOTIC

New York Journal, January 25, 1900, p. 8.

In *UW* (1963).

STEPHEN CRANE SEES FREE CUBA
> *Chicago Tribune,* August 28, 1898, p. 4. "They Favor Annexation."
> *New York Journal,* August 28, 1898, p. 43.
> *San Francisco Examiner,* August 28, 1898, p. 17. "Havanese for Annexation."
> In *UW* (1963); reprints *New York Journal.*
> In *War Dispatches* (1964); reprints *New York Journal.*

STEPHEN CRANE'S OWN STORY / HE TELLS HOW THE COMMO-
DORE WAS WRECKED / AND HOW HE ESCAPED. / FEAR-CRAZED
NEGRO NEARLY SWAMPS BOAT
> *Chicago Record,* January 7, 1897, pp. 1–2. "Out of the Sea. / Novelist
> Crane Tells of His Ship- / wreck and Narrow Escape / from Death."
> *Chicago Tribune,* January 7, 1897, p. 1. "As Told by Stephen Crane. / Ex-
> periences of the Novelist / on the Commodore. / At Mercy of the
> Waves / Story of the Wreck of the Cuban / Filibuster." A considerably
> cut version.
> *New Orleans Times-Democrat,* January 7, 1897, p. 1. "Crane Tells the Story."
> *New York Press,* January 7, 1897, pp. 1–2. This is the full version, except
> for one cut which has not previously been known. *See RW* (1971), item 17.
> *Philadelphia Press,* January 7, 1897, pp. 1, 3. "Stephen Crane Tells the Tale."
> *Boston Record,* January 8, 1897, p. ? "Stephen Crane's Story of His Ship-
> wreck."
> *New Bedford Mercury,* January 9, 1897.
> *Pittsburgh Leader,* January 20, 1897.
> *London Daily Mail,* January 21, 1897. "S. S. Commodore, Fillibuster. / Her
> Loss Described by Mr. Stephen Crane." Excerpts from *Chicago Record.*
> In *Omnibus* (1952); *New York Press* here reprinted for the first time.
> In *UW* (1963); reprints *New York Press.*

STEPHEN CRANE'S PEN PICTURE OF C. H. THRALL
> *New York World,* May 8, 1898, p. 19.
> *Omaha Daily Bee,* May 8, 1898, p. 1. "Condition of Things in Havana."
> This variant text omits the first sentence given in text of *New York World*
> and contains a paragraph not in *World,* which presents on same p. 19
> Thrall's own account, "Thrilling Adventures of World Scout in Cuba." *See*
> *War Dispatches* (1964).
> *Philadelphia Press,* May 8, 1898, p. 2. "The American Blockade as Viewed
> From Havana."
> In *UW* (1963); reprints *New York World.*
> In *War Dispatches* (1964); reprints *New York World.*

STEPHEN CRANE'S PEN PICTURE OF THE POWER'S FLEET OFF
CRETE
> *See* IMPRESSION OF THE "CONCERT."

STEPHEN CRANE, STEPHEN CRANE, CHAUNCEY DEPEW
> *Fine Arts Magazine,* vol. 3, no. 1 (April, 1958). Reproduces in facsimile as
> cover design to the magazine of the University of Connecticut the
> scribblings of Crane made on a paper cardtable cover during one of his
> several games of poker. "Like Stephen Daedalus in Joyce's *Portrait of the
> Artist,* Stephen Crane scribbled his name over and over again: 'Stephen
> Crane, Chauncey Depew, Stephen Crane, Chauncey Depew.'" Here repro-
> duced for the first time from the original in BCC.

STEPHEN CRANE'S VIEWS OF HAVANA
> *Chicago Tribune,* September 7, 1898, p. 1. "No Warship, / No Cash."

New York Journal, September 7, 1898, p. 7.

In *UW* (1963); reprints *New York Journal.*

In *War Dispatches* (1964); reprints *New York Journal.*

STEPHEN CRANE'S VIVID STORY OF THE BATTLE OF SAN JUAN

Boston Globe, July 14, 1898, p. 4.

Chicago Tribune, July 14, 1898, p. 3. "How San Juan Was Taken / Stephen Crane's Graphic Story / of American Valor Be- / fore Santiago."

New York World, July 14, 1898, p. 3.

Harper's Weekly, 42 (July 23, 1898), 722. "In Front of Santiago." A shortened version.

In *Omnibus* (1952); reprints *New York World.*

In *UW* (1963); reprints *New York World.*

In *War Dispatches* (1964); reprints *New York World.*

STEPHEN CRANE TELLS OF WAR'S HORRORS AND TURKEY'S BOLD PLAN

See STEPHEN CRANE AND JULIAN RALPH TELL OF WAR'S HORRORS AND TURKEY'S BOLD PLAN.

STORIES TOLD BY AN ARTIST

See GREAT GRIEF'S HOLIDAY DINNER.

STORMING OF BADAJOS

AMsS., 6 pp., mainly in Edith Richie's hand. BCC.

Lippincott's Magazine, 65 (April, 1900), 579–585.

In *Great Battles of the World.* Philadelphia: J. B. Lippincott Co., 1901.

In *Great Battles of the World.* London: Chapman & Hall Limited, 1901.

In *Great Battles of the World.* London: Hodder & Stoughton, 1914.

STORMING OF BURKERSDORF HEIGHTS

Lippincott's Magazine, 66 (November, 1900), 781–794.

In *Great Battles of the World.* Philadelphia: J. B. Lippincott Company 1901.

In *Great Battles of the World.* London: Chapman & Hall Limited, 1901.

In *Great Battles of the World.* London: Hodder & Stoughton, 1914.

STORY OF A GIRL ARRESTED FOR STEALING

See ELOQUENCE OF GRIEF.

STOVE

AMs., 9 pp. CUCC.

Harper's Magazine, 100 (April, 1900), 798–804.

In *Whilomville Stories.* New York: Harper & Brothers, 1900.

In *Whilomville Stories.* London: Harper & Brothers, 1900.

In *Work,* vol. 5 (1926).

In *CSS&S* (1963).

In *TWH* (1969).

STREET SCENE IN NEW YORK ("WHEN A MAN FALLS A CROWD GATHERS")

TMsS., 5 pp., with autograph corrections, Stephen Crane's signature, and the title in Cora Crane's hand. Notation—"finished by Mrs. Stephen Crane"— cancelled. BCC.

First draft portion of this sketch is in the Crane Notebook, originally in the BCCC, now in BCC. The Crane Notebook is listed in the BCC catalogue, but many sketches in the Pocket Notebook are not listed therein. *See Bulletin,* 60 (September, 1956), 455–462.

TMs., 5 pp., "A Street Scene in New York." Also page proofs, 3 pp., bearing
in Crane's hand the title "When Men Stumble." CUCC.

New York Press, December 2, 1894, p. 5. "When a Man Falls a Crowd
Gathers." This version derives from a lost Ms.

In *Last Words.* London Digby, Long & Co., 1902. "A Street Scene in New
York."

In *Work,* vol. 11 (1926). "A Street Scene in New York."

In *CSS&S* (1963).

In *NYCS* (1966). "When a Man Falls."

In *Notebook* (1969).

SUCCESSFUL MAN HAS THRUST HIMSELF

AMsS., 1 p., poem; inscribed: "Stephen Crane / Dec 5th, 1897." TMs., 1 p.
CUCC.

In *War Is Kind* (1899).

In *Work,* vol. 6 (1926).

In *Poems* (1930).

In *Poetry* (1957).

In *Poems of Stephen Crane* (1966).

SULLIVAN COUNTY BEARS

New York Tribune, April 19, 1892, p. 16 [unsigned].

In *SCTS* (1968).

SHR, 2, no. 1 (Winter, 1968), 24–28.

SULLIVAN COUNTY EPISODE*

See EXPLOSION OF SEVEN BABIES.

SURRENDER OF FORTY FORT

TMsS., 5 pp., signed for Stephen Crane by Cora Crane; one of the Wyoming
Valley tales. BCC.

In *Last Words.* London: Digby, Long & Co., 1902.

In *CSS&S* (1963).

SWEDE'S CAMPAIGN†

In *Great Battles of the World.* Philadelphia: J. B. Lippincott Company, 1901.

In *Great Battles of the World.* London: Chapman & Hall Limited, 1901.

In *Great Battles of the World.* London: Hodder & Stoughton, 1914.

TALE OF A DARK-BROWN DOG

See DARK-BROWN DOG.

TALE OF MERE CHANCE

TMsS., 4 pp., with autograph corrections, signed for Stephen Crane by Cora
Crane. BCC.

Chicago Sunday Tribune, March 15, 1896, p. 41.

Dallas Morning News, March 15, 1896, p. 12.

Galveston Daily News, March 15, 1896, p. 12.

Nebraska State Journal, March 15, 1896, p. 4.

New Orleans Daily Picayune, March 15, 1896, p. 26.

---

* As given erroneously in *W-S Bibliography,* p. 125. The correct title is "An
Explosion of Seven Babies: A Sullivan County Sketch."

† *W-S Bibliography* does not list this title under The Writings of Stephen
Crane.

St. Louis Globe-Democrat, March 15, 1896, p. 41.

Minneapolis Tribune, March 22, 1896, p. 11.

English Illustrated Magazine, 14 (March, 1896), 569–671.

Pocket Magazine, 1 (April, 1896), 115–122.

Current Literature, 19 (June, 1896), 516. "The White Tiles."

In *Best Things from American Literature.* New York: The Christian Herald, 1899.

In *Last Words.* London: Digby, Long & Co., 1902.

In *Work,* vol. 11 (1926).

In *CSS&S* (1963).

In *NYCS* (1966).

TALK OF LONDON

New York Journal, March 11, 1900, p. 27.

San Francisco Examiner, March 11, 1900, p. 27.

In *UW* (1963).

TARANTULA

Mexican story done at Brede in September, 1899, and said to have been destroyed.

TELL ME NOT IN JOYOUS NUMBERS

AMs., 1 p., poem on verso of an unfinished letter inscribed: "To the editor of the Gazette, Sir:— / I compelled to / enter a feeble and tottering protest." CUCC.

In *Poems of Stephen Crane* (1966).

"TENDERLOIN" AS IT REALLY IS—BY STEPHEN CRANE. THE FIRST OF A SERIES OF STRIKING SKETCHES OF NEW YORK LIFE BY THE FAMOUS NOVELIST

New York Journal, October 25, 1896, pp. 13–14.

Literary Digest, 14 (November 7, 1896), 13. "A Picture of the Tenderloin." This quotes a portion of the *New York Journal,* and the quoted portion is sheer Hemingway. My discovery of "The 'Tenderloin' As It Really Is" obtained by tracing it in the *Journal* through the *Literary Digest's* mention of its quoted portion as deriving from that newspaper. I withheld publishing this find until 1966.

In *UW* (1963). Olov W. Fryckstedt, editor of *UW,* also discovered "The Tenderloin As It Really Is" and published it in *UW* for the first time since its 1896 appearance.

In *NYCS* (1966).

TENDERLOIN STORY BY NOVELIST STEPHEN CRANE—YEN-NOCK BILL AND HIS SWEETHEART

New York Journal, November 29, 1896, p. 35.

In *CSS&S* (1963). Same title as in *UW.*

In *UW* (1963). "Yen Nock Bill and His Sweetheart."

In *NYCS* (1966). "A Tenderloin Story, by Novelist Stephen Crane. / Yen-Nock Bill / And / His Sweetheart. / The Distinguished Author of 'The Red Badge of Courage' Writes a / Character Sketch of a Famous / Tenderloin Confidence Man and Shoplifter, a Man 'Who Never Did / a Crooked thing Since He was Born.'"

This sketch relates to Crane's unsigned "Opium's Varied Dreams" and to "Diamonds and Diamonds." Crane locates his play "The Blood of the Martyr" (1898) in China and cites "The City of Yen-Nock."

TENT IN AGONY
  Cosmopolitan, 14 (December, 1892), 241–244.
  Golden Book Magazine, 10 (July, 1929), 59–60.
  World Review, 9 (October 26, 1929), 6.
  In *Men, Women and Boats.* New York: Boni and Liveright, 1921.
  In *Work,* vol. 11 (1926).
  In *Maggie, and Other Stories.* New York: The Modern Library, [1933].
  In *The Pace of Youth and Other Stories.* Girard, Kans.: Haldeman-Julius
    (n.d.).
  In *SCS* (1949).
  In *CSS&S* (1963).
  In *SCTS* (1968).

TERRIBLE CAPTAIN OF THE CAPTURED PANAMA
  New York World, April 28, 1898, p. 3.
  Philadelphia Press, April 28, 1898, p. 3. "Stephen Crane's Picture of the
    Spanish Downfall."
  In *UW* (1963).

TEXAS LEGEND
  See FREIGHT CAR INCIDENT.

THAT WAS THE ROMANCE, / THIS IS THE REALITY, / A BATTLE
TO-DAY IN GREECE / —A FACT. / BY / STEPHEN CRANE
  See IMPRESSION OF THE "CONCERT"; FRAGMENT OF VELESTINO.

THERE EXISTS THE ETERNAL FACT OF CONFLICT
  AMs., 1 p., poem. CUCC.
  In *Poetry* (1957).
  In *Poems of Stephen Crane* (1966).

THERE IS A GREY THING THAT LIVES IN THE TREE-TOPS
  AMs., 1 p., poem. TMs., 1 p. CUCC.
  In *Poetry* (1957).
  In *Poems of Stephen Crane* (1966).

THERE WAS A MAN WITH TONGUE OF WOOD
  AMs., 1 p., poem. CUCC.
  In *War Is Kind* (1899).
  In *Work,* vol. 6 (1926).
  In *Poems* (1930).
  In *Poetry* (1957).
  In *Poems of Stephen Crane* (1966).

THERE WAS ONE I MET UPON THE ROAD
  AMs., 1 p., poem. CUCC.
  In *Black Riders* (1895).
  In *Work,* vol. 6 (1926).
  In *Poems* (1930).
  In *Poetry* (1957).
  In *Poems of Stephen Crane* (1966).

"THE TALE PROPERLY BEGINS WITH"
  This title is first draft of ADVENTURES OF A NOVELIST.

THE WAY IN SULLIVAN COUNTY
New York Tribune, May 8, 1892, p. 15 [unsigned].
In *SCTS* (1968); reprinted here for the first time.
SHR, 2, no. 1 (Winter, 1968), 28–29.

THIRD VIOLET
Prior to publication, this work was tentatively entitled "The Eternal Patience."
Philadelphia Inquirer, October 25, November 1, 8, 15, 1896, p. 29 in each issue.
Pittsburgh Leader, October 26; November 1, 8, 15, 1896; p. 23 in each issue.
Portland Oregonian, October 25; November 1, 8, 15, 1896; p. 16 in each issue.
San Francisco Chronicle, October 25; November 1, 8, 15, 22, 29; December 6, 13, 20, 27, 1896; January 3, 10, 17, 24, 1897; pp. 14, 14, 14, 14, 12, 14, 14, 13, 18, 15, 40, 13, 13, 13.
Chicago Inter Ocean, October 25, November 1, 8, and 15, 1896, p. 16 in each issue.
New York Evening World, November 4–14, 1896.
London: William Heinemann, 1897.
New York: D. Appleton & Co., 1897.
In *The Complete Novels of Stephen Crane*. Garden City, N.Y.: Doubleday & Company, 1967.
Ridgewood, N.J.: The Gregg Press, 1968.

THIS MAJESTIC LIE
Cincinnati Enquirer, June 10, 1900, p. 9.
Chicago Tribune, June 24, 1900, pp. 41–42; July 1, 1900, p. 43.
New York Herald, June 24, 1900, section 6, p. 10; July 1, 1900, supplement, p. 3.
St. Louis Globe-Democrat, June 24, 1900, part 3, pp. 4–5.
In *Wounds in the Rain*. London: Methuen & Co., 1900.
In *Wounds in the Rain*. New York: Frederick A. Stokes Company, 1900.
In *Work*, vol. 2 (1925). "His Majestic Lie," whereas in *New York Herald* and in *Wounds* it is titled "This Majestic Lie."
In *CSS&S* (1963).
In *TW* (1970).

THREE LITTLE BIRDS IN A ROW
AMs., 1 p., poem. BCC.
In *Black Riders* (1895).
In *Work*, vol. 6 (1926).
In *Poems* (1930).
In *Poems of Stephen Crane* (1966). Not in *Poetry* (1957).

THREE MEXICAN SKETCHES
See CITY OF MEXICO.

THREE MIRACULOUS SOLDIERS
Omaha Daily Bee, March 14, 1896, p. 12.
Omaha Evening Bee, March 14, 1896, p. 6.
Boston Globe, March 15, 1896, p. 34.
Chicago Inter Ocean, March 15, 1896, part 4, pp. 33–34.

Denver Republican, March 15, 1896, p. 17.
Kansas City Star, March 15, 1896, p. 16.
Philadelphia Inquirer, March 15, 1896, p. 26.
Pittsburgh Leader, March 15, 1896, p. 22.
Saint Paul Pioneer Press, March 15, 1896, p. 24.
San Francisco Examiner, March 15, 1896, p. 25.
Omaha Weekly Bee, March 18, 1896, p. 1.
English Illustrated Magazine, 15 (May, 1896), 104–115.
In *The Little Regiment.* New York: D. Appleton & Co., 1896.
In *The Little Regiment.* London: William Heinemann, 1897.
In *Pictures of War.* London: William Heinemann, 1898.
In *Pictures of War.* London: William Heinemann, 1916.
In *Work,* vol. 2 (1925).
In *Twenty Stories.* New York: Alfred A. Knopf, 1940.
In *Twenty Stories.* Cleveland & New York: World Publishing Company, 1945.
In *Omnibus* (1952).
In *CSS&S* (1963).
In *TW* (1970).

THREE POEMS ("A MAN ADRIFT ON A SLIM SPAR," "CHANT YOU LOUD OF PUNISHMENTS," "A NAKED WOMAN AND A DWARF")

Bookman, 69 (April, 1929), 120–122. Reproduces holograph Ms. of "A Man Adrift On a Slim Spar," p. 120.
In *Poems* (1930).
In *Poetry* (1957).
In *Poems of Stephen Crane* (1966).

TOMMIE'S HOME COMING

An incomplete and unpublished sketch once owned by Corwin Knapp Linson. A new portion quoted in *MSC,* pp. 40–41. Reprinted in *NYCS* (1966).

TO THE MAIDEN

TMs., 1 p., poem. Included with "What says the sea, little shell?" CUCC.
Philistine, 2 (April, 1896), 152.
Roycroft Quarterly, 1 (May, 1896).
In *War Is Kind* (1899).
In *Work,* vol. 6 (1926).
In *Poems* (1930).
In *Poetry* (1957).
In *Poems of Stephen Crane* (1966).

TRAMPS AND SAINTS

Untraced. A projected book about which nothing is known. Possibly it never got beyond the title.

TRANSFORMED BOULEVARD

See NEW YORK'S BICYCLE SPEEDWAY.

TRAVELS IN NEW YORK: THE BROKEN-DOWN VAN

New York Tribune, July 10, 1892, part 1, p. 8 [unsigned]. Crane's first published New York City sketch. In same *Tribune,* p. 14, appeared a review of Zola's *La Débâcle.*
In *CSS&S* (1963).
In *UW* (1963).
In *NYCS* (1966). *See* note, p. 3.

TREES IN THE GARDEN RAINED FLOWERS

TMs., 1 p., poem. CUCC.

In *War Is Kind* (1899).
In *Work,* vol. 6 (1926).
In *Poems* (1930).
In *Poetry* (1957).
In *Poems of Stephen Crane* (1966).

TRIAL, EXECUTION, AND BURIAL OF HOMER PHELPS

AMs., 3 pp., incomplete holograph of Whilomville story. CUCC.
Harper's Magazine, 100 (May, 1900), 963–968.
In *Whilomville Stories.* New York: Harper & Brothers, 1900.
In *Whilomville Stories.* London: Harper & Brothers, 1900.
In *Work,* vol. 5 (1926).
In *CSS&S* (1963).
In *TWH* (1969).

"TRUTH," SAID A TRAVELLER

In *Black Riders* (1895).
In *Work,* vol. 6 (1926).
In *Poems* (1930).
In *Poetry* (1957).
In *Poems of Stephen Crane* (1966).
Reprinted by *SCraneN,* Columbus, Ohio, 1967. Brochure.

TURKISH ARMY

See TURKS AS FIGHTERS.

TURKS AS FIGHTERS

AMs., 1 p., incomplete and untitled article begun by Cora Crane and finished
by Stephen Crane. CUCC. Quoted from in *Cora Crane.*

TWELFTH CAVALRY AND THE INDIAN WARS

AMs., 17 pp., untitled and unfinished. CUCC. In CUCC catalogue: "In an
unidentified hand." However, it is very clearly in Crane's hand.
In *Exhibition,* p. 55, titled "Indian Fighters in the 12th Cavalry." Again, "Ms.,
written by an amanuensis, 17 pp. Story." *Exhibition* is in error—it is in
Crane's hand.

TWELVE O'CLOCK

Page proofs, 15 pp. (title page and pp. 193–206), with autograph corrections
(in Cora Crane's hand?). BCC.
Pall Mall Gazette, 19 (December, 1899), 462–468.
In *The Monster and Other Stories.* London: Harper & Brothers, 1901.
In *Work,* vol. 12 (1927).
In *CSS&S* (1963).

TWO MEN AND A BEAR

New York Tribune, July 24, 1892, part 2, p. 17.
SHR, 2, no. 1 (Winter, 1968), 33–35.

TWO OR THREE ANGELS

In *Black Riders* (1895).
Philistine, 4 (March, 1897), 118.
In *Work,* vol. 6 (1926).
In *Poems* (1930).
In *Poetry* (1957).
In *Poems of Stephen Crane* (1966).

UNCLE JAKE AND THE BELL-HANDLE
See SKETCHES FROM LIFE: UNCLE JAKE AND THE BELL-HANDLE.

UNTITLED POEM
AMsS., in xerox copy, 1 p., poem laid in his *Red Badge of Courage*. BCC.

UNWIND MY RIDDLE
See CLAN OF NO-NAME, to which this poem is appended.

UPTURNED FACE
TMsS., 6 pp., with autograph corrections by Cora Crane. BCC. Facsimile re-
production of the typescript, p. 1, in *The Works of Stephen Crane*, ed.
Fredson Bowers, vol. VI, *Tales of War* (1970).
Ainslee's Magazine, 5 (March, 1900), 108–110.
Crystal Palace Magazine, 1 (1900).
In *Last Words*. London: Digby, Long & Co., 1902.
In *Men, Women and Boats*. New York: Boni and Liveright, 1921.
In *Work*, vol. 9 (1926).
In *Maggie, and Other Stories*. New York: Modern Library, 1933.
Girard, Kans.: Haldeman-Julius (n.d.).
In *Omnibus* (1952).
In *CSS&S* (1963).
In *TW* (1970).

VASHTI IN THE DARK
A short story written in February, 1895, and said to have been destroyed in
1898. The story is alleged to have been rejected by Harpers. Crane had the
story with him in Cuba, where it was seen by some of his associates. It concerned a rape.

VERY SINCERELY / YOUR FRIEND / S. T. CRANE / NEW YORK
CITY / C. C. & H. R. I. / MARCH 27, 1888
Inscribed in AUTOGRAPHS, a booklet for collectors of autographs, owned
by E. L. Gray, Jr., presumably a colleague of Crane at Claverack College &
Hudson River Institute. At right corner of Crane's inscription is the word
"Whist." The important thing about this item, however, is that Crane here
signs himself "S. T. Crane."
   On the mystery about Stephen Crane's middle name *see Crane,* chap. 2
and Notes, p. 566.
See SCraneN, 3, no. 4 (Summer, 1969), 2. "Stephen Crane's Middle Name,"
by Stanley Wertheim. Agrees with *Crane* that the middle initial was T and
stood for Truesdell.

VETERAN
Proofsheets of *McClure's Magazine*. CUCC.
McClure's Magazine, 7 (August, 1896), 222–224.
Chicago Tribune, December 22, 1896, p. 10.
St. James's Budget, December, 1896, pp. 81–82.
In *The Little Regiment*. New York: D. Appleton & Co., 1896.
In *The Little Regiment*. London: William Heinemann, 1897.
In *Pictures of War*. London: William Heinemann, 1898.
In *Pictures of War*. London: William Heinemann, 1916.
In *Work*, vol. 1 (1925).

In *CSS&S* (1963).
In *TW* (1970).

VICTORY OF THE MOON

TMsS., 3 pp., with autograph corrections. CUCC.
TMsS., 3 pp., with autograph corrections by Cora Crane. BCC.
Nebraska State Journal, July 24, 1895, p. 4.
Pocket Magazine, 4 (July, 1897), 144–152.
In *Last Words.* London: Digby, Long & Co., 1902.
In *Work,* vol. 11 (1926).
In *CSS&S* (1963).

VIRTUE IN WAR

Frank Leslie's Popular Monthly, 49 (November, 1899), 88–101. "West
Pointer and Volunteer."
Cincinnati Enquirer, June 10, 1900, p. 9.
Illustrated London News, 116, (June 16, 1900), 809–811.
In *Wounds in the Rain.* London: Methuen & Co., 1900.
In *Wounds in the Rain.* New York: Frederick A. Stokes Company, 1900.
In *Work,* vol. 2 (1925).
In *CSS&S* (1963).
In *TW* (1970).

VITTORIA

AMs., 1 p., fragment of three sentences. CUCC.
Lippincott's Magazine, 66 (July, 1900), 140–150.
In *Great Battles of the World.* London: Chapman & Hall, Limited, 1901.
In *Great Battles of the World.* Philadelphia: J. B. Lippincott Company,
1901.
In *Great Battles of the World.* London: Hodder & Stoughton, 1914.
SCraneN, 3, no. 2 (Winter, 1968), 5–6. Reproduces the holograph Ms.

VOICE OF THE MOUNTAIN

TMsS., 2 pp., with corrections. CUCC. TMsS., 2 pp., with corrections in
Cora Crane's hand. BCC.
Nebraska State Journal, May 22, 1895, p. 4. Under "Mexican Tales."
Pocket Magazine, 3 (November, 1896), 136–142.
In *Last Words.* London: Digby, Long & Co., 1902.
In *Work,* vol. 11 (1926).
In *CSS&S* (1963).

WAITING FOR THE SPRING

See NEBRASKANS' BITTER FIGHT FOR LIFE.

WAR CORRESPONDENTS

See GREEK WAR CORRESPONDENTS.

WAR IS KIND

New York: Frederick A. Stokes Company, 1899.
New York: Frederick A. Stokes Company, 1902.
In *An American Anthology: 1787–1899. Selections Illustrating the Editor's
Critical Review of American Poetry in the Nineteenth Century.* Boston
and New York: Houghton, Mifflin and Company, 1900, pp. 733–734. Re-
prints "In the night" (titled "The Peaks"), "The wayfarer" (titled "The

Wayfarer"), "There was a land where lived no violets" (titled "The Violets"), and "I explain the silvered passing of a ship at night" (titled "I Explain"). And five poems from *The Black Riders.*

In *Work,* vol. 6 (1926).

In *Poems* (1930).

In *Poetry* (1957).

In *Poems of Stephen Crane* (1966).

Consult the collation of this title for separate appearances of individual poems in the collection.

WAR IS KIND ("DO NOT WEEP, MAIDEN, FOR WAR IS KIND")
See DO NOT WEEP, MAIDEN, FOR WAR IS KIND.

WAR MEMORIES

Anglo Saxon Review, 3 (December, 1899), 16–38.

In *Wounds in the Rain.* London: Methuen & Co., 1900.

In *Wounds in the Rain.* New York: Frederick A. Stokes Company, 1900.

In *Work,* vol. 9 (1926).

In *Amateurs at War.* Boston: Houghton Mifflin Co., 1943, pp. 296–323. Excerpts titled "Well, Begawd, We Done It." Reprints text of *Work,* vol. 9, pp. 201–202, 205, 206, etc. Not indicated are the passages deleted pp. 201, 202, etc.

In *War Dispatches* (1964), pp. 267–295, excerpts.

In *TW* (1970).

WAR'S HORRORS AND TURKEY'S BOLD PLAN
See STEPHEN CRANE AND RALPH JULIAN TELL OF WAR'S HORRORS AND TURKEY'S BOLD PLAN.

WAYFARER

TMs., 1 p., poem; included is the typescript of "A Slant of Sun on Dull Brown Walls." CUCC.

In *War Is Kind* (1899).

In *Work,* vol. 6 (1926).

Golden Book, 5 (June, 1927), 764. "Road to Truth."

In *Poems* (1930).

In *Poetry* (1957).

In *Poems of Stephen Crane* (1966).

WEST POINTER AND VOLUNTEER
See VIRTUE IN WAR.

WHAT SAYS THE SEA, LITTLE SHELL?

TMs., 1 p., poem (included on this page is typescript of "To the maiden"). CUCC.

AMsS., 3 pp. Titled "The Shell and the Pine." BC.

Fair copy tipped into a copy of *The Red Badge of Courage* inscribed "Stephen Crane / To my friend, Dr. A. L. Mitchell. / Hartwood, N.Y. Dec. 28, 1895." In Lilly Library, Indiana University.

Philistine, 2 (February, 1896), 94–95.

Roycroft Quarterly, 1 (May, 1896), 31.

Fra, 5, no. 4 (July, 1900), xxv.

In *War Is Kind* (1899).

In *Work,* vol. 6 (1926).

In *Poems* (1930).

Corwin Linson's 1893 photograph of Stephen Crane.
(Courtesy Syracuse University Library)

gained by having been initiated into the secret rites of Misraim and of Memphis. Among them are several women, one of whom lately seceded from the sect, and published a book dealing with her experiences, entitled "Mrs. Diable au Dix-otber, the high priestess of Lucifer, who claims to be the great-great-grandmother of the future Antichrist.

"The number of popes"—she proclaims—"of Adonai ('The Lord') is, according to the prophets, limited. At the age of thirty-three I shall be the mother of a daughter, who, herself, will give to the world another daughter, who, in her turn, will be the mother of the Antichrist." The lady's reason is

---

RISE TO FAME OF STEPHEN CRANE.

A Sketch of a Literary Light Who Is Winning Unusual Success in His Early Youth. His Birth, Education and Characteristics.

The success of Stephen Crane, whose work, especially the "Red Badge of Courage," has attracted so much atten-

recognition in England than in the United States. It is not rather humiliating? Why should we wait for London to report back to us that we have been entertaining a genius unawares? The side note is descended from a long line of Methodist clergymen, of the order of the saddle-bag. Possibly this heredity, also, may be traced in his work; his style is curiously introspective and analytical.

Is this a betrayal of confidence? I trust not. I recall a certain story that Mr. Crane once showed us, in which two pistols were drawn, and on the trigger of each an angry finger trembled. But no explosion followed; those pistols hung fire for some twenty pages; the scene had shifted to the inner consciousness of one of the actors. Who would not laugh—and admire, too? Like Nathaniel Hawthorne, this author, whatever his theme, always treats "the tragedy of a soul."

Mr. Crane studied more or less at Lafayette College and Syracuse University, but took no degree. Like several other authors of to-day, he appears to have found it hard to stick to the curriculum. Perhaps it is precisely because college courses are so perfectly adapted to the average mind that exceptional minds rarely prosper with them. Stephen Crane's mission was to write, and he began at the age of 16. At 20 he produced his first novel, "Maggie." It met, on the whole, a rather cold reception, but brought him the commendation and friendship of William Dean Howells, Hamlin Garland and a few other appreciative critics. One of his sketches presently found its way into the "Cosmopolitan."

Of his remarkable "lines," published in the volume called "The Black Riders," it need only be said that they are original in the highest degree, and as full of "reason" as they are lacking in rhyme and metre.

The credit of first recognizing the extraordinary merit of "The Red Badge of Courage," and giving its author an effective introduction to the American public, is due to a syndicate, which brought out this story, upon which Mr. Crane's reputation still chiefly rests, in December, 1894, in serial form, and its appearance in "The Press" at that time will be remembered. From that time his success was assured. The story was republished in book form, crossed the sea, and has won the author much praise—and some British gold. He has just completed a novel entitled "The Third Violet," treating of art life in New York. May it prosper no less!

Mr. Crane is one of the founders of "The Sign of the Lanthorn"—a unique literary club in a historic building on William Street, New York, the great attractions being "two old fireplaces and good company." He is still an enthusiastic member; and among

STEPHEN CRANE.

---

body exclaimed. He forgot that the gander would never acknowledge this; the gander, or the friends of the gander. A learned professor tells how somebody once complained that a certain journal was intellectual side down. The professor said that he regretted that the periodical imitated the personalities against Lord Beaconsfield. "Oh, that is a very different thing," said the other. And when at dinner the professor repeated this to an eminent Liberal, expecting him to laugh, the eminent Liberal said: "Why, yes, of course, it is very different." This is always the way. The Tories abused Keats in a disgraceful fashion; nobody ever forgave them. Eternal disapprobation was the sauce for these geese. But the Whigs had already treated Coleridge in precisely the same fashion.

Nobody ever mentions the circumstance, which is entirely new to me, and, being much struck by it, I name it. The Whig goose has just bestowed on the Tory gander. The Stuart Kings were not extremely continent and moral in private life. Charles II was sold to the French, and a bad bargain, for he took the money without giving full value. Every child knows these enormities, but does not know that Sidney and Russell were also vendible. The inconsequences of the Georges, their mistresses and their jobs are slurred over for the young, who are not kept in the dark about the Stuarts.

George I might have des maitresses as he pleased, or George II; but a whisper against James III (upon my word I believe quite unjust and unfounded) may like thunder over Europe, and the Pope sent Cardinals to preach at the exiled Prince. What was sauce for the Stuart goose was not sauce for the Guelph goose. I know not why, but so it is. William III was rather less of a moral character than James II, but it was the Stuart gliding over the topic! Queen Elizabeth was in some very black hankering after all knew, but she did not receive the sauce with which Queen Mary has been freely basted.

This was plain to the humorist (still hankering after allen cattle) who first said that one man might steal a horse while another might not look over a fence. This proverb corrects and mitigates that other erroneous culinary one about the goose and the gander. Neither of these is primitive; they imply inclosure of land, domestication of animals, some culinary science and so forth. The whole subject of proverbs demands the attention of comparative science. We should begin with those of Zulus, Red Men and Hottentots, examining our own more found taking on more civilized would soon find themselves. Similar thoughtful own soon found taking on more civilized expression; we might occasionally catch a proverb on its travels. But we can hardly hope ever to be present at the birth of a proverb.

---

vertically from the landing until, by a series of automatic clutches, it is suspended to the pulleys on the four carrying cables. It will then be propelled by a system of tug cables and pulleys across to the opposite tower, traveling at the rate of 1200 feet a minute. At the opposite end it will be lowered to a landing and the passengers will disembark.

Some idea of the immensity of the undertaking may be gained when it is known that the towers will be higher than any building in the world and that a whole day is involved in an outlay of over $100,000. It will require two miles of two-inch cable and eight miles of running cable.

The plans for the aerial carrier have been sent to the Secretary of War for his inspection, as his permission is required for the erection of any structure crossing a navigable river.

AN OSTRICH TALE.

A Tale the Moral of Which Will Be Useful to Poker Players.

An ostrich, who was closely pursued by a hunter, suddenly thrust his head deep down into the sand, says a writer in "Life."

"Ah! ah!" exulted the hunter, "I have the silly fool at last." He advanced to place a rope around the bird's legs; but the ostrich, who had accurately timed his arrival landed a kick in the pit of his stomach that sent him into the hereafter like a bullet through a fog-bank.

Immoral:

"Umph," said the ostrich as he surveyed his victim, "because a man looks sad at the opening of a Jack-pot, it doesn't necessarily follow that he's only got ace-high."

Never Recovered.

Chollie—"I had fevah once and for three weeks I positively didn't know anything."

Kittie—"That was dreadful, but don't you think you'll ever get over it?"—"Life."

Stephen Crane
on horseback,
probably at
Brede Place.

Portrait of Crane by
David Ericson in
Bookman, May, 1895.

(Left) Charles K. Gaines' story in *Philadelphia Press*,
March 15, 1896.

STEPHEN CRANE

Whilomville
Stories

by

Stephen Crane

Illustrated by
Peter Newell

New York and London
Harper & Brothers
Publishers
1900

Frontispiece and title page to
Whilomville Stories.

" 'IF YOU AIN'T AFRAID, GO DO IT THEN' "

THE MONSTER

AND

OTHER STORIES

BY

STEPHEN CRANE

ILLUSTRATED

LONDON AND NEW YORK
HARPER & BROTHERS PUBLISHERS
1901

Frontispiece and title page of the
London edition of *The Monster
and Other Stories.*

With Stephen Crane in this newly discovered photograph is Lew Boyd, famous bear hunter, holding a Winchester rifle and standing to the right of a bear shot by John F. Whitehead. His little dog that ran the bear was named Buster.

The identity of Crane in this photograph hinges upon the identity of old man Whitehead's rifle. He carries a Savage Arms rifle. If his rifle were vintage 1899, the young man to the left of the bear could not be Stephen Crane because he was in England in 1899. However, Savage Arms (Westport, Massachusetts) reports that their 1899 model had been issued in 1895, that rifle and the 1899 model being identical. So Crane here holds a Winchester rifle, vintage 1892. Lew Boyd holds a Winchester rifle, vintage 1894. In sum, Crane went hunting with Whitehead and Boyd in the winter of 1894–1895, or in the winter of 1895–1896.

"My uncle," said Stephen Crane's niece Edith, "was a good shot. He seemed to enjoy target practice and tramped through the woods a great deal at Hartwood, but he was not as keen about hunting and fishing as my father [Edmund Crane]."
(*Crane,* pp. 38–39.)

Nor was Crane as keen about hunting as his brother William who took Stephen with him on some of his Hartwood Club hunting parties. Although Crane may not have been keen about hunting, he liked to hunt partridge and here he is shown with a party of bear hunters.

Crane was opposed to hunting down animals wantonly; he had a deep respect for life, and he admired the courage not of the hunter but of the hunted. In several of his Sullivan County tales and sketches he exposes the cowardice of the hunter.

For research on the identity of the rifles held by Crane, Whitefield, and Boyd, I am indebted both to Mrs. Stevens and Victor Cassella, student in my 212 class at the University of Connecticut (1969). As for Lew Boyd, he figures in Crane's "The Mesmeric Mountain": "There's Boyd's house and the Lumberland Pike."

This photograph is the gift of Mrs. Richard L. Stevens to whom I am also indebted for its background history (letters to R. W. S., 1969–1970).
Copyright, 1971, R. W. Stallman.

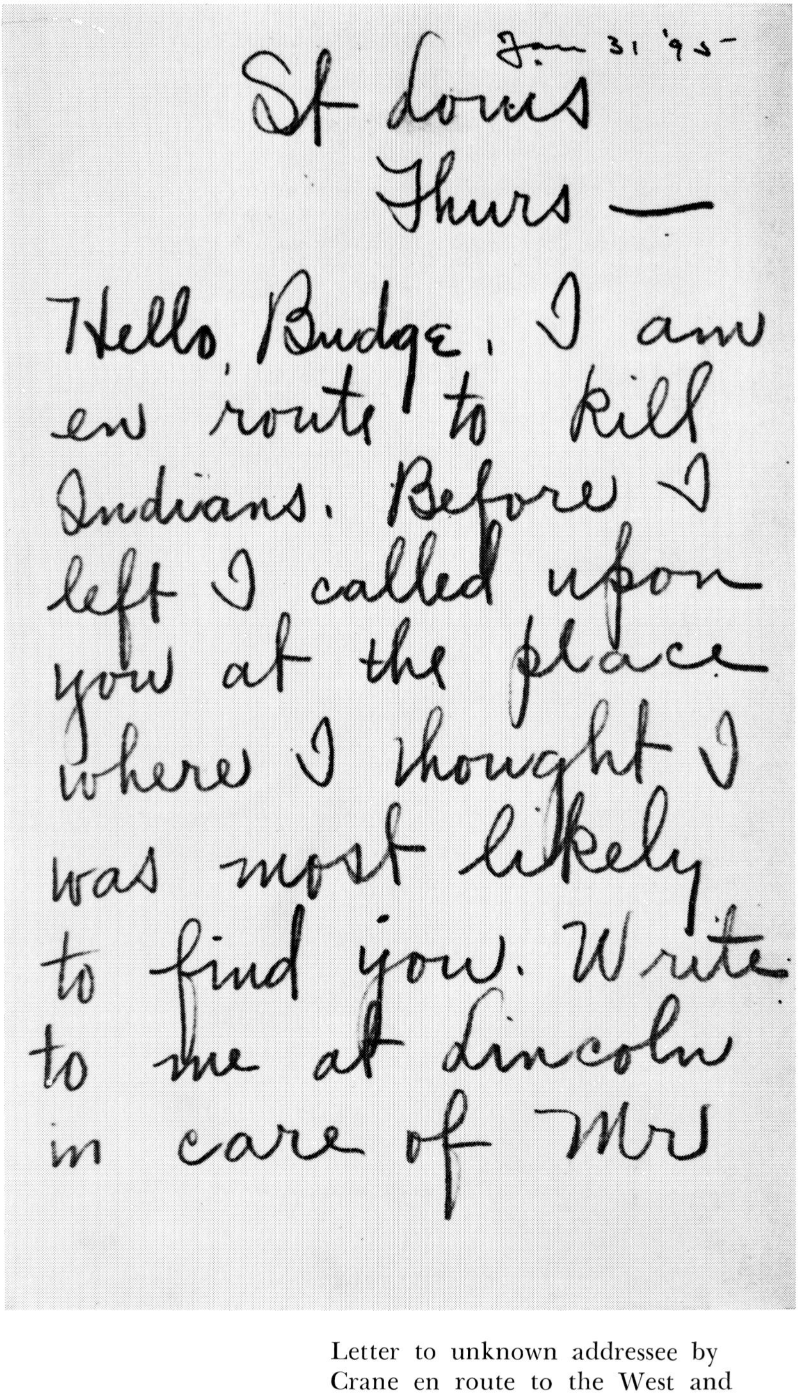

St Louis
Thurs —

Jan 31 '95

Hello, Budge. I am
en route to kill
Indians. Before I
left I called upon
you at the place
where I thought I
was most likely
to find you. Write
to me at Lincoln
in care of Mr

Letter to unknown addressee by
Crane en route to the West and
Mexico, January 31, 1895.
(*Courtesy Barrett Crane Collection*)

Will Owen Jones of the
State Journal.

Lincoln, Nebraska,
I mean.

My distinguished
consideration

Yours as ever

Crane

A man adrift on a slim spar
A horizon smaller than the rim of a bottle
Tented waves rearing lashy dark points
The near whine of froth in circles.
        God is cold.
The incessant raise ~~of~~ and swing of the sea
And growl after growl of crest
The sinkings, green, seething, endless
The upheaval, half-completed.
        God is cold
The seas are in the hollow of The Hand;
Oceans ~~are~~ may be turned to a spray
Raining down through the stars
~~Because~~ of a gesture of pity toward a ~~child~~ babe.
        ~~God is cold~~
Oceans may become
~~The seas took to~~ grey ashes,.
Die with a long moan and a roar
Amid the tumult of the fishes
And the cries of the ships,
Because The Hand beckons the mice.

A horizon smaller than a doomed assassin's cap.
Inky, surging tumults
A reeling, drunken sky and no sky
A pale hand sliding from a polished spar
        God is cold.
The puff of a coat imprisoning air:
A face kissing the water-death
A weary slow sway of a lost hand
And the sea, the moving sea, the sea.
        God is cold. ~~God is cold~~

        Stephen Crane

Holograph MS. of "A Man Adrift
on a Slim Spar" reproduced from
the *Bookman,* April, 1929.

In *Poetry* (1957).

In *Poems of Stephen Crane* (1966).

WHAT? / YOU DEFINE ME GOD WITH THESE TRINKETS? ("A LITTLE INK MORE OR LESS!")

Holograph Ms., 1 p. Inscribed "Stephen Crane / Oh, Hubbard, mark this well. Mark it well! If / it is over-balancing your discretion, inform me. / S. C." This Ms., with inscription, was reproduced in *Fra*, 5, no. 4 (July, 1910), p. xxv. AMsS., in photocopy. BCC.

In *War Is Kind*, (1899).

In *Work*, vol. 6 (1926).

In *Poems* (1930).

In *Poetry* (1957), together with Crane's postscript to Elbert Hubbard.

In *Letters* (1960), pp. 297–298. Quotes the poem and Crane's postscript.

In *Poems of Stephen Crane* (1966), p. 85; postscript, pp. 158–159.

WHEELS ("RUMBLING, BUZZING, TURNING, WHIRLING WHEELS")

Philistine, 8 (December, 1898), front wrapper.

American Literature, 15 (November, 1943), 283.

In *Poetry* (1957).

In *Poems of Stephen Crane* (1966). Not in *Poems* (1930).

WHEN A MAN FALLS A CROWD GATHERS

See STREET SCENE.

WHEN A PEOPLE REACH THE TOP OF A HILL

See BLUE BATTALIONS.

WHEN EVERY ONE IS PANIC STRICKEN ("FIRE")

TMs., 4 pp., titled "The Fire" (Sketch).

TMsS., 4 pp. CUCC.

New York Press, November 25, 1894, part 4, p. 6.

Fire! a pamphlet privately printed with only 100 copies by Ames W. Williams. Alexandria, Va., n.d. [1954].

In *CSS&S* (1963).

In *UW* (1963).

In *NYCS* (1966).

WHEN THE PROPHET, A COMPLACENT FAT MAN

TMs., 1 p., poem. CUCC.

In *War Is Kind* (1899).

In *Work*, vol. 6 (1926).

In *Poems* (1930).

In *Poetry* (1957).

In *Poems of Stephen Crane* (1966).

WHILE THE COLUMBIA AND THE SHAMROCK

AMs., 3 pp. CUCC.

WHILOMVILLE STORIES

Harper's Magazine, 99, 100, 101 (August, 1899 to August, 1900) inclusive.

New York: Harper & Brothers, 1900.

London: Harper & Brothers, 1900. Not included: "His Mittens" and "The Monster."

In *Work*, vol. 5 (1926).

In *TWH* (1969).

London: Garrett Press, Inc., 1969.

WHITE TILES
See TALE OF MERE CHANCE.

WHY DID THE YOUNG CLERK SWEAR?*
TMsS., 3 pp., with autograph corrections in Cora Crane's hand. BBC. Press clipping in CUCC.
Truth, 12 (March 18, 1893). All of Crane's contributions to Truth are signed.
In Last Words. London: Digby, Long & Co., 1902.
In CSS&S (1963).
In NYCS (1966).

WISDOM OF THE PRESENT
No. 10 in Crane's holograph list of titles of his works, the journal publishing the given title, the location of the Ms., and the word count. Here the wordage is 500, and Crane notes "MS with me." List in CUCC.

WISE MEN
Ludgate Monthly, April, 1898, pp. 594–603.
In The Lanthorn Book. New York: The Sign O' The Lanthorn, 1898, pp. 1–19.
In The Open Boat and Other Stories. London: William Heinemann, 1898.
In The Open Boat and Other Tales of Adventure. New York: Doubleday & McClure, 1898.
In The Open Boat and Other Tales of Adventure. New York: Doubleday, Page & Co., 1905.
In Work, vol. 12 (1927).
In CSS&S (1963).
In TA (1970).

WITH GREEK AND TURK
See IMPRESSION OF THE "CONCERT."

WITH THE BLOCKADE ON THE CUBAN COAST
New York World, May 9, 1898, p. 7.
Philadelphia Press, May 9, 1898, p. 3. "At the Gates of Havana."
In UW (1963); reprints New York World.
In War Dispatches (1964); reprints New York World.

WOMAN WITHOUT WEAPONS
See GEORGE'S MOTHER.

WONDERS OF PONCE
See GRAND RAPIDS AND PONCE.

WOOF OF THIN RED THREADS
See PRICE OF THE HARNESS.

WRECK OF THE NEW ERA
Typescript, 5 pp., copied from Crane's AMs. by Edith Crane. BCC. In Stallman Crane Collection, gift of Bacon Collamore. BCC also has AMs. of 14 leaves. Not listed in BCC catalogue, which also errs in claiming it unpublished.

---

* One of the three Crane pieces in Truth discovered by William R. Linneman. In "Stephen Crane's Contributions to Truth," American Literature, 31 (May, 1959), 196–197. The others are "A Night at the Millionaire's Club" and "Some Hints for Play-Makers." A fourth sketch in Truth, "At Clancy's Wake," discovered by Stallman, first appeared in NYCS. UW reprints only two of these pieces, CSS&S only one; NYCS all four.

Fine Arts Magazine (University of Connecticut), 1 (April 28, 1956), 1, 19, 20. Note by R. W. Stallman.*

YALE MAN ARRESTED

Buffalo Evening News, May 14, 1897, p. 5. "American Arrested. / But He was the Correspondent / of a London Newspaper / and wore a Fez."
Chicago Tribune, May 14, 1897, p. 3. "American is Arrested in Greece."
New York Journal, May 14, 1897, p. 3.
Philadelphia Press, May 14, 1897, p. 2. "American Arrested."
In *UW* (1963); reprints *New York Journal.*
In *War Dispatches* (1964); reprints *New York Journal.*

YELLOW UNDERSIZED DOG

Boston Globe, August 16, 1896, supplement, p. 2. "Only a Yellow Dog."
Denver Republican, August 16, 1896, p. 18.
Pittsburgh Leader, August 16, 1896, p. 21. "A Yellow Under-Sized Dog."
In *UW* (1963).
In *NYCS* (1966).

YEN-NOCK BILL AND HIS SWEETHEART

See TENDERLOIN STORY BY NOVELIST STEPHEN CRANE—YEN-NOCK BILL AND HIS SWEETHEART.

"YOU MUST!" "WE CAN'T!"

New York Journal, November 8, 1898, p. 6.
In *UW* (1963).
In *War Dispatches* (1964).

YOUSE WANT "PETEY," YOUSE DO

New York Herald, January 4, 1893, p. 3 [unsigned].
In Berryman's *Crane* (1950). Quoted here for the first time, but source not identified.
In *NYCS* (1966).

YOU TELL ME THIS IS GOD? ("LINES")

TMs., 1 p., poem. Included on the same page is "On the Desert." CUCC. Also in CUCC is proof sheet of the *Philistine.*
See ON THE DESERT.
Philistine, 6, no. 5 (April, 1898), 95 (back wrapper). "Lines."
In *War Is Kind* (1899).
Fra, 7, no. 6 (September, 1911).
In *Work,* vol. 6 (1926).
In *Poems* (1930).
In *Poetry* (1957).
In *Poems of Stephen Crane* (1966).

* A notice about this publication appears in *American Literature,* 28 (November, 1956), 414.

F

WRITINGS BIOGRAPHICAL, BIBLIOGRAPHICAL
AND CRITICAL ABOUT
STEPHEN CRANE

1888

[Anon.]. [Stephen Crane], *Asbury Park Shore News,* January 6, 1888, p. 1.*
A notice that Stephen Crane of Asbury Park took the courses of preparation for university studies at Claverack Military Institute.

1890

[Anon.]. [Stephen Crane], *Delta Upsilon Quarterly,* 9 (Holiday number, 1890), 57.
"Our initiates from '94 are: Stephen Crane of Asbury Park, New Jersey, prepared at the Hudson River Institute [The Claverack College and Hudson River Institute]. . . ."

———. [Stephen Crane], *Lafayette* (Lafayette College), 17 (October 30, 1890).
Lists Crane as an incoming freshman.

———. [Stephen Crane], *Vidette* (Claverack College), 1 (March, 1890), 12.
The Battalion Notes lists promotions of officers: "Adjutant–1st Lieutenant–Stephen Crane."

———. [Stephen Crane], *Vidette* (Claverack College), 1 (May, 1890), 7.
Reports that Crane vacationed at his home in Asbury Park this April.

———. [Stephen Crane], *Vidette* (Claverack College), 1 (May, 1890), 11.
"Crane, catcher, was tendered the office of captain, but declining, Jones, 1st base, was elected Captain."

———. [Stephen Crane], *Vidette* (Claverack College), 1 (June, 1890), 12.
Promotions for the following year include "1st Lieut. Crane, promoted to Captain."

1891

[Anon.]. [Stephen Crane], *Delta Upsilon Quarterly,* 9 (February, 1891), 157.
"At the beginning of the winter term, Brother Stephen Crane, '94, of La-

---

* Many of these early entries draw from research articles by such scholars as Jean Cazemajou and Lyndon Upson Pratt, whose *American Literature* article, "The Formal Education of Stephen Crane" (1939), furnished the *Vidette* and *Lafayette* entries.

fayette, entered the University [Syracuse University], making a valuable addition to our freshmen delegation."

———. [Stephen Crane], *Lafayette* (Lafayette College), 17 (January 30, 1891).
" '94. Stephen Crane, after a few months residence here, has entered Syracuse University. He is one of our youngest alumni."

———. [Crane at Syracuse University], *The Onondagan of '92*, 8 (Spring Term, 1891), 98, 148, 157, 167, 172, 204.

The Onondagan, an annual first issued by the students at Syracuse University in March, 1883, refers to Crane in *The Onondagan of '92* (published by the Junior Class in Spring Term, 1891): Crane is listed as an undergraduate member of the Syracuse Chapter of Delta Upsilon, class of Ninety-four (p. 98). Crane is named as a member and Secretary and Treasurer of the Claverack College and Hudson River Institute Alumni Association (p. 148). Crane is listed as Captain of the Delta Upsilon Cricket Club (p. 157). Crane is named as a member of one of the Delta Upsilon Coasting Clubs called "The Nut-Brown Maiden" (p. 167). Crane is named as a member of the Tooth Pick Club of Delta Upsilon fraternity house on Ostrum Avenue (p. 172).

In the section entitled "Grinds" Crane's name appears among the Freshmen (p. 204), followed by these verses:

> Sweet drop of pure and pearly light,
> In thee the rays of virtue shine,
> More calmly clear, more mildly bright
> Than any gem that gilds the mine.

The above data are recast here from *Courier* (Syracuse University Library Associates), no. 29 (Spring, 1968), 8.

———. "The Syracuse Bugs," *Syracuse Daily Journal*, June 2, 1891.

Reprints the editorial in *New York Tribune*, June 2, 1891, which treats jokingly Crane's unsigned spoof: "Great Bugs in Onondaga," *New York Tribune*, June 1, 1891. The *Tribune* editorial for June 2 is undoubtedly by Crane's friend Willis Fletcher Johnson.

The above data are summarized and quoted in the *Courier* (Syracuse University Library). *See* Mayfield (1963). Crane's "Great Bugs in Onondaga" was first reprinted in the *Courier*, 3, no. 1 (March, 1963), pp. 1–7, in an article by Lester G. Wells: "The Iron Monster." However, Wells does not identify who discovered this Crane sketch. And Ames W. Williams, who did discover it, does not claim himself its discoverer. Consequently, no citation is made in *NYCS*, where "Great Bugs in Onondaga" was reprinted in the Preface, pp. xiv–xvi. Nor is any acknowledgement made by Fryckstedt in *UW*.

Lillian Gilkes claimed that the discoverer of Crane's spoof was John S. Mayfield, editor of the *Courier*. *See* Gilkes (1968).*

———. "Huge Electric Light Bugs. / What a Wild-Eyed Patriot from the Sand Hills Thought He Saw," *Syracuse Standard*, June 1, 1891.

Quotes a portion of "Great Bugs in Onondaga," unsigned [by Stephen Crane], *New York Tribune*, June 1, 1891. With editorial comment in *Syracuse Standard*.

---

* However, this surmise ignores the *Courier* for September, 1963, wherein Ames W. Williams hints that he discovered Crane's *Tribune* spoof. Mayfield declared (1968) to R. W. S. that Ames W. Williams discovered it.

1892

[Anon.]. [Stephen Crane], *Melange* (Lafayette College) (1892), pp. 35, 60, 132.

Canfield, E. A. [Letter to the Editor]. *New York Daily Tribune,* May 24, 1892.
   In *NYCS,* pp. 272–274, here for the first time. In complaint against the *Tribune's* "slur" on the parade at Asbury Park on Sunday, an outing by the Junior Order of American Mechanics. The author of the *Tribune's* sketch of the parade is not named; it was unsigned. It was "On the New Jersey Coast . . . Parades and Entertainments . . .," by Stephen Crane.

1893

Garland, Hamlin. "An Ambitious French Novel and a Modest American Story," *Arena,* 8 (June, 1893) xi–xii.
   The first important review of a Crane work, *Maggie.*

1894

[Anon.]. "Uncut Leaves," American Press Association Release, May 1, 1894.

———. [Uncut Leaves Society], *New York Daily Tribune,* April 26, 1894.
   "John D. Barry read several unnamed poems from the pen of Stephen Crane, who, according to Mr. Barry, was too modest to read them himself; in fact, the poet made the assertion that he 'would rather die than do it.'"

———. Editorial, *New York Press,* December 10, 1894.
   This *Press* anniversary number mentions Stephen Crane.

———. Editorial, *Philadelphia Press,* December 7, 1894.
   "If you have not been reading *The Red Badge of Courage* by Stephen Crane, the story which has been running in 'The Press' for three or four days, you have been missing one of the best war stories going. Stephen Crane is a new name now and unknown, but everybody will be talking about him if he goes on as he has begun. . . ." (*See* "Holland," "The Work of Stephen Crane" (1894), which refers to this editorial.)

"Holland" (E. J. Edwards). "'Uncut Leaves,'" *Philadelphia Press,* May, 1894. Unidentified clipping in Crane scrapbook inscribed by Crane: "American Press Association."
   At Mr. Barry's reading of Stephen Crane's poems, "People asked, 'Who is Stephen Crane?' but there were some in that company who knew that in a recent article Mr. Howells had praised the work of no new man for many years, and that Mr. Howells would give his formal approval by way of introductory note to the volume of poems of this young man which is soon to be published." (However, Howells did not contribute any introductory note, and *The Black Riders* was not published until 1895.)

"Mr. Barry read the poems with delightful elocution, suggesting their perfect rhythmical quality, although they are not arranged in metrical form. . . . Stephen Crane is a New York lad, for he is scarcely more than a lad, who plunged into the miseries of tenement life in New York and associated with the tramps and the outcasts for many months so that he might see them as they are and paint them thus. Mr. Howells has said that in the single book which Mr. Crane has written [*Maggie*, 1893] he has revealed a power of realism, a capacity to paint with almost brutal force and directness, which suggests much of the power of Tolstoi."

Holland [E. J. Edwards]. "The Work of Stephen Crane," *Philadelphia Press*, December 8, 1894.

Reprinted for the first time in *Letters*, pp. 295–296. Reprinted in Katz's edition of the 1894 *Red Badge of Courage* (1967), with no citation of its discovery in *Letters* (1960).

Marshall, Edward. "Greatest Living American Writer [Howells]," *New York Press*, April 15, 1894, p. 2.

An interview with W. D. Howells, who says that among the most strikingly American writers we have today, " 'There is another whom I have great hopes of. His name is Stephen Crane, and he is very young, but he promises splendid things. He has written one novel so far—*Maggie*. I think that as a study of East Side life in New York *Maggie* is a remarkable book. There is so much realism of a certain kind in it that unfits it for general reading, but once in a while it will do to tell the truth as completely as *Maggie* does.' Stephen Crane, the young writer whom Mr. Howells praises in such an unusual manner, is still in the very early twenties and wrote *Maggie* several years ago.* The little book, which is sold by the Arena Company of Boston, is the story of the life and death of a girl of the tenements. It aims at exact truth in painting an unpleasant side of life, and approaches nearer to realizing it than any other book written by an American ever has. A review of *Maggie* will be found in another column of today's *Press*."

1895

[Anon.]. "Stephen Crane," *Bookman*, 1 (May 1895), 229 Portrait.

Reprinted in *Omnibus*, pp. 610–611.

Quotes Crane's inscription to the Reverend Thomas Dixon on a copy of the 1893 *Maggie*. The *Bookman*'s unsigned article says that Crane wrote this inscription "a few months ago, before the author went West on a journalistic trip to Nebraska" (January, 1895).

———. [Crane letter to the editor], *Leslie's Weekly*, November?, 1895.

Reprinted in *Brooklyn Daily Eagle*, June 5, 1900, p. 3.

---

* Marshall's statement adds credence to the dating of Crane's having begun *Maggie* in Spring, 1891. *See* Peaslee (1896), Johnson (1926), and Noxon (1928).

Marshall says that the Arena Company sold *Maggie* copies; whereas Williams-Starrett state that Marshall's article contains an erroneous statement implying that *Maggie* was published by Arena Company. The *Arena* (magazine) reviewed *Maggie* in June, 1893, but did not publish *Maggie*.

Reprinted in *Letters*.

———. "An Extraordinary Work: Stephen Crane's Talent Recognized by the Reviews and Newspapers of the United States," *Port Jervis Union*, November, 1895.
Reprinted for the first time in *Letters*, pp. 296–297.

———. [Stephen Crane], *Vidette* (Claverack College), 5 (December, 1895), 33.
"Among the holiday books recently published is *The Red Badge of Courage, a Tale of the Cruel [sic] War*, by Stephen Crane, non-grad, '87' [error for 1888]."

Howells, W. D. "Life and Letters," *Harper's Weekly*, 39 (June 8, 1895), 532–533.
On Crane's *Maggie*.

———. "Life and Letters," *Harper's Weekly*, 39 (October 26, 1895), 1012–1013.
Review. *See The Red Badge of Courage*.

Hubbard, Elbert. "Comments on Stephen Crane in a Periodical of Protest," *Philistine*, 1 (June, 1895), 27.

———. *Philistine*, 1 (October, 1895), 157, editorial. *See also Philistine*, 1 (August, 1895), 99–100.
Members of the Society . . . See [PHILISTINES' DINNER IN HONOR OF STEPHEN CRANE].

Ruotf, J. H. "Mr. Crane's Mistakes," *Philadelphia Press*, July 21, 1895, p. 33.
Mr. Ruotf, who was an American resident in Mexico, corrects Stephen Crane's mistakes on Mexican cuisine and prices given in his sketches of Mexico.

Sadler, John W. [On *The Red Badge*], *Syracuse University Herald*, January, 1895.
"*The Red Badge of Courage* is the title of a new novel by Stephen Crane, ex-'94. The story has attracted considerable attention, and Mr. Crane is looked upon as one of the most promising young writers before the public by such an able critic as William D. Howells." In *Letters*, p. 113, *n*40.

Souvenir and a Medley . . . See [PHILISTINES' DINNER IN HONOR OF STEPHEN CRANE].

LANTHORN CLUB

Tribune (New York), December 29, 1895, p. 22.
[Anon.]. "Lanthorn Dinner for Crane," *New York Daily Tribune*, April 8, 1896, p. 12.

———. [Stephen Crane], *Vidette* (Claverack College), 6 (May, 1896), 85.
"The Lanthorn Club, of which Mr. Stephen Crane, Class of '90, and author of *The Red Badge of Courage*, is a member, recently gave a dinner at their club house, 126 William Street, New York City to Mr. Crane. Among the guests present were William Dean Howells, Ripley Hitchcock, John Swinton, Henry Loomis Nelson, E. S. Van Zile, Francis F. Brown, editor of the *Dial*, Chicago, and others. The dinner was a very brilliant affair."

Marshall, Edward [unsigned]. "Realists at the Lantern Club," *New York Press,*
September 27, 1896.

Reports a banquet honoring Garland, Cahan, and Crane, at which even
Crane read a manuscript. (On some earlier occasion in 1895 Crane had read
parts of *The Red Badge of Courage* before four or five members of the Lantern
Club.)

————. [Bacheller and the Lantern Club], *Bookman,* 12 (November, 1900), 220–
221.

————. "Authors' Associations," *The Manuscript,* 1 (May, 1901), 32–34.

Reminiscences of W. D. Howells and Irving Bacheller on the "Lanthorne
Club"; Crane mentioned.

PHILISTINES' DINNER IN HONOR OF STEPHEN CRANE

The Society of the Philistines printed—"In Honor of Mr. Stephen Crane"—
a banquet menu-folder presenting three dozen tributes and the regrets of authors and journalists who were unable to attend, including messages from William Dean Howells, Hamlin Garland, Louise Imogen Guiney, Bliss Carmen,
and Ambrose Bierce: "Were it not for the miles which separate us, I would
be with you." There were notes from Richard Harding Davis, Ripley Hitchcock, and S. S. McClure, and a pert one from the editor of the *Albany Express:*
"I have a profound admiration for a man who, casting to the winds rhyme,
reason and metre, can still write poetry." From Amy Leslie of the *Chicago News*
there was a more personal note: "My most gentle thoughts are tinged with
envy of you who are so lucky as to meet Stephen Crane." There was also a
verse parody of Crane by Hayden Carruth ("I saw a Man reading an Invitation"), and quotations from Crane's poems appeared on the back cover of
the menu-folder.

To commemorate the event Hubbard printed three pamphlets of souvenir
stuff: (1) *The Members of the Society,* presenting the letters of invitation and
acceptance: (2) *The Time Has Come,* which reprints the menu and additional
responses and an unsigned new Crane poem ("I have heard the sunset song of
the birches"); and (3) *A Souvenir and a Medley,* with more tributes to Crane
and some poems of Crane, as well as "A Great Mistake" and "A Prologue." Hubbard exploited the whole thing to the utmost.

The above is recast from *Omnibus,* pp. 641, 642. On the Philistine affair *see
Bookman,* 2 (February, 1896), 468–470; Daly (1916), an important eye-witness
report here reprinted for the first time; Noxon (1928); Bragdon (1905, 1929);
Berryman's *Crane,* pp. 90 and 124; *Letters;* Dirlam (1964); and *Crane.*

The *W-S Bibliography* describes the pamphlets thus:

"*The Members of the Society* . . . [East Aurora, New York: The Roycroft Printing Shop, 1895].

An invitation sent to prospective guests of the Society of the Philistines to a
dinner to be held in honor of Stephen Crane on Thursday evening, December 19, 1895, in East Aurora, New York. Actually, the dinner was held at the
Genesee House in Buffalo.

This pamphlet of eight pages contains a reprint of a letter dated November

10, 1895 inviting Stephen Crane to dine with the membership and Crane's reply (twenty lines) to the letter. It is unbound and unsewed. Pages [1–2] and [7–8], which may be regarded as the wrappers, are on fine deckle-edge paper watermarked 'Rye Mill'; the interior pages are of a cheaper paper, with all edges cut."

" 'The Time Has Come,' . . . [East Aurora, N.Y.: The Roycroft Printing Shop, 1895].
    Souvenir menu of the Society of the Philistines' banquet in honor of Stephen Crane on December 19, 1895, in Buffalo. A companion leaflet to *The Members of the Society* (1895). The eight pages, sewed, consist of a title-page, responses of guests unable to attend the Stephen Crane dinner, the menu, and eleven lines of verse by Stephen Crane, unsigned, beginning, "I Have Heard the Sunset Song of the Birches." The verse appears here for the first time in print. The entire leaflet is on "Ruisdael" watermarked paper; top edges cut, others uncut. A full-page design in black and white, signed 'Collin,' is identical with that on cover of *A Souvenir and a Medley*."

* * *   * * *   * * *

MacIntosh, William [unsigned]. "The Philistine Dinner," *Evening News* (Buffalo), December 20, 1895.*

Philistine, 2, no. 2 (January, 1896), 72.
    "The Society of the Philistines gave a dinner in honor of Mr. Stephen Crane on Thursday evening, December 19. It was a large time, and much good copy was passed off into space that otherwise might have been used to enrich publishers."

Critic, 28 (January 11, 1896), 24.

Bookman, 2 (February, 1896), 468–470. Portrait.
    Reports the banquet given Crane by the Society of the Philistines on December 19, 1895, as having been "a very hilarious affair, at which he made a speech that scintillated with flashes of wit, to the merriment of all. In introducing the guest of honor, Mr. Elbert Hubbard spoke of the strong voice now heard in America—the voice of Stephen Crane."

Philistine, 2, no. 3 (February, 1896), 104. Unsigned [by Elbert Hubbard].
    "A whole half column of heavy criticism is leveled at the Philistines by the *New York Tribune* because, as alleged, they 'Lauded Stephen Crane to the Skies' at the recent Square Meal. I don't think it's necessary to defend Mr. Crane against the Serious Critic, but one thing may be said in his favor by way of contrast: he knows a joke at sight."

Lotus, 1, no. 7 (March 1, 1896), 181. "Comment."
    "Stephen Crane need depend no longer on a stray poem or a prismatic flash of pen for his reputation. The author of the *Black Riders* and *The Red Badge of Courage* has been dined by the Philistines and has been the butt of the sparkling wit of some of our best litterateurs, who do not understand his poetry any more than they understand the hieroglyphics on the monolith in Central Park. These same critics can have no such fear of his last book, *The Red Badge of Courage*, which is free from the obscurity of much of his

---

* On the identity of MacIntosh *see* Henry Taber (1923). He was the author of *A Message to Garcia* and editor of the *Buffalo News*.

poetry, and so full of the fire of genius that it promises to be the novel of the hour in the English market."

A Souvenir and a Medley: Seven Poems and a Sketch by Stephen Crane. With Divers and Sundry Communications from Certain Eminent Wits. East Aurora, N.Y.: The Roycroft Printing Shop. *The Roycroft Quarterly.* no. 1 (May, 1896).

The *W-S Bibliography* describes *A Souvenir and a Medley* thus:

"This booklet, containing forty-eight pages, was in the nature of a souvenir, six months after the fact, of the dinner given in honor of Stephen Crane by the Society of the Philistines.

"It consists of tributes by friends and from newspapers, and the following contributions by Crane: Seven poems (pp. 27–33); A Great Mistake (pp. 34–37), a prose sketch; A Prologue (p. 38). Issued in gray cartridge-paper wrappers, lettered in black and red. Decorative design in black symbolizing *The Black Riders,* signed 'Collin.' "

Lotus, 2, no. 1 (June, 1896), 24. "Comment."

"Stephen Crane is now in the woods near East Aurora caging blue air, and I predict, that with a sympathetic sky and a red background, the effect of those approaching Lines will be unparalleled."

[Anon.]. "Bubble and Squeak," *Lotus,* 2, no. 5 (September, 1896), 177. *See also Lotus,* 2, no. 4 (August, 1896), 136–137; 2, no. 5 (September, 1896), 172–173; and 3, no. 2 (February, 1897), 62. On Elbert Hubbard.

(All these *Lotus* articles are newly discovered pieces, not known to Hubbard's biographers.)

"What is the particular legend and moral aim of the rowdy and vulgar rag of Philistia these days: The East Aurora village sheet that disseminates tap-room and parlor gossip among the lewd and illiterate of the submerged tenth.

"It used to be a periodical for Protest . . . and its intense vulgarity and lack of all sense of the decency obtaining among gentlemen gave it a singular reputation in the backwoods for wit and pungency. After a while the Eminent Eclectic, purveyor of literature from all sources purveyed under the style and firm trade-mark of E. Hubbard conceived a fancy for the conceit on the cover of 'The Fly Leaf,' and he appropriated it forthwith, without so much as asking by your leave. It was made 'a Periodical for Curious Persons.' Then, to reveal the extent of his originality, this was changed to 'a Periodical for Peculiar Persons.'

"The readers who enjoy this extraordinary little compendium of pickings and small beer must be peculiar persons indeed. Their sense of humor and appreciation of wit is reserved for the lowest and coarsest tap-room banter. We can only exercise some measure of charity toward them when we remember that the 'E. Hubbard Literature Association' is really a bottling establishment, and the Eminent believes in his own adulteration. Good liquor is spoiled there in a mixture of his gas. The goods under this well known trademark are nearly all stolen or 'Lifted'—the E. E. Hubbard's favorite euphemism—or 'borrowd'; and God knows the whereabouts of all the original creators and owners; but here is one, filled with grateful remembrances for unexpected publicity afforded some of his little things in 'Little Journeys' and 'The Study of the Song of Solomon.'

"I propose to form a club of 'Originals' of E. Hubbard Eclectic Literature Association' if other poor and simple authors will co-operate and send me their

names, care *The Lotus*. I expect to enroll Stephen Crane and Harry P. Taber
on the foundation. 'We shall dine once a year'—every member paying his own
way. 'Tis a fair deal—The 'Thunder' only fell when the dinner was eaten
at that Crane affair."

1896

[Anon.]. "The Rambler; Comments on Stephen Crane and His Work," *Book
Buyer*, 13 (April, 1896), 140–141.

——. "Chronicle and Comment," *Bookman*, 3 (March, 1896), 1.
Thomas Hardy and Crane.

——. Editorial note, *Bookman*, 3 (April, 1896), 196–197, 206.
Introduces the specimen drawings of a young artist, Miss Melanie Elisabeth
Norton, "who has made marginal illustrations to Mr. Stephen Crane's
'Legends' on page 206. Miss Norton has caught to perfection the spirit of
Mr. Crane's unique imaginings. . . ."
Also with "Legends" appear two *Black Riders* poems: "I stood upon a high
place," no. ix, and "Should the wide world roll away," no. x, pp. 196–197.

——. [On *The Red Badge* and other Crane works], *Bookman*, 3 (April, 1896),
111–112.

——. [Sephen Crane], *Book News*, 15 (September, 1896).
Reports that Crane intends to do a study of the metropolitan policeman.

——. [On Hitchcock's note in *A Souvenir*], *Critic*, n.s., 25 (January 11, 1896),
24–25.

——. "Notes," *Critic*, n.s., 25 (February 22, 1896), 24–25.
On *Maggie*.

——. [Stephen Crane], *Critic*, n.s., 25 (March 7, 1896).
A note on Crane which quotes from Crane's letter to the Editor of the *Critic*,
February 15, 1896. The letter appears in facsimile in *Colophon* for 1930.
Vincent Starrett in *Colophon* (July, 1931), appraised this remarkable autobio-
graphical letter as possibly "the most important Crane discovery of recent
years." (The original handwritten letter is in the Barrett Crane Collection.)
Reprinted in *Omnibus* and in *Letters*.

——. "Stephen Crane," *Inter Ocean*, March 15, 1896, p. 24.
Quotes from Crane letters, first published Hilliard's review of *The Red
Badge of Courage, Rochester Post Express*, February 8, 1896.
Reprinted in *Literary Digest*, 12 (October 29, 1896), pp. 520, 671.
Collate with Edwin Watts Chubb, *Stories of Authors* (1910).
Reprinted in *Letters*, pp. 520, 671.

——. *Journal* (Indianapolis), September 9, 1896.
" 'I really believe that Stephen Crane is color blind,' said the girl who is
given to cogitation. 'Why?' asked the chorus. 'I just believe that all the red
he sees is only greenness.' "

——. [Verse, comments on], *Literary Digest*, 12 (February 29, 1896), 520, 671.

——. [Crane letters], *Literary Digest*, 12 (October 29, 1896), 520, 671.

Presents quotations from Crane letters. Collate with *Inter Ocean,* March 15, 1896, p. 24.

———. "A Picture of the Tenderloin," *Literary Digest,* 14 (November 7, 1896), 13.

"Mr. Stephen Crane, who has, as the newspapers have told us all, been making some pretty close studies of life in the 'tenderloin' and 'slum' districts of New York, comes forth with the following scene, which has rather more of verity than animation, of men trying to 'see the town' and not knowing exactly how to do it."

Reprints a portion of "The Tenderloin as It Really Is," from the *New York Journal,* October 25, 1896, a portion which reads nowadays like sheer Hemingway. The *Literary Digest* did not identify the date of the *Journal,* but its clue provided basis for search and discovery of "The Tenderloin as It Really Is."

———. "Comment," *Lotus,* 1, no. 12 (May 15, 1896), 338.

"The nineteen-days fiasco from which came that wonderful *Philistine-Fly Leaf* and which ended in Mr. Walter Blackburn Harte pouring his troubles into the public ear, has given the world some delicious morsels. 'If we would consolidate "The Fly Leaf" and the *Philistine,* and you come on here (East Aurora), we could by hard work make a life-work of the thing, and thus do a John Ruskin-William Morris work or better. Issuing our manifestos to the world direct, we will stand or fall on our merits. . . . As far as printing is concerned, if we get out one book for you, one for me, and one for Stephen Crane in a year, it is all we should try to do. . . . We could do much better fighting the world together than apart.' "

———. "Comment," *Lotus,* 2, no. 3 (July, 1896), 98.

"It is rumored that Mr. Elbert Hubbard, self-appointed manager of Stephen Crane, will return to America sooner than he expected, owing to the unfavorable criticism which *George's Mother* is receiving from the press. He will give another banquet for his protégé, after which the publishers will put this highly colored story of New York slum life in its twentieth edition. Mr. Hubbard is getting local color for his forthcoming introduction to the book of Deuteronomy in Scotland."

———. "Bubble and Squeak," *Lotus,* 2, no. 4 (August, 1896), 135.

"I say it is a little odd and significant of the attitude of the cliques in the East that no notice has been taken of the arrival of Ambrose Bierce in the literary capital. It is true he is the master of a certain department of fiction, in which Stephen Crane, heralded far and wide, has proved himself such a brilliant experimenter. But Bierce, on the contrary, writes out of real knowledge."

———. "Stephen Crane and His Slum Stories," *Munsey's Magazine,* 15 (August, 1896), 630.

———. "A Genuine Jerseyman," *Newark Sunday Call,* May 3, 1896, p. 20.

Contains Crane's letter to the editor of the *Newark Sunday Call,* dated April 29, 1896. In *Omnibus,* where it was reproduced for the first time. On the Crane heritage: "The family is founded deep in Jersey soil (since the birth of Newark), and I am about as much of a Jerseyman as you can find." H. G. Wells said that Crane was "a New Englander of Puritan lineage." And Edward Garnett made the same mistake.

————. [Ambrose Bierce and Crane], *New York Press,* July 25, 1896.

————. "Literary Notes," *New York Tribune,* October 29, 1896.
Comment on Crane's English reception.

————. "London Has Discovered Stephen Crane," *Pall Mall Gazette,* October 22, 1896, p. 4.

————. [Stephen Crane], *Public Opinion,* 21 (August 27, 1896), 282.
Quotes the *Springfield Republican* on the "slump" in the Crane "boom," suggesting that Crane take five years off to learn his craft.

————. "Different Views of Crane's Genius," *St. Louis Republic,* August 25, 1896.

————. [Stephen Crane], *Syracuse University Herald,* December, 1896.
"Mr. Stephen Crane, ex-'94, left New York for Cuba on Friday, November 13, to report the Cuban war news for the *New York Journal.* He postponed his journey a week in order to defy superstition by starting on a so-called unlucky day."

Bright, Edward. "The Literary Den." *Illustrated American,* 20 (June 27, 1896), 32.
A note on the 1896 *Maggie. See* his review on July 11.

————. "The Literary Den," *Illustrated American,* 20 (August 8, 1896), 219.

Davenport, Homer. "Concerning Mr. Crane," *Echo,* 2 (January 1, 1896), 5.

Frederic, Harold. "Stephen Crane's Triumph: London Curious about the Identity of America's New Writer," *New York Times,* January 26, 1896, p. 22.
"If there were in existence any books of a similar character, one could start confidently by saying that it was the best of its kind. But it has no fellows. It is a book outside of all classification. So unlike anything else is it, that the temptation rises to deny that it is a book at all. When one searches for comparisons, they can only be found by culling out selected portions from the trunks of masterpieces and considering these detached fragments one by one, with reference to the *Red Badge* which is itself a fragment, and yet is complete. Thus one lifts the best battle pictures from Tolstoi's great *War and Peace,* from Balzac's 'Chouans,' from Hugo's *Les Miserables,* and the forest fight in '93' from Prosper Mérimée's assault of the redoubt, from Zola's *Le Débâcle* and 'Attack on the Mill,' (it is strange enough that equivalents in the literature of our own language do not suggest themselves) and studies them side by side with this tremendously effective battle painting by the unknown youngster. Positively they are cold and ineffectual beside it. The praise may sound exaggerated, but really it is inadequate. These renowned battle descriptions of the big men are made to seem all wrong. *The Red Badge* impels the feeling that the actual truth about a battle has never been guessed before."

[Gaines, Charles K.]. "Rise to Fame of Stephen Crane," *Philadelphia Press,* March 15, 1896, p. 34. Photograph.
On the two-stranded threads in Crane's heritage, the soldier and the clergyman; an important point restated by Clarence Loomis Peaslee in *Monthly Illustrator* (August, 1896).* (Also in Crane to Hilliard letter in *Critic,* 1896). "The ancestry of a writer of marked originality is always interesting. The Cranes were a family of note in colonial days—a fact to which every line in

---

* Crane's two-stranded heritage is central to Hoffman's thesis in *Poetry,* but he makes no mention of the Gaines and Peaslee articles.

the young author's face bears witness—and several of his progenitors played heroic parts in the great struggle for American independence. In view of this it seems a singular turn of fortune that Mr. Crane's work has received more general recognition in England than in the United States. . . . On his mother's side Mr. Crane is descended from a long line of Methodist clergymen, of the order of the saddle-bag* Possibly this heredity, also, may be traced in his work; his style is curiously introspective and analytical."

The photograph of Crane is the one taken by F. H. King of New York City, first published in the *Critic* (March 7) and reprinted in *Inter Ocean,* March 15, 1896. Reproduced in the *Chicago Record,* January 16, 1897. Crane here wears a high-winged collar and cravat; he has here no moustache.

Higginson, Thomas Wentworth. [On *The Red Badge of Courage*], *Philistine,* 3 (July, 1896), 33–38.

Hilliard, John Northern. "The Hideousness of War: Stephen Crane and *The Red Badge of Courage,"* *Rochester Union and Advertiser,* February 8, 1896.

An important survey of Crane's career by a journalist friend of Crane. *See* Hilliard (1900) for letters of Crane published in *Rochester Post Express, New York Times Literary Supplement,* and the *London Academy. See also Literary Digest* (June 23, 1900); [Anon.] "Stephen Crane" (1896), which requotes Crane's letter from the *Rochester Union and Advertiser,* February 8, 1896. The full text of this *Rochester Union* letter—dated January 2, 1896—was first reproduced from the original in *Letters,* pp. 93–96.

Howells, W. D. "Life and Letters," *Harper's Weekly,* 40 (January 25, 1896), 79. Review. *See The Black Riders.*

———. "An Appreciation," in *Maggie: A Child of the Streets.* London, 1896, pp. v-viii. [Reprinted in *Prefaces to Contemporaries; see* Howells (1957).]
Not included in Appleton's 1896 *Maggie: A Girl of the Streets.*

———. "New York Low Life in Fiction," *New York World,* July 26, 1896. Reprinted with a phrase changed in the opening sentence in Howells, "An Appreciation," *Maggie: A Child of the Streets* (1896).

Crane's *Maggie* "was in the hands of a few in an edition which the author could not even give away three years ago; and I think it is two years, now, since I saw [in 1894] *George's Mother,* which Edward Arnold has brought out, in the manuscript. . . .†

"As pieces of art they [*Maggie* and *George's Mother*] are altogether superior to it [*The Red Badge of Courage*], and as representations of life their greater fidelity cannot be questioned. In *The Red Badge of Courage* there is a good deal of floundering, it seems to me. The narration repeats itself: the effort to imagine, to divine, and then to express ends often in a huddled and confused effect; there is no repose, such as agony itself assumes in the finest art, and there is no forward movement. But in these other books the advance is relentless; the atmosphere is transparent; the texture is a continuous web where all the facts are wrought with the unerring mastery of absolute knowledge. . . .

"There is a curious unity in the spirit of the arts; and I think that what

———
* That phrase is Crane's, as given in his letter to Hilliard on January 2, 1896 (*Letters,* p. 94). Professor Gaines of St. Lawrence University interviewed Crane at the Lantern Club in New York City.
† *George's Mother* was begun on verso of the manuscript of "The Holler Tree" in the spring or early summer of 1893.

strikes me most in the story of *Maggie* is that quality of fatal necessity which dominates Greek tragedy. From the conditions it all had to be, and there were the conditions. I felt this in Mr. Hardy's *Jude,* where the principle seems to become conscious in the writer; but there is apparently no consciousness of any such motive in the author of *Maggie.* Another effect is that of an ideal of artistic beauty which is as present in the working out of this poor girl's squalid romance as in any classic fable."

See also *World,* July 26, 1896, on *The Red Badge of Courage* (1895) and *George's Mother* (1896).

Hubbard, Elbert. "As to the Man," *A Souvenir and a Medley: Seven Poems and a Sketch by Stephen Crane. With Divers and Sundry Communications from Certain Eminent Wits.* East Aurora, N.Y.: The Roycroft Printing Shop. *The Roycroft Quarterly,* 1 (May, 1896), pp. 16–26.

Contents lists seven poems, but on verso of title page an eighth poem appears, reprinted from *The Black Riders.*

Hubbard pronounces Stephen Crane a genius and complains how reviewers and critics mistreat their genius.

"During the latter half of 1895 no writing man in America was so thoroughly hooted and so well abused as Stephen Crane. I have a scrap-book of newspaper clippings that is a symposium of billingsgate mud balls with Crane for the target.* Turning the leaves of this scrap-book, I find these words used in reference to a plain little book called *The Black Riders*: Idiocy, drivel, bombast, rot, nonsense, puerility, untruth, garbage, hamfat, funny, absurd, childish, drunken, besotted, obscure, opium-laden, blasphemous, indecent, fustian, scant, bassoon-poetry, swell-head stuff, bluster, balderdash, windy, turgid, stupid, pompous, gasconade, gas-house ballads, etc. etc. There are also in this scrap-book upward of a hundred parodies on the poems. Some of them are rather clever, but they differ from Crane's work in this that there is not a line of earnest thought in one of them; while there is a great moral truth taught in each of Crane's poems. . . .

"Personally I do not greatly admire *The Black Riders,* but I have no quarrel with the book. I accept it and give thanks. But admitting for argument's sake that *The Black Riders* is 'rot,' it then must be admitted that it was a great stroke of worldly wisdom. For Stephen Crane now has the ear of the world. Publishers besiege him with checks in advance, and the ms. of a story he has just completed has been bid on by four different firms, with special offers for the English copyrights."

Hubbard reports that once when Crane was called upon to recite in the psychology class, he argued with the teacher, who "sought to silence him by an appeal to the Bible: 'Tut-tut, what does St. Paul say, Mr. Crane, what does St. Paul say?' asked the old Professor. 'I know what St. Paul says,' was the answer, 'but I disagree with St. Paul.' 'Take your seat, Sir!' roared the Professor as soon as he got his breath. Of course no Methodist College wanted a student like that, and young Crane wandered down to New York and got a job reporting on the *Herald.* Since then he has worked on the editorial staff of various papers. He is now however devoting his whole time to literature,

* However, no such scrapbook exists among Hubbard's papers (letter of Elbert Hubbard II to R. W. S.), and the known reviews of *The Black Riders* do not employ the epithets which Hubbard attributes to them. John Berryman's account of the reception of *The Black Riders* in Berryman's *Crane* accepts Hubbard's statement on good faith.

living at Hartwood, Sullivan County, New York. Hartwood has a store, a blacksmith shop and a tavern. When the train comes in all of the citizens go down to the station to see 'er. Should you ask one of these citizens who Stephen Crane is, he would probably answer you as he did me: 'Mr. Crane, Mr. Crane? You mean Steve Crane?' 'Yes.' 'Why, he's—he's Steve Crane, an' a dam' good feller!' "

However, Hartwood never had a store, a blacksmith shop, and a tavern (according to the Dimocks of Hartwood). John Berryman repeats this fabrication of Elbert Hubbard in Berryman's *Crane* and locates Hartwood fifty miles from Port Jervis. As Hubbard's veracity is impugned on this account, so also the nonexistent scrapbook was undoubtedly sheer fabrication.

Hubbard, Elbert. [His invitation to Crane to attend the Society of the Philistines' banquet in Crane's honor], *Roycroft Quarterly*, 1 (May, 1896), 5, 16–26.*
See also *Philistine*, 2, no. 2 (January, 1896), 72.

Kennedy, Sidney R. "Bachelor Kingdom," *Yale Courant*, 31, no. 2 (November, 1896?), 81.

Lewis, E. St. Elmo. "Stephen Crane," *Book News*, 15 (September, 1896), 10–11. Photograph.

Norris, Frank. "Stephen Crane's Stories of Life in the Slums," *San Francisco Wave*, July 4, 1896, p. 3.

Peaslee, Clarence L. "The College Days of Stephen Crane," *Monthly Illustrator*, 13 (August, 1896), 27–30. Portrait.

A most important sketch of Crane's college days at Syracuse, but also of paramount importance for defining the two strands in Crane's heredity: clergymen and soldiers. Crane himself declared the double-stranded heritage in his 1896 letter to John Northern Hilliard. It is repeated by Professor Gaines in the *Philadelphia Press*, March 15, 1896. Neither Peaslee nor Gaines is cited in Berryman's *Crane* or *Poetry*. Both Gaines and Peaslee are listed in the *W-S Bibliography*, however.

Peaslee reports that Crane "has just signed a contract to write for *McClure's Magazine* on a salary, which is a very comfortable arrangement indeed."

Penn, Jonathan. "A Little Study of Stephen Crane," *Lotus*, 2, no. 6 (October, 1896), 208–211.

Pollard, Percival. "In the Matter of a Badge," *New York Journal*, May 22, 1896. On Bierce and Crane.

Pollock, Sir Frederick. [Letter to Oliver Wendell Holmes], *Holmes-Pollock Letters, The Correspondence of Mr. Justice Holmes and Sir Frederick Pollock 1874–1932*. Cambridge, Mass., 1941, 2 vols.

On February, 1896, Pollock writes, ". . . I have read *The Red Badge of Courage*—the psychology seems to me artificial and forced. If a recruit did go through all those complex emotions he would never remember them. For the general picture you can bear witness—but I guess the discipline must have been better in your regiment. . . ." (I, 68)

Thompson, Vance. "The Art of Stephen Crane," *Commercial Advertiser*, August 7, 1896.

---

* For this entry and many subsequent entries I am indebted to David H. Dickson, "Stephen Crane and *The Philistine*," *American Literature*, 15 (March, 1943–January, 1944), 279–287.

Warner, C. D. [Colors in literature], *Harper's Magazine,* 90 (May, 1896), 962.

Way, W. Irving. "Some Historical Documents," *A Souvenir and a Medley, The Roycroft Quarterly,* no. 1 (May, 1896), 39–46.

On the Philistine banquet in honor of Crane, at which affair 31 "Philistines of the sterner sex sat 'round the festal board."

Wells, H. G. "The New American Novelists," *Saturday Review* (London), 82 (September 5, 1896), 263.

Welch, J. Herbert. "The Personality and Work of Stephen Crane," *Leslie's Weekly,* May 28, 1896. Portrait.

Contains an important Crane letter, a pen sketch of Crane, and remarks on the English reception of *The Red Badge.*

Williams, Herbert P. "Mr. Crane as a Literary Artist,"* *Illustrated American,* 20 (July 18, 1896), p. 126. Portrait.

An important on-the-spot interview by Williams of the *Boston Herald.* Compares Crane with Verestchagin in his interest in impressionistic landscapes. Williams describes Crane's enormous room at the top of a house near the heart of the city. Williams errs in saying that Crane attended Rochester University.

"DAN EMMONDS"

["Dan Emmonds"], *Book Buyer,* 13 (October, 1896), 511.

["Dan Emmonds"], *Bookman,* 3 (May, 1896), 201.

Mr. Edward Arnold will have "a new novel by Mr. Stephen Crane ready for publication in June, with the probable title *Dan Emmonds.* In this story Mr. Crane returns to the satiric vein of his *Black Riders.* Mr. Thompson, who is Mr. Arnold's representative in America, and Mr. Crane were schoolmates; and a curious circumstance about the renewal of their early association is that Mr. Thompson had lost sight of Mr. Crane since they parted at school, but on the former observing the portrait of Crane in the February *Bookman* he immediately recalled him and hunted him up. Needless to add that a common enthusiasm for the baseball and football field was a closer bond than that usually derived from books. Mr. Edward Arnold arrives in New York as we go to press."

["Dan Emmonds"], *Bookman,* 3 (June, 1896), 301.

"We understand that Stephen Crane's forthcoming novel, *Dan Emmonds,* which was announced for publication in June, will not be ready until the autumn. Mr. Edward Arnold will publish immediately, however, a new story by Mr. Crane entitled *George's Mother.* Mr. W. D. Howells has expressed the opinion that this story is altogether the best bit of work Mr. Crane has yet done. The book will sell for seventy-five cents, and a first edition of 10,000 copies is being printed."

["Dan Emmonds"], *Bookman,* 3 (August, 1896), 201.

---

* One of the Crane letters said to be addressed to Williams in *Crane,* p. 214, was in fact addressed to Harry Thompson, an error to be corrected in the third printing of *Crane.*

["Dan Emmonds"], *Book News*, 15 (October, 1896), 49–50.

"Mr. Stephen Crane sails for England this month for a brief stay, returning probably a short time before the holidays. This will interrupt his work on his new novel 'Dan Emmons,' [*sic*] and will probably postpone its publication until spring. He will, however, be only the gainer thereby, for with *Maggie* and *George's Mother* following close on *The Red Badge of Courage* and *The Third Violet*, forthcoming at an early date, the public will have had in a year as much as it is well to have in that time from one author. A few chapters of 'Dan Emmons' [*sic*] have been written and they give promise of something quite unlike any of Mr. Crane's former work. Dan is an Irish boy, and the story as far as written deals with life in New York City.

"Mr. Crane's publishers, the Appletons, have expressed a desire to correct the impression that still prevails in some quarters that Crane was first appreciated in England, and that his popularity here came after and in consequence of the cordial endorsement of his *Red Badge of Courage* by the English press. *The Red Badge,* the publishers state, was published in America on October 1, 1895. It met with immediate success here. It was received at once with enthusiasm by many of the leading American reviewers and it sold extensively from the start. Its popularity here was assured when, two months later, in December, it was published in England and met with favor there. Its course of success was from West to East, not from East to West."

["Dan Emmonds"], *Critic*, 28 (April 25, 1896), 302.

"Mr. Edward Arnold will publish a new novel by Mr. Stephen Crane, called 'Dan Emmons [*sic*].' "

["Dan Emmonds"], *Dial,* 20 (March 16, 1896), 181.

Listed for Edward Arnold's forthcoming publications.

["Dan Emmonds"], *Dial,* 21 (September 16, 1896), 160.

Listed for Edward Arnold's forthcoming publications.

["Dan Emmonds"], *London News,* 108 (April 18, 1896), 494.

["Dan Emmonds"], *New York Press,* May 3, 1896, p. 30.

Mentioned as Crane's next novel.

[Crane letter], *Stephen Crane Newsletter,* 1, no. 3 (Spring, 1967), 8.

"Have you noticed an [*sic*] ms devoted to the adventures of a certain Irishman? Try to get it." Stephen to Edmund from County Cork, Ireland, September 9 [1897].

As this likely refers to "Dan Emmonds," it tends thus to support the theory (Stallman's) that "Dan Emmonds" was an early writing which Crane recast in 1897. A ten-page typescript, it was published for the first time in *SinSF* 1, no. 1 (Fall, 1963): "New Short Fiction by Stephen Crane," ed. R. W. Stallman. It is there described as "an early Crane voyage fantasy in imitation of Defoe."

POLICE ENCOUNTERS

[Stephen Crane], *Book News* (September, 1896). Reports that Stephen Crane intends to do a study of the metropolitan police.

"Saved From a Fine by Stephen Crane: Novelist Testifies in Behalf of a Woman Accused of Soliciting," *New York Daily Tribune,* September 17, 1896.

"Stephen Crane as Brave as His Hero," *New York Journal,* September 17, 1896.

"Stephen Crane and Dora Clark," *New York Sun,* September 17, 1896.

"Stephen Crane as Champion," *New York Times,* September 17, 1896.

"Stephen Crane, Novelist," *Boston Herald,* September 18, 1896.
    This new article was traced for me by Mr. Michael J. Venezia of the Boston Public Library. Listings on Police Encounters do not include dozens of newspaper accounts which do not name Stephen Crane. A considerable number of articles on the Dora Clark affair exist in press clippings which Crane pasted into a scrapbook, now in the Columbia University Crane Collection. Crane was a subscriber to AUTHOR'S CLIPPING BUREAU, Boston. For additional articles *see NYCS.*

Editorial, *Boston Herald,* September 21, 1896.

"No Reply From Mr. Crane," *New York Daily Tribune,* September 29, 1896.

"The Letter Reached the Wrong Crane," *New York Daily Tribune,* September 30, 1896.

"Stevie Crane," *Boston Traveler,* October 2, 1896: Stevie Crane seems to have gotten into warm water by his valiant defence of a young woman in police court at New York. The chances are that the youthful literary prodigy was on a genuine "lark," and, when his companion was apprehended, invented the tale about searching for book material. That is the way it looks to a cold and unprejudiced world.

"Dora Clark Makes Startling Charges," *New York Journal,* October 8, 1896.

"Novelist Crane a Hard Man to Scare," *New York Journal,* October 11, 1896.

"Novelist Was True-Blue," *New York Journal,* October 16, 1896.

"Stephen Crane on the Stand," *New York News,* October 16, 1896.

"Crane Under Fire," *New York Sun,* October 16, 1896.

"Crane Had a Gay Night," *New York World,* October 16, 1896.

"Mr. Crane and the Police," *Brooklyn Daily Eagle,* October 17, 1896: This editorial (to quote *W-S Bibliography*) "presents an excellent summation of the Dora Clark incident and Crane's persecution by the New York Police Department for testifying in her behalf."

"Crane Risked All to Save a Woman," *New York Journal,* October 17, 1896.

"Red Badge Man on a Police Rack," *New York Press,* October 17, 1896.

"Novelist Crane Racked," *New York Sun,* October 17, 1896.

"A Police Outrage on a Gallant Gentleman," *New York Journal,* October 18, 1896.

"Stephen Crane Not an Opium Fiend," *New York Press,* October 24, 1896.

Bright, Edward. "The Literary Den," *Illustrated American,* 20 (October 31, 1896), 607.
    On Crane's police court adventure; he made a great error "in flying into print to justify his conduct. I should have been much better pleased, and have been much more disposed to consider his motives disinterested, had he

allowed the episode to pass unnoticed." Police Commissioner Roosevelt, I might add, thought likewise.

"Dora Clark in Court," *New York Times,* November 3, 1896.

"Stephen Crane: The Unfortunate Girl," *Rochester Times,* November 3, 1896.

Ford, James L. "Tried by the Police Commissioners," *New York Journal,* October 18, 1896: Reprinted for the first time in *NYCS,* this parody of the police trial against Dora Clark and Crane, was written by the editor of *Truth,* who had published four of Crane's New York City Sketches in 1893–1894.

1897

[Anon.]. [On Ambrose Bierce], *Anti-Philistine,* 3 (August 15, 1897), 169–170.
Crane "writes a good penny dreadful, but Ambrose Bierce etches in words . . . Bierce's stories of the American Civil War, stories ghastly in their terrible intensity, were written years before young Mr. Stephen Crane scored a meretricious success. . . ."

———. [Note], *Bookman* (London), August, 1897.
Remarks that Mr. Stephen Crane is stopping in our country "for an indeterminate time."

———. [On Stephen Crane at the French Ball in New York], *Boston Globe,* January 21, 1897.

———. [On Stephen Crane at the French Ball], *Boston Record,* January 21, 1897, p. 3.
Press clipping in Cora Crane's green scrapbook. BCC.

———. [Note], *Brooklyn Daily Eagle,* January 23, 1897.
"Stephen Crane has written a story of the Western plains, under the title 'A Man and Some Others.' It is said to be in a different style from his previous work. This will give an increased interest to the matter, for now we shall see what Crane can do outside of his 'New Realism' vein."

———. "Modern Literary Fame," *Fitchburg Mail,* January 23, 1897. Undated clipping in Columbia University Crane Collection.
"Stephen Crane is rapidly becoming famous. Brought into early notoriety by the undoubted merit of his first book, *The Red Badge of Courage,* he later distinguished himself by defending the character of an alleged Magdalen, with whom he had struck up an acquaintance, and who had been involuntarily brought into court. Soon after he was heard of on board a Cuban filibusterer, which was conveniently wrecked, drowning him just enough to give him the experience of a 'narrow escape,' which he availed himself of to write up in a thrilling newspaper narrative, still further advancing his fame as an author.

"His last appearance was as a star attraction at the late French ball in New York, which was reported to be so 'deadly respectable' that the women who attended could only while away the time by sliding down the bannisters. Crane is evidently no gosling."

———. [Crane and Davis], *Chap Book,* 7 (August 15, 1897), 233.
Mr. Crane and Mr. Richard Harding Davis intend to make London their

home. "Mr. Crane, Mr. Davis, and John Hay—all gone from U.S. in one year. I truly think London is the Literary Center of America." *See* Waugh (1897).

——. "The Lounger," *Critic*, n.s., 27 (March 20, 1897), 201.

——. "London Letter," *Critic*, n.s., 27 (April 17, 1897), 277. Crane in London enroute to Crete. An important report (*versus* Gilkes).

——. "The Lounger," *Critic*, n.s., 27 (May 15, 1897), 340.

——. "Stephen Crane Still Here," *Florida Citizen* (Jacksonville), February 24, 1897.

——. "Stephen Crane Back / He is Still Confident of Reaching the Shores of Cuba," *Florida Times Union*, February 10, 1897.

——. [On Crane's attempts to get to Cuba], *Florida Times-Union*, February 16, 1897.

——. "Crane is Off for Cuba," *Florida Times-Union*, February 24, 1897.
For this article and some other *Times-Union* entries, I am indebted to William Randel's "From Slate to Emerald Green," *Nineteenth Century Fiction*, 19 (March, 1965), 357–368.

——. "The Literary Boom," *Hartford Courant*, March 29, 1897.
Clipping in Cora Crane's green scrapbook. BCC.

——. [On Crane and Rider Haggard], *Hartford Courant*, March 29, 1897. Press clipping in Cora Crane's green scrapbook. BCC.

——. [Note], *Nashville American*, January 24, 1897.
"Stephen Crane, author of *The Red Badge of Courage*, who was recently shipwrecked on a filibustering vessel while on his way to Cuba, has written a story in a new vein for the February *Century*. It is called 'A Man and Some Others,' and is a tale of the Western plains."

——. "Stephen Crane: The English as So-Called Discoverers of his Talent," *New York Times*, April 3, 1897, p. 7.

——. [On Stephen Crane], *New York Tribune*, January 20, 1897.

——. [Note], *Peoria Herald*, May 17, 1897.
"If Steve Crane could have got over to Greece a little sooner the result of the war might have been different, particularly if he had attacked the Turks with half the vigor that he has the English language."

——. [Stephen Crane and *The Philistine*], *Public Opinion*, 22 (March 25, 1897), 377.

——. "American Style: David Christie Murray on Contemporary American Writers," *Public Opinion*, 23 (October 28, 1897), 563.
Condensed from the *Canadian Magazine*. *The Red Badge* is the "truest picture of the war of the north and south yet written."

——. [On Stephen Crane], *Rochester Post Express*, February 22, 1897.

——. "Mr. Stephen Crane as War Correspondent—Forthcoming Letters to the *Westminster Gazette*," *Westminster Gazette*, April 28, 1897, p. 1.

Bass, John. "How Novelist Crane Acts on the Battlefield," *New York Journal*, May 23, 1897.
Reprinted for the first time in *War Dispatches*, pp. 42–43.

Bright, Edward. "The Literary Den," *Illustrated American*, 21 (May 29, 1897), 732.

———. "The Literary Den," *Illustrated American,* 22 (October 2, 1897), 442.

On Crane's "London Impressions" in the London *Saturday Review,* 84 (1897). Complains that Crane is quoting himself in "London Impressions."

Cather, Willa [unsigned]. "Magazines of the Month," *Leader* (Pittsburgh), October 18, 1897.

On Crane's "Flanagan and His Short Filibustering Adventure" in *McClure's* (October, 1897).*

"If Stephen Crane chose to sacrifice enough, to wait and work enough, he might come nearer the skill of Maupassant than any man of English tongue has ever done. And the world has been waiting for a Maupassant so long."

Harte, William Blackburn. "Why American Novels are Flabby," *Anti-Philistine,* 4 (September 15, 1897), 273.

The Red Badge of Courage "certainly belongs to permanent literature . . ."

Hubbard, Elbert. *Philistine,* 4 (February, 1897), 84 ff., editorial.

On the death of Crane. However, in this same issue appears a retraction: "LATER: Thanks to Providence and a hen-coop, Steve Crane was not drowned after all—he swam ashore."

Lande, Dora, trans. *Maggie das Strassenkind.* Leipzig: Georg H. Wigland's Verlag, 1897.

Loomis, Battel. [Parody of Crane], *Month in Literature, Art and Life: A Journal of Cultivation,* 1–2, no. 2 (January–August, 1897). Also in *Critic,* May 1, 1897.

Morahan, Michael F. "Rejoinder to Mr. Stephen Crane," *Westminster Gazette,* December 3, 1897.

Takes issue with Crane for his errors about the Irish policemen as portrayed in Crane's "Ballydehob." Quoted for the first time in *Crane.* Also quotes, pp. 598–599, the *New York Sun's* November 6 article jesting at Crane's *Westminster Gazette* portrait of Irish policemen.

Norris, Frank. "The Green Stone of Unrest, by S——n Cr——e." *San Francisco Wave,* December 24, 1897.

A parody, reprinted in *Frank Norris of the "Wave,"* ed. Oscar Lewis (1931), pp. 82–85.

Reprinted in *War Dispatches,* pp. 52–53.

Sturgis, Justin [Frank Norris]. "Crane in London: The American Novelist Investigating England with a Microscope," *San Francisco Wave,* September 18, 1897.

Traill. H. D. "The New Realism," *Fortnightly Review,* n.s., 61 (January, 1897), 63–66.

Traill dismisses Howells's praise of Crane's *Maggie,* in Howells's "An Appreciation" prefacing the London edition 1896 of *Maggie: A Child of the Streets.* Traill dismisses Crane as no realist in *Maggie;* nor in *George's Mother;* nor in *The Red Badge.*

* For this and other Cather articles mentioning Crane in contemporary periodicals I have drawn upon Bernice Slote, "Stephen Crane and Willa Cather," *Serif,* 6, no. 4 (December, 1969), 3–15. George Monteiro read the galleys of Part F and contributed many additions.

———. *The New Fiction and Other Essays on Literary Subjects.* London, 1897, pp. 2–5. Reprints his *Fortnightly Review* (1897) essay on Crane and the New Realism.

Waugh, Arthur. "London Letter," *Critic,* 27 (April 17, 1897), 277.

———. "London Letter," *Critic,* 27 (June 26, 1897), 442.
Reports Crane on the Strand on June 10. Richard Harding Davis was also in the neighborhood.

Commodore, WRECK OF

The *New York Press* in January, 1897, claimed that its *Press* articles furnished "a complete account of the sinking of the *Commodore,*" and on that assurance John Berryman, who failed to research other newspaper accounts (there were two dozen variant accounts not known to Berryman) conjectured that there must have been five men in the dinghy, although Crane stated four men in the dinghy both in his *Press* interview, "Stephen Crane's Own Story," and in "The Open Boat."

Since 1950, then, Crane's integrity as journalist has remained impugned, no Crane scholar attempting to refute Berryman's conjecture. That nonexistent fifth man or ghost was removed from the dinghy by Stallman. *See* Stallman, "Journalist Crane in That Dinghy" (1968) and *Crane,* chap. 14.

The present listing includes only the newspaper articles in which Crane is named. For additional background articles *see Crane,* pp. 548–551, and checklist 3, pp. 634–636: "The *Commodore* Disaster," "Logs of *Boutwell* and *Newark,*" Weather Reports, etc.

Daily Florida Citizen, December 14, 1896.
Reports that "Sylvester Scovel of the *New York World* has been here for several days with Stephen Crane, the novelist, all thirsting for fame and glory on the battlefields of Cuba as non-combatants."

"*Commodore* Clears for Cuba," *Florida Times-Union,* January 1, 1897, p. 6.
Listed by names here, the crew and passengers total 28. "Stephen Crane is a young and famous author. He has gone to Cuba as the representative of a syndicate of northern newspapers. He will not be employed as a newsgatherer, but will write Sunday letters to the papers of New York, Philadelphia, Chicago, Pittsburg and Boston. He was asked how long he expected to stay in the island, and replied that he could not tell. He shipped as a seaman at a salary of $20 a month."

"The Wreck of *The Commodore,*" *Florida Times-Union,* January 3, 1897, p. 1.
The steamer *Commodore,* which left Jacksonville on Thursday night, December 31, with an expedition for the Cuban insurgents, "is now resting on the bottom of the sea twenty fathoms below the surface, about eighteen miles northwest of Mosquito Inlet. All of the men on the vessel, twenty-eight in number, reached the shore in safety, and twelve of them arrived in Jacksonville last night over the Florida East Coast railway. The other six-

teen are still down the coast, but are expected to arrive here on a special train this morning."*

"Filibuster Sunk—Crane Missing," *New York Press*, January 3, 1897, pp. 1, 2.

"Steamer *Commodore* Sunk," *Boston Evening Transcript*, January 4, 1897, p. 1. Quotes C. B. Montgomery's version.

"Twelve Men Lost Through Treachery," *Florida Times-Union*, January 4, 1897, p. 1.

"Sixteen of *The Commodore*'s Men Were Lost," *New York Herald*, January 4, 1897, p. 3.

Quotes Steward Montgomery, who correctly has it that twelve Cubans got off in one lifeboat and four others in another. (These sixteen Cubans reached shore on Saturday morning, January 2.) The *Commodore* lost seven men— not sixteen as given in the *Herald*. When their lifeboat was shattered against the *Commodore* in high seas, the seven men climbed back aboard the *Commodore,* and then some of them took to makeshift rafts while Mate Gaines chose to stay on deck and go down with the ship. Captain Murphy with a broken arm was in the dinghy with Crane, Higgins, and Montgomery when the *Commodore* sank nearby.

"The *Commodore* Was Scuttled," *New York Journal*, January 4, 1897, pp. 1–2.

Dictated to the *Journal* "By C. B. Montgomery." He here names the four men who took to the dinghy. (The *Press* for January 4 claimed that five men came ashore in the dinghy.)

"More of the Filibusters Safe," *New York Press*, January 4, 1897, pp. 1–2.

"Five men came ashore at Daytona this noon—Captain Murphy, Stephen Crane (the novelist), the cook [H. B. Montgomery], and two sailors. One of the latter, William Higgins of Rhode Island [he was in fact from Salem, Mass.] died soon after reaching land. . . ." By this account there were, then, five men in the dinghy—as given in Berryman's *Crane*. By other newspaper accounts, however, there were four men in the dinghy. The conclusive proof exists in the log of the *Boutwell*.

The above account includes "Praise for Crane" by Captain Murphy. This *Press* dispatch was first reprinted in *Omnibus*.

"Stephen Crane and His Work. How He Came to be on the Unlucky *Commodore*," [Unsigned; by "Holland," who is E. J. Edwards]. *New York Press*, January 4, 1897, p. 2.

Reprinted for the first time in *Omnibus*.

"Mr. Crane was on the way to Cuba to write about the war there. He will get to Cuba as soon as he can. He is not of the sort who are frightened by an experience in a lifeboat. His letters will appear in *The Press* as soon as they arrive."

"Young New York Writer Astonishes the Sea Dogs by his Courage in the Face of Death," *New York Press*, January 4, 1897.

"*Commodore* Men Adrift," *New York Sun*, January 4, 1897.

"The party of eight men on the life-raft left the vessel before Capt. Murphy's

---

* Much of the data here are in error. The number of persons aboard the *Commodore* was twenty-seven. (Most newspaper accounts said twenty-eight.) Twelve Cubans in one boat and four Cubans in another boat reached shore. *See Crane.*

party and have not been heard of since the vessel went down. Collector of Customs, C. R. Bisbee, has requested the commander of the warship *Newark* to have the ship go with *The Three Friends* and use its flashlight in finding the raft if possible. The beach is being patrolled from St. Augustine to New Smyrna by bicyclists."

In the *Sun's* account the dinghy was twenty-seven hours at sea, high seas were breaking half a mile from shore, and there were twenty-eight members of the crew. There were in fact twenty-seven—by the log of the *Boutwell*. And the number aboard the *Commodore* just before she sank was seven, not eight.

"Loss of the *Commodore*," *New York Times*, January 4, 1897, p. 1.

"C. B. Montgomery (the steward), Stephen Crane, and William Higgins remained with the Captain, and with him launched the dinghy and stood by the tug until 7 o'clock, when the *Commodore* sank." (That puts four men in the dinghy.) The dinghy "was 27 hours at sea, Montgomery and Crane holding Capt. Murphy's overcoat as a sail until the beach was sighted. High seas were breaking a half mile from shore. Montgomery, Crane, and Murphy were washed to the beach, where citizens provided them with medical attendance. Higgins was killed by the overturning of the boat which made ten Americans and six Cubans lost." (Not counting Higgins's death in the surf, seven men were lost at sea, of whom two were Negroes.)

"Crane Knocks Down a Coward," *New York World*, January 4, 1897.

Some display of cowardice: "One man tried to get out a boat and was promptly knocked down by Stephen Crane, the novelist. Mr. Crane stood on the bridge, glasses in hand, peering through the darkness trying to discern a ray of light, as the tug was known to be near Mosquito Inlet light. . . . A big coal-heaver got into the hold and came out with a package of dynamite and told the Captain that they might as well let that off at once. The dynamite was carefully taken from him, and then Capt. Murphy's fist did the rest. 'Lie there, you cowardly dog!' shouted Capt. Murphy. 'Obey orders, and we'll all get off.'" (Crane in his *New York Press* story makes no mention of these incidents.)

"Seven Are Missing," *New York World*, January 4, 1897, p. 7.

"This account was reported to the *World* by C. B. Montgomery, one of the passengers on the *Commodore*, who came ashore today [January 3]." Factual contradictions abound in this account. "The seven Americans lashed to a raft when last seen were rapidly drifting out to sea and are undoubtedly all lost [That much was true.]."*

"Captain Murphy's Shipwrecked Crew," *Florida Times-Union*, January 5, 1897, p. 6.

Reprinted for the first time in *Omnibus*.

When the big lifeboat was stoven against the *Commodore*, Captain Murphy told the seven men to construct a raft. They made three rafts and got on these. Meanwhile, the dinghy—with the Captain, Higgins, Montgomery, and Crane—remained distant about 200 yards. The men on the rafts begged Murphy to take them in tow, and a towline was fastened to the dinghy; but the sea parted the rafts, and some of the men returned to the *Commodore* just before she sank. "Three men went down with her, like heroes with no cry of despair,

---

*These seven men become "the seven mad gods" in Crane's story "The Open Boat."

not a murmur." However, there are discrepancies between Murphy's account and Crane's account (as well as between variant versions of Captain Murphy's story). *See* "Stephen Crane's Own Story," *New York Press,* 1897.

"Were Traitors on *The Commodore?* Some of the Survivors Say There Were and Others Stoutly Deny It. . . . Number of Lost Reduced to Eight Americans Who Were in the Crushed Lifeboat," *New York Herald,* January 5, 1897, p. 9.

Reports "Captain Murphy's Story," which is the same as in his *Florida Times-Union* account, but which differs from his story in *New York World.*

"*Commodore* Said to be Overladen. Many Think That Fact, and not Treachery, Sunk [*sic*] Her," *New York Press,* January 5, 1897, p. 2.

Reprinted for the first time in *Omnibus.* Not quoted by Beer's *SC* or by Berryman's *Crane.*

Captain Murphy's story reports Crane's bravery: " 'That man Crane is the spunkiest fellow out,' said Captain Murphy to-night to *The Press* correspondent, in speaking of the wreck and incidents pertaining to it. 'The sea was so rough that even old sailors get seasick when we struck the open sea after leaving the bar, but Crane behaved like a born sailor.' "

"Capt. Murphy's Story," *New York World,* January 5, 1897.

Erroneously reports that Captain Murphy's left arm was in a sling as the result of injuries he received when he landed through the surf at Daytona. (He had a broken arm on leaving the sinking *Commodore* for the dinghy.) This *World* report quotes Captain Murphy that "The waves were tremendous, as high as I have ever seen hereabouts." Also his comment on Crane's courage: "And right here I want to say that Crane is a man every inch of him, and he acted throughout with grit." Last seen were seven men (not eight, as given in other reports) who were drifting out to sea on a raft. They included Mate Gaines and Chief Engineer James Redigan (erroneously accused of drunken negligence by Paul Rojo). These seven men drowned. After their lifeboat was stoven against the ship, these seven men made three rafts (not one raft as given in the *World*). Collate this account with Captain Murphy's story in the *Florida Times-Union:* "Captain Murphy's Shipwrecked Crew."

"Stephen Crane Safe," *New York World,* January 5, 1897, p. 1.

"Stephen Crane, the novelist, was reported by several afternoon newspapers yesterday to have been drowned on the ill-fated *Commodore* filibustering expedition, which was wrecked off the coast of Florida last Saturday [January 2]. But Mr. Crane is safe and is slowly recovering from his long immersion in the waters of the Gulf. He telegraphed to *The World* last night: 'I am unable to write a thing yet, but will later.' "

The *World* for January 5 also reported that "Stephen Crane, the novelist, said tonight that he had no direct knowledge of the alleged scuttling of *The Commodore.* He added: 'The *Commodore* was a fine boat.* She carried her load like a cork and breasted the waves like a duck, and she was buoyant and did not seem to strain at all. It is rather queer, to say the least, that such a leak occurred.' "

"Stephen Crane's Own Story," *New York Press,* January 7, 1897.

Reprinted in *Chicago Record* and in *London Mail,* of which a press clip-

---

* Crane's statement thus contradicts Thomas Beer's notion that "Crane thought the ship no more seaworthy than an ice-house."

ping for January 21 is in the Crane scrapbook at Columbia University Crane Collection. [Reprinted for the first time since 1897 in *Omnibus*.]

Crane's *Press* account says that there were four men in the dinghy. However, *see* Berryman's *Crane. See also* Stallman, "Journalist Crane in That Dinghy" (1968) and *Crane*.

"One of the Dead," *Florida Times-Union*, January 8, 1897.

"The body of Wm. Higgins, one of the men who left the *Commodore* in company with Captain Murphy, Stephen Crane and Steward Montgomery and was afterwards killed while trying to swim through the surf to the beach, by a stroke from the capsized boat, has been ordered to Salem, Mass., by his relatives. . . . The citizens of Daytona buried Higgins at their expense, which was considerable."

Florida Times-Union, January 12, 1897.

"Stephen Crane left Jacksonville for Tampa yesterday. He will go to Cuba via the Plant steamer *Olivette*, if he cannot make the trip in any other way." However, Crane did not go to Tampa. *See* Randel (1965). Crane was working on "The Open Boat" in Jacksonville in mid-January.

"Stephen Crane," *Academy*, 51 (January 16, 1897), 76.

"It is sincerely to be hoped that there is no truth in the report of Mr. Stephen Crane's death in Cuba. He is—we are loth to write in the past tense— emphatically a young man with a future, and the new literature could ill afford to lose him." Here follows a sketch of Crane's publication career. On *Maggie*.

"It was not until *The Red Badge of Courage* was brought out in this country, in the autumn of 1895, that America 'found' its author. Mr. Crane would be the first to acknowledge his indebtedness to the English critics and the English public, who, with one accord, forced his name into well-deserved prominence." "Mr. Crane has at least four new volumes in the hands of the publishers. *The Little Regiment,* a war story, will appear almost immediately; followed by *A Woman Without Weapons* [*George's Mother,* as it was then known]. *The Third Violet,* and another novel of slum life may be expected very shortly." (This other novel of slum life is the same novel as *George's Mother.*)

"S. S. *Commodore*, Filibuster, Her Loss Described by Mr. Stephen Crane," *London Mail*, January 21, 1897.

Quotes the *Chicago Record*'s reprinting from the *New York Press* of "Stephen Crane's Own Story" for January 7. The *London Mail* article contains a photograph of Crane.

Hubbard, Elbert. [On the death of Stephen Crane], *Philistine* (February, 1897).

"So here's to you, Steve Crane, wherever you may be! You were not so very good, but you were as good as I am—and better, in many ways—our faults were different, that's all. . . . And so, Stevie, good-bye and good-bye!"

Hubbard in this same *Philistine* corrected himself with a note on Crane's resurrection. "Thanks to providence and a hen-coop Steve Crane was not drowned after all. He swam ashore."

Florida Times-Union, February 10, 1897.

Reports that Crane has returned from Tampa, "having remained very close [to Jacksonville] since his *Commodore* episode. He is on his way to Cuba. He is confident of making the shores of that island before the war is ended, and, if indications are what they seem, it is probable that Mr. Crane will be on the scene of conflict in a very short time writing his Sunday stories for a syndicate of northern papers."

Florida Times-Union, February 16, 1897.

Reports that Stephen Crane and Charles Michelson are quoted as saying that they are going to Cuba on "the smart craft that now lies in the harbor," but Theodore Hilborn, who is in charge of the *Buccaneer,* "states that they had no authority for making the statement." Deprived of this opportunity, Crane went back to plans for filibustering with Captain Murphy. *See Florida Times-Union,* February 24, 1897, and Randel (1965).

Florida Times-Union, February 24, 1897.

Reports that Stephen Crane and Charles Michelson (here given as N. A. Michelson) and Captain Murphy left the city "clandestinely, and nothing has been heard of them since their departure." It is supposed that they left on the tug *Buccaneer* of the *Journal.* (However, nothing came of Crane's many attempts to get to Cuba.)

Richmond Times, April 4, 1897.

"The erroneous reports of the loss of Stephen Crane's life at the time of the shipwreck of the Cuban filibusters occasioned great solicitude in England. The *London Chronicle* spoke of him as 'the one young writer of genius that America possesses'—a most flattering tribute. . . ."

[Hathaway, Odell]. "The Day Stephen Crane was Shipwrecked," *Daytona Beach News-Journal,* April 22, 1962. Recast from essay submitted by Odell Hathaway, unacknowledged by *News-Journal* reporter.

Hathaway interviewed persons in 1961–62 who were at Daytona Beach in January, 1897, when the dinghy came ashore. Quoted in *Crane. See also* [Anon.] [Odell Hathaway] (1962).

THE GRECO-TURKISH WAR

See Beer's *SC* (1923); Berryman's *Crane* (1950); *Letters* (1960); *Cora Crane* (1960); Fryckstedt's *UW* (1963), pp. xxxix–xlvi; Crane (1968), chap. 16; and *The Works of Stephen Crane,* vol. IX: *Reports of War,* ed. Fredson Bowers. The Text: History and Analysis: War Dispatches: Greece, pp. 411–466. Also Textual Notes, pp. 565 ff., by Fredson Bowers.

1898

[Anon.]. [Crane in England], *Academy,* 55 (October 15, 1898), 64. Also in *Bookman,* 19 (March, 1904), 39. Portrait of Crane in his study at Ravensbrook, **Oxted, Surrey.**

——. "Concerning the English Academy Awards for 1897," *Bookman*, 7 (March, 1898), 22–24.

——. [On Crane's "The Men in the Storm"], *Commercial Advertiser*, January 11, 1898.
"There is no doubt that Stephen Crane's sketch in *The Philistine*, 'The Men in the Storm,' is one of the most powerful pictures he has ever drawn of the tragedies of life among the poor of New York."

——. [Crane and Frederic], *Critic*, n.s., 29 (May 7, 1898), 318.
Comments on the exchange of courtesies between the two American authors who were then friends in England.

——. "Picture Shows." [Crane as another Verestchagin], *Glasgow Sunday Times*, March 28, 1898.

——. [On Crane's journalism], *Literary Digest* (October 15, 1898).
Remarks that Crane's Cuban War dispatches are out of place in the yellow journalism of Pulitzer *World:* "If they had appeared in a more literary medium they would have carried more weight."

——. [Portrait], *Literature*, 2 (July 13, 1898).
"A Full-Page Portrait of Stephen Crane as a Supplement to this Issue." (Inserted into this issue with no pagination.)

——. "War Vignettes: A Run to Cuba," *London Daily Chronicle*, June 18, 1898.
"In the evening we sat in the stern under the awning spinning yarns and singing [on the *Somers N. Smith*]. Sylvester Scovell has a very good tenor voice and an immense repertoire of songs, and Stephen Crane sings a good second." In *SCraneN*, 4, no. 2 (Winter, 1969), 11.

——. "More 'Black Riders' by Crane." *Louisville Courier-Journal*, November 12, 1898, p. 7.

——. "Books and Bookmen," *Manchester Guardian*, March 26, 1898.
Compares *The Red Badge of Courage* with Whitman's *Specimen Days*. V. S. Pritchett makes the same point of comparison in his *Living Novel* (1949).

——. "The Author of *The Red Badge*," *Munsey's Magazine*, 20 (October, 1898), 147–148.

——. "Stephen Crane Sued," *New York Daily Tribune*, January 4, 1898, p. 3.
Amy Leslie, Chicago drama critic and former dancer, brings suit against Crane to recover the sum of $550, which she alleged Crane had misappropriated.*

——. *Outlook* (London), 1 (April 9, 1898), 313.
Mr. Crane "left last week for Cuba to jointly represent the *New York Journal* and the *London Daily Chronicle. . . .*"
However, in *Crane* (1968) I say Crane sailed on the *Germanic* on April 14, which squares with the arrival of Crane in Manhattan on April 22 as given by Ames W. Williams in *New Colophon*, 1 (1948). Jean Cazemajou in his *Écrivain journaliste* (1969), p. 151, seemingly agrees with the *Crane* dating of April 14, albeit he does not commit himself.

* See *Cora Crane; Letters;* and *Crane.*

———. [Editorial announcement], *Philistine*, 6 (February, 1898), 77. Unsigned [by Elbert Hubbard].

"Arrangements have been made with Stephen Crane (there's only one) to supply 'Lines' for the back of every *Philistine* for a decade. Stevie has sent me enuff of the Choice Stuff to last several lustrums (as he may be shipwrect any time) and the matter will be duly printed regardless of cancellations."

———. "Lines to Pegasus and Stephen Crane," *Philistine*, 7 (July, 1898), back cover. Drawing of Crane on a wooden rocking horse.

———. *Saturday Review* (London), 86 (August 27, 1898), 280.

Ridicules George Wyndham for his warlike writings in which he tries to write like Stephen Crane and fails—under "the spell of Mr. Crane's lurid and dominating style."

Cather, Willa. [Review of Ambrose Bierce's *In the Midst of Life*], *Leader* (Pittsburgh), March 25, 1898.

"Utterly devoid of the sentiment and poetry of war, they freeze the blood as Mr. Stephen Crane's stories never do."

———. "The War and the Magazines," *Leader* (Pittsburgh), July 8, 1898.

"Mr. Stephen Crane could still get a few tips from the *Anabasis*, though he professes to despise the classics."

However, Crane did not despise the classics, as we know from his "List of Books / Brede Place."

Frederic, Harold. "The Open Boat," *New York Times*, May 1, 1898, p. 19.

Garnett, Edward. "Mr. Stephen Crane: An Appreciation," *Academy*, 55 (December 17, 1898), 483–484. Photograph.*

Reprinted in *Friday Nights* (1922), pp. 201–217: "Stephen Crane and His Work." Variant texts. The London *Academy* essay is quoted from and commented on by *Literary Digest*, 18 (January 21, 1899), 69: "An English Appreciation of Stephen Crane."

"What Mr. Crane has got to do is very simple: he must not mix reporting with his writing. . . . In his art he is unique. Its certainty, its justness, its peculiar perfection of power arrived at its birth, or at least at that precise moment of its life when other artists—and great artists too—were preparing themselves for the long and difficult conquest of their art. I cannot remember a parallel case in the literary history of fiction. Maupassant, Meredith, Mr. James, Mr. Howells, Tolstoi, all were learning their expression at the age where Mr. Crane had achieved his, achieved it triumphantly. Mr. Crane has no need to learn anything. His technique is absolutely his own, and by its innate laws of being has arrived at a perfect fulness of power. What he has not got he has no power of acquiring. He has no need to acquire it. . . .

"His art is strictly limited. We would define him by saying that he is the perfect artist and interpreter of the surfaces of life. And that explains why he so swiftly attained his peculiar power, what is the realm his art commands, and where his limitations come in. . . . The rare thing about Mr. Crane's art is that he keeps closer to the surface than any living writer, and, like the great portrait-painters, to a great extent makes the surface betray the depths. . . . In 'The Bride Comes to Yellow Sky,' for example, the art is simply immense. . . .

* Crane in a greenhouse, England, in early 1898. Reproduced in *Crane* (1968).

"Foolish people may call Mr. Crane a reporter of genius; but nothing could be more untrue. He is thrown away as a picturesque reporter, a secondary style of art. . . .* Mr. Crane's technique is far superior to Mr. Kipling's, but he does not experiment ambitiously in various styles and develop in new directions, as Mr. Kipling has done. I do not think that Mr. Crane will or can develop further. Again, I do not think that he has the building faculty, or that he will ever do better in constructing a perfect whole out of many parts than he has arrived at in *The Red Badge of Courage*. . . . [However, he had previously constructed a perfect whole from episodic parts in *Maggie*, a work which escaped Garnett's notice.]

"He is the chief impressionist of this age, as Sterne was the great impressionist in a different manner, of his age. If he fails in anything he undertakes, it will be through abandoning the style he has invented. . . . Mr. Crane's talent is unique; nobody can question that. America may well be proud of him. . . . And undoubtedly of the young school of American artists Mr. Crane is the genius—the others have their talents."

Stallman, in *Critiques* (1952) and in *Omnibus*, attempted a rejoiner to Garnett's charge that Crane's *Red Badge* lacks architectonics.

"That Crane is incapable of architectonics has been the critical consensus for over a half century: 'his work is a mass of fragments'; 'he can only string together a series of loosely cohering incidents'; *The Red Badge of Courage* is not constructed—it is 'not a sustained narrative, but a sequence of extraordinary tableaux' (*Book Buyer*, July 1896). That Crane lacks the great artist's arrangement of complex effects, as Edward Garnett pointed out in his 1898 appraisal of Crane, is certainly true. We look to Conrad and Henry James for 'exquisite grouping of devices'; Crane's figure in the carpet is a much simpler one. What it consists in is the very thing Garnett failed to detect— a schemework of striking contrasts, alternations of contradictory moods. Crane once defined a novel as a 'succession of sharply-outlined pictures, which pass before the reader like a panorama, leaving each its definite impression.' His own novel, nonetheless, is not simply a succession of pictures. It is a sustained structural whole. Every Crane critic concurs in this mistaken notion that *The Red Badge of Courage* is nothing more than 'a series of episodic scenes,' but not one critic has yet undertaken an analysis of Crane's work to see *how* the sequence of tableaux is constructed."

Gwynne, Stephen. "Novels of American Life," *Edinburgh Review*, 187 (April, 1898), 411–414.

The Little Regiment is a better book than *The Red Badge*. *The Third Violet* "is simply amazing in its futility." "We have no objection to stories of slum life; Mr. R. H. Davis's 'Gallegher' is a wonderful and attractive picture of the New York street-arab. But *Maggie* does not seem to us to justify its existence. . . . As a work of art we disbelieve in it. Take Mr. Maugham's 'Liza,' a work equally unsparing and in some ways more revolting; here you have at least credible human beings, with natural affections. . . . The admiration for work of this sort savours of the latest modern cant, which preaches that to see

---

* Garnett's example here is the great English reporter G. W. Steevens, author of *With the Conquering Turk* (1897).

Conrad wrote Garnett about his essay in the *Academy:* "The Crane thing is just—precisely just a ray flashed in and showing all there is." Garnett's critical study and H. G. Well's appraisal of 1900 are the best essays on Crane during the span of the next several decades.

things artistically you must see them disagreeably. Mr. Crane has seen a piece of life in a hard superficial way, and rendered it in the spirit of caricature. That is the true formula for producing what, in the cant of the day, is called uncompromising realism."

Huneker, James. [By Stephen Crane, a parody], *Musical Courier,* 37 (August 3, 1898), 20.
    Parody of Crane as Cuban War correspondent.
    Reprinted in Schwab (1963), pp. 115–116.
    Reprinted in *War Dispatches,* p. 54, with this note from the *Musical Courier* introducing the unsigned parody: "The *Buffalo Enquirer* prints the following war correspondence from the front. It neglects to state whether the dispatches were received by wire or freight." This note is not in Schwab.

————. "The American Language," *Musical Courier,* 37 (September 21, 1898), i.

McCready, Ernest, and Stephen Crane [unsigned]. "In the First Landing 4 of Our Men are Killed," *New York World,* June 13, 1898.
    Dictated by Crane to McCready of the *Herald* at Guantánamo Bay on June 12 and filed by McCready. *See Crane,* quoting for first time McCready's letter of 1934 to Stolper (in R. W. S. files). Crane's dispatch was first reprinted in Louis L. Snyder and Richard B. Morris, eds. (1949) titled "A *World* Correspondent Immortalizes an Incident on the Shores of Guantánamo Bay."

O'Connor, Joseph [unsigned]. "Gossip of the Authors," *Rochester Post-Express,* August 2, 1898, p. 10.*
    "Mr. Crane has no word record. He paints his stories on canvas and has them transcribed into language by a force of stenographers—which may account for some of the eccentricities of his English."

Quiller-Couch, Arthur. [Review of Conrad's *The Nigger of the "Narcissus"*], *Pall Mall Magazine,* 14 (January, 1898), 425.
    There is something of Crane in Conrad's *Nigger.*

Traill, H. D. "The New Realism," in *The New Fiction and Other Literary Subjects.* New York and London, 1898, pp. 4–5.
    Makes a ferocious hashing of Crane's sordid New Realism in *Maggie* and *George's Mother.*
    Reviewed: Fortnightly Review. See Traill (1899).

Wyndham, George. Introduction, "An Appreciation." In Stephen Crane, *Pictures of War.* London (1898), pp. ix–xxiv. Reprinted from *New Review,* 14 (January, 1896), 30–40.
    See The Red Badge of Courage, New Review.

CUBAN WAR

Norris, Frank. "News Gathering at Key West," *New McClure's Magazine,* 11 (May–October, 1898).
    Reprinted in *Letters of Frank Norris,* ed. Franklin Walker, 1956, pp. 10–18.

    * O'Connor resumed his connection with the *Post-Express* on August 1 and had charge of the literary department of the paper (said an editorial for August 1, 1898).

Reprinted in *War Dispatches*.
Crane in Norris's account figures as "The Young Personage" and Sylvester Scovel as "The Press."

Kenealy, Alexander? [unsigned]. "First American Newspaper to Open Headquarters on Cuban Soil in the *World*," *New York World*, June 20, 1898.
Reprinted in *War Dispatches*.

Davis, Richard Harding. "How Hamilton Fish and Allyn Capron Died, Fighting Bravely," *New York Herald*, June 26, 1898, p. 3.
"Stephen Crane, who, with J. P. Dunning of the Associated Press, and myself, witnessed the ambuscade, is looking after him. Mr. Marshall is badly hurt and may not live."

Steep, Thomas W. "First Fighting Days in Cuba," *Leslie's Weekly*, July 14, 1898.
On the death of Assistant Surgeon Gibbs at Guantánamo. Collate with Crane's account in "War Memories" (1899).

[Anon.] [Arthur Brisbane?]. "Some Men Who Have Reported This War," *Cosmopolitan*, 25 (September, 1898), 556–557.*
Compares Crane and James Creelman as reporters. "Mr. Crane's interest in life is not so much to tell what happens as to make telling it interesting." Quotes Langdon Smith of the *Journal*, who described Mr. Crane's conduct under fire "as entirely worthy of the coolest hero that Mr. Crane's imagination ever devised. 'Crane was standing under a tree, calmly rolling a cigarette,' says Mr. Smith; 'some leaves dropped from the trees, cut away by the bullets; two or three men dropped within a few feet. Crane is as thin as a lath. If he had been two or three inches wider or thicker through, he would undoubtedly have been shot. But he calmly finished rolling his cigarette and smoked it without moving away from the spot where the bullets had suddenly become so thick.'"
The Langdon Smith pen-portrait of Crane is important. Quoted in *Crane*.

Graham, George E. "The Destruction of Cervera's Fleet," *McClure's Magazine* (September, 1898), pp. 403–421.
Mentions Crane.

Marshall, Edward. "A Wounded Correspondent's Recollections of Guásimas," *Scribner's* (September, 1898).
Recast, together with his *Cosmopolitan* article ("How It Feels to Be Shot"), in his *Story of the Rough Riders* (1899).

[Anon.]. "Newspaper Men in the War," *Literary Digest*, 17 (October 15, 1898), 455–457. Photographs of correspondents; of Crane, p. 457.
Quotes John D. Barry from *The Literary World* (Boston) that the literary honors of the war have so far been won by Richard Harding Davis, although "Mr. Davis has been notoriously inaccurate." Quotes Edward Marshall's September *Scribner's* article ("A Wounded Correspondent's Recollections of Guásimas") and remarks on Crane's assisting Marshall when Marshall was wounded.
It seems odd, says Barry in *Literary World*, "that Mr. Crane should have

* For discovery of this article I am indebted to Miss Roberta Smith, Reference Librarian at the University of Connecticut.

given so slight a literary evidence of his presence at the war. It is true that he wrote a number of articles for *The World;* but they made very little impression. And yet he applied to the fight the method he used so successfully in his famous book; that is, he chose suggestive incidents and treated them realistically. But in *The World* this work seemed insignificant, at times almost puerile. I have heard it said that the articles lost effectiveness by being out of place in *The World,* and that if they had appeared in a more literary medium they would have carried more weight. Before the war ended, Mr. Crane, knowing that it could not last much longer, returned to England, where he has been living for many months."

However, Crane at this time was hiding out in Havana and did not return to England until early January, 1899. Barry, who had read Crane's poems before the Uncut Leaves Society in April, 1894, had become more critical of Crane in subsequent reviews of his works, an estrangement between them no doubt owing to Crane's characteristic neglect of his friends.

Chicago Record's War Stories. Chicago, 1898.
Important eye-witness reports of the battles by Billman, Harris, James Langland, and Henry Chamberlin, who saw Crane sleeping in the trench while the marines were firing all around him. In "With Sampson Off Santiago," by Henry Barrett Chamberlin. On the death of Surgeon Gibbs *see also* Crane in "War Memories," *War Dispatches.*

Davis, Richard Harding. *The Cuban and the Puerto Rican Campaigns.* New York, 1898, pp. 237–241.

——. *A Year from a Reporter's Notebook.* New York, 1898.

Harris, Kenneth F. "Cavalrymen at Guásimas," in *Chicago Record's War Stories.* Chicago, 1898, pp. 64–70.
An important article in relation to the scarcity of coffee-beans at Siboney on June 23, a situation which echoes the opening scene of Crane's "An Episode of War." For further background materials on the Cuban War *see* the checklist in *Crane,* pp. 637–641.

Hereford, Kenneth. "Crane, America's Greatest Genius," *Saturday Evening Post,* 171 (April 8, 1899), 649.

Davis, Richard Harding. "Our War Correspondents in Cuba and Puerto Rico," *Harper's Magazine,* 98 (May, 1899), 941–943. Retold in Davis, *Notes of a War Correspondent* (1910).
"Crane was the coolest man, whether army officer or civilian, that I saw under fire at any time during the war. He was most annoyingly cool, with the assurance of a fatalist." On Crane at San Juan hills with James Hare of *Collier's.* How Crane took Juana Diaz. Retold in *In Many Wars by Many War Correspondents* (1904). *See* Davis (1904).

McIntosh, Burr. *The Little I Saw of Cuba.* London and New York, 1899, pp. 68, 72, 103, 124–127, 132–133, 165. Photographs of Crane.
One of the liveliest accounts of the Cuban War; important recollections of Crane.

Marshall, Edward. *The Story of the Rough Riders.* New York, 1899, pp. 76, 85, 143.
On Crane at Las Guásimas.

Roosevelt, Theodore. *The Rough Riders.* New York, 1899.
Roosevelt disdains to mention Crane's presence in Cuba.

The Spanish-American War . . . by Eye-Witnesses. Chicago and New York, 1899, pp. 98, 112. Photographs.

Important. Here are multiple points of view by newsmen, some of them reporting also in the *Chicago Record's War Stories:* Chamberlin, Billman, Harris. Useful are Langdon Smith's "Landing of General Shafter's Men," Harris's "With Grimes' Battery," and H. J. Whigham's "Fighting at Guantánamo."

On Crane, p. 98; but Whigham's account is in error. Also in gross error is Malcolm McDowell's fabrication that "one of the Seventy-first New York men, Scovill by name, brought a wounded comrade to the field hospital. He stooped over to aid the surgeon when a Spaniard in a tree 200 yards away put a bullet in Scovill's head, and he fell dead." *Contra* McDowell, Sylvester Scovel headed the *World* staff and had no connection with the 71st New York Volunteers. Crane—not "Scovill" (Scovel)—brought Ed Marshall to the field hospital at Sibony. Scovel never "fell dead." He ended his career as newsman after punching General Shafter in the jaw.

Hilliard, John Northern. "Letters to a Friend," *New York Times Supplement,* July 14, 1900, p. 5407.
Quotes Crane at Guantánamo by Richard Harding Davis.

King, W. N. *The Story of the Spanish-American War and the Revolt in the Philippines.* New York, 1900, p. 161.

Davis, Richard Harding. "How Stephen Crane Took Juana Dias," in *In Many Wars by Many War Correspondents,* ed. George Lynch and Frederic Palmer. Tokyo, 1904, pp. 43–45.
Reprinted in *War Dispatches,* pp. 196–199.

———. *Notes of a War Correspondent.* New York, 1911, pp. 125, 127, 128.
On Crane at San Juan Hill. Important.

[Anon.]. "Adventure Filled Life of Richard Harding Davis," *New York Evening Post,* April 15, 1916.
An obituary on Davis in which is retold Davis's story of Crane at Siboney.

Davis, Charles Belmont, ed. *Adventures and Letters of Richard Harding Davis.* New York, 1917, pp. 200–207 (Crane in Greece), 234–235 (Crane in Cuba).

Starrett, Vincent. "Stephen Crane: An Estimate," *Sewanee Review,* 28 (June, 1920), 405–413.
On Crane with Burr McIntosh in Cuba. *See also* Starrett (1931).

Paine, Ralph D. *Roads of Adventure.* Boston and New York, 1922.
Important; much here on Crane and Ernest McCready.

Beer, Thomas. *Stephen Crane.* New York, 1923.
Claims that Crane could not report. Beer likely obtained this notion from Don Seitz of the *World,* whose malicious grudge against Crane instigated the false charges about Crane as reporter which Walter Millis and subsequent historians repeated (echoing Millis are Mason, Leech, and Swanberg). Beer, who never read Crane's war dispatches, expends but eight pages on Crane in Cuba.

Boyd, Thomas. "Semper Fidelis," *Bookman,* 60 (December, 1924), 409–412.
Retells the story of Sergeant John Quick at Cuzco in the Cuban War, told by Crane in *Wounds in the Rain* (1900), and relates another act of heroism by Sergeant Major Quick—witnessed by Boyd—in World War I.

Seitz, Don Carlos. *Joseph Pulitzer.* New York, 1924, p. 241.

Deliberately charged Crane falsely as having written only a few *World* dispatches, of which one was the *World* article claiming panic among the 71st New York Volunteers, whereas Seitz as business manager of Pulitzer's *World* could readily have ascertained that the author was Sylvester Scovel and that Crane submitted more than twenty dispatches to the *World*. Seitz, who had known Crane at the Lantern Club in 1895 and evidently disliked him, influenced Thomas Beer's unfounded notion in Beer's *SC* that Crane could not report. Seitz's mistaken account of Crane as reporter has damaged Crane's reputation as reporter for three decades, since Millis (1931) repeated Seitz's errors in *The Martial Spirit*. Millis's error is repeated by Mason (1939), by Leech (1959), and by Swanberg (1961), one historian copying the error of his predecessor without investigating any scholarship on Crane.

Cather, Willa. Introduction, *The Work of Stephen Crane,* vol. 9, ed. Wilson Follett. New York, 1926.

Michelson, Charles. Introduction, *The Work of Stephen Crane,* vol. 7, ed. Wilson Follett. New York, 1927.

Millis, Walter. *The Martial Spirit.* Boston, 1931.

Misidentifies Crane as author of the article in the *World* reporting panic among the 71st New York Volunteers. (Sylvester Scovel wrote it.)

Brooks, Van Wyck. *Sketches in Criticism.* New York, 1932.

Quotes an eye-witness of Crane's bravery.

Palmer, Frederick. *With My Own Eyes.* Indianapolis, Ind., 1932, p. 242.

Rubens, Horatio S. *Liberty: The Story of Cuba.* New York, 1932.

On Crane in Jacksonville in January–March, 1897.

Walker, Franklin. *Frank Norris.* Garden City, N.Y., 1932.

Seitz, Don Carlos. "Stephen Crane: War Correspondent," *Bookman,* 76 (Februray, 1933), 137–140.

Seitz here repeats his unfounded charges against Crane made in his *Joseph Pulitzer* (1924). *See* Ames W. Williams, "Stephen Crane: War Correspondent" (1948).

Downey, Fairfax. *Richard Harding Davis and His Day.* New York, 1933, pp. 137, 147–148, 160, 171.

Brown, Curtis. *Contacts.* London and New York, 1935.

Mason, Gregory. *Remember the Maine.* New York, 1939.

A very lively account of the Cuban War. On Crane, however, Mason repeats Millis's false charge that Crane wrote the *World* article charging panic among the 71st New York Volunteers.

Carnes, Cecil. *Jimmy Hare: News Photographer.* New York, 1940.

An eye-witness report on Crane in Cuba; important.

Berryman, John. *Stephen Crane.* New York, 1950, pp. 217–234.

Covers Crane in the Cuban War in twenty pages.

Caster, Henry. *The Year of the Spaniard.* New York, 1950, 1963.

A historical novel with Stephen Crane depicted in the Cuban War.

Walker, Franklin, ed. *The Letters of Frank Norris.* Book Club of California, 1956.

Churchill, Allen. *Park Row*. New York, 1958, pp. 116–117, 128–130.
Misattributes to Crane the *World* article on the 71st New York Volunteers, which was written by Sylvester Scovel. The quotation from Crane's description of the death of Surgeon Gibbs (from "War Memories") is badly misquoted, p. 129.

Freidel, Frank. *The Splendid Little War*. Boston, 1958. Photographs.
Although mainly a picture book, this is the best short summary of the Spanish-American War. Quotes Crane frequently. The photograph of correspondents at Tampa which claims "Stephen Crane in white suit" does not contain Crane, p. 66.

Leech, Margaret. *In the Days of McKinley*. New York, 1959, pp. 304–305.
Leech repeats Millis's error on Crane and the 71st New York Volunteers (Millis, *The Martial Spirit*, 1931).

Gilkes, Lillian. *Cora Crane*. Bloomington, Ind., 1960.

Stallman, R. W., and Lillian Gilkes, eds. *Stephen Crane: Letters*. New York, 1960.

Manchester, William. "The Spanish American War," *Holiday*, 30 (September, 1961), p. 97.

Azoy, A. C. M. *Charge! The Story of the Battle of San Juan*. New York, 1961, p. 145.
A splendid little book—one of the best of the thirty-five or more books on the Spanish-American War.

Langford, Gerald. *The Richard Harding Davis Years*. New York, 1961.
For commentary *see* Langford (1961).

Swanberg, W. A. *Citizen Hearst*. New York, 1961.
On Crane; repeats the erroneous charges which Walter Millis instigated among historians in 1931.

Stallman, R. W., and E. R. Hagemann, eds. *The War Dispatches of Stephen Crane*. New York and London (1964).

Brown, Charles H. *The Correspondents' War*. New York, 1967.
An important book, but superficial in its account of the Santiago campaign. The bibliography's omission of A.C.M. Azoy's *Charge! The Story of the Battle of San Juan* is inexcusable, and the listings on R. H. Davis are incomplete.

Stallman, R. W. *Stephen Crane: A Biography*. New York, 1968, chaps. 21–25, pp. 350–442.
Checklist on Cuban War, pp. 637–641.
Collate with Crane's *Wounds in the Rain* and with his *War Dispatches*. Identifies for the first time the persons and places of battle or skirmish, dating the occasion, which data Crane disguised in his fictional Cuban War tales and in "War Memories."

Bowers, Fredson, ed. *The Works of Stephen Crane*, vol. IX. *Reports of War*. The Text: History and Analysis: War Dispatches: Cuba, pp. 476–510. Also, Textual Notes. Also Editorial Emendations in the Copy-Text, pp. 565 ff. Introduction by James B. Colvert, pp. xix–xxix. Charlottesville, Va., 1971.

1899

[Anon.]. [Cora Crane and Harold Frederic], *Munsey's Magazine,* 20 (January, 1899), 655.

Beerbohm, Max. *Works and More.* London, 1899. Reprinted 1969.
On Crane's review of Ouida's *Under Two Flags.*

Davis, Richard Harding. "Our War Correspondents in Cuba and Puerto Rico," *Harper's Magazine,* 98 (May, 1899), 941–943. Retold in Davis, *Notes of War Correspondent* (1910).

Garnett, Edward? [unsigned]. "Stephen Crane," *Academy,* 58 (1899), 491.

Garnett, Edward. "An English Appreciation of Stephen Crane," *Literary Digest,* 18 (January 21, 1899), 69.
Quotes portions of Garnett's *Academy* essay of December 17, 1898.

Hereford, Kenneth [unsigned]. "Crane, America's Greatest Genius," *Saturday Evening Post,* 171 (April 8, 1899), 649.
On Brede Manor and the legend of Sir Goddard Oxenbridge. *See also* Hereford, "Young Blood—Stephen Crane" (1899).
Reports a story of Crane in Cuba told by George Lynch, war correspondent for the *London Chronicle* and a visitor in 1899 at Brede Manor.
"A company under fire was badly in need of water, and water was seven miles away, down hill at that. Stephen collected all the tin canteens he could find and trotted off for the refreshment. Coming wearily back, there was a sharp ping against one of the cans, and it began to leak. Stephen turned up the can and tried to stop the leak. An officer in the woods near by shouted to him:
" 'Come here, quick! You're in the line of fire!'
" 'If you've got a knife, cut a plug and bring it to me,' replied the young man, and, as he spoke, bang went a bullet against another can.
" 'Come under cover, or you'll lose every can you've got!'
"This warning had its effect. The loss of the precious fluid terrified him in a way that the danger to himself had failed to do. He finally brought the water up to the thirsty company, and then fainted through exhaustion.
"Coming back from turmoil and stress you might imagine he was writing stories of the war. As a matter of fact, he is at the present moment engaged in a series of stories in which boys are the heroes, giving the character of the small boy as it actually is. He is also about one-third on with a novel, commenced before the Cuban campaign, the scene of which is Greece."
Crane experienced here what he had already described in "A Mystery of Heroism" (1895).

———. "Young Blood—Stephen Crane," *Saturday Evening Post,* 172 (November 18, 1899), 413. Portraits.
On Crane at Brede Manor.

Higginson, Thomas Wentworth. *Book and Heart.* New York, 1899.

Howells, W. D. "Problems of Existence in Fiction," *Literature,* n.s., 1 (March 10, 1899), 193–194.

King, W. N. *The Story of the Spanish-American War and the Revolt in the Philippines.* New York, 1900, p. 161.

London, Jack. [Letter June 7, 1899 to Clouderly Johns], *Letters from Jack London*, ed. King Hendricks and Irving Shepard. New York, 1965, p. 41.

"Find enclosed a take-off on Stephen Crane's style, which, in turn, I deem to be a take-off on that of Walt Whitman's. Whiled a way a few minutes on it, just for fun."

McIntosh, Burr. *The Little I Saw of Cuba*. London and New York, 1899, pp. 68, 72, 103, 124–127, 132–133, 165.

Photograph of Crane.

Marshall, Edward. *The Story of the Rough Riders*. New York, 1899, pp. 76, 85, 143.

On Crane at Las Guásimas.

Maurice, Arthur Bartlett. "New York in Fiction," *Bookman*, 10 (September, 1899), 33–49.

In *New York of the Novelists* (1917), chap. 9. Photographs especially fine.

Plarr, Victor Gustave. *Men and Women of the Time*. London, 1899, pp. 246–247.

Biographical note on Crane, which erroneously lists "The Eternal Patience" as a published title.

The Spanish-American War . . . by Eye-Witnesses. Chicago and New York, 1899, pp. 98, 112. Photographs.

Traill, H. D. "The New Realism," *Fortnightly Review*, 67, n.s., 61 (January, 1899), 63–66.

Dismisses Howells's praise of *Maggie* in "An Appreciation," prefacing the London edition (1896), and dismisses Crane as no realist in *Maggie, George's Mother*, and *The Red Badge*.

Whigham, Henry James. "The Battles of Las Guásimas, San Juan, and El Caney," in *The Spanish-American War by Eye Witnesses*. Chicago and New York, 1899, pp. 102–106.

At the burial of Hamilton Fish, Jr., and other Rough Riders, Chaplain Brown read the beautiful Episcopal burial service for the dead and announced the hymn, "Nearer, My God, to Thee."

Quite different is the burial service uttered by Timothy Lean in Crane's "The Upturned Face," which is likely recast from the burial of Surgeon Gibbs at Guantánamo.

Wyndham, George. *Diary of a Cavalry Officer*. London, n.d.

1900

[Anon.]. [On "The Ghost" at Brede Place], *Academy*, January 6, 1900.*

Reproduces in facsimile the first page of the printed program of the play "The Ghost."

* *See also* C. Lewis Hind, *Authors and I* (1921); H. G. Wells, *Experiment in Autobiography* (1934); John D. Gordon, "The Ghost at Brede Place" (1952) and *The Ghost of Brede Place* (1953); Edith Richie Jones, "Stephen Crane at Brede" (1954); *Letters* (1960): *Cora Crane* (1960); and *Crane* (1968).

The holograph manuscript of "The Ghost" is reproduced from the BCC in *Letters* and in *Crane*.

————. [Report on Crane's health], *Academy*, April 14, 1900, p. 1.

————. "Some Letters of Stephen Crane," *Academy*, 59 (August 11, 1900), p. 116.

Quotes portions of Crane letters published by John N. Hilliard in Literary Supplement of the *New York Times*, July 14, 1900.

"When one looks back at Crane's short life, packed as it was with action, his output of work seems curiously large. And when one considers how good in its way everything he published was—how tense, and studied, and complete—this output assumes a very serious air. To die at thirty-one and to have done so much with one's talents is a great achievement. It is possible that his work was done; that as he grew older he would have lost the desire, the zest of writing, would have asked himself: 'Is it worth while?'—that paralysing question. The sardonic in his nature would have had time to develop and might have stifled further energy. This is merely conjecture, of course. Meanwhile his work exists for our admiration and pleasure, and as a noble example to young authors in a hurry.

"Stephen Crane's *Whilomville Stories*, those studies of boy and child life which he wrote with such intense interest towards the close of his brief life and believed in so thoroughly—he told Mr. Alden, the Editor of *Harper's Magazine*, that his best was in them—will be issued in book form very shortly. We are also to have his Irish novel, and two collections of short stories—*Wounds in the Rain* and *The Monster*. And there is a series of studies of great battles also to be published."

————. "Stephen Crane's Artist Friends," *Art News*, October, 1900.

Reports that Crane had been discharged by the *Tribune* because he had given offense to an organization of working-men by writing satirically of their parade at Asbury Park in August, 1892. Did the *Tribune* fire Crane? *See Crane*. On Crane and the French symbolists *see Omnibus* and Peck, "Stephen Crane and Baudelaire" (1965).

————. "The Work of Stephen Crane," *Book Buyer*, 20 (July, 1900), 433–444.

————. [Crane and the Great American Novel], *Bookman*, 11 (March, 1900), 405.

Reports that Robert Barr, less than two years ago, ventured the opinion in a magazine article that Stephen Crane among all the writers before the public was the one most likely to produce the Great American Novel.

————. [Portrait and five views of Brede Place], *Bookman* (London), 18 (July, 1900), 104–105.

————. *Bookman* 11 (July, 1900), 405–406. Photograph.

"In some respects *The Red Badge* is inferior to *Maggie*. There is real power in the latter book. Here and there a phase of proletarian life is caught with photographic fidelity. On the other hand, it is too strained—too intense—it is all out of proportion. Truck-drivers are torn with Promethean woes and stirred with Homeric passions. They bellow—they exchange epithets—and the universe resounds. The sordid squabbles of a besotted tenement-house family become Titanic struggles, and mud-puddles are magnified to measureless oceans."

Quotes Robert Barr on Crane as the one most likely to produce the Great American Novel.

————. [Bacheller and the Lantern Club], *Bookman*, 12 (November, 1900), 220–221. Photograph.

"Late in 1884 Mr. Bacheller gave up his reportorial position to start the Bacheller Syndicate. This organisation was from the first a success and did a great deal toward the revolutionising of literary methods. He was the first to see the power in *The Red Badge of Courage,* and in the winter of 1894 he and Crane and Willis B. Hawkins hung out 'The Sign o' the Lantern' at the little chalet on Monkey Hill, described in Eben Holden."

————. [Crane letter of November 1895], *Brooklyn Daily Eagle,* June 5, 1900, p. 3. Reprints Crane's letter to an editor of *Leslie Weekly,* November (?), 1895.

————. [Style of Stephen Crane], *Chautauquan,* 31 (July 1900), 323.

————. " 'Browsing' and Stephen Crane," *Criterion,* n.s., 1 (July 1900), 31. Appearing in same *Criterion,* also p. 31, is "Stephen Crane's Splendid Imagination."

————. "Stephen Crane's Splendid Imagination," *Criterion,* n.s., 1 (July, 1900), 31.

————. "Stephen Crane," *Cyclopedia of American Biography,* vol. 10. New York, 1900, p. 113.

————. [Report on Crane's health], *Daily Chronicle* (London), April 10, 1900.

————. "Brede: Mr. Stephen Crane Enlivens the Holidays," *Kent Mail,* January 5, 1900, and *Surrey Standard, Sussex Express.*

On the production at Brede Place of *The Ghost.*

On *The Ghost see* Hind (1921), Wells (1934), Gordan (1952), Jones (1954), *Cora Crane, Letters,* and *Crane,* pp. 556–557.

————. "The New Art of Description in Fiction," *Literary Digest,* 20 (February 10, 1900), 183.

————. "Stephen Crane: A 'Wonderful Boy,' " *Literary Digest,* 21 (June 23, 1900).

Quotes Crane letters from the *Rochester Post-Express,* April 18, 1900, p. 4.

————. "English Views of Stephen Crane," *Literary Digest,* 21 (July 7, 1900), 12.

Quotes the *Westminster Gazette* for June 5. *The Red Badge of Courage* "was the outcome of an intensely vivid imagination joined with exhaustive study of all available documents and expressed as to its literary form in language which, if occasionally over-laboured, was for the most part picturesque and powerful to the last degree. Mr. Crane's indebtedness to Kipling was not difficult to detect, while Bret Harte and Mark Twain were other writers suggested by certain qualities of his work." The *Literary Digest* repeats its appraisal of *The Open Boat* volume: "You can scarcely find a wasted stroke or a random stroke in the whole volume."

————. "The Last of Stephen Crane," *Literary Digest,* 21 (December 1, 1900), 647.

————. "A Bit of Stephen Crane's Front Yard," *Literary Review* (Boston), April, 1900.

————. [On "The Ghost" at Brede Place], *Manchester Guardian,* January 13, 1900.

———. [Crane letter], *Newark Sunday Call,* June 17, 1900.

Quotes Crane's letter to the New Jersey Historical Society. A press clipping for June 10, 1900, source not identified, is in Newark Public Library. *See* note on *New York Sun,* June 10, 1900.

———. "Stephen Crane: Jersey Man," *New York Sun,* June 10, 1900, p. 5.

Letter of Crane to New Jersey Historical Society. A press clipping for June 10, 1900, source not identified, is in Crane Collection, Newark Public Library. Crane's letter was reprinted in *Newark Call,* June 17, 1923, and in *Bulletin,* 64 (June, 1960), 339. *See* Part C, Published Letters, where it is quoted, p. 70. Not in *Letters.*

———. "Stephen Crane's Letters to a Friend About His Ambition, Art, and Views of Life," *New York Times,* Supplement, 19, July 14, 1900, p. 466.

———. "Stories About Steve Crane," *Omaha Daily Bee,* June 17, 1900, p. 16.

Reprinted in the *Omaha Weekly Bee,* June 20, 1900, p. 11.

Reprinted in *Prairie Schooner,* 43 (Summer, 1969).

Recounts the Philistine banquet honoring Crane (1895) and quotes Otto Carmichael, Washington correspondent of the *Minneapolis Times,* who sketches here some peculiarities of Crane. He "to a certainty was a Bohemian. He was absolutely worthless except for what he did. The city editor of a modern newspaper would not have had him around the city room for a week. He was irresponsible and unmanageable. There was nothing vicious about him or even reckless; he was serenely indifferent; trifles would change him and big things would not stop him; fancy would hold him to a place and money would not move him from it."

Recounts Crane's hiding out days in Havana, when General Wade, then Chairman of the American Evacuation Commission, asked Carmichael to carry word to Crane that he had a London cablegram. Crane showed no interest.

"He did nothing with regularity. He ate and slept when he could not longer do without these necessary comforts. He would remain in the streets and in the cafes until his friends and chance acquaintances were tired out. He lived with a former filibustering associate in a pair of rooms not far from the downtown hotels and when other places were closed to him he would go there in hopes of finding some stragglers. If he did he would sit and listen to their chatter until they were tired of it. Then he would go to work. When I saw him he was doing 600 words a day. This was the only thing he did with regularity. He was very particular about his work. He wrote somewhat slowly and was whimsical about words. He would spend a long time in trying to find what suited him. Inasmuch as he had no dictionary or books of reference, his search for words and information consisted in chewing his pencil and waiting until they came to him.

"When his 600 words were written he would rouse some of his straggling guests—if they would stand for it—and if not he might read or go to bed. To take care of his health never occurred to him. He had the Cuban fashion of drinking light drinks and coffee, but he did not indulge to excess in alcohol. This was somewhat remarkable at a time and place of excessive drinking. This was two years ago and his health then was wretched. There was no chance for him to live unless he mended his ways.

"I have heard many army officers say he was the bravest man they ever saw. He apparently did not think of danger. Death to him was nothing more than the next breath, or the next breakfast or sleep. Bullets were nothing to him, moving or in cartridges, except something to make copy about. This was not affected. It was the quality of the fellow. To see others suffer tore his tender heart. He was almost girlish in his sympathies. But it apparently did not bother him to be hungry himself or to be in pain. He never grumbled about taking his share.

"So far as I could note, courage was the only thing he admired. If he cared anything for the Cuban cause he never showed it. He had a boundless admiration for the men who did the real fighting. The only time I ever saw him really enthusiastic was when he was trying to prove to a cafe crowd that the filibusterers who landed on the enemy's shore had more courage than any of them.

"Crane had seen all kinds of fighting. It had a fascination for him. Danger was his dissipation. He was really grieved when he learned he had left a cafe just a few minutes before a noisy shooting scrape.

"A strong man could not help feeling sorry for Crane. He seemed on the verge of collapse for lack of strength. His arms were as thin as one who had been ill for a long time. In a dim light Crane's face was handsome to the point of being exquisitely beautiful. In the full light his face had a sick and miserable look. His drawn lips, his yellowish, haggard face, his tired eyes, and generally wornout appearance combined to make a picture not particularly attractive. But he was so simple and genuine that one soon forgot all about these. . . .

"I remember one time where he was drumming up some friend to play hearts with him. Finally he made up his party and they went to a club. The usual stakes were 5 cents a heart. Even 5 cents a heart is sufficient to make this game interesting. The counters were being distributed when Crane suddenly said: 'Let's play for centens.'

"This was startling. Centens were $5 gold pieces. With such stakes it would be possible to lose $65 on a hand, and very easy to get rid of a few hundred dollars at a sitting. Not a member of the party had any right to be playing for such stakes, but for some reason they did. They just fell into a helpless sort of way.

"And no one would have thought that Crane was not used to playing friendly games of hearts for gold centens. It was to be seen, however, that he was taking keen note of the nerve of the others. Courage was always in his mind. He was looking for it in big and little ways.

"The only man who lost much was his friend, the bartender and ex-filibuster. He was the one who could least afford it. That pleased Crane immensely. A book could be written about the comaraderie of these two. They had been in all sorts of tight places together. The 'bartender' knew the Cuban coast by night and day. He had been the pilot on the Three Friends, and later on the Dos Hermanos—the Two Brothers. He was no bartender, but Crane called him that because he once got him a position in a cafe and then had him discharged because he was late in the morning getting to work."

———. "Theatricals at Brede," *South Eastern Advertiser* (Sussex), January 5, 1900.

"The inhabitants of Brede have every reason to be thankful to Mr. and Mrs. Stephen Crane, of Brede Place, for providing them with such a treat as they enjoyed on Thursday week, when a performance of 'The Ghost' was given in the Brede Hill Schoolroom by the Brede Place Christmas House Party and their friends. The play, which is a combination of farce, comedy, opera, and burlesque, is founded on a local legend, and was said to be the production of the following eminent literary men:—Mr. Henry James, Mr. Robert Barr, Mr. Geo. Gissing, Mr. Rider Haggard, Mr. Joseph Conrad, Mr. H. B. Marriott-Watson, Mr. H. G. Wells, M. Edwin Pugh, Mr. A. E. W. Mason, and Mr. Stephen Crane."

Identifies the persons acting various parts in the play (Mason was the ghost) and the authors present in the audience. Describes the play in considerable detail. "No charge was made for admission, the whole of the expenses being defrayed by Mr. Stephen Crane, including an addition to the stage, which he has since presented to the School." (Crane was in debt, however, for nearly $5,000.)

(Photostat of this article is in Stallman files; the original clipping was owned by Roger Frewen.)

————. [On "The Ghost" at Brede Place], *Sussex Express,* January 5, 1900.

————. "The Will of Stephen Crane," *Springfield Daily Republican,* August 25, 1900.

————. "Stephen Crane and the Cubans," *Washington Post,* July 22, 1900, p. 17.

On Crane's astonishing influence over the Cubans, his popularity with the revolutionary element in Havana.

Barr, Robert. [Letter], *New York Herald,* June 21, 1900, p. 10.

Reprinted in Starrett (1921) and *Letters.*

Letter written from Hillhead, Woldingham, Surrey, to Karl Edwin Harriman a few days after Crane's death. It contains a description of Crane's last days, a six-line quotation, and refers to the completion of *The O'Ruddy.*

————. "Stephen Crane's Master Work," *New York Times,* Supplement, July 14, 1900, p. 467.

On the history of publication of *The Red Badge,* an article prompted by Ripley Hitchcock's 1900 edition. *See* Hitchcock (1900).

Belasco, David. "The Genius of Stephen Crane," *Metropolitan Magazine,* 12 (November, 1900), 666.

Reports his intention to dramatize *The Red Badge,* for which purpose he sought an interview with Mr. Crane's widow shortly after Crane's death. (The interview never took place.) When Belasco first read *The Red Badge,* "I dwelt vaguely upon its possibilities for the stage. Stephen Crane, by his directness and wealth of imagination, possesses eminently the qualities of a dramatic writer. He reveals the great human drama, its struggles and tragic climaxes, in a flash of the pen. His creations seem to rise in the flesh, vibrating with life and pulsating with passion. This is dramatic instinct *par excellence.*"

Bothim-Edwards, M. [unsigned]. "Stephen Crane," *Sussex Express,* June 16, 1900.*

"Already months ago . . . it was easy to see that Stephen Crane's years, if not months, were numbered. In February last I met him at the house of a friend—bibliophile, ornithologist, and amateur artist—living at Hastings. Painful was the contrast between the young author of *The Red Badge of Courage*

* A press clipping in Berg Collection contains Cora's script: "An account of my literary tea . . . in Hastings. . . . This notice was written by Miss M. Bothim-Edwards."

and the other guests, all of whom were in good health and spirits. Poor Stephen Crane had that white, worn-out, restless look betokening complete nervous exhaustion. He took no tea, and did not join in general conversation, but moved about uneasily as if in search of something he could not find. Among the guests present was 'that sombre genius,' as 'Shirley' has called the author of 'Mark Rutherford.' But although the two men spent an hour in each other's company, they did not exchange so much as a syllable.

"Brede Place, near Battle, the novelist's last home, is a big straggling, weird old manor house, of which, doubtless, had he lived, he would have made good use. There he lived after the manner of 'a fine old English gentleman,' with plenty of servants, horses and carriage, dogs, and the rest, and exercising before his illness the lavish hospitality in which his countryfolks delight. Last Christmas no less than sixty guests were lodged in the old house, and no less than forty plum puddings were prepared for the Yuletide banquet. 'We like the place so much we never wish to leave it,' Mrs. Crane observed to an acquaintance. It will be interesting to see if Brede Place figures in the forthcoming, and now, alas! posthumous work of its latest tenant."

Cather, Willa ["Henry Nicklemann"]. "Children's Part in a Great Library," *Library* (Pittsburgh), July 7, 1900.

Quoted with commentary by Slote, "Stephen Crane and Willa Cather" (1969).

Cather, Willa. "When I Knew Stephen Crane," *Library* (Pittsburgh), 1 (June 23, 1900), 17–18. Under the pen name of "Henry Nicklemann."

Reprinted under Willa Cather's name in *Courier* (Lincoln), July 14, 1900. Reprinted in *Prairie Schooner*, 23 (Fall, 1949), 231–237, and in Bassan (1967).

"Chelifer" [Rupert Hughes]. "The Genius of Stephen Crane," *Criterion*, 22 (January 6, 1900), 24.

A wonderful appraisal of Crane's works. Hughes credits Crane with having written some of the best pages America has contributed to literature, but he thinks *War Is Kind* is a "crazy nightmare."

"The scene of the fire in the laboratory [in "The Monster"] is a most glorious study in high colors that ought to be quoted for its high beauty. The second story, 'The Blue Hotel,' is a wonderful thing in its way, full of action and most subtly motivated. A big genius, this young fellow Crane!"

Crane, Ellery Bicknell. *Genealogy of the Crane Family,* vol. 2. Worcester, Mass., 1900, pp. 467–519.

However, *see Crane*, Notes, p. 563. *Crane* draws mainly on the Newark Chart, which differs radically from the *Genealogy* in respect to the names of the four children who immediately preceded Stephen. The Newark Chart's author or source is not known. My copy was the gift of the Newark Public Library, Newark, N.J., two decades ago.

Crane, Mrs. George. "Stephen Crane's Boyhood," *New York World,* June 10, 1900, p. E 3.

Stephen's sister-in-law here adds some notes to our knowledge of the boyhood period and confirms that his fondness for things military induced his mother to send him to the Claverack Military College.

Emerson, Edwin, Jr. *Pepys' Ghost.* Boston, 1900, pp. 149–151.

Trivial note on Crane in Havana.

Findlater, Jane H. "The New Art of Description in Fiction," *National Review,*

January, 1900. Quoted in *Literary Digest*, 20 (February 10, 1900), 182.
On Crane's style.

Garland, Hamlin. "Stephen Crane: A Soldier of Fortune," *Saturday Evening Post*, 173 (July 28, 1900), 16–17. Portrait.

Reprinted in *Letters*, pp. 299–305.

In *Book Lover*, 2 (Autumn, 1900), 6–7. "Stephen Crane." Quotes a Crane letter to Garland.

Collate with Garland's variant account: Garland, "Stephen Crane As I Knew Him" (1914).

Another variant account is Garland, "Stephen Crane the Bohemian" (1930).

All these accounts are confusing, the one contradicting the other on the dates and the sequence of Crane's visits with the manuscripts of his poems and of his *The Red Badge of Courage*. Not listed in *W-S Bibliography* are the 1914 and 1930 accounts; hence they were unknown to Berryman in Berryman's *Crane*. See Pizer (1960). Pizer sets straight (from new Garland materials) Garland's tangled accounts. The record of these events follows Pizer's sequence in *Crane*.

Garnett, Edward [unsigned]. "Stephen Crane," *Academy*, 59 (June 9, 1900), 116, 123.

On Crane's *Whilomville Stories*.

———. "Stephen Crane," *Littell's Living Age*, 226 (August 4, 1900), 320–321.

Reprints Garnett's unsigned *Academy* article (June 9, 1900).

Gilder, Joseph B. "Stephen Crane," *Harper's Weekly*, 44 (June 16, 1900), 560. Portrait.

Reprinted in *Outlook*, 65 (July, 1900), 323.

On Crane's life and the history of his publications. Cordial and prompt as was his welcome by the critics of England, "his earliest recognition came from the press of his own country." His is "an extraordinary record of literary productivity. To what extent it is a record of growth is another question."

It cannot be said that greater power is disclosed in any of the eight books that followed *The Red Badge*. "The latest of these, *The Monster*, while it is strong in both matter and manner, is better than *The Red Badge* only by virtue of its greater reticence. The earlier book struck a note that sounded new in English literature. It expressed vividly the author's personality, and this did not find more vivid expression in his later work."

Harriman, Karl Edwin. "A Romantic Idealist—Mr. Stephen Crane," *Literary Review* (Boston), 4 (April, 1900), 85–87. With photographs of Brede Place and of nearby Bodiam Castle.

Describes in detail Crane's life at Brede Place during the writing of *The O'Ruddy*, "having gained the material on the bogs last autumn [in Ireland]." Crane ranks first his *Monster*, second *George's Mother*, and after these, in order of merit, a tiny tale entitled "An Old Man Goes Wooing," and *Maggie*. (However, Crane elsewhere ranked his *Black Riders* at the top; Harriman's list omits *The Red Badge*.) A sentimental tribute by a college admirer who visited with the Cranes at Brede. Harriman repeats the standard myths that Crane wrote *The Black Riders* in three days and *The Red Badge* in nine days "on pulpy copy paper." He also errs in saying that Crane is twenty-nine years of age.

See Critic, 37 (1900), 14–16. Comment on Crane by Harriman. Photos of Crane and Brede Manor.

Hawthorne, Julian. [On Crane], *Book News,* 18 (February, 1900), 337–338.

Hilliard, John Northern. "Stephen Crane: Letters to a Friend," *New York Times,* Supplement, July 14, 1900, p. 407.

One of these Crane letters first appeared in *Rochester Post-Express,* April 18, 1900, p. 4. Portions of these Crane letters are quoted, rather extensively, in the *Academy,* 59 (August 11, 1900), 116.

Reprinted in *Letters* (1960).

————. "Literary Notes," *Rochester Post-Express,* April 18, 1900, p. 4.

Quotes a Crane letter. Another Crane letter appears in same issue of *Post-Express.* The latter and a portion of the former letter were reprinted in *Literary Digest,* June 23, 1900. Hilliard published this second letter as one of the Crane letters he published in his "Stephen Crane: Letters to a Friend," *New York Times,* Supplement, July 14, 1900.

The Crane letter appearing under "Literary Notes" was misassigned to Joseph O'Connor in *Omnibus* (1952), pp. 688–690. It was written to Hilliard, from Brede Place. Excerpts from both letters reappeared in E. W. Chubb's *Stories of Authors* (1910). *W-S Bibliography* cites only Chubb for source of these letters.

Hitchcock, Ripley. Introduction, *The Red Badge of Courage.* New York, 1900. Reissued 1901, 1916, 1917.

Reviewed in *New York Times,* Supplement, July 14, 1900, p. 467. "Stephen Crane's Master Work." Quotes Hitchcock's account of the publication of *The Red Badge.*

Howells, H. D. "Literary Week," *Academy,* 59 (August 18, 1900), 123.

Quotes a portion of a letter of Howells to Mrs. Stephen Crane; the complete text is in *Letters,* pp. 306–307.

Hubbard, Elbert. "Heart to Heart Talks," *Philistine,* 11 (September, 1900), 123–128.

Compares Crane with Frederick Chopin. Claims that Crane "boycotted the tribe of Romeike," because he knew that the clippings of a clipping bureau "would be unkind, and his sensitive soul shrank from the pin-pricks." However, Crane in fact subscribed to a Boston clipping bureau and pasted the clippings in a scrapbook. He did not shrink from them, but rather he gloated over the reviews and found them rather amusing (according to Edith Crane in a letter to Thomas Beer). In R. W. S. file of Edith Crane letters, formerly in Alfred A. Knopf files.

Huneker, James. "The Raconteur," *Musical Courier,* 40 (June 13, 1900), 20–21.

Kauffman, Reginald W. "The True Story of Stephen Crane," *Modern Culture,* 12 (October, 1900), 143–145. Photograph.

Narrates "the real story of this author's introduction to the public," dismissing the gossip and myths about it. How *The Red Badge* got into the *Philadelphia Press:* "The men who first praised his book were not New York but Philadelphia journalists. Chancellorsville only suggested the battle-scene, and the publication of the story in book form occurred in this country five months before it occurred in London. It was its American success that first brought the work to the attention of the English critics." (Kauffman's article errs in several matters, including his misdating of the English edition of *The Red Badge,* published in London during the week of November 30, 1895, although the title-page is dated 1896. In America it was published on October 1, 1895.)

Marshall, Edward [unsigned]. "Stories of Stephen Crane," *Literary Life,* no. 24 (December, 1900), 71–72. Reprinted from *San Francisco Call.*

Recalls his hiring Crane to write sketches for the *New York Press.* His article "on tenement-house fire panics was one of the best things that he or any other man ever did." (Unknown to Marshall, that sketch was a journalistic hoax.) One day he brought Marshall a package of manuscript, which Marshall lost on an elevated train and which he recovered the next day "from the lost property office of the Manhattan L. The manuscript was that of *The Black Riders,* which had a tremendous vogue in England." At the Lantern Club Crane read parts of his *Red Badge of Courage.* Other important incidents briefly related here.

"In losing Crane America lost one of her most promising young writers. But his friends lost more. They lost a chap whom they all knew to be a real man as well as a talented acquaintance."

Wells, H. G. "Stephen Crane From an English Standpoint," *North American Review,* 171 (August, 1900), 233–242.

Reprinted in Wilson, *The Shock of Recognition* (1943), pp. 661–671.

Reprinted in *Letters* (1960), pp. 309–316.

Wells's appraisal struck Wilson as the only one worth reprinting, and it is the richest appreciation until Berryman's *Crane* (1950).

Westminster Gazette, June 5, 1900.

On Crane and Kipling.

DEATH OF STEPHEN CRANE: OBITUARIES AND TRIBUTES

NOTE: For many entries here I am indebted to Professor Jean Cazemajou of the University of Bordeaux, author of *Stephen Crane, 1871–1900, écrivain journaliste* (Paris, 1969). Not mentioned by Cazemajou is the scrapbook of newspaper clippings on the death of Crane at Dartmouth College Library. *See* Herbert Faulkner West, *A Stephen Crane Collection.* Hanover, N.H.: Dartmouth College Library, 1948, p. 23. The Cora Crane scrapbooks in CUCC and in BCC contain additional obituary press clippings, which, however, often lack full bibliographical data. Some additional obituaries, undated, are cited or quoted in *Crane,* pp. 560–561. *See also* West (1948).

Brooklyn Daily Eagle, June 5, 1900, p. 18. "Stephen Crane is Dead." Ink-drawing.

Errs in claiming that Crane died "aged 30 years." "As an author he had but one notable success, *The Red Badge of Courage.* He wrote in a slovenly manner, but the incidents which he created were always picturesque, and he paid most careful attention to their minutest detail."

Reprints Crane's letter to the editor of *Leslie's Weekly* (November, 1895), here unacknowledged. (Quoted in *Letters,* pp. 78–79.)

Brooklyn Daily Eagle, June 5, 1900, p. 3. "Warm Tributes to Crane."

Datelined: "London, June 5—The afternoon papers refer to the death at Badenweiler, Baden, today, of Stephen Crane, the American novelist, in terms of warm admiration.

"The *St. James Gazette* says: 'The loss of one of the most brilliant of present day writers will be as deeply felt by the English as by the American nation.' "

London Evening News, June 5, 1900, p. 13.

Daily Chronicle (London), June 6, 1900. "Death of Stephen Crane."

"Before he had reached even the 'fatal age' of thirty-five—fatal to so many men of genius—Stephen Crane passed away; leaving behind him a legacy of brilliant work accomplished, and the promise of more solid and enduring work in the future. He was only thirty, yet he looked more like a boy of eighteen, and, with his fragile physique and shy and sensitive disposition, he was the last man who might be expected to figure in the stress and storm of battle. Yet 'little Stevey'—as his friends and colleagues delighted to call him—was possessed of the highest and truest courage, the courage of the man of keen imagination, and he proved it on more than one stricken field. Those who have read with him 'in the open book of Death' can recall one memorable scene in the Cuban campaign—his first experience of real war. It was outside Guantánamo, and a company of American soldiers were surrounded by Spaniards. Crane was close to the fighting line—for he never shirked danger in the discharge of duty—and he saw that the soldiers had run out of water. The temperature was something like 108, and there was a high, steep hill to climb before water could be brought to the men. Yet Stephen Crane never hesitated. Collecting about a dozen big bottles he retired to the rear, filled them, and turned to climb the hill again—'his little person festooned with bottles,' as one who saw the incident described it afterwards.

"When he reached the fighting line he dropped exhausted and this gave rise to the report that he had been shot. Happily it was not true. The soldiers were too busy to cheer him at the moment, but they repaid him afterwards with the warmest admiration. That was only one of several occasions on which he showed his genuine pluck. Once during the same war he was in a dispatch boat rowing to the shore. The sailors in the boat began to quarrel and there was a lively prospect of blood being shed. But Crane intervened, and before the boat reached land the would-be belligerents had shaken hands and were vowing that the peacemaker was the 'best little fellow alive.' Like all tender-hearted men he was passionately fond of children and of animals, and his affection was reciprocated. During the Cuban campaign he had as a sort of personal attendant a quaint little 'nigger' boy—nicknamed 'The Bosun'—whom he rescued from some hard fate, and treated with good-humored indulgence."

Globe (London), June 6, 1900, p. 4.

New York Journal, "Stephen Crane's Death is the Untimely End of a Distinct Genius," June 6, 1900, p. 8. By Walter Howard.

New York Sun, June 6, 1900, p. 5. "Stephen Crane Dead."

By special cable to the *Sun* from Berlin, June 5. "Stephen Crane died of exhaustion at 3 o'clock this morning at Badenweiler in the Black Forest. His illness was said to be due to fever contracted in Cuba. . . .

"It has been noted as a curious manifestation of genius that Mr. Crane's imaginative story of a war that was over before he was born should excel his description of the scenes of actual conflict which he witnessed, but it is a fact that his accounts of the wars which he saw were less vigorous and less vivid pictures of strife than those in his work of fiction. He saw the advance of the Rough Riders and the Regulars who were supporting them from Daiquiri and the battle of Las Guásimas, but walking over the trail and the field the next day he was unable to describe the fighting except in a most perfunctory way. 'To tell you the truth there was too much going on,' he said, 'the details escaped me.' "

New York Times, June 6, 1900, p. 6.

New York Tribune, June 6, 1900, p. 9. "Stephen Crane." *Datelined:* "Baden-weiler, Baden, June 5—Stephen Crane died here today."

Cites that Crane "was mentioned in the official dispatches for gallantry under fire with the marines near Guantánamo."

New York World, "Stephen Crane is Dead in a Foreign Land," June 6, 1900, p. 7.

Springfield Daily Republican, June 6, 1900, p. 5. "Death of Stephen Crane." Ink-drawing.

Errs in claiming Crane "aged 29 years." "Stephen Crane, the American author and war correspondent, died at Badenweiler, Baden, at 3 o'clock yesterday morning, aged 29 years. . . . His health was seriously affected by hardships which he underwent while acting as correspondent during the Spanish war."

New York Tribune, June 7, 1900, p. 2.

Sussex Express, June 8, 1900. "Death of Mr. Stephen Crane."

"Although enjoying a world-wide reputation, the death of Mr. Stephen Crane is of peculiar local interest. The deceased gentlemen, for some time, was the occupant of Brede Place, and took a lively interest in the affairs of the village. A few weeks ago, however, his state of health became so precarious as to necessitate his immediate removal to the continent, but he expired on the 4th instant at Badenweiler, in the Black Forest. Mr. Crane, was only thirty years of age,* was a native of Newark, New Jersey, and received his education at Syracuse University. He first charmed the world with *The Red Badge of Courage,* a work of the purest and most vivid imagination; and, then, as a War Correspondent, particularly in the Greco-Turkish War, showed that his grasp of fact was as vivid as his imagination was true. The greatest sympathy is expressed with Mrs. Crane in her very sad bereavement."

Academy, 58 (June 9, 1900), 491. "Stephen Crane," by Edward Garnett [unsigned].

"As we write, his last journey is beginning. He is being taken to his home in America."

Crane's sketch "A Detail" is quoted here.

"He was the type of the nervous, nimble-minded American, slight in figure, shy and kind in manner, speaking little, with a great power of work, a fine memory, and an imagination of astonishing psychological insight. Latterly

---

* He died at 28.

his health had been bad, partly constitutional, and partly through malarial fever contracted in the Cuban campaign."

In *George's Mother,* as in most of his other stories, "The environment grows round the characters. He takes them at some period of emotional or physical stress and, working from within outwards, with quick, firm touches, vivifies them into life. . . . His longer novels, though not wanting in passages that show him at his best, suggest that in time he would have returned to the earlier instinct that prompted him to work on a small canvas. As a writer he was very modern."

Black and White (London), 19 (June 9, 1900), 3.
Photograph.*

Globe (London), June 9, 1900, p. 6.

Graphic (London), 61 (June 9, 1900), 830.

Illustrated London News, June 9, 1900, p. 767. "Personal." Photograph (Crane with the Stevenson moustache).
Errs in saying that Crane died at thirty and that he was born in 1870. Rightly states, however, that Crane never recovered from the malaria he contracted in Cuba. Cora always called it "the yellow fever."

Outlook (London), (June 9, 1900), 604.
An., 1 p. written in Sidney Pawling's hand (the *Outlook*'s commentary on Crane's death). CUCC.

Spectator (London), 84 (June 9, 1900), 795.

Brooklyn Daily Eagle, June 10, 1900, p. 18.

New York Herald, June 10, 1900, p. 8, section 6. "Loss of Stephen Crane—a Real Misfortune For All of Us," by Edward Marshall.

New York Sun, June 10, 1900. "Stephen Crane, Jerseyman."
Crane's family background. Traces Crane's ancestry, particularly Jasper Crane of the company of men who founded Newark in 1666, and reprints Stephen Crane's letter of April 29, 1896, to the editor of the *Newark Sunday Call,* May 3, 1896. Corrects errors in Crane's letter. His letter was reprinted (in shortened form) in *Omnibus,* p. 651, and in *Letters,* p. 124. The *Sun* article was reprinted in the *Newark Sunday Call,* June 17, 1923.

New York Tribune, June 10, 1900, p. 2. "Tributes to Crane."
Quotes the *London Spectator:* "Crane was a writer of singular force and originality, whose studies in the psychology of peril had the quality of clairvoyance nothing short of magical." *See also Tribune,* Illustrated Supplement, p. 10.

New York World, June 10, 1900, p. E 3. "Madcap Genius: Stephen Crane."

Independent, 52 (June 14, 1900), 1453.

Public Opinion, 23 (June 14, 1900), 757. "Death of Stephen Crane."

Springfield Daily Republican, June 15, 1900, p. 5. "The Standing of Stephen Crane."

Harper's Weekly, 44 (June 16, 1900), 560, by Joseph Gilder.

* In this photograph—by Elliott and Fry—Crane wears the Robert Louis Stevenson moustache by which he best became known in subsequent years. Reproduced in *Crane* and on jacket of *Omnibus.*

New York Tribune, June 16, 1900, p. 8.

"Now that Stephen Crane is dead a good deal is being said about his character as a man. His best attribute seems to have been physical courage, which was conspicuously displayed in Cuba during the Spanish-American War. It is said to have been accompanied by qualities not altogether admirable. In spite of his success and in spite of the five years of hard working following it, Mr. Crane died poor. None of his books had apparently one of those sales that nowadays bring fortunes to their authors. Such success as was obtained by *The Red Badge of Courage* was important to Mr. Crane as given value to his future work, yet that novel that he next published, *George's Mother,* proved to be a great failure, in this country at any rate. He had some college training, but it left little impression on him. At the time when he wrote *The Red Badge of Courage* he was a curiously unformed and ignorant boy. He had not only read little, but he deliberately avoided reading for fear of being influenced by other writers. His friends in New York consisted chiefly of young artists, who, as a class, are not noted for their literary attainments. That they probably influenced him, however, was shown by his extreme fondness for impressionism and for the fantastic in art, then exemplified by Aubrey Beardsley.

"The first friend he made among writers was Mr. Hamlin Garland. He had sent to Mr. Garlin [*sic*] a copy of *Maggie,* cheaply printed between paper covers by a publisher of religious books, who at the last moment was afraid to put the firm's imprint on the volume. Mr. Garlin [*sic*] wrote an enthusiastic review of the story in 'The Arena' and introduced Mr. Crane to Mr. W. D. Howells. On one occasion Mr. Howells read aloud to young Crane some of Emily Dickinson's poems. He was greatly stirred by them. Three days later he had completed about thirty of the poems, or 'Lines,' as he called them, which were later to form the volume known as 'The Black Riders.' It was through those verses that he secured his first publisher. A friend called attention to them of M. Fred Holland Day, of the Boston firm of Copeland & Day, now dissolved, and shortly afterwards they were accepted. It is odd that the source of their inspiration should have escaped the notice of the critics. These lines were in no sense imitative; but the fact remains that Emily Dickinson's queer temperament, expressing itself in the symbolism that Mr. Crane loved, had caused them to be written."

Newark Sunday Call, June 17, 1900.

Quotes a Crane letter.

New York Herald, June 21, 1900, p. 10. Barr, Robert [Letter].

See also Birss, "Stephen Crane:" (1933), Bohnenberger (1933), and Stolper (1933).

Literary Digest, 20 (June 23, 1900), 750. "Stephen Crane: A Wonderful Boy." Portrait.

Prints portions of Crane's letters to Hilliard. Collate with letters in *Rochester Post Express,* April 18, 1900, p. 4; in *New York Times Literary Supplement,* July 14, 1900, p. 407 (*see* Hilliard above); and in *Academy* (London), 59 (August 11, 1900), 116. *See Letters* (1960).

The same title—"Stephen Crane: A Wonderful Boy"—is used by Vincent Starrett in his essay on Crane in *Buried Caesars* (1923).

New York Journal, June 28, 1900, p. 5. "Crane's Body Here to Rest With Kin."

Press clipping dated June 28, 1900, unidentified source, titled "Stephen Crane Laid at Rest." CUCC.

New York Times, June 28, 1900, p. 15.

New York Tribune, June 28, 1900. "Funeral of Stephen Crane," by Wallace Stevens [unsigned].

On his first assignment as *Tribune* reporter Stevens attended Crane's funeral service at Central Metropolitan Temple and wrote in his journal for June 28, 1900: "The whole thing was frightful." In *Wallace Stevens: Letters* (1966), p. 42. Not noticed by editor of *Letters* (Holly Stevens) is that Stevens wrote the *Tribune* obituary.

The tone of this *Tribune* review is that of an upstart and arrogant reporter belittling Crane's achievements. In his new assignment of reporting the funeral, the *Tribune* reporter failed to attend the burial grounds and, presumably, that is why he erroneously reported that Crane is buried in Elizabeth, N.J.

However, Crane is buried at Hillside, N.J. This error persists from 1900 to 1960 in Berryman's *Crane,* 1950, and in *Cora Crane,* 1960. For the facts see [Anon.] (1936).

New York Tribune, June 28, 1900, p. 8. "Stephen Crane's Body Here."

New York Times, June 29, 1900, p. 14.

New York Tribune, June 29, 1900, p. 8. "Funeral of Stephen Crane."

"The funeral of Stephen Crane, the author, who died in Badenweiler, Germany, on June 5, and whose body arrived in this city on Wednesday by the steamship Bremen, took place yesterday morning in the Metropolitan Temple—at Seventh-ave. and Fourteenth-st. There was a large attendence.

"The Reverend Dr. James M. Buckley, Editor of 'The Christian Advocate' and lifelong friend of the Crane family, was in charge of the services. He was assisted by the Rev. S. Parkes Cadman, of the Temple, and by Dr. F. J. Beicher.

"Dr. Buckley delivered a eulogy, in which he spoke of the life and work of Mr. Crane and of the inheritance of many of the traits of character of his father. He said that Stephen Crane's career might well be said to have been like that of a meteor which gleams brilliantly in the sky for a time and then sinks to rest.

"The body was taken to Evergreen Cemetery, in Elizabeth, N.J. The pallbearers were Colonel William C. Church, Ripley Hitchcock, J. D. Champlin, John Kendrick Bangs, Arthur B. Hawkins and J. Hamblin Sears."

Bookman, 11 (July, 1900), 405–406.

"The success won by *The Red Badge of Courage* was almost as great in England as it was in this country.* The book was commonly accepted as having been written by one who had lived through the War of Secession, and the discovery that its author had been born five years after the termination of that struggle provoked universal surprise. Just what place this book holds in American literature the future alone can say. It is undoubtedly a remarkable bit of imagination and of word-painting, and it is also certainly marred by its evident immaturity and its frequent lapses into bad taste."

Book News, 18 (July, 1900), 677.

"Stephen Crane, author and war correspondent, died in Badenweiler, Baden,

---

* However, the *Bookman* (February, 1896), said just the opposite, namely that Crane had not received due recognition in his own country. In April, 1900, the *Bookman* rated Frank Norris over Crane.

June 5th. He was born at Newark, N.J., November 1, 1871, and was the son
of the Rev. D. J. T. Crane, a Methodist clergyman. He attended Lafayette
College for a time, and during 1890–91 studied literature at Syracuse University. At sixteen years of age he began doing newspaper work, and at eighteen
wrote fiction. Some of his early newspaper work appeared in *The Tribune.*
When he dropped out of college he resumed newspaper work and wrote extensively for the *Bacheller Syndicate.* In 1897 he was correspondent for the
Westminster Gazette and the *New York Journal,* in the Turko-Grecian War.
In the same year he went on a filibustering expedition to Cuba. On this occasion the steamer was wrecked and he was one of three men who escaped in an
open boat, in which they spent several days. In 1898 he went to Cuba and
Puerto Rico for *The New York World,* and was mentioned in the official dispatches for gallantry under fire with the marines near Guantánamo.

"During recent years Mr. Crane devoted himself chiefly to story writing,
and for some time lived in England. His earliest book, *Maggie: A Girl of the
Streets,* was first published at his own expense. His first successful story was
The Red Badge of Courage. Among his other books were *George's Mother,
The Little Regiment,* 'The Open Boat,' 'The Third Violet,' 'Active Service,'
'The Eternal Patience' [*George's Mother*], and 'Pictures of War.' "

Critic, 37 (July, 1900), 14–16. Comments on Crane by Karl Edwin Harriman.

Review of Reviews, 22 (July, 1900), 93–94. "The Late Stephen Crane." Photograph.

Sussex Daily News, July 13, 1900.

Saturday Evening Post, 173 (July 28, 1900), 19. "Ghosts of Brede Place."

Current Literature, 29 (August, 1900), 149–150.

Living Age, 226 (August 4, 1900), 320–321. "Stephen Crane."
    Recasts (unacknowledged) the London *Academy* obituary (probably by
Edward Garnett) for June 9, 1900.

Academy, 59 (June 9, 1900), 116. "Stephen Crane," by Edward Garnett [un-
signed].

Springfield Republican, August 25, 1900, p. 10.

Literary Digest, 21 (December 1, 1900), 647. "The Last of Stephen Crane."

1901

Adams, O. F. *Dictionary of American Authors.* Boston, 1901, p. 79.

[Anon.] [Crane and Cora]. *Critic,* n.s., 35 (March, 1901), 198–199. Portraits.
    On Cora as co-author of Crane's last writings.

———. "Authors' Associations," *Manuscript,* 1 (May, 1901), 32–34.
    Reminiscences of W. D. Howells and Irving Bacheller on the "Lanthorne
Club." Crane mentioned.

Barry, John D. "A Note on Stephen Crane," *Bookman,* 13 (April, 1901),
    148.

Reports that the *New York Evening Post* in an editorial on "The Decay of Decadence" recently grouped poet Stephen Crane with the Symbolists of France and England. Believes that Crane had never heard of the Symbolists; "it is pretty certain that he had never read them. He was then about twenty-one years of age, and he was woefully ignorant of books. Indeed, he deliberately avoided reading from a fear of being influenced by other writers." Shortly after W. D. Howells read him Emily Dickinson's verses, Crane showed Barry thirty poems in manuscript, "written, as he explained, in three days. These furnished the bulk of the volume entitled *The Black Riders.*"

Contra Barry, however, there is evidence of Crane's wide reading in his "List of Books / Brede Place." *See Crane,* pp. 554–555. Barry says Crane associated with "a group of young American painters, who had brought from France the impressionistic influences, which with him took literary form." *See* McBride (1950), Kwiat (1952), *Omnibus,* and *Crane.*

Daskam, Josephine D. "The Distinction of Our Poetry," *Atlantic,* 87 (May, 1901), 696–705.

Howells, William Dean. [Appreciation of Stephen Crane], *Delta Upsilon Quarterly* (March 1, 1901).

Morris, Harrison S. Introduction, *Great Battles of the World.* Philadelphia and London, 1901.

Vosburgh, R. G. "The Darkest Hour in the Life of Stephen Crane," *Criterion,* n.s., 1 (February, 1901), 26–27. Also in *Book Lover,* 2 (Summer, 1901), 338–339.

The "darkest hour" followed his publishing of *Maggie* at his own expense, sinking into its printing the money he had inherited from his mother's estate. Crane at that time was sharing Vosburgh's studio in the Art Students' League Building and writing *The Red Badge of Courage.* He always wrote at night, "generally beginning after twelve o'clock and working until four or five o'clock in the morning, then going to bed and sleeping the greater part of the day." Crane often declared he would be famous, and sometimes he would doodle his name on loose sheets of paper.

Wolfe, T. F. *Literary Rambles at Home and Abroad.* Philadelphia, 1901, p. 46. Describes Crane's birthplace.

1902

Davis, Richard Harding. "A Derelict," in *Ransom's Folly.* New York, 1902.
A reviewer of "A Derelict," published in 1901, detected a resemblance between the reporter Channing and Stephen Crane. *See Crane,* pp. 293, 596. *See also* Osborn (1956).

Howells, William Dean. *Literature and Life.* New York, 1902, p. 178.

———. "Frank Norris," *North American Review,* 175 (December, 1902), 770–771.
On Crane's vibrant achievement. His physical slightness "reflected the

delicacy of energies that could be put forth only in nervous spurts in impulses vivid and keen, but wanting in breadth and bulk of effect. Curiously enough, on the other hand, this very lyrical spirit, whose freedom was its life, was the absolute slave of reality. It was interesting to hear him defend what he had written, in obedience to his experience of things, against any change in the interest of convention. 'No,' he would contend, in behalf of the profanities of his people, 'that is the way they *talk*. I have thought of that, and whether I ought to leave such things out, but if I do I am not giving the thing as I *know* it.' He felt the constraint of those semi-savage natures, such as he depicted in *Maggie* and *George's Mother,* and was forced through the fealty of his own nature to report them as they spoke no less than as they looked. When it came to *The Red Badge of Courage,* where he took leave of these simple aesthetics, and lost himself in a whirl of wild guesses at the fact from the ground of insufficient witness, he made the failure which formed the break between his first and his second manner, though it was what the public counted a success, with every reason to do so from the report of the sales. . . .

"The true Stephen Crane was the Stephen Crane of the earlier books, the earliest book; for *Maggie* remains the best thing he did. All he did was lyrical, but this was the aspect and accent as well as the spirit of the tragically squalid life he sang, while *The Red Badge of Courage,* and the other things that followed it, were the throes of an art failing with material to which it could not render an absolute devotion from an absolute knowledge. He sang, but his voice erred up and down the scale, with occasional flashes of brilliant melody, which could not redeem the errors. New York was essentially his inspiration, the New York of suffering and baffled and beaten life, of inarticulate or blasphemous life; and away from it he was not at home, with any theme, or any sort of character. It was the pity of his fate that he must quit New York, first as a theme, and then as a habitat; for he rested nowhere else, and wrought with nothing else as with the lurid depths which he gave proof of knowing better than any one else. Everyone is limited, and perhaps no one is more limited than another; only, the direction of the limitation is different in each. Perhaps George Douglas, if he had lived, would still have done nothing greater than *The House with the Green Shutters,* and might have failed in the proportion of a larger range as Stephen Crane did. I am not going to say that either of these extraordinary talents was of narrower bound than Frank Norris; such measures are not of the map. But I am still less going to say that they were of finer quality because their achievement seems more poignant, through the sort of physical concentration which it has. Just as a whole unhappy world agonizes in the little space their stories circumscribe, so what is sharpest and subtlest in that anguish finds its like in the epical breadths of Norris's fiction."

Joline, Adrian F. *Meditations of an Autograph Collector.* New York, 1902, p. 14.
     Reproduces a Crane letter in reply to a request for his autograph: "HART-FORD, N.Y., February 6th DEAR SIR,—I don't thing it possible to get my photograph. They have been mostly ameteur things. Very truly yours, Stephen Crane."
     Joseph Katz reprints this letter in *SCraneN* (1967) although it appeared in *Letters,* p. 113, exactly as given above. The edited version in *Letters* corrects the punctuation of "dont" and the spelling of "ameteur" so as to spare the text "*sic*" and other editorial correction notes. Katz's reason

for reissuing this letter is his claim of "errors in transcription," whereas they are not errors but deliberate editorial corrections. *Letters,* heading it "TO AN ADMIRER OF HIS WORK," prints the text thus: "Hartford [*sic*], N.Y., February 6th [1896] Dear sir: I don't thing [*sic*] it possible to get my photograph. They have been mostly amateur things. Very truly yours, *Stephen Crane.*"

Katz does not refer in *SCraneN* to Vincent Starrett's having cited this letter in *Colophon* (July, 1931).

1903

Hubbard, Elbert. [Crane and Howells], *Philistine,* 17 (August, 1903), 88–89.

Linson, Corwin Knapp. "Little Stories of 'Steve' Crane," *Saturday Evening Post,* 177 (April 11, 1903), 19–20.

Linson's memoir is the most important biographical document published since the Peaslee and Gaines articles of 1896 summing up the double strands in Crane's heritage. On Crane's writing "The Reluctant Voyagers" in 1893 (a dating which has importance for dating of *George's Mother*); his writing *The Red Badge of Courage* in 1893; and his writing "Men in the Storm" in 1894. Linson says he first met Crane in the winter of 1892–1893, whereas in *MSC* Linson says they first met shortly after *Maggie* was published. Contains passages not in *MSC*, which was edited by Edwin Cady without mention of this 1903 memoir. However, *W-S* does not list this Linson article.

Perry, Bliss. *Study of Prose Fiction.* Boston, 1903, p. 315.

1904

Anderson, Harold MacDonald. "The War Correspondent," *Bookman,* 19 (March, 1904), 39. Photograph of Crane (at his desk at Ravensbrook).

"The late Stephen Crane, at the time of the war between Greece and Turkey, had not yet made himself a journalist in the full sense in which the term is understood among practical newspaper men. As a war correspondent he lacked the faculty of organisation. So the paper employing him sent with him a manager. All that Crane had to do was to write the story of a battle as he saw it. The manager looked after all the details, found the horses, secured rations and fodder and places in which to sleep, and finally hurried Crane's written copy to the wire and cabled it to the United States."

[Anon.]. "Redeeming the *Red Badge of Courage,*" *Bookman,* 35 (May, 1904), 235–236.

Davis, Richard. "How Stephen Crane Took Juana Dias," in *In Many Wars by Many War Correspondents,* ed. George Lynch and Frederick Palmer. Tokyo, 1904, pp. 43–45.

John T. Winterich (1933) makes bibliographical comment on *In Many Wars.*

Reprinted in *War Dispatches,* pp. 196–199.

Higginson, Thomas Wentworth. [Comments on Crane], *Philistine,* 19 (November, 1904), 172; 20 (April, 1905), 142.

In the latter *Philistine* he links Crane with Keats, Chatterton, and Chopin, as one of those geniuses "who do their big stunts and die before they are encored into unseemliness."

1905

Bragdon, Claude Fayette. *Merely Players.* New York, 1905.

Reprinted 1929, 1965.

On Crane at the Society of the Philistines' banquet, December 19, 1895. *See also* Bragdon, "The Purple Cow Period" (1929).

Hubbard, Elbert. [Crane, Keats, Chopin, and Chatterton], *Philistine,* 20 (April, 1905), 141–142.

1907

Poole's Index to Periodical Literature. Supplements, 1882–1906. Vol 4, p. 138; vol. 5, p. 141.

1909

Hubbard, Elbert. "The Open Road—Afoot with the Fra," *Fra,* 3, no. 2 (May, 1909), 29–30.

Stanton, Theodore, ed. *A Manual of American Literature.* New York and London, 1909, pp. 230–231, 444.

1910

Chubb, Edwin Watts. "Stephen Crane: A Wonderful Boy," in *Stories of Authors.* New York, 1910, pp. 361–363.

Contains excerpts from two Crane letters written to the literary editor of the *Rochester Post Express* (John Northern Hilliard).

Davis, Richard Harding. *Notes of a War Correspondent.* New York, 1910, pp. 125, 127, 128.

On Crane at San Juan hills.

Hines, Earl Remington. "Stevie Crane," *Fra*, 6, no. 3 (December, 1910), 77.
Poem for Crane.

Hubbard, Elbert. Editorial note, *Fra*, 6 (July, 1910), xxv.
"A few weeks before his passing, Stevie Crane sent me this manuscript. I thought it tipped a bit too much to t' other side, when I first read it. But I got it out the other day and read it again. I liked it better. The *Fra* readers shall judge."
The Crane poem—"What? / You define me God with these trinkets?"—is signed Stephen Crane and carries this inscription: "Oh, Hubbard, mark this well. Mark it well! If it is over-balancing your discretion, inform me. S. C."
Hubbard published the poem without acknowledging that it had appeared in *War Is Kind* (1899). It is no. 4, which begins "A little ink more or less."
Except for the first stanza, the poem with Crane's inscribed note to Hubbard exists in holograph manuscript at Syracuse University Library. It was published in *Letters*, pp. 297–298. However, *Letters* did not identify its published source in the *Fra*. Daniel Hoffman in *Poetry* quotes the poem from the Syracuse MS., but he concludes, p. 79, that Hubbard never published the poem.*

1911

Hueffer, Ford Madox. *Memories and Impressions*. London, 1911, pp. 58–59.
"I remember once hearing Stephen Crane, the author of *The Red Badge of Courage* and of *The Open Boat*, which is the finest volume of true short stories in the English language—I remember hearing him, with his wonderful eyes flashing and his extreme vigor and intonation, comment upon a sentence of Robert Louis Stevenson that he was reading. The sentence was: 'With interjected finger he delayed the motion of the timepiece.' 'By God, poor dear!' Crane exclaimed.† 'That man put back the clock of English fiction fifty years.' "

Vielé-Griffin, Francis, and Henry D. Davray, trans. *La conquête du courage*. Paris: Mercure de France, 1911.
Reissued in 1939, Paris, Les libertés françaises; in 1945, Brussells, Éditions N.R.B.; in 1960, Paris, Le club français du livre; and published in Livre de poche, Paris, 1967. Other translations include: Russian, *Alyi znak doblesti*, with an introduction by Evgeni Lann and preface by Joseph Conrad, Moscow and Leningrad: ZIF, 1930; Italian, *Rosso è l'emblema del coraggio*, Milan and Rome: Jandi Sapi, 1947; German, *Das Blutmal*, Mannheim: Kessler, 1954; Spanish, *La insignia roja del valor*, Barcelona: Ediciones G.P., 1959.

* For copy from the *Fra* I thank John Baker of Minneapolis (letter to R. W. S., September 17, 1969), and also for another copy sent me by Austin M. Fox (April 7, 1968). Professor Fox also sent me a list of Crane publications in the *Fra*.

† However, it was not Crane who said this. It was Harold Frederic. *See Crane*.

Also *Un joven héroe*, Barcelona: Editorial Mateu-Barcelona, 1958. Drawn from Jean Cazemajou's study, *The Red Badge of Courage* (1969).

1912

[Anon.]. "Redeeming *The Red Badge*," *Bookman*, 35 (May, 1912), 235–236.

A story of Crane's *Red Badge*, "which we believe has never before been printed, and which, in its way, is quite worthy of incorporation in a chapter of Henri Murger's *Scènes de la Vie de Bohême*. . . . There was one time in its history when a certain number of chapters had been ransomed from the typewriter agency and submitted to a publisher. To Stephen Crane's delight, they were received with enthusiasm and the book practically accepted, on condition that the remaining chapters were up to the same standard. Crane was absolutely confident that he had not fallen below the level he had set himself in the first part. But there was one serious complication. The balance of the book was practically in pawn at the typewriter's for fifteen dollars. In despair he wrote to a friend:

> Dear Dicon: Beg, borrow or steal fifteen dollars.
> _____ like the *Red Badge* and want to make a contract for it. It's in pawn at the typewriter's for fifteen. Thine, Steve

Unfortunately, the friend was equally hard up for money. Fortunately, he was accustomed to do hack work upon occasion for a successful journalist who happened to be in his debt for thirteen dollars. Rushing round to collect this magnificent fund, he [Dicon, who was John Henry Dick] suggested that it would be a great accommodation if the cheque could be made out for fifteen dollars. He would 'work out' the extra two dollars. The journalist complied with the request, and the cheque was endorsed and despatched to the waiting Crane. But it happened that Crane had already applied to the journalist and the latter had refused the loan. When the cheque came back with Crane's endorsement, there were recriminations. Nothing would make the journalist believe that the hack-worker was innocent of conspiring against him. . . . The journalist refused to be placated and the 'literary underwriter' received no more commissions, after having pawned his only pair of sleeve-links to make good that part of the fifteen dollars that was not his."*

Conrad, Joseph. *A Personal Record*. London, 1912, pp. 103–104.

Sees Crane as "a man almost childlike in the impulsive movements of his untutored genius, the most singleminded of verbal impressionists, using his great gifts of straight feeling and right expression with a fine sincerity and a strong, if, perhaps, not fully conscious conviction. His art did not obtain, I fear, all the credit its unsophisticated inspiration deserved. . . . It was an individual and complete talent, which obtained but a grudging, somewhat

---

*Crane did not repay John Henry Dick ("Dicon"), and his guilt so troubled his conscience that in "A Mystery of Heroism" he depicts Collins as doubting his heroism ("He was then a hero") because heroes do not default on their debts: "He was not a hero. Heroes had no shame in their lives, and, as for him, he remembered borrowing fifteen dollars from a friend and promising to pay it back the next day, and then avoiding that friend for ten months." In *Stephen Crane: Stories and Tales*, ed. R. W. Stallman (1955), p. 182. *See also* Crane.

supercilious recognition from the world at large. For himself one hesitates to regret his early death. Like one of the men in his 'Open Boat,' one felt that he was one of those whom fate seldom allows to make a safe landing after much toil and bitterness at the oar.

"I confess to an abiding affection for that energetic, slight, fragile, intensely living and transient figure. He liked me even before we met on the strength of a page or two of my writing, and after we had met I am glad to think he liked me still."*

1913

Grabo, Carl H. *The Art of the Short Story.* New York, 1913, pp. 161–163.

Macy, John. *The Spirit of American Literature.* New York, 1913, p. 16.

Mencken, H. L. *Smart Set,* 40 (July 1913), 159.
    Praises "The Blue Hotel" for its "sense of brooding disaster, of cruel and immutable fate, of the general meaninglessness of life—in five words, tragedy in the Greek sense."

1914

[Anon.]. "How Stephen Crane 'Drew Off' His Poems," *Current Opinion,* 56 (June, 1914), 460.
    Garland's story here retold from his *Yale Review* account (1914).

———. "Topics of the Week," *New York Times Book Review,* April 5, 1914, p. 166.
    "Mr. Hamlin Garland's appreciation of Stephen Crane, in the April number of *The Yale Review,* indicates that he retains to this day his earliest impressions of the genius of that erratic and lazy writer, whom he put in the way of making an honest living and who showed his gratitude by dedicating to Mr. Garland a volume of verse of very dubious quality. It is a singularly sweet-tempered article, full of expressions of admiration for Crane. There is no gainsaying the remarkable gifts of that short-lived writer. His *Red Badge of Courage,* which was by far his most notable achievement, however, was never a popular book, and when it was published here by Appletons, in the consulship of Ripley Hitchcock, it fell flat although more than one reviewer praised it highly. When Crane went to England,

---

* What Crane had read was Conrad's *The Nigger of the "Narcissus,"* appearing in *New Review* (August, 1897). Conrad had read *The Red Badge of Courage,* which had been published in London by William Heinemann in the week of November 30, 1896. Conrad in writing *The Nigger* (finished by February 19, 1897) was influenced by *The Red Badge of Courage,* although Conrad denied any such influence. He and Crane met in London in October, 1897—not in June when Crane first settled in England, as Conrad elsewhere states it. "I saw Stephen Crane a few days after his arrival in London," says Conrad: Conrad, "Stephen Crane: A Note Without Dates" (1921). Also in *London Mercury,* 1 (December, 1919), 192–193.

Harold Frederic discovered him anew and managed to give new life to the book. But even that did not last." *See* however, Howells (1915).

"Mr. Garland thinks more highly of Crane's 'queer little poems' than the rest of us. Crane died young, but he seems to have finished all the work he had to do before he passed away. Perhaps there will be a revival of interest in his remarkably descriptive prose if not in his verse. Mr. Garland's article might inspire a re-examination of *The Red Badge of Courage*."

Cf. Joseph Conrad to Peter Somerville in 1912: "Believe me my dear Sir no paper, no review, would look at anything that I or anybody else could write about Crane. They would laugh at the suggestion. Crane? Who cares for Crane?" (*Letters*, p. 321.)

Bullard, F. Lauriston. *Famous War Correspondents*. Boston, 1914, pp. 417–419, 423.

Garland, Hamlin. "Stephen Crane as I Knew Him," *Yale Review*, n.s., 3 (April, 1914), 494–506.

Reprinted in the *Syracusan* (December 1, 1917). Photograph.

Garland here reports Crane's bringing him the manuscript of *The Red Badge of Courage* and *then* the manuscript of his poems. The sequence was just the reverse according to Garland's *Roadside Meetings* (1930). That version being John Berryman's sole source, his *Stephen Crane* (1950) is correct about the sequence of Crane's visits to Garland; namely first with the poems and *then* with *The Red Badge* manuscript. By collating Garland's divergent and contradictory accounts in *Yale Review* (1914), in *Saturday Evening Post* (1900), in *Bookman* (1930), and in *Roadside Meetings* (1930), Stallman in *Omnibus* concluded incorrectly the sequence of these events. Garland's tangled accounts are set into proper sequence (from new Garland materials) by Donald Pizer in "The Garland-Crane Relationship," *Huntington Library Quarterly* (November, 1960). Garland's vignette of Crane's 1892 visit when he announced that he had been fired by the *New York Tribune* here expands upon Garland's *Saturday Evening Post* version of 1900. Garland's account here squares with Oliver's (1931). At odds with Crane's claim and Garland's report is Johnson's memoir (1926). On the question of whether or not Crane was fired by the *Tribune* because of his sketch of a parade of the American Mechanics in Asbury Park *see also* Honce (1942), Elconin (1948), Schoberlin (1949), and *Crane*. Garland's *Yale Review* essay silently contradicts the facts given in his first version in *Saturday Evening Post* for July 28, 1900: "Stephen Crane: A Soldier of Fortune." For another variant account *see* Garland, "Crane, the Bohemian" (1930).

The *Yale Review* memoir is commented on by *New York Times Book Review*, April 5, 1914, p. 166.

Garnett, Edward. "Some Remarks on English and American Fiction," *Atlantic Monthly*, 114 (December, 1914), 747–756.

Laments the grudging, inadequate recognition of the most original genius America has produced in story-telling, Stephen Crane. (Howells replies in *Harper's Magazine* [April, 1915].)

1915

Howells, William Dean. "Editor's Easy Chair," *Harper's Magazine* 130 (April, 1915), 797.

Replies to Edward Garnett (1914). Contends that Crane's talent "was valued by our criticism long before he was known in England; his *Red Badge of Courage* was almost the best-seller of its day, possibly because it was his worst book."

——. "Editor's Easy Chair," *Harper's Magazine*, 131 (September, 1915), 634.

"We have not forgotten the *Black Riders* of Stephen Crane, very powerful things in the beat of their short lines, rhymeless, meterless. Yet were they quite shredded prose, like Miss Amy Lowell's *vers libre*, in her *Sword Blades and Poppy Seeds,* or the epitaphs of Mr. Edgar Lee Masters's *Spoon River Anthology?* Not quite, however, for though the *Black Riders* did not prance or curvet, they did somehow march; they did keep time as prose never does at its best." (Here Howells contradicts his standpoint in *Harper's Weekly* review of *The Black Riders* [January 25, 1896].)

Pattee, F. L. *History of American Literature Since 1870.* New York, 1915, pp. 397–398, 412.

Sandburg, Carl. [Letter of March 20, 1915, to Harriet Monroe], *Letters of Carl Sandburg,* ed. Herbert Mitgang. New York, 1968, p. 102.

". . . the quickest way to convince them [editors] that free verse is worth-while is to show them that Stevie Crane and other crack newspapermen did some terribly serious work in libertarian rhythms."

Wells, H. G. *Boon.* London, 1915.

" 'America,' said Boon, 'can produce such a supreme writer as Stephen Crane—the best writer of English for the last half-century. . . . But America won't own such children. . . . She'll sit never knowing she's had a Stephen Crane.' "

Wyatt, Edith. "Stephen Crane," *New Republic,* 4 (September 11, 1915), 148–150.*

Reprinted Wyatt, *Great Companions* (1917), pp. 31–40.

Reassesses Crane's achievement—in *Maggie* and in "The Monster." In his faculty of penetrating social criticism Crane "excels and interests. We have no more spirited portrait of the mob-meanness of our democracy—the peculiarly American disgrace that shames us among nations—than his short story, 'The Monster,' a chronicle of the cruelty of the people of an eastern town [Port Jervis, N.Y.] to a Negro maimed in recovering from a fire the child of the town's best doctor."

Crane's *Black Riders* and *War Is Kind* "have just now a timely interest from their achievement in a certain art of poetic expression regarded by numbers of persons—though certainly not, one believes, by the Imagists themselves—as only recently attempted. As both Stephen Crane and most of the Imagists are American poets it is curious to compare their likeness and

* Not the same essay titled "Stephen Crane as the American Pioneer of the Free Verse Army," *Current Opinion* (March, 1917), which is erroneously assigned to Wyatt in *New Republic* (1915) by *W-S Bibliography,* p. 161. This error is repeated in numerous references, including the Crane bibliography by Hudspeth in *Thoth: Hudspeth* (1963).

divergence on this special point—'direct treatment of subject'—which is, according to Mr. Richard Aldington, the Imagists' first tenet."

However, the art of direct treatment in which Crane's verse excels is absent from the aim of most of the Imagists. They have the same brevity, exactitude, and simplicity of outline that characterize Crane's verses; but they treat situations "by no means in the method of a straightforward, first-hand understanding, but very indirectly, and through the media of the spirit and manner of certain remote, approved civilizations and habits of thought." Their charm of classic echo has the grace of a Wedgewood design. But Crane's poems "evince a far deeper and better conception than the Imagists' of direct expression in poetry."

Wyndham, Guy, ed. *George Wyndham: Letters.* Edinburgh, 1915.

1916

[Anon.]. "Adventure Filled Life of Richard Harding Davis," *New York Evening Post*, April 15, 1916.

Obituary on Davis. Related here is Davis's story about Crane at Siboney following the return of Lt. Richard Robson to the American lines. *See Crane.*

Daly, Tom. "Who's the Philistine?" *Philadelphia Evening Ledger*, July 27, 1916, p. 10; July 28, 1916, p. 8. In "Tom Daly's Column."

"It's a foolhardy thing to attempt to handicap success. It can't be done. The achievement, the basic fact, will emerge from the ruck and wiggle derisive fingers at you amid the laughter of a numerous public, always ready to admire the end, regardless of the means.

"Elbert Hubbard is reported to have accumulated not less than one and a half million dollars in 20 years or so, and he is known, beyond question, to have achieved a certain reputation as a man of letters. Now the man is dead—his passing having been as dramatic as he himself could have wished—and it isn't well to speak unkindly of the dead; but there are things that must be told.

"We could wish that all this might have been brought out while the chief actor was still alive, but during his lifetime there was no occasion for publishing what here is set forth. For while Hubbard was not at all averse to being considered the original Philistine, he was rather careful to make no such sweeping claims for himself as his friends have been making for him since his death.

"The founder of the *Philistine* and of the Roycroft community was Harry Persons Taber, a native of East Aurora, N.Y., and at present engaged in business in Wilmington, Del., into which quiet cove he has come after as varied a life as any newspaperman ever had—and survived.

"The beginnings of the *Philistine* were in the old City Hall—in the Police Department—of Denver in the winter of 1892–93. The police reporters of the city newspapers who, perforce, were there the greater part of the time, had a typewritten—and handwritten—sheet, which was pasted on the wall for the edification of the patrolmen, and even the dignified Chief Farley and good old Sam Howe, then chief of detectives. Johnnie Leyden, now chief of detectives, was on the force at the time, and he helped to furnish news notes for 'The Daily Copper.'

"The men who furnished the material for the paper sassed everybody who needed sassin', and the sheet became somewhat of an institution in the days when 'Soapy' Smith ran his gambling house and the regular evening tragedy of murder and suicide was part of the day's work.

"Finally, it was proposed that a magazine be published in which those of the boys who thought they could write could say just what they pleased. That their efforts found no response from the editors of the regular periodicals is neither here nor there, but when it came to a showdown there didn't seem to be enough money in the bunch to finance the proposition, so it went away from there.

"In March, 1893, it became necessary for Taber to go to his native town of East Aurora, N.Y. There he achieved an interest in the *East Aurora Citizen,* a local newspaper, with Newell W. White and Harry S. Waggoner. The print shop was run under the name of the White & Waggoner Company. The old idea of the magazine which had been proposed in Denver was still current, and with a printing establishment at his disposal the carrying out of the plan seemed an easy matter to Taber.

"The proposition was made to the late William MackIntosh, then the managing editor of the *Buffalo Evening News;* David Gray, of the *Buffalo Times;* Mark Hubbell, City Clerk of Buffalo; Eugene Richard White, John and Frank O'Brien and a few other Buffalo newspapermen. The idea met with approval and the first number of the *Philistine* appeared on June 1, 1895. Taber set it all in type with his own hands and printed every sheet of it with the help of his brother. To this number Elbert Hubbard contributed a short essay.

"Five thousand copies of the first number were printed—and then came a fatal mistake. Instead of sending the little magazine out through the channels of the American News Company, it was sent out to individual newsdealers throughout the country. The magazine was apparently an instant success, for repeat orders poured in, and the July edition was something more than 10,000 copies, still distributed through individual dealers. This was kept up for three or four months, until there came a time when the promoters had more than a thousand accounts due them, ranging from 50 cents to $5 each. These are pretty difficult accounts to collect, and late August brought the publishers to the end of their financial rope. It became necessary to raise money to meet current bills.

"Mr. Hubbard had often expressed a wish to get into the game, and when this crisis came Taber went to him with a proposition to take an interest in the business. He consented to take the affair over if he could become the sole owner of the periodical, agreeing that Taber was to remain as editor-in-chief and keep a half interest in the business. As the crisis was real, and there seemed to be no other way out, Taber agreed to this and things went on as before, Mr. Hubbard taking care of the financial end of the business. This continued until February, 1896, when the split came. This was brought about by Taber's refusal to print an essay of Hubbard's which he did not consider a proper article for a magazine of the type of the *Philistine.*

"Meanwhile, Taber had established the Roycroft Printing Shop for the purpose of making books after the manner then much in vogue, and of which attitude William Morris and his Kelmscott Press were the chief apostles. The only hand-printed book ever turned out of the Roycroft shops was set in type by Taber and printed on an old Washington hand press by him and his brother. This was Mr. Hubbard's 'Song of Solomon.' "

* * *   * * *   * * *

"It will be remembered that we were talking yesterday about the beginning of the *Philistine* and we had come to that part of our story which dealt with the dissolution of the partnership between Mr. Harry Persons Taber, the founder, and Mr. Elbert Hubbard, the financier. The split came in February, 1896.

"At this time Walter Blackburn Harte was publishing in Boston a little magazine similar in form to the *Philistine*. It had been established for some time, and as the Fly Leaf had gained many friends. Mr. Hubbard made an arrangement with Harte to merge his magazine with the *Philistine* and become the editor of the combined publications. Harte came to East Aurora and all went merrily for about five months. The Fly Leaf was wiped out. Then came some disagreement and Harte was dropped from the rolls. His spirit was broken. He went into a decline and lived but a short time after the crash.

"Then came Michael Monahan, and his spectacularly brilliant career as editor of the *Philistine* is a matter of history. When his position became no longer tenable he left the works, hired the opera house and delivered an address which is still remembered with delight by those who love the picturesque in oratory. Then he took the 4 o'clock train. Afterward he established the *Papyrus* and the *Phoenix,* and the work of the brilliant Irishman may still be found on the newsstands monthly. When the memorial meeting was held in East Aurora on July 4, 1915, Mr. Monahan delivered an address of eulogy for Mr. Hubbard, whose tragic end on the *Lusitania* is well remembered.

"But to go back to the stirring days.

"It was in December, 1895, shortly before the general tragedy, that the Society of the Philistines gave its first dinner. This was in honor of Stephen Crane, whose *Black Riders* was the first of the vers libre to attract general attention. At the dinner were men well known in newspaper and magazine work from all over the United States, and the affair was marked by one peculiarly remarkable incident. The attitude of the *Philistine* in the beginning was that of a free lance—one should say what he pleased about any man or thing he pleased, so long as he maintained a frame of mind that was right and proper from the point of view of the framers of libel laws and the tenets appertaining to good taste. During the dinner one of the speakers assailed Crane's work, not indecently, not with bad taste, but with a certain bitterness that brought one of the guests to his feet with a distinct protest. This guest interrupted the speech with a tirade which became historic, and for a few moments the situation was tense. Then rose Robert Mitchell Floyd, of Delaware, and saved the day by jeering at both the speakers for their grouch.

"Crane was called upon then to speak, and the calm, slight (in stature), brilliant genius told a few truths which were summed up in his final phrase: 'The man who can't stand the gaff isn't a man at all; he's a hell of a bum sport.'

"The hand-printing of 'The Song of Solomon,' to which reference has been made, was finished in January, 1896, and in February came the disagreement which resulted in Taber's retirement. With his former associates in newspaper work in Buffalo he formed a company, and asked Mr. Hubbard his price for his interest in the Roycroft Printing Shop and the *Philistine*. Mr. Hubbard named his price. The ambitious company rented a new building, purchased a full new outfit of machinery and type and was ready to go ahead as an individual corporation, separating the affair from the White & Waggoner Company, and went to Mr. Hubbard, offering him a certified check for the price he had named.

"Mr. Hubbard said he had changed his mind, and refused to sell any part of his interest. As it would have cost an interminable legal battle, the new company gave up, and Mr. Hubbard continued the work under his own name.

"When the split came there was in Taber's desk in the office a manuscript written by the late William Mackintosh, which was, in effect, the essay which appeared some years afterward as 'A Message to Garcia.' Certain details were necessarily changed, but 'The Message to Garcia' was really written by Mr. Mackintosh.

"The first real dollar paid for a subscription to the *Philistine* was sent to Taber by the late Samuel Bancroft, of Wilmington, Del., in June of 1895. That was long before Taber ever thought that Delaware would become his adopted State—but when he went to Wilmington 10 years ago this was remembered, and he presented to Mr. Bancroft the original copyright certificate, which is in his library at this time.

"Also there is the matter of *Little Journeys*. The idea of them was suggested to Hubbard by Taber, as is shown by Mr. Hubbard's dedication, reproduced here. Taber set the first ones in type and wrote three or four others—or, rather, rewrote them. He also suggested a few publishing firms that might take the publication, which was finally taken over by Putnam, and he illustrated *No Enemy* with the help of Mr. James B. McCreary and his brother. Then, too, the first chapters of *The Legacy* were planned and set in type by Taber.

"All these facts, as set forth above, were gathered of a pleasant summer evening in a roof garden above an old mansion in Wilmington, where Mr. Taber now makes his home. He told the story without show of heat, without bitterness, as a thing of no great moment that had passed and left him no regrets."*

Garnett, Edward. "A Gossip on Criticism," *Atlantic Monthly,* 117 (February, 1916), 174–185.

Keet, Alfred Ernest. "Stephen Crane, a New York Poet," *Bruno's Weekly,* 3 (September 2, 1916), 951–953.
  A pastiche of quotations; nothing new here.

———. *Stephen Crane: In Memoriam.* New York, n.d. Limited to 50 copies.

Maurice, Arthur Bartlett. *The New York of the Novelists.* New York, 1917.
  Chapter 9 discusses the locale of Crane's New York City sketches.

---

* Daly's report of Taber's exposé of Hubbard is published here through the kindness of Austin Fox, who brought it to my attention. It is not noticed by any biography of Elbert Hubbard, including Champney (1968). The *W-S Bibliography* lists Harry P. Taber's "Chant After Battle" as In preparation, but nothing came of that project. Collate Daly with Taber (1923) and Taber (1940).

Sandburg, Carl. "Letters to Dead Imagists . . . Stevie Crane," in *Chicago Poems*. New York, 1916, p. 176.
"*Stevie Crane:*
War is kind and we never knew the kindness of war till
      you came;
Nor the black riders and clashes of spear and shield
      out of the sea,
Nor the mumblings and shots that rise from dreams on call."

1917

[Anon.]. "Stephen Crane as the American Pioneer of the Free Verse Army," *Current Opinion*, 62 (March, 1917), 202–203.
" 'He was our most original genius since Poe, with the single exception of Frank Norris. He anticipated most of the things which the more attractive wing of the Free Verse army, Miss Amy Lowell's wing, is striving after.' Such is the claim put forward in the *N. Y. Evening Sun* by Harry Esty Dounce for the somewhat eclipsed genius of Stephen Crane. In calling our attention to Crane as a verse [*sic*] libre pioneer, Mr. Dounce takes care to characterize Crane's own experiments in free verse as 'commonplace.' He refers to Stephen Crane's prose, however, in laudatory terms."

Davis, Charles Belmont, ed. *Adventures and Letters of Richard Harding Davis*. New York, 1917, pp. 200, 207 (Crane in Greece), 234–235 (Crane in Cuba.)

Dounce, Harry Esty. "Stephen Crane as a Craftsman," *New York Evening Sun*, January 8, 1917, p. 14.
Quoted in [Anon.] (1917).
A perceptive essay of many important insights, a short study of Crane's achievement reprinted for the first time in *The Art of Stephen Crane: A Critical Symposium*, ed. R. W. Stallman (1973), vol. 1. In preparation, vol. 2.

Empey, A. G. Introduction, *The Red Badge of Courage*. New York, 1917.

Garland, Hamlin. "Stephen Crane as I Knew Him," *Syracusan* (December 1, 1917).
Reprints Garland's *Yale Review* essay (1914).

Hackett, Francis. "Another War," *New Republic*, 11 (June 30, 1917), 250–251.
The Red Badge of Courage "is seldom mentioned even now without a strong word of praise. But is it read? . . .
"The account of the little fight that brims up the youth with war-experience is perhaps more vivid than anything else in the novel, though such segregated pictures as that of the four southern prisoners excels the account of the battle by reason of the humorous sharpness that marked Crane's appreciation of men. The description of the fighting is almost more rhythmic than is tolerable. It is, in fact, poetry in its scansions. This is a blemish, but one of eager youth, like the delight in pressing against the edge of fear. And the proud, solemn tones at the end of *The Red Badge of Courage* are compensatory for horror and anguish. Written in depths of peace by one who never saw warfare, they are more valid than most of the pages written in these days in the ink of fresh blood."

On Hackett's hint that Crane's prose is in fact poetry in its scansions, Schoberlin (1949) scanned some of *The Red Badge* prose in the Introduction to
SCS.

Hitchcock, Ripley. Introduction, *The Red Badge of Courage.* New York, 1900,
1917.

Pattee, F. L. *A History of American Literature Since 1870.* New York, 1917.

Smith, M. Ellwood. "Stephen Crane Ex '94," *Syracuse,* 10 (December 1, 1917),
2–7, 32.
Reprints "Intrigue" (poem) from *War Is Kind.*

Wells, H. G. Introduction, Frank Swinnerton, *Nocturne.* New York, 1917.

Wyatt, Edith. *Great Companions.* New York, 1917, pp. 31–40. Reprinted from
"Stephen Crane," *New Republic,* 4 (September 11, 1915), 148–150.
The best critical assessment of Crane since H. G. Wells (1900). *See* Wyatt
(1915) for annotation.

1919

Conrad, Joseph. "Stephen Crane: A Note Without Dates," *London Mercury,* 1
(December, 1919), 192–193. Also in *Bookman,* 50 (February, 1920), 529–531.
Also in *Current Opinion,* 68 (April, 1920), 537–538.
Reprinted in Conrad, *Notes on Life and Letters* (1921).
Reprinted in *Novelists on Novelists,* ed. Louis Kronenberger (1962), pp.
249–263. Conrad's "A Note Without Dates" became (in much expanded form)
the Introduction to Beer's *SC.*
Reports that Sydney Pawling of the publishing firm of William Heinemann
remarked that Stephen Crane had arrived in England and that when asked if
there was anyone he cared to meet he had named Conrad, whose *The Nigger
of the "Narcissus"* he had read. As *The Nigger* did not appear in *New Review*
until August, 1897, Crane's meeting with Conrad in London occurred not in
June when Crane first settled in England, as stated in Conrad's account: "I
saw Stephen Crane a few days after his arrival in London. . . .
"On my next visit to town we met at a lunch [in early October]. I saw a
young man of medium stature and slender build, with very steady, penetrating
blue eyes, the eyes of a being who not only sees visions but can brood over
them to some purpose. . . . His manner was very quiet, his personality at
first sight interesting, and he talked slowly with an intonation which on some
people, mainly Americans, had, I believe, a jarring effect. But not on me.
Whatever he said had a personal note, and he expressed himself with a graphic
simplicity which was extremely engaging. He knew little of literature, either
of his own country or of any other. . . . His impressionism of phrase went
really deeper than the surface.* In his writing he was very sure of his effects.
I don't think he was ever in doubt about what he could do. Yet it often
seemed to me that he was but half aware of the exceptional quality of his
achievement.

* Conrad in 1897–1898, echoing Edward Garnett, had described Crane as an impressionist of the surface of things; here he concedes that he "went really deeper
than the surface."

"This achievement was curtailed by his early death. It was a great loss to his friends, but perhaps not so much to literature. I think that he had given his measure fully in the few books he had the time to write."*

Monroe, Harriet. "Stephen Crane," *Poetry*, 14 (June, 1919), 148–152.

How far was Crane a pioneer? "Of course Crane was something of an innovator in his poetic experiments. His free verse was different from Whitman's; his use of the short line especially was a presage, and it may have influenced some of the poets—the Imagists, for example—who are now trying out its tunes. Ezra Pound, indeed, has somewhere spoken of him appreciatively. But if he rebelled against the older verse forms and took up a new instrument, he never quite became a master at it. He struck a few slight strains, and then passed it on. And it is for his work in prose that he will be longest remembered."

1920

Conrad, Joseph. "Stephen Crane: A Note Without Dates," *Bookman*, 50 (February, 1920), 529–531. Also in *Current Opinion*, 68 (April, 1920), 537–538.

Reprinted in Conrad, *Notes on Life and Letters* (1921).

Huneker, James Gibbons. *Steeplejack,* vol. 2. New York, 1920, pp. 128, 268–271.

Mencken, H. L. *Prejudices: Second Series.* New York, 1920, p. 42.

Starrett, Vincent. "Stephen Crane: An Estimate," *Sewanee Review*, 28 (July, 1920), 405–413.

Reprinted as Introduction to his *Men, Women and Boats* (1921) and to *Maggie: A Girl of the Streets and Other Stories* (1933).

Reprinted in his *Buried Caesars* (1923).

Reviews briefly Crane's works. Quotes a portion of Crane letter to an unidentified editor (John Northern Hilliard). Reprints here for the first time Robert Barr's letter to an unidentified recipient (Karl Harriman), written from Hillhead, Surrey, on June 8, 1900, and published first in the *New York Herald* for June 21, 1900. *See* Birss (1933), Bohnenberger (1933), and Stolper, *Saturday Review of Literature* (1933).

On Crane with Burr McIntosh in Cuba; also in Starrett (1931).

1921

[Anon.]. [Crane memorial dedication], *Freeman*, December 7, 1921.

———. "Literary Notables Honor Stephen Crane's Memory," *Newark Star-Eagle*, November 8, 1921, p. 4.

* A different viewpoint is taken by Liebling (1961).

————. 'Rare Books, Autographs and Prints," *Publisher's Weekly*, November 12, 1921.

————. [Crane memorial dedication], *Times Literary Supplement*, October 27, 1921.

Beer, Thomas. [On Stephen Crane], *New York Evening Post*, December 17, 1921, p. 474.

Conrad, Joseph. "Stephen Crane: A Note Without Dates," in *Notes on Life and Letters*. London and New York, 1921, pp. 49–52. Reprinted from *London Mercury*, 1 (December, 1919), 192–193.

Dreiser, Theodore. "A Letter About Stephen Crane," *Michigan Daily Sunday Magazine* (Ann Arbor), November 27, 1921, p. 1.

"It pleases me no little to learn that the Schoolmen's Club is to honor Stephen Crane with a bronze tablet. He was among the very earliest of my purely American literary admirations and one of the few writers who stood forward intellectually and artistically at a time when this nation was as thoroughly submerged in romance and sentimentality and business as it is today. At that time, in so far as America was concerned, there were but James and Howells and Mark Twain among the elder realists and Garland and Fuller and Crane as beginners. Of this younger group Crane was a peer. . . .

"He took our hampering hurdles without a thought or a care. The *Red Badge of Courage* is a fine picture of war. And it is not pleasant. There is not much sweetness about it and very little uplift. It ends as it begins, grimly, and without any solution, moral or spiritual standards. If you doubt it study our current books and magazines."

Ford (Hueffer), Ford Madox. "Two Americans—Henry James and Stephen Crane," *New York Evening Post Literary Review*, March 19, 1921, pp. 1–2; March 26, 1921, pp. 1–2. Signed Ford Madox Hueffer.

Recast in "Henry James, Stephen Crane, and the Main Stream," in *Thus to Revisit* (1921). *W-S Bibliography*, p. 142, omits the first installment of March 19, and the checklist in *SCraneN* copies Beer's omission of the first installment and errs in paging the March 26 issue for p. 6. The above Ford article does not get included in Gullason's "Criticism of Crane" (checklist) in *Modern Fiction Studies*, 5 (1959).

————. *Thus to Revisit*. London, 1921, pp. 17, 39, 69, 106–113, 118–120, 210. London and New York, 1921. Reprints "Two Americans" from *New York Evening Post Literary Review*, March 19 and 26, 1921.

Ford's first visits with the Cranes at Limpsfield and Oxted, Surrey. On Henry James, Conrad, and Crane. On Brede Manor. On Stevenson and Crane, who said the most illuminating things.

Recalls the night Crane returned to Ravensbrook from a visit with agent Pinker, who had just then guaranteed him "£20 per thousand words for everything that he chose to write and had advanced him a sum of money sufficient to pay his Oxted debts."

Hind, C. Lewis. *Authors and I*. London and New York, 1921, pp. 70–74.

Continues the legend, usually attributed to Beer (1923), that all Crane got out of his war experiences was proof that *The Red Badge* "is all right." Hind had written in *Academy* "with admiration of this young American who captured literary England," and so it was natural that he should wish to see him. Hind thought that Crane's imagination "worked better in a room than in a battlefield," an opinion held also by Hamlin Garland, H. G. Wells, and Harold Frederic. The same standpoint is taken by Follett, Introduction, *Work*, vol. 3, and by Stallman in *Omnibus*.

Morris, L. B. "The Discourse of the Elders," *Outlook*, 119 (September 14, 1921), 67–68.

A review of Starrett's *Men, Women and Boats* (1921).

Phelps, William Lyon. *"The Scarlet Letter* or *Huckleberry Finn?" New York Times Book Review*, August 7, 1921, p. 3.

Remarks that Crane's "The Monster" is "one of the most painful but one of the most powerful of Crane's writings."

Starrett, Vincent. Introduction, *Men, Women and Boats*. New York: Modern Library, 1921, pp. 9–20.

Reprinted from *Sewanee Review*, 28 (July, 1920), 405–413.

The table of contents for *Men, Women and Boats* groups three pieces as "Sullivan County Sketches," the titles of these three being indented ("A Tent in Agony," "Four Men in a Cave," "The Mesmeric Mountain"). Flush to the margin, however, is "The Snake." Why so? Is not "The Snake" a Sullivan County sketch?

Since that title is not indented under the heading "Sullivan County Sketches," it seems not to have been considered as belonging to that category in the table of contents. However, in the text itself there is no demarcation to indicate that "The Snake" does not belong to "Sullivan County Sketches." The same ambiguity of intention, namely whether or not it is a Sullivan County sketch, obtains in Starrett's *Maggie: A Girl of the Streets and Other Stories* (1933), whose table of contents is the same as in *Men, Women and Boats*—except for the addition of *Maggie*.

The same ambiguity of intention obtains in Wilson Follett's *Work*, vol. 11, where again "The Snake" immediately follows "The Sullivan County Sketches." Follett, but not Starrett, has it thus in his table of contents: I. A Tent in Agony. II. Four Men in a Cave. III. The Mesmeric Mountain. (Next is "The Snake," and then a New York City sketch, "A Self-Made Man," which has no possible affinity to "The Snake," although "The Snake" has kinship with the Sullivan County sketches.)

Starrett's *Men, Women and Boats* is the first Crane collection since Crane's *Last Words* (1902). No Crane revival followed until after the *W-S Bibliography*. Neither Beer's *SC* nor Follett's twelve-volume edition of Crane's works (1925–1927) stirred up any Crane revival. It began in the universities among New Critics after the publication of Berryman's *Crane* and *Omnibus*. European interest in Crane, notably in France and Germany, began with the publication of the English edition of *Omnibus*, shortly after 1954.

See also Beer (1921), Morris (1921), and Brooks (1922), all of whom reviewed this edition.

1922

Beer, Thomas. "Stephen, Henry, and the Hat," *Vanity Fair*, 18 (August, 1922), 63, 88.

The adventures of Pete, coachman to a rich bachelor, composed in a parody of Crane's style with mock quotations from *Maggie* and *The Red Badge of Courage*.

[Brooks, Van Wyck]. "A Reviewer's Notebook," *Freeman*, 4 (January 18, 1922), 455.

An unsigned article prompted by the Starrett edition of *Men, Women and Boats* (1921). Crane's notes "are the notes of irony and pity, which Anatole France has recommended as most worthy of the humane spirit; and while pity is to be found elsewhere in our fiction, in such novels as *Jennie Gerhardt*, for instance, the combination of the two is in him unique. 'An Experiment in Misery' is full of this irony and this pity, and so are the war sketches, particularly 'The Upturned Face'; and as for 'The Open Boat,' it is precisely the irony and the pity in it that makes this grey little tale one of the minor masterpieces of our latter-day literature. The possession of these qualities indeed constituted the very special promise of Stephen Crane—a slight figure only because his years were so few." (Hemingway's characteristic note of irony and pity derives from Crane.)

Brooks's article of two paragraphs is the most illuminating of any appraisal of Crane since H. G. Wells's 1900 study. He points out Crane's "ruling passion was curiosity, and this passion of the artist overruled the normal instincts of the man." This stands in opposition to Beer's 1923 thesis in *Stephen Crane* that "the mistress of this boy's mind was terror."

Garnett, Edward. "Stephen Crane and His Work," *Friday Nights: Literary Criticisms and Appreciations*. New York, 1922, pp. 201–217. Reprinted in enlarged form from Garnett's "Mr. Stephen Crane: An Appreciation," *Academy* (December 17, 1898).

Garnett praises the psychology of *The Red Badge of Courage,* and the realistic description of the battle scenes, but questions the "realism" of so much introspection by a young soldier, although perhaps this may be excused on the grounds of esthetic licence. Garnett's essay is important not only as an appraisal of Crane's artistry, but also because it poses questions still not satisfactorily answered among some 2,000 articles on Crane since 1898. Garnett's charge that *The Red Badge* is not really constructed is one such instance of present-day critical indecision.

On the architectonics of *The Red Badge* see Stallman, *Critiques* (1952) and *Omnibus;* Marcus, "The Unity of *The Red Badge of Courage*" in Lettis (1960). *See also* Bradley (1962); and *Crane.*

Griffith, O. L. "Stephen Crane: 1870–1900," *Publisher's Weekly,* 102 (September 16, 1922), 813.

Guntzer, J. Henry, Jr. "A Memorial to Stephen Crane," *Delta Upsilon Quarterly,* 40 (January, 1922), 36–38.

"On Monday, November 7, 1921, a bronze tablet was unveiled in Brother Crane's honor on the exterior wall of the Free Public Library in Newark, N.J., to commemorate the 50th anniversary of his birth in that city on November 1, 1871. The tablet was paid for by the school children of Newark who took part in the exercises conducted by the Schoolmen's Club in the auditorium of the Burnet School. In the evening the main exercises of the celebration took place in the Old First Presbyterian Church. . . ."

Among those who spoke were Hamlin Garland; ex-Congressman Edward T. Townsend, creator of "Chimmie Fadden"; City Commissioner Thomas L. Raymond of Newark; and Don Seitz of the *New York World*.* Among those who sent letters were Joseph Conrad, H. G. Wells, Arnold Bennett, Edwin Markham, Colonel E. M. House, Irving Cobb, and S. S. McClure.

Among the letters here quoted Bennett's letter says that Crane "must rank with the best writers that America has produced and as one of the finest descriptive experts of modern times." Wells says: "I do not think that criticism has yet done justice to the unsurpassable beauty of Crane's best writing. And when I write these words, magnificent, unsurpassable, I mean them fully; this is not mere commemorative eloquence. He was, beyond dispute, the best writer of his generation, and his untimely death was an irreparable loss to our literature." Edwin Markham wrote: Crane in his *Red Badge of Courage* "ripped away the gilt and glitter that had so long curtained the horror of war and with a stern realism pictured for us the bloody grime of it all."

Guntzer's memorial article concludes with a short sketch of Crane's life. He errs in listing *"Dan Emmonds, novel, 1898,"* and in saying that Crane's body "was brought to Elizabeth, N.Y., for interment." Crane was buried at Hillside, N.J. (*See* "Misplaced Writer," in *The New Yorker* [November 7, 1936].) Guntzer says that Crane, because his satirical description of a labor parade in Asbury Park offended his employers, was dismissed by the *Tribune* and that he then worked for a time on the staff of the *Newark Morning Times* for $10 a week. Since 1895 thirty thousand copies of *The Red Badge of Courage* have been printed in America.

Huneker, James Gibbons. *Steeplejack,* vol. 1, p. 270; vol. 2, p. 128. New York, 1922.

Huneker, Josephine, ed. *Letters of James G. Huneker.* New York, 1922.

Paine, Ralph D. "Bright Roads of Adventure," *Popular Magazine* (March 7, 1922).

———. *Roads of Adventure.* Boston and New York, 1922, pp. 162–170, 174, 192–194, 215, 222–228, 236–238, 243–246, 251–256, 260–261. Photograph of Crane at his desk at Ravensbrook.

Dedicated to Ernest W. McCready, "my old comrade afloat and ashore, and to the memory of Stephen Crane." Important for tracing Crane's whereabouts during the Cuban War. Also on Crane's Jacksonville days and the *Commodore* disaster.

Pattee, F. L. *Sidelights on American Literature.* New York, 1922.

* Don Carlos Seitz, who knew Crane at the Lantern Club and disliked him, undoubtedly said good things about Crane on this occasion, but in 1924 he defamed Crane's reputation as journalist (in *Joseph Pulitzer*) and in 1933 he repeated his deliberate falsifications in his *Bookman* article on Crane as journalist. Midway through the Cuban War Seitz, then business manager of the *New York World*, fired Crane, who then switched from Pulitzer's *New York World* to Hearst's *New York Journal*. (*See Seitz,* 1924 and 1933.)

Raymond, mayor of Newark, wrote a short biographical sketch of Crane in 1923.

1923

[Anon.]. "Lost Souls of Stephen Crane and His Sussex Days," *Bookman's Journal and Print Collector,* 8 (August, 1923), 145–147.

————. 'Stephen Crane," *Library* (Newark), 1, no. 9 (April, 1923), 11.

————. [Stephen Crane: Jerseyman], *Newark Sunday Call,* June 17, 1923.
Reprints an obituary from the *New York Sun,* June 10, 1900: "Stephen Crane: Jerseyman."

Beer, Thomas. *Stephen Crane: A Study in American Letters.* Introduction by Joseph Conrad, pp. 1–33. Garden City, N.Y., 1923; London, 1924.
Reprinted in *The Borzoi Reader,* ed. Carl Van Doren. New York, 1936.
Reprinted in Thomas Beer, *Hanna, Crane, and the Mauve Decade.* New York, 1941.
Reviewed:
Floyd Dell, *Nation,* 119 (December 10, 1923), 637–638.
Ralph D. Paine, *Bookman,* 58 (December 23, 1923), 470–471.
Stanton A. Coblentz, *New York Times Book Review,* 72 (December 30, 1923), 8.
Edmund Wilson, *New Republic,* 37 (January 2, 1924), 153–154.
Thomas Craven, *Freeman,* 8 (January 22, 1924), 475–477.
Carl Van Doren, *Century,* 107 (January, 1924), 476.
Current Opinion, 76 (January, 1924), 39–40.
TLS, September 4, 1924.
Margaret Whipple, *Bookman,* 67 (June, 1928), 538–541.
Malcolm Cowley, *New Republic,* 105 (September 29, 1941), 409–410. "The trouble is that the style is a continuous barrier between the reader and what he wants to know about American literature during the 1890's. The style is always flaunting itself, sometimes in a gold-filled coronet and sometimes in a freshman cap. 'They laid Jesse James in his grave and Dante Gabriel Rossetti died immediately.' Pow! Zam!"
Mina Curtiss, *Nation* (December 27, 1941), 676–677, compares Beer with Lytton Strachey.
Alfred Kazin, *On Native Grounds* (1942), echoes Cowley on Beer's style. In spite of his "undergraduate archness" Beer attained "an oblique irony that he welded into a successful principle of composition" and "he could sound unutterably wise."
Remarked on in *TLS,* June 8, 1951: "[Beer's *SC*] published in 1924, did not bring him to the front again."
Edmund Wilson, *The Shores of Light* (1952) says that Beer imitated not Strachey's style but Henry Adams's style. (In *The Shock of Recognition* [1943] Wilson said: "Thomas Beer's *Stephen Crane* is valuable, but it is simply a sort of memoir written by one who did not know him well.")
Stallman, *Omnibus,* 1952, p. xi: "Literary biography is here lifted to the level of art. But Beer is not reliable. The facts are distorted, and gaps in the chronology are disguised by Beer's tricks of camera, by kaleidoscopic effects and cinematic shadow-work."
See also Mencken (1949).

Callender, L., ed. *The Windmill: Stories, Essays, Poems and Pictures.* London, 1923.

Reprints some Crane writings.

Conrad, Joseph. Introduction, Thomas Beer, *Stephen Crane: A Study in American Letters.* New York, 1923; London, 1924, pp. 1–33.

Paine, Ralph D. "The Life and Art of Stephen Crane," *Bookman,* 58 (December, 1923), 470–471.

Memoirs of his friend, a review of Beer's *SC.* "His life was brief and careless. He left the scantiest material for a biographer, and yet this book portrays the man with candor and fidelity. Through its pages he moves as a wistful figure in shadows often sombre." On Beer's "candor" *see* the Preface, *Crane.*

Partington, Wilfred [unsigned]. "The 'Lost Souls' of Stephen Crane and his Sussex Days," *Bookman's Journal and Print Collector,* 8 (August, 1923), 145–147. Interview with Ford Madox Ford.

On Crane at Brede Manor, as Ford describes it; on "The Squire's Madness." On the "lost souls" in the Crane canon, titles of work for which there exist no manuscripts such as "The Merry Go Round," "Flowers in Asphalt," and "The Cat's March."

Pattee, Fred Lewis. *The Development of the American Short Story: An Historical Survey.* New York and London, 1923, pp. 305, 311, 337, 341–343, 355.

Raymond, Thomas L. Lynch. *Stephen Crane.* Newark, N.J.: Carteret Book Shop, 1923. Introductory Note by J. C. Dana.

The first biography of Crane. Chronology and checklist of books. Dana's Note states that a tablet to Stephen Crane was installed on November 7, 1921, in the Newark Public Library by the Newark Schoolmen's Club in memory of the fiftieth anniversary of Stephen Crane's birth.

Smith, James Walter. "Joseph Conrad—Master Mariner and Novelist," *Boston Evening Transcript,* May 12, 1923.*

Starrett, Vincent. "Stephen Crane: A Wonderful Boy," in *Buried Caesars: Essays in Literary Appreciation.* Chicago, 1923, pp. 73–86. Reprinted from "Stephen Crane: An Estimate," *Sewanee Review,* 28 (July, 1920), 405–415.

The same title appeared in an unsigned obituary in *Literary Digest,* 20 (June 23, 1900), 750. The same title was used by E. W. Chubb in *Stories of Authors* (1910).

———. *Stephen Crane: A Bibliography.* Philadelphia: The Centaur Book Shop, 1923. Introduction by Vincent Starrett: "On Collecting Stephen Crane," pp. 5–11.

The first bibliography on Crane. First editions, pp. 13–40. Critical notices, essays, and books, pp. 41–46.

Taber, Harry P. Letter to Thomas Beer, December 19, 1923.

"My dear Mr. Beer:—I don't know of a better day to write you than on the twenty-eighth anniversary of the dinner we gave Stevie Crane: the nineteenth of December, 1895. Primarily the reason for writing lies in the fact that I want to thank you for the delight I have found in the book you made about the boy a few of us loved devotedly before a very large number of folks came to know the Genius,—for I believe he was that. I believed it one morning when he was visiting me at my home in East Aurora. It was a day or so after the dinner

* For this article I am indebted to Dale B. J. Randall of Duke University.

in Buffalo, and we went together for a walk over the hills and through the snowy woods. We came to a brook. The stream was swift and was not frozen over. We sat down and he began digging with his stick among the stones in the water. Presently he reached into the water with his hand and brought something out. 'What have you found?' I asked him. 'This,—and God,' he said. He held in his hand a tiny crawfish.

"Somehow the situation made a very deep impression on me, for suddenly a wind came swooping out of nowhere and the limbs of frozen trees crackled uncannily. 'The Death Demon in the Tree Tops again,' he said. This referred to some lines he had written for me the Summer before, and which I had published in *The Philistine*. I am enclosing a copy of them.

"As this leads up to something I want to say later, it may be well to explain that I established *The Philistine* in June, 1895. My name did not appear on it as editor in that month, but it did on the second number, and thereafter till February, 1896. In an evil moment I had asked Elbert Hubbard to become associated with the enterprise, and published a short paper of his in the first number. How the split came in February following, and all the other incidents of a rather tragic episode for me, need not be detailed here. Tom Daly published the story in his column in the *Philadelphia Evening Public Ledger* in July, 1916. If memory is serving accurately, I printed the first of Crane's lines in July, and three or four times during that year—1895. *The Riders* was published in October.

"My associate, Eugene Richard White, had become greatly interested with me in Crane and his promise. Late in the Fall White suggested that we get Stephen up to East Aurora, give a dinner for him, and ask some of our friends— and his—to josh him a whole lot, but incidentally show him that we believed in him and his work and his pioneering. I believe that subsequent events proved that our idea was quite right, but in any case it was not Hubbard, as you suggest in your study, who gave the dinner for him in Buffalo, or even had much of anything to do with it except to talk somewhat discursively upon his favorite topic: Love and Himself. Nor was Bragdon, as you say, 'master of ceremonies.' I, as editor of the magazine acted as toastmaster, but Bragdon, who somehow gathered the idea that our jollying of Crane was a bit overdone, made a speech which came near breaking up the show. Robert Mitchell Floyd came to the rescue and saved the situation.

"Crane came up from New York with his close friend Willis B. Hawkins. Irving Way came on from Chicago. Frank Noxon, who had been Crane's classmate at Syracuse, came on, and among the others there were William Mac-Intosh, then editor of the *Buffalo News,* and incidentally the real author of 'A Message to Garcia;' John O'Brien, afterward of *The Sun,* and his brother Frank, now one of the editors of *The Herald;* Samuel G. Blythe, John Northern Hilliard, Dick White, Dwight Collin, Bragdon, Floyd and perhaps twenty more men who were more or less interested in that curious movement of the mid-nineties which found a certain expression in the making of small magazines and the development of such men as Crane, Percival Pollard, Walter Blackburn Harte and a few other protestants.

"I was talking with Byrne Hackett the other day in New York, and he suggested that there was every probability of your delightful book being reprinted and possibly revised somewhat. If this is done, I believe that you might get some rather interesting material from Frank Noxon, who is secretary of the American Railway Association, with his office in the Liberty Building,

Philadelphia. Further, I was talking of Crane with Riley Hatch at the Lambs when I was over last week, and he seemed greatly distressed in that your letter to him did not reach him until long after it should have. He was away at the time on a picture location in Bermuda, and his mail was not forwarded. He has a lot of information that might be valuable in case your biography is extended in future editions.

"I am sending with this a little volume of my friend's verse which I got out, as the preface indicates, after his death. Perhaps you may see in his work something of the spirit of a man who could prophecy with some directness as to Crane and his possibilities. I forget whether it was White or I that discovered *Maggie*. Anyway, one of us brought it to the other, and we started to dig out the boy that wrote it. I was glad, therefore, when I saw what Wells wrote of Crane in his bit of introduction to one of Swinnerton's stories,—glad, in that it proved that we were right—and a quarter-century in advance. I sent to Mr. Wells a letter or so of Crane's and had some correspondence with him."*

Trent, William Peterfield, John Erskine, Stuart P. Sherman, and Carl Van Doren, *The Cambridge History of American Literature.* New York, 1923, pp. 92–93, 309.

1924

[Anon.]. "The Revival of Interest in Stephen Crane," *Current Opinion*, 76 (January, 1924), 39–40. Photograph.

Review of Beer's *SC* and Starrett's *Buried Caesars* (1923). Crane's reputation "is already established. A tablet to his memory has been set in the Free Library at Newark. William Dean Howells and Henry James, as well as Conrad, have sung his praises and H. G. Wells has styled him 'one of the most brilliant, most significant and most distinctly American of all English writers.' But in spite of these panegyrics, Stephen Crane is for many only a legendary figure. . . . He was an imagist, as Mr. Starrett puts it, before our modern imagists were known, and his style was imitated by many of his successors. The delicate dissection of the soul of a recruit, the business of the lady who turns over a letter of farewell to a friend before a battle, a flowery advance of banners and a description of fires by night have all appeared in adaptations; and Alan Seeger's graceful poem, 'I have a rendezvous with death,' is known to have been suggested by the tenth chapter of the novel."

———. "Stephen Crane Home Acquired," *Newark Evening News*, May 18, 1924.

———. "Stephen Crane," *Times Literary Supplement*, September 4, 1924.
Comments on Beer's *SC* and Conrad's Introduction.

Beer, Thomas. "Stephen Crane," *New York Evening Post Literary Review*, July 19, 1924, pp. iv, 910.

* This letter, here published for the first time, is the kind gift of Austin Mc-Cracken Fox of Buffalo, to whom I am again indebted for the related Tom Daly article (1916) and for the Taber to David Balch letter (1940), also here published for the first time.

Beer corrects Ford Madox Ford's statement in *Thus To Revisit* (1921) that Crane earned £20 per thousand words and Ford's statement in "Stevie" (1924), that Crane earned £10 per thousand words. But in 1932, Ford, forgetting Beer's correction note and forgetting what he himself had said, reinstated the terms of £20 per thousand words in his *Return To Yesterday* (1932). *See also* Ford (1937).

James Stronks discusses Crane's earnings in "Stephen Crane's English Years: The Legend Corrected" (1963).

Boyd, Ernest. *Portraits: Real and Imaginary.* New York, 1924.
On Thomas Beer's literary personality and his *Stephen Crane* as an expression of it.

Boyd, Thomas. "Semper Fidelis," *Bookman*, 960 (December, 1924), 409–412.
On Crane and Sergeant John Quick at Cuzco, near Guantánamo Bay, Cuba, in June, 1898. Quotes Crane's account in *Wounds in the Rain.*

Calverton, V. F. *The Newer Spirit: A Sociological Criticism of Literature.* New York, 1924.
Declares that the future lies with "proletarian literature," a literature which will be realistic and comprehensive of all experience, permeated with a sense of the collective as opposed to the individual. He includes Frank Norris and Stephen Crane as "continuators" of a trend which he traces back to Whitman.

Dell, Floyd. "Stephen Crane and the Genius Myth," *Nation*, 119 (December 10, 1924), 637–638.

Ford, Ford Madox. "Literary Causeries: IV. Escape . . . ," *Chicago Tribune* (Paris), no. 4 (March 9, 1924), 3, 11.

——. "Literary Causeries: V. Revivals and Revivalists," *Chicago Tribune* (Paris), no. 5 (March 16, 1924), 3, 11.
Some anecdotes about Crane and Henry James.

——. "Literary Causeries: VII. Pullus ad Margaritan," *Chicago Tribune* (Paris), no. 7 (March 30, 1924), 3, 11.
Remarks on *The Black Riders* that Crane "had all the hard exactness of language of a French writer but managed nevertheless to get into his *vers libre* a great deal of conversational fluidity. . . ."

——. "Literary Causeries: X. Mystifications," *Chicago Tribune* (Paris), no. 10 (April 20, 1924), 3.

——. *Joseph Conrad.* London, 1924; Boston, 1924, pp. 9, 247.

——. "Stevie," *New York Evening Post Literary Review*, July 12, 1924, pp. 881–882.
Reprinted in *Return to Yesterday* (1932).
Thomas Beer replies in "Stephen Crane," same journal, July 19, 1924, p. 910.

Horwill, Herbert W. "American Books and English Readers," *New York Times Book Review*, 74 (November 9, 1924), 6.
A London report on Rebecca West's lecture at National Liberal Club: "Some Thoughts on American Writers," in which Miss West expressed the opinion "that Stephen Crane at his best was superior to Rudyard Kipling at his best."

Overton, Grant. *Cargoes for Crusoes.* New York and Boston, 1924, p. 242.

Preston, Hayter. "The Real Stephen Crane," *First Edition and Book Collector,* 2 (September–October, 1924), 75–77.

Pugh, Edwin. "Stephen Crane," *Bookman,* 67 (December, 1924), 162–164.

Attempts to undercut Joseph Conrad's friendship with Crane, claiming that Conrad patronized Crane, who, for his part, was ironic toward Conrad's affected humility. Claims that Crane "was much more frank and generally in sympathy with me than he seems to have been with any of his other friends." (However, Pugh was one of the parasites at Brede Place.) Pugh characterizes Crane as another Poe.

Seitz, Don Carlos. *Joseph Pulitzer: His Life and Letters.* New York, 1924, pp. 240–242.

Attributes wrongly to Crane the authorship of an unsigned *New York World* dispatch charging panic among the 71st New York Volunteers. Sylvester Scovel wrote that undiplomatic dispatch, not Crane. *See* Williams, "Stephen Crane: War Correspondent" (1948).

Seitz, business manager of the *World,* claims that Crane sent the *World* "only one dispatch of any merit and that, accusing the Seventy-first New York regiment of cowardice at Santiago, imperilled the paper. It was seized upon by Hearst as a slander on heroes and bade fair to do much damage, which was arrested by an official report confirming Crane's account of the command's conduct. Mr. Pulitzer sought to counteract the clamor by raising a fund for a memorial." Seitz knew that Crane had submitted more than twenty *World* dispatches, not just one.

Midway through the Cuban War Crane was fired by Seitz and John Norris, financial manager of the *World.* Crane had known Seitz at the Lantern Club, where Seitz in 1895–1896 had been treasurer. During the memorial services for Crane in 1921 at Newark, New Jersey, Seitz appeared there as his friend. However, in his 1933 *Bookman* critique of Crane as war correspondent he repeated his 1924 defamation of Crane.

Beer's notion that Crane "could not report" derives from Don Carlos Seitz. Seitz's misinformation in *Joseph Pulitzer* has damaged Crane's reputation for forty years because all the historians repeat it: Millis (1931), Mason (1939), Margaret Leech (1958), and W. A. Swanberg (1961).

Van Doren, Carl. "Stephen Crane," *American Mercury,* 1 (January 1924), 11–24.

Reprinted in *American Mercury: Readings from the American Mercury,* ed. Grant C. Knight (1926), pp. 97–106. Reprinted as the Introduction to *Twenty Stories by Stephen Crane,* ed. Carl Van Doren (1940), pp. v–xvii. The best critical appraisal of Crane's works since Edward Garnett's *Academy* summing up in December, 1898, and H. G. Wells's survey in April, 1900.

"Modern American literature may be said, accurately enough, to have begun with Stephen Crane thirty years ago."

———. "Books and Affairs," *Century,* 107 (January, 1924), 476.

Wilson, Edmund. "A Vortex in the Nineties: Stephen Crane," *New Republic,* 37 (January 2, 1924), 153–154.

Reprinted in *The Shores of Light* (1952), pp. 109–114.*

Beer in *Stephen Crane* (1923) imitates not Lytton Strachey but Henry Adams.

The effect of Beer's study is "to bring out in these barren decades in which

---

* Quoted passages in this note are from the text of *Shores of Light.*

Stephen Crane lived a certain importance and interest which they owe to Stephen Crane's having lived in them. The happenings and habits of the era— the Bowery, the Cuban War, Clyde Fitch and Lillian Russell, the debaucheries of the Haymarket and the racing days on the Jersey coast—though they may have for us a charm of memory, do not usually wear for us the aspect of having been in themselves enchanting; but they take on a certain literary glamor when we watch them through Stephen Crane's eyes. What is exciting is to see this life experienced and criticized by a man of first-rate intelligence who was also living in the thick of it—to see its literature tried by the touchstone of a practicing artist who could feel the hollowness of Stevenson and the value of Henry James, who realized that *Huckleberry Finn* was spoiled as a perfect novel by its final pages of farce and—as I learn from another source than the biography of Mr. Beer—sometimes amused himself by trying to cut down specimens of contemporary American poetry to the minimum of idea or emotion that, on scrutiny, he found them to contain. . . .

"Stephen Crane was a vortex of intensity in a generally stagnant sea. He was an artist not as the age understood that word but as the world at large understands it. I do not say that he was a great artist or that he was even of the first rank, but what he had was the real thing and he adulterated it with nothing else. Stephen Crane had arrived in prose, apparently without having read Maupassant or knowing anything of the school of Flaubert, at precisely their objective method and their ironic point of view, and in poetry, at a terse vers libre which at its best has scarcely been surpassed by any of the more profuse vers librists who have since received more liberal publicity; and he managed to practice his art without any journalistic infection." (However, *see* Garnett [1898]).

Wilson in *The Shores of Light* (1952) adds this footnote: "I should certainly say today that Stephen Crane was an artist of the first rank, but I have left this opinion of the twenties as typical of our contemptuous attitude toward the nineties and our diffidence in making claims for the American writers of the past. . . ."

However, for the influence of Flaubert's *Madame Bovary* on Crane's *Maggie* *see* Stallman, "Stephen Crane's Primrose Path" (1955).

Woollcott, Alexander. *Enchanted Aisles.* New York and London, 1924, pp. 130–135.
Calls Beer's *SC* "the most enthralling book which 1923 brought this way."

1925

[Anon.]. *"The Red Badge of Courage,"* Harper's Magazine, December, 1925.

——. [Hall of Fame], *Literary Digest International Book Review,* April, 1925.

——. "Book Sales and Rare Books," *New York Evening Post Literary Review,* January 24, 1925.
On sale of first editions of *Maggie,* letters by Crane, and Beer's *SC.*

——. "Books and Authors," *New York Times Book Review and Magazine Section,* March 15, 1925.

Quotes Max J. Herzberg urging Crane's election to the Hall of Fame, letter to New York University.

————. [Hall of Fame], *Step Ladder*, May, 1925.

————. "Reprints," *Times Literary Supplement*, May, 1925, p. 371.

Beer, Thomas. "The Princess Far Away," *Saturday Review of Literature*, 1 (April 25, 1925), 702.

"Bah," said Joseph Conrad across a shoulder to Alfred Knopf. "James did not know what Stevie was talking about! It was beyond his limitation." What did he really like in Stephen Crane's work? "In the *Third Violet*," he dictated to Willis Clarke, "we have our boy coming to the right thing." The right thing for James was—according to Beer—the chatter of artists; charming pictures of lakes and hills; a rich girl sought by a poor painter—that was the "right thing."

————. "Fire Feathers," *Saturday Review of Literature*, 2 (December 19, 1925), 425–427. Also in Beer, *Design for Reading* (1934), pp. 253–262.

Review of *Work*. Beer's notion that "Nothing much has been omitted and nothing of any value" is rather presumptive in view of the tomes of Crane writings which have been subsequently brought to light and published as *Letters, War Dispatches, NYCS, SCTS,* and manuscripts by the dozens.

It is true that Follett's edition "shows a noble restraint in the face of Crane's experimental punctuation and battered infinitives," but this remark camouflages the truth about the edited texts. They have been tampered with to conform to British spellings, that being the practice of American published houses at that time (as Follett explained in letter to R. W. S.) and so they possess no textual validity.

Borg, Dorothy. "Newark Remembers Stephen Crane," *New York World*, November 8, 1925. Portrait.

Stephen's birthplace, No. 14 Mulberry Place, is an austere red brick front with five uncertain steps leading to the old wooden door and a dignified frieze. "The halls are dark, the rooms large with fireplaces, big windows, and high ceilings bearing old time scroll work."

Mrs. O'Connor, living next door, reports in Dorothy Borg's interview that Bishop Darlington lived at Mulberry Place in the 1870s, "and the Windsors, the Fitzgeralds, the Kents, the Gruets—all old families, now dead. Every one on the block knew each other. 'I've heard them speak of the Cranes,' she said after a while, 'but they weren't people you would mention as much as two or three times. I can only remember that they said Mrs. Crane was a fine woman, but she spent so much time doing good work outside her home that her children and the house were not as well looked after as they should have been.' "

The Stephen Crane Association, started by Mr. Thomas L. Raymond, Mayor of Newark, hopes to buy the Mulberry Place house and turn it into a "town hall of the arts." It intends to fix to the house a plaque of Crane by Seumas O'Brien, bearing the inscription: "novelist, short story writer, poet and author of '*The Red Badge of Courage.*' "

See [Anon.], "Playlot to Rise" (1940).

Conrad, Joseph. "His War Book," Preface to *The Red Badge of Courage*. London: William Heinemann, 1925.

"His War Book: A Preface to Stephen Crane's *The Red Badge of Cour-*

age," in *Last Essays*. London and Toronto: J. M. Dent, 1926, 1928, 1955. Reprinted as Preface to *The Red Badge of Courage*. London: Jonathan Cape, 1937.

"One of the most enduring memories of my literary life is the sensation produced by the appearance in 1895 of Crane's *Red Badge of Courage* in a small volume belonging to Mr. Heinemann's Pioneer Series of Modern Fiction—very modern fiction of that time, and upon the whole not devoid of merit. I have an idea the series was meant to give us shocks, and as far as my recollection goes there were, to use a term made familiar to all by another war, no 'duds' in that small and lively bombardment. But Crane's work detonated on the mild din of that attack on our literary sensibilities with the impact and force of a twelve-inch shell charged with a very high explosive. Unexpected it fell amongst us; and its fall was followed by a great outcry."

Davis, Robert H. Introduction, *Tales of Two Wars*. In *The Work of Stephen Crane*, vol. 2, ed. Wilson Follet. New York, 1925, pp. ix–xxiv.
Important for his report of his interview with Crane in 1896.

Follett, Wilson, ed. *The Work of Stephen Crane*. New York, 1925–1927. Twelve volumes. Reprinted in six volumes by Russell and Russell, 1963.
See Hergesheimer, 1925; Cather, 1926; Michelson, 1927.

Galsworthy, John. "Reminiscences of Conrad," *Scribner's Magazine*, 77 (January, 1925), 9.

Hergesheimer, Joseph. Introduction, *The Red Badge of Courage* and "The Veteran." In *The Work of Stephen Crane*, vol. 1, ed. Wilson Follett. New York, 1925, pp. ix–xvii.
Recounts his experience in 1895 on first reading *The Red Badge,* which was then regarded as "fantastically modern." One image in it became particularly celebrated: "The red sun was pasted in the sky like a wafer." That image came to be regarded "in one camp as a superb piece of imagery, a line which invested one of the oldest of observations with a new and living freshness and vigour; and by the other as a strained and artificial figure." Hergesheimer thought of it as "an actual red wafer such as druggists fixed to their bottles. . . . The sun itself diminished, in the sky like a wafer, a wafer of glazed vermilion paper with a regularly serrated edge."
Edmund Wilson in 1953 thought of it as "obviously the small red sticker that is affixed to legal documents." (In *The New Yorker* [May 2, 1953], unsigned review of *Omnibus.)*
Williams in *Courier* (1962) says that wafers were commonly used in Crane's time, but the fact is that the sealing wafer had long gone out of use since the Civil War, as Dounce points out (1917).
That Crane derived his image of the red sun pasted in the sky like a wafer from a literary source, namely Rudyard Kipling's image of the sun in *The Light That Failed* (1891), was first noticed by Osborn (1951).

Herzberg, Max J. "Stephen Crane and the 'Mulberry Blues,'" *Newark Sunday Call,* July 18, 1925.

———. Introduction, *The Red Badge of Courage*. New York, 1925, pp. v–xli. Introduction and Notes to *The Red Badge of Courage*. New York, 1926, Appleton Modern Literature Series.
Reprinted New York, Pocket Books editions, 1942, 1954.

Errs in claiming that Crane in 1890 "spent two terms at Lafayette College, and the next year he was at Syracuse University." Quotes Clarence N. Goodwin on Crane at Syracuse and Ripley Hitchcock's 1900 Introduction to *The Red Badge*. Also Irving Bacheller, Thomas L. Masson, and Ralph D. Paine. Presents Stephen's letter to his namesake, Stephen Crane of Port Jervis, son of Edmund. Herzberg errs in stating Crane was buried in the family plot at Elizabeth, N.J. (He makes the same error in his sketch of Crane in the *Encyclopaedia Britannica*.) Quotes appraisals of Crane by H. G. Wells, Arnold Bennett, John Galsworthy, Theodore Dreiser, Floyd Dell, and Rebecca West.

————. "Stephen Crane: A Pioneer Novelist," *World Review*, 1 (October 19, 1925), 74.

Hunter, Irene, ed. *American Mystical Verse: An Anthology*. Preface by Zona Gale. New York, 1925.

Littledale, Clara S. "Newark Discovers a Little Brick Shrine," *New York Herald Tribune* (Book Supplement), November 15, 1925, p. 4.

Crane's Birthplace, No. 14 Mulberry Place, Newark, N.J. "The vivid outlines of the men, women and children who live in his books must have come to him as he spent long evenings before the open fire of 14 Mulberry Place." (However, youngster Stephen could hardly have had such thoughts when he lived here for the first four years of his life!) *See also* [Anon.], "Playlot to Rise" (1940).

Macy, John. *The Story of the World's Literature*. New York, 1925 and 1950, p. 538.

Nash, Ogden. "Little and Better," *Book Dial*, Autumn, 1925.

A note on *The Red Badge of Courage*.

Overton, Grant. *Portrait of a Publisher*. New York and London, 1925, pp. 76–77.

Pennell, Joseph. *The Adventures of an Illustrator*. Boston, 1925, p. 105.

". . .the best story of the Battle of the Wilderness, or any battle, is Stephen Crane's *Red Badge of Courage*."

Van Doren, Carl and Mark. *American and British Literature Since 1890*, New York, 1925.

Van Doren, Mark. "First Glance," *Nation*, 121 (December 23, 1925), 736.

Review of *Work*. "I admit that Crane is a most difficult author to write about critically. . . . The precise excellence of *The Red Badge of Courage* deserves analysis. It has never got it, and Mr. Hergesheimer does not give it. . . . The analysis I speak of would begin, I suspect, with a more particular analysis of the one passion which Crane from his first story to his last was concerned with dissecting. Mr. Beer and others have pointed out that this was his fear, and obviously *The Red Badge of Courage* is among other things a study of fear." This was Beer's thesis in *SC;* it became Berryman's thesis in his biography, which again lacks any analysis of *The Red Badge of Courage*.

1926

Anderson, Sherwood. Introduction, *Midnight Sketches*. In *The Work of Stephen Crane*, vol. 11, ed. Wilson Follett. New York, 1926, pp. xi–xv.
"Writers in America who do not know their Stephen Crane are missing a lot. Suppose he did put a pretty little patent-leather finish on some of his later tales. Take him for what he was—his importance. Think of what was going on all around him then. All the painters of that day painting in low tones—going in for facile brush work. The arts all grey. Grey cities, grey people. A young man coming along, not too strong physically, touched with consumption, broke most of his life. Standing up against the almost universal greyness of the art expression of his day. Putting in great splashes of colour. . . . He did a lot. He was an explosion all right. It's about time people began to hear the explosion."

[Anon.]. "First Editions in Demand for the Last Four Years," *Biblio*, July, 1926.

——. "Recollections of Stephen Crane," *English Journal*, June, 1926.

——. "The All Star Literary Vaudeville," *New Republic*, 47 (June 30, 1926), 162–163.
When we consider Henry James, Stephen Crane, and lesser novelists like Howells, we are struck with their superiority over writers of today. They were better craftsmen. "Note the intense artistic integrity, the incapacity for careless work of even Stephen Crane, who passed for a clever newspaper man and an outlaw to respectable literature; but whose work astonishes us now by its quality, by no means incomparable—as how much of our present fiction is?—to the best European work in the same kind."

Aubry, Georges Jean, ed. *Twenty Letters to Joseph Conrad*. London, 1926. Contains two letters from Stephen Crane.

Beer, Thomas. *The Mauve Decade*. New York, 1926. Introduction by Leonard Bacon.
Reprinted in Beer, *Hanna, Crane, and the Mauve Decade* (1941).
On Crane, pp. 59, 92, 114, 126, 139, 152, 182–183, 191, 198, 214, 224, 226, 250. *Reviewed: See* under Beer's SC (1923).

——. Introduction, *The O'Ruddy*. In *The Work of Stephen Crane*, vols. 7–8, ed. Wilson Follett. New York, 1926, pp. ix–xv.

Cather, Willa. Introduction, *Wounds in the Rain*. In *The Work of Stephen Crane*, vol. 9, ed. Wilson Follett. New York, 1926, pp. ix–xiv.
"The sketches in this volume are most of them low-pressure writing, done during, or soon after, Crane's illness in Cuba. He hadn't the vitality to make stories, to pull things together into a sharp design—though 'The Price of the Harness' just misses being a fine war story." Echoes Edward Garnett (1898) and Joseph Conrad in pronouncing Crane to be one of the first post-Impressionist painters in prose.
" 'The red sun was pasted in the sky like a wafer,' that careless observation which Mr. Hergesheimer admires so much, isn't exceptional with Crane. (He wrote like that when he was writing well.) What about the clouds, and the light on the hills, and the background, and the foreground?

Well, Crane left that for his successors to write, and they have been doing it ever since: accounting for everything, as trustees of an estate are supposed to do, thoroughly good business methods applied to art; 'doing' landscapes and interiors like house-decorators, putting up the curtains and tacking down the carpets. . . . He is rather the best of our writers in what is called 'description' because he is the least describing."

Conrad, Jessie. "Recollections of Stephen Crane," *Bookman*, 63 (April, 1926), 134–137.

Reprinted, but with portions expunged, in Conrad, *Joseph Conrad and His Circle* (1935).

Conrad, Joseph. "His War Book," in *Last Essays*. New York, 1926, pp. 93–124. London, 1926, pp. 119–124. *See also* Conrad (1925) (1928) (1937).

———. "Stephen Crane: A Preface to Thomas Beer's *Stephen Crane*," in *Last Essays*. London and New York, 1926, 1928, 1955.

On Crane's method of composition; on their first meeting in London in October, 1897; Conrad sees Crane off for Cuba. Prints Crane's letter of March 17, 1898, misdated for 1899. In *Letters*, pp. 176–177. "The happiest mental pictures my wife and I preserve of Crane is on the occasion of our first visit to Brede Place when he rode to meet us at the Park Gate. He looked at his best on horseback."

Crane, Helen. "In New Jersey," *Newark Star-Eagle*, July 7, 1926, p. 10. Recast from the *New Orleans Picayune*.

Reprinted in the *Kansas City Times*, July 22, 1926.

———. "In New Jersey," *Newark Star-Eagle*, July 8, 1926, p. 12.

"Stephen Crane, my uncle, possibly never saw the Bowery until he went there in search of color." Mrs. Crane, in her capacities as president of the Women's Christian Temperance Union, "found her duties sometimes a bit strenuous for her tiny, frail body; for besides her newspaper work and temperance lecturing there were the many calls made upon a popular preacher's wife. . . . When too sorely pressed she would turn the column over to the charge of her son. He loved his mother very sincerely, but could not resist teasing her now and then.

"My father [Wilbur] told us how my grandmother, not being in any sense a horse-woman, never appreciated the difference between forelock and fetlock. She always planned her work and campaigns like a general marshaling his forces in review before battle, and in her planning said she was trying to 'catch Time by the fetlock.' She never could quite remember, even though Stephen solemnly assured her several times that she would get her head kicked off if she were not more careful."

Davis, Robert H. *Over My Left Shoulder*. New York, 1926.

The dust jacket claims that Davis, editor of *Munsey's Magazine*, is a famous editor who "has influenced the careers of such celebrities as . . . Stephen Crane." Davis, however, met Crane only once in 1896 and influenced Crane not in the slightest. *See* Davis's Introduction to *Work*, vol. 2 (1925).

Follett, Wilson. Introduction, *The Monster* and *The Third Violet*. In *The Work of Stephen Crane*, vol. 3, ed. Wilson Follett. New York, 1926, pp. ix–xxii.

"He was at bottom so little of a realist that it remained to the end impossible for him to make any significant, beautiful, or even graceful use of his own experiences until he had got so far away from them that they might as well have been anybody's experiences. . . . Crane was greatest when imagination and intuition enabled him to present experiences which he never had. He was next greatest when this or that experience of his own made its strongest appeal to his impersonal qualities, his power of excited spectatorship, while leaving his more intimate feelings unaroused. He was least great when he mixed his ink with some animus of his own, or when, pressed for material and working in haste, he merely flung in details from the mental notebook of an ex-reporter." Shellfire and bayonets "had nothing of surpassing value to give to the boy who had written 'The Little Regiment' and *The Red Badge of Courage* without experience of them, and . . . artistically speaking, it was a waste and therefore a mistake for him to go to Greece and to Cuba." The same standpoint is Stallman's in *Omnibus,* pp. xxiv–xxxi: "Crane wasted his genius."

Liebling (1961) takes issue with that claim.

Reviewed: Ford Madox Ford, *New York Herald Tribune,* January 2, 1927.

Herman Mankiewicz, *New York Times Book Review,* January 10, 1927. And its publication prompted other essays on Crane, such as Robert Littell's article, *New Republic* (May 16, 1928).

Herzberg, Max J. *Stephen Crane and the Stephen Crane Association.* Leaflet. Newark, N.J., 1926.

Includes a bibliography.

Hind, C. Lewis. *Naphtali.* New York, 1926, pp. 121–122.

A scant notice about Crane. *See* Hind, (1921).

Hunt, Violet. *The Flurried Years.* London, 1926, p. 41.

Calls Crane the "cranky" Stephen Crane.

Johnson, Willis Fletcher. "The Launching of Stephen Crane," *Literary Digest International Book Review,* 4 (April, 1926), 288–290.

Claims Crane brought him two Sullivan County sketches in the summer of 1891. Also: "One day in the summer of 1891 he brought me a big bundle of manuscript and asked me to read it and tell him what to do with it. I found it to be not a Sullivan County sketch, but a tale of the slums of New York; the first draft of *Maggie: A Girl of the Streets.* It was in some respects crude, but powerful and impressive. Three features were conspicuous. One was the writer's mastery of the speech and manners of the denizens of the New York slums, altho he had spent little time in that city and had enjoyed little opportunity for observation of its ways. . . ." (However, the size of the bundle indicates that it was not the first draft which Peaslee and Noxon testify was written in their Delta Upsilon house at Syracuse University in the Spring of 1891.)

Johnson discredits Beer's account of the report of the parade of American Mechanics at Asbury Park by Crane in the *Tribune,* August 21, 1892, and also Max Herzberg's speculations about the consequences of that article, "On the New Jersey Coast." However, Johnson errs in calling it a Labor Day parade.

He insists that neither he nor Stephen was fired by the *Tribune.* However, research shows that nothing by Crane appeared in the *Tribune* for 1893, nor after September, 1892. William declared that Townley was fired and that this crisis broke him. *See* Oliver (1931), Honce (1942), Elconin (1948), and Crane.

Lowell, Amy. Introduction, *The Black Riders and Other Lines.* In *The Work of Stephen Crane,* vol. 6, ed. Wilson Follett. New York, 1926, pp. ix–xxix.

"If Emily Dickinson cannot be made to stand for Crane's form, where did he find it? I think in the Bible. The son of a mother who was also a Methodist preacher must have been extremely familiar with the Bible. . . . Crane was so steeped in the religion in which he was brought up that he could not get it out of his head. He disbelieved it and he hated it, but he could not free himself from it. A loathed and vengeful God broods over *The Black Riders*. Crane's soul was heaped with bitterness, and this bitterness he flung back at the theory of life which had betrayed him. . . .

"Crane's theme in *The Black Riders* is two-fold. It is at once the cruelty of universal law, and the futility of hope. It is a creed of gall and aloes, and Crane believed it. It is the key to his life."

These insights have earned permanence, but Miss Lowell cannot resist sentimentalizing the young poet dying before his time: "He died too soon. He did much, but the temperature of the world he lived in was unsuitable. He ranks in America somewhat as Chatterton ranks in England. A boy, spiritually killed by neglect. A marvellous boy, potentially a genius, historically an important link in the chain of American poetry."

Mankiewicz, Herman J. "The Literary Craft of Stephen Crane," *New York Times Book Review*, January 10, 1926, p. 7.

A review of *Work*, vol. 1, *The Red Badge of Courage* and *The Veteran* (1925). Introduction by Joseph Hergesheimer.

The Red Badge is far more than a war book; it is "a literary exercise on the grand scale. . . . But Crane was clearly little interested in his hero, or in whether war be good or evil; it was the business of words, of applying them to the canvas, of putting them one after the other, that concerned him." Joseph Hergesheimer* recognizes that it is rather an exercise of some sort. He remembers the ado made in his own youth about Crane's "The red sun was pasted in the sky like a wafer," which "can mean nothing if Crane really meant it to mean anything actual," and he "decides that Crane was being universal, symbolical and allegorical. The words symbolical and allegorical, to be sure, are not Mr. Hergesheimer's, though the sense is his. And thus Mr. Hergesheimer would make of *The Red Badge of Courage*, great in its outpourings of a mind that loved words and thoughts, their color and their movement, a book that tells a great truth, the American *Passing of the Third Floor Back*, perhaps, or even our own *The Light That Failed*."† "There are to *The Red Badge of Courage* those ironies, that inherent cynicism and sardonic eye, that there are in everything Crane wrote. (It is in these things, for instance, that there lies the difference between the *Whilomville Stories* and Mr. Tarkington's pleasant and devitalized tales.)

"Even the central character of *The Red Badge of Courage* is a bloodless creature, a literary device. . . . And there he is, that the red sun might be pasted in the sky like a wafer, that there might appear upon the glazed vacancy of his eyes a diamond point of intelligence, that the distance might splinter and blare with the noise of fighting, that the moon might be lighted and hung in a treetop, that the red sun might be pasted in the sky like a wafer. . . .

---

* My reading of religious symbolism in *The Red Badge* in the Introduction to the Modern Library edition (1951) was encouraged by Hergesheimer's suggestive comments; also by Willa Cather's in her Introduction to vol. 9 and by Amy Lowell's insights on *The Black Riders*, vol. 6.

† *See also* Osborn (1951) and Stallman, "The Scholar's Net: Literary Sources" (1955).

"There will be more of Crane. And in the meantime the business of starting off each new year with a reprinting of *The Red Badge of Courage* would give the succeeding twelve-month an interesting and, for the most part, an unattainable goal to strive for."

Mencken, H. L. Introduction, *Major Conflicts.* In *The Work of Stephen Crane,* vol. 10, ed. Wilson Follett. New York, 1926, pp. ix–xiii.

Contra Amy Lowell in Introduction to vol. 6 of *Work,* Mencken rightly points out that Crane, like most writers of the nineties, "suffered sorely, not from neglect, but from too much appreciation. The magazines bombarded him with orders, and he was also beset by the newspaper syndicates, then on a high tide of prosperity, and more often than not he succumbed to them. The result was a great deal of hurried and third-rate work. There was no time to ponder and revise; sometimes there was not even time enough to get an idea firmly by the tail."

The appearance of *The Red Badge,* which was "at once unprecedented and irresistible," gave the whole movement of the nineties "a sudden direction and a powerful impulse forward. At one stroke realism was made its goal— not the old flabby, kittenish realism of Howells's imitators, with its puerile labouring of trivialities, but the sterner, more searching realism that got under the surface—the new realism that was presently to flower in *McTeague* and then in *Sister Carrie,* and then in a whole procession of books. . . ." And more, perhaps than any other book, *The Red Badge* "made the thing we call American literature to-day."

Phelps, William Lyon. Introduction, *Whilomville Stories.* In *The Work of Stephen Crane,* vol. 5, ed. Wilson Follett. New York, 1926, pp. ix–xiii.

"Stephen Crane was a curious compound of patience and impatience. As a man he was wildly impatient with hypocrisy, cant, pretence, falsehood, brutality, sentimentalism, injustice, and cruelty; as an artist, he was unendingly patient in dealing with these very things." However, on Crane's *Whilomville Stories* Phelps says nothing worth quoting.

Shay, Felix. *Elbert Hubbard of East Aurora.* New York, 1926, pp. 41–43, 365, 384, 508. Foreword by Henry Ford.

Shay edited the *Philistine* and the *Fra,* from which he reprints two W. W. Denslow caricatures of Crane. On Crane's visit at East Aurora. On Hubbard *see* Daly (1916).

Sidbury, Edna Crane. "My Uncle, Stephen Crane, as I Knew Him," *Literary Digest International Book Review,* 4 (March, 1926), 248–250.

Important. Errs in claiming that Mrs. Mary Helen Peck was a graduate of the College of the City of New York. Stephen's mother was not educated in any university or college. Gullason (1963) repeats Sidbury's error.

Two Letters from Stephen Crane to Joseph Conrad. London: First Editions Club, 1926.

Pamphlet consisting of four unnumbered pages bound in orange-red paper wrappers, printed at the Curwen Press in a limited edition, 220 copies. The first letter is in praise of *The Nigger of the "Narcissus,"* and the second is an invitation to visit at Oxted.

Van Doren, Carl. "Stephen Crane," in *American Mercury: Readings from the American Mercury,* ed. Grant C. Knight. New York, 1926, pp. 97–106. Reprinted from *American Mercury,* 1 (January 1924), 11–24.

———. Introduction, *Active Service*. In *The Work of Stephen Crane*, vol. 4, ed. Wilson Follett. New York, 1926, pp. ix–xv.

Warren, Dale. "The Posthumous Fame of Stephen Crane," *Boston Transcript*, September 4, 1926. With photograph of a plaque of Crane's profile by Seumas O'Brien.

Wickham, Harvey. "Stephen Crane at College," *American Mercury*, 7 (March, 1926), 291–297.

Important memoirs of Crane at Claverack College by a schoolmate who disliked him. "The vaunted Crane realism was never of the photographic sort. Thus the only incident which really happened [in *George's Mother*] was George's amazing lunch—a charlotte russe and a beer." Claims that Crane wrote some *Black Riders* poems while camping at Twin Lakes, Pennsylvania. However, the lunch of a charlotte russe and beer occurs in *Maggie*, not in *George's Mother*.

1927

Aubry, George Jean, ed. *Joseph Conrad: Life and Letters*, vol. 1. Garden City, N.Y., 1927, pp. 166, 211, 220, 228, 235, 294–295. *Lettres françaises*. Paris, 1929.

Conrad to Edward Garnett, December 5, 1897, is quoted below in Garnett (1928).

"To R. B. Cunningham Graham 7th Jan. '98 'The man [Crane] sees the outside of many things and the inside of some.'

"To E. L. Sanderson 3rd. Feb. '98. 'Stephen Crane is worrying me to write a play with him. He won't believe me when I swear by all the gods and all the muses that I have no dramatic gift. Probably something will be attempted but I would bet nothing shall be done.'

"To —— 23rd April, 1898 'It is a sore temptation, but I don't think I ought to review Crane's last book. The excellent fellow in the goodness of his heart has been praising me beyond my merits on his own side of the water and his generous utterances have been quoted here. I've not enough standing and reputation to put me above the suspicion of swinging back the censer. Consequently my review would do not good to Crane's work [*The Open Boat and Other Stories*], which deserves a warm appreciation.'

"To John Galsworthy Thursday, May [7], 1900. 'Went to see Crane yesterday at Dover. Been with him 20 minutes. . . . I was awfully shocked of course and had to put on jolly manners. He may yet escape.' See *Letters*.

Beffel, John N. "The Fauntleroy Plague," *Bookman*, 65 (March, 1927), 135–141.

Ford, Ford Madox. "Stevie & Co.," *New York Herald Tribune* (Book Supplement), January 2, 1927, pp. 1, 6.

Reprinted in Ford, *New York Essays* (1927), pp. 21–32.

Memoirs of Crane in England prompted by the publication of *Work* in twelve volumes for $90. "But who is going to be able to possess it? Only the most fortunate!" Ford prefers *The Third Violet* to *The Monster*. On Crane and Henry James. Cf. Ford, "Two Americans" (1921), Ford, "Stevie" (1924), and Ford, "Stephen Crane" (1936).

———. *New York Essays*. New York, 1927, pp. 21–32. Reprints "Stevie & Co. from the *New York Herald Tribune*.

Johnson, Merle. "My Adventures with Stephen Crane," *Bookseller and Print Dealers Weekly*," 2, no. 63 [*Bookseller and Collector*] (December 8, 1927), 6.
  The real boom in the Crane market began with Beer's *SC* (1923) because of its Introduction by Joseph Conrad—that is why collectors bought the Beer book about Crane. "American collectors discovered Crane by way of Conrad!"

Maurice, Arthur Bartlett. "Old Bookman Days," *Bookman*, 66 (September, 1927), 20–26.

Michelson, Charles. Introduction, *The Open Boat and Other Tales*. In *The Work of Stephen Crane*, vol. 15, ed. Wilson Follett. New York, 1927, pp. ix–xxiv.
  With Crane in the Puerto Rican campaign, off San Juan on a tugboat and at Ponce. Crane never got seasick. How Crane "captured" the town of Juana Diaz. On Crane as journalist compared with Richard Harding Davis. *See also* Davis (1904), and Michelson (1944).

Sheridan, Claire. *Nuda Veritas*. London, 1927.

Sherman, S. P. *The Main Stream*. New York, 1927, p. 160.
  Refers to Crane in his chapter on Beer, "Our Petronius at Last."

Wells, H. G. "Wells Assays the Culture of America," *New York Times Book Review*, May 15, 1927.

1928

Bacheller, Irving Addison. *Coming Up the Road*. Indianapolis, Ind., 1928, pp. 236, 276–279, 292–293, 298, 305.
  On Crane's bringing him the *Red Badge of Courage* manuscript—"a bit soiled from much handling. It had not been typed." On the founding of the Lantern Club, pages 280–284. On sending Crane to Cuba with $700 in Spanish gold, after his trip to Mexico for Bacheller's syndicate, pages 292–293. Bacheller errs in saying that Sylvester Scovel was with Crane on the *Commodore* and in the open boat.

Conrad, Joseph. "His War Book," in *Tales of Hearsay and Last Essays*. London: Dent, 1928, 1955, pp. 119–124. In *Last Essays* (1926).
  On *The Red Badge of Courage*, his Preface to the London edition, 1925.

Garnett, Edward, ed. *Letters from Joseph Conrad: 1895–1924*. Indianapolis, Ind., 1928, pp. 11–12, 26, 115, 118–119, 128, 130, 148, 276, 289–290.
  "[October 14, 1897.] 'I shall go to town tomorrow to meet P[awling] and Crane. I *do* admire him. I shan't have to pretend. I'm having a tussle with the *Rescue*.'
  "5th Dec. 1897. 'I had Crane here last Sunday. We talked and smoked half the night. He is strangely hopeless about himself. I like him. The two stories are excellent. Of course *A Man and Some Others* is the best of the two but the boat thing [*The Open Boat*] interested me more. His eye is very individual and his expression satisfies me artistically. He certainly is *the* impressionist and his temperament is curiously unique. His thought is concise, con-

nected, never very deep—yet often startling. He is *the only* impressionist and *only* an impressionist. Why is he not immensely popular? With his strength, with his rapidity of action, with that amazing faculty of vision—why is he not? He has outline, he has colour, he has movement, with that he ought to go very far. But—will he? I sometimes think he won't. It is not an opinion—it is a feeling. I could not explain why he disappoints me—why my enthusiasm withers as soon as I close the book. While one reads, of course he is not to be questioned. He is the master of his reader to the very last line—then—apparently for no reason at all—he seems to let go his hold. It is as if he had gripped you with greased fingers. His grip is strong but while you feel the pressure on your flesh you slip out from his hand—much to your own surprise. That is my stupid impression and I give it to you in confidence. It just occurs to me that it is perhaps my own self that is slippery, I don't know. *You* would know. No matter.

"January 15, 1898. 'Crane wrote me, also, a penitent letter for not replying to mine at Xmas. He says he finds it easier to write *about* me than to me. Says he has written about me, but *where* he says not.

"[February 2, 1898] 'The Cranes have invited the lot of us man woman and child to stay with them ten days—from 19th February—and I've accepted for I feel that if there is no break I will go crazy or go out altogether.'

"[December 18, 1898.] 'The Crane thing [*Stephen Crane: An Appreciation*] is just—precisely just a ray flashed in and showing all there is.'

"'17.1. '21. 'I agree with your opinion of these "War pieces." Oh yes! They are good. And truly in all the work he left behind him there is nothing that could be dismissed as rubbish. For even the *Third Violet* is merely a characteristic failure.'

"March 10, 1923. 'Life is full of surprises! One of them certainly was Mr. Beer, who had communicated with me through dear old Hamlin Garland some time last July or August. I was under the impression I had told you something about it; but truth to say I attached no importance whatever to the episode which had something to do with a batch of Mrs. Crane's letters.* Anyway I knew that there was such a person, and that a biography of Crane was in contemplation.' "

Howells, Mildred, ed. *Life in Letters of William Dean Howells,* vol. 2. New York, 1928, p. 42.
  Crane's letter of gratitude to Howells, January 1, 1896.
  Reprinted in *Letters,* p. 93.

Littell, Robert. "Notes on Stephen Crane," *New Republic,* 54 (May 16, 1928), 391–392.
  "The American Dozen—no matter how you choose the team of writers, Crane is one of them. Squabble over the eleven other All-Americans, write down Poe and scratch him out, accept Mark Twain, and William James and Abraham Lincoln, be ruthless with Longfellow, and doubtful about Bierce and Howells, but you will have to keep Stephen Crane."

McCormick, Lawler [Peter Molyneaux]. "If Stephen Crane Had Returned to Texas," *Bunker's Monthly,* 1 (February, 1928), 316–318.
  See Molyneaux (1929).

* In his biography of Crane (1923) Thomas Beer deliberately slighted Crane's connection with Cora Taylor and mentions her only a few times; he knew her past but preferred to ignore Cora so as not to offend the Crane family. *See* Crane.

Marble, Annie Russell. *A Study of the Modern Novel.* New York, 1928 and 1930, pp. 7, 264–266, 364.

Noxon, Frank W. "The Real Stephen Crane," *Chicago Step-Ladder,* 14 (January, 1928), 4–9.

This was originally a letter addressed to Max J. Herzberg of the Stephen Crane Association, December 7, 1926, which was published in *Letters,* pp. 334–339.

"He told me that a passage in Goethe analyzed the effect which the several colors have upon the human mind. Upon Crane this had made a profound impression, and he had utilized the idea to produce his effects."

Maggie, "at least in its early form, was wholly or in part written at Syracuse. With typical carelessness the author left the sheets lying about in the front corner room with Norton Goodwin. Some of these pages were picked up and read by droppers-in."

On the first draft of *Maggie* see Peaslee (1896) and Johnson (1926).

Whyte, Frederic. *William Heinemann: A Memoir.* London, 1928, pp. 147, 170.

Winkler, John K. *W. R. Hearst: An American Phenomenon.* New York, 1928, pp. 68, 102, 108, 133.

1929

[Anon.]. "Stephen Crane Confounds His Doctor," *New York Times Book Review,* May 26, 1929, p. 8.

Photograph of the water color by George Van Werveke, showing Crane in bed during his last illness; original owned by C. W. Barrett. *See* Barrett (1969).

Bohnenberger, Carl, and Norman Mitchell Hill, eds. "The Letters of Joseph Conrad to Stephen and Cora Crane," *Bookman,* 69 (May, 1929), 225–235, (June, 1929), 367–374.

Reprinted in *Letters.*

Bragdon, Claude. "The Purple Cow Period," *Bookman,* 69 (July, 1929*), 475–478.

On Elbert Hubbard and the little magazines of the 1890s. A pen-portrait of "Fra Elbertus," Hubbard: "pungent, abusive, witty, knowing, vulgar. Hubbard apparently dramatized himself as a sort of composite of Ralph Waldo Emerson and William Morris, but his chief claim to fame is that of being the Father of Modern Advertising." Important is Bragdon's account of Hubbard's Philistine Society banquet intended for honoring Crane on December 19, 1895. *See also* Harry Tabor's account in the Tom Daly article (1916), a recently discovered exposé of Hubbard not noticed by Freeman Champney in *Art and Glory (1968). See also Crane* on Hubbard, and Taber (1923, 1940).

———. *Merely Players.* New York, 1929, pp. 67–70. Reissued 1965. First published in 1905.

On Crane at the Society of the Philistine's banquet.

* Not 1928 as given in *W-S Bibliography.*

See also Daly (1916), Bragdon (1929), *Letters*, Dirlam (1964), Champney (1968), and *Crane*.

Conrad, Joseph. [Conrad's letters to Stephen Crane and Cora Crane], *New York Times Book Review*, April 21, 1929.
    Advertisement by *Bookman* for the forthcoming Conrad letters. Portrait of Crane. See Bohnenberger (1929).

Follett, Wilson. "The Second Twenty-Eight Years: A Note on Stephen Crane," *Bookman*, 68 (January, 1929), 532–537.
    Also published as a leaflet by the Stephen Crane Association, Newark, N.J. (January, 1930).

Ford, Ford Madox. *The English Novel*. Philadelphia, 1929, pp. 142–149.
    The three names in the nineties having importance for the student of the English novel are Henry James, Stephen Crane, and Joseph Conrad. About that triad "there was a certain solidarity, a certain oneness of method and even a certain comradship. They lived in the same corner of England, saw each other often and discussed literary methods more thoroughly and more frequently than can ever at any other time in England have been the case." This triad, says Ford, "Techniques" (1935), was "almost equally the protagonists of literary impressionism in Anglo-Saxondom." (In sum, the three authors, in effect, subscribed to the credo Conrad expressed in his Preface to *The Nigger of the "Narcissus."*)

Grattan, C. Hartley. *Bitter Bierce*. Garden City, N.Y., 1929, pp. 44–45, 132, 143, 273.
    Grattan doubts that Bierce had any influence on Crane. However, for the influence of Bierce on Crane *see* Stallman, "Stephen Crane: A Revaluation" (1952) and *Omnibus; see also Poetry, SCTS*, and *Crane*.

Johnson, Merle. *American First Editions*. New York, 1929, pp. 54–56.
    A checklist of first editions.

——. *High Spots of American Literature*. New York: Bennett Book Studies, 1929, pp. 25–26.
    Notes on *The Red Badge of Courage* and *War Is Kind*.

Kennel, R., trans. *Stephen Crane: Pace of Youth*. Preface, R. Kennel. Moscow, 1929.
    Contains also "The Snake," "A Tent in Agony," and "Four Men in a Cave."

Lemperly, Paul. *Among My Books*. Cleveland, Ohio, 1929, p. 44.
    Crane's inscription in an 1893 *Maggie* (August 29, 1896), quoted in *Letters*, p. 129, was to Paul Lemperly, whereas *Letters* says To an Unknown Recipient. *Letters* quotes from C. W. Barrett's copy, which does not identify the former owner of this *Maggie*. See Monteiro, "Paul Lemperly's *Maggie* (1893)" (1969). *See also* Lemperly (1940).

Manly, John Matthews, and Edith Richert. *Contemporary American Literature: Bibliographical and Study Outlines*. New York, 1929, p. 27.
    "Of the group consisting of Stephen Crane (1871–1900), Frank Norris (1870–1902), and Jack London (1876–1916), the work of Stephen Crane seems to be of greatest absolute and historical interest. He combined a poetically sensitive observation and an unfashionable creed of unqualified realism that make him seem a creature born out of his time."

Molyneaux, Peter. "Had Stephen Crane Returned," *Texas Monthly,* 3 (April, 1929), 503–507. Reprinted from *Bunker's Monthly,* 1 (February 1928) under Lawler McCormick [Peter Molyneaux].
 See McCormick (1928).

Munson, Gorham. "Prose for Fiction: Stephen Crane," in *Style and Form in American Prose.* New York, 1929, pp. 159–170. Reprinted Port Washington, N.Y., 1969.
 A perceptive scrutiny of "The Open Boat."

Overton, Grant. *An Hour of the American Novel.* Philadelphia and London, 1929, pp. 72–76, 79–80, 104, 109.

——. *High Spots of American Literature.* New York, 1929, pp. 25–26.

——. "Do You Remember? *The Red Badge of Courage,*" *Mentor,* 17 (October, 1929), 45, 62.

Ridge, W. Pett. *I Like to Remember.* New York: n.d. [1929?], pp. 210–211.

 "When, after he had written *Maggie,* and the still more wonderful *Red Badge of Courage,* Crane paid his visits to England, he never seemed to be closely accompanied by good health. Once, at Rye, he was taken ill, and the local doctor came in.

 'Now, Mr. Crane,' said the doctor breezily, 'let us take the question of meals. What is your appetite like in the early morning, eh?'

 'Fine, doc., fine.'

 'That's very good to hear. Tell me, what did you have for breakfast this morning?'

 'Double the usual quantity.'

 'Oh, splendid!' cried the local man, with something like rapture.

 'I had,' Stephen Crane went on, 'two brandies and soda instead of one.' "

Taupin, René. *L'influence des symbolistes français sur la poesie americaine de 1910 à 1920.* Paris, 1929.

1930

Adams, George Matthew. "I Buy a Rare Book," *News,* September 25, 1930.

American Art Association: Anderson Galleries. March 11–12, 1930. Sale 3827.
 No. 76. "The Rarest Book in Modern American Literature: A Presentation Copy with a Long Inscription by the Author." A copy of the 1893 *Maggie* (sold to Dr. Isaac Rosenbach for $3,700).
 The catalogue is here quoted: "The excessively rare privately printed first edition. Presentation copy, inscribed on the front wrapper: 'Stephen Crane to Budgon [Lucius L. Button]. [Same inscription as to Lucius L. Button, transcribed in John T. Winterich's *23 Books* (1939), p. 124; in *Omnibus,* 1952, p. 594; in *Letters,* p. 14. Quoted in "A Census (Part III)," *SCraneN,* 3, no. 3 (Spring, 1969), 10–11.] It is inevitable that you will be greatly shocked by this book but continue, please, with all possible courage, to the end. For it tries to show that environment is a tremendous thing in the world and

frequently shapes lives regardless. If one proves that theory one makes room in Heaven for all sorts of souls, notably an occasional street girl, who are not confidently expected to be there by many excellent people. It is probable that the reader of this small thing may consider the author to be a bad man, but obviously that is a matter of small consequence to The Author.' At the top of the wrapper the recipient, Lucius L. Button, has written his name. . . .

"Presentation copies of even Crane's common books are virtually unobtainable. Some time before the publication of *Maggie,* Crane took up residence at a boarding house in Eastern Avenue [Avenue A] where lived a group of young medical men. Here began the friendship between the young reporter and Lucius L. Button. Not long after, Crane, discouraged by the innumerable rejections of *Maggie,* and having come into the possession of about a thousand dollars, determined to issue it in a cheap, paperback form designed to appeal to those who were dependent upon the news-stands for literary nourishment. The first copy from the bindery he brought home and presented to Button. . . . Button insisted upon the privilege of being the first to purchase the little book and dutifully paid its author the fifty cents. Such is the history of this book as related by Mrs. Button.

"The story of the reception of this, the first American ironic novel, is well known: it failed even to attain the notoriety of a news-stand circulation, and has now become THE RAREST BOOK IN MODERN AMERICAN LITERATURE. IT IS CERTAIN THAT NO MORE DESIRABLE COPY EXISTS THAN THE PRESENT ONE, WITH ITS LONG AND PERTINENT INSCRIPTION." *(See* frontispiece.)

Items 79, 80, 81, and 83 (Crane letters to Lucius L. Button, 1894, 1895, and 1896) were omitted from *Letters,* since their existence wasn't then known.

[Anon.], trans. *Das blaue Hotel.* Berlin: F. A. Herbig, 193–?

———. "Delta U's in the News," *Delta Upsilon Quarterly* (October 1930).
A note about the "discovery" of an unpublished Crane manuscript ("The Cry of a Huckleberry Pudding").

———. "Rare Book by Stephen Crane," *Delta Upsilon Quarterly,* October, 1930.
Note of sale of *Maggie* by Lucius Button's estate.

———. "When Genius Markets its Wares: Stephen Crane," *Golden Book,* 12 (September, 1930), 59.
On *Maggie: A Girl of the Streets.*

———. "Who's Who in the *Golden Book,*" *Golden Book,* 12 (December, 1930), 4–5.
Vincent Starrett and Stephen Crane.

———. "Notes on Rare Books," *New York Times Book Review and Magazine Section,* March 9, 1930.
Dr. Lucius Button's estate to sell a first edition of *Maggie.*

———. [Review of *The Collected Poems*], *Times Literary Supplement,* August 21, 1930, p. 671.
"His moods were often and reasonably embittered, but he tended merely to relieve his bitterness in verse instead of expressing it with an intensity that transcended the personal reaction. Much of his verse therefore was a kind of exasperated prose. . . ."

Cairns, William B. *A History of American Literature.* New York, 1912, pp. 484, 485–486, 487, 488, 505, 525. Rev. ed., 1930.

Campbell, Charles A. *Traditions of Hartwood.* Winter Park, Fla., 1930, p. 34.

Cox, Mrs. Martin L. "New Hero of Springfield Battle Revealed," *Sunday Call Magazine Section* (Newark), April 20, 1930.
  Fictionalized account of the heroism of one of Stephen Crane's ancestors during the American Revolution.*

Drake, J. F. "A Stephen Crane Letter," *Colophon,* 4 (December, 1930), 1–4.

Garland, Hamlin. "Crane the Bohemian," *Bookman,* 70 (January, 1930), 523–528. In "Roadside Meetings of a Literary Nomad."
  Reprinted in Garland, "Stephen Crane" (1930).

———. [Inscribed in *George's Mother,* 1896 edition], n.d.
  "As I read this book, now it appears an unimportant youthful venture. It is a lengthened, artificially colored transcript of life. It is Crane, the boy, telling of things he has seen but putting his own psychology into his observations. The English is admirable, concise, vivid and unfaltering. It will live only as a literary phase of a brilliant young literary man, whose later phrases were not much more important. Crane never quite grew up in any sense. Disease came in to weaken his will and death cut it short. His marvellous command of simple English words in his chief claim to distinction to me now as it was in the days when I first knew him."†

———. "Stephen Crane," in *Roadside Meetings,* New York, 1930, pp. 189–206. Reprinted from *Bookman,* 70 (January, 1930), 523–528.
  Collate with Garland's "Stephen Crane: A Soldier of Fortune," *Saturday Evening Post,* 173 (July 28, 1900), and with Garland's "Stephen Crane as I Knew Him," *Yale Review,* 3 (April, 1914). Reprinted in the *Syracusan* (December 1, 1917). Garland's *Roadside Meetings* is not listed in the *W-S Bibliography.*
  Did Crane bring Garland first the manuscript of his poems and then the manuscript of *The Red Badge,* or was it in reverse sequence? Garland in these variant and contradictory accounts has it both ways. Berryman's *Crane* ignored all accounts but that given in *Roadside Meetings;* Stallman in *Omnibus* collated Garland's variant memoirs and thereby erred, also in his note *versus* Berryman, p. 214. Not until Donald Pizer, having the advantage of Garland's journal and papers, disentangled Garland's confused chronology of events was the Crane chronology for early 1894 set straight. *See* Pizer, "The Garland-Crane Relationship" (1960). The Pizer data, an invaluable contribution to Crane scholarship, are incorporated in *Crane.*

Green, M. L. "The Stendhal of American Publications," *Revue de littérature comparee,* 10 (April, 1930), 311.
  Compares Crane's *The Red Badge of Courage* with Stendhal's *La Chartreuse de Parma.*

Gregory, Horace. "Stephen Crane's Poems," *New Republic,* 63 (June 25, 1930), 159–160.
  Review of *The Collected Poems of Stephen Crane,* ed. Wilson Follett. New York, 1930.

---

* For this annotation and many others in the period of 1920–1937, mainly Newark items, I am indebted to Carol Decker, compiler of the Crane catalogued collection at the Public Library of Newark, N.J. (1956). I am also indebted to Miss Decker for the gift of a copy of the catalogue (1956).

† Quoted here from University of Southern California Library.

The percentage "of genuinely youthful, spontaneous poetry is remarkably small. The production of such poetry demands technical precocity, and Stephen Crane was decidedly precocious in many ways. His work seems to anticipate many of the characteristics which the Imagists were destined to advertise some fifteen years after his death. There are times when Stephen Crane seems to resemble Ezra Pound most strikingly. . . .

"His talent is irresistible. . . . There is every reason to suppose that this will not be the last rediscovery of Stephen Crane's poems. That they will be lost again or neglected seems certain, for many of them are in the nature of a personal aside by a very young man of greater potentialities than he had time to develop. He was, however, a genuine artist; even the least important examples of his gift have a special quality of excellence."

Gurvic, V. *The Red Badge of Courage. Review of The Red Badge of Courage.* Moscow and Leningrad: Kniga and Revolutzia, 1930.

Herzberg, Max J. Introduction, *The Red Badge of Courage.* New York and London, 1930. First published 1925.

Reprinted in Modern Library edition, 1942.

Reprinted in Pocket Book edition, 1942. Quotes Clarence N. Goodwin, a classmate of Crane at Syracuse University with whom Crane shared a room in the Delta Upsilon fraternity-house in spring of 1891. "He somehow managed to combine perfect poise and assurance with a very gentle and diffident way of speaking. . . . He had a keen sense of the dramatic, and his countenance usually displayed an amused, satirical, but kindly grin. His keen mind instantly caught the absurd, bizarre, or ridiculous aspect of any incident, and he would draw out an account of it in his own entertaining fashion. . . . He saw into and through the conceits, hypocrisies, weaknesses, and selfishness of mankind, but continued to smile with amusement and without bitterness."

Quotes appraisals of Crane by Arnold Bennett, John Galsworthy, and Theodore Dreiser. A Crane letter to his namesake (twin son of Edmund) here quoted for the first time. Herzberg errs in saying that Crane spent two terms at Lafayette College in 1890 and that "the next year he was at Syracuse University." He also errs in saying that Crane was buried "in the family plot at Elizabeth, N.J." (The family plot was filled, and so Crane was buried at Hillside, N.J.)

———. "Stephen Crane and His Reputation." Introduction to *Stephen Crane: A List of His Writings and Articles About Him Compiled by B. J. R. Stolper for The Stephen Crane Association.* Newark, N.J., 1930.

Johnson, Allen, and Dumas Malone, eds. *Dictionary of American Biography,* vol. 4. New York, 1930, pp. 506–508.

Lists *Genealogy of the Crane Family* by E. B. Crane (1900). However, this book's genealogy of the Crane family is at radical odds with the "Newark Chart," an unidentifiable printed torn page in possession of the Newark Public Library. *Crane* draws mainly from this "Newark Chart" for data on the Crane family, and thus it stands at odds with other accounts, that given in Louis Zara's *Dark Rider,* for instance.

Josephson, Matthew. "The Voyage of Stephen Crane," in *Portrait of the Artist as American.* New York, 1930, pp. 232–263.

An interesting commentary on Crane's life, considering its early 1930 dating. Rightly corrects Beer's notion that Crane's preoccupation with fear "shows him an instinctive coward. It is more likely, however, in view of the premonitions that come to persons of tubercular predispositions, that he was morbidly interested in death as a theme which lent significance to life, which gave it form and style. . . ."

Versus Beer's thesis of fear—reiterated by Berryman—see *Omnibus*, pp. 188–189. *See also* Leaver (1962).

Lanna, Eugene. Introduction, *The Red Badge of Courage*. Trans. from English by A. V. Krivcova and Eugene Lanna. Preface by Joseph Conrad. Moscow and Leningrad: Zemljai Fabrika, 1930.

Mangione, Jerre G. "Stephen Crane's Unpublished Letters," *Chap Book* [Syracuse University Literary Magazine], 2 (May, 1930), 8–10.

On first looking into the Nellie Crouse letters, which Mangione was not permitted to quote from. They left him with the thought that author Crane differed radically from Crane the human being "who could not refer to his own life without suggesting a tense struggle going on within himself. It is the struggle between uncompromising realities and deeply rooted ideals, one which filled Crane's soul with irony and despair." An important insight here, although somewhat overstated on the given evidence of these letters. *See Letters*, p. ix.

Mims, Ella Puryear. "Stephen Crane's 'A Dark-Brown Dog' is My Favorite Story,' " *Golden Book*, 12 (December, 1930), 56.

Parrington, Vernon Louis. "The Beginnings of Critical Realism in America: 1860–1920," in *Main Currents in American Thought*, vol. 3. New York, 1927, 1930, pp. 327, 328–329, and *passim*.

The emergence of Naturalism ("a pessimistic realism that sets man in a mechanical world") is seen in Crane (p. xii). Sees *The Red Badge* as Naturalistic, because the individual is caught "between the external war machine and the inner instinct machine. . . . The hero is at the mercy of the crowd psychology and blind chance." A *tour de force*, it was inspired by Zola's *Le Débâcle*, "but more by Tolstoi—*War and Peace* and perhaps *Sebastopol*."

Pattee, F. L. *The New American Literature: 1890–1930*. New York and London, 1930, pp. 9, 54, 57, 64–72, 106, 211, 318, 358, 410.

Stolper, Benjamin J. R. *Stephen Crane: A List of His Writings and Articles About Him. . . .* Newark, N.J.: Public Library of Newark, N.J., 1930. (Compiled and published for the Stephen Crane Association.) *See also* Herzberg, "Stephen Crane and His Reputation" (1930).

Reviewed: "A Stephen Crane Bibliography," *Library* (Newark), March, 1931.

Walton, Eda Lou. "Stephen Crane: A Poet in Parables," *New York Times Book Review*, September 14, 1930, section 4, p. 2.

Review of *The Collected Poems of Stephen Crane*. New York, 1930.

"The truth is that Crane was not so much a poet as he was a writer of parables. His verses all take this old form: the balanced lines, the condensation of statement, the paradoxical suggestiveness in meaning; all conform to the old pattern of the parable. . . . But such precision of language alone cannot make poetry. Crane had no command of rhythm; his verse is utterly lacking in rhythmical persuasion. He had no very unique or telling imagery. He is always, moreover, rather more interested in being prophet than in being poet. . . . These parables will be read for their wisdom and their skepticism and not for their poetic quality."

Winterich, John T. "Romantic Stories of Books: *The Red Badge of Courage,*" *Publisher's Weekly,* 118 (September 20, 1930), 1303–1307.
    Reprinted in *23 Books and the Stories Behind Them* (1938).
    Recounts Crane's career, making the common error that Crane married Cora Taylor (in Greece). On the first edition of *The Red Badge of Courage,* bibliographical problems.

Winther, Sophus K. "The Realistic War Novel," *University of Washington Chapbooks,* no. 35 (1930).

1931

[Anon.]. "A Stephen Crane Bibliography," *Library* (Public Library, Newark, N.J.), March, 1931.
    A note on B. J. R. Stolper's Bibliography of Crane (1930).

Barney, E. C., "Stephen Crane," *Overland Monthly,* 90 (December, 1931), 309.

Bates, H. E. "Stephen Crane: A Neglected Genius," *Bookman,* 81 (October, 1931), 10–11. Portrait.
    The whole volume of *The Open Boat* "is like a collection of bright audacious paintings. Sometimes the stories remind one forcibly of the stories of Ernest Hemingway. . . . Yet to-day who reads Crane?" He has a steady following among Americans, "who thirty years ago would not look at him; it appears to be in England that he lacks attention, where thirty years ago he was lionised and spoilt by a blaze of popularity."

Blankenship, Russell. *American Literature as an Expression of the National Mind.* New York, 1931, pp. 521–527, and *passim.*
    Rev. ed., 1949, pp. 513, and *passim.*

Book Prices Current, 46 (November, 1931), 228.
    The sale of a presentation copy of *Maggie* brought $230.

Ford, Ford Madox. "Three Americans and a Pole," *Scribner's Magazine,* 90 (October, 1931), 379–386.

——. *Return to Yesterday.* London, 1931. Reprinted New York, 1932.
    Reviewed: New Statesman and Nation, 2 (November 14, 1931), 615–616.

Gray, Charleson. "The Splendid Years," *College Humor,* January, 1931.
    A note on Crane's personal courage.

Hazlitt, Henry. Introduction, *Maggie, together with George's Mother and The Blue Hotel.* New York, 1931, pp. vii–xi.
    On Crane's bringing the manuscript of *Maggie* to *The Century*'s editor, Richard Watson Gilder, in early 1892, and then locking it up in a box at brother Edmund's house after rejection from other publishers. "Then, as fall came on, he took heart; he worked on his manuscript again, borrowed $1,000 from his brother William, and took the revised story of 'Maggie' to New York." Quotes Howells's defense of *Maggie* in 1913. Quotes Beer's claim that Maggie was "the first ironic novel ever written by an American."*

---

* However, the first ironic novel was *Huckleberry Finn.* Hazlitt's legend of the $1,000 Crane supposedly borrowed from William is explained in *Crane.*

Hazlitt contends that the characters in both *Maggie* and *George's Mother* "are less individuals than types. . . . These generalized characters are not the result of an inability on Crane's part to create sharp individual portraits; they reflect his intention. . . . Critics often make the mistake of supposing that to create such generalized persons is less important and less difficult than to create individualized characters, even though the latter may have no significance beyond themselves. This is plainly nonsense. The whole value of Mr. Lewis's George F. Babbitt lay in his appalling typicality. And if one asks for a higher and more secure example of the purely generalized figure, there is Bunyan's Christian." (Critical discussions of Crane's characters as types or not types ignore Hazlitt's 1931 essay.)

Herzberg, M. J. "New and Old Data on Stephen Crane," *Torch*, 4 (April, 1931), pp. 36–38.

Knight, Grant C. *The Novel in English*. New York, 1931.

Lewis, Oscar. *Frank Norris of the "Wave."* San Francisco, 1931, pp. 82–85.
     Parody of Crane reprinted from the *San Francisco Wave*, December 24, 1897. Reprinted in *War Dispatches*, pp. 52–53, "The Green Stone of Unrest, by S——n Cr——e."

Living Authors: A Book of Biographies. New York, 1931.

McLean, David, and Shane Leslie. "Brede Place, Sussex, and America," *Sussex County Magazine*, 5 (July and August, 1931), 488–493, 540–544. Photographs.
     An important history of Brede Manor, on the Frewens, and on Crane and *The Ghost*.

Millis, Walter. *The Martial Spirit*. Boston, 1931.
     Misidentifies Crane as author of the article in the *World* reporting panic among the 71st New York Volunteers (Sylvester Scovel wrote it). This error is repeated by Mason (1939), Leech (1959), and Swanberg (1961).

O'Brien, Edward S. *The Advance of the American Short Story*. New York, 1931, pp. 176–182, 186, 187.

Oliver, Arthur. "Jersey Memories—Stephen Crane," *Proceedings of the New Jersey Historical Society*, 16 (October, 1931), 454–463.
     A firsthand account of Crane's *Tribune* report of the Asbury Park parade by the American Mechanics in the *New York Tribune*, August 21, 1892. In subsequent versions of this story Oliver's account is ignored—by Elconin (1948) and by Schoberlin (1949). An important memoir. Crane's 1892 *Tribune* sketch of the parade was first reprinted in *Library*, 5, no. 1 (1932).

Rothenstein, Sir William. *Men and Memories*, vol. 1. London, 1931.

Starrett, Vincent. "Stephen Crane: Notes Biographical and Bibliographical," *Colophon*, 2 (September, 1931), part 7, [1–8]. Photograph of Crane on horseback.
     Discusses some writings on Crane new to Stolper's *Stephen Crane* (1930) and Starrett's 1923 Crane bibliography, which items supply missing data in Beer's *SC*. Quotes from Colonel Edwin Emerson's *Pepys' Ghost* (1900) and from a conversation Starrett had with Henry Cary, who found it difficult to "get any work out of Stevie" and who considered him "an amusing little cuss."
     Describes a unique copy of the Appleton *Maggie* "in buff wrappers, without the final advertisements, and with a tipped-in title page. The front wrapper

reproduces the Appleton title page, in Old English (Starrett no. 8), even to the publisher's device, but omits the imprint. . . ."*

Sussex County Magazine, 5 (May, July, and August, 1931).

A series of articles on Brede Manor by Viscountess Wolseley; on Brede Place by Shane Leslie and David McLean.

Taylor, Harvey. [Manuscripts of Crane], *New York Herald Tribune,* November 22, 1931.

"A large packet of unpublished writings by Stephen Crane has been discovered, of the first interest. The material includes notes for *Maggie: A Girl of the Streets, The Red Badge of Courage,* sketches, short stories, poems and dialogues. They are to be published in the spring of 1932. As literary manager of Crane's estate, I should like to communicate with those who have in their possession any Stephen Crane material, letters included."

Nothing came of this project other than the publication in 1932 of "A Lost Poem by Stephen Crane," a leaflet issued in one hundred copies "for the friends of Harvey Taylor." Reprinted in the *Golden Book,* 19 (February, 1934), 189.

Walpole, Hugh. "Books Abroad," *New York Herald Tribune* (Book Supplement), November 1, 1931.

"The masterpieces of Stephen Crane—are dead and forgotten." (However, nowadays what is dead and forgotten are the masterpieces of Hugh Walpole.)

1932

[Anon.]. "Henry James: Two Views," *Bookman,* 75 (October, 1932), 581.

One of the two photographs here is a snapshot of Henry James eating a doughnut at the charity bazaar given in Brede Place in August 1899 (not "at a garden party given by Stephen Crane at his English home, Brede Place"). Reproduced in *Cora Crane,* and in *Crane.*

———. "Limited Edition of Stephen Crane Book," *Delta Upsilon Quarterly,* January, 1932.

Quotes a brief article about *The Red Badge of Courage* in *New York Herald Tribune* by Lewis Gannett.

———. "Presidential Parade: A Newsstory by Stephen Crane," *Library* (Public Library, Newark, N.J.), 5, no. 1 (September, 1932), 3.

Reprints the Asbury Park parade sketch "On the New Jersey Coast," *New York Tribune,* August 21, 1892. Claims its discoverer was B. J. R. Stolper, compiler of a Crane bibliography for the Stephen Crane Association of Newark, N.J., published by the Newark Library in 1930. The *W-S Bibliography,* p. 69, says its first book appearance was in *The Public Papers of a Bibliomaniac,* by Charles Honce (1942). *Library* errs in claiming that this sketch is "the earliest known writing of Stephen Crane."

* The London title page was tipped in by Heinemann in June, 1896, according to investigation by R. W. S. However, *see* Bowers, 1969.

Barney, E. C. "Stephen Crane," *Overland Monthly*, n.s., 90 (December, 1932), 309.

Beach, Joseph Warren. *The Twentieth Century Novel: Studies in Technique.* New York, 1932, p. 321.

Brooks, Van Wyck. *Sketches in Criticism.* New York, 1932, pp. 156–158.
   On Crane's bravery at Guantánamo Bay. *See also* Brooks (1952).

Calverton, V. F. *The Liberation of American Literature.* New York, 1932, p. 407.

Chamberlain, John. *Farewell to Reform.* New York, 1932, pp. 117–118.
   "The sharpest commentator of the nineties was a man who never considered his age, so far as his fiction went, in economic terms—in fact, he once seriously told Gustavus Myers never to attack the upper crust. This person who couldn't see the economic application of his own fiction was Stephen Crane, an atomic person who instinctively rejected all the values of his society. . . . Crane was, of course, the best of his generation so far as sheer *writing* went. But architectonics were beyond him." Garland said that he couldn't see Crane developing "as Booth Tarkington has developed." Chamberlain agrees: "The seeds of development were not in him; and perhaps it is fortunate for his young reputation that he died before he commenced to repeat himself. In any case, Crane stands as symbol of America's literary luck as the decade of muck drew nigh."

Dreiser, Theodore. "The Great American Novel," *American Spectator*, 1 (December, 1932), 1.

Dudley, Dorothy. *Forgotten Frontiers: Dreiser and the Land of the Free.* New York, 1932.

Ford, Ford Madox. *Return to Yesterday.* New York, 1932, pp. 26, 27, 33, 35–39, 53–57, 61–63, 66–70, 206, 209–210.
   Memoirs of Conrad, H. G. Wells, Henry James, and of Crane at Ravensbrook in Surrey and at Brede Manor in Sussex. Crane "used to declare at one time that he was the son of an uptown New York bishop; at another that he had been born in the Bowery and there dragged up. At one moment his voice would be harsh, like a raven's, uttering phrases like: 'I'm a fly-guy that's wise to the all night push,' if he wanted to be taken for a Bowery tough; or 'He was a mangy, sheep-stealing coyote,' if he desired to be thought of cowboy ancestry. At other times, he would talk rather low in very selected English. That was all boyishness."
   Collate *Return to Yesterday* with Ford, *Thus to Revisit* (1921). *See* Goldring (1949) on Ford.
   Reviewed: Edward Gannett, "Books and Things," *New York Herald Tribune*, January 15, 1932.

Garland, Hamlin. *My Friendly Contemporaries.* New York, 1932, pp. 369–370, 499.

Hill, Edwin B., ed. *Joseph Conrad on Stephen Crane.* Ysleta, Texas, 1932. (Privately printed, only 31 copies.)
   Conrad's letter to Peter Somerville, privately printed for Vincent Starrett. In *Letters.*

Knight, Grant C. *American Literature and Culture.* New York, 1932, pp. 395–400.

Lewisohn, Ludwig. *Expression in America.* New York, 1932.

Palmer, Frederick. *With My Own Eyes.* Indianapolis, Ind., 1932, p. 242.
"The realities of war hampered Crane's imagination, his gift of picturing reality."

Rubens, Horatio S. *Liberty: The Story of Cuba.* New York, 1932.
On Crane in Jacksonville in January–March, 1897.

Smith, Col. Ernest G. "Comments and Queries" [Stephen Crane], *Lafayette Alumnus,* 2 (February, 1932), 6.
Ernest Smith of the class of '94 relates how freshman Crane confronted in his East Hall room the fraternity hazing sophomores at Lafayette College. They forced his door and found him backed into a corner "with a revolver in hand. He was ghastly white as I recall and extremely nervous. There was no time to escape what might have proved a real tragedy until Crane unexpectedly seemed to wilt limply in place and the loaded revolver dropped harmlessly to the floor."

Walker, Franklin. *Frank Norris.* Garden City, N.Y., 1932, pp. 177–180, 236–238, 282–285, 308. New York: Russell and Russell, 1963. Photographic reprint.

1933

[Anon.]. "Milestones," *Time,* 21, no. 10 (March 6, 1933), 30.
Note on the death of Edward Marshall.

Bacheller, Irving Addison. *From Stores of Memory.* New York, 1933, pp. 110–112. *See also* Bacheller (1928).

Birss, J. H. "Stephen Crane: Letter and Bibliographical Note," *Notes and Queries,* 165 (October 7, 1933), 243.
"Letters of Stephen Crane, accounted by collectors to be among the scarcest of modern literary manuscripts, have been rearing their heads occasionally from hidden corners (a number of friendly communications to Conrad recently came to light), and it is to be hoped that they will be gathered together for a collected edition. Definite information about Crane's movements is so meagre that letters are often important in weaving together fragmentary data. Unknown connections are sometimes revealed—as in the notation of the epistle here noted, dated March 22, 1893, addressed to the critic, Julius F. Chambers. It is recorded in Henkel's catalogue (no. 934, item 830)* for the auction sale of the William Ritter collection of autograph letters and historical documents. With this letter were sent a paper-bound copy of *Maggie* (at the suggestion of Hamlin Garland) and a request for criticism. Whether Chambers wrote a review is not indicated in the Crane biographies, none of which, however, is an attempt at exhaustive compilation.
"This copy of *Maggie* ought to be included in the census of the very few early copies of the privately-printed first edition, which left Crane's own hands. *Maggie* used to be the rarest book in modern American literature, but

* It is not recorded in Henkel's catalogue no. 934, however; it remains untraced.

since the discovery of a *cache* of copies the book is fairly accessible and obtainable."

———. "The Death of Stephen Crane," *Saturday Review of Literature,* 10 (November 25, 1933), 288.

Complains that in Beer's *SC* "the factual outline of his life remains comparatively slight" and offers to fill in the gaps by a letter of Robert Barr (dated June 8, 1900), which "has escaped Crane's biographers and bibliographers" and which he has rescued from the *New York Herald,* June 21, 1900. However, unknown to Mr. Birss, this Robert Barr letter, whose "original recipient is unknown," was first made known by bibliographer Vincent Starrett in his Introduction to *Men, Women and Boats* (1921). The recipient of Barr's letter, not then known to Starrett, was Karl Harriman.

The letter by Robert Barr first appeared in the *New York Herald,* June 21, 1900. Reprinted in *Letters.*

See the rejoinders to Birss's article by Bohnenberger (1933) and Stolper (1933). *See also* Birss, "A Letter of Stephen Crane" (1934).

Bohnenberger, Carl. "Stephen Crane and Robert Barr," *Saturday Review of Literature,* 10 (December, 1933), 350.

Points out that the Crane letter, which John H. Birss thought a new letter, was reproduced in Vincent Starrett's sketch of Crane in *Buried Caesars. See* Stolper (1933), another rejoinder to Birss (1933).

Cargill, Oscar, ed. *The Social Revolt: American Literature from 1888 to 1914.* New York, 1933.

Downey, Fairfax. *Richard Harding Davis—His Day.* New York, 1933, pp. 137, 147–148, 160, 171.

Crane as a war correspondent.

Hicks, Granville. *The Great Tradition: An Interpretation of American Literature Since the Civil War.* New York, 1933, pp. 99, 133, 159–163, 169, 210, 302.

Crane "hated the poor because they could consent to the ugliness of their surroundings, the brutality of their lives, the defeat of their hopes, because they continued to live on such terms. . . . Hatred is a healthier emotion for the artist [or for the reviewer, like Hicks in the *Saturday Review*]." However, *contra* Hicks, in Crane there is no hatred—only irony and pity.

Hicks complains that we never know what sort of person Maggie appeared to herself. "As in *George's Mother,* the author stands on the outside. He could not enter into the characters' lives because he did not understand them, and he did not understand them because he did not understand how they had come into existence. We see them merely as they present themselves to Crane, a symbol of everything he feared. As a result there is something dry and harsh in all Crane's work, even in *The Red Badge of Courage.*" Hicks concludes that Crane's writings are "arid." Also that other writers of comparable historical importance have been neglected, while Crane has been singled out for admiration. However, what is admired in Crane transcends his historical importance, namely his aesthetic importance in achieved perfections of art, an ingredient seemingly irrelevent to Marxian critic Hicks. *(See* p. 304: "the only clue to the tangled web of life in the last century is the Marxian analysis.") In the above quotation Hicks echoes Beer's thesis of fear in Crane, and what Hicks says of *Maggie* and *George's Mother* is lifted from Frank

Norris. From some other mistaken source Hicks obtained his error that Crane died at twenty-nine—in England!

Reviewed: James T. Farrell, "Mr. Hicks: Critical Vulgarian," *American Spectator,* 4 (April, 1936), 21–26.

Madigan, Thomas F. *Autograph Album,* 1 (October, 1933), 35.

Quotes the late Arnold Bennett: "In my opinion, he [Crane] must rank with the best writers America has produced and is one of the finest descriptive writers of modern times." This new Crane letter (not in *Letters*) is here reprinted for the first time.

A.L.S., 6 pp. 12 mo. New York, March 2, 1896. To Miss Daisy D. Hill. [She had expressed her admiration for him and offered to exchange her photograph for his.]

"I have been wondering if you are not making game of me. And yet I suppose the egotism of the average man is large enough to make it all appear perfectly sincere. Assuming then that you mean what you say, your letter makes me mournful. In the first place, I am such a small pale-yellow person with a weak air and no ability to pose, that your admiration, or whatever it may be—if admiration is too strong a term—causes me to feel that I am an imposter and am robbing you of something. Of course, your letter appeals to me. It is the expression of a vibratory sensitive young mind reaching out for an ideal. But then I can not for a moment allow you to assume that I am properly an ideal. Ye Gods! I am clay—very common uninteresting clay. I am a good deal of a rascal, sometimes a bore, often dishonest. When I look at myself I know that only by dint of knowing nothing of me are you enabled to formulate me in your mind as something of a heroic figure. If you could once scan me you would be forever dumb.

"Your mind must be a finer mold than the minds around you or the figures of your soul would never so reach into the distance. This is why I am glad to write to you and tell you the truth as I know it. Of course, I wish for the sake of the episode that I could tell you that I am a remarkable person, but, alas, poor romance, I am most hideously ordinary." Etc. *See* Cady (1969).

Parry, Albert. *Garrets and Pretenders.* New York, 1933, pp. 67, 89–90, 101–102, 258.

Seitz, D. C. "Stephen Crane: War Correspondent," *Bookman,* 76 (February, 1933), 137–140.

Repeats the unfounded charges, first made in his *Joseph Pulitzer* (1924), that Crane wrote the *World's* unsigned dispatch exposing panic among the 71st New York Volunteers. Reports the unfounded rumor that Crane "brought out the fact that he had a sister who was a chambermaid in Omaha," a story which got into the *World's* editorial page and which pleased Crane's enemy, Seitz.

Midway through the Cuban War Crane got fired by the *World's* financial manager, John Norris. On his way downstairs at the *World's* offices, says Seitz, "I met John Norris, the Financial Manager, coming out of his office, rubbing his hands gleefully. 'I have just kissed your little friend Stephen Crane good-bye,' he said with a full-face grin."

Starrett, Vincent. Introduction, *Maggie: A Girl of the Streets and Other Stories.* New York, 1933.

"Stephen Crane: An Estimate" is here reprinted from *Sewanee Review*, 28 (July, 1920).

Stolper, Benjamin J. R. "Unpublished Crane Material," *Saturday Review of Literature*, 10 (December 30, 1933), 380.

A rejoinder to Birss, "The Death of Stephen Crane" (1933). Stolper points out that the "new" Robert Barr letter "is not so unknown as Mr. Birss fancies." He notes also that *The Black Riders* was set to music by William Schuyler. *See also* Bohnenberger, "Stephen Crane and Robert Barr" (1933).

Winterich, J. T. *"The Red Badge of Courage," Publisher's Weekly*, 118 (September 20, 1933), 1303–1307.

———. "Made in Japan," *Saturday Review of Literature*, 9 (January 28, 1933), 406.

Bibliographical comment on *In Many Wars by Many War Correspondents* (1904).

1934

[Anon.]. "Stephen Crane: 'A Mystery of Heroism,'" in *American Short Novel, Twentieth Century*. Moscow, 1934.

Angoff, Charles. "A Fiction Without Women," *American Mercury*, 33 (November, 1934), 375–376.

Barrett, Richmond. "Correspondence" [on Cora Crane], *American Mercury*, 33 (May, 1934), xxi–xxii.

An important note on Cora in Jacksonville. *See also* Beer, "Mrs. Stephen Crane" (1934) and *Crane*.

Beer, Thomas. "Mrs. Stephen Crane," *American Mercury*, 31 (March, 1934), 289–295.

Presents a portrait of "Mrs. Stephen Crane"—not in Beer's *Stephen Crane* (1923)—drawn from unpublished letters having considerable importance. However, here again Beer suppresses the identity of Cora (hostess of the Hotel de Dream in Jacksonville who, after Crane's death, reopened her business at The Court there). Beer's article is a defense of Cora in the face of Helen R. Crane's 1934 *American Mercury* exposé of her identity. *See also* Barrett (1934).

———. "The Works of Stephen Crane," in *Designed for Reading: An Anthology Drawn from the Saturday Review of Literature, 1924–1934*, ed. Henry Seidel Canby, Boston, 1934, pp. 253–262. Reprinted from "Fire Feathers," *Saturday Review of Literature*, 2 (December 19, 1925), 425–427.

———. "Sunny Blue," in Carl C. Van Doren, *Modern American Prose*. New York, 1934, pp. 285–297. Reprints a chapter of Beer's *SC*.

Birss, J. H. "A Letter of Stephen Crane," *Notes and Queries*, 166 (April 7, 1934), 240–241.

See Birss, "The Death of Stephen Crane" (1933).

Collamore, H. Bacon. "The Collector's World," *Literary Observer*, 1, no. 2
(June–July, 1934), 57.
 Quotes an 1895 letter of Crane to Copeland and Day, publishers of *The
Black Riders*. Reprinted in *Omnibus*, p. 602.

Crane, Helen R. "My Uncle, Stephen Crane," *American Mercury*, 31 (January,
1934), 24–29.
 Wilbur's daughter here got her revenge against the Crane family who had
ostracized her parents, father Wilbur having married the maid in William's
Port Jervis household. Their "nicely laundered lives," into which rebel
Stephen did not at all fit, were now stirred into disbelief by Helen's exposé
of the identity of "Mrs. Stephen Crane" as in fact the hostess of a Jacksonville
"house of joy."
 "I hope the part about Cora being the owner of a 'house of joy' is not true,
and if it isn't Mr. Beer should be assured that his book is authentic." So
Florence wrote Edith in their 1934 correspondence about outcast Helen's
American Mercury revelations about Stephen and Cora. They appealed to
Thomas Beer, who replied that "most of what Helen has written is bosh." In
his *Stephen Crane* (1923) he had suppressed the truth about Cora so as not to
offend the Crane family, and now in silent reply to Helen's *American Mercury*
sketch he issued there in March 1934 a portrait of Cora drawn from unpublished letters which again whitewashed her past by ignoring it. However,
Richmond Barrett in the *American Mercury* upset Beer's intent by pinpoint-
ing her identity in Jacksonville.
 See Barrett (1934).

Foerster, Norman, ed. *American Poetry and Prose*. Boston, 1934 and 1947,
p. 1171 (note on Crane), pp. 1171–1200. Reprints "The Open Boat" and some
poems. A popular textbook, among the first to reprint Crane.

Ford, Ford Madox. *It Was the Nightingale*. Philadelphia, 1933. London, 1934,
p. 102.

French, Mansfield J. "Stephen Crane: Ball Player," *Syracuse University Alumni
News*, 15 (January, 1934), 1, 4.

Harriman, Karl Edwin. "Last Days of Stephen Crane," *New Hope*, 2 (October,
1934), 12–14.
 Memoirs of Crane at Brede Manor by a 23-year-old journalist of the *Detroit
Free Press* visiting the Cranes in the summer of 1899. *See also* Harriman
(1900).

Hartwick, Harry. *The Foreground of American Fiction*. New York and Cincinnati, 1934, pp. 21–29, 31–44 [on impressionism].
 "Because he was an enemy to the moralizing that afflicted his age, it is hard
to trace Crane's philosophy." Since Crane's day "sentences have tended to
grow shorter (and even elliptical), as in Ernest Hemingway's. . . . How far
Crane was influenced in his impressionism, it is hard to say. . . . It is also
hard to decide whether Crane caught any of his verbal pointillism from
modern theories of painting. . . . Nor is it any easier to name other authors
who might have influenced him, either in theme or technique, because of the
fact that his reading experience was so limited. His appetite for adventure
may have been prompted, to an extent, by the popularity of Kipling. . . ."

Hartwick errs in every one of the following statements: That Crane's journal-istic experiences "had provided him with material for a lame, febrile novel entitled *Maggie: A Girl of the Streets* (1892)." That Maggie, finding herself quickly deserted, "tried in vain to become a prostitute." That Crane, focus-sing "his clairvoyant fancy," wrote *The Red Badge* in ten days. And that Crane sailed for Cuba in 1896, was shipwrecked by Spaniards, and the next year left "to cover a Balkan disturbance, fell sick, and on his way home, lingered a while in England, making friends and writing, until in 1898 the *Maine* disaster sent him flying down to Cuba again," and that when the war ended he returned to England "and the wife he had married in Athens." "In pursuit of his thesis Mr. Hartwick goes so far as to maintain that the bewildered hero of *The Red Badge of Courage* is a rampaging superman who has adopted the ruthless policy of laissez-faire. Thus a false theory ham-strings criticism" [to quote Walcutt, 1946].

Lucock, Halford E. *Contemporary American Literature and Religion.* Chicago, 1934, pp. 32, 56, 190.

Rosene, M. R. "The Five Best American Books Published Since 1900," *Writer,* 46 (October, 1934), 370–371.

Refers to Hemingway's "The Undefeated" as "the best American short story since Crane's 'Open Boat.'" (However, "The Undefeated" is no match for Crane's incomparable "The Open Boat.")

Wells, H. G. *Experiment in Autobiography.* New York, 1934, pp. 522–525, 529, 531. Reissued in 1967.

On the Christmas party at Brede Manor, 1899. Agent James B. Pinker "had *fixed* some stories for him. 'I got to do them,' he said, 'I got to do them.' The tragic entanglement of the highly specialized artist had come to him. Sensa-tion and expression—and with him it had been well nigh perfect expression—was the supreme joy of his life and the justification of existence for him. And here he was, in a medley of impulsive disproportionate expenditure, being pursued by the worthy Pinker with enquiries of when he could 'deliver copy' and warnings not to overrun his length. The good thing in his life had slipped by him."

Wimberly, Charles Lowry. "How a Dull Western City Takes on Class," *Ameri-can Mercury* 32 (July, 1934), 368.

On Crane in Lincoln, Nebraska, in February, 1895.

1935

American Art Association, Anderson Galleries, New York. Catalog no. 4175. Sale of April 24–25, 1935. Items 71–72. No. 71 is quoted here:

"From March 11, 1930, to Dec. 5, 1934, 11 copies of this work [the pri-vately printed first edition of *Maggie: A Girl of the Streets*] appeared at public sale in America, three of which were presentation copies; some of the volumes were in very poor condition. Nine of the eleven were sold in these

Galleries, the first (a presentation copy) on March 11, 1930, and the last (also a presentation copy) on Dec. 5, 1934.

"Only two, however, of the nine that we have sold were the property of the owner of the present copy, Mrs. Florence Crane Coughlan. When Mr. Coughlan came to the Galleries to negotiate the sale of the present copy, we gave it as our opinion that it would be unwise to offer it for sale unless a definite statement was made in the catalogue regarding the exact number of copies still held by him and his wife.

"We are informed that they still hold 11 copies and that the present copy is one of the finest [entirely uncut and unopened], being practically as fresh as on the day it left the printer's hand. . . . An arrangement has been made with Mr. and Mrs. Coughlan whereby these 11 copies are to be sold in these Galleries at the rate of two copies each season hereafter until the entire number has been distributed."

Mrs. Coughlan, at the request of the Anderson Galleries, made the following written statement (January 22, 1935): "After the death of my Father, Stephen Crane's brother William in California several years ago, two copies of *Maggie* were sent to my sister Agnes and me by the estate. Not knowing the value but suspecting that they would bring a few dollars at least, I took them to the Anderson Galleries, where I was congratulated on the possession of these books, and they were put up at auction. The result is book history. Like everyone else, probably, who had ever seen or heard of *Maggie*, I racked my brains to remember any more possible copies in the family library. When our home in Brooklyn was broken up, most of our possessions were stored on my grandfather's farm, and I mentally repacked the books which had been sent there. As far back as I could remember there had always been a small pile of paper-bound *Maggies* in our storage room, but when I spoke of this to my mother she said she didn't believe there were any left as my two eldest sisters had burned them, believing they were 'not nice.' "

On the market prices of the 1893 *Maggie* see Honce (1938). A note recasting the above appears in *Letters*, pp. 12–13.

———. Catalog no. 4194, October 30–31, 1935, item 40.

An unlocated letter, 1 p., dated Hartwood, N.Y., February 17, n.d. (1894 or 1896?). Crane's note on this letter is quoted by the *Stephen Crane Newsletter* 3, no. 3 (Spring, 1969), 7.

[Anon.]. "Good Reading," *New York Herald Tribune*, December 10, 1935, p. 10.

———. *Stephen Crane: The Red Badge of Courage*. Moscow, 1935.

Contains also "The Little Regiment," "A Mystery of Heroism," "Three Miraculous Soldiers," "Gray Sleeve," "The Open Boat," and "The Price of the Harness."

———. "Stephen Crane: 'The Reluctant Voyagers,' " in *30 Days*, no. 1 (1935), 49–59.

Brown, Curtis. *Contacts*. New York, 1935, pp. 260–266; London, 1935, pp. 222–227.

The publication of *The Red Badge* in the Sunday *Press*, in December, 1894, and Brown's encounter with Crane. *The Black Riders* inscribed: "To Curtis Brown—not at all reluctantly, but with enthusiasm—From Stephen Crane, May 16, 1895." Brown visits Brede Place a week after the Christmas-New

Year's party, and calls on the undertaker's shop in Baker Street to view Crane's body in a horse-stall of the stable-yard. Describes Brown's subsequent visit with Cora Crane in London. "To show respect we went. Mrs. Crane, a generously-built blonde with curiously unresponsive pale blue eyes, sat in a rocking chair by the door from the hall, and rose to say merely: 'You will find chairs over there,' and then sat down again. . . . Most of the occupants did not appear to know each other, and sat in silence, deriving their entertainment from hearing each new-comer greeted with 'You will find a chair over there.' There were no refreshments, and there was not much walking about. Mrs. Crane did not leave her chair except to rise—and quickly sit. She did not appear to wish for conversation. . . . I learned afterwards that Mrs. Crane and her inseparable lady-companion had packed all their possessions into trunks and boxes before the party. The moment the last guest left, they called a van and a taxi, hurried the luggage aboard, closed the house and drove off for a steamer for New York. We never heard of them again."

Brown reports that Crane had sent him *The Third Violet,* "a novel of no quality," in the hope that the *New York Press* would publish it serially. "We couldn't. Here is a letter from him about it:—"

> My Dear Curtis,
>   Thank you for your kind words and for your *Sketch* clipping. I hear the damned book [*The Red Badge of Courage*] is doing very well in England. In the meantime I am plodding along. I have finished my new novel—'The Third Violet'—and sent it to Appleton and Co., as per request, but I've an idea it won't be accepted. It's pretty rotten work. I used myself up on the accursed 'Red Badge.'
> > Yours as ever,
> > Stephen Crane*
> Hartwood, N.Y.
>   Dec. 31st, 1896.

Conrad, Jessie. *Joseph Conrad and his Circle.* New York and London, 1935, pp. 56–58, 72–75. Photographs.† Reissued 1964.
      The Conrads visit the Cranes at Ravensbrook in Surrey with the baby Borys and Jessie's young sister Dora. Photograph. On Crane at Dover waiting for a calm sea. Cora's queer telegram: "God took Stephen at 11.5, make some arrangement for me to get the dog home." Collate with Mrs. Conrad's *Bookman* article for April, 1926, containing passages not in *Joseph Conrad.*

Damon, S. Foster. *Amy Lowell: A Chronicle with Extracts from Her Correspondence.* Boston and New York, 1935, pp. 104, 175, 176, 177, 284, 311, 651, 652, 665.

Ford, Ford Madox. "Good Reading," *New York Herald Tribune,* December 10, 1935, p. 19.

———. "Techniques," *Southern Review,* 1 (July, 1935), 20–35.
      On techniques of impressionism. Flaubert, Henry James, Conrad. On Crane as prose impressionist, pp. 26, 29, 31–32.

---

* This letter was inadvertently omitted from *Letters.*
† The photograph of Crane at his desk is not at Brede Place.

Hatcher, Harlan. *Creating the Modern American Novel.* New York, 1935; London, 1936, pp. 12–20.

Hemingway, Ernest. "Monologue to the Maestro: A High Seas Letter," *Esquire,* 4, no. 4 (October, 1935), 21, 174a–174b.
Among the books a writer should read are *The Open Boat* and *The Blue Hotel.*

Jones, Claude. "Stephen Crane at Syracuse," *American Literature,* 7 (1935), 82–84.

———. "Stephen Crane: A Bibliography of His Stories and Essays," *Bulletin of Bibliography,* 15 (September-December, 1935), 149–150.
Designed as a supplement to Stolper's handlist of Crane's "writings and articles about him." Stolper (1930) made little effort to trace the original appearance of the short prose works or their subsequent publication. *See also* Jones (1936).

Martin, T. E. "Stephen Crane: Athlete and Author," Syracuse University *Argot,* 3 (March, 1935), 1–2.
Reproduces a Crane graffito burned into the east side wall in the cupola of the Delta Upsilon house at Syracuse one afternoon early in May, 1891: "Sunset 1891 May / Steph Crane."

Mitchell, Edwin V. *The Art of Authorship.* New York, 1935, pp. 69–70.
On Crane's Notebook, "Anton Tchekhov said that a writer should never keep a notebook, but should depend solely upon his memory. When he died the drawer of his writing-table was found to be stuffed with notebooks." Conrad said that Crane never kept a diary or owned a notebook. But Crane kept a notebook, "and it lies at my elbow as I write this."
See Stallman, "Stephen Crane: Some New Stories (Part I)," (1956). Reproduced from the Notebook of Stephen Crane; here for the first time, are: "Matinee Girls," "The Art Students' League," and "Election Night: New York 1894" ("Heard in the Street Election Night"). *See* Greiner, *The Notebook of Stephen Crane* (1969).

Perry, Bliss. *And Gladly Teach.* Boston, 1935, p. 142.

1936

[Anon.]. "Misplaced Writer," *The New Yorker* (November 7, 1936), p. 14.
Where is Crane buried? "The *Encyclopaedia Britannica* says that Crane is buried in 'the cemetery of Elizabeth, New Jersey.' Thomas Beer, in his biography of Crane which Knopf published in 1923, says Crane is buried 'at Elizabeth.' Max J. Herzberg, in his introduction to *The Red Badge of Courage* (Appleton-Century), says Crane is buried in Elizabeth.* Well, come to find out, this is a lot of vaporing. Elizabeth has three cemeteries, and although one of them holds the remains of three Stephen Cranes, not one of

* John Berryman in his *Stephen Crane* (1950) has Crane buried in the wrong cemetery; so does Lillian Gilkes in *Cora Crane* (1960). Max Herzberg wrote the *Encyclopaedia Britannica* article.

these Cranes is the author of *The Red Badge of Courage,* not one is the author and poet about whom the *Britannica* is so glibly informative. . . . Crane lies in the neighboring township of Hillside, in Lot 168, Section C, of Evergreen Cemetery. The grave is marked by a large gray granite stone, inscribed: 'Stephen Crane—Poet—Author—1871–1900.' At first our investigator supposed that Hillside must once have been a part of Elizabeth, and that this would account for the error in the *Britannica* and elsewhere. Such is not the case. Hillside stands separate, and has never been Elizabeth.

"The First Presbyterian churchyard in Elizabeth holds the three other Cranes, all of them Stephen. One died in 1780 at the age of seventy, one died in 1796 at the age of fifty-eight, and one died in 1846 at the age of sixty-four."

Not noticed by *The New Yorker*'s investigator is that the tombstone has engraved on it also J. T. Crane, next to whom brother Stephen Crane is buried. Jonathan Townley Crane, Jr., died—according to the tombstone—in 1908. However, his death certificate at Binghamton, N.Y., says he died in 1909. *See Crane.*

However, *See* Gilkes (1970), pp. 7–11.

Beer, Thomas. "Sunny Blue," in *The Borzoi Reader,* ed. Carl Van Doren. New York, 1936. Reprinted from Beer's *SC.*

Boynton, Percy. *Literature and American Life.* Boston, 1936, pp. 677, 678, 751, 754, 860, 880–881.

Cather, Willa. *Not Under Forty.* New York, 1936, p. 91.
"He died young, but he had done something real. One can read him today."

Ford, Ford Madox. "Stephen Crane," *American Mercury,* 37 (January, 1936), 36–45.
Reprinted in *Portraits From Life.* Boston, 1937.
Reprinted in *Mightier Than the Sword.* London, 1938.
"One awakened one morning in the Nineties in England and *The Red Badge of Courage* was not; by noon of the same day it filled the universe." On Crane at Limpsfield Chart, at Ravensbrook in Oxted, Surrey, and at Brede Manor. An extraordinary memoir, albeit not to be trusted in one detail or another. For instance, Ford says that he did not know that Stephen was buried in Elizabeth, N.J., until he read Thomas Beer's "painstaking biography." However, Beer's painstaking biography is misinformed; *see* [Anon.], "Misplaced Writer" (1936).

Hemingway, Ernest. *Green Hills of Africa.* London, 1936.
" 'The good writers are Henry James, Stephen Crane, and Mark Twain. That's not the order they're good in. There is no order for good writers. Crane wrote two fine stories. *The Open Boat* and *The Blue Hotel.* The last is best.' "

Herzberg, Max J. "Newark's Great Man of Letters," *Newarker* (bulletin marking the 100th anniversary of the incorporation of Newark, N.J.), May 1, 1936.
Sketch of Crane and photograph of a diorama of Crane writing *The Red Badge of Courage.*

Jones, Claude. "Stephen Crane: A Bibliography of His Stories and Essays," *Bulletin of Bibliography,* 16 (January–April, 1936), 170.
See also Jones, "Stephen Crane:" (1935).

Plekhanov, George V. *Art and Society.* New York: Critic's Group, 1936.

Quinn, Arthur Hobson. *American Fiction: An Historical and Critical Study.* New York, 1936, pp. 532–538.

That "Crane went down into the depths so often would not have mattered if, like Eugene O'Neil, he had had the power to draw beauty from the struggles of dwarfed souls striving upward to the light. But Crane too often left them in the mud, content to describe them in that state which has no justification in art except as a place from which to rise." (That the criterion of literary value is spiritual uplift was the credo of George Woodbury in the decade of the 1910s.)

Taylor, W. F. *A History of American Letters.* New York, 1936, pp. 281–283, 362. Rev. ed., Chicago, 1956.

Watson, Elmo. *A History of Newspaper Syndicates in the United States.* Chicago, 1936, p. 43.

On the manuscript of *The Red Badge of Courage* and its serial publication in newspapers by the Bacheller and the Kellog Newspaper Company.

On the shortened newspaper version of *The Red Badge of Courage* see Werner (1945), Katz (1968), *SCraneN*, 2 (Spring, 1968), and *Crane.*

1937

[Anon.]. "Letters of a Shortstop," *The Month at Goodspeed's,* 9 nos. 1–2 (September and October, 1937), 10–14.

Quotes Thomas Beer's opinion that Crane's "scarce letters are not often interesting. They have a formal running tone, now and then lifted by a phrase."* Quotes from the present group of eight Crane letters—each one an A.L.S.—to Copeland and Day in 1894 and 1895, priced at $350. The letter of June 8, 1895, written on printed stationary of The Hartwood Club, has importance: "I returned from Mexico some days ago but have come up here [to Port Jervis, N.Y.] for a time because I am not in very good health."

Seven of the eight letters listed here were published for the first time in *Omnibus; see* p. 601. *The Month at Goodspeed's* errs in saying that *The Black Riders* was published in the autumn of 1894.

———. [Stephen Crane and Lew Wallace], *Saturday Review of Literature,* 15 (January 16, 1937), 10. Portrait of Crane.

Crane, "who had not seen a battle" wrote *The Red Badge of Courage,* "and Lew Wallace, who served in two wars, wrote *Ben Hur.*"

Baker, Ernest. *History of the English Novel.* London, 1937.

Conrad, Joseph. Preface, *The Red Badge of Courage.* London: Jonathan Cape, 1937. Reissued from the Heinemann edition, 1925.

See also Conrad (1925), Conrad, "His War Book" (1926) and Conrad (1928).

De Voto, Bernard. "Fiction Fights the Civil War," *Saturday Review of Literature,* 17 (December 18, 1937), 3–4, 15–16.

* Beer's knowledge of Crane letters was limited; even these business letters to Copeland and Day were not known to him.

The Red Badge is set in the battle of Chancellorsville "But neither the processes nor the events of history have any part in it, and Chancellorsville might as easily have been any battle in any war. For *The Red Badge of Courage* is a portrayal of an individual in battle—what he felt, what he thought, what he did—and it is nothing more. Its theme is a man in battle, as another novel's theme might be a man in marriage or in business or in the church. We cannot properly call it a Civil War novel. But it established a way of writing about battle that in our own time has had a decisive influence. Whenever, in fiction of the last ten years, a Civil War battle crosses the story's path you may see Stephen Crane's seal on it. In making the individual the conscious, sentient focus of battle scenes he did a great service to our fiction."

Ford, Ford Madox. *Portraits from Life*. Boston, 1937, pp. 21–37, 206–208.

Reprinted in paperback edition, Chicago, n.d., pp. 28–40. "Stephen Crane." On Crane also pp. 274–276.

Reissued as *Mightier Than the Sword*. London, 1938, pp. 38–58, 267–269. Photograph.

"When he descended on me in the troglodytic cottage on Limpsfield Chart where I lived severely browbeaten by Garnetts and the Good generally, though usually of a Fabian or Advanced Russian variety, I took him at once to be a god—an Apollo with starry eyes." (However, this romanticized legend, repeated by Amy Lowell and others, is undercut by the fact that Ford on first meeting Crane took an immediate dislike of him because of his arrogant tone in a lecture Crane gave before the Limpsfield Chart audience in June, 1897.)

Reports his visit with Cora at Ravensbrook when Crane returned from London after a session with agent Pinker, who promised him "twenty pounds for every thousand words he chose to write." (On how much Crane earned *see* Stronks [1963]). Crane's happy London session with Pinker occurred on December 15, 1897. *See Crane*. Ford describes Crane's life at Ravensbrook, Crane shooting at flies on a lump of sugar, and at Brede Place, where he visited for the last time on January 2, 1900. "Thomas Beer said that Crane did not have a very tumultuous reception in England. He was wrong, for that was exactly the type of reception that poor Crane did get once he was settled at first in Oxted and afterwards in Brede."

Kearny, Thomas. *General Philip Kearny: Battle Soldier of Five Wars*. New York, 1937, p. 267.

"Crane born in Newark, while resident in Asbury Park and later before he became famous visited 'Kearny Castle' ['Belle Grove']. When his fame was achieved he again visited General [John Watts] Kearny and told the General the symbolic meaning hidden under the title of his famous book." (John Watts was the son of General Philip Kearny.)

Crane was thus familiar with the well-known insignia of the red patch worn by soldiers under General Philip Kearney in the Third Corps of the Army of the Potomac, and that special badge of honor was the source of Crane's metaphoric title for his Civil War novel, *The Red Badge*. See Cecil D. Eby, Jr., in *American Literature* (May, 1960).

Lewis, Oscar, ed. *Frank Norris of the "Wave."* San Francisco, 1937.

Loggins, Vernon. *I Hear America Singing: Literature in the United States Since 1900*. New York, 1937, pp. 23–31.

Major, Stanley B. "No. 14 Mulberry Place," *The Polymnian* (Newark Academy), 40 (March, 1937), 4–7.
> Sketch of Crane's life. Drawing of Crane. Picture of Crane's birthplace.

Müller, Herbert J. *Modern Fiction: A Study of Values.* New York, 1937, pp. 200–201, 202.
> "Conspicuous in the first litter of naturalists was Stephen Crane. In *Maggie: A Girl of the Streets* he plunged into muddier waters than had yet been explored and rose from the bottom with uglier specimens than had yet been exhibited. It is indeed an amateurish performance that today seems ludicrous in its self-conscious and almost gloating display of brutal detail. . . ."

Stresau, Hermann, and Haus Reisiger, trans. *Das blaue Hotel.* Berlin, 1937.

Woollcott, Alexander. "Stephen Crane's *Whilomville Stories*," *Saturday Review of Literature*, 16 (October 23, 1937), 14.
> Quotes a letter of Booth Tarkington about the *Whilomville Stories,* on which Woollcott contributes his own memoir.

1938

Bragdon, Claude Fayette. *More Lives Than One.* New York, 1938.

Collamore, H. Bacon. "Some Notes on Modern First Editions," *Colophon,* n.s., 3 (Summer, 1938), 358.
> On *The Open Boat,* New York ed., 1898.

Federal Writers' Project. *Stories of New Jersey.* New York, 1938, pp. 146–153. Compiled and written by the Federal Writers' Project of the Works Progress Administration for the State of New Jersey. Photograph of a bust of Crane at the Newark Public Library.
> A short sketch of Crane's life, not without errors.

Ferguson, Delancey. *Men and Moments: A Book of Living Narratives.* New York, 1938.

Ford, Ford Madox. *The March of Literature.* New York, 1938, p. 839.

———. *Mightier Than the Sword.* London, 1938, pp. 146, 158, 163, 267–269. First issued as *Portraits from Life.* Boston, 1937, pp. 21–37, 206–208.
> Of extraordinary interest for Ford's pen-portraits of Crane, Conrad, H. G. Wells, Henry James, the Garnetts, and others. *See also* Ford (1936).

Honce, Charles. "Stephen Crane's 'Maggie,'" in *A Sherlock Holmes Birthday.* Mount Vernon, Va.: The Golden Eagle Press, 1938, pp. 104–108. Limited edition, one hundred copies.
> An inscribed copy of the 1893 edition of *Maggie* fetched at an Anderson Gallery auction in 1930 one of the highest prices ever paid for a book of an American author: $3,700. "Only Edgar Allan Poe's *Tamberlaine* has topped *Maggie*'s auction record among books of the last century. But since 1930, when the book was described as 'the rarest in modern literature,' enough additional copies have come to light to bring about a startling drop in the sales record." A few days ago at the Anderson Galleries a copy sold for $150. The high spot of $3,700 was for the copy inscribed by the author to Lucius L. Button

of Rochester. Two months later in 1930 an uninscribed *Maggie* fetched $2,100, and in October of that year a copy inscribed to Elbert Hubbard was sold for $1,125.

"A few years ago a niece of Crane's discovered 11 copies stored with family books on her grandfather's farm. These are being auctioned at the rate of two a season, and usually one or two from other sources make their appearance each year. Prices realized since 1935 have included $475, $275, $280 and $150, depending on condition."

See American Art Association Catalog (1935).

Kunitz, S. J., and Howard Haycraft, eds. *American Authors: 1600–1900.* New York, 1938, pp. 188–190.

Lawrence, T. E. *The Letters of T. E. Lawrence,* ed. David Garnett. London, 1938, 1964, pp. 778, 779. On *Maggie,* pp. 384, 603, 708, 777; on *Wounds in the Rain,* p. 779.

His library now finally includes in 1933 Crane's *Maggie,* difficult to obtain, and *The Red Badge of Courage.* "I remember him as a man of astonishment —one who surprised and shocked, by turns of incident and vivid phrases. Rather that, than a sustained artist."

Lüdeke, Henry. "Stephen Crane's Gedichte," *Anglia,* 62 (May, 1938), 410–422.

Reprinted in Henry Lüdeke, *The Democracy of Henry Adams and Other Essays.* Bern, Switzerland, 1950, pp. 111–122.

Considers to what extent Emily Dickinson and Walt Whitman appear in Crane's verses as influences. "The basic force of Crane's poetry, after all, is not a free lyrical emotion, but a moral passion shaped in irony." In the love poems one element stands out, namely "the consoling and healing part that women have in his murky picture of life." Love gets a whole cycle to itself in *War Is Kind* (1899), in the Intrigue poems.

Not until after World War I, when the Imagists "had brought the free-rhythm movement into power and proclaimed Emily Dickinson's importance, did *The Black Riders* attract any attention and was their position as precursors of the modernists recognized. Harriet Monroe's judgment of them was not unfair; but the note of almost unwilling concession that her article emits can now be supplanted by a greater warmth of appreciation. Crane had admittedly no influence on his contemporaries; but is it really true that Edgar Lee Masters, when he wrote his *Spoon River Anthology* in short paragraphs of free rhythms, had no knowledge of Crane?" Ezra Pound took Crane's poems as the point of departure for his own early work. "Poems such as 'N. Y.' and 'The Garret' are Crane's form in Pound's tonality." An important study.

The Modern Library in First Editions. New York, 1938, p. 53.

Reports a presentation copy of *Maggie:* "It is indeed a brave new binding and I wish the inside were braver." To DeWitt Miller, July 3, 1896. Crane's letter-inscription is reprinted in *Letters,* p. 125. Facsimile reproduction in *SCraneN,* 2, no. 2 (Winter, 1967), 6. Katz, p. 4, claims that *Letters* makes "a distortion in transcription" and that this is "wrong and misleading," which is nonsense in that *Letters* reprints a faithful copy of the original. " 'It is indeed a brave new binding and I wish the inside were braver.' Stephen Crane." There is no distortion in transcription. What is "wrong and misleading" is Katz's note: "DeWitt Miller's *Maggie:* A Correction." The sole point of Katz's note is that this Crane inscription was in an 1893 *Maggie,* a point not identified in *Letters*. Katz says: "Because all this can lead a critic astray, a correction is necessary."

The necessary correction [lest bibliographers like Katz go astray] is that this Crane inscription was first published in *The Modern Library of First Editions* and that Katz fails to acknowledge in *SCraneN* (1967) this prior publication. That this book is unkown to Katz is evidenced by the fact that it misdates *Maggie* for 1891.

Rothenstein, William. *Men and Memories*, vol. 3. London, 1938, p. 28.

Stories of New Jersey. See Federal Writer's Project (1938).

Winterich, John T. "*The Red Badge of Courage*," in *Twenty-three Books: The Stories Behind Them*. Berkeley: Book Arts Club of the University of California, 1938, pp. 121–131. A reprint of his *Publisher's Weekly* article (1930). Republished New York, 1939.

Points out that the price of fifty cents for *Maggie* in 1893 was highly priced when the newsstands were "thick with novels in wrappers at twenty-five cents each—novels much longer than *Maggie*, and written by men and women much better known than Johnston Smith." Quotes Crane's inscription to Lucius L. Button: "It is inevitable that you will be greatly shocked by the book but continue, please, with all possible courage, to the end. . . ." Winterich does not say so, but this same inscription occurs in slightly variant versions again and again, as in his copy of *Maggie* to the Reverend Thomas Dixon quoted in *Bookman* (May, 1895). *See Letters*. To his close friend Button it must have seemed too formal and impersonal.

On bibliographical problems of the text of the first edition. Important. Winterich's essay discusses also the history of *Maggie*'s publication, the *Commodore* disaster, and Crane in Greece. Speculates that the revival of interest in Crane began with the outbreak of hostilities in World War I. "This very fact, as Vincent Starrett ingeniously points out in his bibliography of Crane, may have a good deal to do with the present rarity of the first edition of *The Red Badge*. When compassionate men and women were ransacking shelves and garrets in response to the American Library Association's appeal for camp reading, what more inevitable than that they should choose copies of *The Red Badge of Courage* if they had them?"

Reviewed: New York Times, January 15, 1939.

1939

Blankenship, Russell. *American Literature*. New York, 1939.

Garnett, David, ed. *The Letters of T. E. Lawrence*. New York, 1939, pp. 384, 603, 708, 777–779. London, 1938.

Brief comments on several of Crane's books.

Haight, Gordon S. Introduction, *Miss Ravenel's Conversion from Secession to Loyalty*, J. W. DeForest. New York, 1939.

Collate with *Omnibus* on the realism of Crane as compared with the realism of DeForest.

Honce, Charles. *Authors in Falseface: Diverse Details on Anonymity and Pseudonymity in Literature*. Mount Vernon, Va.: The Golden Eagle Press,

Christmas, 1939, pp. 7–8. Portrait (woodcut) by Mathew Zimmer.
On Crane as "Johnston Smith."

Mason, Gregory. *Remember the Maine*. New York, 1939.

Pattee, Fred Lewis. Letter to Alfred A. Knopf, December 19, 1939.*
"Your letter concerning your proposed volume of selections from the short story work of Stephen Crane interests me. Such selections would make an interesting volume for readers and would be helpful for students of the art of Stephen Crane. However, I could not use the book in my short story classes as a required text and I doubt if many other teachers could use it, save as a book to be referred to and consulted in the college library. As I define the short story, Crane was not a short story writer at all. In my *History of the American Short Story*, Harpers [*sic*], I say this:

> Whether this Stephen Crane type of short narrative is a short story or not depends wholly upon definitions. Of plot, as plot is usually defined, it has none; of love element, of women indeed, none; of problems, or of dramatic dilemma, or struggle between contrasted forces, none at all. It is a running series of moving pictures, each picture moving and intense; it is a forced growth in the field of modern journalism. . . .

> "The Open Boat," perhaps his most praised story, is the day's work of a newspaper correspondent intent only [in] reproducing graphically the experience through which he has just passed. The style is staccato, short of sentence, compressed like a night letter, stripped bare of all but essentials. Every detail must be made vivid by an epithet or a picturing phrase. Details seemingly trivial are made important. Expressionism is pushed to the extreme; the picture is everything.

"There are no characters: only types, so soulless that they do not even have names: 'the oiler,' 'the correspondent,' etc. A whole volume like *The Red Badge of Courage* and not a single individual with a name: type figures. A short story should have what I have elsewhere called a 'soul.' Crane is a mere newspaper camera set up for movie use or for the daily journal column, alive to-day; tomorrow in the ash barrel.

"There is not much use to choose among the short narratives he has left. All are of the same piece. All of the *Whilomville Stories*, however, show the signs of haste and slap-dash workmanship. I advise dropping them from the collection.

"Crane's influence has been bad. The present group of young writers, who use newspaper methods and who despise all rules, learned their methods in some degree from Crane. I am glad to see that the influence on the short story of these young literary journalists is declining."

Pratt, Lyndon Upson. "The Formal Education of Stephen Crane," *American Literature*, 10 (January, 1939), 460–471.
On Claverack College, "one of New York State's superior collegiate institutions, whose classical graduates could step directly into the junior year at Yale, Syracuse, Cornell, or Wesleyan." *Contra* Thomas Beer's statement that Crane arrived at Claverack in February, 1887, Crane's signature first appears on the school register for January 4, 1888. He registered again on September 10, 1888, and on September 9, 1889. His first signed publication, an article on the explorer Henry M. Stanley, appeared in the school's *Vidette* (February, 1890). Instead of returning to Claverack in the autumn of 1890, Crane entered

---

* From the files of A. A. Knopf, Inc. Now in the files of R. W. S., the gift of Knopf's editor, the late Herbert Weinstock.

Lafayette College, registering on September 12. On the courses he took there and at Syracuse University in the spring of 1891, where the only mark he received was an *A* in English literature. Pratt errs in saying that Crane spent two semesters at Syracuse.

On Claverack College *see* Wickham (1926), and on Syracuse University *see* French (1934), and Peaslee (August, 1896). On Crane at Lafayette College *see* Smith (1932) and Chamberlin (1961).

Pratt's article is of considerable biographical importance. For new data from the files of Claverack College *see SCraneN* (Summer, 1968).

―――. "A Possible Source of *The Red Badge of Courage*," *American Literature*, 11 (March, 1939), 1–10.

Pratt rightly conjectures the debt Crane owed for his *Red Badge of Courage*, for certain scenes in it, to the Civil War reminiscences of his Claverack College history teacher, the Reverend General John Bullock Van Petten, who fought at Antietam and was wounded at the battle of Winchester in Virginia. The latter item is supplied in O'Donnell's subsequent data buttressing Pratt's undocumented conjecture. In *American Literature*, 27 (May, 1955): "John B. Van Petten: Stephen Crane's History Teacher." Both the Pratt and O'Donnell articles attain importance because they provide, in retrospect, evidence which puts into question the standard claim that the battlefield in *The Red Badge* is solely Chancellorsville. *See* Hungerford (1963).

―――. "An Addition to the Canon of Stephen Crane," *Research Studies of the State College of Washington*, 7 (March, 1939), 55–58. Reprints for the first time from the *Vidette*, 1, no. 3 (February, 1890) Crane's article "Henry M. Stanley," signed "S. Crane" in the student publication of Claverack College and Hudson River Institute.

Randall, D. A., and J. T. Winterich. "One Hundred Good Novels: Crane, Stephen, *The Red Badge of Courage*," *Publisher's Weekly*, 136 (October 21, 1939), 1625–1626.

Small, Major Abner B. *The Road to Richmond*, ed. Harold Adams Small. Berkeley, Calif., 1939, 1957, p. 185. *See* Anderson (1961).

"*Bravery and courage.*—These remain deep mysteries. In the heat and turmoil of a fight, the word 'bravery' has no significance to the combatants; men are heroes or cowards in spite of themselves. All the demands of active service call for courage; but the real test comes before the battle—in the rear line, under fire, waiting. The true perspective of danger is observed and comprehended by the man attached to the edge of a battle—not in it, but near enough to feel its fierce pulsations and get an occasional shock of its power.

"A young author, his boyish fancy stimulated by books, has written a story in which he takes a raw recruit into, through, and out of a battle and represents him with a brain fully alive to reason and revealing a cunning course of deception, all in a way apparently realistic, and intensely interesting, but only possible in an imaginative mind before a parlor grate.

"That any man in my regiment, or in the army, analyzed his feelings and marked out any specific line of conduct while under fire, or even thought for five consecutive minutes of the past, present, or future, or measured out or acted upon any theoretical course of conduct irrespective of the arbitrary military law which held him in obedience, is absurd. Afterthoughts are in a sense real, and give a correct résumé of what might have been; but to put an endless and connected train of thought in the brain of a green soldier, so thoroughly scared—by his own admission—that he is not accountable, and set it in systematic motion which shall develop the *Red Badge of Courage,* is sheer rot.

"The bravest front, bolstered by pride and heroic resolution, will crumble in the presence of the agony of wounds. Wading through bloody fields and among the distorted dead bodies of comrades, dodging shells, and posing as a target to hissing bullets that whisper of eternity, is not conducive to continuity of action, much less of thought. The shock from a bursting shell will scatter a man's thoughts as the iron fragments will scatter the leaves overhead."

Smith, Bernard. *Forces in American Criticism.* New York, 1939.

Webster, H. T. "Wibur F. Hinman's *Corporal Si Klegg* and Stephen Crane's *The Red Badge of Courage,*" *American Literature,* 11 (November, 1939), 285–293.

No Crane scholar disputes Webster's claim of influence on *The Red Badge* by Hinman's *Corporal Si Klegg,* a parallelism first discussed in *Omnibus.*

1940

[Anon.]. "Playlot to Rise at Birthplace of Stephen Crane," *New York Herald Tribune,* January 1, 1940, p. 20.

The W.P.A. (Work Projects Administration) plans to demolish the dilapidated brick and graystone house at 14 Mulberry Place, where Stephen Crane was born. The site will become the Stephen Crane Playground, of which the first unit will be an outdoor roller-skating rink for children.

Former members of the Stephen Crane Association, a victim of the Depression, intend to put up a tablet honoring Stephen Crane. Except for that tablet in the Free Public Library of Newark, "the playground will be the first public memorial in the United States to the man who Joseph Conrad and other European authors believed to be the first modern American writer of genius."

Applejoy, Petronius. "Stephen Crane Is News," *Catholic World,* 151 (August, 1940), 586–594.

Crane in *The Red Badge* "practiced the methods of psychoanalysis long before its vocabulary had become the argot of the intellectual market-place."

Balch, David Arnold. *Elbert Hubbard: Genius of Roycroft, A Biography.* New York, 1940, pp. 183–184, 217–220.

Misdates the Society of the Philistine banquet for Crane for December 19, 1896 (1895). "Crane earned his keep at the Roycroft Shop during those early days by writing cryptic epigrams for the covers of *The Philistine.* . . ." However, Crane did not earn his keep by contributing to the *Philistine;* for Hubbard paid Crane nothing for his many contributions.

See Taber (1940).

Barr, Mark. "Stephen Crane's Memorial," *New York Herald Tribune,* January 2, 1940, section 11, p. 9.

On the memorial of a playground on the site of his birthplace, 14 Mulberry Place, Newark, N.J.; mention of it prompts Mark Barr to write this tribute to Stephen Crane. He had "a rare trait—he disliked publicity and he made an enemy of the 'yellow press' reporters." They told Richard Harding Davis that Crane was a drug addict, and he flatly denied it. So, too, were all the other libels against Crane "a stinking lie." Henry James at Rye told Mark Barr: " 'We love Stephen Crane for what he is; we admire him for what he is going to be.' He meant that while Crane's writings in his early twenties showed talent, he would later become one of the great writers of America." At Brede Place "Stephen and his wife received many friends, and the joy we had was indescribable."

Brooks, Van Wyck. *New England Indian Summer: 1865–1915*. New York, 1940, pp. 500–501, 504, and *passim*.

    Reports that Barrett Wendell in one of his lectures described *The Red Badge* as "sensational trash."

Carnes, Cecil. *Jimmy Hare: News Photographer*. New York, 1940, pp. 53, 60–63, 70–75, 77–78, 128, 291.

    An important and lively account: Crane playing poker aboard the *Somers N. Smith* with Scovel, Meriwether, and others; Crane's encounter with Reuben McNab (his Claverack College classmate) at Bloody Bend;* and Rough Rider Teddy Roosevelt's disapproval of Crane on moral grounds.

Honce, Charles. "Farewell to Stephen Crane," in *Mark Twain's Associated Press Speech*. Mount Vernon, Va., 1940, pp. 120–121.

Kazin, Alfred. "American fin-de-siècle," *Saturday Review of Literature*, 21 (February 3, 1940), 11–12.

    Reprinted in *On Native Grounds* (1942), pp. 51–72.

Kramer, Sidney. *A History of Stone and Kimball and Herbert S. Stone and Co.* Chicago, 1940, p. 21.

Lang, Martin. *Character Analysis Through Color*. Westport, Conn., 1940.

Lemperly, Paul. The *Library of the late Paul Lemperly, Lakewood, Ohio*. New York, 1940, pp. 38–39.

    See also SCraneN (Spring, 1969) pp. 7–9.

Nye, Russell B. "Stephen Crane as a Social Critic," *Modern Quarterly*, 11 (Summer, 1940), 48–54.

    See Westbrook, "Stephen Crane's Social Ethic" (1962), who takes issue with Nye and also with Walcutt (1956).

Taber, Harry P. Letter to David Balch (n.d., ca. 1940).

    "Through an error on my part in making up the type pages, my name was left off the masthead of that first number [of the *Philistine* (June, 1895)]. I owned the copyright and the original of the grant to me from the Library of Congress is in the collection of the late Samuel Bancroft, Jr., of Wilmington, who sent the first dollar for a subscription to the magazine which remained under my editorial direction until February, 1896. At that time a violent altercation concerning editorial policy and other matters brought to an end my association with Hubbard. Our old crowd made a proposition to him: would he buy my interest in the concern or would he sell his? He said he would sell, and named a price based on the then estimated value of the property. A dozen or so of us got together and funds were subscribed for the purchase. I went to New York and contracted for a complete new outfit of

    * Reuben McNab is not the name of the barber in Crane's "The Angel Child," as mistakenly given in *Omnibus*. This error was not caught in the second edition of *Crane*, p. 397.

presses and equipment, and these were shipped to East Aurora where my brother had prepared a building for the plant.

"With me in New York was Eugene White and we had a meeting with Stephen Crane at the Hotel Imperial. We laid our plans before him—told him that we proposed to publish books as well as the magazine. He promised that for our first book from the new plant (Roycroft, by the way), we should have one on which he was then working. With this as a nucleus we felt that we were on firm foundation for the name of Crane would give us tremendous prestige. But when we returned to East Aurora Hubbard had changed his mind. He refused to sell. Would he buy, then? Yes. So it was understood that my estimated share—matter of approximately $8,000.00—should be paid to me. It never was. The equipment purchased in New York was returned and that was that.

"The *Philistine* and the Roycroft Shop were sold to Hubbard by me on November 29, 1895. By the terms of this contract I was to remain editor of the magazine and manager of the Roycroft and receiving one-half the net profits of the concerns, payments to be made every six months. That contract is in my desk. It has been there for forty-five years. As is noted in your book, Hubbard's conception of a contract reserved the right to break it whenever either party thereto became dissatisfied with it. And this, too, reminds one of Hitleric procedure. Good enough if you can get away with it, and The Genius did in my case, for I could not go into court and fight as Fred Gardner could—and did, and won his suit. Never mind the rest of the story of the *Journeys*. It is too sad. It is not tuned to polite ears. The truth of it is, however, far removed from the one you relate. Somebody's been kidding you.

"You say on page 159 that Hubbard could be 'personally vindictive to an extreme, an almost venomous extent.' God bless my soul! You are telling *me?* Didn't I get a dose of it? Didn't poor Walter Blackburn Harte, the last of the great American essayists, die from the impact? And didn't one of the gentlest souls on earth, Stephen Crane, suffer from it? And then didn't Hubbard, after having administered one of his subtle purges, keen with the doleful sound of some professional mourner when Stephen died? I'll say he did. He had crucified Harte's *Fly-Leaf* and brought the editor of that little magazine from Boston to East Aurora as editor of the *Philistine* . . . but you do not, I think, touch on that matter. It would pay you, perhaps to read Percival Pollard's 'Their Day in Court.'

"The description of Hubbard's association with Crane is a soothing bedtime story. Crane did not earn his keep, as you say, by writing cryptic epigrams for the covers of the *Philistine* and contributing free verse. (The lines you quote as being a fragment of one of these Crane did not write. It was a parody, appearing in The Onlooker's columns of Town Topics.) Nor did Crane spend much time in East Aurora 'walking and talking for long hours with Hubbard.' He was too busy down on the Florida coast observing the filibusters and writing of them. You by inference lead us to believe that Crane wrote *The Red Badge of Courage* subsequent to his East Aurora visits. That phenomenal book was written early in 1893 and sold to the Bacheller Syndicate for a hundred dollars. It was published in book form by Appletons in October, 1895,—two months before Crane came to Buffalo (and East Aurora) for the first time. That visit was on the occasion of the dinner for him to which you refer as 'an unheard of thing!' Details concerning the dinner may be found in a chapter I have written in my own account of the Hubbardian period. The dinner, by the way, was on December 19, 1895—not 1896, as you say.

"Of the affairs treated of in your book occurring after February, 1896, I have nothing to say. I had nothing to do with them. Two men within the past few years have come to me for some part of the story of the Roycroft and the *Philistine*. I offered them what help I could. I did not discourage their efforts, but for some reason they gave up their plan for writing a biography of the Dispenser of Loving Kindness. As I have said, I have no grievance now against the man; nor have I even the slightest hint of one against you for the rather contemptuous treatment of my part in the play. The *Philistine* and the Roycroft began with a spirit which died when the Great Showman took control and cast high hopes into some abysmal depths. My associates and I had no part in the Success which Hubbard made out of our ideas. We couldn't have made that sort of Success and continued orisons arise in thankfulness for that. We were at least honest, and though our output may have been skim-milk, it did not 'masquerade as cream.' But yes. I have one grievance. You said I wrote poetry which was innocuous. If I ever wrote poetry—which God forbid!—I hope somebody could find some fiercer word to apply to it. 'Innocuous' sounds sort of silly."

Relate Taber's letter to Balch (1940) with Taber's letter to Beer (1923) and to Taber's account of Hubbard as told in Tom Daly's 1916 article.*

Van Doren, Carl. *The American Novel: 1780–1939.* New York, 1940, pp. 228–233. Rev. ed.

————. Introduction, *Stephen Crane: Twenty Stories.* Selected with an Introduction by Carl Van Doren. New York: Alfred A. Knopf, Inc., 1940. Reprinted by World Publishing Company, Cleveland and New York, 1945. Notes, pp. 501–507.

The Introduction, an excellent essay, quotes from Van Doren's interview with Willa Cather. She told him that of Crane's Western stories she preferred "The Bride Comes to Yellow Sky." One must disagree with Van Doren's claim that of the Cuban War stories "The Price of the Harness" is of the same quality as Crane's best Civil War stories. As Cather elsewhere said, "The Price of the Harness" "just misses being a fine war tale." Van Doren's Crane selection while larger in scope than Starrett's *Men, Women and Boats* (1921), includes much second-rate Crane. Of his twenty selected Crane pieces, *Omnibus* reprints but seven. *Omnibus* established the canon of Crane's best works, whcih has remained chiefly the same works in reprint-editions since 1952 with the exception of "The Monster," not included in *Omnibus*. Van Doren's *Twenty Stories* included it.

Reviewed:

Margaret Marshall, "Books and the Arts," *Nation,* 151 (September 21, 1940), 247. Contends that the quality of Crane's stories is uneven. However, Crane's work doesn't deserve the obscurity with which most of it, except *The Red Badge*, seems fated. *Maggie* "is interesting now only as one of the first examples of realism." See Alfred Kazin (1942) and Marcus Cunliffe (1955), who share the same viewpoint as Marshall's.

However, *contra* Kazin, see Stallman, "Crane's Primrose Path" (1955), contending that by its art *Maggie* transcends the dustbin of mere realism. On

---

* For these letters and the Daly article, all published here for the first time, I am indebted to Professor Austin McCracken Fox.

Maggie again *see Houses* (1961), an expanded version of the *New Republic* essay. *See also Crane* (1968).

New York Herald Books, September 29, 1940, p. 29.

Booklist, 37 (November 1, 1940), 90.

Springfield Republican, February 2, 1941, p. 7E.

1941

[Anon.]. "Biographical Note on Stephen Crane," *Scholastic,* 38 (February 17, 1941), 30.

Reprints "A Mystery of Heroism," pp. 29–30, 34–35.

Ayshiskina, N. "Stephen Crane: *Twenty Stories,*" *Literaturnoc Obozrenie* (Moscow), no. 1 (1941), 83–84.

A review of Carl Van Doren's *Twenty Stories by Stephen Crane.*

Bates, H. E. *The Modern Short Story: A Critical Survey.* New York, 1941, pp. 64–71.

Beer, Thomas. *Hanna, Crane, and the Mauve Decade.* New York, 1941.

In *The Mauve Decade* (1926), pp. 44, 70, 86, 96, 117, 139, 140, 146 (Crane and Norris), 150, 153, 164, 179, 193n. For reviews *see* Beer (1923).

Bennett, Whitman. *A Practical Guide to American Book Collecting* (1663–1940). New York: Bennett Book Studies, 1941.

Note on *The Red Badge;* also on *Maggie.* "Crane was only 29 when he died. Frank Norris, born a year earlier, died two years later at 32. Crane was the more brilliant; Norris the more powerful and deliberately constructive. Neither ever reached his prime." (Crane died at 28, not at 29.)

Brooks, Cleanth, and Robert Penn Warren, eds. *An Approach to Literature.* New York, 1941, pp. 45–46.

On Crane's "An Episode of War"; questions of critical insight such as: "What makes this more than a mere sketch?" "What is the function of the last lines of the story?"

Cargill, Oscar. *Intellectual America.* New York, 1941, pp. 84–89, 107, 351, 352, 361, 362.

Concedes "that only two pieces of writing from the pen of Stephen Crane possess that finish which marks the maturity of a writer, and these are both short stories: 'The Open Boat' and 'The Blue Hotel.'" As for *The Black Riders* and *War Is Kind,* "whether these pieces are poetry is debatable."

Contra Cargill, Crane did not marry Cora Taylor, *Maggie* was not published in 1892, and Henry James's journalist in *The Wings of the Dove* bears no resemblance to Stephen Crane.

As for *Maggie* (says Cargill), "There is no question whatsoever about Crane's inspiration for the book: it is wholly the product of reading Zola's *L'Assommoir.* Yet we ought not to have mentioned them in the same breath, for in comparison with Zola's great document *Maggie* reads like a burlesque. . . . It is painful to estimate this little book fairly, for Crane was roundly abused for writing it, and our sympathies are wholly with him. Yet to rank *Maggie* with any of the genuine masterpieces of Naturalism is ridiculous."

On the influence of Zola's *L'Assommoir* on Crane *see* Cunliffe (1955) and Stone (1963). On the influence of Flaubert's *Madame Bovary* on *Maggie see* Stallman, "Stephen Crane's Primrose Path" (1955). *Versus* Cargill's thesis that Naturalism is pessimistic determinism *see* Walcutt (1946) and (1956).

Honce, Charles. [Stephen Crane], *The Papers of the Bibliographical Society of America*, 35 (Fourth Quarter, 1941), 297.
   A collation of *Tales From Town Topics*, no. 33 (September, 1899), which contains "In the Tenderloin."

Short, Raymond, and Richard B. Sewall, ed. *Short Stories for Study*. New York, 1941, pp. 134–138, 591–592. Reprints "The Upturned Face." The note misdates *Maggie* ("written 1893, published 1896") and *The Red Badge of Courage* ("1896").

1942

Berenson, Bernard. *One Year's Reading for Fun*. New York, 1942.

Blanck, Jacob. *Merle Johnson's American First Editions*. New York, 1942, pp. 128–130.
   Checklist of Crane first editions. However, no collection of British first editions exists in any American library, nor in BCC (only in Stallman's Crane collection), said Blanck in letter to R. W. S. (1950s).

Fletcher, John Gould. "Homage to Ford Madox Ford," in *New Directions*, no. 7. New York, 1942, p. 473.

Gregory, Horace, and Marya Zaturenska. "A Note on Stephen Crane," in *A History of American Poetry: 1900–1940*. New York, 1942, pp. 133–137.
   Collate with Gregory (1930).

Hemingway, Ernest, ed. *Men at War: The Best War Stories of All Time*. Introduction by Ernest Hemingway. New York, 1942, p. xvii.
   The Red Badge of Courage "is one of the finest books of our literature, and I included it entire because it is all as much of one piece as a great poem is." Cf. V. S. Pritchett (1946).

Herzberg, Max J., ed. *The Red Badge of Courage*. New York, 1942. London: Penguin Books, 1942.
   Reviewed: Pritchett (1942).

Honce, Charles. "Legends of Stephen Crane," in *The Public Papers of a Bibliomaniac*. Mount Vernon, Va., 1942, pp. 115–125. An edition of one hundred copies.
   First book publication of Crane's report of the parade of the American Mechanics at Asbury Park in the *New York Tribune*, August 21, 1892. Cited in *Bulletin of Bibliography* (January–April, 1936) by Claude Jones. B. J. R. Stolper listed it in his Crane bibliography (1930), simply as an "unsigned article dated from Asbury Park giving the news from that resort with lists of people at hotels. Said to be earliest known writing of Crane." First reprinted in *Library* (Newark, N.J.), 5, no. 1 (September, 1932), 3.
   Oscar Cargill in *The Social Revolt* (1930) misdated Crane's parade sketch

for 1891. Other versions of the story include Hamlin Garland's in *Yale Review* (April, 1914) and in *Roadside Meetings* (1930); John D. Barry's in *Bookman* (April, 1901); Max Herzberg's in his Introduction to *The Red Badge of Courage* (1925); and Thomas Beer's in his *Stephen Crane* (1923), pp. 89–90.

Willis Johnson in "The Launching of Stephen Crane" (April, 1926) insists that Crane was not fired by the *Tribune* because of this *Tribune* article, "On the New Jersey Coast." And Victor Elconin agrees in his 1948 essay on Crane at Asbury Park agrees. However, not known to Elconin was Arthur Oliver's "Jersey Memories—Stephen Crane," in the *New Jersey Historical Society Magazine* (October, 1931). Oliver quotes Crane first hand and George Wheeler's report of the news: "Townley Crane was fired by mail and Stevie by wire!"

Melvin Schoberlin, while ignoring Oliver and Honce, takes issue with Johnson and flatly declares that both Stephen and Townley were summarily discharged by the *Tribune*. Townley got reinstated, but William Crane said that Townley never recovered from this crisis and that he ended a broken man. (Journalist Townley ended his career in Port Jervis as superintendent of streets and died in Binghamton, N.Y., in 1908.)

Subsequent research of the *Tribune* for 1892 and 1893 has turned up nothing by Stephen Crane (under the dateline Hartwood, N.Y.); as the *Tribune* published nothing of Crane after September, 1892, it is evident that—*contra* Willis Fletcher Johnson—Crane was fired. *See Crane.* Crane's sketch of the Asbury Park parade, "On the New Jersey Coast," was reprinted in *Omnibus*.

Kazin, Alfred. *On Native Grounds.* New York, 1942, pp. 10, 32, 34, 67–72, 87–88, 97–98 [Crane and Frank Norris], 240, 320, 322.

Well-phrased but sweeping judgments founded not on the whole body of Crane's works nor on scrutinies of individual works: "No one in America had written like him before; but though his books precipitately gave the whole esthetic movement of the nineties a sudden direction and a fresher impulse, he could contribute no more than the intensity of his spirit. Half of him was a consummate workman; the other half was not a writer at all." (One half of Kazin is also missing in this gross misjudgment.) Kazin calls "The Open Boat" drawn "from an almost direct report of experiences in the Caribbean," a "great show piece." (The "great show piece"—unknown to Kazin—occurred not in the Caribbean but off the coast of Daytona Beach, which is in Florida.)

Innovator Crane ("he proved himself the first great pyrotechnician of the contemporary novel"), also "wrote more trash than any other serious novelist of his time." However, Crane—according to Kazin (p. 97)—somehow seems "so significantly a symbol of the fin de siècle, the last glowing ember of a dying century. . . ."

Kazin, one concludes, dislikes Crane, underrates his achievement ("Crane's best work was curiously thin and, in one sense, even corrupt"), and seems puzzled that Crane fits neatly into no one pigeon-hole. Nothing in Kazin's essay is documented; p. 67 echoes Amy Lowell, and p. 239 on Beer's style is lifted from Malcolm Cowley's review of Beer's *Hanna, Crane, and the Mauve Decade* in *New Republic* (September 29, 1941).

Kazin, p. 69, contends that Crane was "essentially uneducated. . . . He read very little. . . ." However, that Crane read a great many books is evidenced by "List of Books / Brede Place" (1899). *See Crane.*

Kunitz, S. J., and Howard Haycraft, eds. *Twentieth Century Authors.* New York, 1942.

Luckey, Robert. "Apreciación del poeta Stephen Crane," *Revista Ibero-americana*, 5 (October, 1942), 317–343.

Marchand, Ernest. *Frank Norris: A Study*. London, 1942, pp. 53, 184, 206, 224, 235, 236, and *passim*.

Pritchett, V. S. [unsigned]. *"The Red Badge of Courage:* Epitaph for Romantic Wars," *New Statesman and Nation*, 24 (August 8, 1942), 95.
     Review of the Penguin edition of *The Red Badge of Courage*, ed. Max J. Herzberg.
     Reprinted in Pritchett's *The Living Novel* (1949), pp. 172–178.

Van Doren, Mark. "Work of Stephen Crane," in *Private Reader: Selected Articles and Reviews*. New York, 1942, pp. 156–158.

1943

Arms, George, and William M. Gibson. "Five Interviews with William Dean Howells," *Americana*, 37 (April, 1943), 257–295.
     Reprints here for the first time Crane's signed interview in the *New York Times*, October 28, 1894, "Fears Realists Must Wait."
     Reprinted in *Omnibus* (1952), pp. 169–172. "Howells Fears Realists Must Wait." (The *Americana* was then unknown to Stallman.)

Barbosa, A. Rolmes. *Escritores norte-americans e outros*. Pôrto Alegre: Ediçâo Globo, 1933, pp. 153–157.
     Includes among 100 important American books of the previous ten decades Carl Van Doren's edition of Crane's "Best Tales" [*Stephen Crane: Twenty Stories* (1940)] and Thomas Beer, *The Mauve Decade*.

Cabell, Branch, and A. J. Hanna. "Cora Comes Back," in *The St. John's*. New York, 1943, pp. 275–286.
     Their claim that Cora, on returning to Jacksonville after Crane's death had her brothel "The Court" modelled after Brede Manor has no foundation in fact. It bore no resemblance to that ancient manor house in Sussex. This error—repeated in *Omnibus*—is corrected in *Letters*.
     Cabell and Hanna reported in *The St. John's*, the local Jacksonville legend subscribed to by librarian Carl Bohnenberger (d. 1934). See *Cora Crane*. Bohnenberger published Conrad's letters to Stephen and Cora Crane in *Bookman* (May, 1929).

Dickason, David. "Stephen Crane and the *Philistine*," *American Literature*, 15 (November, 1943), 279–287.
     Surveys Crane's publications in Hubbard's *Philistine*, but neglects to trace what Crane pieces the *Philistine* and the *Fra* published subsequent to Crane's death. Not noted by Dickason is the fact that Hubbard did not pay his contributors. Unknown to Dickason are the following data:
     Harry P. Taber's name did not appear on the first 1895 number of the *Philistine* as editor, but it did appear in the second number and thereafter until February, 1896. "At that time a violent altercation concerning editorial policy and other matters brought to an end my association with Hubbard."

For new light on Hubbard, the *Philistine,* Taber's Roycroft Shop, and the the banquet tendered Crane by the Philistine Society *see* Taber (1923) and (1940). *See also* Daly (1916).

Millett, Fred B. *Contemporary American Authors.* New York, 1943, p. 30.

"Of the work of the pioneers in naturalism that of Stephen Crane seems likely to be of the greatest historical and aesthetic interest. His audacious stylistic experimentation is a continuing influence on the contemporary literary impressionists. Crane's combination of poetically sensitive observation and unqualified realism makes him seem a creature born before his time."

Salvan, Albert J. *Zola aux États-Unis.* Providence, R.I., 1943, p. 163.

"*Dans la question toujours délicate d'établir un rapport d'influence définie entre Zola et Stephen Crane, nous sommes forcés de rester sur une note evasive. Il n'est guère douteux que l'auteur de* Maggie *manquait d'une connaissance très entendue de la littérature française du XIXe siecle en genéral.*"

Opposition to this thesis is the sum of Lars Ahnebrink's study of Crane: Ahnebrink (1950).

Silveira, Brenno. *Pequena história da literatura norte-americana.* São Paulo, Brazil: Martins, 1943, pp. 175–177.

Wells, H. G. "Stephen Crane From an English Standpoint," in *The Shock of Recognition,* ed. Edmund Wilson (1943). Reprinted from *North American Review,* 171 (August, 1900), 233–242.

Reprinted in *Letters,* pp. 309–316.

Who Was Who in America, vol. 1, 1897–1942. Chicago, 1943, p. 273.

Williams, Ben Ames, ed. *Amateurs at War: The American Soldier in Action.* Boston, 1943, pp. 290–323. Reprints Crane's "War Memories" under the title: "'Well, Begawd, We Done It' / The Santiago Campaign / By / Stephen Crane."

Erroneously reports, pp. 294–295, that Crane in 1898 "was still in his thirties."

Wilson, Edmund, ed. *The Shock of Recognition.* New York, 1943, pp. 659–660. Reprints H. G. Wells's "Stephen Crane From an English Standpoint." *See* Wells (1900).

"It has been difficult to find anything about Stephen Crane for the purposes of this book. Thomas Beer's *Stephen Crane* is valuable, but it is simply a sort of memoir written by one who did not know him; and though the collected edition of Crane includes prefaces by Amy Lowell, Willa Cather, Sherwood Anderson and Howells, these are brief and deal with special aspects. One has to go abroad for something better." However, Wilson does not mention Garnett's "Mr. Stephen Crane" (1898), or Vincent Starrett's "Stephen Crane: An Estimate," *Sewanee Review* (June, 1920). Wilson errs in that Crane died on June 5, not June 4, and Howells did not contribute an introduction to *Work.*

Reprinted 1955, pp. 661–671. Reprinted in *Letters* (1960), pp. 309–316.

1944

Allen, Frederick Lewis. *Paul Revere Reynolds*. New York, 1944. Introduction
by Frederick Lewis Allen: "The Agent and An Author: Stephen Crane,"
pp. 48–62.
   Crane's letters to agent Reynolds here for the first time. With related letters
by R. W. Gilder and Walter H. Page. Crane's letters are reprinted in *Letters*.
   Errs in stating that Crane was dead at "thirty-four," p. 62. And then for
Paul Reynolds "there remained only the duty of collecting payments for the
settlement of his meager estate."

[Anon.] (trans.). *La roja insignia del coraje* [*The Red Badge of Courage*].
Buenos Aires, Argentina: Emecé Editores, 1944.
   An Argentine translation into the Spanish.

Bushman, John C. "The Fiction of Stephen Crane and Its Critics." Dissertation,
University of Illinois, 1944.

Frewen, Hugh. *Imogene: An Odyssey*. Sydney, Australia, n.d. [1944], pp.
99–100.
   On Crane and Brede Place; quotes Crane's poem "The Wayfarer."

Michelson, Charles. *The Ghost Talks*. New York, 1944, p. 89.
   A brief glimpse of Crane enroute to the Spanish-American War. Nothing
new here. However, *see* Michelson's Introduction, *Work* (1927).

Trilling, Lionel, John Mason Brown, and Richard Sewell. *Invitation to Learning* (a recording). New York, 1944.
   Discussion about *The Red Badge of Courage*.

Van Doren, Carl. Introduction, *The Red Badge of Courage*. New York, 1944,
pp. vii–xiii. Illustrated by John Curry.
   A simple-minded version of a very complicated novel for simple-minded
readers, appropriately printed in large type.

Whitehead, Jean V. "The Art of Stephen Crane." Dissertation, Cornell
University, 1944.

1945

Baker, Ray Standard. *American Chronicle*. New York, 1945, pp. 78, 99, 317.

Beer, Thomas. "Henry James and Stephen Crane," in *The Question of Henry
James*, ed. F. W. Dupee. New York, 1945, pp. 105–107. Reprinted from
Beer's *SC*.

Fitzgerald, F. Scott. *The Crack-Up*. New York, 1945, p. 274.
   Writes J. P. Bishop that his novelette, *The Cellar*, is "right up with the very
best of Crane and Bierce."

Sewall, R. B. "Crane's *The Red Badge of Courage*," *Explicator*, 3, no. 7 (May,
1945), item 55.
   Parallelisms between *The Red Badge* and *Lord Jim*. Questions the conclusion of *The Red Badge*. Crane "gives us no hint that his moral victory is

anything but complete. As Henry turns 'with a lover's thirst to images of tranquil skies, fresh meadows, cool brooks—an existence of soft and eternal peace,' one wonders if Crane has not left him in a state of complacency, which, in terms of Henry's moral struggle as Crane has represented it, seems undeserved and arbitrary." However, Crane does not give Henry Fleming any final moral triumph, as pointed out by Lynskey (1949).

With Sewall's article and Lynskey's rejoinder the critical warfare about *The Red Badge of Courage* begins.

Sheridan, Clare. *My Crowded Sanctuary.* London, 1945.
On Crane at Brede Manor. Of footnote interest.

Silveira (Junior), Alarico, trans. *A novia chega a yellow sky,* in *Os norte americanos antigos e modernos,* ed. Vinicius de Morais, Origenes Lessa, and Tati de Melo Morais. Rio de Janeiro Brazil: Companhia Editôra Leitura, 1945, pp. 179–187.

Werner, W. L. "Stephen Crane and *The Red Badge of Courage,*" *New York Times Book Review,* September 30, 1945, p. 4.
An illuminating and useful discussion of the history of the much shortened newspaper version of *The Red Badge* appearing in December, 1894, in the *New York Press* and the *Philadelphia Press.*

Werner's important short study is ignored by Joseph Katz in his facsimile edition of the 1894 *Red Badge of Courage* (1967). Thomas A. Gullason, in *The Complete Novels of Stephen Crane* (1967), omits mention of Werner's important article in his preface of acknowledging "my indebtedness to all previous Crane criticism. . . ."

1946

[Anon.]. "Stephen Crane," in *American Short Novel, Nineteenth Century.* Moscow, 1946.
Contains "An Experiment in Misery," "An Episode of War," and "A Dark Brown Dog."

Burlingame, Roger. *Of Making Many Books.* New York, 1946, pp. 72, 133, 327.

Gregory, Horace, and Marya Zaturenska. "Note on Stephen Crane," in *A History of American Poetry: 1900–1940.* New York, 1946, pp. 133–137. Recast from *New Republic,* 63 (June 25, 1930).
Gregory's 1930 study of Crane's place as poet and his influence was a landmark and remains so to this day. In some points he was anticipated by Edith Wyatt (1915). Gregory's standpoint on Crane's historical importance as poet against the background of his time and against subsequent trends in poetry is echoed in *Omnibus.*

Phillips, William. Introduction, *Great American Short Novels,* ed. by William Phillips. New York, 1946, pp. x–xi. Reprints *Maggie,* 1896 ed. (not 1893 as given).
Rightly claims that *The Red Badge* "is realistic only in a thematic sense, for its style and sensibility have little in common with the method of additive detail associated with the modern realistic school. It is rather *Maggie,* a some-

what earlier novel that created less of a stir than *The Red Badge of Courage,* that foreshadowed the development of truly naturalistic writing not only of the serious but of the popular variety as well. And it seems to me an act of remarkable creative discipline on Crane's part to have maintained a genuine literary integrity and spareness in a story that contains all the sentimental ingredients of the five-and-dime novel. . . . We observe also in *Maggie* all the pathos, sometimes shallow and only dimly conscious, of the underdog, that makes up the mood as well as the subject of what we now call 'social realism.' "

Quotes Mencken on Crane's method as being "grossly ill-adapted to the novel, properly so-called. He had, so to speak, no literary small talk; he could not manage what the musicians call passage work. His superlative skill lay in the handling of isolated situations; he knew exactly how to depict them with a dazzling brilliance, and he knew, too, how to analyze them with a penetrating insight. . . ."

Pritchett, V. S. "Two Writers and Modern War" [Whitman and Crane], *The Living Novel.* London, 1946 and 1949, pp. 167–178. New York, 1947, pp. 167–178. Recast from *New Statesman and Nation* (August 8, 1942), p. 95.

Reprinted in *The Living Novel and Later Appreciations.* New York, 1964. "*The Red Badge of Courage* is a *tour de force.* Crane starts a bugle call and sustains it without a falter to the end of the book. . . . There is no plot in this book; it is a collection of episodes. . . . The whole thing is almost as anonymous as a poem or a piece of music and has the same kind of tension and suspense." Cf. Hemingway in *Men at War* (1942): *The Red Badge* "is all as much of one piece as a great poem is."

Shipley, Joseph T., ed. "United States Literature," *Encyclopedia of Literature,* vol. 2. New York, 1946, p. 981.

Trent, W. P., John Erskine, and others, eds. *The Cambridge History of American Literature,* vol. 3. New York, 1946, pp. 92–93, 309.

Walcutt, Charles C. "From Scientific Theory to Aesthetic Fact: the 'Naturalistic' Novel," *Quarterly Review of Literature,* 3, no. 2, n.d. [October, 1946], 167–179.

Toward a definition of literary Naturalism in the novel. This definition differs from Walcutt's subsequent definition of literary Naturalism in *American Literary Naturalism* (1956), a difference which Walcutt silently corrects in the latter version. His definition in *QRL* is, I think, the more correct version.

Compare Walcutt with Hartwick (1934) on *The Red Badge* and with Cargill (1941); is *The Red Badge* or is it not a work exemplifying literary Naturalism?

Wells, Lester G. "Stephen Crane—Syracusan Extraordinary," *Syracuse University Alumni News,* 27 (October, 1946), 14–15.

1947

Austen, Edmund. *Brede, the Story of a Sussex Parish.* Rye, Sussex, England, 1947, p. 33.

Casey, Alfredo, ed. and trans. *Dos siglos de poesia norteamericana.* Buenos Aires, Argentina: Editorial Claridad, 1947, pp. 85–86.

Translates *Black Riders,* no. 3, "En el desierto" ("In the Desert") and *Black Riders,* no. 24, "He visto a un hombre siguiendo el horizonte" ("I Saw a Man Pursuing the Horizon").

Cowley, Malcolm. " 'Not Me': A Natural History of American Naturalism," *Kenyon Review,* 9 (Spring, 1947), 414–435.

Reprinted in *Critiques and Essays on Modern Fiction: 1920–1951,* ed. John Aldridge. New York, 1952, pp. 370–387.

Reprinted in *Evolutionary Thought in America,* ed. Stow Persons. New Haven, Conn., 1950.

Defines Naturalism as "pessimistic determinism" and then applies the category to Crane by referring not to examples of determinism, but rather to nature's indifference in "The Open Boat." As Max Westbrook says (1959): "A quick check of Crane's obedience to the basic tenets of naturalism shows that he has been distorted on the sometimes Procrustean bed of literary history." On Crane and literary Naturalism *see also* Spiller (1948), Ahnebrink (1950), Walcutt (1956), and James T. Cox (1957).

Elconin, Victor A. "Studies in the Fiction of Stephen Crane." Ph.D. dissertation, Ohio State University, 1947.

Leary, Lewis, ed. *Articles on American Literature Appearing in Current Periodicals, 1920–1945.* Durham, N.C., 1947, p. 61. Reissued for 1900–1950 under same title, 1954.

Morris, L. R. "The Skepticism of the Young," *Postscript to Yesterday.* New York, 1947, pp. xxii, 54, 107–110, 233.

Schoberlin, Melvin, ed. New Year's card reproducing the holograph of Crane's poem, "I explain the silvered passing of a ship at night." Baltimore: Mogollon Press, 1947. One hundred copies.*

Snell, George. "Naturalism Nascent: Crane and Norris," in *The Shapers of American Fiction.* New York, 1947, pp. 223–226, and *passim.*

Crane in England was divorced from his roots, like Bret Harte, Joaquin Miller, Harold Frederic, and other Americans; "He scattered his powers and wrote little once he had broken ties with his origins. The short stories and poems remain as fragmentary evidence of a continuing creative function, but Crane died young without fulfilling his wonderful promise—a rebel to the end; as an artist, instinctive, often irrational, more highly gifted than any in his generation, and cut off by death long before he had arrived at artistic maturity."

However, Crane attained artistic maturity almost from the start in *Maggie, The Red Badge, George's Mother, The Little Regiment,* "The Open Boat," and also in *The Black Riders.* The standard tombstone legend that he died young without fulfilling his promise is confounded by his achievements.

Starrett, Vincent. "Mrs. Stephen Crane," *Books and Bipeds.* New York, 1947, pp. 101–102.

Wilson, Edmund. *The Wound and the Bow.* New York, 1947, p. 150. On Crane, Kipling, and Conrad.

Wilson, Rufus R., and E. Wilson Otilie. *New York in Literature.* Elmira, N.Y., 1947.

* The above entry derives from *Poetry,* p. 123.

1948

Brooks, Van Wyck. *A Chilmark Miscellany*. New York, 1948.

Cowie, Alexander. *The Rise of the American Novel*. New York and Cincinnati, 1948, pp. 469, 508, 520, 699, 749, 853.

Only passing notes on *The Red Badge*. "Stephen Crane brilliantly united a naturalistic attitude with impressionistic technique."

Elconin, Victor A. "Stephen Crane at Asbury Park," *American Literature*, 20 (November, 1948), 275–289.

Presents some new Crane sketches of Asbury Park, while simultaneously the *W-S Bibliography* (1948) lists some Asbury Park sketches by Crane not mentioned by Elconin. Additions to the Crane canon of Asbury Park sketches include "Asbury Park as Seen by Stephen Crane," *New York Journal*, August 16, 1896, reprinted in *UW* (1963); and in *NYCS* (1966) is the *Journal's* variant text: "Stephen Crane at Asbury Park," *Kansas City Star*, August 22, 1896. The above account intends to point out that Elconin did not discover all of Crane's Asbury Park sketches. *Contra* Gullason in *CEA Critic* (1969).

Elconin reprints Crane's *Tribune* report of the parade by the American Mechanics, appearing in *New York Tribune* for August 21, 1892, and he corrects the accounts of Crane's sketch as given by Beer, Garland, Willis Fletcher Johnson, and others. However, Elconin agrees with Johnson (1926) that Crane was not discharged. But the fact is that the *Tribune* fired Crane—as well as brother Townley. *See Crane* (1968). Research of the *Tribune* shows that nothing by Stephen Crane appeared in the *Tribune* after September, 1892; nothing in 1893.

Elconin's version as to whether Crane was fired by the *Tribune* ignores Arthur Oliver's firsthand news of that event. *See* Oliver (1931).

Fabian, R. C. "Stephen Crane Collection: Report for 1948," *Syracuse University News*, 30 (December, 1948), 11; (January, 1949), 11.

Frierson, William C., and Herbert Edwards. "Impact of French Naturalism on American Critical Opinion: 1877–1892," *Publications of the Modern Language Association*, 63 (September, 1948), 1007–1016.

On the critical bias of the 1890s against contemporary American novelists who were influenced by the French literary naturalists: Crane, Garland, and Norris. "In America the pivotal year in the acceptance of Zola was 1888. In England it was 1893." Up to 1879 Zola's novels were available only in French.

Errs in claiming that Crane "unsuccessfully sought for three years to find a publisher for *Maggie* before deciding to publish it himself." Errs also in claiming that the 1893 *Maggie* had appended to it "a laudatory Introduction by Howells."

Gibson, William M., and George Arms. *A Bibliography of William Dean Howells*. New York: New York Public Library, 1948, pp. 120, 121, 122, 123, 128.

Goldring, Douglas. *The Last Pre-Raphaelite: A Record of the Life and Writings of Ford Madox Ford*. London, 1948, p. 93. *Trained for Genius: The Life and Writings of Ford Madox Ford*. New York, 1949.

Herzberg, Max J. "Stephen Crane," *Encyclopaedia Britannica*, vol. 6. Chicago, 1948, p. 634.

Herzberg has Crane buried "in the cemetery of Elizabeth, New Jersey," whereas Crane is buried in Hillside, N.J. The same error is made by Berryman (1950) and Gilkes (1960).

Hunter, Dard. "Elbert Hubbard and 'A Message to Garcia,'" *The New Colophon,* 1, part 1 (January, 1948), 33.

Crane's letter to Hubbard concerning A. S. Rowan who carried the famous message. However, as to the author of "A Message to Garcia," Harry Taber claims that Hubbard did not write it. *See* Daly (1916).

Reisiger, Hans, trans. *Im Rettungsboot* ["The Open Boat"] Bergen II, Upper Bavaria, Germany, 1948. In the series "Die Weltliteratur" [World Literature], vol. 33.

Spiller, Robert. "Stephen Crane," *Literary History of the United States,* vol. 2, ed. Robert Spiller, *et al.* New York, 1948, chap. 62, section 3, pp. 1020–1026; bibliography, vol. 3, pp. 458–461.

Academic criticism has firmly attached to Crane's writings the literary label Naturalism, and as the naturalist of the school of Zola is theoretically indifferent to style critics seldom pursue the question of Crane's language. Spiller's account here of "The Open Boat," as James Colvert observes (1958), summarizes the established attitude. "To Spiller, Crane's 'masterpiece' is a 'simple record of the actual wreck of a filibustering vessel off the coast of Florida,' an account which 'achieves its effect by understatement.' The significant meaning, the meaning which strikes deepest into Crane's world view, Spiller says, is expressed in the revelation that nature is indifferent to man. 'This,' he remarks, 'is [to Crane] the meaning of life, in so far as it has a meaning.'"

Spiller's reading of Crane, as Max Westbrook remarks (1959), has become the conventional dogma. *The Literary History of the United States* calls Crane one of the four American writers who at the turn of the century most nearly practiced the Naturalistic beliefs of Zola. Westbrook contends that Crane is not a pessimistic determinist, *contra* Malcolm Cowley (1947), James T. Cox (1957), and other critics.

West, Herbert Faulkner. *A Stephen Crane Collection.* Hanover, N.H.: Dartmouth College Library, 1948.

A catalog of the George Matthew Adams collection with an Introduction and Notes. Includes a scrapbook of newspaper clippings on the death of Crane, p. 23.

Reviewed: Williams (1948).

Williams, Ames W. "A Stephen Crane Collection," *Antiquarian Bookman* (May 1, 1948), pp. 717–718. Facsimile of the 1893 *Maggie* cover.

Reviews Herbert Faulkner West's *A Stephen Crane Collection* (1948), pointing out that the letter of Stephen to William is misdated. The letter of October 29 was written in 1897, not 1898 as printed. Agrees with Beer's refutation of the legend that Channing in Richard Harding Davis's "The Derelict," a short story in *Ransom's Folly* (1902) resembles Crane. Clark's illustration of Channing could conceivably resemble Crane, but then likewise so could a host of other correspondents, says Williams. "In point of fact, Channing is a noble if over-generous character, and those who have read 'The Derelict' will agree that if any resemblance was intended, the result is a tribute and not a derogation." However, *see Crane,* pp. 293, 596n21.

———. Letters to Lily Brandon Munroe, by Crane. "In preparation," 1948, by Ames W. Williams. Not published.

Reproduced in *Letters* from the photocopies supplied by Frederick B. Smillie. (Exceptions as to first printing are letters numbered in *Letters* as nos. 75 and 234.)

Ames Williams interviewed Lily Brandon Smillie, and this important document informed *Letters*. New portions of it are cited in *Crane*. A copy of Williams's interview is owned by Stallman, but is not in the Arents Library of Syracuse University.

———. "Stephen Crane: War Correspondent," *New Colophon*, 1 (April, 1948), 113–124. Photograph of Cora Taylor.

Crane's journalistic experiment in the Greco-Turkish War was a disappointment. Contends that Crane "was not a successful reporter or correspondent." He had no talent for news of the type demanded by his editors. Williams is mistaken about Crane's marrying Cora Taylor in Greece.

Refutes Don Carlos Seitz's charge that Crane wrote the *World* dispatch accusing the 71st New York Volunteers of cowardice. *See* Seitz (1924) and (1933). (That Crane did not write it and that Sylvester Scovel did was first stated by Edward Marshall in his *Story of the Rough Riders,* 1898). That Crane wrote only one or two dispatches for the *World* is confounded by Williams's list of Crane's contributions to the *World*. Reproduces for the first time Cora Crane's letter to the Secretary of War (September 25, 1898) from our National Archives. An important essay.

Williams, Ames, and Vincent Starrett. *Stephen Crane: A Bibliography.* Glendale, Calif., 1948.

Incorporated into *Stephen Crane: A Critical Bibliography* by permission of Williams and Starrett in letters of 1955 to R. W. S. The 1948 edition, long out of print and impossible to obtain, is now available in facsimile reissue from Burt Franklin Bibliography and Reference Series 298, New York, N.Y., 1970.

1949

[Anon.]. [Portrait of Stephen Crane], *Saturday Review of Literature,* 32 (July 9, 1949), 9.

Berryman, John. "The Style of Babel," *Commentary,* 7 (January, 1949), 92–93.

Compares Isaak Babel, Chekhov, and Crane as forerunners and models of modern modernity (in a review of Isaak Babel's *Benya Krik, The Gangster and Other Stories*).

Blankenship, Russell. *American Literature as an Expression of the National Mind.* New York, 1949, p. 513, and *passim.* First ed., 1931.

Cather, Willa. "When I Knew Stephen Crane," *Prairie Schooner,* 23 (Fall, 1949), 231–237. Reprinted from *Library,* 1 (June 23, 1900), 17–18.

A valuable pen-portrait of Crane in Lincoln, Nebraska, in February, 1895.

———. "Stephen Crane's *Wounds in the Rain and Other Impressions of War,*" in *On Writing: Critical Studies on Writing as an Art.* Foreword by Stephen

Tennant. New York, 1949, pp. 67–74. Reprints Cather's Introduction, *Work,* vol. 9 (1926).

Coan, Otis W., and Richard G. Lillard. *America in Fiction.* Stanford, Calif., 1949, pp. 26, 86, 102, 118.

Goldring, Douglas. *Trained for Genius: The Life and Writings of Ford Madox Ford.* New York, 1949, pp. 65, 87, 93, 95.

Gordon, Caroline. "Stephen Crane," *Accent,* 9 (Spring, 1949), 153–157.
> Reprinted in *The House of Fiction,* ed. Caroline Gordon and Allen Tate (New York, 1950), pp. 308–312.
> In error is Caroline Gordon's notion, repeated in *The House of Fiction* (1950 and again 1960), which reprints her *Accent* mistake: "Crane tells us that the battle scenes in Stendhal's *La Chartreuse de Parma* inspired him to write his masterpiece, *The Red Badge of Courage.*" Crane said nothing of the kind. As pointed out in Stallman, "Stephen Crane: A Revaluation" (1952) and in *Omnibus,* Crane never read *La Chartreuse de Parma* and was angered when told he had. *See* Beer's *SC.*
> On "The Open Boat"; however, far more perceptive is Munson (1929).

Imbert, André, trans. *Maggie: fille des rues.* Monaco: Edition du Vieux Monaco, 1949.

Lynskey, Winifred. "Stephen Crane's *The Red Badge of Courage,*" *Explicator,* 8 (December, 1949), item 18.
> "Crane does not betray his readers by giving Henry Fleming a 'moral victory' at the close. Henry's so-called 'moral victory' is 'complete' and 'complacent' only to himself. . . . The powerful and insensate forces of war which both pose and resolve Henry's 'moral problem of conduct,' are as meaningless as his 'moral victory' in the sense that both are irrational and sub-human. Men, guns, and conflicts are likened to savage or monstrous animals. . . . Every figure in the book supports the atmosphere of un-reason."
> *See also* Sewall (1945).

Mencken, H. L. "Stephen Crane," *A Mencken Chrestomathy.* New York, 1949, pp. 496–497. Reprinted from the *Baltimore Sun,* 1924.
> Reprinted in *Literature in America,* ed. Philip Rahv (1957), pp. 303–304.

Overstreet, H. A. "Antimilitarists Like Stephen Crane," *The Mature Mind.* New York, 1949, p. 138.

Schoberlin, Melvin, ed. Introduction, *The Sullivan County Sketches of Stephen Crane.* Syracuse, N.Y., 1949, pp. 1–20.
> Rightly declares that Crane and his brother Townley were discharged by the *Tribune* for Stephen's report of the American Mechanics' parade in Asbury Park on August 20, 1892 *(Tribune,* August 21). In supporting evidence is Arthur Oliver's important article in *Proceedings of the New Jersey Historical Society* (October, 1941), which Schoberlin does not cite. *See* Johnson (1926) and Elconin (1948), who contend that Crane was not fired. However, Elconin ignores Oliver's account.
> Schoberlin and Elconin reprint Crane's undiplomatic parade sketch, which was reprinted for the first time in *Library,* 5, no. 1 (1932); a fact not noticed by Honce (1942), by Elconin (1948), and by Schoberlin (1949).
> The Crane letter to Lily Brandon Munroe, here published for the first time, which Schoberlin dates February 29, 1896, is redated on internal evidence March, 1894, in *Letters.*

Reviewed:
Herbert Barrows, "Sketches in Terror," *New York Times Book Review,* May 8, 1949, pp. 4, 20. Contends that "almost every one of these sketches is at least in part a study in the transcriptioin of terror." The same reading, only slightly qualified, is repeated by Berryman in *Stephen Crane* (1950).

Robert Halsband, "Pseudo-Ghosts," *Saturday Review of Literature,* 32 (July 9, 1949), 9–10. The *SCS* "contain revealing clues to the evolution of his genius."

For recently discovered Sullivan County sketches *see SCTS.*

Snyder, Louis L., and Richard B. Morris, eds. *A Treasury of Great Reporting.* New York, 1949, 1962, pp. 236–240.

Editor's note, pp. 236–237. Reprints, pp. 238–239, the passage from *Wounds in the Rain* describing the death of surgeon Gibbs, in "War Memories."

Reprints, pp. 237–238, a dispatch from the *New York World,* June 13, 1898, for which the editors invent here the title: "A *World* Correspondent Immortalizes an Incident on the Shores of Guantánamo Bay." However, this dispatch —unsigned—had in fact the simple title: "In the First Land Fight 4 of our Men are Killed." Dictated by Crane to Ernest McCready of the *Herald* aboard *The Three Friends* off Guantánamo on June 12 (1898), McCready describes the occasion in one of his letters to B. J. R. Stolper (1934), quoted for the first time in *Crane.*

Welty, Eudora. "The Reading and Writing of Short Stories," *Atlantic Monthly,* 183 (February, 1949), 54–58; continued (March, 1949) pp. 46–49.

Calls "The Bride Comes to Yellow Sky" a "playful story, using two situations like counters."

West, Ray B., Jr., and Robert Wooster Stallman. *The Art of Modern Fiction.* New York, 1949, 1962, pp. 53–58.

Reprinted in *Forms and Focus,* ed. Robert F. McDonnell and William E. Morris. New York, 1961, pp. 364–368.

On "The Open Boat." The author of this essay is Ray B. West, Jr.

Wright, W. F. *Romance and Tragedy in Joseph Conrad.* Lincoln, Nebr., 1949, p. 107.

1950

Ahnebrink, Lars. *The Beginnings of Naturalism in American Fiction: A Study of the Works of Hamlin Garland, Stephen Crane, and Frank Norris.* Uppsala, Sweden: A. B. Lundequista Bokhandeln, 1950; Cambridge, Mass., 1950.

Contends that Zola's *L'Assommoir* and *La Débâcle* were important sources for Crane's *Maggie* and *The Red Badge of Courage.* This thesis of French and Russian influences is undermined by Cunliffe (1955) and by Colvert (1955). Cf. Salvan (1943). The problem of Crane influences is discussed in *Omnibus.*

On the influences of Flaubert's *Madame Bovary* on *Maggie see* Stallman, "Stephen Crane's Primrose Path" (1955). On literary Naturalism, *see* Cowley (1947), Shroeder (1950), Walcutt (1956), and James T. Cox (1957).

Reviewed: Walcutt (1950).

Barrows, Herbert. *Suggestions for Teaching "15 Stories."* Boston, 1950.

Bates, H. E. *Edward Garnett.* London, 1950, p. 21.

Berryman, John. *Stephen Crane.* New York: William Sloan Associates (American Men of Letters Series), 1950. London: Methuen, 1951. Toronto: George J. McLeod, 1951. Cleveland: World Publishing Company, 1962. New York: Meridian Books, 1962. London: Transatlantic, 1962. Photograph of Crane on *Three Friends* off Cuba, 1898.

A short biography of 260 pages with two essays appended: "Crane's Art," pp. 263–293, and "The Color of This Soul," pp. 297–325. Covers Crane in the Cuban War in twenty pages and erroneously puts Crane in the wrong cemetery and silently impugns Crane as journalist by claiming that there were five men in the dinghy. The Hartwood that Berryman describes never existed. Not noticed by Berryman's reviewers and subsequent Crane critics is the fact that Berryman's *Crane* omits critical commentary on *The Red Badge* and provides no redaction of what the novel is about except by way of contemporary reviews.

Reviewed:

Newsweek, 36 (December 11, 1950), 97–99: "Crane's life is of more general interest than that of the others in the American Men of Letters Series. It is closer to the present, less well known, and it has not, like the lives of Hawthorne or Melville, hardened into a myth that the biographer must accept or try to correct." The lack of a consistent point of view robs Berryman's book "of the narrative interest of Thomas Beer's biography of Crane, even though Berryman had material unavailable to Beer, and his last chapters of psychoanalytic appraisal are almost incoherent. His extravagant praise of his subject's work in general (a fault of all the books in the series) lessens the impact of his comments on Crane's masterpieces. The weakness of Berryman's biography is that he does not discriminate between them."

Clara Stillman, *New York Herald Tribune Book Review,* December 17, 1950, p. 5: Berryman's is "an ambitious undertaking, for almost everything concerning Crane is fantastically involved."

Time, 56 (December 25, 1950), 58: Crane "never achieved that summit of craft where art appears to be artless," says *Time's* reviewer. "His oddly arresting similes and metaphors jut up like boulders deflecting the clear stream of his narratives. Many a sentence of Crane's is beaded with the sweat that went into its construction. Despite these deficiencies, his pages twang with an intense, nervous conviction of actuality." (*Time* has Crane's prose jutted with boulders, beaded with sweat, and twanging!) "Biographer Berryman glibly discerns an Oedipus complex, but there are more things in heaven and earth than are dreamed of in Freudian psychology."

Robert E. Spiller, *Saturday Review of Literature* (January 27, 1951), p. 11: The inclusion of Crane in the American Men of Letters Series emphasizes the place that Carl Van Doren assigned to Crane in the Twenties: "He is as timeless as any novelist in English. Modern American literature began with him." Berryman, says Spiller, "has somewhat confused his own discovery of Crane with a supposed but unfounded previous neglect by the critical world at large. His bibliography is conspicuous for its neglect of the literary historians, although he is correct in pointing out that up to now the impressionistic method of criticism has not been applied to this pioneer in American impressionistic fiction."

Spiller takes issue with Berryman's opinion that Crane " 'owes nothing whatever, apparently, to painting.' Mr. Berryman adds very little to our knowledge as derived from the account of Thomas Beer and a handful of articles and letters published since . . . the total portrait is very little altered and Crane's place in literary history is obscured rather than clarified by the attempt to divorce him from the literary movements of his time. This is not therefore the careful biography that the critics of Beer have long called for. It is rather, like Beer's, an essay in criticism written in a biographical frame, and it only supplements Beer."

Berryman makes two new and important points, each in his concluding chapters. He demonstrates that Crane's art is ironic and he attributes Crane's system of symbolism, "by Freudian analysis, to two childhood experiences. . . . The fear which Beer and others have always stressed as central in Crane's mind is here provided with sources in the subconscious and with specific results in art. Stephen Crane is now a conspicuous figure moving across a light that comes from nowhere."

Andrews Wanning, *Partisan Review*, 18 (May, 1951), 358–361: Berryman's portrait is not likely to be definitive. "His treatment proposes the wider question of the uses of psychoanalysis to the biographer of the dead writer, or perhaps more exactly, of the nature of the evidence which will justify such uses." There is the anticlimax of "arriving at promised revelation in the form of an Oedipus complex, even a special and ingenious pattern of an Oedipus complex. What is more serious is the question of the criteria for proof. Much depends, in Berryman's account, on a single incident whose source is Thomas Beer (not elsewhere regarded as particularly reliable) about Crane's fright at seeing at the age of twelve a white girl stabbed by her Negro lover. But the conscientious analyst can do little with an isolated epidsode. . . .

"There is also in question the utility of the life as an illumination of the work. From the point of view of the reader who is interested simply in the impact of the story I cannot see that it is less than distracting to learn that 'The Upturned Face' represents 'the father's death, even the father's defiled death'; or that of the six delineated characters in 'The Blue Hotel' four are masks of Crane himself. The general question is wider; but Berryman, at any rate, seems to me most illuminating—as in the exceedingly perceptive account of 'The Open Boat'—when the critic and the biographer are least involved with one another."

Claude E. Jones, *Nineteenth Century Fiction*, 6 (June, 1951), 74–76: Berryman is notably successful in that section of his book which is properly biographical, notably on Crane's liaison with Cora. Unlike Beer, Berryman "does not feel that he is obliged to be either coy or snide about Crane's relationships with women. . . . To the present reviewer it seems, however, that Berryman pays too much attention to Crane's parents and their effect on a boy who was essentially an independent, unfilial, and introverted character." Jones objects to Berryman's treatment of Crane's war writing and seafaring materials. "One has the impression that to Berryman battle experience is rather carefully compartmented according to the results of psychoanalysis, and his treatment of this material is unconvincing."

The "semiscientific gobbledegook" in Berryman's Section Five, a pseudo-psychoanalytic treatment of Crane with the title "The Color of the Soul," blights the art of criticism. "It seems most unfortunate that a biographer with as much new material and clear, sensitive interpretation as Mr. Berryman provides for the first 260 pages of his study should have wasted his and the reader's time in so unrewarding a final act."

TLS (1951), p. 356: Beer's *SC* did not bring Crane to the front again. Crane anticipated the current vogue for the cynical, the violent and the brutal, and his manner of voicing it prompted other writers from Conrad to T. E. Lawrence and Hemingway to indite it in a like manner.

"Mr. Berryman turns this searching ray into Crane and finds enough hidden to make a reader recoil from the very masterpieces he ought to respect. No more than an umbrella seen in one of the tales is, after all, a phallic symbol. There is also a pack of cards; almost anything can be a symbol with that import. It looks as if painters of still life in future will have to be more careful in choosing subjects. And that is not the worst of it. . . .

"When viewed in a more penetrating light we see, says Crane's latest biographer, that his 'general war on Authority . . . was rooted rather in jealousy and hatred of his father.' As a child, he wished to 'rescue' his mother and save her for himself. Critics of letters, on this showing, will have to begin all over again. From Longinus on they have been deceived by the suppressed hatred of little children for parents. What vistas now open for new evaluations? What, for instance could be done with the *Divine Comedy!* But had we not better forget it? Would it not be more fun to read Crane as if, when he named things, he meant what he wrote?"*

Charles Poore, *New York Times*, July 14, 1951.

Morgan Blum, *Poetry*, 78 (August, 1951), 298–307: One flaw of Berryman's *Crane* is lack of documentation. "In particular we would like to know where he gets his actual quotations from the Crane letters." The reader "has no way of distinguishing between those instances where Beer is sole authority and those in which Mr. Berryman has been able to confirm the earlier quotation. The point is not without importance. Why should Beer have abandoned his habits of 'grand inaccuracy, expurgation and distortion' only when it came time to quote?"†

"Mr. Berryman is regularly rewarding when he treats those areas where criticism and biography meet. Nowhere is this more persuasively demonstrated than in his brilliant tracing of the images and situations that recur obsessively in Crane's writings. Not surprisingly, Mr. Berryman develops repeated images and situations into a psychoanalytic thesis. What does seem surprising is how little additional illumination emerges from this attempt."

Daniel Aaron, *Hudson Review*, 4 (Autumn, 1951), 471–473: In the more purely biographical portions of *Stephen Crane* Berryman "pays Crane the questionable compliment of emulating his tone and manner, but the elliptical phrasing, the wrenched antithesis that so often give distinction to Crane's stories are not well-suited to conventional biography." Berryman has brought Beer's biography up to date, corrected old mistakes, and introduced new material, but large portions of his book "merely retell less engagingly what

---

* The same point is made by Liebling (1961).

† This dilemma is unavoidable because Beer's book is the sole source for most of the letters he quotes; as not a single one of them has ever appeared on the market, one is forced to conclude that Beer destroyed the originals and/or copies. This point is set down in Stallman's Preface to *Crane; see also* the Notes. *Letters* redates many letters misdated by Beer.

Beer had already recorded." Beer's *SC* "as biography is far better than
Mr. Berryman's study, but the newer book is the first truly critical treatment
of Crane as a writer."

Life (September 5, 1951), p. 108.

John T. Flanagan, *American Literature*, 23 (January, 1952), 510–511.

Brom Weber, *Western Review*, 16 (Summer, 1952), 329–334.

Granville Hicks, *Sewanee Review*, 60 (Winter, 1952), 149–155: Hicks finds
the book fresh and "sometimes irritating." Its tone is not judicious; "it makes
large and belligerent claims. But it is exciting reading, and in spite of the
way we react against its almost hysterical enthusiasms, it compels us to recognize Crane's stature."

The book is "a full-dress Freudian analysis of Crane's personality in its
relation to his writings. Although the analysis rests on rather meager evidence,
it seems certain that Berryman has found in the unconscious the origins of
some of Crane's recurring themes and symbols and has shown how others may
have developed. Application of the Freudian method proves valuable in that
it lifts certain phenomena of Crane's writing out of the realm of mystery; if
it does not 'explain' them, at least it relates them to other phenomena with
which we have become familiar. But there is one point, and that the most
important, at which the mystery is unresolved. As Trilling has said, the
important thing about an artist is not that he has a neurosis but that he is
able to do something quite distinctive and valuable with it. That Crane of
all persons could accomplish this transformation seems, after a reading of
Berryman's book, nothing less than miraculous."

On Berryman's *Crane* see *Omnibus* (1952), p. 188; Geismar (1953), regards
The Red Badge of Courage as a psychiatric case study which reflects Crane's
childhood traumas. Solomon (1956): The wound motif in Crane's war stories
"has given Freudian critics a field-day opportunity to expound on 'castration
complexes' and subconscious 'Oedipal repressions,' as though Crane were not
a conscious author, but an unthinking instrument through which instinctual
and emotional patterns are poured into a fixed mould. Indeed, one recent
study alleges that Crane's 'best work sprang in effect from . . . the episode of
childhood and infancy,' and that his life was a 'a classic instance of the
"prostitute complex" in Freudian thought.' " *Poetry*, 1957, p. 116, which
contradicts p. 9; Greenfield (1958): "Berryman's interpretation of Crane as a
whole is vitiated by his peculiar psychoanalytical view of Crane."

Chase (1960), p. xxii: "Although Mr. Berryman's book is not the complete
study one would like, its generally Freudian account of Crane's personality,
and thus of the origins of his art, seems essentially convincing." Liebling
(1961): "Freudian criticism reaches full frenzy" in Berryman's obsession with
Freudian symbolism in Crane's writings.

Weiss (1965), buttresses and extends Berryman's Freudian reading of Crane,
notably on *The Red Badge* (not scrutinized by Berryman in his *Stephen
Crane*). Compares *The Red Badge* and *Oedipus Rex*. Henry Fleming's search
for reunion with omnipotence is, in Oedipal terms, "a reunion through a
masochistic identification with the mother."

However, *see* Cady (1962) and the Preface to *Crane*. Cady finds Berryman's
case for identifying Crane with the victims portrayed in Freud's "Special Type
of Choice of Object Made by Men" very shaky. Berryman "plays fast and
loose with the evidence. The sole example, finally, is Cora. It was not true
that Helen Trent and Lily Brandon Munroe were 'sexually discredited' any

more than that Crane was in love with Dora Clark, Dorris Watts, or Amy Leslie, or any more than Crane fell in love with Cora because he knew of Captain Stewart as a necessary 'injured third party.' There is no evidence of 'an exceptional concern with prostitutes.' What has happened is a juggling of evidence to make Crane prove out Freud—the method of the exegete, of the fundamentalist. This is, it seems to me, an abdication of the responsibility of the biographer. Instead of bringing ideas, information, and insights to elucidate the life, this method employs notions about the life to justify the Master. This same arbitrary, essentially irrelevant method vitiates the criticism, turning it always away from art and back to conjectural biography. It explicates not the literature but the critic's notion of Freudian ideas."

Carter, Everett. *Howells and the Age of Realism.* Philadelphia, 1950, 1954, pp. 19, 231–232, 237, 269.
Carter is the first biographer of Howells to mention Crane. On Howells and Crane *see Omnibus.*

Caster, Henry. *The Year of the Spaniard.* New York, 1950, 1963, pp. 82–83, 102–103, 124–132, 141–143, 147–151, 176–177, 180–184, 187–188.
A novel based on the Cuban War with Stephen Crane as one of the main characters. "Warren sighed. 'If only I could write like Stephen Crane. He writes what he sees—not what languid females want for hammock reading' " [p. 25].

Commager, Henry Steele. *The American Mind.* New Haven, Conn., 1950, pp. 43, 109.

Cowley, Malcolm. In *Evolutionary Thought in America,* ed. Stow Persons, New Haven, Conn., 1950, pp. 300–333. Reprinted from *Kenyon Review* (1947).

Farrell, James T. "Some Observations on Naturalism, So Called, in Fiction," *Antioch Review,* 10 (Summer, 1950), 247–264.
Dismisses as irrelevant the criterion of Naturalism. Crane's *Red Badge of Courage* could be cited as a Naturalistic novel, but what insight do we gain by subsuming it under that loose category?
(The much applied test of literary Naturalism, which has to do with the philosophical outlook in the given work, tests not at all whether or not the given literary work is a work of art. Farrell is quite right.)
However, not in agreement with the Farrell standpoint are numerous professors of American literature, including Ahnebrink (1950), Shroeder (1950), and Walcutt (1950).

Feldman, Abraham. "Crane's Title from Shakespeare," *American Notes and Queries,* 8 (March, 1950), 185–186.
Suggests that Crane's title *Red Badge of Courage* may have derived from Shakespeare's "murder's crimson badge" in *Henry VI: Part III.*
Feldman's suggested source is plausible because Crane owned in separate editions the complete works of Shakespeare as given in "List of Books / Brede Place." However, the indisputable source is the well-known red patch worn on the caps of Union soldiers under General Philip Kearny, a diamond-shaped red patch signifying a badge of honor. *See* Eby (1960).

Gibson, William. Introduction, *Stephen Crane: Selected Prose and Poetry.* New York, 1950. Reissued 1956, titled *The Red Badge of Courage and Selected Prose and Poetry.*

Gordon, Caroline, and Allen Tate, eds. *The House of Fiction: An Anthology of the Short Story.* New York, 1950, pp. 308–312. Reissued 1960.

The 1960 reissue of this textbook does not correct the 1950 error in Caroline Gordon's mistaken notion that Stendhal inspired Crane to write his *The Red Badge of Courage.*

Honan, William H., ed. *The Greenwich Village Guide.* New York, 1950, p. 23.

Crane lived at Number 61 on the south side of Washington Square in the Greenwich Village rooming house of Marie Branchards, a French-Canadian mother of six children who had run a boarding house in Syracuse, Crane staying there in January, 1891, just before moving into the Delta Upsilon fraternity. Her Washington Square house became famous because Crane had stayed there, "as had Willa Cather when she was writing her verses, and later Frank Norris, when he was working on the final draft of *McTeague*." In *Crane,* p. 27. (However, the above source is not cited in Notes to chap. 2.)

Kazin, Alfred. "American Naturalism Reflections from Another Era," in *The American Writer and the European Tradition,* ed. Margaret Denny and William H. Gilman. Minneapolis, 1950, pp. 121–122.

Contends that *Maggie,* a social exposé, is "rather a trick, the book of a precocious and restless young reporter who has found an untouched subject in the slums. It has nothing of the daemonic sincerity of *The Red Badge of Courage.* . . . Morally Norris is not *in* his book at all, just as Crane, led to *Maggie* by its scandalousness, is not in his; everything [in *McTeague*] seems just a little too deliberately planned. . . ."

Stallman, taking issue with Kazin, explores Crane's artistry in *Maggie; see* Stallman, "Stephen Crane's Primrose Path" (1955).

Kirk, Clara Marburg, and Rudolf Kirk, eds. *William Dean Howells: Representative Selections, with Introduction, Bibliography, and Notes.* New York, 1950 and 1961, rev. ed., pp. cxxxvii, 385–386.

Lüdeke, Henry. "Stephen Crane's Poetry," in *The Democracy of Henry Adams and Other Essays.* Berne, Switzerland, 1950, 111–112.

Reprints in translation Lüdeke's "Stephen Crane's Gedichte," *Anglia,* 62 (1938), 410–422.

McBride, Henry. "Stephen Crane's Artist Friends," *Art News,* 49 (October, 1950), 46.

An important article on Crane's association with artists, which "may explain some of his own essential artisticness." Crane "dined regularly every night for two or three years with a certain coterie which had managed to incorporate a little bit of France into a dingy but quite clean tenement somewhere in the Thirtieth Streets west of Broadway. This coterie revolved around the Pike brothers. . . ." Relate to *Omnibus, MSC,* Kwiat (1952), and *Crane.*

McBride facetiously calls his little article a "little chapter in the life of the novelist Stephen Crane," and Berryman's *Crane* asserts that McBride intended to write a biography of Crane; but there is no foundation for this speculation, and McBride denied having any such intention.*

Okubo, Yasuo, trans. *Chimata no musume [Maggie: A Girl of the Streets].* Tokyo Tōzai Shobo, 1950.

Remords, Georges. "Un précurseur des romanciers américains contemporains:

---

* Letter from Charles Feinberg to R. W. S.

Stephen Crane (1871–1900): sa renommee et son influence," *Bulletin de la Faculté des Lettres de Strasbourg,* 28 (March, 1950), 190–202; (April, 1950), 249–262; (May–June, 1950), 351–367; and 29 (December, 1950), 158–166; (January, 1951), 182–195.

Sandburg, Carl. "Letters to Dead Imagists," in *Complete Poems.* New York, 1950, p. 73.

Schorer, Mark, ed. *The Story: A Critical Anthology.* New York, 1950, pp. 20, 35. Reprints, pp. 21–34, "The Bride Comes to Yellow Sky."
Schorer's note, p. 20, is a keen comment on the structure of Crane's story.

Shively, James R., ed. *Writings from Willa Cather's Campus Years.* Lincoln, Nebr., 1950, pp. 22–24.

Short, Raymond W., and Richard B. Sewall. *A Manual of Suggestions for Teachers Using "Short Stories for Study,"* rev. ed. New York, 1950.
On "The Upturned Face," pp. 19–21.

Shroeder, John W. "Stephen Crane Embattled," *University of Kansas City Review,* 17 (Winter, 1950), 119–129.
"The Open Boat," "The Monster," and "Death and the Child" represent Crane's artistic victory. Concerned with the antagonism of man and nature, they exemplify literary Naturalism and thus earn Crane "a place among the significant American writers." For Shroeder a work exemplifying the philosophy of literary Naturalism is thus and therefore an "artistic victory," which is to confound the one thing with the other. As *The Red Badge of Courage* fails in the former, so then it fails in artistry. While this may be true it is not for that reason. Naturalism is no criterion for literary merit. "Death and the Child," which Shroeder considers "a triumph of Naturalistic thought and of art," is in fact an artistic failure. Meanwhile, *Maggie* gets no mention.

Walcutt, Charles C. *"Red Badge of Courage* as Literary Naturalism," *Arizona Review,* 1950, pp. 371–373.
Review of Ahnebrink's *The Beginnings of Naturalism in American Fiction* (1950). *See* Ahnebrink (1950).

Welty Eudora. *Short Stories.* New York, 1950, pp. 18–20.
Reprinted ("The Reading and Writing of Short Stories") in *Modern Prose: Form and Style,* ed. William Van O'Connor. New York, 1959, pp. 434–435.
Remarks on Crane's "The Bride Comes to Yellow Sky," pp. 57–58, that it is a "playful story, using two situations like counters." On "The Bride" *see* Berryman (1950), Stallman, *Omnibus* (1952), Barnes (1958), Cady (1961), G. W. Johnson (1963), Solomon (1966), Gibson (1968), and *Crane. See also The Stephen Crane Reader,* ed. R. W. Stallman (1972).

Wilson, Edmund. *Classics and Commercials.* New York, 1950, pp. 35, 107, 138, 424.

1951

Aaron, Daniel. "Stephen Crane," *Hudson Review,* 4 (Autumn, 1951), 471–473.
A review of Berryman's *Crane;* here is an essay of considerable insight.

"Thomas Beer's *Stephen Crane*, as biography, is far better than Mr. Berryman's study, but the newer book is the first truly critical treatment of Crane as a writer. . . . [True, but not noticed by any reviewer or subsequent critic on Berryman's *Crane* is that his book is devoid of critical scrutiny of *The Red Badge*, a most curious omission.]

"In the more purely biographical portions of the book, he pays Crane the questionable compliment of emulating his tone and manner. . . . [So does Beer, Aaron might have added.]

"Mr. Berryman stands in front of Stephen Crane and explains him too solicitously; it is not always clear whether he is quoting or paraphrasing him. Even though he has brought Beer's biography up to date, corrected old mistakes and introduced some new material, large portions of his book merely retell less engagingly what Beer has already recorded. He departs from Beer and makes his real contribution when he drops his role of biographer and pauses to comment on particular stories and poems.

"In the last two concluding chapters especially, free at last from the burden of the narrative, he has many brilliant things to say. No one, in my opinion, has looked so closely at Crane's prose or analysed his poetry and fiction so intelligently. I am not referring to the Freudian probings, or to the suggestive but sometimes heavy-handed psychologizing, but rather to Mr. Berryman's understanding of Crane's intent, to his sense (to paraphrase Edward Garnett) of what the surface betrays. Crane, he says, 'is simultaneously *at war with* the people he creates and *on their side*'; his characters have 'to run a gauntlet to the author's sympathy.' In Crane's stories, he observes, pathos and irony, horror and humor are indistinguishably blended, and the 'consequences of these recognitions, bitterness and horror, disguise themselves in his grotesquerie of concept and style, his velocity, his displacement of rage.'

"Mr. Berryman also points out that unlike Frank Norris ('a romantic moralist,' he calls him, 'with a style like a great wet dog'), Crane was not a naturalist, in the sense that naturalism accumulates laboriously and omits nothing, but a selective writer and an impressionist so far as method is concerned. The distinction is a good one even though Crane shares more of the attitudes of the so-called American Naturalists than Mr. Berryman is ready to admit.

"In disproving Conrad's contention that Crane was only an impressionist, however, and after noting Crane's inclusion of the realistic and the fantastic, Mr. Berryman maintains that Crane owed 'nothing whatever, apparently, to painting.' This may or may not be true, but his remark that Crane 'does not use color in the least like a painter' is more dubious. . . . Such matters as his feud with the New York police, his reporting of the Spanish-American war, his vignettes of the Bowery, are conceived of as literary episodes, and Mr. Berryman, who does not hesitate to speculate freely on the psycho-analytical implications of Crane's writings, is surprisingly reticent when it comes to Crane's social or religious beliefs."

[Anon.]. "A Boy and a Battle: Film Version of *The Red Badge of Courage* Gives Handsome Panorama of Civil War Battle," *Life*, 31 (September 10, 1951), 102–108. Illustrated by Bill Mauldin; also photographs.

———. [Crane's *Maggie*], *New York Times*, July 14, 1951, p. 11.

Beach, Joseph Warren. "Five Makers of American Fiction," *Yale Review*, 40, no. 4 (June, 1951), 746–747.

Bennett, Mildred R. *The World of Willa Cather*. New York, 1951, pp. 205–208.
Recounts Crane's meeting with Willa Cather in *Nebraska State Journal* offices, but misdates it "Spring of 1894," whereas they met in February, 1895.

Blum, Morgan. "Berryman as Biographer: Crane as Poet," *Poetry: A Magazine of Verse*, 78 (August, 1951), 298–307.

Bogan, Louise. *Achievement in American Poetry*. Chicago, 1951, pp. 17–18.

Breit, Harvey. "Talk With Wright Morris," *New York Times Book Review*, June 10, 1951, p. 19.
On Crane and Frank Norris.

A Century of Books: 1851–1951. *New York Times*, Supplement, 1951. Reprints the 1896 *New York Times* review of *Maggie: A Girl of the Streets*.

Cowley, Malcolm. *Exile's Return*. New York, 1951, p. 45.

Dempsey, David. "Tough and Tormented," *New York Times Book Review*, February 25, 1951, p. 5.
Review of James Jones's *From Here to Eternity*. "In pushing forward the limits of naturalism while looking into the hearts of men, Mr. Jones does for our time what Stephen Crane did for his in *The Red Badge of Courage*."

Farber, Manny. "Films" [*The Red Badge of Courage*], *Nation*, 173 (November 10, 1951), 409.

Fatout, Paul. *Ambrose Bierce: The Devil's Lexicographer*. Norman, Okla., 1951, p. 220.
Quotes Bierce on Crane in the *San Francisco Examiner*, July 26, 1896.

Gibson, William. Introduction, Van Wyck Brooks, *Indian Summer*. New York, 1951, pp. vii, viii.

Gohdes, Clarence. "Facts of Life Versus Pleasant Reading," in *Literature of the American People: An Historical and Critical Survey*, ed. Arthur Hobson Quinn. New York, 1951, pp. 737–762.

Herzberg, Max J. Introduction, *The Red Badge of Courage*. New York, 1951.

———. "Fiction Reprints," *Times Literary Supplement*, November 2, 1951, p. 699.

Herzberg, Max J., ed. *This Is America*. New York, 1951, pp. 104–106.

Hoffman, Frederick J. *The Modern Novel in America: 1900–1950*. Chicago, 1951, pp. 31, 32, 33, 39, 86–87, 92, 144.
"Even in his important Civil War novel, Crane had often been clumsily 'artistic' where Hemingway was rigidly faithful to his material. It is doing more than justice to compare the opening paragraph from *The Red Badge of Courage* with that of *A Farewell to Arms*." (However, quite a different reading results from scrutiny of the two novels in *Omnibus*.)

Knight, Grant C. *The Critical Period in American Literature*. Chapel Hill, N.C., 1951, pp. 107–118, 126–140, 153–161, and *passim*.
Reviewed: TLS, February 29, 1952, p. 160: "The Nineties in America."
"This book is a necessary and informative introduction to those close and detailed studies of Crane, Norris, Garland and others which are sure to come from the intense and mighty hive of American criticism and to which—if they

can be written with such lack of pretension as Mr. Knight's book—we look forward with confident expectation."

Leary, Lewis. *Articles on American Literature: 1900–1950.* Durham, N.C., 1951, pp. 61–63. First ed., 1947.

Lowe, Mervin R. "Stephen Crane's *The Red Badge of Courage:* A Study of a Novel." Dissertation, University of Pennsylvania, 1951.

Matthiessen, F. O. *Theodore Dreiser.* New York, 1951, pp. 91–92.
Matthiessen's comment on *Maggie* is, "it now appears both forced and callow."

Mizener, Arthur. "How to Write for Practically Nothing a Year," *Western Review,* 16 (Autumn, 1951), 22.

Morison, Elting E., *et al.,* eds. The Letters of Theodore Roosevelt, vol. 1. Cambridge, Mass., 1951, p. 550.
"I spent three nights in town, and the others out here; a Professor Smith, a friend of Bob's, turned up and dined with me—also Jacob Riis & Stephen Crane. . . ." Letter to Anna Cowles, July 26, 1896.

Morris, Lloyd. *Incredible New York.* New York, 1951, pp. 179–180.

Osborn, Scott C. "Stephen Crane's Imagery: 'Pasted Like a Wafer,'" *American Literature,* 23 (November, 1951), 362.
Points out the resemblance of Crane's famous image to Kipling's in *The Light That Failed* (1891): "The fog was driven apart for a moment, and the sun shone, a blood-red wafer, on the water."
Discussed by Stallman, "The Scholar's Net:" (1955) and by Colvert (1955).

Quinn, Arthur Hobson, ed. *The Literature of the American People.* New York, 1951, p. 573 and *passim.*

Stallman, R. W. Introduction, *The Red Badge of Courage.* New York, 1951, pp. v–xxxiii. Trans. into Greek; Athens, Greece, n.d. [1956].
Interprets (in "Notes Toward an Analysis of *The Red Badge of Courage*") biblical allusions in Crane's war novel, a reading which has instigated much critical warfare.
Reprinted in "Stephen Crane: A Revaluation," in *Critiques and Essays on Modern Fiction,* ed. John Aldridge (1952); in *Omnibus;* in *Houses;* in *The Red Badge of Courage: Text and Criticism,* ed. Richard Lettis (1960); in *The Red Badge of Courage: An Annotated Text, Backgrounds and Sources, Essays in Criticism,* ed. Scully Bradley (1962); *Stephen Crane: A Collection of Critical Essays,* ed. Maurice Bassan (1967), pp. 128–138, with new material appended, pp 138–140, drawn from an unpublished doctoral thesis by Donald Thomas.

Targ, William. Introduction, *The Red Badge of Courage.* Illustrated with wood engravings from drawings by Winslow Homer. Cleveland and New York, 1951, pp. v–xii.

Troy, William. "The Authority of Failure," in *F. Scott Fitzgerald,* ed. Alfred Kazin. Cleveland, 1951, p. 190.
The Great Gatsby has the pattern and meaning of a Grail-romance or of the initiation ritual. Like *The Red Badge of Courage* "it is a record of the strenuous passage from deluded youth to maturity."

Van Doren, Mark. Introduction, *The Best of Hawthorne*. New York, 1951, p. 5.

Winterich, John. "Stephen Crane: Lost and Found," *Saturday Review of Literature*, 34 (February 3, 1951), 21, 43.
>   Reprinted in *Saturday Review Reader* (1951), pp. 177–181.
>   "Stephen Crane has been subjected to more rediscoveries than any other American writer."

———. Introduction, *The Red Badge of Courage*. London: The Folio Society, 1951, pp. 5–19. A note on this edition, pp. 21–25. Photographs by Matthew Brady.
>   Reproduces for the first time the final manuscript, but the text is incomplete and erroneous. It has nevertheless been used or quoted as text by certain critics, including Chase (1960), who thus ignore the existence of the early draft. Both manuscripts appeared for the first time in *Omnibus,* and again, with five new manuscript pages, in Stallman, *The Red Badge of Courage and Selected Stories,* (1960). In *Omnibus* footnotes reproduce passages crossed out by the author in MS. SV, the early and short version, and canceled passages in MS. LV, the final and long version; these passages appear here for the first time. Uncanceled passages in MS. LV are restored to the text by the use of square brackets, as in Winterich's text. The *Omnibus* (1952) and Signet Edition (1960) texts supersede as authoritative the reprinting of the 1895 First American Edition in *Work,* vol. 5 (1926), as well as Winterich's edition.
>   Crane wrote "The End" at the phrase "walking sticks," but then he added some fifty-five words, extending the ending of the story through "soft and eternal peace." He wrote this on second thought because it is in a subsequent handwriting done with a different and apparently new pen. The third ending—"Over the river a golden ray of sun came through the hosts of leaden rain clouds"—is not in the final holograph. Winterich says that this sentence "bears the unmistakable spoor of the editor—an editor not too happily inspired."
>   In *Omnibus,* p. 370, Stallman contends that the third ending was added to the typescript by Crane himself and that it is prepared for by the second ending. "That Crane plotted the entire novel by images and situations evoking contradictory moods of despair and hope is evidenced not only in this terminal image of the book but in the opening image of Chapter I, or again in Chapter VII with its flat statement of conscious intention (notably in the word *again*): 'Again the youth was in despair.'" *See also Omnibus,* pp. 201–224: "The Original Manuscripts of *The Red Badge of Courage.*"

Zolotow, Maurice. *No People Like Show People*. New York, 1951.
>   *Reviewed:* Charles Poore, *New York Times,* July 14, 1951: "Discussing Jimmy Durante's conversational style, Mr. Zolotow says that, to get the pure flavor, 'you have to go back to some of Stephen Crane's short stories, written fifty years ago, in which the dialogue spoken by slum characters sounds exactly like Jimmy Durante's.'
>   "So we ups to da bookie case ('Evvybody wants tuh get inta da act! It's a conspiracy—dat's what it is') and take down 'Twenty Stories by Stephen Crane,' edited by Carl Van Doren (Knopf, 1940), and find that in 'An Experiment in Misery' such a line as 'Now, yeh know how a respecterble gentlem'n feels when he's down on his luck,' or 'me t'roat feels like a fryin'-pan' certainly shows the connection Mr. Zolotow has pointed out between two great artists."

1952

Aldridge, John W., ed. *Critiques and Essays on Modern Fiction: 1920–1951: Representing the Achievement of Modern American and British Critics.* With a Foreword by Mark Schorer. New York, 1952. "Stephen Crane: A Revaluation," by R. W. Stallman, pp. 244–269. Checklist, "Stephen Crane," prepared by Sy Kahn for the "Selected Bibliography of Criticism of Modern Fiction," pp. 578–579.

> *Reviewed:* Harry T. Moore, *Notes and Queries* 7 (September, 1952), 145.

[Anon.]. "Unconventional Son of a Parson," *Life*, 31 (September 10, 1952), 108.

[Anon.], trans. *The Red Badge of Courage,* translated into the Siamese language. Bangkok, Thailand, 1952.

Baker, Carlos. *Hemingway, the Writer as Artist.* Princeton, N.J., 1952, pp. 27, 176, 179, 181, 182, 203.

Berenson, Bernard. *Rumour and Reflection: 1941–1944.* London, 1952.

Brooks, Van Wyck. *The Confident Years: 1885–1915.* New York, 1952, pp. 133–143, and *passim.*

> "Crane's ruling passion was curiosity. Eager for sensations, he was always ready to risk his own existence in order to know 'how it felt'. . . . How slight were the subjects of many of his sketches—a man meets a snake on a mountain path, a bear falls off a precipice entangled in a tent, some soldiers hesitate to throw the earth on the upturned face of a dead comrade; but, slight as they were, these events assumed, because of the acuteness of his own sensibility,—at once, in the reader's mind,—a prodigious importance. Crane's touch, moreover, was invariably light and swift. To use one of his own phrases, he wrote with the 'pace of youth.' "

> Brooks errs in misidentifying the Davis whom Crane advised in 1896 to read Ambrose Bierce; it was Robert Davis, not Richard Harding Davis.

Cross, Leslie [unsigned]. "Stephen Crane 'Find' by Former Milwaukeean," *Milwaukee Journal*, August 24, 1952, p. 4.

> On the discovery by Stallman of the manuscripts of *The Red Badge,* not known to exist, by John Berryman (1950), and of the Crane pocket Notebook "in the possession of a Hartford (Conn.) collector"—Bacon Collamore.*

Goldman, Eric. *Rendezvous with Destiny.* New York, 1952, p. 79.

> On Crane's *Maggie.*

Goodrich, Lloyd. *John Sloan.* New York, 1952.

> Notes that Sloan's color print of "Three A.M."—done in 1909—might have been intended to illustrate the collected works of Stephen Crane.

> *Reviewed:* Charles Poore, *New York Times*, February 9, 1952.

Gordan, John D. *"The Ghost* at Brede Place," *Bulletin of the New York Public Library,* 56 (December, 1952), 591–595.

> Reproduces the printed program for the performance of *The Ghost* at Brede School House (December 28, 1899) and discusses Crane's conception of the

---

* The Bacon Collamore Crane Collection is now in the Barrett Crane Collection. It includes the pocket Notebook, subsequently misclaimed to have been lost or misplaced, from which Stallman published many Crane manuscripts in "Stephen Crane: Some New Stories" (1956–1957).

play, its collaborators, and the staging of the little play which added a third act not given in the printed program.

Williams and Starrett expressed scepticism of a "play supposedly written in collaboration with Joseph Conrad and others. Unpublished and manuscript probably lost." Gordan speculates that the manuscript may some day turn up; it turned up in the Crane Collection at Columbia University Library. In *Columbia Library Columns* (February, 1953), Hoffman announced existence of some pages (five pages, of which three are in holograph) in Columbia University Crane Collection and reproduced the autographed program of *The Ghost*. Seven pages in typescript are in the Berg Collection. A facsimile of the first page of the printed program appeared in the London *Academy*, January 6, 1900.

On *The Ghost* see Hind (1921), Wells (1934), Jones (1954), *Letters*, and *Crane*.

Horton, Rod W., and Herbert W. Edwards. *Backgrounds of American Literary Thought*. New York, 1952, pp. 258–259.

Kazin, Alfred. [On Crane's *Maggie*], *New York Times Book Review*, September 30, 1952.

"What, after all, is it that keeps alive with such savage force a period piece like *Maggie*, though as a social study it is hilariously out-dated?"

See Stallman, "Stephen Crane's Primrose Path," *New Republic*, 83 (September 19, 1955), 17–18. The answer to Kazin's question is the art by which Crane constructed *Maggie*.

Kwiat, Joseph J. "Stephen Crane and Painting," *American Quarterly*, 40 (Winter, 1952), 331–338.

Crane made use of the techniques of painters in his prose, as well as writing about artists in his New York City sketches, and knew graphic artists very early in his career. In "War Memories" he indicated he was attempting in words what the French Impressionists were striving for in color.

Kwiat thus contradicts John Berryman's statement in Berryman's *Crane* that Crane "owes nothing whatever, apparently to painting" and that he knew few real painters.

A short but detailed study of Crane and painting appeared—a few months before Kwiat's article—in *Omnibus*, pp. 185–187: "Crane's style is prose pointillism. It is composed of disconnected images, which coalesce like the blobs of color in French Impressionist paintings, every word-group having a cross reference relationship. . . ."

Locke, Alain. "The Negro in American Literature," *New World Writing*, New York, 1952, p. 28.

Article referring to "The Monster."

Loew's Incorporated. Report of Annual Meeting, April 29, 1952, pp. 5, 13.

"The Chairman informed the meeting that only *The Red Badge of Courage*, which had been named as one of the best pictures of the year, did not make any money and explained that although it was a beautiful picture concerning a soldier in the Civil War, it apparently did not appeal to the general public."

Lynskey, Winifred, ed. *Reading Modern Fiction*. New York, 1952, pp. 173–175. Fourth ed., 1968.

On "The Blue Hotel."

Mackenzie, Aeneas. "Face to Face" (Crane's "The Bride Comes to Yellow Sky" and Conrad's *The Secret Sharer).* Theasquare Productions; released by R.K.O. Radio Pictures, 1952. Screen adaptation by Aeneas Mackenzie. Direction by John Brahm and Bretaigne Windust.

O'Connor, William Van. "The Novel as a Social Document," *American Scholar,* 4 (Summer, 1952), 172–173.
    Crane's *Red Badge of Courage* is not a document of the Civil War. (However, other than O'Connor, no critic thought it worthwhile to propose such a misreading.)

O'Donnell, Thomas F. "A Note on the Reception of Crane's *The Black Riders,*" *American Literature,* 24 (May, 1952), 233–235.
    The belief that *The Black Riders* was received with laughter and philistine scorn and little else has become the standard viewpoint. "The myth that *The Black Riders* was dismissed as a collection of freakish lines began, perhaps, in 1923,* with the publication of Beer's biography of Crane. In it, Beer grants the volume only two favorable reviews—those in the *Lotus* and the *Bookman*—and records that 'the reading nation was told at once that Stephen Crane was mad.' Crane's most recent biographer, John Berryman, helps to continue the myth in an indirect way when he states vaguely: 'The ferocity of the attacks on *The Black Riders* has been, if anything, understated, but from the beginning there were powers of opposition.' Who these 'powers of opposition' were, Mr. Berryman does not say." Berryman quotes only the *Bookman.* O'Donnell quotes only the *Nation* and *Atlantic Monthly,* both favorable, to refute the Beer and Berryman distortion. Katz in *The Poems of Stephen Crane* (1966), p. xxxiii, says that it would be equally mistaken "to agree with O'Donnell's suggestion that Crane's reception was enthusiastic," but O'Donnell's little article does not suggest that Crane's *Black Riders* received an enthusiastic reception. Katz misrepresents O'Donnell. For *The Black Riders* in review *see Crane.*

Poore, Charles. "Books of the Times," *New York Times,* February 9, 1952, p. 11.
    On John Sloane and Crane.

Prescott, Orville. [*The Red Badge* and Shelby Foote's *Shiloh*], *New York Times,* April 11, 1952, p. 21.

Ross, Lillian. "Onward and Upward with the Arts," *The New Yorker,* 27 (May 24, 31 and June 7, 14, 21, 1952).
    Reprinted in *Picture.* New York, 1952.
    Reprinted in *Reporting.* New York, 1964, pp. 223–379. Reissued 1969.
    On the filming of *The Red Badge of Courage.*

Stallman, R. W. "Stephen Crane: A Revaluation," in *Critiques and Essays on Modern Fiction,* ed. John W. Aldridge. New York, 1952, pp. 244–269.† "A Selected Bibliography of Criticism of Modern Fiction," compiled by R. W. Stallman, pp. 553–610.
    On Crane, pp. 578–579.
    "*Maggie* is a tone painting rather than a realistic photograph of slum life,

---

    * However, it began with Elbert Hubbard's article on Crane in *Roycroft Quarterly* (May, 1896). Beer popularized Hubbard's fabrication.
    † Intended for the Introduction of *Omnibus,* this essay was written prior to knowledge of *The Red Badge* manuscripts. It incorporates "Notes Towards an Analysis of *The Red Badge of Courage,*" reprinted from the Modern Library edition of *The Red Badge of Courage* (1951), which was written in 1950. The Crane checklist in *Critiques* was compiled by Sy Kahn.

but it opened the door to the Norris-Dreiser-Farrell school of sociological realism. In *The Red Badge of Courage* and 'The Open Boat,' that flawless construct of paradox and symbol, Crane established himself among the foremost technicians in American fiction. 'The Open Boat' is a perfect fusion of the impressionism of *Maggie* and the symbolism of *The Red Badge of Courage.* The two main technical movements in modern American fiction—realism and symbolism—have their beginnings here in these early achievements of Stephen Crane" (p. 245).

On realism and *The Red Badge of Courage* (p. 249). On Crane's use of colors and the method employed by the French Impressionists (the law of Simultaneous Contrast); both use pure colors and contrasts of colors (pp. 252–254). Crane's relation to Joseph Conrad and Henry James (p. 252), Chekhov (p. 257), Tolstoy, Kipling, Bierce, and others. *The Red Badge* and Melville's "Benito Cereno" (p. 259), and Conrad's *Lord Jim* (pp. 256–257), and Hemingway's *A Farewell to Arms* (p. 255).

"Irony is Crane's chief technical instrument. It is the key to our understanding of the man and of his works. He wrote with the intensity of a poet's emotion, the compressed emotion which bursts into symbol and paradox. All his best works are built upon paradox. They are formed upon ironic contrasts between ideals of romantic illusions *and* reality." (Pp. 245–246.)

——. "Letters of Stephen Crane," *London Times Literary Supplement,* August 8, 1952, p. 517.

Request for new Crane letters. "Thanks to the extraordinary kindness of Mr. Clifton Waller Barrett, of Garden City, I have in my possession photoduplications of 30 new Crane letters and two manuscripts of *The Red Badge of Courage.* Until very recently the existence of these manuscripts remained unknown or was denied. . . . Crane wrote several hundred letters—not just a few, as Thomas Beer believed."*

——. "Letters of Stephen Crane," *New York Times Book Review,* April 27, 1952, p. 18.

Stallman, R. W., ed. *Stephen Crane: An Omnibus.* Selected and Edited with Critical Introductions and Notes by Robert Wooster Stallman. New York: Alfred A. Knopf, 1952. Reissued in London by William Heinemann, 1954, without the frontispiece portrait of Crane by C. K. Linson. Reissued in much shortened form as *Stephen Crane: Stories and Tales.* New York: Alfred A. Knopf, Vintage Books, 1955.

Omnibus, said Kazin, presents "virtually all of Crane that any one except specialists will want to read, and several things by Crane that not even specialists have seen before." The two manuscripts of *The Red Badge of Courage* are brought here together for their first published occasion. The essential canon of Crane's best fictional works is here established and critically appraised; here also is the first collection of Crane's letters.

Reviewed:

TLS, August 8, 1952, p. 517.

Kirkus, 20 (September 1, 1952): "After reading the provocative introductory and critical material contributed by the editor, I defy anyone to leave unread the carefully chosen selections from Stephen Crane's output . . . and an intriguing lot of letters which give glimpses of the man, his moods, his loves and

---

* *Omnibus,* published on November 4, 1952, presented the first collection of Crane letters, 120 in all, 57 of them here for the first time.

friendships, his pecuniary difficulties, his sensitivity. Some of the letters have never before been published, and the interpretations put upon them—and others read but not used—show up quite a different Crane from some of his biographers. The critical commentary on the writings makes one wonder whether Crane is due for the sort of revival that James, Hawthorne and Melville had."

Publisher's Weekly (September 20, 1952). Reproduces from *Omnibus* a Crane letter from the Berg Collection but announces it as from the Barrett Collection.

Taylor Glenn, *Bridgeport Sunday Post* (November 9, 1952): "As exhilarating as it is erudite, a long-needed addition to American letters—and the finest testimonial one could wish to the genius of one of the western world's great writers."

Lewis Ball, *Richmond Times Dispatch* (November 9, 1952): "The introduction is stimulating without being effusive. In no other one-volume collection is it possible to get anything like so much of Crane's work, and it cannot be denied that it is representative."

Hartford (Connecticut) *Times* (November 10, 1952): "To each of these Works Mr. Stallman has contributed an enlightening introduction. . . . and he succeeds quite well, I think, in setting Crane in his proper historical perspective as not only the first of modern realists (with Hemingway as a descendent) but also as one of our finest symbolic imaginations."

Albert J. Guerard, Jr., *Saturday Review of Literature* (November 11, 1952); p. 27: "The present very handsome volume—containing the best of Crane's work and some 50,000 words of bristling commentary by Robert W. Stallman —may well provoke the critical attention long over-due. It is one of Mr. Stallman's established virtues that he leaves no reader indifferent. He sends one back to the texts one had no intention of rereading—perhaps puzzled, perhaps angry, but in any event interested. Mr. Stallman's principles are the right ones: attention to the work and not the man, and only the best of the work. . . . Mr. Stallman is frankly embarrassed by Crane's 'veritism' and eager pursuit of 'experience.' Why not stay at home and get one's material from other books? For the only significant honesty is fidelity to one's inward vision. Mr. Stallman's viewpoint has its value, and to insist on the religious symbolism of *The Red Badge of Courage* is certainly more rewarding than to see it only as a chronicle of the Civil War. Stephen Crane is lively reading, and so too is Mr. Stallman. I want to say this without irony. Mr. Stallman is a critic to be reckoned with, and this particular book is an angry labor of love. He shows, in criticism, much of Crane's energy as a novelist. But of the two, the editor remains for me the more paradoxical and the more puzzling. The writing seems clear and vivacious, yet presents insoluble contradictions. But no matter: the bewilderment Mr. Stallman created sent me back to Crane's great novel, and for this I sent up thanks."

Thomas Ripley, *Atlanta Constitution*, November 16, 1952: "Always symbol and paradox marked his writings, the irony of opposites like the man himself."

Vincent Starrett, *Chicago Tribune*, November 16, 1952. The Crane letters "illuminate and correct the standard biographies, by Beer and Berryman, in important particulars."

John Wyllie, *Richmond* (Virginia) *News-Leader*, November 17, 1952: "But there isn't really a bona fide introduction in the lot that I would eliminate. There is too much that is good in them. Stallman has a knack of nailing down the significant things in Crane's life and writings. . . . On the critical side, Mr. Stallman is also most acute. Though I have read and reread both *The Red Badge of Courage* and Hemingway's *Farewell to Arms,* it had never occurred to me that Hemingway's hero, Frederic Henry, was a straight and intentional inversion of Crane's hero, Henry Fleming, the one dealing with 'disenchantment with withdrawal, and the other with quest and triumph!' For much criticism of this sort, the Crane admirer will be greatly indebted to Mr. Stallman. But most of all, he will be indebted for all the best prose of Stephen Crane beautifully printed in one handsome and inexpensive volume."

Max Herzberg, *Newark News,* November 19, 1952: Presents "the most coherent and credible Stephen Crane we have as yet encountered."

Washington Star, November 23, 1952: "This volume . . . is beyond much doubt exactly what it purports to be. It is a selection which has long been needed."

Boston Herald, November 30, 1952: "Excellent selections, intelligently edited with fine critical commentary. . . . A fine gift and a literary item."

Hartford Courant, November 30, 1952.

Burton Rascoe, *Literary Journal* (n.d.): "This book may signalize a new trend—or a return to the right principles—in literary evaluation."

Alfred Kazin, *New York Herald Tribune,* November 30, 1952: "As a labor of scholarship, Mr. Stallman's collection is admirable; he has given us virtually all of Crane that anyone except specialists will want to read, and several things by Crane that not even specialists have seen before. Mr. Stallman has given us, along with so much else that is interesting and genuinely useful, more of Crane's letters than have ever been gathered together before. And the whole collection is all the more remarkable when one remembers how few of our classics have been served this well. He is an expert on the subject, and no doubt one of the incidental uses of this volume—though it contains no compact biographical sketch—is that it helps to correct some of the many misstatements and idle rumors about Crane that still persist. No one who plows through all of Mr. S's notes is ever likely to forget that many other commentaries on Crane were conceived in error and born in corruption. . . ."

Crane seems to Kazin "the one novelist in his age of triumphant science who accepted metaphysically, with shattering completeness, the new dogma that the human intelligence must remain apart from the objects it studies. To the already existing division between man and nature, between nature and purpose, he added that single drop of acid which ate through man's heart to make the final and searing alienation: man cannot even respect the universe which ignores him. The other 'realists' or 'naturalists' of the period were either too easygoing, like Howells, to reach these depths, or were too cynical, like Frank Norris; Dreiser too often identified himself with the objects of his compassion."

H. G. Kinchelce, *Raleigh* (North Carolina) *Observer,* November 30, 1952: "As for some of the critical opinions expressed in the introductory essays, Professor Stallman is likely to run into vigorous opposition from his critical contemporaries. Opinionated or not, the essays are stimulating to read; and the volume as a whole is excellent one for us to have."

St. Louis Globe Democrat, November 30, 1952: "Stallman's critical introduction and notes give us background and point up the tales, but always let the stories speak for themselves. As a consequence, Crane emerges in a new light."

Walter Havighurst, *Cleveland News,* December 3, 1952: "The stories are accompanied by Mr. Stallman's vigorous and arresting criticism. He sees more symbolism in Crane's work than many readers will agree to. . . . Now it is good fortune to have it (a volume of Crane) prepared by an editor of Mr. Stallman's judgement, taste, and insight."

Charles Poore, *New York Times,* December 4, 1952: "This is the best book by and about Crane that has ever been put together. It displays his astonishing genius, its faults and excellence, in full range. Mr. Stallman has collected here an interesting lot of Crane's letters. Fifty-seven of these have not been published before, and their appearance should stir the consciences of persons in America and Europe who may be hoarding others. Although Mr. Stallman shows a proper prudence in reminding us that 'letters serve the critic only as corroborative evidence,' he shows that these letters do reveal the man, and throw vivid light on Crane's character."

Tom Duncan, *Lexington Herald-Leader,* December 7, 1952: "This picture is enhanced by Stallman's introductory material. Most readers will disagree with some of his opinions, but few should cast them aside as worthless or dull. Stallman's speculations on the value of actual experience to Crane's art probably will cause more controversy than any of his other opinions. Crane 'wasted his genius,' the editor argues. The real value of Stallman's introductions is his evaluation of Crane and the discussion of his importance to American literature."

Tulsa World, December 7, 1952: "In *Stephen Crane: An Omnibus,* edited by Robert Wooster Stallman, America can read for the first time the complete version of *The Red Badge of Courage,* as it appears in Crane's original manuscript of his classic. Stallman, a professor of English at the University of Connecticut, has provided informative and critical introductory material."

John Aldridge, *New York Times Book Review,* December 8, 1952: "The virtue of Mr. Stallman's *Omnibus* is that it states the terms in which such a reckoning must one day be made. The introductory notes represent the closest and most complete reading of Crane's basic works we have had so far; and that is where a serious criticism must begin, in the heretical assumption that Crane, like any other literary artist, can be read with more profit than he can be psychoanalyzed or bibliographed or excavated for the sludge of historical influence. The reward of this most arduous because most sensible of all approaches to Crane is no more or less than the truth about him. The old botched portrait of Crane the realist, Crane the naturalist, Crane the boy reporter of a war he never saw, goes out with the rest of the rubbish; and what remains is the naked work of a man who, if he belongs anywhere, belongs well up in the second rank of that great company of ironic impressionists—. . . . This is Mr. Stallman's achievement, and it is high indeed . . . clearly a labor of literary love. . . . In plain terms, Mr. Stallman has done more than any other man to clarify our view of Crane's achievement as an artist; and he has defined the course which future Crane criticism must inevitably follow."

Houston Press, December 12, 1952: "If anything will make Crane's current 'discovery' stick, then it is this *Omnibus* so ably edited, with a Crane autobiographical and critical appraisal and notes and explanations no end. *The Red Badge of Courage* is published here complete from the original manuscripts for the first time in America. There is a total of 703 pages of Crane, including the enlightening and down-to-earth comment of editor Stallman."

Edward Wagenknecht, *Chicago Tribune,* December 14, 1952: "This is a very important book. . . . Moreover, he gives us a new text of *The Red Badge* based on two newly discovered manuscripts. This is accompanied by elaborate introduction and notes, importantly illuminating the growth of the novel and Crane's intentions regarding it. All in all, the editor himself has contributed some 125 pages of critical and scholarly interpretation to this volume."

Cincinnati Enquirer, December 14, 1952: "As a man almost ferocious in his enthusiasm for the best of Crane, Mr. Stallman, the critic, is heartless in the rejection of the poor stuff, of which there is not little. I should take care not to be within his reach when I say I find *Maggie: A Girl of the Streets* unreadable, but then in doing so I am expressing a personal taste, a deed which I am told runs counter to the canons of the 'new' criticism."

Book List, 49 (December 15, 1952), p. 49.

Christian Science Monitor, December 18, 1952.

Denver Post, December 21, 1952: "Stallman is regarded as the foremost authority on Stephen Crane and his collection is a notable and a valuable piece of work."

Nashville Tennessean, December 21, 1952: "Truly 'the heart of the Crane canon,' and the editor adds much valuable information in notes and critical introductions."

San Antonio Express, December 21, 1952: "A rich packet: *Stephen Crane: An Omnibus,* edited and critically annotated by R. W. Stallman, more than 100 Crane letters never published before, and 100-plus pages of critical appraisals by Stallman."

William Griffin, *Nashville Banner,* January 2, 1953: "Unlike most books described as omnibuses, this collection from the works of Stephen Crane is carefully planned, copiously annotated, and seriously evaluated. For most readers, the significance of this volume will not be found in the Crane texts, but in Mr. Stallman's essays. In addition to a general introduction that attempts to assess virtues and shortcomings of the author, there are illuminating introductions to each of the seven sections of the book. A helpful bibliography appears at the end."

David Stocking, *Milwaukee Journal,* January 4, 1953: Presents "a revaluation of Crane as a literary artist, emphasizing his mastery of impressionist technique and of symbol. Stallman offers the interesting idea that Crane, like Hemingway, learned much about writing from painting and painters. He also points to many parallels between Crane's works and Hemingway's both in structure and in theme."

L. S. Munn, *Springfield* (Massachusetts) *Republican,* January 18, 1953: "Unlike most admirers of literary geniuses, Stallman is willing to admit that Crane wrote considerable 'trash.' In combining the life of Crane with his stories, and in inclusion of inconsequential letters, as well as able analyses of the tales, *An Omnibus* marks a turning in the right direction of the appreciation of a remarkable man who indubitably is one of the foremost of America's creative writers."

Washington Post, January 18, 1953: "Professor Stallman corrects some of the unbalance by giving us a generous sampling of Crane's other stories (including *Maggie,* which has relapsed into limbo after a brief interval in the '30s), some of his better poetry, the cream of his reporting and a group of letters never before published. Not all of it is worth exhuming, but taken as a whole it gives a much more rounded picture of Crane's production. The editor's notes are most informative. Students will note that *The Red Badge* is printed here from the original manuscript, which differs from the text customarily used."

Kansas City Star, January 24, 1953: "Stallman's plan for the book is an excellent one. First there is a foreword and the editor's introduction. Then, before each novel, group of stories, and collections of poems, letters or sketches, Stallman supplies critical and biographical notes. In all there are around 125 pages of writing contributed to the book by Stallman himself, and as a result one feels saturated in information and opinion on Crane."

San Francisco Chronicle, January 25, 1953: "The editor does a fine job in showing the influences on Crane, and Crane's influences on other writers. . . . Mr. Stallman has admirably achieved his purpose of representing the achievement, rather than the range in the prolific Stephen Crane."

Norfolk Pilot, February 1, 1953: "This is a prize package for the general reader and for the student of American literature. Stallman's introduction and analyses of each major grouping of Crane's works is a brilliant piece of scholarly criticism. Robert Stallman has done a major service to American letters in rescuing the artist from the myth, in evaluating the works and not the man, in a creative criticism of what Crane wrote, rather than psycho-analyzing his vagaries."

West Australian (Perth, Australia), February 28, 1953.

United States Quarterly Book Review, 9 (March, 1953) 31: "The inclusion of a number of Crane's letters and the scholarly setting down of such details of the author's life as are needed to explain his writings makes this book not only a first-rate anthology, but also probably the best biography of Crane to date."

Clarence Ghodes, *American Literature,* 25 (March, 1953), 125: "The editorial material—unusually copious—represents a curious combination of the interests of the scholar and of the subjective type of critic. Unsupported statements jostle side by side with elaborately detailed accounts of the inaccuracies of Beer, Berryman, and others."

Nineteenth Century Fiction, 7 (March, 1953), 311: "No group of collectors and executors, unless it be that of Emily Dickinson, has ever so baffled scholarship as the 'protectors' of Stephen Crane. . . . It is rarely that the editor of an anthology emerges on this basis alone as the leading authority on his subject, but this is without doubt Mr. Stallman's achievement."

Isaac Rosenfeld, *Kenyon Review,* 15 (Spring, 1953), 310, 312–314: On Crane's image of "The red sun was pasted in the sky like a wafer," Rosenfeld observes: "Mr. Stallman remarks of this simile, 'I do not think it can be doubted that Crane intended to suggest here the sacrificial death celebrated in the Communion.' I, for one, do not doubt it, and even if the statement about Crane's *intention* can never be verified, one cannot deny that the line in question functions in this manner." *(Contra* Wilson in *The New Yorker.)*

The New Yorker (May 2, 1953): Unsigned [Edmund Wilson]. Mr. Stallman's commentary and the introduction "are full of ineptitudes. We find Mr. Stallman, for example, giving in to the current fashion of religious interpretation to the extent of informing us that when Stephen Crane writes that 'The red sun was pasted in the sky like a wafer,' he means by 'the sun' 'the Son' and that the wafer is the wafer of the Mass, though Crane's parents were not Catholics but Methodists, and the wafer is obviously the small red sticker that is affixed to legal documents." *See* Dounce on the wafer as sticker (1917).

Cresset, (June, 1953), pp. 43–44: "Editor Stallman has done a model job in adding notes throughout the text. His introductions come close to being a sane appraisal of Stephen Crane's worth."

Louis Kronenberger, *Partisan Review*, 19 (June, 1953), pp. 348–351: It is "not with most of Professor Stallman's specific judgments that one has any quarrel. He happens to be among the most exacting of the New Critics. . . ." However, "there is nothing very controversial about Stephen Crane himself. . . ."

Capital Times (Madison, Wisconsin), (August 7, 1953): "Thus, within these covers appears for the first time in America the complete version, from the original ms., of *The Red Badge* . . . with a bibliography, and a brilliant introduction. Certainly this is an important collection; it takes precedence over all other works mining the same field. Mr. Stallman places Crane not in the first rank with 'Hawthorne, and Melville and Henry James,' but in the second rank 'with Poe and Howells and Mark Twain,' which is eminently respectable company indeed; moreover, he holds that Crane 'perfected more works than either Poe or Twain,' which I daresay some readers would dispute. But let them first read this *Omnibus* and Professor Stallman's comments."

New Statesman and Nation (July 10, 1954), p. 16: ". . . Crane's new American editor, Mr. Stallman, who has done an exhaustive critical inspection of the Crane texts and has brought together a collection of Crane's best work. One volume has been squeezed out of the twelve volumes of stories, newspaper articles, war reports which Crane left behind him. His subject lies in his ironical attitude to the will to attack and survive and, as Mr. Stallman says, in his moral sensibility to shame, guilt and conscience. . . . Mr. Stallman properly looks at Crane from an American point of view. He has some good things to say, and others that puzzle me extremely. He says, truly, that Crane was an impressionist and influenced by painters, that his style can be called pointillist. . . . It is a good judgement of Mr. Stallman's that, in his best work, Crane's characters are occupied less with the casuistries of fear or the uncomprehending simplicities of aggressiveness than with a quest for self-identity. What they fear more than fear is incredulity. They cannot believe that life can treat them in this and that fashion. They wish to find themselves and to form a soul."

London Observer, July 11, 1954.

Spectator, July 23, 1954: "Mr. Stallman is illuminating on Crane's symbolism and on Crane's central theme in his best work, that only by immersing himself in experience does man become purified. It could be asserted that Stephen Crane not merely wrote masterpieces but also tried to live one."

Time and Tide (August 7, 1954): "It is certainly one of the most substantial guinea's worth any publisher has produced lately. Well known as Crane is, little of his work is easily available. Here, however, we have not only a critical edition of *The Red Badge*, with numerous deleted passages added from the manuscript. . . . This is, in Professor Stallman's opinion—he exhibits a rare degree of candor about his opinions—the best of Crane's work, for the selection has been determined by critical standards, not by mere personal taste. One can hardly ask more of an editor than that; unless, perhaps, that he might be a little more indulgent to his author's weaker moments."

The Scotsman (August 26, 1954): ". . . this collection confirms Mr. Stallman in his contention that Crane left behind him more than enough perfections to place him solidly among the half-dozen major artists of American fiction in the nineteenth century. . . ."

On *The Red Badge* Mss. *see* Scully Bradley (1962) and Howarth (1965); *also Crane.*

————. "Notes Toward an Analysis of *The Red Badge of Courage*," in *Stephen Crane: An Omnibus,* New York, 1952; London, 1954, pp. 191–193, 221.

"Ernest Hemingway's remark that *The Red Badge of Courage* 'is all as much one piece as a great poem is' is doubly revelatory because it defines not only Crane's novel but Hemingway's own *Farewell to Arms. A Farewell to Arms* is an inverted *Red Badge of Courage:* the one deals with disenchantment and withdrawal, the other with quest and 'triumph.' Hemingway's novel starts, as it were, where Crane's left off: Frederic Henry, the already maimed hero, is the idealistic Henry Fleming turned cynic. It is significant that both are without father and are virtually nameless. Crane's hero is always just 'the youth,' and it is not until halfway through the book (on the last page of Chapter XI) that the youth discloses what his name is, and then, ashamed because he has fled the battlefield, he utters his name only to himself. Hemingway's hero has for surname a given name. Both heroes undergo change and insight through wounds, but in opposite directions. Where Crane's Henry progresses upward toward manhood and moral triumph, Hemingway's Henry descends toward moral and spiritual degeneration. In both novels the education of the hero ends as it began: in self deception. Frederic Henry renounces war, society, and the 'comforting stench' of comrades and makes a 'separate peace.' But his farewell to arms is as illusory as Henry Fleming's farewell to vain ideals and compromising illusions. Both heroes are deluded, the one believing he can turn his back upon the battle of life, the other believing that he has triumphed in facing up to it shorn of all romantic notions.

"Both novels are ritualistic, mythic, symbolic. The dominant symbolism is religious.* Henry Fleming's forest chapel transposes into the mountain sanctuary of the lovers in *A Farewell to Arms.* As in *The House of the Seven Gables* and *Huckleberry Finn,* the alternating episodes of *Farewell* and *The Red Badge of Courage* concern withdrawal and return, the quest for self-identity, and insight or recognition through wound or suffering.' The central theme of *Farewell*—everyone has to 'get down off the mountains'—harks back through *The Red Badge* to *Huckleberry Finn.* And Twain's 'You Can't Pray a Lie,' the leitmotiv of deception in *Huckleberry Finn,* vibrates through both *The Red Badge* and *A Farewell to Arms.*

"Like Henry Fleming, Frederic Henry has romantic illusions about war. The opening scene of the novel delineates this 'picturesque front'. . . . Hemingway begins his novel exactly as Crane begins his: the opening picture manifests motifs of change and deception. . . .'' (pp. 191–192 ff.)

"Both *The Red Badge of Courage* and *A Farewell to Arms* close with the same image that their opening scenes prepared for. In both it is an image of fog or rain. . . .'' (p. 222.)

Omnibus' note comparing *The Red Badge of Courage* and *A Farewell to Arms* is not mentioned by Earle Labor, who discusses the differences between the two novels. *See* Labor (Summer, 1959).

————. [Crane and the French Impressionists], in *Stephen Crane: An Omnibus.* New York, 1952; London, 1954, pp. 185–187.

---

* In *"A Farewell to Arms:* Frederic Henry's Rejected Passion," *Renascence,* 14 (Winter 1961), John J. McAleer writes a very convincing case arguing for the grail quest motif through Christ symbolism in *Farewell to Arms.*

"Crane's style is prose pointillism [in *The Red Badge of Courage*]. It is composed of disconnected images, which coalesce like the blobs of color in French impressionist paintings, every word-group having a cross-reference relationship, every seemingly disconnected detail having interrelationship to the configurated whole. The intensity of a Crane work is owing to this patterned coalescence of disconnected things, everything at once fluid and precise. A striking analogy is established between Crane's use of colors and the method employed by the impressionists and the neo-impressionists or divisionists, and it is as if he had known about their theory of contrasts and had composed his own prose paintings by the same principle. Their principle, as one writer defines it, is this: 'Each plane of shade creates around itself a sort of aura of light, and each luminous plane creates around itself a zone of shade. In a similar way a coloured area communicates its "complementary" to the neighbouring colour, or heightens it if it is "complementary".'* In almost every battle scene in *The Red Badge of Courage* the perspective is blurred by smoke or by the darkness of night. Here is one example of the former contrast: namely, dark masses circled by light; and of the latter contrast: namely, a luminous spot circled by darkness. (The former contrast is created in the first sentence of Crane's description, and the latter contrast in the second.)

> The clouds were tinged an earthlike yellow in the sunrays and in the shadow were a sorry blue. The flag was sometimes eaten and lost in this mass of vapor, but more often it projected, sun-touched, resplendent.

"Crane's perspectives, almost without exception, are fashioned by contrasts—black masses juxtaposed against brightness, colored light set against gray mists. At dawn the army glows with a purple hue, and 'In the eastern sky there was a yellow patch like a rug laid for the feet of the coming sun; and against it, *black and pattern-like,* loomed the gigantic figure of the colonel on a gigantic horse.' Black is juxtaposed against yellow or against red. Smoke wreathes around a square of white light and a patch of yellow shade. Smoke dimly outlines a distance filled with *blue* uniforms, a *green* sword, and a *sapphire* sky. Further examples of color-contrast, particularly white versus black, occur throughout *The Open Boat,* and blue is used symbolically in *The Blue Hotel.* Crane had an extraordinary predilection for blue, which Hamlin Garland took to be the sign manual of the impressionists. It seems likely that Crane read Garland's *Crumbling Idols* (1894), but in any case he wrote a novel about an impressionistic painter—the hero of *The Third Violet.* And in one of his sketches he wrote:

> The flash of the impression was like light, and for this instant it illumined all the dark recesses of one's remotest idea of sacrilege, ghastly and wanton. I bring this to you merely as an effect, *an effect of mental light and shade,* if you like; something done in thought *similar to that which the French impressionists do in colour;* something meaningless and at the same time overwhelming, crushing, monstrous.†

"Crane paints with words 'exactly' as the French impressionists paint with pigments: both use pure colors and contrasts of colors. Black clouds or dark

---

* Cited in *Painting in France: 1895–1949,* by G. di San Lazzaro (1949), p. 28n.
† "War Memories," *Anglo Saxon Review,* 3 (December, 1899). Reprinted *War Dispatches,* p. 288.

smoke or masses of mist and vapor are surrounded by a luminous zone; or, conversely, specks of prismatic color are enclosed by a zone of shade. Shifting gray mists open out before the splendor of the sunrays. Or, conversely, billowing smoke is 'filled with horizontal flashes'; 'the mist of smoke [is] gashed by the little knives of fire.' Inside the surrounding darkness the waters of the river appear wine-tinted, and campfires 'shining upon the moving masses of troops, brought forth here and there sudden gleams of silver and gold. Upon the other shore a dark and mysterious range of hills was curved against the sky.' Cleared atmospheres, unimpeded vision of perspective, are rarely delineated; and where they occur the precision of vision is equated, symbolically, with revelation or spiritual insight. One instance of this symbolic use of color appears on page 248. Dark mists and vapors represent the haze of Henry's unenlightened mind ('He, the enlightened man who looks afar in the dark, had fled because of his superior perceptions and knowledge.'). Darkness and smoke serve as symbols of concealment and deception, vapors masking the light of truth. Sunlight and changing colors signify spiritual insight and rebirth. Henry is a color-bearer, but it is not until he recognizes the truth of his self-deception that the youth keeps 'the bright colors to the front.' In the celebrated impression of the red sun 'pasted in the sky like a wafer' Crane is at once an impressionist painter and a symbolic artist."

Stevenson, John W. "The Literary Reputation of Stephen Crane, *South Atlantic Quarterly*, 51 (April, 1952), 286–300.

Surveys some of the contemporary reviews of *The Red Badge of Courage* and of Crane's literary standing at the time of his death; briefly traces his subsequent reputation. Nothing new here.

Sutton, Walter. "Pity and Fear in 'The Blue Hotel,'" *American Quarterly*, 4 (Spring, 1952), 73–76.

On the social level the individual is isolated; "the idea of collective security is illusory"; in Sutton's view, the Swede and the Easterner are "a projection of the double vision of the writer . . . which distinguishes 'The Blue Hotel' as the expression of a tragic point of view operating within the framework of reference of literary naturalism." However, *see also* Satterwhite (1956), James T. Cox (1957), Gleckner (1959), and MacLean (1959).

One of the best studies is Gibson (1964).

On the two endings of "The Blue Hotel" (whether the first ending contradicts the second), *see Omnibus* and *Crane*.

Trilling, Lionel. "The Roots of Modern Taste and William Dean Howells," *Adelphi* (First Quarter, 1952), pp. 499–516.

Wagenknecht, Edward. *Cavalcade of the American Novel*. New York, 1952, pp. 212–216.

Walcutt, Charles C. "Sherwood Anderson: Impressionism and the Buried Life," *Sewanee Review*, 60 (January, 1952), 28–47.

Crane's belief in social determinism is shown in *Maggie*. *See* Max Westbrook (1962), who debates this topic, and Fitelson (1964), who takes issue with Westbrook's discussion of *Maggie*.

West, Ray B., Jr. *The Short Story in America: 1900–1950*. Chicago, 1952, pp. 29–30, and *passim*.

Wilson, Edmund. "A Vortex in the Nineties: Stephen Crane," in *The Shores of Light.* New York, 1952, pp. 109–114. Reprinted from *New Republic,* 37 (January 2, 1924), 153–154.

Young, Phillip. *Ernest Hemingway.* New York, 1952, pp. 161–169. Enlarged edition: *Ernest Hemingway: A Reconsideration.* University Park, Pa., and London, 1966, pp. 175, 188, 191–196, 198, 238, 250.

1953

Adler, Elmer. "An Informal Talk by Elmer Adler at the University of Kansas," April 17, 1953. In Stephen Crane Collection, Lafayette College.
On *Maggie.*

Arnavon, C. "Stephen Crane (1871–1900)," *Histoire littéraire des Etats-Unis.* Paris: Hachette, 1953, pp. 271–274.

Barrett, Clifton Waller. *The Stephen Crane Society at Lafayette.* Easton, Pa., n.d. Reprinted from *Antiquarian Bookman* (July 11, 1953).

Brooks, Van Wyck. *The Writer in America.* New York, 1953, p. 37.

Brown, E. K. *Willa Cather: A Critical Biography.* Completed by Leon Edel. New York, 1953, pp. 74–76.
For Cather's full account of Crane see *Library* (1900) or Cather, "When I Knew Stephen Crane" (1949).

Colvert, James B. "Stephen Crane: The Development of His Art." Dissertation, Louisiana State University, 1953.

Dimock, E. J. "Stephen Crane and the Minisink Valley." Unpublished address to the Minisink Valley Historical Society, February, 1953. In the George Arents Crane Collection, Syracuse University. Copy in R. W. S. Crane Collection.
Interesting anecdotes about Crane's life at Hartwood in Sullivan County. Reports the register of the Hartwood Club signed by *Stephen, William, Edmund, J. Townley,* and *Mrs. Helen Peck Crane* on September 30, 1891. Stephen signed it again in March and in May of 1892. Quoted for the first time in *Crane.*

Fitzgerald, F. Scott. "How to Waste Material: A Note on My Generation," in *Afternoon of an Author,* by F. Scott Fitzgerald. New York, 1953.

Garnett, David. *The Golden Echo.* London, 1953. New York, 1954, pp. 62–63, 63–64.

Geismar, Maxwell. "Stephen Crane: Halfway House," in *Rebels and Ancestors.* Boston, 1953, pp. 68–136.
In *The Red Badge of Courage* Jim Conklin walks stiffly in his death throes, "as if he were taking infinite care not to arouse the passion of his wounds." Geismar remarks: "And the famous tag line of this chapter 'The red sun was pasted in the sky line a wafer'—a line which became in its time the slogan of Crane's modernism—actually referred of course to the flesh and the blood of the martyred God, or the bleeding Son." (The same reading appeared in the

Introduction by Stallman to the Modern Library edition of *The Red Badge of Courage*.) *See* Stallman (1951).

Geismar also echoes John Berryman's 1950 psychoanalytical interpretation: Crane as a classic instance of the "prostitute complex" in Freudian thought. In Crane's works the oedipal drama is central and predominant. In "The Monster" a fire destroys Negro Johnson's face. "So the fire in Crane's heart (or in his wounded psyche) had at last destroyed the writer's sense of his own tradition, family, name, honor, as well as his place in society." Crane's illegitimate relationship with Cora put him outside of social conventions and made him "a faceless monster" in his own mind, too. Etc.

Reviewed:

London Magazine, 1, no. 6 (July, 1954), 88, 91.

Fred B. Millett, *American Literature,* 26 (January, 1955), 584–587. "Even more disconcerting than Mr. Geismar's amateur psychoanalyzing is the slovenliness of the writing in many passages in the book."

Gordan, John D. *The Ghost at Brede Place.* New York. The New York Public Library, 1953. Printed wrapper.

An account of the unpublished play, *The Ghost.*

Gullason, Thomas A. "Some Aspects of the Mind and Art of Stephen Crane." Dissertation, University of Wisconsin, 1953.

Hart, John E. *"The Red Badge of Courage* as Myth and Symbol," *University of Kansas City Review,* 19 (Summer, 1953), 249–256.

Reprinted in *Myth and Literature,* ed. John Vickery (1965).

The Red Badge of Courage as the discovery of the self, i.e., the unconscious self which when identified with the universal life forces, enables man to understand the nature of his world and what moves it. This is the Jungian approach. The basic sequence in what is generally a dream pattern is separation, initiation, and return. According to Hart, the youth ventures from his known environment into a region of naturalistic, if not supernaturalistic wonder; he encounters monstrous forms of war and death, is transformed through a series of rites and revelations into a hero, returns to identify his new self with the deeper communal forces of the group and to bestow the blessings of his findings on his comrades.

Hart defines his thesis on the basis that, in spite of its "realistic" style, much of the meaning of the novel is revealed through metaphor and symbol. He cites the use of soubriquets instead of names; the use of color; the use of paraphernalia of myth-religion and sacrificial rites: dancing, dragons, menacing landscape, entombment, the unexpected guide, and so on.

Hart sees the conflict between conscious fear and unconscious desire as preventing Henry from coming to terms with his new environment. Henry needs to face the enemy in the light of day and perceive his relationship to the group—which is clear in the darkness of his unconscious mind. When he flees he physically isolates himself from the source of energy which impels heroic achievement.

According to Hart this isolation is caused by Henry's unwillingness to give up his individual self and achieve his full self. His rebirth of identity is helped by outside agents—the dead man in the forest, the tattered man, Jim Conklin. The receiving of the wound, however ironic, helps him to atone and reach the group. He dies, in a sense, and is guided back. His triumphant return is followed by a new landscape the next day and victories.

He wins the goddess—the enemy flag—and is a hero. His individual strength becomes the collective strength of his comrades, which the flag exemplifies. He had faced and for a time subdues death.

Crane shows how the moral and spiritual strength of the individual springs from that of the group and, Hart states, how through the identification of the self with the group, the individual can be reborn in identity with the whole of the universe.

There is no doubt that Henry does eventually translate his early romantic dreams into a happy ending for his first campaign, and that romantic notions are constantly drifting through his mind and modifying his thoughts on past actions. The general myth pattern fits, but cannot be taken to cover all that the novel is.

"The value of Mr. Hart's analysis is limited by his purpose, which is to compare Henry Fleming to the mythic hero, thus reflecting more the anthropological interests of 20th Century criticism than the naturalism of the late 19th Century fiction." Cox (1959).

Hoffman, Daniel G. "An Unwritten Life of Stephen Crane," *Columbia Library Columns,* 2 (February, 1953), 12–16.

Reviews the important newly acquired Crane materials at Columbia University Butler Library. The collection includes letters addressed to Stephen and Cora, mirroring the literary life of a whole decade, but it does not contain a single letter from Stephen Crane. (The letters of importance and interest appear for the first time in *Letters.*)

Reproduces the autographed program of *The Ghost,* of which several pages of the script for this Brede Place play are in the Columbia Crane Collection. *See* Gordan (1952) and (1953).

———. "Stephen Crane's New Jersey Ghosts: Two Newly Recovered Sketches," *Proceedings of the New Jersey Historical Society,* 71 (October, 1953), 239–253.
Reprinted in *A New Jersey Reader* (1961).

Reprints for the first time two press clippings preserved in Cora Crane's scrapbook in Columbia University Crane Collection: "Ghosts on the New Jersey Coast," *New York Press,* November 11, 1894, p. 2, and "The Ghostly Sphinx of Metedeconk," *New York Press,* January, 1895, p. 1. The former relates to Crane's "The Wreck of the New Era," first reproduced from the holograph manuscript by R. W. Stallman. *See* Stallman, "The Wreck of the New Era" (1956).

Kwiat, Joseph J. "The Newspaper Experience: Crane, Norris, and Dreiser," *Nineteenth Century Fiction,* 8 (September, 1953), 99–117.

Reprints and comments on Crane's report of the American Day parade of the Junior Order of United American Mechanics at Asbury Park, in the *New York Tribune,* August 21, 1892. "There is evidence that the *Tribune* not only dismissed him, but that its management attacked and maligned him as well." Kwiat, however, provides nothing as evidence.

The evidence (in addition to William Crane's statement that Townley was a broken man after his dismissal by the *Tribune* for Stephen's undiplomatic sketch of the parade and the Asbury Park onlookers) is the fact that nothing by Stephen Crane appeared in the *Tribune* in 1893, a fact ascertained by recent researching of the *Tribune* for 1892–1893.

McCaffrey, John K., William G. Rogers, and Lyman Bryson. "Stephen Crane: *The Red Badge of Courage*," in *Invitation to Learning*, ed. George D. Crothers. New York, 1953, pp. 272–281. Reissued 1966, pp. 127–235.

Originally a broadcast discussing the quality of fear in *The Red Badge of Courage*, described here as a novel of the common man as distinguished from the novels of war by Tolstoy and Zola, in which the individual has no real part.

O'Donnell, Thomas F. "Charles Dudley Warner on *The Red Badge of Courage*," *American Literature*, 25 (November, 1953), 363–365.

Parks, Ed Winfield. "Crane's 'The Open Boat,' " *Nineteenth-Century Fiction*, 8 (June, 1953), 77.

Poore, Charles. "Books of the Times," *New York Times*, January 24, 1953, p. 13.

Review of *My Brother Bill*, by Ruth Mitchell. "There is a touch here of Carl Sandburg's way of reminiscing over his adventures in the Spanish-American war. There are also touches of Richard Harding Davis and of the young Stephen Crane, who was only a few years older than Billy Mitchell."

———. "Books of the Times," *New York Times*, February 7, 1953, p. 13.

Remords, Georges. "Stephen Crane et son *Red Badge of Courage*," *Bulletin de la Faculté des Lettres de Strasbourg*, (March, 1953), 237–248.

Rosenfeld, Isaac. "Stephen Crane as Symbolist," *Kenyon Review*, 15 (Spring, 1953), 310–314.

A review of *Omnibus*. "The most consistent interpretation that he works out for Crane's symbolism has to do with Jim Conklin's death (in *The Red Badge*), and Henry Fleming's emotion at witnessing it. Henry, deep in the guilt of his desertion, cannot help but regard Jim Conklin as a Christ figure; for all one knows, he has been wounded in place of Henry and is dying in his stead. The wound, moreover, is in the side, like Christ's, and Henry's regeneration begins with this death. Over the scene stands the sun, red with the youth's shame and anger, red with blood, 'pasted in the sky like a wafer.' Mr. Stallman remarks of this simile, 'I do not think it can be doubted that Crane intended to suggest here the sacrificial death celebrated in communion.' I, for one, do not doubt it, and even if the statement about Crane's *intention* can never be verified, one cannot deny that the line in question functions in this manner. But I see no evidence for the further claim Mr. Stallman makes for this interpretation, that it is 'the key to the symbolism of the whole novel,' as much of the symbolism of *The Red Badge* does not have any reference to Christianity. Yet if this broader claim be true, and *The Red Badge* is, in essence, a Christian novel, then even the detail of the dead soldier leaning against a tree and staring like a fish, must participate in the symbolism. 'That looks merely realistic,' says Mr. Stallman, 'but the dead man is a symbol.' Again he neglects to say what he is a symbol of, but if the 'sacrificial death celebrated in communion' is really the key to the symbolism of the *whole* novel, there can be no doubt that the dead soldier's *fishy* stare is a further reference to Christ, the fisher of men. Perhaps this will pass, and so, perhaps, will Mr. Stallman's attempt to clinch the identification of Jim Conklin by calling attention to his initials. But I must draw the line at his footnote to the sentence that Henry screams out when he encounters the wounded Jim: 'Gawd! Jim Conklin!' This, says Mr. Stallman, 'suggests an identification of

Jim Conklin with God.' It suggests even more strongly that the critic is working his poor horse to death.''[*]

However, a great many incidents in *The Red Badge* are echoes from the Bible, from the Gospels in the first half of *The Red Badge* and from the Book of Revelation in the second half. *See* Thomas, "The Long Logic" (1967) and Stallman, "Notes Toward an Analysis" (1967).

Roth, Russell. "A Tree in Winter: The Short Fiction of Stephen Crane," *New Mexico Quarterly*, 23 (Summer, 1953), 188–196.

Saillet, Maurice. "Paul Valery et 'La Conquête du Courage,'" *Mercure de France*, 317 (February 1, 1953), 376–378.

Shane, Marion L. "Spiritual Poverty in Selected Works of Four American Novelists: Mark Twain, Crane, Fitzgerald, Dreiser." Dissertation, Syracuse University, 1953.

Spiller, Robert, *et al., Literary History of The United States.* New York, 1953, pp. 1020–1027.

There is "little in his life or reading to account for the pessimism and the sensibility of his tales and poems. . . . It is the familiar story of romantic youth seeking escape from life into art and achieving a fleeting mastery before the overtaxed body gives way. The term of twenty-nine years, the late marriage to an older woman, and the death by consumption at a health resort follow an almost classic formula. . . . His slim volumes of epigrammatic and symbolic verse give him a minor but significant place in American poetry. The appearance of an original artist, springing without antecedent into life, is always illusion, but the sources of Crane's philosophy and art are as yet undeciphered."

Spiller's notion of the romantic youth achieving "a fleeting mastery" belittles Crane's achievement. The "romantic youth seeking escape from life" was in fact a cynical anti-romantic war correspondent risking his life in Greece and Cuba, not escaping from life but facing into it.

Wells, Lester G. "Off the Press," *Delta Upsilon Quarterly*, 71 (April, 1953), 89.

Wilson, Edmund [unsigned]. [On *The Red Badge of Courage*], *The New Yorker*, 29 (May 2, 1953), 124.

A review of *Omnibus.* Contends that Crane could not possibly have intended to represent the wafer of the Mass in the image of the "red sun pasted in the sky like a wafer" occurring at the death-scene of Jim Conklin in Chapter 9 of *The Red Badge.* Crane could not possibly have intended or employed the symbolism of Catholic ritual because Crane's parents were Methodists, not Catholics.

However, consider the converses of this Wilson proposition: if an author uses Catholic ritual then he or his parents subscribe to the Catholic faith, and if an author employs Catholic symbolism then you thereby know what church denomination he subscribes to. As a matter of fact, in the ritual of the Mass there was only nominal difference between the Catholic Church and the Methodist Church during the 19th Century.

The Methodist Church sometime in the late 19th Century used grapejuice

---

[*] Reprinted here by permission of Mrs. Isaac Rosenfeld, letter to R. W. Stallman (1969).

instead of wine *and* bread instead of a wafer, "but otherwise the Methodist and Catholic ritual was essentially the same ritual." (Letter of Bishop Herbert Welch of New York to R. W. S.)

1954

Adams, Richard P. "Naturalistic Fiction: 'The Open Boat,'" *Tulane Studies in English,* 4 (1954), 137–146.

Crane's use of color imagery here is hardly very systematic or consistent, albeit there are nearly a hundred "more or less distinct terms referring to some kind or aspect of color" in "The Open Boat." On color imagery in *The Red Badge see Omnibus,* pp. 185–187, and Wogan (1960).

[Anon.]. "News and Ideas," *College English,* 16 (October, 1954), 59–60.

Brooks, Van Wyck. *Scenes and Portraits: Memories of Childhood and Youth.* New York, 1954, pp. 110, 125, 152.

Mentions that Stephen Crane had lived on Twenty-third Street, across the way from where Brooks lived a dozen years later. "His housemate Edward Marshall, the crippled correspondent, lived there still, nursing his recollections of the mercurial Crane, a name to me almost as vague then as Edwin Arlington Robinson's name or the name of Theodore Dreiser, who was also in New York."

Cady, Edwin H., and Lester G. Wells, eds. *Stephen Crane's Love Letters to Nellie Crouse.* Syracuse, N.Y., 1954. Photographs.

Presents the seven Nellie Crouse letters first remarked on by Mangione in 1930, and six Crane letters to friends, all here for the first time except for Crane's letter to the Philistine Society (November 15, 1895) which first appeared in *Omnibus.* Noxon's *Step Ladder* letter of 1928 also obtained publication prior to this volume of *Crane's Love Letters to Nellie Crouse,* and the Crane letters to Hawkins were published in *Omnibus* for the first time, *not* reprinted there (as claimed by the editors Cady and Wells). Except for their notes and appendix matters, *Letters* (1960) reprints the entire volume of *Crane's Love Letters to Nellie Crouse,* including Frank Smalley's letter to Mrs. Crane and Charles Little's letter to Crane.

Cunliffe, Marcus. *The Literature of the United States.* Baltimore, 1954, pp. 204–207. Also, pp. 185–186, 208, 241, 271, 272.

Considers *Maggie* "dated and violent and absurd like a primitive film; and its most remarkable feature—a descriptive vocabulary similar to that in Crane's poems—has nothing to do with orthodox naturalism."

To discuss *The Red Badge of Courage* "as an example of naturalism is to miss its mood. Crane is preoccupied with the personal reaction to fear: so while Fleming, judged by his conversation, is loutish, his inward turmoil is that of the sensitive man (a discrepancy less evident in the book as printed than in the manuscript draft)."*

    * One manuscript draft was first made known in John T. Winterich's Folio Society edition (London, 1951), while both Ms. SV and Ms. LV drafts appeared together for the first time in *Omnibus. See* Bradley (1962) and Howarth (1965).

Dixson, Robert J., ed. *The Red Badge of Courage.* Simplified and Adapted for Greater Reading Pleasure. New York, 1954.

> With exercises and vocabulary drill (the vocabulary range is 2,600 words).

Emery, Edwin, and Henry Ladd Smith. *The Press and America.* New York, 1954, pp. 350, 423, 443, 479.

Gelfant, Blanche H. *The American City Novel.* Norman, Okla. 1954, pp. 63, 237.

Gillis, E. A. "A Glance at Stephen Crane's Poetry," *Prairie Schooner,* 28 (Spring 1954), 73–79.

> Quotes Berryman's claim that Crane's poems "accumulated upwards of a hundred parodies and certain good-natured epithets. Not only were they 'absurd,' 'besotted,' 'idiotic,' 'lunatic,' but they were 'hamfat,' 'garbage,' 'rote,' and also 'opium-laded,' . . . gas-house ballads.' "
>
> However, none of these epithets appears in the known reviews of *The Black Riders.* Their claim to "fact" rests solely on Elbert Hubbard's statement that they appeared in reviews he pasted into a notebook, but no such notebook survives among Hubbard's papers. Gillis's essay is as superficial as his title indicates.

Herzberg, Max J. Introduction, *The Red Badge of Courage.* New York: Pocket Books, 1954. Reprint of 1925 edition.

Jones, Edith R. "Stephen Crane at Brede," *Atlantic Monthly,* 114 (July, 1954), 57–61.

> Describes in considerable detail the life at Brede Manor in the summer and fall of 1899; "the house radiated with the happiness of the Cranes." She never heard money mentioned while she was there, and she never saw an uninvited guest. Takes issue with Ford Madox Ford's account in *Mightier Than the Sword* (1938).
>
> Crane said that most of his Whilomville Stories were founded on stories that Cora had told him of her childhood. "One day he told us that he had had a dream which he thought would make a good story. He dreamed that he was acting on the stage of some theater and in the play he was a prisoner. He had been handcuffed and his ankles were bound together. Suddenly there was a cry of 'Fire!'. . . . I don't know whether he published the story, but he lived it and wrote it."
>
> That story, to identify it, was "Manacled," published in *Argosy* (August, 1900). *See Crane.*

Leary, Lewis, ed. *Articles on American Literature 1900–1950.* Durham, N.C., 1954, pp. 61–62, 63.

Nojiri, Yoshinoshin. " 'The Open Boat' o chūshin ni mita Stephen Crane no riarizumu" [Stephen Crane's realism, mainly on "The Open Boat"], *Hokkaido Daigaku Gaikokugo Gaikoku-bungaku Kenkyu,* no. 2 (1954), pp. 69–79.

Osborn, Scott C. "Stephen Crane and Cora Taylor: Some Corrections," *American Literature,* 26 (November, 1954), 416–418.

> From Richard Harding Davis letters here quoted, the question whether Cora traveled with Crane from Athens to Velestino and Volo is answered. She accompanied Crane north from Athens on April 29, 1897. Relate to Osborn (1956).

Pound, Ezra. *Literary Essays.* London, 1954, p. 384.

> In a 1914 review of Robert Frost's poetry, Pound says, "a sane man knows that a prose story can't be much better than the short stories of de Maupassant or of 'Stevie' Crane."

Pritchett, V. S. "Books in General," *New Statesman,* 48 (July 10, 1954), 46–47.

Review of *Stephen Crane: An Omnibus,* ed. R. W. Stallman (1952; London, 1954).

"Stephen Crane is one of those writers of short, original performance whose intense life and early death (at the age of 28) create a personal legend. The natural comparison is with Stevenson, and the two men had, in fact, an astonishing physical resemblance. There are other resemblances: a certain ironical, moral dandyism of temperament which comes out also in their styles, for Crane is a very literary writer and has, in consequence, been compared—as he complained—to everyone from Tolstoy to Loti. As H. G. Wells said in one of his accurate moments, Crane really suggested Whistler rather than Tolstoy. This game is quickly dropped by Crane's new American editor, Mr. Stallman, who has done an exhaustive critical inspection of the Crane texts and has brought together a collection of Crane's best work. . . .

"Many European critics have said that Crane's subject was fear (here Mr. Stallman dissents), but this fear is a good deal the fear of not being tough, which runs openly or implicitly through American realism and which gives it, again and again, so many sentimental overtones. It is evident from the images used in his *Bowery Tales* that Crane shares the radical preoccupation with aggressiveness. . . . It is a good judgment of Mr. Stallman's that, in his best work, Crane's characters are occupied less with the casuistries of fear or the uncomprehending simplicities of aggressiveness than with a quest for self-identity. What they feel more than fear is incredulity. They cannot *believe* that life can treat them in this and this fashion."

Pritchett disbelieves Stallman's notion that when Jim Conklin ignores the rumours of the coming battle and goes off and washes his shirt in the dirty river (in the opening chapter of *The Red Badge of Courage*) he is performing the act of absolution, or that when Conklin dies the young narrator at sight of the red wafer-like appearance of the sun "partakes of the sacramental blood and body of Christ." This seems to Pritchett to carry symbolism to very dubious lengths. However, *see* Rosenfeld (1953).

Stallman, R. W. *Stephen Crane: An Omnibus.* London, 1954.

Reviewed, 1954:
London Daily Express, June 11.
News Chronicle, June 17.
The Listener, June 24.
TLS, July 9.
John Davenport, *The Observer,* July 11.
Dublin Irish Times, July 17.
Anthony Powell, *Punch,* July 21.
Daily Worker, July 22.
Dal Stivens, *The Spectator,* July 23.
Foyles Bookshop Magazine, July.
Douglas Newton, *Time and Tide,* August 7.
London Evening Standard, August 19.
The Poet, September 9.
Bucher aus Amerika, November (reprints the London *Spectator* review).
See also Pritchett (1954).

Stallman, R. W., and R. E. Watters. *The Creative Reader.* New York, 1954, 1962, pp. 366–367, 488.
> Reprints "The Upturned Face," pp. 59–62; "The Open Boat," pp. 216–231 [1962 ed. only]; and newspaper reports of the *Commodore* disaster, pp. 216–241.

Umstätter, Hans, trans. *Das Blutmal* [*The Red Badge*]. Mannheim, Germany: Kessler, n.d. [1954].

Yamamoto, Hiroshi. "Stephen Crane to shizenshugi" [Stephen Crane and Naturalism], *Shizuoka Daigaku Bunrigaku-bu Kenkyu Hokoku (Jinbun Kagaku),* no. 5 (January, 1954), 55–74.

1955

Archibald, Elizabeth. "A Study of the Imagery in Stephen Crane's 'The Open Boat'," *Exercise Exchange,* 2 no. 2 (1955), 3–5.

Brooks, Van Wyck. *John Sloan: A Painter's Life.* New York, 1955, pp. 32, 54–56, 235.
> Sloan illustrated Crane's *Great Battles of the World* (1901), but he knew nothing of his fiction until years later; he then liked *Maggie* and "The Open Boat," but he did not care for *The Red Badge.* Sloan said: "Crane's attitude was human rather than socially conscious," adding, "I think he really loved the down and outs on the Bowery, out of his love for all life." This might be said of Sloan himself, says Van Wyck Brooks.

Chase, Richard. *Walt Whitman Reconsidered.* New York, 1955, pp. 126, 127, 162, 167.

Clark, H. H., Richard Fogle, and others, eds. *The Development of American Literary Criticism.* Durham, N.C., 1955, p. 148, and *passim.*
> Reviewed: R. W. Stallman, *Modern Language Notes,* 71 (Summer, 1956), 227–229.

Colvert, James. "The Origins of Stephen Crane's Literary Creed," *University of Texas Studies in English,* 34 (1955), 179–188.
> Reprinted in *A Mirror for Modern Scholars,* ed. L. A. Beaurline. New York, 1966, pp. 156–165.
> Two theories commonly are advanced to explain Crane's phenomenal literary development: one is that he had no origins at all, and the other is that he sprang directly from the tradition of the French and Russian Naturalists. "Unlike Frank Norris, who once referred to himself as 'Mr. Norris, Esq. (The Boy Zola)!' Crane seems to owe little, if anything, to nineteenth-century French and Russian naturalism."
> Colvert thus takes issue with Ahnebrink (1950) and Spiller (1948); he agrees with Salvan (1943). However, Colvert subsequently qualified this standpoint on finding evidence that Crane more than likely read Zola's *La Débâcle. See* Colvert (1956). In 1955 Stallman identified parallelisms between *Madame Bovary* and *Maggie,* in "Stephen Crane's Primrose Path."
> Colvert, spotting a review of Kipling's *The Light That Failed* in the *Literary*

News (1891), examines Kipling's novel about artist Dick Heldar and points
out parallelisms between Dick Heldar's artistic aims and Crane's own conception of the art of fiction. "Since the evidence for the influence of the
[French] naturalists upon Crane's literary theory is unconvincing, and since
he knew neither Howells' nor Garland's theory of realism and veritism until
after 1892, before which time he had read *The Light That Failed,* it seems
likely indeed that Kipling is Crane's chief literary ancestor." In *The Light
That Failed* is a whole literary credo "which exactly parallels Crane's," namely
that art is grounded in actual experience, that even ugly and unpleasant experience is material for the artist, and that honesty is indispensable for the
artist.

However, *contra* Colvert, the same credo was expounded by Hamlin Garland—prior to his *Crumbling Idols* (1894)—in his Asbury Park lectures of
1891–1892, and thus Kipling's *Light That Failed* (1891) was not Crane's
sole source.

Scott C. Osborn first cited that Crane knew Kipling's *The Light That Failed,*
noting that Crane's famous image in *The Red Badge of Courage*—"The sun
was pasted in the sky like a wafer"—echoes a similar image in Kipling's novel.
See Osborn (1951) and Stallman's rejoinder in 'The Scholar's Net: Literary
Sources" (1955).

Cunliffe, Marcus. "Stephen Crane and the American Background of *Maggie*,"
American Quarterly, 7 (Spring, 1955), 31–44.

Discusses Émile Zola's *L' Assommoir* and other possible sources for *Maggie*
and concludes that Zola's novel does not explain Crane's *Maggie*. Agrees with
Stallman in *Omnibus* that Crane wrote a first draft in the spring of 1891 and
then "knew very little about the Bowery, slum life, and prostitutes," and so
Crane either invented *Maggie* or borrowed something from other writers, says
Cunliffe.

Crane could have gotten the idea for Maggie's suicide from Charles Loring
Brace's *The Dangerous Classes of New York* (1872) and his thesis that environment "frequently shapes lives regardless" might have come from reform clergymen like Thomas DeWitt Talmage. In his *Night Side of New York City Life*
(1878) a forgiving mother greets her dying girl with the cry of "Oh, Maggie!"
Cites other points of parallelism with Crane's *Maggie*. He reproduces here a
woodcut entitled "The Street Girl's End," and on this item alone Professor
Jack Levenson asserts that this woodcut "vividly supports" Cunliffe's thesis
"that Stephen Crane was not influenced by the French naturalists. *(See* Levenson [1962]). *Contra* Levenson *and* the woodcut, Crane was influenced by
Flaubert's *Madame Bovary* by the evidence of parallelisms noticed in Stallman's studies of *Maggie* (1955 and 1959).

Cunliffe identifies in *Maggie* the Broadway Gardens, but not noticed by
Cunliffe is the fact that that place was identified by a reviewer of *Maggie* in
1896: A. H. Lewis in *New York Journal,* March 8, 1896.

Dor, Milo, and Elisabeth Moltkau, trans. *Die Flagge des Mutes.* Frankfurt am
Main, Germany, and Wien, Austria: Forum, 1955.

Edel, Leon, ed. *The Selected Letters of Henry James.* New York, 1955, p. xx.

Fiedler, Leslie. "Images of Walt Whitman," in *Leaves of Grass: One Hundred
Years After,* ed. Milton Hindus. Stanford, 1955, p. 66.

Whitman at his best was "a singer of urban life, like Baudelaire," and surely

Crane in prose was likewise "dedicated to redeeming for the imagination . . .
the life of the cities."

Gwynn, Frederick. Editorial note, *College English,* 16 (April, 1955), 427.
Scoffs at the notion that the initials of Jim Conklin in *The Red Badge of
Courage* can possibly signify that Jim Conklin is Jesus Christ.
However, while true that the initials *J. C.* would not warrant such an identification, Gwynn ignores for the sake of his jest here the internal evidence
such as "the passion of his wounds," and the external evidence such as the
fact that any number of other Crane works are loaded with biblical allusions,
echoes, and parallelisms.

Haight, Gordon S., ed. *Miss Ravenel's Conversion,* by John William De Forest.
New York, 1955, pp. xv–xvii. First edition, 1939.
Contrasts De Forest's realism with Crane's: "Everything that Crane sees
looks like something else; De Forest describes things as they are. He never
sees a wood as a chapel, boughs as a door, and pine needles as carpet, nor do
his corpses remind one of the exhibits in Madame Tussaud's chamber of
horrors." In Crane's *Red Badge* campfires dot the night "like red, peculiar
blossoms," and tents spring up "like strange plants"; whereas De Forest's
"tents are canvas, usually rotten enough to let the rain through, and campfires
are lit for warmth. That is the difference between a somewhat decadent impressionism and true realism. . . . There is no doubt that Crane knew De
Forest's battle scenes; no discriminating reader can believe that he has improved them." The discriminating critic, however, recognizes the fallacy in
Haight's misguided premise that presumes realism (art as photocopyistic of
reality) to be the criterion of evaluation in literary art. Realism is not enough,
said Conrad. "You stop just short of being absolutely real," said Conrad in his
1902 letter to Arnold Bennett, "because you are faithful to your dogmas of
realism. Now realism in art will never approach reality. And your art, your
gift, should be put to the service of a larger and freer faith."
See also O'Donnell (1956) and *Crane.*

Hart, Andrew W. "Stephen Crane's Social Outlook as Revealed in His Writings."
Dissertation, Michigan State University, 1955.

Hoffman, Federick J. *The Twenties: American Writing in the Postwar Decade.*
New York, 1955, pp. 55–56, 61, and *passim.* Rev. ed., 1962, pp. 75–76.
The influence of Crane's Naturalism on Hemingway. Hemingway and the
writers of the 1920s inherited from Crane an interest in violence and the
graphic description of physical action; his portrayal of courage in *The Red
Badge of Courage* was of particular interest to them. However, Crane and
Hemingway disagreed on the definition of courage. Hoffman sees courage in
The Red Badge as accidentally issuing from cowardice, as an emotion governing an action or the man who is to act, the result in this case being bathed
in deserved irony. In Hemingway he finds courage the term for a decision
which may take a man towards *or* away from the battlefield; flight and refusal
to fight become natural reactions, and this change in attitude toward war and
cowardice by the 1920s (in American fiction) denies these writers the perspective of irony.

Howard, Leon, Louis B. Wright, and Carl Bode, eds. *American Heritage: An
Anthology and Interpretive Survey of our Literature,* vol. 2. New York, 1955,
pp. 458–460, 478.

Reprints *Maggie* (1896 edition). The editorial notes contain several errors: Beer's *SC* is 1923; Brom Weber wrote on Hart Crane, not Stephen Crane; *Maggie* is incorrectly given as 1892; "The Open Boat" is 1897 and *The Open Boat* is 1898. Crane spent not a year at Lafayette College but only one semester, and he was age 28 when he died, not 29.

Kahn, Harry, trans. *Männer im Boot und andere Erzählungen*. Basel, Switzerland, 1955.

Contains the title work ("The Open Boat"), "Experiment in Misery," "The Bride Comes to Yellow Sky," "The Blue Hotel," and two newspaper reports on the *Commodore*'s shipwreck. In translation into the German.

O'Brien, Edmond. *The Red Badge of Courage*, a recording. Caedmon (1955).

Reviewed: Thomas Lask, *New York Times*, August 4, 1957: "Mr. O'Brien gives a virtuoso performance. His pacing, range of mood and handling of the dialogue combine to make the reading of this chronicle thoroughly absorbing."

O'Donnell, Thomas F. "John B. Van Petten: Stephen Crane's History Teacher," *American Literature*, 27 (May, 1955), 196–202.

Buttresses and expands Lyndon Upson Pratt's supposition in "The Formal Education of Stephen Crane" (1939) that Crane in *The Red Badge* was influenced by the war reminiscences of his Claverack College history teacher, the Reverend General John B. Van Petten. *Contra* Berryman, Van Petten was far more than just a "white-haired old elocution teacher" given to sentimental memories of the past. As chaplain of the 34th New York Volunteers he saw his regiment distinguish itself at Fair Oaks in May of 1862, and what happened there compares with the final victorious charge of Crane's fictitious 304th New York in Chapter 23 of *The Red Badge*. Later at Antietam on September 17, 1892, the 15th Massachusetts, fighting in the same line with the 34th New York, captured from the hands of the enemy a battle flag, "wrenching it from the grasp of its wounded bearer." Compare the last "grim fight" of Henry Fleming's rival color-bearer. At Antietam, Van Petten may have seen panic, but at Winchester (Opequon Creek) on September 19, 1864, it is certain that he did. General Van Petten's accounts of that battle, O'Donnell concludes, "could have provided Crane with all the necessary details he needed to authenticate the panic scenes in his great novel."

Compare Hungerford (1963). In retrospect O'Donnell's evidence remains as a corrective of Hungerford's theory of Chancellorsville for the original site of the battlefield in *The Red Badge*, which undoubtedly combines with Chancellorsville something of Winchester and Antietam. On Van Petten *see also* O'Donnell (1956).

Pizer, Donald. "Crane Reports Garland on Howells," *Modern Language Notes*, 70 (January, 1955), 37–39.

A note on Crane's reporting of a lecture by Hamlin Garland in the summer of 1891 in "Howells Discussed at Avon-by-the-Sea," *New York Tribune*, August 18, 1891, p. 5. Crane's article is here reprinted for the first time.

Poore, Charles. [*The Red Badge* and MacKinlay Kantor's *Andersonville*], *New York Times*, October 27, 1955, p. 35m.

Richards, R., ed. *Concise Dictionary of American Literature*. New York, 1955.

Richie, Donald. "Eight American Writers: III. Stephen Crane," *The Study of Current English* (Tokyo), 10 (October, 1955), 33–41.

Spiller, Robert E. *The Cycle of American Literature.* New York, 1955, pp. 145, 155, 157–158, 167, 171, 221. Reissued, 1967.

"Somewhere, somehow, Crane had felt the force of analytical psychology before anyone had appeared to formulate its principles. . . . Diffused in other stories and finally lost in an effort to court the public, Crane's mastery of theme and form in his early and best work was in the tradition of Poe and Hawthorne and Ambrose Bierce rather than in that of Whitman and Norris. As his discipline was derived from art rather than from experience, it did not develop beyond its first sharp distillation, and the forces released so briefly into expression were soon turned inward again to consume the artist himself."

Spiller's contention that Crane, like Frank Norris, knew the paintings and painters of the Impressionist school stands in agreement with Stallman in *Omnibus,* with Kwait (1952), and in disagreement with Berryman in his *Crane.*

Stallman, R. W. "Stephen Crane's Revisions of *Maggie: A Girl of the Streets,*" *American Literature,* 26 (January, 1955), 528–536.

Discovers a new passage not reprinted in the Appleton 1896 edition (the new passage precedes the final paragraph of Chapter 17):

" 'When almost to the river the girl saw a great figure. On going forward she perceived it to be a huge fat man in torn and greasy garments. His grey hair straggled down over his forehead. His small, bleared eyes, sparkling from amidst great rolls of red fat, swept eagerly over the girl's upturned face. He laughed, his brown, disordered teeth gleaming under a grey, grizzled moustache from which beer-drops dripped. His whole body gently quivered and shook like that of a dead jelly fish. Chuckling and leering, he followed the girl of the crimson legions. . . .'

"The leering fat man represents a mockery of Maggie's plight, and his attribute of 'dead jelly fish' prepares for the death by drowning that occurs subsequent to Maggie's encountering him. That he is a 'dead jelly fish' anticipates, to put it another way, the death of Maggie."

However, a cogent reason toward explaining why Crane expunged this passage is given by Gibson (1956), pp. xvi–xviii. *See also* Bowers (1969).

———. "The Scholar's Net: Literary Sources," *College English,* 17 (October, 1955), 20–27.

Relates to Kipling's image in *The Light That Failed* (1891) as the source for Crane's "The red sun was pasted in the sky like a wafer." Discovery of this Crane source was made by Scott C. Osborn (1951). Kipling's image: "The fog was driven apart for a moment, and the sun shone, a blood-red wafer, on the water."

Osborn thinks these images seem "nearly identical," but they bear only a surface resemblance because each is utilized for wholly different purposes; at their metaphoric level there is no resemblance whatsoever. At their literal level both images, says Osborn, seem to compare the sun "to a red wafer of wax used to seal an envelope." However, what was used for sealing envelopes during the nineteenth century was a red wafer of glue, not wax; a small, round, orange-red stickable sealing-wafer. Kipling fashioned it "blood-red," and Crane has it properly "pasted." In Kipling the blood-red sun is the wafer of a coin, which mocks artist Dick Heldar because he has sold himself out for bloody money. In Crane, on the contrary, the blood-red sun suggests the wafer of the Communion at which Henry Fleming curses on the moment of Jim Conklin's death.

James Colvert (1955) finds in Kipling's *The Light That Failed* the origins of Crane's literary creed.

——. "Stephen Crane's Primrose Path," *New Republic*, 133 (September 19, 1955), 17–19.

Reprinted in expanded form as "Crane's *Maggie*: A Reassessment," in *Modern Fiction Studies*, 5 (1959).

Recast as "A Critique of *Maggie*," in *American Literature: Readings and Critiques*, ed. Stallman and Waldhorn (1961), pp. 712–717.

Reprinted in *Houses*, pp. 72–81; and in *Stephen Crane's Maggie: Text and Context*, ed. Maurice Bassan (1966), pp. 139–144.

Contends that Crane wrote *Maggie* prior to experiencing the Bowery, while at Syracuse University in spring of 1891, and that he invented the plot (as Beer first observed). Identifies here for the first time parallelisms between *Maggie* and Flaubert's *Madame Bovary*. On *Maggie* see *Crane*.

——. "*The Red Badge of Courage*: A Collation of Two Pages of Manuscript Expunged from Chapter XII," *Papers of the Bibliographical Society of America*, 49 (Third Quarter, 1955), 273–277.

The Signet edition of *The Red Badge* in *The Red Badge of Courage and Selected Stories*, ed. R. W. Stallman (1960) provides the above two MS. pages and three additional MS. pages, here for the first time, together with MS. LV and MS. SV. These five new pages are reprinted in *The Stephen Crane Reader*, ed. R. W. Stallman (1972).

Stallman, Robert Wooster, ed. *Stephen Crane: Stories and Tales*. New York: Knopf Vintage Book, 1955.

A shortened paperback version of *Stephen Crane: An Omnibus* (1952), without *The Red Badge of Courage*, the poems and letters, and related introductory matters.

Stresau, Hermann, trans. *Stephen Crane: Das blaue Hotel*. München, Germany, Albert Langen–Georg Müller, 1955.

Untermeyer, Louis. "Stephen Crane," in *Makers of the Modern World*. New York, 1955, pp. 444–449.

Van Abele, Rudolph, and Walter Havighurst. "Symbolism and the Student," *College English*, 16 (April, 1955), 424–434.

"But it is unjustifiable for Robert Wooster Stallman to say that the celebrated line about the sun pasted in the sky like a wafer, in Crane's *Red Badge of Courage*, is a symbolic prophecy of redemption; for the word 'pasted' clearly shows that the wafer is not the Host but the seal affixed to a document attesting its having been completed."

However, the wafer of the Host is also pasted. Why should the red sun appear at Jim Conklin's death as the seal affixed to a document? No legal imagery exists anywhere in *The Red Badge;* if it exists as such here, it is an isolated instance, whereas all other images in *The Red Badge* are patterned, repeated again and again.

Von Abele's notion of the wafer sun as a sealing wafer echoes Scott Osborn (1951) and Edmund Wilson (1953), and in turn all three are echoed by Eric Carlson (1958), Cecil Eby (1963), and Joseph Katz in *Portable Stephen Crane* (1969), p. 246. Neither Carlson nor Katz acknowledge that their idea has been anticipated by any previous critic, and not one in the above list offers any interpretation as to what contributing function the wafer sun as sealing wafer could possibly have in relation to Jim Conklin's death-scene and/or to any other incident in the narrative.

Katz says "but it is necessary to note its function and reference." However, the only "function" he indicates is legal "symbolism," but he does not trace it —because legal symbolism is nonexistent. As for the referent of wafer sun, Katz says: "but this wafer is 'pasted,' like a seal." No, the original seal was not pasted; it was glued; Crane has it "pasted." True, Crane may have known about such seals through lawyer William Crane, according to Katz, but these seals were not limited to legal documents.

All these critics—from Osborn and Wilson to Katz and Eby—confound the referent with its function in the novel. Katz's notion of legal symbolism is nonsense. As for the referent, possibly its referent *is* the red round seal (a copy of which I own as gift of Bertram Rota, Ltd.), but there is the testimony of H. E. Dounce in "Stephen Crane as Craftsman" that sealing wafers had disappeared from use before the Civil War and that "Crane had not seen a wafer of the kind to which he refers." *See* Dounce (1917).

On the wafer sun image as the Host wafer, *see* Isaac Rosenfeld (1953), Daniel Hoffman in his Harper Modern Classics *Red Badge of Courage* (1957), Edward Stone, "The Many Suns of *The Red Badge of Courage*" (1957), and James Colvert (1958 and 1959).

On *The Red Badge* as a religious allegory or as a work infused with biblical allusions, *see also* Maxwell Geismar (1953), Bernard Weisberger (1958), Olov Fryckstedt (1961), James Tuttleton (1962), Robert Detweiler (1964), Donald Thomas (1967), and John McDermott (1968).

Wheeler, Post, and Hallie Ermine Rives. *Dome of Many-Coloured Glass.* New York, 1955, pp. 4, 21–22, 98–101, 142, 175.
   Memoirs of Crane at Asbury Park.

Winkler, John K. *William Randolph Hearst: A New Appraisal,* New York, 1955.
   On Crane in Greece; nothing on Crane in Cuba.

1956

Adams, J. D. [Stephen Crane and New York City], *New York Times Book Review,* July 1, 1956.

[Anon.]. "Stephen Crane Exhibit," *Columbia Library Columns,* 6 (November, 1956), 44.

Baum, Joan H., ed. *Stephen Crane (1871–1900): An Exhibition of His Writings Held in the Columbia University Libraries September 17–November 30, 1956.* Arranged and described by Joan H. Baum. Foreword by Professor Lewis Leary. New York: Columbia University Libraries, n.d. [1956]. Frontispiece: Portrait of Crane by Corwin Knapp Linson, 1894, from the original oil painting in the BCC. Photographs. Crane aboard *The Three Friends* "after his ordeal at sea following the sinking of the *Commodore*," p. 51. Crane and John Bass in Greece, 1897, p. 52. The photograph of Crane aboard *The Three Friends* is wrongly attributed to the BCC; the original is at Yale University Library.

Reproduces in facsimile: the first page of *Maggie* (1893) and Crane's inscription, p. 16; the holograph manuscript of the first page of *The Red Badge of Courage* (MS. LV), p. 24; and the printed program for *The Ghost,* with signatures of eight of its ten authors.

This work is an important bibliographical account of Crane's publications and of Crane's manuscripts, typescripts, letters, etc. However, it does not list the holograph of "Corporal O'Connor's Story," which belongs to Appendix 1, pp. 55–56. Appendix 4 (Writings on Crane Since 1948), errs both in its listings and grossly in its omissions (by 1956 some 1,250 articles had been published on Crane). Miss Baum's additions to the *W-S Bibliography* comprise but a small fraction of the writings on Crane 1948–1956, pp. 59–61.

Appendix 1 lists titles of unpublished Crane writings. Most of them have since been published. Appendix 2 lists clippings and proofs in CUCC, titles not in *W-S Bibliography*. All of them have since been published. Appendix 3 lists titles of clippings in Crane's scrapbooks in CUCC and in the BCC, titles of pieces published in journals not listed in *W-S Bibliography,* or titles known but published in unlisted journals.

Bosquet, Alain. *Anthologie de la poésie americaine des origenes à nos jours.* Paris, 1956.

Three Crane poems in translation. Crane, *"concis et rageur, est de ceux qui ont fait le plus pour dénouncer l'absurdité d'un monde matérialiste; il n'est pas sans rappeler Corbière et LaForgue."*

Bremmer, Robert H. *From the Depths: The Discovery of Poverty in the United States.* New York, 1956, pp. 105–106.

Colvert, James B. *"The Red Badge of Courage* and a Review of Zola's *La Débâcle,"* *Modern Language Notes,* 71 (February, 1956), 98–100.

The *New York Tribune,* July 10, 1892, reviewed Zola's *La Débâcle* (in a French edition and in a translation of the book into English). Colvert quotes the review and concludes that Crane probably read it because his sketch "The Broken-Down Van" appeared in the same issue of the *Tribune.* He was also appearing in the *Tribune* this summer with his Sullivan County sketches. Crane always denied any connection with Zola and was annoyed when his English friends insisted on his discipleship to the French Naturalists. "Yet *The Red Badge* so closely resembles *La Débâcle* in general plan, design, and intention that literary historians have always suspected that Crane had some knowledge of the precedent that had been set for him."

Commented on in *College English* (1957), p. 333.

Decker, Carol Joan. "A Bibliography of the Stephen Crane Collection in the Free Public Library, Newark, N.J." M.A. thesis, Columbia University, 1956.

Emmanuel, Caesar, trans. *Stephen Crane: The Red Badge of Courage.* Introduction, Robert Wooster Stallman, pp. vii–xxx, translated into Greek. Athens, "Atlantis," n.d. [1956].

Friedrich, Otto. "The Passion of Death in Ambrose Bierce," *Zero,* 2 (Spring, 1956), 72–94. On Crane, pp. 77–79, 82–83, 91–92.

"Bierce was a master of the kind of realism that manages to imply a great deal, and to establish a pervasive mood, without the devices of symbolism." In both Bierce and Crane the atmosphere of battle is one of chaos, but Bierce transcends descriptive realism in "a surrealistic, supernatural concentration of horror, chaos and death. . . . His mind was too scarred and crippled to reach the dimensions that Stephen Crane's unhampered imagination achieved in *The Red Badge of Courage*. Much of the best war writing has been done by men whose contact with actual fighting was brief or peripheral."

Contends that Bierce, not Crane, anticipated Hemingway, despite Hemingway's admitted admiration for Crane and his ignoring of Bierce. Discusses Bierce's "Chickamauga" without recognizing the affinity of Crane's "Death and the Child." An excellent little study of Bierce.

Gibson, William. Introduction, *Stephen Crane: The Red Badge of Courage and Selected Prose and Poetry*. New York, 1956, pp. iii–xx. Revised and enlarged version of *Selected Prose and Poetry of Stephen Crane* (1950). Textual and Bibliographical Note, pp. xvi–xx.

Reprints *The Red Badge* MS. LV from the London Folio Society edition (1951), which text is inaccurate and does not include MS. SV, first published in *Omnibus*.

Gibson surveys briefly highpoints in publications on Crane. "Old controversies, new materials, and known though unpublished work suggest that a full biography is yet to be written."

Compares 1893 and 1896 texts of *Maggie* (first collated by Stallman in *American Literature* [1955]); he points out why Crane expunged from the 1896 text the passages where Maggie is met by the "huge fat man in torn and greasy garments" and by two other men of brief dialogue. "Thus in Crane's revised text, Maggie no longer solicits the last two men she meets, and the 'huge fat man' whom she might accept has wholly disappeared: she has, plainly, made up her mind to drown herself. The ambiguity is gone and the logic of Crane's chapter and his whole story is improved, or remains unimpaired. One may of course question that logic on larger grounds, but if one accepts Maggie as a girl who 'blossomed in a mudpuddle' and was capable of deep shame and remorse, the last events of Crane's story in its final version seem inevitable."

Gibson's reading has gone unnoticed by critics of *Maggie,* including Joseph Katz, who agrees with Sallman's 1955 proposal to include the missing passage ("the leering fat man"): "The *Maggie* Nobody Knows" (1966).

Greene, Graham. *The Quiet American*. London, 1955. New York, 1956, p. 38.
"Stephen Crane could describe a war without seeing one. Why shouldn't I?"

Hackett, Alice Payne. *Sixty Years of Best-Sellers 1895–1955*. New York, 1956, p. 104.

Hagemann, E. R. "Crane's 'Real' War in His Short Stories," *American Quarterly,* 8 (Winter, 1956), 356–367.
"A serious, important effort to analyze Crane's vision of war" (Cady, 1962). Crane's vision of war in the short stories is analyzed under six categories: (1) the individual soldier, (2) the lure of violence, (3) the effect of warfare on the soldier, (4) heroism and duty, (5) death, and (6) the destruction of the "nature scene by the machines—and man—of battle."

Hart, James D. "Stephen Crane," in *The Oxford Companion to American Literature*. New York, 1956, pp. 165–166.

Hayashi, Nobuyuki. "On Stephen Crane's Novels," *Studies in English Language and Literature* (Tokyo, Japan: in Japanese), no. 4 (December, 1956), 1–16.

Hayashi, Nobuyuki, and Shiro Yokozawa, trans. *Akai bukunsho* [*The Red Badge of Courage*]. Tokyo, Japan: Shin-eisha, 1956.

Hoffman, Daniel G. "The Poetry of Stephen Crane." Dissertation, Columbia University, 1956. Published as *The Poetry of Stephen Crane* (1957).

Kanno, Masaaki. "S. Crane no shi" [The Poems of Stephen Crane], *Tenri Daigaku Gakuho*, no. 56 (December, 1956), 47–68.

Kindilien, Carlin T. *American Poetry in the Eighteen Nineties.* Providence, R.I., 1956, pp. 155–161, 165–168.

Reports Hubbard's record of newspaper comments on *The Black Riders,* kept in a scrapbook, which comments—according to Hubbard—included such epithets as "idiocy," "drivel," "rot," etc. However, no such scrapbook exists among Hubbard's papers, and no reviews containing such epithets have turned up; so that one concludes that they were Hubbard's invention, as was also the scrapbook.

Kindilien discusses *The Black Riders'* theme of the relation of man and his god; his account is superficial.

Leary, Lewis. "Stephen Crane, 1871–1900," in *Stephen Crane: An Exhibition of his Writings.* . . . New York: Columbia University Libraries, 1956, pp. 3–10.

"But except for the studies of John Berryman, Robert Wooster Stallman, and Daniel G. Hoffman, little has been done by students of our day to supplement the pioneer work of Thomas Beer in discovering why or how Stephen Crane wrote in the manner he did."

Matsumoto, Masaharu. "Stephen Crane no konkyu: kankyo to ningen" [A study of Stephen Crane: environment and man], *Mukogawa Gakuin Joshi-daigaku Kiyo,* no. 3, part 2 (February, 1956), 151–170.

Mayfield, John S. "Stephen Crane's Curious Conflagration," *American Book Collector,* 7 (December, 1956), 6–8, and "Letters to the Editor," *ABC,* 7 (January, 1957), 2.

On Crane's sketch of a tenement fire in "When Every One Is Panic Stricken," *New York Press,* November 25, 1894. Reissued by Ames W. Williams in a pamphlet, n.d. [1954], titled "Fire!"

"The facts are: there was no fire at all, no baby, no hysterical mother, no brave policeman, no nothing, except Crane's magnificent and, in this instance, impish imagination, and the great William Dean Howells was so taken in that he pronounced Crane's article 'a piece of realistic reporting.'" Anyone who consults the several newspapers published in New York City around the date 25 November, 1894, "will find nothing at all about any fire having taken place, much less anything about any policeman rescuing a child from a burning building."

Beer in *Stephen Crane* quotes a portion of this *Press* sketch in connection with Crane's statement: "The *Herald* fired me last week." Beer concludes: "Crane's shadowy term with the *New York Herald* exactly prophesied his whole career as a journalist. He could not report. Apparently he did not even try to report." However, the *Herald* did not discharge Crane because of his tenement-fire sketch, which appeared not in the *Herald* but in the *Press* (in 1894). Edward Marshall praised it for a fine piece of realistic reporting; *see* Marshall, "Stories of Stephen Crane," *Literary Life* (1900).

Norris, Frank. "Crane in London," and "News Gathering at Key West," in *The Letters of Frank Norris,* ed. Franklin Walker. San Francisco: The Book Club of California, 1956, pp. 9–18.

The former reprinted from *San Francisco Wave,* September 18, 1897, and the latter reprinted from *McClure's Magazine* (May, 1898).

A portion of "News Gathering at Key West" is reprinted in *War Dispatches,* p. 123, titled: "Frank Norris' Pen Portrait of Stephen Crane Aboard *The Three Friends.*"

O'Donnell, Thomas F. "DeForest, Van Petten, and Stephen Crane," *American Literature,* 27 (January, 1956), 578–580.

Did Crane know about DeForest's *Miss Ravenel's Conversion?* Gordon Haight in his Introduction to his edition of DeForest's novel (Haight [1955]) concludes that "there is no doubt that Crane knew DeForest's battle scenes." O'Donnell establishes the fact that DeForest and the Reverend John B. Van Petten, Crane's history teacher at Claverack College, were comrades-in-arms in several battles, including the battle of Winchester in Virginia. *See* O'Donnell's article in *American Literature* (May, 1955): "John B. Van Petten: Stephen Crane's History Teacher."

On DeForest and Crane, their realism compared, *see Omnibus.*

Ohashi, Kenzaburo, trans. *Aoi hoteru (ta)* [The Blue Hotel]. Tokyo, Eihosha, 1956. Eibei Meisaku Library.

Includes "The Open Boat," "The Upturned Face," and "An Experiment in Misery."

Osborn, Scott C. "The 'Rivalry-Chivalry' of Richard Harding Davis and Stephen Crane," *American Literature,* 28 (March, 1956), 50–61.

Crane and Richard Harding Davis first met in London in late March, 1897, says Osborn. (However, they had first met at the Lantern Club in 1895.) Quotes from unpublished Davis letters having importance for the Crane chronology. For instance, did Crane go to Crete? In Athens on April 28, 1897, Davis met Crane and wrote home to his mother: "Stephen Crane came in last night having been searching for me all over Albania and to my satisfaction told me he had been in Crete all this time that I have been in Florence." Davis's initial liking for Crane in 1897 changed into dislike by 1898. "Crane violated Davis's sense of decorum; Crane did not think, talk, dress, or act like the gentlemen with whom Davis felt most at ease."

Contra Beer, in Davis's "A Derelict," Channing's character is in large part founded on Davis's conception of Crane. In his comedy "The Galloper" (in *Farces,* 1906), based on the Greco-Turkish War, "Davis possibly modeled one of the characters upon Cora Taylor; in it an actress, 'an attractive, dashing-looking woman of the adventuress type,' who is pursuing her divorced war correspondent husband in an attempt to collect alimony, resembles Davis's conception of Cora." *See Crane.*

Rahv, Philip. "Fiction and the Criticism of Fiction," *Kenyon Review,* 18 (Spring, 1956), 276–299.

Reprinted in Rahv's *The Myth and the Powerhouse.* New York, 1965, pp. 33–60.

Reprinted in his *Literature and the Sixth Sense.* New York, 1969. Rahv *versus* Stallman, pp. 227–230.

A literal-minded Marxian critic, Rahv denies that there is any irony or any symbolism in Crane's writings. Stallman replies in "Fiction and Its Critics: A Reply to Mr. Rahv," *Kenyon Review* (1957) and in his *Houses* he replies by a much expanded version of his argument for the poetic use of language in the novel.

Against the critical reading of fiction as though it were a poem, "This recent infection of the prose-sense by poetics." Denies Stallman's claim that Crane, like Conrad, "puts language to poetic uses," that Crane converts realistic details in *The Red Badge* into symbols, and that there is any irony in "The Open Boat." Stallman "professes to see a poetic paradox in the phrase 'cold, comfortable sea-water,' but in point of fact within the context of the story the juxtaposition of 'cold' and 'comfortable' cannot strike us as paradoxical but rather as wholly natural . . . the water *in* the boat feels 'comfortable' as against the waves beating *at* the boat," etc.

Rahv, as answered in *Houses,* strikes Stallman as "not only absurd in his turn," but arrogant. He accuses Stallman of "having made this image [the "cold, comfortable sea-water"] paradoxical by sequestering it from its context in Crane's story. . . . On the contrary, I think it must be read as paradoxical if you do not sequester it from its context. For this image shares with other images in 'The Open Boat' a mockery of the plight of the men in their God-forsaken dinghy. . . .

"Rahv's literal reading ignores the over-all play of Crane's ironic point-of-view through which this image must be read. Establish this relationship and you cannot fail to see that the image of 'cold, comfortable sea-water' represents that contradiction of emotions or paradox which I've ascribed to it. . . . The men in the boat are mocked by the gulls sitting on the sea near patches of seaweed: 'The birds sat *comfortably* in groups, and *they were envied* by some in the dinghy, for the wrath of the sea was no more to them than it was to a covey of prairie chickens a thousand miles inland.' The men envy the gulls for being comfortable; hence their own plight, obversely, is uncomfortable and the sea-water in the boat is cold-comfortable therefore in the ironic sense. One of the gulls tries to alight upon the captain's head: 'His black eyes were *wistfully* fixed upon the captain's head.' The epithet 'wistfully' transfers to the captain, for it is he and not the gull who is in fact thinking wistfully. The gull has no reason to think wistfully as he is already comfortably situated.

"Again, Crane writes with irony: 'It is almost certain that if the boat had capsized he would have tumbled comfortably out upon the ocean as if he felt sure that it was a great soft mattress.' I don't see how it can be doubted that 'comfortably' is here used ironically, and as in this instance so likewise in the above companion-images—notably in 'cold, comfortable sea-water.' What is meant, Mr. Rahv, is just the opposite of what is stated. Obviously, the ocean is anything but 'a great soft mattress'; actually, were the men tumbled into the ocean they'd find its cold water 'sad' and 'tragic.'

"Rahv contends that 'the water *in* the boat feels "comfortable" as against the waves beating at the boat,' that the water-in-the-boat 'seems positively domesticated. Hence the adjective "comfortable"'. I shall answer this notion under two heads: (a) In what sense can the water at the bottom of the boat be considered more comfortable than the water outside? And (b) in what sense is it 'domesticated'?

"(a) Whereas the oiler, 'a wily surfman,' is the spokesman for the hard cruel facts and is the only realist in the group, the others are given to illusions. Even the hurt captain and the cynical correspondent are given to illusions. It is the correspondent who imagines the water-in-the-boat as comfortable (or, to be precise, as cold-comfortable). That he so imagines it is an ironic illusion, this one being patterned by all the other ironic illusions. No sooner is the correspondent spelled by Billie than he falls asleep, and he falls asleep not comfortably but 'despite the fact that his teeth played all the popular airs.' What Mr. Rahv, is *comfortable* about that?

"Only to the gulls, Mr. Rahv, is the January sea-water (icy literally both in the boat and outside it) comfortable *naturally.*

"(b) The cold boat-water seems to the correspondent 'domesticated' not 'positively' but rather ironically. You will notice that the men are given to domestic thoughts and that these domestic images mock their plight quite as much as do the comfortable gulls. The men are mocked also by the indifferent shore with its windmill turning its back upon their plight. Things viewed by the men at sea are viewed as though they were men on land. Thus the cold-comfortable sea-water image is patterned by the same ironic outlook as is everything else in the story, by the contrast between what is and what seems. Land images impinge upon their situation at sea; the waves seem like a mountain-cat, each crest seems but a hillside ('Viewed from a balcony'), seagulls remind them of a covey of prairie chickens a thousand miles inland, and their dinghy seems like a wild colt ridden by circus-men. They are so 'comfortable' in the cramped and cold dinghy that even the icy sea-water seems 'domesticated,' but of course not literally so. Thus the ocean is said to be their mattress, two lights on the sea look like 'the furniture of the world,' and their grotesque domicile is even furnished with a stove, but of course not literally so. The cook 'seemed almost stove-like.' The stove-like shape of the cook provides the frozen correspondent a semblance of warmth and domesticity.

"Non-literal readers will recognize the above items as metaphors having a grotesque ironic intent. Huddling against the stove-like shape of the cook provides the correspondent the only warmth that the icy boat-water affords; namely (1) on the literal level, a semblance of bodily warmth from huddling against the cook's cork lifebelt, and (2) on the spiritual level the warmth of brotherhood. While literally the boat-water is as cold as the ocean outside the boat, what makes the boat-water seem cold-comfortable is that brotherhood which their plight has effected in an otherwise uncomfortable dinghy. It is 'comfortable' only in this spiritual sense, but even this is ironic; for their brotherhood is earned through the bitter experience of their plight. It is furthermore ironic because of the fact that the men in the boat cannot comprehend the full meaning of that brotherhood, the reality of it, until they are safe on land. And again it is ironic that even on land their comfort and their brotherhood are spoiled by grief at the loss of the oiler.

"He alone held no illusions. And perhaps that is why he, the wily surfman, meets his death on the surf. Or, as your literal reader will likely prefer, it is because Higgins, the original for Crane's oiler, met his death precisely in this way."

On *The Red Badge of Courage* Rahv falsifies Stallman's account of the identity of Jim Conklin with Christ by sequestering a single item of identity, the initials *J. C.* in Jim Conklin's name, whereas Stallman's account involves far more evidence in Crane's text than Rahv admits to.

Opposition to Rahv's literal-minded reading of Crane is expressed by West (1956), James T. Cox (1957), and Colvert (1958).

Remords, Georges. "Les lettres américaines et la critique universitaire française," *Bulletin de la Faculté des Lettres de Strasbourg,* 36 (December, 1956–January, 1957), 160–177.

Rideout, Walter. *The Radical Novel in the United States: 1900–1954.* Cambridge, Mass., 1956.

The author of that radical novel *Maggie* obtains only a slight reference here.

Satterwhite, Joseph N. "Stephen Crane's 'The Blue Hotel': The Failure of Understanding," *Modern Fiction Studies,* 2 (Winter, 1956–1957), 238–241.

"The cash-register legend, 'This registers the amount of your purchase,' is misleading because it implies the Swede has deliberately sought and deserved his death [by other readings he has done just that, and the register says just that]; actually he has been destroyed by a social environment which has refused or has been unable to understand him." On "The Blue Hotel" *see also Omnibus,* James T. Cox (1957), and Colvert (1958).

Siebold, Dr. F. K. "Stephen Crane: Ein Lebensbildnis des amerikanischen Schriftstellers, der in Badenweiler starb," *Badenweiler,* 27 (September 15, 1956), 3–4.

Propaganda by Dr. von Siebold, Bürgermeister of Badenweiler, for his plan of commemorating Crane's sixtieth anniversary at Badenweiler on June 5, 1960.

See also Helm, "In Memory of Stephen Crane," and "Stephen Crane: ein Vergessener?" (1959) and Ingeborg Hecht (1959).

Solomon, M. [pseudonymn; identity not known] "Stephen Crane: A Critical Study," *Masses and Mainstream,* 9, nos. 1 and 2 (January and March, 1956), 25–42, 31–47.

Critical of John Berryman's thesis that Crane's life was "a classic instance of the 'prostitute complex' in Freudian thought." A fresh and original survey, brief but illuminating on *The Red Badge, George's Mother,* and Crane's social criticism. "Crane shared the aristocratic view of the poor so common among radicals of his time. The intellectual of conscience looked at the oppressed asking only why they did not rebel against injustice."

Stallman, R. W. "Stephen Crane's Letters to Ripley Hitchcock," *Bulletin of the New York Public Library,* 60 (July, 1956), 318–332.

Reproduced here for the first time*; reprinted in *Letters.*

———. "Stephen Crane: Some New Stories (Part 1)," *Bulletin of the New York Public Library,* 60 (September, 1956), 455–462.

Reproduces for the first time first drafts from the Crane Notebook in the BCC, formerly in the BCCC: "The Art Students' League," "Matinee Girls," "Election Night: New York 1894," and "Literary Notes." Also "Gustave and Marie," written on the back of page 137 of the final handwritten manuscript of *The Red Badge of Courage* (a fragment numbered page 3.)

———. "Stephen Crane: Some New Stories (Part 2)," *Bulletin of the New York Public Library,* 60 (October, 1956), 477–486.

Reproduces for the first time "The Raft Story" from the holograph manuscript in the BC. An unidentified newspaper proof-sheet is in CUCC, dated "For Aug. 2" [1896]. Reproduces for the first time "Diamonds and Diamonds" from the typescript corrected in the author's hand, in the BCC. Also comments on other manuscript fragments.

---

* Crane's letters to Hitchcock were quoted in Berryman's *Crane* in spite of refusal of permission to quote them by John D. Gordan, Head of the Berg Collection, New York Public Library.

——. "'The Wreck of the New Era' (An Unpublished Sketch by Stephen Crane)," *Fine Arts Magazine* [University of Connecticut], April 28, 1956, pp. 1, 2, 19–20.

Reproduced here for the first time from the holograph manuscript (14 leaves); typed copy in the BCC, originally in the BCCC.

Noticed:

American Literature, 28 (November, 1956), 414.

——. Introduction, *The Red Badge of Courage,* trans. into Greek. Athens, Greece [n.d., 1956], Modern Library ed. (1951).

Stock, Irvin. *William Hale White: Mark Rutherford.* New York, 1956, pp. v, 3.

Taylor, W. F. *The Story of American Letters.* Chicago, 1956, pp. 281–283, 362.

Walcutt, Charles Child. "Stephen Crane: Naturalist and Impressionist," in *American Literary Naturalism, A Divided Stream.* Minneapolis, 1956, pp. 66–86, 222–223, 296.

Indecisive in defining literary Naturalism because he begs his terms. Collate with Walcutt (1946).

On *Maggie,* "The Blue Hotel," and *The Red Badge of Courage.* Walcutt ignores "The Open Boat" in his discussion of literary Naturalism. In error on date of *Maggie* (1893, not 1892).

Walker, Franklin, ed. *The Letters of Frank Norris.* Book Club of California, 1956.

West, Ray B., Jr. [Editorial], *Western Review,* 20 (Summer, 1956), 258–260, 335–336.

"If Mr. Stallman's discovery of symbols in Crane and Conrad went too far for the sensibility of Mr. Rahv, Stallman is still probably nearer the truth about these two authors than Mr. Rahv who, by implication, seems to be saying that there is little or no symbolism." On Rahv (1956) *see* Stallman "A Reply to Mr. Rahv" (1957).

Wilson, Edmund. *A Literary Chronicle: 1920–1950.* New York, 1956, pp. 90, 123, 230, 264.

1957

[Anon.]. [On Crane and Zola], *College English,* 18 (March, 1957), 331.

The fact that Zola's *La Débâcle* appeared under review in the same issue of the *Tribune* as Crane's "The Broken-Down Van" indicates that Crane read the review, but it does not prove that Crane read the book. "The point remains moot." *See* Colvert (1956).

Asselineau, Roger. "Realism, rêve et expressionnisme dans *Winesburg, Ohio,*" *Archives des Lettres Modernes,* 1–2 (April, 1957), 22.

Ayers, Robert W. "W. D. Howells and Stephen Crane: Some Unpublished Letters," *American Literature,* 28 (January, 1957), 469–477.

The Howells letters, reserved for first publication in *Letters,* were here published without the permission of the Howells estate and inaccurately reproduced. Ayers thus scooped *Letters*. *American Literature*'s apology appears in the November, 1957, issue, p. 326.

Blanck, Jacob. *Bibliography of American Literature*, vol. 2. New Haven, Conn., 1957, pp. 329–338.
   Describes nonperiodical publications on and by Crane.

Breit, Harvey. "In and Out of Books," *New York Times Book Review*, March 24, 1957, p. 8.

Chase, Richard. *The American Novel and Its Tradition*. Garden City, N.Y., 1957, pp. 4, 139, 142, 200, 208.
   Except for occasional mention of his name, nothing of Crane's achievement figures in Chase's theory of American fiction.

Cox, James M. "*The Pilgrim's Progress* as a Source for Stephen Crane's *The Black Riders*," *American Literature*, 28 (January, 1957), 478–487.
   Crane's "reliance on the form and furniture of Bunyan's world discloses an important aspect of his poetic nature: he is far more moralist and mechanic preacher in his poetry than he is imagist or free versifier or symbolist. As deeply and furiously rebellious as this Byronic war seeker appears, he still rants in the anguished tones of an inspired Methodist minister; his manner and style come from the world he can no longer believe in. But he wants that lost world again, this figure who is so absurdly out of place among the naturalists with whom he is frequently grouped."
   Cox's thesis stands in opposition to Daniel Hoffman's in *Poetry*, namely that Crane was ignorant of Bunyan's *Pilgrim's Progress*. *See also* Kindilien (1957).

Cox, James Trammell. "Stephen Crane as Symbolic Naturalist: An Analysis of 'The Blue Hotel,'" *Modern Fiction Studies*, 3 (Summer, 1957), 147–158.
   "The limitations of labels are less apparent when the term, like *naturalism*, has clearly definable boundaries than when it suffers from an excess of meaning, as in the much discussed omnibus *romanticism*. But they are no less real and no less critically inhibiting. . . . R. W. Stallman is almost alone in perceiving a fundamental difference in the fictional method of Crane and that of other naturalists in American fiction. . . ." Opposes Philip Rahv, who denies that Crane's fictional method includes irony and symbolism. Scrutinizes in detail "The Blue Hotel" as example of his thesis that Crane's fictional method "is that of the symbolist rather than the naturalist."

Day, Cyrus. "Stephen Crane and the Ten-Foot Dinghy," *Studies in English* (Boston University), 3 (Winter, 1957), 193–213.
   Contends that "The Open Boat" must be reappraised in the light of his findings, based on wind-velocity charts made in January, 1897, at Florida weather stations, that no heavy seas prevailed when the *Commodore* sank and Crane in the dinghy tried to reach shore through the surf. It is not true that "These waves were most wrongfully and barbarously abrupt and tall," as Crane describes them in "The Open Boat." And the heavy seas Crane reported in his *New York Press* article, January 7, 1897, did not exist.
   This latter charge impugns Crane as a journalist. However, *contra* Day, charted wind velocities are no accurate prediction of the condition of the seas at Daytona because the Gulf Stream (not reckoned in Day's account) could cause heavy seas irrespective of gentle winds recorded at weather stations located at New Smyrna and at Jacksonville. Furthermore, heavy seas did prevail on the night of January 1, 1897, as given in the journal of the

Newark—evidence not noticed by Day, nor by Berryman (1950), nor by Randel (1962). *See* Stallman, "Journalist Crane in That Dinghy" (1968), and *Crane*.

Gilkes, Lillian, and Joan H. Baum. "Stephen Crane's Last Novel: *The O'Ruddy*," *Columbia Library Columns*, 6 (February, 1957), 41–48.

Gordon, Caroline. *How to Read a Novel*. New York, 1957, 1964, pp. 91–93, 97, 205, 233.

Commits the same error made in her *Accent* article (1949) (reprinted in *The House of Fiction*, 1950): "Crane tells us somewhere that he got the idea for his famous *Red Badge of Courage* from one of the battle scenes in *The Charterhouse of Parma*." (However, Crane never read *La Chartreuse de Parma* and was angered when told that he had. Caroline Gordon is much mistaken.)

Gullason, Thomas. "New Sources for Stephen Crane's War Motif," *Modern Language Notes*, 72 (December, 1957), 572–575.

On Crane's Wyoming Valley tales.

See Arnold (1959). *See also* Gullason in his Introduction to *CSS&S* (1963), pp. 29, 34–35.

———. "New Light on the Crane-Howells Relationship," *New England Quarterly*, 30 (September, 1957), 389–392.

"While the young Crane worshipped Howells as a 'progressive realist' in 1891, he renounced him as the epitome of the bourgeois dullness in 1900—and for good reason."

———. "Additions to the Canon of Stephen Crane," *Nineteenth-Century Fiction*, 12 (September, 1957), 157–160.

One of his proposed additions to the canon—"Harvard University Against the Carlisle Indians, Described by Stephen Crane" *(New York Journal,* November 1, 1896)—is genuine. The other—"Veterans' Ranks Thinner by a Year" *(New York Press,* May 31, 1894)—is not the work of Crane. *See* Hoffman (1959).

Gullason persists (Gullason, "Thematic Patterns" [1961]) in his claim that "Veterans' Ranks" is by Crane and that Hoffman has demonstrated no real proof that it isn't. Hoffman's claim that "The Gratitude of a Nation" was written by Crane (Hoffman [1959]) does not convince Gullason even though its holograph manuscript is in Crane's hand—in the CUCC.

Hayashi, Nobuyuki. "Stephen Crane no shōsetsu ni tsuite" [On Stephen Crane's novels], *Tokyo Toritsu Daigaku Eibungakkai Eigo to Eibungaku,* no. 4 (February, 1957), 1–16.

Herzberg, Max J., ed. *The Red Badge of Courage and Other Stories*. New York, 1957.

With biographical illustrations and pictures of the settings of the stories.

Hoffman, Daniel G., ed. *Poetry of Stephen Crane*. New York, 1957.

Represents "a very considerable advance over the earlier biographies by Thomas Beer and John Berryman," says Kenneth Rexroth in *Saturday Review* (July 5, 1958). However, it is nothing of the kind since it is not a biography. One of the main contributions to Crane criticism and scholarship, Hoffman's book is a brilliant close reading of the poems, some of which are reproduced here for the first time from manuscripts in CUCC.

In 1896 articles by Gaines and Peaslee pointed out the all important fact that Crane's ancestry included several clergymen and soldiers. Hoffman traces mainly the thread of Crane's religious heritage as it shows up in the poetry. He expands upon the theme first announced by Clarence Loomis Peaslee in *Monthly Illustrator* (August, 1896), although he mentions neither Peaslee nor Gaines. Peaslee declared: "It is an interesting study in heredity to note the influence of these two professions [clergymen and soldiers] in Mr. Crane's literary work, the one furnishing the basis of style, the other of incident."

Hoffman adopts Berryman's theories about Crane's love poems, but elsewhere he is original and useful in his insights on Crane's poems. The best short scrutinies of Crane's poems are by Harland Nelson (1963) and Ruth Miller (1968).

————. Introduction, *The Red Badge of Courage and Other Stories*. New York, 1957.

Reproduces for the first time the untitled manuscript here titled "The Gratitude of a Nation," in CUCC.

"Although Crane is often thought to have introduced Zolaesque naturalism into American writing, he liked none of Zola's works. And, as John Berryman observes, Crane had no sympathy whatever for Zola's worship of force, nor did he share the French writer's addiction to scientific method. His debt to Zola, if it may be so called, was for providing fictional examples of a human world completely ruled by deterministic forces. Crane hated these forces, but he believed that they exist. Yet Crane in *The Red Badge* was no naturalist."

In Tolstoy's *Sebastopol*, which Crane read in 1888 or 1889, conflicts between appearance and reality, between opinion and fact, between truth and self-deception, appear intermittently. Crane in *The Red Badge* systematized them into a coherent structural framework to give greater thematic unity. "Crane's story is surely better unified than Tolstoi's report of the defeat in Crimea." "The recently recovered manuscript of *The Red Badge of Courage* includes several passages omitted from the text of the first edition which make possible a clearer view of one of the important themes of the book. This theme is the ethic of redemption, reminiscent of Tolstoi's, whose morality Crane once remarked 'is simply that of Christ.' "*

In one of these manuscript passages Henry's mother, who links with the theme of redemption, gives Henry Fleming a Bible. "It is the presence of Jim Conklin in Henry's company which makes unnecessary his reading of the Bible, for, as R. W. Stallman has observed, Jim, with his tall spectral bearing, his wounded side and bloody hand, and the very initials of his name, 'is intended to represent Jesus Christ. . . . The religious symbolism . . . radiates outward from Jim Conklin.' Jim's appearance in *The Red Badge* is both symbolically and literally a Second Coming. . . . As Professor Stallman remarks, these religious images reach their climax in the famous metaphor which sacramentalizes the death of the Son: 'The sun was a red wafer pasted in the sky [*sic*].' *The Red Badge of Courage,* then, is an apocalyptic novel in which war is not so much the subject as the source of the governing metaphors." (Hoffman's reading buttresses Stallman's in *Omnibus* and in his Modern Library Introduction, 1951.)

Howells, William Dean. "An Appreciation," in *Prefaces to Contemporaries*, ed.

---

* Hoffman says that the restored passages were first published in the Folio Society edition of *The Red Badge of Courage* (1951), but that text reproduced only the final manuscript. Both MS. LV and MS. SV were first reproduced in *Omnibus*.

William Gibson, George Arms, and Frederic Marston, Jr. Gainesville, Fla., 1957, pp. 62–64. Reprinted from Howells' Introduction to *Maggie: A Child of the Streets*. London, 1896, pp. v–viii.

Kindilien, C. T. "Stephen Crane and the 'Savage Philosophy' of Olive Schreiner," *Studies in English* (Boston University), 3 (Summer, 1957), 97–107.

"The sound and the fury of Crane's lines are, of course, far removed from Olive Schreiner's calm scene, just as her soft didacticism has little in common with Crane's typical tone. But there are points of comparison beyond the allegorical method and setting. The repetition of phrase, the alliterative effects, and the imagery of light and wind are characteristic of both works, and if the mood and message of Olive Schreiner's introductory allegory are foreign to Crane, the journey motif and the terrain could well be his." The journey through a wasteland to the mountains is the most obvious common denominator between Olive Schreiner's *Dreams* (1891) and Crane's *Black Riders* (1895) and the *War Is Kind* (1899) poems.

Collate this study with *Poetry*. Crane probably "learned to handle" his biblical images from Olive Schreiner "rather than from the Bible itself." Schreiner's "cloying *Dreams* did give him clues and hints which, as was true of his 'use' of the Bible, he inverted to express his own sensibility. Ignorant of *Piers Ploughman* or *Le Romaunt de la Rose*—even, it seems, of *Pilgrim's Progress*—Crane found in this ill-written fantasy [in Schreiner's *Dreams*] his first example of secular allegory." *See* James M. Cox (1957).

LaFrance, Marston. "Stephen Crane's 'Private Fleming: His Various Battles,'" in *Patterns of Commitment in American Literature*, ed. M. LaFrance. Toronto, 1957, pp. 113–133.

Taking the stand that Crane is a great ironist, LaFrance proceeds to attack both the Naturalist and symbolic schools of thought on *The Red Badge of Courage*. He sees Henry Fleming as possessing both will and conscience. Far from having his actions determined by his environment or heredity, Henry actually determines his environment.

LaFrance demolishes one by one the three claims of the "Naturalist" school concerning animal imagery, "moving box" episode and the view that Henry neither changes nor develops.

As part of his central argument, LaFrance takes an excerpt from one of Crane's letters to illustrate Crane's own view of Henry Fleming and his "battles." Crane stated that (1) a man is responsible not for his vision but for his personal honesty; (2) "There is a sublime egotism in talking of honesty."; (3) This condition of personal honesty is the only worthwhile goal in life and "A man is sure to fail at it, but there is something in the failure." Therefore Henry Fleming is to be held responsible.

LaFrance dismisses symbolic criticism on the basis that the symbols exist only in context; the wafer is the seal of finality, the sign that the separation between man and external nature is complete. He sees emblematic imagery rather than symbolism, the result of "craftsmanship, not primarily the conceiving imagination."

LaFrance makes an important distinction in quality between the three combats in which Henry engages, the last of which brings him the total experience.

LaFrance sees no irony in the last passages. He sees a moral victory for Henry, or at least the ingredients for it as evident in the text. Henry reviews his past actions, balancing the good against the bad in an honest and practical way. Rather than ironic, the peaceful end is seen as emblematic of the end of his moral battle.

Reprinted in his *A Reading of Stephen Crane* (1971).

Leal, Isa Silveira, trans. *O barco aberto* ["The Open Boat"], in *Obras primas da novela universal,* ed. Mário da Silva Brito, São Paulo, Brazil: Livraria Martins Editôra, 1957, pp. 115–141.

Brazilian translation into the Portuguese.

Lively, Robert. *Fiction Fights the Civil War.* Chapel Hill, N.C., 1957, pp. 12, 14, 33–34, 136–137, 152–155.

On Crane's *The Red Badge of Courage,* Harold Frederic in *Copperhead* and De Forest's *Miss Ravenel's Conversion.* Crane as realist "cut a channel which has been utilized ever since." This echoes Bernard De Voto in *Saturday Review* (De Voto, [1937]). However, on Crane as realist *versus* De Forest *see* Haight (1955) and *Omnibus* (1952).

Matthews, Joseph J. *Reporting the Wars.* Minneapolis, 1957, p. 135.

Mencken, H. L. "Sketches in Criticism: Stephen Crane," in *Literature in America,* ed. Philip Rahv. New York, 1957, pp. 303–304. Reprinted from *A Mencken Chrestomathy* (1949), pp. 496–497.

Morooka, Hisashi. "Stephen Crane no 'kaibutsu' ni tsuite" [On Stephen Crane's *The Monster*], *Rikkyo Daigaku Eibei Bungaku,* no. 18 (1957), 83–104.

Ohashi, Kenzaburo, trans. *Machi no onna Magi* [*Maggie: A Girl of the Streets*]. Tokyo, Kenkyusha, 1957. Amerika bungaku senshu series.

Includes "Kaibutsu" [*The Monster*].

———. "Amerika shizenshugi to Stephen Crane—'kankyo' to 'jokyo' " [American Naturalism and Stephen Crane—'environment' and 'situation'], *Tokyo Gaikokugo Daigaku Eibei Kenkyu,* no. 4 (December, 1957), 35–39.

Rosenblum, Arlette, trans. *Les vingt meilleures nouvelles américaines.* Paris: Seghers, 1957.

Includes "Le Canot" ("The Open Boat").

Small, Major Abner R. *The Road to Richmond.* Berkeley, Calif., 1957, p. 185.

See Anderson (1961).

Stallman, R. W. "Stephen Crane: Some New Stories (Part III)," *Bulletin of the New York Public Library,* 61 (January, 1957), 36–46.

Reproduces for the first time "Across the Covered Pit," a Sullivan County tale, from the holograph manuscript in the BCC. Also "A Foreign Policy, in Three Glimpses," from holograph manuscript in the BCC. Quotes from "Greed Rampant" from the typescript originally in BCCC. Describes briefly "The Ghost."

———. "Fiction and Its Critics: A Reply to Mr. Rahv," *Kenyon Review,* 19 (Spring, 1957), 290–299.

A reply to Rahv's "Fiction and the Criticism of Fiction," *Kenyon Review* (Spring, 1956). "Fiction and Its Critics" is reprinted in much expanded version in *Houses,* pp. 232–252. (This expanded version restores the passages expunged by *Kenyon Review.*)

Rahv "indicts my whole view of *The Red Badge* because of the way I interpreted, 'The red sun was pasted in the sky like a wafer.' He contended that in the first edition of Crane's novel the word 'wafer' was preceded by the word 'fierce.' What this tells me is that Rahv has not looked at the reconstructed texts of *The Red Badge* as presented from the original manuscripts in my *Omnibus*. The hard fact is that the word 'fierce' preceded the word 'wafer' in the shortened newspaper version (1894), but this is not the first edition of *The Red Badge*. The word 'fierce' was expunged from the first edition (1895) and did not appear in any subsequent American edition until the *Omnibus*, where it is given in brackets as follows: 'The [fierce *cancelled*] red sun was pasted in the sky like a fierce wafer.' Scholarship is the prerequisite of the critic; able critics check on their facts. . . .

   " 'The absurdity of Mr. Stallman's reading of Crane becomes all too apparent,' says Rahv, 'when you look up the text to check on his quotations.' 'Moreover, in the first edition of the novel "wafer" was preceded by "fierce," a modifier hardly suggestive of the Christian communion.' Crane's notorious metaphor, notorious inasmuch as it has been ridiculed or praised by a dozen critics before my own appearance on the scene, is used at a crucial point in the narrative, the death of Jim Conklin, and it is used with symbolic intent—the wafer of the Mass. Mr. Rahv argues that the word 'fierce' is proof against my reading, by which the novel 'is transmogrified into a religious allegory.'

   "Apparently Crane thought first of the red sun as 'fierce,' and then added the same epithet to 'wafer' so as to give 'wafer' the same attribute. A wafer is conceivably fierce when it is emblematic of the dying God. Red connotes the red wine of the sacrament—the white wafer which was to have been the flesh has been saturated by the red of Christ's blood. And I might mention that Mr. Isaac Rosenfeld wrote in his review of the *Omnibus* which appeared in the pages of this journal: 'Mr. Stallman remarks of this simile "I do not think it can be doubted that Crane intended to suggest here the sacrificial death celebrated in the Communion." I, for one, do not doubt it, and even if the statement about Crane's *intention* can never be verified, one cannot deny that the line in question functions in this manner.' " *See* Rosenfeld (1953). *See also* Stone (1957).

Stone, Edward. "The Many Suns of *The Red Badge of Courage*," *American Literature*, 29 (November, 1957), 322–326.
   Interprets the sun symbol in *The Red Badge of Courage* as operating in six instances characterized by: (1) with one exception reference to sun is made at end of chapter where the sun has appeared; (2) color of sun underscores mood of the actors on whom it looks down; (3) varied appearances of sun almost precisely spaced suggest that they were meant to "provide a supplementary interpretation of the stages of the interior action of the story." (4) Henry's spiritual course can be chartered in the sky, e.g., the sun may be alternately "a friend, a cruel foe, or merely indifferent."
   Stone traces the sun's appearance and the mood of men on whom it looks down upon. "But the 'red sun . . . pasted in the sky like a wafer' at the end of Chapter 9 is like no other sun in the book." It seems red to Henry Fleming "because it is now the symbol of a celestial partisan, of an *enemy*, agent of man's misery and violent ends. It is red in the *sense* that it (war, that is) was in Chapter 3 and will be again in Chapter 12—'the red animal, war, the blood-swollen god.' "
   Stone neglects to collate the printed text of *The Red Badge* with the new manuscript passages, MS. LV and MS. SV in *Omnibus*.
   On sources of the red sun as wafer image *see* Stallman, "The Scholar's Net: Literary Sources" (1955). *See also* Von Abele (1955).

Woodress, James, ed. *Dissertations in American Literature: 1891–1955*. Durham, N.C., 1957, p. 11.

1958

Ando, Shoichi. "Stephen Crane ron: ninshiki to bungaku (sono 1)" [Stephen Crane's viewpoint and his works], *Ritsumeikan Daigaku Gaikoku Bungaku Kenkyu*, no. 1 (December, 1958), 99–113.

[Anon.]. "Stephen Crane," in *American Short Novel, Nineteenth Century*. Moscow, 1958.
    Contains "An Experiment in Misery," "An Episode of War," "The Blue Hotel," and "A Dark Brown Dog."

———. "Some Prominent Members of Delta Upsilon," *Manual of Delta Upsilon* (1958), p. 125.

Barnes, Robert. "Crane's 'The Bride Comes to Yellow Sky,'" *Explicator*, 16 (April, 1958), item 39.
    Expands on the obvious cultural conflict of East *versus* West and twice quotes Crane's text inaccurately. Replied to by Ferguson (1963).

Cady, Edwin H. *The Realist at War: The Mature Years, 1885–1920, of William Dean Howells*. Syracuse, N.Y., 1958, pp. 211–218, 222, 224, 239, 258.

Carlson, Eric. "*The Red Badge of Courage*, IX," *Explicator*, 16 (March, 1958), item 34.
    Suggests that the image of the red sun "pasted in the sky like a wafer" derives from the common nineteenth-century wafer used for sealing documents. However, not noticed by Carlson is the fact that his standpoint was anticipated by *The New Yorker*'s reviewer (Edmund Wilson, unsigned) of *Omnibus*. Not noticed by Carlson is Isaac Rosenfeld's agreement of Stallman's interpretation of the wafer as a religious emblem having the significance of the Communion wafer (Rosenfeld [1953]).
    "When Henry cuts short his oath of protest, he does so from a sudden awareness that Jim's fate is *sealed* by the 'wafer' of a blindly irrational or malevolent power that knows no mercy." A blood-thirsty Moloch is implied. "That such a barbaric god or universe exacts the life-sacrifice of Jim Conklin is suggested by both the verbal and the dramatic contexts of Chapter IX. 'There was something rite-like in these movements of the doomed soldier. And there was resemblance in him to a devotee of a mad religion, blood-sucking, muscle-wrenching, bone-crushing.' Certainly this cannot be a Christian death, as claimed by Hoffman (p. xix) and Stallman (p. 199), who cite 'mad religion' without the descriptive adjectives that follow. . . . In short, there seems to be no Christian symbolism intended, not even for ironic purposes."
    However, Carlson fails to recognize the likelihood of Crane's ironic use of the Christian religion as "a mad religion, blood-sucking, muscle-wrenching, bone-crushing," which aptly describes the history of the Church in its warfares against contending factions and infidels throughout the centuries. Or that Henry Fleming figures as the raw recruit in the Army of the Lord and at Jim Conklin's death revolts against the Chief of Staff, as it were. "He shook his fist. He seemed about to deliver a philippic. 'Hell—' The red sun was pasted in the sky like a wafer."

Carlson flatly claims that "since his protest [Henry Fleming's] is not directed at the sun, it seems pointless to speculate on Jim's alleged blasphemy against the sun as a symbol of his conscience or of his faith." However, *contra* Carlson, it is a point of question whether or not Henry Fleming shakes his fist at the battlefield. Carlson's claim that Henry Fleming does not protest against the sun is contradicted by MS. SV, reproduced for the first time in *Omnibus*. Not noticed by Carlson is this MS. LV passage: "He turned in tupenny fury upon the high, tranquil sky. He would have like [*sic*] to have splashed it with derisive paint." So, then, Henry's philippic is directed to the sky and against the sun, and not to the battlefield.

By ignoring the manuscripts in *Omnibus* Carlson's interpretation remains impugned. The same criticism applies to critics who explicated *The Red Badge* subsequent to Stallman's Signet edition of *The Red Badge of Courage* (1960), for they thus ignored the five manuscript pages here presented for the first time. Carlson uses for his text the 1956 Rinehart edition, edited by William Gibson, in spite of his knowing *Omnibus*, which he mentions. Gibson's text copies the erroneous Folio Society edition (1951), edited by John Winterich. It omits MS. SV and is not a faithful copy of its presentation of MS. LV. Both manuscripts were first published in *Omnibus*. Carlson adds that Crane had originally written "the fierce red sun was pasted in the sky like a fierce wafer." Carlson could obtain this phrasing only from *Omnibus*, but he does not acknowledge *Omnibus* as his source of text!

Carlson opines that "the adjective 'fierce' shows that Crane had in mind a primitive, naturalistic quality and power, in keeping with the symbolism of 'red,' with the animal metaphors that dominate the novel, with the nature of Conklin's death, and with the shock and indignation felt by Henry. In short, there seems to be no Christian symbolism intended, not even for ironic purposes."

However, *see* Rosenfeld (1953), Hoffman, "Introduction, *The Red Badge of Courage*" (1957), and *Modern Fiction Studies* (1959). *See also* Pritchett (1960). *Contra* Carlson, Olov Fryckstedt (1961) says that Jim Conklin's "final struggle parodies the rites of a religion in order to bring out the cruel irony of death's total lack of significance in an indifferent naturalistic universe. Under these circumstances any protest against the order of things is futile."

Churchill, A. *Park Row*. New York, 1958, pp. 116–117, 194–204.
The Correspondents' War (as the Spanish-American War was known); Crane and Richard Harding Davis.

Colvert, James B. "Style and Meaning in Stephen Crane: *The Open Boat*," *Texas Studies in English*, 37 (1958), 34–45.
Contra Philip Rahv, "Crane does in this sense put language to poetic uses, and it would seem that the techniques of poetry analysis . . . are valid and necessary if we are to grasp the full meaning and significance of his writing." *See* Rahv (1956) and Stallman's reply, "Fiction and Its Critics (1957).

Edel, Leon, and Gordon N. Ray, eds. *Henry James and H. G. Wells*. Urbana, Ill.: 1958, pp. 17, 67.
"You will have felt, as I have done, the miserable sadness of poor Crane's so precipitated and, somehow, so unnecessary extinction. I was at Brede Place this afternoon—and it looked conscious and cruel." James to Wells, June 17, 1900.)

Freidel, Frank. *The Splendid Little War*. Boston, 1958, pp. 56–57, 150, 156, 162–163, 171, 238, 240–242, 276.

A picture book with excellent narrative and useful bibliography. Some factual errors are in Freidel's story of the Cuban War. The person identified as Stephen Crane in the photograph, page 66, is not Stephen Crane. The best full account of the Spanish-American war is by Charles H. Brown (1967), but Brown slights the Santiago campaign and slights also A. C. M. Azoy's *Charge! The Story of the Battle of San Juan Hill* (1961), which is the best account of that battle. Azoy is not listed in Brown's bibliography.

Friedman, Norman. "Criticism and the Novel," *Antioch Review*, 18 (Fall, 1958), 343–370.

Friedman, intentionally dismissing a symbolic interpretation, argues with great uncertainty that Henry Fleming does not undergo any change of character in *The Red Badge of Courage*, but does undergo a change in thought, that is, "in his conceptions of himself in relation to war as an experience." Friedman sees no evidence that Henry acts from deliberate moral choice after Conklin's death. During much of the plot, Henry acts with ambivalence because of his "lack of consciously purposeful behavior." His change occurs when, at the end, he emerges from battle; the change, Friedman submits, is from ignorance to knowledge, not from cowardice to heroism, not from irresponsibility to maturity.

Fryckstedt, Olov W. *In Quest of America: A Study of Howells' Early Development as a Novelist*. Cambridge, Mass., 1958, p. 262, and *passim*.

Greenfield, Stanley B. "The Unmistakable Stephen Crane," *PMLA*, 73 (December, 1958), 562–572.

An onslaught against reading *The Red Badge of Courage* as myth or symbolism, notably Stallman's interpretation of religious allusions and biblical parallelisms. To understand the novel (says Greenfield), "we must realize Crane's handling of *behavior* and *attitude*. We may begin with the former. Its deterministic side has so often been commented on that a brief summary will suffice." Greenfield's summary is as brief as a diaper hung upon the washline of his thesis, a washline which is a rope readily shredded. By the rope of his bias he misreads Crane. His reading of "The Blue Hotel," for instance, is an entirely erroneous reading, as Donald Gibson observes (1964).

"I must examine at greater length the criticism of Crane by Robert Stallman. We are indebted to a great degree to Stallman for the revival of an interest in Crane. But his critical method and interpretation I find very disturbing." Greenfield is disturbed also to learn that Stallman's Modern Library Introduction to *The Red Badge of Courage* (1951) has been appearing since 1956 in a Greek edition of the novel published in Athens. He is disturbed because its translation into the Greek indicates "perseverance of the same argument and method of criticism" which has "led to converts" of Stallman's reading of *The Red Badge of Courage*. Greenfield here cites James T. Cox (1957) as a reader buttressing Stallman and dismisses Cox's essay in a footnote citation. He ignores also Hoffman (1957) whose reading of *The Red Badge* stands in agreement with Stallman and Cox. Greenfield remarks that "though the best criticism of his own time reveals a careful reading and understanding of his works, most recent criticism has seen Crane through a glass darkly."

Stallman's claims that Jim Conklin's rumor that the army is going into action the next day, that the army is to cross the river and come at the enemy from behind, is, Greenfield contends, "an error of fact that is *not* negligible." Says Greenfield: Jim Conklin's rumor is *not* the gospel truth, or any truth at all, for the first sentence of Chapter II clearly states that "The next morning the youth discovered that his tall comrade had been the fast-flying messenger of a mistake." A literal-minded reader like Greenfield ought to check on the facts of the literal level of the novel's action. *Contra* Greenfield, Conklin's prophesy *is* the gospel truth; the army does cross the river and come behind the enemy. And so Conklin is not "the fast-flying messenger of a mistake." What Conklin prophesies comes true.

At Conklin's death, according to Stallman *(Omnibus,* p. 223), Henry blasphemes against the wafer-like sun. Greenfield contends—without having studied Crane's manuscripts' variant readings in the *Omnibus Red Badge* edition—that Henry "is not even aware of the sun" and "is blaspheming against the battlefield." However, MS. SV—unknown to scholar Greenfield—states that Henry Fleming, immediately following the death-dance of Jim Conklin in Chapter IX, "turned a tupenny fury upon the high, tranquil sky. He would have like [*sic*] to have splashed it with a derisive paint. . . . And he was bitter that among all men, he should be the only one sufficiently wise to understand these things." Greenfield can hardly be expected to know these things inasmuch as he remains ignorant of the manuscript passages quoted above. Fleming shakes his fist at the sun and is "about to deliver a philippic" not at the battlefield but at the sun itself. That unnoticed fact, unnoticed not only by Greenfield but by all subsequent Crane critics of this crucial passage in *The Red Badge of Courage,* undercuts Greenfield's presumption.

"It is interesting to observe that Stallman, after examining the earlier manuscripts of *The Red Badge of Courage,* seems to have had a change of mind about Henry's 'salvation.' He sees the 'images of tranquil skies' at the end of the novel as flatly sentimental and feels that they are given an ironic turn by the sun-through-clouds image: '[Henry] has undergone no change, no real spiritual development' *(Omnibus,* p. 221)." However, *contra* Greenfield, that Henry has undergone no real spiritual development, *that* is from our reader's point of view, whereas from Henry's point of view he has achieved manhood and heroic stature. *Omnibus,* unfortunately, did not specify again and again this double point of view and thus it opens itself to the charge of contradiditions, as by Frederick Crews and others. The ironic interpretation about Henry Fleming's "salvation" first appeared in Stallman's Modern Library Introduction (1951), p. xxiv. It next appeared in his "Stephen Crane," in John Aldridge's *Critiques and Essays on Modern Fiction* (1952), and later that year in *Ominbus.* The MSS. of *The Red Badge of Courage* were not available until December, 1951, by which time the *Critiques* essay had gone to the printer; hence, Greenfield's charge that Stallman had a change of mind about Fleming's salvation after he examined the manuscripts is unwarranted, not true.

Greenfield admits that "There *is* irony in the end of the novel; in fact, if one examines the longer version in the earlier manuscript of *The Red Badge of Courage,* he can have no doubt that there is." So I said in my *Critiques* essay (1952) and in *Omnibus.* However, the longer version of the manuscript is Ms. LV, not—as Greenfield mistakes it—the "earlier manuscript," Ms. SV. This ignorance of the manuscripts faults Greenfield as scholar and critic.

For instance, Greenfield claims: "Even more damning to Stallman's 'salvation' is the following: 'The rescue of the men from the sea [in "The Open Boat"] has cost them "a terrible grace"—the oiler lies face-downward in the shallows.' Where does the 'grace' quotation appear in the story? On the second page, in the following context: 'There was a terrible grace in the move of the waves, and they came in silence, save for the snarling of the crests.' " In the context of Greenfield's *PMLA* essay, p. 563, he is charging me with lifting phrases out of context or refashioning things "highly misleading." A literal-minded critic, Greenfield objects to the transfer of "terrible grace" from page 2 (even had that phrase been paginated in my essay) to the end of "The Open Boat," whereas I contend that any phrase or image in a work of poetic fiction, which uses language poetically (metaphorically, reflexively), is immediately transferable by the reader's cognizance—the critical reader sees the relationship—from the place where it occurs in the text to any other place where it occurs in the text. The "terrible grace" phrase at the beginning of "The Open Boat" anticipates the death of the oiler at the very end of the story, albeit no such phrase ("terrible grace") occurs at the death scene of oiler Higgins. Not noticed by literal-minded readers of Crane like Greenfield is the artistry of Crane. His "terrible grace in the move of the waves" serves as transferred epithet to the plight of oiler Higgins and foreshadows it. *See* Marcus (1960). *See Houses,* pp. 101, 102–103.

Guidi, Augusto. "Realtà e allegoria nella narrativa di St. Crane," in his *Occasioni americane*. Roma, Ediz. Moderne, 1958, pp. 63–73.

Gullason, Thomas. "Stephen Crane: Anti-Imperialist," *American Literature,* 30 (May, 1958), 237–241.

No American writer "was a more ardent anti-imperialist, a more serious, defiant, sincere humanitarian than Stephen Crane." He had a good working knowledge of history and current affairs and was "vitally concerned with international politics." Gullason traces this political concern of Crane in "The King's Favor" (1891), in "A Foreign Policy, in Three Glimpses," and in his closet-drama "The Blood of the Martyr" (1898); a satire on German imperialism and on American missionaries.

———. "Tennyson's Influence on Stephen Crane," *Notes and Queries,* n.s., 5 (April, 1958), 164–165.

The poem "War Is Kind" closely parallels in stanzas two and three a passage in Tennyson's "The Charge of the Light Brigade." "Continually, Crane's ironic lines destroyed the romantic tenor of Tennyson's poem," says Gullason. An impossible proposition absurdly phrased; Tennyson's poem survives Crane's ironic intent, of course. Gullason's notion that Crane reacted strongly against "The Charge of the Light Brigade" because he had to recite it in school and that this "laid a foundation" for Crane's later antiromantic attitude toward war is, to my mind, implausible, nonsense.

Hagemann, E. R. " 'Correspondents Three' in the Greco-Turkish War: Some Parodies," *American Literature,* 30 (November, 1958), 339–344.

Parodies of Kipling, Richard Harding Davis, and "St—ph—n Cr——n," in the *Critic* (1897), by Charles Battell Loomis. The parody of Crane is reprinted in *War Dispatches.*

Linson, Corwin Knapp. *My Stephen Crane,* ed. and with an Introduction by Edwin H. Cady. Syracuse, N.Y., 1958. Photographs.

"It was Crane's painter's touch that most impressed Linson. 'The painter's color sense is born—so was his.' Himself a painter, Linson confirms the fact that 'Steve reveled in the use of words as a painter loves his color' and that Crane was a consciously symbolic artist: 'As to color, it always stood in his mind for a symbol, and so apt was his use of color-words that ever after they would image the thing defined.' " (Stallman, "Friendly Reminiscence" [1958])

Linson's memoirs have extraordinary importance. They confirm that Crane wrote *Maggie* in the spring of 1891, as was claimed by Peaslee and Noxon. Linson dates his first meeting with Crane just after *Maggie* was published, and by that fact we can date "The Reluctant Voyagers" for May–June, 1893, the script of that tale being written on verso of "The Holler Tree" (1892). Also written on verso of that Sullivan County tale (the manuscript of "The Holler Tree") is the beginning of *George's Mother,* which we can thereby date for May–June, 1893, at about the same time of his writing "The Reluctant Voyagers." Here also are accounts of Crane's life among struggling artists, his explorations of the Bowery for writing "Men in the Storm," enduring thus his own "Experiment in Misery," his researching Scranton coalmines for *McClure's Magazine* (1894), his turning the poetic spout on for poems he showed Linson, his submitting *The Red Badge* to Bacheller's syndicate in late February, 1894, and so on.

Editor Cady fails to collate *MSC* with Linson's "Little Stories of Stevie Crane" in *Saturday Evening Post* (April 4, 1903), an important memoir not mentioned by Cady and containing passages not included in *MSC.* The editor also fails to mention that Linson's book contains several new Crane letters and bits of manuscripts. Linson's errors in various matters, including Crane's age in 1897 (for instance), are left uncorrected by the editor. Reproduced here as frontispiece is Linson's oil painting of Crane belonging to the BCC, and several new photographs.

Letters (1960) failed to include the new Crane letters in Linson's *My Stephen Crane.*

Martin, Harold C. "The Development of Style in Nineteenth Century American Fiction," *English Institute Essays.* New York, 1958, p. 133.

Mayer, Grace M. and Byron. *Once Upon a City.* New York, 1958. Foreword by Edward Steichen.

Quotes, p. 10, Crane's "In the Broadway Cars."

Miyata, Hitoshi. "Stephen Crane no zokugo" [Slang of Stephen Crane], *Waseda Daigaku Eibungaku,* no. 15 (1958).

Owen, Guy, Jr. "Crane's 'The Open Boat' and Conrad's 'Youth,' " *Modern Language Notes,* 73 (February, 1958), 100–102.

Marlow, Conrad's spokesman in "Youth," resembles Crane's correspondent in "The Open Boat," and both stories center upon the testing of a young man by an ordeal at sea. Conrad's source is his own experience on the barque *Palestine,* but some of his phrasings recall, consciously or unconsciously, Crane's.

Pizer, Donald. "Romantic Individualism in Garland, Norris, and Crane," *American Quarterly,* 10 (Winter, 1958), 463–475.

Pulos, C. E. "The New Critics and the Language of Poetry," *University of Nebraska Studies,* 19 (March, 1958), 10, 12–13.

Rexroth, Kenneth. " 'Is Anybody Out There.' " *Saturday Review,* 41 (July 5, 1958), pp. 19, 30.

Silveira, Brenno, trans. *O emblema rubro da coragem* [*The Red Badge of Courage*]. Rio de Janeiro, São Paulo and Bahia, Brazil, Editôra Civilização Brasileira, 1958.

Brazilian translation into the Portuguese.

Reprinted in a separate series: *Biblioteca Universal Popular,* vol. 23. Rio de Janeiro, Ficção Estrangeira, 1963.

Solomon, Eric. "Another Analogue for *The Red Badge of Courage,*" *Nineteenth Century Fiction,* 13 (June, 1958), 63–67.

The analogue suggested is Joseph Kirkland's *The Captain of Company K* (1891), which had appeared serialized in the *Detroit Free Press* in 1890.

See also his article, "Yet Another Source for *The Red Badge of Courage,*" *English Language Notes* (1965).

Stallman, R. W. [Crane's cardtable cover], *Fine Arts Magazine* (University of Connecticut), 3, no. 1 (April, 1958), 64.

The cover design is a facsimile reproduction of the cardtable cover on which Crane scribbled his name over and over again: " 'Stephen Crane, Chauncey Depew, Stephen Crane, Chauncey Depew.' He had millionaire Chauncey Depew on his mind because Crane needed money—he was in desperate need of winning this poker game." The original cardtable cover—in the Barrett Crane Collection—is reproduced here for the first time.

———. "Friendly Reminiscence," *New York Times Book Review,* October 5, 1958. Portrait (oil), 1894, by Linson.

Review of Corwin Knapp Linson's *My Stephen Crane* (1958).

"These collected reminiscences of the only person still living who knew Stephen Crane intimately cover four important years—1893–97—in the writer's brief life. Corwin K. Linson was doing drawings for illustrated magazines when Crane first met him in his studio in the winter of 1892–3 (not 1891, as the editor, Edwin H. Cady, Professor of English at Syracuse University has it).

"While Linson's memoirs bring to light no new phases of Crane's personality and aims as a writer, they have at least the importance of confirming the chronology of events as conjectured by some Crane scholars. The memoirs show, for instance, that *Maggie: A Girl of the Streets,* which Crane published at his own expense in 1893 under the pseudonym 'Johnston Smith,' was written in the spring of 1891 when Crane was 20 and a student for a single semester at Syracuse University. This proves that Crane invented the plot of *Maggie* and had written one or two drafts before becoming acquainted with the Bowery.

"It was the same with *The Red Badge of Courage,* a war novel invented by a youth with no experience of war. Crane's source was a set of the *Century* magazines containing *The Battles and Leaders of the Civil War,* which he read in Linson's studio. 'He was squatting like an Indian among the magazines when he gave one a toss of exhausted patience and stood up: "I wonder that *some* of those fellows don't tell how they felt in those scraps. They spout eternally of what they *did,* but they are as emotionless as rocks." ' ...

"In chapter 3, Linson reads Crane's short story 'The Pace of Youth' (1893) as a symbolic work; and in chapter 6, he retells the genesis of some of Crane's syndicated newspaper sketches (1894), of which a few were illustrated with Linson's drawings. These two chapters strike me as particularly interesting. The editor fails to mention that this book contains several new Crane letters and bits of manuscripts. New also are the conversational pieces Linson records up to his last meeting with Crane in March, 1897, just before Crane sailed for Greece as a Hearst war correspondent to cover the Greco-Turkish

War. 'He was now a bit over 26,' says Linson, whereas in fact Crane was then 25. Linson is constantly in error about Crane's age. Reprinted here as frontispiece is Linson's magnificent oil painting of Crane."

Stein, William Bysshe. "New Testament Inversions in Crane's *Maggie*," *Modern Language Notes*, 73 (April, 1958), 268–272.

Stein contends, *contra* Stallman: "It is not enough, for instance, to say that the novel is the sum of 'innocence thwarted and betrayed by environment.' " Stein documents some New Testament inversions in *Maggie*, but these biblical inversions do not contradict Stallman's *Omnibus* reading; contrary to Stein, they provide additional evidence that Maggie is trapped by her environment.

Stewart, Randall, *American Literature and Christian Doctrine*. Baton Rouge, La., 1958, pp. 109–113.

Suggests that in so far as Henry Fleming in *The Red Badge* has become something of a hero at the end Crane falls short of being a Naturalist. Stewart places Crane with the Naturalists on the opposite pole from the Romantics, such as Emerson and Whitman, but he notes that Crane and Norris were not complete Naturalists—only half-way Naturalists—because they refused to deprive their characters of all responsibility or all traces of heroism.

Stone, Edward. "Crane's 'Soldier of the Legion,' " *American Literature*, 30 (May, 1958), 242–244.

Suggests parallelisms between the plight of Henry Fleming in *The Red Badge* and that of "bingen" in Caroline E. S. Norton's poem "Bingen on the Rhine," a lachrymose ballad used in Crane's "The Open Boat":—"A soldier of the Legion lay dying in Algiers."

Weisberger, Bernard. *"The Red Badge of Courage,"* in *Twelve Original Essays on Great American Novels*, ed. Charles Shapiro. Detroit, 1958, pp. 96–123.

The Red Badge of Courage as realistic and modern in its handling of "interior action." Weisberger discusses the marks of modern fiction in *The Red Badge of Courage*: (1) environmental symbolism; (2) its relation to symbolist poetry and to modern painting in the breakdown of barriers between sensory images; (3) Naturalistic attitude; (4) the theme of the individual will against the collective personality; (5) "realism" as seen in fidelity to detail, dialect.

Weisberger gives a critical summary of events in the novel, recognizing three steps in redemption in what he calls a "negation of Christian conversion." The first step is the wound which is essentially self-inflicted as it follows a crisis of guilt and is inflicted by an image of his fugitive self. The second step is his memory of a pool soon after the wound. Following this baptism comes a redeemer whose conversation emphasizes that there is no ultimate purpose in life, not even a defining line between good and evil. The redeemer vanishes without trace, so that this has been a journey of self-discovery after a self-inflicted wound with no saviour to help, no devil to blame. Henry's return is his final step towards salvation. Jim Conklin is the representative of his old ideal and the old standards. Henry is reconciled with himself and can take things as they come as there *is* no explanation.

Yanagi, Kiichiro. "Stephen Crane to 'The Open Boat' " [Stephen Crane and 'The Open Boat'], *Osaka Furitsu Daigaku Eibei Bungaku*, no. 6 (May, 1958), 1–18.

1959

Arnold, Hans. "Stephen Crane's 'Wyoming Valley Tales': Their Source and Their Place in the Author's War Fiction," *Jahrbuch für Amerikastudien,* 4 (1959), 161–169.

On the three tales set in Wyoming Valley, Pennsylvania: "Ol' Bennett and the Indians," "The Battle of Forty Fort," and "The Surrender of Forty Fort." Crane's source was *Wyoming: Its History, Stirring Incidents and Romantic Adventures* (1858), by his maternal grandfather, the Rev. Dr. George Peck of Scranton, Pennsylvania. Old Bennett was Stephen Crane's own great-great grandfather. Mary Helen Peck contributed a picture to the illustrations in her father's book, *Wyoming*. "Crane may well have had this pious work at his disposal during the later years in England. . . . But it is unlikely that he wrote the 'Wyoming Valley Tales' at such a late date."

Not noticed by Arnold or by Gullason (1963) is the fact that Crane's "List of Books / Brede Place" does not include Peck's *Wyoming*, a fact which puts into doubt Gullason's assertion that Crane in his last years in England "borrowed vastly from his grandfather's *Wyoming*." The holograph manuscripts show an early hand, as Arnold suggests, and additional testimony that these Wyoming Valley tales belong to Crane's earliest writings is found in Beer's statement that Crane sent Wallis McHarg "the curt, compressed tales of the Wyoming valley." (Beer adds that they had appeared in the *New York Tribune* but they are not to be found there.)

Baughman, Roland. *Manuscript Collections in the Columbia University Libraries.* New York, 1959.

Briefly describes the contents of the Crane collection, which includes seventy-four books from Crane's library, many of them signed. "Manuscripts and letters of Stephen and Cora Howorth Crane, ca. 1895–1908, approximately 1,200 items." However, the collection contains not a single Crane letter.

Beebe, Maurice, and Thomas A. Gullason. "Criticism of Stephen Crane: A Selected Checklist with an Index to Studies of Separate Works," *Modern Fiction Studies,* 5 (Autumn, 1959), 282–291.

Valuable for its listings of studies of individual Crane works of fiction.

This checklist is brought up to date in *The Stephen Crane Reader,* ed. R. W. Stallman (1972).

Brooks, Van Wyck. *Howells: His Life and World.* London and New York, 1959, pp. 53, 94, 196, 208, 218, 257, 268–271, 275.

On Crane's meetings with Howells.

Buitenhuis, Peter. "The Essentials of Life: 'The Open Boat' as Existentialist Fiction," *Modern Fiction Studies,* 5 (Autumn, 1959), 243–250.

Also in *Form and Focus,* ed. R. F. McDonnell and William Morris. New York, 1961, pp. 392–399.

"Berryman's work is the starting point for the most recent discussions of Crane, while Stallman has made the first intensive study of the text [of "The Open Boat"]. Greenfield, in his recent article [*PMLA,* December, 1958], criticized Stallman for 'distortions' in his reading. He [Greenfield] commented on the 'richness' of the story, but ignored some of its elements. I believe also that he has overemphasized the role of fate in 'The Open Boat.'" *See also Omnibus,* Satterwhite (1956), and Colvert (1958).

Chambers' Encyclopedia, vol. 4. London, 1959, p. 210. The checklist mentions only Beer's *SC* and *Work.*

Colvert, James B. "Structure and Theme in Stephen Crane's Fiction," *Modern Fiction Studies,* 5 (Autumn, 1959), 199–208.

A significant study, one of the best in the whole body of writings on Crane. The Crane story "again and again interprets the human situation in terms of the ironic tensions created in the contrast between man as he idealizes himself in his inner thought and emotion and man as he actualizes himself in the stress of experience. In the meaning evoked by the ironic projection of the deflated man against the inflated man lies Crane's essential theme: the consequence of false pride, vanity, and blinding delusion."

Colvert notes the "close thematic kinship of *Maggie* and the earlier Sullivan sketches. The basic conceptual pattern is the same. *Maggie,* like the sketches, is an ironic study of vanity and conceit, and like the *Tribune* pieces it depends for its structural coherence upon the ironic sense of situation and event. Crane brought to bear upon his slum study essentially the same attitude and the same literary idea and method he applied to his study of 'the little man'; the chief difference is that in the dark and grim *Maggie* he elaborated the moral consequences of the human perversities he comically satirized in the earlier pieces."

Colvert sees the 1892 Sullivan County pieces as "hardly more than crude groping toward a fictional subject and manner," throwing nevertheless "valuable light on Crane's mature work." However (*contra* Colvert), they were written at the same time as *Maggie,* which was "begun perhaps as early as 1891 when Crane was a student at Syracuse University, but not finished in its final version until the winter of 1892, several months after the Sullivan County sketches were published in the *New York Tribune.*" Frank W. Noxon (1928) and Clarence Peaslee (1896), Crane's fraternity brothers, testify that they saw the manuscript of *Maggie* at the Delta Upsilon house in the spring of 1891, and Willis Johnson (1926) says that Crane brought him the manuscript that summer. Crane boasted that he wrote *Maggie* in ten days before Christmas. That is in December of 1892, as other scholars have very recently pointed out. The fact remains that Crane was writing *Maggie* at the same time that he was writing his Sullivan sketches and tales (1892). It follows, then, that Crane's "groping toward a fictional subject and manner" occurred within the short period of a few months at most; or rather it occurred simultaneously with his first drafts of *Maggie.* This fact upsets the commonly held assumption—by Schoberlin (1929), as well as by Colvert and others—that the Sullivan sketches "point forward to his own mature writings" or exhibit "Crane's first steps toward the evolution of a method and a style" which culminated in *Maggie* and *The Red Badge* (to quote 1949 reviewers of Schoberlin's book). In sum, the period of Crane's "development" into maturity as artist was much shorter than supposed; so short in fact that, in one sense, he developed not at all. As Howells rightly observed: "Here is a writer who has sprung into life fully armed." (This question of Crane's development is treated in *Crane,* 1968.)

The Red Badge "treats four stages in Fleming's growth toward moral maturity. In the beginning he is unable to distinguish between his heroic dreams and hopes and the actual condition of war. Then follows a period of confusion and doubt as reality begins to intrude upon his dream world. Next he goes through a period of desperate but futile struggle to preserve, through deceit and rationalization, his pseudo-heroic image of himself and the world. In the

end, he solves his problem . . . when he is finally able to bring his subjec-
tivity into harmony with the reality which his experience makes clear to him.
The structure of the novel is characteristically a series of loosely related, ironic
episodes built up in the contrast between two points of view toward reality, a
subjective interpretation originating in vanity, pride, and illusion, juxtaposed
against an 'objective' reality originating in the superior long view of the
narrator."

Colvert adds that a similar point about the structure of *The Red Badge*,
namely that it is built by alternating moods of hope and despair, illusion and
reality, was made by Stallman in *Omnibus* ("Notes Toward an Analysis of
The Red Badge of Courage," pp. 191–201). "But by his reading the religious symbolism that 'radiates outwards from Jim Conklin' is the key to the
structure of the novel. The difference between my reading and Mr. Stallman's
is a matter of emphasis at this point, but the implications of Mr. Stallman's
claim for religious symbolism leads away, in my opinion, from the core of
Crane's true meaning."

Cox, James Trammell. "The Imagery of *The Red Badge of Courage*," *Modern
Fiction Studies*, 5 (Autumn, 1959), 209–234.

Focusing primarily on a Naturalistic "endless struggle to survive" as the
theme of the novel, Cox discusses the symbolism of color, the role of the sun,
the association of smoke with man's tendency to hide his fear, and the ironic
implications in the resemblance of Conklin to Christ. Discusses the function
of nature imagery, machine imagery, and Christian and pagan imagery. Henry
Fleming does not change; within the action of the novel he does not learn
much, but he maintains to the end a great deal of his pride and dignity. To
his world he is a success.

The imagery insists upon the irony of Henry's discovery of courage through
the wounded vanity of egocentrism; the "decided growth in moral behavior"
which Greenfield (1958) finds in Fleming's development ignores this basic
irony. Cox agrees with Stallman, *Omnibus*, that Christian symbolism is present, but sees it as used negatively. As Bernard Weisberger (1958) put it:
"There is going to be rebirth, indeed, but not a supernatural one. Here is a
negation of the Christian conversion." . . .

"On the question of Crane's fictional method, Stallman is still significantly
right in his recognition of the extent to which 'Crane puts language to poetic
uses, which is to use it reflexively and symbolically.' And it is past time that
this fundamental question be considered apart from any given interpretation,
for a full understanding and appreciation of the better works of Stephen
Crane are absolutely dependent upon an awareness of this method." *See also*
James T. Cox (1957).

Gargano, James W. " 'A Mystery of Heroism': A Possible Source," *Modern
Language Notes*, 74 (January, 1959), 22–23.

Crane's "A Mystery of Heroism" is indebted to the biblical passage in 2
Samuel 23: 13–17. Crane "derides the notion of heroism enshrined in
romantic fiction" and "identifies heroism with the ideal of brotherhood, most
effectively dramatized in 'The Open Boat.' Obviously, the conventional Old
Testament idea of bravery is repudiated in favor of the more responsible and
humane code of conduct advanced by the New Testament." An important
insight worth tracing throughout Crane's works.

Gleckner, Robert. "Stephen Crane and the Wonder of Man's Conceit," *Modern
Fiction Studies*, 5 (Autumn, 1959), 271–281.

Studies the two worlds of "The Blue Hotel," the hotel and the saloon world, as does MacLean in this same issue of *MFS*. Argues that the much criticized last section is a necessary conclusion to everything that has gone before. *See* Shroeder (1950), *Omnibus*, Sutton (1952), Satterwhite (1956), James T. Cox (1957), and Gibson (1964).

Gohdes, Clarence. *Bibliographical Guide to the Study of the Literature of the U.S.A.* Durham, N.C., 1959.

Gullason, Thomas A. "Stephen Crane's Private War Against Yellow Journalism," *Huntington Library Quarterly*, 22 (May, 1959), 201–209.

――――. "The Significance of *Wounds in the Rain,*" *Modern Fiction Studies,* 5 (Autumn, 1959), 235–242.

"The unity and control of purpose that Stephen Crane achieved in *Wounds in the Rain* explodes another myth. Contrary to popular belief, he did not show any failing or weakening of his craftsmanship in the last few years of his short life. For when one reads the original version of *Wounds* and compares it with his earlier writings, like the romantic *Red Badge,* one can see a more mature, realistic Stephen Crane at work. His writing gained in depth; his style was no longer obtrusive; his cynicism gave way to a mellow worldliness; his vision and range of perspective showed gains by his broader, more skillful blending of political, social, and individual insights. Real war gave Crane *real* experience—and this filled an irksome void in his quest for the truth."

Contra Gullason, however, *see* Willa Cather (1926).

――――. "The Sources of Stephen Crane's *Maggie,*" *Philological Quarterly,* 38 (October, 1959), 497–502.

Parallelisms between *Maggie* and Jacob Riis's *How the Other Half Lives* (1890), which Gullason misdates and which he misclaims as one of "two never-mentioned sources" for *Maggie. See Omnibus.* The other source consisted of books by Crane's father, previously noticed by Hoffman in *Poetry* (1957). Gullason's claim that Crane "did not need further inspiration" other than such native sources as these is a theory which will not bear scrutiny.

See Cunliffe (1955) for a much more important study of *Maggie*'s sources.

Haffley, James. " 'The Monster' and the Art of Stephen Crane," *Accent,* 19 (Summer, 1959), 159–165.

An excellent study included in *The Art of Stephen Crane: A Critical Symposium,* vol. 1, ed. Robert W. Stallman (1973).

Hagemann, E. R. "The Death of Stephen Crane," *Proceedings of the New Jersey Historical Society,* 77 (July, 1959), 173–184.

Reports the events surrounding Crane's journey to Badenweiler, Germany; new data on Dr. Albert Fraenkel. Crane's death certificate, which is *not* quoted here, states his death occurred at 3:00 A.M. the morning of June 5, 1900. This fact thus corrects Cora's telegram, as quoted here from Jessie Conrad's *Conrad and His Circle,* "God took Stephen at 11:05, make some arrangement for me to get the dog home." [The telegram was to "their man of business," who was Alfred Plant.] Hagemann says that John Berryman, "in his often mysterious way, without reference or authority, wrote that 'the body was on London view in a stall between champing horses, off a littered stableyard, where it looked to an old friend as if its tenant had suffered horribly.' " [The old friend was Curtis Brown, whose *Contacts* is the source Berryman paraphrased.]

The missing all in Hagemann's article is the death certificate, produced for the first time in *Notes and Queries*, vol. 7, no. 4 (April, 1960), by John O. Eidson: "The Death Certificate of Stephen Crane." (An original in photocopy is in the Crane files of R. W. S., gift of Dr. F. K. von Siebold of Badenweiler, 1958.) A variant death certificate was reproduced in facsimile in *SCraneN*, 1, no. 4 (Spring, 1967). However, no acknowledgment of the variant certificate in *Notes and Queries* is made.

Hecht, Ingeborg. "Badenweiler entdeckt Stephen Crane," *Baditche Zeitung* (Freiburg, Germany), December 5–6, 1959, p. 12.

Helm, Johannes. "In Memory of Stephen Crane," *The American-German Review*, 26 (October–November, 1959), 16–17, 36.

Reprinted in translation from *Badenweiler*, 13 (May 30, 1959), 5–6. Also in *Die Markgrafschaft*, August, 1959, pp. 8–10.

Sketches his life, not without errors (on his marriage and on his burial place), mentions American scholars of Crane, and observes that *Maggie, das Strassenkind* appeared in 1897 in a German translation by Dora Lande.

——. "Stephen Crane: ein Vergessener?" *Baden Württemberg*, November, 1959, pp. 31, 46. Reprinted from *Sandtchaffler* (Basel, Switzerland), July 21, 1959, p. 2.

"To give the poet and author Stephen Crane, whose course of life ended at Badenweiler, the literary position he deserves in this country also, there is a commemoration planned at Badenweiler for the 60th anniversary of his death on the 5th of June, next year. . . . It would be a fine gesture of the American Crane Friends if . . . the acquisition of a Crane bust could be made possible through a magnanimous donation."

(The articles by Frau Helm and by Dr. F. K. von Siebold, Bürgermeister of Badenweiler, propagandize Mayor Siebold's scheme to bolster tourist trade. They appeal for donations from American Crane friends—not from Germans. The plan for commemorating Crane's sixtieth anniversary at Badenweiler did not succeed.)

Herron, Ima H. *The Small Town in American Literature*. New York, 1959, pp. 184–186.

On *Whilomville Stories*.

Hoffman, Daniel G. "Crane's Decoration Day Article and *The Red Badge of Courage*," *Nineteenth-Century Fiction*, 14 (June, 1959), 78–80.

Disputes Gullason's claim in "Additions to the Canon of Stephen Crane" (1957) that Crane wrote "Veteran's Ranks Thinner By a Year," in the *New York Press*, May 31, 1894. Gullason replies in "Thematic Patterns in Stephen Crane's Early Novels" (1961) that it is in Crane's ironic style, whereas "The Gratitude of a Nation," which was not published in Crane's day is not in Crane's style. However, it exists in holograph manuscript in the CUCC, together with its prefatory poem. Hoffman published "The Gratitude of a Nation" in 1957 in his edition of *The Red Badge of Courage and Other Stories*, but without the prefatory poem ("A soldier, young in years").

Not noticed by Gullason and Hoffman is that the unknown author of "Veterans Ranks Thinner by a Year" witnessed what he wrote about, whereas Crane's "The Gratitude of a Nation" is not an eye-witness report; it was written weeks before Decoration Day, 1894. That fact fits what Crane wrote Hamlin Garland on May 9, 1894: "I wrote a Decoration Day thing for the *Press* which aroused them to enthusiasm. They said in about a minute, though, that I was firing over the heads of the soldiers." (Garland, *Roadside Meetings* [1930], and *Omnibus.*)

Hough, Robert. *The Quiet Rebel: W. D. Howells as Social Commentator.* Lincoln, Nebr., p. 2.

Howells, William Dean. "New York Low Life in Fiction," in *Criticism of Fiction and Other Essays,* ed. Clara M. Kirk and Rudolph Kirk. New York, 1959, pp. 271–275. Reprinted from the *New York World,* July 26, 1896, p. 18.

On Crane's realism. Reviews *Maggie* and *George's Mother* and ranks them superior to *The Red Badge of Courage* on their greater fidelity to life.

Kanazeki, Hisao. "Stephen Crane no inshōshugi-teki shuho ni tsuite" [On the Impressionistic technique of Stephen Crane], *Osaka Shiritsu Daigaku Bungakkai Jinbun Kenkyu,* 10, no. 7 (July, 1959), 132–147.

Kirk, Clara M. and Rudolph, eds. *Criticism of Fiction and Other Essays,* by William Dean Howells. New York, 1959, pp. 267–271. Reprints Howells's "New York Low Life in Fiction," from *New York World* (July 26, 1896), pp. 271–275.

The editors survey Crane's relations with Howells in "Stephen Crane (1871–1900)," pp. 267–271.

Klotz, Marvin. "Crane's *The Red Badge of Courage,*" *Notes and Queries,* 6 (February, 1959), 68–69.

Suggests as analogues Henry Morford's *The Coward: A Novel of Society and the Field in 1863* (1863), and *Red-Tape and Pigeon-Hole Generals* (1864), by William H. Armstrong, in which few of the characters are named except by such sobriquets as the "Vociferous Colonel," etc. Klotz's half-hearted case for these books as having "some bearing on aspects of *The Red Badge*" is unconvincing.

Labor, Earle. "Crane and Hemingway: Anatomy of Trauma," *Renascence,* 11 (Summer, 1959), 189–196.

Probably the most valid statement Labor makes is in the second paragraph of his essay where he is comparing *A Farewell to Arms* and *The Red Badge of Courage:* "Most notable are the basic tonal similarities in the two works: the same attitude of author toward his materials is vividly defined in the opening paragraphs of both. Hemingway's reference to landscape—particularly to the roads, the trees, the distant mountains, and the river—is very much like Crane's. The mutual importance of setting can hardly be over-emphasized. Of both books one is tempted to say that setting not only provides mood and theme but also becomes central character. Certainly there is the similar underplaying of the roles of the human protagonists."

From that point, however, Labor's article becomes a curiously mixed salad of grail quest, family life, and spiritual values, spiced liberally with the salts of amateur psychology. For example, Labor contends that Frederic Henry remains disillusioned because of his inadequate childhood training. "Unlike Henry Fleming's parents, those of the Hemingway hero have failed to ensure the stability so essential to his subsequent orientation into the multiple experiences of violence." Near the end of his article Labor says of Frederic Henry, "Certainly his premature initiation to suffering and the lack of family security account considerably for his inability to make a satisfactory adjustment." I am curious to know exactly what kind of family security Labor would consider adequate to enable a man to "make a satisfactory adjustment" to a chaotic and meaningless war and the gratuitous deaths of his lover and child. And of what does that "satisfactory adjustment" consist?

The above annotation was written by James Harstad, University of Hawaii (English 780). On *A Farewell to Arms* and *The Red Badge of Courage* see also Stallman, *Omnibus*, pp. 191–193, 221.

Landor, M. "Stephen Crane and University Study," *Foreign Literature* (Moscow), no. 6 (1959), 267–268.

———. "Portrait of Stephen Crane," *Voprosy Literature* (Moscow), no. 8 (1959), 228–233.
    Review of C. K. Linson's *My Stephen Crane.*

Leech, Margaret. *In the Days of McKinley.* New York, 1959, pp. 304–305.
    New Yorkers "were especially touchy about their gallant Seventy-first, whose prowess the newspapers had glorified without regard to the facts. The *World*, in an inadvertent moment, had printed a truthful account of the panic in this regiment under fire, as described by a young correspondent named Stephen Crane, who was known as the author of a cynical novel about the Civil War."
    Leech repeats the error of Don Carlos Seitz who in 1924 attributed this *World* dispatch to Crane, whereas it was written by Sylvester Scovel. The same error is made by historians Walter Millis (1931), Gregory Mason (1939), and W. A. Swanberg (1961).

Lewis, R. W. B. *The Picaresque Saint.* Philadelphia and New York, 1959, p. 92.

Linneman, William R. "Stephen Crane's Contributions to *Truth*," *American Literature*, 31 (May, 1959), 196–197.
    Discovers in *Truth* two Crane sketches, but he misses in *Truth* a third sketch: "At Clancy's Wake"—reprinted from *Truth* (March 18, 1893) and in *NYCS,* for the first time. "At Clancy's Wake" is cited in the *W-S Bibliography* with *Last Words* for its sole publication; not listed are Linneman's discoveries, additions thus to the Crane canon: "Some Hints for Playmakers" and "A Night at the Millionaire's Club."

Ludwig, Richard M., ed. *Literary History of the United States: Bibliography Supplement.* New York, 1959, pp. 100–102.
    Supplements vol. 3, Bibliography, *The Literary History of the United States,* ed. Robert Spiller, *et al.* (1948). A highly selective listing.

MacLean, Hugh N. "The Two Worlds of 'The Blue Hotel,'" *Modern Fiction Studies,* 5 (Autumn, 1959), 260–270.
    "The blue hotel is the world of 'what might be,' isolated, mysterious, highly symbolic. . . . The saloon represents the world of 'what is,' at the heart of society, realistic, all but nonsymbolic, and essentially amoral, 'naturalistic.'" *See also* Sutton (1952) and James T. Cox (1957).
    MacLean quotes from *Omnibus* a letter of Crane to Hilliard and a letter of Crane to Joseph O'Connor, contending that "The Blue Hotel," finished by February, 1898, should be read in the context of these letters. "Their common denominator is Crane's insistence that man must fight." However, the 1898 letter to O'Connor is misdated in *Omnibus* and is reassigned to Hilliard in *Letters.*

Marcus, Mordecai, and Erin Marcus. "Animal Imagery in *The Red Badge of Courage*," *Modern Language Notes*, 74 (February, 1959), 108–111.
    "Animal images and animal comparisons are used throughout the novel to

convey changes in states of mind and the pattern of their development. Most important is Crane's use of them in presenting the theme of change from cowardice to wild courage, and finally from immaturity to manhood."

Marshall, Thomas F., ed. *An Analytical Index to American Literature*, 1–30 (March, 1929–January, 1959). Durham, N.C., 1963, pp. 29–30.

Milne, W. Gordon. "Stephen Crane: Pioneer in Technique," *Die Neuren Sprachen*, 8 (July, 1959), 297–303.
  On Crane's style.

Modern Fiction Studies: Stephen Crane Special Number, vol. 5, no. 3 (Autumn, 1959), ed. Maurice Beebe. Lafayette, Ind., 1959.
  The first collection of critical studies on Crane; most important. *See also* Maurice Bassan's collection of critical essays, *Stephen Crane* (1967). In preparation is *The Art of Stephen Crane: A Critical Symposium*, vol. 1, ed. R. W. Stallman (1973).

Ohashi, Kenzaburo, trans. "Shishu (sho)" [Poems, a selection], in *Sekai Meishishu Taisei*, vol. 11. Tokyo: Heibonsho, 1959, 135–138.
  Includes seventeen poems from *The Black Riders* and six from *War Is Kind*.

Solomon, Eric. "The Structure of *The Red Badge of Courage*," *Modern Fiction Studies*, 5 (Autumn, 1959), 220–234.
  "Even the most sympathetic critics have been unable to call the book a unified whole. It has usually been passed off as an impressionistic novel." "It is equally an oversimplification to think of Crane's book merely in terms of naturalistic fiction." One of the most illuminating passages that Crane expunged from the final version represents war in Naturalistic terminology. "From his pinnacle of wisdom, he regarded the armies as large collections of dupes. Nature's dupes who were killing each other to carry out some scheme of life." However, neither impressionism nor Naturalism is the dominant mode; Henry's actions are those of a free individual.
  Unlike Friedman (1958), Solomon sees Henry as a matured individual; however, there is the element of irony in this conclusion. He discusses the five comrades who help in bringing about Henry's change. While recognizing the irony which allows the sinner to succeed without changing his ways, Solomon excuses Henry from the familiar charges of cowardice and guilt. The memory of the tattered man will always block Henry's return to his ignorant beginnings. Henry received his wound from a coward while Henry was in the act of striving to rally fugitives and moving towards the battle himself. The first twelve chapters marks the completion of Henry's isolation; the second half of the book shows Henry's understanding of war and of his own nature.
  Stallman "comes closest to understanding the nature of the novel's structure. He describes *The Red Badge of Courage* as a series of fluctuations between hope and despair, a group of withdrawals and engagements. This is accurate. . . ." However, it is difficult to accept Stallman's view of Conklin as a Christ figure. "The inconsistency of Crane's religious symbolism which mixes Biblical and pagan phrases without any apparent order would seem to vitiate a theory of controlled religious structure. It would be safer to say that there are religious overtones to Crane's novel." (*See* Colvert [1959], p. 205.)

Stallman, R. W. "Crane's *Maggie*: A Reassessment," *Modern Fiction Studies*, 5 (Autumn, 1959), 251–259.
  Reprinted in *Houses*.

Reprinted in *Stephen Crane's Maggie: Text and Context,* ed. Maurice Bassan (1966), pp. 139–144.

First published in shortened form in *New Republic,* 33 (September 19, 1955), 17–19.

"A tone-painting, rather than a realistic photograph, *Maggie* is the painter's novel, the poet's novel—the art-novel." Double mood, the contrast of contradictory moods, and bathos pattern *Maggie.* It is "a Bowery version of Flaubert's *Madame Bovary.*"

Crane proves his theme "to show that environment is a tremendous thing in the world"—by fashioning *Maggie's* environment to grow round his characters. "By paired and contrasted images he reinforces his theme, and he quickens his characters into 'life' by metaphor. His plot is less impressive than his theme, and the theme less impressive than the style, the metaphoric language that shapes the whole book. His plot is a sentimental melodrama, like Norris's *McTeague,* but in style *Maggie* is not sentimentalized. The ironic viewpoint from which Crane designs his forthright moral and social intent makes the crucial difference. That difference is what saves *Maggie* from the dustbin of outdated sociological novels."

Stein, William Bysshe. "Stephen Crane's *Homo Absurdus,*" *Bucknell Review,* 8 (May, 1959), 168–188.

Crane "holds no brief for the social code of courage that dedicated itself to the exhibition of superior manhood—however stupidly, sincerely, modestly, or accidentally, as exemplified in the respective conduct of Conklin, Wilson, the tattered soldier, and Fleming himself."

Ueno, Naozo, and Nobunao Matsuyama, trans. *Stephen Crane: Text and Translation.* Gendai Sakka Series, 27. Tokyo: Nan' undo, 1959.

Includes "The Open Boat," "The Blue Hotel," and "His New Mittens."

Ward, J. A. " 'The Blue Hotel' and 'The Killers,' " *CEA Critic,* 21 (September, 1959), vi, 7–8.

Wells, Lester G. "The Syracuse Days of Stephen Crane," *Syracuse 10,* 2 (1959), 12–14, 40–42. Photograph.

Nothing new here.

Welty, Eudora. "The Reading and Writing of Short Stories," in *Modern Prose: Form and Style,* ed. William Van O'Connor. New York, 1959, pp. 434 ff.

West, Ray B., Jr., ed. *American Short Stories.* New York, 1959, pp. 6, 7, 8, 9, 143.

Westbrook, Max. "Stephen Crane: The Pattern of Affirmation," *Nineteenth-Century Fiction,* 14 (December, 1959), 219–229.

Contra literary historians, Crane does not subscribe to the tenets of literary Naturalism. The conventional interpretation of Crane, as found in *The Literary History of the United States* (1948), labels him a literary Naturalist, but this is a one-sided view. The attitude toward life in Crane's writings "is basically affirmative" and the moral struggle "is considered both noble and real."

"Traditionally, the naturalist has no heroes, and yet one could marshal from the Crane canon an impressive army of heroes, ranging from the oiler (a classic hero) to Dr. Trescott (a social hero) and including the frequently romantic heroes of *The Little Regiment.*"

1960

Alberts, Frank. "The Blue Hotel: A Play in Three Acts, by Frank Alberts, based on the story by Stephen Crane," *Theatre*, 2 (October, 1960), 27–42.

[Anon.]. "The Beautiful War," *London Times Literary Supplement*, November 25, 1960, p. 758.

    Review-essay prompted by *Letters* (London, 1960), and *The Red Badge of Courage and Other Stories*, ed. with a note on the texts by R. W. Stallman with an Introduction by V. S. Pritchett (London, 1960).

    Compares Crane and Dylan Thomas. On *Active Service:* "It would almost be possible to apply one of Hemingway's titles, *Men Without Women*, to a volume containing the essential Crane." On the women in Crane's life, and their letters and Crane's. Up to the last his was "all strongly wrought work and for all the pressures he never became a hack, but somehow one cannot find it in oneself to regret the books he might have written had he lived his proper span." The same standpoint was expressed by Joseph Conrad and by Stallman in *Omnibus*. The contrary standpoint is taken by Liebling (1961).

    On *The Red Badge of Courage:* "What this particular youth cannot see then is that in becoming a veteran—and Crane's characters can nearly all be divided into youths and veterans—he will at the same time fail the test."

———. "Stephen Crane Read," *New York Sun*, June 6, 1960, p. 5.

Aury, Dominique, trans. *Stephen Crane: L'insigne du courage*. Lausanne, Switzerland: La Guilde du Livre, 1960. Brady's photographs of the Civil War battlefields, hand-pasted onto the text of each chapter.

Baines, Jocelyn. *Joseph Conrad: A Critical Biography*. New York, 1960, pp. 203–205, 207–208, and *passim*.

    Mistakenly disclaims the influence of *The Red Badge* on Conrad's *The Nigger of the "Narcissus,"* p. 205. See *Omnibus*, Bruce Johnson (1963), and *Crane*. Mistakenly repeats Berryman's error in Berryman's *Crane*, p. 207, that out of Crane's collaboration with Conrad on a play came *The Blood of the Martyr*. See *Crane* for evidence to the contrary.

    On the Conrad-Crane relationship *see* Bruce Johnson (1963); Solomon, *Stephen Crane in England: A Portrait of the Artist* (1964); and *Crane*. Baines's account is perfunctory. *See* Reviews of *The Red Badge of Courage*, Part D, especially Courtney (1897).

Berryman, John. "Commentary" [on "The Open Boat"], in *The Arts of Reading*, by Ralph Ross, John Berryman, and Allen Tate. New York, 1960, pp. 279–287. Reprints "The Open Boat," with Berryman's commentary.

    Cites Cyrus Day's query into the ethics of the captain's having left his ship at all and the condition of the seas judged by wind velocity charted at weather stations at Jacksonville and New Smyrna. "But all this has nothing really to do with the story at all, important though it certainly may be from a *biographical* point of view."

    How important it is from a biographical point of view is seen in the fact that Crane's integrity as journalist was impugned by Berryman in Berryman's *Crane* and by Day in his "Stephen Crane and the Ten-foot Dinghy" (1957). Berryman's mysterious fifth man in the dinghy and Day's denial of Crane's claim of heavy seas demanded investigations and brought about the conclusions reached by Stallman on new evidence in "Journalist Crane in That Dinghy," *Bulletin* (1968). Also in *Crane.*

Blackmur, R. P. "Introduction," *American Short Novels.* New York, 1960, pp. 8–9.

On Crane's *Maggie.* Blackmur in this short note defines it as a burlesque allegory of reality.

Brennan, Joseph X. "The Imagery and Art of *George's Mother*," *College Language Association Journal,* 4 (Winter, 1960–1961), 106–115.

An excellent reading. However, Brennan's theme that the mother and the son are representative of larger opposed forces—the Church *versus* the city of Mammon—was first stated by Stallman in *Omnibus,* p. 20: "The conflict between George and his mother is summed up in Crane's symbolic picture of city and church. The conflict between them (reality *versus* illusion) is symbolically pictured in Part XI." Insofar as Brennan's essay expands on that earlier insight, acknowledgement was due.

Brooks, Cleanth, and Robert Penn Warren, eds. *The Scope of Fiction.* New York, 1960, p. 147.

On the structure of "The Bride Comes to Yellow Sky." *See also* Mark Schorer (1950).

Brooks, Van Wyck. Introduction, *Maggie: A Girl of the Streets and George's Mother.* Greenwich, Conn., 1960, pp. 5–8.

Cahoon, Herbert. *A Brief Account of the Clifton Waller Barrett Library.* Charlottesville, Va., 1960, pp. 29–30.

Chase, Richard. Introduction, *The Red Badge of Courage and Other Writings.* Boston, 1960, pp. vii–xxi.

Considers Crane a Naturalist, even in *The Red Badge,* though by comparison with Norris and Dreiser, "Crane is a *romancer,* and his naturalism remains relatively poetic, abstract, pure, and impressionistic. With few exceptions— Pete, the bartender, in *Maggie,* and perhaps the mother and son in *George's Mother*—Crane's characters strike us as being *figures* or ideas *about* people rather than real people. His settings tend to be barely adequate to authenticate the action that occurs in them—as in *The Red Badge.*"

A tale teller and romancer rather than a novelist, Crane "is not a symbolist of the sort Mr. Stallman makes him out to be. If he is a symbolist at all, it is only in the sense that any writer with a poetic turn of mind will inevitably introduce symbols into his writing. But the symbols are local and limited in reference, and sometimes they seem no more than decorative. They are not, like the symbols in *Moby-Dick,* richly connotative and mutually interwoven in a structure of meaning. The well-known test case in Crane comes at the end of Chapter 9 of *The Red Badge,* in the truly marvelous scene where Jim Conklin, 'the tall soldier,' dies in a kind of crucifiction, or at least a death dance, the last line in the chapter being 'The red sun was pasted in the sky like a wafer.' There is undeniably a Christian feeling and some Christian imagery in this scene, including the initials of the tall soldier. But it seems we are going pretty far if we accompany Mr. Stallman on his explanations of the 'wafer' as a communion wafer. Why shouldn't it just as well be a wafer of wax, such as is affixed to legal documents?"

No, Crane's symbols "are not like those in Melville; they do not mean so much. Religious symbolism does not, as Mr. Stallman alleges, 'toolmark the whole book.' *The Red Badge* is not a 'symbolic construct.' In fact it is hard to think of so episodic and wayward a volume as being a 'construct' of any kind."

However, that *The Red Badge* is toolmarked by biblical allusions and parallelisms is evidenced by Thomas's study "Stephen Crane:" (1967). *See also Omnibus* and *Houses;* Hoffman (1957); Colvert (1959); and Fryckstedt (1961).

Chase ("A Note on the Text," pp. xxiii–xxiv) claims that the text of *Maggie* is here reprinted from the "revised first edition, New York, 1896." But it isn't. The Appleton 1896 *Maggie* has "dirt disguised her" (in Chapter 5, p. 38), same as in the 1893 *Maggie;* whereas Chase's text in this Riverside edition, p. 15, has it "dirt disgusted her." Chase's text of *Maggie* copies the error of Heinemann's clothbound 1896 *Maggie,* an error made in all subsequent editions in England and in America until 1966. Chase reprints the text of the first edition of *The Red Badge of Courage* (1895), but he omits the manuscript passages in *Omnibus* as inferior and unnecessary. "In claiming that the deleted passages point us along 'the directional line of the author's concealed intention' Mr. Stallman is wrong or at least inscrutable." However, not all of the deleted passages were marked for cancellation by Crane in his manuscripts, and in any case they do reveal Crane's concealed intentions. Their value is appraised by Marcus (1960) and by Fryckstedt (1961), appraisals standing in contradiction to Chase.

———. Introduction, *The Red Badge of Courage.* Boston, 1960.

The same Introduction and text as in the above title: *The Red Badge of Courage and Other Writings* (1960).

Craig, H. A. L., director. Third Program, London radio, adaptation of *The Red Badge of Courage.* London, March 15, 1960.

Cramer-Nauhaus, Barbara, and Anneliese Dangel, trans. *Kleine Romane und Erzählungen.* Leipzig, East Germany, 1960, 1967. In Sammlung Dieterich, vol. 222.

Contains translations into the German of *Maggie, George's Mother,* "The Men in the Storm," "An Experiment in Misery," "A Mystery of Heroism," "The Upturned Face," "An Episode of War," "The Open Boat," "The Blue Hotel," "The Bride Comes to Yellow Sky," and "The Monster."

Eby, Cecil D., Jr. "The Source of Crane's Metaphor, '*The Red Badge of Courage,'*" *American Literature,* 32 (May, 1960), 204–207.

The source of the phrase "red badge of courage" was possibly Shakespeare's "murder's crimson badge" in *Henry VI: Part III,* as Abraham Feldman suggested in *American Notes and Queries* (March, 1950). However, for any Union veteran with service in Virginia, "red badge of courage" would have brought to mind both the New Jersey General Philip Kearny and his famous "red badge" (also called "red diamond" and "red patch") division of the Third Corps, Army of the Potomac. Kearny, whose family home was in Newark during Stephen Crane's lifetime, ordered his men "to wear a red patch in shape of a diamond on the crown or left side of their cap, while enlisted men were to wear theirs in front of the cap." From the first the patch was a "sign of good character and a badge of honor." A Kearny red medal, designed by his successor, General David B. Birney, was awarded soldiers who distinguished themselves by acts of heroism in battle.

Crane before he became famous visited Kearny's mansion, Belle Grove, on the Hudson County side of the Passaic River, and when his fame was achieved he again visited Kearny's son, General John Watts Kearny, at Belle Grove "and told the General the symbolic meaning hidden under the title of his famous book." Unfortunately nothing more is said of this "symbolic meaning." Union veterans would associate Crane's title with Kearny and the red badge division; "therefore it is little wonder that the novel was bitterly criticized by former soldiers who resented the author's wholly unexpected and unflattering exploration of the nature of courage."

Ellison, Ralph. Introduction, *The Red Badge of Courage and Four Great Stories*. New York, 1960, pp. 7–26.
Reprinted in *Shadow and Act* (1964), pp. 74–88; (1967), pp. 60–76.
Feeling Crane "revealed a unique vision of the human condition and an unusual talent for projecting it," Ellison argues that Crane "turned from religion but transferred its forms to his art." But as with several of his generalizations, Ellison neglects to support this with specific evidence from Crane's work. He briefly surveys Crane's life, discusses several of his works, and praises Crane's remarkable talent. In particular, he sees Crane's use of the Civil War in *The Red Badge of Courage* as appropriate for a sensitive young man who had a "questioning attitude toward every aspect of the nation's self-image."

Feidelson, Charles, Jr. "Three Views of the Human Person: *The Scarlet Letter, Walden,* and *The Red Badge of Courage*," *Yale Conference on the Teaching of English*. New Haven, Conn., 1960, pp. 48–49, 52.

Fiedler, Leslie. *Love and Death in the American Novel*. New York, 1960, pp. 125, 126, 175, 239–240, 324, 347, 367, 454, 459.
On Crane's "The Monster," p. 367: "No other story in our literature defines so clearly the opposition between the demands of male loyalty and the claims of polite female society; and in none is the Negro more brutally portrayed at the limits of mindlessness and nauseating horror."

———. *No! In Thunder: Essays on Myth and Literature*. Boston, 1960, p. 278.

Fox, Austin M. Introduction, *Maggie and Other Stories*. New York, 1960, pp. v–xviii.

Gilkes, Lillian. *Cora Crane: A Biography of Mrs. Stephen Crane*. Bloomington, Ind., 1960.
An important contribution to Crane's biography since it makes use of much new material in CUCC.
However, Gilkes' bias is for Cora, and certain situations or facts are slanted so as not to damage Cora's image or to make her appear unimportant. For instance, Gilkes omits the fact that Cora's extravagances included her renting a railway coach to take the dying Crane from Calais on his journey to the Black Forest. It is to enhance Cora's importance that Gilkes claims Crane was with Cora on the overland route to Constantinople and Greece, whereas no proof exists. Gilkes misreads Cora's diary to say *"Steve* named him," whereas the diary says "Have named him. . . ." *See* the Stallman-Gilkes exchange in Stallman, "Was Crane's Sketch of the Fleet Off Crete a Journalistic Hoax?" (1964), and Gilkes, "No Hoax: A Reply to Mr. Stallman" (1964).
See Gilkes (1969), *Crane,* and Stallman, "How Stephen Crane Got to Crete," *American Literature,* 44 (May, 1972), 308–313.
Reviewed:
Alfred Kazin, *Reporter,* 23 (November 24, 1960), 53–54, 56. Reprinted in Kazin (1962), pp. 60–64. Kazin in previous writings on Crane (1942 and 1950),

downgraded Crane's importance; here he upgrades Cora as portrayed by Gilkes.

TLS, March 16, 1962. The truth about Cora "is that she was downright silly and that her principal contribution to Stephen Crane's character and career was to encourage him in his own silliness. . . . The feeling of irritation with the heroine [Cora Crane] is reinforced by irritation with the author, whose thoroughness is not as real as it is apparent."

Edwin Cady (1962), p. 172, points out that Gilkes "seems to have made some arbitrary decisions about the dates, handwriting, authorship, and perhaps the meaning of some very ambiguous documents. Nor is her treatment of Cora's 'husband' impeccable. Miss Gilkes's attitude toward Stephen, in fact, comes through as characteristically what lawyers call 'adversary.' She defends Cora by denigrating Crane. Like most good biographers, she has fallen in love with her subject. She seems to wish to ignore the fact emphasized in her title, as in the structure of the book. . . . Nevertheless, from Miss Gilkes's point of view, Cora can do no real wrong. Did she make money off the flesh, nerves, and psyches of her girls? Well, at least in 1896 they didn't sleep in. Did Crane make efforts to escape from her? He was a heel. The possibilities that Cora may have been fatal to Crane's art and health are never entertained: Cora was literary too."*

Gullason, Thomas A. "The Symbolic Unity of 'The Monster,'" *Modern Language Notes,* 85 (December, 1960), 663–668.

Hoffman, Daniel G. "Stephen Crane's First Story," *Bulletin of the New York Public Library,* 64 (June, 1960), 273–278.

The manuscript—written in Crane's large, open, clearly readable hand on lined tablet-paper—is dated 1885. As the punctuation is written with printer's symbols, Hoffman conjectures that "Sketches From Life: Uncle Jake and the Bell-Handle" may have appeared in one of the newspapers with which Crane's brother Townley was connected, possibly the *Asbury Park* (N.J.) *Journal.*

———. "Stephen Crane's Last Novel," *Bulletin of the New York Public Library,* 64 (June, 1960), 337–343.

A projected story about the Revolutionary War which Crane outlined in his last year in "Plans For New Novel" and "Plans For Story," of which the originals are in the CUCC. The letter here reproduced from the *Newark Call* which Hoffman says is not included in the Stallman-Gilkes edition of Crane's correspondence appears in fact as no. 293 in *Letters,* pp. 224–225.

Holloway, Jean. *Hamlin Garland: A Biography.* Austin Tex., 1960, pp. 71–74, 91, 103, 291.

Rather interesting here is Garland's "awed incredulity" on reading Crane's manuscripts of poems and of the war novel in early 1894. Holloway does not risk it to declare the precise dates in 1894 for Crane's visits to Garland with these manuscripts.

Itazu, Yukisato. "Stephen Crane ron: Hitotsu no kōsatsu" [On Stephen Crane], *Tokyo Toritsu Daigaku Eigo to Eibungaku,* no. 7 (September, 1960), pp. 94–104.

Jones, Joseph, Ernest Marchand, and others, eds. *American Literary Manuscripts.* Austin, Texas, 1960, p. 88.

* In a forthcoming essay on Cora and Crane, Gilkes argues that except for Cora Stephen probably never would have written "The Bride Comes to Yellow Sky," "The Monster," and some Whilomville stories.

Kagami, Eizo. "Amerika shizenshugi bungaku no taidō to kussetsu—S. Crane bungaku e no joron" [The formation and refraction of Naturalistic literature in America—an introduction to S. Crane's literature], *Gifu Daigaku Gakugei-gaku-bu Kenkyu Hōkoku (Jinbun Kagaku)*, no. 9 (December, 1960), pp. 1–8.

Karl, Frederick R. "Joseph Conrad's Literary Theory," *Criticism*, 2, no. 4 (Fall, 1960), 328.

Katz, Joseph. "The *Maggie* Nobody Knows," *Modern Fiction Studies*, 12 (Summer, 1966), 200–212.

Rightly argues that the 1893 *Maggie* is a superior text, as Stallman had claimed in "Stephen Crane's Revisions of *Maggie: A Girl of the Streets*" (1955). Katz says: "My indebtedness to this pioneering study is great," and he traces why this is so. He acknowledges also his debt to William Gibson for his collation of the 1893 and 1896 *Maggie* in *The Red Badge of Courage and Selected Prose and Poetry* (1956).

Katz's article brings together the Stallman and Gibson readings of the variant passages in the 1893 *Maggie,* and he makes one keen point. "In the 1896 edition the religious overtones are present but the coherence is lost. No longer do the characters invoke in their speech the suggestions of hell, damnation, and the futility of calling upon God."

Kawakami, Tadao. "Stephen Crane no bungaku—sono shizenshugi ni tsuite no kōsatsu" [The literature of Stephen Crane—a study of its Naturalism], *Osaka Joshidaigaku Joshidai Bungaku Gaikoku Bungaku-hen,* no. 12 (March, 1960), pp. 15–25.

Keating, Clark L. "Francis Viele-Griffin and America," *Symposium,* 14 (Winter, 1960), 277–285.

Lettis, Richard, Robert F. McDonnell, and William E. Norris, eds., *Stephen Crane's The Red Badge of Courage: Text and Criticism*. New York, 1960.

Reprints contemporary reviews and a selection of subsequent studies of the novel, beginning with Winifred Lynskey (1949), Shroeder (1950), and Stallman (1951). Mordecai Marcus's essay ("The Unity of *The Red Badge of Courage*"), published here for the first time, stands in contradiction to Richard Chase's opinion. *See* Chase (1960). Not available to Marcus were five additional pages of the final manuscript. *See also* Stallman (1960).

Text and Criticism reproduces "those parts of *The Red Badge of Courage* which are found in the manuscript but were omitted from the first American edition." However, not included here is the earlier manuscript designated MS. SV in *Omnibus.*

"The first interesting controversy centering about this novel (carried on primarily in early reviews and notices) was evaluative; the critics argued whether or not Crane's novel was good art. The second controversy, begun by Robert Wooster Stallman's interpretation in his Introduction to the Modern Library edition of the novel [1951], is interpretive and explicatory. This controversy still rages."

Marcus, Mordecai. "The Unity of *The Red Badge of Courage,*" in *Stephen Crane's The Red Badge of Courage: Text and Criticism*, ed. Richard Lettis, Robert F. McDonnell, and William E. Morris (1960), pp. 189–195.

Of recent publications aiding towards a reassessment of *The Red Badge,* most important is the publication in *Omnibus* "of passages which Crane canceled or later excised from a manuscript of the novel. These passages provide clues to some of Crane's intentions and problems, and throw light on the novel's often criticized resolution. . . . These passages suggest that Crane planned a terminal irony both about Henry's early cowardice and later delusions of his importance to the universe. That Crane later changed his plan, as other excisions also indicate, suggests something more basic than the attempt to 'redress the tonal balance' which Greenfield [1958] sees in these revisions. It suggests an ambiguity in Crane's attitude toward his material, an ambiguity he probably found it difficult to resolve."

Marcus's essay, here for the first time, appeared simultaneously with Richard Chase's Introduction to *The Red Badge of Courage and Other Writings* (1960). Chase argues against including in his text the expunged passages, "not to restore what Crane himself wanted left out (not of great bulk, in any case) because, as it seems to me, every passage he expunged, without exception, is inferior to the whole, being either inept, sententious, thematically misleading, or merely superfluous. . . . In claiming that the deleted passages point us along 'the directional line of the author's concealed intention' Mr. Stallman is wrong or at least inscrutable." Marcus thus answers Chase. *See also* Fryckstedt (1961).

Neves-Pedro, António, trans. *A glória de um cobarde* [A Coward's Glory]. Lisbon, Portugal: Editora Ulisseia, 1960.
The Red Badge of Courage, Portuguese translation.

Nordell, Rod. "Stephen Crane," *Christian Science Monitor,* June 23, 1960, p. 13.
Essay prompted by *The Red Badge of Courage and Selected Stories,* ed. R. W. Stallman.

Nyren, Dorothy. "Stephen Crane," in *A Library of Modern Criticism: Modern American Literature,* ed. Dorothy Nyren. New York, 1960, pp. 120–124.

Osborn, Scott C. "Richard Harding Davis: Critical Battleground," *American Quarterly,* 12 (Spring, 1960), 84–92.

Parke-Bernet catalogue, March 22, 1960.
See SCraneN, 3, no. 1 (Fall, 1968).

Pizer, Donald. *Hamlin Garland's Early Work and Career.* Berkeley and Los Angeles, Calif., 1960, pp. 28, 123, 130, 178n.

———. "The Garland-Crane Relationship," *Huntington Library Quarterly,* 24 (November, 1960), 75–82.
An important biographical essay. Pizer, using new Garland materials, readjusts the sequence of Crane's visits with the manuscript of his poems and with the manuscript of his Civil War novel in early 1894. Corrects thereby all previous accounts, including Stallman's in *Omnibus.*

Garland's tangled accounts of Crane's visits with these manuscripts is the result of his divergent and contradictory memoirs of those meetings in the *Saturday Evening Post* (July 28, 1900), in *Book-Lover* (Autumn, 1900), in *Yale Review* (April, 1914), in *Bookman* (January, 1930), and in *Roadside Meetings* (1930).

See Stanley Wertheim (1968) on *Maggie,* correcting Pizer and Stallman.

Potter, N. A. J. (Review of *Stephen Crane: Letters*), *New Mexico Quarterly,* 30 (1960), 208.

Prial, Frank J. "Littered Lot His Memorial," *Newark Evening News,* June 5, 1960.

Pritchett, V. S. Introduction, *The Red Badge of Courage and Other Stories.*
London: The World's Classics, 1960, pp. vii–xii. With "A Note on the Texts
of *Maggie* and *The Red Badge of Courage*," by R. W. Stallman, pp. xiii–xvi.
Reissued in paperback, London: Oxford; New York, 1969.

"Stephen Crane is one of those writers who, after one startling *tour de force,*
burn themselves out. American journalism seized him, labelled him, thrust
him into 'real life' as a war correspondent and annulled his imaginative talent
and health. At 28 he was dead. Fittingly he has become a legend, a symbol of
the misused artist." Compares Crane and Robert Louis Stevenson. "Crane's
Methodist background is matched by Stevenson's Calvinist upbringing and
both men, we notice, moved to an ironical, unbelieving, moral dandyism
which affected their prose. They believe in the word and not the Word and
are constantly surprising us with phrases that come to an ear trained by the
pulpit and the Bible."

Pritchett agrees with Wells's remark (1900) that Crane's writing suggested
Whistler rather than Tolstoy; "Wells is the only European critic to have kept
in mind the distinguishing American character of Crane's work. The fact is
that Crane was as profoundly American in his disposition for writing fable or
poetic romance, as were Hawthorne, Poe, Melville, and Henry James. *The Red
Badge of Courage* is not simply one of the earliest realistic novels about war
written in Tolstoy's sceptical and anti-romantic spirit; it is a poetic fable
about the attempt of a young man to discover a real identity in battle."

In *The Red Badge:* "The battle itself is compared at times with a mad
religion, a sectarian conflict. The story might well be an artist's transposition
of a dilemma of religious conscience;* he has been romantically committed to
'fight the good fight,' is frightened into running away, and then has to reas-
semble his self-respect out of fear, doubt, and lies and learn how to live with
his experience. It is quite true that all Crane stories are concerned with fear,
but with fear as a moral ferment, fear as the question put to the American
dream of toughness, the emotion natural to the lonely uncertainty about who
or what one is. The desire of all the Crane heroes is to find an identity by
belonging to something. The theme is at the heart of *Maggie;* in the early
Bowery tales; in *The Red Badge of Courage;* and even in the short, half-comic
stories like 'The Bride Comes to Yellow Sky,' 'The Blue Hotel,' and the
dramatic report of 'The Open Boat.'

"In his psychological observation and in his ear for speech Crane is one
of the founders of American realism as we have known it since his time. In
him it moves towards the fabulous and poetic; occasionally it sprawls and
becomes rhetorical—see the end of *Maggie.* He appears to have been bedev-
illed by the theory that a writer must know from personal experience the
thing he is writing about†—a theory he certainly did not stick to in *The Red
Badge of Courage* except in an esoteric sense, and did stick to in 'The Open
Boat' and his war reporting. . . .

"Crane was a brilliant impressionist and has strong affinities with the
Impressionist painters."‡

---

* Mr. Pritchett's reading here suggests his possible agreement, in general terms,
with that of American critics who find in *The Red Badge's* Henry Fleming a "religious conscience" and in the novel, religious symbolism.

† This thesis on Crane is argued by Stallman, *Omnibus,* a standpoint ridiculed
by Liebling (1961).

‡ A standpoint first argued by Stallman, *Omnibus,* and Kwiatt (1952); Berryman
had contended that Crane owed nothing to the Impressionist painters.

On Pritchett's reading of Crane, *see* Bradbury and Goldman (1963).

Randel, William Pierce. "Stephen Crane," in *Collier's Encyclopedia*. Crowell-Collier Publishing Company, New York, 1960, pp. 616–617.

Schumacher, Theo, trans. *Realistische Erzählungen*. Ebenhausen bei München, Germany, 1960. Edition Langewiesche-Brandt, vol. 46.

Contains translations into the German of "The Bride Comes to Yellow Sky," "Lynx-Hunting," "The Men in the Storm," and "A Mystery of Heroism."

Solomon, Eric. "A Gloss on *The Red Badge of Courage*," *Modern Language Notes*, 75 (February, 1960), 111–113.

For a full understanding of the conclusion of *The Red Badge of Courage*, "The Veteran" must be taken into consideration.* The question of whether or not Henry Fleming has indeed matured from coward to hero, with a gain in moral integrity, is left ambiguous in the novel for the sake of realism; however in later short stories, "The Veteran" (1896) and "Lynx-Hunting" (1899) Crane vindicates Henry Fleming.

According to Solomon, Crane felt that Henry Fleming was identified with himself and that the later vindication was also a defense of the author. The old Henry Fleming is allowed to admit his fears in his first battle; he also forgives a boy for lying because he was afraid. Solomon feels Crane distinguishes between the selfish avoidance of truth—the refusal to explain his wound—and the white lie or Henry's forgetting the past after proving himself. The veteran Henry dies calmly, doing his duty.

But it is also possible to argue that the youth Henry Fleming at the time of his first battle and the old veteran are really two different people. Also, to accept this theory is to agree that the novel is incomplete.

Stallman, R. W. A Note on the texts of *Maggie* and *The Red Badge of Courage*, in *The Red Badge of Courage and Other Stories*. London: Oxford University Press (World Classics), 1960. Introduction by V. S. Pritchett, pp. vii–xii.

Stallman, R. W., ed. Foreword, *The Red Badge of Courage and Selected Stories*. New York: New American Library, 1960, pp. vii–x. Notes, pp. 206–224.

Reproduces MS. LV and MS. SV with the text of the First American Edition, together with five new manuscript pages here brought together for the first time: Houghton 98, Berg 98, Columbia 99, Columbia 101, and Houghton 102. (In "Footnotes to *The Red Badge of Courage*," pp. 209–220.) The history of the manuscripts is briefly commented on in "Notes to the Text of *The Red Badge of Courage*," pp. 206–208. This Signet edition of *The Red Badge of Courage*, copyright 1960 by Stallman, constitutes the complete, but not yet definitive edition.

Reprinted in *The Stephen Crane Reader,* ed. R. W. Stallman (1972). With new Notes to the Text of *The Red Badge of Courage*.

On MSS. LV and SV *see* Howarth (1965).

Reviewed by René Rapin in *Études des Lettres* (Lausanne), 2, no. 4 (October–December, 1960), 221–224 (also contains review of *Letters*).

---

* Solomon here adds: "John Berryman has noticed that the hero of the novel appears in the short story, but Berryman does not show the connection between the two works." See Berryman's *Crane*, p. 324. However, Solomon ignores Carl Van Doren's Introduction to *Twenty Stories* (1940).

Solomon's critical fallacy is the assumption that "The Veteran" proves something about Henry Fleming in *The Red Badge of Courage*, whereas the implications of Fleming's plight are contained within *The Red Badge* without reference to "The Veteran" or any other work in which Fleming reappears.

Stallman, R. W., and Lillian Gilkes, eds. *Stephen Crane: Letters*. With an Introduction by R. W. Stallman. New York and London, 1960. Crane to Howells letter in holograph; frontispiece, C. K. Linson's painting of Crane. *See* Published Letters, Part C.

Reviewed:

D. E. McCoy, *Christian Science Monitor*, February 4, 1960: Considerable new insight into Crane the man is here revealed. "We see a man whose life always seemed dominated by the fierce inner struggle between actuality and ideals, whose spirit seemed pervaded by irony and despair—a man whose rest- lessness and discontent constantly drove him to plans for travels never under- taken, to seek the sociability of city life when secure in the country, and to yearn for the country when in the city. The letters reveal a character alter- nately humble, even shy and self-deprecatory, and unabashedly arrogant. . . ."

Granville Hicks, *Saturday Review*, 63 (February 6, 1960), 14: The editors are both authorities, "and the reader is not likely to forget it. . . . Stallman himself skimmed off the cream in the *Omnibus*, in which he included 120 letters. . . . Here are all the letters in one volume, and here also is a mass of valuable material pertaining to Crane's life and work. One does get, in the end, a sense of the man."

Chicago Tribune, February 7, 1960.

Charles Poore, *New York Times*, February 16, 1960: Crane "was an artist and a rebel. He spent an incomparable talent prodigally." The editing in this "wonderfully interesting new book about him" is "infinitely meticulous." As for Beer's *SC*, "it is truer to Crane's spirit than anything else anyone has written about him. Therefore, the thing to do when you encounter justified cluck-clucking over Beer's vivid, Crane-like impressionism is to adapt some lines of Housman's and say:

> But Beer does more than others can
> To justify S. Crane, the man."

James B. Stronks, *Commonweal*, 71 (February 19, 1960), 578–579: "Anno- tated here are about 230 Crane letters, but more are sure to turn up."

Thomas Gullason, *New York Times Book Review*, March 6, 1960: "One sees more deeply than ever before the soul of an intense artist who is more contradictory than ever but no longer fragmentary." "The editors have pre- sented capsule biographies of people little known yet intimately connected with Crane (like Lily Brandon Munroe, a woman he loved and once asked to elope with him) to further explain him. By this method, the editors have successfully filled in many biographical gaps, corrected dates and facts previ- ously misdated and misrepresented, and what is most important, sharpened the focus on the real Crane."

Chattanooga Times, March 6, 1960.

New Orleans Picayune, March 20, 1960.

Providence Journal, March 20, 1960.

St. Louis Post Dispatch, March 20, 1960: *Letters* results in almost a biog- raphy. "Consequently this book is much more valuable than either of the inadequate undocumented works by Thomas Beer and John Berryman."

Richmond Times Dispatch, March 20, 1960.

Chicago Sun Times, March 27, 1960.

Samuel F. Morse, *Hartford Courant* Magazine, May 15, 1960: "An extremely valuable book, it belongs, obviously, to the still small body of permanently useful work on one of America's most extra-ordinary writers."

San Francisco Chronicle, May 29, 1960: "The editorial interventions of Mr. R. W. Stallman are tactful and revealing." *Letters* "give us a life of Crane which supersedes Beer's and Berryman's, and prepares the way for a final biography. Mr. Stallman is the man to write it."

James T. Cox, *Western Humanities Review,* 14 (Spring, 1960), 236–237: "The cumulative effect of this composite view is a sense of intimacy and authenticity conspicuously lacking in any single effort previous to *Letters.* Paradoxically the Stephen Crane that emerges from these pages would seem to confirm in some sense all of the divergent views we have had of him from Beer's boy knight to Berryman's Oedipal coward, but the value of this volume is that it clearly reveals a larger Crane, more capable both of sustained human relationships and of single-minded devotion to his art than any picture we have had of him yet."

Yale Review (Spring, 1960): " 'A new biography is needed,' notes Stallman in his introduction; until someone responds to this scholarly challenge, *Stephen Crane: Letters* will remain the most complete and accurate record we have of the facts of Crane's life and the nature of his personality."

DeLancey Ferguson, *New York Herald Tribune,* June 5, 1960: "Chronic shortage of cash is not the only Crane trait to receive new emphasis. 'He was a gentleman,' says Mr. Stallman, 'and he was also a smart aleck and an irresponsible heel.' "

Manchester Guardian Weekly, June 30, 1960.

Nineteenth-Century Fiction, 15 (June, 1960), 90–91.

Florida Times-Union, August 7 and 14, 1960.

London Spectator, August 19, 1960.

American Scholar, 34 (Summer, 1960).

Modern Fiction Studies (Summer, 1960).

Robert L. Hough, *Prairie Schooner,* 34 (Summer, 1960), 175–176. "The letters are primarily important not as ethics or as criticism but rather as a chronological record of certain periods of Crane's life (something that Crane criticism has long needed) and as a means of affording some insight into the complexities of Crane the man." They show a man "who is by turns conceited and shy, callous and understanding, fickle and loyal. The Crane that emerges is quite different from the rebellious romantic pictured in the biographies by Thomas Beer and John Berryman. The romantic is there, to be sure, but also present is the perceptive young man who was older than his years and who did not live to tell all that he knew. . . .

"Editorially, Miss Gilkes and Professor Stallman have resisted the temptation to comment on the obvious and succeeded in the formidable task of arranging the letters, sometimes only peripherally touching Crane, into a meaningful sequence. There are problems of course. Professor Stallman believes the book 'presents all the letters that are known to exist,' yet he mentions Melvin Schoberlin's claim to own 600 letters by (or about?) Crane without clearly reconciling the two statements.* Despite such objections, this collection is a significant piece of scholarship. It brings more fully into view a puzzling and contradictory biography. On the basis of recent interest, it

---

* The 600 letters owned by Schoberlin (letter to R. W. S.) comprise copies of those in the Columbia University Crane Collection drawn upon in *Letters.*

seems certain that Crane will be a much explored writer in the next few years. This book provides a starting point for some vitally needed information."

René Rapin, *Études de Lettres* (Lausanne), 2, no. 4 (October–December, 1960), 222–224.

James Stronks, *College English,* 22 (October, 1960), 66. These letters "make it possible for Beer's undocumented, unobjective portrait and Berryman's derivative, thesis-ridden Freudian one to be superseded by a definitive critical biography."

TLS, November 25, 1960.

James Colvert, *American Literature,* 32 (November, 1960), 336–338. The editors have presented much more than a collection of letters and notes; they have provided "a documentary history of his life and career." *Letters* is the most useful book yet to appear as a guide to the facts which are often confused in the Beer and Berryman biographies. *Letters* "corrects the impression given in Beer's and Berryman's biographies that he [Crane] was an infallible critical intelligence in caustic revolt against the cant and unreason of his times. He was superbly gifted, of course, and his performance as a man and writer testifies to his high moral courage and devotion to his craft. But he could also be, as Mr. Stallman puts it, 'a smart aleck and an irresponsible heel.' His carelessness with dates and appointments was symptomatic of a deeper carelessness, and he sometimes appeared indifferent and unsympathetic in his relations with others. He was capable of shallow, even fatuous, self-dramatization, as parts of his letters to Nellie Crouse show; and his picture of himself as a lonely victim of world-weary despair suggests how much indebted to one side of his own personality his famous antiromantic irony really was. Crane's *Letters* will be indispensable to the literary critic; for the more credible, more human Crane revealed in these admirably assembled materials reveals new and significant relationships between the writer and his work."

Waggoner, Wyatt H., *Criticism,* 3 (Winter, 1961), 62–65.

Earle G. Labor, *Renascence,* 13 (Spring, 1961), 153–155. What emerges clearly from this volume "is the portrait of a hectic, tragic life confronted with 'desperate resolution.' "

A. J. Liebling, *New Yorker,* 37 (August 5, 1961), 48–60, 63–66, 69–72. Liebling laments that the American Library Association's list of forty-six Notable Books of 1960 failed to include *Letters.* "This saddened me."

Guy J. Forgue, *English Studies,* 49 (February, 1968), 1: "This volume complements Dr. Stallman's first collection of Crane letters (*Omnibus,* 1952) and Miss Gilkes' 1959 biography of Cora Howorth Crane. Practically all the Crane letters and inscriptions extant as well as a number of letters from Cora and Stephen's friends are brought together here for the first time. Most of the letters printed here are concerned with Crane's writing and publishing problems and, as such, are of great value to specialists, if only because they provide new chronological landmarks toward the biography of Crane that someone will have to write to supersede Thomas Beer's work, now largely obsolete, and the more recent and interpretative study by John Berryman who, however, used the same documents as Beer. The letters afford many valuable insights into Crane's family and his hitherto neglected relationship with Cora. The volume, in fact, comes near to being a biography in itself, for Editor Stallman has provided many short chapters which comment on the salient events of Crane's career or elucidate the conditions in which some of the letters were written. Oddly enough, the Appendix is not far from being the most interesting section of the book, for Crane's intimate friends and acquaintances almost steal the show from him and represent him in a more vivid light than he ever did himself. Dr. Stallman's editorial work is as thorough and learned as the most exacting critic might demand; his footnotes contain a wealth of information. We may ascribe his sometimes cramped, uninspired style to the uneasiness brought on by limitation of space, but in that case, why not have tried to brighten up the book through typographical devices? As it is printed it lacks artistry or even plain clarity, thus emphasizing the text's inherent monotony. The letters are supplemented by a complete index preceded by a catalogue which conveniently indicates the origin, location and history of each letter."

Ueno, Naozo and Nobunao Matsuyama, trans. *Kaibutsu (ta) (The Monster)*. 20 Seiki no Shugyoka Series, Tokyo, Nan'undo, 1960.

Vielé-Griffin, Francis, and Henry-D. Davray. Preface. *Stephen Crane: la conquete du courage: épisode de la guerre de sécession*. Paris, 1960. (Copyright 1939 by *Mercure de France*.) First published in 1911.

Wogan, Claudia C. "Crane's Use of Color in *The Red Badge of Courage*," *Modern Fiction Studies*, 6 (Summer, 1960), 168–172.

Remarks that John Berryman's statement in Berryman's *Crane*, p. 289, that Crane "owes nothing whatever, apparently, to painting" has little evidence to support it. On Crane's use of color *see* Kwiat (1952); Stallman, "Stephen Crane:" (1952); *Omnibus;* and *Crane*.

1961

Anderson, David D. "Major Small and *The Red Badge of Courage*," *Lincoln Herald*, 63 (1961), 191–192. (Lincoln Memorial University, Harrogate, Tenn.)

Quotes Major Abner B. Small's view of *The Red Badge of Courage* in his memoirs, *The Road to Richmond* (1939 and 1957) pp. 185–186. Major Small, who served in the 16th Maine Volunteer Infantry, Army of the Potomac, comments: The common soldier "simply takes his chances, always believing that as an individual he is immune." Small makes this pronouncement on Crane's psychological realism:

> That any man in my regiment, or in the army, analyzed his feelings and marked out any specific line of conduct while under fire, or even thought for five consecutive minutes of the past, present, or future, or measured out or acted upon any theoretical course of conduct irrespective of the arbitrary military law which held him in obedience, is absurd. Afterthoughts are in a sense real, and give a correct résumé of what might have been; but to put an endless and connected train of thought in the brain of a green soldier, so thoroughly scared—by his own admission—that he is not accountable, and set it in systematic motion which shall develop the "Red Badge of Courage," is sheer rot.

Literary historians see the novel in relationship to American literature, whereas Major Small saw it "against the emotional intensity of his own combat service. While Small's view is narrower and less objective, it cannot be rejected solely on these grounds. Rather, it remains as a vivid personal reaction to a work that has long been considered a classic of realistic fiction."

Ando, Shoichi. "Stephen Crane no *Akai bukunsho*" [Stephen Crane's *The Red*

Badge of Courage], *Kyoto Daigaku Kyoyo-bu (Jinbun),* no. 7 (1961), pp. 135–155.

[Anon.]. "Proclamation Pays Honor to Author Stephen Crane," *Union-Gazette* (Port Jervis, N.Y.), November 8, 1961.

Azoy, A. C. M. *Charge! The Story of the Battle of San Juan Hill.* New York, London, and Toronto, 1961, pp. 145–146.

> One of the best books on the Cuban War, not noticed by Charles Brown in his *Correspondents' War* (1967).

Baasner, Peter. "Stephen Crane and Joseph Conrad," *Kleine Beitrage,* 21 (Winter, 1961), 34–39.

Bache, William B. *"The Red Badge of Courage* and 'The Short Happy Life of Francis Macomber,' " *Western Humanities Review,* 15 (Winter, 1961), 83–84.

Balch, David. "Fire Across the Sky," *The Villager,* 34 (November, 1961), 16–17, 33.

Beck, Henry Charlton, ed. *A New Jersey Reader.* New Brunswick, N.J., 1961.

> Reprints "Ghosts on the New Jersey Coast" and "The Ghostly Sphinx of Metedeconk."

Bergonzi, Bernard. *The Early H. G. Wells.* Manchester, England, 1961, p. 130.

Cady, Edwin H. "Stephen Crane and the Strenuous Life," *ELH,* 28 (December, 1961), 376–382.

> Cady's Theory of the Gentleman, into which he fits Crane (cf. *The Gentleman in America* and Cady's writings on Crane), seemingly gets contradicted here by his admission that in Crane "we are dealing with a vivid and significant writer who cannot be categorized simply—perhaps not at all." Here, Cady argues that "the trope basic to Crane's vision was that of the game." Crane began with the game of hunting in his Sullivan County tales and sketches, and then in *Maggie* the slum children play "King of the Hill," and then in the poems life is a game God plays with man; etc.
>
> "His experience of sports brought Crane knowledge. . . . It gave him the experience of testing his courage and thence personal knowledge of pain and fear, victory and defeat. From that vantage point he commanded the cosmic gambler's stoic outlook: despising the petty, safe and comfortable; prizing the chance-taking, the enterprising, the seeking, aggressive and tough. In this he was at one with the prophets of the strenuous life. But he went beyond them in the depth of his forceful but ambivalent compassion for losers. He was anxious that their courage or at least their agony be defended against and registered upon the smug and ignorant. But he would not defend them against the law, against the rules of the game of life." Cady here provides a penetrating diagnosis of the enigmatic Crane.
>
> However, while Crane was again and again a gentleman he was also again and again an irresponsible heel. I do not see Crane fitting into any theory of the gentleman. Berryman in his 1962 Preface to the Meridian edition of Berryman's *Crane,* p. xi, says: "From Stallman, who considers Stephen Crane an 'irresponsible heel' (*Letters,* p. x), will no doubt crawl forth in due time one more satisfying [biography of Crane]." In *SC* (1923) Beer calls Crane an ass.
>
> As for Cady's trope of the game, the more relevant trope is warfare. Crane saw city life as warfare, not as a game; etc.

Chamberlin, Ralph. "Lafayette's Most Notorious Flunk Out," *Marquis* (Lafayette College), February, 1961, pp. 16–17, 27.

Chambers' Biographical Dictionary, ed. J. O. Thorne. New York, 1961, p. 327.
Mistakes Beer's *SC* publication date for 1936.

Franchere, Ruth. *Stephen Crane: The Story of an American Writer.* New York,
1961.
Fictionalized biography for younger readers. The description of Ravensbrook errs in certain details.

Fryckstedt, Olov W. "Henry Fleming's Tupenny Fury: Cosmic Pessimism in
Stephen Crane's *The Red Badge of Courage,*" *Studia Neophilologica* (Uppsala,
Sweden), 33, no. 2 (1961), 265–281.
An important study of *The Red Badge,* text and manuscript. Fryckstedt
sees Jim Conklin's death struggle as a grotesque ritual mocking religion. That
climactic moment in the book "parodies the rites of a religion in order to
bring out the cruel irony of death's total lack of significance in an indifferent
naturalistic universe." This reading squares with, but refines, Stallman's
Introduction, *The Red Badge* (1951), his essay in *Critiques and Essays* (1952),
and with the *Omnibus*'s reading of *The Red Badge. See also* Rosenfeld (1953),
and Hoffman, Introduction, *The Red Badge* (1957). Oppositions to this
reading include Rahv (1956), replied to by Stallman, "Fiction and Its Critics:"
(1957). *See also The Red Badge* casebooks edited by Lettis, *et al.* (1960) and
by Bradley (1962).
In the "Tupenny Fury" passage of *The Red Badge* manuscript Henry
shakes his fist at the sky (as given in Stallman's reading of Conklin's death
dance scene). Fryckstedt does not notice this fact. Other critics claim that
Henry Fleming shakes his fist at the battlefield, but they ignore the *Red Badge*
manuscripts because the manuscripts upset their fixed idea. Colvert (1958)
agrees and is the only critic declaring that Henry's fist is directed at the sky.
The point is of considerable importance in interpreting the notorious image
of the red sun "pasted in the sky like a wafer."
Fryckstedt's essay is reprinted in Bassan (1967).

Gazarra, Ben. *The Red Badge of Courage.* A TV reading on "Legacy of Light,"
sponsored by the Union of the American Hebrew Congregations. New York,
1961.
Reading of *The Red Badge of Courage* by Ben Gazarra, with illustrations
by Brady photographs. Introduced by Rabbi Maurice N. Eisendrath and
R. W. Stallman.

Gerstenberger, Donna, and George Hendrick, eds. *The American Novel 1789–
1959: A Checklist of Twentieth Century Criticism.* Denver, 1961, pp. 49, 50–
52, 53.

Gullason, Thomas A. "Thematic Patterns in Stephen Crane's Early Novels,"
Nineteenth Century Fiction, 16 (June, 1961), 59–67.
Traces Beer's theme of fear in *Maggie* and *George's Mother,* the war motif
in both novels (the battle of slum life), and the religious motif in *George's
Mother* and in *The Red Badge.* Nothing new here. "The celebrated wafer
image in Chapter IX symbolizes the culminating point of Henry's religious
conflict."
Gullason also traces the theme of ideals *versus* realities, previously traced by
Mangione (1930) and by Stallman in *Omnibus.* Again, nothing new here.
"If one accepts the judgment of a few of the early critics—that *George's*

Mother and not *The Red Badge* followed *Maggie*—then Crane's pattern of development becomes all the clearer."*

————. "The Jamesian Motif in Stephen Crane's Last Novels," *Personalist*, 42 (Winter, 1961), 77–84.

Hassan, Ihab. *Radical Innocence: Studies in the Contemporary American Novel*. Princeton, N.J., 1961, pp. 42–43.

Heilbrun, Carolyn G. *The Garnett Family*. New York, 1961, pp. 77, 101, 102, 128–130.

Henderson, Dion. "The Dark Splendor of Genius," *Milwaukee Journal*, September 1, 1961, part 1, p. 12.

    Surveys Crane's career, prompted by Louis Zara's novel *Dark Rider* (1961), "which is probably a better re-creation of the man and his works than most biographies."†

Hoffman, Daniel G. *Form and Fable in American Fiction*. New York and London, 1961, pp. 275, 359.

Hough, Robert L. "Crane's Henry Fleming: Speech and Vision," *Forum*, 3 (Winter, 1961), 41–42.

Kagami, Eizo. "S. Crane no 'The Monster' ron e no kokoromi" [On "The Monster" of S. Crane: an attempt], *Nagoya Daigaku Ivy*, no. 2 (1961), 1–8.

Kahn, Sholom J. "Stephen Crane and Whitman: A Possible Source for 'Maggie,'" *Walt Whitman Review*, 7 (December, 1961), 71–77.

    Traces certain resemblances in the lives of Crane and Whitman, as well as between *George's Mother* and Whitman's *Franklin Evans*, or again between *Maggie* with its 28 women and 28 tables in Chapter 14 and Whitman's "Song of Myself" (Section 2) with its "Twenty-eight men bathe by the shore." "The analogy between the two situations is not so close, of course, that it would have suggested itself readily without the allusion to the number twenty-eight; and even with the number, it does not seem to have been noticed by reader-critics. Am I, then, making too much of a mere coincidence"‡

Klotz, Marvin. "Stephen Crane: Tragedian or Comedian: 'The Blue Hotel,'" *University of Kansas City Review*, 27 (Spring, 1961), 170–174.

    "How shall Stephen Crane be read? The approach engendered by R. W.

---

* However, Crane's "pattern of development" occurred within the short span of two years, 1891–1893, when almost simultaneously he was writing *Maggie* and the Sullivan County tales and sketches (1891–1892), and then the next year he began *George's Mother* on verso of the manuscript of "The Holler Tree," just after *Maggie* was published, and he wrote (1893–1894) *The Red Badge*, possibly begun in late 1892. He returned to *George's Mother* in May of 1894. See *Crane* and *SCTS*.

† However, in writing *Crane* (1968) I found it dangerous to utilize anything in Zara's novel because it is impossible to distinguish therein between fact and fiction. By fictionalizing a situation Zara falsified it. No fact thus remains a fact. Had novelist Zara utilized his extensive research on Crane for writing a biography of Crane, he would have blocked me from writing *Crane*.

‡ Stallman, *Stephen Crane: Stories and Tales* (1955), "relates Crane's prose to two major streams of American literature: the 'quest for and immersion in experience' and the relation of this to 'innocence'—without however finding any links to Whitman." (Kahn would have found, however, some links between Crane and Whitman in *Omnibus*, but he chose to use instead the selected Crane *Stories and Tales*, a shortened version of *Omnibus*.)

Stallman in 1951 has gained many converts who have made of Crane an in-
credibly subtle and sophisticated symbolical writer—downright allegorical—a
crafty writer whose metaphors and images need to be examined with the
intensity required in an examination of Kafka, of Joyce, or Faulkner. The
ingenuity of these critics is surpassed only by their proliferation and their
refusal to take correction."

In opposition to James Cox (1957), Stein (1959), and Roth (1953), Klotz is
also opposed, on the other hand, to the literary Naturalist reading of "The
Blue Hotel" (as by Walcutt [1956]) and considers the story to be "a deliberate
burlesque of literary naturalism."

Kudo, Kozo. "Crane 'Sekishoku bukosho' no mittsu no 'shi' no sowa" [Three
episodes of 'death' in *The Red Badge of Courage* by Stephen Crane], *Yamagata Daigaku Eigo Eibungaku Kenkyu*, no. 6 (February, 1961), 69–84.

Langford, Gerald. *The Richard Harding Davis Years*. New York, 1961, pp. 15,
109, 110, 186, 187, 188, 194, 201–202.
Covers the Cuban War in eleven pages (Beer does it in eight pages and
Berryman in twenty pages in their biographies of Crane). Consequently, there
is nothing new here on Crane; nor anything new on Davis in Chapter 13:
"War in Cuba and Greece." Langford says that Davis met Crane for the first
time in London in 1897, but in fact they had met at the Lantern Club in
1895. *See Crane.*

Liebling, A. J. "The Dollars Damned Him," *The New Yorker*, 37 (August 5,
1961), 48–60, 63–66, 69–72.
An important and useful biographical study, surveying Crane scholarship
and criticism from *Letters* back to Beer, Berryman, and *Omnibus*. "The letters
clearly show us that Crane was the victim not of self-indulgence or a death-
wish, as it has been popular among critics to assume, but of his situation,
which was banal. He died, unwillingly, of the cause most common among
American middle-class males—anxiety about money." What killed Crane was
the malady of money worry, which "is constant in societies wherein the Western
Nonconformist Protestant culture sets the pattern." In England Cora ran up
bills until they were seriously in debt to the tune of nearly two hundred
pounds, or almost a thousand dollars. [However, Crane at his death owed
Pinker $5,000.] "This and not a patch on his lungs, was the first lesion of
Crane's terminal disease. . . ." (Liebling's thesis is documented in *Letters*.)
   " 'Crane wasted his genius,' Professor Stallman wrote nine years ago. 'What
killed Crane was . . . his own will to burn himself out, his Byronic craving
to make his body a testing ground for all the sensations of life.' Stallman
adds, like a sensible uncle, 'He could have retreated from life to calculate it
at a distance, as Hawthorne and James did. Instead, he got as close to life as
possible.' *Bref*, Crane died because he neglected to put on his overshoes—a
truly academic mode of suicide. Professor Stallman, incidentally, in his
otherwise valuable *Omnibus*, descants interminably on the benefits, for an
author, of personal inexperience. To describe well, he implies, nothing is so
essential as not to have seen. Stallman would have made a great foreign-news
editor for Hearst or Luce. . . . For a clincher, he advances the argument that
'Crane reproduced the immediacies of battle in *The Red Badge of Courage*
long before he had seen and suffered actual shellfire.' This is to argue that if
a man can tie his shoelaces with one hand he couldn't do it better and faster
and more easily with two. . . . Most important, Crane did not 'reproduce the

immediacies of battle;' he made a patterned, a rhetorical war such as never existed, to test the heart of his hero. The readers who wasted their admiration on his backdrop were the ones who raved over the scenery in David Belasco's productions of Civil War plays—'so natural you would have thought it was real'—and who bought paintings because the Spanish dancers' mantillas made you think that if you touched them they would feel like lace. The luxurious detail was a concession to the only taste, besides his own, that Crane knew then. It is extraneous to the true merit of the book, which is about a boy in a dragon's wood, and timeless."

Liebling speculates on the kind and quality of work Crane would have done had he recovered his health while at Brede Place, where he produced too much and kept repeating himself (said *Omnibus*, and Liebling agrees). "The quality of the work admittedly fell off," says Liebling. He thinks Crane might have written novels as original as *Maggie* and *The Red Badge,* but concedes that Crane's problem was to keep free "of another syndrome of advances and effort to catch up with them." (However, it was impossible for Crane to write another work comparable to *Maggie* while issuing hack work to pay the housekeeping bills at Brede Manor. Liebling, who argues it both ways, might have revised his standpoint had he known that Crane in 1900 owed $5,000.) "I cannot agree with Professor Stallman's opinion, expressed in 1952, that Crane's 'death at twenty-eight resulted in no loss to literature. He had exhausted his genius.' Stallman supported this by quoting Garland . . . a congenital stuffed shirt [who] couldn't write for free seeds. It is perhaps unfair to tilt against the Stallman of 1952."

Liebling on Beer: "Beer, a slick-fiction writer turned informal (another way of saying careless) biographer, picked up and continued the pair of unfounded suppositions—that Crane was 'unfulfilled' and that it didn't matter, because he lacked the capacity to improve. Beer was sympathetic, in the sloppy fashion of the early twenties. He made Crane a romantic figure, like Dick Diver."

Liebling on Berryman: In his biography of Crane he said that Crane had an interest in horses that showed him pregnant with violence, of which the horse is a symbol. "It had not occurred to Berryman that a man whose 'idea of happiness' is a saddle might just like horses, or that if a man is much with horses, rides horses, covets horses, and thinks a good deal about horses, a high percentage of the images in his prose and verse are likely to be horse images. . . . Freudian criticism reaches full frenzy in Berryman's assertion that when Crane, in an unpublished play,* called a mythical city in Yen Hok—it was a humorous play—he was still dominated by the horse cult. 'Hock,' Berryman reminds the reader, means a 'horse's ankle'—violence again. 'Now Crane had already written the story of a dying dope fiend named "Yen-Nock Bill."' . . . Nothing just like these names have I found: Crane evidently invented them.' " However, the fact is that "yen hok" and "yen nock" are variant spellings for the Chinatown word for "opium pipe." It is obvious from Crane's spoofing dateline to his drama—"Opium Pipe, China"—that "Opium Pipe Bill" is a pseudonym for "hophead," as Crane well knew. "The word 'hock' in 'yen hock' has no more to do with a horse than the 'hock' in a Rhine-wine bottle. Again, when Berryman notes, with the air of a discoverer, that another character in the Yen-Nock Bill story is named Swift Doyer, and that a swift is a

---

* "The Blood of the Martyr," *New York Press,* April 3, 1898, pp. 9–11.

bird (also an adjective and a brand of bacon), which, it seems, has even direr significance than a horse, it appears that he does not know that Doyers Street is one of the three thoroughfares of New York Chinatown (Mott and Pell are the others), and that because of its indirection it gave rise to the old New York gag description of a dishonest fellow: 'As crooked as Doyers Street.' Swift Doyer, then, is as obviously a joke name as Yen Hock, or Yen-Nock Bill."

Manchester, William. "The Spanish-American War," *Holiday,* 30 (September, 1961), 97.
An interesting story, but too short to be more than clever and superficial; not comparable to Freidel's commentary to his picture book *The Splendid Little War* (1958).

Mayfield, John [unsigned]. "Ames W. Williams," *Courier* (Syracuse University Library), 1 (December, 1961), 7–10.
On the Ames Williams collection of volumes and letters by Harold Frederic. Frederic's description in *In the Valley* of the battle in the Mohawk Valley during the French and Indian wars, says editor Mayfield, "is as good writing as found anywhere in Stephen Crane's combat scenes in *The Red Badge of Courage.*"

McColly, William. "Teaching *The Red Badge of Courage,*" *English Journal,* 50 (November, 1961), 534–538.
Crane's "dialogue is dialectal, incoherent, banal, and profane; but the exposition is lofty, dramatic and colorful; these qualities establish a mode of irony that pervades almost every line. *The Red Badge* is thus a travesty; if Crane makes a travesty of the words, thoughts, feelings, and actions of Henry and his comrades, he therefore intends a travesty of his theme—courage. And so he does; there is no getting around it. Crane's hero finds courage in these steps: egocentrism and self-pity; desertion; dispassion (rejecting the tattered soldier); lying and deception; and finally foolhardiness. The sublime expression of this unheroic spectacle results in comedy and satire."

McDonnell, Robert F., and William E. Morris, eds. *Form and Focus: A Rhetorical Reader.* New York, 1961, pp. 364–368, 368–371, 371–378, 378–389, 389–392, 392–399.
Interpretations of "The Open Boat," pp. 363 ff., by Ray B. West, Jr.; by Robert Wooster Stallman; by Richard P. Adams; by James B. Colvert; by S. B. Greenfield; and by Peter Buitenhuis.

Meredith, Robert C., and John D. Fitzgerald. *The Professional Story Writer and His Art.* New York, 1961, pp. 105–111, 114, 175, 193, 217.

Molitor, Suzanne, trans. *Le sceau du courage.* Verviers, Belgium: Collection Marabout, 1961.

O'Donnell, Thomas F., and Hoyt C. Franchere. *Harold Frederic.* New York, 1961, pp. 20, 33, 68, 105, 106, 147, 152, 157, 158, 160, 161, 163.

Osborn, Neal J. "Crane's 'The Monster' and 'The Blue Hotel,' " *Explicator,* 23 (October, 1961), item 10.

Pearce, Roy Harvey. *The Continuity of American Poetry.* Princeton, N.J., 1961, p. 255.
Contends that Crane did not count for much as poet in his time, nor should he now.

Ray, Gordan N. "H. G. Wells's Contributions to the *Saturday Review*," *Library*, 16 (March, 1961), 33.
   A factually ridden essay (as distinguished from the equally common thesis-ridden essay).

Reed, Jared. *The Red Badge of Courage*. A reading for Folkways. New York, 1961.

Ross, Danforth. *The American Short Story*. Minneapolis, 1961, pp. 32–33.

Rubin, Louis, and John Moore. *The Idea of an American Novel*. New York, 1961, pp. 84–85, 273–279, 314–315.

Santos, Therson, trans. *A Noiva Chega a Yellow Sky,* in *Os mais belos contos norte-americanos*. Rio de Janeiro, Brazil: Edições Caravela, 1961, pp. 210–216.
   Brazilian translation into the Portuguese.

———. *O barco aberto* ["The Open Boat"], in *Os mais belos contos norte-americanos*. Rio de Janeiro, Brazil: Edições Caravela, 1961, pp. 26–40
   Brazilian translation into the Portuguese.

Schneider, Robert W. "Stephen Crane and the Drama of Transition," *Journal of the Central Mississippi Valley American Studies Association*, 2 (Spring, 1961), 1–16.

Schorer, Mark. *Sinclair Lewis: An American Life*. New York, 1961, p. 552.

Scott, W. T. [on *The Red Badge* and Howard Fast's *April Morning*], *New Mexico Pasatiempo,* May 28, 1961.

Solomon, Eric. "Stephen Crane's War Stories," *Texas Studies in Literature and Language,* 3 (Spring, 1961), 67–80.
   On "A Mystery of Heroism," "Death and the Child," "The Price of the Harness," and "The Upturned Face." Nothing deeply perceptive here.

Stallman, R. W. A Note about the holograph manuscript, Crane's "A small black and white and tan hound," reproduced in facsimile on the covers of this issue of *Fine Arts Magazine* (University of Connecticut), 6 (1961). Reproduced here for the first time from the original in CUCC. Note, p. 47.

———. " 'The Open Boat': A Symbolic Interpretation," in *Form and Focus*, ed. Robert F. McDonnell and William E. Morris. New York, 1961, pp. 368–371. Reprinted from *Omnibus*, pp. 416–419.
   On "The Open Boat" *see also* Stallman in *Houses*, pp. 248–251. *See also* Adams (1954), Colvert (1958), and Greenfield (1958). On the *Commodore* disaster *see* Stallman in *Bulletin* (1968), a study refuting the claims of Berryman (1950) and Day (1957), by which Crane as journalist was impugned. In *Crane*.

———. *The Houses That James Built and Other Literary Studies*. East Lansing, Mich., 1961, pp. 63–72, 72–81, 81–103, 103–110, 149, 232–252.
   "Crane's *Maggie* in Review," pp. 63–72, collects for the first time contemporary reviews, of which only a few are listed in the *W-S Bibliography*.
   Reprinted in *Crane*. "Crane's *Maggie*: A Reassessment" first appeared in *Modern Fiction Studies* (Autumn, 1959). Revised and expanded from the short version in *New Republic* (1955): "Stephen Crane's Primrose Path." Reprinted from *Omnibus* is the section, pp. 103–110, "Crane's Short Stories."
   "*The Red Badge of Courage*," pp. 81–103, includes "Notes Toward an Analysis of *The Red Badge of Courage*," which first appeared in the 1951

Modern Library edition of *The Red Badge of Courage*, then in 1952 in *Critiques and Essays on Modern Fiction*, ed. John Aldridge (1952), with very slight alterations, and again in *Omnibus* (1952) with no alterations, but with much additional critical commentary surrounding the essay itself.

"Fiction and Its Critics," pp. 232–252, is an expanded version of Stallman's reply to Philip Rahv in *Kenyon Review* (Spring, 1957).

Stallman, R. W., and Arthur Waldhorn. *American Literature: Readings and Critiques*. New York, 1961, pp. 675–676, 712–717, 819–822, 824–827.

Reprints *Maggie* (1896 text), "The Bride Comes to Yellow Sky," "The Upturned Face," and a selection of poems with "A Critique of Crane's Poetic Structure." The critique is recast from *Omnibus*. "A Critique of *Maggie*," pp. 712–717, is recast from Stallman, "Stephen Crane's Primrose Path" (1955) and "Crane's *Maggie*: A Reassessment" (1959).

Swanberg, W. A. *Citizen Hearst*. New York, 1961, pp. 107, 159, 160.

Swanberg, like Mason (1939) and Leech (1959), copies the errors of Millis (1931) on Crane; namely that in Cuba "Crane had sent only one dispatch. This one proved a boomerang, for it told of the shaky conduct of the 71st at San Juan." Swanberg and Leech have not done their homework on Crane. Not Crane but Scovel wrote that undiplomatic dispatch about the 71st; *see* Williams (1948).

Wegelin, Christof. "Crane's 'A Man Said to the Universe,'" *Explicator*, 20 (September, 1961), item 9.

Reprinted in the *Explicator Cyclopedia* (1966).

Wright, Austin McGiffert. *The American Short Story in the Twenties*. Chicago, 1961, pp. 26–29.

Yoshida, Hiroshige. "A Note on Stephen Crane's Use of Colloquial and Slangy Words and Idioms," *Kansai Daigaku Anglica*, 4, no. 3 (January, 1961), 59–71.

Zara, Louis. *Dark Rider: A Novel Based on the Life of Stephen Crane*. Cleveland and New York, 1961.

Reviewed:

Anne Duchene, *Chicago Sunday Tribune*, August 27, 1961: "Another one of those polished, fictionalised biographies in which the less creative batten on the more so—in this case, Stephen Crane. It exudes solemnity, satisfied minor scholarship and an acceptance of the superficial, its level of inquiry and speculation staying steadily round that of 'Reader's Digest.'"

J. K. Hutchens, *New York Herald Tribune Books*, September 10, 1961: "Here is a fat novel based on Crane's life, a life so improbable that Crane himself, for all the daring of his imagination, not to say his genuine humility, could hardly have dreamed of such a thing as a book about it. . . . Page after page of the *Dark Rider* might well seem, to a reader who happened to know little of Crane's life, like a straight biography—here and there marked by a bit of guess-work, and heightened by a melodramatic touch, but in general tracing his course with substantial accuracy from point to point. When Mr. Zara has no choice but to imagine his writing takes on a tone at which one must think that Crane himself, a writer of fine-edged precision and with a loathing for clichés, would wince. . . ."

H. T. Moore, *New York Times Book Review*, September 17, 1961: "Unfortunately, biographical fiction tends to be self-defeating when it takes on an author who wrote so much about his own experiences with the force and color that Stephen Crane had at his command. Louis Zara gamely faces up to such hazards; he even tries to suggest the workings of his hero's consciousness in moments of visionary intensity. . . . The finest part of the book is its middle section, which deals with the youthful Crane's precarious life as a reporter. . . . A definitive biography may one day give us the great story inherent in all this material; Mr. Zara's novel doesn't succeed in doing so because of its own shortcomings as fiction and because it inevitably has to compete with the glaring fact that Crane—so far—is the best novelist who has written about Crane."

G. W. Allen, *Saturday Review,* 44 (September 23, 1961), 18: "There are few scenes that are overdramatized or sentimentalized and the emotional tensions of Crane's Methodist family, the pathos of his Bowery period, and his final tragic months in England are presented with great vividness and skill. A biography in novel form, however, has its disadvantages. The most serious is that the reader does not know where fact ends and imagination begins. . . . *Dark Rider* gives the spirit of Stephen Crane's life, and is as interesting to read as a well-written, suspense-filled novel."

Richard McLaughlin, *Springfield Republican,* October 22, 1961: "Even in the hands of veteran novelist Louis Zara, the stirring story of the life of the author of *The Red Badge of Courage* reads like a carbon copy of the raw and colorful stuff of Crane's crowded career. . . . In fact, here is one time when empathy for Stephen Crane the artist rather than adhering to the straight facts might have produced something more than a pedestrian monograph."

Noted by Edwin H. Cady in *Stephen Crane* (1963), p. 171. In *Dark Rider* Zara "exercises the privileges of a fictional biographer by appropriating and intensifying a number of Berryman's ideas and then projecting his own sexual fantasies upon Crane until the poor author's life reads like a Kinsey case-study."

See Henderson (1961).

1962

[Anon.]. "The Civil War at Home," *New York Times,* September 30, 1962.
  Notes on phonograph records containing readings of Stephen Crane stories.

———. "Honor Crane, Famed Author," *Union-Gazette* (Port Jervis, N.Y.), June 6, 1962, p. 6.

Baskett, S. S., and T. B. Strandness, eds. *The American Identity.* Boston, 1962, pp. 301–305.

Berryman, John. *Stephen Crane.* Cleveland and London, 1962. New York: Meridian Books, 1962. Reissue of the 1950 edition with new Preface and added bibliographical Note. "Additional Bibliography" (1962), pp. 331–332.
  "The most substantial contributions to the biography" are to be found in *Stephen Crane: Letters* "edited with prolix commentaries by Stallman and Lillian Gilkes (1960); supersedes earlier collections of the letters to Nellie Crouse and others." Berryman's "Additional Bibliography" (a checklist of one page) concludes with the slick notion that "Many literary histories, critical

studies, and textbooks now contain brief accounts." (There are in fact 1,040 writings on Crane 1952–1962; the Crane revival continues.)

Berryman, 1950 ed., p. 94, had then declared that the manuscript of *The Red Badge of Courage* does not exist, although two pages of the first draft "are said to be among Cora Crane's papers." (There were five pages, all belonging to the final draft, and they were brought together for the first time in Stallman's Signet edition of *The Red Badge of Courage,* 1960.) Berryman notes in this edition that his 1950 opinion is now "out of date; manuscripts of *The Red Badge* turned up and are fully handled in Stallman's *Omnibus.*" He lists, among other writings on Crane since 1950, Cyrus Day on Crane's shipwreck experiences in *Studies in English* (1957) and adds: "but see my comments in *The Arts of Reading*" (1960).

"Preface to the Meridian Edition," pp. ix–xii. Here Berryman lists some of his errors in the 1950 edition, but the errors he admits are not the important ones. (*Crane* corrects many of Berryman's errors, often silently.) Berryman here regrets that in his 1950 Crane biography there was "an absence of consecutive detailed critical investigation of the major works"—including *The Red Badge of Courage.*

That absence, which no reviewer noticed, was filled in by Berryman's 1965 article on *The Red Badge of Courage,* which regards Crane's novel as a success story. *See* Berryman, 1965. There is nothing new in that Berryman article, nor in his essay on "The Open Boat" in *The Arts of Reading* (1960). In both essays Berryman evades the crucial issues raised by other critics of *The Red Badge of Courage* and "The Open Boat," issues central to our interpretations of these Crane works.

"Stallman's intelligence as a critic," says Berryman in his Meridian Preface (1962), "may be judged in the light of his thinking, apparently, that the famous 'wafer' in *The Red Badge* is sacramental; I blush to report this, but he has good remarks, also." However, there is no need for Berryman to "blush" in reporting the "wafer" mystery in that dozens of critics have encamped on Stallman's side of the river of this controversy. *See* Berryman (1965), where again he hedges on this issue.

Bradley, Sculley, Richmond Crome Beatty, and E. Hudson Long, eds. *The Red Badge of Courage: An Annotated Text, Backgrounds and Sources, Essays in Criticism.* New York, 1962. Bibliography, pp. 342–344.

A Note on the Texts: "Robert W. Stallman, in *Stephen Crane: An Omnibus* (1952), pp. 225–270, discusses the textual problems and shows them by footnotes in his text of *The Red Badge.* The final manuscript was first published in the Folio Society edition in 1951, but the text of that London edition is incomplete and erroneous. In *Omnibus* appeared for the first time both manuscripts of *The Red Badge,* the final holograph and the earlier draft, and here Mr. Stallman showed that certain uncanceled passages in the final manuscript were somehow omitted from the printed first edition of 1895. Mr. Stallman's *Omnibus* text shows 26 of these passages—uncanceled but not printed—by restoring them between square brackets wherever they appeared in the manuscript. . . . none of the omissions altered the meaning of the novel, but they have a certain interest for the critic."

The text here is the first American edition, with passages from the manuscript not given in the text but in the section entitled "The Manuscript: Unpublished Passages" (pp. 113–117). However, not included here are the five new manuscript pages which were published for the first time in the Signet edition of *The Red Badge of Courage and Selected Stories* (New American Library, 1960), ed. R. W. Stallman.

Brennan, J. X. "Irony and Symbolic Structure in Crane's *Maggie*," *Nineteenth-Century Fiction*, 16 (March, 1962), 303–315.

Notices how Crane interlinks the sections of *Maggie* "by an ironic inversion of some key phrase or circumstance." Notices also in Chapter 17, where Maggie briefly plies her trade as a streetwalker, that Maggie has prospered after a few months' activity and yet she commits suicide. "And if she is really seriously interested in engaging profitable attention, why does she enter into 'darker blocks than those where the crowd traveled' to solicit less numerous and less well-to-do customers?" (A good question, but Brennan does not answer it at the literal level of Maggie's situation.) The problems raised in Chapter 17 cannot be resolved by Brennan's bypassing them in saying that the scene must be taken "as a drastic foreshortening or symbolic telescoping of the inevitable decline and ruination to which Maggie and all the women of her order must come." For Brennan it is "a panoramic and symbolic view of the prostitute's career," but this overrides the hard fact of Maggie's suicide at a time when as prostitute she has prospered, as evidenced by the costly garments she wears. Not mentioned by Brennan is William Gibson's explanation (1956).

Brennan begins his essay thus: "It is rather symptomatic of the scant attention scholars have accorded Stephen Crane that in the sixty-seven years since its publication no adequate formal analysis has yet appeared of his telling short novel *Maggie: A Girl of the Streets*." This statement ignores the fact that 1,527 books and articles, not counting contemporary reviews, had been published by 1962 and that on *Maggie* an "adequate formal analysis" appeared in the *New Republic* for 1955 and in *Modern Fiction Studies* for 1959 (the Stephen Crane number), reprinted in 1961 in *Houses*.

In Brennan's essay, one must conclude, there is little that is new. New, however, is his reading of Maggie's last night. With no acknowledgement to Brennan, Brennan's idea gets echoed by Cady (1962 and 1969), by Katz (1966), and by Bruccoli, who labels the situation of Maggie's last night as a "two-time scheme" (*that* is precisely Brennan's insight). *See also* Bowers (1969); under Bowers is Stallman's radically (1969) different reading of Maggie's last night. Reprinted in *The Stephen Crane Reader,* ed. R. W. Stallman (1972).

Burke, W. J., and Will D. Howe. *American Authors and Books: 1640–Present Day*, rev. ed. New York, 1962, p. 165.

Cady, Edwin H. *Stephen Crane.* New York, 1962. Selected Bibliography, pp. 169–180.

One of the Twayne United States Authors Series, a biographical and critical study limited in scope by the designed pattern of the series. Useful, although it lacks original probings in both categories. Presents the first annotated Crane bibliography, a highly selective one.

"In dealing with Crane," says Cady (p. 47), "one is forced inevitably to guess." And so there is much guesswork in Cady's *Stephen Crane.* Overriding the whole book is Cady's personal version of what perhaps happened. He says, for instance, that "there is no evidence that Crane was upset" at the fiasco of the banquet honoring him in Buffalo, December 19, 1895. Contrary to Crane's own camouflaging of that fiasco, there is much evidence to contradict Cady's reading. *See* Bragdon (1929), *Letters,* and new evidence now supplied here by Daly (1916) and Taber (1923, 1940).

"But once again an examiner runs into a thick fog of ignorance about Crane's life. . . . What did Crane ever read?" asks Cady (p. 69). Well, we know what he read by his "List of Books / Brede Place."

Contends rightly that *The Red Badge of Courage* "is not a work of naturalism" (p. 131), and he argues against Walcutt's "Stephen Crane: Naturalist and Impressionist" essay in *American Literary Naturalism* (1956). Cady contends that Walcutt's case for making Crane out to be the complete Naturalistic artist is "not proven—or provable" (pp. 109–110). Neither here nor in Cady's *Maggie* essay in *Landmarks of American Writing,* ed. Hennig Cohen (1969) does Cady come at *Maggie* for its artistry. Critics of "The Blue Hotel" explain away portions of the text, Cady rightly contends, "in order to make the story conform with the critics' predetermination that it shall be a work of naturalism. Actually, however, 'The Blue Hotel' is no more purely naturalistic than any of Crane's other major work. . . . There is no evidence in the story that it is nature or any other deterministic force which kills the Swede" (p. 155). Cady's discourse is thus keenly perceptive here and there, with many dull spots in the journey and too much lecturing the reader.

Perversely, Cady denies the Christ-figure of Jim Conklin in *The Red Badge of Courage,* but contrariwise he suggests that oiler Billy Higgins in "The Open Boat" "is certainly no less a Christ-figure than Melville's Billy Budd" (p. 154)! And he contradicts his standpoint that the loss of Crane "was a real tragedy to the development of our literature" and agrees with A. J. Liebling (1961) that Crane might have gone on to write long novels of originality; whereas Cady also says, p. 67, "But creative growth was at an end"—in 1900, or even in 1899.

Cady has an interesting discussion of the Mss. LV and SV of *The Red Badge of Courage,* in which he doubts any religious symbolism. Nor could Crane think of the red sun wafer as eucharistic wafer because his religious background was "anti-Catholic," a mistaken notion indeed. Cady here echoes Edmund Wilson (1953). However, the mass as celebrated by the Methodist Church was almost identical with the mass as carried out by the Catholic Church. *See* Stallman *versus* Wilson (1953). Cady claims that Crane is not truly a symbolist; "the test case may be 'The Open Boat.' " However, Cady has picked the wrong test case in that there is plenty of symbolism in "The Open Boat." And Cady himself spots something symbolic therein, pp. 152–153, which passage contradicts Cady, p. 137.

Reviewed:

Vincent Starrett, *Chicago Tribune Magazine of Books,* March 3, 1963: "Dr. Cady is more concerned with Crane as an artist than as an 'impressionist,' a 'Naturalist,' a 'symbolist,' or any other sort of 'ist.' Freudian explanations of Stephen's genius leave him cold, as they do me. The result is a brief and balanced account of our first modern novelist, a work of scholarship that I can recommend heartily as the best study of Crane now available."

Paul R. Stewart, *College English,* 25 (November, 1963): "Professor Cady (Indiana), who acknowledges the 'thick fog of ignorance' surrounding Crane's life, has concentrated on the essential nature of the brilliant and rebellious *isolato,* as revealed chiefly in his works. Because Crane's masterpieces are few and generally familiar, Cady is able to explore them in depth, establishing Crane as a master of irony symbolism, and psychological realism."

On Maggie's last night *see* Cady and Bruccoli (1967). *See also* Stallman, ed. *The Stephen Crane Reader* (1972).

Carruth, Gorton, and associates, eds. *The Encyclopedia of American Facts and Dates.* New York, 1962, pp. 364, 372, 380.

Conrad, Joseph. "Stephen Crane: A Note Without Dates," in *Novelists on Novelists,* ed. Louis Kronenberger. New York, 1962, pp. 259–263.

Cross, Leslie. "In Quest of Young Mr. Crane," *Milwaukee Journal,* March 18, 1962.

On Mark Schorer of Sauke City, whose biography of Stephen Crane "will be published by Knopf.* The publisher has announced no date for its appearance." Stallman's biography of Crane is in preparation for Holt, Rinehart & Winston. He "hopes to publish in the fall of 1963."

Current-Garcia, Eugene, and Walton R. Patrick, eds. *Realism and Romanticism in Fiction: An Approach to the Novel.* Chicago, 1962.

Davidson, Dorothy P., ed. *Book Review Digest.* New York, 58 (March, 1962– February, 1963), 1337–1338.

Dieckmann, Edward A., Jr. "The Hemingway Hypnosis," *Mark Twain Journal,* 11 (Summer, 1962), 3–4.

Dolch, Martin. *Insight I: Analysis of American Literature.* Frankfurt, Germany, 1962, pp. 36–41.

Eble, Kenneth E., ed. *Howells: A Century of Criticism.* Dallas, Tex., 1962, pp. 127, 129, 139, 148, 161, 229, 232, 240.

Fadiman, Clifton, ed. *The Red Badge of Courage.* Illustrated by Herschel Levit. New York and London, 1962. With an Afterword by Clifton Fadiman, pp. 203–205.

The text with final manuscript passages is pirated from the Folio Society edition (1951).

Farlekas, Christopher. "Stephen Crane of Port Jervis," *Views* (the official publication of the Orange County Community of Museums and Galleries), 1, no. 3 (October, 1962), 3–5. Oil portrait by Paul Zavorskas from an old family picture of Crane now at Syracuse University.

Mentions the lynching of the Negro Robert Lewis at noon of June 2, 1892, "by an angry mob on a high tree in front of the Port Jervis Baptist Church. Crane had tried in vain to stop this, but his voice and fists were lost against the 5,000 in the mob." *See* Farlekas (1965). These two articles are my source for my account of the lynching of Negro Lewis in *Crane* (1968), together with *New York Tribune* articles (not mentioned by Farlekas), which are here listed under Farlekas (1965).

Farlekas, Christopher, ed. *Stephen Crane: An Appreciation.* Port Jervis, N.Y., 1962.

---

* Subsequently, in mid-June, 1962, Mr. Knopf broke off negotiations with Prof. Mark Schorer for the Knopf biography of Crane, and a few years later Holt's new editor broke off contract on Crane with Stallman, whose publisher then became George Braziller, thanks to Editor Edwin Seaver.

A pamphlet containing "The Anatomy of a Memorial" [unsigned]; "Stephen Crane: The First of the Moderns," by Wallace Stegner; "Stephen Crane and *The Red Badge of Courage*," by Robert Luther Clark; and "In Search of Light: Three Poems for Stephen Crane," by John Chesley Taylor.

Fryckstedt, Olov W. "Crane's *Black Riders*: A Discussion of Dates," *Studia Neophilologica*, 34, no. 2 (1962), 282–293.

A closely studied and very sensitively rendered account of the history of Crane's writing his *Black Riders* poems. Retells the earlier accounts by Berryman and Stallman on Crane's bringing the manuscript of his poems to Hamlin Garland. Fryckstedt, reporting Stallman in *Omnibus*, says that Stallman finds in Garland's *Yale Review* version (1914) "further weighty, almost conclusive evidence that Crane wrote the first poems for *The Black Riders* early in April 1893." John Barry, Garland, Beer, and Stallman have it that way, whereas Berryman dates the poems for February, 1894. C. K. Linson had it February, 1894, in his *MSC*, the manuscript of which was used by Berryman in 1950. Fryckstedt says that Beer "did not have access to this source of information." He could have added that neither did Stallman. In 1952 there was no other evidence but Garland's various and contradictory accounts, four in all. Berryman cited only one Garland account, the one which squared with the then-unknown-to-exist Linson manuscript; had Berryman declared in 1950 his Linson source my *Omnibus* account would have taken a different stance. In any case it is now corrected in *Crane*—thanks to Donald Pizer's "The Garland-Crane Relationship" (1960), which sets the record straight by making known Garland's journals for the first time.

Fryckstedt in his summing up says that "the available facts show almost beyond doubt that Stephen Crane began to write poetry sometime during the winter of 1894." However, he is mistaken. Crane's earliest poems were written in the winter of 1891–1892 to Helen Trent.

Fryckstedt's data on C. K. Linson are limited to *MSC*, Linson being one of the four main witnesses to Crane's manuscript of the poems. However, Linson also published in the *Saturday Evening Post* an article on Crane (1903), passages of which are not incorporated in *MSC*, or noticed by either the editor Edwin Cady, or Fryckstedt.

———. "Stephen Crane in the Tenderloin," *Studia Neophilogica*, 34 (1962), 135–163.

On the Dora Clark, Crane, and Charles Becker affair; an expanded version drawing upon many newspaper articles not listed in the *W-S Bibliography*. Another selection of newspaper articles on the Dora Clark-Crane-Becker affair appears in *NYCS*.

Gibson, William M., Introduction, *The Red Badge of Courage and Selected Prose and Poetry*. New York, 1962.

Reprints, with additions, the 1956 edition.

Gibson's text of *The Red Badge of Courage* is the faulty Folio Society text, ed. by Winterich (London, 1951), which is MS. LV—minus any mention of the existence of MS. SV. (Both manuscripts appeared for the first time in *Omnibus*.)

Gibson in his textual note discusses the 1893 and 1896 *Maggie* editions, in which he differs "very considerably" from Stallman's reading of the variants. *See* Stallman, "Stephen Crane's Revisions of *Maggie: A Girl of the Streets*"

(1955). Our difference of opinion is whether *Maggie* should include or ex-
punge from the text the paragraph describing "a huge fat man in torn and
greasy garments." He appears only in the 1893 edition, Chapter 17.

Gibson here provides a cogent probing of the situation in Chapter 17, in
explanation of Crane's deletion of this pen-portrait. In Crane's revised text
(1896) "Maggie no longer solicits the last two men she meets, and the 'huge
fat man' whom she might accept has wholly disappeared; she has, plainly,
made up her mind to drown herself. The ambiguity is gone and the logic
of Crane's chapter and his whole story is improved, or remains unimpaired."
Collate with Pizer, Introduction, *Maggie* (1968) and Cady on *Maggie* (1969).

Cady's standpoint is that the 1893 *Maggie* is preferable to the 1896 *Maggie*,
a point of view first expressed by Stallman (1955); he prophesies that "the
1896 edition will simply disappear; and good riddance, too." If so, then the
1896 deleted passage on the "huge fat man" will become known once more.

See also Katz (1966); Bruccoli (1967); and Bowers (1969); with Stallman's
(1969) version of Maggie's last night (reprinted in *The Stephen Crane
Reader*, ed. R. W. Stallman, 1972).

Goethals, Thomas. Introduction, *The Red Badge of Courage.* New York, 1962,
pp. 7–12.

Defines *The Red Badge* as a romance-novel with its theme of a young man's
initiation, a theme equally central to Cooper's *The Deerslayer,* Twain's
Huckleberry Finn, Hemingway's *In Our Time,* and Faulkner's *The Bear.*

Citing Richard Chase, Goethals separates the romance from the novel. He
finds their chief difference is in their attitudes towards reality: the novel
deals with reality more closely, social relationships, character rather than
action, the realistic and the plausible; the romance emphasizes the symbolic
and the ideological, idealized relationships, action rather than character. He
also cites Tocqueville on the dichotomy between ideals and practice in the
American mind. Upon this he builds a theory of the romance-novel in American fiction to which the works of Hawthorne also belong.

Harvey, David, *Ford Madox Ford, 1873–1939: A Bibliography of Works and
Criticism.* Princeton, N.J., 1962. Annotated; p. 204 and *passim.*

Heath, Monroe. *Great American Authors at a Glance.* Menlo Park, Calif.,
1962, p. 28 and *passim.*

Honig, Donald. Introduction, *Stephen Crane: "An Illusion in Red and White"
and Ten Other Stories Not Available in Any Other Book in Print.* New York,
1962, pp. 7–13.

A drug-store paperback of Crane's minor tales, a selection which contradicts
Honig's bold claim that "Crane must be read at every level of quality; if one is
to strive for a better understanding of the man one must read beyond the
paltry handful of Crane's work that has generally been before the public's eye."

Hough, Robert L. "Crane's Henry Fleming: Speech and Vision," *Forum,* 3
(Summer, 1962), 41–42.

———. "Crane and Goethe: A Forgotten Relationship," *Nineteenth-Century
Fiction,* 17 (September, 1962), 135–148.

Crane's indebtedness to French Impressionist painters was generally accepted
until 1949 when Melvin Schoberlin disputed this interpretation; Berryman
(1950) agreed that Crane borrowed nothing from the Impressionists. (They
had obtained their standpoint from C. K. Linson, whose *MSC* was then in

manuscript.) Almost immediately Stallman, in "Stephen Crane:" (1952) and in *Omnibus,* argued that the influence of the studio on Crane could be readily demonstrated and that Crane's techniques were too close to those of the Impressionists to be accidental. *See also* Kwiat (1952).

Hough restudies Frank Noxon's 1928 remark that Goethe's *Theory of Colors* (London trans., 1840) influenced Crane. Red is purely descriptive in Crane's *Whilomville Stories,* written 1898–1900, whereas in the earlier Sullivan County tales and sketches, in *Maggie,* and in *The Red Badge* "red is usually metaphoric, sometimes synesthetic, and almost always used to heighten emotion or to imply violence." Crane used red "in conformity with its effect," which is Goethe's theory of the symbolic application of color.

"R. W. Stallman, who first commented on Crane's use of contrast, believes it definitely links the author with the nineteenth century impressionistic painters who employed similar devices of juxtaposition and perspective. (Stallman gives several examples of Crane's use of contrast between light and dark, warm color and cold color.*) But it is quite possible that Crane first studied this technique while reading Goethe." Hough thinks that Crane knew the work of the French Impressionists, but that "some of the influence usually credited to them probably originated with Goethe" and that he knew Goethe in all likelihood before he knew about the Impressionist painters (no article in American magazines appeared until mid-1892). "The stress on the emotional reaction to color, the concern with contrast and complementarism, the interest in light and shade, and the whole concept of a scientific approach to the problems of light may be found in both Goethe and the French painters." *See also* Wogan (1960).

————. "Crane on Herons," *Notes and Queries,* 9 (March, 1962), 108–109.

Hough asserts that the light blue legs of the heron described in the opening of "The Blue Hotel" designate the age of a heron rather than a species of heron as Crane supposed. "What Crane knew and used in 'The Blue Hotel' was a young heron, not a particular kind of heron." This raises the competence of Crane as a bird-watcher; but Hough is mistaken, as C. T. Peterson points out in *Notes and Queries* (Peterson [1963]). So, then, "Stephen Crane, for the honour of cranes and herons, was accurate in his observations."

Jones, Winifred W., ed. Preface, *Stephen Crane's The Red Badge of Courage,* adapted with Notes and Exercises by Winifred W. Jones. Englewood Cliffs, N.J., 1962, pp. v–viii.

An adaptation with the shortened novel rewritten within a 3,000-item word list for students of English as a second language.

Kagami, Eizo. "S. Crane no War Tales ni tsuite" [On War Tales of S. Crane], *Gifu Daigaku Kenkyu Hōkoku (Jinbunkagaku),* no. 11 (1962), 20–27.

Kazin, Alfred. "Stephen Crane's Scarlet Woman," in *Contemporaries.* Boston, 1962, pp. 60–64.

An essay prompted by Gilkes' *Cora Crane.*

Klein, Eduard, and Klaus Marschke, trans. *Das rote Siegel.* East Berlin: Volk und Welt, 1962.

Contains in translation into the German *The Red Badge of Courage* (the title work), "The Bride Comes to Yellow Sky," "Shame," "His New Mittens," "An Ominous Baby," "The Men in the Storm," *Maggie,* "The Monster," "A

———————————
* In *Omnibus,* pp. 184–187.

Mystery of Heroism," "An Episode of War," "The Blue Hotel," and "The Open Boat."

Klotz, Marvin. "Romance or Realism? Plot, Theme, and Character in *The Red Badge of Courage*," *College Language Association Journal*, 6 (December, 1962), 98–106.

"Had Crane wished, he might have written an epilogue of judgment on Henry—but he chose not to. He nowhere really judges Henry, or evinces the slightest desire to, and this, finally, is the most realistic attribute of the entire novel, an attribute rarely found in nineteenth century American fiction at any level, despite the fact that the theory of realism requires just such a suspension of judgment on the part of the author."

Kuspet, Donald B. "Charles Dana Gibson's Girl," *Jahrbuch für Amerikastudien*, 7 (1962), 183–187.

Comments on Crane's *Maggie*.

La Point, Charles. "The Day That Stephen Crane Was Shipwrecked," *Daytona Beach News Journal*, April 22, 1962. Photographs of Ocean Avenue and "Surfcrest," the house where Crane and the dinghy's survivors were taken, and a drawing of the *Commodore* by R. Stevens.

Recast from an unpublished article by Odell S. Hathaway, who interviewed in 1962 the persons aiding the survivors of the dinghy at Daytona Beach: Mrs. Spalding of the "Surfcrest" cottage and John Kitchell. Also Fred Nivens, telegraph operator. (La Point rewrote Hathaway's article, thus scooping him.)

Lassen, Uwe, trans. *Das Monstrum*. Hamburg, Germany, 1962.

Leaver, Florence. "Isolation in the Work of Stephen Crane," *South Atlantic Quarterly*, 61 (Autumn, 1962), 521–532.

"Crane's modernity in his insisting upon isolation as the common lot of common men is evident." Fear is but a symptom of personal isolation. "Much can be said in support of Robert Stallman's statement that the 'reading of fear as the "theme" of everything he [Crane] wrote ignores about as many of his short stories as, superficially, it accounts for.' There are indeed various themes, and certainly some of the better pieces 'have nothing to do with fear.'"

Levenson, J. C. "Stephen Crane: 1871–1900," in *Major Writers of America*, vol. 2. Ed. Perry Miller. New York, 1962, pp. 383–397. Selections of Crane's works include "The Monster" and "Death and the Child."

Nothing new here, and no sources cited. Errs in misdating *Maggie* for 1892 and in the notion that Crane "was a kind of innocent in a fallen world, free from the burdens of the past. . . ." This ignores Crane's burden of the past, namely his military and religious heritage (first cited by Gaines and Peaslee in 1896). "While his short life partly accounted for his being a man without a historical shadow, his peculiar innocence must be attributed partly to failure of mind.

"Too much the legendary innocent, he was slow to learn that culture is man's substitute for experience, and that without it a young man is prey to deceptions that arise as much from his own ignorance as from the falsity of the world." Levenson thus lectures his author.

Linneman, William R. "Satires of American Realism, 1880–1900," *American Literature*, 34 (March, 1962), 80–93.

"The work of Crane provides a touchstone for deciding what the humor magazines preferred in literature." They "wished for a literature that was realistic in manner but romantic in material. Their ideal novel would fall somewhere between the dime novel and realistic fiction." They praised *The Red Badge of Courage,* although *Life* parodied it: "The sun hung like a custard pie in a burnt blanket." James Ford's *Truth* said that Crane in *Maggie* was wasting his talent in describing such grim reality. "This opinion is exactly opposite that of Howells, who thought Crane in *The Red Badge of Courage* 'wronged the finer art' he had shown in his earlier writing [*Maggie*]."

Marcus, Mordecai. "The Threefold View of Nature in 'The Open Boat,' " *Philological Quarterly,* 61 (April, 1962), 511–515.

The men in the dinghy have a three-fold view of nature, and it grows out of their changing experience. They see nature "first as malevolently hostile, then as thoughtlessly hostile, and finally as wholly indifferent." *Contra* Greenfield (1958) "the idea that nature is indifferent does not come as 'a revelation to the correspondent when the men are stalled within sight of land,' as Greenfield maintains [p. 564], but rather grows out of a progressive change of thought." The three-fold view of nature, as revealed in the characters' thoughts, is accompanied by the men's deepening concept of brotherhood. Previous critics do give attention to a conflict between the ideas of a hostile and an indifferent nature, but "they neglect its stages, its psychological meaning, and its resolution." The previous critics Marcus cites are West (1949), Adams (1954), Greenfield (1958), and West and Stallman. However, the author of the essay on "The Open Boat" by West and Stallman was written by Ray B. West, Jr., not by Stallman.

Meixner, John A. *Ford Madox Ford's Novels.* Minneapolis, Minn., 1962, pp. 3, 19, 24, 40, 280.

Metzger, Charles R. "Realistic Devices in Stephen Crane's 'The Open Boat,' " *Midwest Quarterly,* 4 (Summer, 1962), 47–54.

Molitor, Lucienne, trans. *Maggie, fille des rues et six nouvelles de Stephen Crane.* Verviers, Belgium: Collection Marabout, 1962.

Contains translation into the French of "The Upturned Face," "The Knife," "His New Mittens," "The Bride Comes to Yellow Sky," "The Blue Hotel," "The Open Boat," and the title story, *Maggie.*

Moore, Harry T. "Speaking of Books" [on Norris and Crane], *New York Times Book Review,* September 16, 1962, p. 2.

Mott, Frank Luther. *American Journalism: A History, 1690–1960.* New York, 1962, pp. 521, 534, 580.

Nichols, Lewis. "In and Out of Books," *New York Times Book Review,* November 4, 1962, p. 8.

Quotes an unidentified source which ranks Booth Tarkington's *Penrod Stories* far below Mark Twain's *Tom Sawyer* and *Huckleberry Finn* and Crane's *Whilomville Stories.*

O'Connor, Richard. *The Scandalous Mr. Bennett.* Garden City, N.Y., 1962, pp. 90–91.

Overmeyer, Janet. "The Structure of Crane's *Maggie,*" *University of Kansas City Review,* 29 (October, 1962), 71–72.

Peter, Jr., Emmett. "Fiction or Fact on the Life of Cora Crane," *Tampa Tribune* (February 25, 1962).

Pizer, Donald. "Frank Norris' Definition of Naturalism," *Modern Fiction Studies*, 8 (Winter, 1962–1963), 408–410.

Randel, William. "The Cook in 'The Open Boat'," *American Literature*, 34 (November, 1962), 405–411.

Impugns the character of Charles Montgomery, the steward of the *Commodore*, by claiming that cook Montgomery lied in stating that there were five men in the dinghy, in the *New York Press*, January 4, 1897. John Berryman, not mentioned by Randel, concluded—solely on the evidence of the *Press*—that five men were in the dinghy in contradiction of Crane's own *Press* version that there were four men in the dinghy, including himself. Since Berryman's *Crane* no Crane scholar has refuted Berryman's conjecture. Day (1957) ignores the issue, and Randel provides not the slightest evidence in factual proof one way or the other.

The point has importance because Crane's integrity as journalist is impugned by the claim of Berryman and of cook Montgomery; but the *Press* undoubtedly misquoted Montgomery, a point not considered by Berryman or by Randel, whose research is limited to the *Press* and the *Florida Times-Union and Citizen*. Randel, quoting the *Times Union*, January 1, 1897, says that the total signed aboard the *Commodore*, officers and crew, was twenty-eight. However, he ignores the *Florida Times-Union*, January 5, reporting Captain Murphy's statement that there were twenty-seven passengers aboard the *Commodore*. That would put four men in the dinghy; no need then to impugn Montgomery, whatever his character.

Murray Nobles quit the crew of the *Commodore* at the last minute, "and it is not known if anyone took his place," says Randel—solely on the evidence of the *Times-Union*, January 4. However, Murray Nobles was replaced, according to Captain Murphy's account variously reported in New York papers such as the *Herald, Journal,* and *World*. If he was replaced, then there were twenty-eight persons aboard the *Commodore*. That would put five men in the dinghy. Randel asks, "Which number is correct?" His essay fails to answer the question he raises, a question which can be answered only by ascertaining the number of persons aboard the *Commodore*. The conclusive proof that the dinghy held only four men is provided by the log of the *Boutwell:* Number of persons aboard the *Commodore:* 27. Stallman, "Journalist Crane in that Dinghy" (1968), answers the problems raised but not solved by Randel, Day, and Berryman. In *Crane*.

Smirnov, B. A. *Stephen Crane: Scarlet Sign of Valor: Stories.* Translation from the English. Moscow and Leningrad, 1962.

Introduction translated from the Russian by Mrs. W. S. Woytinsky (for R. W. S.) "The evolution of Crane is one of the mysteries of American literature. True, the amazing mastery of young Maupassant in French literature was also striking, but everyone knew that he had learned his art under the tutelage of the great master, Flaubert. . . . The sensitiveness and intuition of Crane are supernatural. He stands out by reason of the fact that not for one moment is he torn away from life. The austere sharpness of his creative art was prompted by his time and the literary tradition which he had selected. Marx stressed that just when people seemed to be occupied in changing everything around them, they were trapped by the tenacious claws of tradition. This is true also with respect to literary innovation."

Crane gave his greatest attention to the work of Tolstoy. "This was the only writer among the contemporaries who fascinated him unreservedly. Following the precepts of Tolstoy, he tried to develop principles of American realism." Some of his novels and short stories are masterpieces; "they laid the foundation for the American literature of the twentieth century." Three subjects stand out and form a unity in his writings: life in the slums, the tragedy of war, and the misfortunes of a child. "The subject of *Maggie* was rather a pretext for him to express his bitterness toward his compatriots."

A. P. Chekhov, in formulating his poetic principles, said: "The subject must be new, but the plot may be absent." Crane, says Smirnov, "could not have known these words, but in his own way he followed the same road, rejecting the traditional Anglo-Saxon 'fabulism.' Honesty compels one to add that he was not alone in fighting that tradition. Ambrose Bierce mobilized the poetry of nightmares and horrors for that same purpose, and later O. Henry treated entertaining plots ironically by the stunning illogicality of his denouements." Points out that Scratchy Wilson in "The Bride Comes to Yellow Sky" was "brother to Bret Harte's heroes and also a direct precursor of the figures of O. Henry, who exemplified the idea of the sentimental education of lawbreakers in 'Resurrection of Calliope.' " The lyrical tendencies of this type of narrative were, "on the one hand, full of drama and, on the other, assured its distribution in a country where the problem of human rights had become particularly important."

In "The Blue Hotel" appears "the whole system of man's destruction in American life. In spite of Crane's aversion to comments, the ideological features in this story are presented sharply. Man is wolf to man—this is the formula of the American Way of Life. . . .

"Crane was a realist-writer who wanted to pull the romantic veil from the face of war. His contemporaries were sure that America was different from other countries, that she did not have the features of approaching Imperialism. But Crane saw in war (perhaps not without the influence of Tolstoy and Stendhal) the terrible force, the tragic atmosphere of human life in the twentieth century. He depicted war as an unnatural state of society, which distorted the true image of humanity. . . . Like Tolstoy, from whom he had learned much, Crane did not see in war any conscious art of the military leader, any purposeful action of the soldiers. No, these were spontaneous, mostly unconscious and disunited actions of different people. How and what a man feels on the battlefield, what impulses dominate him—these are the questions with which Crane concerns himself. . . ."

Snyder, Louis L., and Richard B. Morris, eds. "Stephen Crane Pins the Red Badge of Courage on Surgeon Gibbs," in *A Treasury of Great Reporting*. New York, 1949. Rev. ed., 1962, pp. 236–240.

Reprints Crane's *World* dispatch, June 13, 1898 ("In the First Landing 4 of Our Men Are Killed") under the invented and fictitious title: "A *World* Correspondent Immortalized an Incident on the Shores of Guantánamo Bay," pp. 237–238. Reprints from "War Memories" in vol. 9 of *Work* his account of the death of Surgeon Gibbs, pp. 238–240.

"In the First Landing 4 of Our Men Are Killed" is an unsigned *World* dispatch, dictated by Crane to Ernest McCready. *See War Dispatches.*

Stallman, R. W. "Stephen Crane," in *The Reader's Encyclopedia of American Literature,* ed. Max Herzberg. New York, 1962, pp. 219–223. (Also Crane's works in summary sketches listed alphabetically throughout the volume.)

Stone, Edward. "Introducing Private Smithers," *Georgia Review,* 16 (Winter, 1962), 442–445.

Bill Smithers, an unnoticed soldier who enters the story anonymously in Chapter 2 of *The Red Badge,* emerges as a true-to-life characterization. His experience in the hospital "had proved no more a sanctuary for him than the church in the forest had for Henry. . . . Thus even he is changed by war; he is neither the loud, fearful soldier (Wilson) who has grown soft-spoken; nor the quiet, fearful soldier (Fleming) who has grown loud-mouthed; but the eternal type of not-quite-brave, not-quite-cowardly soldier who gets through the war creditably enough. . . . His name is legion."

Thorne, J. O., ed. *Chamber's Biographical Dictionary.* New York, 1962, p. 327.

Tuttleton, James W. "The Imagery of *The Red Badge of Courage,*" *Modern Fiction Studies,* 8 (Winter, 1962–1963), 410–415.

"*The Red Badge of Courage* continues to provoke the liveliest kind of criticism. . . . That Stallman's interpretation of the novel has proved unacceptable to so many serious critics of the novel, however, suggests that the imagery he has isolated (and it *is* there) is either meaningless or coincidental, or that it has some other function in the novel." On the pagan religious imagery and the Christian imagery, which is primarily concentrated in the first half of the book. On "He was a man," a statement which sounds suspiciously like the "brass and bombast of his earlier gospels." If so, then Fleming at the end is the same as at the beginning. The manuscript supports this conclusion, as given in *Omnibus,* p.369. "Such a conclusion is not the wisdom of a man who has, after such battle experience, grown, matured, been initiated, enlightened, or saved. Crane's irony gets in the way of the conclusion he is driving toward. If Henry's soul does change, it is only much, much later than the conclusion of the novel that it does so. Crane only states that Henry Fleming has changed; he does not demonstrate from the boy's actions that actual change has occurred. In this respect, the novel fails of its intention." Collate with Friedman (1958).

Tuttleton suggests that Crane deliberately juxtaposed Christian and pagan religious imagery so as to "evoke an irony of opposites."

Weale, Emma Jane. "Stephen Crane—Man of Letters," *Union-Gazette* (Port Jervis, N.Y.), June 8, 1962, p. 4.

The Stephen Crane Memorial Program, held in the public library of Port Jervis on June 5, was the first official recognition of Crane by the city.

Weeks, Robert P. "The Power of the Tacit in Crane and Hemingway," *Modern Fiction Studies,* 8 (Winter, 1962–1963), 415–418.

Parallelisms between *The Red Badge of Courage* and *For Whom the Bell Tolls.*

West, Ray B., Jr. "Stephen Crane: Author in Transition," *American Literature,* 34 (May, 1962), 215–228.

Reprinted in his *Writer in the Room.* East Lansing, Mich., 1968.

Discusses conflicts in Crane's life and works.

Westbrook, Max. "Stephen Crane's Social Ethic," *American Quarterly,* 14 (Winter, 1962), 587–596.

"*Maggie: A Girl of the Streets* offers the best supporting evidence for critics who contend that Stephen Crane believed in social determinism."* Further evidence is found in *George's Mother*, "The Blue Hotel," and "An Experiment in Misery." The central theme of each, according to critical consensus, is that environment shapes lives "regardless" (to quote Westbrook). Westbrook's thesis is that Crane's social ethic "is based on a universal which holds all men responsible for doing the best they can with what they are given. The customary assumption is that a writer who stresses environment is a relativist, and usually the assumption is correct, and certainly Crane does stress environment. When Crane concluded that 'environment is a tremendous thing,' however, he did not throw away ethics and take up social determinism. Rather, he worked out a realistic ethic."

Westbrook takes issue with Nye (1940); with Walcutt (1956); with Gleckner (1959); and McLean (1959). Walcutt says that Crane's works are an early and unique flowering of "pure naturalism." "When Walcutt encounters a non-naturalistic passage in Crane, he says, typically, that 'Crane's technique flags for a moment.'"

Fitelson (1964) takes issue with Westbrook's discussion of *Maggie*.

———. "Stephen Crane and the Personal Universal," *Modern Fiction Studies*, 8 (Winter, 1962–1963), 351–360.

"The discussion of Fleming's salvation has centered around the interpretation of Jim Conklin. R. W. Stallman's analysis of Conklin as a Christ figure has divided critics of *The Red Badge* into two camps: those who agree that Conklin is a Christ figure and that religious imagery is the center of the novel; and those who deny that Conklin is a Christ figure and locate the values of the novel in an ethical context. Stallman's evidence has merit. . . . Those critics who disagree center their attention, not on a denial of Stallman's specific points, but on Stallman's extension of the Christ analogy into an interpretation of the whole novel as a study in spiritual salvation. While the anti-Stallman critics are probably correct in objecting to this emphasis on the religious theme, the Christ analogy, apart from Stallman's extensions, is left dangling. . . . Granted that the language of *The Red Badge* forces a comparison between Jim Conklin and Jesus Christ, there remains the question of significance. In what sense is Conklin a Christ figure?"

Westbrook briefly answers this query, and subsequently Donald Thomas answers it in an excerpt of his doctoral thesis, appearing on pp. 138–140 of *Stephen Crane: A Collection of Critical Essays. See* Bassan (1967).

Williams, Ames W. "On Collecting the Writings of Stephen Crane," *Courier* (Syracuse University Library), 2 (December 1962), 1–11.

Personal reminiscences; the history of his partnership with Vincent Starrett in preparing the *W-S Bibliography*. Notes incidentally that Nightingale and Nightingale, a solicitor's firm in Surrey, "still maintained a file on Crane: overdrawn bank accounts, dishonored drafts, and tradesmen's pleas for remittances." (Noted during Mr. Williams' researches on Crane in England during World War II.)

Williams here mentions the discovery of Crane's "Great Bugs in Onondaga."

---

* "Of primary importance is the work of Stallman. *See* especially *Stephen Crane: An Omnibus* (New York, 1952), pp. 3–20, and 'Crane's *Maggie*: A Reassessment,' *Modern Fiction Studies*, 5 (Autumn, 1959), 251–259." Two critics who object to this standard interpretation are Berryman (1950) and Sutton (1952). "Berryman's subject, however, is Crane's mind (p. 211), not his fiction. . . ."

However, he phrases it somewhat ambiguously; he himself made the discovery. Gilkes, in *Saturday Review* (August 31, 1968), scolds Stallman for not crediting Mayfield in *Crane* with the discovery of Crane's "Great Bugs in Onondaga." However, not Mayfield but rather Williams discovered that Crane sketch. *See* Case (1963).

Wilson, Edmund. *Patriotic Gore: Studies in the Literature of the American Civil War*. New York, 1962, pp. 500–501, 584, 684, 701.

Notes influences on Crane by Emily Dickinson and Ambrose Bierce, and, on *The Red Badge,* by the Reverend John Van Petten of Claverack College, a fellow campaigner of De Forest, who mentions Van Petten in *A Volunteer's Adventures*. In sum, nothing on Crane here that is new.

1963

Bassan, Maurice. "Misery and Society: Some New Perspectives on Stephen Crane's Fiction," *Studia Neophilologica,* 35 (1963), 104–120.

On "An Experiment in Misery." "Crane seems closer in his social thought to the *Arena* group of radicals dominated by B. O. Flower than to any other of the theorists and observers who wrote on the problem of the derelicts." Surveys contemporary writings on tramps and slum life.

Becker, George J., ed. *Documents of Modern Literary Realism*. Princeton, N.J., 1963, pp. 431, 435, 437, 443, 447, 449, 450.

Berryman, John. "Crane's Art," in *Modern American Fiction: Essays in Criticism,* ed. A. Walton Litz. New York, 1963, pp. 32–44. Reprinted from *Stephen Crane* (1950).

Contends that Crane "scarcely made a type in all his work. At the same time, he scarcely made any characters." One of the great stylists of the language, "Crane wrote several styles. . . . He began with the somber-jocular, sable, fantastic prose of the 'Sullivan County Sketches' and the jagged, colored, awkward, brilliant *Maggie*. . . ." For his technical revolution Crane is "indispensable. By a margin he is probably the greatest American story-writer, he stands as an artist not far below Hawthorne and James, he is one of our few poets, and one of the few manifest geniuses the country has produced. . . . Whether Tolstoy's [*Master and Man*] is a better story than Crane's fantastic 'The Blue Hotel' it is less easy to decide. *The Red Badge of Courage* is much better than *Sevastopol*." (There is no critical scrutiny or even a redaction of *The Red Badge* here, nor in *Stephen Crane,* from which this essay derives.) Contends that Crane "owes nothing whatever, apparently, to painting." However, *see* Wells (1900), Kwiat (1952), Stallman, "Stephen Crane:" (1952), *Omnibus,* and *Crane*.

On the claim that Crane does not create types, the opposite standpoint is made by Hazlitt (1931).

Bradbury, Malcolm, and Arnold Goldman. "Stephen Crane: Classic at the Crossroads," *British Association for American Studies Bulletin,* n.s., 6 (June, 1963), pp. 42–49.

A review of *Stephen Crane: Letters* (1960) and of the World's Classics edition of *The Red Badge of Courage,* with an Introduction by V. S. Pritchett and a Note on the texts by R. W. Stallman (London, 1960).

"Vain, pushing, pretentious and unquestionably naive, Stephen Crane emerges from the collected letters as something less than one's idea of a literary genius. As Professor Stallman says in his introduction, the letters do give us 'a new perspective' on Crane. Artists are notoriously self-contradictory, Professor Stallman tells us; but there is something disturbing about the contradictoriness of these letters, where Crane says one thing to one friend and something very different to another, makes high claims for himself in one letter and low ones in the next. The letters, indeed, tempt the reader to make an overall hypothesis about them; they may have the variousness of the complicated mind that makes an interesting personality (Stallman's reading of the case) or they may be the letters of a man whose largest aim in life was to dramatize himself and to impress others. . . .

"'Never trust the artist. Trust the tale,' cries Professor Stallman at this point, reminding us that not all artists have been great or wise or even nice men. There is indeed a remarkable gap between Crane's observations about his work and the work itself. It is easy to be put off by the aesthetic theory which these letters adumbrate; he had all too plainly borrowed from Howells, Hamlin Garland and even Henry James, and he has not even digested his borrowings well. . . .

"In fact, all the pretensions to providing the moral or lesson are there in Crane's work, and one can't help but suspect that—as with Hemingway in *The Old Man and the Sea*—Crane hides his logic because the further out of sight it is, the more 'artistic' the story seems to be, and the more possible meanings can be projected into it. This is the point, surely, of Crane's hedging—he is a man seeking desperately to elevate what he has to offer into art. Far from being 'slices of life' Crane's stories often seem to be contrived in the worst sense of the word, that is, tricked out in a pretentious vocabulary and described with a considered abstractness in order that the reader can find what he cares to put in. Why else should characters always be 'the tall soldiers' or 'the Swede,' why else is Crane so generous with charged 'biblical' landscapes, why else does he grant so much weight to colours and extended similes—why else save to give his tales the charged quality of poetry, the hint of meaning that lies beyond meaning? The reason that the long logic is better kept out of sight is that it is discouraging for the reader to see, in fact, what it is; when he gives the game away, as he does in 'The Blue Hotel' (compare it with Hemingway's 'The Killers'). In Hemingway there is implied in the murder of the Swede a larger universe in which humanity learns from anguish something about the human condition; in Crane, where, likewise, all the characters are involved against their will in the murder of the Swede, the lesson offered is one not in responsibility but in causality), we see how slender this logic is, and how it is in fact a simple mechanistic account of the small man in the large universe.

"Yet in spite of all this, Crane has kept a high reputation; and *The Red Badge of Courage* has long been recognised as a classic—it is now an official *World's Classic.* There is a somewhat reserved introduction by V. S. Pritchett, in which he notes that Crane's feeling for 'life' is related to an anxiety about toughness and to the American approval of aggressiveness and to fighting as an initiation rite. This is a singularly good observation, for in a sense Crane is a primitive Hemingway. Not only is experience what life and literature are about; it is also what a man has to have. Crane's work is both about experience and about his own attitude toward it. That attitude, as we have said, is hedging; and the hedging is very much the substance of his tales. Thus Pritchett goes on to make an illuminating comparison between Tolstoy's and Crane's way of describing battles. Crane wanted his battle to be 'real'—he claimed to have got the experience for it on the football field—but in fact, says Pritchett, it is described at second hand from literature, and is presented in order to enact a drama of personal salvation:

> Wars do not occur for the purpose of providing moral tests. We would not gather from Crane's little masterpiece that he was describing a battle in a civil war. . . . where large, public moral issues profoundly affecting the growth and spirit of a nation were being decided. The war appears to be meaningless. We have no strong impression that the soldiers he describes are really civilians. The result is that the tale has length, very much in the manner of picaresque writing, but no depth—or at any rate no more than a bias towards privacy. His tale is a marvellous one for a very young man to have constructed out of nothing, but it remains a brilliant collection of impressions and surfaces. Perhaps he felt a romantic guilt in not having known the real thing. . . .

Its real interest, Pritchett says, lies in the fact that it is a tale about a man trying to find an identity by belonging to something. This is the logic behind the tale—a logic that is indeed long rather than deep. . . .

"It is this immersion in the destructive element which Stallman posits as the 'heroism' of Henry Fleming—'moments when he loses his soul in the flux of things.' [*Omnibus*, p. 199] 'Losing one's soul' is indeed the nature of the case, and the blind instinctual response is surely the ideal that Crane is holding up unconsciously to his readers. It is not in fact the final achievement of Henry Fleming; he then goes one step further—he bears the regimental banner. At this moment he is simultaneously 'doing' and 'knowing'; he is in the action, and able to observe at the same time, an actor and a thinker—and the cynosure to boot. Crane is careful to note that the colour in the flag which stands out is red—the flag is the ultimate 'red badge' and its bearer the real man of courage. By being the standard-bearer, Henry Fleming solves his dilemma."

Bridgewater, William, and Seymour Kurtz, eds. *Columbia Encyclopedia*, 3d ed. New York and London, 1963, p. 506.

Budd, Louis J., "Howells and Crane," in *American Literary Scholarship 1961*, ed. James L. Woodress. Durham, N.C., 1963, pp. 112–117.

Carpeaux, Otto Maria. *História da literatura ocidental*, 5. Rio de Janeiro, Brazil: Edições O Cruzeiro, 1963.

The poet of Naturalists, Crane employed the methods of Impressionism; hence his own valid recognition that his talent was not that of the novelist but that of the short story writer. (Annotation by Professor George Monteiro.)

Case, Richard G. " 'Great Bugs of Onondaga' invented by Crane / Famed Writing Style Gives him Away," *Syracuse Standard*, May 26, 1963. Photographs of Crane and two illustrations by Fred Heyman.

Labels Crane a hoaxer for his "Great Bugs in Onondaga," reprinted in *Courier* (March, 1963), by Lester G. Wells, who refrained from identifying Crane as the author and Ames W. Williams as the discoverer of Crane's hoax. Not noticed by Case is that Hoffman had identified Crane as the author and Williams as the discoverer in *Poetry*. The same omission occurs in John S.

Mayfield's edition of *Courier* (September, 1963): "Stephen Crane's Bugs." Here various Crane scholars argue for the identity of Crane as author of "Great Bugs in Onondaga," a point already made by Hoffman in 1957. *See* Williams (1962).

Chandler, George F. "I Knew Stephen Crane at Syracuse," *Courier* (Syracuse University Library), 3 (March, 1963), 12–13.

A letter prompted by Ames W. Williams' article in *Courier* (December, 1962) Mr. Chandler (aged 90) reports that Crane at Syracuse University "was not popular but I liked him. He always talked about how hard life was and how unfair it all seemed to him. He certainly was unusual and all along showed me that he intended to do as he pleased with his life, and would not be bossed by any one."

However, Crane ended his life by being bossed by the indomitable Cora Taylor, the tigress Nora in *Active Service* to Crane as the "mouse." (Cora in her 1897 journal wrote of Crane: "mouse ill.")

Delvaille, Bernard, trans. *L'hotel bleu.* Paris: Seghers, 1963.

Dillingham, William B. "Insensibility in *The Red Badge of Courage*," *College English*, 25 (December, 1963), 194–198.

"*The Red Badge* has frequently been read as the story of how a young soldier achieves some sort of spiritual salvation. One critic sees Henry Fleming's 'growth toward moral maturity' [Colvert (1959)]; another, his 'redemption' through 'humility and kindness.'* His initiation has been called the successful search for 'spiritual and psychological order,' the discovery of a 'vision of pattern' [Labor (1959)]. Some readings emphasize Henry's new sense of brotherhood and call the book the story of a young man's developing awareness of social responsibility [Hart (1953)]." Such views "tend to obscure the central irony of the novel, that of the nature of courage. . . . The chief purpose of the novel is to objectify the nature of heroism through Henry Fleming."

As Henry becomes more accustomed to battle, "He sinks into a subhuman dullness and is thereby able to act courageously. He does not learn to know himself, as one critic asserts [Friedman (1958)], but to escape himself—to make his mind blank, to become a 'spectator.' Otherwise, Henry remains essentially unchanged during the course of the novel. It is a mistake to think of him as having become rejuvenated through humility or in any way changed into a better person morally. . . . The Christian references, which have so frequently been a subject of controversy, do not point to 'rebirth' or 'salvation' for Henry. The pattern of religious imagery . . . is part of the pervasive irony of the book." (All critic-readers of *The Red Badge* are thus mistaken, but no one more so than Dillingham in his insensibility to the fact that many critics have long ago pointed out the pervasive irony of the book, an irony by which Henry's notion of rebirth and salvation is undercut again and again.)

Eby, Cecil D., Jr. "Stephen Crane's 'Fierce Red Wafer,'" *English Language Notes*, 1 (December, 1963), 128–130.

Eby notes that those critics who disagree with Stallman's interpretation of Crane's wafer-like sun "have not tried to explain Crane's use of the word

---

* Dillingham here footnotes Stallman's Introduction to the 1951 Modern Library *Red Badge of Courage*, without reference to his 1952 essay in Aldridge's *Critiques* and the 1952 *Omnibus*, wherein more emphasis is made of the double point of view, Crane's irony impinging upon Henry Fleming's thoughts of maturity.

fierce" in the earlier drafts of *The Red Badge of Courage* manuscript. Eby shows that red in Crane's *Active Service* suggests "some fiery or 'fierce' quality." But unfortunately Eby's dogmatic insistence that therefore there is nothing symbolic about it contributes little to the critical discussions of this "most controversial [metaphor] in American Literature."

Farlekas, Chris. "Stephen Crane of Port Jervis," *York State Tradition*, 17 (Summer, 1963), 11–14.

Contains a Crane poem beginning "On the ridge-top a dismal choir." Undoubtedly a fake. *See* Farlekas (1964).

Ferguson, S. C. "Crane's 'The Bride Comes to Yellow Sky,'" *Explicator*, 21 (March, 1963), item 59.

Corrects Barnes in *Explicator* (April, 1958), on the East-West conflict. In structure and tone Crane's story is "a spoof on the 'penny dreadful' literature of the school of Ned Buntline, whose delineations of the romantic, danger-ridden careers of Annie Oakley and Wyatt Earp and their kind titillated youngsters of Crane's generation."

Follett, Wilson, ed. *The Works of Stephen Crane.* New York: Russell and Russell, 1963. Reprints in six volumes the Knopf twelve-volume edition of 1925–1927.

Free, William J. "Smoke Imagery in *The Red Badge of Courage,*" *College Language Association Journal,* 7 (December, 1963), 148–152.

An extended footnote to a passage in *Omnibus,* p. 187: "Cleared atmospheres, unimpeded vision of perspective, are rarely delineated; and where they occur the precision of vision is equated, symbolically, with revelation or spiritual insight. . . . Dark mists and vapors represent the haze of Henry's unenlightened mind. . . . Darkness and smoke serve as symbols of concealment and deception, vapors masking the light of truth. Sunlight and changing colors signify spiritual insight and rebirth." No acknowledgement is made to *Omnibus* in Free's article.

Fryckstedt, Olov W. Introduction, *Stephen Crane: Uncollected Writings.* Uppsala: Uppsala University Press *(Acta Universitatis Upsaliensis),* 1963, Introduction, pp. xvii–lxvii. Note on the Text, pp. lxviii–lxxviii.
Reviewed:
   TLS, July 9, 1964, p. 588.
   Antioch Review (June, 1965).
   Maurice Bassan, *The Mad River Review,* 1, no. 2 (Spring-Summer, 1965), 85–90.

Gullason, Thomas A., ed. Preface and Introduction, *The Complete Short Stories and Sketches of Stephen Crane.* New York, 1963, pp. 1–45.

Gullason's title is misleading in that the *complete* short stories and sketches would comprise another forty pieces in the category of short stories and sketches. As to the difference between short story and sketch, Gullason is silent. As editor of *CSS&S,* Gullason might have marked the distinction of the one from the other.

Gullason's texts are also questionable in that the cited source is not the source of his text. His texts are the tampered texts of Follett's *Work.* But Gullason appends to each Crane story or sketch *the journal where it first appeared,* a citation indicating that the given Crane writing is here faithfully quoted from the cited source. For "The "Upturned Face" he cites *Ainslee's*

Magazine, but his text is not from *Ainslee's Magazine.* It is from *Work,* not from the original source as cited. Thus, Gullason's texts are spurious, as are his citations of source.

Reviewed:

Library Journal, 88 (December, 1963): "The stories taken as a whole might be thought to have diminished our respect for Crane, as many of them were written when he was a student and others as articles for newspapers; but, rather, the reverse takes place. Crane was an extremely competent writer and, on occasion, an inspired writer with a style as modern as Hemingway's."

Joseph Katz, *Antioch Review,* 25 (Summer, 1965), 337–341.

Mad River Review, 1, no. 2 (Spring-Summer, 1965).

Jean Cazemajou, *Études Anglaises,* 18, no. 2 (1965), 213–214: "*Au total, cet ouvrage rend accessible, sous un format commode, un grand nombre de récits dispersés dans des recueils de morceaux choisis, des magazines, des journaux, ou des collections de manuscrits, et toutes nos louanges vont au professeur Gullason pour la minutie de son travail de collation. Il est regrettable qu'aucun appareil critique (index ou notes paginales) n'accompagne les textes, mais l'introduction, riche et nuancée, donne sur l'auteur de ces nouvelles des vues personnelles qui fourniront au profane un guide précieux, et conduiront le spécialiste vers de fructueuses discussions.*"

Hudspeth, Robert N. "A Bibliography of Stephen Crane Scholarship: 1893–1962," *Thoth* (Syracuse University, English Graduate Group), 4 (Winter, 1963), 30–58.

Subsequent annual entries under Hudspeth: "The *Thoth* Annual Bibliography of Stephen Crane Scholarship." The bibliographical data are frequently unreliable, misleading, or in error; especially in the early *Thoth* issues. Not annotated.

Hungerford, Harold R. "That Was Chancellorsville: The Factual Framework of *The Red Badge of Courage,*" *American Literature,* 34 (January, 1963), 520–531.

However, collate with Pratt, "A Possible Source of *The Red Badge of Courage*" (1939). Pratt suggests that the battle is partly based on Antietam as does O'Donnell (1955).

Johnson, Bruce. "Joseph Conrad and Crane's *The Red Badge of Courage,*" *Papers of the Michigan Academy of Science, Arts, and Letters,* 48 (March, 1963), 649–655.

A shrewd survey of the charge by contemporary reviewers of Conrad's *The Nigger of the "Narcissus"* that Conrad had been influenced by Crane's *The Red Badge of Courage,* a charge to which Conrad reacted peevishly. The reviewers had touched a sore spot. In his Introduction to Beer's *SC,* Conrad coyly hinted that he had not encountered *The Red Badge* until after *The Nigger* was appearing in the *New Review* (1897) but Jessie Conrad says that Joseph began *The Nigger* in April, 1896,—four months after *The Red Badge* was published in England. Crane's influence is seen not only in *The Nigger,* but also in *Lord Jim*—as given in *Omnibus* and in *Letters.*

Johnson maintains that Conrad's Preface to *The Nigger* was a deliberate attempt by Conrad to claim for his own visual and moral Impressionism "an important depth missing in Crane." Conrad and Edward Garnett labeled Crane an Impressionist who dealt only with surfaces; in 1919, however, Conrad admitted that Crane "really went deeper than the surface."

The missing all in Bruce Johnson's article, which says nothing new to any scholar of Conrad and Crane, is that Johnson provides no evidence of the influence of Crane on Conrad in either *The Nigger* or *Lord Jim*.

Johnson, George W. "Stephen Crane's Metaphor of Decorum," *PMLA*, 78 (June, 1963), 250–256.

A brilliant essay on the contradictions in Crane. To Nellie Crouse, who wanted a "man of fashion," Crane proclaimed himself "a savage," "docile . . . only under great social pressure," "by inclination a wild shaggy barbarian." At the same time, however, "this rebel against middle class conventionality strove to remain a gentleman, gallant if only to street-walkers, chivalric to the déclassé, ministerial to reckless youth, and grandly hospitable at Brede Place to friend and stranger alike."

After *The Red Badge* "his imagination hardly moved at all. For there he had already discovered that the game of the strenuous life had no goal, that men were nothing without rules but that the rules killed them." Reprinted in Bassan (1967).

Kahn, Sy. "Stephen Crane and the Giant Voice in the Night: An Explication of 'The Monster,'" *Stetson Studies in the Humanities*, 1 (1963), 35–45. Also in *Essays in Modern Literature*, ed. Richard E. Langford. DeLand, Fla., 1963.

Koyama, Toshisaburo. "Stephen Crane no tokushitsu" [Some aspects of Stephen Crane], *Aoyama Gakuin Daigaku Eibungakkai Eibungaku Shicho*, 35 (December, 1962), 177–194 and 36 (December, 1963), 157–174.

On *Maggie* and Naturalism, the theme of resurrection in *The Red Badge of Courage*.

Levin, Harry. *Contexts of Criticism*. Cambridge, Mass., 1957. New York, 1963, pp. 61, 167, 192.

Lombardo, Agostino. Introduction, *Stephen Crane: romanzi brevie e racconti*. Milan, 1963.
Reviewed:
Enzo Golino, *Il Monde*, 11 (1964), 11.
Tommaso Pisanti, *Nuova Antologia* (1964).
Sergio Perosa, *Il Verri*, 10 (1964), 114–119.

Lyon, Peter. *Success Story: The Life and Times of S. S. McClure*. New York, 1963, pp. 129, 140, 156–157, 159.

Matsumoto, Tadashi. "Shi to shōsetsu no kōsa: S. Crane no baai" [The intersection of poetry and fiction: Stephen Crane's case], *Hosei Daigaku Kyoyo-bu Kenkyu Hōkoku*, no. 7 (March, 1963), 62–68.

Maxwell, D. E. S. *American Fiction: The Intellectual Background*. New York, 1963, pp. 294–299.

Mayfield, John S. "Stephen Crane's Bugs," *Courier* (Syracuse University Library), 3 (September, 1963), 22–31.

Further discussion about Crane's "Great Bugs in Onondaga," first presented in *Courier* (March, 1963), by Lester G. Wells. A note by Ames W. Williams, pp. 29–30, contains a statement indicating that he discovered this Crane literary hoax. See Case (1963). See Crane.

Mayfield, John S. [unsigned]. "Stephen Crane's Copy of *Maggie*," *Courier* (Syracuse University Library), 3 (December, 1963), 11–13.

A unique copy of the 1893 *Maggie* in that it bears twice Crane's signature.

He gave his signed copy to Charles J. Pike with an inscription dated May 10th, 1896. This copy was sold at auction on March 31, 1930, for $3,700.

Meyers, Robert. "Crane's 'The Open Boat,'" *Explicator*, 21 (April, 1963), item 60.

"Crane toys with inversions of Christian themes in his novel *The Red Badge of Courage* and in his short religious poems. But 'The Open Boat' may be read in such a way that mockery of traditional Christianity, although never explicit, is woven into almost every event."

Moers, Ellen. "Teddy Roosevelt: Literary Feller," *Columbia University Forum*, 6 (Summer, 1963), 10–16.

Important. On Jacob Riis, Crane, and Roosevelt, who wrote articles for the *Cosmopolitan* when Howells was editor in 1892. "But Roosevelt was alarmed by the increasing 'morbidity' of Howells' fiction, which he rightly associated with the novelist's move toward the political left. Howells had suffered, T. R. wrote his friend Brander Matthews at Columbia, by taking a 'jaundiced view of life. This is not an uncommon development of the reform spirit.' With even greater suspicion Roosevelt at first approached Howells' leading critical disciple, Hamlin Garland."

Crane sent Brander Matthews a copy of the 1893 *Maggie* with a note describing the novel as "a very small book which Mr. Hamlin Garland thinks will interest you." Matthews' *Vignettes of Manhattan* (1894) imitates or spoofs Crane's *Maggie* in "Before the Break of Day." The tenement girl named Maggie in Matthews' tale ends not as a prostitute, but as a loyal and heroic wife.

On Crane's relationship with Roosevelt in 1896 and briefly in Cuba (1898). In *Crane*.

Molitor, Lucienne, trans. *L'école du courage*. Paris: Seghers, 1963.

Monteiro, George. "Stephen Crane's 'The Bride Comes to Yellow Sky,'" in *Approaches to the Short Story*, ed. Neil Isaacs and Louis Leiter. San Francisco, 1963, pp. 221–238.

Morgan, H. Wayne. "Stephen Crane: The Ironic Hero" in *Writers in Transition: Seven Americans*. New York, 1963, pp. 1–23.

Bibliographical discussion of Crane appears on pp. 165–166.

Nelson, Harlan D. "Stephen Crane's Achievement as a Poet," *Texas Studies in Literature and Language*, 4 (Winter, 1963), 564–582.

The poems which Nelson regards as Crane's best are, in form, the bare unadorned parables that Hoffman in *Poetry* (1957) "thinks are his slightest achievements. Hoffman values most highly the symbolistic poems, and of them the more formally developed ones, as I have said: overvalues them, I think. . . ." The anthologists of verse have done Crane pretty well; Crane's talent was for slighter things. The poems of complex organization generally result in poorer poems; among these is "The Blue Battalions," which Hoffman thinks is among Crane's best. Nelson shows why it isn't. Not only is Hoffman mistaken about the kind of poem that Crane did best, but also he has not "quite grasped the full significance for Crane's poetry of his religious background." Nelson contends that Crane's best poems are those in which "by some technique of restraint and indirection" Crane embodied his most deeply felt beliefs: "certain convictions and attitudes that he derived from his religious tradition. . . .

"Crane made his poetry out of his losses; and in his poetry, too, he needed a mask. When he wrote without one—without some sort of technical restraint —his hurts showed in extravagances of defiance or bathos. But when he could employ such a device in conjunction with the beliefs that he had salvaged from his tradition, Crane was in a position to do his best work." Nelson's essay is among the very best studies of Crane's poetry.

Peterson, Clell T. [Reply to Robert L. Hough's "Crane on Herons"], *Notes and Queries*, 10 (January, 1963), 29.

Hough, "Crane on Herons" (1962) correctly identifies Crane's heron in "The Blue Hotel" as the Little Blue Heron. But he asserts that (1) the legs of the immature Little Blue Heron are light blue and that (2) "the adult of no species of heron has light blue legs." For confirmation of (1) he refers to Audubon's picture of a Little Blue Heron in *Birds of America*. But Audubon's picture is grossly inaccurate. As for (2), the legs of the adult Little Blue Heron, as shown in Thomas Gilliard's *Living Birds of the World* (1958), are of "precisely the shade of light blue that I have always supposed the Blue Hotel to be painted." So, then, Stephen Crane, "for the honour of cranes and herons, was accurate in his observations." He cannot be impugned as bird-watcher!

Pritchett, V. S. "American Soldiers," *New Statesman*, 65 (February 8, 1963), 207.

On James Jones's *The Thin Red Line* and Crane and Hemingway, masters of the battle piece.

Randel, William. "Stephen Crane's Jacksonville," *South Atlantic Quarterly*, 62 (Spring, 1963), 268–274.

Some new data about the night-life in Jacksonville during Crane's four months there; for other data no acknowledgement is made to *Letters* or to *Cora Crane*.

Schroeder, Fred. "America's First Literary Realist: Horatio Alger, Junior," *Western Humanities Review*, 17 (Spring, 1963), 129–137.

Alger foreshadows, among others, Crane.

Schwab, Arnold T. *James Gibbons Huneker*. Stanford, Calif., 1963, pp. 114–117, 180, 209.

Smillie, C. M. Letter to Miss Mary Benjamin, February 15, 1963. A typed letter on stationery of Mrs. Frederick B. Smillie in the BCC.

On Lily Brandon Munroe; important. Also important is Ames W. Williams' interview with Mrs. Frederick B. Smillie, the former Lily Brandon Munroe. This interview is not in the Ames W. Williams papers at Syracuse University Library; a copy is in the files of R. W. S.

C. M. Smillie claims that Corwin Linson made a sketch of Lily that he never finished; but it was David Ericson who never completed the sketch he made of Lily, a painting.

Spiller, Robert E., Willard Thorp, Thomas H. Johnson, and Henry Seidel Canby, eds. *Literary History of the United States*, 3d. ed., rev. New York and London, 1963, pp. 458–461. *Bibliography Supplement*, ed. Richard M. Ludwig, 1963, pp. 100–102. (A very selective listing.)

Stallman, R. W. "Stephen Crane as Dramatist," *Bulletin of the New York Public Library*, 67 (October, 1963), 495–511.

Presents here for the first time "Drama in Cuba," pp. 498–511, from the typescript in CUCC. A play in two acts, not completed.

Reprinted in *War Dispatches,* pp. 318–334.

"Successful as novelist and short-story writer and as journalist, Crane from the start hankered to achieve also a name for himself as dramatist; and from the start he cast some pieces in dramatic dialogue-form. . . ." Nothing by Crane got onto the stage except *The Ghost.*

"Lillian Gish, it was once announced in the papers, proposed to appear in the film version of *Maggie: A Girl of the Streets,* but Alfred Knopf squashed the project. Thomas Beer, writing to Miss Edith Crane (Stephen's niece) on 2 January 1923, said that Mr. Knopf 'has moved to prevent any such catastrophe without Mr. William Crane's consent and the necessary contracts. If Miss Gish would provide a suitable and honest version of the story, it might not be a bad thing, but you doubtless have observed what happens to good literature when it falls among thieves and movies belong in the same category.' (William was Judge Crane of Port Jervis, New York; Stephen's oldest brother.) The Crane family considered *Maggie* improper, 'not nice.' In 1951 when Gottfried Reinhardt (Max Reinhardt's son) produced *The Red Badge of Courage,* directed by John Huston, Crane finally got onto the screen. And in November 1962 Crane's *Red Badge* was produced on TV in a reading by Ben Gazzara (synchronized with Brady photographs of the Civil War) and introduced by Rabbi Eisendrath's brief interview with R. W. Stallman concerning *The Red Badge* in a program entitled 'Legacy of Light' (produced by Westinghouse Broadcasting Company)."

———. "New Short Fiction by Stephen Crane: I, 'Dan Emmonds,' " *Studies in Short Fiction,* 1, no. 1 (Fall, 1963), 1–7.

Reproduces here "Dan Emmonds" from the typescript in CUCC. Reproduced also at the same time—in *CSS&S* (1963).

A Crane voyage fantasy in imitation of Defoe, Crane called it "a satirical sketch of mine—an old thing, strong in satire but rather easy writing." Gilkes, "Stephen Crane's 'Dan Emmonds' " (1964) and Stallman, "Was Crane's Sketch . . . a Journalistic Hoax? A reply to Gilkes" (1964) debate the problem as to whether "Dan Emmonds" was an early or late Crane writing. Again in Gilkes, "No Hoax" (1964). Colvert, Introduction to *Maggie* (1969) agrees with Stallman that "Dan Emmonds" was an early writing. Of course, it might have been later recast from that "old thing." See *Crane* (1968), pp. 537–539, on "Dan Emmonds." *See also* Monteiro, "The *Illustrated* American" (1969).

Stone, Edward. "Crane and Zola," *English Language Notes,* 1 (September, 1963), 46–47.

Confirms Berryman's belief that Crane was influenced by *L'Assommoir* (in translation), in *The Red Badge.* Henry Fleming trudges "from the place of blood and wrath," and "his soul changed. He came from *hot plowshares* to prospects of clover tranquilly, and it was as if *hot plowshares* were not." In *L'Assommoir* Gervaise's alcoholic husband dances "as if on *burning* plowshares."

Other correspondences are between Jim Conklin's death-dance and Coupeau's *Totentanz.* "Not only does a close study of the Zola alcoholic's strenuous final fit in Chapter XIII at last disclose a model for the hitherto unexplained and apparently gratuitous horror of Jim's throes in Chapter IX of *The Red Badge,* but even the details seem to match in several places. . . .

"It may also be true that, as Professor Robert W. Stallman maintains,* the dying soldier is meant to suggest Christ, with his resemblance, as Jim strides toward his death site, 'to a devotee of a mad religion.' We may suppose that it would not have struck Crane as irreverent to use as a model for the final act of his Passion play the last rites of the mad religion of drink as he had seen them described in the padded cell of the Asylum of Saint-Anne.'"

Stronks, James B. "Stephen Crane's English Years: The Legend Corrected," *Papers of the Bibliographical Society of America,* 57 (Third Quarter, 1963), 340–349.

Reassesses the rate of pay Crane earned per one thousand words; a useful study. Stronks does not mention Thomas Beer's article in the *New York Evening Post Literary Review,* July 19, 1924, correcting Ford Madox Ford's statement in that same journal, June 12, 1924, that Crane earned £20 per thousand words. *See also Letters* and *Crane.*

Wells, Lester G. "The Iron Monster, the Crackling Insects of Onondaga County, and Stephen Crane," *Courier* (Syracuse University Library), 3, no. 1 (March, 1963), 1–7.

Presents a newly discovered Crane sketch, unsigned in *New York Tribune,* June 1, 1891. It is Crane's literary hoax, "Great Bugs in Onondaga." Also, here is the *Tribune's* editorial on that sketch, an editorial undoubtedly written by Willis Fletcher Johnson. In *Tribune,* June 2, 1891.

Quotes appraisals by Olov Fryckstedt, Edwin Cady, and Walter Sutton as judges of whether this unsigned sketch is by Crane. The Sutton letter of appraisal cites images of insects and arc light in "The Monster" (1898) which echo Crane's Great Bugs sketch.

Cranes "Great Bugs in Onondaga" is reprinted in Fryckstedt's *UW* without acknowledgement to the discoverer of that sketch. However, Lester G. Wells failed to say who discovered it. Nor did John Mayfield, editor of *Courier,* say who discovered it. It was reprinted in *NYCS,* appearing there as the coda to Stallman's Introduction, and again without acknowledgement to the discoverer of Crane's hoax. Stallman's footnote disappeared in the galley. And the printer's error has it June 18 instead of June 1, 1891, for the *New York Tribune.*

However, the identity of the discoverer was made known by Daniel G. Hoffman in *The Poetry of Stephen Crane* (1957), a point not noticed by Gilkes in "Some Omissions," *Saturday Review,* August 31, 1968. The discoverer was Ames W. Williams. In "Stephen Crane's Bugs," *Courier,* September, 1963, Ames W. Williams hints that he discovered Crane's sketch; but he does not flatly say so. *Contra* Gilkes (1968), Williams was author of a portion of that *Courier* article and Stallman's *Crane* (1968) rightly credits Williams.

On Crane's "Great Bugs in Onondaga" *see also* Case (1963).

Westbrook, Max. "Stephen Crane's Poetry: Perspective and Arrogance," *Bucknell Review,* 11 (December, 1963), 24–34.

"Crane's readers, however, have failed to distinguish two quite different

---

* Introduction, *The Red Badge of Courage,* The Modern Library (1951), xxxiii–xxxiv.

voices in the poems. The voice of perspective, with reasonable consistency, is affirmed; the voice of arrogance, without exception, is mocked. Behind both voices lies a single and coherent standard of values. . . . Failure to distinguish the two voices has led critics to impose a preconceived theology on Crane's poems, to assume that if God is indifferent then man's pursuit of truth must be without purpose, and the God who 'whispers in the heart' must be a comfort merely, not a reality. In Crane's poetic world, however, there are two Gods." One is the Old Testament God, and the other is the god of internal conscience.

See Berryman's *Crane*, p. 114; Gillis (1954); *Poetry* (1957); Nelson (1963); and Wertheim (1964).

Williams, Ames W. "Stephen Crane's Bugs," *Courier* (Syracuse University Library), 3, no. 3 (September, 1963), 22–31. Part 2 of *Courier* article (March, 1963): "The Iron Monster," by Lester G. Wells. (Crane's unsigned *Tribune* sketch was discovered by Ames W. Williams.)

Crane's "Great Bugs in Onondaga," in the *Tribune*, June 1, 1891, was followed by Johnson's editorial on June 2. The *Syracuse Standard* on June 1 quoted part of Crane's sketch under the title: "Huge Electric Light Bugs" and commented on it. That same day, June 2, the *Syracuse Daily Journal* reproduced Johnson's *Tribune* editorial under the title "The Syracuse Bugs / New York Tribune." Crane's journalistic hoax was commented on by Richard G. Case in the *Syracuse Standard*, May 26, 1963, under the heading: " 'Great Bugs of Onondaga' Invented by Crane / Famed Writing Style Gives Him Away."

The likely source inspiring Crane's sketch was an article in the *Syracuse Sunday Herald*, May 24, 1891: "Caterpillars Delay Trains." The editor of the *Courier*, John Mayfield, quotes the reference to locusts in *The Revelation of St. John the Divine*, and suggests that Crane was familiar with these biblical bugs, locusts as big as horses, with breastplates of iron, "and the sound of their wings was as the sound of chariots of many horses running to battle."

1964

Anderson, Warren D. "Homer and Stephen Crane," *Nineteenth-Century Fiction*, 19 (June, 1964), 77–86.
On Homeric hints in *The Red Badge of Courage*.

[Anon.]. "Kinds of Courage and Realism," *London Times Literary Supplement*, July 9, 1964, p. 588.
Review-essay prompted by *Stephen Crane: Uncollected Writings*, ed. Olov W. Fryckstedt (1963).
On Crane as a journalist. His war dispatches from Greece "show how accurate he had been in his anticipation of the actual effects and scenes of war." On Willa Cather's remark that Crane "was one of the first post-impressionists; that he began it before the French painters began it, or at least as early as the first." "*Maggie* and *George's Mother,* and the related stories and sketches, are certainly realistic in the sense of both confronting the harsh realities of society and describing them factually; but rather than the realism of Zola, Crane's is

more the realism of the Salvation Army. . . . Crane describes the setting of these stories adequately, but his concern is with individuals rather than with the scene itself or social classes."

The forms assumed by the challenge confronting Crane's heroes are various. "The tides in 'The Open Boat,' which will not allow the survivors from the shipwreck to come easily ashore . . . are the readiest illustration of the challenge in nature. That such natural obstructions are to be understood symbolically is made plain in a remarkable sketch, 'The Mesmeric Mountain.' The 'little man' sets off down the forest track, in spite of his friends having told him that it leads only to Jim Boyd's. When the mountain attacks him, he counterattacks and desperately gains the top, only to find the world unchanged beneath him. . . . Or the challenge can assume a human shape: a pugnacious schoolboy in the *Whilomville Stories;* a gunman run berserk in such a tale as 'The Bride Comes to Yellow Sky.' But in its most serious form the challenge is embodied in the hero. The entire theme of *The Red Badge of Courage* is Henry Fleming's attempt to reckon with his cowardice under the inexorable circumstances of battle. While the challenge is being presented, all that is malignant in nature seems to combine intently upon the predestined victim, but at the moment of inevitable destruction, the tension may inexplicably relax and life return to its ordinary calm appearance. . . . The trial by ordeal is finished; the customary once more takes command—until the next time."

[Anon.], trans. *Das blaue Hotel: Erzählungen.* Cologne and Olten, Germany, 1964.

Contains translations into the German of "The Blue Hotel" (the title work), "The Bride Comes to Yellow Sky," *The Red Badge of Courage,* and "The Open Boat."

Askew, Melvin. "Psychoanalysis and Literary Criticism," *Psychoanalytic Review,* 51 (Summer, 1964), 43–50.

On "The Blue Hotel," a story about paranoia; but from Askew's standpoint a story *because* of paranoia.

Bassan, Maurice. "A Bibliographical Study of Stephen Crane's Poem, 'In the Night,'" *Papers of the Bibliographical Society of America,* 63 (Second Quarter, 1964), 173–179.

"Are Stephen Crane's poems worthy of critical attention? A brilliant case for the affirmative is offered by Daniel G. Hoffman *(The Poetry of Stephen Crane,* 1957); on the other hand, Roy Harvey Pearce, in the course of attempting to define our major poetic traditions *(The Continuity of American Poetry,* 1961), neatly damns Crane by omission."

However, all this has nothing to do with Bassan's attempt here "to arrive at the best text of one of Crane's most carefully structured poems, 'In the Night,' and to suggest implicitly along the way some of the pitfalls which may lie in the path of future editors and commentators on Crane's 'lines.'"

———. "Crane, Townsend, and Realism of a Good Kind," *Proceedings of the New Jersey Historical Society,* 82 (April, 1964), 128–135.

Townsend and Crane at the Lantern Club; *A Daughter of the Tenements* (1895), and *Maggie.*

———. "The Design of Stephen Crane's Bowery Experiment," *Studies in Short Fiction,* 1 (Winter, 1964), 129–132.

On the fusion of structure and imagery in "An Experiment in Misery."
Reprinted in Bassan, *Stephen Crane* (1967), pp. 118–122.

Budd, Louis J. "Stephen Crane," in *American Literary Scholarship 1962*, ed. James L. Woodress. Durham, N.C., 1964, pp. 117–119.
N.C., 1964, pp. 117–119.

"The only mark of academic prestige now lacking for Crane is a newsletter. Under the editing of Robert N. Hudspeth, the second installment for an annual bibliography of Crane scholarship *(Thoth, V, 85–87)* has appeared. A leader in the search for rare items, Robert W. Stallman has printed three interesting sketches as 'New Short Fiction by Stephen Crane' *(SSF, I, 1–7, 147–152);* biographical commentary on one of these sketches, by Lillian B. Gilkes, 'Stephen Crane's "Dan Emmonds": A Pig in a Storm' *(SSF, II, 66–71),* elicited a stinging rejoinder by Stallman ('Was Crane's Sketch of the Fleet Off Crete a Journalistic Hoax?' *(SSF, II, 72–76)* and a softer reply ('No Hoax: A Reply to Mr. Stallman,' *(SSF, II, 77–83).* With E. R. Hagemann, Stallman has also edited *The War Dispatches of Stephen Crane* (New York, New York Univ. Press), which brings together scarce and unknown items and fresh background materials, mostly to his clear credit as both a human being and a writer."

Cazemajou, Jean. "Stephen Crane et ses esquisses de vie newyorkaise," *Caliban* [*Annales de la Faculté des Lettres de Toulouse*], no. 1 (January, 1964), 7–24.

Concise Dictionary of American Biography. New York, 1964, pp. 198–199.

Crews, Frederick. Introduction and Annotation, *The Red Badge of Courage.* Indianapolis, New York, and Kansas City, 1964, pp. vii–xxiii. With battle maps of Chancellorsville.

Briefly discusses *The Red Badge* as an account of the battle of Chancellorsville and, under Some Critical Considerations, he questions: "Does Henry Fleming 'develop' in the course of the novel? Different answers to this question have led critics to see the book variously as a tale of growing courage and maturity, a study of Christian virtue, and a denunciation of all the uses of war. Most readers would agree that there is development of *some* sort in Henry's character. . . . Crane's ironic handling of Henry's ego becomes not less but more pronounced in the closing sentences of the novel. The tone there becomes idyllic—much too idyllic to be taken seriously—as Henry begins to turn from 'the red sickness of battle' to delusive 'images of tranquil skies, fresh meadows, cool brooks—an existence of soft and eternal peace.' Surely this is blatant irony, and the irony is directed precisely at Henry's capacity for forgetting the conditions under which his courage has been forced upon him. Crane, unlike Henry, keeps his focus on the capricious fate that has permitted Henry's existence to be prolonged thus far."

Crews says that *Omnibus* develops the same allegorical reading given in Stallman's 1951 edition of *The Red Badge,* "but the same evidence now yields an opposite conclusion: Henry 'has undergone no change, no real spiritual development.'" However, this seemingly contradictory reading is obtained by ignoring the stated references in *Omnibus* to Crane's ironic rendering of Henry's *presumed* moral development or spiritual triumph. It is his illusion, but not Crane's. *Omnibus,* p. 222: "Crane's ironic method presents the mocked hero as 'a-blaze with desire to change. He saw himself a sun-lit figure upon a peak, pointing with true and unchangeable gesture.' . . . His self-contradiction is summed up in this single turnabout."

There is, then, no contradiction between Stallman's standpoint in *Omnibus* and that in his 1951 Modern Library Introduction. Here (p. xxiv) the ending of the novel is likewise viewed as ironic. "This sun-through-rain image, which epitomizes the double-mood pattern dominating every tableau in the whole sequence, is a symbol of Henry Fleming's moral triumph *and is an ironic commentary upon it.* Crane is a master of the contradictory effect." Crews's "blatant irony" is a variant echo of that same point.

The Selected Bibliography's annotations are slanted in favor of the editor's own literal-minded reading of *The Red Badge,* squaring with Rahv's anti-symbolic-and-religious interpretations. (For Rahv *The Red Badge* "is actually 'about' what it seems to be, war and its impact on human beings moved by pride, bravado, fear, anxiety and sudden panic.") Not mentioned is Stallman, "Fiction and Its Critics:" a reply to Rahv (1957), or Hoffman, Introduction, *The Red Badge of Courage* (1957) which buttresses and extends the symbolic-religious interpretation. Crews's annotations for James Colvert and Isaac Rosenfeld silently ignore their support of that same reading. The Selected Bibliography, by claiming to list "only the most prominent or controversial treatments of *The Red Badge* in English," contradicts itself by including works which contain no scrutiny of the novel, no discussion of it other than its contemporary reception, namely Beer's *SC* and Berryman's *Crane.* Berryman discussed *The Red Badge* not in his Crane Biography. but only in his short essay contributed to Stegner's *The American Novel* (1965). On the usefulness of *The Red Badge* MSS. *see* Bradley (1962).

Current-García. Eugene and Walton R. Patrick, eds. *American Short Stories.* Chicago, 1964, pp. 319–320.

Reprints "A Mystery of Heroism" and "The Bride Comes to Yellow Sky." Errs in the notion that Crane lived 29 years and that he spent "a year of college training at Lafayette College and a second year at Syracuse University"!

Detweiler, Robert. "Christ and the Christ Figure in American Fiction," *Christian Scholar,* 47 (Summer, 1964), 117–122.

A detailed discussion of the Christ figure in American fiction. Artist can work with Christ figure as sign, myth, symbol, or allegory. Indicates that Jim Conklin was one of the earliest Christ symbols in American fiction. Henry learns three important lessons from Conklin's death: (1) a vicarious experience of the horror of death; (2) ritual aspect of Jim's death; (3) Jim's courage. However, it would be going too far to suggest that Conklin is the instrument of Henry's salvation. "Crane's Christ symbol acts as the vehicle for introducing a pivotal point in the novel." Like Christ he interprets death, thereby helping the protagonist to save himself. Detweiler's treatment of the various aspects of the Christ figure in American fiction seems both more detailed and substantial than most discussions of the same subject.

Detweiler, seemingly unaware that the topic of Conklin as a Christ figure has occupied Crane scholarship and criticism since 1951, mentions no critic whatsoever.

———. "Christ in American Religious Fiction," *Journal of Bible and Religion,* 32 (January, 1964), 8–14.

Dillingham, William B. " 'The Blue Hotel' and the Gentle Reader," *Studies in Short Fiction,* 1 (Spring, 1964), 224–226.

Dirlam, H. Kenneth, and Ernest E. Simmons. *Sinners, This Is East Aurora: The Story of Elbert Hubbard and the Roycroft Shops.* New York, Washington, and Hollywood, 1964.

On Crane at the banquet honoring him as guest of the Society of the Philistines in Buffalo on December 19, 1895. *See also* Bragdon (1929), Berryman's *Crane*, pp. 90, 124, *Letters*, and *Crane*. However, for new data recently brought to light (by Austin Fox) *see* Daly (1916). On Philistines' Dinner *see* Dirlam, pp. 24–29.

Eble, Kenneth. Introduction, *The Awakening*, by Kate Chopin. New York, 1964, p. xi.

"Only Stephen Crane, among her contemporaries, had an equal sensitivity to light and shadow, color and texture, had the painter's eye matched with the writer's description of character and incident."

Ellison, Ralph. "Stephen Crane and the Mainstream of American Fiction," in *Shadow and Act*. New York, 1964, pp. 74–78. London, 1967, pp. 60–76. Reprinted from his Introduction to *The Red Badge of Courage and Four Great Stories* (1960).

Encyclopedia Americana, vol. 8. New York, 1964, p. 155.

Errs in saying that *Maggie* was published in 1892. Nothing here on Cora, nor on Crane's burial place. The checklist ends at 1950 with Berryman's *Crane*.

Farlekas, Chris [unsigned]. "The Day Between," *Times Herald Record* (Middletown, N.Y.), March 28, 1964, p. 11.

Here is a "new" Crane poem—"The Day Between," a poem discovered by Frederick Mears "among the papers of Crane's niece" last summer. However, in my opinion, "The Day Between" is *not* a new Crane poem but a literary fabrication in the echoed style of T. S. Eliot. By Mears or by poet Farlekas?

Wander sometime through the wild, shocked streets,
Clear with cold when death
Drains the umber blood of sunsets
Into gutters, numb and crisply still
The light flakes like old plaster
And dark is windowed
His stark cry to forgive them
For they know not what they do,
Is reduced to the winds moaning
Wander the pallid swindle of the sidewalk
By windows reflecting flocked skies,
By tinkling women insisting
By tumbling boys crushing egg-shelled puddles
Or scribbling arabesques on the asphalt
With their wheeled feet
Cities are only sepulchures
We are the fault of eden,
It is the day between and we shrivel
The lean crosses relieved of their burdens,
Drape the wind in scalloped assembly
And the skull is scraped bitter
Yesterday we watched the swarming storm
The sleeping, oil storm that came sniffing the winter city
Smothering the frowzy sky for our noon darkness
Now our flesh shudders horse-like
Beneath the touch of our lovers
Our teeth are besequined
And we bicker with passion
And our ears are hidden
The day between is settling on the city like sin.

Farlekas, Chris. "Port Marks Stephen Crane Day," *Times Herald Record* (Middletown, N.Y.), July 5, 1964. Photographs of William Crane's house on East Main Street in Port Jervis.

On Mayor Cole's proclamation that June 5 is Stephen Crane Day "to commemorate the anniversary of the death of one of America's great writers." Mentions Stallman's visit in Hartwood with the Dimock brothers, 1964.

Fitelson, David. "Stephen Crane's *Maggie* and Darwinism," *American Quarterly,* 16 (1964), 182–194.

Fuchs, Daniel. "Ernest Hemingway, Literary Critic," *American Literature,* 36 (1964–1965), 431–451.

Like Crane, Hemingway burlesqued heroic rhetoric, story-book endings. and chivalric displays.

Gibson, Donald B. " 'The Blue Hotel' and the Idea of Human Courage," *Texas Studies in Language and Literature,* 6 (Autumn, 1964), 388–397.

A finely reasoned rereading. Some critics see the central theme to be the brotherhood of man; others see the tale as meaning that we are determined creatures. By the former theme we are all responsible to and for each other; by the latter, no one is then responsible; these two possibilities are antithetical. The best support of either position is to be found in the conclusion. The conclusion is not tacked on, as some critics have contended. Prior to the last section "there is little to suggest determinism, or that 'men's wills do not control their destinies!' " (Gibson here corrects Walcutt [1956].) Greenfield (1958) makes "an entirely erroneous reading of the last section. . . . There is no reason to suspect that the Easterner interprets the preceding events wrongly."

However, Crane errs in the execution of the reader's sympathies by his bias against the Swede.

Gibson relates the Swede's problem to that of the little man in the Sullivan County tales, to George in *George's Mother,* and to Fleming in *The Red Badge of Courage;* to Maggie on the one hand, and on the other hand to "The Open Boat" with its theme of brotherhood. Gibson's essay is among the very best on "The Blue Hotel."

Gilkes, Lillian. "Stephen Crane's 'Dan Emmonds': A Pig in a Storm," *Studies in Short Fiction,* 2 (Fall, 1964), 66–71.

Agrees with Stallman's notes on "Dan Emmonds," first published in vol. 1, no. 1, of *SinSF* (Fall, 1963), that it is a "Crane voyage fantasy in imitation of Defoe," but disagrees that it is early. Cora's near shipwreck on her Black Sea voyage "when she and Stephen narrowly missed drowning, enroute to Constantinople and the Greek war," is copied in Crane's Crusoe-tale; therefore "Dan Emmonds" must be a late writing.

However, even if it were a late writing, it does not prove that Crane experienced that near shipwreck with Cora. There is no evidence in Cora's journal or diary that Crane was with her, and he himself declared that he was going to Greece by way of Crete. *See* Stallman's rejoinder in this same issue of *SinSF:* "Was Crane's Sketch of the Fleet Off Crete a Journalistic Hoax? A Reply to Miss Gilkes." And Gilkes' reply, pp. 77–83. *See* Randel (1965).

———. "No Hoax: A Reply to Mr. Stallman," *Studies in Short Fiction,* 2 (Fall, 1964), 77–83.

Here Gilkes reverses her standpoint in *Cora Crane* (1960) by declaring that Crane's "Pen Picture of the Powers' Fleet Off Crete" was not the hoax she claimed it was in *Cora Crane,* p. 91. "But it is also quite possible that he may have faked the Cretan dispatch." Also, on p. 91 of *Cora Crane* she says that Crane "had obviously not been near Marseilles." She thus impugns Crane's integrity as a journalist. Again, p. 91, Gilkes says: 'Moreover, it appears from the wording of the dispatch that, *if he was on it at all,* he remained aboard ship for the *Guadiana*'s return trip to Athens without even going ashore." Gilkes' *Cora Crane* account of Crane and Cora in getting to Greece is the most mixed-up speculation ever written by *any* biographer; notably pp. 81–83, 91.

In spite of that standpoint, Gilkes, who had thus impugned Crane's integrity as journalist, now claims "No Hoax," dismissing her *Cora Crane* charges. In Gilkes' "Stephen and Cora Crane," *American Literature* (1969) she again reverses herself by claiming that Crane and Cora got to Crete from Athens, in which case Crane fabricated his Cretan dispatch. It is once more a hoax. Stallman replies in "How Stephen Crane Got to Crete," *American Literature* (1972).

Not known to Gilkes is the London Letter in the *Critic* (London), 27 (April 17, 1897), reporting that Mr. Stephen Crane flitted through London "this week on his way to the scene of the insurrections in Crete. . . ." Since Crane went directly to Crete, he was not—*contra* Gilkes—with Cora on the overland route to Constantinople.

In Stallman's rejoinder in *SinSF* (1964) he contends that Crane got to Crete from Marseilles aboard the *Guadiana* en route to Athens and that Cora and Mathilde got to Greece by the overland route. "The conclusive proof that Crane was not with Cora is that he figures not at all in Cora's written account of her journey to Constantinople. It is impossible for Miss Gilkes to substantiate her theory because nowhere in Cora Crane's loose-leaf sheets, notebook or so-called diary, does she mention Stephen by name. Later at Volo she alludes to him as 'mouse ill.'" In *Cora Crane,* p. 96, Gilkes says that Cora and Crane breakfasted at Volo with "a French officer they had met at a wayside station," but she cleverly omits to quote what Cora says in her journal; namely that the French officer was from the *Guadiana.* That being so, they breakfasted with him because Crane had met him aboard the *Guadiana* sailing from Marseilles. In his Cretan dispatch Crane mentions a French lieutenant. But for Gilkes to mention him would damage her theory; namely that Crane did not get to Crete from Marseilles.

Miss Gilkes' scholarship is impugned again by the fact that she misreads several times what's what in Cora's journal. "Many are the stories told by the guides—we have one who is a character. *Steve* named him Alabasta Serbastopoli." *That* puts Steve in Constantinople—until one reads precisely what Cora wrote: "*Have* named him Alabasta Serbastopoli." Gilkes misquotes Cora's journal in *Cora Crane,* p. 82. In "No Hoax," *SinSF,* pp. 78–79, she says, "I am perhaps in error in my earlier reading, 'Steve.' But as Cora's handwriting admits of some doubt, reproduction here given [in facsimile of Cora's prose] must decide the question." There can be no question, however, since Roland Baughman, then Head of Special Collections at Columbia University Libraries, confirmed my reading of "Have," instead of "Steve." Four letters instead of five!

Gilkes desperately wants it known that Crane was with Cora all the way to Greece so as to slant the importance of Cora's relationship with Crane, her theory being that it was a "second honeymoon"—although Cora did not share the cabin on the *Danae* with "S," whom Gilkes designates as Stephen. What kind of a "honeymoon" was *that?* Well, Gilkes can unriddle any problem so as to substantiate her fixed idea. "That he did not occupy the cabin with Cora is, in my judgment, pretty nearly conclusive indication that he *was* there.

For with another correspondent in the party bound for Athens, Sylvester Scovel, *to advertise his intimacy with Cora* by sharing a room with her is exactly what the thin-skinned Crane, dreading gossip, would *not* have done. Especially not after Davis's coldshouldering [of Cora] on the dock at Dover!" What a perversion of the evidence! Crane was there, in effect, because he wasn't in Cora's cabin; she shared Sylvester Scovel's cabin. However, Gilkes' identification of the "S.S." in Cora's journal as Sylvester Scovel is erroneous, as we discover from Randel's article "From Slate to Emerald Green," *American Literature* (1965); Gilkes' "S. S." was then in Missouri. And Crane, by my account, was en route to Crete and Athens on the *Guadiana* from Marseilles. *See Crane,* chap. 16 and pp. 537–539; and Gilkes (1969), and Stallman (1972).

Gullason, Thomas A. "The Short Story: An Underrated Art," *Studies in Short Fiction,* 2 (Fall, 1964), 15–17.
   "At present there are two biographies of Crane, and at least two new ones are in the making."

Hemingway, Ernest. *A Moveable Feast.* New York, 1964, p. 133. Moscow, 1965.

Hague, John A., ed. *American Character and Culture: Some Twentieth Century Perspectives.* DeLand, Fla., 1964, pp. 86, 87.

Hoffman, Hester, ed. *The Reader's Adviser and Bookman's Manual,* 10th ed. New York, 1964.

Hohenberg, John. *Foreign Correspondence: The Great Reporters and Their Times.* New York, 1964, pp. 134, 135, 137, 283.

Hudspeth, Robert N. "The *Thoth* Annual Bibliography of Stephen Crane Scholarship," *Thoth,* 5 (Spring, 1964), 85–87.

Huffman, Grant, ed. *Six Scripts for Three Media: Television, Movies, Theatre.* Toronto and Montreal, 1964, pp. 181–195.
   Reprints "The Bride Comes to Yellow Sky."

Itabashi, Yoshie. "Shizenshugi bungaku to gikō—Stephen Crane no baai" [Naturalistic literature and its technique—in the case of Stephen Crane], *Amerika Bungaku,* no. 3 (Septmeber, 1964), 6–14.

Katz, Joseph. "Some Light on the Stephen Crane–Amy Leslie Affair," *Mad River Review,* 1 (Winter, 1964–1965), 43–62.
   New background information on Amy Leslie.

———. "Cora Crane and the Poetry of Stephen Crane," *Papers of the Bibliographical Society of America,* 58 (Fourth Quarter, 1964), 469–476.
   Queries the authenticity of Cora Crane's transcriptions of Crane's poems. "Since this woman had both opportunity and motive for altering the work of her husband, may one assume that her copies of that work are faithful transcriptions of Crane's intentions?" Notes that in the Columbia University Crane Collection "there is an edition of several of Stephen's poems prepared by Cora at the height of her financial need." Katz studies this "edition" of typescripts not noticed by Hoffman in *Poetry,* or by Gilkes (1960).
   However, all seven typescript poems in Cora's "edition" have been published, and the typescripts vary from the published versions by slight or insignificant changes in punctuation or in spelling.

Kazin, Alfred. "A Procession of Children," *American Scholar,* 33 (Spring, 1964), 171–173, 176–178, 180–183.

Klein, Eduard, and Klaus Marschke, trans. *Das blaue Hotel.* Cologne: Jakob Hegner, 1964.

Kramer, Maurice. "Crane's *Maggie: A Girl of the Streets,*" *Explicator,* 22 (February 6, 1964), item 49.
On the religious imagery in *Maggie.*

Leary, Lewis, ed. *Articles on American Literature: 1900–1963.* Durham, N.C., 1964.

MacShane, Frank, ed. *Critical Writings of Ford Madox Ford.* Lincoln, Nebr., 1964, pp. ix, 63–67.

Mane, Robert. "Une rencontre litteraire: Hamlin Garland et Stephen Crane," *Études Anglaises,* 17, no. 1 (January–March, 1964), 30–46.

Meyers, Robert. "Crane's 'The Open Boat,'" *Explicator,* 21 (April, 1964), item 60.

Ohasi, Kensaburo, trans. *Machi no onna Magi* [*Maggie: A Girl of the Streets*]. Tokyo, Chikuma Shobo, 1964. *Kindai Shosetsu-shu* Sekai Dungaku Taikei Series, vol. 91, 398–437.

———. "Aoi Hoteru," *Sekai tanpen bungaku zenshu 13: Amerika bungaku, 19 seiki,* ed. Masami Nishikawa. Tokyo: Shueisha, 1964.

Osborn, Neal. "Crane's 'The Monster' and 'The Blue Hotel,'" *Explicator,* 22 (October, 1964), item 10.

Perosa, Sergio. "Stephen Crane fra naturalismo e impressionismo," in *Annali di Ca' Foscari,* 3 (1964), 119–142.
Reprinted with minor changes in *Le vie della narrativa americana.* Milano: Mursia, 1965.
Reprinted, in abridged and slightly revised version, titled "Naturalism and Impressionism in Stephen Crane's Fiction," in *Stephen Crane: A Collection of Critical Essays,* ed. Maurice Bassan. Englewood Cliffs, N.J., 1967, pp. 80–94.
On Crane's use of Impressionism in *The Red Badge of Courage* as an "instrument for the representation of the moral and psychological inner life of the protagonist."
Perosa gives a sensitive analysis of how the subjective vision is reconciled with objective reality. The action in the novel is filtered through a single consciousness which it also illuminates. The gradual process of perception which goes on and which, Perosa believes, helps Henry to achieve a moral victory over himself, is revealed in a number of stylistic devices—terms of visual perception, auditory verbs, verbs of inner feeling, innumerable sense impressions and rhythms of perception. Perosa sees it as the truth of life revealed in the incessantly repeated "moment of vision."
Perosa emphasizes his observation that the "peculiar feature of Crane's fiction" is the dialectic relation of Naturalism and Impressionism. Contrast Perosa's essay with Walcutt's "Stephen Crane: Naturalist and Impressionist." *See also* Walcutt (1956).

Pizer, Donald, ed. *The Literary Criticism of Frank Norris.* Austin, Tex., 1964, pp. 159–166, 172–174. Reprints, pp. 164–166, Norris's "Stephen Crane's Stories of Life in the Slums," *San Francisco Wave,* 15 (July 4, 1896), 13.

Pritchett, V. S. *The Living Novel and Later Appreciations.* London, 1964. First edition, 1947.

Ross, Lillian. *Reporting*. New York, 1964, pp. 223–379. First issued 1952. Reissued 1969.

On the making of the motion picture of *The Red Badge of Courage*. The publisher's blurb claims it is one of the most famous books ever written on the cinema.

Slote, Bernice. "Stephen Crane: Waiting for Spring," *Prairie Schooner,* 38 (Spring, 1964), 15–26.

Reprints a variant title in *Nebraska State Journal,* February 24, 1895, for "Nebraskans' Bitter Fight for Life," in *Philadelphia Press,* February 24, 1895, and in *New York Press,* same date, titled "A State's Hard Fight." These known appearances, listed in *W-S Bibliography,* are not mentioned in Slote's editorial note, p. 15, to "Waiting for Spring."

Solomon, Eric. "The Bitterness of Battle: Ambrose Bierce's War Fiction," *Midwest Quarterly,* 5 (Winter, 1964), 147–165.

Bierce as a precursor of Crane.

———. *Stephen Crane in England: A Portrait of the Artist.* Columbus, Ohio, 1964.

Solomon does not bring together "all the more important information relating to Crane in England." He has bypassed volumes of pen portraits of Crane by Conrad, Ford, H. G. Wells, and other eye-witnesses of his life at Ravensbrook and at Brede Place, and as biography he has simply recast *Letters.* What is new in his book consists almost entirely of book reviews not in the *W-S Bibliography.* While scratching but the surfaces of Crane's relationships with Conrad, Ford, Wells, and Henry James, Solomon's slim book of 118 pages (about 28,000 words) contains numerous errors. *Contra* Solomon (p. 8), Crane started writing *George's Mother* in 1893 (on verso of "The Holler Tree"); he fell in love with Cora Taylor not "after reporting the Cuban insurrection," but before 1897 (p. 9); Ford Hueffer was not four years younger than Crane (p. 51); **Crane** did keep a notebook (p. 82); Jessie Conrad's *Joseph Conrad and His Circle* was first published in 1935, not in 1926 (p. 95); Wells called "The Open Boat" not "the cream" of all Crane's work, but rather the "crown" (p. 49); and what is quoted (pp. 58–59) as Crane's remark on Stevenson, as Ford erroneously reported it, was made not by Crane but by Harold Frederic.

See Crane, chapter 22 ff., for a full account of Crane's English years.

Reviewed:

Modern Fiction Studies, 10 (Winter, 1964–1965): "The portrait that emerges from this slim monograph is that of 'an author among authors,' an image of Crane quite different from those held by his American contemporaries."

TLS, May 20, 1965: "Mr. Solomon has nothing especially new to offer on either Crane's critics or his friends, but by bringing neatly together all the more important information relating to Crane in England, he has produced a pleasant and helpful essay."

Joseph Katz, *Antioch Review* (September, 1965).

Nineteenth-Century Fiction, 20 (September, 1965): "Solomon skillfully traces the English experience, piecing out the events from fragments of information. Of chief interest is the analysis of Crane's relationship to Conrad, James, Wells, and Ford Madox Ford, who regarded the young writer not as an untutored genius who scarcely knew how he achieved his startling effects but as a sophisticated and highly self-conscious artist."

Jean Cazemajou, *Études Anglaises*, 18, no. 2 (1965), 212-213.

James Stronks, *English Language Notes*, 3 (December, 1965), 154-157: Solomon's book assembles the facts with 283 footnotes. "And as a starter it refutes the obsolete view that Crane was a facile genius who fell into a few lucky successes and then conveniently died. Repeatedly this study argues, for whose information it is not clear, that Crane was in fact a serious, self-conscious artist, with sophisticated theory and disciplined craft. It surveys Crane's British critical reception, and then gives a chapter each to reconstructing his friendships with such discerning fellow professionals, most of them his neighbors and houseguests in Surrey [and Sussex], as Harold Frederic, Edward Garnett, H. G. Wells, Ford Madox Ford, Henry James, and Joseph Conrad. The study is only incidentally biographical, however, adding little to what we learned in 1960 from Gilkes' thoroughly researched *Cora Crane* and the annotated *Letters.*"

American Literature, 37 (1965), 231: "Mr. Solomon never quite proves his general assumption that Howells and Garland, for example, never understood Crane as thoroughly as did his British friends and acquaintances." His generalizations about Crane's connections with Wells, Ford, Conrad, and James are based on an insufficiency of material.

Stallman, R. W. "A Soldier Young in Years" [by Stephen Crane], *Fine Arts Magazine* (University of Connecticut), 1964.

Reproduces here for the first time facsimile of the holograph manuscript of Crane's poem in CUCC. Here for the first time is the photograph of Crane aboard *The Three Friends* after the *Commodore* disaster, from the original at Yale University Library.

The poem was published by Hoffman (1957). And by Katz (1966), without citation to its previous publication—understandably so—in the above not known to exist undergraduate journal.

———. "New Short Fiction by Stephen Crane: II," *Studies in Short Fiction*, 1, no. 2 (Winter, 1964), 147-152.

Reproduces here for the first time "Art in Kansas City" from the holograph manuscript in CUCC. It is one of a group of Uncle Clarence sketches and belongs in the category of fables such as "In the Country of Rhymers and Writers," which is also reproduced here for the first time from the holograph manuscript in CUCC. So too is "The Camel," which exists in a two-page typescript in CUCC. "The Camel," intended to be published in this series but previously published in 1963 by Gullason, shows Crane once more influenced by Kipling. In "The Second Generation" (1899) Casper Cadogan—so named because he is a cad again—remarks that he didn't know "what a commissary officer was until I *was* one." That word "was intimately associated in my mind with camels. Funny, eh? I think it came from reading that ryme of Kipling's about the commissariat camel" *(Wounds in the Rain*, 1900, p. 316).

"Art in Kansas City" also seems to be an early writing, but it isn't. In the holograph manuscript Crane spells words after the British spelling: "colour," for instance, tells us that he wrote "Art in Kansas City" while living in England, 1897-1900; for when he lived in America he spelled it "color."

Reprinted by Joseph Katz in *SCraneN* (Fall, 1967) without acknowledgement to its prior publication in *SinSF*. Typescripts of "Art in Kansas City"—

typed by Edith Crane—belonged to H. B. Collamore, from whom Stallman obtained copy in 1953.

———. "Was Crane's Sketch of the Fleet Off Crete a Journalistic Hoax?" *Studies in Short Fiction,* 2 (Fall, 1964), 72–76.
Gilkes in *Cora Crane* (1960), p. 91, opines that Crane "may have faked the Cretan dispatch." She uses Crane's "Dan Emmonds," a voyage fantasy in imitation of Defoe, to support her theory that Crane was with Cora on her overland journey and experienced the near-shipwreck Cora recorded in her journal or diary. In Gilkes, "Stephen Crane's 'Dan Emmonds'; a Pig in a Storm," *SinSF* (Fall, 1964). In that same *SinSF* Gilkes seemingly agrees with Stallman by the very title of her rejoinder, "No Hoax: A Reply to Mr. Stallman" (1964). However, the titles of our articles belie our standpoints and differences. We differ radically on how Crane got to Greece, Stallman contending that Crane was not with Cora on the Orient Express land route and not with Cora on the *Danae*'s near shipwreck in the Black Sea. "Dan Emmonds" figures in the debate because it includes a shipwreck described in terms similar to Cora's description of the *Danae*'s near shipwreck. "Dan Emmonds" was published in *SinSF* (Fall, 1963). See *Crane,* chap. 16 and pp. 537–539.
See Gilkes (1969) and Stallman's rejoinder, "How Stephen Crane Got to Crete," *American Literature,* 44 (May, 1972).

Stallman, R. W., and E. R. Hagemann. *The War Dispatches of Stephen Crane.* New York: New York University Press; London: Peter Owen, 1964. Maps and three portraits of Crane.
Reviewed:
Alan Pryce-Jones, *New York Herald Tribune,* July 11, 1964, p. 24: "A most important addition to existing Crane studies. All of it is unfamiliar, much has never been republished, and the texts have been most scrupulously edited, to make a highly readable collection of (on the analogy of action-painting) action-writing."
Joseph Haas, *Chicago Daily News,* July 11, 1964: The editors "deserve great praise for their painstaking research. Not satisfied with merely reprinting Crane's stories as they appeared in the British and American press, they have run down, whenever possible, Crane's original copy. . . . A reading of his [Crane's] coverage of the Greco-Turkish War of 1896 and, two years later, of the Spanish-American War, should convince any skeptic that Crane must be ranked with Melville and Twain as the great precursors of 20th Century prose writing. Not only are his descriptions of war as vivid as anything Hemingway did a generation later, but Crane proves himself the master of the techniques of crisp, realistic dialog such as were to help make Hemingway famous."
Charles Shapiro, *Louisville Courier-Journal,* July 12, 1964: This volume "is a fine example of distinguished scholarship at work. Stallman and Hagemann function well together, and their brief introductions and notes are precise and, what is even rarer, well-written."
Robert Cromie, *Chicago Tribune,* July 21, 1964.
Morse Allen, *Hartford Courant,* July 26, 1964: "Crane reported the Cuban War for a United States which seems to us immature, and Crane's style shares in its youth. He could sound boyishly artificial."
Joseph Brandt, *Los Angeles Times,* July 26: "The editors made a solid

contribution to American letters in bringing together for the first time in one volume much of Crane's best writing. He is a precursor of Ernie Pyle, because he writes primarily about people rather than bullets. Probably no other war correspondent used such colorful language to describe action and people."

Los Angeles Herald-Examiner, August 2, 1964.

Arno Karlen, *Nation,* 199 (August 10, 1964), 54–55: The war dispatches are "especially interesting in the light of Crane's entire work. The editors have to some extent suggested this by their inclusion of 'The Price of the Harness' and 'Death and the Child,' but they did not closely examine the relationship between reporting and fiction, observation and imagination, Naturalist theory and practice; so they failed to give greater significance to the reprinting of the dispatches. And if they were going to include well-known and widely re-printed stories, why not also 'The Open Boat' and 'The Men in the Storm' and the journalism on which they were based?"

This book "slows down the general reader and scamps the literary questions it raises. It is also useless as a literary source book, as literary history or as military history. The most uncharitable inference is that the editors and publishers packed the book with extra material, cheap reprints and pre-tentious but useless notes to make it fat, expensive and seemingly authoritative. The most charitable is that their planning was without intelligence or taste. But Mr. Stallman has already become known as an authority on Crane because of what seems to me embarrassingly wrong-headed criticism. Still, the reader who plows through this opaqueness will be rewarded by a hundred new pages of Crane at his best, a precious addition now available for the first time."*

Harrison E. Salisbury, *New York Times,* August 21, 1964: "Stephen Crane possessed one of the true—but small—talents of turn-of-the-century American literature. He wrote a war classic, *The Red Badge of Courage;* a dramatic human sketch, 'The Open Boat,' and a first-class social document, *Maggie: A Girl of the Streets.* Unfortunately, Crane possessed neither the style nor the philosophy to support broad scholarly research—a fact that this exercise in pedantic petit point makes painfully evident."

The New Yorker, 40 (September 19, 1964), pp. 214–215: "Crane's war dis-patches are surprisingly readable, the reason being that most of them are not news stories at all but vignettes, and the best of these are stamped with his peculiar genius."

Nineteenth-Century Fiction, 19 (December, 1964): "Though it is good to

---

* *In reply to Karlen: War Dispatches* does not include "The Open Boat" and "The Men in the Storm" because they are not war dispatches. As for "the journal-ism on which they are based," "The Men in the Storm" is not—as Karlen thinks—a sea-story, and so there exists no journalism on which it is based. Mr. Karlen is also wrongheaded in his notion that Crane as journalist was "strictly self-disci-plined," that Crane died at the age of 29, that *The Red Badge* "was the first great Naturalist novel by an American," that his " 'Naturalist objectivity' was a mask for his outrage at social injustice," and that Crane's war dispatches might just as well have been written by one man and his fiction and poetry by another. *Contra* Karlen, the war dispatches are infused with the same poetic use of language, the same painterly and metaphoric style, as Crane's fiction. The same incidents Crane had imagined in his war fiction he later experienced and they recur in his war dispatches; the same Crane wrote both accounts, and only Crane could have writ-ten them. *Contra* Karlen, the texts of *War Dispatches* are faithful reproductions of original first newspaper and magazine publications; they are not "cheap re-prints."

have these journalistic pieces readily available, few readers are likely to go along with the publisher's assertion that 'they add a new dimension to [Crane's] reputation.' Indeed, one has the feeling that the recent hard-driving search for additional items for the Crane canon has not only reached but passed the point of diminishing returns."

Jean Cazemajou, *Études Anglaises*, 17, no. 3 (1964), 308–310: *"Si le titre du livre ne convient qu'à une partie de son contenu, le travail de collation et d'érudition des professeurs Stallman et Hagemann place néanmoins entre les mains du spécialiste un ouvrage indispensable."*

TLS, December 31, 1964: All the pieces are usefully annotated, but "the collection will not be quite so surprising, however, as its editors obviously hoped it would be. Of the forty-seven dispatches by Crane—the bulk of the book—which they claim to be reprinting from the journals for the first time, all but one have in fact recently appeared in Mr. O. W. Fryckstedt's admirable edition of Crane's *Uncollected Writings*.* . . . The texts chosen by the rival editors are not always the same, which could lead later to some confusion in references."

Modern Fiction Studies, 10 (Winter, 1964–1965), 395: It is fitting "that the editors include not only Crane's own dispatches, but related articles by other correspondents, views of Crane as journalist, several parodies of his war stories and other material. The result is a substantial book of undoubted importance for students of Crane's life and writings."

Julian Rayford, *American Book Collector* (February, 1965): "Far from being a poor reporter, an inept reporter, Crane was a great reporter. Stephen Crane was one of the few real individuals who has ever worked successfully at being a reporter. He was a great war correspondent, a gallant man and always a superb human being in his writing. Several myths about him are swept away in this book. For 65 years, people have credited Crane with the story that the men of the 71st New York Regiment were cowards. William Randolph Hearst believed that story. Joseph Pulitzer believed it. Even Teddy Roosevelt believed it. But Crane did not write that story. Sylvester Scovel wrote it. It is not often you find a book worth going overboard for—this one is that rare exception—there is a certain splendor about it—it is a magnificent book!"

Oliver Knight, *Journalism Quarterly*, 42 (Spring, 1965), 303–304: "Stephen Crane is beneath notice in the history of American journalism . . . , but a collection of war dispatches commands some attention nonetheless. . . . Although the editors do not specify their purpose, the general tone of the book and the fact that they are specialists in American literature (Stallman is a Crane scholar) imply that they approach Crane's war reporting with reference to the total picture of Crane the creative writer. Consequently, they have not bothered to analyze his war reporting as such. No one could argue with their not doing so, considering their interests. But the omission of such analysis sterilizes this volume insofar as the journalism historian is concerned."

Antioch Review (June, 1965).

---

* Published in Uppsala in 1963, this work does not include all of Crane's uncollected writings and it presents no new Crane manuscripts. His book was made possible by an eighteen months' sojourn in America (1960–1962) "by a generous research grant from the United States." The "rival editors" meanwhile, without benefit of such a research grant, completed *War Dispatches* in 1963 only to have its publication unfortunately postponed.

Cecil Eby, *Roanoke Times*, June 9, 1965: "Perhaps the quality about Crane's dispatches which makes them memorable is his careful description of minute details actually within his field of vision. Instead of telling about what was happening on a battlefield at large—the perspective of a general—Crane focussed upon a limited and therefore specific area immediately in front of him. His subject is not war as seen by a military leader but war as felt and seen by the little man holding a rifle. In this sense Crane foreshadows later masters of battlefield prose such as Hemingway, Herbert Matthews, and Alvah Bessie. Or the camera technique of Robert Capa."

Maurice Bassan, *Mad River Review*, 1, no. 2 (Spring-Summer, 1965), 85–90: "The student will need both *War Dispatches* and Fryckstedt's *Uncollected Writings* for the following reasons. Fryckstedt includes five Cuban dispatches unaccountably omitted by his rivals (nos. 75, 77, 80, 84, and 90), not to mention three later discussions by Crane of the Boer War which might be thought at least relevant to a volume of war dispatches. On the other hand, the Stallman-Hagemann texts are in several respects more complete where the editors wisely use English rather than American texts; in addition, there are three new manuscript pieces. . . . Both books, incidentally, omit the *World* dispatch dated June 13, 1898, almost certainly by Crane, dealing with the death of surgeon John Blair Gibbs later treated in *Wounds in the Rain*."

James Stronks, *English Language Notes*, 3 (December, 1965), 154–157: "Thus, *War Dispatches* unearths from newspaper files about sixty-five 'new' Crane pieces—a major addition to the canon. A dozen of these were not even known to exist in 1948 when the Williams-Starrett bibliography appeared, and three of them have never before seen print in any form. Indexed, and with their topical allusions well footnoted, the *Dispatches* make a companion volume to Stallman's edition (with Lillian Gilkes) of *Stephen Crane: Letters* (1960), having the same jacket design outside and editorial method inside. The forthcoming Stallman-Hagemann edition of Crane's *New York City Sketches* will complete a trio of matched volumes making accessible nearly a thousand more pages from Crane's pen than we had as recently as 1959.

"Besides its autobiographical value, Crane's war reporting is of interest because he was not really a reporter. Ill-suited to the flashy front page of Hearst and Pulitzer, he was a special correspondent, a literary man with a celebrated style, free to write about whatever interested him. . . . To show this transmuting of experience into reportage into literature, the present editors place some later Crane stories among his war dispatches at appropriate spots (for example 'The Price of the Harness,' which derived from the Kettle Hill action in Cuba). By this juxtaposition they invite study of this transmutation process, a study which might well consider also Hemingway's comparable practice in the interchapters of *In Our Time*."

Stone, Edward. *The Battle and the Books: Some Aspects of Henry James*. Athens, Ohio, 1964, pp. 5, 28, 41, 44, 69, 70, 150, 173, 181.

On Christ figures in *The Grapes of Wrath* and in *Light in August*, p. 150. "There is yet a third characterization in American fiction of a man with the initials of J and C who has been associated by literary criticism with Jesus Christ—namely the Jim Conklin of Stephen Crane's *Red Badge of Courage*. (And we are all familiar with Professor Stallman's interpretation of the 'fierce wafer' of the sun in that novel as the eucharistic wafer.) But I agree with H. G. Wells' judgement that one of the 'certain enormous repudiations' in

Crane's art is this very eschewing of images of the fabulous: 'Any richness of the allusion . . . the half quotation that refracts and softens and enriches the statement, the momentary digression that opens like a window upon beautiful or distant things, are not merely absent, but obviously avoided.' "

Stronks, James B. "A Realist Experiments with Impressionism: Hamlin Garland's 'Chicago Studies,' " *American Literature*, 36 (March, 1964), 38–52.
    Garland preached the theory of Impressionism ("vertism"), but Crane had from the first practiced it "instinctively and with ease" (to quote Robert Spiller, 1949). In his unpublished "Chicago Studies" (1895) Garland's style is influenced by Crane's colorful Impressionism.

Thiffault, George F. "Stephen Crane: UConn Author Sheds New Light on Great Writer," *Hartford Courant*, May 17, 1964. Photographs.
    Stallman interviews E. J. Dimock and Judge George E. Dimock and L. B. Watson, dining with them at the home of David Balch near the Hartwood Club and the Stephen Crane Pond, and taking notes on their reminiscences of the Crane they knew when they were boys.
    Subsequently, *The New York City Sketches of Stephen Crane and Related Pieces,* ed. R. W. Stallman and E. R. Hagemann, 1966, bears this dedication: "For three gentlemen who as boys knew the young Stephen Crane at Hartwood, New York, and at Twin Lakes, Pennsylvania: E. J. Dimock, George E. Dimock, L. B. Watson."

Tsunematsu, Masao. "Stephen Crane kanken" [My view of Stephen Crane], *Shimane Daigaku Ronshu (Jinbunkagaku),* no. 13 (February, 1964), 38–50.

Uema, Kamemasa. "Stephen Crane no 'The Monster' ni tsuite" [*The Monster* of Stephen Crane], *Ryukyu Daigaku Bunrigaku-bu Kiyo (Jinbun),* no. 8 (June, 1964), 159–190.

Vedro, Stephen S. Biographical Note and Introduction, *The Red Badge of Courage.* New York, 1964, pp. v–xiv.
    Text printed in very large type with the Introduction written for young readers.

Wertheim, Stanley. "Stephen Crane and the Wrath of Jehova," *Literary Review,* 7 (Summer, 1964), 499–508.
    "The theme of the revolt against the father is exemplified more clearly in the life and the work of Stephen Crane than in any other American writer. His clerical forbears had insisted that the heart was loathsome and the source of all evil, and Crane nowhere denied that man was a fallen sinner. Yet, as an artist it was essential for him to express that which was within his heart, although it was bitter, and he preferred to identify with fallen humanity rather than to worship transcendent injustice. The wrathful Jehova who issued from the pens of Jesse Peck and Jonathan Crane created man with desires and then proceeded to condemn him for expressing them. Crane's sense of justice was outraged by his cosmic dilemma. Against the brutal villain of the Old Testament he set an interior God of simple human compassion. . . .
    "This inner voice of mercy takes men out of the Christian churches where ministers threaten in the name of a menacing Jehova. It allows them to recognize their brotherhood in sin. However, it is not a shield against the indifference or hostility of the natural and social universe. For the Peck family and for Jonathan Crane, the God of Wrath was a mighty fortress, a bulwark against the black riders of sin, but a vague bond of sympathy offered inade-

quate protection. Guilt, anxiety, and psychic isolation were the penalties which Crane paid for his defiance. 'You must go alone before the bar of God,' Jesse Peck had warned. 'You must answer for your own life of guilt, and you yourself must, if finally impenitent, obey the terrific words, "Depart ye cursed, into everlasting fire." You alone must suffer for your obstinate rebellion.' Crane cut himself off from the ancestral ties which threatened his independence and stifled his aspirations as a writer but which had been the original basis of his childhood security. His rejection of the firm moral code embodied in the manual of piety compiled by his father was essential, but it left him with a feeling of isolation in a hostile universe which found expression in all his writings and culminated in the desperate soul searching of *The Red Badge of Courage.*

"Crane's loss of faith in religious orthodoxy and traditional ethical values occurred at an early age, and his rejection of the angry Jehova precipitated strong feelings of uncertainty and guilt. Because of this there is an oppressive repetitiveness in the themes of futility, self-deception, and isolation which permeate his writings. Lost in a world in which appeared to be a maze without a plan, he submerged himself in nihilism, viewing with chilling objectivity the barren schemes of men who seek to impose patterns of order upon an arbitrary universe. Individuals remain estranged from one another since there are no absolutes, and men cannot coordinate their egocentric desires in a meaningful social community. In the end, Crane stressed personal awareness and self-reliance—the ability to observe the absurd chaos of life unflinchingly, fearing neither the wrath of God nor the judgement of man. . . ."

On Crane's gods and his rejection of the angry Jehovah *see* Hoffman, *Poetry* (1957), Nelson (1963), and *Crane,* which quotes Wertheim.* Also, Robert Schneider's essay (1965) relates to Wertheim's essay. *See also* Westbrook (1963).

Ziff, Larzer. "The Other Lost Generation: The Strange Story of a Literary Eclipse," *Saturday Review,* 47 (December 5, 1964), 15–18.
   See Ziff's *The American 1890's* (1966).

1965

Aaron, Daniel. "Howells' *Maggie,*" *New England Quarterly,* 38 (March, 1965), 85–90.
   On Howells' *Suburban Sketches,* one of which is here reproduced: "The Scene," reporting the suicide by drowning of a Fallen Woman. "Written twenty years before Stephen began his first draft of *Maggie* in a Syracuse fraternity house, it anticipates the subject if not the theme of Crane's Bowery novel and (whether or not Crane knew of it) may have some relevance to the not entirely easy association of the 'Dean' and his professed disciple."

Abstract of English Studies, 8, no. 10 (December, 1965), items 3089–3090.

   * Quoted and paraphrased, but the footnote on Wertheim got misplaced, and the Checklist of Sources was expunged in galley because it would have made *Crane* too bulky. Acknowledgement to Wertheim appeared in the second printing (August, 1968).

Corrects the inexact accounts given in *AES*, 8, no. 8 (September, 1965) for Stallman's "Was Crane's Sketch of the Fleet off Crete a Journalistic Hoax? A Reply to Miss Gilkes." And for Gilkes' "No Hoax: A Reply to Mr. Stallman." Both articles in *SinSF*, 2 (Fall, 1964).

Agee, James. [Letter to Malcolm Lowry], *Selected Letters of Malcolm Lowry,* ed. Harvey Breit and Margerie Lowry. Philadelphia and New York, 1965, p. 444.

Agee writes, "I'm ending nearly six months' stay out here mainly involved revising a script I wrote last summer of Crenes [*sic*] *Blue Hotel.*"

[Anon.], trans. *Ein Wunder an Mut: sieben Erzählungen und der Roman "Maggie."* Cologne and Olten, 1965.

Contains "A Mystery of Heroism" (the title work), *Maggie,* and seven other stories, in translation into the German.

Bassan, Maurice. "An Early Draft of *George's Mother,*" *American Literature,* 36 (January, 1965), 518–522.

Reproduces here for the first time the first draft of *George's Mother* appearing on verso of "The Holler Tree," holograph manuscript in the Barrett Crane Collection, and for collation the opening portion of Chapter 2 of the published novel. Bassan claims that this early draft "provides" almost certain evidence that the novel was begun either in 1892 or earlier," *but* he makes no mention of the fact that *also* on verso of "The Holler Tree" holograph manuscript, p. 3, is the beginning of "The Reluctant Voyagers," an omission which damages his conclusions. Linson in *MSC* says he first met Crane sometime after *Maggie* was published, and so the earliest possible date for "The Reluctant Voyagers," which Linson illustrated, is May–June of 1893. It follows that Crane wrote *George's Mother* also in 1893—not in 1892 as Bassan surmises. In 1893 Crane began here that portion which in the published novel is the opening passage of Chapter 2. Prior to writing these first fragments of *George's Mother* and of "The Reluctant Voyagers," he wrote his Sullivan County sketch "The Holler Tree" and used the clean backs of that manuscript for these starts at his Bowery novel and of his "Reluctant Voyagers." Having reused the manuscript of "The Holler Tree" in this way, Crane—one conjectures— probably misplaced the manuscript; *that* seems probably why "The Holler Tree" was not published during his lifetime. ("The Holler Tree" was first published in *Golden Book* [February, 1934].)

———. "Stephen Crane and 'The Eternal Mystery of Social Condition,' " *Nineteenth-Century Fiction,* 19 (March, 1965), 387–394.

Benet, William Rose, ed. *The Reader's Encyclopedia.* New York, 1965, pp. 232–233.

Berryman, John. "Stephen Crane, *The Red Badge of Courage,*" in *The American Novel from James Fenimore Cooper to William Faulkner,* ed. Wallace Stegner. New York, 1965, pp. 86–96.

"Perhaps many readers take it as a novel of development, a sort of success story, and this view is encouraged by the climatic passage: 'He felt a quiet manhood. . . . He was a man.' " (This view of *The Red Badge* as a success story is echoed by Stegner in his Preface. p. xii.)

Berryman adds cautiously: "It is possible to feel very uncomfortable with this way of looking at the book. . . . I find it hard to believe that in this passage Crane is exonerating his hero without irony." (The passage, in which Henry Fleming half-reproaches himself for his cowardice, begins: "He saw that he was good. . . .") On the image of the red sun "pasted in the sky like a wafer," Berryman evades the problems it raises: "A wafer is thick nourishment, too, is it not?" He is positive only in denying that Crane was a Naturalist. He is surprised at the "absence of interest in religion in *The Red Badge of Courage.*"

However, there is no absence of interest in religion by critics of Crane's writings. *See* Rosenfeld (1953); Hoffman, Introduction, *The Red Badge of Courage* (1957); Weisberger (1958); Colvert (1959); James T. Cox (1959); Tuttleton (1962); Detweiler (1964); and Thomas, *Stephen Crane: A Collection* (1967), pp. 137–140.

Berthoff, Warner. *The Ferment of Realism: American Literature 1884–1919.* New York, 1965.

Bruccoli, Matthew J. "Cora's Mouse," *Papers of the Bibliographical Society,* 59 (Second Quarter, 1965), 188–189.

Kipling's *The Seven Seas* given Cora by Stephen Crane.

Budd, Louis J. "Stephen Crane," in *American Literary Scholarship 1963,* ed. James L. Woodress. Durham, N.C., 1965, pp. 67, 129, 137–140, 141, 152.

Butterfield, Roger. Foreword, *First Books by American Authors.* New York: Seven Gables Bookshop, 1965, pp. 25–26. Catalogue 30. Illustrated.

Lists an 1893 *Maggie* for $1,000. Quotes Stallman from *Letters,* pp. 12–13. "Published in mustard-yellow covers, this paper-bound *Maggie,* priced at 50 cents, sold not at all. In 1930, however, this first edition was described as the rarest in modern literature, an inscribed copy then fetching $3,700. Having given away about a hundred copies to friends (out of the 1,100 copies printed in 1893), and having used the remainder to kindle his boardinghouse stove, Crane himself possessed only one copy in 1896. The number of extant copies known to collectors was reported in 1937 to be fewer than thirty. In 1935 Mrs. Florence Crane Coughlan brought eleven copies for auction at the Anderson Galleries, to be sold at the rate of two each season thereafter, but most of these copies were chipped, stained, or torn. They had been stored in a wagon house for twenty years and mice had nibbled them. There had been other copies too, but Mrs. Coughlan's two eldest sisters had burned them, believing they were not nice. *Maggie* remained unchristened until William Howe Crane, Stephen's brother, gave the book that name."

Cajado, Octavio Mendes, trans. *Histórias de Stephen Crane* [Short Stories by Stephen Crane], selection and notes by José Paulo Paes. São Paulo, Brazil: Editôra Cultrix Ltda., 1965.

Translated into the Portuguese from texts selected from *Omnibus.*

Contents: Nota Liminar, pp. 7–9. *The Men in the Storm,* pp. 9–16; *Maggie: A Girl of the Streets,* pp. 17–90; A Mystery of Heroism, pp. 91–101; The Upturned Face, pp. 102–107; An Episode of War, pp. 108–112; The Open Boat, pp. 113–142; The Blue Hotel, pp. 143–178; His New Mittens, pp. 179–192.

Cazemajou, Jean. "A propos de quelques parodies de l'oeuvre de Stephen Crane." *Caliban,* 1, no. 1 (April, 1965), 65–86.

Colvert, James B. Introduction, *Great Short Works of Stephen Crane.* New York: Harper and Row, 1965, pp. vii–xv. Biography, pp. 355–357, and Bibliogra-

phy, p. 358, by Frank N. Magill. In short version edition 1965 not included
are *Maggie*, "The Monster," "An Experiment in Misery," and "The Pace of
Youth." Enlarged edition, 1968.

"Although Stephen Crane's fiction is often described as 'realism' (especially
in literary histories), the term is inappropriate and misleading." In *The Red
Badge of Courage* Crane's Henry Fleming identifies himself with Nature, and
in so doing he touches upon a basic religious problem—one that Crane attacked
more directly in his book of poems, *The Black Riders*. Henry thinks "in terms
of a victory, *not* over the confederate enemy or his fear of them, but of a
victory over Nature, as if he sees his new condition as a vengeful triumph
over the hostile forest which refused him solace in the cathedral-like bower.
Henry's real enemy is Nature or, by extension, the whole universe."

Cook, Robert G. "Stephen Crane's 'The Bride Comes to Yellow Sky,'" *Studies
in Short Fiction*, 2 (Summer, 1965), 368–369.

DeBrito, Maria Fernanda, trans. *A insignia rubra da coragem*. Porto: Livaria
Civilização, 1965.

Besides *The Red Badge of Courage* in Portuguese translation, this volume
contains translations of seven additional short pieces by Crane.

Farlekas, Chris [unsigned]. "Then and Now. Port Jervis Lynching: Part II,"
Times Herald Record (Middletown, N.Y.), May 5, 1965, p. 48.

Retells the story of the lynching of the Negro Robert Lewis in Port Jervis
73 years ago this month. "Some men tried to pull the rope down, among
them Judge William H. Crane and his brother Stephen. . . . They were all
pushed aside." Here is my source for claiming in *Crane* (1968) that William
and Stephen participated in this event. *Crane* recasts this tragic event from
the following sources (not mentioned by Farlekas): *New York Tribune*, June 3,
1892: "The Lynching Denounced." It is probable that J. Townley Crane
wrote this article. *New York Tribune*, June 4, 1892, p. 1: "Mob-Law in New
York." *New York Tribune*, June 4, 1892, p. 6: "The Port Jervis Lynching."
New York Tribune, June 5, 1892, p. 6: "Depravity, Not Justice." *New York
Tribune*, July 10, 1892, p. 8: "To Sue the State for the Lynching of Lewis"
(under "Legal Proceedings" section).

Farlekas mentions "Judge Crane" in his *Times Herald Record* recast of
these *New York Tribune* sources, but in 1892 William Howe Crane was not
yet the Judge Crane he makes him out to be.

Fuchs, Daniel. "Ernest Hemingway, Literary Critic," *American Literature*, 36
(January, 1965), 431–451.

Like Crane, Hemingway burlesqued heroic rhetoric, story-book endings,
and chivalric displays.

Going, William T. "William Higgins and Crane's 'The Open Boat': A Note
about Fact and Fiction," *Papers on English Language and Literature*, 1 (Winter, 1965), 79–82.

Gordan, John D. "Stephen Crane," in *An Anniversary Exhibition: The
Henry W. and Albert A. Berg Collection*. New York: New York Public
Library, 1965, p. 48.

On *Maggie*.

———. "Novels in Manuscript: An Exhibition from the Berg Collection,"
Bulletin of the New York Public Library, 69 (June, 1965), 403–404.

Gordon, Noah. *The Rabbi.* New York, 1965.
Crane is the rabbi's favorite writer.

Hart, James D. *The Oxford Companion to American Literature,* 4th ed. New York, 1965, pp. 192–193.

Hart, John E. "*The Red Badge of Courage* as Myth and Symbol," in *Myth and Literature,* ed. John Vickery. Lincoln, Nebr., 1965, pp. 221–227. Reprinted from *University of Kansas City Review,* 19 (Summer, 1953), 249–256.

Hausermann, H. W. *Moderne amerikanische Literatur.* Bern and Munich, 1965, pp. 99, 137, 140.

Howarth. William L. "*The Red Badge of Courage* Manuscript: New Evidence for a Critical Edition," *Studies in Bibliography,* 18 (1965), 229–247.

An important restudy of the manuscripts, correcting Stallman's pioneer account in *Omnibus.* There are 57 leaves for the earlier draft, not 56 nor 58 first-draft leaves. In the second draft of *The Red Badge* Crane used five different kinds of legal-sized paper, not identical kinds of paper as given by Stallman and by Winterich, Introduction, *The Red Badge* (1951).

"Stallman mistakenly estimates the length of the first draft 'from the fact that one of its pages is numbered 149,' (*Omnibus,* p. 216). Yet '149,' although it appears on the verso of page 163, is merely a false start for 149 of the *second* draft, not the first: '149' is on paper E, a paper which does not appear in the first draft." (In *Omnibus* the first draft is designated Ms. SV, and the second or final draft as Ms. LV.)

Alterations in the manuscripts are either in Crane's hand or in a later non-authorial hand. Stallman "does not distinguish between authorial and non-authorial changes. Evidently he was unable to recognize the different states from his photostatic copies, for he assumes that Crane alone was responsible for all notations appearing in the manuscript [Ms. LV, that is]."

Howarth retraces the history of the documents that reportedly stand between the second or final draft (Ms. LV) and the first edition: a typescript, a condensed newspaper version, a printer's typesetting copy, and a set of page proofs. "The major sources are in reminiscences by Hamlin Garland and Irving Bacheller, the Beer and Berryman biographies, Stallman's somewhat disjointed survey in his *Omnibus* (pp. 201–217), and the volume of Crane's collected letters." (*See Letters.*) Subsequent to Howarth's essay there is Stallman's account in *Crane.*

"Stallman once speculated that the manuscript Crane sent to Hitchcock was 'probably the typescript copy or page proof, rather than the actual handwritten manuscript' (*Omnibus,* p. 645n.). Yet the fact that Crane took the manuscript to Bacheller in November and submitted newspaper clippings to Hitchcock in December is good evidence for assuming that the typescript no longer existed and had probably been lost at McClure's." Howarth speculates that Crane got the manuscript back from Bacheller and gave it to the Appleton editor "just before he left New York in January. As for whether page proof or the manuscript was sent to New Orleans, Hitchcock himself says that publication of the book was held off until Crane returned to New York to correct the proofs (Hitchcock, p. vi). It seems hardly probable that Hitchcock would have had proofs made before major authorial revision. . . . In all probability, he sent the second-draft manuscript to New Orleans, not proofs. In a later account, Stallman abandons his conjectural typescript and adopts this position (*Letters,* pp. 45, 51, 53)."

Howarth notes that, since *Omnibus* in 1952, four editions of *The Red Badge* have reprinted the unpublished passages which first appeared in the Winterich and Stallman editions, whose copy-text is the 1895 edition. However, Howarth fails to note that Winterich's Folio Society edition (1951) presents only the second or final draft, MS. LV and not at all MS. SV. Gibson (1956) reprints the Folio text. Lettis, *et al.* (1960) reprints the *Omnibus* text, but not accurately. Bradley, Beatty, and Long's *The Red Badge of Courage: An Annotated Text, Backgrounds and Sources, Essays in Criticism* (1962) reprints the *Omnibus* text with several explanatory and interpretive notes by the editors. The fourth edition in Howarth's list is Stallman, *The Red Badge of Courage and Selected Stories* (1960). This reprints the *Omnibus* text and adds to it five new manuscript pages belonging to the expunged Chapter 12. *See* "Textual Notes," pp. 207 ff., in this Signet Classic edition, copyrighted by R. W. Stallman (1960).*

Hudspeth, Robert N. "The *Thoth* Annual Bibliography of Stephen Crane Scholarship," *Thoth*, 6 (Spring, 1965), 31–33.

Inoue, Kenji. "Akai bukunsho—sono shudai to kōsei" *(The Red Badge of Courage*—its theme and construction), *Meiji Daigaku Kyoyo Ronshu*, no. 31 (1965), pp. 98–111.

Itabashi, Yoshie. " 'To Be a Man'—A Study of Fear and Courage in Stephen Crane's Stories," *Tsuda Review*, no. 10 (November, 1965), 1–48.

Izzo, Carlo. "Aspetti del simbolismo di Stephen Crane," in *Il simbolismo nella letterature americana,* ed. M. Pagnini. Firenze, Nuova Italia, 1965, pp. 191–204.

   Reprinted in Carlo Izzo's *Civilta americana.* Roma, Ediz. di Storia e Letteratura, 1967, vol. 1, pp. 207–222. Titled: "Stephen Crane: Dal realismo sperimentale all' impressionismo simbolista."

Kagami, Eizo. "Stephen no 'The Third Violet' ni tsuite" (On Stephen Crane's "Third Violet"), *Gifu Diagaku Kyoyo-bu Kenkyu Hokoku*, no. 1 (1965), 28–119.

Kato, Tadahiko. "S. Crane no shi—sono ichi kōsatsu" (About the poetry of S. Crane), *Rikkyo Daigaku Eibei Bungaku*, no. 26 (March, 1965), 101–120.

Katz, Joseph. "Toward a Descriptive Bibliography of Stephen Crane's *The Black Riders,*" *Papers of the Bibliographical Society of America*, 59 (1965), 150–157.

Kerscher, Rudolf. *"Whilomville Stories:* Stephen Crane's vergessene Kindheitserzählungen," *Die Neueren Sprachen*, 14 (1965), 77–80.

Klein, E., and K. Marschke, trans. *Sieben Erzahlungen und der Roman Maggie.* Koln: Jakob Hegner, 1965.
   Reviewed: Christoph Burgauner, "Stephen Crane: Ein Wunder an Mut," *Neue Deutsche Heft*, 13, ii (1966), 164–166.

LaFrance, Marston. "A Few Facts about Stephen Crane and 'Holland,' " *American Literature*, 37 (May, 1965), 195–202.

   * It claims to be "the only correct and complete manuscript text . . . the definitive edition." However, by the printer's error a 12-word passage was omitted from the text of Houghton 102 MS., p. 217. It is "definitive" only in the sense that it presents all manuscript pages here for the first time.
   The Stephen Crane Reader, ed. R. W. Stallman (1972), incorporates the Signet text of *The Red Badge of Courage* with the five new MS. pages and new editorial notes to the 1895 edition.

Important new data, identifying "Holland" as E. J. Edwards. Reprints two press "letters" by "Holland," one of which—"The Work of Stephen Crane"—was first reprinted in *Letters*. Marston points out that "The Work of Stephen Crane" was a subhead to an overall title in the *Philadelphia Press* and that it appeared on December 8, 1894 (not on December 4, as given in *Letters*). The other "Holland" column appeared in the *Philadelphia Press*, April 22, 1894 (not on April 15, as given in *Letters*): "Society Leaders' Suffrage Crusade."

Ignored by Marston, however, is what Crane wrote in his scrapbook, p. 18, about E. J. Edwards and his article on the Suffrage Crusade. "This is a fake—not only a fake but a wretched, unartistic fake written by a very stupid man." *See SCraneN*, 1, no. 4 (Spring, 1967). *See Crane*.

Lainoff, Seymour. "Jimmie in Crane's *Maggie*," *Iowa English Yearbook*, 10 (1965), 53–54.

Leed, Jacob, and Robert Hemenway. "Use of the Computer in Some Recent Studies of Literary Style," *Serif*, 2 (June, 1965), 17.

Ludwig, Richard M., ed. *Letters of Ford Madox Ford*. Princeton, N.J., 1965, pp. 125, 236, 243, 248, 302.

McCormick, Edgar L. "Thomas Wentworth Higginson, Poetry Critic for the *Nation*, 1877–1903," *Serif*, 2 (September, 1965), 18, 19.
See also Katz, "The 'Preceptor' and Another Poet:" (1968).

Macdonald, Ross. *Black Money*. New York, 1965.

MacShane, Frank. *The Life and Work of Ford Madox Ford*. New York, 1965, pp. 31, 32, 87, 197, 238n, 249.

Marsh, John L. *"The Red Badge Revisited,"* *Exercise Exchange*, 13 (November, 1965), 17–18.

Normand, Jean. "Sous le signe du centaure: la 'bataille' de Stephen Crane," *Études Anglaises*, 18 (July–September, 1965), 269–284.

Osborn, Neal. "Optograms, George Moore, and Crane's 'Silver Pageant,' " *American Notes and Queries*, 4 (November, 1965), 39–40.
On George Moore's influence on Crane in "The Silver Pageant."

———. "William Ellery Channing and *The Red Badge of Courage*," *Bulletin of the New York Public Library*, 69 (March, 1965), 182–196.
Osborn points out a number of parallels between Channing's 1816 discourse on "War" and *The Red Badge of Courage*. Parallel passages in both works reveal that Channing and Crane shared similar ideas about military courage, "the moral independence of the individual and his moral duty to the universal brotherhood of man," the celebration of Christian heroes, whose lives have been devoted to peace and service instead of legalized murder, etc. In Osborn's view Fleming's true conversion ends the novel; Conklin's function in *The Red Badge of Courage* is that of a horrible example (pagan militarism) and is contrasted with Wilson's conversion to Christian ideals.
"Killing in war tends in itself to produce the 'pagan' motives of bloody revenge, as Channing notes and Fleming illustrates. (The rejection of the pagan ideals of war through individual spiritual progress toward the Christian ideals of peace is the remedy Channing recommends and the one Fleming is to achieve.)" Channing "predicts" something of the theme and even the title of *The* [Delusive] *Red Badge of* (Military) *Courage:* "If men must fight, let

them wear the badges which become their craft." In sum, Channing anticipates the course of Henry Fleming's spiritual progress from childish devotion to pagan ideals of military glory to manly acceptance of the Christian ideals of peace. Channing's view of the young soldier is exemplified by one or another of Crane's triad of youth: Jim Conklin, who shares the role of the pathetic victim "marginally associated with Christ," Wilson with his "Christlike behavior," and Henry Fleming with his new "gospel of peace"—the acceptance of the Christian ideals of brotherhood and peace was Channing's credo. "Despite some cross-purposes in Crane's irony, it is Henry Fleming's true conversion which ends the novel. . . .

"Put very generally, Conklin's function is that of the horrible example, a painful proof that the pagan religion of military courage and unthinking obedience is the wrong way. And there is a sense in which his friend's terrible death is the price Fleming must pay for his own complicity in that 'religion.' But Wilson's conversion to Christian ideals exemplifies the right way. . . . What Channing hoped to teach youth was that these two models and a reflective command of his own experience taught Henry Fleming." *The Red Badge of Courage* is thus "an almost perfect 'exemplum' to Channing's 1816 sermon."

————. "The Riddle in 'The Clan': A Key to Crane's Major Fiction," *Bulletin of the New York Public Library*, 69 (April, 1965), 247–258.

An over-extended treatise, but not without useful insights; notably the link between Crane's poem which prefaces his Cuban War story "The Clan of No-Name" *and* a passage in Dr. J. T. Crane's *Popular Amusements* (1870), p. 194. Also, Osborn cites Ellery Channing's "The Philanthropist." *See* Osborn, "William Henry Channing" (1965).

As Osborn rightly observes: "Anyone familiar with the body of Crane's work will be aware that he makes a considerable use of biblical allusion."

Overton, James P. "The 'Game' in 'The Bride Comes to Yellow Sky,'" *Xavier University Studies*, 4 (1965), 3–11.

Peck, Richard E. "Stephen Crane and Baudelaire: A Direct Link," *American Literature*, 37 (May, 1965), 202–204.

A direct link exists between Crane's *The Black Riders* and the French Decadents, a link hitherto unnoticed. Crane's "A naked woman and a dead dwarf" restates the content of Baudelaire's "The Buffoon and the Venus," a prose poem translated into the English and published in *Pastels in Prose* (1890).

Not noticed by Peck is John D. Barry's *Bookman* article (1901) with his denial that Crane had ever heard of the French Symbolists.

————. "A 'New' Stephen Crane Poem," *Notes and Queries*, n.s., 12 (February, (1965), 64–66.

Opines that since "A Prologue" appeared entirely in capitals unlike the prose in Elbert Hubbard's *Roycroft Quarterly* (titled "A Souvenir and A Medley"), it is poetry and not prose; it thus remains today "an 'undiscovered' prose-poem, a 'new' addition to the total body of Crane's poetry."

Joseph Katz disposes of Peck's proposition in *Notes and Queries; see* Katz, "A New Stephen Crane Poem:" (1966), and *The Portable Stephen Crane* (1969).

On the source of "A Prologue" *see Crane*, pp. 545–546.

Perosa, Sergio. *The Art of F. Scott Fitzgerald.* Ann Arbor, Mich., 1965, pp. 76, 191, 194–195, 207.

Piper, Henry Dan. *F. Scott Fitzgerald: A Critical Portrait.* New York, 1965, pp. 35, 61–62.

Pizer, Donald. "Nineteenth-Century American Naturalism: An Essay in Definition," *Bucknell Review,* 13 (December, 1965), 4, 12–17, 18.

> On *The Red Badge* and Frank Norris's *McTeague.*

———. "Stephen Crane's *Maggie* and American Naturalism," *Criticism,* 7 (Spring, 1965), 168–175.

> *Maggie* is "a novel primarily about the falsity and destructiveness of certain moral codes. . . . But Crane's ironic technique suggests that his primary goal was not to show the effects of environment but to distinguish between moral appearance and reality, to attack the sanctimonious self-deception and sentimental emotional gratification of moral poses. He was less concerned with dramatizing a deterministic philosophy than in assailing those who apply a middle class morality to victims of amoral, uncontrollable forces in man and society." *Maggie* is thus like *The Red Badge of Courage,* which "seeks to demonstrate the falsity of a moral or romantic vision of the amorality which is war." Pizer's reading expands upon what has already been noticed (briefly) in essays by Stallman (1959), Cady (1962), and others.

Rahv, Philip. *The Myth and the Powerhouse.* New York, 1965, pp. 33–60. Reprints his *Kenyon Review* essay (Spring, 1956): "Fiction and the Criticism of Fiction."

> Reprinted in *Literature and the Sixth Sense.* New York, 1969.

> Rahv conveniently ignores all writers who took issue with his 1956 literal-minded reading of Crane. *See* Rahv (1956) and Stallman's reply, "Fiction and Its Critics," *Kenyon Review* (1957) and *Houses.*

Randel, William. "From Slate to Emerald Green: New Light on Crane's Jacksonville Visit," *Nineteenth-Century Fiction,* 19 (March, 1965), 357–368.

> Corrects *Letters* by redating Crane's notes to Cora for December 4 instead of Crane's mistaken November 4, 1896. *See also* Joseph Katz, "Stephen Crane, 'Samuel Carlton,' and A Recovered Letter" (1968).

> Randel provides much new data about Crane's whereabouts in Jacksonville during January to March, 1897.

> Randel assumes that Crane was with Cora on the trip to Greece, by train from Munich to Varna, Bulgaria; but he shows proof that the American correspondent whom Cora identified as "S. S." on this Orient Express trip could not have been Sylvester Scovel, as Lillian Gilkes proposed in her *Cora Crane.* Stephen Crane is presumed by Gilkes to have shared the overland route with Cora, but it is impossible for Miss Gilkes to substantiate her theory because nowhere in Cora Crane's loose-leaf sheets, notebook or so called diary, does she mention Stephen by name, as Stallman points out in "New Short Fiction by Stephen Crane: II" (1964). "The conclusive proof that Crane was not with Cora is that he figures not at all in Cora's written account of her journey to Constantinople. Miss Gilkes misquotes Cora's text thus: 'Many are the stories told by the guides—we have one who is a character. *Steve* named him Alabasta Sebastopoli.' *That* puts Stephen Crane in Constantinople with Cora—until one reads precisely what Cora wrote: '*Have* named him Alabasta Serbastopoli.'"

Schneider, Robert W. "Stephen Crane: The Promethean Revolt," in *Five Novelists of the Progressive Era.* New York, 1965, pp. 60–111.

Points out that Van Wyck Brooks "was perhaps the first to make a clear distinction between the two Gods that appear in *The Black Riders,* an insight that was developed by Daniel Hoffman." (However, Hoffman does not cite Van Wyck Brooks.) On the two Gods in Crane's poetry *see* Nelson (1963) and Wertheim (1964).

On Crane as a social critic; his sympathy for the Bowery underdog. Was Crane a reformer? No. He was critical of the characteristic self pity of the Bowery underdog and defined pity as "a virtue almost useless." Did Crane reject environment as a determinative power? Etc. "The heart of Crane's viewpoint seems to be that man in society is subject to illusions that are at variance with reality, and that human conduct is sometimes directed by a moral code which has little applicability to the lives of the participants. Man can break the code, he can depart from the social norm, and to this extent he has free will; but if he does so he must expect defeat at the hands of social prejudices. This Crane has certainly learned from his own experience. Still, man can exert his free will in defiance of society and Crane's position here was in line with the old American tradition that the individual is essentially free from the control of institutions and traditions. So, while it is true that Crane expressed indignation over social and economic injustice, it is not true that he felt these were the cause of the human dilemma."

On the Intrigue Poems he remarks that they express "the themes of love as a sacrifice, love as momentary joy and ceaseless remorse, and love as violence." On the Intrigue Poems *see Crane,* chap. 25.

Schneider is mistaken in claiming that Crane "had no use for Ambrose Bierce's work," and the letter of Crane to Joseph O'Connor is in fact to John Northern Hilliard, an error made in *Omnibus* and corrected in *Letters.*

Slavov, Georgi, ed. *The Red Badge of Courage.* Sophia, Bulgaria, 1965. Postword, pp. 140–144.

Translated into the Russian from the Modern Library edition of *The Red Badge of Courage* (1951), with Introduction by R. W. Stallman.

Sloan, John. *John Sloan's New York Scene,* ed. Bruce St. John. New York, 1965.

"It bothers me that scholars writing about the period from 1890 to 1920 assume I was influenced in my thinking and working habits by Stephen Crane and Theodore Dreiser. I never liked their idea about the artist needing to have experiences in order to understand or to gather subject matter from life. . . . I have never gone slumming to get subject matter." (Sloan's diary shows he read *The O'Ruddy* in August, 1908.)

Solomon, Eric. "Yet Another Source for *The Red Badge of Courage,*" *English Language Notes,* 11 (March, 1965), 215–217.

Suggests that Crane's treatment of courage and cowardice in *The Red Badge* may have derived from Horace Porter's "The Philosophy of Courage," appearing in *Century Magazine* (June, 1888).

———. "Stephen Crane, English Critics, and American Reviewers," *Notes and Queries,* n.s., 12 (February, 1965), 62–64.

Starrett, Vincent. *Born in a Bookshop: Chapters from the Chicago Renascence.* Norman, Okla., 1965, pp. 92, 125, 160, 211, 223.

Thorp, Carol, and Christine Baker [unsigned]. "Stephen Crane at Syracuse," *Daily Orange,* November 12, 1965. Illustrated.

Commented on in the *Courier* (Syracuse University Library) no. 25 (1966):

"This essay is interesting, informative, and accurate, and answers many questions about Crane's career as an erstwhile student at Syracuse University." The *Daily Orange* is the newspaper published by the students there.

Tibbetts, A. M. "Stephen Crane's 'The Bride Comes to Yellow Sky,'" *English Journal*, 54 (April, 1965), 314–316.

Treats the story as a comedy. West (1962) calls it a comedy of manners; G. W. Johnson (1963) refers to "the comic aspects of the 'transaction' which occurs between two different conventions"; and Cady (1961) calls the story "a hilariously funny parody of neo-romantic lamentations over 'the Passing of the West.'" *See also* Solomon, *Stephen Crane: From Parody to Realism* (1966).

Tibbetts thinks that Stallman in *Omnibus* misreads the story by not appreciating it as comedy. "R. W. Stallman believes, for example, that the marshal and the badman 'represent two opposite worlds or points of view: the idealistic world of spiritual values whose force lies in its innocence, and the non-imaginative world of crass realities.'" Compare Eudora Welty's remark (1949) that "The Bride" is a "playful story, using two situations like counters."

Tsunematsu, Masao. *"The Red Badge of Courage"* (in Japanese), *Shimane Daigaku Ronshu (Jinbun-kagaku)*, no. 14 (February, 1965), 51–62.

———. "Shakai hihyoka to shite no Stephen Crane" [Stephen Crane as a social critic], *Shimane Daigaku Ronshu (Jinbun-kagaku)*, no. 15 (December, 1965), 45–59.

Vanderbilt, Kermit, and Daniel Weiss. "From Rifleman to Flagbearer: Henry Fleming's Separate Peace in *The Red Badge of Courage*," *Modern Fiction Studies*, 11 (Winter, 1965–1966), 371–380.

"The present confusion over the unity of *The Red Badge of Courage* might have been partly avoided had Crane's later critics been more willing to accept his own stated intention, to present 'a psychological portrayal of fear.' Cosmic issues aside, *Red Badge* is clearly what Crane said it was, an extended dramatic portrayal of fear."*

Vanderbilt and Weiss, noting the wide disagreement over the meaning of the world of Henry Fleming, feel that an understanding of his self-appointed commission as flagbearer will disclose the structural and psychological unity of *The Red Badge of Courage*. In Part I, they review Henry's action up to his continuous firing at the retreating enemy. Their "understanding" of Henry, however, is based on two conclusions: that Jim's death has not produced any significant change in Henry and that Crane in no way hints that Henry will change from "fearful youth" to "happy warrior" after his first day of battle. In Part II, they continue to review Henry's action, emphasizing his role as flagbearer. In Part III, they summarize Henry's alternating actions and conclude that Crane's final chapter does not show Henry as seasoned soldier, mythical hero, optimistic humanitarian, nor confident Christian.

Vanderbilt and Weiss quote Stallman in his "Notes Toward an Analysis of *The Red Badge of Courage*" (1951): the novel "is about the self-combat of a youth who fears [*sic*] and stubbornly resists change, and the actual battle is symbolic of this spiritual warfare against change and growth." (The novel is

---

* However, that *The Red Badge* contains far more than solely "a psychological portrayal of fear" is evidenced by the critical warfare in interpretations of that novel. As for any author's declared intentions, "Never trust the author; trust the tale" (to quote D. H. Lawrence).

that, but it is not just that—and nothing more. Beer and Berryman settle for the thesis of fear throughout Crane's works. On *The Red Badge* they report contemporary reviews, but neither Berryman nor Beer scrutinize—or even summarize—*The Red Badge of Courage,* a point ignored by all Crane critics.)

Vasilievskaya, Olga B. "Evolution in the Art of Stephen Crane," *Izvestiya, Academy of Sciences of the U.S.S.R., Series of Literature and Language,* 24, no. 3 (1965), 226–236.

In translation by Mrs. W. S. Woytinsky:* "Unfortunately, very little has been written about Crane in the Soviet press, though his writings are included in the programs and textbooks of the universities and enjoy the interest of Soviet readers. The current American articles about the work of Crane do not reveal how his talent and his work have developed in the course of time. Beer and Linson limit themselves to the description of the most personal features of Crane's life, while Berryman offers a rather superficial survey of Crane's writings, projected against the background of his life story largely taken from the book of Beer. Stallman offers an apparently erroneous concept, namely that Crane's creativeness did not grow with the years but on the contrary it did deteriorate. Not convincing is also the attitude of Wilson Follett. . . ." Follett scattered through twelve volumes Crane's works which had appeared originally in one volume. "By doing this, Follett not only has changed the intention of Crane in his volume *Wounds in the Rain,* but has also deprived this book of its accusatory powers."

The main significance of *Maggie* "is in the fact that Crane, against his own will, had found the explanation of the horrible life-conditions in the Bowery—social inequality, unequal distribution of income, capitalistic exploitation and the passivity of those who by their patience permit others to exploit them, thus enabling the exploiters to enrich themselves by fantastic profits."

The war of 1898 did not interrupt the growth of Crane's creative strength; it helped him to reappraise his previous attitude toward American politics. "He saw the American soldiers wounded, hungry, sick from malaria, dying not only from the enemy's bullets but from the neglect by their commanders. In contrast to Mark Twain, Crane did not understand the meaning of that war. Too strong was the propaganda which confused even many of those who were much more experienced in politics than was Crane." His writings during the second period of his development, 1897–1900, consisting mainly of correspondence from the war front, are not second to those published earlier; they are characterized by a growing tendency towards realism. "In contrast to his previous war writings Crane had learned by then what war really was. His best writings of the more mature period contain the condemnation of the political structure that breeds wars."

Walker, Warren S. *Twentieth-Century Short Story Explication.* Hamden, Conn., 1965.

Weiss, Daniel. "*The Red Badge of Courage,*" *Psychoanalytic Review,* 52 (Summer, 1965), 32–52 (176–196), 130–154 (460–483).

* In letter to R.W.S. (December 21, 1965): "While O. B. Vasilievskaya criticizes everybody who has written about Crane, her article is no more penetrating than would have been any article written by other Soviet writers. Naturally, Crane is great to her, as he would be to other Soviet writers, because he has revealed the depth of poverty in the United States, social injustice and inequality, the criminal irresponsibility of the American High Command, and so on."

Part I consists of five sections. In Section 1, Weiss assumes "that Hemingway's formulation of the steps by which one becomes a veteran (or at any rate masters fear) is empirically correct and that it follows with reasonable accuracy Crane's own formulation . . . [Weiss also assumes] that both writers have in their own way struck on a psychological process whose accuracy may be objectively determined." In Section 2, after stating that psychoanalysis "succeeds in giving the work of art its fullest measure of importance," he remarks that John Berryman fails in his biography of Crane to "attempt to account psychoanalytically for the habitual motifs in Crane's fiction." Weiss prefers "to neglect the artist in considering his work." In Section 3, he notes Henry Fleming's two predictable anxieties: his anticipation of danger and his consideration of his relationship to the group. When Henry enters battle as a spectator, a "psychological naturalism" asserts itself in his conditioned response of defense and aggression. In Section 4, he discusses the overall motif in *The Red Badge of Courage:* Henry's obsessive need to purge himself of fear, exercising his "anxiety-defense mechanisms." Henry flees when his anxiety turns to panic, a bad adjustment to fear. Weiss sees similarities in Hemingway's Frederick Henry: in Henry Fleming's sense of invulnerability by projecting war into the past and into literature and by projecting his own fears onto his friend Wilson. In presenting the Oedipal family involvement in a military situation, which "provides a moratorium on maturity," Crane extends Henry's concept of his mother in the collective security of the regiment and of his father in certain men who represent aggression, assurance, and omnipotence. In Section 5, he affirms that Henry achieves "oceanic reunion" in his first battle sleep. With Jim Conklin as his ego ideal, Henry confronts the idea of death when the enemy rises up against him, and he flees.

Part II consists of seven sections (6–13). In Section 6, Weiss remarks that Henry "overcomes his fear of death by the strength of his identification with Conklin." His struggle in seeking reunion with omnipotence is, in Oedipal terms, "a reunion through a masochistic identification with the mother." In Section 7, aware of unity in *The Red Badge of Courage* and consistency in Henry's character, Weiss interprets the failure of Henry's rationalization as a signal for his flight toward death, "whereupon it loses its terror for him and he returns to life." *The Red Badge of Courage* may "be described as a rhythm of alternating 'flights.'" In Section 8, continuing comparisons between *The Red Badge of Courage* and *Oedipus Rex,* Weiss notes. however, Henry's anger and sense of revenge in his second stand in battle. In Section 9, Weiss considers Henry's moral and emotional sensibilities, his role as spectator in seizing the flag that he endows with "intermingled trappings of maternity and divinity," his new invulnerability in seizing the rivals' flag, and finally his repudiation of that which he had struggled to achieve. In Section 10, Weiss discusses some analogies between Crane's and Hemingway's lives and fiction. In Section 11, he extends his argument to Crane's other fiction to show the same psychological texture: Crane's creation of an uneasy sense of invulnerability in war, of father images, of maternal regiments, and of passive neophytes. In Section 12, he focuses on the Swede in "The Blue Hotel" to illustrate the framework of "the game syndrome," implied in Henry's reaction to war "first as a 'blue demonstration' and finally as a 'matched game.'" Mastering his own homosexual aggressions, the Swede, like Henry, moves from "apprehensive depression to manic elation." "Crane's vision of normality [is] a mind turned outward upon the world, away from its own crippling presentiments." *See* Wertheim (1971).

West, Ray B., Jr. "Stephen Crane: Author in Transition," in *Critical Approaches to American Literature,* ed. Ray B. Browne and Martin Light. New York, 1965, pp. 166–178. Reprinted from *American Literature,* 34 (May, 1962), 215–228. *See* West (1962).

1966

Albrecht, Robert C. "Content and Style in *The Red Badge of Courage,*" *College English,* 27 (January, 1966), 487–492.
   A derivative footnote; nothing new here.

Bassan, Maurice, ed. Preface and Textual Note, *Stephen Crane's Maggie: Text and Context.* Belmont, Calif., 1966.
   Reprints short excerpts from all critics of *Maggie,* beginning with Howells. Portions of essays by Berryman, Stallman, and others have been deleted; intact are David Fitelson's "Stephen Crane's *Maggie* and Darwinism" (1964) and William Lenehan's "The Failure of Naturalistic Techniques in Stephen Crane's *Maggie,*" published here for the first time. *See* Lenehan (1966). Quotes passages of Crane's letters relevant to *Maggie* and a short passage from Crane's manuscript "City of Mexico," here for the first time.*
   Reproduces for the first time the 1893 text of *Maggie.* Not noticed by the editor is the fact that all editions—English and American—subsequent to the 1893 *Maggie*—reproduce an error which crept into Heinemann's hardcover *Maggie: A Child of the Streets,* published in September, 1896. This misprint occurs in the opening paragraphs of Chapter 5: "Dirt disgusted her," which reads in the 1893 *Maggie:* "Dirt disguised her."
   Bassan has it that Crane began *Maggie* in the Delta Upsilon house at Syracuse University in the spring of 1891. This squares with Stallman (1952) and *Omnibus.*

Bridgman, Richard. *The Colloquial Style in America.* New York, 1966, pp. 137–140.

Budd, Louis J. "Stephen Crane," in *American Literary Scholarship/1964,* ed. James Woodress. Durham, N.C., 1966, pp. 117, 119.

Burgauner, Christoph. "Stephen Crane: Ein Wunder an Mut," *Neue Deutsche Heft,* 13, ii (1966), 164–166.

Burns, Lando, Jr. [On "The Open Boat"], *Studies in Short Fiction,* 3 (Summer, 1966), 455–458.

Carruth, Gorton, and associates. "Stephen Crane," *The Encyclopedia of American Facts and Dates,* 4th ed. New York, 1966, pp. 364, 372, 380.

---

* From "Three Mexican Sketches" reproduced for the first time from the holograph manuscript in Columbia University Crane Collection in Stallman, "Stephen Crane: Some New Sketches" (1967).

Cazemajou, Jean. "Impressions et images de la charge de San Juan," *Caliban,* no. 3 (January, 1966), 215–234.

Colvert, James B. "The Origins of Stephen Crane's Literary Creed," in *A Mirror for Modern Scholars,* ed. L. A. Beaurline. New York, 1966, pp. 156–165. Reprinted from *Studies in English* (1955).

Delvaille, Bernard, trans. *Couleurs locales, treize nouvelles regionales americaines.* Paris: Seghers, 1966.

> Contains translation into the French of "The Bride Comes to Yellow Sky."

Denny, Neville. "Imagination and Experience in Stephen Crane," *English Studies in Africa,* 9 (March, 1966), 28–42.

Ellison, Ralph. "Stephen Crane and the Mainstream of American Fiction," in *Shadow and Act.* New York and London, 1966, pp. 74–88. Reprinted from his Introduction to *The Red Badge of Courage and Four Great Stories* (1960).

> One of the best essays in the book, says the *TLS,* January 18, 1968: "Mr. Ellison shows that after the abandonment of reconstruction and the consequent blurring of 'the line between civil war and civil peace' it is Stephen Crane who takes on the burden of every responsible American, 'a questioning attitude toward every aspect of the nation's self-image.' That is his greatness."

Gale, Robert L. *Crane's The Red Badge of Courage* [and Other Works], Woodbury, N.Y.: Barron's Educational Series, 1966.

> Barron's simplified approach to *The Red Badge* simplifies what occurs in the novel. Gale's summary of Chapter 2 says that "In the morning it becomes obvious that the tall soldier's rumor of their moving was false." However, not noticed by Gale in his chapter by chapter summary is the fact that the tall soldier's prophecy comes true. This error, p. 23, is repeated in Gale's discussion of Jim Conklin, pp. 59–60 ("Main Characters Analyzed"). Jim "is a fist-fighter who spreads false rumors."
>
> Gale's statement that Henry Fleming "seems unaware of the wafer-like sun" ignores the manuscript passage: "He turned in tupenny fury upon the high, tranquil sky." *(Omnibus,* p. 292.) Gale's text analysis makes no reference to the existence of MS. SV and MS. LV (in *Omnibus,* and in the Signet *Red Badge of Courage,* 1960).

Gibson, D. B. "Crane's *The Red Badge of Courage,*" *Explicator,* 24 (February, 1966), item 49.

> Gibson observes at least thirty references, mostly metaphors, to fairytales and myths in Crane's *Red Badge of Courage.* These references to tales and legends in which a hero battles a dragon or monster and then, if successful, rewarded, "indicate an awareness on Crane's part of the archetypal nature of the experience Henry Fleming undergoes, and they show us how Henry conceives of himself and his situation." Gibson sees these analogies as centering around Chapter 12 in which the "cheery soldier" functions as the figure in myth who lends aid to the hero confronted by tasks beyond his capacities. The use of the third person restricted point of view in the novel allows Crane to employ mythology without "committing himself to the proposition that the universe is so constituted that the supernatural does in fact intervene in the affairs of men."

Harada, Keiichi, ed. *The Open Boat and Other Stories.* Tokyo: Shimizu Shoin, 1966.

Holman, C. Hugh. *The American Novel Through Henry James*. New York, 1966, pp. 23–25.

"A seriously deficient 'Goldentree Bibliography,' " according to Katz in *SCraneN*, 1, no. 2 (1966).

Honig, Donald. "Stephen Crane: The Boy Genius," *Caper*, 12, no. 1 (January, 1966), 53, 60.

A sketch of Crane's life in *Caper*, a girlie magazine.

Hudspeth, Robert N. "The *Thoth* Annual Bibliography of Stephen Crane Scholarship," *Thoth*, 7 (Spring, 1966), 76–77.

Kagami, Eizo. "Stephen Crane no 'Active Service' ni tsuite" [On *Active Service* of Stephen Crane], *Gifu Daigaku Kyoyo-bu Kenkyu Hokoku*, no. 2 (1966), 49–58.

Kanno, Masaaki. "Stephen Crane no ningen zo—kare no shokanshu yo ri mita" [Image of man in Stephen Crane—seen in his letters], *Tenri Daigaku Gakuho*, no. 52 (June, 1966), 1–35.

Kaplan, Justin. *Mr. Clemens and Mark Twain*. New York, 1966, p. 504 (index).

Lists Crane, Stephen, for p. 377. However, there is nothing about Crane, p. 377, nor anywhere throughout Kaplan's book. For the relationship of Crane and Twain *see Crane* (1968).

Katz, Joseph. Introduction, *Maggie: A Girl of the Streets (A Story of New York)*. Gainesville, Fla., 1966.

A facsimile reproduction of the first edition of 1893. Bassan's reproduction of the 1893 text appeared simultaneously. *See* Bassan, *Stephen Crane's Maggie: Text and Context* (1966).

———. The *Maggie* Nobody Knows," *Modern Fiction Studies*, 12 (Summer, 1966), 200–212.

Contends against the textual theory that because the 1896 edition was the last authorial revision it should stand as definitive. This theory is defective "since it ignores the circumstances under which the revision was made, circumstances in which Crane evidently subordinated artistic concerns."

Because Appleton editors imposed house styling on the novel, a house styling based on the English tradition,* "*Maggie* became a strange mutant, an American novel on an American theme in a local dialect—in English orthography. But more important, the Appleton house styling interfered with Crane's stylistic effects."

The *Maggie* "nobody knows" is the 1893 text, first made known in Stallman, "Stephen Crane's Revision of *Maggie*:" a collation of the two editions (1955), and in Gibson, Introduction, *The Red Badge of Courage* (1956). An omission from the 1896 text, first noted by Stallman's collation, is the portrait of the leering fat man, the tenth man Maggie meets on her journey in 1893. "Mr. Stallman continued: 'The leering fat man represents a mockery of Maggie's plight, and his attribute of "dead jelly fish" prepares for the death by drowning that occurs subsequent to Maggie's encountering him. That he is a "dead jelly fish" anticipates, to put it another way, the death of Maggie. On both accounts, as I see it, this unreproduced passage from the 1893 edition of *Maggie* deserves to be incorporated into future editions on the grounds of its artistic relevance to what precedes and follows it.' " Katz agrees: "The

---

* The same English tradition prevailed in the 1920s at Alfred A. Knopf, and consequently *Work* consists of tampered texts.

grotesque great figure that she meets at the river certainly does suggest the end that she will meet." Unnoticed by Katz, however, is William Gibson's shrewd commentary on Maggie's end (1962).

——. "A 'New' Stephen Crane poem: An Evaluation," *Notes and Queries*, 13 (September, 1966), 346–349.

Argues against the claim that "A Prologue" belongs in the canon of Crane's poetry.* It isn't a poem; it is "an attempt to compress drama to its fundamentals."

Neither Katz nor Peck, who claims "A Prologue" is a poem (1965), notice that the source of "A Prologue" is Talmage's dramatic prose sketch in *Night Side of New York Life* (1878), as cited for the first time in *Crane.*

——. "SC to Elbert Hubbard: A New Letter," *Stephen Crane Newsletter*, 1, no. 2 (Winter, 1966), 2.

——. "SC to Mr. Richards: A New Letter at the Hamilton Sale," *Stephen Crane Newsletter*, 1, no. 2 (Winter, 1966), 5.

——. "'The Blue Battalions' and the Uses of Experience," *Studia Neophilologica*, 38, no. 1 (1966), 107–116.

Rightly redates "The Blue Battalions" for 1897, rather than 1896, as Hoffman opined in *Poetry.* The poem can be dated with a high degree of probability by the kind of paper it was written on, but also by collating the poem with his Greco-Turkish War dispatches; the parallels are "extensive, revealing, often startling." An excellent essay transcending its starting point in bibliographical data. However (a minor note), Katz neglects to state that "The Blue Battalions" made its appearance in *Spanish-American War Songs* (1898), when in fact it was not a Spanish American War Song!

Katz, Joseph, ed. *The Poems of Stephen Crane: A Critical Edition.* New York: Cooper Square, 1966. With sample facsimiles of manuscripts. Portraits.

Katz, p. xxxiii, says "It would be a distortion to say with Thomas Beer that 'the reading nation was told at once that Stephen Crane was mad,' but it would be equally mistaken to agree with O'Donnell's suggestion that Crane's reception was enthusiastic." However, Katz himself has committed a distortion of O'Donnell's statement in that O'Donnell stated nothing of the kind. *See* O'Donnell, "A Note on the Reception of *The Black Riders*" (1952).

The source is not identified for the Crane photograph used as frontispiece and on the jacket. The photograph appeared in *"S. S. Commodore,* Filibuster," *Mail and Express,* January 21, 1897. On a copy of that photograph in Lilly Library, Indiana University, appears on verso this new Crane letter published in *Poems.*

> "My dear Doctor: I was in Virginia when your letter came to Hartwood and so did not get it until yesterday. You delight me with your appreciation and yet too it makes me afraid. I did not bend under the three hills of ridicule which were once upon my shoulders but I dont know that I am strong enough to withstand the kind things that are now sometimes said to me. I have a strong desire to sit down and look at myself. Always your friend / Stephen Crane."

Katz's *Poems* could not have been published without clearing the project with Stallman, but there is no admission of that specific and large debt in Katz's Acknowledgements, pp. vii–viii.

* *See* Peck, "A 'New' Stephen Crane Poem" (1965), an article of miniskirt importance.

Not cited by Katz is the source of the Crane photograph used on the back of the dust jacket. It obtains from Jessie Conrad's *Joseph Conrad and His Circle* (1935). It is of no use to the Crane scholar to be told, for instance, that the Crane photograph in his edition of the 1894 *Red Badge of Courage* (1967) is "From the proof in the collection of Joseph Katz."

Error occurs p. 195, where Katz claims that "What? / You define me God with these trinkets?" appeared in Hubbard's *Fra* in 1900. Katz says that Hubbard's note preceding this fragment of the poem beginning in *War Is Kind* "A little mile more or less!" provides "the possibility for distorting the dating of the poem." However, this is not true in that Hubbard's note was written in 1910, his *Fra* publishing lines 7–19 of the complete poem in July, 1910, not in 1900 as Katz mistakenly has it. (For this item I am indebted to John Baker of Minneapolis.)

Reviewed:

Maurice Bassan, *American Literature*, 39 (January, 1968), 575–576.

Olov Fryckstedt, *Studia Neophilologica*, 40 (April, 1968), 255–258.

Katz, Joseph, and Matthew J. Bruccoli. "A Colonial Edition of *Great Battles of the World*," *Stephen Crane Newsletter* 1, no. 2 (Winter, 1966), 3–4.

Kerscher, Rudolph. "*Whilomville Stories*: Stephen Crane's vergessene Kindheitserzählungen," *Die Neueren Sprachen*, 15 (February, 1966), 76–80.

Kissane, Leedice. "Interpretation through Language: A Study of the Metaphors in Stephen Crane's 'The Open Boat,'" *Rendezvous*, 1, no. 1 (1966), 18–22.

"'In "The Open Boat" things viewed by the men at sea are viewed as though they were men on land,' says R. W. Stallman. Furthermore, could we not say, things at sea are described in terms of specific experiences the men have undergone on land. . . .'" Some interesting insights on "The Open Boat" from several diverse approaches, such as the notation that Crane "maintains a jeering attitude toward women throughout his tale. . . ." A worthwhile article.

Kudo, Kozo. "Stephen Crane's Psychologism," *Yamagata Daigaku Eigo Eibungaku Kenkyu*, no. 11 (February, 1966), 27–60.

Kurita, Ariyasu. "Stephen Crane no kenkyu—violence to shi ni kansuru ichi kōsatsu" [A study of Stephen Crane on violence and death], *Chuo Gakuin Daigaku Ronso*, 1 (November, 1966), 23–28.

Lavers, Norman. "Order in *The Red Badge of Courage*," *University of Kansas City Review*, 32 (Summer, 1966), 287–295.

Superimposes upon Crane's works a pattern which he believes fits "with great precision. . . . If R. W. Stallman's attempts to fit the Christian myth over this basic pattern seem unsuccessful, it is only because of his consistently misplaced emphasis. Actually, no doubt due to Crane's early religious environment, the movement of his work readily translates into Christian terminology. The pattern leads from (1) a sense of sin, through (2) awareness of mortality, (3) the sacrifice of an innocent, (4) atonement through suffering and 'good works' (in a vividly depicted purgatory) to (5) ultimate redemption through self-knowledge." All three of Crane's major works follow the same pattern: separation from the mother in order to achieve full development as an individual; they are strikingly parallel in theme and structure. (However, Lavers does not mention *Maggie* because it evidently does not fit his scheme.)

Crane in *George's Mother*, written some years before Freud's first mention of the Oedipus complex, leads us "without a false step" through the history of a terrible mother who possesses her son "all but physically, so that the covert carnal temptations of their relationship have obsessed them both with guilt, paralyzed the son's development, and bred in him what may be reasonably called a latent homosexuality. This sounds glib. . . ." (I quite agree.)

The same pattern of separation from the mother is seen—according to Lavers—in "The Open Boat" and in *The Red Badge*. In the former, "separation from mother is represented archetypically in the men's attempts to escape 'the fierce old mother' of Whitman, the maternal sea. Without pressing for a homosexual interpretation, I can point out that once more the first step away from the mother is taken with the assistance of other men, with whom the protagonist has an especially close fellow-feeling." (In other words, the oiler is a slick homosexual!)

As for *The Red Badge*, Lavers says that other critics agree that it is pattern-less, a mere series of brilliant and inconsequential episodes, "at best ordered by alternating moods."* He says that Crane is "entirely unaware of what he is about. . . .

"Nonetheless, the story has a firmly articulated structure, and it pursues a consistent course to an unequivocal conclusion." To see this, says Lavers, "we have to give Crane's famous imagery our *shrewdest* attention." However, "The imagery *per se,* operating so perfectly on the descriptive level, is not going to concern us here. . . ."

Lavers nevertheless studies *The Red Badge* solely through its animal imagery,† tracing through it the ebb and surge of Henry Fleming's courage during his progress from sin to redemption, from painful separation to triumphal return, "which I have all along been suggesting is central to Crane's major work." His courage parallels (somehow) Crane's own efforts "to become free of an Oedipal fixation."

Leeb, David, ed. *The Red Badge of Courage*. Philadelphia, 1966. Study guide-book of Educational Research Associates.

Biographical sketch; summary of the chapters: 1–4, The Novice; 5–9, The Initiate; 10–18, The Conflict; 19–24, The Veteran. Recent criticism, "starting with Stallman, seems to revolve not around the change in styling (convention *versus* 'realism' or 'impressionism'), but around the more specific factors of interpretation and explanation. Critics are now absorbed in the extent and meaning of the symbolism within *The Red Badge of Courage* (particularly that which surrounds the figure of Jim Conklin), the question of ironic overtones in the book (i.e., was Crane's use of irony, if indeed it was irony, intentional?), and Henry Fleming's achievement of maturity. This interpretative trend has, in turn, led to more speculation about the construction of the book."

On the image of the red sun "pasted in the sky like a wafer," which image "is probably the strongest argument for the symbolic identification of Jim Conklin with the Christ figure, Stallman's interpretation is opposed by Greenfield (1958). Leeb concludes that Crane does not actually equate Jim Conklin with Christ, but that he "does seem to want to utilize certain Christlike similar-

---

* However—*contra* Lavers—a work may be composed of episodes and simultaneously patterned one to another (however inconsequential the episodes). That *The Red Badge* is patterned by alternating moods was first said in *Omnibus* and in Stallman (1951).

† On animal imagery in *The Red Badge see* Marcus (1959).

ities in describing the stoic, almost martyr-like death of Jim Conklin. . . . In spite of Jim's sacrificial death (if the reader chooses to consider it that), Henry has had no rebirth of spirit and no moral regeneration." Leeb concludes that Jim Conklin's death "does have some qualities of a redemptive and sacrificial nature," but his death-dance negates the sacrificial symbolism by Crane's savage thrust "at the fanaticism in religion. The symbolic role of Jim Conklin, such as it is, is a revelation of Crane's ambivalent attitude toward religion, much as he preferred to remain the detached observer."

Lenehan, William T. "The Failure of Naturalistic Techniques in Stephen Crane's *Maggie*," in *Stephen Crane's Maggie: Text and Context,* ed. Maurice Bassan. Belmont, Calif., 1966, pp. 166–173.

Leslie, Anita. *Mr. Frewen of England.* London, 1966, pp. 158–162.
    Of Moreton Frewen, Crane wrote: "He seemed like a search-light on a hungry boat at sea." New Crane letters here. Claims that Moreton Frewen let Crane have Brede Place for a rent of £40 a year on condition that Crane continue restorations of the manor-house, but the rent was £120. The new Crane letters are quoted in *Crane,* by permission of Anita Leslie.

Leyris, Pierre, trans. *La bateau ouvert [The Open Boat].* Paris: Mercure de France, 1966.
    Reviewed:
        Claude Michel Cluny, *Nouvelle revue Française,* 14 (November 1, 1966), 913–914.
        Michel Boulanger, *Esprit,* 35 (February, 1967), 411–412.

Lytle, Andrew. " 'The Open Boat': A Pagan Tale," in *The Hero with the Private Parts.* Baton Rouge, La., 1966, pp. 60–75.

McCaffrey, John K., William G. Rogers, and Lyman Bryson. "Stephen Crane: *The Red Badge of Courage,*" in *Invitation to Learning,* ed. George D. Crothers. New York, 1966, pp. 127–235. First published 1953.

Marcus, Mordecai. "Structure and Irony in Stephen Crane's 'War Is Kind,' " *College Language Association Journal,* 9 (1966), 274–278.
    Neither Berryman (1950), nor Hoffman, *Poetry* (1957) notice "the complex structure of the poem, the subtlety of its ironies, nor the ways in which these technical features create a persona." Marcus cites Stallman as "the first critic to have applied the concepts of alternation of mood to Crane's fiction and poetry.* Certainly it is a major technique in the poem 'War Is Kind,' and thorough understanding of the poem requires exploration of its variety of voices and their relationship to its structure."

Marsh, John, and John Dove. *On Televising American Literature: A Report.* American Studies Association of the Middle Atlantic States, 1966.

Martin, Jay. "*The Red Badge of Courage:* The Education of Henry Fleming," in *Twelfth Yale Conference on the Teaching of English.* New Haven, Conn.: Yale University Office of Teacher Training, 1966, pp. 75–85.
    Martin feels that Hawthorne, James, and Crane "form a clear line in the tradition of American fiction which has continued through Faulkner, Hemingway, and Ralph Ellison." All explore "external action and the inward meaning," as well as "states of mind" and "moral behavior." Martin then skillfully

---

* In "Stephen Crane: A Revaluation" (1952) and in *Omnibus* (1952), p. 571. The concept of "alternation of mood" or Double Mood derives from Kenneth Burke's *Counterstatement* (1931).

develops each of "six states of consciousness in which Crane shows Henry's mind disengaged from a sense of reality": (1) "unreasoning fear of death," (2) "feeling of the utter helplessness of the human condition," (3) "savage response to war," (4) "dwelling upon death," (5) "curious but cold regard for war," (6) excessive and grotesque self-confidence "because compensating for fears expressed on other occasions." He concludes with brief reference to "The Veteran" as "the truly heroic conclusion to Henry Fleming's education."

Mayfield, John S. "To Stephencraneites," *Courier*, 25 (1966), 26.

Mohrt, Michel. "Le poeme rouge de la guerre," *Figaro Litteraire*, October 27, 1966, p. 6.

Monteiro, George. "Cora Crane to John Hay: A New Letter on Stephen Crane's Havana Disappearance," *Stephen Crane Newsletter*, 1, no. 3 (Spring, 1967), 2–3.
 See Crane, p. 415.

Morita, Masaru. "Stephen Crane kenkyu" [A study of Stephen Crane], *Hiroshima Daigaku Bungaku-bu Phoenix*, no. 4 (1966), 36–41.

Napier, James J. "Indifference of Nature in Crane and Camus." *CEA Critic*, 28 (February, 1966), 11–12.
 Crane's universe in "The Open Boat" is flatly indifferent to man's plight; Camus in *The Stranger* reflects "benign indifference."

Neilson, William Allan, ed. "Stephen Crane" in *Webster's Biographical Dictionary*. Springfield, Mass., 1966, p. 363.

Nose, Toshi. "On Stephen Crane's *The Red Badge of Courage*," *Okayama Daigaku Kyoyo-bu Kiyo*, no. 2 (1966).

O'Donnell, Bernard. "Stephen Crane's *The O'Ruddy*: A Problem in Authorship Determination," in *The Computer and Literary Style*, ed. Jacob Leed. Kent, Ohio, 1966, pp. 107–115.
 Crane probably wrote Chapter 24 of *The O'Ruddy*.

O'Donnell, Thomas F., ed. *Harold Frederic's Stories of York State*. Introduction by Edmund Wilson. Syracuse, N.Y., 1966.
 Editor's foreword, p. v., on Crane.

Oshitani, Zen-ichiro. " 'Maggie' ni tsuite" [On Stephen Crane's *Maggie*], *Wakayama Daigaku Kyoikugaku-bu Kiyo (Jinbun)*, no. 16 (December, 1966), 31–48.

Overland, Orm. "The Impressionism of Stephen Crane: A Study in Style and Technique," in *Americana Norvegica*, ed. Sigmund Skard and Henry H. Wasser. Oslo, Norway, and Philadelphia, 1966, pp. 239–285.
 Crane as an Impressionist. As in *The Red Badge*, Crane's use of detail evokes the Impressionist's attitude to experience as a succession of detached and momentary impressions. "The author does not introduce order where there is only confusion." As Overland admits, "this paper may not have come up with sensational news." Missing from Overland's 46-page survey with its 80 footnotes is citation of *Omnibus* with its detailed analysis of *The Red Badge* and the French Impressionist's method, as in Seurat; also Stallman, "Stephen Crane: A Revaluation" (1952), and *Houses. See also* Kwiat (1952), Hough, "Crane and Goethe:" (1962), and *Crane*.

Peper, Jurgen. "Das Erleben im 'Eindruck': Stephen Crane," in *Bewusstsein-*

lagen des Erzahlens und Erzahlte Wirklichkeiten. Leiden, E. J. Brill, 1966, pp. 77–94.

Pizer, Donald. *Realism and Naturalism in Nineteenth Century American Literature.* Carbondale, Ill., 1966, pp. 88–98, 121–131. Recast from Pizer's "Stephen Crane's *Maggie* and American Naturalism," *Criticism,* 7 (Spring, 1965), 168–177.

Price, Lawrence M. *The Reception of U.S. Literature in Germany.* Chapel Hill, N.C., 1966, pp. 123, 157.

Raasch, Albert. *"Whilomville Stories:* Stephen Crane's vergessene Kindheitserzählungen," *Die Neueren Sprachen,* 15 (1966), 77–86.

Sansom, William. Introduction, *Maggie: A Girl of the Streets.* London, Cassell, 1966, pp. vii–xiv. Ed. Herbert Van Thal for Cassell's "First Novel Library." However, the text is not that of the 1893 *Maggie,* which is misdated for 1892. And the title is the American version.

   Sansom errs in saying that Crane—after *The Red Badge*—wrote "no further novel." (The flyleaf lists other novels by Crane.) He errs also in saying that Crane was the youngest of fourteen "sons" of a Methodist moralist preacher, that Crane "married in Greece," and that Crane was a "prose writer of small output." Crane wrote enough to fill twelve volumes in *Work* and three more volumes in *Letters, War Dispatches,* and *NYCS.* Crane, in fact, wrote far more than James Joyce, whose total output is contained, or almost so, in the *Portable Joyce.*

Solomon, Eric. *Stephen Crane: From Parody to Realism.* Cambridge, Mass., 1966.

   Solomon, unfortunately, uses for Crane's texts the tampered texts in *Work.* However, for the text of *The Red Badge* he uses *Omnibus.* "Far from being a reporter, or a war novelist, or an uneducated genius, Stephen Crane was, I contend, that most conscious of literary artificers, a parodist." Whereas the traditional success novel recounts the rise in fortune of the young hero, Crane's failure novel—*George's Mother*—"tells of the fall of the young antihero. The plot, then, is plainly parodic. Within the context of the novel, moreover, Crane seems to laugh at another genre, the temperance novel" (p. 51). "There is another element of parody in the verbal texture of *George's Mother.* Here, as in the first section of *Maggie,* Crane leans heavily on war imagery. . . . In *George's Mother,* however, there seems to be a crucial difference in Crane's employment of these images, and we may conjecture that he is parodying himself, the author of *The Red Badge of Courage*" (p. 57). "When we consider the bare plot of *George's Mother* we can understand Crane's parodic approach that reverses the American type of success saga. Like the Alger hero, George is strong, has a job, is recently from the country, and provides sole support for his widowed mother. There the resemblance ends" (pp. 50–51). It does indeed!

   Solomon's thesis forces him into claiming that "The Open Boat" is "a sport in the Crane canon," admitting that the tale is not "essentially parodic." A good many of Crane's major works, and minor ones as well, are not parodies. "An Illusion in Red and White" is a parody, but Solomon does not mention that tale.
Reviewed:

   Charles Poore, *New York Times,* December 22, 1966: "Crane's bladed

phrasing, his wild humor, his deadly irony, convey the shock of excellence."
Mr. Solomon "rides his chosen hobby horse too hard. But then, what else
are scholarly hobby horses for, ladies and gentlemen? A less stately word for
parody as Mr. Solomon uses it to dramatize Crane's blistering scorn for
triteness would, I suppose, be debunking. But right now the in word is parody.
We encounter it wherever even the most inept manifestations of image-
breaking are currently rampant." Mr. Solomon sprinkles his pages with jab-
berwocky. "Deep in the research-tangled wildwood of citations, enumerations
and footnotery there is a built-in target for parody. What is it? Why, it's Mr.
Solomon himself parodying the higher criticism in America."

Matthew J. Bruccoli, *SCraneN*, 1, no. 3 (Spring, 1967): The thesis of *From
Parody to Realism* "will not stand up under scrutiny of Crane's work. He did
not serve an apprenticeship through parody, not if a parody still is a burlesque
imitation with exaggeration of the content and technique of the thing being
imitated. Like most young writers, Crane reacted against certain models, but
it is inaccurate to claim that he parodied them. *Maggie* may well have been
a rejection of sentimental fiction about slum-flowers, and *The Red Badge* rejects the melodrama of heroic war stories. But they do not parody: they
ironically reject the clichés of popular fiction while expressing Crane's own
visions of reality." Bruccoli finds Solomon's misreadings of "The Open Boat"
and of *The Red Badge* "appalling." Laments his use of Crane texts from
Work, because they are tampered texts.

Burton Sabol, *Northwest Review*, 9 (Summer, 1967), 108–110.

Claude Simpson, *Nineteenth-Century Fiction*, 22 (September 1967), 204–206.

Gerald Manning, *Queen's Quarterly*, 74 (Autumn, 1967), 537–538: Manning states that Solomon's critical study of Crane will not disappoint
because it analyzes the full scope of Crane's fiction while maintaining a unified approach. Solomon's central thesis, "that Crane is to a large extent a
conscious parodist and that his creative genius develops from this technique,"
remains flexible enough to "allow us to grasp something of the diversity of
Crane's art. . . ."

David H. Hirsch, *Novel: A Forum on Fiction*, 1, no. 1 (Fall, 1967): Criticizes Solomon's confused meaning of parody and his failure to come to
terms "with the crucial question of how Crane's parody is related to his use
of irony. The problem is that in some ways parody and irony intermingle, and
it becomes difficult to tell one from the other. . . . The concept of parody
as imitation of a literary work also suffers, when applied to Crane, from the
mystery surrounding his reading. Since no one is quite certain what Crane
read, and since he does not provide telltale clues to any individual novels or
stories he may be parodying, Solomon is forced to fall back on general categories. Unable to identify any specific book that Crane parodied (though he
makes a few guesses), he concludes that Crane was parodying such vague entities as the slum novel, the war novel, the success novel, the temperance
novel, and so on. And occasionally, the definition of parody as imitation of a
literary work disappears altogether, and the word returns to its popular
meaning as a ludicrous copy."

By limiting what Crane "parodies" to the popular and sentimental fiction
of his own time Solomon thus makes "a mockery of his statement that 'the
finest parody can retain the force of the original while criticizing it.' All the
originals Solomon posits have no force to begin with. But Stallman has made
a strong case for parallels between *Maggie* and *Madame Bovary;* 'The Bride

Comes to Yellow Sky' offers interesting echoes of *Beowulf,* and 'The Blue Hotel' might be profitably compared to medieval romance. If such parallels were worked out in detail they might reveal how Crane used parody, not simply to attack the tenth-rate fiction of the day but to transplant ancient myth to a new environment and age."

Another weakness of this book is its lack of any critical context. His "tacit claim to independence" both "requires and suggests a greater originality than is to be found in this book. Solomon is in greater debt to his predecessors than he realizes, especially to Stallman for his understanding of *The Red Badge.* A close examination will show that almost all the passages Solomon chooses to use as examples or to quote for comment are passages that have already been singled out by Stallman. In addition, there are some striking verbal echoes. . . ." (p. 82). The absence of even one acknowledging footnote is "a disturbing oversight."

Max Westbrook, *American Literary Realism: 1870–1910,* 1 (Fall, 1967), 100–103: Solomon omits from his thesis that Crane is a conscious literary parodist in all of Crane's poetry. What Solomon means by "parody" is obscured by frequent contradictions. " 'In the fullest sense of the term,' he writes, 'Crane parodied the familiar themes of fiction, but not always, nor even primarily for comic effect.' Yet Crane 'was always a humorist.' Crane was neither an Impressionist nor a Naturalist; he had, as parodist, no need for 'the fully developed philosophy with which some recent interpreters [unnamed] have sought to supply him. . . .' "

Westbrook rightly adds that Solomon never traces Crane's supposed movement from parody to realism, and therefore "Solomon is left with the impossible task of trying to explain the fiction of Crane by means of a term without content, a term that seems to mean little more than 'unlike' popular stereotypes (167). The Easterner in 'Horses—One Dash,' for example, is said to be a travesty (satire, irony, travesty, mockery are interchangeable with parody) of the fearless Western hero, with—since the horse is noble—a touch of naturalism. But, as Solomon himself points out (24), the Easterner is a dude and not a Westerner, whereas the Westerner in the story is unstintingly and even fanatically brave.

"Solomon insists that Crane 'wrote only as an observer' (27), which makes it awkward to discuss, as Solomon does, the moral position of Crane in 'The Open Boat,' 'The Monster,' *The Red Badge,* etc. 'As always,' Solomon writes, 'Crane refuses to moralize' (55), and yet moralizing passages are discussed (119, 271), and 'Showin' Off' and 'Making an Orator' are said to fail because the moral is too obvious: 'Crane is preaching' (217)."

Paul Witherington, *American Literature Abstracts,* 1 (December, 1967): Concludes that reviewers find Solomon's thesis unacceptable, with some reviewers not objecting to the thesis; they find his study offers insights into the individual works and has value for showing Crane's relationship to his times.

Thomas A. Gullason, *American Literature,* 40 (March, 1968), 93–94: "Mr. Solomon warns about the danger of overreading Crane's work. Then he overreads and overrates, underreads and underrates. He finds the average sketch, 'In the Tenderloin: A Duel . . . ,' one of Crane's best. He sees the entire *Maggie* as 'an emendation, a cutting . . . of traditional slum fiction,' the plot of *George's Mother* 'plainly parodic,' and *Active Service* beginning as a 'full-scale parody' (his evidence here is thin). Even when the parodic effect is 'very faint' in 'The Open Boat,' Mr. Solomon is tempted to say 'perhaps a note of parody of traditional endings' exists at the close of the story."

In sum, Solomon distorts Crane's art. However, Solomon has some good things to say about Crane's art, although from Gullason's review no one would guess it.

Walton Patrick, *SinSF,* 5 (Spring, 1968), 297–299: A favorable review, ending with Patrick's conjecture that Solomon's book "likely is destined to become a landmark in Crane scholarship."

Modern Fiction Studies, 13 (Summer, 1967), 275: "Solomon finds 'The Blue Hotel' as the culminating work in Crane's parodic approach, 'for the Swede is a living parody, a badly scared Don Quixote nurtured on dime-novel fiction, whose death, in the finest irony of all, is both a parody and the sole reality of his life. . . .' "

See Frohock (1970).

Stallman, R. W. "Crane's *Maggie:* A Reassessment," in *Stephen Crane's Maggie: Text and Context,* ed. Maurice Bassan. Belmont, Calif., 1966, pp. 139–144. Reprinted from *Houses.*

Stallman, R. W., and E. R. Hagemann. Preface, *The New York City Sketches of Stephen Crane: And Related Pieces.* New York: New York University Press, 1966, pp. lx–xvi. Preface reprints Crane's "Great Bugs in Onondaga," *New York Tribune,* June 1, 1891.

Reviewed:

Robert Cromie, *Chicago Tribune,* May 17, 1966.

Guy Savino, *Newark Sunday News,* May 22, 1966, p. 24: The Crane-Dora Clark case suggests "a striking parallel between police department conditions then and now."

Robert Stilwell, *Louisville Courier-Journal,* May 29. 1966: Several pieces in this book "have never before seen publication in any form; others have not previously been reprinted; and some are now definitely attributed to Crane for the first time." This collection "ought to prove of considerable interest and importance. . . . There is an intrinsic worth about certain of these writings, entirely aside from their bibliographical value." Another reason for its importance is that this book "rounds off another large phase in the fantastically complicated task of establishing the canon of Crane's writings."*

Thomas Buckley, *New York Times,* June 22, 1966.

Stuart B. James, *Denver Quarterly,* Summer, 1966, pp. 127–128.

Ralph Williams, *Hartford Courant Magazine,* September 18, 1966, p. 13: Crane wrote brother William Howe Crane that "Some of my best work is contained in short things which I have written for various publications, principally the *New York Press* in 1893 or thereabouts. There are some 15 or 20 short sketches of New York street life and so on which I intended to have published in book form under the title of 'Midnight Sketches.' " This is the first collected edition of Midnight Sketches.

---

* An addition to the Crane canon is readily identified, however, by the fact that the given Crane title or manuscript is not listed in the *W-S Bibliography.*

(Stilwell notices that the Preface "seems confused as to the precise title of the volume that it is introducing." The title "And Other Pieces," as stated in the Preface, p. x, had been injected at galley proof stage by New York University Press's editor, who consented at page proof stage to change it to "And Related Pieces"—as given in the title page.)

Edwin Cady, *American Literature,* 38 (January, 1967), 570–571. *See* Stallman, "Reply to Reviewer Cady" (1968).

Chicago Choice (January, 1967): "More and more fugitive Crane material continues to appear, and every shred, of course, adds some significant, if not new, light on the total work of this major literary figure. This collection offers further revelations into Stephen Crane's talent as a journalist and erratic talent of Lower Manhattan's Bohemian colony of the early 1890's. . . . Short pieces dealing with gamblers and drug addicts, 'fly' cops and fallen women, resort life and prison days give young Crane opportunity to indulge in the often bizarre virtuosity that characterized a poignant strain in the history of American journalism in the gaslight era. There are compiled here 67 sketches by Crane and 17 relevant articles by others of his contemporary circle. The editors have included an adequate scholarly apparatus."

Robert Rutland, *Quill* (January, 1967): Crane "was not a do-gooder out to rake the muck and reform society in the bargain. This volume deals with the tarnished side of big-city life as a reporter with under-dog sympathies saw it. It lacks the sustained interest of the earlier collection of Crane's war dispatches [1964], but it does enlighten us on how the reporter's craft has evolved historically."

James B. Stronks, *SinSF* (Winter, 1968), 195–196: "From the beginning he is the complete ironist, nearly every line meaning more than it says, or less. And his nerveless understatement, a species of irony as he uses it, is already a confirmed way with him." Stronks notes Crane's "wizard technical mastery" and that Crane wrote most of this material in his early twenties when he already possessed "one all important quality that his critics never seem to have noticed: his superior intelligence." Also that Crane anticipated the Ash-Can School of Manhattan canvasses.

Stephen Crane Newsletter, 1, no. 1 (Fall, 1966), 1–7. Ed. Joseph Katz. Initiates a quarterly letter on Crane scholarship with a checklist of writings on Crane. This and subsequent issues are annotated here only for important items.

Discusses the third printing of the 1896 *Maggie.* Prints an unknown review of *Maggie* in *Yale Courant,* 33 (November, 1896?), and presents a new Crane letter to Mr. Appleton, July 16, 1896.

———. 1, no. 2 (Winter, 1966), 2–8.

Two new Crane letters here for the first time. The one to Elbert Hubbard, February 13 (1896), has been privately known, however.* The letter to Mr. Richards from Crane at Hartwood for January 4 (undated) includes this statement: ". . . of the notices of me which have appeared from time to time, the one in *The Tribune* of December 28, is the one I prefer above all others." Crane asks Mr. Richards to send him a few copies of the "Dec. 28 issue of your papers." (However, I find that the *Tribune* contains no article on Crane for that date in 1896, nor in 1895.)

Quotes Crane's letter from Jacksonville, March 11, 1897, with the recipient William and not Edmund—as given in *Letters.* Matthew Bruccoli provides bibliographical description of a colonial edition of *Great Battles of the World,* by Joseph Katz and Matthew J. Bruccoli, and Eric Solomon reviews *The American 1890's* by Larzer Ziff.

Stevens, Wallace. [On Crane's funeral], in *Wallace Stevens: Letters,* ed. Holly Stevens. New York, 1966, p. 42.

* Hence, *SCraneN* is not cited in *Crane,* p. 584, for this item.

On his first assignment as *New York Tribune* reporter Stevens attended Crane's funeral service at the Central Metropolitan Temple and wrote in his journal for June 28 (1900): "The whole thing was frightful."

For Wallace Stevens's *Tribune* account of the Crane funeral and his appraisal of Crane's achievement as writer, *see* Obituaries (1900). Unsigned is the *Tribune's* "Funeral of Stephen Crane," June 29. *Not* noticed in *Wallace Stevens: Letters*. First noticed in *Crane* as by Wallace Stevens.

Stone, Edward. *Voices of Despair: Four Motifs in American Literature.* Columbus, Ohio, 1966, pp. 52–57, 120–122, 129, 130, 163–164.

Walcutt, Charles Child, and J. Edwin Whitesell, eds. *The Explicator Cyclopedia,* vol. 1: Modern poetry. Chicago, 1966, pp. 34–35.

Crane's "A Man Said to the Universe" explicated by Christof Wegelin.

Weimer, David R. "Landscape of Hysteria: Stephen Crane," in *The City as Metaphor.* New York, 1966, pp. 52–64.

Westerfield, Nancy G. "At Rye: Henry James' House," *College English,* 28 (October, 1966), 50.

Quotes a new Crane poem.

Winterich, John T., and David A. Randall. *A Primer of Book Collecting,* 3rd ed. New York, 1966, pp. 46, 78–82, 126–150.

The famous "collector's progress" has been repriced, and the front wrapper of Garland's first copy of the 1893 *Maggie* is in facsimile.

Wycherly, H. Alan. "Crane's 'The Blue Hotel': How Many Collaborators?" *American Notes and Queries,* 4 (February, 1966), 88.

Young, Philip. *Ernest Hemingway: A Reconsideration.* University Park, Pa., and London, 1966, pp. 175, 188, 191–196, 198, 238, 250. (New and enlarged from the 1952 edition.)

The influence of Crane on Hemingway. "In Crane he could find his own strict sense of personal integrity and honesty, exercised in a rigorous effort to look for himself directly and immediately at things, so that he might see them as if they had not been seen before." Young mentions the fact that "The Blue Hotel" bears resemblances to "The Killers," "An Alpine Idyll," and *The Fifth Column;* and that "A Clean Well-lighted Place" clearly establishes Hemingway's debt to Crane in "An Episode of War." Not mentioned is the parallelism between the opening of *A Farewell to Arms* and *The Red Badge of Courage,* first discussed in *Omnibus,* pp. 192–193, 222.

Ziff, Larzer. *The American 1890's: Life and Times of a Lost Generation.* New York, 1966, pp. 185–205.

Reviewed:

Warner Berthoff, *American Literature,* 39 (March, 1967), 110–112. Its "best chapters are on what are already well established as its most important particular topics. The description of Crane's brief progress and of Dreiser's shocking achievement in *Sister Carrie* are solid additions to critical understanding." (On the contrary, the criticism of Crane's writings is perfunctory and secondhand. On Crane, pp. 185–205, nothing new here; several errors of fact.)

American Literature Abstracts, 1 (December, 1967), which concludes that Ziff's study "is undistinguished in its criticisms of individual authors and works and that it fails to establish its thesis concerning the peculiar importance of the nineties."

TLS, February 1, 1968, which remarks that "the one truly *fin de siècle* American who stands out is Stephen Crane."

1967

American Literature Abstracts, ed. James K. Bowen and Richard Van Der Beets. Vol. I, no. 1 (December, 1967). Published semiannually, December and June.
A review of current scholarship in the field of American literature, it reviews also important books. *See* Bowen (1967) for annotations.

Bassan, Maurice, ed. Introduction, *Stephen Crane: A Collection of Critical Essays.* Englewood Cliffs, N.J., 1967, pp. 1–11.
"While Berryman's effort to explain Crane's psychic makeup has struck some readers as amateurish, the psychoanalytic approach of recent critics such as Daniel Weiss has produced more satisfactory results. Daniel Hoffman's *The Poetry of Stephen Crane* (1957) was another landmark, for the first time establishing the influence of Crane's Methodist heritage upon his themes and craft,* and tracing relationships between Crane's poems and the poetic traditions of his time and our own. Much of the criticism of the past decade, including the very close readings that Crane's major novels and stories have received, has been in the form of intelligent footnotes to the work of Berryman, Stallman, and Hoffman."
Here for the first time: "Stephen Crane's Magic Mountain," by James B. Colvert; Biblical parallelisms in *The Red Badge,* Donald Thomas, incorporated in "Notes Toward an Analysis of *The Red Badge of Courage,*" R. W. Stallman.

Bernard, Kenneth. " 'The Bride Comes to Yellow Sky': History as Elegy," *English Record,* 17 (April, 1967), 17–20.

Bowen, James K., and Richard Van Der Beets, eds. *American Literature Abstracts,* 1, no. 1 (December, 1967), 47–48, 128–129, 133–135.
Published semiannually (December and June) at Stockton, California, it reviews current scholarship in American literature. Provides abstracts of the following articles: Fraser, "Crime and Forgiveness" (1967); Ives, "The Little Regiment" (1967); and Monteiro, "Whilomville as Judah" (1967).

Bradley, Sculley, Richmond Croom Beatty, and E. Hudson Long, eds. *The American Tradition in Literature,* vol. 2, 3d ed., New York, 1967, pp. 940–942, 943–977.
Preface, pp. 940–942: "Among the *avant garde* writers of the 1890's, Crane was most clearly the herald of the twentieth-century revolution in literature. Had he written *Maggie: A Girl of the Streets* (1893) or *The Red Badge of Courage* (1895) twenty-five years later, he would still have been as much a pioneer as Sherwood Anderson then was. Even more than Garland, Norris, Dreiser, or Robinson—his contemporaries—he made a clean break with the past in his selection of material, his craftsmanship, and his point of view. It was his nature to be experimental. At twenty he wrote *Maggie,* our first completely naturalistic novel. By the age of twenty-four he had produced, in his earliest short stories and his masterpiece, *The Red Badge of Courage,* the first examples of modern American impressionism. That year, in his collected poems, he was the first to respond to the radical genius of Emily Dickinson,

---

* However, the double strand in Crane's heritage—clergymen and soldiers—exploited by Hoffman, was first announced in the 1896 articles by Peaslee and by Gaines; also by John Northern Hilliard. Hoffman's insight derives thus from Peaslee, Gaines, and Hilliard, none of whom is acknowledged by Hoffman.

and the result was a volume of imagist impressionism twenty years in advance of the official imagists. He was in every respect phenomenal."

Reprints some poems, plus "The Open Boat," and "The Bride Comes to Yellow Sky."

Brown, Charles H. *The Correspondents' War.* New York, 1967, Bibliography. Photocopy of the *New York Press's* front page for January 7, 1897. Photographs.

An excellent and lucid account, but quite superficial on the Santiago campaign; not mentioned are many incidents and reports by correspondents there. The best account of the battle of San Juan Hill is by A. C. M. Azoy (1961), in *Charge!*—not mentioned in Brown's bibliography.

Bruccoli, Matthew J. "Maggie's Last Night," *Stephen Crane Newsletter,* 2, no. 1 (Fall, 1967), 10–11.

On chap. XVII, *see also* Cady (1962), pp. 105–106. A similar point of view about Maggie's last night was issued by J. X. Brennan, "Ironic and Symbolic Structure in Crane's *Maggie*" (1962). Cady again discusses Maggie's last night in his essay on *Maggie* (1969). Again discussed by Katz, *MFS* (1966). Katz's notion is dismissed by Fredson Bowers in his restudy of the puzzle in chap. XVII of *Maggie*, in his Textual Introduction to *The Works of Stephen Crane: Bowery Tales* (1969), pp. lxxx–xci. *See* commentary by R.W.S. in this entry.

Brennan's insights get no mention by Cady, Katz, and Bruccoli.

Budd, Louis J. "Stephen Crane," *American Literary Scholarship, 1965,* ed. James Woodress. Durham, N.C., 1967, pp. 137–141.

Cady, Edwin H. [Review: *The New York City Sketches of Stephen Crane,* ed. Stallman and Hagemann], *American Literature,* 38 (January, 1967), 370–371. *See* Stallman, "Reply to Reviewer Cady," *American Literature,* 40 (March, 1968), 83–85.

Cazemajou, Jean. "Stephen Crane et la petite ville americaine," *Caliban,* no. 4 (March, 1967), 85–93.

———. "Stephen Crane: Pennington Seminary: Étape d'une éducation Méthodiste," *Études Anglaises,* 20, no. 2 (April–June, 1967), 140–148.

Surveys with much new information Crane's years at Pennington from September, 1885, to December, 1887, with an announcement in Asbury's Park's *Shore Press,* January 6, 1888, on his attending Claverack Military Institute.

A most important piece of research because Cazemajou has uncovered in the *Asbury Park Journal* and the *Shore Press,* March, 1886, notices that Mrs. M. Helen Crane, "who has been very ill for several months, is now suffering from a temporary aberration of the mind, and is in a critical condition." Not noticed by Cazemajou is the link between Mrs. Crane's mental illness and that of Mrs. Kelcey in *George's Mother. See Crane.*

Colvert, James B. "Stephen Crane's Magic Mountain," in *Stephen Crane: A Collection of Critical Esays,* ed. Maurice Bassan (1967), pp. 95–105.

Not previously published and important. Weaknesses in *The Red Badge of Courage* all stem from Crane's inability to control his recurring image (employed in both poetry and prose) of the "little man in conflict with the hostile mountain." The novel might appear to be a story of a self-centered youth who comes to a measure of redeeming wisdom through war experiences. But the ending of the novel is confused and unconvincing. How has Henry changed? Hasn't his conflict with Nature been too rapidly dispatched at the conclusion? Crane's failure in *The Red Badge of Courage* is twofold; a failure in tone and theme. In tone—how can Crane portray Henry as a genuine hero when his own conception of heroism is undermined by a naive and spurious sentimentalism? At the end of *The Red Badge of Courage* Crane has no solution to this problem.

Colvert's insights in this brilliant essay, one of the very best ever written on Crane, point out Crane's own confusion in his artistic conception of *The Red Badge.* No other critic has done just that, an attack on Crane's failures as artist. Other critics, ignoring this crucial standpoint, contend one against the other to champion their singular interpretation of a novel faulty in its conceptional scheme and faulty in its execution from start to finish. The war over the critical reading of *The Red Badge* continues since 1950, and what a critical warfare it has been! What explosions of contempt by one camp of critics for another, and much of this unnecessary warfare owing to Crane's own confused intentions!

Dahlberg, Edward. "Stephen Crane: American Genius," in *The Leafless American,* ed. Harold Billings. New York, 1967, pp. 58–61.

Dillingham, William B. "Crane's One-Act Farce 'The Upturned Face,'" *Research Studies of Washington State University,* 35 (December, 1967), 324–330.

Ehrlich, Miguel, trans. *Stephen Crane: hombres en la tormenta y otros relatos. Introductión general de A. D. van Nostrand. Introducciónes parciales de Robert Wooster Stallman.* Buenos Aires, Argentina: Ediciones Troquel, 1967.*

    Contents: Introducción general de A. D. Van Nostrand, pp. 7–28. Parte I— Cuentos del bowery. Introducción de R. W. Stallman, pp. 31–46. Hombres en la tormenta (Men in the Storm), pp. 49–57; Maggie, una chica de la calle (Maggie, a Girl of the Street), pp. 61–141; Howells teme que los realistas deban aguardar (Howells Fears Realists Must Wait), pp. 145–149.

    Parte II—Un cuento del mar. Introducción de R. W. Stallman, pp. 153–159. El bote abierto (The Open Boat).

    Parte III—Cuentos de whilomville. Introducción de R. W. Stallman, pp. 199–201. La navaja (The Knife), pp. 205–219; Los mitones nuevos (His New Mittens), pp. 223–237.

———. *Stephen Crane: la insignia roja del valor y otros relatos. Introducciónes parciales de Robert Wooster Stallman.* Buenos Aires, Argentina Ediciones Troquel, 1967†.

Evans, David L. "Henry's Hell: The Night Journey in *The Red Badge of Courage,*" *Proceedings of the Utah Academy of Sciences, Arts and Letters,* 44 (1967), 159–166.

Ferreiro, Wamberto Hudson, trans. *O hotel azul,* in *7 novelas classicas,* ed. Philip Rahv. Rio de Janeiro, Editôra Lidador, 1967, pp. 109–133. Brazilian translation into the Portuguese.

Fraser, John. "Crime and Forgiveness: 'The Red Badge' in Time of War," *Criticism,* 9 (Summer, 1967), 243–246.
    See Bowen, (1967).

Fujimoto, Sachio. "Guzohakai to jissenteki aironi—*Sekishoku bukunsho* to *Bukiyo saraba* ni tsuite" [Iconoclasm and practical irony—*The Red Badge of Cour-*

---

* The texts and the introductions by R. W. Stallman are selected from *Omnibus.*

† The texts and the introductions by R. W. Stallman are selected from *Omnibus.*

age and *Farewell to Arms*], *Kyushu Sangyo Daigaku Kyoyo-bu Kiyo*, vol. 4, no. 1 (December, 1967).

Garner, Stanton. "Some Notes on Harold Frederic in Ireland," *American Literature*, 39 (March, 1967), 60–74.
> On Stephen and Cora in Ireland, pp. 64–65.

Grebstein, Sheldon Norman. "Hemingway's Dark and Bloody Capital," in *The Thirties: Fiction, Drama and Poetry*, ed. Warren French. Gainesville, Fla., 1967.
> Compares Hemingway's "The Capital of the World" and Crane's "The Blue Hotel."

Gullason, Thomas A., ed. Preface and Introduction, *The Complete Novels of Stephen Crane*. Garden City, N.Y., 1967, pp. vii–xvi, 3–97.
> Gullason grossly errs in claiming that here (in Appendix 2: The Major 1893 Variants from *Maggie*) "is the first publication and collation of the most important variant readings from the 1893 and 1896 *Maggie*." The missing all in Gullason's collation occurs in the opening paragraph of *Maggie*'s episode for Chapter 5.

>> The girl, Maggie, blossomed in a mudpuddle. She grew to be a most rare and wonderful production of a tenement district, a pretty girl. None of the dirt of Rum Alley seemed to be in her veins. . . . When a child, playing and fighting with gamins in the street, dirt *disgusted* her.

> Not noticed by Gullason in his collation is the fact that the 1893 text has: "dirt disguised her." Not noticed by Gullason is that all editions of *Maggie* —both English and American—subsequent to the 1893 *Maggie* have it wrongly "dirt disgusted her." This error first appeared in Heinemann's 1896 edition and has remained there ever since in all editions of the 1896 *Maggie*. Gullason, p. 798, fails to include this very important variant, and Katz, in his edition of the 1893 *Maggie* (1966), also ignorant of its significance, mentions it not at all. The one exception is the 1896 Appleton *Maggie*.
> *See* Stallman's collation of the 1893 and 1896 *Maggie* in *American Literature* (1955) and William Gibson's collation (1956).
> *Reviewed:*
>> Granville Hicks in *Saturday Review* (July 22, 1967).
>> *Modern Fiction Studies*, 13 (Summer, 1967), 275. Gullason "has rendered a major service to scholars on many counts. His volume is the first to contain the final 1896 version of *Maggie* along with the variant readings from the privately printed 1893 manuscript and the first to provide the newspaper version of *The Red Badge*, which appeared in 1894 in the *Philadelphia Press*."*
>> *Choice*, 5 (March, 1968), 48: "An appendix gives the 'uncanceled' variant readings of *The Red Badge*, available also in R. W. Stallman's *Stephen Crane: An Omnibus* (1952)." However, Gullason's text does not include the canceled passages, nor the five new MS. pages first brought together in Stallman's Signet *Red Badge* (1960).
>> Marston LaFrance, *SinSF*, 6 (Winter, 1969), 221–222: LaFrance here quotes what he said of Gullason's companion book *(CSS&S)* in his review of that book in *Modern Language Journal* (February, 1965): "If Mr. Gullason were not

---

* Katz in 1967 also issued *The Red Badge of Courage* in the 1894 newspaper version, the one preceding the other by a matter of some months.

hampered by having to write for the general reader, one might accuse him of a certain insensitivity to the *inner* life of a profoundly creative artist. Because he tries to include too much material within too brief a compass Mr. Gullason's ideas seem somewhat disconnected, and Crane, the ironic, organizing imagination, seems to evade capture by disappearing behind a screen of facts.

"This caveat applies to the present Introduction the more regrettably because the compass is here much wider. Mr. Gullason, quite reasonably, is committed to the historical approach by way of facts, sources, and influences; and while he has as good a command of Crane's factual background as any scholar now writing, he seems insufficiently aware of two pitfalls that make Crane one of the most elusive subjects in American literature. One is that the sources of these facts, most often remembrances imperfectly recalled by decidedly fallible human beings some two or three decades after Crane's death, are extremely questionable. Beer is admittedly untrustworthy, but it seems to me that Ford, Harriman, Hilliard, Bass, and yet others are even less reliable than Beer is. The memoirs by Crane's two nieces often contradict each other and are obviously colored by each writer's own view of the Crane family relationships. And, so far as I can determine, the only person whose writings about Crane imply an innocence even more astonishing than Garland's is Lillian Gilkes. . . ."

————. "Four Men in a Cave: A Critical Appraisal," *Readers and Writers*, 1 (April–May,1967), 30–31.

Hallam, George W. "Some New Stephen Crane Items," *Studies in Bibliography*, 20 (1967), 263–266.

The important item is Crane's holograph note, undated:

> Wounds in the Rain.
> A collection of stories relating to the Spanish-American war
> of 1898
> By Stephen Crane.

> Note: The intermediate descriptive phrase should certainly appear on the cover of the book as well as on the title page. Otherwise, *rain* rhymes atrociously with *Crane* and ruins the entire effect of the singular and sinister brutality of the title. The intermediate sentence should also be made to appear in any advertisement.
> S. C.

This Crane note was affixed to the inside of the front cover of Cora's copy of *Wounds in the Rain*. As Hallam points out, "the cover of the book reads exactly the way Crane did *not* wish it to read: '*Wounds in the Rain* / By Stephen Crane.' " Relate Crane's note to *Letters*, p. 264.

Hanneman, Audre. *Ernest Hemingway: A Comprehensive Bibliography*. Princeton, N.J., 1967, pp. H248, 1082, 1137, 1209, 1434₁.

Hashiguchim, Yasuo. " 'The Open Boat' ni okeru Billie" [Billie in "The Open Boat"], *Kyushu Daigaku Eigo Eibungaku Ronso*, no. 17 (1967), 63–74.

Hasley, Louis. "On Reading Verses by Stephen Crane" [poem], *Prairie Schooner*, 41 (Winter, 1967), 409.

Hawkins, Willis Brooks. "All in a Lifetime," *Stephen Crane Newsletter*, 1, no. 3 (Spring, 1967), 3–5. Part II in *Stephen Crane Newsletter*, 3, no. 1 (Fall, 1968), 6–7.

Hicks, Granville. "The Short Story Was His Medium," *Saturday Review*, 50 (July 22, 1967), 31–32.

"Our literary history is full of writers whose powers declined in their later years, but I know of no case quite like Crane's. . . . That he needed to write books that might sell, and therefore, tried to cater to popular taste, is understandable. Men of even greater genius have written potboilers, but there has almost always been a touch of genius in the work that kept the pot boiling. Now that I realize to what depths Crane fell in these late novels, I find the problem of his life and work doubly perplexing."*

Hillman, Hans, trans. *Stephen Crane: Das blaue Hotel: Erzählungen.* Frankfurt am Main and Hamburg, Germany: Fischer Bucherei, 1967.

Contains translations into the German of the title story ("The Blue Hotel"), *Das rote Siegel (The Red Badge of Courage)*, and *Im Rettungsboot* ("The Open Boat").

Hudspeth, Robert N. "The *Thoth* Annual Bibliography of Stephen Crane Scholarship," *Thoth*, 8 (Spring, 1967), 98–99.

Isaacs, Neil D. "Yojimbo Comes to Yellow Sky," *Kyushu American Literature*, 10 (1967), 81–86.

Itabashi, Yoshie. "Stephen Crane no kenkyu doko" [The trend of Stephen Crane criticism], *Eigo kyoiku* (Taishukan), 16, no. 4 (July, 1967), 29–31.

———. "The Modern Pilgrimage of *The Black Riders:* An Interpretation," *Tsuda Review*, no. 12 (November, 1967), 1–41.

Ives, C. B. " 'The Little Regiment' of Stephen Crane at the Battle of Fredericksburg," *Midwest Quarterly*, 8, no. 3 (1967), 247–260.

The details of the story identify the battle as Fredericksburg and probably identify "the little regiment" as the 69th New York, "one of the five regiments of the then famous 'Irish Brigade' and now known as the 'Fighting 69th,' still famous, still reputedly Irish."

See Bowen (1967).

Jakes, John. *Great War Correspondents.* New York, 1967, pp. 35–51.

Katz, Joseph. "The Wondrous Painting Cow of Old K. C.," *Kansas City Star*, December 31, 1967, section D, p. 1. A reissue of Crane's "Art in Kansas City." Reprinted from Katz, *SCraneN* (Fall, 1967), pp. 3–4, which fails to mention that "Art in Kansas City" was first published by Stallman. *See* Stallman, "New Short Fiction by Stephen Crane" (1964).

Katz, Joseph, ed. "Whitman, Crane, and the Odious Comparison," *Notes and Queries*, 14 (1967), 66–67.

———. *"The Red Badge of Courage" by Stephen Crane: A Facsimile Reproduction of the New York Press Appearance of December 9, 1894.* With an Introduction and Textual Notes. Gainesville, Fla., 1967. Photographs. Illustrations.

Katz's text of *The Red Badge of Courage* is in blurred type and is scarcely readable. The illustrations include those in the text of the *Philadelphia Press* (1894), an editorial in the *New York Press*, December 10, 1894 (new here), and an editorial in the *Philadelphia Press*, December 7, 1894, which appears

---

* Hicks on Crane is again perplexed in his 1968 review of *Crane.*

as though new here but which was first reproduced in *Letters*, pp. 295–296. The latter is "The Work of Stephen Crane" by Holland, whose identity is not mentioned by Katz. *See* LaFrance (1965).

Katz's Introduction discusses the history of the *Red Badge* manuscripts with no citation of its discussion in *Omnibus*. He says there "is a manuscript *now* at the Alderman Library" (italics mine) but this acquisition by the Alderman Library, University of Virginia, occurred many years ago, and the bound volume contains manuscripts first made known to exist in *Omnibus*. He says "The deleted Chapter XII (which survives in pages scattered among the New York Public Library, the Butler Library at Columbia University, and the Houghton Library of Harvard University) is a long philosophical construction. . . ." Katz fails to cite the identity of these MSS., collected by Stallman in his 1960 Signet edition of *The Red Badge of Courage and Selected Stories*. They were collected there, all five, for the first time.

Everything in Katz's Introduction appears as if there were no antecedent for its appearance here. The photograph of Crane in his military uniform, which derives from the *W-S Bibliography* (1948), is said to derive "From a proof in the collection of Joseph Katz." We want to know where the Crane photograph first appeared, not that Katz owns glossy copies. (Unidentified are the photographs of Crane used on the jacket of Katz's *The Poems of Stephen Crane* [1966]). We especially need to know the source of the new photograph of Crane as a baby, p. 12, but to ascertain its validity as a true photograph of baby Crane one must apply to Katz since its source is given simply: "From a proof in the collection of Joseph Katz."

New here is the two-page MS. of "Corporal O'Connor's Story," pp. 16–17. Reproduced from CUCC.

At no point in the history of the composition of *The Red Badge of Courage* does Katz probe the situation and come up with new facts or insights, while at the same time he acknowledges no previous Crane scholar's probing these very problems. On that "minor crux in the history of *The Red Badge of Courage*" which occurred when Crane borrowed $15 to retrieve the typescript, Katz glibly camouflages that puzzling affair and cleverly avoids thus engaging himself in scholarly probings of it. He is superficial and he is not exempt from errors. He says that the Bacheller, Johnson, and Bacheller Syndicate was incorporated in May, 1896 (p. 37); whereas the syndicate began some years earlier, as given in *Omnibus*. Katz says that the chronology of *The Red Badge of Courage*'s composition "seems reasonably clear" (p. 11); whereas—*contra* Katz—Crane might have begun writing that Civil War novel in late 1892. *See Crane.*

Katz includes "Textual Variants," pp. 45–56, which is addressed to the scholar, whereas his Introduction is addressed to the general reader by the fact that it is a slick popularization. Gullason (1967) scooped by some months Katz's edition of the 1894 *Red Badge of Courage*.

It is inexcusable of bibliographer Katz not to acknowledge W. L. Werner's important pioneer study of the 1894 *Red Badge* newspaper shortened version. *See* Werner (1945) and also Winterich (1951). *See also Omnibus.*

———. "Stephen Crane and 'Holland,' " *Stephen Crane Newsletter*, 1, no. 4 (Spring [Summer], 1967), 1.

    See LaFrance (1965).

———. "*Maggie: A Girl of the Streets* (1893): A Census (Part I)," *Stephen Crane Newsletter*, 2, no. 2 (Winter, 1967), 9.

Katz's error here is corrected by George Monteiro, article in *SCraneN*, 3, no. 3 (Spring, 1969), 7–9.

Katz, Joseph, and Matthew J. Bruccoli. "Toward A Descriptive Bibliography of Stephen Crane: 'Spanish-American War Songs,'" *Papers of the Bibliographical Society of America*, 61 (Third Quarter, 1967), 267–269.

Kilchenmann, Ruth J. *Die Kurzgeschichte: Formen und Entwicklung*. Sprache und Literatur, Band 37. Stuttgart, Germany, 1967, pp. 90–98 and *passim*.

Klein, Eduard, and Klaus Marschke, trans. *Das blaue Hotel und andere Erzählungen*. Frankfurt am Main and Hamburg, Germany, 1967. Vol. 819 in the "Fischer Bücherei" series.

Contains translations of the title work, *The Red Badge of Courage*, and "The Open Boat."

Kurita, Ariyasu. "Stephen Crane no kenkyu—Tanpen ni okeru shuhō to sōsakuteki sōzōryoku ni tsuite" [A study of Stephen Crane on technique and creative imagination in his short stories], *Chuo Gakuin Daigaku Ronso*, 2, no. 1, (November, 1967), 111–139.

Kuroiwa, Shun-ichi. "Stephen Crane no futatsu no tanpen" [Two short stories of Stephen Crane], *Keiogijuku Daigaku Kogaku-bu Hiyoshi Kiyo* (1967), pp. 34–42.

LaFrance, Marston. "Stephen Crane's Private Fleming: His Various Battles," in *Patterns of Commitment in American Literature*, ed. Marston LaFrance. Toronto, 1967, pp. 113–133.

Reprinted in *A Reading of Stephen Crane* (1971).

A Critical Bibliography by Theodore Gross and Stanley Wertheim (1971), p. 274, notices that LaFrance dismisses too lightly Henry Fleming's belief that he has become a man *versus* that belief as Henry's self-delusion. "It is indeed puzzling that while LaFrance considers Crane primarily an ironist, one who maintains a double vision of reality, he is unable to find even a trace of such irony in the ambiguous concluding paragraphs of *The Red Badge of Courage* which describe Henry Fleming's change of soul. But as Clark Griffith put it, 'if Henry succeeds in fooling himself (and, apparently, some of his critics), Stephen Crane knows better.'" So, then, Griffith and Gross-Wertheim agree with Stallman's reading of the ambiguous concluding paragraphs of Henry's plight, as given in *Omnibus* (1952), p. 221 ff. LaFrance ignores the *Omnibus* reading, which apparently the Gross-Wertheim annotators haven't read for their *Critical Bibliography;* for otherwise they would have cited it instead of Griffith, who also makes no mention of this antecedent reading.

Omnibus, p. 221, is worth quoting here. "The 'sun-through-rainclouds' image gives an ironic twist to the flat sentimental 'images of tranquil skies, fresh meadows cool brooks—an existence of eternal peace.' Henry has not attained eternal peace, and though the sun shines, it pierces 'hosts of leaden rain clouds.' It is interesting to notice that Hemingway's hero in *A Farewell to Arms* also makes his 'separate peace'—that too an illusion not unlike Henry Fleming's. From the start Henry Fleming recognizes the necessity for change of heart but wars against it, and at the end he is the same Henry Fleming. He has undergone no change, no real spiritual development."

Levin, Gerald, ed. *The Short Story: An Inductive Approach*. New York, 1967, pp. 356–378, 378–380.

Reprints "The Blue Hotel." In Suggestions for Study, pp. 378–380, question no. 6 asks: "Is a deterministic view in which environment and circumstance shape men's destinies consistent with the statement on responsibility at the conclusion? A critic has commented:

> . . . Crane has here violated his own artistic canon. He intrudes to preach a deliberate moral. The story ends with the grotesque image of the murdered Swede whose eyes stare "upon a dreadful legend that dwelt atop of the cash-machine: 'This registers the amount of your purchase.' " This point marks the legitimate end of the story. Crane spoiled the whole thing by tacking on a moralizing appendix.*

Lorch, Thomas M. "The Cyclical Structure of *The Red Badge of Courage*," *College Language Association Journal*, 10 (March, 1967), 229–38.

Malkin, Sol M. "Mail Box," *Bookman's Weekly*, 40, no. 9 (1967), 652–653.

Martin, Jay. "The Great American Novel" [De Forest, Howells, Crane, and Norris], in *Harvests of Change: American Literature: 1865–1914*. Englewood Cliffs, N.J., 1967.

Martin, John. "Childhood in Stephen Crane's *Maggie*, 'The Monster,' and *Whilomville Stories*," *Midwestern University Quarterly*, 2 (1967), 40–46.

Marushige, Kenzo. "The New York City Sketches ni okeru Stephen Crane no ningen-byōsha ni tsuite" [Stephen Crane's description of man in the New York City sketches], *Yamanashi Daigaku Gaikokugo Kankei Ronbun-shū*, no. 7 April, 1967), 1–5.

Maurer, Leonard. *A Bookman's Weekly*, 40 (August 28, 1967), 652–653.

Mito, Osamu. " 'Inshō' no bungaku—Stephen Crane (sono 1)" [Impressionism—Stephen Crane 1], *Kyoto Joshidaigaku Eibungaku Ronso*, no. 11 (November, 1967), 26–43.

Monteiro, George. "Whilomville as Judah: Crane's 'A Little Pilgrimage,' " *Renascence*, 19 (Summer, 1967), 184–189.

An important article on one of Crane's seemingly unimportant Whilomville stories. Jimmie Trescott in Sunday School, where hangs behind the superintendent's chair a "lithograph of the martyrdom of St. Stephen." This lithograph, as Monteiro notes, "has a relevance which pervades the entire story." Crane chose his text from Jeremiah.

See Bowen (1967).

——. "Ralph Paine and 'The Memory of Stephen Crane,' " *Stephen Crane Newsletter* 2, no. 1 (Fall, 1967), 6–7.

Nabuco, Caolina. *Retrato dos Estados Unides à luz da sua literatura*. Rio de Janeiro, Brazil: Livraria José Olympio Editôra, 1967, pp. 60–64. The realism of *The Red Badge* is a high watermark in the evolution of Western war fiction.

Napier, James J. "Land Imagery in 'The Open Boat,' " *CEA Critic*, 29, no. 7 (April, 1967), 15.

The reader "can easily overlook the originality of Crane's conception in which the sea is rendered in terms of earth, animal and domestic life. Illustrations are numerous."

---

* R. W. Stallman, editor. *Stephen Crane: An Omnibus*. New York: Alfred A. Knopf, Inc., 1952, p. 482 [Levin's footnote].

Napier repeats what has already been published by Stallman. *See* Stallman, "The Land-Sea Irony in 'The Open Boat' " (1968).

O'Connor, Richard. *Ambrose Bierce*. Boston, 1967, pp. 6, 155, 262.

Patrick, Walton R. "Poetic Style in the Contemporary Short Story," *College Composition and Communication*, 18 (May, 1967) 77–84.
On "A Mystery of Heroism."

Perosa, Sergio. "Naturalism and Impressionism in Stephen Crane's Fiction," in *Stephen Crane: A Collection of Critical Essays*, ed. Maurice Bassan (1967), pp. 80–94.
An abridged and slightly revised version of Perosa's original essay in *Annali di ca' Foscari*, 3 (1964), 119–142.
Reprinted with minor changes in *Le vie della narrativa americana* (1965).

Safranek, William P. "Crane's *The Red Badge of Courage*," *Explicator*, 26 (November, 1967), item 21.
In both Henry Fleming and in Wilson, the loud soldier, the character development is marked by three changes: each soldier has new eyes, sees himself as insignificant, and appears and feels himself to be much older.
Abstracted, *American Literature Abstracts* (June, 1968).

Sasatani, Taku. " 'Akai bukunsho' ni okeru hi to mizu no imeji" [Fire and water images in *The Red Badge of Courage*], *Silvan* no. 12 (December, 1967), 34–43.

Spiller, Robert E. *The Cycle of American Literature: An Essay in Historical Criticism*. New York, 1967. First published 1955.

Stallman, R. W. "Stephen Crane and Cooper's Uncas," *American Literature*, 39 (November, 1967), 393–396.
Reprints from the *New York Tribune*, February 21 (Sunday), 1892, an unsigned sketch new to the Crane canon: "The Last of the Mohicans," here published for the first time.*
Uncas, the noble warrior of Cooper's fiction, ended his days in Sullivan County, New York; but the original for Cooper's fictional bronze god Uncas, so Sullivan County storytellers insist, ended his life there not as a noble warrior who had yearned after the blood of his enemies but as a derelict begging from house to house a drink of the white man's rum. "He was a veritable 'poor Indian.' He dragged through his wretched life in helpless misery."
The pathos about Uncas lies in the contrast: "His Aspect in Fiction Contradicted by His Fame in Folk-Lore." In Crane's life, likewise, the pathos lies in the contrast between Crane's expectations and ideals *and* their collapse into rather banal trivialities and disappointments. In *Maggie* and *George's Mother* and in his Midnight Sketches of the city Crane exposed life's grim realities, the truth undercutting the fiction, exactly as here in his first Sullivan County sketch. As *The Red Badge of Courage* is designed by ironic contrasts of illusions undercut by crass realities, so too is Crane's 1892 sketch of the contrasted Uncas: Cooper's falsely glorified version and the real thing.

---

* Subsequent to this discovery in 1966, five more new Crane pieces were traced in the *New York Tribune* for 1892 by the clue of the dateline: "Hartwood, Sullivan County, N.Y." *American Literature* in the above article failed to print this data in the submitted footnote. *See* Gullason in *SHR* (Winter, 1968) and in *CEA Critic* (May, 1969). Stallman's discoveries were collected, together with other Sullivan County and related pieces, in *SCTS* (1968).

———. "Stephen Crane: Some New Sketches," *Bulletin of the New York Public Library,* 71 (November, 1967), 554–562.

Reproduces here for the first time "Three Mexican Sketches" from the holograph manuscripts—written on lined sheets and signed but untitled—in CUCC.

MS. no. 3 was subsequently issued in January, 1968, in pamphlet form by J. Katz ("for the friends of Mr. and Mrs. Joseph Katz, January 1968") without acknowledgement to its previous publication. In *Above All Things / By Stephen Crane.*

A portion of MS. no. 3 was quoted by Maurice Bassan in his *Maggie: Text and Context* (1966), p. 96.

———. "Notes Toward an Analysis of *The Red Badge of Courage,"* *Stephen Crane: A Collection of Critical Essays.* ed. Maurice Bassan (1967), pp. 128–140. Reprinted from *Houses,* here abridged, with a coda, pp. 137–140, recast from Thomas, "The Long Logic:" (1967).

Starrett, Vincent. "Stephen Crane," *Chicago Tribune Books Today,* June 4, 1967, p. 15.

———. "Stephen Crane at Claverack," *Stephen Crane Newsletter,* 2, no. 1 (Fall, 1967), 4.

Stephen Crane Newsletter, 1, no. 3 (Spring, 1967), 1–8.

Presents two new Crane letters to Edmund [1897], from Edith Crane transcript made in 1960, and a new Cora letter to John Hay from Ravensbrook, September 24, 1898 (discovered by George Monteiro at Brown University Libraries). Reprints from an unidentified newspaper one of the articles on Crane by Willis Brooks Hawkins, column 13, in his column entitled "All in a Lifetime."

Matthew J. Bruccoli reviews Eric Solomon, *Stephen Crane: From Parody to Realism* (1966).

———. 1, no. 4 (Spring, 1967 [misprint for Summer, 1967]), 1–8.

Reproduces a new Crane to Mrs. Moreton Frewen letter from the BCC, Crane remarking on his *Active Service:* "may heaven forgive it for being so bad."

Prints in facsimile Crane's Badenweiler death certificate. Not cited is the variant death certificate first published by John Eidson on *Notes and Queries,* 7, no. 4 (April, 1960), 148–150: "The Death Certificate of Stephen Crane." This variant certificate supplies new information and is utilized in *Crane.**

Prints the entry in the Rev. Dr. J. T. Crane's diary for November 1, 1871, from a transcript made by Edith F. Crane in 1960.†

Wednes. Nov. 1 [1871]

This morning at 5:30 our fourteenth child was born. We call him Stephen, the name of the ancestor of the Elizabethtown Cranes, who was one of the company of "Associates" who settled at E town in 1665; also of S. Crane of Revolutionary times, who was prominent in patriotic labor and counsels for 15 years. Afternoon: called

---

* My copy, obtained in 1958 at Badenweiler through Dr. F. K. von Siebold, Mayor of Badenweiler, is the same as Eidson published two years later.

† However, this note was transcribed by Edith Crane a decade previously and was known in the 1950s through BCCC. My copy, deriving from that source, appears in *Crane.*

on Bro. Cookman, who is sick.
Evening: heard Drs. Read & Hatfield on the Chicago fire.

Reprints from Crane's scrapbook an unidentified press clipping signed by
E. J. Edwards, reporting John Barry's reading of Crane's poems in April, 1894
—the "Uncut Leaves" affair. Quotes Crane's marginal note about his friend
E. J. Edwards on page 18 of the scrapbook. "This is a fake—not only a fake
but a wretched, unartistic fake written by a very stupid man. But it was a
great benefit." Crane here refers to the press clipping of "Society Leaders'
Suffrage Crusade" by Holland," the pen name of E. J. Edwards, whose identity
was first made known by LaFrance (1965).

In sum, all the above "new" Crane items have been known to Crane researchers for many years; nothing new here.

————. 2, no. 1 (Fall, 1967), 1–12.

A new letter by John D. Barry to Crane, March 22, 1893. Articles on Crane
at Claverack College by Vincent Starrett* and by Stanley Wertheim; a new
Crane letter to Copeland & Day, and a new Copeland & Day letter to Crane;
and a new Crane letter to William, March 16, 1897. M. J. Bruccoli in his
discussion of why Maggie commits suicide ignores William Gibson's insights
about that Maggie problem. So does Edwin Cady in *Landmarks of American
Writing*, ed. Hennig Cohen (1969), p. 176. *See* Gibson's Introduction, *The Red
Badge of Courage and Selected Prose and Poetry* (1956, 1962), pp. xvii–xviii.

Published here is Crane's "Art in Kansas City" as "A New Clarence Story"
with no acknowledgement to *SinSF*, where "Art in Kansas City" was published
by Stallman for the first time. *See* Stallman, "New Short Fiction by Stephen
Crane: II" (1964).

————. 2, no. 2 (Winter, 1967), 1–12.

Two new Crane letters to the editor of *Chap-Book,* snippits of no worth
or interest. Crane inscription to Jim Moser written in Gordon's studio on
November 14, 1894; an interesting item. Also, Crane's reply to the editor of
The Youth's Companion (November 5, 1895), whose letter of October 31st is
in *Letters*. Also, a letter dated Sunday, 27 June (1898) from "Near Santiago,"
which consists of this fragment: "My dear sir: I have forgotten everything just
now. Sorry."

The editor of *SCraneN*, Joseph Katz, remarks that the date and place of
this Crane letter "make it intriguing, but it might be even more so if one
knew what it was about and to whom it was sent. Anyone know?" The answer
to Crane's whereabouts for the week of June 27 (1898) is to be found in
Crane, chap. 22.

Katz reprints Crane's letter to DeWitt Miller, July 3, 1896, which was first
reproduced in *Letters*, p. 125. Katz claims that the version of this Crane
inscription in *Maggie* as given in *Letters* contains "a distortion in transcription" and is "wrong and misleading." However, the holograph which Katz
here reproduces is identical with the text of Crane's inscription letter to De-
Witt Miller given in *Letters*. Consequently, Katz's reprinting of this item is
pointless. Not acknowledged also is that this letter appeared in *Modern
Library First Editions* (1938), p. 53. On Katz's neglect to acknowledge previous
publication of letters in *SCraneN see* Joline (1902) for another instance.

* Everything in Starrett's article is in Harvey Wickham's memoirs (1926); so,
nothing new here.

The same criticism applies to Katz's reprinting of this Crane letter: "Dear Sir,—I don't thing it possible to get my photograph. They have been mostly ameteur things." Except that in *Letters* the word "ameteur" was silently edited for correction into "amateur," the text of Katz's reprint here is identical with the text given in *Letters*—including the heading with "Hartford [*sic*]" for Hartwood, N.Y. *See* Joline (1902).

Letters, p. 129, quotes Crane's inscription to the 1893 *Maggie* (dated August 29, 1896): "And the wealth of the few shall be built upon the patience of the poor / Prophecy not made B.C. 1090." Katz claims that this has been "transcribed with an error in Stallman and Gilkes, *Letters*, p. 129." My holograph copy disproves Katz's claim—except that "B.C. 1090" appears without the periods in Crane's holograph. The missing periods do not justify Katz's accusation of error.

Stanley Wertheim contributes an interesting article: "Franklin Garland's *Maggie*."

Thomas, Donald. [Biblical parallelisms in *The Red Badge of Courage*], in *Stephen Crane: A Collection of Critical Essays*, ed. Maurice Bassan (1967), pp. 137–140.
    An excerpt from Thomas's 1966 doctoral dissertation ("The Long Logic"), used as coda to Stallman's "Notes Toward An Analysis of *The Red Badge of Courage*," an essay reprinted in Bassan's *Stephen Crane*. Thomas's thesis attempts to establish biblical parallelisms throughout *The Red Badge*. See Thomas, "The Long Logic:" (1967).

———. "The Long Logic: A Symbolic Interpretation of Stephen Crane's *The Red Badge of Courage*." Ph.D. dissertation, University of Connecticut, 1967.
    Henry Fleming is symbolically a soldier in the Army of the Lord; his salvation is achieved by a change from selfishness to selflessness. Jim Conklin is both the suffering Christ and—in the role of the Cheery Soldier—the risen and returned Christ. His characterization is developed by biblical echoes and parallelisms to Christ. The first half of *The Red Badge of Courage* echoes again and again the Gospels, while the second half of the book echoes or is based upon the Book of Revelation.

Tsunematsu, Masao. "Toward Man in Society—A Study of Stephen Crane," *Shimane Daigaku Bunrigaku-bu Kiyo (Jinbunkagaku Hen)*, no. 1 (December, 1967), 78–89.

Turnbull, Andrew. *Thomas Wolfe*. New York, 1967, p. 137.

Vasilievskaya, O. B. *The Creative Works of Stephen Crane (1871–1900)*. Moscow: Nauka, 1967. 313 pages, indexed. Photograph of Crane.
    A thoroughly documented study of Crane and his works, with many footnotes in English detailing sources.

Wertheim, Stanley. "Crane and Garland: The Education of an Impressionist," *North Dakota Quarterly*, 35 (Winter, 1967), 22–28.
    Relate to Kwiat (1952), pp. 331–338 and to Mane (1964), pp. 30–46. Mane, says Wertheim, makes "some interesting speculations about the personality conflicts between the two writers and their attitudes toward one another. No one, however, has hitherto discussed the influence of Garland's impressionistic theories upon the development of Crane's style."
    Not noted by Wertheim is Stallman's analysis of Crane's style as prose poin-

tillism and its cross-identity with French Impressionist paintings, as given in *Omnibus,* pp. 185–187.

———. "Why Stephen Crane Left Claverack," *Stephen Crane Newsletter,* 2, no. 1 (Fall, 1967), 5.

———. "Franklin Garland's *Maggie,*" *Stephen Crane Newsletter,* 2, no. 2 (Winter, 1967) 1–3.

Westbrook, Max. [Review of Solomon's *Stephen Crane: From Parody to Realism*] in *American Literary Realism: 1870–1910,* 1 (Fall, 1967), 100–103.

Wright, Elizabeth, and George Hendrick. "Bibliography of explications of short fiction," *Studies in Short Fiction,* 6 (Summer, 1969), 491–493.
A wrongly designed checklist, worthless.

Yoshimura, Akio. "S. Crane: Maggie, A Girl of the Streets (1893)—Maggie no shi o megutte—" [—Maggie and her death—], *Hiroshima Nogyo Tanki-daigaku Kenkyu Hokoku,* 3, no. 2 (December, 1967), 87–92.

1968

Agrawal, D. C. "Vision and Form in *The Red Badge of Courage,*" *Banasthali Patrika,* 11 (July, 1968), 86–90.

Andrews, Anthony. *The Splendid Pauper.* Philadelphia, 1968.
Review article on Ralph Ellison's *Shadow and Act;* on Crane, p. 50.

[Anon.]. "Crane Biography," *Hackettstown Gazette,* August 22, 1968.
On Stephen Crane's father, who served in Hackettstown as pastor of Trinity Methodist Church in 1867.
Triggered by the publication of *Crane,* this article contains some new data; but it errs in the notion that Crane died at 29 and also in misnaming Edmund Crane as Edward.

———. "Romantic Realist [Stephen Crane]," *M.D., Medical Newsmagazine,* 12 (June, 1968), 153–158. Photographs.
The sources for this sketch, mainly *Omnibus,* are not cited. The photograph said to be of Crane at his desk at Brede Place is of Crane at his desk at Ravensbrook. Errs in stating that Crane died at "the age of 29."

———. "An American, A Negro," *Times Literary Supplement,* January 18, 1968, pp. 49–50.

Bowen, James K., and Richard Van Der Beets, eds. *American Literature Abstracts,* 1, no. 2 (June, 1968), 194–196.
Provides abstracts of the following articles: Gullason, "The Cranes at Pennington Seminary" (1968); Pelletier (1968); Safranek (1967); and Stallman, "Stephen Crane and Cooper's Uncas" (1967).

———. *American Literature Abstracts,* 2, no. 1 (December, 1968), 58–63.
Provides abstracts of the following articles: Grenberg, "Metaphysic of Despair" (1968); Gullason, "The First Known Review of Stephen Crane's *Maggie*" (1968); Gullason, "The Last Will of Mrs. Mary Helen Peck Crane" (1968); Miller, "Regions of Snow" (1968); Stallman, "Journalist Crane in That

Dinghy" (1968); Stallman, "The Land-Sea Irony in 'The Open Boat'" (1968); and Van Der Beets, "Character as Structure" (1968).

Bradbury, Malcolm. "Art and Reality in Stephen Crane," *Journal of American Studies,* 2 (April, 1968), 117–120.

An excellent essay reviewing Eric Solomon's *Stephen Crane in England* (1966) and his *Stephen Crane: From Parody to Realism* (1967).

Braunstein, Simeon. "A Checklist of Writings by and about Stephen Crane, in *The Fra,*" *Stephen Crane Newsletter,* 3, no. 2 (Winter, 1968), 8.

Cady, Edwin. "Stephen Crane," *Encyclopaedia Britannica,* vol. 6. Chicago, 1968, pp. 695–696.

Cady's sketch includes such errors as misdating the death of Crane ("at the age of 29") and asserting that Crane married Cora Taylor. Cady's sins of omission include the burial place of Crane and the identity of Cora as madame of the Hotel de Dream in Jacksonville, first woman war correspondent in Greece, and commonlaw wife of Crane at Ravensbrook and then at Brede Manor. Cady's sketch omits even her name.

Cazemajou, Jean. "*The O'Ruddy,* Robert Barr et *The Idler,*" *Caliban,* no. 5 (January, 1968), 69–78.

Champney, Freeman. *Art and Glory: The Story of Elbert Hubbard.* New York, 1968, pp. 68–69, 219, 223, 234.

Nothing new here about the Crane-Hubbard relationship, pp. 68–69. Champney's *Story of Elbert Hubbard* is by no means the full story. *See* Daly (1916) and Taber's letters to Beer (1923) and to Balch (1940). These new data, thanks to Austin M. Fox, appear for the first time in *Stephen Crane: A Critical Bibliography.*
Reviewed:

Simeon Braunstein, *SCraneN,* 2 (Fall, 1968). He is quite mistaken in claiming that Champney "has researched his subject carefully" and that the evidence is in his "excellent bibliography and extensive chapter notes." Braunstein opines that Champney's treatment of the Hubbard-Crane relationship "is considerably kinder to Crane than biographers of Crane have been to Hubbard." These, the author states, "have treated Hubbard as a blatant idiot, whose relationship with Crane was explosive and brutal. The evidence is meager, but it doesn't support such a reconstruction." However, the evidence against Hubbard is not meager. The scholar is referred to the Buffalo and Erie County Public Library, where the Harry Taber papers reside.

Champney, p. 54, has Elbert Hubbard in New York City in 1894, but he also has Hubbard in England, p. 68, and back in East Aurora, N.Y., p. 49. It is a most confusing account of Hubbard's whereabouts. Stallman in *Crane* has Hubbard meeting Crane in New York City in early 1894 (on other evidence, not Champney's).

Colvert, James B. Introduction, *Great Short Works of Stephen Crane.* New York, 1968, pp. vii–xv. With a short biography by Frank N. Magill.

Reprints the 1896 *Maggie,* but corrects that edition's error in chap 5, substituting the 1893 phrase "dirt disguised her" for "dirt disgusted her."

Magill is mistaken, p. 357, in claiming that Stephen and Cora "were married in Greece." In England they held a mock marriage, witnessed by H. G. Wells, but they could not obtain a legal marriage because Cora could not obtain a divorce from her second husband. *See Crane* (1968). Magill's note errs in saying that Crane at Lafayette College distinguished himself "at boxing," that his mother's death ended his college career, and that he wrote *Maggie* in two days before Christmas in 1891; also he errs in opining that Crane was not a successful reporter.

Dendinger, Lloyd N. "Stephen Crane's Inverted Use of Key Images of 'The Rime of the Ancient Mariner,'" *Studies in Short Fiction,* 5 (Winter, 1968), 192–194.

   The incidents of the gulls and the shark and the windtower in "The Open Boat" strike Dendinger as inversions of images in Coleridge's poem; he admits, however, that "there is no evidence of a deliberate parody on Crane's part."

   See Bowen, *American Literature Abstracts* (June, 1968).

Dusenbery, Robert. "The Homeric Mood in *The Red Badge of Courage,*" *Pacific Coast Philology,* 23 (April, 1968), 31–37.

Fleming, Thomas J. "The Press at War," *This Week Magazine,* in *Milwaukee Journal,* June 2, 1968, pp. 5–6.

   On Crane at San Juan. Fleming is mistaken about Roosevelt; he charged up Kettle Hill, not San Juan. On Creelman at El Caney. On Edward Marshall at Siboney. On the Cuban War; *see Crane.*

Fraser, Robert S., ed. "The *Thoth* Annual Bibliography of Stephen Crane Scholarship," *Thoth,* 9, no. 2 (Spring, 1968), 58–61.

Frederick, John T. "The Fifth Man in 'The Open Boat,'" *CEA Critic,* 30 (May, 1968), 1, 12–14.

   The title refers to Frederick himself as the imaginary fifth passenger in the dinghy of "The Open Boat." A more pertinent inquiry would be the fifth man in the dinghy of Crane's press dispatch, "Stephen Crane's Own Story," *New York Press,* January 7, 1897. Crane, to be sure, said there were four men in that dinghy, but John Berryman in his *Crane* conjectured a fifth man in the dinghy of the press dispatch and of "The Open Boat," and no Crane scholar since 1950 has troubled to remove that ghost and thereby absolve Crane from the impugnment of his integrity as journalist.

   That ghost is removed from the dinghy by Stallman in "Journalist Crane in That Dinghy" (1968). Reprinted in *Crane.*

Gallagher, Robert S. "Stephen Crane's Tenderloin Adventure," *New York, N.Y., An American Heritage Extra,* 1968.

Gemme, Francis R. Introduction, *Maggie and Other Stories.* New York, 1968.

   Contents: Virtue in War, The Monster, The Angel Child, The Pace of Youth, The Knife, The Bride Comes to Yellow Sky, The Open Boat, *Maggie: A Girl of the Streets,* His New Mittens, A Mystery of Heroism.

Gibson, Donald B. *The Fiction of Stephen Crane.* Carbondale, Ill., 1968. Preface by Harry T. Moore.

   "But what is this true importance of Crane?" asks Harry T. Moore. "Robert Wooster Stallman, who has written most frequently and most usefully about him, began an Introduction to *The Red Badge of Courage* with the statement, 'I think the most important thing to say about Stephen Crane is that he is a great stylist. He puts language to poetic use, which is to use it reflexively and symbolically.' Elsewhere Mr. Stallman has noted, and the emphasis is his, 'The works that employ this reflexive and symbolic language constitute what is *permanent* of Crane.'" Moore, Preface, pp. v–vi.

What H. T. Moore quotes here stands at odds with the Donald B. Gibson contention in his Introduction, pp. xvii–xviii, that we should resist the temptation to regard Crane as a symbolist. "For the most part he is no more a symbolist than one must be who uses language, a symbolic medium. . . . Most of the symbolism in Crane's work is universal and unconscious. Often what has been taken for symbolism is no more than the thing itself."

Gibson contends that the critic must consider whether a particular symbolic reading contributes toward "some over-all meaning, whether it leads anywhere." He admits that in "The Open Boat" Crane "has quite obviously intended the reader to interpret symbolically. But even in these tales ["The Open Boat" and "The Blue Hotel"] it would seem that some limitations should be put on symbolic reading."

On symbolism in the minute particulars of "The Open Boat" see *Houses* and Stallman, "Stephen Crane: A Revaluation" (1952).

Gibson contends that Crane knew few literary works and discusses Crane's unusual deficiencies in reading; but Gibson's opinion fails to mention "List of Books/Brede Place," which listing of his library must be cited before pronouncing on his deficiencies in reading.

On *The Red Badge:* "Most commentators have generalized from one or two battles, not apparently realizing that in each encounter Henry is different; not realizing that each battle has a separate function in the novel." Gibson on this point corrects Walcutt's generalization (1956), p. 81. He also corrects Greenfield (1958).

Reviewed:

George Monteiro, *Brown Alumni Monthly,* 69 (April, 1969), 43.

Modern Fiction Studies, 15 (Summer, 1969), 273–274.

Stanley Wertheim, "The Fiction of Stephen Crane," *Literature and Psychology,* 19, no. 2 (1969), 125–128: An excellent essay. "Gibson's study of 'The Blue Hotel' makes an impressive attempt to bridge the logical gap between the Swede's obvious responsibility for bringing about his own death and the Easterner's final statement that 'Every sin is the result of a collaboration.'

"In *The Red Badge of Courage* Crane wavered in his decision," says Wertheim, "whether or not to show growth of any kind in his protagonist and consequently presented contradictory deterministic and volitional points of view toward human behavior. Gibson feels that deletions in the manuscript reveal that Crane realized the novel lacked unity and struck out many passages of absurd posturing in which Henry Fleming considers himself the victim of a naturalistic universe. Crane's final emphasis is on 'the traditional story of the hero, beset by great odds, who through fortitude and endurance is able to achieve his ends' (p. 68). However, while Gibson is correct in maintaining that many of the passages expunged from the manuscript were antithetical to the maturation theme, this does not necessarily indicate that Crane was attempting to unify the novel. The excised passages differ more in tone than in content from the considerable number of statements remaining in the published text that show strong irony of manner in Henry's concept of self. Crane apparently attempted to exclude from the later parts of the novel the doctrinaire naturalistic tirades that resemble 'the brass and bombast' of Henry's 'earlier gospels'. Thus there is a quantitative lessening of the irony as *The Red Badge* draws to a close, but Crane still views his protagonist as a deluded youth who has failed to resolve the contradictions in his thoughts, feelings, and actions. There seems to be a mocking quality rather than a deep human sympathy in Crane's treatment of Henry's final musings. His happiness is based on a conviction of superiority to his comrades rather than empathy with them, and his pride is restored through a false evaluation of his spurious red badge of courage. 'He had performed his mistakes in the dark, so he was still a man.' Crane does not allow Henry to realize the absurdity of this position, but his self-satisfaction is a sham which illustrates the conceit of man at which Crane marvelled in 'The Blue Hotel.' "

Thomas A. Gullason, *American Literature*, 41 (May, 1969), 293–294: Complains that Gibson does not credit Gullason and others in stating that the *Sullivan County Sketches* comprise "the burden of the corpus of Crane's writing." However, *contra* Gullason, any Crane critic knows this much without reference to Gullason, who himself does not make any distinction between tale and sketch, evidently ignorant of the distinction. The Sullivan County pieces consist of tales *and* sketches. *See* Stallman, Introduction to *SCTS* (1968).

"There are, unfortunately, so many limitations to Mr. Gibson's approach to the interpretation and evaluation of Crane's fiction that his contribution to Stephen Crane scholarship is negligible." Gullason has here confounded critical reading of texts with scholarship, which has nothing to do with evaluation and critical interpretation. To Gullason they are all one and the same thing, which is why Gullason is no literary critic. Secondly, Gibson makes no pretense of engaging in Crane scholarship and would be the first to admit that his contribution in it is negligible. Gullason, on the other hand, because he confounds his contributions in Crane scholarship, which are considerable, with his contributions in Crane criticism, which are indeed negligible, feels embittered that other writers on Crane neglect to mention Thomas A. Gullason. As critic he thus ends mainly as a critic of those who ignore to mention his Crane writings.

"Mr. Gibson also has an inadequate grasp of Crane's arts and themes when he tries his hand at interpretation and evaluation. For example, he misrepresents Crane's portrait of the Swede in 'The Blue Hotel' (pp. 111, 113); supposedly Crane dislikes the Swede the most in the story."

Is Gullason saying that Crane likes the Swede? By Crane's tone we know his bias, as in the cash-register's declaration. *Contra* Gullason, Gibson has written a very sensitive reading of "The Blue Hotel," one of the best studies of "The Blue Hotel" in the history of Crane criticism.

Marston LaFrance in *SCraneN*, 3, no. 3 (Spring, 1969), 9–10. Another nitpicking "review" typical of *SCraneN* reviewers; smart-aleck in tone, LaFrance can find nothing good in Gibson's book. However, Gibson's chapter on "The Blue Hotel" is splendid. LaFrance scoffs at Gibson's considering *Maggie* as an example of literary Naturalism. "*Maggie* is not deterministic unless one is able to ignore all of Crane's bludgeoning irony in it." However, that is a debatable notion.

Gibson, William, Introduction, *The Red Badge of Courage and Selected Prose and Poetry*, 3d ed. New York, 1968. First edition, *Selected Prose and Poetry*, 1950, did not include *The Red Badge of Courage*. Second edition, *The Red Badge of Courage and Selected Prose and Poetry*, 1956, reproduced in bracketed passages the final manuscript of *The Red Badge* from the faulty text of the Folio Society edition, ed. John Winterich (1951). Frontispiece, "Mr. Stephen Crane in His Study, from a newspaper sketch; source unknown."

In the Introduction and Postscript to the Third Edition, pp. v–xxiii, Gibson makes many sharp points or queries. However, on "The Blue Hotel" with its second ending confounding the first ending, Gibson takes an ambiguous viewpoint, stating that "Except for Crane's afterword, the story ends with a sardonic tableau. . . . 'This registers the amount of your purchase.'" Implied here is that the cash register ending is the rightful ending of "The Blue Hotel." I agree. However, Donald Gibson in *The Fiction of Stephen Crane* (1968) brilliantly reconciles the seemingly conflicting double endings.

Selected Bibliography, by Stanley Wertheim. pp. xxv–xxxiv. Annotated. Fails to list the facsimile edition of *Maggie*, 1893, ed. Donald Pizer (1968). Fails to cite the refutation of Cyrus Day's "Stephen Crane and the Ten-Foot Dinghy" (1957) in Stallman's "Journalist Crane in that Dinghy" (1968). And again in *Crane* (1968). Fails to cite Stallman's "Stephen Crane: A Revaluation," in *Critiques and Essays on Modern Fiction*, ed. John Aldridge (1952). Ignores his "Crane's *Maggie* in Review," in Stallman's *The Houses That James Built* (1961).

Wertheim annotates Gullason's *Complete Short Stories and Sketches* (1963) thus: "The most reliable collection of Crane's shorter fiction." However, the texts are not reliably the sources cited; for example, the cited source for "An Experiment in Misery" is *New York Press*, but Gullason's text is not that of the *Press;* nor is "The Upturned Face" from *Ainslee's Magazine*, although appended to the story is Gullason's misleading citation of *Ainslee's Magazine*. Nor is Gullason's title for this collection reliable in that it is not *The Complete SS&S* it pretends to be—it omits more than forty tales, sketches, and stories.

Wertheim lists *Omnibus* under Stallman's Introduction to *The Red Badge of Courage* (1951), saying that this seminal essay was "incorporated with additions and revisions into Stallman's *Stephen Crane: An Omnibus* (New York: Alfred A. Knopf, Inc., 1952)." However, no revisions were made in that reprinting of "Notes Toward an Analysis of *The Red Badge of Courage*," nor in any subsequent reprinting. Additions to that essay, dealing with other Crane works, amount to more than 100 pages in *Omnibus*, which deserved a separate entry under Editions and Collections, as well as an annotation of its contents. And *Omnibus* was published in London by Heinemann, 1954.

"Stallman argues that *The Red Badge* is mythical and ritualistic, and its dominant symbolism is religious. For an impressive refutation of this point of view, see Philip Rahv, 'Fiction and the Criticism of Fiction,' *Kenyon Review*. XVIII (Spring, 1956), 276–299." However, Rahv not only denies symbolism in *The Red Badge*, but also irony in "The Open Boat." I doubt that Wertheim fully subscribes to the palpable nonsense of Marxian critic Rahv, or would subscribe to it had he read my refutation of Rahv and Marxian criticism in my "Fiction and Its Critics," *Kenyon Review*, 19 (1957), 290–297. Or the longer and original version printed in *The Houses That James Built* (1961). There is no excuse for Wertheim's failure to know about and cite my *Kenyon Review* reply to Rahv by the fact that it is listed in the *MFS* Crane checklist (1959).]

Gilkes, Lillian. "Some Omissions," *Saturday Review*, 51 (August 31, 1968), 20.

Claims that *NYCS* published Crane's "Great Bugs in Onondaga" with no mention that Lester G. Wells first published it in *Courier* (1963). However, there is no claim by Wells that he discovered that literary hoax; nor does Mayfield claim it in a subsequent *Courier* (1963). Nor does Gilkes here state who discovered it. Williams is cited as its discoverer in *Crane,* and this is correct. Gilkes thus errs in saying that *Crane* leaves "the impression that Stallman was its discoverer."

However, no such impression can possibly exist from Notes, p. 567. Crane's sketch is here footnoted to say that it was first reprinted in the *Courier* for March, 1963. There is no need to cite Wells. Where this Note errs is in mis-identifying the essay "Stephen Crane's Bugs" as authored by Ames W. Williams, whereas it is an unsigned piece (by Mayfield), with a portion of it by Ames W. Williams, pp. 29–30. It is here–unnoticed by Gilkes–that Williams admits that he discovered Crane's "Great Bugs." Everyone involved in the publication of Crane's "Great Bugs" had been very skittish about who had discovered it and whether Crane was its author.

It is true that *Crane* does not mention Melvin Schoberlin's *The Sullivan County Sketches of Stephen Crane,* but under writings *by* Crane there was no need to list that outdated and misnamed edition, and under writings *on* Crane the Schoberlin Introduction is cited in *Crane,* p. 440. *Stephen Crane: A Biography* is not a bibliography. (Schoberlin's book is misnamed in that these are tales, not sketches.) Gilkes laments that *Crane*'s checklist does not list Gullason's *CSS&S,* nor Fryckstedt's *UW,* but *UW* contains no new Crane MSS., and so there was no need to mention *UW. Crane* could not afford space to list in its checklist, pp. 625–641, reprints of Crane's works such as Gullason's *CSS&S,* which is forty sketches and stories short of being "complete." Also, Gullason's texts are not those he cites as his source; "An Experiment in Misery" is from *Work,* not from the *New York Press* as Gullason claims.

Grenberg, Bruce L. "Metaphysics of Despair: Stephen Crane's 'The Blue Hotel,'" *Modern Fiction Studies,* 14 (Summer, 1968), 203–213.

Griffith, Clark. "Stephen Crane and the Ironic Last Word," *Philological Quarterly,* 47, no. 1 (January, 1968), 83–91.

On "The Open Boat," "The Blue Hotel," and *The Red Badge of Courage* in defining Crane's technique of undercutting by the ironic last word. On Crane's ironic vision *see also Omnibus* and Colvert (1959).

Gullason, Thomas A. "The Cranes at Pennington Seminary," *American Literature,* 39 (January, 1968), 530–541.

The students' register at Pennington Seminary "contains names identical with some which appear in *Maggie* (Nellie, Maggie, Mary) and in *The Red Badge of Courage* (Conklin, Wilson).

Not noticed by Gullason is Cazemajou's "Stephen Crane: Pennington Seminary," *Études Anglaises* (April, 1967), which is a much more important study of the same topic. *See Crane.*

Gullason's study is abstracted in Bowen, *American Literature Abstracts* (June, 1968).

For the sources of the names of Henry Fleming and of Hasbrouck in *The Red Badge of Courage,* as well as the source for Crane's title *Active Service, see Crane.*

———. "The Last Will and Testament of Mrs. Mary Helen Peck," *American Literature,* 40 (May, 1968), 232–234.

See Bowen, *American Literature Abstracts* (December, 1968).

———. "The First Known Review of Stephen Crane's 1893 *Maggie,*" *English Language Notes,* 5 (June, 1968), 300–302.

A review in Port Jervis *Union* for March 13, 1893.

————. "A Stephen Crane Find: Nine Newspaper Sketches," *Southern Humanities Review* (Auburn University, Alabama), 2, no. 1 (Winter, January, 1968), 1–37. Editorial note, p. iii. Preface, pp. 1–10.

Contents: The Last of the Mohicans*; Hunting Wild Hogs; The Last Panther; Not Much of a Hero; Sullivan County Bears; The Way in Sullivan County; A Reminiscence of Indian War; Bear and Panther; Two Men and a Bear.

This list contains three new Crane sketches, new to Stallman's *SCTS* (May, 1968), not then known to exist: They are "Not Much of a Hero," "A Reminiscence," and "Two Men and a Bear." They appear here for the first time in *SHR*, but by their publication in that relatively unknown journal they remained unknown (as Gullason's findings) until his article obtained listing in *PMLA Bibliography, PMLA*, 84 (June, 1969), 889.

The six new Crane pieces discovered by Stallman in 1966 obtained galley by December, 1967, for *SCTS. See* Stallman, "Stephen Crane and Cooper's Uncas" (1967).

Hagemann, E. R. "Stephen Crane in the Pages of *Life* (1896–1901), A Checklist," *Stephen Crane Newsletter,* 3, no. 3 (Spring, 1969), 1, 3–5.

————. "Stephen Crane Faces the Storms of *Life,* 1896–1900," *Journal of Popular Culture,* 2 (Winter, 1968), 347–360.

Hepburn, James. *The Author's Empty Purse and the Rise of the Literary Agent.* London, New York, and Toronto, 1968, pp. 57, 74, 75.
Reviewed: TLS, July 11, 1968, p. 734. "Middlemen."

Holroyd, Michael. *Lytton Strachey: A Critical Biography,* vol. 2. New York, 1968, p. 133.

Itabashi, Yoshie. "Comedies of Love: A Study of *The Third Violet* and *Active Service,*" *Tsuda Review,* no. 13 (November, 1968), 15–63.

Katz, Joseph. "Stephen Crane: Muckraker," *Columbia Library Columns,* 17 (February, 1968), 3–7.

Recasts from Linson's *MSC* the visit of Linson and Crane to the Scranton coal-mines which Crane reported in *St. Louis Republic* (July 22, 1894): "Down in a Coal Mine." The variant version appeared in *McClure's Magazine* (August, 1894): "In the Depths of a Coal Mine." (Reprinted in *NYCS.*) Quotes a passage which never saw print, given in *MSC.* There is thus nothing new in Katz's article except the fact of a deed dated January 24, 1893, by which Stephen sold to brother William his share in the coal-mine stock (at Kingston, Pennsylvania) he inherited on his mother's death in 1891.

————. "Stephen Crane, 'Samuel Carlton,' and a Recovered Letter," *Nineteenth-Century Fiction,* 23 (September, 1968), 220–225.

Reproduces for the first time the complete text of the Crane letter to William H. Crane (November 29, 1896). *See Letters,* pp. 135–136. Collate Katz's article with Randel (1965).

————. "The 'Preceptor' and Another Poet: Thomas Wentworth Higginson and Stephen Crane," *Serif,* 5 (March, 1968), 17–21.

---

* First reprinted by Stallman in *American Literature* (November, 1967) from the *Tribune,* February 21, 1892. This priority is not cited by Gullason in his Notes, p. 37.

A biographical sketch of Higginson and commentary on his reviews of Crane works in *The Nation*. See McCormick (1965).

——. "An Early Draft of 'The Blue Hotel,'" *Stephen Crane Newsletter*, 3 (Fall, 1968), 1–2.

——. "*Maggie: A Girl of the Streets* (1893): A Census (Part II)," *Stephen Crane Newsletter*, 3 (Fall, 1968), 6.

Kurita, Ariyasu. "Stephen Crane kenkyu—'Sullivan County Sketches' no ichi kōsatsu" [A study of Stephen Crane—on "Sullivan County Sketches"], *Chuogakuin Daigaku Ronsō*, 3, no. 1 (November, 1968), 27–47.

LaFrance, Marston. "The Ironic Parallel in Stephen Crane's 1892 Newspaper Correspondence," *Studies in Short Fiction*, 6 (Fall, 1968), 101–103.
See Bowen, *American Literature Abstracts* (June, 1969).

McDermott, John L. "Symbolism and Psychological Realism in *The Red Badge of Courage*," *Nineteenth-Century Fiction*, 23 (December, 1968), 324–331.
See Bowen, *American Literature Abstracts* (June, 1969).

Mane, Robert. *Hamlin Garland: l'homme et l'oeuvre (1860–1940)*. Études Anglaises 30: Paris: Didier, 1968.

Martins, Heitor. "Crane, Xavier, Chocano: Un caso de plagio inter-americano," *Revista de Cultura Brasileña*, 25 (1968), 173–181.

Maxwell, D. E. S. *American Fiction: The Intellectual Background*. New York, 1968, pp. 294–299.

Mayfield, John [unsigned]. "S. C. at S.U.," *Courier* (Syracuse University Library), no. 29 (Spring, 1968), 8.
Lists the references to Crane in the *Onondagan* of '92. See [Anon.] (1891).

Miller, Ruth. "Regions of Snow: The Poetic Style of Stephen Crane," *Bulletin of the New York Public Library*, 72 (May, 1968), 328–349.
Takes issue with Daniel G. Hoffman in *Poetry*: Crane's poetry is neither realistic nor sensuous nor metaphorical, and Hoffman is in error.
For a nonmetaphoric reading of Crane's poems, especially the Intrigue poems, see *Crane*. On Crane's poetry *see Omnibus*.
See Bowen, *American Literature Abstracts*, (December, 1968).

Mitgang, Herbert, ed. *The Letters of Carl Sandburg*. New York, 1968, p. 92.

Monteiro, George. "Bernard Berenson's Notes on Stephen Crane," *Stephen Crane Newsletter*, 2, no. 3 (Spring, 1968), 1–2.

——. "A Capsule Assessment of Stephen Crane by Hamlin Garland," *Stephen Crane Newsletter*, 3, no. 1 (Fall, 1968), 2.

Noble, David W. "Norris, Crane, Dreiser," in *The Eternal Adam and the New World Garden: The Central Myth in the American Novel Since 1830*. New York, 1968, pp. 101–132.
A worn out thesis-ridden book flatly claims that *Maggie: A Girl of the Streets* presents Maggie as "the symbol of the American dream of innocence" and that her death indicates that "There is no place for innocence in the world of reality." George Kelsey in *George's Mother* is "the American Adam who has lost his idyllic home in the American countryside." In the urban nightmare George and his mother "will try to preserve the myth of innocence. . . . The dream of arcadian simplicity has dissolved into the reality of the

urban nightmare. This is the setting for the moral testing of the last American Adam, George Kelsey."

Crane, of course, never heard of the American Adam, but that is the way it goes nowadays, even by a professed historian of American letters and history. "Since I am a historian," says Noble, professor of history at the University of Minnesota; but historian Noble damages his case by having eschewed documentation of his sources, and so on Crane we get a monologue devoid of import historically or biographically and devoid of import critically speaking. There is here no contribution on Crane.

Pelletier, Gaston. *"Red Badge* Revisited," *English Journal,* 57 (January, 1968), 24–25, 99.

Crane's diction explodes and overwhelms this reader with too much color and too much noise. "Once overpowered by such diction, it is difficult to hear Crane's message sounding out somewhere within that verbal din."

See Bowen, *American Literature Abstracts* (June, 1968).

Phelps, Robert, and Peter Deane. *The Literary Life: A Scrapbook Almanac of the Anglo-American Literary Scene from 1900–1950.* New York, 1968.

Pizer, Donald. Introduction, *Maggie: A Girl of the Streets.* San Francisco, 1968. Facsimile of the 1893 *Maggie.*

Pizer, Donald, ed. *Hamlin Garland Diaries.* San Marino, Calif., 1968, p. 121.

Mark Barr "again spoke of Stephen Crane's marriage. He quoted Crane as saying, 'I brought Cora back.' He married her over here in the presence of [H. G.] Wells and one or two others. 'Conrad wrote about him saying that he was surrounded by a lot of third-class people.' He was never given to really fine associations. Barr considered Cora Crane a woman of education, 'an ample "negro mammy" sort of person.' The fact of Wells being a witness at the wedding would not add anything to its legal aspect, for so far as I know he does not believe in the home or marriage [so said Garland].

"In looking back on Crane, I can now see that he had not the power of growth. He had a gift but not the attributes of a big writer. He made no advance over *The Red Badge.* In truth he retrograded. With all his endowments he was not an admirable character. He gave out the effect of being an alley cat so far as habit went. And during the days when I first knew him in New York City he was living like an outcast. Although not a drinking man, he smoked incessantly and I sometimes thought used a drug of some kind. Of this I was never sure, and though the police found an opium pipe in his rooms, there was no proof that he used it for himself." *See Crane.*

Reid, B. L. *The Man From New York: John Quinn and His Friends.* New York, 1968, p. 124.

Ruber, Peter. *The Last Bookman: A Journey into the Life and Times of Vincent Starrett. . . .* Introduction by Christopher Morley. New York, 1968.

Scriba, Jay. "His 'Pot Boiler' Became a Classic," *Milwaukee Journal,* August 14, 1968, p. 20. Photograph.

Stallman, R. W. "Notes Toward an Analysis of *The Red Badge of Courage,*" in *Adventures in American Literature,* ed. James Early and Robert Freier. New York, 1968. With Teachers' Manual.

———. "Reply to Reviewer Cady," *American Literature,* 40 (March, 1968), 83–85.

"Cady says that *NYCS* 'was almost entirely anticipated' by Gullason's *Complete Short Stories and Sketches of Stephen Crane* (1963). However, *NYCS* "anticipated" both Gullason and Fryckstedt by publishing 35 pieces not in Gullason's *CSS&S* and a dozen pieces not in Olov Fryckstedt's *Uncollected Writings of Stephen Crane* (Uppsala, 1963)."*

"Cady says that 'only three writings' by Crane appear in *NYCS* which were not in Fryckstedt; 'none is significant.' However, to correct Cady's miscount of three, *NYCS* presents *also* 'Why Did the Young Clerk Swear?' (significant because Crane here portrays himself as a shop-clerk); 'Diamonds and Diamonds' (significant as evidence that Crane knew his Maupassant); 'When Every One is Panic Stricken' (significant as one of Crane's two journalistic hoaxes); and 'At Clancy's Wake,' which is in neither Fryckstedt nor Gullason because I discovered it—in *Truth!*

"In sum, *NYCS* has these 7 pieces plus 8 new SC MSS not in Fryckstedt's *UW*. As for Gullason, not noticed by Edwin Cady is the fact that his title is grossly misleading since his *Complete SS&S* lacks more than three dozen SS&S. Cady complains that 'it has clearly become a prime duty of scholars to get the facts straight concerning the canon, text,' etc.; but as shown in the above Cady's own facts are amiss. The fact is that Gullason's texts are not those of his stated source (his text for 'The Upturned Face' is not *Ainslee's Magazine*), whereas the texts in *NYCS* are precisely those they claim to be, namely their first periodical publication. Gullason's texts are often copies of the tampered texts of Follett's spurious edition of *The Work of Stephen Crane*.

"Cady complains that the design of *NYCS* seems "extraordinarily confused, as the lame trailer *And Related Pieces* of the title acknowledges." N.Y.U. Press added that trailer in galley against my protest; but even so *NYCS* is a self-contained unit and not—like Gullason's *CSS&S*—a baggy monster of pieces chronologically—and thus indiscriminately—juxtaposed.

"Cady objects to *NYCS*' categories of 'On the New Jersey Coast' and 'Excursions' as unnecessary because these sketches were 'printed in New York City papers and hardly ever discuss events a hundred miles away.' By Cady's criterion Fryckstedt is in error, although Cady does not say so, because he lists under 'Syracuse' a sketch of New York City ('Broken-Down Van'), which is more than one hundred miles from Syracuse, and under 'Cuba' he lists Crane's play which is situated in China, which is more than one hundred miles from Cuba and from New York City! Here he also includes Crane's Asbury Park sketch, which by Fryckstedt's own confused design obviously belongs under his category 'Syracuse and Asbury Park.'

"Cady opines that *NYCS* 'provides interesting documentation for Olov Fryckstedt's (unacknowledged) articles on the Dora Clark episode.' However, when Olov sent me his 1962 article I wrote him that I had already researched Dora Clark and had found a dozen additional items, including a new piece by James Ford (a parody of police commissioners); that exempted my making any acknowledgements. Gullason in his *CSS&S* acknowledges two bibliographies and Gullason himself, a fact which Cady ignores. Also the fact that

* Fryckstedt, as he states in his Preface, spent eighteen months in the U.S. on a grant by our state department to compile his volume of Crane. Meanwhile, two American scholars were compiling their Crane volumes for New York University Press. The state department thus undercut the New York Press project, begun by Stallman in 1956.

Gullason while citing where new Crane manuscripts first appeared slights the names of the scholars who first published them."

In "Mr. Cady's Reply," p. 85, Cady says: ". . . I agree, now as in the review, with Professor Stallman that the state of Crane's minor, scattered writings, often in unreliable texts, is deplorable. His 'Rejoinder,' like his book, confirms me in the belief that the determination of the canon and the establishment of the texts must be done by the on-going Virginia Edition of Stephen Crane."

————. "Stephen Crane and Cooper's Uncas," *American Literature Abstracts*, 1, no. 2 (June, 1968), 196.

Summarizes the article published in *American Literature* (November, 1967): "Stephen Crane and Cooper's Uncas," which presented the text of Crane's 1892 *Tribune* sketch "The Last of the Mohicans," there for the first time. *Abstracts* here publishes the footnote which *American Literature* did not print: "Subsequent to this discovery, five more Sullivan County sketches were traced in the *Tribune* for 1892 by the clue of its dateline: 'Hartwood, Sullivan County, N.Y.' They are reproduced for the first time, together with several related pieces, in *Stephen Crane: Sullivan County Tales and Sketches*, edited by R. W. Stallman. . . ."

Priority in publishing these new Sullivan County pieces would have been confirmed had *American Literature* printed that footnote, and the publisher of *SCTS* would have been spared the embarrassment of Thomas Gullason's letter (October 10, 1968): "I trust you realize that I published all the 'unknown' sketches you mention (and more) in *Southern Humanities Review* (Winter, January, 1968)."

————. "*A bas* Justin Kaplan," *Atlantic Monthly*, 222 (November, 1968), 48. With "Mr. Kaplan replies."

————. "Journalist Crane in That Dinghy," *Bulletin of the New York Public Library*, 72 (April, 1968), 260–277. With illustrations.

If there were twenty-eight pasengers aboard the *Commodore*, well, *then*, because sixteen Cubans made it to shore and seven men in a third lifeboat which cracked up against the ship's side were drowned, there may have been five men in the dinghy. The *New York Press* reported that five men reached shore at noon of January 3: Stephen Crane, Capt. Murphy, the Cook, and *two* sailors. Because John Berryman knew only the *Press* account, he conjectured in *Stephen Crane* (1950) that there were five men in the dinghy—not four as Crane declared in his *Press* dispatch: "Stephen Crane's Own Story." However, such a conjecture cannot be pressed this way without evidence, for it impugns Crane as journalist.

Since 1950 Crane's integrity as journalist has remained impugned not only by Berryman, but also by scholars William Randel and Cyrus Day. For eighteen years no scholar has questioned Berryman's speculation. For the biographer of Crane here was a crucial issue.

Randel's main source was the *Florida Times-Union*, which declared the *Commodore* had twenty-eight passengers; so Randel fell into Berryman's trap. However, they both ignored some three dozen newspaper accounts, including the New York *World*, wherein Capt. Murphy lists the crew as twenty-seven— therefore four in the dinghy, just as Crane said in his *Press* dispatch.

However, these various newspaper accounts contradict each other. And so my job was to unriddle the mystery. It was solved when I obtained from our National Archives copy of the log of the *Boutwell:* Number of passengers on board: twenty-seven. That fact puts four men in the dinghy. It also puts into dry dock scholars John Berryman and William Randel.

Scholar Cyrus Day contended in 1957 that Crane had falsified the stormy condition of the sea, and so once more Crane's integrity as journalist was impugned. He contended that the hardship supposedly endured by the men in the dinghy had been "grossly exaggerated." At this point in my investigations I obtained the logs of the steamers *Newark* and *Roland.* The *Newark,* standing forty miles northeast of Daytona Beach at midnight of January 1 (1897), was "rolling from 21 degrees to port to 19 degrees to starboard." With that *biased* roll, it is evident that a strong sea was running.

This reading was confirmed by the log of the *Roland,* which reads: "Moderate gale, rough sea." Then for Jan. 2: "Moderate gale and strong breeze . . . chopping sea." Then for Jan. 3: "Strong breakers. . . . Sea rough High from east." So then, Crane—*contra* Cyrus Day (in *Boston University Studies in English,* 1958), did not exaggerate the condition of the sea, neither in his *Press* dispatch nor in his "The Open Boat" short story, where he rightly has it that "These waves were most wrongfully and barbarously abrupt and tall." And that's the way it was.

See Bowen, *American Literature Abstracts* (December, 1968).

————. "The Land-Sea Irony in 'The Open Boat,'" *CEA Critic,* 30 (May, 1968), 15.

What James J. Napier overlooks in his "Land Imagery in 'The Open Boat'" (*CEA Critic:* April, 1967) is that the substance of his article is identical with Stallman's 1952 reading of land-sea imagery in "The Open Boat," in Aldridge's *Critiques and Essays on Modern Fiction:* "Things viewed by the men at sea are viewed as though they were men on land. This double vision in the point of view manifests the two-part contrast of Crane's theme, sea and land symbolizing two ways of life." Restated in *Omnibus* and in expanded form in "Fiction and Its Critics," *Kenyon Review* (1957). Reprinted in *Houses* thus: "Things viewed by the men at sea are viewed as though they were men on land. Thus the cold-comfortable sea-water image is patterned by the same ironic outlook as is everything else in the story, by the contrast between what is and what seems. Land images impinge upon their situation at sea; the waves seem like a mountain-cat, each crest seems but a hillside ('Viewed from a balcony'), seagulls remind them of a covey of prairie chickens a thousand miles inland, and their dinghy seems like a wild colt ridden by circus-men."

Napier replies in *Critic* for May, 1968: "The similarity of my observations to Professor Stallman's is indisputable; I see I should have consulted his article before writing my short piece. . . ."

See Bowen, *American Literature Abstracts* (December, 1968).

————. *Stephen Crane: A Biography.* New York, 1968. Photographs and illustrations. First printing: May, 1968. Second printing: August, 1968.
Noticed:
Leslie Cross, *Milwaukee Journal,* January 7, 1968.
New Britain (Connecticut) *Herald,* January 17, 1968.
Reviewed:
Virginia Kirkus Bulletin, March 1, 1968, p. 320: "Stephen Crane may be con-

sidered the forerunner of the modern American writer. Youthful ardor, rebellion against the middle class, bravado mixed with cynicism—all that we associate with Hemingway, Fitzgerald and Wolfe were incarnated in this late 19th century figure, famous at twenty-four, dead four years later, the author of *The Red Badge of Courage,* that totally imaginary and classic novel of the Civil War. His life, as Professor Stallman comprehensively demonstrates in a striking and definitive biography, was based on a code of personal integrity that had little to do with the Puritan outlook of Melville or Hawthorne, or the strict Methodist home of his clergyman father. Indeed, the conflict of generations, so fashionable now, seems to have been the compelling factor behind Crane's turbulent life, from his early experiences with red light districts (epitomized in *Maggie: A Girl of the Streets*) to his bizarre, ill-fated marriage to a 'woman with a past.' His rise in the literary world was meteoric but rarely without attendant hardships. This milieu is given an exacting and panoramic evocation by Stallman, and the story of Crane's various and complicated relations with Conrad, James, Wells, Howells, and Hamlin Garland is one of the most interesting and valuable sections in the book. Stallman's scholarship is often so dense and painstaking that Crane's colorful personality doesn't always emerge. Nevertheless, the essential portrait is here at last."

Publisher's Weekly, June 3, 1968: "This graphic, haunting and skillfully written book is a meticulous and authoritative biography of Stephen Crane. It is haunting because it faithfully and sensitively conveys Crane's charm, genius and tragedy in his brief life. The Crane writings are analyzed and tied in with their sources in Crane's experiences (for poignant example, take the shipwreck off Florida, a brush with death which fashioned into the story 'The Open Boat' and which obsessed him when he lay dying of tuberculosis several years later).

"Here is Crane the reporter; the seeker after life and real, however degraded, experience, the lover of many women; the spinner of many tales and user of vivid language; the happy summertime playmate of his young nieces; the desperately poor and struggling young writer; the friend of literary greats. R. W. Stallman, professor of literature at the University of Connecticut, who is also the editor of Crane's letters, has immersed himself in his subject and incorporated much new material—letters, sketches and poems—which he has found. A very fine book; a literary event."

Nard Jones, *Seattle Post Intelligencer,* June 16, 1968: "Unquestionably this is the definitive biography of Stephen Crane. It is splendidly researched, with much fresh material, and it corrects at last the unfortunate *Stephen Crane* which Thomas Beer issued in 1923.

"Yet somehow the subject never quite comes alive, and neither do the men and women who surrounded the American genius. This is not entirely the fault of the biographer. Crane's life was tragically brief (he died at 28) and certainly neither the author nor his writings were fully developed at his death. On the other hand, Mr. Stallman shows little empathy for Crane or those closest to him. It may be sure that this large volume (530 pages plus appendix and notes) suffers by comparison with other recent biographies of later American authors: Hemingway, Scott Fitzgerald, Lewis and others. However, the biographers of these writers had the tremendous advantage of being able to talk with the people who knew their subjects. The biographer of Fitzgerald knew him personally."

Parade Magazine, July 28, 1968.

Arnold Smithine, *The Library Journal,* July and August, 1968.

Book Buyer's Guide, August, 1968.

William Coyle, *Springfield* (Ohio) *Sun,* August 3, 1968: An "authoritative biography. He corrects many errors and presents new facts. That is not to say that the result is an altogether satisfactory book. Stallman's somewhat dogmatic tone is suggested by the closing sentence of an appendix in which he discusses a minor controversy about one of Crane's stories: 'And that settles that.' Nevertheless, this is a major work of scholarship and will hereafter be the starting point for anyone working on Crane."

Dick Schaap, *Chicago Sun-Times Book Week,* August 4, 1968, and *San Francisco Chronicle,* August 4, 1968.

Jack Conroy, *Chicago Sun-Times Book Week,* August 4, 1968.

Abe C. Ravitz, *Cleveland Plain Dealer,* August 4, 1968: He "warily approaches the personality of this adventurous writer with feeling and insight—not with the fixed mind to make a Freudian case study. With the manuscript collections at his complete disposal, Stallman could now deal conclusively with the women in Crane's life: Nellie Crouse, Dora Clark, and Cora Taylor, proprietress of the Hotel de Dream, who later became the writer's notorious wife. Now chronologies are straight, relationships are identified and Stephen Crane steps clearly before the footlights, revealed in fullest texture. The supreme sense of isolation that Crane so poignantly expressed in his fiction was, as Stallman determines, the flywheel of his very life."

Virginia Pasley, *Newsday,* August 10, 1968: Even now many of Crane's writings are ignored. Stallman's "comprehensive and understanding biography ought to change all that. It is a thick volume to cover the life of a man who lived so few years; but Stallman has searched out the sources of all his works, discusses them in detail, relating them to incidents in his life and telling enough of the story to whet the appetite to go to the original. Stallman's book spends perhaps too much time on contemporary criticism. The inclusion of quotes from almost every periodical about almost every novel slows up the action and could have been better cut. On the whole, however, Stallman has done an incredible job of research and writing."

Granville Hicks, *Saturday Review* 51 (August 10, 1968), pp. 29–30: Finds Crane a puzzling person. "By digging up and bringing together a great mass of materials, Stallman may have simplified the task of subsequent scholars, but he himself has not penetrated very far into the mystery." Complains that *Crane* "is made out of facts" (whereas Hicks prefers a biography of speculations?). Justin Kaplan makes the same criticism of *Crane* in the *Atlantic* (September, 1968).

Stallman's rejoinder to Hicks, "Inflated by Facts," *Saturday Review,* August 31, 1968, p. 20, is here quoted: "I wish to clear up a few criticisms in Granville Hicks's review of my *Stephen Crane: A Biography (SR,* Aug. 10).

1. Mr. Hicks says that the book 'is made out of facts,' whereas he presumably prefers a book to be made out of theory (Freudian, like John Berryman's *Stephen Crane;* or Marxian, like G. Hicks's *The Great Tradition).*

2. Mr. Hicks thinks my account of Crane in Cuba (ninety pages against the eight pages by which Beer surveys Crane in Cuba) is 'inflated,' but any new account of Crane in the Cuban War would have to be 'inflated' by comparison with Berryman (twenty pages) or Beer, who—never having read Crane's war

dispatches—blithely declared that Crane could not report! My account is 'inflated'—in the sense that it presents for the first time multiple eyewitness reports of Crane on Cuban battlefields.

3. Mr. Hicks also thinks my account of the shipwreck is 'inflated,' and maybe it is. But meanwhile it deflates Berryman's conjecture that there were five men in the dinghy and reinstates thus Crane's integrity as journalist, which Berryman's distorted account had impugned."

Jay Bail, *Patriot Ledger* (Quincy, Mass.), August 10, 1968, and *San Francisco Chronicle*, August 11, 1968: "But what is not expected are sharp and true judgments of Crane that are not often admitted in literary circles. . . ."

John Barkham, *Grand Rapids* (Mich.) *Press*, August 11, 1968: "It is a pleasure . . . to be able to announce that justice has at last been done to Stephen Crane in R. W. Stallman's massive new biography. It is a work which shows every sign of wide-ranging research (Crane was a global wanderer), meticulous documentation and informed judgment."

Carlos Baker, *New York Times Book Review*, August 11, 1968: "Not the least among Mr. Stallman's achievements is his portrait of Cora Stewart, the golden-haired hostess of the Hotel de Dream, sporting house in Jacksonville. . . . this life story probably comes as close to being a definitive biography as we are likely to get. . . . If the central test of a biography is to recreate a vanished personality, Mr Stallman has admirably succeeded."

Jean Stafford, *Washington Post*, August 11, 1968.

Day Thorpe, *Washington* (D.C.) *Star*, August 11, 1968.

Raymond A. Sokolov, *Newsweek*, August 12, 1968: Crane "would have been his own ideal biographer, but others have had to do it for him." Stallman "is the third to try, also the best, and because of this, probably the last."

Christian Century, August 14, 1968.

Wayne E. Gibbs, *Camden* (N.J.) *Courier-Post*, August 14, 1968: "The book is a scholarly biography that presents Crane as the records have him. But what Professor Stallman has done is to add a new book by gleaning from articles and documents found since 1950. The book is an invaluable tool for scholars; it is an enjoyable enlightenment for general readers."

Donald Stanley, *San Francisco Examiner*, August 14, 1968.

Austin M. Fox, *Buffalo Evening News*, August 17, 1968: "For his carefully documented account of the adventure-laden life of one of the most baffling personalities in American Literature, Prof. Stallman should be awarded a front-rank place in the blue battalions of eminent American literary historians. His sections on Crane's almost incredible reportorial activities during the Spanish-American War are especially fascinating not only for the new material Dr. Stallman has unearthed but also for the order and understanding he has managed to bring out of this material. The biography has much new information, too, on Crane's swing through the West and into Mexico for the Bacheller newspaper syndicate, on Crane's shipwreck at the time of the *Commodore* disaster, on Crane's war correspondence experience during the Greco-Turkish War, and on his literary baronetcy in England during his last years. Dr. Stallman has handled all this material with much scholarly competence, and his estimate of Crane can be regarded as judicious, accurate and highly readable."

Van Allen Bradley, *Chicago Daily News*, August 17, 1968: "While there is still much to be learned about Stephen Crane, it is likely that Mr. Stallman's exhaustive study will remain the most illuminating life of *The Red Badge*'s author for a long time to come . . . Professor Stallman's chapter on *The Red Badge* and how it was written is one of the best in the book."

Martha MacGregor, *New York Post,* August 17, 1968: "What sort of writing would Crane have done if he had lived on? 'A. J. Liebling did a long essay in which he argued that Crane might have written another *Red Badge of Courage.* I don't think so. He was so terribly in debt. Cora was so extravagant. He owed $5,000 to his agent, a lot of money then. I think he would have gone on writing drivel, turning out more hack work to try and pay the bills.' If Crane were a young man today, would he take drugs? Professor Stallman thinks not: 'He would experiment once with LSD, write it up, as he did with opium in his own day. He had to experience everything; to write about the Bowery he dressed up like a bum and slept in flop houses. And yet he wrote *The Red Badge* without ever seeing a battle.' "

Sidney Thomas, *Atlanta Constitution and Journal,* August 18, 1968.

Wirt Williams, *Los Angeles Times,* August 18, 1968: Stallman's "new critical biography is, beyond question, the definitive one. Sympathetically but without sentimentality, he unfolds the great young writer's struggle and pain."

Louis Zara, *Philadelphia Inquirer,* August 18, 1968.

Wayne Robinson, *Philadelphia Sunday Bulletin,* August 18, 1968: Stallman refutes "Beer's curious summation: 'A thoroughly romantic lover who had not made exactions in love and probably knew precious little about women.' The professor leaves no doubt how wrong Beer was. In his solid narrative and voluminous notes at the back of this thick book, he documents nearly every step of Crane's short life from Nov. 1, 1871 to June 5, 1900, private and public. He includes and analyzes almost everything Crane wrote—including society notes from Asbury Park. Novelists (Louis Zara was one, with *Dark Rider,* in 1961) have tried to convey the spirit of Crane. This biography reads better than most novels, and no one will put it down without knowing Crane as completely as the written word can bring the whole substance of a poet-journalist-novelist who burned the candle at both ends, famous at 24 and dead at 28."

N. G. Flous, *Pittsburgh Press,* August 18, 1968: "Mr. Stallman has had to outdo two other first rate Crane biographies—the Thomas Beer (1923) and the John Berryman (1950). This he does. Through a prodigious collection of detail, fact and quoted comment, Mr. Stallman seems to have abolished the need for another book on Mr. Crane's life."

Bliss Buchanan, *New Orleans Times-Picayune,* August 25, 1968.

Leslie Cross, *Milwaukee Journal,* August 25, 1968.

Edmund Fuller, *The Wall Street Journal,* August 28, 1968: Stallman's biography "is a model of its kind—absorbingly readable, exhaustively thorough, perceptively critical and supported by a solid substructure of notes and bibliography. It corrects the errors and fills in omissions of earlier biographies.

"The chronicle of the English years is particularly rich in collateral portraits. The picture of Joseph Conrad, long Crane's close friend, is the best we've seen outside of full-scale lives of Conrad, and is a contribution to the studies of that writer. Mr. Stallman demonstrates convincingly that Crane had a marked influence on Conrad's literary development, . . . He recognizes, however, that Conrad, whose concentration on his main work was greater than Crane's, went on after his friend's early death to pile up a body of work that considerably surpasses Crane. . . . No section of this book is finer than the long account of Crane in the field as a war correspondent in Cuba. . . ."

August Derleth, *Capital Times* (Madison, Wis.), August 29. "Stallman does not quite solve the enigmas of Crane's personality and life, but he goes farther toward doing so than any other Crane biographer."

Times Literary Supplement (London), August 29, 1968: "The earlier, well-known biographies by Thomas Beer and Mr. John Berryman will still be read for their own sakes, but Mr. Stallman's will be the one that is consulted and quoted in support of biographical arguments. . . . Here is a book that will be mined, by critics of Crane and literary historians of the period, and it is better to be serviceable for years than brightly entertaining for months."

Time, August 30, 1968: "The result unquestionably is the most exhaustive biography ever written about Crane—or likely to be written. Nothing is ignored. . . ."

William Kiefer, *Hartford Times*, August 31, 1968.

Serrell Hillman, *Saturday Night* (Toronto, Canada), August, 1968.

Richard Lehan, *Boston Sunday Herald-Traveler*, September 1, 1968: "Stallman wanted to tell the whole story. This he succeeded in doing, and no one is ever going to tell it more completely."

James F. Light, *Nation*, September 2, 1968, pp. 183–184.

Dorothy Tyler, *Detroit News*, September 7, 1968: "The chapters on Crane's life in England are among the most interesting in the book."

Daniel Aaron, *New Republic*, September 7, 1968, pp. 33–34: "And yet if Stallman can't resolve all of the mystery surrounding Crane, his super-saturated, sympathetically objective biography convincingly detaches the authentic writer from the lurid legend, and establishes itself as the best source for understanding him."

Thomas Lask, *Arizona Phoenix*, September 8, 1968, and *New York Times*, August 13, 1968, p. 37: "What Stallman's biography does prove is that everything about Crane is intriguing and puzzling—his life and his work in equal measure."

The New Yorker, September 28, 1968, p. 180: "Its virtues are comprehensiveness, accuracy . . . , honesty . . . , and a real enthusiasm for the subject."

Daniel Greene, *National Observer*, September 30, 1968.

Justin Kaplan, *Atlantic*, 222 (September, 1968), 121–123: "The book is loaded with repetitions. . . . A seven-line passage about the pseudonymous Ouida contains two terrible errors in the rendering of her real name and one substantive error which vitiates Crane's review of her work by implying that *Under Two Flags* was one of her later novels. Edward Waterman Townsend, the author of Chimmie Fadden . . . appears correctly the first time, the second time as Edward E. Townsend, and the third time as the author of 'Jimmie Fadden.' We are given a brief description of a certain barfly by a writer named 'O' Henry,' but the only bar I associate this 'O' Henry' with is a candy bar."

In *"A bas* Justin Kaplan," *Atlantic*, 222 (November, 1968), 48, Stallman replies that Kaplan "unjustly nit-picks some errors in my 'factuality,' errors which reviewer Kaplan—a former editor in trade publishing—knows full well are typos. . . . One of the two terrible errors is the obvious printer's error of 'Lousie' for the intended Louise. Another error—almost as terrible—is the misprint of 'O' Henry' instead of O. Henry. This O. Henry misprint and many other typos have already been corrected in the June second printing of my *Stephen Crane*. How unjust of Justin to quibble about such petty typos!"

Kaplan in his review of *Crane* "complains that I have 'pretty consistently avoided or suppressed speculations of anything other than a purely circumstantial nature,' but in the biography as history speculations are precisely what ought to be avoided." Reviewers of Kaplan's *Mr. Clemens* found his penchant for psychoanalysis its major weakness. "Throughout the book," said one reviewer, psychoanalytical probings and pronouncements are often more than speculative; they are wildly speculative." Kaplan, said another reviewer, "knows how to please readers," and that is the main merit of his book. "Mr. Kaplan, he told the truth, mainly, but there are some things he stretched."

Atlantic expunged from my reply what the reviewers complained about in Kaplan's *Mr. Clemens and Mark Twain* (1966), namely "numerous inaccuracies, documentation that leaves much to be desired, and questionable interpretations." *Atlantic* expunged also the fact that Kaplan's *Mr. Clemens* errs in citing in the Index, page 377, Stephen Crane; whereas there is no mention of Stephen Crane on p. 377, nor anywhere else in Kaplan's book. Mr. Cyril Clemens, editor of *Mark Twain Journal*, submitted his letter to the *Atlantic* making the same criticism, but the *Atlantic* refrained from publishing it.

John K. Hutchens, *Book of the Month Club News*, October 28, 1968: Crane "emerges fully drawn in a readable work of scholarship. Professor Stallman's book is surely among the superior literary biographies of our time."

Choice, October, 1968.

Arlin Turner, *Virginia Quarterly Review*, 44 (Autumn, 1968), 678–682.

R. Weber, *Louisville Times,* November 20, 1968, p. 9.

James Mellow, *Commonweal*, November 29, 1968, pp. 322–323.

Alfred Kazin, *New York Review of Books*, December 5, 1968.

Thomas Lask, *New York Times,* December 28, 1968: Includes *Crane* among the best biographies of 1968.

Stanley Wertheim, *Literature and Psychology*, 18 (1968), 179–182: Berryman's *Crane* "is less reticent about Crane's personal life" than Beer's *SC*.

"Berryman is able to cite only occasional instances in Crane's writings and isolated incidents in his life, such as that reported by Robert Davis in which Crane gallantly offered to show a streetwalker 'the way' to indicate compulsive desires to rescue sexually discredited women or that because of an Oedipal fixation these were the only women he could love. . . .

"R. W. Stallman makes no attempt to impose an arbitrary theoretical structure upon Crane's complex and enigmatic life or to find rigid thematic patterns in his work. The tenor of *Stephen Crane: A Biography* is reportorial and objective. The book incorporates a wealth of primary and secondary material unknown or unavailable to John Berryman—letters, memoirs, tales, sketches, and poems—much of which Mr. Stallman himself brought to light in previous publications. Virtually all the known facts about Stephen Crane are gathered together here, and many puzzling questions are resolved. There are also a good number of relatively minor but interesting new discoveries such as the source for the title *Active Service* in Tolstoy's *War and Peace* (a novel Crane may have read, at least in part since he professed himself unable to finish it, before or during the composition of *The Red Badge of Courage*) and the revelation that *The Black Riders* was not universally condemned by American reviewers as indicated by Beer and Berryman, but was for the most part well received.

"Whenever possible, Stallman allows Stephen Crane to tell his own story through biographically relevant material in his fiction and poetry and, more frequently, through his journalism. This method conveys a sense of immediacy, but extended summaries of the minor creative writing and travel and war correspondence often clog the narrative and inordinately swell the bulk of the volume. Crane's self-portrait is counterpointed by the perspectives of literary friends and acquaintances: Hamlin Garland, William Dean Howells, Richard Harding Davis, Joseph Conrad, Ford Madox Ford, Henry James, and many others. Their testimony at times contradictory, is tested and reconciled in the alembic of Stallman's comprehensive knowledge, acquired in the course of over twenty years as the dean of Stephen Crane studies. There are occasional inaccuracies, e.g. the manuscript subtitle of *The Red Badge of Courage* which should read "An Episode of the American Civil War," is misquoted (p. 582); it is implied that Crane spent only a single semester at Pennington Seminary (p. 18). . . .* Nevertheless, this will probably remain the standard Crane biography for many years to come. As never before, Crane's life is presented in full, without notable gaps or contradictions. . . .

"Although the scholarly quality of this monumental biography is generally very high, sporadic documentation and the absence of an adequate bibliography sometimes preclude recognition of the achievements of previous scholars and critics.† Analyses and evaluations of Crane's most important works of fiction (there is relatively little criticism of the poetry) are concise and perceptive. Stallman has modified but not abandoned his controversial interpretation of *The Red Badge of Courage* as a Grail quest in which Jim Conklin assumes the role of a sacrificial God and he now concedes that the religious imagery of the novel does not follow a consistent allegorical pattern. *The Red Badge* is a study in human conceit which begins with motifs of change and growth but ends in self-deception. The final image of the golden sun gleaming through leaden rain clouds recapitulates the despair-hope contrast of the first chapter. This circular design with its ironic implications, Stallman emphasizes, is paralleled in 'The Open Boat,' which ends as it begins with the contrast of hope and despair."

Louis Budd, *Modern Fiction Studies,* 14 (Winter, 1968–1969), 490–492: "Sections grow out of proportion if more material happens to be available, as on the months in Cuba or the closing years in England, and Stallman excerpts heavily from Crane's lesser-known pieces and sometimes quotes copiously from negligible reviews. I find this biography definitive only in the sense that it forced me to reassess Crane's character, to separate my unstinted admiration for his best work from the legend of another rejected and mistreated genius.

"Even after allowing for human frailty, it is now hard to idolize Crane, who must have finally lost much of his self-respect. . . .

"Far too casually, Stallman observes that Crane 'was influenced by Kipling, notably at the beginning of his career but also even at the end, and he owned a good many of Kipling's books.' Someday a study of Crane may be entitled *The Light That Failed.*

"A fairer title would be *The Red Light That Failed,* for a study of his years with Cora Crane. The sentimental notion is that though they met in her

---

* Here Wertheim cites Gullason in *American Literature* (January, 1968) for the dates of Crane at Pennington Seminary, whereas the dates were known to me from Cazemajou, *Études Anglaises,* April, 1967. The implication cited above is caused by an ambiguity of phrasing (p. 18): Crane "had spent the previous fall semester at the Pennington Seminary. . . ." The dates for Crane at Pennington—September, 1885, to December, 1887—are given p. 566, a fact not noticed by Wertheim.

† The checklist of writings on Crane was expunged at galley time by the editor's decision that it would overload an already bulky book. The "sporadic documentation" was injected into the galley of Notes, pp. 563 ff., an expensive and time-pressured ordeal.

discreet 'sporting house,' she turned out a 'good wife' for him—loyal, support-ive, devoted to his writing career, and selfless at nursing him. All in all she was his fatal disaster. Justice to her must admit that Crane, while clearly tempted at least once, failed to save himself; the record never shows that he seriously tried to curb her spending, which strapped him to an accelerating wheel of debt, especially after she put and helped to keep Brede Manor on his frail back, though a photograph in Stallman's book reveals that the estate was much huger than I had imagined and though its upkeep made their chances for solvency not grim but hopeless. . . .

"A handy cliché is to discover that a novelist's life mimicked one of his plots, yet Crane never wrote anything so sourly tragic as his own undoing. This judgment does not echo Stallman but is rather inherent in the materials he has gathered. Knowing his strong-handedness as a critic, I expected him to be obtrusive. Essentially, he stays content to pile up and synthesize the facts, which he has been digging for very persistently and widely. After taking short-cuts he still ends up with sixty pages of notes, and the bibliography he has amassed had to be held over for a forthcoming volume. Nobody will—or any-way should—try soon to do another full-scale biography of Crane.

"Likewise, explication of his major work has laid out most of the approaches possibly valid for our time; the unrefined gold in the minor pieces that Stall-man plays up will not pan out to even a scholar's fortune. . . .'"

M. J. Bruccoli, *Stephen Crane Newsletter*, 3, no. 2 (Winter, 1968), 8–9.

Joseph Katz, *American Literature*, 40 (January, 1969), 565–567.

Eric Solomon, *Nineteenth-Century Fiction*, 23 (March, 1969): Stallman's *Crane* "is, without question, a remarkably complete biography of the novelist. It remains questionable, however, whether the young man who died at age 28 can sustain as intense a biographical treatment as fits the short life of a Byron or a Keats. . . . [See *TLS*, August 29, 1968, wherein the same question is raised.]

"His nearly two decades of research into the mysteries of Crane's brief life have culminated in a successfully organized narrative that brings together nearly every known detail of the novelist's circumstances.

"The biographical externals are gathered with finesse and care. But Stall-man does not reveal the color of Crane's soul. The fault lies not in the biog-rapher but in the star, the brightly lit, elusive star of Crane's early success; as Henry McBride once warned Thomas Beer: 'I spent ten years planning a study of Crane and ended by deciding there was no such animal, although I knew him for eleven years.'*

"Stallman adopts the best possible strategy for his biographical approach. He mixes the known facts, materials from the letters and from memoirs of Crane's friends, with substantial chunks of Crane's occasional journalism. The technique can work effectively as in the two solid Cuban War chapters. By joining Crane's reports with the comments of other war correspondents, Stall-man measures Crane's perceptions and reveals a good deal about his writing methods. Momentarily an aspect of his personality flashes forth as when Stall-man quotes Crane's rationale for his admiration of the regular as opposed to the volunteer soldier, and we realize that he is discussing his view of the pro-fessional author's commitment. . . .

---

* However, McBride denied to Charles Feinberg that he had ever planned to write any study of Crane.

"Stallman is excellent on the self-contradictions of Stephen Crane's attitudes, at once arrogant and humble, slap-dash and careful.

"Stallman's *Stephen Crane* adds some pertinent facts, narrates the sad, short story of Crane's life from every available source. The book displays first-rate-scholarship, taste and order as it balances probabilities against certainties; what it lacks is that one quality its subject possessed most remarkably—imagination.

"Discussing a recently discovered sketch, Stallman mentions the irony of Crane's life, and this irony also applies to the difficulties of capturing his essence in a biography. His life was built 'upon mountains which collapsed into banal troughs again and again, and the pathos lies in the contrast between his expectations and ideals and their collapse into disappointments, disillusionments and grim ironies.' "

Richard Peck, *Georgia Review*, 23 (Spring, 1969), 105–107: "The impressive scholarship obvious in these early chapters represents this biography's greatest virtues.

"Such thoroughness informs even more Mr. Stallman's untangling of the confusing events which surround the sinking of the *Commodore* and Crane's subsequent use of those hectic events in 'The Open Boat.' Having checked weather station records, ships' logs, and varying newspaper reports, Mr. Stallman clears away the apparent contradictions, presents a factual and persuasive account of the entire disaster, and—in the process—offers a fast-paced and dramatic narrative.

"The Greco-Turkish War and Crane's Cuban adventures also move quickly, in spite of the mass of information presented. Mr. Stallman has gathered the reports of journalists who covered those campaigns and reveals Crane through such reports as well as through Crane's autobiographical writings. Allowed thus to talk of Crane, several minor figures come alive themselves, notably Richard Harding Davis, who—for all his dislike and apparent jealousy of Crane—frequently defended Crane from the malicious gossip of his many detractors. By affording his reader this many-sided view of Crane, the author adopts a method not unlike Crane's own literary impressionism.

"As critic rather than biographer, Mr. Stallman appears content to reassert positions he has taken in the past (e.g., his reading of the religious symbolism in *The Red Badge of Courage*). A few of Crane's minor works are treated at unnecessary length, given the author's knack for the occasional epigrammatic statement, often worth paragraphs of analysis: 'The only remarkable thing about *Active Service*,' Mr. Stallman comments, 'is that the author of *The Red Badge of Courage* wrote it.'

". . . the biography is corrective enough, and should stand as authoritative. It is inconceivable that the research here represented will be overthrown in any major way. Willing to point out errors in his own earlier edition of Crane's *Letters*, Mr. Stallman will himself note corrections in the details of his portrait by future scholars.

"He may also—should this biography ever undergo revision—wish to read proof carefully. Individually of little import, minor (and often merely typographical) errors accumulate in annoying aggregate. To cite a few: some of Crane's poems are silently modified (*Intrigue* IX, p. 429) or misquoted (pp. 131, 158, 174); it is confusing to find in a Lincoln, Nebraska barroom fight in February of 1895 the 'germinal situation' for *Black Riders* XXX (p. 131), a poem on which Crane had read proof in December of 1894 (p. 126)—a verbal slip corrected later (p. 159).*

"But minor lapses are perhaps inevitable in so long a book. Until the promised appearance of Mr. Stallman's annotated bibliography of Crane makes unnecessary some of this volume's cumbersome notes, nothing can surpass it as a source for Crane scholars. It is certainly the best available Crane biography; more, it is a good book which, because of its too inclusive nature, contains an even better one."

The error of "consumptive now" appears instead of "consumptive nun," p. 69, an error of typesetting corrected in the second printing (August, 1968). The Index has it Henry Thompson Peck, an error Mr. Peck notices. However, the text rightly has it Harry Thurston Peck, a point of collation not noticed by Mr. Peck in his otherwise very favorable review.

Bernice Slote, *Prairie Schooner* [Vol. 2] 43, no. 1 (Spring, 1969), 140–142: ". . . R. W Stallman's biography, *Stephen Crane*, is a major work of finding, assessing, and relating an enormous body of detail about Crane's world, his friends, his movements, his writings. It is a dogged, tough, brilliant job of research and brings us at last upon the shore of a time and place where Stephen Crane actually lived.

"Stallman has gathered an incredible amount of factual detail and contemporary statement, and a very large part of what he has found is entirely new. What is astonishing is that there is so much information, when we thought we had so little. The fact is that no one had done much looking. . . . Stallman's emphasis is quite different. His aim has been to gather fact, contemporary comment, statements of eyewitnesses—all with a scrupulous accounting of the truth. The result has been to realize the weather and shape of a real world, with all its kaleidoscopic differences, and to show a man of several dimensions in whom some secrets still lie. If Crane is not as vividly narrated as in Beer, or as much interpreted as in Berryman, he may be more like a man alive for us to see and hear. If we should ask what Crane was like, for example, we have numerous vivid glimpses. . . .

"Not the least valuable parts of the book are the summaries of reviews and contemporary criticism of Crane's writing, more than eight pages (pp. 180–188) on *The Red Badge of Courage,* for example. Important sections in the appendix do the same for *Maggie* (pp. 539–545) and *The Little Regiment* (pp. 546–548). Other valuable sections in the appendix are the notes on the *Commodore* disaster; accounts of the writing of *The O'Ruddy* and of Crane's play *The Ghost;* lists of parodies of Crane and books at Brede Place. The extensive notes add much material not in the text, and are readable for themselves.

---

* *Contra* reviewer Peck, *Crane,* p. 131, says that in Lincoln, Nebraska, Crane recited some lines from his forthcoming *The Black Riders,* "then in preparation for May, 1895, publication: 'One man feared that he might find an assassin; / Another that he might find a victim. / One was more wise than the other.' The poem has the same germinal situation as 'The Blue Hotel.'" On p. 159 I say that this syllogistic three-line poem anticipates the germinal situation Crane developed in "The Blue Hotel." On p. 130 I say that the barroom fight on February 12 Crane later transposed "into the fight between the Swede and the hotel owner's son in 'The Blue Hotel.'" I say only that the barroom fight was the germinal situation for "The Blue Hotel"—*not,* as Mr. Peck misreads my text, for the poem in *Black Riders,* which I number rightly (p. 159) as No. LVI. Mr. Peck has misnumbered it *BR XXX.*

There are checklists not only of Crane's writings but of related background material on the Greco-Turkish War, the Spanish-American War, and other subjects.

"In *Stephen Crane*, R. W. Stallman has done a very great service in letting Crane's world speak in its many voices. We can find all of its mingled elements, important or inconsequential, relevant to Crane's work. Some biographies conclude a subject, but this one opens the way to new studies which can be based upon its solid foundation. It is another indispensable book."

Thomas A. Gullason, *CEA Critic,* 31 (May, 1969).

See (for reply) Stallman, "Stallman's *Crane*," *CEA Critic* (1970).

Lewis Leary, *Sewanee Review,* 77 (Spring, 1969), 294–300: [An excellent essay on Crane.] " 'He was too brilliant, too fickle, too erratic to last.' That was the testimony of Hamlin Garland thirty years after Stephen Crane's death, and it is testimony which almost forty years later Robert Stallman reinforces in a biography which is mortised and tenoned in the granite of dedicated and meticulous investigation. Few have delved more deeply into records than Mr. Stallman, or read more widely in what Crane wrote or in what has been written about him, or been more resolute in appraisal, more spirited in speculation. The bibliography attached to his biography is complicated and enormous, and do not overlook his rear-clustered notes which contain delightfully well-mannered rebukes to people who have preceded him and who have mishandled fact or intepretation. That is not to say that his book is only a reference tool (though it is that also), to be read backwards, from index to text. It moves and it is moving; it tells a good story and it limns a convincing portrait. Unlike John Berryman and Daniel Hoffman, whose critical studies of Crane are extended rather than superseded, Mr. Stallman patiently reveals a whole man, pausing even over journeyman hack work to fit it to its place.

"Mr. Stallman is generous throughout in supplying quotations of this kind. He finds evidence in plenty that 'Crane smoked and drank and had a hankering for women,' and that most of his women were older than he, more experienced, and not always untarnished: 'He could afford to court innocent young girls only in his fiction.' He invited ladies of uncertain virtue to his room—'took up with many a drab and was not overly particular,' recalled one unfriendly acquaintance, 'as to her age, race, or color,' and during one fortunate summer lived in a boarding house of ill-repute where girls where more conveniently accessible. 'A 'conceited youth,' Mr. Stallman finds him, 'also sometimes a smart-aleck and an irresponsible heel,' but charming withal, for his was a 'fine nature,' another friend is allowed to testify, 'and his appreciation of the charm and frankness of true womanhood and the innocence of young girlhood was chivalry itself.

". . . Crane had shot overnight from obscurity toward a reputation which he was unable to sustain. It must not be thought that he did nothing praiseworthy after that: Mr. Stallman makes this plain amid the slough of newspaper reportage which is presented in such kindly detail that whole chapters become a kind of résumé-anthology of everything that Crane wrote (and with Mr. Stallman often writing better in summary explanation than Crane, cheating on his talent, had hurriedly written before)—even amid such scrub growth an occasional bright bloom appears, and in displaying these Mr. Stallman is at his critical best, though it may be that he holds up for admiration more than many admirers of the best in Crane can in honesty admire. . . .

"But much that he wrote after 1895 was trash, and he must have known it to be trash. *George's Mother,* in which in 1896 he attempted to catch again some of the spirit and tone and vocabulary of the Bowery which he had so successfully set forth three years before in *Maggie: A Girl of the Streets,* remains, at best, a source book for collectors of native colloquialisms. *The Third Violet,* a year later, may well be the worst novel ever written by a talented man of letters and exists, if at all, as part of the penitential reading yawned through by students of art in America. *Active Service,* in 1899, was a potboiler, slipshod and clumsy. Crane did better in the *Whilomville Stories* which, published the year before his death in 1901, captured something of boy life as he had known it in and around Port Jervis, but Crane created no Huck, not even a Penrod, certainly not a Holden Caulfield. He was too much concerned with complications of misery, including by this time his own, to be convincing about complicating simplicities of boyhood.

"Much of Mr. Stallman's best attention is turned toward Stephen Crane's war years. . . . The dispatches which he sent from battle areas are uneven, distorted perhaps by censorship or editorial intrusion, but they breathe impatience, excitement, intimations of cowardice and courage, even (perhaps especially) in the summary accounts which Mr. Stallman patiently presents. . . .

"My single quarrel with Mr. Stallman is in his description of 'An Episode of War' as 'one of Crane's masterpieces,' and without presenting even a small piece of it to demonstrate why.* To have sent Crane to report actual warfare, said Hamlin Garland, was a mistake: 'His genius lay in depicting battles which never saw the light of day, and upon which no eyes but his own had ever gazed.'

". . . But if throughout his brief career he remained the gloriously mixed-up kid, brilliant, erratic, intellectually unsure, spoiled and magnificently rebellious, in his life and writings he did sketch outlines which would define and confine all the Fitzgeralds and Hart Cranes and Hemingways and Allen Ginsbergs who followed him. Carl Van Doren was right when many years ago he said that much that is brilliant and troublesome in recent American writing derives from Stephen Crane. But he did not have it for the long haul. As Mr. Stallman so honestly reveals, he cheated more than most; money and ambition and rebellion had him in thrall, and he wrote too often the kind of thing which Hemingway once defined as slop. . . .

"As biographer, Mr. Stallman wisely sticks to his proper task—to set forth Stephen Crane entire, reconstructing from evidence of every available kind what he did and when he did it, and sometimes why, and limiting commentary to brief evaluation of those tales and those poems in which Crane seems to him to be at his best. He does this so well that he tempts again to the further step: to find in Crane, his writings and his career, intimations of where a person of his temperament and his talent goes wrong, of what fault in western experience tempts toward disillusion and distraction. Such seeking is old hat perhaps, embarrassingly old, and better put aside, it can be thought, for other concerns. Van Wyck Brooks introduced it many years ago; Lionel Trilling has spoken to it, and Richard Blackmur, and many another; but it troubles still, elusive, talked about, but unresolved—those brilliant first books, and then the fumbling, the depths, the disappointments, the dispersal of talent, the waste. Perhaps Mr. Stallman, his present task done, will turn to the

---

* For an explication of "An Episode of War" *see The Stephen Crane Reader,* ed. R. W. Stallman (1972).

other, for certainly in all pertinent respects he understands as much about Stephen Crane as Stephen Crane ever did."

Daniel R. Buerger, *American Literature Abstracts*, 2, no. 2 (June 1969), 335–337: A biographer, said Arnold Stein, is " 'obliged to assemble the external facts and to give them a narrative organization, yet no sincere biographer is likely to undertake his task without at least one conviction and supplementary hope—that the story of the life will yield some of the satisfaction of good narrative, and that the external account may succeed in striking through to the inner life.' In general, the appraisals of Stallman's book have indicated his admirable success in the former objective, while a good many have reservations concerning the latter."

Buerger concludes his appraisal-survey of a dozen reviews of Crane (selected from the six dozen reviews appearing into June, 1968): "Judgment of this biography, then, must be based on the crucial decision whether to give precedence to the historian, who is to be held accountable for his scholarship, or the poet, who is to be judged by his fidelity to the inner life and 'mystery' of the subject."

Max Westbrook, *American Literary Realism* (Summer, 1969): "Perhaps more satisfactory as 'Life Records' than as a definitive biography, R. W. Stallman's study of Stephen Crane is nonetheless a major contribution to scholarship. Any subsequent work on the life of Crane will owe a great debt to Stallman's diligent research. Earlier biographical studies—Thomas Beer, John Berryman—are made almost irrelevent. Critical studies not heretofore possible are now invited by publication of this much-needed book and by the recent editorial work of Stallman and others. . . .

". . . too much space is devoted to Crane's minor reporting and sketches (usually with summary or paraphrase), topics on which Stallman has done a great deal of work. When scholarly disputes and new or neglected minor writings are kept in perspective, as in the splendid chapters on the Dora Clark affair and on Crane as a reporter in Cuba, Stallman focuses attention on Stephen Crane and writes biography of the highest order.

"The chief disappointment of this major work is that Stallman's criticism of Crane's art does not progress substantially from the position he had already taken in the *Omnibus*. . . .

"Still, it would not be just or accurate to allow such objections to obscure the central worth of this biography. The information and materials Stallman has made available to others will constitute for a long time the basis of Crane scholarship. Professor Stallman has earned recognition as a distinguished scholar."

James B. Colvert in *Novel: A Forum on Fiction*, 3, no. 2 (Winter, 1970), 177–178. "This tendency to tack on and pile up is actually of no serious consequence except in those cases where it tends to distort the sense of the author's arguments and demonstrations. A passage discussing Crane's method of composition illustrates the tendency:

> Conrad speaks of Crane's unsophisticated inspiration and describes him as a writer "who in his art (as indeed in his private life) was the least 'contriving' of men," but he concedes that Crane contrived *The Red Badge*, every impression in it being preconceived and patterned, one image with another. His was not a studied technique, however, and he agreed with Linson that self-conscious work was bad as art. Vosburgh testifies that in *The Red Badge* "almost every impression was pre-

conceived" and that Crane in the Needham studios studied with much care his daring phrases and metaphors and then, after he had trimmed them to final form, he would repeat them aloud and "dwell on them lovingly."

It is hard to know what conclusion is to be drawn from this. Stallman's comment, 'His was not a studied technique, however,' seems to contradict Conrad in part and Vosburgh altogether. One suspects that the purpose of the passage is not so much to clarify the point as to get into the record—for the sake of completeness—the opinions of three contemporary witnesses.

"But from one point of view Stallman's passion for getting things into the record is a distinct virtue. It makes his biography, whatever its weaknesses, the single most useful book on Crane in existence. It gives us the choice between Beer's graceful inaccuracies and Stallman's information; between Berryman's cryptic irony and psychologizing and Stallman's predominant straightforwardness. It clears up mysteries in the chronology of Crane's life and brings his personality into sharper focus than any writer has been able to give it. There are long stretches of splendid narrative writing, as in the account of Crane's troubles over his defense in court of the prostitute Dora Clark, a crisp, dramatic description which reveals Crane's idealism and integrity . . . more clearly than it has ever been revealed. It is by far the most informative book on Crane to date, and future biographers and scholars will be inescapably indebted to Professor Stallman for this encyclopedic accumulation of data and information."

———. "A Prologue," in *Stephen Crane: A Biography* (1968), Appendix 3, pp. 545–546.

Identifies the source of "A Prologue," which Crane wrote sometime after the Society of the Philistines' banquet (December 19, 1895).

3. " 'A PROLOGUE' "

"Sometime after the Philistine banquet Crane dashed off 'A Prologue,' which Hubbard published in *A Souvenir and a Medley:*

A gloomy stage. Slender curtains at a window, centre. Before the window, a table, and upon the table, a large book, opened. A moonbeam, no wider than a sword-blade, pierces the curtains and falls upon the book.

A moment of silence.

From without, then—an adjacent room in intention—come sounds of celebration, of riotous drinking and laughter. Finally, a swift quarrel. The din and crash of fight. A little stillness. Then a woman's scream:

'Ah, my son, my son.'

A moment of silence.

CURTAIN

In its dramatic form 'A Prologue' echoes a passage in the Reverend Thomas de Witt Talmage's *Night Side of New York Life* (1878):

Act the first of the tragedy: A young man starting off from home; parents and sisters weeping to have him go. . . . Ring the bell and let the curtain fall. *Act the second:* The marriage altar. Full organ. Bright lights. . . . *Act the third:* a woman waiting for staggering steps. Old garments stuck into the broken window pane. Marks of hardship on the face. . . . Ring the bell and let the curtain drop. *Act the fourth:* Three graves in a dark place. . . . Oh, what a blasted heath with three graves! Plenty of weeds, but no flowers. Ring the bell and let the curtain drop. *Act the fifth:* A destroyed soul's eternity. No light. No music. No hope. . . ."

On whether "A Prologue" is or is not a poem *see* Peck (1965) and Katz (1966).

———. Introduction, *Stephen Crane: Sullivan County Tales and Sketches*. Ames, Iowa, 1968. Illustrated with ink drawings by "W. W."

Presents seven new Sullivan County pieces, of which five are here published for the first time.* Included among the 25 best designed books of 1968 by American Association of University Presses.

"At the same time that Crane was writing *Maggie* in 1891 and rewriting it in 1892, he was also writing his Sullivan County pieces. This conjuncture of events has importance in that it contradicts the commonly held assumption that the Sullivan County writings anticipated *Maggie* and *The Red Badge,* whereas the gap between them spans less than a year and in the writing of *Maggie* there was no time gap at all. In largeness of conception and design the gap between these masterworks and his rather inept Sullivan County tales is immense, but the fact remains that he was simultaneously bringing *Maggie* to completion while publishing his Sullivan County pieces in 1892. . . . [And, furthermore, he was engaged in writing *The Red Badge* in early 1893 and at that same time he began *George's Mother*.]

"*The Sullivan County Tales and Sketches* ask for and reward our reappraisal of the evolution of Crane's genius. They contain the seeds of themes that sprouted almost simultaneously in the grotesqueries of *Maggie* and *The Red Badge,* wherein he rapidly developed his gift for the psychological probing of character and related scene. They contain the seeds of his painterly and impressionistic style with its addiction to color adjectives, metaphor and symbol. William Dean Howells rightly remarked of the author of *Maggie* in 1893: 'Here is a writer [who has] sprung into life fully armed.' " (Introduction, pp. 12 and 24, dated 27 September, 1967.)†

Reviewed:

Joseph Katz in *SCraneN*, 2 (Fall, 1968) argues that it is a mistake to include pieces which are merely geographically located in Sullivan County. He would limit the pieces to the tales. However, Katz confounds the distinction between a tale and a sketch. He says that "The Sullivan County Sketches have an integrity obtaining from Crane's apprenticeship attempt at constructing a world defined only in part by the setting that parallels the real Sullivan County." Its basis "is the posture of their narrator, its consistent cast of characters, and its quality of events. All these show just how significant they are in defining the group's integrity when they are preceded by the very different group of the six *New York Tribune* feature pieces which Stallman discovered."

However, *SCTS* clearly defines which pieces are tales and which are sketches; the inclusion of sketches with the tales contradicts neither the integrity of the tales nor of the sketches. Katz's criticism is also niggling in his contention that "The Snake" is not a Sullivan County sketch. It is, first of all, a sketch (not a tale). Secondly, whether the germinal situation of "The Snake" occurred in Pike County or in Sullivan County, that academic hair-splitting of boundaries is irrelevant to the general catgory of "The Snake" as a Sullivan County sketch.

---

* Simultaneously discovered by Thomas A. Gullason and published in an unknown to exist journal, *Southern Humanities Review*, 2, no. 1 (Winter, 1968).

† This dated Introduction was written prior to Gullason's "A Stephen Crane Find, Nine Newspaper Sketches," *SHR* 2, no. 1 (Winter, 1968) and disproves Gullason's unwarranted notion that Stallman published Gullason's findings (1968) in *SCTS* (1968).

In *Men, Women and Boats* (1921) Vincent Starrett seemingly conjoins three Sullivan County tales with "The Snake." No dividing title-page separates the latter from the former. In the Table of Contents, however, the titles of the three tales are indented, whereas "The Snake" is not. The same ambiguity of intention obtains in Starrett's *Maggie* edition (1933), which reprints all four pieces. In *Work*, 11 (1926) Follett conjoins the same three tales under the heading "Sullivan County Sketches," followed by "The Snake." Neither Starrett nor Follett, one concludes, was certain where to locate "The Snake" and thus hedged.

Katz asserts that my Preface is wrong in suggesting that "Across the Covered Pit" is " 'new' here; it appeared in Gullason's *CSS&S*, pp. 107–109" (1963). Bibliographer Katz is mistaken. "Across the Covered Pit" was first published by Stallman, "Stephen Crane: Some New Stories," *Bulletin* (1957). That source is not cited by Gullason. Also, it is a new Sullivan County piece since it is new to the Melvin Schoberlin *SCS* (1949).

Courier Journal (Louisville, Ky.), October 6, 1968.

Hartford Courant, October 9, 1968.

Long Beach Press-Telegram, October 24, 1968.

Dave Peyton, *Herald-Advertiser* (Huntington, W. Va.), November 3, 1968.

Ralph Williams, *Hartford Courant*, November 7, 1968.

The Oregonian, November 17, 1968.

The New Yorker, November 23, 1968.

Jean Cazemajou, *Études Anglaises*, 1 (1969), 98–99.

Bernice Slote, *Prairie Schooner*, 43 (Spring, 1969), 142: "Its pages are beautifully designed and the illustrations are strong and eloquent drawings by 'W. W.' (William Wooster Stallman). Six new sketches, published from February 21 to July 17, 1892, are included in this edition, with eleven other Sullivan County stories and a coda of two later fables that relate to the early stories. With these additions to the Stephen Crane canon and a new arrangement of contexts, more is available for the study of the evolution of Crane's art. As Stallman says in his introduction, the Sullivan County pieces 'contain the seeds of themes that sprouted almost simultaneously in the grotesqueries of *Maggie* and *The Red Badge*, wherein he rapidly developed his gift for the psychological probing of character and related scene.' "

Clarence Ghodes, *American Literature*, 41 (March, 1969), 141: "On page 27 the year [for the appearance of 'The Last of the Mohicans' in *American Literature*, November, 1967] is erroneously given as 1957 and the texts of the two printings are not exactly the same." This obviously is a printer's error of 1957 for 1967.

Thomas Gullason, *CEA Critic*, 31, no. 8 (May, 1969), 8–9. Much of Katz's complaint (cited above) is here echoed by Gullason. Gullason claims that Stallman has sequestered some data from his Crane publications in *SCTS* and in *Crane*. However, the statement that Mrs. Crane was "vice-president of the W.C.T.U. for New Jersey" derived not from Gullason but from Helen Crane's *American Mercury* article (1934), not noted by Gullason.

"When Stallman says that 'Hunting is warfare too,' he acts as though he is the first to notice this in the sketches; others, including myself, pointed this out before." It's a petty complaint in that it is a rather obvious thing to say about Crane's Sullivan County hunting sketches, having in mind Crane's remark that city life is warfare too! The student who researched the *New York*

Tribune in quest of new Crane sketches missed "A Reminiscence of War," which Gullason simultaneously found "and reproduced in the *SHR* [Winter, 1968], and which Stallman knows nothing about. . . ." He is quite right. I knew nothing about Gullason's findings, not having at any time heard of that obscure journal, which *PMLA* Bibliography did not list and which first announced Gullason's article, "A Stephen Crane Find," in 1969. *See SCraneN,* (Winter, 1968).

Year's Work in English Studies (1969), pp. 378, 393.

Arthur E. Jones, Jr. *New York History* (New York Historical Association) 52 (January, 1971), 98–99: "In his introductory account the author of the best biography of Stephen Crane describes the accidental discovery which, in 1966, led to the identification of six more Sullivan County tales in the 1892 pages of the *New York Tribune*. . . . Whether they are tales or sketches doesn't really matter. They are here attractively presented with a useful introduction and intriguingly anonymous pen-and-ink drawings. True, they cannot be acclaimed great literature, but they have a real interest for anyone concerned with the artistic development of Stephen Crane or for anyone attracted to the local history and legend of the Sullivan and Orange County sections of New York State. . . .

"Crane's principal themes are well represented in the collection: fear and courage, man against the order of things, and the impersonality of nature. Clearly he was experimenting with extravagant metaphors, vivid images, active adjectives. He seldom named his characters and he increasingly tended to represent states of mind by oblique observations. The opportunity to see a young man becoming a writer is one of the pleasures of reading these Sullivan County sketches. It makes up for some of their deficiencies as fiction."

Stephen Crane Newsletter, 2, no. 3 (Spring, 1968), 1–12.

Important for letters of Elbert Hubbard to Crane, not in Freeman Champney's *Art and Glory* (1968). Katz opines "From these letters it is evident that Hubbard learned of Crane through a review copy of *The Black Riders* in April, 1895." (However, the formality of Hubbard's June 11, 1895, letter does not rule out the likelihood that they had met in New York City in 1894. *Contra* Katz, Champney has Hubbard in New York City in early 1894. Stallman's *Crane,* unknown to Katz and Champney, also has Hubbard in New York City in early 1894 and meeting Crane then, on other evidence.)

Reprints and discusses Elmo Watson's recollection of *The Red Badge of Courage.* George Monteiro quotes Bernard Berenson's opinions on Crane, and Sister Mary Anthony Weinig writes on "Heroic Convention in 'The Blue Hotel.'"

———. 2, no. 4 (Summer, 1968), 1–12.

Reproduces the Appleton contract for *The Red Badge of Courage,* and two new Crane letters (new, that is, to *Letters*). The original for the letter to Miss Daisy D. Hill is unlocated. Dated March 2, 1896, it was cited in *The Autograph Album,* 2 (October, 1933), 35. This important source is not noticed by Katz. Also his mistaken version of this letter gets corrected in *SCraneN,* 4, no. 2 (Winter, 1969).

The second "new" letter is from Crane to Irving Bacheller for March 24, 1896; it was first quoted in *Crane* (May, 1968), p. 202. *See* p. 584, Notes: "Crane's letter to Bacheller (the only one known to be extant) is quoted here for the first time from the original in the St. Lawrence University Library."

"Stephen Crane at Claverack College and Hudson River Institute," pp. 1–5, reprints data from the files of that institution. *See also* Pratt, "The Formal Education of Stephen Crane" (1939). Katz says the originals of these items seem to have been among Edith Crane's papers, 1959; however, they were not in the BCCC, which included the Edith Crane papers when I saw them, 1951.

The item dated January 30, 1888, misidentifies Crane's middle initial thus: "Stephen *M.* Crane. An item for January 31, 1890, has it: "Stephen *T.* Crane." Quotes the autograph album inscribed: "Very sincerely / Your Friend / S. T. Crane / New York City / CC&HRI / March 27, 1888." This item was quoted in *Crane,* "here for the first time." *See Crane,* chap. 2 and the Notes, p. 566, where the puzzle of Crane's middle name is investigated through research into possible sources in Newark, N.J. Stallman concludes that Crane's middle initial was T. for Townley, perhaps, but more likely T. for Truesdell.

Not noticed by Katz is the fact that the New York City Directory for 1892–1893 lists under Crane: "Stephen H. author, h[ouse] 1604 Av. A." The directory for the previous year lists Stephen Crane as a janitor living on W. 24th Street. Nowhere else than in the above instances did Crane sign himself with a middle initial. What was his middle name?

"One conjectures that the 'H' in the New York City Directory was a misprint and that Stephen's middle name was Truesdell, after Bishop Jesse Truesdell Peck, uncle of Stephen's mother." *Crane,* p. 566. *See* William's letter to Stephen, p. 472. He speculates "how much Stephen owed to the Peck side of his make-up for his literary abilities."

See Wertheim (1969).

———. 3, no. 1 (Fall, 1968), 1–12.

Reproduces in "An Early Draft of 'The Blue Hotel' "—a fragment from verso of the first page in Cora Crane's manuscript of "Peter the Great." Reproduces C. K. Linson's holograph note tipped into a copy of the 1897 *The Third Violet,* and Crane's passport for November 21, 1896. (Crane's passports were first quoted in Stallman's *Crane* which was published May, 1968.)

Quotes a letter by Garland about Crane, undated, and snippits of Crane letters or notes to Lucius L. Button as given in *American Art Association—Anderson Galleries* for March 11 and 12, 1930. Katz says that these three notes are not in *Letters* but they are not in *Letters* because they are snippits of the originals.

Reprints Part II of "Stephen Crane Flinches," being Willis Brooks Hawkins' account of Crane's ordeal at the Society of the Philistines' banquet honoring Crane on December 19, 1895, in Buffalo. *See SCraneN,* 1, no. 3 (Spring, 1967) for Part I.

Reproduces a Hubbard letter to Lyman Chandler on Crane's verses, dated September 25, 1895, and reprints Crane's letter to Harry Thompson as a "new" letter, under the heading: "Stephen Crane to Harry Thompson: A 'New' Letter." This is the same letter as first published in *Crane,* p. 214, except that in *Crane* the salutation is misidentified as Herbert P. Williams.*

Simeon Braunstein here reviews Freedman Champney's *Art and Glory,* and Katz reviews *SCTS.*

---

* My copy derived from Mr. Charles Feinberg, but his gift of three Crane letters was *not* accompanied by "a typewritten note, apparently prepared by a former owner, correctly identifying its recipient." My misidentification owes to a xerox sheet containing the letter and the wrong envelope, one addressed to Mr. Herbert P. Williams.

————. 3, no. 2 (Winter, 1968), 1–12.

Contains a useful article on "The Saga of March 23rd: Garland, Gilder, and Crane" (pp. 1–3), a discussion of Pizer and Stallman on *Maggie* by Stanley Wertheim. *See* Wertheim (1968) which annotation paraphrases Wertheim's letter to Stallman, February 21, 1969.

Katz reproduces another Crane passport, already quoted in *Crane*, p. 604. As usual, Katz claims it has "an error in quotation." Reproduces manuscript snippits of "Vittoria" and "The Battle of Bunker Hill." That Kate Lyons Frederic wrote almost all of Great Battles of the World was first claimed in *Crane*, not noted in Katz's discussion, "Manuscripts and Method." A new Crane letter (to John Lee) consists of a single sentence of no importance. Simeon Braunstein contributes a short checklist of writings by and about Crane in Hubbard's *Fra*. *See* Braunstein (1968).

Katz, in "A Note on *Stephen Crane: Sullivan County Tales and Sketches*" says that its new pieces were not first found by Stallman but by Gullason "ten months before Stallman's book was published." Gullason's "A Stephen Crane Find" first appeared in *SHR* (Winter, 1968). *SCTS* was in book form in May, 1968, but not published until October; it was in galley late 1967. My findings were made in the *New York Tribune* in 1966, and one of them—"The Last of the Mohicans"—was published prior to Gullason's article of January, 1968, in *SHR*, a journal not known to me until it was first listed in *PMLA* Bibliography in June, 1969. Katz does not mention this prior publication of this Sullivan County sketch in *American Literature*, "Stephen Crane and Cooper's Uncas" (1967). And *American Literature* failed to print the footnote noting the future publication in *SCTS* of the other five new Crane discoveries.* Katz's checklists in *SCraneN*, 3, nos. 1 and 2, do not list that article, nor several other Stallman publications. Katz's intent to show that Stallman must have known Gullason's findings is unwarranted.

M. J. Bruccoli reviews *Crane* by simply listing typos and presumed errors. One of the letters Beer used in Beer's *SC* has turned up in Katz's "Stephen Crane, Samuel Carlton" (September, 1968) since publication of Stallman's *Crane*, but this is the only letter in Beer's *SC* that has appeared on the scene in forty years, and its appearance does not disprove the conjecture that Beer perhaps destroyed the Crane letters quoted in his 1923 book. *See* Preface, p. viii, *Crane*: "I reluctantly came to this conclusion and tested it before the Bibliographical Society of America in an address at the Pierpont Morgan Library in January, 1963. To date my inference has not been disproved." Mr. Charles Feinberg of Detroit attended that meeting and assured me that I was quite right.

Bruccoli says *Crane* "is not a reliable scholarly job." By his definition, neither is *SCraneN* "reliable." For instance, Bruccoli, who is Katz's co-editor of *SCraneN*, says that Crane's inscription to DeWitt Miller was on the 1893 *Maggie*, not the 1896; however, *SCraneN* reproduces that letter (1967), although it was first reproduced in *Letters*. Nor does Katz's *SCraneN* acknowledge its prior publication in *Modern Library First Editions* (1938), p. 53. Bruccoli lists *Crane*, p. 445—"'Lynch Hunting' should be 'Lynx Hunting.'" That is, of course, a typo and it appears as "Lynx Hunting" in the second edition of *Crane* (August, 1968).

---

* A contents listing of *SCTS* was in the publisher's hands April 28, 1967. *American Literature Abstracts* (June, 1968) published such a footnote. *See* Stallman, "Stephen Crane and Cooper's Uncas" (1967).

Bruccoli claims there is no source for the statements in *Crane,* pp. 29 and 69, that Crane was offered a job by a "major baseball team" and that Crane "labored at typesetting" the 1893 *Maggie.* However, these statements occur in memoirs published by Crane's former schoolmates, all of whose articles are listed in *Stephen Crane: A Critical Bibliography.* The important sources— all of them—are listed in *Crane.* The bulk of a complete listing of sources would have overbalanced the book. *Contra* Bruccoli *Crane* is not "carelessly documented." It is simply by necessity not footnoted for every source; but for every statement there is a source.

In *Crane,* p. 74, one of the men Maggie encounters mistakes "young Maggie for her mother, a well-known prostitute." Bruccoli says "Twice wrong." However, he mistakenly calls her "Mary," by which she is cross-identified with Mary Johnson, her mother. So it is that everyone in *Maggie* is mis-identified or cross-identified with another, Maggie with her mother, Jimmie with Pete, the bar-theatre with the church, etc., including the mission-house preacher with Christ!

In *Crane,* p. 170, "It is the gospel truth, but Henry is one of the doubting apostles," Bruccoli in his list of "errors" comprising his "review" says. "But the text says, 'The next morning the youth discovered that his tall comrade had been the fast-flying messenger of a mistake.'" If Bruccoli reads further into *The Red Badge of Courage* he will find that Jim Conklin's prophecy that the army is going to cross the river finally takes place, a fact which proves his having uttered at the start "the gospel truth."

Tanner, Tony. "Stephen Crane's Long Dream of War," *London Magazine,* n.s., 8 (December, 1968), 5–19. Photograph.

Surveys Crane's career. Nothing new here, and no sources are cited for any critical standpoint or insight. On "The red sun was pasted in the sky like a wafer," Tanner remarks that this "was taken as a perfect example of the new impressionism, but, as so often in Crane, the impressionism contains a symbol. Red is the colour of war and blood; and the wafer evokes the sacrifice of the crucified Christ, thus in turn reminding us of all the massacred innocents in human history."

Tanselle, Thomas. "The Descriptive Bibliography of American Authors," *Studies in Bibliography,* 21 (1968), 1–24.

The *W-S Bibliography* (1948) is cited as being "above the level of the average bibliography."

Thomas, Donald. "The Long Logic: A Symbolic Interpretation of Stephen Crane's *The Red Badge of Courage,*" *Dissertation Abstracts,* 28 (1968).

A portion of this University of Connecticut dissertation is paraphrased and quoted in the coda to Stallman's "Toward an Analysis of *The Red Badge of Courage,*" in Bassan's *Stephen Crane: A Collection of Critical Essays* (1967), pp. 138–140.

Van Der Beets, Richard. "Character as Structure: Ironic Parallel and Transformation in 'The Blue Hotel,'" *Studies in Short Fiction,* 5 (Spring, 1968), 294–295.

The characters in the saloon scene are to be taken as ironic parallels to the characters in the hotel scene. *See* Bowen, *American Literature Abstracts* (December, 1968).

Wager, Willis. *American Literature: A World View.* London and New York, 1968, pp. 168–170.

Brief comments on *Maggie, The Red Badge,* "The Blue Hotel," and "The Open Boat." "Though there are many details throughout [*The Red Badge*] that suggest a primitive Christian intention, perhaps the religious aspect is but one of the many overtones, as in the late James novels. Another is the aesthetic: the color indications, for example, are handled quite carefully and sensitively. In many ways a *tour de force,* it has a spare, lithe, modern air."
Notes that Billy the oiler is a Christlike figure, comparable to Melville's Billy Budd and that "The Blue Hotel" "suggests the general human responsibility in the slaying of an innocent victim—as, for example, in the Crucifixion."

Waggoner, Hyatt H. *American Poets: From the Puritans to the Present.* Boston, 1968.
Abstracted, *American Literature Abstracts,* 2, no. 2 (June, 1969), 343–345.

Walcutt, C. C., and J. E. Whitesell, eds. *Explicator Cyclopedia,* vol. 3. Chicago, 1968, pp. 22, 23.

Wasserstrom, William. "Cagey John: Berryman as Medicine Man," *Centennial Review,* 12, no. 3 (1968), 334–354.

Weinig, Sister Mary Anthony. "Heroic Convention in 'The Blue Hotel,'" *Stephen Crane Newsletter,* 2, no. 3 (Spring, 1968), 6–7.

Wertheim, Stanley. "The Saga of March 23rd: Garland, Gilder, and Crane," *Stephen Crane Newsletter,* 3, no. 2 (Winter, 1968), 1–3.
"Stallman concluded that Crane had substituted for it [for the MS. Crane brought to Gilder with Garland's note: "I want you to read a great M.S. of Stephen Cranes making."] the first draft of *The Red Badge of Courage* and therefore that Garland read *Maggie* only in book form." However, Editor Katz has here changed Wertheim's manuscript to suit his purposes.
Editor Katz changed "Gilder" in Wertheim's manscript to "Garland," which change makes it that Stallman said Garland read *Maggie* only in book form, whereas it should read Gilder read *Maggie* only in book form.
Editor Katz again changed Wertheim's manuscript thus: Wertheim submitted that Stallman "reinstates without qualification Beer's account of Gilder's rejection of a manuscript of *Maggie* and the date of March 23, 1892, for this event." Editor Katz changed the date to 1893, as given in *SCraneN,* p. 2. He also altered Wertheim's "in different years" to "in succeeding years," lines 10–11, p. 2. Both the date 1892 and the word *different* were essential to the accuracy and consistency of Wertheim's essay.
Editor Katz furthermore injected into Wertheim's manuscript for the word "Ostensibly" the phrase "The incredible suggestion" by Stallman. Wertheim in what he submitted to Katz's *SCraneN* had said simply that Gilder had "ostensibly" refused "both *Maggie* and *The Red Badge of Courage* for the *Century* and both on the same date of March 23rd, although in different years." Not—as Katz's tampered version has it—in succeeding years.
In *SCraneN,* 3, no. 3 (Spring, 1969) Katz—requested by Wertheim to acknowledge his errors—admits three nonsensical statements.
Katz's admission begins: "Through no fault of its author, Stanley Wertheim's 'The Saga of March 23rd: Garland, Gilder, and Crane" in the last *SCraneN* made three nonsensical statements." It would be honest of Katz to declare flatly that he himself made three nonsensical statements, and even more honest to include the fourth about Stallman's "incredible suggestion," a point Stall-

man never suggested; but Katz cannot risk to declare that the fault is his. Instead, he ambiguously says it's not through any fault of author Wertheim. His acknowledgement note is limited to citing the three nonsensical statements: "P. 1, lines 3–4 from the bottom, should read 'Gilder read *Maggie* only in book form'; p. 2, line 8, should read '23rd March, 1892'; and p. 2, lines 10–11, should read 'in different years.'"

Wertheim's article has importance because it points out contradictions in Donald Pizer's Introduction to *Maggie* (1968) about the roles played by Garland and Gilder in relation to *Maggie,* 1893 edition.

West, Ray B., Jr. "The Use of Action in 'The Bride Comes to Yellow Sky,'" in *Reading the Short Story.* New York, 1968, pp. 17–23.

——. *The Writer in the Room.* East Lansing, Mich., 1968. Reprints "Stephen Crane: Author in Transition," *American Literature,* 34 (May, 1962), 215–228.

1969

[MY QUEST for Writings on Stephen Crane ended in 1969 for titles published in 1968. What entries occur for 1969 derive, but not entirely so, from the *1969 PMLA International Bibliography,* vol. 1 (1970) and the *American Literature Abstracts* (1969). To the 1968 entries, then, the listings for 1969 and 1970 might be considered a coda, possibly rather inclusive for 1969 and obviously fragmentary for 1970, the year when this manuscript was concluded.

Except for entries in foreign language fields, I have read everything written on Crane and own same either in photostat or xerox copy, or in the original book or journal. However, I cannot claim the same for writings on Stephen Crane for 1969 and 1970; not at this writing: August, 1970. RWS]

[Anon.]. "Types of Realism," *Times Literary Supplement,* October 23, 1969, p. 1231.

Barrett, C. Waller. *The American Writer in England: An Exhibition Arranged in Honor of the Sesquicentennial of the University of Virginia.* With a Foreword by Gordon N. Ray and an Introduction by C. Waller Barrett. Charlottesville, Va., 1969, pp. xxxii–xxxiii, 110–114. Photograph of C. K. Linson's oil portrait of Stephen Crane in 1894.

List of first editions, photographs of Crane, autograph MS. of "Storming of Badajos" and of *The Red Badge of Courage,* autograph MS. and printer's copy. Crane's letter to Collis (typed) is reproduced, p. 111, and quoted, p. 112. This letter was first published in *Letters.* A new ALS, Crane to Mrs. Moreton Frewen, May 5 (1899) is quoted, p. 112.

Item 283 lists "Stephen Crane at Rye." Original water color by George Van Werveke, showing Crane in bed during his last illness. Published in the *New York Times Book Review,* May 26, 1929, p. 8. This should be titled "Stephen Crane at Brede Place."

Beards, Richard D. "Stereotyping in Modern American Fiction: Some Solitary Swedish Madmen," *Moderna Språk* (Göteborg, Sweden), 63 (1969), 329–337.

Traces the degree to which four American fiction writers "are trapped by a single cultural stereotype involving the Swede." The four works are Crane, "The Blue Hotel"; Hemingway, "The Killers"; Katherine Anne Porter, "Noon Wine"; and Ken Kesey, *One Flew Over the Cuckoo's Nest.*

Beerbohm, Max. *Works and More*. London, 1899. Grosse Pointe, Mich., 1969. On Crane's review article of Ouida's *Under Two Flags*.

Bowen, James K., and Richard Van Der Beets, eds. *American Literature Abstracts*, 2, no. 2 (June, 1969), 253–257.
    Provides abstracts of the following articles: Ives, "Symmetrical Design in Four of Stephen Crane's Stories" (1969); LaFrance, "The Ironic Parallel in Stephen Crane's 1892 Newspaper Correspondence" (1968); McDermott, "Symbolism and Psychological Realism in *The Red Badge of Courage*" (1968); Rathbun, "Structure and Meaning in *The Red Badge of Courage*" (1969); and Witherington, "Stephen Crane's 'A Mystery of Heroism' " (1969).

———. *American Literature Abstracts*, 3, no. 1 (December, 1969), 23. *See* Gilkes (1969) and Stallman's rejoinder (1972).

Bowers, Fredson. "Crane's *The Red Badge of Courage* and other 'Advance Copies,' " *Studies in Bibliography*, 22 (1969), 273–277.

Bowers, Fredson, ed. *The Works of Stephen Crane*, 10 volumes, 1969–(1974). The University of Virginia Edition of The Works of Stephen Crane. Charlottesville, Va.: The University Press of Virginia.
    Vol. I, *Bowery Tales*, Introduction by James B. Colvert, 1969.
    Vol. VII, *Tales of Whilomville*. Introduction by J. C. Levenson, 1969.
    Vol. V, *Tales of Adventure*. Introduction by J. C. Levenson, 1970.
    Vol. VI, *Tales of War*. Introduction by James B. Colvert, 1970.
    Vol. IV, *The O'Ruddy*. Introduction by J. C. Levenson, 1971.
    Vol. IX, *Reports of War*. Introduction by James B. Colvert, 1971.

———. *The Works of Stephen Crane*, vol. I, *Bowery Tales: Maggie* and *George's Mother*. Introductions by James B. Colvert. Textual Introductions and Notes by Fredson Bowers. Charlottesville, Va., 1969. Frontispiece, C. K. Linson's oil painting of Stephen Crane. Dedication page, "To / Clifton Waller Barrett."
    Contents: Foreword, pp. vii–viii; The Text of the Virginia Edition, pp. xi–xxix. *Maggie: A Girl of the Streets*. Introduction, by James B. Colvert, pp. xxxiii–lii; Textual Introduction, by Fredson Bowers, pp. liii–xcviii. Publisher's Note (prefixed to the 1896 edition), p. 3; An Appreciation, by William Dean Howells (prefixed to the London 1896 edition), pp. 4–5. The Text, pp. 7–77.
Appendixes, pp. 79–98.
    George's Mother. Introduction, by James B. Colvert, pp. 101–108; Textual Introduction, by Fredson Bowers, pp. 109–112; facsimile reproduction of two manuscript pages of early draft of *George's Mother*. The Text, pp. 115–178. Appendixes, pp. 179–184.
    Colvert's introductions to *Maggie* and *George's Mother* must not go unnoticed. "But even if it could be shown that *Maggie* derived from *L'Assommoir*, it would explain very little about Crane's book as a work of art." In sum, Crane transcended his sources, whatever they were. One of them was (I contend) Flaubert's *Madame Bovary*. Colvert says that Stallman "cites Flaubert's *Madame Bovary* as the source of *Maggie* (Crane, pp. 77–78), arguing the point chiefly on the inconclusive evidence of similarities in the characterizations of Emma and Maggie. Stallman also reaffirms the influence of Zola's determinism in *L'Assommoir* (p. 74)."
    The latter idea was first advanced in Frank Norris's review of *Maggie* in the *San Francisco Wave* (July 4, 1896). The former idea was first advanced

in Stallman's *New Republic* essay, "Stephen Crane's Primrose Path" (1955). Crane's *Maggie* again and again echoes almost word for word passages in *Madame Bovary*, unmistakably so in Maggie's reveries of Joy at a Distance.

Points out that Crane's "The Black Dog" was influenced by Bierce's "The Suitable Surroundings" (1891) and that other Sullivan County pieces show the influence of Mark Twain. Also: "Kipling provided a creed of art and showed Crane the possibilities of an impressionistic method, and Garland provided a theory for both the creed and the method." That is keenly put. "Edgar Fawcett exploited the master plot two years before Crane began his study for *Maggie* in his novel of the slums, *The Evil That Men Do* (1889)." That is a new item. "Crane invented the plot of *Maggie* in its details, but the large patterns were given." Thomas Beer (1923) was first to say that Crane invented the plot of *Maggie*, a standpoint repeated in Stallman (1952).

In his Textual Introduction, Bowers reexamines the 1893 *Maggie*, which is reproduced here, p. 7 ff., and the textual changes made in the 1896 *Maggie*. He cites Stallman (1955): "Stallman conjectures that the excisions and substitutions of blasphemous epithets and swearing phrases were Crane's own work but says 'It was probably the editor who turned what "damns" and "hells" remained in the text into such ellipses as mark the 1896 edition. . . .' This is plausible, but we have no evidence."

Why does Maggie drown herself when she has a handsome cloak and well-shod feet? She has thus not failed in her profession. What motive then exists for her death? This question has importance. In chap. XVII "she is moving swiftly forward on a predetermined journey, and the solicitation of men is not the primary purpose of her movement. It is scarcely necessary to point out that she neither patrols the glittering district where her customers have provided her with a handsome cloak and good shoes nor does she pause at any time in her flight to attempt to persuade a man to change his mind. The only inference suitable to draw from the details offered us is that from the beginning she has been in progress toward a planned suicide in the river. Since her motives are not financial, we are required in literal terms to assume that they must stem from what might be termed moral or spiritual despair."

Precisely so, and that moral despair is triggered anew by the fact that Maggie is misidentified and crucially cross-identified with her mother when the "belated man says: 'Hi, there, *Mary*, I beg your pardon! Brace up *old girl*.'" Unstated but implicit in that subtle cross-identification is the recognition that Maggie's life is her mother's life all over again, and that the only escape is in suicide. There is no other escape possible because the only alternative given in the Bowery perspective is the Island of the prison where "a worm of yellow convicts came from the shadow of a grey ominous building and crawled slowly along the river's bank" (chap. I). This point is not noticed by Bowers, nor by Cady (1962), Bruccoli (1967), or Katz (1966).*

The crucial encounter with unknown men in the 1893 version is Maggie's accosting the clergyman who rejects her: "He did not risk [his respectability] to save a soul" (chap. XVI). This rejection undermines her, and this situation echoes that of Emma Bovary's moral decline once she has been ignored by the priest to whom she appeals; they are both undermined by the Church. In *Maggie* the Church undermines the whole Bowery world by the fact that

---

* Bowers rightly dismisses Joseph Katz's notion in "The Maggie Nobody Knows" (1966) that Maggie chooses country visitors to town, etc. Katz's views "distort Crane's intentions."

it exists mainly in mission houses doling out soup and maudlin sentiment. Or again in imitation church staged in the theatre with "happy-hued church-windows," with the fake choir singing within "Joy to the World." "To Maggie and the rest of the audience this was transcendental realism. Joy always within, and they, like the actor, inevitably without" (chap. VIII). *See* Stallman (1955); also *MFS* (1959); also *Houses* (1961). The crucial point here is that Maggie's meeting with the clergyman decides her fate, or as Bowers puts it, decides her to turn prostitute (p. lxxxvi).

Another climactic meeting is with the fat man, the last of the encountered men in chap. XVII, whom Crane expunged from the 1896 edition. Bowers notices a parallel between the clergyman and the expunged fat man. In the *AL* collation of the 1893 and 1896 *Maggie* Stallman (1955) contended that the expunged fat man portrait should be reinstated in future editions. Unfortunately, he has disappeared from Bowers' text, for the rather dubious reasons—critically regarded—footnoted pp. xc–xci.

Reviewed:

William Randel, *American Literature*, 42 (March, 1970), 109–110.

"Tales of the Ur-Hemingway," *Times Literary Supplement*, April 12, 1969, p. 1377.

———. *The Works of Stephen Crane*, vol. VII, *Tales of Whilomville:* "The Monster," "His New Mittens," *Whilomville Stories*. Introduction by J. C. Levenson. Textual Introductions by Fredson Bowers. Charlottesville, Va., 1969. Frontispiece photograph, Stephen Crane as a boy.

Contents: Foreword, pp. v–vi; Introduction, by J. C. Levenson, pp. xi–lx; Textual Introduction (to "The Monster") by Fredson Bowers, pp. 3–6; Text of "The Monster," pp. 9–65; Appendixes, pp. 69–72; Textual Introduction (to "His New Mittens") by Fredson Bowers, pp. 75–79; Text of "His New Mittens," pp. 83–93; Appendixes, pp. 97–99; Textual Introduction (to *Whilomville Stories*, by Fredson Bowers, pp. 103–126; Text of the *Whilomville Stories*, pp. 12–239; Appendixes, pp. 243–277.

An early draft of "The Monster," a short fragment, is reproduced from the single leaf in CUCC, p. xxxi, and a new Crane letter, p. xxxviii: Crane to William (undated), in which Crane tells William: "Yes, it is true I am married to an English lady. . . . Love to all from the wayward brother." Not noted by Levenson here is the fact that Cora was not an English lady by birth but only by marriage to a British officer and the fact that no marriage between Cora and Crane ever occurred.

Photocopy of the single leaf of "The Monster" is reproduced in Bowers' Textual Introduction, pp. 4–5, with Bowers saying here that this one leaf "could be the final manuscript version of 'The Monster'. . . ."

Facsimile reproductions also of the first page of the manuscripts of "The Lover and the Tell-Tale," facing p. 133, and of the fourth page of "Making an Orator," manuscript showing both Stephen and Cora Crane's handwriting, facing p. 148.

The text, beginning with Bower's Textual Introduction to *Whilomville Stories,* is headed "Whilomville Stories," p. 104 through p. 276, since it comprises the original contents of *Whilomville Stories* (1900). "The Monster" and "His New Mittens," because they were omitted from the first edition, are not designated by the head title "Whilomville Stories," and that is accurate. *However,* the entire volume is titled *Tales of Whilomville,* whereas (a) every piece in this volume is a short story and not a tale, and (b) no distinction between what differentiates a story from a tale is mentioned. Are these tales or are they stories? Bowers, Levenson, and Colvert ignore the question, which ought to be answered; especially in this volume by Levenson's Introduction, since in this volume especially the question occurs by the contradiction cited above. *Tales of Whilomville* is, I repeat, a misnamed title for what are stories.

Reviewed:

Donald Pizer, *Modern Philology*, 68 (November, 1970), 212–214. Questions whether the eclectic text of *Maggie* constructed by Bowers, which accepts the 1896 stylistic changes, rejects his 1896 omissions of profanity, and accepts his omission of the "huge fat man" (given only in the 1893 *Maggie*), is of use to any critic. "The 1893 *Maggie* is one kind of book, the 1896 another, and Bowers's is a third. A responsible critic will still have to read the 1893 and 1896 texts independently in order to sense the distinctive qualities of each. . . . The Virginia text of *Maggie* may indeed be the best possible coalescing of the 1893 and 1896 editions, but it is nevertheless primarily a bibliographical curiosity rather than an aid to criticism."

On that "huge fat man" passage in the 1893 *Maggie*, Pizer mistakenly claims that he is "successfully solicited by Maggie." There is no proof that she solicits him.

Bradbury, Malcolm. "Sociological and Literary Studies, II. Romance and Reality in *Maggie*," *Journal of American Studies*, 3 (1969), 111–121.

"The new world of style leads not simply to a more accurate reportage, but to impressionism. And the nature of this structure is ironic; indeed in many senses it leads not to an understanding of society and how it works, but to an awareness of how it is *unreal*. Crane's in fact becomes a kind of negative vision, perplexed between realism and impressionism, which we can take as the breeding ground of the modernism that was to follow."

Brennan, Joseph X. "Stephen Crane and the Limits of Irony," *Criticism*, 11 (1969), 183–200.

Briggs, Austin, Jr. *The Novels of Harold Frederic*. Ithaca and London, 1969, pp. 7–8 and *passim*.

Bruccoli, Matthew J. " 'The Wonders of Ponce': Crane's First Puerto Rican Dispatch," *Stephen Crane Newsletter*, 4, no. 1 (Fall, 1969), 1–3.

Reprints an unrecorded war dispatch in the *Kansas City Star*, August 21, 1898, p. 5.

Bruccoli, M. J., and Joseph Katz, "Scholarship and Mere Artifacts: The British and Empire Publications of Stephen Crane," *Studies in Bibliography*, 22 (1969) 277–287.

Cady, Edwin H. "Stephen Crane's *Maggie: A Girl of the Streets*." In *Landmarks of American Writing*, ed. Hennig Cohen. New York and London. 1969, pp. 172–181.

Nothing new here; not even the commentary on Maggie's last night (in chap. XVII), an insight which had been first issued by J. X. Brennan. *See* Brennan, "Irony and Symbolic Structure in Crane's *Maggie*" (1962).

Most of Cady's main points about *Maggie* echo previous critics, including Stallman (1955, 1959, 1961). Cady agrees with Bassan and Katz that the 1893 *Maggie* is the text we should today read, not the 1896 *Maggie*. However, that point was first made by Stallman in "Stephen Crane's Revisions of *Maggie: A Girl of the Streets*," *American Literature* (1955).

Cady, Elizabeth W. "Stephen Crane to Miss Daisy D. Hill: The Letter Recovered," *Stephen Crane Newsletter*, 4, no. 2 (Winter, 1969). Corrects the inaccurate and incomplete version of this letter published in *SCraneN*, 2 (Summer, 1968). *See* Madigan (1933).

Cazemajou, Jean. "Stephen Crane: deux décennies de redécouverte (1948–1968)," *Les Langues Modernes*, 63 (January–February, 1969), 54–58.

———. *Stephen Crane.* Pamphlets on American Writers, no. 76. Minneapolis, Minn., 1969. Selected Bibliography, pp. 43–47.
An excellent short introduction to Crane. "In Crane's war novel religious imagery prevails, centered on an itinerary of spiritual redemption which leads not to eternal salvation but to a blissful impasse. . . . Besides this procession of religious images there appears here and there a scattering of scenes with animal characters which seem to be fables in miniature. The style abounds in symbolic rabbits, squirrels, horses, cows, and snakes which form a conventional bestiary by the side of a Christian demonology swarming with monsters directly borrowed from Biblical literature." *See* Stallman, "Notes Toward an Analysis of *The Red Badge of Courage*" (1951, 1952) and *Houses.*
Reviewed: Stanley Wertheim in *SCraneN*, 3, no. 4 (Summer, 1969), 8–9.

———. *Stephen Crane (1871–1900) écrivain journaliste. Études Anglaises,* no. 35. Paris: Librairie Didier, 1969.
A richly documented history of Crane's life and works. Much new data here, especially in book reviews contemporary with Crane's works. There are some holes in the biography (*viz.,* Crane in Athens at conclusion of the Greco-Turkish War), but Crane's chronology is pinpointed accurately. Cazemajou agrees with Stallman's *Stephen Crane* (1968) that Crane did not get to Greece by the overland route with Cora, but rather that Crane got there alone via Marseille, sailing on the *Guadiana* to Athens, with half a day enroute off the coast of Crete, as given in Crane's dispatch in the *New York Sun:* "Half a Day in Suda Bay." It would thus seem that Lillian Gilkes is in error in her *Cora Crane* (1960) on how Crane got to Greece.
Cazemajou's book is indispensable to the Crane scholar and, like his bibliography, pp. 533–564, it is full of surprises.
See Gilkes (1969) and Stallman (1972).
Reviewed: Le Nouvelle Littéraire, June 4, 1970, p. 5.

Colvert, James B. Introduction, *The Works of Stephen Crane,* ed. Fredson Bowers, vol. 1, *Bowery Tales: Maggie* and *George's Mother,* 1969.

Davidson, Richard Allan. "Crane's 'Blue Hotel' Revisited: The Illusion of Fate," *Modern Fiction Studies,* 15 (Winter, 1969–1970), 537–539.
See American Literature Abstracts, 3, no. 2 (June, 1970), 115.

Dekle, Bernard. *Profiles of Modern American Authors.* Tokyo, 1969.

Dillingham, William B. *Frank Norris: Instinct and Art.* Lincoln, Nebr., 1969, pp. 18–19, 35–36, 37, 51, 83, 85–86, 115–116.

Edel, Leon. *Henry James: The Treacherous Years: 1895–1901.* Philadelphia and New York, 1969.
Nothing here on James's associations with and friendship for Stephen Crane. See, however, Edel, vol. 5 (1972).

Forster, Imogen, ed. "The Thoth Annual Bibliography of Stephen Crane Scholarship," *Thoth,* 10, no. 2 (Spring, 1969), 25–27.

Ford, Philip H. "Illusion and Reality in Crane's *Maggie*," *Arizona Quarterly*, 25 (Winter, 1969), 293–303.

Fox, Austin M. "New Crane Letter Links Him to Hubbard, WNY," *Buffalo Evening News*, December 20, 1969.

Fox recounts the banquet of the Society of the Philistines in honor of Crane in Buffalo, December 19, 1895. The new Crane to Hubbard letter was discovered pasted inside a first edition of *The Little Regiment*, belonging to Elbert Hubbard's daughter, Mrs. Howard D. Roelofs of East Aurora, whom Professor Fox interviewed. I am indebted to Austin M. Fox for copy of this article with the following new Crane letter:

c/o William Heineman[n]
21 Bedford St., W.C.
London
Oct. 29. [1897]
My dear Hubbard: It is a dangerous thing to forget to communicate with one's friends. Soon it becomes hard to retrace. I am glad you wrote to me because I have been believing myself an ass in your respect and now I have opportunity to say so.

As for your damned friends I have lost the card but if you send me another one with the address I shall call there as soon as I can afford a top-hat. It is somewhere in Russel Sq I know and I am thinking of calling from house to house.

Sometime ago I sent a thing to The Bookman with instructions in a circuitous way, that if they could not use ($) it, they should forward it to The Philistine. I think you will get it since McArthur cant tell good stuff from hot clam broth. Remember me vividly to Mrs. Hubbard, to the doctor and his wife and to Marie and to the hoodlums who played Indian on your lawn.

                                   Yours faithfully / Stephen Crane

————. "Stephen Crane and Joseph Conrad," *Serif*, 6, no. 4 (December, 1969), 16–20.

Fox traces various interrelationships between the fiction of Crane and Conrad, and certain influences of Crane's work on Conrad's. A useful article.

Furnas, Joseph Chamberlain. *The Americans: A Social History of the United States, 1587–1914*. New York, 1969, pp. 873–874.

Gilkes, Lillian. "Stephen and Cora Crane: Some Corrections, and a 'Millionaire' Named Sharefe," *American Literature*, 41 (May, 1969), 270–277.

Gilkes summarizes this article in *American Literature Abstracts*, 3 (December, 1969), 23, her argument being that Stephen and Cora took the *Guadiana* at Constantinople "and were aboard her in Suda Bay bound for Athens. This corrects my previous account in *Cora Crane*." The journey was thus "westbound," according to Gilkes' new version, whereas Stallman has contended that Crane took the *Guadiana* at Marseilles and on an eastbound voyage to Athens stopped half a day in Suda Bay, Crete.

In *ALA*, as in *AL*, Gilkes claims that Crane's Cretan dispatch "is the giveaway" because he says his "expected glimpse of Greece . . . appeared to the north. Actually, says Gilkes, "on a southeasterly course from Marseilles it must have appeared to the south. . . ." However, Gilkes fails to quote the full text of Crane's Cretan dispatch, "Stephen Crane's Pen Picture of the Powers' Fleet Off Crete," wherein he says that on the early morning "of the fourth day" [from Marseilles] a ponderous headland appeared to the north and we knew it to be the expected glimpse of Greece." Gilkes misconstrues the headlands to belong to Crete, whereas they belong to the mainland of Greece, and they would appear to the north, as Cape Akritas or Cape Tainaron.

Gilkes aims to show that Crane falsified his entire voyage so as to prove by hook or crook that Crane got to Crete from Constantinople with Cora, of course, a theory which in turn would lend credence to her other theory that Stephen was with Cora on the overland route to Constantinople. (*See Cora Crane*, p. 91, which is a most mixed-up bag of speculations.)

However, Crane clearly defines those first headlands as off the mainland of Greece, saying that "some hours later another ponderous headland appeared to the southward," whereupon he discovered that the ship had changed her course and that "we were not bound for the Pieree [Athens], but for the Bay of Suda in Crete." (In *War Dispatches*, p. 12.) Crane says he journeyed eastward from Marseilles; Gilkes says "poor Stevie piled one lie upon another, hoping to create the impression that he had come to Greece by the sea route from Marseilles." (In *AL*, p. 275.) She has Crane fabricating an entire dispatch in order to conceal from Richard Harding Davis that "he had traveled across the continent with Cora Taylor, ex-mistress of the Hotel de Dream, whom Davis remembered from Jacksonville." But Crane and Davis detested each other; so why should he concoct a journalistic hoax when he couldn't care less what Davis or any other reporter thought of him? He did not lie to Davis about having been to Crete, nor did he lie to his brother in writing him that he intended to get to Crete.

According to Gilkes, Crane is lying in saying—in "Half a Day in Suda Bay" (a variant title to his Cretan dispatch)—that he boarded the *Guadiana* at Marseilles, was off Crete on the fourth day, and had listened to "the thin wail of a baby that had objected without pause from Marseilles to the roll and heave of the ship," and had noticed that some freight which had been brought "from Marseilles" was towed to the *Guadiana* by French sailors. To satisfy Gilkes' theory Crane had to invent all these statements, a palpable impossibility!

Additional evidence that Crane wrote his dispatch before reaching Athens, not after touching port there (*contra* Gilkes), is indicated by the fact that an Englishman aboard the *Guadiana* was cocksure that the Cretans could never be conquered by the Turks, whereas (as I pointed out in my *Stephen Crane: A Biography*, p. 593n), "unknown to him and to Crane the island had already been subdued." That explains why the Greek passengers stared at a tiny blood-red banner, the Turkish flag over a redoubt. (In *Crane*, p. 270.) Nobody aboard the *Guadiana* knew about the defeat of the Cretans two weeks previously. However, Crane would have known about it had he come from Constantinople and Athens. Gilkes' version has the *Guadiana* dipping past Pieree (Athens) to visit Crete and then returning to Athens, which is an unlikely excursion trip if the *Guadiana* knew about the Cretan defeat and Turkish control of the island. Nor do I believe that such an excursion exists in the records of the *Guadiana*'s routine and scheduled voyage from London and Marseilles to Batum on the Black Sea. In his *Stephen Crane Écrivain Journaliste* (Paris, 1969), p. 128, Jean Cazemajou supports Stallman's standpoint that Crane was not with Cora on the overland route and that he got to Crete from Marseilles.

In *Cora Crane* (1960), p. 91, Gilkes claimed that Crane "had obviously not been near Marseilles," also that he had never been in Turkey, and that it's quite possible that he may have faked the Cretan dispatch. However, Crane was in Epirus on April 18, which Epirus was then Turkey, an error which Gilkes does not admit in her *AL* account. She is more positive in *AL* that

Crane faked his dispatch, being desperate to prove that Crane got to Athens not from Marseilles but from Constantinople, "not by the last leg of the Balkan route—as I earlier thought—but aboard the *Guadiana* on the return from her last port of call, Batum. . . . This corrects my previous account." However, Gilkes' admission of errors only serves to camouflage her crucial errors, and there remains no radical change in her *AL* account and *Cora Crane*. Both accounts are solely conjectures, not based on evidences and documented research.

Utter conjecture is her claim that Crane got to Crete from Constantinople and Athens and that Cora was with him off Crete, as well as her fixed idea that Sylvester Scovel and Crane accompanied Cora and Mrs. Mathilde Ruedy on the Orient Express to Varna and then on the *Danae*, "a terrible tub" on which the passengers endured near shipwreck. That Sylvester Scovel cannot figure as the "S. S." in Cora's diary—an important point ignored by Gilkes in her *AL* account—is indicated by the fact that he was in St. Louis in April, 1897, just then getting married. William Randel happens to mention this fact in his article on Crane's "The Open Boat" in *Nineteenth-Century Fiction*, 19 (March, 1965). To make the "S." in Cora's diary figure as Stevie, Gilkes transposed the word "Have" into "Steve" in her misreading of the holograph manuscript of Cora's diary—in *Cora Crane*, p. 79. *See* Stallman, "Was Crane's Sketch of the Fleet Off Crete a Journalistic Hoax?" *See* Gilkes' reply in same issue of *SinSF*.

In her "No Hoax: A Reply to Mr. Stallman," *SinSF* (1964), Gilkes agrees with my standpoint that Crane's Cretan dispatch was no hoax, as implied in my inept title. I was saying—*contra* Gilkes—that it was no hoax, although my questioning title casts possible misinterpretation on my standpoint, and indeed it was so misinterpreted in a published abstract by a hack scholar who never read the substance of my attack on Gilkes. Ironically, Gilkes in *AL* now claims Crane's Cretan sketch was a complete hoax, in contradiction of her *SinSF* article "No Hoax." She reverts to her standpoint in *Cora Crane* without admitting in *AL* its numerous errors, including the crucial one that Crane got to Marseilles to get to Crete and was not with Cora enroute to Varna and Constantinople. She does not admit in her *AL* account that it could not possibly have been for Crane and Cora "their second honeymoon," says *Cora Crane*, p. 78. But how could it be any honeymoon with "S." sleeping in a hen coop and Cora sleeping with Ferris on the *Danae*? What Gilkes recasts as a honeymoon Cora described as a nightmare. That "S." is not Stevie and that Stevie was not with Cora is made obvious by the very fact that Cora took along at her expense Mrs. Ruedy as travel companion, whereas there would be no excuse for her presence were Cora accompanied by Crane.

Gilkes concludes her *AL* article with a rehash of that puzzling "Memorandum of trip from N.Y. to Paris to Marseilles, A. N., 1 p.," in Columbia University Crane Collection, where it is designated thus. If read from the top to the bottom, this Crane notation traces his journey to Marseilles. However, because Gilkes cannot tolerate the fact that Crane did just that, proceeding from New York to Paris to Marseilles (*that* fact contradicts her theory), Gilkes reads this note from the bottom upwards to the top—both in *Cora Crane*, pp. 109–110, and in her *AL* article. Her aim is to persuade us that Crane never got to Marseilles except on his homeward journey and that when homeward bound he wrote at the bottom of a piece of paper "Arrested in

Marseilles. No tickets," and then added upwards on the scrap of paper other notations ending with (at the top) "New York 290 / 261." However, only the Chinese write from the bottom upwards, and Crane was not Chinese.

Gilkes' contention is utterly implausible. It is explainable that she distorts the evidence only in view of her necessity to defend her *Cora Crane* thesis (as cited above), which no Crane scholar can possibly substantiate by any evidence. As surmised in my *Crane*, "New York 290 / 261" refers to the two cabins on the *Etruria* from New York to Liverpool, Cora and Mrs. Ruedy sharing one cabin and Crane the other. (For this insight I am indebted to E. R. Hagemann's researches many years ago.) If so, then—*contra* Gilkes—even from the start of their voyage to Greece it was no honeymoon. And if so, then the Greek boys were not aboard the *Etruria,* the Greek boys whom Crane rescued from Greece and took to England at the war's end. And if so, which is the way it was, then Gilkes' speculations that Crane was called by the Greek boys "shereef" or prince is nonsense because Crane—enroute to Marseilles—had not yet encountered these Greek chaps—if you read Crane's memorandum scrap of paper simply and logically from top to bottom.

Suppose, says Gilkes in her *AL* article, that Crane, "for whatever reasons, was not telling the truth? As I am convinced he was not." Whom are we to believe: Gilkes or Crane?

See also Stallman (1972).

——. "A Recent Book about Stephen Crane," *Courier* (Syracuse), 31 (Spring, 1969), 1–6.

——. "Stephen Crane and the Harold Frederics," *Serif*, 6, no. 4 (December, 1969).

——. "Corrections of R. W. Stallman's *Stephen Crane: A Biography,*" *Stephen Crane Newsletter*, 3, no. 3 (Spring, 1969), 6–7.

"Stallman has Cora, at Pharsala, noting 'Mass desertion.' She wrote 'Bass desertion' in the diary . . . , referring to John Bass leaving the party in which she travelled. Stallman's error is unfortunate first because it is error, and again because it makes a reader suppose that there was a defection of some of those 'curious officers.' . . . It is trebly unfortunate because it ultimately obscures the already foggy note to all this on p. 594: 'Bass deserted Cora's project to interview Prince Constantine in Pharsala.' Who did what?" *Contra* Gilkes, the latter statement clarifies the previous quotation in *Crane*, p. 277, and suggests that "Mass desertion" is a printer's error.

Gilkes knows it is a printer's error, by the evidence of "Bass deserted Cora's project," p. 594, and exploits this Mass for Bass error to embarrass me by her falsified account painfully explaining that there was no mass desertion; I never said there was—the printer said it. James Stronks caught a hundred printer's errors in the first edition of *Crane*, which were corrected in the second edition, thanks to his kind letter. Unlike friend Stronks, Gilkes has chosen to nitpick *Crane,* while professing: "It is a painful experience but an undeniable duty to list factual errors in the latest work. . . ." *Crane* is painful to Gilkes because it upsets her biased view of Cora at the expense of Crane and it disturbs her versions of some crucial events in the chronology. As the *Times Literary Supplement* put it (March 16, 1962, p. 183), "The feeling of irritation with the heroine is reinforced by irritation with the author (of *Cora Crane*, 1960), whose thoroughness is not as real as it is apparent. For example, Rembrandt's 'Anatomy School' has been owned by the Mauritshuis in The Hague since 1828, and if the Cranes saw it in Brussels in 1899 one would like to know how it came to be there. . . . Who are these London publishers called Castle? Presumably Cassell. And what is 'English citizenship,' of which we hear from time to time in the book?"

"Stallman says that Ralph D. Paine and E. W. McCready spent Christmas, 1896, in Key West, and so McCready was wrong in remembering a Jacksonville dinner then. 'That was surely on Thanksgiving Day,' he concludes of the dinner (p. 241). But McCready's testimony is in a letter of 1934—and it is contradicted by testimony twelve years fresher: Paine's memory in *Roads of Adventure* (Boston, 1922), p. 121, that he and McCready spent a 'cheerful Christmas Day' on the Key of No Name. . . .'' So, then, they were at Key of No Name according to Paine, whereas according to McCready they were at Key West. Gilkes pits Paine against McCready so as to produce another "error" in *Crane*, whereas it matters not at all where they were in Florida, but only that they were not in Jacksonville for Christmas. (In *Letters*, p. 340, our fn. 85 says that McCready confused the chronology in that the turkey dinner occurred on Thanksgiving Day, 1896. That is the main point.)

Of far more importance is the fact that Sylvester Scovel was not in Greece* at the time Gilkes has him figuring as "S. S." in Cora's diary and thereby sharing Cora's overland train trip to Varna on the Black Sea, in *Cora Crane*, p. 79. Her book is loaded with errors, which no Crane scholar has troubled himself to notice or cite. Cora's diary, she says, was written "on loose sheets of lined legal cap paper," p. 79. But it isn't lined legal cap paper. The passage Gilkes mistranscribes includes such errors as "foresight" for "forethought," "advantage of it to go" instead of "advantage of it and go," "clothes" instead of "cloth," "needed in Europe" for "needed traveling in Europe," etc. Where Cora wrote "F. S.," Gilkes inserts between these letters a bracket for a comma to divide F from S, so as to preserve her fixed theory of "S" as representing Stephen, and all of these errors and tampering with the text occur on one half page of p. 79. "S" is not Stephen, and "S. S." is not Sylvester Scovel. Gilkes' errors are unfortunate first because they are errors, and again because they mislead the innocent reader into thinking that Stephen and Scovel were with "F. S." and Cora and Mathilde (Mrs. Ruedy). These Gilkes errors are—to use her phrase—"trebly unfortunate" because they obscure the truth.

"It is a painful experience but an undeniable duty to list factual errors" (to quote Gilkes above) in her *Cora Crane*, as well as to admit them in my *Crane*, including "Marjory" for "Margery" and "The Brown Hotel" for "Brown's Hotel," pp. 660 and 332. *Crane* errs also in saying that the Frewens never visited the Cranes at Brede Place, p. 498; I forgot or mislaid Mrs. Frewen's 1904 letter to Cora. All in all, none of the errors Gilkes makes so much of here amount to more than minor embarrassments at not being invulnerably correct on every one of *Crane's* 664 pages.

In this already extensive rejoinder I've space perhaps to reply to her claim that "Stallman unaccountably—and inaccurately—demotes Smolenski to Colo-

* Richard Harding Davis on May 16 wrote that Scovel reached Greece when the war was almost over. In *Adventures and Letters of Richard Harding Davis* (1917), pp. 210–211. Randel also points out that Scovel married in St. Louis on April 5 and was not scheduled to sail from New York until the eighth. It would have been a miracle could Scovel have possibly caught up with Cora before the eighteenth of April. Randel rightly concludes that "S. S." in Cora's diary is—*contra* Gilkes—not Scovel. In "From Slate to Emerald Green," *Nineteenth-Century Fiction*, 19 (March, 1965), 367.

nel from the rank of General he properly held the page before—in the same
paragraph." The paragraph begins with "General Smolenski" on April 30,
p. 279, and ends with "Colonel Smolenski" on May 18, whereas the former
should read Colonel and the latter General in that he was in between time
promoted, not, of course, demoted!

Gonnaud, Maurice, Jeanne-Marie Santraud, and Jean Cazemajou. *Stephen
Crane: étude de Maggie et The Red Badge of Courage.* Paris: Librairie
Armand Colin, 1969.

Greiner, Donald J., and Ellen B. Greiner, eds. *The Notebook of Stephen Crane.*
Charlottesville, Va., 1969.

Reproduces Crane's Pocket Notebook (1892–1894), which contains the poem
"Little Birds of the Night," Literary Notes, and seven major sketches, all seven
published in *NYCS* (1966). The editors do not provide notes to indicate the
differences between these seven sketches and their printed texts. "The Art
Students' League," "Matinee Girls," and "Election Night" ("Heard on the
Street Election Night") were first reproduced from the Notebook of Stephen
Crane in *Bulletin* (September, 1956). *See* Stallman, "Stephen Crane: Some
New Stories (Part I)." They were reprinted in *NYCS* with errors in punctua-
tion, spelling, and sometimes word sequence, as the editors Greiner point out.

However, a note in *NYCS*, p. 14, claimed the Notebook "was lost almost a
decade ago while being transferred from the Collamore Crane Collection to
the Barrett Crane Collection. A photocopy is all that remains of it." This was,
namely, my photocopy taken in the early 1950s. The transfer to BCC occurred in 1956, and at the conclusion of the exhibition of Crane's Writings
held in Low Library, Columbia University, rumor had it that the Notebook
was lost. If it was lost, I could not collate it anew for texts in *NYCS* (*contra*
the Greiners). And lost it was! "The real excitement behind that missing
pagination in the Notebook is this—Mr. Barrett could not find the Notebook
nor any of the manuscripts of these things you are describing and quoting
[in *Bulletin:* September, 1956]. He said he was sure he had given them all
to Columbia last spring; the Columbia people are equally sure that they never
received any such box of manuscripts and in fact they were quite surprised to
learn of the existence of these things on your list. . . . I suppose this is all
to be kept very much on the q.t." (Dr. David Erdman, Editor of *Bulletin,* to
R. W. S., September 18, 1956.)

Fortunately, the Notebook was found and is here published as a whole for
the first time.

The editors' Introduction, pp. v–xxi, observes that the Notebook contradicts Crane's claim that revisions are a sign of dishonesty in the writer (a point
first made in *Omnibus*) and that the Notebook "verifies his affirmation of impressionism." It also "supports the claims of Crane's biographers that he was
more of a conscious artist than he sometimes liked to admit." Here the editors
refer, p. viii, to Joseph Conrad in his Introduction to Beer's *SC*, which they
misdate 1924 when it is 1923 (and 1924) and to *Omnibus*, pp. xxx–xxxii, which
they misdate, q.v., for 1957, when the true date is 1952.

Gullason, Thomas A. "The Letters of Stephen Crane: Additions and Corrections," *American Literature,* 41 (March, 1969), 104–106.

Issues a letter of Joseph Conrad to Edith Crane, January 24, 1912, and the
full text of a Crane letter to Edmund Crane, July 22, 1897, a portion of which
was published in *Letters* (1960), the only portion then available. A third

Crane letter (inscribed on a card) "shows that the editors of *Stephen Crane: Letters* have inaccurately dated and quoted from it." The date is not, as given in *Letters,* April but January 31, 1900.

Says Gullason, p. 106: "In at least two other places, Stallman quotes from portions of Stephen Crane's letters in his footnotes (he does not reproduce them in the body of his text), and he never reveals his sources." However, it is Gullason who never reveals his sources, the sources of these very letters—in what library or Crane collection do the originals exist? I am surprised that the Editor of *American Literature* permitted Gullason's sin of omission.

Secondly, Gullason notes, p. 105, that the maiden name of Edmund Crane's wife was Fleming, "the name Stephen Crane took for the hero of *The Red Badge of Courage.*" However, there are two possible sources for this statement, one being the Newark Chart in the Newark Public Library and the other my *Stephen Crane: A Biography* (1968), where this fact is first made known (page 646 and elsewhere). Gullason acknowledges neither of these sources, silently claiming the identification as his own.

Thirdly, all the new letters Gullason quotes, since they are dated 1897, 1900, and 1912, belong to the editorial province of Lillian Gilkes, to whom Gullason's complaints should have been addressed—not to Stallman. Gilkes' share of responsibility began where Cora Crane entered. *Letters* (1960).

Our sources are given in the Catalogue, which states that our footnotes of quoted portions of letters do not get included in List of Letters. Our Crane snippits quoted in footnotes obviously derived from Beer's *SC* (1923). No other source was possible. Gullason says that Stallman "refers to Crane's letter of September 9, 1897, to Edmund Crane; he quotes a part of a sentence as though it were the whole sentence, and it is not." However, it is a snippit from Beer and therefore it was relegated to a footnote, p. 144, *n*102. "Stallman quotes: 'Finished a novelette of 20,000 words—*The Monster.*' In the original letter, the entire sentence reads: 'I have just finished a novelette of 20000 words—*The Monster.*'" The complete letter is reproduced in the *SCraneN,* 1 (no. 3), 8 (Spring, 1967); it is based on a transcription by Edith Crane. Miss Crane sent me some new things, but this was not included in my correspondence with her; nor was it in the files of Alfred A. Knopf containing Edith Crane letters. But no matter that the sentence lacks the first two words ("I have"); so what?

SCraneN has become notorious for issuing "new" Crane letters which already exist in *Letters,* for issuing them because of discrepancies of a missing comma or phrase (as in the above Gullason item), and also for issuing them as though for the first time without acknowledging their prior publication. Gullason here in *American Literature* emulates Joseph Katz's constant attempts to undercut the texts and overall integrity of *Letters.*

———. "The New Criticism and the Older Ones: Another Ride in 'The Open Boat,'" *CEA Critic,* 31 (June, 1969), 8.

Gullason takes Mordecai Marcus to task for claiming that Stallman "seems to be the first critic to have applied the concepts of alternation of mood to Crane's fiction and poetry."

Says Gullason: "All one has to do is read Mr. Munson to see this is not true." He quotes in italics this passage from Gorham B. Munson's *Style and Form in American Prose* (1929): "On the emotional plane the development [of "The Open Boat"] proceeds by alternation, the alternation of hopefulness and despair." Says Gullason: "In his several readings of Stephen Crane's *The Open Boat*, Mr. Stallman overlooks yet repeats Mr. Munson. In his *Stephen Crane: An Omnibus* (1952) Mr. Stallman says: '*The Open Boat* and *The Red Badge* are identical in form, in theme, and even in their patterns of leitmotivs and imagery. In *The Open Boat* the despair-hope mood is established (and the point of view prepared for) in the opening sentence. . . .' "

Again, says Gullason: In Stallman's Modern Library edition of *The Red Badge of Courage* (1951) "Mr. Stallman writes: 'The form of *The Red Badge of Courage* is constructed by repetitive alternations of contradictory moods. The opening scene establishes the same despair-hope pattern as the very last image of the book. . . .' " Again, says Gullason: "In comments on Crane's poetry, Mr. Stallman again points to the 'contrast of moods,' to despair and hope (*Omnibus*, p. 571). He draws on hope-despair in his reading of *Maggie* (*The Houses That James Built*, p. 77)."

To pay me a compliment is the last thing Gullason is aiming at, and yet he unwittingly has done it. For it requires more ingenuity than I possess to have constructed the categories of form in Crane's poetry and fiction from my friend Munson's little phrase about alternations of hopefulness and despair. No, my source was not Munson, whose insight is limited to "The Open Boat," whereas my reading of Double Mood extends throughout Crane's major writings in prose and poetry.

Contra Gullason—my reading of Crane's designs of structuring poems and short stories (some designed logically and some psychologically in the interrelationship of their parts) derived not at all from Munson, but rather from Kenneth Burke.

And this debt to Burke's *Counter-Statement* (1931), which is reprinted in large portions in my *Critiques and Essays in Criticism: 1920–1948* (1949), is acknowledged in my "Stephen Crane: A Revaluation," in *Critiques and Essays on Modern Fiction,* ed. John Aldridge (1952), p. 259. "Burke's categories of forms have never before been applied to fiction. They provoke the most illuminating key to the nature and form of fiction that I know of." Gullason does not admit that I make this acknowledgement to Burke. Marcus is right, and Gullason is wrong: I believe I was first in applying Burke's categories of forms to Crane's fiction and poetry.

Not noticed and admitted by Gullason is that Munson's *Style and Form* is acknowledged in *Omnibus* (1952). Again, it is listed in the *Critiques* bibliography (1949) and again in my "Selected Bibliography of Criticism of Modern Fiction," in *Critiques and Essays on Modern Fiction,* ed. John Aldridge (1952).

The proof that I owed no debt to Munson is that I use the terms Double Mood and Syllogistic Form in my analysis of Crane's fiction and poetry, whereas Munson does not mention them in his *Style and Form.* What Burke calls Qualitative Progression is refined by Yvor Winters as Double Mood in his unknown essay, "The Extension and Re-integration of the Human Spirit Through the Poetry, Chiefly French and American, Since Poe and Baudelaire," in *The Third Caravan.* A summary of Winters' theory appears in my *Critic's Notebook* (1950), which reprints Flint's review-essay from *Symposium,* 1 (July, 1930). Related to the topic of literary form is Burke's *Counter-Statement,* of course, and Edgell Rickword's "The Use of 'Negative' Emotions" (1925), the latter reprinted in my *Critiques and Essays in Criticism.* It was with this background of critical theory of the forms of fiction and poetry, of which Gullason is obviously ignorant, that I approached Crane's fiction and poetry in 1950–51. As for my reading of the land-sea imagery in *The Open Boat*, I know of no source for that reading, which is, I think, crucial to any interpretation of that work. Implied in Gullason's attack is that here, too, I am indebted to Munson, which is nonsense. The closest thing to the land-sea imagery is the Rome-Egypt situation in *Antony and Cleopatra:* When we are in Rome, then Egypt is described, and when we are in Egypt, then Rome is invoked. Cf. G. Wilson Knight, *The Imperial Theme* (1931).

———. "Stallman's *Crane*," *CEA Critic*, 31 (May, 1969), 8–9. *See* Stallman (1970) for reply to this article.

Haack, Dietmar. "Stephen Crane und die 'kühne' Metapher," *Jahrbuch für Amerikastudien,* 14 (1969), 116–123.

Hemingway, Ernest. *A Moveable Feast.* New York, 1969, p. 131.
"Tolstoi made the writing of Stephen Crane on the Civil War seem like the brilliant imagining of a sick boy who had never seen war but had only read the battles and chronicles and seen the Brady photographs that I had read and seen at my grandparents' house."

Holton, Milne. "The Sparrow's Fall and the Sparrow's Eye: Crane's *Maggie*," *Studia Neophilologica,* 41 (1969), 115–129.

Hyde, H. Montgomery. *Henry James at Home.* New York, 1969, pp. 179, 183–188.

Itabashi, Yoshie. "Stephen Crane ni okeru Shizenshugi no Henyo," *Eigo Seinen* (The Rising Generation) (Tokyo, Japan), 115 (1969), 352–353.
On the transformation of Naturalism in Crane.

Ives, Chauncey B. "Symmetrical Design in Four of Stephen Crane's Stories," *Ball State University Forums,* 10 (Winter, 1969), 17–26.
See Bowen (1969).

Jackson, Agnes Moreland. "Stephen Crane's Imagery of Conflict in 'George's Mother,' " *Arizona Quarterly,* 25 (Winter, 1969), 313–318.

Jackson, John A. "Sociology and Literary Studies: I. The Map of Society: America in the 1890's," *Journal of American Studies,* 3 (1969), 105–110.

Katz, Joseph. *Checklist of Stephen Crane.* Columbus, Ohio, 1969, pp. 1–41.
"The student will find the Merrill Checklists especially useful if he records library call numbers next to entries for the writings as he uses them." The library call numbers are useful, but not this checklist, which is untrustworthy and eccentric. It is eccentric because under the heading *The Monster* Katz lists writings on "The Blue Hotel," and "The Bride Comes to Yellow Sky" is listed under the heading *The Open Boat.* The beginning student will not readily unriddle Katz's puzzling mixup, nor will he be interested in any of the entries—mainly by Katz—in *SCraneN,* such as "Manuscripts and Method" *(Great Battles of the World).* He would profit most not from Katz and his *SCraneN,* but from Sergio Perosa's "Naturalism and Impressionism in Stephen Crane's Fiction" (1964), but he won't find that splendid essay listed here.
Katz lists himself thirty-four entries, while under *Poetry* he omits listing the best essays on Crane's poetry by Harland Nelson (1963), Max Westbrook (1963), and Ruth Miller (1968). Katz's checklist is of course highly selective, but it is not selective of Katz's own published things. His things are *Articles,* but he subsumes under *Articles* what are in fact *essays* by Crane critics and scholars.

Daniel Aaron's "Stephen Crane" (1951) is a review-essay, not an article. Considering his space of 41 pages, it tells against his organizing talent that John Martin gets listed under three separate categories, under *Maggie*, "The Monster," and *Whilomville Stories*, whereas no other essay dealing with multiple Crane titles obtains recurrent mention. Jay Martin's *Harvest of Change* (1967) is not mentioned.

Dendinger is misspelled *Deninger* and his essay's title is also incorrectly given, p. 28.

While Katz errs on Jay Martin, he also errs on Harold Martin in that his entry has no publication date. Neither has the Randall Stewart entry, p. 19. A bibliography, especially when issued by a bibliographer, ought to state the date of publication for any given work and rightly, if possible. Katz's checklist has Norman Friedman's essay (not an "article") appearing Fall, 1969, whereas it appeared Fall, 1968. And Vincent Starrett, "Stephen Crane: An Estimate," was published in June, 1920, not in July, 1920. And Starrett's *Men, Women and Boats*—says my first edition—is dated 1921, not as Katz has it erroneously, 1923. Donald Pizer's essay on *Maggie* in *Realism and Naturalism* (1966) requires pp. 88–98 to be added to Katz's pp. 121–131.

The overall trouble with Katz's *Stephen Crane Checklist* is that it squints, being neither constructed for nor addressed to the beginning Crane student on the one hand, nor, on the other, to the graduate student. For the latter, it is hopelessly untrustworthy and inadequate and eccentric. The student—graduate or undergraduate—cannot attach "library call-numbers" (as Katz advises him to do) to essays on Crane's works that are not included in Katz's pretentious checklist. There exist more than 2,000 essays, articles, and books of writings on Crane, of which only a small fraction get mentioned in Katz's checklist.

———. "Stephen Crane," *Collier's Encyclopedia*, vol. 7. New York, 1969, pp. 418–420.

Katz is mistaken in his notion that *The Red Badge of Courage* "remains a model of naturalism." Because we share Fleming's mental process and point of view, we observe him attempting to manipulate his own destiny, and insofar as he possesses mind and will to do so the protagonist is not trapped by his environment. *Contra* Katz, the exemplar of literary Naturalism is *Maggie*.

———. "Two Uncollected Articles," *Prairie Schooner*, 44 (Winter, 1969), 287–296.

———. Introduction, *The Red Badge of Courage*. Columbus, Ohio, 1969, pp. v–xiii.

A simplified account, evidently intended for high school students, on the writing of *The Red Badge,* here in facsimile of the first impression, first edition (1895). "From a copy in the collection of Joseph Katz."

Katz's comments about the manuscripts of *The Red Badge* oversimplify their history, and no mention is made of their publication by Winterich (1951) and by Stallman (1952). The phrase "in his twenty-nine years" errs by the fact that Crane was not twenty-nine when he died.

———. *Stephen Crane: The Blue Hotel*. Columbus, Ohio, 1969. A casebook with "General Instructions for a Research Paper," pp. v–xii.

———. "An Early Draft of 'Death and the Child,'" *Stephen Crane Newsletter*, 3, no. 3 (Spring, 1969), 1.

On verso of p. 2 of Cora Crane's manuscript *Peter the Great* is a draft—in

Cora's hand—of paragraphs nine through thirteen of "Death and the Child." On verso of p. 1 is an early draft of "The Blue Hotel." *See SCraneN,* 3, no. 1 (Fall, 1968).

———. "An Early Draft of 'Moonlight on the Snow,'" *Stephen Crane Newsletter,* 3, no. 4 (Summer, 1969), 1–2.

MS. is on verso of a sheet of hotel letterhead in CUCC, which Columbia University Crane Collection is arbitrarily designated by Katz "NNC."

———. "John William de Forest on Stephen Crane," *Stephen Crane Newsletter,* 4, no. 1 (Fall, 1969), 6.

———. "Stephen Crane's Passport Applications: Part IV," *Stephen Crane Newsletter,* 4, no. 1 (Fall, 1969), 4–5.

———. "Stephen Crane to an Unknown Recipient: A New Letter," *Stephen Crane Newsletter,* 3, no. 3 (Spring, 1969), 5.

Facsimile reproduction of a printed card by the Author's Club, dated May 28, 1896, signed Stephen Crane. It is rather far fetched of Katz to call an autographed card "A New Letter."

———. "Stephen Crane to the *Atlanta Journal:* A New Letter," and "Stephen Crane to the American Press Association: A New Letter," *Stephen Crane Newsletter,* 4, no. 1 (Fall, 1969), 3, 6.

Katz, Joseph, ed. *The Portable Stephen Crane.* New York, 1969.

Katz's Editor's Note says certain emendations in Crane's writings "have been made silently." However, Katz criticizes *Letters* (1960) for doing precisely the same thing. *Letters,* he says, p. xxiv, "is standard, but its transcriptions are unreliable, its datings are not always trustworthy, and it omits many important letters by, to, and about Crane." However, since *Letters* fewer than two dozen new ones have come to light, and of these issued in Katz's *SCraneN* (1966–1968) six are reprinted almost exactly as given in *Letters* except for variant punctuation or an altered salutation, and the rest of the new letters are mainly of a sentence or two each or unimportant.

Katz cites only the libraries of *Letters'* sources and not at all *Stephen Crane Letters* (1960), and by this device Katz creates the misleading impression that these letters were *not* previously published and are new to his *Portable Stephen Crane.*

Of *SCTS,* Katz says only "its first six pieces" make the collection worthwhile; the rest of them "are *not* Sullivan County tales and sketches in the sense in which Crane created the group." However, the first six pieces in *SCTS* are "The Last of the Mohicans" and five hunting sketches. Then follow ten Sullivan County tales which form a group, beginning with "Killing His Bear." Katz cannot possibly mean what he says about the first six pieces making "the collection worthwhile," because he elsewhere objects vigorously against confounding the so-called integrity of the tales by conjoining them with the sketches, which is nonsense since the tales remain as a group in *SCTS,* and again it is nonsense because the "first six pieces" are not the most interesting Sullivan County sketches. Neither are the grotesque little tales of the woods, as Crane called them, the most interesting pieces, except for "The Holler Tree" and "The Mesmeric Mountain." *SCTS* presents seven new pieces.

Katz errs in claiming that Cora Stewart "later became Mrs. Stephen Crane." All the evidence is to the contrary. *See* Gilkes' *Cora Crane, versus* Katz, p. 329.

No acknowledgement is made to the discovered passages new to the text of

"An Experiment in Misery" in *Omnibus,* in Katz's reprinting of these passages which open and close that sketch. Nor does Katz acknowledge prior publication of "Heard on the Street Election Night," nor of the data used in his note, p. 176, which Crane article was first published in "Stephen Crane: Some New Stories (Part I)," *Bulletin* (September, 1956). Katz claims, p. 246, that the wafer sun in *The Red Badge of Courage* is " 'pasted' like a seal" and that Stephen "would have been aware of both the legal wafer and its symbolism." However, he does not explain the kind of symbolism intended. There is no legal symbolism in the book.

Katz says that Berryman's *SC* "loses from inaccuracies and from a Freudian interpretation of Crane that seems irrelevant." However, this is not true. Irrelevant it is not; it is simply that psychological criticism is not the whole story, nor literary criticism, as Berryman himself admits (1962). As for *Crane* Katz claims it "draws widely from a host of unacknowledged sources." However, all the main sources are cited in *Crane,* and what by editorial decree had to be expunged gets included in the companion-volume, *Stephen Crane: A Critical Bibliography.* Katz says *Crane*'s style is "confusing" and "its criticism quirky." Perhaps so. Its style does involve quirks, sudden twists, clever sallies, quips, and strikes with the sudden jerk of a whip. (That is the Webster definition of "quirk.")

"There is no definitive text of Crane's short prose," says Katz, adding that *The Portable Stephen Crane* "provides authoritative texts of that material." However, for the text of "An Experiment in Misery" he reprints the text of that sketch from *The Open Boat and Other Stories* (London, 1898), while at the same time he also prints the *Press*'s opening and closing portions which were omitted in *The Open Boat's* version of that sketch. Katz thus has it both ways. Nor does he acknowledge that the New York Press version was first made known in *Omnibus.* Nor is there any acknowledgement that "Heard on the Street Election Night" was first made known in *Bulletin* (1956). Elsewhere Katz has argued that "A Prologue" is not a poem, but here he includes it under Posthumously Published Poems.
Reviewed: Austin M. Fox, "Hubbard Gives Impetus to Stephen Crane Career," *Buffalo Evening News,* August 2, 1969: Complains that the last two categories of the contents—"A World of Ironies" and "A World of Miniature" —"seem a little ambiguous and strained." They are, indeed, ridiculous categories coming after "A World of Shipwreck," which is also forced. "Unfortunately, the anthology omits all Spanish-American War materials, especially regrettable because some of Crane's best works appear in his dispatches. . . ."

Knapp, Daniel. "Son of Thunder: Stephen Crane and the Fourth Evangelist," *Nineteenth-Century Fiction,* 24 (December, 1969), 253–291.
   See *American Literature Abstracts,* 3, no. 2 (June, 1970), 115–116.
   "Criticisms of Crane's fiction have suffered from a failure to grasp firmly the importance and the nature of his relationship to New Testament narrative. The narrative structure of 'The Monster' is modelled after the last of the Gospel of John. . . ."

Levenson, J. C. Introduction, *The Works of Stephen Crane,* ed. Fredson Bowers, vol. VII, *Tales of Whilomville:* "The Monster," "His New Mittens," *Whilomville Stories.* Charlottesville, Va., 1969.
   On the identity of Henry Johnson *see* Sidbury (1926), which Levenson ignores.

Moers, Ellen. *Two Dreisers*. New York, 1969.

Monteiro, George. " 'Grand Opera for the People': An Unrecorded Stephen Crane Printing," *Papers of the Bibliographical Society of America*, 63 (First Quarter, 1969), 29–30.

Discovers a reprint of "Grand Opera in New Orleans," in *Public Opinion*, 18 (July 4, 1895), 770, from *Galveston Daily News*, March 25, 1895, p. 4. "A Century of Music."

―――. "The *Illustrated American* and Stephen Crane's Contemporary Reputation," *Serif*, 6, no. 4 (1969), 49–54. Photograph of Crane, 1898, inside front cover, *Serif*.

The *Illustrated American* for June 24, 1898, characterized Crane at Tampa, Florida, as "a quiet, unassuming fellow and well liked by his associates." Monteiro says that this appraisal "offers evidence that qualifies, although it does not necessarily controvert, R. W. Stallman's characterization of Crane in Key West and Tampa as both testy and difficult in his relations with contemporaries—that at the time 'Crane had a chip on his shoulder.' " In *Crane*, p. 356. However, the evidences for my characterization of Crane at this time are the Ernest McCready letters to Stolper (1934). Crane was usually a quiet, unassuming fellow; but he often was arrogant, boastful, indifferent, testy, and difficult. McCready knew Crane intimately, whereas the correspondent interviewing him for the *Illustrated American* did not.

The Herbert P. Williams article, "Mr. Crane as a Literary Artist," in the *Illustrated American*, 20 (July 18, 1896), is not a discovery by Monteiro. It is quoted, and Williams' interview with Crane is discussed, in *Crane*. Not listed in *W-S Bibliography*.

―――. "Stephen Crane's 'Dan Emmonds': A Case Reargued," *Serif*, 6, no. 1 (1969), 32–36.

"Stallman and Miss Gilkes agree that Crane in 'Dan Emmonds' recast what Cora [Crane] told him about *her* near-shipwreck [en route to Constantinople in 1897], and [that] he fused what she reported with what he had himself experienced of shipwreck in the *Commodore* disaster of 1 January 1897." *See* Stallman's argument that "Crane's Sketch of the Fleet Off Crete" was not a journalistic hoax, *SinSF*, 2 (Fall, 1964); Gilkes' "Reply to Mr. Stallman," *ibid.*, pp. 78–80. *See* also Stallman (1972).

Monteiro, then, rightly concludes that there existed a novel *Dan Emmonds*, which was a different work from the manuscript fragment "Dan Emmonds," published by Stallman in *SinSF*, 1 (Fall, 1963), 1–7. Crane wrote brother Edmund from Ireland (September 9, 1897): "Have you noticed an ms devoted to the adventures of a certain Irishman? Try to get it." This is a new letter in *SCraneN*, 1, no. 3 (Spring, 1967), 8, where Joseph Katz suspects that the manuscript is the sketch "Dan Emmonds," not a novel. I had contended that the sketch was an early writing which Crane recast in 1897, and so Katz's conjecture echoes mine of 1963.

Monteiro traces notices in various journals of a forthcoming novel by Crane "to be published in the fall of 1896," titled *Dan Emmonds*. He agrees with Stallman's contention that it has nothing to do with *George's Mother*, *contra* John Berryman (1950).

―――. "Brazilian Translations of Stephen Crane's Fiction," *Stephen Crane Newsletter*, 4, no. 2 (Winter, 1969), 7–8.

———. "Paul Lemperly's *Maggie* (1893), and a New Stephen Crane Letter," *Stephen Crane Newsletter*, 3, no. 3 (Spring, 1969), 7–9.

The Crane inscription in *Letters*, p. 129, was made in a copy of the 1893 *Maggie* originally owned by Paul Lemperly and now owned by C. W. Barrett. Monteiro's article corrects Joseph Katz's Census (Part I) in *SCraneN*, 2, no. 2 (Winter, 1967), 9.

Narveson, Robert. " 'Conceit' in 'The Blue Hotel,' " *Prairie Schooner*, 43, no. 2 (Summer, 1969), 187–191.

O'Donnell, Thomas F. "Hall Caine, R. W. Stallman, and the Kate Lyon Fund," *Frederic Herald*, 2, no. 3 (1969), 4.

Pizer, Donald. "A Primer of Fictional Aesthetics," *College English*, 30 (April, 1969), 572–580.

"Crane chose to tell *The Red Badge* in the third person, with his omniscience almost entirely confined to two units of action and consciousness. . . . Moreover, Crane's use of both Henry and his regiment as 'intelligences' permits him to develop two additional major themes. The first such theme is the psychological dependence of the individual upon the group. Thus, Crane is able to establish that Henry's heroism has its source not in Henry's own belief that he is courageous but in the belief of his regiment that he is. The second such theme arising out of a dual point of view is that of the ironic interplay between individual feeling and group action. . . . In short, the critic who concerns himself with Crane's choice and method of point of view in *The Red Badge* is able to come to grips with the twofold stress of the novel—that its themes concern not only an individual's response to battle (an oft-noted theme) but also (and less obviously) the interdependence of individual and group response. He is able to recognize that *The Red Badge* is both a psychological and a social novel."

This is fine, but not entirely new in that the insight about the two units of action and consciousness with the ironic dual point of view was first made in the *Saturday Review*, 81 (January 11, 1896). It was also made by Joseph Conrad (1923), not noticed by Pizer, Conrad pointing out that *The Red Badge of Courage* treated the relations of the individual to the group and that—to quote Solomon's paraphrase,—"the story belonged as much to the regiment as to the young soldier—a fact that almost no other critic noticed." Solomon, in *Stephen Crane in England* (1964), does not cite here the priority of the *Saturday Review* critic. And Pizer cites neither Solomon, nor Conrad, nor *The Saturday Review*.

The Red Badge of Courage, says Pizer, "can be interpreted as containing two mythic symbolic structures. . . . A second interpretation of mythic structural symbolism in *The Red Badge* is that which posits a Christian myth as the center of the novel. Critics prone to find Christian myth in ostensibly nonreligious works have several defenses of this method. . . . The interpretation of *The Red Badge* as a Christian myth is in somewhat bad odor because its principal proponent has been judged guilty [by Greenfield, 1958] of taking out of context and wrenching the meaning of various images and incidents in order to support his reading." However, that charge of wrenched meaning of incident and image, etc. is a gross distortion. Pizer adds that *The Red Badge of Courage* "is the kind of novel which would appear to lend itself to stylistic analysis. . . . Any such analysis would undoubtedly lead to a study of Crane's stance as an ironic narrator." Some stylistic analysis, however, forms part of "Notes Toward an Analysis of *The Red Badge of Courage*," in *Omnibus*, which reading treated "Crane's stance as an ironic narrator." Again, in "Stephen Crane: A Revaluation," in *Critiques* (also 1952).

Rahv, Philip. *Literature and the Sixth Sense*. New York, 1969, pp. 222–242. Reprinted from *The Myth and the Powerhouse*. New York, 1965. Reprinted from *Kenyon Review* (1956).

Rahv's important essay "Fiction and the Criticism of Fiction" (1956) was replied to by Stallman, "Fiction and Its Critics," *Kenyon Review* (1957) and again in *Houses* (1961). Rahv makes no mention of these rejoinders in the above collections of essays. In *Literature and the Sixth Sense* his attack on Stallman's reading of Crane appears pp. 227–230.

Randall, David A. "Stephen Crane," *Dukedom Large Enough: Reminiscences of a Rare Book Dealer, 1929–1956*. New York, 1969, pp. 220–229.

A sketch of sales and prices obtained for first editions of *Maggie* (1893) and *The Red Badge* manuscripts, with remarks on various Crane collectors. Bacon Collamore, for instance, had pursued Crane for years and had a remarkable collection—"he was way ahead of his time."

Randall says he recently purchased a good unpublished Crane letter for $750, but he does not quote its contents. An unpublished Crane to Paul Reynolds letter is quoted here for the first time. Dated from Ravensbrook, Jan. 27th, 1899, it hangs framed in the office of literary agent Paul Reynolds, Jr., where I saw it two decades ago and mistakenly presumed it had been published in Frederick Lewis Allen, *Paul Revere Reynolds* (1944). Randall discovered that it wasn't in that book. The original still hangs there.

Identifies the source of the manuscript of *The O'Ruddy*—it belongs to Mrs. Donald Klopfer. And discovers that "It is completely in Crane's hand with a few pages by Cora till about a quarter through Chapter XXV. In his work Barr excluded a few of Crane's paragraphs but did nothing else except finish it." Randall scoffs, pp. 228–229, at my error in *Crane* that only a fourth of *The O'Ruddy* is Crane's writing, saying it is an example of "amateur pseudo-scholarship," since Stallman's "opinion [is] based upon I don't know what evidence (none was supplied). . . ." That is not true. My source is cited in *Crane*, p. 560; namely, Robert Barr's claim to Willis Clarke that only a fourth of *The O'Ruddy* was really Crane's.

Not known to me in 1967–1968 was Bernard O'Donnell's *An Analysis of Prose Style . . . The O'Ruddy. . . .*, published in the Hague in 1970.

Nor could I have known that Robert Barr wrote Miss A. E. Trent of Buffalo in 1904: "Here follows the part of 'The O'Ruddy' which I wrote," and that—*contra* Barr's claim to Willis Clark that only a fourth of *The O'Ruddy* was really Crane's—Barr wrote chapters XXVI–XXXIII. This note by Barr appears on the corrected proof sheets of *The O'Ruddy* and is made known in *Stephen Crane 1871–1971: An Exhibition from the Collection of Matthew J. Bruccoli* (1971).

Rathbun, John W. "Structure and Meaning in *The Red Badge of Courage*," *Ball State University Forum*, 10 (Winter, 1969), 8–16.

See Bowen, (1969).

Ridgely, Joseph V. "Stephen Crane," *American Literary Scholarship*, 1967, ed. James Woodress. Durham, N.C., 1969, pp. 145–147.

Rogers, Rodney O. "Stephen Crane and Impressionism," *Nineteenth-Century Fiction*, 24 (December, 1969), 292–304.

"R. W. Stallman goes farthest of all when he calls Crane's style 'prose pointillism' because 'it is composed of disconnected images, which coalesce like blobs of color in French impressionist painting,'* a remark illustrating how easily such a line of argument can be made to finesse the question it proposes to address. For unless Stallman actually means that Crane learned to write a certain way of conceiving literary images as dots of paint, his statement, however thought-provoking, suggests not a causal connection but only an analogy between these two widely divergent art techniques. While such an analysis is helpful to a point, a more meaningful relation of Crane to impressionism would seem to await the admission that painting can exert influences upon writing which do not primarily depend upon the use of similar stylistic techniques by artists working in vastly different art media. I will suggest that Crane's sense of the nature of reality is what most convincingly implies his link with impressionism. If Crane in fact owes anything substantial to the French school, it consists mainly in his having adopted the world view upon which impressionism as a painting style depends. . . .

". . . nevertheless, Crane without doubt was familiar with the work of the French impressionists, and it therefore seems entirely likely that their sense of the physical world at least buttressed and strengthened his own metaphysical notions, whatever their origins. Moreover, though ultimately an attempt to link Crane to impressionist painting can be no more than tentatively conclusive, it would seem to be justified if it helps identify and explain Crane's characteristic techniques for modulating a point of view, since these techniques in large part are responsible for creating the meaning in his fiction."

Santraud, Jeanne-Marie, and Jean Cazemajou. *Stephen Crane: Maggie: A Girl of the Streets,* by Jeanne-Marie Santraud; *The Red Badge of Courage,* by Jean Cazemajou. Presentation by Maurice Gonnaud. Paris: Librairie Armand Colin, 1969.

Schellhorn, G. C. "Stephen Crane's 'The Pace of Youth'" *Arizona Quarterly,* 25 (Winter, 1969), 334–342.

Serif (Kent State University Library Quarterly), 6, no. 4 (December, 1969). Special Issue: Stephen Crane.
    New photograph of Crane from *The Illustrated American.*
    Contains: "Stephen Crane and Willa Cather," by Bernice Slote; "Stephen Crane and Joseph Conrad," by Austin M. Fox; "Stephen Crane and the Harold Frederics," by Lillian B. Gilkes; "*The Illustrated American* and Stephen Crane's Contemporary Reputation," by George Monteiro.

Seyersted, Per, ed. *The Complete Works of Kate Chopin,* vol. 1. Baton Rouge, La., 1969. Foreword by Edmund Wilson, p. 13. Introduction by Per Seyersted, pp. 30, 33.

Seymour-Smith, Martin. *Fallen Women.* London, 1969, pp. 182–185.
    Compares Charles-Louis Phillippe's *Bubu de Montparnesse* with Crane's *Maggie.*
    Reviewed: TLS (London), December 3, 1970, p. 278. "Tumbled Ladies."

Shima, Hideo. "Nature, Love, and Solitude in Stephen Crane's Poems," in *Collected Essays by the Members of the Faculty.* No. 13. Kyoritsu, Japan, 1969, pp. 82–102.

----

* *Omnibus*, p . 185.

Slote, Bernice. " 'San Antonio': A Newly Discovered Stephen Crane Article," *Prairie Schooner*, 43, no. 2 (Summer, 1969), 176–183.

———. "Stephen Crane in Nebraska," *Prairie Schooner*, 43, no. 2 (Summer, 1969), 192–199.

———. "Stephen Crane: Two Uncollected Articles," *Prairie Schooner*, 43 [not 44 as printed] no. 3 (Fall, 1969), 287–296.

Presents here for the first time Crane's "Filibustering," from the *Pittsburgh Leader*, May 2, 1897. Datelined from Jacksonville, Fla., April 28, 1897, although Crane was then covering the Greco-Turkish War in Greece.

Another new Crane find is from the *Pittsburgh Leader*, May 16, 1897, p. 21. It is "The War Correspondents."

———. "Stephen Crane and Willa Cather," *Serif*, 6, no. 4 (1969), 3–15.

Cather's "When I Knew Stephen Crane" was published in the *Library* (Pittsburgh weekly), June 23, 1900, under the pen name "Henry Nicklemann." It was reissued under Cather's name in the *Courier* (Lincoln weekly), July 14, 1900. Reprinted in *Prairie Schooner* (1949) and in Bassan (1967).

Cather's 1900 article, says Slote, "is incorrect if we take it as autobiography." It is essentially true, but the article "needs to be approached with some caution. . . ." Most of the circumstantial facts are wrong "and many of the comments on Crane may be borrowed."

The situation which Slote unriddles here is too complicated to detail in the present redaction of her important article. All in all, it is a very interesting summary of the Crane-Cather relationship; much new material here.

———. "Stephen Crane in the *Nebraska State Journal*, 1894–1896," *Stephen Crane Newsletter*, 3, no. 4 (Summer, 1969), 4–5.

Lists twenty appearances of Crane in *Nebraska State Journal*, many with variant titles.

Slote, Bernice D., ed. "Stephen Crane: *A Portfolio*," *Prairie Schooner*, 43, no. 2 (Summer, 1969), 175–204.

Reprints here for the first time "Patriot Shrine of Texas" from the *Omaha Daily Bee*, January 8, 1899, p. 15. It was reprinted in the *Omaha Weekly Bee*, January 11, 1899, p. 12. It was datelined January 6, from San Antonio; but of course Crane was there in 1895, not in 1899. In the *Pittsburgh Leader*, January 8, 1899, p. 23, its title was "Stephen Crane in Texas."

Reproduces here for the first time "Apaché Crossing," from the manuscript in Columbia University Crane Collection. In *Exhibition* it is listed as "The Grave-Yard of Apaché Crossing." The text is followed by "Note on 'Apaché Crossing,' " by R. W. Stallman.

Contains a biographical sketch of Crane in Havana by Otto Carmichael, in an unsigned article—"Stories About Steve Crane," *Omaha Daily Bee*, June 17, 1900, p. 16. Reprinted in the *Omaha Weekly Bee*, June 20, 1900, p. 11. The Carmichael article is here titled "Stephen Crane in Havana," pp. 200–204. These new data fit in with Stallman's account of Crane in Havana; *see Crane*, p. 418.

Robert Narveson contributes " 'Conceit' in 'The Blue Hotel,' " pp. 187–191. Bernice Slote writes an interesting survey, "Stephen Crane in Nebraska," pp. 192–199.

Stallman, R. W. "Stephen Crane's 'Apaché Crossing.' The Text of an Unfinished Story," *Prairie Schooner*, 43, no. 2 (Summer, 1969), 186.

———. "A Note on the Texts," in *Stephen Crane: The Red Badge of Courage and Other Stories*. With an Introduction by V. S. Pritchett. London and New York. World's Classics (paperback), 1969. First edition, 1960.

Stephen Crane Newsletter, 3, no. 3 (Spring, 1969), 1–12.

Articles include "Stephen Crane in the Pages of *Life* (1896–1901): A Checklist," by E. R. Hagemann; "Corrections of R. W. Stallman's *Stephen Crane: A Biography*," by Lillian Gilkes; "Paul Lemperly's *Maggie* (1893), and a New Stephen Crane Letter," by George Monteiro; and a review of Donald B. Gibson's *The Fiction of Stephen Crane* (1968), by Marston LaFrance. The Editor supplies a note on "An Early Draft of 'Death and the Child' "; "Stephen Crane to an Unknown Recipient: A New Letter"; and a note on an unlocated Crane letter listed in Anderson Galleries Catalog 4194, p. 9, for October 30–31, 1935.

———. 3, no. 4 (Summer, 1969), 1–12.

Includes "Stephen Crane's Middle Name," by Stanley Wertheim; "Stephen Crane in the *Nebraska State Journal*, 1894–1896," by Bernice Slote; and a review by Wertheim of Jean Cazemajou's *Stephen Crane* (pamphlet, 1969). Editor Katz contributes: "An Early Draft of Moonlight on the Snow" (a note), Crane's "Passports Applications: Part III," which item was quoted in *Crane*, p. 604. Here a facsimile copy of passport issued April 23, 1898. Also facsimile copy of new Crane inscription to J. G. Widrig, dated Havana, Nov 24 1898; and facsimile copy of Crane's holograph manuscript of the contents and dedication pages of *The Open Boat and Other Stories*. The usual Quarterly Checklist is, as usual, extraordinarily selective, incomplete, and negligent about reviews of books on *Crane*.

———. 4, no. 1 (Fall, 1969), 1–8.

Contains a new Crane letter from Jacksonville, January 6 (1897), stating to the *Atlanta Journal*, "The ship probably was not scuttled."* Editor Katz also issues "Stephen Crane's Passport Applications: Part IV," in facsimile copy, passport May 19, 1900. Katz says this passport is mentioned in *Crane*, p. 604, "where it is claimed to state that Crane's 'mouth had no moustache.' " Other Crane passports have written in, "*Mouth:* with moustache." This passport

---

* J. C. Levenson, in his scrambled misaccount of my case history of the *Commodore* disaster in *Crane*, wonders "how the accident could have happened at all except by treachery." In his Introduction, *The Works of Stephen Crane: Tales of Adventure*, vol. 5, p. lix, note 49. The answer to Levenson is that Crane himself did not give credence to rumors of treachery, as again given in the new Crane letter to *Atlanta Journal*.

That Levenson's summary of Stallman's account is scrambled is indicated by this sample. Another one is that Levenson says that Stallman "dismisses the cook's mention of five men in the dinghy on the ground that to take that evidence seriously 'impugns Crane as a journalist' " (p. 249). No such statement exists on p. 249 of *Crane*. Who impugns Crane as journalist is John Berryman, not the cook. Levenson replaces Berryman with the cook to spare Berryman. *Crane*, p. 249, says Berryman puts five men in the dinghy. "But such a conjecture cannot be pressed this way without evidence, for it impugns Crane as journalist."

The bias of Levenson blinds him. He praises the Crane Special Issue of *Prairie Schooner* for reprinting (in Fall, 1969) two unrecorded newspaper pieces of Crane, but he omits in his "Preface" to note in *SCraneN*, 4, no. 1 (Fall, 1969), Bernice Slote's newly discovered "San Antonio" and Stallman's "Stephen Crane's 'Apache Crossing.' " Both of these new Crane pieces are more important than the reprints "Filibustering" and "The War Correspondents."

reads: *"Mouth:* ordinary." So, then, it is exactly as stated in *Crane, contra* Katz's implication. Katz fails to notice that this May 19, 1900, passport errs in stating *"Age: 29 years."*

Other items are "John William de Forest on Stephen Crane," from *New York Times Book Section,* December 17, 1898, p. 856, and a new Crane letter to the American Press Association, a single sentence accompanying a manuscript submitted; original in "University Library, MiU," which is the code for Alderman Library, University of Virginia!

There is also in this issue of *SCraneN* a jointly edited article by Katz and Matthew J. Bruccoli: " 'The Wonders of Ponce': Crane's First Puerto Rican Dispatch."

————. 4, no. 2 (Winter, 1969), 1–12.

Corrects the incomplete and inaccurate Crane letter to Miss Daisy D. Hill (March 2, 1896) in *SCraneN,* 2 (Summer, 1968), in "The Letter Recovered," by Elizabeth W. Cady. "Of course your letter appeals to me. It is the expression of a vibratory sensitive young mind reaching out for an ideal. But then I cannot for a moment allow you to assume that I am properly an ideal. Ye Gods! I am clay—very common uninteresting clay. I am a good deal of a rascal, sometimes a bore, often dishonest. . . ."

G. L. Williams, "Henry Fleming and the 'Cheery Voiced Stranger.' " George Monteiro, "Brazilian Translations of Stephen Crane's Fiction."

Stone, Edward. *A Certain Morbidness: A View of American Literature.* Preface by Harry T. Moore. Carbondale, Ill.: 1969.

Crane: "The Blue Hotel," pp. xii–xiii, 53–69; "The Open Boat," pp. 32, 62–63, 84; *The Red Badge of Courage,* pp. 53, 57, 62–63, 67–68, 172; "The Monster," p. 57; "The Men in the Storm," p. 58; *Maggie,* pp. 68, 173; mentioned, pp. xi, 14, 172.

Taylor, Gordon O. *The Passages of Thought.* London, 1969, pp. 4, 16, 109, 111–119, and *passim.*

Tebbel, John. *The Compact History of the American Newspaper.* New York, 1969, pp. 200, 203.

Thomas, Donald S. "Crane's *The Red Badge of Courage,*" *Explicator,* 27 (May, 1969), item 77.

The troops pass the body of a dead soldier, and Henry Fleming stares at the corpse: "the impulse of the living to try to read in dead eyes the answer to the Question." In *Omnibus,* p. 249. Thomas links this Question to *What Must I Do To Be Saved?* by Bishop Jesse Truesdell Peck, Mrs. Crane's uncle.

Wertheim, Stanley. "Stephen Crane's Middle Name," *Stephen Crane Newsletter,* 3, no. 4 (Summer, 1969), 2, 4.

Decides that his middle initial was "T." This agrees with *Crane,* p. 566, where the puzzle of Crane's middle name was first unriddled with "T" for Truesdell, instead of for Townley.

White, W. M. "The Crane-Hemingway Code: A Revaluation," *Ball State University Forum,* 10, no. 2 (1969), 15–20.

Williams, G. L. "Henry Fleming and the Cheery Voiced Stranger," *Stephen Crane Newsletter,* 4, no. 2 (Winter, 1969), 4–7.

Witherington, Paul. "Stephen Crane's 'A Mystery of Heroism': Some Redefini-
tions," *English Journal*, 58 (February, 1969), 201–204, 218.
    See Bowen, (1969).

Wright, Elizabeth, and George Hendrick. [Checklist], *Studies in Short Fiction*,
6 (Summer, 1969), 491–495.

1970

Bewley, Marius. *Masks and Mirrors: Essays in Criticism*. London, 1970, pp.
256–259.
    On the influence of Crane on L. Frank Baum's "The Girl in the Chicken
Coop," in *Ozma of Oz* (1907).

Bowers, Fredson. "The New Look in Editing," *South Atlantic Bulletin*, 35
(1970), 3–10.

Bowers, Fredson, ed. *The Works of Stephen Crane*, vol. V, *Tales of Adventure*.
Introduction by J. C. Levenson. Textual Introduction by Fredson Bowers.
Charlottesville, Va., 1970. Frontispiece, Crane after his rescue from the
sunken *Commodore*.* Photographs: Autograph dedication for *The Open
Boat* and contents list for the English edition (CUCC). Autograph inventory
list, about July, 1897 (CUCC). Includes "The Loss of an Arm," 1500 words,
for *Youth's Companion,* wherein it never appeared. Here is the source for
Bowers' discovery that "An Episode of War" is a Civil War story written
prior to Crane's experiences in the Cuban War. It is included in *Tales of
War,* vol. VI of *The Works of Stephen Crane*. Facsimile reproduction of the
holograph manuscript of "The Five White Mice", page 1, printer's copy
(Huntington). Two early autograph starts at "Moonlight on the Snow"
(CUCC). Typescript of "A Poker Game," prepared by Cora Crane (BCC).
"Death and the Child": unique page of early version dictated to Cora Crane
(CUCC). "The Blue Hotel": unique page (numbered 8) dictated to Cora
Crane (CUCC). Crane in his study at Brede Place, September, 1899 (Roger
Frewen). Crane in 1899 (reproduced from *Napthali*, by C. L. Hind).
    Contents: Foreword, pp. vii–xi; Introduction, J. C. Levenson, pp. xv–
cxxxii. Provides collation of the draft version and final text of "Death and
the Child" and of "The Blue Hotel."† Textual Introduction, by Fredson
Bowers, pp. cxxxiii–cxcv.
    Tales of Adventure: The Pace of Youth, pp. 3–12; One Dash—Horses,
pp. 13–25; The Wise Men, pp. 26–38; The Five White Mice, pp. 39–52; A
Man and Some Others, pp. 53–67; The Open Boat, pp. 68–92; Flanagan and
His Short Filibustering Adventure, pp. 93–108; The Bride Comes to Yellow
Sky, pp. 109–120; Death and the Child, pp. 121–141. [Why is this war story
not in *Tales of War,* vol. VI, where it belongs?] The Blue Hotel, pp.
142–170; Twelve O'Clock, pp. 171–178; Moonlight on the Snow, pp. 179–191;
A Poker Game, pp. 192–194.

    * This photograph was considered too horrible by my editor at Knopf to be used
in *Omnibus* (1952). I discovered it at Yale and deposited copy in the BCC, 1951–52.
    † For commentary on Levenson's Introduction to vol. V, *see* Levenson (1970).

Appendixes, pp. 197–242. These appendixes include Textual Notes, pp. 197–210; Editorial Emendations in the Copy-Text, pp. 211–223; World-Division, pp. 224–225; and Historical Collation, pp. 226–242.

This vol. V, *Tales of Adventure,* is grossly misproportioned in the relation of Crane texts, 191 pages, to editorial commentary of 224 pages, of which Levenson's Introduction consumes 117 pages and Bowers' commentaries consume 107.

——. *The Works of Stephen Crane,* vol. VI, *Tales of War: The Little Regiment, "An Episode of War," Wounds in the Rain, "Spitzbergen Tales."* Introduction by James B. Colvert. Charlottesville, Va., 1970. Frontispiece, photograph of Crane at Brede Place, 1899.

Contents: Foreword, pp. vii–viii; Introduction, James B. Colvert, pp. xi–xxxvi. Photocopies pp. xxxii ff. Autograph inventory for *Wounds in the Rain;* p. 9 of an early draft of "The Little Regiment"; typescript, p. 1, " 'And If He Wills, We Must Die' " a manuscript page of "The Kicking Twelfth" in Edith Richie's hand; a manuscript page of "The Shrapnel of Their Friends" in an unknown hand; first page of a typescript of "The Upturned Face." Photograph of Crane on *The Three Friends* off Cuba, and a new photograph of Crane and others on board ship for Puerto Rico, 1898.

Textual Introduction, by Fredson Bowers, pp. xxxvii–cxci. Bowers establishes the identity of "An Episode of War" as a Civil War story written possibly in late 1896 or not later than early 1897, for it is listed in Crane's inventory for 1897 (spring?) titled "The Loss of an Arm." This is, of course, an important find.

Notes that Crane hoped to get "The Upturned Face" dramatized, a point which I first pinpointed in *Letters* (1960). Contends that Crane's letter to Reynolds about a "personal anecdote thing" has to do with "Marines Signaling Under Fire," rather than with "This Majestic Lie," as given in *Crane* (1968), p. 525.

The Little Regiment: The Little Regiment, pp. 3–21; Three Miraculous Soldiers, pp. 22–47; A Mystery of Heroism: A Detail of an American Battle, pp. 48–56; An Indiana Campaign, pp. 57–66; A Grey Sleeve, pp. 67–81; The Veteran, pp. 82–86.

An Episode of War, pp. 89–93.

Wounds in the Rain: The Price of the Harness, pp. 97–113; The Lone Charge of William B. Perkins, pp. 114–118; The Clan of No-Name, pp. 119–136; "God Rest Ye, Merry Gentlemen," pp. 137–154; The Revenge of the *Adolphus,* pp. 155–171; The Serjeant's Private Mad-House, pp. 172–179; Virtue in War, pp. 180–193; Marines Signaling Under Fire at Guantánamo, pp. 194–200; This Majestic Lie, pp. 201–221; War Memories, pp. 222–263; The Second Generation, pp. 264–284.

Spitzbergen Tales: The Kicking Twelfth, pp. 287–296; The Upturned Face, pp. 297–300; The Shrapnel of Their Friends, pp. 301–306; "And If He Wills, We Must Die," pp. 307–312.

Appendixes, pp. 315–400. Addendum, p. 401.

Tales of War collects all of Crane's short stories dealing with war except "Death and the Child," which is in *Tales of Adventure,* vol. V.

Bruccoli, Matthew J. "Robert Barr's Proofs of *The O'Ruddy," Stephen Crane Newsletter,* 4, no. 3 (Spring, 1970), 8–9.

———. "An Unrecorded Parody of Stephen Crane," *Stephen Crane Newsletter*, 4, no. 4 (Summer, 1970), 7.

Burns, Landon C. A Cross-Referenced Index of Short Fiction and Author-Title Listing. *Studies in Short Fiction*, 7, no. 1 (Winter, 1970), 1–218.
For anthologies reprinting Stephen Crane stories *see* pp. 143–144.

Casey, Alfredo, trans. [Poems of Stephen Crane], in *Dos siglos de poesia norte-americana,* ed. Alfredo Casey. Buenos Aires, Brazil: Ediciones Antonio Zamora, 1970.

Colvert, James B. Introduction, *The Works of Stephen Crane,* ed. Fredson Bowers. Vol. VI, *Tales of War: The Little Regiment, "An Episode of War," Wounds in the Rain, "Spitzbergen Tales."* Charlottesville, Va., 1970.

Conrad, Borys. *My Father: Joseph Conrad.* London, 1970, p. 31.

Curtin, William M., ed. *The World and the Parish: Willa Cather's Articles and Reviews, 1893–1902.* Lincoln, Nebr., 1970, pp. 585, 587, 700–702, 771, 778.

Dameron, J. Lasley. "Symbolism in the Poetry of Poe and Stephen Crane," in "Poe Symposium," ed. Richard P. Benton, *Emerson Society Quarterly,* 60 (1970), 22–28.

Edelstein, Arthur. Introduction, *Three Great Novels by Stephen Crane: Maggie, George's Mother, The Red Badge of Courage.* Greenwich, Conn., 1970.

Frohock, W. M. *"The Red Badge* and the Limits of Parody," *Southern Review,* n.s., 6 (January, 1970), 137–148.
A study of Crane's language in *The Red Badge of Courage;* parody doesn't account for Crane's achievement here. *See* Solomon (1966).

Fulwiler, Toby. "The Death of the Handsome Sailor: A Study of *Billy Budd* and *The Red Badge of Courage,*" *Arizona Quarterly.* 26 (Summer, 1970), 101–112.

Garraty, John A. "A Century of American Realism [an interview with Alfred Kazan]." *American Heritage,* 21 (June, 1970), 12–15, 86–90. *See* pp. 14, 87, and 90.

Gilkes, Lillian. "Stephen Crane's Burial Place: Some Inconsequential Ghost Laying," *Serif* (Kent State University Libraries), 7, no. 2 (June, 1970).
On Crane's burial place in Evergreen Cemetery. Questions the statement "Hillside stands separate, and has never been Elizabeth" (New Jersey). *See* [Anon.], "Misplaced Writer" (1936); Decker, "A Bibliography of the Stephen Crane Collection in the Free Public Library, Newark, N.J." (1956); and *Crane.*

Gullason, Thomas A. "To Readers of the *CEA Critic* and to Mr. Stallman." *CEA Critic* 32 (June, 1970), 12–13.
A reply to Stallman's reply to Gullason's review of *Stephen Crane: A Biography. See* Stallman, "Stallman's *Crane*" (1970).

Itabashi, Yoshie. "A Landscape of Complicity: A Study of *Whilomville Stories,*" *The Tsuda Review,* 15 (November, 1970), 37–70.

Jordan, Philip D. Introduction, *Maggie: A Girl of the Streets (A Story of New York).* Lexington, 1970.

Katz, Joseph, ed. *Stephen Crane in the West and Mexico.* Kent, Ohio, 1970.
Pen-portrait of Crane by C. K. Linson.

LaFrance, Marston. "Crane, Zola, and the Hot Ploughshares," *English Language Notes,* 7 (June, 1970), 285–287.

Leary, Lewis. *Articles on American Literature: 1950–1967.* Durham, N.C., 1970.

Levenson, J. C. Introduction, *The Works of Stephen Crane,* ed. Fredson Bowers. Vol. V, *Tales of Adventure.* Charlottesville, Va., 1970.

On the *Commodore* disaster Levenson says that "Stallman seems to have established that the number of men in the dinghy was four." By not mentioning that John Berryman in his *Stephen Crane* (1950) conjectured that there must have been five men in the dinghy, Levenson is silently protecting Berryman. He was the butt of my inquiry, the significance of which is rather lost when in Levenson's report no mention is made as to what provoked my investigation. For twenty years no Crane scholar doubted Berryman's conjectured fifth man in the dinghy.

The sole aim of my investigation was to see if it were possible to exonerate Crane from being impugned as journalist, for Berryman's conjecture impugned Crane. Levenson does not cite my evidence, namely the log of the *Boutwell* (number of passengers: 27), nor the evidence that the seas were indeed rough, namely the log of the *Newark.* He says "Stallman seems to have established that the number of men in the dinghy was four, that the seas were indeed rough, and even that there was no treachery involved in the sinking." However, Levenson retracks on this last item, saying that he wonders "how the accident could have happened at all except by treachery." The answer is simply that the ship had twice struck a sand bar in going out to sea and sprung a leak. That being the situation, there was no occasion for treachery.

Stallman "dismisses the cook's mention of five men in the dinghy on the ground that to take that evidence seriously 'impugns Crane as a journalist'" (p. 249). However, Levenson has mangled carelessly or deliberately what is said in *Crane,* p. 249, wherein I quote Berryman's conjecture about the five men in the dinghy and conclude that "such a conjecture cannot be pressed this way without evidence, for it impugns Crane as journalist." The charge of impugning journalist Crane attaches to Berryman, solely to him and not at all to the cook's notion of five men in the dinghy—an impossibility put into the cook's mouth by the newspaper man interviewing him. Levenson's account, p. lix, gives the impression that my evidence is solely the newspaper accounts, which is not true. Because they contradict each other, they are unreliable and must be collated with other evidence where that is available. Levenson says that "the basic documents of the episode are reprinted in *Stephen Crane: An Omnibus,* ed. Robert Wooster Stallman (New York, 1958)," but he is careless about the date of *Omnibus* (1952) and mistaken that the *Omnibus* reprintings of *New York Press* and *Florida Times-Union* accounts of the *Commodore* disaster constitute "the basic documents of the episode." These six dispatches and "Stephen Crane's Own Story" represent but a fraction of the total coverage of the episode in that there are more than three dozen newspaper accounts, of which Berryman knew but one or two accounts only. Had he probed the situation he might not have made the conjecture of five men in the dinghy, for some newspapers stated that there were 27 persons aboard the *Commodore,* which would put properly only four men in the dinghy.

As for the cook's claim that there were "heart-rendering cries," whereas Crane claimed that there were "no shrieks, no groans," but only silence when the ship sank, Levenson conjectures that "apparently Crane and the captain refer to the men from the foundered lifeboat who stayed on board the *Commodore* as she sank, and the cook refers to the men who tried the rafts and foundered a second time." However, Levenson's observation is not a newly discovered fact. In *Crane*, p. 251, I make the same point: "In conflict with Crane's report, there may be reason to believe Montgomery's report not of silence, but of 'heart-rendering cries'—*uttered by the raft survivors perhaps.*"

Link, Franz H. "Stephen Crane," in *Stilanalysen amerikanischer Erzählkunst: Eine Einführung mit Übungen* [Stylistic Analyses of American Narrative Art: An Introduction with Exercises]. Frankfurt and Bonn: Athenäum Verlag, 1970, pp. 86–94.

Lynn, Kenneth S. *William Dean Howells: An American Life.* New York, 1970, pp. 38, 58, 140, 163, 203, 311–313, 314, 315.

Miller, E. E. "Trilogy of Irony: Analysis of *War Is Kind,*" *English Journal,* 54 (January, 1970), 59–62.

Miller, Wayne Charles. *An Armed America: Its Face in Fiction: A History of the American Military Novel.* New York, 1970, pp. 10, 54, 57, 58, 60, 70–81, 85, 88, 90*n*, 91*n*, 95, 96, 98, 100, 101, 107, 109, 125, 143, 144, 209.
An interesting and useful book.

Monteiro, George. "With Proper Words (or Without Them) the Soldier Dies: Stephen Crane's 'Making an Orator'," *Cithara,* 9, no. 2 (May, 1970), 64–72.

———. "Cora Crane to John Hay: A Last Communication," *Stephen Crane Newsletter,* 4, no. 3 (Spring, 1970), 8.

———. "Stephen Crane and John Hay: Two Notes," *Stephen Crane Newsletter,* 4, no. 4 (Summer, 1970), 5–6.

Noel, Edgar E. "Stephen Crane: A Realist Who Painted with Words," *Kyushu American Literature* (Fukuoka, Japan), 12 (1970), 20–31.

O'Donnell, Bernard. *An Analysis of Prose Style to Determine Authorship: The O'Ruddy, a Novel by Stephen Crane and Robert Barr.* The Hague: Mouton, Holland, 1970. (Studies in General and Comparative Literature, no. 4.)

Perkins, George, ed. *The Theory of the American Novel.* New York, 1970, pp. xvii, 229–230, 231–233, 234–236, 314.

Reed, Kenneth T. " 'The Open Boat' and Dante's *Inferno:* Some Undiscovered Analogies," *Stephen Crane Newsletter,* 4, no. 4 (Summer, 1970), 1–3.

Ridgely, Joseph. "Stephen Crane," in *American Literary Scholarship: An Annual, 1968,* ed. J. Albert Robbins. Durham, N.C., 1970, pp. 152–155.
"Partisanship and acrimony continue to writhe around studies of Stephen Crane. An unmatched example came with the publication of R. W. Stallman's *Stephen Crane: A Biography* (New York, George Braziller). A big book (664 pages, including appendixes, notes, checklist and index) and the culmination of many years of research, the biography was generally well received in the nonacademic press. Carlos Baker, for example, in a notice in the *New York Times Book Review* (11 August), asserts that 'this life story probably comes as close to being the definitive biography as we are likely to get.' Moreover, 'If the central test of a biography is to re-create a vanished personality, Mr. Stallman has admirably succeeded.' "

Both these judgments were anathema to Matthew Bruccoli and Lillian Gilkes in *SCraneN* (3, no. 2, 9–10, and 3, no. 3, 6–7). Even more sweeping condemnation came from Joseph Katz (*AL*, 40, 1969), Ridgely reports.

Ridgely says that because *Crane* "is likely to remain a standard reference work for some time, a consensus of reaction by its critics so far is useful." However, no such consensus of reviewers exists in his account. Nor is there any evidence in his account that he has even read a representative sampling of the reviews. Nor even that he has noticed the Book Review Consensus by Daniel R. Buerger in *American Literature Abstracts*, 2 (June, 1969), 335–337, wherein *Crane* obtains a fair consensus. Ridgely's is limited to four reviews out of more than eighty across the country. All four are by academic scholars. Ridgely quotes Carlos Baker as his sample of the "nonacademic press," which error indicates his ignorance. Baker is at Princeton, and Gilkes was once upon a time teaching at Columbia. Thus, not a single nonacademic reviewer is represented in Ridgely's "consensus." Because *Crane* differs radically from Gilkes' *Cora Crane* on crucial as well as on minor issues, our differences should have disqualified her as a reviewer of *Crane*. And for that reason I made no attempt to review her *Cora Crane*.

Ridgely quotes Matthew Bruccoli's notion that *Crane* is "carelessly documented." That is a gross misrepresentation. *Crane* is incompletely documented, but not "carelessly." It is incompletely documented by the omission of the detailed checklist of my sources which was expunged shortly before galleys on *Crane*. To salvage the situation, I then had to compose the Notes (61 pages), which I managed to compose during a period of ill health under time pressures for deadline. However, *Crane* contains 101 pages of documentation (61 pages of Notes, 16 pages of Checklist, and 24 pages of Appendix.), and no trade edition could likely tolerate more documentation. John Unterecker's *Hart Crane* (1969) is devoid of any bibliography, but no reviewer has mentioned that Missing All.

Contra Bruccoli, Katz, and Gilkes, my sources—except for minor things—are identified, as noticed by Arlin Turner in his review in *Virginia Quarterly Review*, 44 (Autumn, 1968). He complains, however, that the reader is not always sure "whether phrases and sentences quoted in the biographer's narrative are from Beer or some other, or from a letter, a newspaper report, or a fictional account by Crane." The expunged checklist would have supplied precisely such data for identification of every quoted phrase, but only a university press would publish such a book.

Ridgely says of *Stephen Crane: Sullivan County Tales and Sketches* that "there are misstatements in the claims as to which scholar first printed what where," but no such misstatement is made in *SCT&S*. See Stallman (1970).

For this and other reasons Ridgely calls the book "marred." Ridgely is quite as much biased against fair play in his so-called consensus on *Crane* as the three scholars he cites for reviewers representing the opposition to *Crane*. Ridgely cannot bring himself to admit that there are new things in *Crane*, where the Notes have the recurrent refrain "here for the first time." When did Crane first meet Elbert Hubbard? Or first meet Mark Twain? No biographies of Twain or of Hubbard answer that question. How many men were in the dinghy? How did Crane get to the Greco-Turko warfront? In his Cuban War stories Crane disguised the exact location of battle or skirmish; they are identified in *Crane*. "I admire the narrative style and the easy flow of the action. To read Stallman's chapters on the Cuban War simultaneously with *Wounds in the Rain* is an exciting experience," says Fredson Bowers. Katz, quoted by Ridgely, says of *Crane:* "Untrustworthy as a source of information, this book is no more reliable for its criticism." However, Lewis Leary (Univ. North Carolina) says: "Stallman has certainly done the job, for there is not another book on Crane which touches his, either as biography or as criticism." On Crane and the dinghy, that chapter is "splendid, definitive," says Thomas F. O'Donnell (Utica College). "The most complete and dependable biography of Crane. . . . His book is built on facts carefully gathered and put together. . . . It does what no other biography has done; it makes Crane out to be a man as well as an artist." "The chapters on Crane's life in England are among the most interesting in the book," said Dorothy Tyler in the *Detroit News.* (The quotations from Bowers, Leary, and O'Donnell, together with other appraisals from *Wall Street Journal, London Times Literary Supplement, New Republic,* etc., appeared in an ad sheet in *American Literature* for May, 1969. Ridgely deliberately ignored them.)

I conclude that Ridgely by his superiority complex of disdain for the labors of scholars and critics of Crane, whereas he himself has published not as much as a footnote on Crane, only seemingly deplores "partisanship and acrimony." For he adds to the acrimony writhing around studies of Crane by his partisan and lopsided "consensus" of Crane scholarship for 1968.

Sadler, Elva Elizabeth "Stephen Crane, 1871–1900: Forerunner of the Modern Literary Movement," *English Teaching Forum,* 8 (January–February, 1970), 11–15.

Sharma, D. R. "War and the Individual Man in *The Red Badge of Courage,*" *Literary Criticism,* 9 (Summer, 1970), 56–64.

Sherry, Norman. "A Conrad Manuscript," *Times Literary Supplement,* June 25, 1970, p. 691.

An unknown MS. dated February 12, 1898, in Conrad's handwriting and signed by him, suggests that "as late as 1898 his grasp of the English language was not entirely certain."

Recounts Conrad's meeting with Crane when Sidney Pawling of Heinemann took them to lunch in October, 1897. Quotes Conrad to Crane letters in *Letters,* pp. 155, 167, 175–176, and Conrad's Introduction to Beer's *Crane.* Conrad wrote his siege of Paris notes, which comprise this new Conrad MS., shortly before he took his family to Ravensbrook to stay with the Cranes. " 'I shall bring a lot of paper and you shall find a pen. I am anxious to know what you have done with your idea for a play. A play to write is no play.' (Stallman and Gilkes, pp. 175–176)." Conrad perhaps took with him to Ravensbrook not only paper but his siege of Paris notes "in the hope that they might collaborate on a novel centred round this subject."

Stallman, R. W. "Stallman's *Crane,*" *CEA Critic,* 32 (June, 1970), 11–12. With a reply by Thomas A. Gullason: "To Readers of the *CEA Critic* and to Mr. Stallman," pp. 12–13.

"In *CEA Critic,* 31 (May, 1969) Thomas A. Gullason damns my *Stephen Crane: A Biography* for having 'shirked the basic research tasks expected of any serious biographer' and for 'Stallman's appropriation of the work of other Crane scholars without giving them due right.'

"1. Stallman 'mentions that Crane lifted passages from his grandfather's *Wyoming* for his own fiction and points to Mrs. Crane's art work in her father's volume, but fails to note that these facts were first pointed out by

Mr. Hans Arnold and myself.' However, my source is Helen Crane, 'In New Jersey,' Newark *Star-Eagle,* July 8, 1926. This article, one of two by Helen Crane in *Star-Eagle,* mentions the 'history of the Wyoming valley in Pennsylvania and recounts the wars of the early settlers with the Indians. It is graphically illustrated. . . .' Ironically, in *The Complete Novels of Stephen Crane,* p. 16, Gullason fails to cite the Helen Crane article, which scooped Gullason by forty years.

"2. Gullason wants to be given credit for having noticed that Mrs. Helen Peck Crane was 'national vice-president of the W. C. T. U.' He claims that my source was 'obviously drawn from' Gullason's *The Complete Novels* (1967). However, my source was again this same Helen Crane's Newark *Star-Eagle* article.

"3. 'Before entering Claverack, Stephen had spent the previous fall semester at Pennington Seminary,' says *Stephen Crane,* which provides in supplementary Notes, p. 566, that Stephen attended Pennington from September 1885 to December 1887. 'Characteristically,' says Gullason, 'Stallman does not quote his source for this information, which may be found along with a good deal more of biographical value in an extensive essay on Crane's life at Pennington.' However, I do quote my source; it is not Gullason. It is not Gullason because I couldn't possibly have read Gullason's 'The Cranes at Pennington,' *American Literature* for January 1968 because by then both *Stephen Crane: A Biography* and *The Sullivan County Tales and Sketches* were in pageproof. Neither in his *American Literature* article nor in his *CEA Critic* nitpicking review of both books does Gullason mention Jean Cazemajou's 'Stephen Crane: Pennington Seminary,' *Études Anglaises* for April-June 1967. I quote this for my source on Crane at Pennington in *Stephen Crane,* p. 569.

"4. In my *Sullivan County Tales and Sketches* I say that Willis Fletcher Johnson had been a student at Pennington Seminary, whereas in my *Stephen Crane* I say simply that he was a friend of the Crane family. As for the former fact, Gullason complains that 'Stallman now adds this information and he does not give credit to someone else's recent discovery.' By which Gullason means Gullason. I must disappoint him once more, for here again my source is Cazemajou (1967), an article not known to Gullason's boasted 'basic research.'

"5. It is impossible for any Crane scholar to misdate Mrs. Crane's death because John Berryman in his *Stephen Crane* (1950) made it a rather crucial point in his Freudian reading that Crane began *Maggie* just after his mother's death on December 7, 1891. He was mistaken, and so is Gullason, who says that Stallman's *Stephen Crane* has it that Mrs. Crane 'died in 1899.' That is not true. My copy of *Stephen Crane,* p. 44, says that she died on December 7, 1891.

"6. I find nothing 'ludicrous' about 'Stallman's obsessive scouring for the "correct" facts,' which to Gullason 'borders on the ludicrous, as when he chides Crane himself for having mistaken a gelding for a mare. . . .' However, I do not 'chide' Crane; I simply say 'Crane was mistaken; it was a gelding and a mustang' (p. 199). However, had I not corrected Crane, Gullason would now be correcting me. Gullason wants it both ways.

"7. Gullason damns the book for not including more and more scholarship facts, notably Gullason's facts, and yet he also complains that the book is too bulky. 'Such negligence is unfortunate, yet even more so is Stallman's failure to use, wisely and properly, much available Crane scholarship which would have benefited his research.' However, 'such negligence' is 'unfortunate' for Gullason but not for *Stephen Crane,* which utilizes nothing of Gullason's research and nowhere mentions him. 'But poor Crane suffers . . . from the self-laudatory padding with which Stallman carries over into this volume materials shoveled wholesale out of his earlier *Stephen Crane: An Omnibus* (1952) and *The Houses That James Built* (1961).' However, this spared me from shoveling into my Crane biography all subsequent Crane critical studies, including Gullason's, whose critical insights are too negligible to mention. If you say it's like eating my own heart, I reply in Crane's words: "But I like it / Because it is bitter, / And because it is my heart.'

"8. 'When Stallman says that "Hunting is warfare too," he acts as though he is the first to notice this' in the *Sullivan County Tales and Sketches.* Well, the first person to perceive this theme in the sketches was not Gullason, but rather my research assistant, Miss Kelly Flynn, who spotted it before I had read the new sketches and while she was researching the microfilm of the 1892 *Tribune.* That was in November 1966.

"In November 1967 *American Literature,* I published Crane's 'The Last of the Mohicans.' In January 1968 Gullason published in *Southern Humanities Review* that same sketch *without acknowledgement of Stallman's prior publication.* Sometime in late 1968 Gullason complained to the Director of my publishing house that I had compiled *The Sullivan County Tales and Sketches* from Gullason's discoveries of them in *SHR.* The answer to this outrageous charge is that my *SCT&S* was already in pageproof by January and in book-form by May 1968,* although not issued until October. Secondly, one of the Sullivan County pieces discovered by Gullason (but not by my research assistant, alas) forecasts *The Red Badge of Courage,* says Gullason in his *CEA Critic* onslaught, saying it was published in *Southern Humanities Review,* of 'which Stallman knows nothing about. . . .' Unwittingly, he is quite right. I knew nothing about that most obscure journal, and neither did the bibliographer for the 1968 *P.M.L.A.;* nor was Gullason's article of Sullivan County discoveries listed in *P.M.L.A. Bibliography* until June, 1969. In sum, it was impossible for me to know about a journal that was not known to exist.

"9. 'A chief weakness of the book is its pretentiousness. . . . Similarly, the pretense that he is proving for the first time that Crane wrote "Travels in New York: The Broken-Down Van" will delight many scholars who have for years accepted this piece as Crane's work.' Here again Gullason perverts my obvious intention, which is to state simply: 'Although it is unsigned, it is unmistakably a city version of the same kind of sketch from life that Crane was writing at Asbury Park and Ocean Grove.' The note carries on, p. 570, the stylistic ways it links with the Asbury Park sketches. 'It is identifiable by the same stylistic characteristics: ingredients of color adjectives or of Hawthornesque chiaroscuro; contrast, and the "musical device" of a reiterated leitmotif or a phrase repeated in variant versions.' It is simply a Note about Crane's style bearing his signature even in this unsigned New York City sketch, and as such I do not think other scholars will warm to Gullason's implied charge that I pretend to have discovered 'The Broken-Down Van.' And why should *that* 'delight many scholars'? Gullason's charge is absurd. I couldn't possibly make any such pretended claim since 'The Broken Down Van' is listed in the Williams-Starrett *Bibliography!*

* Furthermore, my Introduction to *SCT&S* is dated "27 September 1967," which is proof of priority and of the untruth of Gullason's charges.

"10. 'Shoddier scholarship than this, however, is evident in Stallman's appropriation of the work of other Crane scholars without giving them due credit. His excuse that he has no room to include a complete checklist of writings on Crane has a hollow ring, for it is inexcusable to use materials discovered by others without giving appropriate documentation over and above a general "acknowledgement" given to sources to which one is "obligated."' I reply that my annotated checklist of writings on Crane was expunged just before galley time by Braziller's Editor-in-Chief because it would swamp the book, already bulky by extensive bibliographical materials (Appendix, Notes, and Checklist), which amounted when printed to 104 printed pages. Enough! However, all my main sources are cited in the text, in the Appendix, Notes, and Checklist of Writings on Stephen Crane, pp. 633–641, wherein I declare it impossible to specify every source or to provide a complete checklist since the more than 2,000 articles on Crane require a book in itself. I then referred the reader to this *Stephen Crane: A Critical Bibliography* (Iowa State University Press, 1972). By editorial decree, I had no other choice; so I followed the device of Barbara Tuchman in *The Guns of August*. Unterecker's *Hart Crane* (1969) has no bibliography whatsoever; the biographer asks his readers to write for a mimeographed copy of his unpublished checklist!

"11. Stallman, says Gullason, 'never mentions Eric Solomon's *Stephen Crane in England* (1964), which any biographer must confront.' However, one confronts here no new materials since *Stephen Crane: Letters* (1960), excepting new book reviews. Even the source materials Solomon cites he has exploited scarcely at all; *that* missing all was a fortunate thing for my *Stephen Crane,* which presents anew Crane's English years with Harold Frederic, Edward Garnett, H. G. Wells, Ford M. Hueffer, Henry James, and Conrad. As I utilized nothing in Solomon's book, I felt no obligation to mention it. Gullason complains that I do not state 'that the majority of the Asbury Park dispatches he uses and then compiles at the end of his volume were discovered by Mr. Elconin.' However, it would clutter the text to cite Elconin for every Asbury Park sketch Elconin discovered, and there are a great many he did not discover. My acknowledgement to Elconin is ample: 'Indispensable is Victor Elconin's 'Stephen Crane at Asbury Park,' *American Literature* (November, 1938).'

"Untruths abound in Gullason's vicious *CEA Critic* review, but limitations of space here make it impossible for me to engage Gullason point by point."

Gullason in his reply refuses to admit that my data for Willis Johnson at Pennington exists in the Cazemajou study, *Études Anglaises* (1967), which I cited in *Crane*. (Cazemajou, not Gullason, was my source for item no. 3.) As for no. 1, Gullason says my claimed source—Helen Crane in *Newark Star Eagle* —does not say that Crane lifted passages from his grandfather's *Wyoming*. Of course Helen Crane did not say that, but it is obvious that Crane did utilize *Wyoming* by simply collating the texts. "Any experienced Crane scholar would quickly note that Helen Crane is not a reliable source of information," says Gullason. However, she *is* reliable for the facts which I utilized from her memoirs.

Gullason on no. 5: "Stallman says it is 'impossible' for any Crane scholar to misdate Mrs. Crane's death. Mr. Stallman has achieved the impossible. On p. 565 of his biography, Stallman says: 'She [Mrs. Crane] spoke probably for the last time in July, 1899. . . .' " However, Gullason deliberately misconstrues this to mean that she died then, whereas it means what it says, note 14, p. 565: "She spoke probably for the last time in July, 1899, at the New Jersey, W.C.T.U. meeting at Ocean Grove, reading a paper there on 'Press Work.' " Furthermore she could not have died in 1899 when it is given in *Crane*, p. 44, that Mrs. Crane died "in December 7, 1891." Nor could she have lectured in 1899 when she died in 1891. Gullason refuses to admit that *Crane* says she died in 1891, both in his *CEA Critic* attack and again in his rebuttal. The date 1899 is obviously a misprint for 1889. This may have been a solecism but Gullason's comment is seemingly nonetheless a deliberate perversion of facts.

Gullason on no. 6 complains that "Stallman should have concerned himself with more important factual matters" than the fact that Crane's horse was a gelding-mare. However, he also complains that *Crane* is too bulky "with extraneous material." However, I took the stand that the mind of Crane is evoked through what he wrote and what he said; *that* is where Crane lives as much as in his life events, about which he mostly said nothing. What Gullason calls extraneous material strikes me as vital.

Stephen Crane Newsletter, 4, 3 (Spring, 1970), 1–12.

Contains articles by the editor, including "Crane's Chapter Headings for *The O'Ruddy*," with facsimile copy of the manuscript in CUCC, which is oddly designated by Katz NNC for Columbia University Crane Collection. Also, "Stephen Crane in *The Fly Leaf*"; *The Red Badge of Courage:* A Preliminary History of the Appleton Printings; "*The Lanthorn Book:* A Census (Part I)"; also, "Elbert Hubbard's Watermark." Points out that the watermarked stationery that Elbert Hubbard used was not used until some years after the Philistine banquet correspondence; however, my information came from Elbert Hubbard II, who supplied me the sample. It is on goldenrod stationery and the watermark also appears colored, although Katz no doubt is correct in saying that the watermark is not colored. The watermark drawing of Hubbard is in the upper quarter of the sheet, and—*contra* Katz—it is "large as half the sheet," as claimed in *Crane*, p. 161. It is approximately as long as one-half a sheet in the reproduced sample in *SCraneN*, p. 10, and in the context of my paragraph in *Crane*, p. 161, what is implied is that Hubbard's ego (to quote Katz) "was as large as the watermark" of his own likeness. Precisely so, and that is why it is appropriate to mention it in any biography of Crane's relationship with Hubbard, an egocentric ass. Katz arbitrarily rules that its mention has no place in a biography of Crane, to which I respond with a Katzian word—"bunk." Apart from the watermarked stationery, Hubbard sent Crane a photograph of himself, "which Crane did not need for identifying the editor of *The Philistine*, since they had already met in New York." That statement is the important thing; when did Crane first meet Hubbard?

Contains articles by Richard M. Weatherford, "Stephen Crane in *The Lotus* and *Chips*"; and by George Monteiro; and "Robert Barr's Proofs of *The O'Ruddy*," by Matthew J. Bruccoli.

———. 4, no. 4 (Summer, 1970), 1–12.

Articles include " 'The Open Boat' and Dante's *Inferno*," by Kenneth T. Reed; "A Manuscript of 'Black Riders Came From the Sea,' " by Richard M. Weatherford; "Stephen Crane and John Hay: Two Notes," by George Monteiro; "An Unrecorded Parody of Stephen Crane," by Matthew J. Bruccoli; and several articles by the editor, Joseph Katz, including "Crane's Interview with William Dean Howells." Contains a list of some persons invited to the Philistine banquet, and two letters by Elbert Hubbard on that affair, and other trivia, issued by Katz. Also a clipping from the *Sacramento Record Union* for September 16, 1900, on *War Is Kind* from Cora Crane's clipping scrapbook.

Thoth, "A Bibliography of Stephen Crane Scholarship: 1893–1969," ed. Robert Hudspeth and others, *Thoth* 11 (Fall, 1970). Special Supplement.
    See Forster for *Thoth,* 10 (1969) and Dennis for *Thoth,* 11 (1971).
    Collate *Thoth's* entries with *Stephen Crane: A Critical Bibliography* for additions, especially under obituaries and reviews of individual works of fiction. *Thoth* lists, for instance, a review of *Active Service* in *Bookman,* 17 (December, 1899), 89, which is not here included in Part D, Contemporary Reviews and Parodies. However, the *Thoth* checklists require rechecking.

Vickery, Olga W. "The Inferno of the Moderns," in *The Shaken Realist: Essays in Modern Literature in Honor of Frederick J. Hoffman,* eds. Melvin J. Friedman and John B. Vickery. Baton Rouge, La., 1970, pp. 147–164.

Walker, Warren S. *Twentieth-Century Short Story Explication.* Hamden, Conn., 1970.

Weatherford, Richard M. "A Manuscript of 'Black Riders Came from the Sea,'" *Stephen Crane Newsletter,* 4, no. 4 (Summer, 1970), 3–4.
    Facsimile reproduction of the manuscript, dated March 19, 1896, signed. In Special Collections, CLU.* (University of California, Los Angeles.)

———. "Stephen Crane in the *Lotus* and *Chips,*" *Stephen Crane Newsletter,* 4, no. 3 (Spring, 1970), 2–3.
    A checklist of writings on Crane in *Lotus* (Kansas City, Mo.), 1896–1897. The list is not quite complete. Writings are briefly commented upon, not quoted. They are amply quoted, most of them, in this work, Parts D and F. Prior to Weatherford's 1970 checklist, they were discovered many years ago by R. W. S. and were incorporated into the manuscript before *SCraneN* appeared.
    Editor Katz appends "Stephen Crane in *The Fly Leaf,*" pp. 3–4. Katz looks into *Fly Leaf* and tells us that it survived five months, 1895–1896, and then in the next sentence illogically adds that *Fly Leaf* "did not fold; it was the victim of some odd deal between its editor, Walter Blackburn Harte, and Elbert Hubbard. What really happened is obscure." However, *contra* Katz, the little *Fly Leaf* folded fast, obviously so—in five months! For clarification of this "obscure" story about Hubbard and Harte, *see* Daly (1916), here published for the first time.

Wertheim, Stanley, ed. *The Merrill Studies in Maggie and George's Mother.* Columbus, Ohio, 1970. Introduction, pp. iii–viii.

Woodress, James Leslie. *Willa Cather: Her Life and Art.* New York, 1970, pp. 68, 69, 89, 213.
    Reviewed: Robert Gorham Davis, *New York Times Book Review,* March 21, 1971.

* CLU is *SCraneN* coding.

Wright, Elizabeth, and George Hendrick, comp. Bibliography, *Studies in Short Fiction,* 7, no. 3 (Summer, 1970), 501–502.

Yardley, Jonathan. "How Papa Grew," *New Republic,* 163 (October 10, 1970), 25–26, 30.

"We Americans are quick to exploit, and quick to ruin, writers who come quickly to fame: Frank Norris, Stephen Crane, Jack London, Fitzgerald, Wolfe, Hemingway."

ADDENDA

1971

[Anon.]. "The Human Flashpoint," *Times Literary Supplement,* October 13, 1971, p. 965.

Review of *The Works of Stephen Crane,* vols. V and VI, ed. Fredson Bowers.

Bowers, Fredson, ed. *The Works of Stephen Crane.* The O'Ruddy, IV. Charlottesville, Va., 1971.

———. *The Works of Stephen Crane. Reports of War,* IX. Charlottesville, Va., 1971.

Dennis, Scott A. "Stephen Crane Bibliography, 1970" *Thoth,* 11, no. 3 (Spring-Summer, 1971), 33–34.

Eichelberger, Clayton L. "Stephen Crane's 'Grand Opera for the People': A Bibliographic Identification and a Correction," *Papers of the Bibliographical Society of America,* 65 (First Quarter, 1971), 70–72.

"In *PBSA* (First Quarter, 1969) George Monteiro called attention to an unrecorded *Public Opinion* printing of a Stephen Crane piece on the New Orleans opera. Noting that the *Public Opinion* version contained three sentences which did not appear in the longer known version published in the *Philadelphia Press,* Monteiro expressed doubt that the sentences were attributable to Crane." *See* Monteiro " 'Grand Opera for the People' " (1969).

The version in *Galveston Daily News,* March 25, 1895, contains four paragraphs omitted from the *Philadelphia Press* version for March 24, 1895. Eichelberger collates these versions and the shorter *Public Opinion,* and concludes that the new passages are by Crane.

Gerstenberger, Donna. " 'The Open Boat': Additional Perspective," *Modern Fiction Studies,* 17, no. 4 (Winter 1971–72), 557–561.

Goetsch, Paul, ed. *Studien und Materialien zur Kurzgeschichte.* Frankfurt, Germany, 1971.

Gullason, Thomas A. "The Fiction of the Reverend Jonathan Townley Crane," *American Literature,* 43 (May, 1971), 263–273.

———. "Stephen Crane and the *Arena:* Three 'Lost' Reviews," *Papers of the Bibliographical Society of America,* 65 (Third Quarter, 1971), 297–299.

They are reviews of "An Ominous Baby" and "The Men in the Storm," both of which the *Arena* published in 1894, and of *The Black Riders.* However, Crane's scrapbook in CUCC contains copies of the first two reviews.

Hall, Charlotte H. "But Is He Relevant?" *Ridgewood Herald News,* November 4, 1971, pp. 2, 21.

An article prompted by the Newark Library's exhibit of Crane memorabilia (supplied from the files of R. W. S.), commemorating Crane's centennial. Reprints a photograph of the Crane house at 14 Mulberry Place, which was razed in 1941 "to make way for a skating rink which was never built. Today the site is a rubble-strewn playground for neighborhood children." Hall recounts Crane's heritage as a Jerseyman, but she errs in claiming that Crane's Jersey heritage "has received little attention in accounts of his short and colorful life. . . ."

Itabashi, Yoshie. "Stephen Crane and the New York City Sketches: Looking for Humanity," *The Tsuda Review,* 16 (November, 1971), 11–41.

Kibler, James E., Jr. "The Library of Stephen and Cora Crane," in *Proof: The Yearbook of American Bibliographical and Textual Studies,* vol. 1. ed. Joseph Katz. Columbia, S. C., 1971, pp. 199–243.

Corrects *Crane;* "List of Books/Brede Place" is in Cora's hand. In *Crane,* p. 12, "R. W. Stallman says that Stephen's brother Wilbur owned a copy of *Wyoming,* brought it to Stephen in 1899, and 'must also have taken it back home with him; it is not listed in Crane's "List of Books at Brede Place." ' Stallman may be correct in saying that Wilbur loaned Crane a copy. However, he is wrong in assuming that because the title does not appear in Cora's List Crane did not have it. For in the Butler Library are two copies of the book which were at Brede." The reason that George Peck's *Wyoming* is not on the List is that the list ends with titles at "T."

Killigrew, Michael, ed. *Your Mirror to My Times: The Selected Autobiographies and Impressions of Ford Madox Ford.* New York, 1971.

LaFrance, Marston. *A Reading of Stephen Crane.* Oxford, 1971.

Reviewed: Times Literary Supplement, December 10, 1971, p. 1548. "Fearful Illusions."

Lynn, Kenneth S. *William Dean Howells: An American Life.* New York, 1971.

Mauldin, William. "A Buddy's Tribute to Audie Murphy," *Life,* 70, no. 22 (June 11, 1971), 77.

On Murphy as the Youth and Mauldin as the Loud Soldier in John Huston's movie *Red Badge of Courage.*

Mizener, Arthur. *The Saddest Story: A Biography of Ford Madox Ford.* New York and Cleveland, 1971, pp. xxi, 38, 67, 68, 95, 255.

Mizener errs in saying, p. 38, "that Ford first saw Stephen Crane, fresh from Cuba." Crane was then fresh from the Greco-Turkish War.

Of Ford's relationship with Crane and of his many commentaries on Crane as writer and as friend, there is nothing in Mizener's biography. For these facts *see Crane* (1968).

Reviewed: New York Times Book Review, May 2, 1971. On Crane, p. 1.

Monteiro, George. "Society and Nature in Stephen Crane's 'The Men in the Storm,' " *Prairie Schooner,* 45, no. 1 (Spring, 1971), 13–17.

Links a passage of Crane's text to the *Old Testament.* "True to his family's Methodism, Crane alludes to the Book of Ecclesiastes."

Moore, Harry T. *Age of the Modern and Other Literary Essays.* Carbondale, and Edwardsville, London and Amsterdam, 1971, pp. 46, 54.

Paredes, Raymund. "Stephen Crane and The Mexican," *Western American Literature,* 6 (Spring, 1971), 31–38.

"There are few characterizations of the Mexican in serious American literature less flattering than Crane's. His Mexicans perpetuate a traditional Yankee stereotype; they are wicked, drunken and cowardly. Their only function in Crane's stories is to provide an odious comparison—to glorify the powerful Anglo by serving as grotesque foils for his tedious exhibitions of courage and ingenuity. The Yankee may have his problems back East, but in the Southwest and in Mexico he is All Man, Crane feels compelled to tell us, and what easier, less painful way to assert his manliness than at the expense of the lowly Mexican." (P. 38)

Pizer, Donald. "Stephen Crane," in *Fifteen American Authors Before 1900: Bibliographical Essays in Research and Criticism,* edited by Robert A. Rees and E. N. Harbert. Madison, Milwaukee, and London, 1971, pp. 97–137.

Not mentioned by Pizer is the catalogue of Columbia University Crane Collection (CUCC), which corrects the many errors in *Exhibition* (1956). Not mentioned by Pizer is the fact that the CUCC contains no Crane letter. Pizer, by this evidence, has neglected to research his subject of MANUSCRIPTS, pp. 97–98. The errors and omissions in *Exhibition* are not entirely corrected by the CUCC catalogue, however. They are supplied in *Stephen Crane: A Critical Bibliography* (1972).

The same is true of the Barrett Crane Collection, which is catalogued but with some omissions yet to be listed (1970), whereas Pizer erroneously claims "no separate list or calendar of its holdings has appeared." Pizer suggests that a census of Crane manuscripts would be helpful because "There is a sufficient amount of Crane manuscript material (particularly letters) in various other private and public collections"; however, Pizer doesn't specify which collections these new manuscripts and letters are to be found in. Presumably, no new manuscripts are likely to show up, and the known ones complete the Crane canon.

Rees, Robert A., and E. N. Harbert, eds. *Fifteen American Authors Before 1900: Bibliographical Essays on Research and Criticism.* Madison, Wis., 1971.

Trillin, Calvin. "What Enormous Problems a Man Can Cause Himself by Answering His Mail!" *New York Times Magazine,* May 2, 1971, p. 31.

Mentions that Crane's niece [Edith] corresponded with H. L. Mencken about her intention "to write a memoir about life with Stephen Crane."

Wertheim, Stanley. "Stephen Crane," in *Hawthorne, Melville, Stephen Crane: A Critical Bibliography,* Theodore L. Gross and Stanley Wertheim. New York and London, 1971, pp. 203–295. Indexed.

Wertheim, p. 211, rightly points out that Gullason's texts in *CSS&S* (1963) are not the texts presented, that "the actual sources of these texts are not always clear, and spot checking discloses occasional inaccuracies." He errs in claiming that *CSS&S* presents "Dan Emmonds" for the first time; it was first published by Stallman in *SinSF* (1963).

Wertheim again errs, p. 214, in stating that the new Sullivan County pieces in Stallman's *SCT&S* (1968) were first reprinted by Gullason. On *War Dispatches* (1964), p. 216: "Place names and geographical areas are identified in maddening detail, and each passing allusion to a warship calls forth a statistical breakdown of its type, tonnage, length, speed, and principal armament." I agree that these footnotes in *WD* consist mainly of irrelevant details—supplied by E. R. Hagemann.

Wertheim's appraisal of Beer's *SC*, p. 218, is excellent, but he is mistaken that Gilkes' *Cora Crane* (1960), p. 220, is "scrupulously researched." *See* under Gilkes (1960) reviews, including the London *TLS* for March 16, 1962. And *see* Gilkes (1969) for Stallman's critique, published in recast form in *American Literature*, 44 (May, 1972). On Garland (1900), p. 230, "the Harlem apartment" of Garland was not in Harlem, although Garland thought it was; Wertheim is mistaken, and so was I in *Crane* (1968).

Wertheim considers Griffith's "S.C. and the Ironic Last Word" (1968), pp. 233–234, "one of the most valuable as well as best-written of the many essays concerned with Crane's narrative technique. . . . Griffith explains that Crane's irony underscores his compassion." However, *Omnibus* (1952) put it this way: Crane's characteristic note is irony fused with pity.

Wertheim rarely traces who said what first, but without this background of scholarship bibliographer Wertheim tends to overrate the given Crane essay. It isn't as original as it seems. This statement applies even more pointedly to Wertheim's commentaries on Joseph X. Brennan's reading of *George's Mother* (1960), as well as to Brennan's "Ironic and Symbolic Structure in Crane's *Maggie*" (1962), because neither essay is without echoes from *Omnibus*. Or from my "SC: A Revaluation" (1952), which gets no mention here. However, much more important is his omitting mention of two of the best short studies of Crane's works; namely the essays by Sergio Perosa and by James B. Colvert collected in Maurice Bassan's *SC: A Collection* (1967). Other splendid scrutinies of Crane's works by Chauncey Ives and Daniel Knapp (1969) appeared after Wertheim completed his bibliographical essay (1968), which in any case is but a selection of 105 entries out of a possible range of more than 2,000 critical writings on Crane.

1 9 7 2

Edel, Leon. *Henry James, the Master: 1901–1916*. Philadelphia and New York, 1972, pp. 23, 44, 57–68, 537.

Gullason, Thomas A. "Stephen Crane: Onward and Upward?" *CEA Critic*, 34, no. 4 (May, 1972), 30–31.

"The Stephen Crane industry continues to flourish at an accelerated pace. This could excite teachers into thinking there is a breakthrough at last in arriving at a fair and full record of the life and writings of America's 'infant precocious.'" Nevertheless, says Gullason, it is clear "that much work remains in terms of resolving major problems that still exist in Crane's life and art." However, Gullason shies from declaring what these major problems might be.

Hubbell, Jay B. *Who Are the Major American Writers?* Durham, N. C., 1972.

Monteiro, George. "Stephen Crane and the Antinomies of Christian Charity," *Centennial Review*, 16 (Winter, 1972), 91–104.

"What began as an important theme in Crane's work—the nexus of social injustice, false philanthropy, and the bankruptcy of charity—was to be put to the test in Crane's own life. His conflict with New York authorities in 1896 over a prostitute falsely accused by the police would eventually lead him to the recognition that the disinterested practice of Christian charity could bring its own bitter fruit—a recognition which would inform his prescient tale, *The Monster* (1898)."

Stallman, R. W. "How Stephen Crane Got to Crete," *American Literature*, 44 (May, 1972), 308–313.

Refutes Gilkes' notion that Crane and Cora got to Crete from Athens and that Crane got to Greece by the overland route instead of by ship, the *Guadiana*, from Marseilles. Crane got to Crete from Marseilles, and Cora was not with him, *contra* Gilkes. *See* Gilkes, "Stephen and Cora Crane," (1969).

———. "Stephen Crane," *Encyclopaedia Britannica*. In press.

Stallman, R. W., ed. *The Stephen Crane Reader*. Glenview, Ill., and London, 1972.

Presents the five new manuscript pages (1960) and the Short Version and the Long Version manuscripts of *The Red Badge of Courage* (1952), together with a newly (1972) annotated text. Presents the 1893 *Maggie* and early drafts of *George's Mother*, "The Blue Hotel," "The Monster." The Notes explain textual inconsistencies in different editions of Crane's works and list the source for each text, whether first book or first periodical publication. Provides critical scrutiny of Crane's works in Introductions to the various sections of the book and an extensive and useful Checklist of Writings on Crane's Fiction and Poetry, indexed by title, pp. 576–604.

LETTERS: SOME ADDITIONS

BARRETT CRANE COLLECTION

ALS, 2 pp. Crane to unknown addressee. Published here for the first time. By permission. N.d. (January 31, 1895). Facsimile, picture section.

> St. Louis
> Thurs—
> Hello Budge. I am / en route to kill / Indians. Before I / left I called upon / you at the place / where I thought I / was most likely / to find you. Write / to me at Lincoln / in care of Mr / Will Owen Jones of the / State Journal. / Lincoln, Nebraska, / I mean. / My distinguished / consideration / Yours as ever / Crane

ALS, 2 pp. Crane to Elbert Hubbard, with envelope addressed to "Mr Elbert Hubbard/East Aurora/N.Y." Postmarked Jan. 2, 1896. Published here for the first time. By permission.

> My dear Haitch: I read your / "No Enemy" today. I always / find that I better appreciate / what books are to us when I / wait for the moment to come / when I want a book and / want it badly. This afternoon / I read "No Enemy" at one / sitting. I like it. Your / manipulation of the life in / Indiana and Illinois is out of sight. There are swift / character sketches all through it that strike me as being / [page 2 begins]

immense. However, I sympathize with the clergy- / man in Chapter I. He stated his case rather / badly but he was better than Hilliard. Hilliard / proved in the rest of the book that he was / not what he indirectly said he was in / Chapter I. Hilliard is a bird. Yet in / Chapter I he was a chump.* Your flowers / on the water—good god, that is mag- / nificent. A thing that I felt in the / roots of my hair. Hell and blazes, but / I do envy you that paragraph. / The book strengthened me and up- / lifted me. It is a peach. Yours sincerely / Stephen Crane.

ALS, 1 p., with envelope addressed to "Mr Shipman / The Player's Club / New York City" Here published for the first time. By permission.

                                        33 East 22 d
                                        [March, 1896 ?]

Dear Mr Shipman: Hope you / can find it your heart / to pardon. I indeed feel too ill this morn- / ing to leave the house / Many regrets. / Yours sincerely / Stephen Crane.

Autograph note on a small piece of paper and on a card bearing the address: 269 West 22nd St (1896).

ALS, 2 pp. Published here for the first time. By permission.

                                        Dec. 27, [1897]
Telegrams.   *Ravensbrook,*
Crane, Oxted   *Oxted,*
                                        Surrey.

Dear sir: In response to your / letter of Dec. 22 d, I would / be glad say [sic] that I have / new book of nine [sic] collected / story coming out probably in / March. The title story will be The Open Boat. They / are all tales of adventure / five of them being Mexican / and Rio Grande border / sketches. We rather expect / it to be my most successful / [page 2 begins] book since The Red Badge. / Faithfully yours / Stephen Crane / Egan New, Esq.

ALS, 2 pp. Here published for the first time. By permission.

Telegrams.   *Ravensbrook,*
Crane, Oxted.   *Oxted,*
                                        Surrey.
                                        Jan. 21 [1899]

My dear John: I am very / anxious to get the originals of / the illustrations to the Bride / Comes to Yellow Sky. Can you / arrange it for me? I am / of course willing to pay for / them. Will you buy them, send / them to me here and charge / it all to my a/c? Also / will you ask Taber

---

* John Northern Hilliard, a journalist who later was editor of the Rochester *Union and Advertiser,* figures in *No Enemy* as "Hilliard." He loaned Crane the suit Crane wore to dinner at William Dean Howells's house in early April, 1893. That winter Hubbard was in New York City. In *No Enemy,* p. 6, he says "I visited the Bethel Home in New York last winter" (1893). He was visiting the city to take notes for his *Arena* article "The Rights of Tramps" (April, 1894). Hubbard persuaded Crane to read Twain's *Huckleberry Finn.* So Crane wrote *Maggie,* and the beginnings of *George's Mother* and *The Red Badge of Courage* before he had read *Huckleberry Finn. See Crane,* pp. 84–85.

No biographer of Hubbard mentions his visit to New York City in late 1893, nor his meeting with Crane then, nor his walks in Union Square with Crane and plump Acton Davies, drama critic of the *New York Sun.*

if it / is possible to buy his il- / lustrations to The Little Regiment? That's a good / boy. / Faithfully yours / S. C.

ALS, 2 pp. Crane to Hugh Frewen. Published here for the first time. By permission.

Telegrams—Crane—Brede Hill
Station—Rye

Brede Place,
Brede,
Northiam,
Sussex.

January 1, 1900

Dear Mr Hugh Frewen: I am desolated / by your request because I fear it is / the result of a misunderstanding. It / is true that we gave a play in the / village school-house but the whole / thing was a mere idle string of rub- / bish made to entertain the villagers / and with music frankly stolen from / very venerable comic operas such as / "The Mikado" and "Pinafore." The whole / business was really beneath contempt / to serious people and it would be / inconsiderate, even unkind, of me / to send it to you. The names of the / authors was more of a joke than / anything. Still, we made it genuine / by causing [sic] all these men really / wrote a mere word or phrase / —such as "It's cold" or, in / fact anything at all—and / in this way we arranged this / rather historic little program. / Allow me to wish you a / very fine shining 1900. / Yours faithfully / Stephen Crane

Holograph manuscript of a note (not a letter), 1 p. Published here for the first time. By permission.

If it were only a movement to / erect a bad statue to Poe, I / suppose there would be a / popular reply. However, if / New York pauses for a moment / to [preser canceled] save [written above the line] this relic, New York / should feel proud. If we cant do it for Poe's sake, we / should do it for our own sake. Stephen Crane

COLUMBIA UNIVERSITY CRANE COLLECTION

Holograph manuscript, 1 p., written on verso of Crane's poem "Tell me not in joyous numbers." An unfinished Crane letter addressed "To the Editor of the Gazette." CUCC lacks a single Crane letter except for this portion.

PUBLIC LIBRARY, MASON CITY, IOWA.

ALS, 1 p. Here published for the first time.

Telegrams.
Crane, New Oxted

Sep. 19 th 97
Ravensbrook,
Oxted,
Surrey.
England

E. Leslie Gilliams / Dear Sir: My terms / for a story of between five and ten thousand words / is $500. This does not include the English rights. I would be willing to / submit to you a story / to be paid for on these terms. / Very truly yours, / Stephen Crane

SYRACUSE UNIVERSITY LIBRARY.

Holograph note:

"May you never lack autographs. / Stephen Crane." For a list of manuscripts and original letters in the George Arents Stephen Crane Collection at Syracuse University, see Stephen Crane's Love Letters to Nellie Crouse, ed. Edwin H. Cady and Lester G. Wells (1954). The above Crane note is not listed.

UNIVERSITY OF TEXAS LIBRARY

Autograph note signed on the title page of the 1893 Maggie. Inscription in the first edition of *The Black Riders and Other Lines:* "To Curtis Brown— / — not at all reluctantly / but with enthusiasm.— / From Stephen Crane / May 26, 1895."

Although this inscription was quoted in *Crane* (1968), p. 151, it is requoted here because its source was not made known.

MISCELLANY

MORGAN LIBRARY

A portion of Crane's will appointing William Howe Crane his American executor and Thomas Plant his British executor. It is dated July 27, 1900. In Contract Book 11, p. 226.

In Contract Books 10 and 11 are letters of Paul R. Reynolds, 1898, 1899, and contracts with Harper and Brothers for the serial use of "The Monster," for serial use of the Whilomville stories, and for *The Monster and Other Stories.* For this data I am indebted to Fredson Bowers.

NEWARK PUBLIC LIBRARY

Two Crane letters and the Newark Chart (so called in *Stephen Crane: A Biography,* 1968), genealogy of the Crane family.*

STALLMAN CRANE COLLECTION

Advertisement of *The Red Badge of Courage* by Stephen Crane, stated within a circle printed on red cardboard, with four triangular spokes projecting from the hub of the encircled *Red Badge of Courage* advertisement. On one such spoke is printed *"Heinemann's Pioneer Series"* and the price, etc. On another spoke of the wheel is printed what *Saturday Review* says: "In the supreme moments of the fight he is possessed with the fiery breath of battle, and finds an inspired utterance that will reach the universal heart of man." On another spoke of the wheel is printed what *The Speaker* says: "Every page is crowded, not merely with incidents such as the war correspondent describes but with the tragedy of life. The reader sees the battle from the inside." And the fourth spoke of the wheel quotes the *St. James Gazette,* which says: "This is not merely a remarkable book; it is a revelation. Mr. Crane has laid the War God on the dissecting-table and exposed to view his every bone, nerve, sinew and artery." The gift of Bertram Rota, Ltd.

H. G. Wells's letter, addressed to Vincent Starrett on stationery printed *Lou Pidou / Saint Mathieu / Grasse A.-M.*

Dec. 8. 27

My dear Sir

I am very sorry to say I can't help you to disinter any unknown *work* (?) by Stephen Crane. I wish I could. But he never talked over his projects with me that I can remember & I lost touch with his wife after his death

Very sincerely yrs

H. G. Wells

* The original of the Newark Chart has been lost or misplaced at the Public Library of Newark (letter to R. W. S., July, 1972). My copy does not identify the author of the Newark Chart, which differs radically from Ellery Bicknell Crane's *Genealogy of the Crane Family* (1900) in respect to the names of the four children who immediately preceded Stephen. See *Crane,* p. 563.

INDEX

[PART E, arranged alphabetically, is not included in this Index. Periodicals and collections entries begin after the general Index entries, p. 636]

PART F ENTRIES BY YEAR

PERIODICALS AND COLLECTIONS